D0744334

AMERICAN
DECADES
PRIMARY SOURCES

1990-1999

AMERICAN DECADES
PRIMARY SOURCES
1990-1999

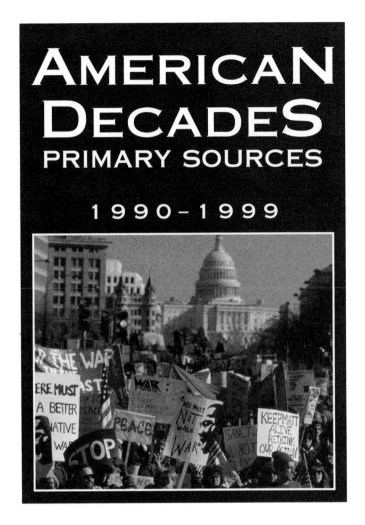

CYNTHIA ROSE, PROJECT EDITOR

GALE®

THOMSON

GALE

Detroit • New York • San Diego • San Francisco • Cleveland • New Haven, Conn. • Waterville, Maine • London • Munich

American Decades Primary Sources, 1990–1999

Project Editor
Cynthia Rose

Editorial
Jason M. Everett, Rachel J. Kain, Pamela A. Dear, Andrew C. Claps, Thomas Carson, Kathleen Droste, Christy Justice, Lynn U. Koch, Michael D. Lesniak, Nancy Matuszak, John F. McCoy, Michael Reade, Rebecca Parks, Mark Mikula, Polly A. Rapp, Mark Springer

Data Capture
Civie A. Green, Beverly Jendrowski, Gwendolyn S. Tucker

Permissions
Margaret Abendroth, Margaret A. Chamberlain, Lori Hines, Jacqueline Key, Mari Masalin-Cooper, William Sampson, Shalice Shah-Caldwell, Kim Smilay, Sheila Spencer, Ann Taylor

Indexing Services
Jennifer Dye

Imaging and Multimedia
Randy Bassett, Dean Dauphinais, Leitha Etheridge-Sims, Mary K. Grimes, Lezlie Light, Daniel W. Newell, David G. Oblender, Christine O'Bryan, Kelly A. Quin, Luke A. Rademacher, Denay Wilding, Robyn V. Young

Product Design
Michelle Dimercurio

Composition and Electronic Prepress
Evi Seoud

Manufacturing
Rita Wimberley

For permission to use material from this product, submit your request via Web at http://gale-edit.com/permissions, or you may download our Permissions Request form and submit your request by fax or mail to:

Permissions Department
The Gale Group, Inc.
27500 Drake Rd.
Farmington Hills, MI 48331-3535
Permissions Hotline:
248-699-8006 or 800-877-4253, ext. 8006
Fax: 248-699-8074 or 800-762-4058

Cover photographs reproduced by permission of AP/Wide World Photos (Mister Rogers, left; President George H. W. Bush, Ross Perot, and Bill Clinton at a 1992 presidential debate, center; Tiger Woods, right), Mambo/Corbis Sygma (Internet computer lab, spine), and Najlah Feaney/Corbis SABA (Demonstrators protest against the Persian Gulf War in front of the U.S. Capitol building, background).

Since this page cannot legibly accommodate all copyright notices, the acknowledgments constitute an extension of the copyright notice.

While every effort has been made to ensure the reliability of the information presented in this publication, The Gale Group, Inc. does not guarantee the accuracy of the data contained herein. The Gale Group, Inc. accepts no payment for listing; and inclusion in the publication of any organization, agency, institution, publication, service, or individual does not imply endorsement of the editors or publisher. Errors brought to the attention of the publisher and verified to the satisfaction of the publisher will be corrected in future editions.

LIBRARY OF CONGRESS CATALOGING-IN-PUBLICATION DATA

American decades primary sources / edited by Cynthia Rose.
   v. cm.
Includes bibliographical references and index.
Contents: [1] 1900-1909 — [2] 1910-1919 — [3] 1920-1929 — [4] 1930-1939 — [5] 1940-1949 — [6] 1950-1959 — [7] 1960-1969 — [8] 1970-1979 — [9] 1980-1989 — [10] 1990-1999.
   ISBN 0-7876-6587-8 (set : hardcover : alk. paper) — ISBN 0-7876-6588-6 (v. 1 : hardcover : alk. paper) — ISBN 0-7876-6589-4 (v. 2 : hardcover : alk. paper) — ISBN 0-7876-6590-8 (v. 3 : hardcover : alk. paper) — ISBN 0-7876-6591-6 (v. 4 : hardcover : alk. paper) — ISBN 0-7876-6592-4 (v. 5 : hardcover : alk. paper) — ISBN 0-7876-6593-2 (v. 6 : hardcover : alk. paper) — ISBN 0-7876-6594-0 (v. 7 : hardcover : alk. paper) — ISBN 0-7876-6595-9 (v. 8 : hardcover : alk. paper) — ISBN 0-7876-6596-7 (v. 9 : hardcover : alk. paper) — ISBN 0-7876-6597-5 (v. 10 : hardcover : alk. paper)
   1. United States—Civilization—20th century—Sources. I. Rose, Cynthia.
E169.1.A471977 2004
973.91—dc21

2002008155

CONTENTS

Entries are arranged in chronological order by date of primary source. For entries with one primary source, the entry title is the primary source title. Entries with more than one primary source have an overall entry title, followed by the titles of the primary sources.

Fashion and Design

Government and Politics

Law and Justice

Lifestyles and Social Trends

The Media

Medicine and Health

Religion

Science and Technology

Sports

ADVISORS AND CONTRIBUTORS

Advisors

CARL A. ANTONUCCI, JR. has spent the past ten years as a reference librarian at various colleges and universities. Currently director of library services at Capital Community College, he holds two master's degrees and is a doctoral candidate at Providence College. He particularly enjoys researching Rhode Island political history during the 1960s and 1970s.

KATHY ARSENAULT is the dean of library at the University of South Florida, St. Petersburg's Poynter Library. She holds a master's degree in library science. She has written numerous book reviews for *Library Journal,* and has published articles in such publications as the *Journal of the Florida Medical Association,* and *Collection Management.*

JAMES RETTIG holds two master's degrees. He has written numerous articles and has edited *Distinguished Classics of Reference Publishing* (1992). University librarian at the University of Richmond, he is the recipient of three American Library Association awards: the Isadore Gibert Mudge Citation (1988), the G.K. Hall Award for Library Literature (1993), and the Louis Shores-Oryx Press Award (1995).

HILDA K. WEISBURG is the head library media specialist at Morristown High School Library and specializes in building school library media programs. She has several publications to her credit, including: *The School Librarians Workshop, Puzzles, Patterns, and Problem Solving: Creative Connections to Critical Thinking,* and *Learning, Linking & Critical Thinking: Information Strategies for the K-12 Library Media Curriculum.*

Contributors

EUGENIA F. BELL is a freelance editor and publication manager who holds a bachelor's in philosophy from Pennsylvania State University. She spent four years as an editor of architecture and design books for the Princeton Architectural Press before working for a year as a publications manager for the Walker Art Center in Minneapolis, Minnesota. She is the author of *The Chapel at Ronchamp* (1999).
Chapter: Fashion and Design.

TIMOTHY G. BORDEN has contributed to such publications as *History Behind the Headlines, Michigan Historical Review, Polish American Studies,* and *Northwest Ohio Quarterly.* He also serves as reader/referee of Notre Dame University at Lebanon's *Palma Journal.*
Chapter: Lifestyles and Social Trends.

DENNIS A. CASTILLO received his doctorate in the history of Christianity from the University of Chicago. Currently an associate professor of Church history at Christ the King Seminary in East Aurora, New York, he is at work on his first book, *The Maltese Cross:*

A Military History of Malta. A Detroit native, he now lives in Buffalo, New York.
Chapter: Religion.

PAUL G. CONNORS earned a doctorate in American history from Loyola University in Chicago. He has a strong interest in Great Lakes maritime history, and has contributed the article "Beaver Island Ice Walkers" to *Michigan History.* He has worked for the Michigan Legislative Service Bureau as a research analyst since 1996.
Chapter: Government and Politics. *Essay:* Using Primary Sources. *Chronologies:* Selected World Events Outside the United States; Government and Politics, Sports chapters. *General Resources:* General, Government and Politics, Sports.

CHRISTOPHER CUMO is a staff writer for *The Adjunct Advocate Magazine.* Formerly an adjunct professor of history at Walsh University, he has written two books, *A History of the Ohio Agricultural Experiment Station, 1882–1997* and *Seeds of Change,* and has contributed to numerous scholarly journals. He holds a doctorate in history from the University of Akron.
Chapter: Science and Technology. *Chapter Chronologies and General Resources:* Business and the Economy, Education, Medicine and Health, Science and Technology.

JENNIFER HELLER holds bachelor's degrees in religious studies and English education, as well as a master's in curriculum and instruction, all from the University of Kansas. She has been an adjunct associate professor at Johnson County Community College in Kansas since 1998. She is currently at work on a dissertation on contemporary women's religious literature.
Chapter Chronology and General Resources: Religion.

DAVID M. HOLFORD has worked as an adjunct instructor at Ohio University, Park College, and Columbus State Community College; education curator for the Ohio Historical Society; and held editorial positions at Glencoe/McGraw Hill and Holt, Rinehard, and Winston. He also holds a doctorate in history from Ohio State University. A freelance writer/editor since 1996, he has published *Herbert Hoover* (1999) and *Abraham Lincoln and the Emancipation Proclamation (2002).*
Chapter Chronologies and General Resources: Lifestyles and Social Trends, The Media.

MILLIE JACKSON is an associate librarian at Grand Valley State University in Allendale, Michigan. She has

previously worked as an English teacher and as the special collections librarian at Oklahoma State University. Dr. Jackson's dissertation on ladies's library associations in Michigan won the American Library Association's Phyllis Dain Library History Dissertation Award in 2001.
Chapters: The Arts, Education, The Media.

JACQUELINE LESHKEVICH joined the Michigan Legislative Service Bureau as a science research analyst in 2000. She earned her bachelor's of science in biochemistry from Northern Michigan University and a master's degree, also in biochemistry, from Michigan Technological University. A contributor to such publications as *Nature Biotechnology* and *Plant Cell,* she is also an amateur astronomer.
Chapter: Medicine and Health.

SCOTT A. MERRIMAN currently works as a part-time instructor at the University of Kentucky and is finishing his doctoral dissertation on Espionage and Sedition Acts in the Sixth Court of Appeals. He has contributed to *The History Highway* and *History.edu,* among others. Scott is a resident of Lexington, Kentucky.
Chapter: Law and Justice.

JESSIE BISHOP POWELL is a librarian assistant at the Lexington Public Library and a cataloger at Book Wholesaler's Inc. She resides in Lexington, Kentucky.
Chapter: Sports.

PATRICK D. REAGAN has taught history at Tennessee Technological University since 1982. He has written over forty book reviews and has contributed to such publications as *Designing a New America: The Origins of New Deal Planning, 1890–1943* and *American Journey: World War I and the Jazz Age.* He is also the author of *History and the Internet: A Guide.*
Chapter: Business and the Economy.

LORNA BIDDLE RINEAR is the editor and co-author of *The Complete Idiot's Guide to Women's History.* A Ph.D. candidate at Rutger's University, she holds a bachelor's from Wellesley College and a master's degree from Boston College. She resides in Bellingham, Massachusetts.
Chapter Chronologies and General Resources: The Arts, Fashion and Design.

AMY ROSE taught at the college level for ten years before becoming a freelance writer, editor, and instructional designer. She has published articles on such topics as ergonomics and labor relations. She holds a bachelor's and doctorate, both in classical studies, from the University of Colorado at Boulder.

Chapter: Fashion and Design.

MARY HERTZ SCARBROUGH earned both her bachelor's in English and German and her J.D. from the University of South Dakota. Prior to becoming a free-lance writer in 1996, she worked as a law clerk in the Federal District Court for the District of South Dakota and as legal counsel for the Immigration and Naturalization Service. She lives in Storm Lake, Iowa.

Chapter Chronology and General Resources: Law and Justice.

ALICE WU holds a bachelor's in English from Wellesley College, as well as an master's in fine art in sculpture from Yale University. An artist and fashion designer, she lives in New York City.

Chapter: The Arts.

ACKNOWLEDGMENTS

Following is a list of the copyright holders who have granted us permission to reproduce material in this volume of American Decades Primary Sources. *Every effort has been made to trace copyright, but if omissions have been made, please let us know.*

Copyrighted material in *American Decades Primary Sources, 1990–1999*, was reproduced from the following periodicals: *Academe, The Magazine of the American Association of University Professors*, v. 84, July/August, 1998. Reproduced by permission. — *Adbusters Magazine*, August, 1998 for "Tibor Kalman" by Allan Casey. Reproduced by permission of the author. — *The American Fertility Society*. 1993. Copyright © 1993 Society of Biological Psychiatry. Reproduced by permission. — *American Journalism Review*, v. 21, July/August, 1999. Reproduced by permission of American Journalism Review. — *The American Prospect*, v. 10, January 1, 1999–February 1, 1999. Reproduced by permission of The American Prospect, 2000 L Street, NW, #717, Washington, D.C. 20036. — *Architectural Record*, April, 1999. Reproduced by permission. — *Art in America*, v. 83, December, 1995 for "The Art World & I Go On Line" by Robert Atkins. Reproduced by permission of the author. — *ARTnews*, October, 1997 for "Perspective: Making the Planet a Better Place" by Dianne H. Pilgrim. Reproduced by permission of the author. — *Cell*, v. 90, July 11, 1997. Reproduced by permission of Elsevier. — *The Christian Century*, v. 108, February 6–13, 1991. Reproduced by permission. — *Columbia Journalism Review*, v. 36, March/April, 1998 for "Is FOX News Fair?" by Neil Hickey. Copyright © 1998 by Columbia Journalism Review. Reproduced by permission of the publisher and the author. — *Communications of the ACM*, v. 41, October, 1998 for "Digital Village: Who Won the Mosaic War?" by Hal Berghel. Reproduced by permission of the publisher and the author. — *Database*, v. 20, February/March, 1997. Reproduced by permission. — *Dissent*, v. 43, Fall, 1996. Reproduced by permission. — *Education Week*, v. 18, March 3, 1999. Reproduced by permission. — *Fortune*, v. 134, December, 1996. Copyright © 1996 Time Inc. All rights reserved. Reproduced by permission. — *Graphis*, May/June, 1998 for "Ken Burns Makes History Happen Now" by Martin Pedersen. Reproduced by permission of the author. — *Harvard Educational Review*, v. 65, Summer, 1995. Copyright © 1995 by the President and Fellows of Harvard College. All rights reserved. Reproduced by permission. — *Journal of American Chemical Society*, v. 116, 1994 for "First Total Synthesis of Taxol" by Lisa Gentile. Copyright 1994 American Chemical Society. Reproduced by permission of the publisher and the author. — *Media Culture & Society*, v. 18, April, 1996; v. 20, July, 1998. Reproduced by permission of Sage Publications, Thousand Oaks, London and New Delhi. —National Public Radio Transcript, April 24, 1999. Reproduced by permission. — *National Review*, v. 49, December 8, 1997. Reproduced by permission. — *New York Magazine*, October 23, 2000 for "Office Culture: Banana Republicans" by Laurie Sandell and Jessica Lustig. Reproduced by permission of Laurie Sandell. — *The New York Review of Books*, October 8, 1998; May 23, 2002. Copyright © 1998, 2002 NYREV, Inc. Reproduced by permission. — *The New York Times*, March 24, 1997; February 15, 1998; November 28, 1999. Copyright © 1997 by The New York Times Co; Copyright © 1998 Hal Espen; Copyright © 1999, Sheryl Gay

Stolberg. Reproduced by permission. — *Newsweek*, v. 129, February 17, 1997. Copyright © 1997 by Newsweek. All rights reserved. Reproduced by permission. — *Phi Delta Kappan*, v. 79, November, 1997 for "The Controversy Over Ebonics" by Steve Fox. Reproduced by permission of the author. — *SACNAS News*, v. 3, Fall, 1999. Reproduced by permission. — *School Library Journal*, v. 42, May, 1996. Reproduced by permission. — *Science Magazine*, v. 265, September 23, 1994; v. 226, October 7, 1994. Reproduced by permission. — *Scientific American*, April, 1992 for "The Multiregional Evolution of Humans" by Alan G. Wolpoff and Alan G. Thorne. Reproduced by permission of the authors./ April, 1992 for "The Recent African Genesis of Humans" by Rebecca L. Cann and Allan C. Wilson. Reproduced by permission of Rebecca L. Cann and the Estate of Allan C. Wilson. — *Southern California Law Review*, v. 66, May, 1993. Reproduced by permission of the Southern California Law Review. —*Sport*, v. 88, April, 1987. Reproduced by permission. — *Sports Illustrated*, v. 91, December 20, 1999. Copyright © 1999, Time Inc. All rights reserved. Reproduced by permission of SPORTS ILLUSTRATED. — *Television Quarterly*, v. 28, 1997; v. 29, 1998. Reproduced by permission. — *The Wall Street Journal*, October 29, 1993 for "The Coming White Underclass" by Charles Murray. Copyright © 1993 by Dow Jones & Company, Inc. All rights reserved. Reproduced by permission of the publisher and the author. — *The Women's Letter*, v. 3, April, 1990; v. 3, December, 1990. Reproduced by permission. — *Time Magazine*, v. 148, December 30, 1996/January 6, 1997; v. 149, April 14, 1997. Copyright © 1997 TIME Inc. Reproduced by permission. — *U.S. Catholic*, v. 57, November, 1992. Reproduced by permission. — *USA Today*, v. 124, March, 1996. Reproduced by permission.

Copyrighted material in *American Decades Primary Sources, 1990–1999*, was reproduced from the following books: Adams, Scott. From *The Dilbert Principle: A Cubicle's Eye View of Bosses, Meetings, Management Fads & Other Workplace Afflictions*. HarperBusiness, A Division of HarperCollins Publishers, 1996. Copyright © 1996 by United Feature Syndicate, Inc. All rights reserved. Reproduced in North America by permission of HarperCollins Publishers, Inc. Reproduced in the rest of the world by permission of United Features Syndicates, Inc. —Armstrong, Lance with Sally Jenkins. From *It's Not About the Bike: My Journey Back to Life*. Copyright © 2000 by Lance Armstrong. All rights reserved. Reproduced by permission of G.P. Putnam's Sons, a division of Penguin Group (USA) Inc. —Barnhart, Joe E. From *Religious Television: Controversies and Conclusions*. Edited by Robert Abelman and Stewart M. Hoover. Ablex Publishing Corporation, 1990. Copyright © 1990 by Ablex Publishing Corporation. All rights reserved. Re-

produced by permission. —Behe, Michael J. From *Darwin's Black Box: The Biochemical Challenge to Evolution*. A Touchstone Book Published by Simon & Schuster, 1996. Copyright © 1996 by Michael J. Behe. All rights reserved. Reproduced by permission of The Free Press, a division of Simon & Schuster Adult Publishing Group. —Berners-Lee, Tim with Mark Fischetti. From *Weaving the Web: The Original Design and Ultimate Destiny of the World Wide Web by Its Inventor*. HarperSanFrancisco, A Division of HarperCollins Publishers, 1999. Copyright © 1999 by Tim Berners-Lee. All rights reserved. Reproduced in North American by permission of HarperCollins. Reproduced in the rest of the world by permission of Fish & Richardson. —Carson, David. From *The End of Print: The Graphic Design of David Carson*. Chronicle Books, 2000. Copyright © 2000 by Lewis Blackwell. All rights reserved. Reproduced by permission of the author. —Carver, Lisa. From *Dancing Queen: The Lusty Adventures of Lisa Crystal Carver*. An Owl Book/Henry Holt and Company, 1996. Copyright © 1996 by Lisa Carver. All rights reserved. Reproduced by permission. —Cleary, Edward J. From *Beyond the Burning Cross: A Landmark Case of Race, Censorship, and the First Amendment*. Copyright © 1994 by Edward J. Cleary. Reproduced by permission of Random House, Inc. —Close, William T. From *Ebola: A Documentary Novel of Its First Explosion*. Copyright © 1995 by William T. Close, M.D. All rights reserved. Reproduced by permission of Ivy Books, a division of Random House, Inc. —Collins, Billy. From *Picnic, Lightning*. University of Pittsburgh Press, 1998. Copyright © 1998 by Billy Collins. All rights reserved. Reproduced by permission. —Coupland, Douglas. From *Generation X: Tales for an Accelerated Culture*. St. Martin's Press, 1991. Copyright © 1991 by Douglas Coupland. All rights reserved. Reproduced by permission of St. Martin's Press LLC. —Crichton, Michael. From *Jurassic Park*. Copyright © 1990 by Michael Crichton. All rights reserved. Reproduced by permission of Alfred A. Knopf, a division of Random House, Inc. —Darden, Christopher A. with Jess Walter. From *In Contempt*. ReganBooks, an imprint of HarperCollins Publishers, 1996. Copyright © 1996 by Christopher A. Darden. All rights reserved. Reproduced by permission of HarperCollins Publishers Inc. —Dees, Morris with Steve Fiffer. From *A Season For Justice: The Life and Times of Civil Rights Lawyer Morris Dees*. Charles Scribner's Sons, 1991. Copyright © 1991 by Morris Dees and Steve Fiffer. All rights reserved. Reproduced by permission of Morris Dees. —Deloria, Vine, Jr. From *For This Land: Writings on Religion in America*. Edited by James Treat. Routledge, 1999. Copyright © 1999 by Vine Deloria, Jr. All rights reserved. Reproduced by permission. —Dershowitz, Alan M. From *Reasonable Doubts: The Criminal Justice System and the*

Reproduced in the rest of the world by permission of Houghton Mifflin Company. —Lewis, Harold J. From *Lift Every Voice and Sing II: An African American Hymnal*. The Church Hymnal Corporation, 1992. Words copyright © 1992 by Harold T. Lewis. Copyright © 1993 by The Church Pension Fund. All rights reserved. Reproduced by permission of the author. —Limbaugh, Rush H., III. From *See, I Told You So*. Pocket Books, 1993. Copyright © 1993 by Rush H. Limbaugh, III. All rights reserved. Reproduced by permission of Atria Books, an imprint of Simon & Schuster Adult Publishing Group. —Limbaugh, Rush H., III. From *The Way Things Ought to Be*. Pocket Books, 1992. Copyright © 1992 by Rush Limbaugh. All rights reserved. Reproduced by permission of Atria Books, an imprint of Simon & Schuster Adult Publishing Group. —Lipinski, Tara as told to Emily Costello. From *Tara Lipinski: Triumph on Ice: An Autobiography as Told to Emily Costello*. Bantam Books, 1997. Copyright © 1997 by Tara Lipinski. All rights reserved. Reproduced by permission of Random House Children's Books, a division of Random House, Inc. —Macdonald, Andrew. From *The Turner Diaries*. Barricade Books, Inc., 1978. Copyright © 1978, 1980 by William L. Pierce. All rights reserved. Reproduced by permission. —Moceanu, Dominique as told to Steve Woodward. From *Dominique Moceanu: An American Champion: An Autobiography as Told to Steve Woodward*. Bantam Books, 1996. Copyright © 1996 by Dominique Moceanu. All rights reserved. Reproduced by permission. —O'Neal, Shaquille with Jack McCallum. From *Shaq Attaq!* Hyperion, 1993. Copyright © 1993 by Shaquille O'Neal. All rights reserved. Reproduced in North America by permission of Hyperion. Reproduced in the rest of the world by permission of Reid Boates Literary Agency. —Perelli, Robert J. From *Guides to Pastoral Care: Ministry to Persons with AIDS: A Family Systems Approach*. Augsburg, 1991. Copyright © 1991 by Augsburg Fortress. All rights reserved. Reproduced by permission. —Proulx, Annie. From *The Shipping News*. Scribner Classics, 1993. Copyright © 1993 by E. Annie Proulx. All rights reserved. Reproduced in North America by permission of Simon & Schuster, Inc. Reproduced in the rest of the world by permission of HarperCollins Publishers Ltd. —Rifkin, Jeremy. From *The Biotech Century: Harnessing the Gene and Remaking the World*. Penguin Putnam Inc., 1998. Copyright © 1998 by Jeremy Rifkin. All rights reserved. Reproduced by permission of Jeremy P. Tarcher, an imprint of Penguin Group (USA) Inc. —Rogers, Fred and Barry Head. From *Mister Rogers Talks With Parents*. Berkley Books, 1983. Copyright © 1983 by Family Communications, Inc. All rights reserved. Reproduced by permission. —Rogers, Fred. From *Dear Mister Rogers, Does It Ever Rain in Your Neighborhood?: Letters to Mister Rogers*. Penguin Books, 1996. Copyright © 1996 by Family Communications, Inc. All rights reserved. Reproduced by permission. —Rogers, Fred M. "Won't You Be My Neighbor?" Family Communications, Inc. Copyright © 1967 by Fred M. Rogers Estate. All rights reserved. Reproduced by permission. —Ross, Andrew. From *The Celebration Chronicles: Life, Liberty, and The Pursuit of Property Value in Disney's New Town*. Copyright © 1999 by Andrew Ross, Ph.D. Reproduced by permission of Ballantine Books, a division of Random House, Inc. —Sizer, Theodore R. From *Horace's School: Redesigning the American High School*. Houghton Mifflin Company, 1992. Copyright © 1992 by Theodore R. Sizer. All rights reserved. Reproduced by permission. —Vance, Sandra S. and Roy V. Scott. From *Wal-Mart: A History of Sam Walton's Retail Phenomenon*. Twayne Publishers, 1994. Copyright © 1994 by Twayne Publishers. All rights reserved. Reproduced by permission. —Vardey, Lucinda. From *The Flowering of the Soul: A Book of Prayers by Women*. Edited by Lucinda Vardey. Beacon Press, 2001. Copyright © 1999, 2001 by Lucinda Vardey. All rights reserved. Reproduced by permission. —Woods, Earl. From *Playing Through*. HarperCollins Publishers, 1998. Copyright © 1998 by Earl Woods. All rights reserved. Reproduced by permission of HarperCollins.

Copyrighted material in *American Decades Primary Sources, 1990–1999*, was reproduced from the following websites: Berry, Lorraine, "One on One with Sheryl Swoopes, Houston Comets." Online at: http://www.gballmag.com/pp_swoopes.html. Published by Gball, December 1999. Reproduced by permission. —Bowden, Larry, "Room For All Science." Online at: http://www.cjonline.com/stories/083099/opi_letters30.shtml. Published by Topeka Capital Journal, August 30, 1999. Reproduced by permission. —"Breaking the Code: A NewsHour with Jim Lehrer Transcript." http://www.pbs.org/newshour/bb/health/july-dec99/dna_12-2.html. Published by PBS.org, December 2, 1999. Reproduced by permission. —"Bt and Monarchs: Monsanto Statement on Bt Corn: Environmental Safety and a Recent Report on the Monarch Butterfly." Online at: http://www.biotech-info.net/monsanto_on_btcorn.html. Reproduced by permission. —"Charter of the New Urbanism." Online at: http://www.cnu.org. Reproduced by permission. —"Debate Transcripts: 1992 Debates: The Second Clinton-Bush-Perot Presidential Debate, October 15, 1992 (First Half of Debate)." Online at: http://www.debates.org/pages/trans92b1.html#q-healthcare. Published by Commission on Presidential Debates. Reproduced by permission. —Farrakhan, Louis, "Minister Farrakhan Challenges Black Men: Transcript From Minister Louis Farrakhan's Remarks at the Million Man March." Online at: http://www-cgi.cnn.com/US/9510/megamarch/10-16/transcript/index.html. Published by CNN.com, October 17, 1995. Reproduced by permission. —From "An Interview with Philip Glass" by Alex Christaki. Online at: http://www.glasspages .org/interview.html. —Fuller, Kevin. From "Media Killers: An Interview with Anna Deavers Smith." Appendx, 1997. Online at: http://www.appendx.org/appendx .htm. Copyright © 1997 by Appendx, Inc. Reproduced by permission. —"Interview Transcript: Richard Seed, Physicist." Online at: http://www.cnn.com/CNN/bureaus /chicago/stories/9801/cloning/index1.htm. Published by CNN.com. Reproduced by permission. —"Karolyi: I'm Old-Fashioned." Online at: http://espn.go.com/otl/athlete /karolyi.html. Published by ESPN.com, January 20, 2000. Reproduced by permission. —NewsHour Transcript: "World Com Together." Online at: http://www.pbs.org /newshour/bb/business/july-dec97/mci_11-10.html. Published by PBS.org, November 10, 1997. Reproduced by permission. —"PBS Life on the Internet: Timeline." Online at: http://www.pbs.org/internet/timeline/timeline-txt .html. Published by PBS.org. Site produced by Cochran Interactive. Reproduced by permission. —Rice, Ellen, "Foundress, Missionary, Bride of Christ: Mother M. Angelica." Online at: http://www.catholic.net/RCC/Periodicals /Dossier/1998-03-04/feature.html. Published by Catholic Dossier Issues in the Round/Ignatius Press, March/April,

1998. Reprinted by permission of Ignatius Press, San Francisco, CA. —Ruden, Douglas, Paulyn Cartwright, and Bruce Lieberman, "Evolution Is Science." Online at: http://www.cjonline.com/stories/070199/opi_letters.shtml. Published by Topeka Capital Journal, July 1, 1999. Reproduced by permission. —Taylor, Humphrey, The Harris Poll #11, "Explosive Growth of a New Breed of 'Cyberchrondriacs.'" Online at: http://www.harrisinteractive.com /harris_poll/index.asp?PID=34. Published by HarrisInteractive, February 17, 1999. Reproduced with permission. — "'The Whisper of AIDS,' Republican National Convention Address, Houston, TX, Aug. 19, 1992." Online at: http://www.pbs.org/greatspeeches/timeline/m_fisher_s1 .html. Published by PBS.org. Reproduced by permission. —Walker, Kara. From "Conversations with Contemporary Artists." Online at: http://www.moma.org/online projects/conversations/trans_kwalker.html. Museum of Modern Art, 1999. Copyright © 1999 by The Museum of Modern Art. Reproduced by permission. —Williams, Venus, "From Russia With Love: Entry 1—10/27/97." Online at: http://www.venustennis.com. Reproduced with permission.

ABOUT THE SET

American Decades Primary Sources is a ten-volume collection of more than two thousand primary sources on twentieth-century American history and culture. Each volume comprises about two hundred primary sources in 160–170 entries. Primary sources are enhanced by informative context, with illustrative images and sidebars—many of which are primary sources in their own right—adding perspective and a deeper understanding of both the primary sources and the milieu from which they originated.

Designed for students and teachers at the high school and undergraduate levels, as well as researchers and history buffs, *American Decades Primary Sources* meets the growing demand for primary source material.

Conceived as both a stand-alone reference and a companion to the popular *American Decades* set, *American Decades Primary Sources* is organized in the same subject-specific chapters for compatibility and ease of use.

Primary Sources

To provide fresh insights into the key events and figures of the century, thirty historians and four advisors selected unique primary sources far beyond the typical speeches, government documents, and literary works. Screenplays, scrapbooks, sports box scores, patent applications, college course outlines, military codes of conduct, environmental sculptures, and CD liner notes are but a sampling of the more than seventy-five types of primary sources included.

Diversity is shown not only in the wide range of primary source types, but in the range of subjects and opin-

ions, and the frequent combination of primary sources in entries. Multiple perspectives in religious, political, artistic, and scientific thought demonstrate the commitment of *American Decades Primary Sources* to diversity, in addition to the inclusion of considerable content displaying ethnic, racial, and gender diversity. *American Decades Primary Sources* presents a variety of perspectives on issues and events, encouraging the reader to consider subjects more fully and critically.

American Decades Primary Sources' innovative approach often presents related primary sources in an entry. The primary sources act as contextual material for each other—creating a unique opportunity to understand each and its place in history, as well as their relation to one another. These may be point-counterpoint arguments, a variety of diverse opinions, or direct responses to another primary source. One example is President Franklin Delano Roosevelt's letter to clergy at the height of the Great Depression, with responses by a diverse group of religious leaders from across the country.

Multiple primary sources created by particularly significant individuals—Dr. Martin Luther King, Jr., for example—reside in *American Decades Primary Sources*. Multiple primary sources on particularly significant subjects are often presented in more than one chapter of a volume, or in more than one decade, providing opportunities to see the significance and impact of an event or figure from many angles and historical perspectives. For example, seven primary sources on the controversial Scopes "monkey" trial are found in five chapters of the

1920s volume. Primary sources on evolutionary theory may be found in earlier and later volumes, allowing the reader to see and analyze the development of thought across time.

Entry Organization

Contextual material uses standardized rubrics that will soon become familiar to the reader, making the entries more accessible and allowing for easy comparison. Introduction and Significance essays—brief and focused—cover the historical background, contributing factors, importance, and impact of the primary source, encouraging the reader to think critically—not only about the primary source, but also about the way history is constructed. Key Facts and a Synopsis provide quick access and recognition of the primary sources, and the Further Resources are a stepping-stone to additional study.

Additional Features

Subject chronologies and thorough tables of contents (listing titles, authors, and dates) begin each chapter. The main table of contents assembles this information conveniently at the front of the book. An essay on using primary sources, a chronology of selected events outside the United States during the twentieth century, substantial general and subject resources, and primary source type and general indexes enrich *American Decades Primary Sources*.

The ten volumes of *American Decades Primary Sources* provide a vast array of primary sources integrated with supporting content and user-friendly features.

This value-laden set gives the reader an unparalleled opportunity to travel into the past, to relive important events, to encounter key figures, and to gain a deep and full understanding of America in the twentieth century.

Acknowledgments

A number of people contributed to the successful completion of this project. The editor wishes to acknowledge them with thanks: Luann Brennan, Katrina Coach, Pamela S. Dear, Nikita L. Greene, Madeline Harris, Alesia James, Cynthia Jones, Pamela M. Kalte, Arlene Ann Kevonian, Frances L. Monroe, Charles B. Montney, Katherine H. Nemeh, James E. Person, Tyra Y. Phillips, Elizabeth Pilette, Noah Schusterbauer, Susan Strickland, Karissa Walker, Tracey Watson, and Jennifer M. York.

Contact Us

The editors of *American Decades Primary Sources* welcome your comments, suggestions, and questions. Please direct all correspondence to:

Editor, *American Decades Primary Sources*
The Gale Group, Inc.
27500 Drake Road
Farmington Hills, MI 48331-3535
(800) 877-4253

For email inquiries, please visit the Gale website at http://www.gale.com, and click on the Contact Us tab.

ABOUT THE VOLUME

Closing out the twentieth century, the 1990s showed no signs that the United States would enter quietly into the next millennium. Under the George H.W. Bush administration, U.S. troops fought in the first Gulf War, liberating Kuwait from Iraq. David Koresh's cult compound in Waco, Texas, was raided by federal agents. President Bill Clinton was impeached by Congress, but remained in office to complete his second term. NASA's *Pathfinder* sent images of Mars back to Earth. The curious could view the images on the rapidly expanding and increasingly accessible Internet. While new technology transformed much of how people communicated and worked, some business-place practices are universal. These were humorously represented in the new *Dilbert* comic strip. The following documents are just a sampling of the offerings available in this volume.

Highlights of Primary Sources, 1990–1999

- Art work by African American artist Kara Walker
- The Preamble to the North American Free Trade Agreement (NAFTA)
- Transcript of National Public Radio broadcast about the Columbine shootings in Littleton, Colorado
- Advertisement for Levi's Dockers pants
- The First Bush-Clinton-Perot Debate
- *The Starr Report, September 9, 1998*
- *Dilbert* cartoon by Scott Adams accompanied by an excerpt from Adams's *The Dilbert Principle*
- "Is Fox News Fair?" an article from the *Columbia Journalism Review*
- President Clinton's Memorandum on Fetal Tissue Transplantation Research
- Speech by Minister Louis Farrakhan at the Million Man March, October 17, 1995
- *Darwin's Black Box,* by Michael Behe
- "From Russia With Love," excerpts from Venus Williams's diary
- Testimony from the confirmation hearings of Clarence Thomas

Volume Structure and Content

Front matter

- Table of Contents—lists primary sources, authors, and dates of origin, by chapter and chronologically within chapters.
- About the Set, About the Volume, About the Entry essays—guide the reader through the set and promote ease of use.
- Highlights of Primary Sources—a quick look at a dozen or so primary sources gives the reader a feel for the decade and the volume's contents.
- Using Primary Sources—provides a crash course in reading and interpreting primary sources.
- Chronology of Selected World Events Outside the United States—lends additional context in which to place the decade's primary sources.

Chapters:

- The Arts
- Business and the Economy
- Education
- Fashion and Design
- Government and Politics
- Law and Justice
- Lifestyles and Social Trends
- The Media
- Medicine and Health
- Religion
- Science and Technology
- Sports

Chapter structure

- Chapter table of contents—lists primary sources, authors, and dates of origin chronologically, showing each source's place in the decade.

- Chapter chronology—highlights the decade's important events in the chapter's subject.

- Primary sources—displays sources surrounded by contextual material.

Back matter

- General Resources—promotes further inquiry with books, periodicals, websites, and audio and visual media, all organized into general and subject-specific sections.

- General Index—provides comprehensive access to primary sources, people, events, and subjects, and cross-referencing to enhance comparison and analysis.

- Primary Source Type Index—locates primary sources by category, giving readers an opportunity to easily analyze sources across genres.

ABOUT THE ENTRY

The primary source is the centerpiece and main focus of each entry in *American Decades Primary Sources*. In keeping with the philosophy that much of the benefit from using primary sources derives from the reader's own process of inquiry, the contextual material surrounding each entry provides access and ease of use, as well as giving the reader a springboard for delving into the primary source. Rubrics identify each section and enable the reader to navigate entries with ease.

Entry structure

- Key Facts—essential information pertaining to the primary source, including full title, author, source type, source citation, and notes about the author.

- Introduction—historical background and contributing factors for the primary source.

- Significance—importance and impact of the primary source, at the time and since.

- Primary Source—in text, text facsimile, or image format; full or excerpted.

- Synopsis—encapsulated introduction to the primary source.

- Further Resources—books, periodicals, websites, and audio and visual material.

Navigating an Entry

Entry elements are numbered and reproduced here, with an explanation of the data contained in these elements explained immediately thereafter according to the corresponding numeral.

Primary Source/Entry Title, Primary Source Type

•1• **"Ego"**
•2• Magazine article

•1• **PRIMARY SOURCE/ENTRY TITLE** The entry title is the primary source title for entries with one primary source. Entry titles appear as catchwords at the top outer margin of each page.

•2• **PRIMARY SOURCE TYPE** The type of primary source is listed just below the title. When assigning source types, great weight was given to how the author of the primary source categorized it. If a primary source comprised more than one type—for example, an article about art in the United States that included paintings, or a scientific essay that included graphs and photographs—each primary source type included in the entry appears below the title.

Composite Entry Title

•3• **Debate Over *The Birth of a Nation***

•1• **"Capitalizing Race Hatred"**
•2• Editorial

•1• **"Reply to the *New York Globe*"**

•2• Letter

•3• **COMPOSITE ENTRY TITLE** An overarching entry title is used for entries with more than one primary source, with the primary source titles and types below.

Key Facts

•4• **By:** Norman Mailer

•5• **Date:** March 19, 1971

•6• **Source:** Mailer, Norman. "Ego." *Life* 70, March 19, 1971, 30, 32–36.

•7• **About the Author:** Norman Mailer (1923–) was born in Long Branch, New Jersey. After graduating from Harvard and military service in World War II (1939–1945), Mailer began writing, publishing his first book, the best-selling novel *The Naked and the Dead,* in 1948. Mailer has written over thirty books, including novels, plays, political commentary, and essay collections, as well as numerous magazine articles. He won the Pulitzer Prize in 1969 and 1979. ■

•4• **AUTHOR OR ORIGINATOR** The name of the author or originator of the primary source begins the Key Facts section.

•5• **DATE OF ORIGIN** The date of origin of the primary source appears in this field, and may differ from the date of publication in the source citation below it; for example, speeches are often given before they are published.

•6• **SOURCE CITATION** The source citation is a full bibliographic citation, giving original publication data as well as reprint and/or online availability (usually both the deep-link and home-page URLs).

•7• **ABOUT THE AUTHOR** A brief bio of the author or originator of the primary source gives birth and death dates and a quick overview of the person's life. This rubric has been customized in some cases. If the primary source is the autobiography of an artist, the term "author" appears; however, if the primary source is a work of art, the term "artist" is used, showing the person's direct relationship to the primary source. Terms like "inventor" and "designer" are used similarly. For primary sources created by a group, "organization" may have been used instead of "author." If an author is anonymous or unknown, a brief "About the Publication" sketch may appear.

Introduction and Significance Essays

•8• **Introduction**

. . . As images from the Vietnam War (1964–1975) flashed onto television screens across the United States in the late 1960s, however, some reporters took a more active role in questioning the pronouncements of public officials. The broad cul-

tural changes of the 1960s, including a sweeping suspicion of authority figures by younger people, also encouraged a more restive spirit in the reporting corps. By the end of the decade, the phrase "Gonzo Journalism" was coined to describe the new breed of reporter: young, rebellious, and unafraid to get personally involved in the story at hand. . . .

•8• **INTRODUCTION** The introduction is a brief essay on the contributing factors and historical context of the primary source. Intended to promote understanding and jump-start the reader's curiosity, this section may also describe an artist's approach, the nature of a scientific problem, or the struggles of a sports figure. If more than one primary source is included in the entry, the introduction and significance address each one, and often the relationship between them.

•9• **Significance**

Critics of the new style of journalism maintained that the emphasis on personalities and celebrity did not necessarily lead to better reporting. As political reporting seemed to focus more on personalities and images and less on substantive issues, some observers feared that the American public was ill-served by the new style of journalism. Others argued that the media had also encouraged political apathy among the public by superficial reporting. . . .

•9• **SIGNIFICANCE** The significance discusses the importance and impact of the primary source. This section may touch on how it was regarded at the time and since, its place in history, any awards given, related developments, and so on.

Primary Source Header, Synopsis, Primary Source

•10• **Primary Source**

The Boys on the Bus [excerpt]

•11• **SYNOPSIS:** A boisterous account of Senator George McGovern's ultimately unsuccessful 1972 presidential bid, Crouse's work popularized the term "pack journalism," describing the herd mentality that gripped reporters focusing endlessly on the same topic. In later years, political advisors would become more adept at "spinning" news stories to their candidates' advantage, but the essential dynamics of pack journalism remain in place.

•12• The feverish atmosphere was halfway between a high school bus trip to Washington and a gambler's jet junket to Las Vegas, where small-time Mafiosi were lured into betting away their restaurants. There was giddy camaraderie mixed with fear and low-grade hysteria. To file a story late, or to make one glaring factual error, was to chance losing everything—one's job, one's expense account, one's drinking buddies, one's mad-dash existence, and the methedrine buzz that comes from knowing stories that the public would not know for hours and secrets that the public would never know. Therefore reporters channeled their gambling instincts into late-night poker games and private bets on the outcome of the elections. When it came to writing a story, they were as cautious as diamond-cutters. . . .

•10• **PRIMARY SOURCE HEADER** The primary source header signals the beginning of the primary source, and "[excerpt]" is attached if the source does not appear in full.

•11• **SYNOPSIS** The synopsis gives a brief overview of the primary source.

•12• **PRIMARY SOURCE** The primary source may appear excerpted or in full, and may appear as text, text facsimile (photographic reproduction of the original text), image, or graphic display (such as a table, chart, or graph).

Text Primary Sources

The majority of primary sources are reproduced as plain text. The font and leading of the primary sources are distinct from that of the context—to provide a visual clue to the change, as well as to facilitate ease of reading. Often, the original formatting of the text was preserved in order to more accurately represent the original (screenplays, for example). In order to respect the integrity of the primary sources, content some readers may consider sensitive was retained where it was deemed to be integral to the source. Text facsimile formatting was used sparingly and where the original provided additional value (for example, Aaron Copland's typing and handwritten notes on "Notes for a Cowboy Ballet").

Narrative Break

•13• I told him I'd rest and then fix him something to eat when he got home. I could hear someone enter his office then, and Medgar laughed at something that was said. "I've got to go, honey. See you tonight. I love you." "All right," I said. "Take care." Those were our last words to each other.

■ ■ ■

Medgar had told me that President Kennedy was speaking on civil rights that night, and I made a mental note of the time. We ate alone, the children and I. It had become a habit now to set only four places for supper. Medgar's chair stared at us, and the children, who had heard

about the President's address to the nation, planned to watch it with me. There was something on later that they all wanted to see, and they begged to be allowed to wait up for Medgar to return home. School was out, and I knew that Van would fall asleep anyway, so I agreed.

•13• **NARRATIVE BREAK** A narrative break appears where there is a significant amount of elided material, beyond what ellipses would indicate (for example, excerpts from a nonfiction work's introduction and second chapter, or sections of dialogue from two acts of a play).

Image Primary Sources

Primary source images (whether photographs, text facsimiles, or graphic displays) are bordered with a distinctive double rule. The Primary Source header and Synopsis appear under the image, with the image reduced in size to accommodate the synopsis. For multipart images, the synopsis appears only under the first part of the image; subsequent parts have brief captions.

•14• "Art: U.S. Scene": *The Tornado* by John Steuart Curry (2 OF 4)

•14• **PRIMARY SOURCE IMAGE HEADER** The primary source image header assists the reader in tracking the images in a series. Also, the primary source header listed here indicates a primary source with both text and image components. The text of the *Time* magazine article "Art: U.S. Scene," appears with four of the paintings from the article. Under each painting, the title of the article appears first, followed by a colon, then the title of the painting. The header for the text component has a similar structure, with the term "magazine article" after the colon. Inclusion of images or graphic elements from primary sources, and their designation in the entry as main primary sources, is discretionary.

Further Resources

•15• **Further Resources**

BOOKS
Dixon, Phil. *The Negro Baseball Leagues, 1867–1955: A Photographic History.* Mattituck, N.Y.: Amereon House, 1992.

PERIODICALS
"Steven Spielberg: The Director Says It's Good-Bye to Spaceships and Hello to Relationships." *American Film* 13, no. 8, June 1988, 12–16.

WEBSITES
Architecture and Interior Design for 20th Century America, 1935–1955. American Memory digital primary source collection, Library of Congress. Available online at http://memory.loc.gov/ammem/gschtml/gotthome

.html; website home page: http://memory.loc.gov
/ammem/ammemhome.html (accessed March 27, 2003).

AUDIO AND VISUAL MEDIA

E.T.: The Extra-Terrestrial. Original release, 1982, Universal. Directed by Steven Spielberg. Widescreen Collector's Edition DVD, 2002, Universal Studios.

•15• **FURTHER RESOURCES** A brief list of resources provides a stepping stone to further study. If it's known that a resource contains additional primary source material specifically related to the entry, a brief note in italics appears at the end of the citation. For websites, both the deep link and home page usually appear.

USING PRIMARY SOURCES

The philosopher R.G. Collingwood once said, "Every new generation must rewrite history in its own way." What Collingwood meant is that new events alter our perceptions of the past and necessitate that each generation interpret the past in a different light. For example, since September 11, 2001, and the "War on Terrorism," the collapse of the Soviet Union seemingly is no longer as historically important as the rise of Islamic fundamentalism, which was once only a minor concern. Seen from this viewpoint, history is not a rigid set of boring facts, but a fascinating, ever-changing field of study. Much of this fascination rests on the fact that historical interpretation is based on the reading of primary sources. To historians and students alike, primary sources are ambiguous objects because their underlying meanings are often not crystal clear. To learn a primary document's meaning(s), students must identify its main subject and recreate the historical context in which the document was created. In addition, students must compare the document with other primary sources from the same historical time and place. Further, students must cross-examine the primary source by asking of it a series of probing investigative questions.

To properly analyze a primary source, it is important that students become "active" rather than "casual" readers. As in reading a chemistry or algebra textbook, historical documents require students to analyze them carefully and extract specific information. In other words, history requires students to read "beyond the text" and focus on what the primary source tells us about the per-

son or group and the era in which they lived. Unlike chemistry and algebra, however, historical primary sources have the additional benefit of being part of a larger, interesting story full of drama, suspense, and hidden agendas. In order to detect and identify key historical themes, students need to keep in mind a set of questions. For example, Who created the primary source? Why did the person create it? What is the subject? What problem is being addressed? Who was the intended audience? How was the primary source received and how was it used? What are the most important characteristics of this person or group for understanding the primary source? For example, what were the authors' biases? What was their social class? Their race? Their gender? Their occupation? Once these questions have been answered reasonably, the primary source can be used as a piece of historical evidence to interpret history.

In each *American Decades Primary Sources* volume, students will study examples of the following categories of primary sources:

- Firsthand accounts of historic events by witnesses and participants. This category includes diary entries, letters, newspaper articles, oral-history interviews, memoirs, and legal testimony.

- Documents representing the official views of the nation's leaders or of their political opponents. These include court decisions, policy statements, political speeches, party platforms, petitions, legislative debates, press releases, and federal and state laws.

- Government statistics and reports on such topics as birth, employment, marriage, death, and taxation.

- Advertisers' images and jingles. Although designed to persuade consumers to purchase commodities or to adopt specific attitudes, advertisements can also be valuable sources of information about popular beliefs and concerns.

- Works of art, including paintings, symphonies, play scripts, photographs, murals, novels, and poems.

- The products of mass culture: cartoons, comic books, movies, radio scripts, and popular songs.

- Material artifacts. These are everyday objects that survived from the period in question. Examples include household appliances and furnishings, recipes, and clothing.

- Secondary sources. In some cases, secondary sources may be treated as primary sources. For example, from 1836 to 1920, public schools across America purchased 122 million copies of a series of textbooks called the McGuffey Reader. Although current textbooks have more instructional value, the Reader is an invaluable primary source. It provides important insights into the unifying morals and cultural values that shaped the worldview of several generations of Americans, who differed in ethnicity, race, class, and religion.

Each of the above-mentioned categories of primary sources reveals different types of historical information. A politician's diary, memoirs, or collection of letters, for example, often provide students with the politicians' unguarded, private thoughts and emotions concerning daily life and public events. Though these documents may be a truer reflection of the person's character and aspirations, students must keep in mind that when people write about themselves, they tend to put themselves at the center of the historical event or cast themselves in the best possible light. On the other hand, the politician's public speeches may be more cautious, less controversial, and limited to advancing his or her political party's goals or platform.

Like personal diaries, advertisements reveal other types of historical information. What information does the WAVES poster on this page reveal?

John Phillip Faller, a prolific commercial artist known for his *Saturday Evening Post* covers, designed this recruitment poster in 1944. It was one of over three hundred posters he produced for the U.S. Navy while enrolled in that service during World War II. The purpose of the poster was to encourage women to enlist in the WAVES (Women Accepted for Volunteer Emergency Service), a women's auxiliary to the Navy established in

COURTESY OF THE NAVAL HISTORICAL FOUNDATION. REPRODUCED BY PERMISSION.

1942. It depicts a schoolgirl gazing admiringly at a photograph of a proud, happy WAVE (perhaps an older sister), thus portraying the military service as an appropriate and admirable aspiration for women during wartime. However, what type of military service? Does the poster encourage women to enlist in military combat like World War II male recruitment posters? Does it reflect gender bias? What does this poster reveal about how the military and society in general feel about women in the military? Does the poster reflect current military and societal attitudes toward women in the military? How many women joined the WAVES? What type of duties did they perform?

Like personal diaries, photographs reveal other types of historical information. What information does the next photograph reveal?

Today, we take electricity for granted. However, in 1935, although 90 percent of city dwellers in America had electricity, only 10 percent of rural Americans did. Private utility companies refused to string electric lines

THE LIBRARY OF CONGRESS.

to isolated farms, arguing that the endeavor was too expensive and that most farmers were too poor to afford it anyway. As part of the Second New Deal, President Franklin Delano Roosevelt issued an executive order creating the Rural Electrification Administration (REA). The REA lent money at low interest rates to utility companies to bring electricity to rural America. By 1950, 90 percent of rural America had electricity. This photograph depicts a 1930s tenant farmer's house in Greene County, Georgia. Specifically, it shows a brand-new electric meter on the wall. The picture presents a host of questions: What was rural life like without electricity? How did electricity impact the lives of rural Americans, particularly rural Georgians? How many rural Georgians did not have electricity in the 1930s? Did Georgia have more electricity-connected farms than other Southern states? What was the poverty rate in rural Georgia, particularly among rural African Americans? Did rural electricity help lift farmers out of poverty?

Like personal diaries, official documents reveal other types of historical information. What information does the next document, a memo, reveal?

From the perspective of the early twenty-first century, in a democratic society, integration of the armed services seems to have been inevitable. For much of American history, however, African Americans were prevented from joining the military, and when they did enlist they were segregated into black units. In 1940, of the nearly 170,000-man Navy, only 4,007, or 2.3 percent, were African American personnel. The vast majority of these men worked in the mess halls as stewards—or, as labeled by the black press, "seagoing bellhops." In this official document, the chairman of the General Board refers to compliance with a directive that would enlist African Americans into positions of "unlimited general service." Who issued the directive? What was the motivation behind the new directive? Who were the members of the General Board? How much authority did they wield? Why did the Navy restrict African Americans to the "messman branch"? Notice the use of the term "colored race." Why was this term used and what did it imply? What did the board conclude? When did the Navy become integrated? Who was primarily responsible for integrating the Navy?

CONFIDENTIAL

DOD Dir. 5200.10, June 29, 1960
NND by *FFB* date *Oct. 5, 1961*

SECRET

DOWNGRADED AT 3 YEAR INTERVALS.
DECLASSIFIED AFTER 12 YEARS
DOD DIR 5200.10 NARS-NT

G.B. No. 421
(Serial No. 201)
SECRET

Feb 3, 1942

From: Chairman General Board.
To: Secretary of the Navy.

Subject: Enlistment of men of colored race to other than
             Messman branch.

Ref: (a) SecNav let. (SC)P14-4/MM (03200A)/Gen of
             Jan 16, 1942.

   1.   The General Board, complying with the directive
contained in reference (a), has given careful attention to the
problem of enlisting in the Navy, men of the colored race
in other than the messman branch.

   2.   The General Board has endeavored to examine the
problem placed before it in a realistic manner.

A.   Should negroes be enlisted for unlimited general service?

        (a) Enlistment for general service implies that the
individual may be sent anywhere, - to any ship or station where
he is needed. Men on board ship live in particularly close
association; in their messes, one man sits beside another; their
hammocks or bunks are close together; in their common tasks they
work side by side; and in particular tasks such as those of a
gun's crew, they form a closely knit, highly coordinated team.
How many white men would choose, of their own accord, that their
closest associates in sleeping quarters, at mess, and in a gun's
crew should be of another race? How many would accept such
conditions, if required to do so, without resentment and just
as a matter of course? The General Board believes that the
answer is "Few, if any," and further believes that if the issue were
forced, there would be a lowering of contentment, teamwork
and discipline in the service.

        (b) One of the tennets of the recruiting service
is that each recruit for general service is potentially a leading
petty officer. It is true that some men never do become petty
officers, and that when recruiting white men, it is not possible
to establish which will be found worthy of and secure promotion
and which will not. If negroes are recruited for general service,
it can be said at once that few will obtain advancement to petty
officers. With every desire to be fair, officers and leading
petty officers in general will not recommend negroes for promotion
to positions of authority over white men.

DOWNGRADED AND
DECLASSIFIED

- 1 -

CONFIDENTIAL

The General Board is convinced that the enlistment of negroes for unlimited general service is unadvisable.

B.   Should negroes be enlisted in general service but detailed in special ratings or for special ships or units?

(a) The ratings now in use in the naval service cover every phase of naval activity, and no new ratings are deemed necessary merely to promote the enlistment of negroes.

(b) At first thought, it might appear that assignment of negroes to certain vessels, and in particular to small vessels of the patrol type, would be feasible. In this connection, the following table is of interest:

Type of Ship	Total Crew	Men in Pay Grades 1 to 4	Men in Pay Grades 5 to 7 (Non-rated)
Battleship	1892	666	1226
Light Cruiser (10,000 ton)	988	365	623
Destroyer (1630 ton)	206	109	97
Submarine	54	47	7
Patrol Boat (180 foot)	55	36	19
Patrol Boat (110 foot)	20	15	5

NOTE: Pay grades 1 to 4 include Chief Petty Officers and Petty Officers, 1st, 2nd and 3rd Class; also Firemen, 1st Class and a few other ratings requiring length of service and experience equal to that required for qualification of Petty Officers, 3rd class. Pay grades 5 to 7 include all other non-rated men and recruits.

There are no negro officers and so few negro petty officers in the Navy at present that any vessels to which negroes might be assigned must have white officers and white petty officers. Examination of the table shows the small number of men in other than petty officer ratings that might be assigned to patrol vessels and in-dicates to the General Board that such assignments would not be happy ones. The assignment of negroes to the larger ships, where well over one-half of the crews are non-rated men, with mixture of whites and negroes, would inevitably lead to discontent on the part of one or the other, resulting in clashes and lowering of the efficiency of the vessels and of the Navy.

- 2 -

CONFIDENTIAL

The material collected in these volumes of *American Decades Primary Sources* are significant because they will introduce students to a wide variety of historical sources that were created by those who participated in or witnessed the historical event. These primary sources not only vividly describe historical events, but also reveal the subjective perceptions and biases of their authors. Students should read these documents "actively," and with the contextual assistance of the introductory material, history will become relevant and entertaining.

—Paul G. Connors

Chronology of Selected World Events Outside the United States, 1990–1999

1990

- On January 1, Vaclav Havel, playwright and former dissident and prisoner of conscience, is sworn in as president of Czechoslovakia.

- On January 3, Panamanian president Manuel Noriega surrenders to American authorities who extradite him to the United States on charges of drug smuggling.

- On January 24, Japan launches the first probe sent to the Moon since 1976.

- In February, Canadian scientists discover 600-million-year-old fossils of multicellular animals, marine invertebrates.

- On February 2, President F.W. de Klerk of South Africa ends a thirty-year ban on the African National Congress (ANC).

- On February 7, the Central Committee of the Communist Party in the Soviet Union votes to end the Party's monopoly on political power.

- On February 11, South Africa releases Nelson Mandela after twenty-seven years in prison.

- On February 21, the Republic of Namibia becomes independent.

- On February 25, a U.S.-backed coalition under Violeta Chamorro wins elections in Nicaragua against Daniel Ortega's Sandinista government.

- On February 26, the Soviet Union agrees to withdraw its troops from Czechoslovakia within sixteen months.

- On March 11, Lithuania declares independence from the Union of Soviet Socialist Republics (U.S.S.R.).

- On March 11, Soviet troops begin to withdraw from Hungary.

- On March 15, Mikhail Gorbachev is sworn in as the first executive president of the U.S.S.R.

- On March 16, Dr. Jonathan Mann, director of the United Nations Global Program on AIDS, resigns over policy disputes with his boss, Dr. Hiroshi Nakajima of the World Health Organization (WHO).

- On March 24, voters return the Labour Party to office for a fourth time in the Australian general elections.

- On March 31, protestors riot and loot businesses in the West End after the police disperse an anti–poll tax demonstration in Trafalgar Square, London.

- On April 1, one thousand inmates riot in Strangeways Prison, Manchester, Britain.

- On April 1, Robert Mugabe wins the presidency in Zimbabwe.

- On April 13, the Soviet government admits responsibility and expresses regret for the 1940 massacre of Polish Army officers in the Katyn Forest near Moscow.

- On May 1, protesters jeer Mikhail Gorbachev at the May Day parade in Red Square, Moscow.

- On May 3, the North Atlantic Treaty Organization (NATO) agrees to admit Germany after its reunification.

- From May 4 to May 8, Latvia and Estonia declare independence from the U.S.S.R.

- On May 15, schools and hospitals in the United Kingdom ban home-produced beef in fear of "mad-cow disease" (bovine spongiform encephalopathy, or BSE).

- On May 20, voters give the National Salvation Front a majority and elect Ion Iliescu president in the first free elections in Romania since 1937.

- On May 22, North and South Yemen merge to form the Yemen Republic.

- On May 29, voters elect Boris Yeltsin president of the Russian Federation.

- On May 30, Alexander Solzhenitsyn receives the Russia State Literature Prize for *The Gulag Archipelago* (1974–1978).

- On June 1, U.S. president George Herbert Walker Bush and Soviet premier Mikhail Gorbachev sign a bilateral agreement to stop producing chemical weapons and to begin destroying stocks of agents by the end of 1992.

- On June 12, the Russian Federation declares independence from the U.S.S.R.

- On June 12, the fundamentalist Islamic Salvation Front wins a majority in Algerian local elections.

- On June 20, Uzbekistan declares independence from the U.S.S.R.

- On June 22, the Canadian provinces of Manitoba and Newfoundland reject the Meech Lake Accord recognizing Quebec as a "distinct society."

- On July 1, East Germany agrees to adopt West German economic and monetary policy.

- On July 8, Indian troops seize Kashmir following violence from those in Kashmir who want independence.

- On July 12, Boris Yeltsin and other reformers in the U.S.S.R. renounce their Communist Party membership.

- On July 16, the Ukrainian Parliament votes independence from the U.S.S.R.

- In August, Iraq invades Kuwait and the Emir flees to Saudi Arabia, raising fears that Iraq would control its and Kuwait's oil reserves.

- On August 1, Pope John Paul II consecrates the largest cathedral in the world in Yamoussoukro, Ivory Coast.

- On August 6, the United Nations (U.N.) Security Council imposes sanctions, including an oil embargo, against Iraq.

- On August 7, U.S. president George Herbert Walker Bush sends the first American troops to Saudi Arabia to prevent Iraq from invading it.

- On August 9, Iraq announces the annexation of Kuwait.

- On August 31, East and West Germany sign a reunification treaty.

- On September 12, the Soviet Union agrees to withdraw all troops from East Germany by 1994.

- In October, the Human Genome Project (HGP) begins to map all human genes on their respective chromosomes.

- On October 2, the German Democratic Republic ceases to exist at midnight, and East and West Germany unite as the Federal Republic of Germany.

- On October 27, the National Party led by James Bolgar defeats the Labour Party of New Zealand in elections.

- On October 27, the European Community (EC) Summit opens in Rome, Italy to discuss economic and monetary union by 1994.

- On October 28, non-communist candidates win elections in the Soviet republic of Georgia.

- On November 7, Mary Robinson becomes the first woman president of the Republic of Ireland.

- On November 27, John Major becomes leader of the British Conservative Party. The next day he replaces Margaret Thatcher as prime minister.

- On December 9, Lech Walesa wins the Polish presidential election.

- On December 9, voters elect Slobodan Milošović of the Serbian Socialist Party president of Serbia in the first free elections in fifty years.

- On December 16, Father Jean-Bertrand Aristide wins the first presidential election in Haiti.

- On December 23, more than 90 percent of voters in Slovenia endorse independence from Yugoslavia.

1991

- On January 16, a United States–led coalition begins an air offensive (Operation Desert Storm) to liberate Kuwait from Iraqi occupation and thereby end Iraqi control of Kuwait's oil reserves.

- On January 18, Iraq launches Scud missiles at Israel.

- On February 24, coalition troops in the Persian Gulf launch a ground offensive against Iraqi forces.

- In March, architects Robert Venturi and Denise Scott Brown complete their work on the Sainsbury Wing, National Gallery, London.

- On March 1, Basra and other Shi'ite cities of Iraq revolt against Sadam Hussein.

- On March 26, hikers discover the five-thousand-year-old remains of a man in the Italian Alps.

- On March 27, the United States begins to withdraw medium-range missiles from Europe.

- On April 9, the parliament of Soviet republic Georgia votes independence from the Soviet Union.

- On April 30, Kurdish refugees in northern Iraq begin to move into Western-protected havens.

- On May 15, Edith Cresson becomes the first woman prime minister of France.

- On May 18, chemist Helen Sharman is the first Briton to go into space, as a participant in a Soviet space mission.

- On May 21, a Tamil extremist assassinates Rajiv Gandhi, son of Indira Gandhi and grandson of Jawaharlal Nehru.

- On May 31, President Dos Santos and Jonas Savimbi, leader of União Nacional para a Independência Total de Angola (UNITA), sign a peace agreement in Lisbon, Portugal, ending the Angolan civil war.

- In June, South Africa rescinds the Land Acts, Group Areas Act, and 1950 Population Registration Act, which had taken land from blacks and segregated them from whites.

- On June 5, President Mikhail Gorbachev of the U.S.S.R. delivers his Nobel Peace Prize lecture.

- On June 25, the republics of Croatia and Slovenia declare independence from Yugoslavia.

- In July, the discovery of fraud and involvement in organized crime, arms dealing, and the drug trade collapses the Bank of Credit and Commerce International.

- On July 1, the Warsaw Pact dissolves.

- On July 31, President George H. W. Bush and President Mikhail Gorbachev sign the Strategic Arms Reduction

Treaty (START) to reduce arsenals of long-range nuclear weapons by one-third.

• On August 8, terrorists release British journalist John McCarthy after 1,943 days of captivity in Lebanon.

• On August 14, scientists report that a worldwide band of volcanic dust from the eruptions of Mount Pinatubo (June/July 1991) in the Philippines could temporarily cool the climate worldwide.

• On August 19, Gennady Yanayev leads communist hardliners in a coup against President Gorbachev and put him under house arrest in the Crimea.

• From August 20 to August 21, Estonia and Latvia declare independence from the Soviet Union.

• On August 21, a military coup to restore communism in the U.S.S.R. collapses following widespread resistance led by Boris Yeltsin.

• On August 24, Mikhail Gorbachev resigns as First Secretary of the Communist Party of the Soviet Union.

• On August 27, Serbian forces take the Croatian city of Vukovar after an eighty-six-day siege.

• On August 30, Azerbaijan declares independence from the Soviet Union.

• On September 6, the Soviet Union recognizes the independence of Latvia, Lithuania, and Estonia.

• On September 8, Macedonia declares independence from Yugoslavia.

• On September 11, researchers announce the discovery of a gene responsible for mental retardation.

• On September 22, Armenia declares independence from the Soviet Union.

• On September 25, an eleven-year civil war in El Salvador ends with the signing of a peace accord.

• On October 19, Albanian legislators declare Kosovo independent from Yugoslavia.

• On December 5, debt and rumors of misappropriated pension funds collapse the business empire of Robert Maxwell.

• On December 8, the leaders of Russia, Belarus, and the Ukraine agree to form the Commonwealth of Independent States.

• From December 9 to December 10, European Community leaders agree to strengthen economic and political ties at a summit in Maastricht, Holland.

• On December 25, Mikhail Gorbachev resigns as president of the Soviet Union, and the U.S.S.R. ceases to exist.

1992

• On January 1, Boutros Boutros-Ghali becomes U.N. Secretary-General.

• On January 15, the European Community recognizes Croatia and Slovenia as independent republics.

• On February 6, Barbara Mills becomes the first woman Director of Public Prosecutions in England and Wales.

• On February 13, Sweden ends its policy of neutrality.

• On March 1, although Bosnian Serbs boycott the proceedings, a referendum in Bosnia-Herzegovina declares independence from Yugoslavia.

• On March 2, Serbs, Croats, and Muslims clash in Sarajevo.

• On March 5, the Council of Baltic Sea States is established to foster economic development and strengthen links with the EC.

• On March 6, a computer virus called "Michelangelo" strikes thousands of personal computers around the world.

• On March 19, Buckingham Palace announces the separation of the Duke and Duchess of York, who had married in 1986.

• On April 6, the Lombard League, the Greens, and the anti-Mafia La Rete Party win the Italian general elections.

• On April 7, the EC recognizes the independence of Bosnia-Herzegovina.

• On April 8, Serb and Yugoslav troops begin to shell Sarajevo.

• On April 9, voters return the Conservatives to power for a fourth term in a British general election.

• On April 27, voters elect Betty Boothroyd the first woman speaker of the British House of Commons.

• On June 9, the largest environmental summit opens in Rio de Janeiro, Brazil, with representatives from 178 nations.

• On August 3, the African National Congress (ANC) demands equality for blacks in South Africa.

• On August 13, the U.N. condemns the Serbs' "ethnic cleansing" (forced removal) program.

• In September, American pharmaceutical firm Merck agrees to pay the Costa Rican National Institute of Biodiversity (*El Instituto Nacional de Biodiversidad,* or INBio) $1 million over two years for the right to search for new drugs in the tropical forests of Costa Rica.

• On September 16, British Chancellor of the Exchequer, Norman Lamont, increases the base rate of the pound.

• On October 12, demonstrators in many Latin American countries protest the five-hundredth anniversary of Christopher Columbus's discovery of America.

• On October 13, despite a huge public outcry, Britain announces an end to coal production at thirty-one of its fifty coal mines.

• On October 31, the Vatican apologies for condeming astronomer and physicist Galileo Galilei in 1633 for advocating heliocentrism, the idea that the Sun rather than Earth is the center of our solar system.

• On November 11, the Church of England General Synod approves the ordination of women priests.

• On November 16, the Goldstone Commission in South Africa exposes a state-operated campaign to discredit the ANC and thereby deny blacks a voice in political and economic affairs.

• In December, the Anglican Church ordains ten Australian women priests despite a ruling by a court of appeals.

• On December 6, Hindu extremists destroy the sixteenth-century mosque at Ayodhya, India.

- On December 9, Operation Restore Hope begins with the arrival of U.S. troops in Mogadishu, Somalia, to supervise the delivery of food to famished Somalians.
- On December 16, the Czech National Council adopts a constitution, effective January 1, 1993.

1993

- Samples of deoxyribonucleic acid (DNA) from the Duke of Edinburgh and other relatives of the Romanov family prove that recently discovered remains are of Czar Nicholas II and his family, whom Bolsheviks executed in 1918.
- On January 1, the countries of the European Community begin operating as a single market.
- On January 1, the Czech and Slovak republics become separate countries.
- On January 3, Russian president Boris Yeltsin and U.S. president George H. W. Bush sign the Start II Treaty to eliminate two-thirds of nuclear weapons in their nations.
- On February 7, Russian authorities announce that they possess the Schliemann Gold, objects found by Heinrich Schliemann at the ancient city of Troy in 1873 and which disappeared from Berlin at the end of World War II.
- On February 11, both Queen Elizabeth II of Britain and the Prince of Wales volunteer to pay income tax and capital gains tax on their private incomes.
- On February 22, the U.N. Security Council creates a tribunal to prosecute war crimes in the former Yugoslavia.
- On February 25, Cubans vote for the first time in elections to the national assembly.
- On March 12, the Russian Congress in an emergency session restricts Boris Yeltsin's powers and rejects his constitutional amendments.
- On March 12, North Korea withdraws from the Treaty on Nuclear Non-Proliferation of Nuclear Weapons.
- On March 16, Britain imposes a value-added tax on domestic fuel in hopes of spurring Britons to conserve fuel.
- On March 27, Jiang Zemin becomes president of China.
- On March 29, Edouard Balladur becomes the prime minister of France, and the Socialist Party loses seats in the national legislature.
- On April 30, the European Organization for Nuclear Research (CERN, *Conseil European pour la Recherché Nucleaire*) announces that the World Wide Web will be free for everyone.
- On May 4, the Scott inquiry begins to examine Britain's export of arms to Iraq.
- On May 6, the U.N. Security Council declares "safe areas" in Sarajevo, Tuzla, Zepa, Goradze, Bihac, and Srebrenica in Bosnia-Herzegovina.
- On May 29, a Neo-Nazi arson attack in Solingen, Germany, kills five Turkish women.
- On May 30, sculptor Rachel Whiteread receives the Turner Prize for *House,* a plaster cast of the inside of a house in London's East End.
- On May 30, Bosnian Serb forces attack Goradze and Srebrenica.

- On June 13, Kim Campbell of the Progressive Conservative Party becomes the first woman prime minister of Canada.
- On June 23, the United Nations imposes sanctions on Haiti.
- In July, British mathematician Andrew Wiles solves "Fermat's Last Theorem."
- On July 18, the Liberal Democrats, in power since 1955, lose the Japanese general elections.
- In August, the Vatican, after fifteen years of refusal, allows scientists to test a tiny portion of the Shroud of Turin in Turin, Italy for the rate at which the isotope carbon fourteen decayed into carbon twelve. The test dates the shroud to 1300 C.E., proving that it could not have been the burial shroud of Jesus.
- On August 2, the European Exchange Rate Mechanism collapses, and currencies fluctuate within 15 percent of the central rates.
- On August 6, Buckingham Palace in London opens to the public.
- In September, an international research team, led by Daniel Cohen of the Center for the Study of Human Polymorphisms (*Centre d'Etude du Polymorphisme Humain* or CEPH) in Paris, produces a map plotting some genes on all twenty-three pairs of human chromosomes.
- On September 6, Canadian Peter de Jager warns in *Computerworld* that computers with a binary code for the year may not function when 2000 begins.
- On September 13, Yasser Arafat of the Palestine Liberation Organization (PLO) and Yitzhak Rabin of Israel sign a peace accord in Washington, D.C.
- On September 21, Boris Yeltsin suspends the Russian parliament and calls for elections, but the Supreme Soviet ignores his order and swears in Alexandr Rutskoi as president.
- On September 27, troops seal off the White House in Moscow, the seat of the Russian parliament.
- In October, the Swedish Royal Academy awards the Nobel Peace Prize to Nelson Mandela and Frederik W. de Klerk for dismantling apartheid in South Africa.
- On October 3, U.S. Special Forces, on a mission to capture two Habr Gidr clan leaders, followers of the warlord Mohamed Farrah Aidid, are ambushed in Mogadishu, Somalia.
- On October 4, the rebels holding out in the Moscow parliament building surrender.
- On October 5, the Vatican releases the Papal encyclical *Veritatis splendor* (The Splendour of Truth), affirming Catholic moral teachings.
- On October 25, the Liberal Party wins Canadian general elections.
- On November 1, the Maastricht Treaty transforms the European Community into the European Union (EU).
- On December 12, Liberal Democrats, led by nationalist Vladimir Zhirinovsky, win a large share of seats in the Russian legislature.
- On November 18, South Africa adopts a new constitution allowing majority rule.

• On December 15, John Major and Albert Reynolds, the prime ministers of Britain and the Republic of Ireland, respectively, make the Downing Street Declaration, the basis for a peace agreement in Northern Ireland.

• On December 15, in Geneva, Switzerland, 117 nations sign the General Agreement on Tariffs and Trade (GATT), a move toward free trade.

1994

• The cleaning of Michelangelo's paintings in the Sistine Chapel in the Vatican reveals the vivid colors Michelangelo had used.

• On January 1, the Zapatista National Liberation Army leads a revolt in Chiapas, Mexico, where peasants support the army.

• On January 1, the United States, Mexico, and Canada begin trading under the North American Free Trade Agreement (NAFTA), which, like GATT, lowers tariffs.

• On January 1, the European Union establishes the European Economic Area in preparation for economic and monetary union in Europe.

• On January 30, Peter Leko becomes the youngest chess grandmaster to date.

• On January 31, Britain grants Gerry Adams, president of Sinn Féin, the political wing of the IRA, a visa to visit the United States.

• On February 11, five astronauts and a cosmonaut return to Earth aboard *Discovery* after the first joint U.S.-Russian space shuttle mission.

• On February 15, North Korea ends a year-long standoff with the International Atomic Energy Agency (IAEA), allowing inspectors to check seven nuclear plants.

• On March 18, Bosnia-Herzegovina and Croatia sign an accord to create a federation of Bosnian Muslims and Croats.

• On March 12, the Church of England ordains the first women priests at Bristol Cathedral.

• On March 24, the factions in Somalia sign a peace agreement.

• From March 26 to March 27, the Freedom Alliance wins parliamentary elections in Italy.

• In April, the presidents of Rwanda and Burundi die in an airplane crash.

• From April 26 to April 29, the African National Congress (ANC) wins the first election in which blacks may vote in South Africa.

• On May 6, the Channel Tunnel between Britain and France opens. The tunnel links Britain and France by a road beneath the English Channel.

• On May 10, Nelson Mandela, who has spent his life crusading for the rights of blacks, is sworn in as president of South Africa.

• On May 12, John Smith, leader of the British Labour Party, dies. Tony Blair replaces him on July 21.

• On May 13, the Palestinian National Authority assumes control of the part of Jericho in the occupied West Bank after Israeli troops withdraw.

• On May 27, Russian novelist and Nobel laureate Alexander Solzhenitsyn returns to Russia after twenty years in exile.

• On June 1, South Africa rejoins the British Commonwealth.

• On June 5, former U.S. president Jimmy Carter visits North Korea to diffuse a crisis over nuclear inspections.

• On July 1, Yasser Arafat, chairman of the PLO, enters Gaza for the first time in twenty-five years.

• On July 2, Colombian soccer player Andrés Escobar is killed in Medellín. Escobar had inadvertently scored a goal against his own team in the game that eliminated Colombia from the World Cup.

• On July 9, China announces an end to the legislative council in Hong Kong when China resumes control of the city in 1997.

• On July 12, the high court in Germany approves the use of German troops outside NATO countries in collective security operations.

• On July 15, Jacques Santer, prime minister of Luxembourg, becomes president of the European Commission of the EU.

• From July 16 to July 22, fragments of the comet Shoemaker-Levy 9 collide with the planet Jupiter.

• On July 18, the Rwandan Patriotic Front claims victory in the Rwandan civil war.

• On July 25, in a ceremony in Washington, D.C., King Hussein of Jordan and Prime Minister Yitzhak Rabin of Israel sign a declaration ending war between their countries.

• On July 31, the U.N. Security Council authorizes "all necessary means" to remove the military regime in Haiti.

• On August 1, the U.N. establishes a commission to investigate human rights violations in Rwanda.

• On August 14, police arrest terrorist "Carlos the Jackal" in Khartoum, Sudan.

• On August 31, the IRA announces an end to violence in Northern Ireland.

• On September 19, American troops invade Haiti.

• On September 28, nine hundred people die when the car ferry *Estonia* sinks in the Baltic Sea off Finland.

• On September 30, Russian president Boris Yeltsin, after landing at Shannon airport, refuses to leave his plane and meet with the Irish prime minister.

• In October, the Swedish Royal Academy awards the Nobel Peace Prize to Yasser Arafat, Shimon Peres, and Yitzhak Rabin.

• On October 15, President Jean Baptiste Aristide returns to Haiti after three years in exile.

• From November 25 to November 26, opposition forces attack the Chechen capital of Grozny.

• On November 28, Norway rejects EU membership.

• On December 11, Russian troops invade the breakaway republic of Chechnya.

• On December 17, the presidents of Argentina, Brazil, Paraguay, and Uruguay sign a pact creating the Southern Common Market (Mercosur), the second-largest customs union in the world.

• On December 31, Russian troops attack Grozny.

1995

- On January 1, Sweden, Finland, and Austria join the EU, bringing its membership to fifteen.

- On January 1, the World Trade Organization (WTO), the successor to GATT, comes into existence with eighty-one member countries.

- On January 11, Pope John Paul II begins an eleven-day tour of Asia and Australia.

- On January 17, an earthquake in Kobe, Japan, kills more than five thousand people.

- On January 19, Russian troops capture the presidential palace in Grozny.

- On January 31, floods inundate northern Europe.

- On February 26, Britain's oldest merchant bank, Baring's, collapses following £600 million in losses.

- On February 28, U.S. and Italian marines begin to evacuate fifteen hundred U.N. troops from Somalia after warring factions refuse to cease fire.

- On March 10, Kostas Stephanopoulos is sworn in as president of Greece.

- On March 19, the Social Democratic Party wins the Finnish general elections.

- On March 20, terrorists release the nerve gas sarin in a Tokyo, Japan, subway, killing twelve and injuring five thousand.

- On March 27, South African president Nelson Mandela dismisses his estranged wife, Winnie, from the government.

- On March 28, delegates from more than 130 nations attend the U.N. World Climate Conference in Berlin, Germany.

- On April 4, Burundi soldiers and Tutsi gunmen kill four hundred Hutu women and children in Rwanda.

- On April 16, Spain and Canada resolve their dispute over fishing rights off the coast of Newfoundland.

- On April 22, the Tutsi-led Rwanda Patriotic Army kills two thousand Hutu refugees at a camp in southern Rwanda.

- On May 1, a four-month United Nations cease-fire expires in Bosnia-Herzegovina, and fighting resumes in Croatia.

- On May 10, in Zaire, health officials report an outbreak of Ebola virus.

- On May 15, police arrest Aum Shinrikyo cult leader Shoko Asahara for the March gas attack in a Tokyo subway.

- On May 16, Serb artillery begins to shell Sarajevo.

- On May 19, the government coalition in Thailand, led by Chuan Leekpai, resigns over a land reform scandal.

- On May 21, Jean-Luc Dehaene retains control of the Belgian government following general elections.

- On May 25, NATO warplanes bomb Bosnian Serb targets after the Serbs refuse to surrender their heavy weapons to peacekeeping forces.

- From May 30 to May 31, the Prince of Wales tours the Republic of Ireland, the first royal visit since 1911.

- From June 2 to June 18, Bosnian Serbs release their U.N. hostages.

- On June 15, an earthquake in Egion, Greece, kills at least twenty-two people and leaves thousands homeless.

- On June 19, Chechen gunmen release Russian hostages in hopes of resuming negotiations with Moscow to end the six-month war in Chechnya.

- On June 29, a department store collapses in Seoul, South Korea, killing five hundred.

- On July 9, French naval commandos storm *Rainbow Warrior II,* flagship of the environmental group Greenpeace, near Mururoa Atoll in the South Pacific, where France planned nuclear testing.

- On July 11, Bosnian Serbs overrun the U.N. safe area of Srebrenica.

- On July 25, the U.N. safe area of Zepa falls to the Bosnian Serbs.

- On July 26, the U.S. Senate votes to lift an arms embargo against Bosnia at the risk of escalating the war.

- In August, Croat troops expel Serbs from the Croatian enclave of Krajina.

- On August 3, Sri Lanka gives the Tamils self-rule in hopes of ending twelve years of civil war.

- On August 10, the U.N. Security Council learns of the massacre of twenty-seven hundred Bosnian Muslim men and boys after the fall of Srebrenica in July.

- On August 15, the fiftieth anniversary of the end of World War II, the Japanese prime minister offers a "heartfelt apology" for the suffering Japan caused.

- On August 24, a Chinese court sentences U.S. human rights activist Harry Wu to fifteen years in jail for spying.

- On August 30, NATO planes and U.N. artillery begin to strike Serb positions in retaliation for attacks on Sarajevo.

- On September 1, factions in Liberia sign a peace agreement to end six years of civil war.

- On September 4, more than five thousand delegates attend the fourth U.N. World Conference on Women in Beijing, China.

- On September 5, France carries out an underground nuclear test at Mururoa Atoll despite international fears that other nations might respond by accelerating their nuclear arms programs.

- On September 28, Israeli prime minister Yitzhak Rabin and PLO chairman Yasser Arafat sign an accord in Washington, D.C., transferring much of the West Bank to Palestinian control.

- On October 12, a sixty-day cease-fire begins in Bosnia.

- On October 21, leaders of more than 140 countries gather in New York City to celebrate the fiftieth anniversary of the U.N.

- On October 25, Israel begins withdrawing troops from West Bank towns.

- On October 30, Quebec voters reject independence from Canada.

- On November 4, a Jewish extremist assassinates Israeli prime minister Yitzhak Rabin at a peace rally in Tel Aviv.

- On November 5, voters reelect Eduard Shevardnadze president of the former Soviet republic of Georgia.

- On November 19, Socialist Aleksander Kwasniewski wins the Polish presidential election.

- On November 21, warring parties sign in Dayton, Ohio an agreement to end four years of war in Bosnia-Herzegovina.

- On November 24, French public workers begin a series of strikes to protest welfare cuts.

- On December 2, Nick Leeson begins a six-year prison sentence in Singapore after pleading guilty to fraud relating to the February collapse of Baring's Bank.

- On December 14, the presidents of Bosnia, Serbia, and Croatia sign a peace accord in Paris, France, ending a war that claimed two hundred thousand lives and left three million homeless.

- From December 15 to December 16, European leaders agree at an EU summit in Madrid, Spain to name the single currency the "Euro."

- On December 20, sixty thousand NATO peacekeepers begin Operation Joint Endeavor to monitor the peace agreement in Bosnia.

- On December 20, reports reveal that Islamic Taleban militia killed thousands in two months of fighting around Kabul, Afghanistan in an attempt to overthrow the government.

1996

- On January 15, Russian troops storm the village of Pervomaiskoye, where Chechen rebels held more than one hundred hostages for a week.

- On January 16, Captain Julius Maado Bio seizes the government in Sierra Leone.

- On January 21, Palestinians elect PLO chairman Yasser Arafat the first president of Palestine.

- On January 29, fire destroys the two-hundred-year-old La Fenice opera house in Venice, Italy.

- On January 31, Tamil Tiger terrorists detonate a truck bomb in central Colombo, Sri Lanka, killing fifty-five and wounding fifteen hundred.

- On February 7, one hundred and eighty-nine people die when a Boeing 757 crashes off the coast of the Dominican Republic.

- On February 9, an IRA bomb kills two in London, ending a seventeen-month cease-fire.

- On February 24, Cuba shoots down two unarmed Cessna planes flown by Cuban Americans, killing four.

- On February 25, two suicide bombers of Hamas, a Palestinian terrorist group, kill twenty-five Israelis in Jerusalem and Ashkelon.

- On March 8, China test fires three M9 ballistic missiles into the sea off Taiwan.

- On March 25, the EU imposes a worldwide ban on exports of British beef amid an outbreak of "mad cow" disease.

- On March 31, President Boris Yeltsin announces a cease-fire and partial withdrawal of Russian troops from Chechnya.

- On April 2, Britain announces the slaughter of 4.6 million cattle in an attempt to end the spread of "mad cow" disease.

- On April 6, government troops in Liberia attack rebel leader General Roosevelt Johnson's compound.

- On April 11, Israeli gunships fire rockets into the southern suburbs of Beirut, Lebanon in their first attack on the city in fourteen years in retaliation for Hizbullah attacks on northern Israel.

- On May 21, six hundred people die when an overloaded Tanzanian ferry sinks on Lake Victoria.

- On May 29, the Likud Party, which rejects any concessions to Palestinians, wins the general elections in Israel.

- On June 4, the *Ariane 5,* a European Space Agency rocket, explodes on liftoff in French Guiana.

- On June 9, King Bhumibol of Thailand, the longest-serving monarch in the world, celebrates fifty years on the throne by granting amnesty to twenty-six thousand prisoners.

- On June 15, an IRA bomb, one of the largest exploded in Britain, injures about 220 people in Manchester, England.

- On June 18, President Yeltsin of Russia dismisses Defense Minister General Pavel Grachev and other hardliners.

- From June 21 to June 23, the Arab League discusses how Arab nations might respond to the election of the Likud Party in Israel.

- On June 25, nineteen U.S. servicemen die in a terrorist bombing near Dhahran, Saudi Arabia.

- On July 4, a bomb explodes on a commuter train in Colombo, Sri Lanka, killing seventy and wounding 450.

- On July 10, Britain sends one thousand troops to Northern Ireland in response to renewed violence.

- On July 19, Bosnian Serb leader Radovan Karadžić, indicted for war crimes, resigns as president of the Bosnian Serb Republic and head of the ruling Serb Democratic Party.

- On July 20, Hutu rebels kill three hundred Tutsis in Burundi in retaliation against the Tutsi slaughter of Hutus in Rwanda.

- On July 25, Tutsi opposition leader Pierre Buyoya, in a military coup, seizes power in Burundi.

- On July 25, Israeli Prime Minister Benjamin Netanyahu offers to withdraw troops from southern Lebanon if Syria will disarm Hizbullah, a terrorist organization.

- On August 21, former president F. W. de Klerk apologizes for the suffering whites caused blacks in five decades of apartheid in South Africa.

- On August 28, a British high court grants a divorce to Charles, Prince of Wales, and Lady Diana, Princess of Wales, ending their fifteen-year marriage.

- On August 29, Russian officials and Chechen rebel leaders sign a peace treaty, ending nearly two years of fighting which killed ninety thousand.

- On September 4, Israeli Prime Minister Benjamin Netanyahu and PLO leader Yasser Arafat hold peace talks for the first time in the Gaza Strip.

- On September 5, Turkish war planes attack rebel Kurd bases in northern Iraq.

- On September 26, Israel declares a state of emergency after the worst fighting in thirty years in the West Bank and Gaza Strip.

- On September 27, the Taleban, a group Islamic extremists, overruns Kabul, deposes the government, and imposes repressive Islamic law in Afghanistan.

- On October 17, President Boris Yeltsin of Russia dismisses security chief General Aleksandr Lebed amid allegations that he was plotting a revolt.

- On October 23, Hutu refugees begin to flee from Zaire to escape fighting between the army and Tutsi tribesmen.

- On November 11, a Saudi Arabian Boeing 747 and Kazakh Airways Ilyushin-76 collide in midair above Delhi, India, killing 350 people.

- From November 18 to November 29, French truckers block roads across France until France grants them higher wages and shorter hours.

- On November 28, General Ratko Mladić, charged with war crimes, resigns as commander of the Bosnian Serb Army.

- On December 11, China names shipping tycoon Tung Chee-hwa chief executive of Hong Kong when China reclaims the city from Britain in 1997.

- On December 13, delegates at the EU summit in Dublin, Ireland, agree to new banknotes of currency in denominations of five, ten, twenty, fifty, one hundred, two hundred, and five hundred Euros.

- On December 17, leftist guerrillas of the Tupac Amarú Revolutionary Movement, demanding the release of their jailed comrades, seize nearly five hundred hostages at the Japanese embassy in Lima, Peru.

- On December 26, five thousand riot police break up an antigovernment demonstration in Belgrade, Serbia.

- On December 27, China and Russia sign an agreement in Moscow to reduce troops along the Sino-Russian border.

- On December 29, the last Russian troops leave Chechnya.

- On December 29, the Guatemalan National Revolutionary Unity (URNG) Movement and the government sign a peace agreement in Guatemala City ending thirty-six years of civil war.

1997

- J.K. Rowling publishes the children's book *Harry Potter and the Philosopher's Stone* in Britain.

- On January 1, a lone Israeli gunman injures six Arabs as Israeli troops prepare to withdraw from the West Bank town of Hebron.

- On January 1, Kofi Annan of Ghana becomes the seventh Secretary-General of the United Nations, replacing Boutros Boutros-Ghali.

- On January 5, more than one hundred thousand people protest against the government in Belgrade, Serbia.

- On January 15, Israeli and Palestinian cabinets approve an agreement in which Israel will return 80 percent of Hebron to Palestinian control.

- On February 4, seventy-three Israeli servicemen die when two helicopters crash near the southern border of Lebanon.

- On February 5, the Swiss government establishes bank funds to compensate Holocaust victims and their heirs.

- On February 12, an Iranian foundation increases the bounty for killing Salman Rushdie, author of *The Satanic Verses* (1989), to $2.5 million.

- In March, the Hale-Bopp comet comes within 122 million miles of Earth.

- On March 2, Albanian leaders declare a state of emergency as antigovernment protests increase.

- On March 6, the Polish shipyard Gdansk, the birthplace of the Solidarity Movement, closes with the loss of thirty-eight hundred jobs.

- On March 11, Russian President Boris Yeltsin dismisses most of his cabinet.

- On March 13, a Jordanian soldier kills seven Israeli schoolgirls at the Hill of Peace in the Jordan Valley.

- On March 19, Italy declares a state of emergency as ten thousand Albanian refugees inundate the country.

- On March 30, riots injure dozens in the West Bank following Israel's decision to build thirty-two thousand Jewish homes in east Jerusalem.

- On April 22, Peruvian commandos rescue the remaining seventy-one hostages held by leftist guerrillas for 126 days at the residence of the Japanese ambassador in Lima.

- On May 2, Tony Blair, at age forty-three, becomes the youngest prime minister in Britain since 1812 after a victory by the Labour Party the previous day.

- On May 7, the United States accuses Switzerland of accepting gold looted by the Nazis from occupied countries during World War II.

- On May 10, an earthquake in Iran, near the Afghan border, kills sixteen hundred people.

- On May 11, the IBM supercomputer Deep Blue makes chess history by defeating Russian Garry Kasparov, the first time a computer beats a reigning world champion.

- On May 17, President Mobutu of Zaire flees to Morocco after thirty-two years in power.

- On May 30, four hundred Westerners evacuate Sierra Leone as fighting intensifies between rebel forces and Nigerian-backed government troops.

- From June 23 to June 27, eighty-five heads of state attend Earth Summit II at the United Nations in New York City to discuss environmental issues.

- On June 30, at midnight Hong Kong returns to Chinese sovereignty after 156 years as a British colony.

- In July, Scottish scientist Ian Wilmut at the Roslin Institute in Scotland announces the cloning of a sheep named Dolly.

- On July 6, a coup topples Cambodian prime minister Prince Norodom Ranariddh.

- On July 8, NATO invites Poland, Hungary, and the Czech Republic to join the alliance in time for its fiftieth anniversary in 1999.

- On July 10, British soldiers shoot an indicted war criminal and arrest another in Bosnia.

- On July 11, a team of U.S. and German molecular biologists announces that Neanderthal DNA is too dissimilar to our DNA for Neanderthal to be our ancestor.

- On July 15, voters elect Serbian leader Slobodan Milosević; president of the Federal Republic of Yugoslavia for a four-year term.

- On July 16, President Jacques Santer of the EU Commission proposes to expand the EU to twenty-one nations.

- On July 20, the IRA announces restoration of the 1994 cease-fire broken last February.

- On July 25, a Khmer Rouge people's tribunal sentences former leader Pol Pot to life imprisonment for ordering the death of two million Cambodians during the 1970s.

- On August 5, a Korean Air Boeing 747 crashes on the U.S. protectorate of Guam, killing 220.

- On August 31, Diana, Princess of Wales, dies in a car crash in Paris.

- On September 13, dignitaries from around the world attend the state funeral in Calcutta, India, of Mother Teresa, who died on September 5.

- On September 25, Briton Andy Green reaches 714 mph, a record, in the jet-powered car *Thrust SSC* in the Nevada desert. On October 17 he becomes the first person to break the sound barrier on land, reaching 764.18 mph.

- On September 26, an earthquake in Italy kills eleven, leaves thousands homeless, and damages the thirteenth-century Basilica of St. Francis.

- On October 1, Israel frees the ailing Shaikh Ahmad Yasin, founder of Palestinian terrorist group Hamas, from jail in exchange for Israeli agents detained in Jordan.

- On October 2, scientists deliberately freeze their ship, the Canadian icebreaker *Des Groseilliers,* into the Arctic ice for a yearlong study of weather changes in the Arctic.

- On October 8, Kim Jong II, son of the late Kim II Sung, becomes the general secretary of the ruling Workers' Party in North Korea.

- On October 9, four hundred Mexicans die when hurricane Pauline strikes the Pacific resort of Acapulco.

- On October 13, Tony Blair meets with Sinn Féin leader Gerry Adams.

- On October 22, President Nelson Mandela of South Africa travels to Tripoli, Libya, to mediate a dispute between Libya and the United States and Britain over extradition of two Libyans suspected of the 1988 Lockerbie bombing over Scotland.

- On November 8, Chinese leaders attend the completion of a dam on the River Yangtse, one of the world's largest hydroelectric projects.

- On November 9, Russia and China sign a declaration defining their joint 2,800-mile border.

- On November 24, Yamaichi Securities collapses with a loss of 3.2 billion yen, the biggest financial failure in Japan since 1945.

- On December 4, delegates from 125 nations at a U.N. conference in Ottawa, Canada, sign an agreement banning the use, production, transfer, and stockpiling of antipersonnel landmines.

- On December 10, representatives of industrial nations pledge at the U.N. Conference on Climate Control in Kyoto, Japan to reduce carbon dioxide emissions by the early twenty-first century in an effort to slow global warming.

- On December 11, in a ceremony at Portsmouth, England, the royal yacht *Britannica* is decommissioned after forty-five years of service.

- On December 22, paramilitary gunmen kill forty-five peasants in southern Mexico.

- On December 30, Islamic militants massacre 412 people in the Algerian province of Relizan.

1998

- On January 5, Amnesty International, a human-rights agency, reports that more than eighty thousand people had died from fighting in Algeria since 1992.

- On January 25, Tamil Tigers bomb Sri Lanka'a holiest shrine, the Temple of the Tooth in Kandy, killing eleven.

- On January 28, an Indian court sentences twenty-six people to death for the 1991 assassination of Rajiv Gandhi, former prime minister, son of Indira Gandhi, and grandson of Jawaralal Nehru.

- On February 3, a U.S. military jet accidentally cuts a wire supporting a cable car at an Italian ski resort. Twenty people fall to their death.

- On February 4, an earthquake kills four thousand people in northern Afghanistan.

- On February 13, a constitutional convention in Australia votes to hold a referendum on ending its participation in the British Commonwealth.

- On February 16, a Taiwanese A-300 Airbus crashes on approach to Taipei, killing 260 people.

- On February 23, U.N. Secretary-General Kofi Annan and Iraqi leaders agree to give U.N. weapons inspectors unrestricted access to all sites in Iraq.

- On February 25, Kim Dae Jung is inaugurated as president of South Korea.

- On February 26, the last total solar eclipse of the millennium is visible from the Western Hemisphere.

- On March 2, Serb police disperse fifty thousand Albanians who petition for autonomy in Pristina, the capital of Kosovo.

- On March 25, the European Commission announces that eleven states will join the monetary union and that the commission will issue the Euro single currency in January 1999.

- On April 1, the Israeli cabinet votes to withdraw troops from southern Lebanon.

- On April 2, a court sentences former French cabinet minister Maurice Papon to ten years in jail for his deportation of Jews to Nazi concentration camps in World War II.

- On April 24, Rwanda executes twenty-two men and women for their part in the 1994 massacres.

- On April 27, Serb police and the Yugoslav Army invade the province of Kosovo to suppress the separatist Kosovo Liberation Army.

- On May 11, India conducts three underground nuclear weapons tests in the Rajasthan desert despite Western threats of international sanctions.

- On May 14, Israeli forces kill eight Palestinians who were attacking Jewish settlements in the Gaza Strip.

- On May 21, following nationwide protests, General Suharto resigns as president of Indonesia after thirty-two years in power.

- On May 30, a second earthquake kills three thousand people in northern Afghanistan.

- On June 4, space shuttle *Discovery* docks with Russian space station *Mir* to collect astronaut Andrew Thomas after he spends four months aboard *Mir*.

- On June 12, world stock markets slump in response to news that Japan is in recession.

- On June 12, Queen Margrethe of Denmark opens the four-mile Storebaelt Bridge between eastern and western Denmark. It is the world's second-longest suspension bridge.

- On June 15, NATO aircraft stage Operation Falcon through Albania and Macedonia, warning Serbia to stop attacks in Kosovo.

- On June 16, the World Bank warns that Japan's recession may spread throughout Asia.

- On June 16, a cyclone kills thirteen hundred in northern India.

- On July 2, the world's largest terminal opens at the Chek Lap Kok Airport in Hong Kong.

- On July 10, floods in the Chinese province of Sichuan kill six hundred.

- On July 17, a tidal wave kills three thousand in Papua New Guinea.

- On July 17, Russia holds a state funeral in St. Petersburg, Russia, for internment of the remains of Czar Nicholas II, his family, and servants, whom Bolsheviks executed in 1918.

- On August 3, Serbian forces burn Albanian towns in Kosovo.

- On August 5, Iraq urges the U.N. to end the oil embargo and to withdraw its weapons inspectors.

- On August 7, a car bomb explodes outside the U.S. embassy in Nairobi, Kenya, killing at least 240 and injuring five thousand.

- On August 11, British Petroleum announces the purchase of U.S. oil company Amoco, the biggest industrial merger to date.

- On August 13, Swiss banks agree to pay £767 million ($1.25 billion) to victims of the Holocaust whose assets the Nazis had stolen.

- On August 15, an IRA car bomb kills twenty-eight and injures two hundred in Omagh, County Tyrone, in Northern Ireland.

- On August 20, the United States launches cruise missiles on terrorist bases in Afghanistan and on a chemical weapons plant in Sudan in retaliation for the August 7 attacks on U.S. embassies in East Africa.

- On August 24, Britain and the United States propose a trial in the Netherlands for the two Libyans accused of bombing a Pan Am airplane over Lockerbie, Scotland, in 1988.

- On September 4, a U.N. International Criminal Tribunal sentences former Rwandan Prime Minister Jean Kambanda to life in jail for genocide.

- On September 14, more than fifty thousand Albanians had fled Kosovo in the past week.

- On September 24, Britain persuades Iran to rescind its 1989 death sentence against author Salman Rusdie.

- On October 18, British authorities arrest former Chilean leader Augusto Pinochet at a London hospital. A Spanish judge had requested his extradition for human rights violations during his 1973–1990 dictatorship in Chile.

- On October 26, Ecuador and Peru sign a treaty ending their one-hundred-year border dispute.

- On October 30, Hurricane Mitch causes flash floods and mudslides in Central America and kills ten thousand people in Honduras and Nicaragua.

- On November 15, the United States calls off cruise missile attacks against Iraq when, at the last minute, Iraq agrees that the U.N. may continue weapons inspections.

- On November 17, the Leonid meteor shower, perhaps the most intense meteor shower in thirty years, threatens five hundred satellites circling Earth.

- On November 24, the Yasser Arafat International Airport opens in the Gaza Strip.

- On November 25, the British House of Lords votes to extradite Augusto Pinochet to Spain to stand trial for atrocities in Chile.

- On November 26, a Tokyo court refuses to compensate former British prisoners of war for Japanese mistreatment during World War II.

- On November 28, Israel shells Hizballuh positions in southern Lebanon after Hizballuh terrorists kill seven Israeli soldiers in an ambush.

- On December 9, voters elect Ruth Dreifuss the first woman president of Switzerland.

- From December 16 to December 20, U.S. and British forces conduct Operation Desert Fox, a series of bombing raids against Iraq for refusing to cooperate with U.N. weapons inspectors.

- On December 17, a British high court rescinds the November 25 decision by the House of Lords to extradite Augusto Pinochet because of a judge's connection to Amnesty International, a human rights agency.

1999

- In January, North and South Korea hold talks on a peace settlement.

- In January, the European Union issues the first Euro, the currency of all EU members.

- On January 25, an earthquake measuring 6.3 on the Richter scale kills at least 1,170 people in Colombia.
- On February 9, the trial of three former government ministers begins in Paris. France charges them with manslaughter for delaying HIV-testing of the blood supply, which led hundreds of people to contract AIDS.
- In March, government and rebel forces clash in northern Chad.
- In March, the Czech Republic joins NATO.
- In March, Iraq accuses the United States of spying and continues to shoot at Allied jets in the "no-fly zones."
- In March, Iceland calls for a resumption of whaling, confident that whales no longer face extinction.
- On March 1, an international treaty banning land mines takes effect.
- On March 21, Swiss psychiatrist Bertrand Piccard and British pilot Brian Jones become the first men to fly around the world in a balloon.
- On March 24, NATO begins Operation Allied Force, a bombing campaign against Yugoslav targets to protect the Albanian majority in the province of Kosovo.
- In April, both India and Pakistan conduct ballistic missile tests, raising fears that should the two clash, they might fire missiles with nuclear warheads at each other.
- In April, the U.N. indicts Radovan Karadžić and Ratko Mladić for war crimes in Bosnia.
- In May, India bombs the bases of Pakistani-backed guerrillas in Kashmir.
- In May, Belgium outlaws the Hell's Angels motorcycle gang.
- In May, France confirms that nuclear tests damaged the coral beds of French Polynesia.
- In May, archaeologists discover a Mayan city in a dense forest on the Yucatán Peninsula, Mexico.
- On May 8, China calls an emergency session of the U.N. Security Council following the U.S. accidental bombing of the Chinese embassy in Belgrade.
- On May 17, voters elect General Ehud Barak Israeli prime minister.
- On May 28, the annual conference of the International Whaling Commission at St. George's, Grenada, reaffirms the thirteen-year ban on whaling.
- On May 29, a civilian government under President Olusegun Obasanjo assumes power in Nigeria.
- In June, Russian officials decide to abandon the *Mir* space station on the grounds that it is too expensive to maintain.
- In June, Indian and Pakistani troops clash in Kashmir, a region each claims as its own.
- On June 10, NATO suspends bombing as Serb forces begin to withdraw from Kosovo.
- On June 20, the last Serb forces withdraw from Kosovo.
- On June 24, Red Cross officials in Brussels, Belgium, state that 1998's natural disasters were the worst on record and predict that catastrophes will increase as the climate changes.

- On June 29, Israeli lawyers announce the application process for Holocaust survivors to receive compensation from two Swiss banks.
- On July 27, the United States bans trade with Afghanistan.
- On August 12, North Korea affirms its right to test a long-range missile capable of reaching the United States.
- On August 17, an earthquake measuring 7.4 on the Richter scale kills seventeen thousand people in Turkey, its worst natural disaster in sixty years.
- In September, East Timor votes, in a U.N.-sponsored referendum, for independence from Indonesia.
- In September, Russia decides to resume whaling.
- On September 21, an earthquake that measures 7.6 on the Richter scale kills more than two thousand people and destroys twelve thousand buildings in Taiwan.
- On September 21, anthropologists declare a woman's skull in Brazil the oldest human fossil in the Americas. The skull is 11,500 years old.
- In October, scientists in Siberia exhume an intact mammoth.
- On October 2, Russia invades the breakaway republic of Chechnya, the second time in the 1990s.
- On October 4, Palestinian and Israeli negotiators agree on opening a "safe passage" route between the West Bank and Gaza Strip.
- On October 12, world population reaches six billion people.
- On October 15, the Swedish Royal Academy awards the 1999 Nobel Peace Prize to Doctors Without Borders, the rapid-reaction group of medical volunteers who have led humanitarian interventions around the world.
- On October 27, gunmen storm the Armenian parliament, killing Prime Minister Vazgen Sarkisian and several others.
- On October 29, a cyclone strikes the east coast of India, kills ten thousand people, and leaves 2.5 million homeless.
- On October 29, an EU panel declares British beef safe for human consumption, rejecting France's desire to continue a ban on exports in fear of bovine spongiform encephalopathy, better known as "mad cow" disease.
- In November, Hong Kong officials approve the construction of a Disney theme park.
- On November 17, scientists report that the Arctic Ocean's ice cap has shrunk more than previously believed. The cap is 4.3 feet thinner than it was in 1976.
- On November 21, China announces the launch of a space vehicle capable of carrying astronauts.
- On December 1, scientists from the United States, Japan, and England announce the first mapping of the human genome, a goal of the Human Genome Project.
- On December 2, Britain transfers power in Northern Ireland to a twelve-member cabinet of Protestants and Catholics.
- On December 3, a World Trade Organization (WTO) meeting ends in Seattle, Washington, after a week of protests by environmentalists and protectionists.

- On December 17, floods in Venezuela cause mudslides that kill ten thousand people.
- On December 17, Germany establishes a $5.2 billion fund to compensate slave laborers and other victims of the Third Reich.
- On December 19, Portugal returns Macau to China after 442 years as a Portuguese colony.

- On December 24, Kashmiri separatists hijack an Indian Airlines jet.
- On December 31, the United States returns the Panama Canal to Panama after eighty-five years of U.S. control.
- On December 31, Boris Yeltsin resigns. Vladimir Putin replaces him as president of Russia.

1

THE ARTS

MILLIE JACKSON, ALICE WU

Entries are arranged in chronological order by date of primary source. For entries with one primary source, the entry title is the same as the primary source title. Entries with more than one primary source have an overall entry title, followed by the titles of the primary sources.

Important Events in the Arts, 1990–1999

1990

- Eight directors (Martin Scorsese, Stanley Kubrick, Woody Allen, Francis Ford Coppola, George Lucas, Sydney Pollack, Robert Redford and Steven Spielberg) found the Film Foundation, dedicated to protect and preserve the American motion picture history.

- The first rap record to top the U.S. singles chart is Vanilla Ice's "Ice Ice Baby."

- A judge in Florida bans the sale of 2 Live Crew's album "As Nasty As They Wanna Be" to minors.

- In February, the New York Public Library launches a major retrospective of the work of Berenice Abbott, the largest exhibit ever accorded a living photographer.

- On March 18, the largest art theft since 1911 occurs at the Gardner Museum in Boston. Among the stolen paintings, which are valued at $200 million, are five by Edgar Degas and *Storm on the Sea of Galilee,* the only known landscape by Rembrandt. The museum is uninsured.

- In September, President George Bush presents a silver National Medal of Arts to artist Jasper Johns for helping to make the United States a "cultural giant."

- On September 27, the Motion Picture Association of America drops its X rating and begins using an NC-17 rating for movies to which no one under seventeen can be admitted.

- In October, President Bush awards artist Andrew Wyeth a Congressional Gold Medal, making him the first artist to receive the award.

- On October 5, the Contemporary Arts Center in Cincinnati and its director, Dennis Barrie, are acquitted of obscenity charges stemming from exhibition of *The Perfect Moment,* a controversial group of homoerotic photographs by Robert Mapplethorpe.

- In November, the Armand Hammer Museum of Art and Cultural Center opens in Los Angeles after Hammer, president of Occidental Petroleum, wins a stockholders' suit challenging his right to use company funds to build the museum.

- On November 14, pop-music group Milli Vanilli admits to lip-synching hits such as "Girl You Know It's True." Its Grammy Award for Best New Artist of 1989 is revoked.

- In December, Congress requires that artists funded by the National Endowment for the Arts (NEA) must return grant money if their works are judged obscene.

MOVIES: *Another 48 Hours,* directed by Walter Hill and starring Eddie Murphy and Nick Nolte; *Awakenings,* directed by Penny Marshall and starring Robert De Niro and Robin Williams; *Bird on a Wire,* directed by John Badham and starring Mel Gibson, Goldie Hawn, and David Carradine; *Dances with Wolves,* directed by and starring Kevin Costner; *Days of Thunder,* directed by Tony Scott and starring Tom Cruise, Robert Duvall, Nicole Kidman, and Randy Quaid; *Dick Tracy,* directed by Warren Beatty and starring Beatty, Al Pacino, and Madonna; *Die Hard 2,* directed by Renny Harlin and starring Bruce Willis and Bonnie Bedelia; *Flatliners,* directed by Joel Schumacher and starring Kiefer Sutherland, Julia Roberts, and Kevin Bacon; *Ghost,* directed by Jerry Zucker and starring Patrick Swayze, Demi Moore, and Whoopi Goldberg; *The Godfather Part III,* directed by Francis Ford Coppola and starring Al Pacino, Diane Keaton, and Andy Garcia; *GoodFellas,* directed by Martin Scorsese and starring Robert De Niro, Ray Liotta, and Joe Pesci; *The Grifters,* directed by Stephen Frears and starring Anjelica Huston, John Cusack, and Annette Bening; *Henry and June,* directed by Philip Kaufman and starring Fred Ward, Uma Thurman, and Maria de Medeiros; *Home Alone,* directed by Chris Columbus and starring Macaulay Culkin, Joe Pesci, and Daniel Stern; *The Hunt for Red October,* directed by John McTiernan and starring Sean Connery, Alec Baldwin, Sam Neill, and James Earl Jones; *Presumed Innocent,* directed by Alan J. Pakula and starring Harrison Ford and Bonnie Bedelia; *Pretty Woman,* directed by Garry Marshall and starring Richard Gere and Julia Roberts; *Reversal of Fortune,* directed by Barbet Schroeder and starring Glenn Close, Jeremy Irons, and Ron Silver; *Teenage Mutant Ninja Turtles,* directed by Steve Barron and starring Michelan Sisti, Leif Tilden, and Dave Forman; *Total Recall,* directed by Paul Verhoeven and starring Arnold Schwarzenegger and Sharon Stone.

FICTION: Nicholson Baker, *Room Temperature;* Frederick Barthelme, *Natural Selection;* Vance Bourjaily, *Old Soldier;* T. Coraghessan Boyle, *East is East;* Frederick Busch, *Harry and Catherine;* Tom Clancy, *Clear and Present Danger;* Patricia Cornwell, *Post Mortem;* Michael Crichton, *Jurassic Park;* Clive Cussler, *Dragon;* Ivan Doig, *Ride with Me, Mariah Montana;* Dominick Dunne, *An Inconvenient Woman;* Richard Ford, *Wildlife;* George Garrett, *Entered from the Sun;* George V. Higgins, *Victories;* Tony Hillerman, *Coyote Waits;* Alice Hoffman, *Seventh Heaven;* Charles Johnson, *Middle Passage;* Barbara Kingsolver, *Animal Dreams;* Elmore Leonard, *Get Shorty;* Robert Ludlum, *The Bourne Ultimatum;* Peter Matthiessen, *Killing Mr. Watson;* Jill McCorkle, *Ferris Beach;* Larry McMurtry, *Buffalo Girls;* Sue Miller, *Family Pictures;* Joyce Carol Oates, *Because It Is Bitter, And Because It Is My Heart;* Tim O'Brien, *The Things They Carried;* Reynolds Price, *The Tongues of Angels;* Thomas Pynchon, *Vineland;* Anne Rice, *The Witching Hour;* Philip Roth, *Deception;* Dori Sanders, *Clover;* Danielle Steel, *Message from Nam;* Scott Turow, *The Burden of Proof;* John Updike, *Rabbit at Rest;* Kurt Vonnegut, *Hocus Pocus;* Joseph Wambaugh, *The Golden Orange;* John Edgar Wideman, *Philadelphia Fire.*

POPULAR SONGS: Wilson Phillips, "Hold On"; Roxette, "It Must Have Been Love"; Sinead O'Connor, "Nothing Compares 2 U"; Bell Biv Devoe, "Poison"; Madonna, "Vogue"; Mariah Carey, "Vision of Love"; Phil Collins, "Another Day In Paradise"; En Vogue, "Hold On"; Billy Idol, "Cradle of Love"; Jon Bon Jovi, "Blaze of Glory."

1991

• Grunge music, based in Seattle, spreads with the success of the bands Nirvana and Pearl Jam.

• Cardinal O'Connor asks the Pope to excommunicate singer Madonna.

• *Terminator 2* is the most expensive movie with production costs over $100 million.

• On March 11, Walter Annenberg announces that on his death his collection of more than fifty Impressionist and Postimpressionist European paintings, watercolors, and drawings—valued at $1 billion—will be donated to the Metropolitan Museum of Art in New York City.

• On March 15, *The West as America: Reinterpreting Images of the Frontier* opens at the National Museum of American Art in Washington, D.C. The controversial exhibit includes works that depict white violence and racism in American history, provoking questions over public funding for such shows. The show goes on to the Denver Museum in August and the St. Louis Art Museum in November.

• On September 24, the Seattle grunge band Nirvana releases *Nevermind.* By January 11 a song from the album, "Smells Like Teen Spirit," has reached number one on the *Billboard* singles charts and has become an alternative rock anthem for "Generation X."

MOVIES: *The Addams Family,* directed by Barry Sonnenfeld and starring Anjelica Huston and Raul Julia; *Backdraft,* directed by Ron Howard and starring Kurt Russell, William Baldwin, Robert De Niro, and Donald Sutherland; *Beauty and the Beast,* animated feature, directed by Barry Trousdale and Kirk Wise; *City Slickers,* directed by Ron Underwood and starring Billy Crystal and Jack Palance; *Dying Young,* directed by Joel Schumacher and starring Julia Roberts, Colleen Dewhurst, and Ellen Burstyn; *Father of the Bride,* directed by Charles Shyer and starring Steve Martin and Diane Keaton; *The Fisher King,* directed by Terry Gilliam and starring Robin Williams, Jeff Bridges and Mercedes Ruehl; *Fried Green Tomatoes,* directed by Jon Avnet and starring Kathy Bates and Jessica Tandy; *Grand Canyon,* directed by Lawrence Kasdan and starring Danny Glover, Kevin Kline, and Steve Martin; *JFK,* directed by Oliver Stone and starring Kevin Costner, Sissy Spacek, Kevin Bacon, and Tommy Lee Jones; *The Naked Gun 2½: The Smell of Fear,* directed by David Zucker and starring Leslie Nielsen, Priscilla Presley, George Kennedy, and O. J. Simpson; *New Jack City,* directed by Mario Van Peebles and starring Wesley Snipes and Ice T; *Point Break,* directed by Kathryn Bigelow and starring Patrick Swayze and Keanu Reeves; *Robin Hood: Prince of Thieves,* directed by Kevin Reynolds and starring Kevin Costner and Morgan Freeman; *The Silence of the Lambs,* directed by Jonathan Demme and starring Jodie Foster and Anthony Hopkins; *Sleeping With the Enemy,* directed by Joseph Ruben and starring Julia Roberts; *Thelma & Louise,* directed by Ridley Scott and starring Susan Sarandon and Geena Davis; *Terminator 2: Judgment Day,* directed by James Cameron and starring Arnold Schwarzenegger; *What About Bob?,* directed by Frank Oz and starring Bill Murray and Richard Dreyfuss; *White Fang,* directed by Randal Kleiser and starring Ethan Hawke.

FICTION: Julia Alvarez, *How the Garcia Girls Lost Their Accents;* Nicholson Baker, *U&I;* Russell Banks, *The Sweet Hereafter;* John Barth, *The Last Voyage of Somebody the Sailor;* Madison Smartt Bell, *Doctor Sleep;* Harold Brodkey, *Runaway Soul;* Frederick Buechner, *Telling Secrets;* Frederick Busch, *Closing Arguments;* Robert Coover, *Pinocchio in Venice;* Don DeLillo, *Mao II;* Pete Dexter, *Brotherly Love;* Stephen Dixon, *Frog;* Bret Easton Ellis, *American Psycho;* Gail Godwin, *Father Melancholy's Daughter;* John Grisham, *The Firm;* Norman Mailer, *Harlot's Ghost;* Richard Moore, *The Investigator;* Walter Mosley, *Devil in a Blue Dress;* Marge Piercy, *He, She, and It;* Philip Roth, *Patrimony: A True Story;* Norman Rush, *Mating;* Sandra Scofield, *Beyond Deserving;* Isaac Bashevis Singer, *Scum;* Jane Smiley, *A Thousand Acres;* Danielle Steel, *Heartbeat;* Amy Tan, *The Kitchen God's Wife;* Anne Tyler, *Saint Maybe.*

POPULAR SONGS: Bryan Adams, "(Everything I Do) I Do It For You"; Color Me Badd, "I Wanna Sex You Up"; C & C Music Factory, "Gonna Make You Sweat"; Paula Abdul, "Hush, Hush"; Timothy T., "One More Try"; EMF, "Unbelievable"; Extreme, "More Than Words"; Hi-Five, "I Like The Way" (The Kissing Game); Surface, "The First Time"; Amy Grant, "Baby, Baby."

1992

• Compact discs surpass cassette tapes as the preferred medium for recorded music.

• On February 21, in the continuing controversy over NEA funding for controversial artists, Republican presidential hopeful Patrick Buchanan accuses the Bush administration of supporting "filthy and blasphemous art," and President Bush responds by firing NEA chairman John E. Frohnmayer.

• Comedian Bob Hope is awarded his fifty-eighth honorary doctorate, by the University of Rhode Island.

MOVIES: *Aladdin,* animated feature, directed by John Musker and Ron Clements; *Basic Instinct,* directed by Paul Verhoeven and starring Michael Douglas and Sharon Stone; *Batman Returns,* directed by Tim Burton and starring Michael Keaton, Danny DeVito, and Michelle Pfeiffer; *The Bodyguard,* directed by Mick Jackson and starring Kevin Costner and Whitney Houston; *Bram Stoker's Dracula,* directed by Francis Ford Coppola and starring Gary Oldman, Winona Ryder, Anthony Hopkins, and Keanu Reeves; *The Crying Game,* directed by Neil Jordan and starring Stephen Rea, Miranda Richardson, and Forrest Whittaker; *Death Becomes Her,* directed by Robert Zemeckis and starring Meryl Streep, Bruce Willis, Goldie Hawn, and Isabella Rossellini; *Far and Away,* directed by Ron Howard and starring Tom Cruise and Nicole Kidman; *A Few Good Men,* directed by Rob Reiner and starring Kevin Bacon, Kiefer Sutherland,

Jack Nicholson, Tom Cruise, and Demi Moore; *Glengarry Glen Ross,* directed by James Foley and starring Al Pacino, Jack Lemmon, Kevin Spacey, Alec Baldwin, Alan Arkin, and Ed Harris; *The Hand that Rocks the Cradle,* directed by Curtis Hanson and starring Annabella Sciorra and Rebecca De Mornay; *Home Alone 2: Lost in New York,* directed by Chris Columbus and starring Macaulay Culkin, Joe Pesci, and Daniel Stern; *Honeymoon in Vegas,* directed by Andrew Bergman and starring James Caan, Nicolas Cage, Sarah Jessica Parker, and Pat Morita; *Housesitter,* directed by Frank Oz and starring Steve Martin and Goldie Hawn; *Howards End,* directed by James Ivory and starring Anthony Hopkins, Emma Thompson, Vanessa Redgrave, and Helena Bonham Carter; *The Last of the Mohicans,* directed by Michael Mann and starring Daniel Day-Lewis and Madeleine Stowe; *A League of Their Own,* directed by Penny Marshall and starring Tom Hanks, Madonna, Geena Davis, and Rosie O'Donnell; *Lethal Weapon 3,* directed by Richard Donner and starring Mel Gibson, Danny Glover, Joe Pesci and Rene Russo; *Malcolm X,* directed by Spike Lee and starring Denzel Washington and Angela Bassett; *My Cousin Vinny,* directed by Jonathan Lynn and starring Joe Pesci and Marisa Tomei; *Passenger 57,* directed by Kevin Hooks and starring Wesley Snipes; *Patriot Games,* directed by Phillip Noyce and starring Harrison Ford and Anne Archer; *The Player,* directed by Robert Altman and starring Tim Robbins and Whoopi Goldberg; *A River Runs Through It,* directed by Robert Redford and starring Brad Pitt, Craig Sheffer, and Tom Skerritt; *Scent of a Woman,* directed by Martin Brest and starring Al Pacino and Chris O'Donnell; *Sister Act,* directed by Emile Ardolino and starring Whoopi Goldberg, Maggie Smith, and Kathy Najimy; *Sneakers,* directed by Phil Alden Robinson and starring Robert Redford, Sidney Poitier, Dan Aykroyd, Ben Kingsley, and River Phoenix; *Under Siege,* directed by Andrew Davis and starring Steven Seagal; *Unforgiven,* directed by Clint Eastwood and starring Eastwood, Gene Hackman, Morgan Freeman, and Richard Harris; *Wayne's World,* directed by Penelope Spheeris and starring Mike Myers and Dana Carvey; *White Men Can't Jump,* directed by Ron Shelton and starring Woody Harrelson and Wesley Snipes.

FICTION: Dorothy Allison, *Bastard out of Carolina;* Paul Auster, *Leviathan;* Nicholson Baker, *Vox;* Richard Bausch, *Violence;* Robert Olen Butler, *A Good Scent from a Strange Mountain;* Joan Didion, *After Henry;* David James Duncan, *The Brothers K;* Ellen Gilchrist, *Net of Jewels;* John Grisham, *The Pelican Brief;* George V. Higgins, *Defending Billy Ryan;* Alice Hoffman, *Turtle Moon;* William Kennedy, *Very Old Bones;* Ken Kesey, *Sailor Song;* Stephen King, *Dolores Claiborne;* W. P. Kinsella, *Box Socials;* Dean Koontz, *Hideaway;* Elmore Leonard, *Rum Punch;* Cormac McCarthy, *All the Pretty Horses;* Alice McDermott, *At Weddings and Wakes;* Thomas McGuane, *Nothing But Blue Skies;* Jay McInerney, *Brightness Falls;* Terry McMillan, *Waiting to Exhale;* Larry McMurtry, *The Evening Star;* James Michener, *Mexico;* Toni Morrison, *Jazz;* Gloria Naylor, *Bailey's Cafe;* Joyce Carol Oates, *Black Water;* Chaim Potok, *I Am the Clay;* Reynolds Price, *Blue Calhoun;* Richard Price, *Clockers;* E. Annie Proulx, *Postcards;* Anne Rice, *The Tale of the Body Thief;* Leslie Silko, *Almanac of the Dead;* Lee Smith, *The Devil's*

Dream; Susan Sontag, *The Volcano Lover;* Danielle Steel, *Mixed Blessings;* Donna Tartt, *The Secret History;* John Updike, *Memoirs of the Ford Administration;* Gore Vidal, *Live from Golgotha;* Alice Walker, *Possessing the Secret of Joy;* Robert James Waller, *The Bridges of Madison County;* Joseph Wambaugh, *Fugitive Nights;* Larry Woiwode, *Indian Affairs.*

POPULAR SONGS: Sir Mix-A-Lot, "Baby Got Back"; Kris Kross, "Jump"; Boyz II Men, "End Of The Road"; Billy Ray Cyrus, "Achy Breaky Heart"; Eric Clapton, "Tears In Heaven"; Right Said Fred, "I'm Too Sexy"; House of Pain, "Jump Around"; Red Hot Chili Peppers, "Under The Bridge"; Nirvana, "Smells Like Teen Spirit"; Guns N' Roses, "November Rain."

1993

• The movie *Lost in Yonkers* is edited on an Avid Media Composer system, the first nonlinear editing system to allow viewing at the "real-time" rate of twenty-four frames per second. It converts film images into digital bits that can be manipulated on a computer.

• *Jurassic Park* is the highest grossing movie of all time.

MOVIES: *Demolition Man,* directed by Marco Brambilla and starring Sylvester Stallone and Wesley Snipes; *Dennis the Menace,* directed by Nick Castle and starring Walter Matthau; *Falling Down,* directed by Joel Schumacher and starring Michael Douglas and Robert Duvall; *The Firm,* directed by Sydney Pollack and starring Tom Cruise and Gene Hackman; *The Fugitive,* directed by Andrew Davis and starring Harrison Ford and Tommy Lee Jones; *Groundhog Day,* directed by Harold Ramis and starring Bill Murray and Andie MacDowell; *In the Line of Fire,* directed by Wolfgang Petersen and starring Clint Eastwood, John Malkovich, and Rene Russo; *In the Name of the Father,* directed by Jim Sheridan and starring Daniel Day-Lewis and Emma Thompson; *Indecent Proposal,* directed by Adrian Lyne and starring Paul Newman, Demi Moore, and Woody Harrelson; *Jurassic Park,* directed by Steven Spielberg and starring Sam Neill, Laura Dern, and Jeff Goldblum; *Last Action Hero,* directed by John McTiernan and starring Arnold Schwarzenegger and F. Murray Abraham; *Lost in Yonkers,* directed by Martha Coolidge and starring Richard Dreyfuss; *Mrs. Doubtfire,* directed by Chris Columbus and starring Robin Williams and Sally Field; *The Pelican Brief,* directed by Alan J. Pakula and starring Julia Roberts and Denzel Washington; *Philadelphia,* directed by Jonathan Demme and starring Tom Hanks and Denzel Washington; *The Piano,* directed by Jane Campion and starring Holly Hunter, Harvey Keitel, and Sam Neill; *Rising Sun,* directed by Philip Kaufman and starring Sean Connery, Wesley Snipes, and Harvey Keitel; *Schindler's List,* directed by Steven Spielberg and starring Liam Neeson, Ben Kingsley, and Ralph Fiennes; *Six Degrees of Separation,* directed by Fred Schepisi and starring Stockard Channing, Will Smith, and Donald Sutherland; *Sleepless in Seattle,* directed by Nora Ephron and starring Tom Hanks and Meg Ryan; *Sommersby,* directed by Jon Amiel and starring Richard Gere and Jodie Foster; *Tombstone,* directed by George P. Cosmatos and starring Kurt Russell and Val Kilmer.

FICTION: Walter Abish, *Eclipse Fever;* Alice Adams, *Almost Perfect;* William Baldwin, *The Hard to Catch Mercy;*

Frederick Barthelme, *Brothers;* Richard Bausch, *Rebel Powers;* Madison Smartt Bell, *Save Me, Joe Louis;* T. Coraghessan Boyle, *The Road to Wellville;* Frederick Buechner, *The Son of Laughter;* James Lee Burke, *In the Electric Mist with Confederate Dead;* Frederick Busch, *Long Way from Home;* Frank Conroy, *Body & Soul;* James Dickey, *To the White Sea;* Ivan Doig, *Heart Earth;* Ken Follett, *A Dangerous Fortune;* Ernest J. Gaines, *A Lesson Before Dying;* David Guterson, *Snow Falling on Cedars;* John Grisham, *The Client* and *A Time to Kill;* Kathryn Harrison, *Exposure;* Ernest Hebert, *Mad Boys;* George V. Higgins, *Bomber's Law;* Oscar Hijuelos, *The Fourteen Sisters of Emilio Montez O'Brien;* Tony Hillerman, *Sacred Clowns;* William Kennedy, *Riding the Yellow Trolley Car;* Barbara Kingsolver, *Pigs in Heaven;* Dean Koontz, *Mr. Murder;* Alan Lightman, *Einstein's Dreams;* Elmore Leonard, *Pronto;* Bobbie Ann Mason, *Feather Crowns;* Larry McMurtry, *Streets of Laredo;* Joyce Carol Oates, *Foxfire;* E. Annie Proulx, *The Shipping News;* Ishmael Reed, *Japanese by Spring;* Anne Rice, *Lasher;* Philip Roth, *Operation Shylock;* Dori Sanders, *Her Own Place;* Joseph Wambaugh, *Finnegan's Week.*

POPULAR SONGS: Whitney Houston, "I Will Always Love You"; Tag Team, "Whoomp! (There It Is)"; Wreck-N-Effect, "Rump Shaker"; Silk, "Freak Me"; Dr. Dre, "Nuthin' But A G Thang"; UB40, "Can't Help Falling In Love"; Snow, "Informer"; Shai, "If I Ever Fall In Love"; Duice, "Dazzey Duks"; H-Town, "Knockin' Da Boots."

1994

- In 1994, veteran rock and roll bands Pink Floyd and the Rolling Stones go on tour—Pink Floyd earns $103 million; the Rolling Stones earn $114 million.

- Director Steven Spielberg forms DreamWorks SKG with David Geffen and Jeffrey Katzenberg.

- From August 12 to August 14, Woodstock '94 commemorates the twenty-fifth anniversary of the original weekend-long concert held near Woodstock, New York. Performers include Bob Dylan and the Allman Brothers, who performed at the 1969 concert, as well as the groups Green Day and Nine Inch Nails.

MOVIES: *Ace Ventura: Pet Detective,* directed by Tom Shadyac and starring Jim Carrey and Courteney Cox; *Clear and Present Danger,* directed by Phillip Noyce and starring Harrison Ford, Willem Dafoe, Anne Archer, and James Earl Jones; *Disclosure,* directed by Barry Levinson and starring Michael Douglas, Demi Moore, and Donald Sutherland; *Dumb & Dumber,* directed by Peter Farrelly and starring Jim Carrey and Jeff Daniels; *The Flintstones,* directed by Brian Levant and starring John Goodman, Elizabeth Perkins, Rick Moranis, and Rosie O'Donnell; *Forrest Gump,* directed by Robert Zemeckis and starring Tom Hanks; *Guarding Tess,* directed by Hugh Wilson and starring Shirley MacLaine and Nicolas Cage; *Interview with the Vampire: The Vampire Chronicles,* directed by Neil Jordan and starring Tom Cruise, Brad Pitt, and Antonio Banderas; *The Lion King,* animated feature, directed by Roger Allers and Rob Minkoff; *The Mask,* directed by Charles Russell and starring Jim Carrey and Cameron Diaz; *Maverick,* directed by Richard Donner and starring Mel Gibson, Jodie

Foster, and James Garner; *Natural Born Killers,* directed by Oliver Stone and starring Woody Harrelson and Juliette Lewis; *Nobody's Fool,* directed by Robert Benton and starring Paul Newman, Jessica Tandy, Bruce Willis, and Melanie Griffith; *The Paper,* directed by Ron Howard and starring Michael Keaton, Glenn Close, Robert Duvall, Marisa Tomei, and Randy Quaid; *Pulp Fiction,* directed by Quentin Tarantino and starring John Travolta, Samuel L. Jackson, and Uma Thurman; *Quiz Show,* directed by Robert Redford and starring John Turturro, Rob Morrow, and Ralph Fiennes; *The River Wild,* directed by Curtis Hanson and starring Meryl Streep and Kevin Bacon; *The Shawshank Redemption,* directed by Frank Darabont and starring Tim Robbins and Morgan Freeman; *Speed,* directed by Jan de Bont and starring Keanu Reeves, Dennis Hopper, and Sandra Bullock; *Star Trek Generations,* directed by David Carson and starring Patrick Stewart and William Shatner; *True Lies,* directed by James Cameron and starring Arnold Schwarzenegger, Jamie Lee Curtis, and Tom Arnold.

FICTION: Paul Auster, *Mr. Vertigo;* John Barth, *Once Upon a Time;* Louis Begley, *As Max Saw It;* Thomas Berger, *Robert Crews;* Doris Betts, *Souls Raised From the Dead;* Harold Brodkey, *Profane Friendship;* Charles Bukowski, *Pulp;* James Lee Burke, *Dixie City Jam;* Robert Olen Butler, *They Whisper;* Caleb Carr, *The Alienist;* Carolyn Chute, *Merry Men;* Tom Clancy, *Debt of Honor;* Mary Higgins Clark, *Remember Me;* Michael Crichton, *Disclosure;* E. L. Doctorow, *The Waterworks;* John Gregory Dunne, *Playland;* Bret Easton Ellis, *The Informers;* Louise Erdrich, *The Bingo Palace;* Irvin Faust, *Jim Dandy;* William Gaddis, *A Frolic of His Own;* Gail Godwin, *The Good Husband;* Ellen Gilchrist, *Anabasis;* William Goyen, *Half a Look of Cain;* Shirley Ann Grau, *Roadwalkers;* John Grisham, *The Chamber;* Jane Hamilton, *A Map of the World;* Mark Harris, *The Tale Maker;* Joseph Heller, *Closing Time;* Alice Hoffman, *Second Nature;* John Irving, *A Son of the Circus;* Stephen King, *Insomnia;* David Mamet, *The Village;* Cormac McCarthy, *The Crossing;* Larry McMurtry, *Pretty Boy Floyd;* Walter Mosley, *Black Betty;* Joyce Carol Oates, *What I Lived For;* Tim O'Brien, *In the Lake of the Woods;* Robert B. Parker, *All Our Yesterdays;* Jayne Anne Phillips, *Shelter;* Marge Piercy, *The Longings of Women;* Anne Rice, *Taltos;* Danielle Steel, *The Gift;* Peter Taylor, *In the Tennessee Country;* John Updike, *Brazil.*

POPULAR SONGS: All-4-One, "I Swear"; Boyz II Men, "I'll Make Love To You"; R. Kelly, "Bump N' Grind"; Bryan Adams, Rod Stewart, and Sting, "All For Love"; Ace of Base, "The Sign"; Celine Dion, "The Power of Love"; Warren G & Nate Dogg, "Regulate"; Coolio, "Fantastic Voyage."

1995

- Singer Sonny Bono of Sonny and Cher becomes a U.S. Congressman.

- *Waterworld* is the most expensive movie ever made with production costs at $200 million.

- On June 1, in a speech delivered in Los Angeles, Republican presidential candidate Robert Dole denounces the American entertainment industry for "debasing U.S. culture with movies, music and television programs that had produced 'nightmares of depravity' drenched in sex and violence."

• On September 1, the Rock and Roll Hall of Fame and Museum, designed by architect I.M. Pei, opens in Cleveland.

• On October 2, at a performance of *Otello* the Metropolitan Opera in New York unveils Met Titles, providing simultaneous translations on screens mounted on audience seats.

• On November 21, Capitol Records releases the much anticipated *Beatles Anthology I,* which includes the previously unreleased recording of "Free as a Bird."

MOVIES: *The American President,* directed by Rob Reiner and starring Michael Douglas, Annette Bening, and Martin Sheen; *Apollo 13,* directed by Ron Howard and starring Tom Hanks, Bill Paxton, and Kevin Bacon; *Babe,* directed by Chris Noonan; *Braveheart,* directed by and starring Mel Gibson; *The Bridges of Madison County,* directed by Clint Eastwood and starring Eastwood and Meryl Streep; *Clueless,* directed by Amy Heckerling and starring Alicia Silverstone; *Crimson Tide,* directed by Tony Scott and starring Gene Hackman and Denzel Washington; *Dead Man Walking,* directed by Tim Robbins and starring Susan Sarandon and Sean Penn; *Devil in a Blue Dress,* directed by Carl Franklin and starring Denzel Washington; *First Knight,* directed by Jerry Zucker and starring Sean Connery and Richard Gere; *Get Shorty,* directed by Barry Sonnenfeld and starring John Travolta, Gene Hackman, Rene Russo, and Danny DeVito; *GoldenEye,* directed by Martin Campbell and starring Pierce Brosnan; *Grumpier Old Men,* directed by Howard Deutch and starring Walter Matthau, Jack Lemmon, Ann-Margret, and Sophia Loren; *Leaving Las Vegas,* directed by Mike Figgis and starring Nicolas Cage and Elizabeth Shue; *Nixon,* directed by Oliver Stone and starring Anthony Hopkins; *Pocahontas,* animated feature, directed by Mike Gabriel and Eric Goldberg; *Sense and Sensibility,* directed by Ang Lee and starring Kate Winslet, Emma Thompson, and Hugh Grant; *Toy Story,* animated feature, directed by John Lasseter; *The Usual Suspects,* directed by Bryan Singer and starring Stephen Baldwin and Kevin Spacey; *Waiting to Exhale,* directed by Forrest Whittaker and starring Whitney Houston and Angela Bassett; *While You Were Sleeping,* directed by John Turteltaub and starring Sandra Bullock.

FICTION: Alice Adams, *A Southern Exposure;* Julia Alvarez, *In the Time of the Butterflies;* Frederick Barthelme, *Painted Desert;* Rick Bass, *In the Loyal Mountains;* Ann Beattie, *Another You;* Madison Smartt Bell, *All Souls' Rising;* T. Coraghessan Boyle, *The Tortilla Curtain;* Nicholas Delbanco, *In the Name of Mercy;* Pete Dexter, *The Paperboy;* Stanley Elkin, *Mrs. Ted Bliss;* Richard Ford, *Independence Day;* William H. Gass, *The Tunnel;* John Grisham, *The Rainmaker;* John Herman, *The Weight of Love;* George V. Higgins, *Swan Boats at Four;* Alice Hoffman, *Practical Magic;* Mary Hood, *Familiar Heat;* John Keene, *Annotations;* David Long, *Blue Spruce;* Sue Miller, *The Distinguished Guest;* Joyce Carol Oates, *Zombie;* Robert B. Parker, *Thin Air;* Richard Powers, *Galatea 2.2;* Reynolds Price, *The Promise of Rest;* Philip Roth, *Sabbath's Theater;* Mary Lee Settle, *Choices;* Jane Smiley, *Moo;* Lee Smith, *Saving Grace;* Amy Tan, *The Hundred Secret Senses;* Anne Tyler, *Ladder of Years.*

POPULAR SONGS: Coolio featuring L.V., "Gangsta's Paradise"; TLC, "Creep"; Mariah Carey, "Fantasy"; TLC, "Waterfalls"; Monica, "Don't Take It Personal"; Shaggy, "Boombastic/In The Summertime"; The Notorious B.I.G., "One More Chance/Stay With Me"; Adina Howard, "Freak Like Me"; Montell Jordan, "This Is How We Do It"; Michael Jackson, "You Are Not Alone."

1996

• On February 13, the musical *Rent* opens to rave reviews on Broadway.

• In March, legal thriller writer John Grisham charges that director Oliver Stone is responsible for the death of Grisham's friend William Savage, because the two teenagers who committed the crime claim to have been inspired by Stone's 1994 movie, *Natural Born Killers.*

• In November, *Marc Chagall 1907–1917* at the Los Angeles County Museum includes early Chagall paintings never before exhibited in the United States.

MOVIES: *The Cable Guy,* directed by Ben Stiller and starring Jim Carrey and Matthew Broderick; *Courage Under Fire,* directed by Edward Zwick and starring Denzel Washington, Meg Ryan, and Lou Diamond Phillips; *The English Patient,* directed by Anthony Minghella and starring Ralph Fiennes and Juliette Binoche; *Evita,* directed by Alan Parker and starring Madonna and Antonio Banderas; *Executive Decision,* directed by Stuart Baird and starring Kurt Russell, Steven Seagal, and Halle Berry; *Fargo,* directed by Joel Coen and starring Frances McDormand; *First Wives Club,* directed by Hugh Wilson and starring Goldie Hawn, Bette Midler, Diane Keaton; *Hunchback of Notre Dame,* animated feature, directed by Gary Trousdale and Kirk Wise; *Independence Day,* directed by Roland Emmerich and starring Will Smith, Robert Duvall, Dennis Quaid, and Jeff Goldblum; *Jack,* directed by Francis Ford Coppola and starring Robin Williams, Diane Lane, Bill Cosby, and Jennifer Lopez; *Jerry Maguire,* directed by Cameron Crowe and starring Tom Cruise and Cuba Gooding, Jr.; *Mission, Impossible,* directed by Brian de Palma and starring Tom Cruise; *The Nutty Professor,* directed by Tom Shadyac and starring Eddie Murphy and Jada Pinkett; *101 Dalmations,* directed by Stephen Herek and starring Glenn Close and Jeff Daniels; *The People vs. Larry Flynt,* directed by Milos Forman and starring Woody Harrelson and Courtney Love; *Primal Fear,* directed by Gregory Hoblit and starring Richard Gere and Frances McDormand; *Ransom,* directed by Ron Howard and starring Mel Gibson and Rene Russo; *The Rock,* directed by Michael Bay and starring Sean Connery and Nicolas Cage; *Shine,* directed by Scott Hicks and starring Geoffrey Rush; *Sling Blade,* directed by Billy Bob Thornton and starring Thornton, John Ritter, and J. T. Walsh; *Tin Cup,* directed by Ron Shelton and starring Kevin Costner and Rene Russo; *Twister,* directed by Jan de Bont and starring Helen Hunt and Bill Paxton.

FICTION: Anonymous [Joe Klein], *Primary Colors;* Richard Bausch, *Good Evening Mr. & Mrs. America,* and *All the Ships at Sea;* Madison Smartt Bell, *Ten Indians;* Thomas Berger, *Suspects;* Wendell Berry, *A World Lost;* Harold Brodkey, *This Wild Darkness;* Larry Brown, *Father and Son;* James Lee Burke, *Cadillac Jukebox;* Fred Chappell,

Farewell, I'm Bound to Leave You; Mary Higgins Clark, *Moonlight Becomes You;* Robert Coover, *John's Wife;* Michael Crichton, *Airframe;* Joan Didion, *The Last Thing He Wanted;* Nicholas Evans, *The Horse Whisperer;* John Grisham, *The Runaway Jury;* George V. Higgins, *Sandra Nichols Found Dead;* Tony Hillerman, *The Fallen Man;* William Kennedy, *The Flaming Corsage;* Jamaica Kincaid, *Autobiography of My Mother;* William Kotzwinkle, *The Bear Went Over the Mountain;* Elmore Leonard, *Out of Sight;* Clarence Major, *Dirty Bird Blues;* Ed McBain, *Gladly the Cross-Eyed Bear;* Jill McCorkle, *Carolina Moon;* Terry McMillan, *How Stella Got Her Groove Back;* Steven Millhauser, *Martin Dressier;* Jacquelyn Mitchard, *The Deep End of the Ocean;* Walter Mosley, *A Little Yellow Dog;* Joyce Carol Oates, *We Were the Mulvaneys;* James Patterson, *Jack & Jill;* Janet Peery, *The River Beyond the World;* E. Annie Proulx, *Accordion Crimes;* Anne Rice, *The Servant of the Bones;* John Updike, *In the Beauty of the Lilies;* Joseph Wambaugh, *Floaters;* John Edgar Wideman, *The Cattle Killing.*

POPULAR SONGS: Los Del Rio, "Macarena (Bayside Boys Mix)"; Mariah Carey & Boyz II Men, "One Sweet Day"; Bone Thugs-N-Harmony, "Tha Crossroads"; 2Pac (Featuring K-Ci & JoJo), "How Do U Want It/California Love"; Keith Sweat, "Twisted"; Toni Braxton, "You're Makin' Me High/Let It Flow"; Whitney Houson, "Exhale (Shoop Shoop)"; Quad City D.J.'s, "C'Mon N' Ride It (The Train)"; Celine Dion, "Because You Loved Me"; LL Cool J, "Hey Lover."

1997

• On June 19, *Cats* stages its 6,138th performance, moving ahead of *A Chorus Line* as the longest-running Broadway show in history.

• On December 19, *Titanic* opens in American movie theaters. The most expensive movie of all time, it cost nearly $300 million to produce and market.

MOVIES: *Absolute Power,* directed by Clint Eastwood and starring Eastwood, Gene Hackman, and Ed Harris; *Air Force One,* directed by Wolfgang Petersen and starring Harrison Ford and Glenn Close; *Anastasia,* animated feature, directed by Don Bluth and Gary Goldman; *As Good as It Gets,* directed by James L. Brooks and starring Helen Hunt and Jack Nicholson; *Austin Powers: International Man of Mystery,* directed by Jay Roach and starring Mike Myers and Elizabeth Hurley; *Batman and Robin,* directed by Joel Schumacher and starring George Clooney, Chris O'Donnell, and Uma Thurman; *Con Air,* directed by Simon West and starring Nicolas Cage and John Cusack; *Conspiracy Theory,* directed by Richard Donner and starring Mel Gibson and Julia Roberts; *Contact,* directed by Robert Zemeckis and starring Jodie Foster and Matthew McConaughey; *Devil's Advocate,* directed by Taylor Hackford and starring Al Pacino, Keanu Reeves, and Charlize Theron; *Face/Off,* directed by John Woo and starring John Travolta and Nicolas Cage; *The Full Monty,* directed by Peter Cantanneo and starring Robert Carlyle, Tom Wilkinson, and Mark Addy; *Good Will Hunting,* directed by Gus Van Sant and starring Matt Damon and Robin Williams; *The Ice Storm,* directed by Ang Lee and starring Kevin Kline and

Sigourney Weaver; *In & Out,* directed by Frank Oz and starring Kevin Kline, John Cusack, Tom Selleck, and Matt Dillon; *The Jackal,* directed by Michael Caton-Jones and starring Bruce Willis, Richard Gere, and Sidney Poitier; *John Grisham's The Rainmaker,* directed by Francis Ford Coppola and starring Danny DeVito and Matt Damon; *L.A. Confidential,* directed by Curtis Hanson and starring Kevin Spacey, Russell Crowe, Danny DeVito, and Kim Basinger; *Lolita,* directed by Adrian Lyne and starring Jeremy Irons and Melanie Griffith; *The Lost World: Jurassic Park,* directed by Steven Spielberg and starring Jeff Goldblum and Julianne Moore; *Men in Black,* directed by Barry Sonnenfeld and starring Tommy Lee Jones and Will Smith; *Soul Food,* directed by George Tillman and starring Vivica A. Fox, Vanessa Williams, and Nia Long; *Titanic,* directed by James Cameron and starring Kate Winslet and Leonardo DiCaprio; *Tomorrow Never Dies,* directed by Roger Spottiswoode and starring Pierce Brosnan.

FICTION: Alice Adams, *Medicine Men;* Julia Alvarez, *Yo;* Frederick Barthelme, *Bob the Gambler;* Doris Betts, *The Sharp Teeth of Love;* Frederick Buechner, *On the Road with the Archangel;* James Lee Burke, *Cimarron Rose;* Frederick Busch, *Girls;* Robert Olen Butler, *The Deep Green Sea;* Caleb Carr, *The Angel of Darkness;* Mary Higgins Clark, *Pretend You Don't See Her;* Nicholas Delbanco, *Old Scores;* Don DeLillo, *Underworld;* Stephen Dobyns, *The Church of the Dead Girls;* Dominick Dunne, *Another City, Not My Own;* Charles Frazier, *Cold Mountain;* Ellen Gilchrist, *Sarah Conley;* Arthur Golden, *Memoirs of a Geisha;* John Grisham, *The Partner;* Allan Gurganus, *Plays Well with Others;* John Hawkes, *An Irish Eye;* George V. Higgins, *A Change of Gravity;* Alice Hoffman, *Here on Earth;* Madison Jones, *Nashville 1864;* Stephen King, *Wizard* and *Glass;* Robert Ludlum, *Matarese Countdown;* Peter Matthiessen, *Lost Man's River;* Jay McInerney, *The Last of the Savages;* Larry McMurtry, *Comanche Moon;* Walter Mosley, *Blue Light;* Joyce Carol Oates, *Man Crazy;* Cynthia Ozick, *Puttermesser Papers;* Thomas Pynchon, *Mason & Dixon;* Philip Roth, *American Pastoral;* John Updike, *Toward the End of Time;* Kurt Vonnegut, *Timequake;* Edmund White, *The Farewell Symphony;* Tom Wolfe, *Ambush at Fort Bragg.*

POPULAR SONGS: Elton John, "Candle In The Wind/Something About The Way You Look Tonight"; Puff Daddy and Faith Evans, "I'll Be Missing You"; Puff Daddy (Featuring Mase), "Can't Nobody Hold Me Down"; LeAnn Rimes, "How Do I Live"; Usher, "You Make Me Wanna"; Spice Girls, "Wannabe"; Hanson, "MMMBop"; Mark Morrison, "Return Of The Mack"; Tim McGraw With Faith Hill, "It's Your Love"; The Notorious B.I.G. (Featuring Puff Daddy & Mase), "Mo Money Mo Problems."

1998

• *Titanic* becomes the highest-grossing movie of all-time, earning more than $580 million in the United States and winning a record-tying eleven Academy Awards, including those for Best Picture and Best Director (James Cameron).

• Movie-theater owners agree to require teenagers to show photo IDs to get in to see R-rated movies.

- Bob Dylan's album *Time Out of Mind* wins a Grammy for Album of the Year.

- Sotheby's auction house in New York sells Pop artist Andy Warhol's *Orange Marilyn, 1964* for $17.3 million.

- On June 16, the American Film Institute announces its list of the top one hundred motion pictures of all time. *Citizen Kane* is number one, sparking a 1,600 percent increase in video rentals of the movie.

- On June 26, *The Art of the Motorcycle* opens at the Guggenheim Museum in New York City; critics charge that industrial design has no place in an art museum, but attendance breaks museum records.

- In November, Volume 200 of the *Dictionary of Literary Biography* is published.

MOVIES: *Affliction,* directed by Paul Schrader and starring Sissy Spacek, Nick Nolte, James Coburn, and Willem Dafoe; *American History X,* directed by Tony Kaye and starring Edward Norton and Edward Furlong; *The Apostle,* directed by Robert Duvall and starring Duvall, Farrah Fawcett, Billy Bob Thornton, and June Carter Cash; *Beloved,* directed by Jonathan Demme and starring Oprah Winfrey and Danny Glover; *A Bug's Life,* animated feature, directed by John Lasseter and Andrew Stanton; *Bulworth,* directed by Warren Beatty and starring Beatty and Halle Berry; *City of Angels,* directed by Brad Silberling and starring Nicolas Cage and Meg Ryan; *A Civil Action,* directed by Steven Zaillian and starring John Travolta and Robert Duvall; *Dancing at Lughnasa,* directed by Pat O'Connor and starring Meryl Streep and Michael Gambon; *Deep Impact,* directed by Mimi Leder and starring Robert Duvall, Tea Leoni, and Morgan Freeman; *Dr. Dolittle,* directed by Betty Thomas and starring Eddie Murphy and Ossie Davis; *Elizabeth,* directed by Shekhar Kapur and starring Cate Blanchett and Geoffrey Rush; *Enemy of the State,* directed by Tony Scott and starring Will Smith, Gene Hackman, and Lisa Bonet; *Fallen,* directed by Gregory Hoblit and starring Denzel Washington, John Goodman, and Donald Sutherland; *Fear and Loathing in Las Vegas,* directed by Terry Gilliam and starring Johnny Depp and Benicio Del Toro; *Great Expectations,* directed by Stuart Walker and starring Ethan Hawke and Gwyneth Paltrow; *He Got Game,* directed by Spike Lee and starring Denzel Washington, Ray Allen, and Ned Beatty; *Hope Floats,* directed by Forrest Whittaker and starring Sandra Bullock and Harry Connick, Jr.; *The Horse Whisperer,* directed by Robert Redford and starring Redford and Kristin Scott Thomas; *How Stella Got Her Groove Back,* directed by Kevin Rodney Sullivan and starring Angela Bassett; *Les Miserables,* directed by Bille August and starring Liam Neeson, Uma Thurman, and Claire Danes; *Meet Joe Black,* directed by Martin Brest and starring Anthony Hopkins and Brad Pitt; *Mulan,* animated feature, directed by Barry Cook and Tony Bancroft; *One True Thing,* directed by Carl Franklin and starring Meryl Streep, Renee Zellweger, and William Hurt; *Out of Sight,* directed by Steven Soderbergh and starring George Clooney and Jennifer Lopez; *Patch Adams,* directed by Tom Shadyac and starring Robin Williams; *Pleasantville,* directed by Gary Ross and starring Tobey Maguire, Jeff Daniels, and Joan Allen; *Primary Colors,* directed by Mike Nichols and starring John Travolta, Emma Thompson, Kathy Bates, and

Billy Bob Thornton; *The Prince of Egypt,* animated feature, directed by Brenda Chapman and Steve Hickner; *Saving Private Ryan,* directed by Steven Spielberg and starring Tom Hanks; *Shakespeare in Love,* directed by John Madden and starring Joseph Fiennes and Gwyneth Paltrow; *There's Something About Mary,* directed by Bobby Farrelly and Peter Farrelly and starring Cameron Diaz, Matt Dillon, and Ben Stiller; *The Thin Red Line,* directed by Terrence Malick and starring Sean Penn and Nick Nolte; *The Truman Show,* directed by Peter Weir and starring Jim Carrey, Ed Harris, and Laura Linney; *The Waterboy,* directed by Frank Coraci and starring Adam Sandler, Kathy Bates, and Henry Winkler; *You've Got Mail,* directed by Nora Ephron and starring Tom Hanks and Meg Ryan.

FICTION: Nicholson Baker, *The Everlasting Story of Nory;* Russell Banks, *Cloudsplitter;* Andrea Barrett, *The Voyage of the Narwhal;* Richard Bausch, *In the Night Season;* Louis Begley, *Mistler's Exit;* T. Coraghessan Boyle, *Riven Rock;* Frederick Buechner, *The Storm;* Robert Coover, *Ghost Town;* Louise Erdrich, *Antelope Wife;* John Grisham, *The Street Lawyer;* George V. Higgins, *The Agent;* Tony Hillerman, *The First Eagle;* John Irving, *A Widow for One Year;* Gayl Jones, *The Healing;* Barbara Kingsolver, *The Poisonwood Bible;* Stephen King, *Bag of Bones;* Wally Lamb, *I Know This Much Is True;* Elmore Leonard, *Cuba Libre;* Cormac McCarthy, *Cities of the Plain;* Jill McCorkle, *Final Vinyl Days;* Alice McDermott, *Charming Billy;* Toni Morrison, *Paradise;* Gloria Naylor, *The Men of Brewster Place;* Joyce Carol Oates, *My Heart Laid Bare;* Reynolds Price, *Roxanne Slade;* Richard Price, *Freedomland;* Anne Rice, *The Vampire Armand;* Philip Roth, *I Married a Communist;* Jane Smiley, *The All-True Travels and Adventures of Lidie Newton;* Nicholas Sparks, *Message in a Bottle;* Anne Tyler, *A Patchwork Planet;* John Updike, *Bech at Bay;* Alice Walker, *By the Light of My Father's Smile;* Bailey White, *Quite a Year for Plums;* John Edgar Wideman, *Two Cities;* Tom Wolfe, *A Man in Full.*

POPULAR SONGS: Brandy & Monica, "The Boy Is Mine"; Next, "Too Close"; Shania Twain, "You're Still The One"; Elton John, "Something About The Way You Look Tonight/Candle In The Wind 1997"; Puff Daddy & The Family, "Been Around The World"; LeAnn Rimes, "How Do I Live"; Usher, "Nice & Slow"; Destiny's Child, "No, No, No"; Usher, "My Way"; Mariah Carey, "My All."

1999

- On April 17, as NATO forces bomb Belgrade, the Yugoslav movie academy awards top honors to *Wag the Dog,* about White House aides who stage a phony crisis in the Balkans to draw attention away from a presidential sex scandal.

- On May 19, *Star Wars: Episode I: The Phantom Menace* is released and breaks a string of box-office records. The movie grosses $102.7 million in five days.

- On July 14, *The Blair Witch Project* is released, becoming a cult-movie classic and grossing more than $140 million. Because the production cost of the movie was only thirty thousand dollars, it is the most profitable motion picture of all time.

- From July 23 to July 25, Woodstock '99 is held in Rome, New York. Concertgoers complain that the spirit of the original Woodstock has been compromised and commercialized. The crowd sets fires and destroys property during the finale, and several sexual assaults are reported.

• In September, Mayor Rudolph W. Giuliani of New York City threatens to cut off funding and cancel the lease for the Brooklyn Museum of Art if it continues with plans to show *Sensation,* an exhibit of works by contemporary British artists that he labels profane and blasphemous.

MOVIES: *American Beauty,* directed by Sam Mendes and starring Kevin Spacey; *American Pie,* directed by Paul Weitz and starring Jason Biggs and Shannon Elizabeth; *Analyze This,* directed by Harold Ramis and starring Billy Crystal and Robert De Niro; *Angela's Ashes,* directed by Alan Parker and starring Emily Watson and Robert Carlyle; *Anna and the King,* directed by Andy Tennant and starring Jodie Foster and Chow Yun-Fat; *Any Given Sunday,* directed by Oliver Stone and starring Al Pacino, Cameron Diaz, Dennis Quaid, and James Woods; *Anywhere but Here,* directed by Wayne Wang and starring Susan Sarandon and Natalie Portman; *Being John Malkovich,* directed by Spike Jonze and starring John Cusack, John Malkovich, and Cameron Diaz; *The Blair Witch Project,* directed by Daniel Myrick and Eduardo Sanchez and starring Heather Donahue and Michael Williams; *The Bone Collector,* directed by Phillip Noyce and starring Denzel Washington and Angelina Jolie; *Buena Vista Social Club,* documentary, directed by Wim Wenders; *The Cider House Rules,* directed by Lasse Hallström and starring Tobey Maguire, Charlize Theron, and Michael Caine; *Double Jeopardy,* directed by Bruce Beresford and starring Tommy Lee Jones and Ashley Judd; *EdTV,* directed by Ron Howard and starring Matthew McConaughey, Jenna Elfman, and Woody Harrelson; *Election,* directed by Alexander Payne and starring Matthew Broderick and Reese Witherspoon; *End of the Affair,* directed by Neil Jordan and starring Ralph Fiennes, Julianne Moore, and Stephen Rea; *The General's Daughter,* directed by Simon West and starring John Travolta and Madeleine Stowe; *Girl, Interrupted,* directed by James Mangold and starring Winona Ryder, Angelina Jolie, and Whoopi Goldberg; *The Green Mile,* directed by Frank Darabont and starring Tom Hanks; *The Hurricane,* directed by Norman Jewison and starring Denzel Washington; *The Insider,* directed by Michael Mann and starring Al Pacino and Russell Crowe; *The Iron Giant,* animated feature, directed by Brad

Bird; *Magnolia,* directed by Paul Thomas Anderson and starring Tom Cruise and Julianne Moore; *Man on the Moon,* directed by Milos Forman and starring Jim Carrey, Danny DeVito, and Courtney Love; *The Matrix,* directed by the Wachowski Brothers, and starring Keanu Reeves and Laurence Fishburne; *Music of the Heart,* directed by Wes Craven and starring Meryl Streep, Aidan Quinn, and Angela Bassett; *Notting Hill,* directed by Roger Michell and starring Julia Roberts and Hugh Grant; *October Sky,* directed by Joe Johnston and starring Jake Gyllenhaal, Chris Cooper, and Laura Dern; *South Park: Bigger, Longer & Uncut,* animated feature, directed by Trey Parker; *Star Wars: Episode I: The Phantom Menace,* directed by George Lucas and starring Liam Neeson; *Stuart Little,* directed by Rob Minkoff and starring Geena Davis, Michael J. Fox, and Gwyneth Paltrow; *Summer of Sam,* directed by Spike Lee and starring John Leguizamo; *Tarzan,* animated feature, directed by Kevin Lima and Chris Buck; *Three Kings,* directed by David O'Russell and starring George Clooney, Mark Wahlberg, and Ice Cube; *Toy Story 2,* animated feature, directed by John Lasseter; *Walk on the Moon,* directed by Tony Goldwyn and starring Diane Lane, Liev Schreiber, and Anna Paquin.

FICTION: Paul Auster, *Timbuktu;* Thomas Berger, *The Return of Little Big Man;* Frederick Busch, *The Night Inspector;* Carolyn Chute, *Snow Man;* Stephen Dobyns, *Boy in the Water;* Ivan Doig, *Mountain Time;* Ralph Ellison, *Juneteenth;* Janet Fitch, *White Oleander;* John Grisham, *The Testament;* Oscar Hijuelos, *Empress of the Splendid Season;* Tama Janowitz, *A Certain Age;* Stephen King, *The Girl Who Loved Tom Gordon;* Peter Matthiessen, *Bone by Bone;* Thomas McGuane, *Some Horses;* Larry McMurtry, *Duane's Depressed;* Sue Miller, *While I Was Gone;* Walter Mosley, *Walkin' the Dog;* Joyce Carol Oates, *Broke Heart Blues;* Anne Rice, *Vittorio.*

POPULAR SONGS: Cher, "Believe"; Deborah Cox, "Nobody's Supposed To be Here"; R. Kelly & Celine Dion, "I'm Your Angel"; Britney Spears, " . . . Baby One More Time"; Christina Aguilera, "Genie In A Bottle"; Whitney Houston (featuring Faith Evans and Kelly Price), "Heartbreak Hotel"; LFO, "Summer Girls"; Jennifer Lopez, "If You Had My Love"; Ricky Martin, "Livin' La Vida Loca"; Monica, "Angel of Mine."

"Media Killers: An Interview with Anna Deavere Smith"

Interview

By: Anna Deavere Smith; Kevin L. Fuller; Andrea Armstrong

Date: August 27, 1993

Source: Fuller, Kevin L., and Andrea Armstrong. "Media Killers: An Interview with Anna Deavere Smith." *Appendx.* Issue 2. Available online at http://www.appendx.org/Issue2 /smith/index1.htm; website home page: http://www.appendx .org (accessed July 6, 2003).

About the Artist: Anna Deavere Smith (1950–), professor, actor, and author, was born and raised in Baltimore, Maryland. With financial support from the Ford Foundation, she founded the Institute on the Arts and Civic Dialogue at Harvard University. Smith has taught at Stanford and Yale, and in 2003 at New York University's Tisch School of the Arts and Law School. In 1996, Smith received a MacArthur "genius" Grant. ■

Introduction

Blending theater, journalism, and social commentary, Anna Deavere Smith is credited for having invented a new theatrical genre consisting of verbatim reiterations of tape-recorded interviews with people from the street, gang members, crack addicts, shop owners, and housewives. Leaving intact all the tics, stutters, and colloquialisms, Smith re-created characters, not only caricatures, and managed to reveal the substance of the individual interviewed. In listening to those she interviewed, Smith looked for things that people say, "that nobody else can say." She looked for the poem within the expressions of each person.

Smith applied her unique method of performance to explore situations of social upheaval. In 1991, Smith performed *Fires in the Mirror: Crown Heights, Brooklyn and Other Identities* based on interviews concerning the heightened tensions between urban blacks and Hasidic Jews in Crown Heights, Brooklyn, after a seven-year-old black boy was hit and killed by a Hasidic driver. In 1994, she performed *Twilight: Los Angeles 1992,* addressing the race riots following the beating of Rodney King. More than propagating a particular social position, Smith sought to encourage understanding in her one-person performances of varied voices. By presenting her "body as the evidence that a human being can take on the identity of another," Smith challenged individuals' fixed positions and identities in order to evoke compassion and insight.

Smith's primary love was language. In the introduction to *Fires,* Smith stated that she was less interested in performance or social commentary than in language and its relationship to character. Smith had been fascinated with the magic of words and of language ever since her early childhood, when her grandfather once told her that if she said a word enough times, it would become her.

Significance

Hailed as "the most exciting individual in American theater," Smith is credited for inventing an original genre of performance art. Her performances combined technology, acting, journalistic investigation, and a unique linguistic sensibility in a provocative form. Although her pieces were definitely not fiction, as they are comprised of the verbatim speech of actual people, they were neither completely documentary or non-fiction—since the speech was reiterated, or performed, and the characters recreated, or acted out. By interpreting the characters with a keen attention to certain aspects of their speech, Smith brings out the poetry that is in them.

Due to its mix of fictional and non-fictional elements, Smith's performances were difficult to categorize as exclusively art or social commentary. Her pieces blended the two, revealing art in the articulation of thoughts of ordinary people and embedding controversial social perspectives in theater. Consequently, although Smith made her pieces for the public "on the street" from which her characters were taken, her work was widely viewed and heavily discussed in elite academic arenas.

Finally, Smith's work is most significant for what it plainly does—giving a voice to those who normally go unheard. In doing so, she did not take sides, but probes and presents as many sides as possible. In *Twilight: Los Angeles 1992,* Smith gave voice to the police officers who had been overwhelmingly condemned by the public. Thus her works went beyond mere character studies, expressing, through a collage of voices, the "spirit, the imagination and the challenges of [her] own time. I started thinking," she said, "that if I listened carefully to people's words, and particularly to their rhythms, that I could use language to learn about my own time." Smith's multifaceted scope derived from her original and lasting love of language, overriding any social agenda. Language, and the poem in each individual, was for Smith the ultimate inspiration and source for her works.

Primary Source

"Media Killers: An Interview with Anna Deavere Smith" [excerpt]

SYNOPSIS: This interview, conducted by Kevin L. Fuller and Andrea Armstrong, took place in New York City on August 27, 1993, a few days after a performance of excerpts from *Fires in the Mirror* and *Twilight* at the Agassiz Theater in Cambridge, Massachusetts. Smith responds to inquisitive questions about characters from her two plays and about her opinion on race issues in America.

Kevin L. Fuller (KLF): Have you ever come close to death?

Anna Deavere Smith (ADS): (Laughter.) No.

KLF: I open with this question because of its relation to your discussion of the areas where language breaks down. In not losing track of some of these silences or distortions, if you will, as they relate to class, gender, sexuality—and with your ability to animate and embody difference—what do you see as some of the breakdowns in language of contemporary theorists in the context of ideological whiteness? (And when I say this, I'm speaking of an array of cultural workers in the mass media, art, theater, and literature of any color, ethnicity, or race.)

ADS: I don't know. I can't answer that. I don't really know enough about contemporary theorists to tell you that.

Andrea Armstrong (AA): What about in the theater? Where do you see silences in the theater?

ADS: I think the biggest silence is from white people—

AA: About?

ADS: Race.

AA: What sort of silence is there—is it about talking about race completely?

ADS: Well, there's that. I think that enough people have told me—people that I know well—have told me that in their private lives they don't really talk about race, whereas in the private lives of black people I know, that takes up 80 percent of every day. It would be rare to find a black person in my experience who didn't make some sort of reference to this, or some sort of reference to power, in the course of a day. What's interesting to me is that the masses of white people don't think about it. They don't talk about it nearly as much as we do. I don't know the case with Latinos or Asians,

Actor, playwright, and teacher Anna Deavere Smith. **AP/WIDE WORLD PHOTOS. REPRODUCED BY PERMISSION.**

if they discuss that, and I'm trying to find that out now. I'm trying to open up my own perspective to be more reflective. And you know, I think that's a dangerous thing to say because I'm learning there are certain turfs and territories and good reasons for those, but even selfishly I would like to know more about their experience so I can understand mine. I wonder if we all have the same image of whiteness, or if it changes—I mean, I was very surprised in the Korean community, for example, this idea that they—the woman at the end of "Excerpts," who says, "I used to think that America was the best." Again, I can't think of very many African Americans who ever thought America was the best; it's in our upbringing to be suspect of our own land where we were born. And so I think that in itself is important for me to try to get my imagination around. It's not that hard because so many people had really difficult situations, whereas in our case we were taught that we came against our will. It's just really interesting, and I don't know if we'll ever be able to resolve it, except that we have to resolve it, but when will we be free enough from those contacts in the past to meet one another in the moment? I think it's really difficult.

AA: That reminds me of something you said during the question-and-answer period of your recent performance, that in Twilight *you were trying to disrupt your own ethnicity, and that blacks—or one black woman in particular—was somewhat suspect of what you were trying to do, not trusting you. So in disrupting your own ethnicity, what is it that leads the black community to distrust?*

ADS: Well, I think that's very general. I mean, she distrusted me for other reasons. This is Georganne Williams, who is the mother of Damian Football Williams. She mistrusted me because she thought I was the same as the media, and she had had, you know, a less than pleasant experience with one magazine, I think. She was disenchanted with something that was written about her, and she mistrusted me as well because she was associating me with a powerful institution, which was the theater I was working for; I was an outsider. I don't even know if she has any idea of this particular ambition I have of going to L.A. It wasn't so much to disrupt my own ethnicity, because I can't do that; I needed to, for a moment, disrupt the idea of race as a black and white issue, because it isn't anymore. But my background, my emotional connection to race, is one of black and white. And it's very, very hard to re-mediate myself of that—very hard. Because that's how I think, that's how I've been created, that's how I'm made up. And in order to get a better idea of what's going on now, even if it comes back to the same thing—which is, this is a black and white issue, and everybody else is visiting—I don't believe that. But even if it came back to that, I still have to make the trip to begin to see this from another person's point of view. From other people's points of view, to see this geography of race, just positioning myself a little bit differently, less from the heart, if you will, less from automatic response and more patient, more like stepping back, stepping back, stepping back, stepping back. And we also have to, in talking about Georganne Williams, be very careful, because here is a woman who is overwhelmed and who is quickly becoming politicized, and she shouldn't be. Who am I? I'm this Stanford professor who's writing a play, and as far as I'm concerned, who am I in her life? What she is dealing with I believe is very, very serious, and it's up to her to decide who she wants to talk to, and if she doesn't want to talk to me, I applaud that, because she has a lot of things going on, and I doubt if she has a staff to orchestrate her days and help her get groceries, clean her house—you know, an assistant or anything. Her sole objective is to protect her son and to be vigilant over this process, and as far as I'm concerned,

she can tell all of us to get away. So I want to make sure it doesn't seem as though I'm advocating for this woman to suddenly pay attention to somebody writing a play. But in the larger context, a play for an American theater . . . no American theater has ever shown any great evidence that it is particularly interested in African Americans—period.

KLF: In the context of a performance, were you able to provoke that level of intensity during the question-and-answer period?

ADS: Well, not just in questions and answers; what's very interesting about this situation, for example, is that there were different people in the L.A. core community, and I tried getting interviews with many of them, and I wasn't successful. And after the play started, we heard from one of them who said, "You know, I want to come see this play and bring some people, and we want free tickets, and we think you should give us free tickets because we don't think that we've been represented well." And the response was, "Well, you haven't been represented because we couldn't get an interview. Why didn't you talk to us? You wouldn't talk to us." "Well, we don't want to have to picket, so we think you better invite us so we can see this." I was very glad, because suddenly this thing, this play which is on the periphery of their experience, becomes important. And I think it's rare that institutional theaters are important to people at the grass roots—rare, rare, rare. It's usually something that you do because you have forty extra dollars. Not something that you believe could be crucial in your life, or it could be making a mistake; it could be helping you and it could be making a mistake.

AA: What is their concern?

ADS: Well, I think I would be concerned—they were afraid that the L.A. Four [the four men involved in the beating of Reginald Denney] were being misrepresented. He came and he liked the show, this particular man. And as it turned out, my play was very popular in Los Angeles and it did play to sold-out audiences, and I think it's a good concern that the audience may be getting some information that isn't going to be appropriate in a trial which is very volatile, very important, and very difficult. That something which is part of theater becomes of concern is rare. I mean, I could see if it was a strike or something.

Further Resources

BOOKS

Goldner, Ellen J., et al. *Racing and (E)racing Language: Living with the Color of Our Words.* Syracuse, N.Y.: Syracuse University Press, 2001.

Hoeveler, Diane Long, et al. *Women of Color: Defining the Issues, Hearing the Voices.* Westport, Conn.: Greenwood Press, 2001.

PERIODICALS

Fitzgerald, Sharon. "Anna of a Thousand Faces." *American Visions,* October-November 1994, 14–15.

Hupp, Steven L. "A Review of *Fires in the Mirror.*" *Library Journal,* February 1, 1994, 125.

Johnson, Pamela. "Anna Deavere Smith: She's Bridging our Vast Racial Divides Through Theater." *Essence,* August 1994, 40–41.

Reinelt, Janelle. "Performing Race: Anna Deavere Smith's 'Fires in the Mirror.'" *Modern Drama,* Winter 1996, 609.

Tobias, Tobi. "Alvin Ailey American Dance Theater." *New York,* January 3, 1994, 56.

Torrens, James S. *"Twilight: Los Angeles, 1992* (A Review)." *America,* June 4, 1994, 23.

WEBSITES

Loyd, Carol. "Voice of America." Available online at http://www.salon.com/bc/1998/12/cov_08bc.html; website home page: http://www.salon.com (accessed July 6, 2003).

Stepanek, Marcia. "Creative Reality: Anna Deveare Smith." *Women in Communications.* Available online at http://www.awic-dc.org/womennews_Deveare-Smith.shtml; website home page: http://www.awic-dc.org (accessed July 6, 2003).

The Shipping News
Novel

By: E. Annie Proulx

Date: 1993

Source: Proulx, E. Annie. *The Shipping News.* New York: Scribner Classics, 1993, 1–3.

About the Author: Edna Annie Proulx (1935–) was born in Norwich, Connecticut. She writes both fiction and nonfiction. Proulx attended Colby College in Maine and the University of Vermont, earning a B.A. in 1969. She also received an M.A. from Sir George Williams University in Montreal. Proulx began her career as a journalist and writing "how-to" books. Her first novel, *Postcards,* won the PEN/Faulkner Award in 1993. She also won the Pulitzer Prize for Fiction in 1994 for *The Shipping News.* ∎

Introduction

Through the development of quirky and eccentric characters, *The Shipping News* explores the challenge of recovery from haunting pasts. The novel's main character is a middle-aged man, Quoyle (pronounced "coil"). Quoyle, lacking self-assurance because of an abusive father, wastes his life in passivity. After his attractive, but unfaithful, wife is killed in an accident, Quoyle and his two daughters move to his old family home in New-

foundland, Canada. Quoyle's estranged aunt, who also recently lost her partner, joins them in the Newfoundland home. There both grieving spouses must deal with the demons of the past. Quoyle gradually adjusts to life in the small coastal town, becoming friends with a woman, Wavey Prowse, who also suffers from loss. Through their friendship, Quoyle learns unexpectedly to overcome his damaged past. Proulx has stated that *The Shipping News* was an "exercise in writing a happy ending," and yet that "happy ending is ironic."

The novel's journalistic style, reflected in Quoyle's stories for the local newspaper, was "purposeful for this book." Proulx was "trying to give the feeling of older style newspapers that had those little subheads, condensed thoughts, little crammed up precedes to events." The style also reflects the speech patterns in Newfoundland.

Proulx uses descriptions of nautical knots and splices as epigrams for chapter headings to provide a flavor of the plot's coastal setting, and also to serve as a metaphor for Quoyle, who "leads a life so entangled in 'over–and–under arrangements' that release seems impossible." Compared, among others, to a love knot, a strangle knot, and a rolling hitch, Quoyle appears bound to a lonely existence. After he meets Wavey Prowse, he becomes part of a "clove and hitch" and discovers his own "need to hold on to someone else for support."

Significance

The Shipping News was Proulx's second novel. It appeared on many of the year's best fiction lists and won the National Book Award and the Pulitzer Prize in 1994.

Although some reviewers were critical of Proulx's style, many appreciated the novel's colorful details. Howard Norman, novelist, wrote that it was a "vigorous, quirky novel" with "surreal humor and . . . zest for the strange foibles of humanity." Further, he says, "her inventive language is finely, if exhaustively, accomplished." Although Verlyn Klinkenborg, a creative writing teacher at Harvard, finds the characters limited, "not enlarged, by what goes unspoken," she generally praises the novel.

According to many critics, *The Shipping News* captured the reading public by exploring the universal theme of recovery from loss and abuse. It also employed a well-tuned linguistic style and provided vivid descriptions of those often-overlooked, small and unusual details in life and human behavior.

Primary Source

The Shipping News [excerpt]

SYNOPSIS: In the opening chapter of *The Shipping News,* the sad life of the main character, Quoyle, is explored. Despised by his family, he dropped out of college and worked at a number of dead–end jobs. In this chapter, Quoyle finds what will ultimately heal his sad, lonely existence—working for a newspaper.

Quoyle

Quoyle: A coil of rope.

"A Flemish flake is a spiral coil of one layer only. It is made on deck, so that it may be walked on if necessary."

THE ASHLEY BOOK OF KNOTS

Here is an account of a few years in the life of Quoyle, born in Brooklyn and raised in a shuffle of dreary upstate towns.

Hive-spangled, gut roaring with gas and cramp, he survived childhood; at the state university, hand clapped over his chin, he camouflaged torment with smiles and silence. Stumbled through his twenties and into his thirties learning to separate his feelings from his life, counting on nothing. He ate prodigiously, liked a ham knuckle, buttered spuds.

His jobs: distributor of vending machine candy, all-night clerk in a convenience store, a third-rate newspaperman. At thirty-six, bereft, brimming with grief and thwarted love, Quoyle steered away to New-foundland, the rock that had generated his ancestors, a place he had never been nor thought to go.

A watery place. And Quoyle feared water, could not swim. Again and again the father had broken his clenched grip and thrown him into pools, brooks, lakes and surf. Quoyle knew the flavor of brack and waterweed.

From this youngest son's failure to dog-paddle the father saw other failures multiply like an explosion of virulent cells—failure to speak clearly; failure to sit up straight; failure to get up in the morning; failure in attitude; failure in ambition and ability; indeed, in everything. His own failure.

Quoyle shambled, a head taller than any child around him, was soft. He knew it. "Ah, you lout," said the father. But no pygmy himself. And brother Dick, the father's favorite, pretended to throw up when Quoyle came into a room, hissed "Lardass, Snotface, Ugly Pig, Warthog, Stupid, Stinkbomb, Fart-tub, Greasebag," pummeled and kicked until Quoyle curled, hands over head, sniveling, on the linoleum. All stemmed from Quoyle's chief failure, a failure of normal appearance.

A great damp loaf of a body. At six he weighed eighty pounds. At sixteen he was buried under a casement of flesh. Head shaped like a crenshaw, no neck, reddish hair ruched back. Features as

Novelist E. Annie Proulx's work, *The Shipping News,* received the National Book Award and a Pulitzer Prize. **MR. JERRY BAUER. REPRODUCED BY PERMISSION.**

bunched as kissed fingertips. Eyes the color of plastic. The monstrous chin, a freakish shelf jutting from the lower face.

Some anomalous gene had fired up at the moment of his begetting as a single spark sometimes leaps from banked coals, had given him a giant's chin. As a child he invented stratagems to deflect stares; a smile, downcast gaze, the right hand darting up to cover the chin.

His earliest sense of self was as a distant figure: there in the foreground was his family; here, at the limit of the far view, was he. Until he was fourteen he cherished the idea that he had been given to the wrong family, that somewhere his real people, saddled with the changeling of the Quoyles, longed for him. Then, foraging in a box of excursion momentoes, he found photographs of his father beside brothers and sisters at a ship's rail. A girl, somewhat apart from the others, looked toward the sea, eyes squinted, as though she could see the port of destination a thousand miles south. Quoyle recognized himself in their hair, their legs and arms. That sly-looking lump in the shrunken sweater, hand at his crotch, his father. On the back, scribbled in blue pencil, "Leaving Home, 1946."

At the university he took courses he couldn't understand, humped back and forth without speaking to anyone, went home for weekends of excoriation. At last he dropped out of school and looked for a job, kept his hand over his chin.

Nothing was clear to lonesome Quoyle. His thoughts churned like the amorphous thing that ancient sailors, drifting into arctic half-light, called the Sea Lung; a heaving sludge of ice under fog where air blurred into water, where liquid was solid, where solids dissolved, where the sky froze and light and dark muddled.

Further Resources

BOOKS

Rood, Karen L. *Understanding Annie Proulx.* Columbia: University of South Carolina, 2001.

Varvogli, Aliki. *Annie Proulx's "The Shipping News": A Reader's Guide.* New York: Continuum, 2002.

PERIODICALS

Flavin, Louise. "Quoyle's Quest: Knots and Fragments as Tools of Narration in *The Shipping News.*" Critique 40, no. 3, Spring 1999, *239–247.*

Klinkenborg, Verlyn. "The Princess of Tides." *The New Republic* 210, no. 2, May 30, 1994, 35–37.

Norman, Howard. "In Killick-Claw, Everybody Reads The Gammy Bird." *The New York Times Book Review,* April 4, 1993, 13.

Turner, Tracy Peterson. "Knots & Metaphors in *The Shipping News. Notes on Contemporary Literature* 27, no. 2, March 1997, 2–3.

WEBSITES

"Imagination Is Everything: A Conversation with E. Annie Proulx." Available online at http://www.theatlantic.com /unbound/factfict/eapint.htm; website home page: http:// www.theatlantic.com (accessed July 5, 2003).

AUDIO AND VISUAL MEDIA

The Shipping News. Original release, 2001. Miramax. Directed by Lasse Hallstrom. VHS/DVD, 2002.

"An Interview with Philip Glass"

Interview

By: Philip Glass and Alex Christaki
Date: July 2, 1994
Source: Glass, Philip, and Alex Christaki. "An Interview with Philip Glass." Available online at http://www.glass

pages.org/interview.html; website home page: http://www .glasspages.org (accessed July 6, 2003).

About the Artist: Philip Glass (1937–) was born in Baltimore, Maryland. He was introduced to classical music by listening to the "offbeat" music of records that sold poorly in his father's radio repair and record shop. He began studying violin at age six and the flute at eight. After graduating from the University of Chicago at nineteen with an A.B. degree in 1956, he studied composition at the Juilliard School in New York City and received an M.S. in 1964. He also studied composition with Nadia Boulanger in Paris, France, in 1964–66. ■

Introduction

One of the most famous American composers of the late twentieth century, Philip Glass describes himself as a "theatre composer who is tonal in orientation." By "theatre composer," Glass clarifies that the source of inspiration for his work is largely non-musical—"the image, movement, story." Although Glass's principal body of work consists of music for film, dance, and opera, he has also written in traditional forms, including symphonies, etudes for piano, and a violin concerto.

Although classically trained, Glass was influenced significantly by traditional Indian music and theater. Glass worked in Paris transcribing the music of the Indian sitarist, Ravi Shankar, into western notation. Subsequently, he researched music in North Africa and India. Traveling in Asia, Glass also studied rhythm structure as the basis of music. Drawing from such non-Western musical traditions, Glass's music typically consists of repetitive, strong, syncopated rhythms with subtle variations.

Glass describes himself as a "mainstream" composer in the broad sense that his music is very popular and enjoyed by heterogeneous audiences. Glass's works have been performed for a variety of audiences. On commission from the New York Metropolitan Opera, Glass produced an opera to commemorate Columbus's arrival in the Americas, *The Voyage.* Later, Glass wrote *The Heroes Symphony* for American choreographer, Twyla Tharp, using themes from popular musicians David Bowie and Brian Eno. He wrote the score for Martin Scorsese's film about the Dalai Lama, *Kundun* (1998), for which Glass received a Golden Globe nomination and an Academy Award nomination for best score.

In 1995, he was made a *Chevalier de l'Ordre des Arts et des Lettres* by the French ministry of culture, and he has received honorary degrees from several American universities. In 1999, he won the Golden Globe Award for best score for the film, *The Truman Show.*

Significance

Although he skeptically questions the meaning of the term, Philip Glass is widely known as one of the founders of American Minimalism in classical music, along with

Steve Reich, Terry Rilley, and John Adams. Glass describes his own works as "music with repetitive structures," producing "soundscapes" more akin to pictures than to more traditional melodic-oriented pieces with clear linear progression.

Defying neat categorization, Philip Glass's music draws from a broad array of sources, from non-Western rhythms to the music of rock musicians. Such breadth has reached audiences beyond those of more traditional "classical music." Despite its apparent accessibility, however, Glass's music is extremely complex and sophisticated musically. He is, therefore, often considered to belong to the contemporary classical music world and credited for bringing contemporary classical music to a broader audience.

Glass's openness to innovation is evidenced in his collaboration with popular musicians including Linda Ronstadt, Paul Simon, and Richard James, otherwise known as Aphex Twin, a techno musician. His collaboration with "pop" musicians is less provocative, but rather reflective of Glass's attitude toward music that tends to reject traditional classifications. Of his collaboration with Aphex Twin, Glass typically failed to see any dichotomy.

Glass's music also makes significant use of technology. He appreciates the possibility of making a full-fledged sound with just a few instruments, as well as the ability to work with an enormous amount of sounds made possible by sampling.

Primary Source

"An Interview with Philip Glass"

SYNOPSIS: This interview, conducted by composer Alex Christaki, was recorded at the Royal Lancaster Hotel in London, England, on July 2, 1994. Christaki approached the interview as a fellow composer and musical admirer of Glass. Accordingly, his questions focused on certain issues reflecting his own personal experiences.

AC: How is your style of composition according, with today's musical development and style?

PG: I am a theatre composer who is tonal in orientation. I feel that I benefited from techniques I learnt from studying traditions in non-western music. However, I also benefited from current contemporary technology. My work involves music for theatre projects to invent a musical language with strategies. That is what is represented in my work.

AC: Would you class your music as mainstream?

PG: Yes, as it is very popular, in that at concerts at the Festival Hall both nights were sell-outs. It is not therefore played in small galleries, alternative galleries and late night clubs which were the venues

in the early sixties and seventies. However I feel that you have to be careful using the word "mainstream"—what is the meaning? For example, popular music and pop music are very different things. Pop music is examined in terms of record numbers. For 1–10 million people, classical music may be popular but maybe only sell 100 thousand copies. It may be only a few decimal point difference but it is a big one. Mainstream suggests that the music is enjoyed by a heterogeneous audience. That of different age groups, economic classes therefore not specialist. In the USA mainstream is Country and Western. However in the context of classical music you need to ask will I be in a concert alongside Mozart and Mendelssohn?, probably not. People may see themselves as classical music lovers but may not hear a lot of music.

AC: In the U.K. an artist such as Michael Tippett could possibly be classed as contemporary classical . . .

PG: By the academics or non-academics? Is it approved by the critics? It is obvious that a certain music style will get good reviews as critics are afraid to give it a bad one. If a piece of music is unprotected by the establishment it becomes much more vulnerable. It may be said that if music does not concede to the academic/honourary society it is a little more aggressive. Tippett I feel has a reputation of being a singing composer, . . . re-evaluated and compared favourably to Benjamin Britten. Twenty years ago it was not the case. Indeed it could be seen as complicated and challenging. The *Midsummer Marriage* works in America and is not easy to listen to, hence it is not very popular. But then can you have something that is mainstream yet fails to be popular? A curious contradiction. However, Tippett could fill a hall on his own, sure of his large following.

AC: I have found that your style has not really changed since around the 70's. Pinpointing North Star *and* Koyaanisqatsi, *how different are they?*

PG: Compared to *Einstein on the Beach*? Between 1966-76 that body of work more or less has an identifiable style, changes can appear normal.

AC: Have all your works been principally for theatre?

PG: There have been 20 ballets, 12 operas, half a dozen pieces for music theatre. Here subject matter is the source of inspiration for work. Gandhi was the character, technology in society in *Koyaanisqatsi,* therefore non-musical material—the image, movement, story is all involved in music theatre. Subject matter is the primary source. I almost write with a story, pictures, etcetera.

American composer Philip Glass in Avery Fisher Hall in New York City, 1997. © 1997 JACK VARTOOGIAN. REPRODUCED BY PERMISSION.

AC: *Trademarks in your music include the extensive use of alternating 4ths and 5ths.*

PG: Certain pieces do and others don't. In *La Belle* there is very little. It is important in dance music which requires abstract rhythmic style. A dancer likes that. However in a narrative like *La Belle,* it is more lyrical as it tells a story, that's the bottom line. The key factors are melody, harmony and rhythm. To be rhythmic it needs to be strong and conditioned. More prominent in non-western music. I shared this experience with Ravi Shankar and we travelled a lot, in particular in Asia where I studied rhythm structure as the basis of music. Harmonic factor can be stylistic, early, or with a sophisticated, single movement as with the recent pieces. My approach to harmony is not traditional. The key centres are "array" creating movement and "variety." The relationship of major thirds or even organic fourths or triads situation creates a tonality, a harmonic language more than a classical harmony. A melody is much more operatic. Vocal lines are handled by voices, determined by the applied text. *La Belle* displays melodic material as it is closely associated with the harmony. The distance is dependant on the text or the place in the music at that moment. In the earlier works such as *Satyaghraha* the melodic material is closer

to the tonal centres in *La Belle* it is different. Range occurs however it is not necessary disjointed. In the twentieth century it is popular to add intervallic situations. In older motets it was melodic writing as opposed to identiphonic and electronic or serialism.

AC: *Did you write the* Solo Piano *music parallel to other works?*

PG: Yes. *Wichita Sutra Vortex* and *Hydrogen Jukebox* is metamorphosis in a film. Mad Rush is a dance piece and is my only recent piano piece not connected to a theatre subject. I began a collection of eight etudes for piano and have written six.

AC: *Where does the* Violin Concerto *fit in to all this?*

PG: I don't think it does. I wrote it in 1987 and it is played a lot. It is basically a traditional violin concerto with three movements, lacking oddly enough a cadenza. As with 19th and early 20th century concertos, it follows rhythm, harmony and melody, etcetera. As a concert piece it has no subject matter.

AC: *Wasn't it written after* Powaqqatsi*?*

PG: The pieces are not always logical, not exact sequences but groups of pieces. A five year period may have a similar order but not necessarily similar matter.

AC: The piece I am concentrating on is Powaqqatsi. *How did you go about writing it?*

PG: I started by looking at the pictures. The film was not completed and we had about twenty hours of film grouped in large categories. The opening "Serra Pelada," the "Gold Mine" was originally thirty minutes but was eventually ten. Working with the subject I generally wrote music which would work well with it, to support and suggest something either public or subtle. The distance or duration of the relationship may have a large range with each section having a large volume of images suggested by the music. The editor used my music to cut the film therefore creating a closeness between image and music as the actual picture was cut to music.

AC: I particularly liked the imitation of the train . . .

PG: Trains are my favourite things. There is a train in *Powaqqatsi* and the first song of *Hydrogen Jukebox.* I grew up in a town with trains and I love the regular rhythm from the wheels. I think I'm "good at trains."

AC: An article describes you as a composer "destined to remain an unrecorded composer for as long as he remains a productive one."

PG: I've done 25 records at least. I've recorded two this year. People are always asking why I haven't recorded more, for example *The Fall of the House of Usher, The voyage.* In fact I'm far behind. People love different records such as *Akhnaten, Glassworks* and *That's Nice.* They're even fun to collect.

AC: I've been compared to yourself, a "post Philip Glass" composer. I've completed a 6 piano piece with a strong signature, a recognisable sound. What were your influences?

PG: Probably Western classical music, the non-Western music for example the Indian music with Ravi Shankar in the 1960's. My time in Africa with Claude Sousot was useful. It helps to explode our own musical hobbies, those you come to naturally without thinking. To confront them with an exotic culture can shake them up.

AC: Do you compose alone?

PG: I can collaborate, but the actual conception of my music I do myself.

Further Resources

BOOKS

Jones, Robert T., ed. *Music by Philip Glass.* New York: Harper and Row, 1987.

Kostelanetz, Richard, ed. *Writings on Glass.* New York: Schirmer, 1997.

WEBSITES

The Official Website of Philip Glass. Available online at http://www.philipglass.com (accessed on July 6, 2003).

Stewart, Brian. "Glass Fragments." Available online at http://www.cyberhalides.com/curator/composer.html; website home page: http://www.cyberhalides.com (accessed July 6, 2003).

Pulp Fiction
Movie still; Poster

By: Quentin Tarantino

Date: 1994

Source: *Pulp Fiction.* Original release, 1994. Miramax Films. Directed by Quentin Tarantino. Collector's edition DVD/VHS, 2002. Buena Vista Home Entertainment.

About the Artist: Quentin Jerome Tarantino (1963–) was born in Knoxville, Tennessee, and grew up in California. The self-taught writer and director dropped out of high school to pursue an acting career. His first feature, *Reservoir Dogs,* premiered at the Sundance Festival in 1992, and it was featured at the Cannes, Toronto, and Montreal film festivals. ∎

Introduction

Pulp Fiction intertwines three stories and uses a unique mixture of humor and violence. One story follows two hit men, portrayed by John Travolta and Samuel L. Jackson, as they go about their work of killing for hire. Another story is based on a boxer, played by Bruce Willis, paid to throw a fight. In the last story, the hit man played by John Travolta is ordered by his frightening boss to entertain the boss's attractive wife without touching her. The familiar plot of each of the stories is subverted and finally brought together.

Although *Pulp Fiction* has been described as "film noir" because of its dark and violent humor, Tarantino compares it more simply to "modern day crime fiction." The film's modernity is highlighted by conspicuous references to popular culture. The prevalence and sheer glare of such popular references create an interesting clash of the banality of everyday life and the fantasy of the fictitious plot lines. The film's hit men characters always have time "to debate such moral quiddities as the meaning of a foot massage or the personality a pig would have to have to be edible."

Conspicuous references to popular culture also serve as a method of subversion. The film offers vignettes on the seemingly trivial details of the characters' daily lives, allowing the audience to relate to and sympathize with characters, not as mere caricatures. Some of the most shocking and comic scenes expose unexpected aspects

Primary Source

Pulp Fiction: Movie still

SYNOPSIS: John Travolta (left) and Samuel L. Jackson portray hit men in a scene from *Pulp Fiction*. The film contains both hilarious and disturbingly violent scenes. Three stories of petty thugs, who are not particularly bright, intersect and overlap at key points. The film reestablished Travolta's presence on the screen and introduced several lesser-known stars to a wide audience. THE KOBAL COLLECTION/MIRAMAX/BUENA VISTA. REPRODUCED BY PERMISSION.

of the characters' humanity, such as utter fear in the intimidating mob boss, shame in his attractive wife, sentimentality in the tough boxer, and endearing pettiness in the hit men. Such subversion is also achieved through the film's script—presenting stream-of-consciousness dialogues concerning random topics, in contrast to the carefully formulated, significance-laden dialogues expected in films.

Significance

Pulp Fiction achieved immense popularity across the globe, winning an Academy Award for best screenplay and Tarantino won the *Palme d'Or,* the top award, at Cannes in 1994. Tarantino's work inspired a number of filmmakers in the 1990s who released films that copied the combination of violence and hip irreverence, though none was as successful as *Pulp Fiction*. Tarantino and his films also helped bring in the greater amount of attention given to independent films during the 1990s.

Pulp Fiction received both praise and sharp criticism for its extreme violence and, more significantly, the unconventionally comic contexts in which the violence is presented. Henry Giroux, a leading writer on culture and education, labels *Pulp Fiction* "hyper-real violence" or the kind of violence that "exploits the seamy side of controversial issues." By "empt[ying] violence of any critical social consequences, [and] offering viewers only the immediacy of shock, humor, and the irony as elements of mediation," the film could be seen as implying the lack of "morality or justice in the patterns of life and death," as one critic claims. According to Giroux, such a world view, including racist and sexist insinuations, is harmful to the viewing public and especially its youth.

The film was also significant in creating a "generic transformation," subverting a myth from the traditional gangster genre. Through the plot, *Pulp Fiction* subverts the myth of the gangster genre suggesting that "violence invokes its own inevitable doom." The film also desta-

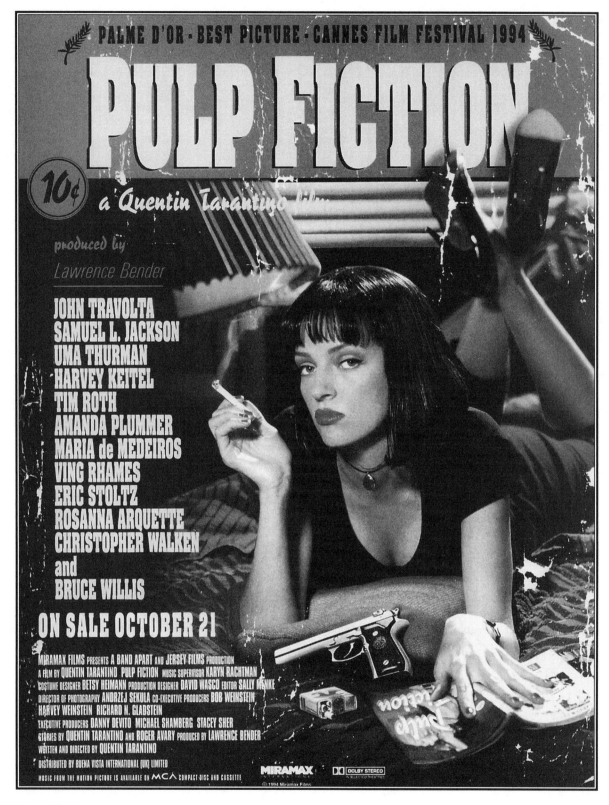

Primary Source

Pulp Fiction: Poster

Uma Thurman on a poster advertising the 1994 movie *Pulp Fiction*. Thurman was nominated for the Academy Award for Best Supporting Actress for her portrayal of Mia Wallace, the wife of a mob boss. THE KOBAL COLLECTION/MIRAMAX/BUENA VISTA. REPRODUCED BY PERMISSION.

bilizes the genre by revealing humanizing characteristics in the genre's usual caricatures of hit men, the boxer, the gangster boss, and his wife. As a result, the film evades both an automatic interpretation by viewers and the critics' natural tendency to categorize—thereby offering a fresh, contemporary view on traditional themes.

Further Resources

BOOKS

Botting, Fred, and Scott Wilson. *The Tarantinian Ethics.* London: Sage, 2001.

Leitch, Thomas. *Crime Films.* Cambridge, United Kingdom: Cambridge University Press, 2002.

Peary, Gerald, ed. *Quentin Tarantino Interviews.* Jackson: University Press of Mississippi, 1998.

Tarantino, Quentin. *Pulp Fiction: A Quentin Tarantino Screenplay.* New York: Miramax Books/Hyperion, 1994.

PERIODICALS

Cawelti, John. "Chinatown and Generic Transformation in Recent American Films." Reprinted in Mast, Gerald, and Marshall Cohen, eds. *Film Theory and Criticism,* 3rd ed. New York: Oxford University Press, 1985.

Davis, Todd F., and Kenneth Womack. "Shepherding the Weak: The Ethics of Redemption in Quentin Tarantino's *Pulp Fiction.*" *Literature/Film Quarterly* 26, no. 1, 1998, 60–66.

Giroux, Henry. "Pulp Fiction and the Culture of Violence—*Pulp Fiction* Directed by Quentin Tarantino." *Harvard Educational Review,* 65, no. 2, Summer 1995, 299–314.

Lipman, Amanda. "Pulp Fiction." *Sight and Sound* 4, no. 11, November 1994, 50–51.

WEBSITES

Chamberlain, Bryn. "Revenge of the Killer Genre." Available online at http://www.film.queensu.ca/Critical/Chamberlain1.html; website home page: http://www.film.queensu.ca (accessed July 5, 2003).

"Untitled #303"

Photograph

By: Cindy Sherman

Date: 1994

Source: Sherman, Cindy. "Untitled #303." Reproduced in *Cindy Sherman: A Retrospective.* Edited by the Museum of Contemporary Art, Los Angeles. New York: Thames & Hudson, 1997.

About the Artist: Cindy Sherman (1954–) was born in Glenn Ridge, New Jersey. She began her artistic career as a painter, but switched to photography during college. Sherman attended the State University of New York at Buffalo, where she earned a B.A. in 1976. At twenty-nine, Sherman was awarded a Guggenheim Foundation fellowship. In 1995, she was awarded a MacArthur "genius" Grant. ■

Introduction

"Untitled #303" is one of Cindy Sherman's later works that portrays women with surreal, sometimes nightmarish, fairy-tale qualities. It is typical of her entire body of work—dating back to the "Untitled Film Stills" from the mid-1970s that brought her wide recognition. The "Untitled Film Stills" provided portraits of females with costumes, makeup, and poses reflective of particular historical styles and genres. However, "Untitled #303" also reflects a marked development from Sherman's well-known earlier photographs of black and white images, imitating the "various female character types from old B movies and film noir" in its lushness of color and hyperbolic mythical aura, according to art critic Amanda Cruz. Although "Untitled #303" differs visually from Sherman's earliest stills, it shares the method of manipulating recognizable images from conventional and historical genres.

A consistent theme running through Sherman's oeuvre focuses on the intimate relationship between costume and identity. As a child, Sherman often played with makeup and costumes in front of the mirror; and sometimes she walked around the neighborhood dressed as an old woman. In college, she was notorious for dressing up in public as Lucille Ball. A certain quality of childlike playfulness emanates even in her most grotesque portraits. Despite the utter seriousness with which her photographs have been approached, they are undeniably absurd. Sherman articulates the intrinsic duality of her works in her theory about her more fantastic, gruesome images. She stated, "It prepares you psychically for the potential for violence in your own life. Or your own death. I think it's also a way to be removed enough from it to even laugh at it."

Instinct is Sherman's *modus operandi.* She tries not to concern herself with the viewer when making her works. Sherman's resistance to titling her photographs lends them a certain thematic ambiguity that allows the intrinsic, irresistible visual quality of her images to strike the viewer.

Significance

Sherman has been called one of the most influential artists of her generation. Her work is unique in consistently developing views of women, challenging prevalent stereotypes drawn from popular culture and history.

Sherman's earliest works played with media-generated archetypes of female characters found in 1950s and 1960s film and television. Her manipulated depiction of these archetypes has led critics to recognize her work as "exemplifying a postmodern culture of simulation [and] a feminist negotiation of the male gaze." Although her portraits seem specifically to address the identity and objectification

Primary Source

"Untitled #303"

SYNOPSIS: This photograph by Cindy Sherman displays a triple-image of a female character with a painted face and wild hair, and adorned in an elaborate costume. © 1997 BY THE MUSEUM OF CONTEMPORARY ART, LOS ANGELES.

of women, they have also been noted for provocatively expressing the more general Freudian phenomenon of "taking other people as objects, subjecting them to a con-trolling and curious gaze." Basically, Sherman's work raises questions of how perception is influenced by culture and society.

"Untitled #224," photograph by Cindy Sherman, 1990. In the early 1990s Sherman produced a series that parodied renowned Renaissance portraits. In this work she spoofs *Sick Bacchus,* (1593–1594), by the Italian painter Caravaggio. **CINDY SHERMAN, UNTITLED #224. COURTESY OF THE ARTIST AND METRO PICTURES.**

Photographer Cindy Sherman. © CORBIS. REPRODUCED BY
PERMISSION.

Sherman's series of sexual, grotesque, and "porno-graphic" images has attracted much controversy. A commissioned series for *Artforum* in 1981 caused such heated debate that eventually it was not published. Her sex pictures "portray pornography as ridiculous" and were created during the early 1990 battles at the NEA over what was obscene art.

In 1997, there were two major exhibits of Sherman's work. One was the Retrospective, which opened in November at the Museum of Contemporary Art in Los Angeles. The other was an exhibition of her first series, "Untitled Film Stills," mounted at the Museum of Modern Art in New York. Sherman's Retrospective exhibit traveled internationally.

Further Resources

BOOKS

Krauss, Rosalind E. *Cindy Sherman: 1975–1993.* New York: Rizzoli, 1993.

Mulvey, Laura. "Visual Pleasure and Narrative Cinema." In *Feminisms: An Anthology of Literary Theory and Criticism.* New Brunswick, N.J.: Rutgers University Press, 1991, 432–442.

PERIODICALS

Fuku, Noriko. "A Woman of Parts." *Art in America,* June 1997, 74–79.

Hoban, Phoebe. "Sherman's March." *Vogue* 187, no. 2, February 1997, 240–243, 278.

WEBSITES

"Cindy Sherman." Available online at http://www.artcyclopedia .com/artists/sherman_cindy.html; website home page: http:// www.artcyclopedia.com (accessed July 6, 2003).

Helfand, Glen. "Cindy Sherman: From Dreamgirl to Nightmare Alley." December 8, 1997. Available online at http://www .salon.com/media/1997/12/08media.html; website home page: http://www.salon.com (accessed July 6, 2003).

Angels in America
Play script

By: Tony Kushner

Date: 1995

Source: Kushner, Tony. *Angels in America: A Gay Fantasia on National Themes.* New York: Theatre Communications Group, 1995.

About the Author: Tony Kushner (1956–) was born in New York City and grew up in Lake Charles, Louisiana. Kushner's parents were classical musicians, and his mother was an actress. He earned a B.A. from Columbia University in 1978, and an M.F.A. in directing from New York University in 1984. Until he was able to support himself in theater, he worked as a switchboard operator at the United Nations. ∎

Introduction

Angels in America was published in two parts, each comprising a full-length play. Part one, *Millennium Approaches,* was first performed in 1991, followed by *Perestroika,* in 1992. The plays, set in New York City from 1985 to 1990, last seven hours combined. They address AIDS and homosexuality in the context of the increasingly-conservative culture and politics of the Ronald Reagan (served 1981–1989) administration.

Angels in America presents more than the contemporary themes of sexuality and AIDS in 1990s America. Walter Benjamin, a philosopher, described the angel in a painting by Paul Klee, *Angelus Novus,* as being caught in the storm "we call progress." The plays are "feverish historical drama about America's immediate and contemporary history, examine many themes, but are held together by [Walter] Benjamin's conception of the ruins of history as the price of progress." Angels appear in the two parts of the play as "apocalyptic harbingers" who "troubled the waters," symbolizing the changes in American society.

Angels in America includes autobiographical aspects from Kushner's life. Five of the eight main characters struggle with homosexuality. Two of the characters repress their homosexuality with denial, and another must confront his boyfriend with the fact that he has AIDS. Kushner himself grappled with his sexuality until his twenties, when he finally told his mother from a phone booth that he was gay.

Significance

Angels in America was unique in boldly tackling controversial contemporary issues. The play dramatized the struggle between conservatives and liberals, as well as the social attitude toward homosexuality and the AIDS epidemic. Through Mormon characters, the play also addressed religious aspects in the social conflicts.

The subtitle, "A Gay Fantasia on National Themes," suggests the play's discussion of political topics. The play was strongly influenced by the conservative political climate in which it was written and performed. Integral themes of power, loyalty, and self-delusion run throughout the story and the characters' lives. The second part of the play uses the Russian word, *Perestroika,* meaning "restructuring," as its title, suggesting the possibility of a social and political revolution—reflecting the revolution taking place at the time in the recently-collapsed Soviet Union.

Reviews focused primarily on the play's presentation of contemporary themes and the particular zeitgeist prevalent in American politics and society. Questioning, "how such a dark and vaguely subversive play could win such wide critical acceptance?" Robert Brustein of *The New Republic* described the play as a "repository of high cultural hopes and great economic expectations." However, the play's focus on actual social and political issues was also criticized. Gerald Weales confessed that watching the play left him feeling "absorbed [and] fascinated, but oddly uninvolved."

Despite such mixed reviews, the play achieved wide critical success. It won the Pulitzer Prize, two Tony Awards, two Drama Desk Awards, the Evening Standard Award, two Olivier Award Nominations, the New York Critics Circle Award, the Los Angeles Drama Critics Circle Award, and the LAMBDA Literary Award for Drama.

Primary Source

Angels in America [excerpt]

SYNOPSIS: In the opening scenes of Part I, Kushner introduces two major themes, corruption of power and religious morals. Act One introduces Roy Cohn, symbolic of the corruption in conservative politics and a reflection of the "red scare" of the 1950s. Cohn uses power as a bully, trying to manipulate those who he thinks will bend to serve him. Joe Pitt, a clerk for a federal justice and a Mormon, is not quite as easy a mark as Cohn thinks he will be. Both men will grapple with being gay during the course of the play.

In Tony Kushner's play, *Angels in America,* the characters try to deal with AIDS in an unaccepting society. AP/WIDE WORLD PHOTOS. REPRODUCED BY PERMISSION.

Scene 3

Later that day. Harper at home, alone. She is listening to the radio and talking to herself, as she often does. She speaks to the audience.

Harper: People who are lonely, people left alone, sit talking nonsense to the air, imagining . . . beautiful systems dying, old fixed orders spiraling apart. . . .

When you look at the ozone layer, from outside, from a spaceship, it looks like a pale blue halo, a gentle, shimmering aureole encircling the atmosphere encircling the earth. Thirty miles above our heads, a thin layer of three-atom oxygen molecules, product of photosynthesis, which explains the fussy vegetable preference for visible light, its rejection of darker rays and emanations. Danger from without. It's a kind of gift, from God, the crowning touch to the creation of the world: guardian angels, hands linked, make a spherical net, a blue-green nesting orb, a shell of safety for life itself. But everywhere, things are collapsing, lies surfacing, systems of defense giving way. . . . This is why, Joe, this is why I shouldn't be left alone.

(Little pause)

I'd like to go traveling. Leave you behind to worry. I'll send postcards with strange stamps and tantalizing messages on the back. "Later maybe." "Nevermore. . . ."

(Mr. Lies, a travel agent, appears.)

Harper: Oh! You startled me!

Mr. Lies: Cash, check or credit card?

Harper: I remember you. You're from Salt Lake. You sold us the plane tickets when we flew here. What are you doing in Brooklyn?

Mr. Lies: You said you wanted to travel . . .

Harper: And here you are. How thoughtful.

Mr. Lies: Mr. Lies. Of the International Order of Travel Agents. We mobilize the globe, we set people adrift, we stir the populace and send nomads eddying across the planet. We are adepts of motion, acolytes of the flux. Cash, check or credit card. Name your destination.

Harper: Antarctica, maybe. I want to see the hole in the ozone. I heard on the radio . . .

Mr. Lies *(He has a computer terminal in his briefcase)*: I can arrange a guided tour. Now?

Harper: Soon. Maybe soon. I'm not safe here you see. Things aren't right with me. Weird stuff happens . . .

Mr. Lies: Like?

Harper: Well, like you, for instance. Just appearing. Or last week . . . well never mind.

People are like planets, you need a thick skin. Things get to me, Joe stays away and now. . . . Well look. My dreams are talking back to me.

Mr. Lies: It's the price of rootlessness. Motion sickness. The only cure: to keep moving.

Harper: I'm undecided. I feel . . . that something's going to give. It's 1985. Fifteen years till the third millennium. Maybe Christ will come again. Maybe seeds will be planted, maybe there'll be harvests then, maybe early figs to eat, maybe new life, maybe fresh blood, maybe companionship and love and protection, safety from what's outside, maybe the door will hold, or maybe . . . maybe the troubles will come, and the end will come, and the sky will collapse and there will be terrible rains and showers of poison light, or maybe my life is really fine, maybe Joe loves me and I'm only crazy thinking otherwise, or maybe not, maybe it's even worse than I know, maybe . . . I want to know, maybe I don't. The suspense, Mr. Lies, it's killing me.

Mr. Lies: I suggest a vacation.

Harper *(Hearing something)*: That was the elevator. Oh God, I should fix myself up, I. . . . You have to go, you shouldn't be here . . . you aren't even real.

Mr. Lies: Call me when you decide . . .

Harper: Go!

(The Travel Agent vanishes as Joe enters.)

Joe: Buddy?

Buddy? Sorry I'm late. I was just . . . out. Walking.

Are you mad?

Harper: I got a little anxious.

Joe: Buddy kiss.

(They kiss.)

Joe: Nothing to get anxious about.

So, So how'd you like to move to Washington?

Scene 4

Same day. Louis and Prior outside the funeral home, sitting on a bench, both dressed in funereal finery, talking. The funeral service for Sarah Ironson has just concluded and Louis is about to leave for the cemetery.

Louis: My grandmother actually saw Emma Goldman speak. In Yiddish. But all Grandma could remember was that she spoke well and wore a hat.

What a weird service. That rabbi . . .

Prior: A definite find. Get his number when you go to the graveyard. I want him to bury me.

Louis: Better head out there. Everyone gets to put dirt on the coffin once it's lowered in.

Prior: Oooh. Cemetery fun. Don't want to miss that.

Louis: It's an old Jewish custom to express love. Here, Grandma, have a shovelful. Latecomers run the risk of finding the grave completely filled.

She was pretty crazy. She was up there in that home for ten years, talking to herself. I never visited. She looked too much like my mother.

Prior *(Hugs him)*: Poor Louis. I'm sorry your grandma is dead.

Louis: Tiny little coffin, huh?

Sorry I didn't introduce you to. . . . I always get so closety at these family things.

Prior: Butch. You get butch. *(Imitating)* "Hi Cousin Doris, you don't remember me I'm Lou, Rachel's boy." Lou, not Louis, because if you say Louis they'll hear the sibilant S.

Louis: I don't have a . . .

Prior: I don't blame you, hiding. Bloodlines. Jewish curses are the worst. I personally would dissolve if anyone ever looked me in the eye and said "Feh." Fortunately WASPs don't say "Feh." Oh and by the way, darling, cousin Doris is a dyke.

Louis: No.

Really?

Prior: You don't notice anything. If I hadn't spent the last four years fellating you I'd swear you were straight.

Louis: You're in a pissy mood. Cat still missing?

(Little pause.)

Prior: Not a furball in sight. It's your fault.

Louis: It is?

Prior: I warned you, Louis. Names are important. Call an animal "Little Sheba" and you can't expect it to stick around. Besides, it's a dog's name.

Louis: I wanted a dog in the first place, not a cat. He sprayed my books.

Prior: He was a female cat.

Louis: Cats are stupid, high-strung predators. Babylonians sealed them up in bricks. Dogs have brains.

Prior: Cats have intuition.

Louis: A sharp dog is as smart as a really dull two-year-old child.

Prior: Cats know when something's wrong.

Louis: Only if you stop feeding them.

Prior: They know. That's why Sheba left, because she knew.

Louis: Knew what?

(Pause.)

Prior: I did my best Shirley Booth this morning, floppy slippers, housecoat, curlers, can of Lit- tle Friskies; "Come back, Little Sheba, come back. . . ." To no avail. Le chat, elle ne reviendra jamais, jamais . . .

(He removes his jacket, rolls up his sleeve, shows Louis a dark-purple spot on the underside of his arm near the shoulder)

See.

Louis: That's just a burst blood vessel.

Prior: Not according to the best medical authorities.

Louis: What?

(Pause)

Tell me.

Prior: K.S., baby. Lesion number one. Lookit. The wine-dark kiss of the angel of death.

Louis *(Very softly, holding Prior's arm)*: Oh please . . .

Prior: I'm a lesionnaire. The Foreign Lesion. The American Lesion. Lesionnaire's disease.

Louis: Stop.

Prior: My troubles are lesion.

Louis: Will you *stop*.

Prior: Don't you think I'm handling this well?

I'm going to die.

Louis: Bullshit.

Prior: Let go of my arm.

Louis: No.

Prior: Let go.

Louis *(Grabbing Prior, embracing him ferociously)*: No.

Prior: I can't find a way to spare you baby. No wall like the wall of hard scientific fact. K.S. Wham. Bang your head on that.

Louis: F— you. *(Letting go)* F— you f— you f— you.

Prior: Now that's what I like to hear. A mature re- action.

Let's go see if the cat's come home.

Louis?

Louis: When did you find this?

Prior: I couldn't tell you.

Louis: Why?

Prior: I was scared, Lou.

Louis: Of what?

Prior: That you'll leave me.

Louis: Oh.

(Little pause.)

Prior: Bad timing, funeral and all, but I figured as long as we're on the subject of death . . .

Louis: I have to go bury my grandma.

Prior: Lou?

(Pause)

Then you'll come home?

Louis: Then I'll come home.

Further Resources

BOOKS

Fisher, James. *The Theater of Tony Kushner: Living Past Hope.* New York: Routledge, 2001.

Geis, Deborah R., and Steven F. Kruger, ed. *Approaching the Millennium: Essays on* Angels in America. Ann Arbor: The University of Michigan Press, 1997.

PERIODICALS

Borreca, Art. "Angels in America, Part I: Millennium Approaches (Royal National Theatre, London, England.)" *Theatre Journal* 45, no. 2, May 1993, 235–238.

Brustein, Robert. "Angels in America. (New York, New York)." *The New Republic* 208, no. 21, May 24, 1993, 29–31.

Weales, Gerald. "Angels in America (Walter Kerr Theatre)." *Commonweal* 120, no. 13, July 16, 1993, 19–20.

Independence Day
Novel

By: Richard Ford

Date: 1995

Source: Ford, Richard. *Independence Day.* New York: Vintage Contemporaries, 1995.

About the Author: Richard Ford (1944–), novelist, essayist, and short story writer, was born and raised in Mississippi. He received a B.A. from Michigan State University in 1966 and an M.F.A. from the University of California, Irvine, in 1970. At Irvine, he studied with E. L. Doctorow and Oakley Hill. ∎

Introduction

Independence Day challenged what Ralph Waldo Emerson termed "the infinite remoteness that separates people." The novel follows Fred Bascombe, a character who debuted in an earlier Ford novel, *The Sportswriter*. It details Bascombe's life during his "Existence Period," a period of refuge from searing pain and regret following a series of dramatic crises, including divorce and the death of his son. To maintain a distance from others and his own past, Bascombe changed his career from sports-writer to real estate agent in a New Jersey suburb. Real estate affords him a superficial sense of permanency and attachment.

Bascombe's equilibrium was shaken, however, on a Fourth of July weekend trip he took with his disturbed teenage son. They visit as many sports halls of fame as possible. Bringing along Emerson's *Self-Reliance*, Bascombe intended to help his son surmount his problems. Yet Bascombe learns, through the relationship with his son, as well as with a woman, that real engagement in other people's lives necessarily involves precisely the emotional and psychological disturbances he had sought to avoid.

Independence Day originated from Richard Ford's notebooks, in which the word "independence" kept recurring. Inspired by a quote from Henry Miller, "never think of a surface except as a volume," Ford explored the true meaning of "independence." In the novel, he offered a definition alternative to independence as a distance from others. In *Independence Day,* independence was eventually understood as the freedom to make contact with others.

Significance

In 1996, Richard Ford won both the Pulitzer Prize and the PEN/Faulkner Award for *Independence Day*. The Pulitzer Prize committee called the novel "a visionary account of American life" and that "*Independence Day* reveals a man and our country with unflinching comedy and the specter of hope and even permanence, all of which Richard Ford evokes with keen intelligence, perfect emotional pitch and a voice invested with absolute authority."

Independence Day was praised for providing a voice for contemporary America. Steve Brzezinski in *The Antioch Review* stated that "[t]hrough Frank's ruminations Ford describes a country that seems to have lost its way in some fundamental sense: hope is put on hold, civility is in disrepair, and violence and ugliness are ubiquitous." Novelist Charles Johnson wrote that "Frank Bascombe has earned himself a place beside Willy Loman and Harry Angstrom in our literary landscape, but he has done so with a wry wit and a *fin de siecle* wisdom that is very much his own;" he alludes to the protagonists of American classics *Death of a Salesman*, by Arthur Miller, and *Rabbit, Run*, by John Updike, also caught in the complexity of living in contemporary American society.

Primary Source

Independence Day [excerpt]

> **SYNOPSIS:** Frank Bascombe's job in the real estate office provides him a window into American life.

What do people want in a home? How can he "sell" that dream to them? In the opening chapters, Frank thinks about his relationship with his son, Paul, a troubled boy who has never fully recovered from his brother's death.

In Haddam, summer floats over tree-softened streets like a sweet lotion balm from a careless, languorous god, and the world falls in tune with its own mysterious anthems. Shaded lawns lie still and damp in the early a.m. Outside, on peaceful-morning Cleveland Street, I hear the footfalls of a lone jogger, tramping past and down the hill toward Taft Lane and across to the Choir College, there to run in the damp grass. In the Negro trace, men sit on stoops, pants legs rolled above their sock tops, sipping coffee in the growing, easeful heat. The marriage enrichment class (4 to 6) has let out at the high school, its members sleepy-eyed and dazed, bound for bed again. While on the green gridiron pallet our varsity band begins its two-a-day drills, revving up for the 4th: "Boom-Haddam, boom-Haddam, boom-boom-ba-boom. Haddam-Haddam, up 'n-at-'em! Boom-boom-ba-boom!"

Elsewhere up the seaboard the sky, I know, reads hazy. The heat closes in, a metal smell clocks through the nostrils. Already the first clouds of a summer T-storm lurk on the mountain horizons, and it's hotter where *they* live than where we live. Far out on the main line the breeze is right to hear the Amtrak, "The Merchants' special," hurtle past for Philly. And along on the same breeze, a sea-salt smell floats in from miles and miles away, mingling with shadowy rhododendron aromas and the last of the summer's staunch azaleas.

Though back on my street, the first shaded block of Cleveland, sweet silence reigns. A block away, someone patiently bounces a driveway ball: squeak . . . then breathing . . . then a laugh, a cough . . ."All *riiight,* that's the *waaay.*" None of it too loud. In front of the Zumbros', two doors down, the streets crew is finishing a quiet smoke before cranking their machines and unsettling the dust again. We're repaving this summer, putting in a new "line," resodding the neutral ground, setting new curbs, using our proud new tax dollars—the workers all Cape Verdeans and wily Hondurans from poorer towns north of here. Sergeantsville and Little York. They sit and stare silently beside their yellow front-loaders, ground flat-teners and backhoes, their sleek private cars—Camaros and Chevy lowriders—parked around the corner, away from the dust and where it will be shady later on.

And suddenly the carillon at St. Leo the Great begins: gong, gong, gong, gong, gong, gong, then a sweet, bright admonitory matinal air by old Wesley himself: "Wake the day, ye who would be saved, wake the day, let your souls be laved."

Though all is not exactly kosher here, in spite of a good beginning. (When is anything *exactly* kosher?)

I myself, Frank Bascombe, was mugged on Coolidge Street, one street over, late in April, spiritedly legging it home from a closing at our realty office just at dusk, a sense of achievement lightening my step, still hoping to catch the evening news, a bottle of Roederer—a gift from a grateful seller I'd made a bundle for—under my arm. Three young boys, one of whom I thought I'd seen before—an Asian—yet couldn't later name, came careering ziggy-zaggy down the sidewalk on minibikes, conked me in the head with a giant Pepsi bottle, and rode off howling. Nothing was stolen or broken, though I was knocked silly on the ground, and sat in the grass for ten minutes, unnoticed in a whirling daze.

Later, in early May, the Zumbros' house and one other were burgled twice in the same week (they missed some things the first time and came back to get them).

And then, to all our bewilderment, Clair Devane, our one black agent, a woman I was briefly but intensely "linked with" two years ago, was murdered in May inside a condo she was showing out the Great Woods Road, near Hightstown: roped and tied, raped and stabbed. No good clues left—just a pink while-you-were-out slip lying in the parquet entry, the message in her own looping hand. "Luther family. Just started looking. Mid-90's. 3 p.m. Get key. Dinner with Eddie." Eddie was her fiancé.

Plus, falling property values now ride through the trees like an odorless, colorless mist settling through the still air where all breathe it in, all sense it, though our new amenities—the new police cruisers, the new crosswalks, the trimmed tree branches, the buried electric, the refurbished band shell, the plans for the 4th of July parade—do what they civically can to ease our minds off worrying, convince us our worries aren't worries, or at least not ours alone but everyone's—no one's—and that staying the course, holding the line, riding the cyclical nature of things are what this country's all about, and thinking otherwise is to drive optimism into retreat, to be paranoid and in need of expensive "treatment" out-of-state.

Richard Ford won both the Pulitzer Prize for Fiction and the PEN/Faulkner Award for *Independence Day,* marking the only time one novel has ever received both prestigious recognitions of excellence. AP/WIDE WORLD PHOTOS. REPRODUCED BY PERMISSION.

And practically speaking, while bearing in mind that one event rarely causes another in a simple way, it must mean *something* to a town, to the local *esprit,* for its values on the open market to fall. (Why else would real estate prices be an index to the national wellbeing?) If, for instance, some otherwise healthy charcoal briquette firm's stock took a nosedive, the *company* would react ASAP. Its "people" would stay at their desks an extra hour past dark (unless they were fired outright); men would go home more dog-tired than usual, carrying no flowers, would stand longer in the violet evening hours staring up at the tree limbs in need of trimming, would talk less kindly to their kids, would opt for an extra Pimm's before dinner alone with the wife, then wake oddly at four with nothing much, but nothing good, in mind. Just restless.

And so it is in Haddam, where all around, our summer swoon notwithstanding, there's a new sense of a wild world being just beyond our perimeter, an untallied apprehension among our residents, one I believe they'll never get used to, one they'll die before accommodating.

A sad fact, of course, about adult life is that you see the very things you'll never adapt to coming toward you on the horizon. You see them as the problems they are, you worry like hell about them, you make provisions, take precautions, fashion adjustments; you tell yourself you'll have to change your way of doing things. Only you don't. You can't. Somehow it's already too late. And maybe it's even worse than that: maybe the thing you see coming from far away is not the real thing, the thing that scares you, but its aftermath. And what you've feared will happen has already taken place. This is similar in spirit to the realization that all the great new advances of medical science will have no benefit for us at all, though we cheer them on, hope a vaccine might be ready in time, think things could still get better. Only it's too late there too. And in that very way our life gets over before we know it. We miss it. And like the poet said: "The ways we miss our lives are life."

This morning I am up early, in my upstairs office under the eaves, going over a listing logged in as an "Exclusive" just at closing last night, and for which I may already have willing buyers later today. Listings frequently appear in this unexpected, providential way: An owner belts back a few Manhattans, takes an afternoon trip around the yard to police up bits of paper blown from the neighbors' garbage, rakes the last of the winter's damp, fecund leaves from under the forsythia beneath which lies buried his old Dalmatian, Pepper, makes a close inspection of the hemlocks he and his wife planted as a hedge when they were young marrieds long ago, takes a nostalgic walk back through rooms he's painted, baths grouted far past midnight, along the way has two more stiff ones followed hard by a sudden great welling and suppressed heart's cry for a long-lost life we must all (if we care to go on living) let go of . . . And boom: in two minutes more he's on the phone, interrupting some realtor from a quiet dinner at home, and in ten more minutes the whole deed's done. It's progress of a sort. (By lucky coincidence, my clients the Joe Markhams will have driven down from Vermont this very night, and conceivably I could complete the circuit—listing to sale—in a single day's time. The record, not mine, is four minutes.)

My other duty this early morning involves writing the editorial for our firm's monthly "Buyer vs. Seller" guide (sent free to every breathing freeholder on the Haddam tax rolls). This month I'm fine-tuning my thoughts on the likely real estate fallout from the approaching Democratic Convention, when the unin-

spirational Governor Dukakis, spirit-genius of the sin-
ister Massachusetts Miracle, will grab the prize, then
roll on to victory in November—my personal hope,
but a prospect that paralyzes most Haddam property owners with fear, since they're almost all Republicans, love Reagan like Catholics love the Pope,
yet also feel dumbfounded and doublecrossed by the
clownish spectacle of Vice President Bush as their
new leader. My arguing tack departs from Emerson's
famous line in *Self-Reliance,* "To be great is to be
misunderstood," which I've rigged into a thesis that
claims Governor Dukakis has in mind more "pure
pocketbook issues" than most voters think; that economic insecurity is a plus for the Democrats; and
that interest rates, on the skids all year, will hit 11%
by New Year's no matter if William Jennings Bryan
is elected President and the silver standard reinsti-
tuted. (These sentiments also scare Republicans to
death.) "So what the hell," is the essence of my
clincher, "things could get worse in a hurry. Now's
the time to test the realty waters. Sell! (or Buy)."

Further Resources

BOOKS

Guagliardo, Huey, ed. *Conversations with Richard Ford.* Jackson: University Press of Mississippi, 2001.

———. *Perspectives on Richard Ford.* Jackson: University
Press of Mississippi, 2000.

PERIODICALS

Brzezinski, Steve. "Independence Day." *The Antioch Review*
54, no. 1, Winter 1996, 114.

Guagliardo, Huey. "A Conversation with Richard Ford." *The
Southern Review* 34, no. 3, Summer 1998, 609–620.

Johnson, Charles. "Stuck in the Here and Now." *The New York
Times Book Review,* June 18, 1995, 1, 28.

Levasseur, Jennifer, and Kevin Rabalais. "Invitation to the
Story: An Interview with Richard Ford." *The Kenyon Review,* 23, no. 3/4, Summer/Fall 2001, 123–143.

WEBSITES

Lee, Don. "About Richard Ford: A Profile." Available online
at http://www.pshares.org/issues/article.cfm?prmarticleID=
4087; website home page: http://www.pshares.org (accessed
July 5, 2003).

"MWP: Richard Ford." Available online at http://www.olemiss
.edu/depts/english/ms-writers/dir/ford_richard/; website home
page: http://www.olemiss.edu (accessed July 5, 2003).

"The Pulitzer Prize Winners 1996: Fiction Richard Ford."
Available online at http://www.pulitzer.org/year/1996
/fiction/works/; website home page: http://www.pulitzer.org
(accessed July 5, 2003).

Cremaster I
Work of art

By: Matthew Barney
Date: 1996

Source: Barney, Matthew. *Cremaster I.* 1996. Available online at http://www.guggenheim.org/barney/cremaster_1/; website home page: http://www.guggenheim.org (accessed July 5,
2003).

About the Artist: Matthew Barney (1967–) was born in San
Francisco, California. He spent his youth in Idaho and New
York City, where his mother introduced him to art. He began
studying medicine at Yale, but eventually concentrated in
visual arts. ∎

Introduction

Matthew Barney's *Cremaster I* is the first video in
a five-part series, *The Cremaster Cycle,* produced and released from 1994 to 2002. *The Cremaster Cycle* presented
highly nontraditional video, mixing various artistic media to portray a parallel mythological world. This world
consisted of symbolic images concerning sexuality.

Cremaster I presented a musical set in an athletic
stadium in Barney's hometown, Boise, Idaho. Hovering
above the blue-surfaced stadium were two blimps, each
attended by four women wearing 1930s uniforms. The
women surrounded two tables, each covered by a white
tablecloth, on which there were grapes—red in one blimp
and green in the other. The centerpiece of each table was
a sculpture of the female reproductive system. Underneath each table is the film's heroine, Goodyear, who
poked through the tablecloth picking the grapes. The
grapes passed through her body, falling onto the floor
from a glass horn protruding from one of her shoes. The
falling grapes formed geometric patterns mirrored by a
chorus line of dancing girls on the football field below.
Finally, Goodyear appeared on the field, pulling the two
blimps on ropes, as the chorus line behind her performs
a wave with their orange hoop skirts. Both the dancing
and the accompanying soundtrack are reminiscent of the
familiar genre of a 1930s musical.

The Cremaster Cycle generally explored the conflicting roles of male and female biology and sexuality.
The "cremaster" is "the muscle that raises and lowers the
testicles in response to warmth, cold or whatever other
stimuli." Barney presented "the stage of fetal development during the first eight weeks of gestation, when the
embryo has not yet been differentiated as male or female"
as a metaphor for extreme potential. Though most of the
films in the cycle concentrate on male sexual desire, *Cremaster I* symbolically portrays the transformation of the
female body.

Primary Source

Cremaster I

SYNOPSIS: Colors are used symbolically in Barney's videos. Pastels are featured in *Cremaster I* and the themes are female-, rather than male-centered. The goal of the first film is to communicate gender ambiguity to the audience. MATTHEW BARNEY.

CREMASTER I: GOODYEAR CHORUS, 1995. C-PRINT IN SELF-LUBRICATING PLASTIC FRAME. 43 3/4 X 53 3/4 INCHES (111.1 X 136.5 CM). COURTESY BARBARA GLADSTONE.

Significance

Called "magisterial" and referred to as "without parallel in contemporary culture," *The Cremaster Cycle* transcended the usual boundaries of the art world, exhibiting at major museums around the world, including the Guggenheim Museum in New York City, and on television—on the *PBS Series, Art: 21.*

Cremaster I displayed a sweeping variety of images taken from many different cultural and historical sources, including the cinema, sports, religion, philosophy, theater, and music. The video also incorporated a broad range of artistic media, from sculpture to song and dance, creating an entirely self-contained, mythological world and iconography—as opposed to a purely representative two or three-dimensional piece. The stadium in *Cremaster I* represented precisely such a contained form. Through such a multifaceted and multidisciplinary composition, *Cremaster I,* along with the rest of *The Cremaster Cycle,* "probes deeply the dilemmas and problems that shape our time," thereby helping us to "understand what we are and where we are going." According to such an accomplishment, Barney has been called the "great hope of an art world always looking for hope."

Further Resources

BOOKS

Barney, Matthew, et al. *Matthew Barney: The Cremaster Cycle.* New York: Guggenheim Museum, 2002.

Barney, Matthew, and Barbara Gladstone. *Cremaster I.* Basel, Switzerland: Museum fur Gegenwartskunst, 1997.

PERIODICALS

Kimmelman, Michael. "The Importance of Matthew Barney." *The New York Times Magazine,* October 10, 1999, 62–69.

Lacayo, Richard. "The Strange Sensation Matthew Barney Can Be a Captivating Oddity." *Time,* March 3, 2003, 66.

Saltz, Jerry. "The Next Sex." *Art in America* 84, no. 10, October 1996, 82–91.

WEBSITES

"Artist Project: Matthew Barney." *Tate Magazine.* Issue 2. Available online at http://www.tate.org.uk/magazine/issue2

/barney.htm; website home page http://www.tate.org.uk (accessed July 5, 2003).

Matthew Barney: The Cremaster Cycle. Available online at http://www.cremaster.net/home.htm (accessed July 5, 2003).

PBS Art 21: Matthew Barney. Available online at http://www.pbs.org/art21/artists/barney/card1.html (accessed July 5, 2003).

Fargo
Movie still

By: Ethan Coen and Joel Coen
Date: 1996
Source: *Fargo.* Directed by Joel Coen. Gramercy Pictures, 1996.
About the Artists: Joel Coen (1955–) and Ethan Coen (1958–) were born and raised in a suburb of Minneapolis, Minnesota. Joel attended Simon's Rock College in Massachusetts and the New York University, and Ethan attended Princeton. The brothers' collaboration dates to their very first film, *Blood Simple,* released in 1984. ∎

Introduction

Fargo is the sixth film by the writing team of brothers Joel and Ethan Coen. It opens with a winter landscape scene from the American Midwest—where the white plains of the sky and snow blend into one another. Snow as a white-washed covering of darker undersides served as a metaphor throughout the film.

Allegedly based on actual events, *Fargo* tells the story of Jerry Lundegaard (played by William H. Macy), a small-town car salesman. Ridden with debt, Lundegaard hired two psychologically unstable men in Fargo, North Dakota, to kidnap his wife to extract a ransom from Lundegaard's wealthy, obtrusive father-in-law. As the two men clumsily carry out the kidnapping, they embark on an escalating spree of cold-blooded violence. Marge Gunderson (played by Frances McDormand), the soft-spoken, seven-month pregnant sheriff of Brainerd, Minnesota, carries out an investigation of the crime. With plain and quiet diligence, she eventually discovers both the factual and emotional reasons for the crimes.

In contrast to their other films, the Coen brothers imbued *Fargo* with "a very dry manner," letting "the camera . . . report the story as an observer." They used only natural light to highlight the starkness of the Minnesota and North Dakota landscape. The characters, exemplified by Marge Gunderson, reflect the expansive northern Midwest culture, with its polite reserve and the folksiness of their Scandinavian-inflected speech. Many reviewers noticed the stark contrast between the utter normalcy of the local townspeople and the horror of the crimes. This contrast was both visually and thematically prevalent throughout the film, creating an unsettling experience for its viewers.

Significance

In the age of large-budget Hollywood films, the Coens produced *Fargo* for only seven million dollars. This demonstrates that films focusing on acting, style, and writing can be highly appreciated and find a large audience.

One original aspect of the film was its presentation of peculiar attributes local to a particular region of the country. The film was shot "on location" in Minnesota and North Dakota during a "warm" Minnesota winter. Also, the Coen brothers created the characters, with their peculiar way of speaking and their even, down-to-earth attitudes, by drawing from their own personal experiences while growing up in Minnesota. Although *Time* magazine thought that the "Coens' attitude toward the Minnesotan characters was condescending," the Coens claim an affectionate intimacy with both the place and the people of the locality in the film.

Fargo presented certain jarring juxtapositions both typical and atypical of the Coen brothers' films. The juxtapositions included the contrast between normalcy and macabre, the obvious and the unexpected, pragmatism and emotionalism, humor and violence, and, finally, warmth and cold. Perhaps the most conspicuous of these juxtapositions is that of humor and violence. The local townspeople—portrayed as endearingly simple, almost laughably normal—are in stark contrast with the kidnappers' psychotic instability. Visually, the bleak, white landscape is occasionally splattered by gruesome butchery. Finally, Marge eventually reveals a concern for emotionally understanding her straightforward and pragmatic investigation. These juxtapositions produce a riveting effect on the viewer.

With *Fargo*'s intriguing story, superb acting, and exquisitely refined style, the Coen brothers once again brought independent film to the mainstream. The film won Best Feature, Best Director for Joel Coen, Best Actor for William H. Macy, Best Actress for Frances McDormand, and Best Screenplay for Joel and Ethan Coen from the 1997 Independent Spirit Awards. McDormand also won Best Actress from the 1997 Academy Awards.

Further Resources
BOOKS

Bergan, Ronald. *The Coen Brothers.* New York: Thunder's Mouth Press, 2000.

Levine, Josh. *The Coen Brothers: The Story of Two American Filmmakers.* New York: ECW Press, 2000.

Primary Source

Fargo

SYNOPSIS: Marge Gunderson, the heroine of *Fargo,* does not enter until a third of the way into the film. From there she calmly takes on a crime investigation that includes a triple homicide in her small town. She is diligent in her search for the solution to the murders and the root of the kidnapping. Gunderson prevails, uncovering the deception. THE KOBAL COLLECTION. REPRODUCED BY PERMISSION.

Russell, Carolyn R. *The Films of Joel and Ethan Coen.* Jefferson, N.C.: McFarland, 2001.

PERIODICALS

Johnson, Brian D. "Fargo." *Maclean's* 109, April 1, 1996, 74.

McKinney, Devin. "Fargo." *Film Quarterly* 50, no. 1, Fall 1996, 31–34.

Toles, George. "Obvious Mysteries in *Fargo.*" *Michigan Quarterly* 38, no. 4, Fall 1999, 627–664.

WEBSITES

Coen Brothers. Available online at http://www.artandculture .com/arts/artist?artistId=69; website home page: http://www .artandculture.com (accessed July 5, 2003).

My Brother

Memoir

By: Jamaica Kincaid

Date: 1997

Source: Kincaid, Jamaica. *My Brother.* New York: Farrar, Straus and Giroux, 1997, 3–7.

About the Author: Jamaica Kincaid (1949–) was born in St. John's, Antigua, in the West Indies. She immigrated to the United States in 1966, and attended a community college in New York City and Franconia College in New Hampshire. She has written for *The New Yorker* and published several fiction and non-fiction books. In 2003 she was the gardening editor for *Architectural Digest.* ∎

Introduction

After twenty years in the United States, Jamaica Kincaid returned to Antigua in the mid-1990s to care for her youngest brother, who was dying from AIDS. Kincaid hardly knew her brothers, whom she regards as her "mother's children." In reencountering them, Kincaid challenged her ideas of kinship and love. "I felt myself being swallowed up in a large vapor of sadness. . . . I became afraid that he would die before I saw him again. It surprised me that I loved him; I could see that was what I was feeling, love for him, and it surprised me because I did not know him at all."

Along with unexpected love, Kincaid faced her disgust for her brother's apathy and carelessness toward life. Such carelessness was poignantly expressed when, "diseased and dying" on a hospital bed, he propositioned a former girlfriend. Through the process of reacquainting herself with her brother and learning about how he may have acquired the disease, Kincaid also wrote about both the economic and cultural poverty in the society she left, but could not completely abandon. In comparing her brother's life to her own, Kincaid dealt with a topic prevalent throughout her works—her intense, complicated relationship with her mother. Finally, maintaining her honest and lyrical style, Kincaid confronted the stark experiences of grief and death.

Kincaid's writing style is deliberately precise and lyrical. Her writing is often compared to a flowing river, a metaphor reflected by her collection of short stories, *At the Bottom of the River.* Her writing is driven by an uncompromising honesty that, with sweet innocence, delves into the most profound depths of often unpleasant emotions and psychological conditions.

Significance

Kincaid's writing is an important contribution to American literature both for its distinctive style and its unique view on contemporary and universal topics. Kincaid's style has been described as precise, spare, and deceptively simple. Her writing is marked by a refreshing honesty that is absolutely unafraid to explore social injustice, the darkest experiences, and the bitterest emotions. Free of hyperbole and affected elaboration, Kincaid's works innocently journey into the heart of areas of human life often avoided and unacknowledged. She thereby provides a distinct voice in the world of English–language literature.

Kincaid's works are also significant for providing a unique view of topics that are prevalent in contemporary American society, in American intellectual culture, and universally. *My Brother,* both directly and indirectly, addressed social problems including poverty and how the spread of AIDS affected post-colonial Antigua. Through her life experiences, she also tackled the universal topics of sexuality, death, kinship, love, and maternal relationships. Her leaving impoverished Antigua and living for more than twenty years in the United States in relative economic comfort distinctly colored the book's views on these universal topics. As an American writer whose works reflect deep roots in a foreign culture, Kincaid offers an alternative view on the world that is invaluable to American cultural life. In an interview about *My Brother,* she criticized the emphasis of happiness in American life and the expectation of happy endings in American literature, stating, "I feel it's my duty to make everyone a little less happy."

Jamaica Kincaid's writing style has been described as precise, spare, and deceptively simple. **GETTY IMAGES. REPRODUCED BY PERMISSION.**

The prevalence of negative topics in Kincaid's work derives from a quest to be frank and honest without regard to external criticism. In the 1990s, her uncompromising artistic integrity caused her to break a long relationship with the important literary magazine, *The New Yorker.* Kincaid disapproved of the magazine's editorial changes during that era. It is precisely such literary and personal integrity that renders Kincaid's writing highly significant in modern American culture.

Primary Source

My Brother [excerpt]

> **SYNOPSIS:** In the first few pages of *My Brother* Kincaid writes of learning that her brother is sick. She remembers the birth of her brother and explains her relationship with her mother, a theme developed more fully in the book.

When I saw my brother again after a long while, he was lying in a bed in the Holberton Hospital, in the Gweneth O'Reilly ward, and he was said to be dying of AIDS. He was not born in this hospital. Of my mother's four children, he was the one born at home. I remember him being born. I was thirteen years of age then. We had just finished eating our supper, a supper of boiled fish and bread and butter, and my mother sent me to fetch the midwife, a woman named Nurse Stevens, who lived on the corner of Nevis and Church Streets. She was a large woman; the two halves of her bottom rolled up and down with each step she took, and she walked very slowly. When I went to give her the message that my mother wanted her to come and assist with my brother's birth, she was just finishing her own supper and said that she would come when she was through. My brother was born in the middle of the night on the fifth of May in 1962. The color of his skin when he was born was a reddish-yellow. I do not know how much he weighed, for he was not weighed at the time he was born. That night, of course, the routine of our life was upset: the routine of my two other brothers and I going to sleep, our father taking a walk to a bridge near the recreation grounds—a walk recommended by his doctor as good for his bad digestive tract and for his bad heart—the heavy black of the streetlampless night falling, our father returning from his walk, a dog barking at the sound of his steps, the door opening and being locked behind him, the click of his false teeth as they were placed in a glass of water, his snoring, and then the arrival of early morning. We were sent to neighbors' houses. I do not remember exactly to whose house my other brothers were sent. I went to the house of a friend of my mother's, a woman whose six-year-old daughter took sick not so very long after this night of my brother's birth and died in my mother's arms on the way to the doctor, exhaling her last breath as they crossed the same bridge that my father walked to on his nightly outing. This was the first person to die in my mother's arms; not long after that, a woman who lived across the street from us, Miss Charlotte was her name, died in my mother's arms as my mother tried to give her some comfort from the pain of a heart attack she was having.

I heard my brother cry his first cry and then there was some discussion of what to do with his after-birth, but I don't know now what was decided to do with all of it; only that a small piece of it was dried and pinned to the inside of his clothes as a talisman to protect him from evil spirits. He was placed in a chemise my mother had made, but because she had two other small children, my other brothers, one of them almost four years old, the other almost two years old, she could not give his chemise the cus-

tomary elaborate attention involving embroidery stitching and special washings of the cotton fabric; the chemises he wore were plain. He was wrapped in a blanket and placed close to her, and they both fell asleep. That very next day, while they were both asleep, he snuggled in the warmth of his mother's body, an army of red ants came in through the window and attacked him. My mother heard her child crying, and when she awoke, she found him covered with red ants. If he had been alone, it is believed they would have killed him. This was an incident no one ever told my brother, an incident that everyone else in my family has forgotten, except me. One day during his illness, when my mother and I were standing over him, looking at him—he was asleep and so didn't know we were doing so—I reminded my mother of the ants almost devouring him and she looked at me, her eyes narrowing in suspicion, and she said, "What a memory you have!"—perhaps the thing she most dislikes about me. But I was only wondering if it had any meaning that some small red things had almost killed him from the outside shortly after he was born and that now some small things were killing him from the inside; I don't believe it has any meaning, this is only something a mind like mine would think about.

That Thursday night when I heard about my brother through the telephone, from a friend of my mother's because at that moment my mother and I were in a period of not speaking to each other (and this not speaking to each other has a life of its own, it is like a strange organism, the rules by which it survives no one can yet decipher; my mother and I never know when we will stop speaking to each other and we never know when we will begin again), I was in my house in Vermont, absorbed with the well-being of my children, absorbed with the well-being of my husband, absorbed with the well-being of myself. When I spoke to this friend of my mother's, she said that there was something wrong with my brother and that I should call my mother to find out what it was. I said, What is wrong? She said, Call your mother. I asked her, using those exact words, three times, and three times she replied the same way. And then I said, He has AIDS, and she said, Yes.

Further Resources
BOOKS

Birbalsingh, Frank. *Jamaica Kincaid: From Antigua to America.* New York: St. Martin's, 1996.

Ferguson, Moira. *Colonialism and Gender Relations from Mary Wollstonecraft to Jamaica Kincaid: East Caribbean Connections.* New York: Columbia University Press, 1994.

———. *Jamaica Kincaid: Where the Land Meets the Body.* Charlottesville: University Press of Virginia, 1994.

PERIODICALS

Ferguson, Moira. "A Lot of Memory: An Interview with Jamaica Kincaid." *Kenyon Review* 16, no. 1, Winter 1994, 163–188.

Muirhead, Pamela Buchanan. "An Interview with Jamaica Kincaid." *Clockwatch Review: A Journal of the Arts* 9, no. 1–2, 1994–1995, 39–48.

Murdoch, Adlai H. "The Novels of Jamaica Kincaid: Figures of Exile, Narratives of Dreams." *Clockwatch Review: A Journal of the Arts* 9, no. 1–2, 1994–1995, 141–154.

WEBSITES

Snell, Marilyn. "Jamaica Kincaid Hates Happy Endings." *Mother Jones,* September/October 1997. Available online at http://www.motherjones.com/mother_jones/SO97/snell .html; website home page: http://www.motherjones.com (accessed July 6, 2003).

Kara Walker

Slavery! Slavery!

Work of art

By: Kara Walker

Date: 1997

Source: Walker Kara. *Slavery! Slavery!* 1997. Available online at http://www.brentsikkema.com/images/artists /karawalker/KW-Slavery-Slavery-1997.html; website home page: http://www.brentsikkema.com (accessed July 6, 2003).

"Conversations with Contemporary Artists: Kara Walker"

Interview

By: Kara Walker

Date: 1999

Source: Walker, Kara. "Conversations with Contemporary Artists: Kara Walker." Museum of Modern Art. Available online at http://www.moma.org/onlineprojects/conversations /kw_f.html; website home page: http://www.moma.org (accessed July 6, 2003).

About the Author: Kara Walker (1969–) was born in Stockton, California. She grew up mostly in Atlanta, Georgia, where her father was an art professor. She received a B.F.A. from the Atlanta College of Art and an M.F.A. from the Rhode Island School of Design. She was awarded the MacArthur Foundation Achievement Award in 1997. ■

Introduction

In "Conversations with Contemporary Artists: Kara Walker" the artist explains the political and personal na-

ture of her art, her influences, intentions, and developments. Although Walker wanted to become an artist "primarily" because her father was one, out of a "slight rebellion" against his abstract paintings, she developed an interest in pictures that told stories of things—genre and historical paintings. As a young artist, she instinctively collected old memorabilia depicting African Americans. She recognized the popular, stereotypical images of blacks in America, in minstrel shows and advertising, as art, and reviewed "them as something more powerful than they were meant to be."

While trying to avoid an "overbearing explanation" in her work, Walker's pieces often deal with historical and political issues, especially concerning race and identity. Growing up as an African American in the South, Walker felt a desire to be a "bearer of some truth of history" through her art. In *The Battle of Atlanta—Being the Narrative of a Negress in the Flames of Desire—a Reconstruction,* one of her earliest works, Walker expresses a collection of negative associations and "vibes" about being black, which "bubble up to the surface of [her] brain and spill out into th[e] work."

Walker's best-known pieces are near life-sized silhouette cut-outs that "encapsulate" complicated issues of race and identity. She recognized silhouette making, in its historical context, as a way for middle-class white people to imagine alternative identities through anonymity and invisibility. Her own silhouettes emerge creating complex historical narratives that are "at once seductive and confrontational," lewd, comic, horrific, and lyrical. They offer visions that "complicate human interactions."

Significance

Walker's works are many things at once—both political and personal, epic and intimate, challenging and hopeful, powerful and refined. The sheer depth and breadth of her art provides both a distinctive personal voice for America and a distinctive American voice for the rest of the world.

Walker's art is heavily influenced by growing up as an African American in the South, where she struggled with the relationship between personal and political identities. Drawing both from her own experiences and the historical iconography of blacks in America, Walker's works profoundly explore the meaning of "blackness." One of her earliest motives was to investigate interracial desire, and she studied "myths about blackness, the [kind of] blackness that's exotic, animalistic, or savage; or noble and strong and forceful."

Walker contributes an invaluably unique voice to the ongoing project of telling and retelling narratives of the American experience. This voice is a result of her

merging personal experiences with a larger political issue or agenda. It also results from Walker's remarkable
ability to weave together infinitely complex narratives
into simple two-dimensional images. Although her
works largely concentrate on narratives derived particularly from the African American experience, their
tremendous depth and eloquence reveal the relevance
of personal and political issues of identity to the entire
American public. Her silhouettes, in contrast to their
simple, black-and-white appearance, refuse to portray
stories with simplified moral dichotomies of black and
white, good and bad, or right and wrong. Their narrative power reveals the shared essence of particular individualized stories with the general story of an entire
nation.

Through their sheer beauty, Walker's works also extend far beyond the American experience. The elegant
lines of her silhouettes, attesting to her works' sheer aesthetic qualities, create an interesting tension with the
scenes of degradation, sex, and violence they are arranged
to form. It is precisely this mixture of fantastic beauty
and hard political reality that distinguishes Walker's
work in the contemporary art world. At twenty-seven, she
was the youngest artist ever to receive the MacArthur
"genius" award.

Primary Source

"Conversations with Contemporary Artists: Kara
Walker" [excerpt]

SYNOPSIS: This conversation with Kara Walker is a
part of the Museum of Modern Art's online project,
Conversations with Contemporary Artists, launched
in 1993. The Conversations allows the public to engage in an informal discussion with contemporary
artists working in various media based on their work
shown at the Museum.

I wanted to become an artist when I was about
three, primarily because my father is also an artist—
he's a painter and teaches and has taught for many
years—of the sort that you might find in The Museum of Modern Art, perhaps, one day . . . Because
of him, I've gained a desire to have an imagination,
which was never very easy for me . . . [and] was
epitomized by being able to fantasize about traveling in time. But I could never really fully imagine myself doing that, because there was always some bit
of brutality, some little hint of reality, that prevented
me from getting very far. . . .

I guess there was a little bit of a slight rebellion, maybe a little bit of renegade desire that made
me realize at some point in my adolescence that I

really liked pictures that told stories of things—
genre paintings, historical paintings—the sort of de-
rivatives we get in contemporary society. And, what
I would ordinarily say about these pictures is that
when I was coming along in Georgia, I became black
in more senses than just the kind of multicultural
acceptance that I grew up with in California. Blackness became a very loaded subject, a very loaded
thing to be—all about forbidden passions and desires, and all about a history that's still living, very
present . . . the shame of the South and the shame
of the South's past; its legacy and its contemporary troubles. Race issues are always at the heart
of these matters. And then I got interested in the
ways that I almost wanted to aim to please . . .
and fulfill these kinds of desires, these assumptions and associations with blackness. I became
very submissive and subservient to myths about
blackness, the [kind of] blackness that's exotic, animalistic, or savage; or noble and strong and forceful—worth putting on display, something grander
than grand.

And so I started a couple of years ago keeping
a notebook of words and ideas and images, and just
about anything that I could to process what blackness was and is all about for me—very personal writings, along with just clippings, nothing that was art,
just a way of getting at ideas. I was, at the time, interested in Adrian Piper's political self-portraits and
maybe the way she could discuss an incident in her
childhood and merge it with a larger political issue
or agenda. Also [in] collecting little bits of . . . Black
Americana from flea markets around the area, but
nothing of the sort that serious collectors might find
. . . sometimes reproductions of older works, things
that are being pulled out of the attics and mass-produced for the benefit of this newly aware black collecting audience . . .

I knew that if I was going to make work that had
to deal with race issues, they were going to be full
of contradictions. Because I always felt that it's really a love affair that we've got going in this country, a love affair with the idea of it [race issues], with
the notion of major conflict that needs to be overcome and maybe a fear of what happens when that
thing is overcome—And, of course, these issues
also translate into [the] very personal: Who am I beyond this skin I'm in? beyond this place where I've
been changed?

This is a picture of an 18th century silhouette-
making device, a little window to the world. While I
was working on drawings, keeping a notebook, I was

Primary Source

Slavery! Slavery!

SYNOPSIS: Kara Walker's *Slavery! Slavery!* is a 12 x 85 feet panorama of silhouettes made from cut-out black paper. Reflective of Walker's most popular works, the panorama presents a picturesque yet disturbing image of plantation life in the American South during the pre–Civil War era. Elegance is accompanied by lewdness, and propriety with shame, revealing an intricate and complex narrative in a beautifully simple form. COURTESY OF BRENT SIKKEMA NYC. REPRODUCED BY PERMISSION.

really searching for a format to sort of encapsulate, to simplify complicated things—it's very difficult to look at words and images over and over again. And some of it spoke to me as: "it's a medium— historically, it's a craft—and it's very middle-class." It spoke to me in the same way that the minstrel show does—it's middle class white people rendering themselves black, making themselves somewhat invisible, or taking on an alternate identity because of the anonymity . . . and because the shadow also speaks about so much of our psyche. You can play out different roles when you're rendered black, or halfway invisible.

The other influence is the cyclorama. What the cyclorama and the silhouette have in common is that they're complete opposites, but they're sort of not relegated to art. The cyclorama is a grand scale painting and diorama in the round, sort of a late 19th century, pre-cinematic entertainment, grand history painting overblown. And where those two meet is somewhere here: [my work] The Battle of Atlanta, which is a 400-foot painting in the round with a diorama in the front, creating an illusion of space, whereas the silhouette, of course, flattens out space and identity.

The Battle of Atlanta

This is a piece of mine called *The Battle of Atlanta: Being the Narrative of a Negress in the Flames of Desire—A Reconstruction.* This was the first piece I did in Atlanta, sort of a homecoming. I guess what happened somewhere in the recesses of my mind was I had appropriated and assimilated all sorts of the detritus of blackness without having searched for it . . . and maybe through years of denial about where we've come from or what we've achieved, at least in my family. All of the bad vibes, the bad feelings, all of the nastiness, and all of the sort of vulgar associations with blackness, and the more base associations in this culture about Black Americans or Africans bubble up to the surface of my brain and spill out into this work. I'm not really about blackness, per se, about blackness and whiteness, and what they mean and how they interact with one another and what power is all about. And I guess with this work, it's the Negress, this semi-artificial artist attempting to usurp power from everybody.

What's the driving force that has you creating this work?

That's a big one. The driving force—there's a lot of them. They're crashing into one another a lot of the time. I wanted to, at first, investigate interracial desire. I think it maybe started from that. And the ways in which it seemed, in my life, to challenge set stereotype notions about blackness and whiteness and how they're operating in Georgia, where I was. Well, let's see, let's be anecdotal [about this]. The feeling of being thrust into history for walking down the street with a white man by some outside force— say a Ku Klux Klan or a guy who leaves a flyer on my car after spotting this illicit liaison. . . . The feeling of walking and talking and having to be historical somehow, bearer of some truth of history. [It's] wanting to make up for the absent 19th century Negress artist who made the cyclorama of the battle of her life. And wanting to take that place and knowing my inability to do that . . . with any sort of real authenticity and knowing that I'm just taking on roles. The way that a picture can inspire lust or bad feelings or distrust or conflict within the viewer—a lot of things.

What are your feelings on race issues?

It's never been anything I can verbalize well, and since I'm not much of a politician . . . It is the grand drama, in a way. It's the thing—"It," racism in general—it's easier to see if you kind of polarize it between color opposites, sort of a dramatic color differentiation, something to that effect. It's very visual, but I don't know if I really want to go into my feelings on that—it's where I go with the work.

Further Resources

BOOKS

Copjec, Joan. *Imagine There's No Women: Ethics and Sublimation.* Cambridge, Mass.: MIT Press 2002.

Harris, Michael D. *Colored Pictures: Race and Visual Representation.* Chapel Hill: University of North Carolina Press, 2003.

WEBSITES

Rosenbaum, Sarah. "Rethinking the Woman as Fetish: The Art of Kara Walker." Available online at http://www.columbia.edu/cu/museo/walker/index.html; website home page: http://www.columbia.edu (accessed July 6, 2003).

Sheets, Hilarie M. "Cut it Out!" Available online at http://www.artnewsonline.com/pastarticle.cfm?art_id=1097; website home page: http://www.artnewsonline.com (accessed July 6, 2003).

"Journal"

Poem

By: Billy Collins

Date: 1998

Source: Collins, Billy. "Journal." *Picnic, Lightning.* Pittsburgh: University of Pittsburgh Press, 1998, 20–21.

About the Author: Billy Collins (1941–) was born in New York, N.Y. He received a B.S. degree in English in 1963 from Holy Cross College, Worcester, Massachusetts, and a Ph.D. degree in 1971 from the University of California in Riverside. Collins was named poet laureate of the United States on June 21, 2001. Collins's poetry has been collected in books and has appeared in anthologies and many periodicals, including *Poetry* and *The New Yorker*. He taught at Lehman College, City University of New York, was a writer in residence at Sarah Lawrence College, and conducted workshops in Ireland during the summer. He was awarded the New York Foundation for the Arts poetry fellow, 1986; National Endowment for the Arts creative writing fellow, 1988; and the Literary Lion Award from the New York Public Library, 1993. ■

Introduction

Billy Collins's poem "Journal" is thematically and stylistically emblematic of the rest of the poems in *Picnic, Lightning.* The poem focuses on ordinary aspects of daily life to demonstrate that adopting a particular attitude and approach to ordinary things can enrich life. "Journal" is described as a "log of the body's voyage" providing room "for the pencil to go lazy and daydream." It offers the narrator a refuge where one is free to experiment with ideas, ruminate the thoughts of writers from bygone eras such as Camus and Catullus, or draw original, yet absolutely useless, contraptions. The poem's clear message is that the world of words, in a journal or a book, fills the seemingly mundane activities of life with satiating meaning. Collins explains, "it's that willingness to slow down and examine the mysterious bits of fluff in our lives that is the poet's interest."

The style of "Journal" is typical of Collins's larger oeuvre. He writes simply with strong narratives, embedding "story in his lyrics, and through narration deliver[ing] the strange music and time of lyric poetry." Writer John Updike described Collins's poetry as "limpid, gently and consistently startling, more serious than they seem."

Collins has been widely admired for his poems' humor and irony. Collins has stated that the "perfect poem is funny and serious at the same time. The reader doesn't know which it is."

Significance

As poet laureate of the United States, Billy Collins attempted to bring poetry into the daily lives of ordinary people. To this end, he instituted a program, "Poetry 180," providing a poem to be read by or aloud to high school students every day. Believing strongly in having people hear poetry, Collins frequently arranged public readings of his poetry.

Collins's motive for making poetry accessible to a broader public is evidenced by the highly narrative, funny, and light style of his own poems. As he is writing, Collins is "always reader conscious," making sure he does not "talk too fast or too glibly." In the beginning of his poems, he tries to create a "hospitable tone." Although his poetry has been criticized by some for being like "elevator music," other have praised his ability to write poems "that appear so transparent on the surface yet become so ambiguous, thought-provoking or simply wise once the reader has peered into the depths."

Collins has undoubtedly succeeded in exposing his own poems to a wider public. In early 1997, a few weeks after publishing, *Picnic, Lightning,* Collins appeared on Garrison Keillor's national radio show, *A Prairie Home Companion* on National Public Radio. Shortly thereafter, Terry Gross interviewed him on her show, *Fresh Air,* another national broadcast on NPR. Sales for his book rose remarkably. Three of his four books of poetry have been among the sixteen top-selling poetry titles on Amazon.com, along with writers e.e. Cummings, Robert Frost, and Walt Whitman. Collins signed with publisher Random House for an unprecedented advance.

Primary Source

"Journal"

> **SYNOPSIS:** Collins transposes ordinary experiences and items into something the reader can interpret with deeper understanding. In "Journal," Collins copies facts and records thoughts. As the writer gazes at a page, inspirational historical figures appear in his thoughts—Camus, Leonardo, as well as images saved for the future.

Journal
Ledger of the head's transactions,
log of the body's voyage,
it rides all day in a raincoat pocket,
ready to admit any droplet of thought,
nut of a maxim,
narrowest squint of an observation.

It goes with me
to a gallery where I open it to record
a note on red and the birthplace of Corot,
into the tube of an airplane
so I can take down the high dictation of clouds,
or on a hike in the woods where a young hawk
might suddenly fly between its covers.

Billy Collins's poems explore the everyday things in life. AP/WIDE WORLD PHOTOS. REPRODUCED BY PERMISSION.

And when my heart is beating
too rapidly in the dark,
I will go downstairs in a robe,
open it up to a blank page,
and try to settle on the blue lines
whatever it is that seems to be the matter.

Net I tow beneath the waves of the day,
giant ball of string or foil,
it holds whatever I uncap my pen to save:
a snippet of Catullus,
a passage from Camus,
a tiny eulogy for the evening anodyne of gin,
a note on what the kingfisher looks like when he
 swims.

And there is room in the margins
for the pencil to go lazy and daydream
in circles and figure eights,
or produce some illustrations,
like Leonardo in his famous codex—
room for a flying machine,
the action of a funnel,
a nest of pulleys,
and a device that is turned by water,

room for me to draw
a few of my own contraptions,
inventions so original and visionary
that not even I—genius of the new age—
have the slightest idea what they are for.

Further Resources

PERIODICALS

Weber, Bruce. "On Literary Bridge, Poet Hits a Roadblock." *The New York Times,* December 19, 1999.

Weeks, Linton. "The Bard of Simple Things." *The Washington Post,* November 28, 2001, C10.

"A Temporary Matter"

Short story

By: Jhumpa Lahiri

Date: 1999

Source: Lahiri, Jhumpa. "A Temporary Matter." In *Interpreter of Maladies.* New York: Houghton Mifflin, 1999.

About the Author: Jhumpa Lahiri (1967–), the daughter of Bengali parents, was born in London, England, and grew up in Rhode Island. She earned a B.A. in English from Barnard College, three Master of Arts degrees (English, Creative Writing, and Comparative Literature) and a Ph.D. in Renaissance Studies from Boston University. Lahiri was awarded the O. Henry Award in 1999 and the Pulitzer Prize for Fiction for *Interpreter of Maladies* in 2000. ∎

Introduction

"A Temporary Matter," the first story in Lahiri's debut collection of short stories, *Interpreter of Maladies,* opened with a notice from the power company informing a young Indian couple in America that the electricity would be shut off for one hour each evening for the next five days. During the first evening, a young professional, and her husband, a Ph.D. candidate, have dinner by candlelight, their first dinner together in months. The wife suggests that they play a game her family played in India during power outages, where each would reveal a secret. Over the ensuing evenings more secrets are revealed, and the couple quietly restore their relationship, which had recently suffered from a stillbirth. "Something happened when the house was dark. They were able to talk to each other again."

"A Temporary Matter," like the other stories in the collection, explored universal themes of loneliness, love, and companionship from the perspective of contemporary American immigrants. The story echoed broader themes of the collection—including alienation, assimilation, and questions about the nature of home and human relationships. Lahiri's explorations of the human condition were accented by thoughtful details of cultural elements particular to the immigrant characters.

Lahiri has been widely praised for her uncluttered style, reflecting a "steady gaze" that penetrated into the world she created. Critic Charles Taylor noted that her "simple, direct prose whose refinement is invisible," al- lows Lahiri to "invest the ordinary with an emotion that makes us feel we're seeing it anew." The book's predominant quality was aptly formulated in its closing line: "As ordinary as it all appears, there are times when it is beyond my imagination."

Significance

Jhumpa Lahiri's *Interpreter of Maladies* offered thoughtful insight into the experiences of contemporary American immigrants. Avoiding stereotypes and clichés, Lahiri portrays characters often ambivalent about both their new and old worlds. Through compelling depictions of apparently exotic but basically human characters, Lahiri's stories explored complex themes such as cultural displacement and loneliness.

Lahiri came up with the title, *Interpreter of Maladies,* from an acquaintance's part-time job interpreting for a doctor's office in a Russian neighborhood of Brooklyn. This vignette aptly conveys Lahiri's skillful use of thoughtful, yet unobtrusive details and metaphors. Although all the main characters in the stories are Indian, the book does not remain fixated on the peculiarities of the immigrant experience or Indian culture. Rather, the stories masterfully use culturally specific details, such as food and marriage customs, as small windows to explore the depths of a fundamentally human predicament— which Lahiri describes as "the dilemma, the difficulty, and often the impossibility of communicating emotional pain and affliction to others, as well as expressing it to ourselves." Lahiri has been widely praised for her stories' ability to express profound and far–reaching sense of humanity both deriving from and transcending cultural peculiarities. In the words of Frederick Busch, "Lahiri honors the vastness and variousness of the world."

Jhumpa Lahiri's stylistic and narrative skills are a source of inspiration to contemporary young writers. Two young writers whose stories debuted in *The New Yorker*'s first fiction issue of 2003 mentioned her as an inspiration. *Interpreter of Maladies* won both the Pulitzer Prize for fiction and the PEN/Hemingway award.

Primary Source

"A Temporary Matter"

> **SYNOPSIS:** "A Temporary Matter," the first story in the collection, tells the tale of a young couple who have grown distant after the stillbirth of their first child. When the power company has to fix a line, their house is dark for one hour each night. In the darkness, they share secrets that heal their relationship after their tragedy.

The notice informed them that it was a temporary matter: for five days their electricity would be cut off for one hour, beginning at eight P.M. A line had gone down in the last snowstorm, and the re-pairmen were going to take advantage of the milder evenings to set it right. The work would affect only the houses on the quiet tree-lined street, within walking distance of a row of brick-faced stores and a trolley stop, where Shoba and Shukumar had lived for three years.

"It's good of them to warn us," Shoba conceded after reading the notice aloud, more for her own benefit than Shukumar's. She let the strap of her leather satchel, plump with files, slip from her shoulders, and left it in the hallway as she walked into the kitchen. She wore a navy blue poplin raincoat over gray sweatpants and white sneakers, looking, at thirty-three, like the type of woman she'd once claimed she would never resemble.

She'd come from the gym. Her cranberry lipstick was visible only on the outer reaches of her mouth, and her eyeliner had left charcoal patches beneath her lower lashes. She used to look this way sometimes, Shukumar thought, on mornings after a party or a night at a bar, when she'd been too lazy to wash her face, too eager to collapse into his arms. She dropped a sheaf of mail on the table without a glance. Her eyes were still fixed on the notice in her other hand. "But they should do this sort of thing during the day."

"When I'm here, you mean," Shukumar said. He put a glass lid on a pot of lamb, adjusting it so only the slightest bit of steam could escape. Since January he'd been working at home, trying to complete the final chapters of his dissertation on agrarian revolts in India. "When do the repairs start?"

"It says March nineteenth. Is today the nineteenth?" Shoba walked over to the framed corkboard that hung on the wall by the fridge, bare except for a calendar of William Morris wallpaper patterns. She looked at it as if for the first time, studying the wallpaper pattern carefully on the top half before allowing her eyes to fall to the numbered grid on the bottom. A friend had sent the calendar in the mail as a Christmas gift, even though Shoba and Shukumar hadn't celebrated Christmas that year.

"Today then," Shoba announced. "You have a dentist appointment next Friday, by the way."

He ran his tongue over the tops of his teeth; he'd forgotten to brush them that morning. It wasn't the first time. He hadn't left the house at all that day, or the day before. The more Shoba stayed out, the more she began putting in extra hours at work

Jhumpa Lahiri's short stories, which mix her Indian background and her American roots, have been included in the *Best American Short Stories*. AP/WIDE WORLD PHOTOS. REPRODUCED BY PERMISSION.

and taking on additional projects, the more he wanted to stay in, not even leaving to get the mail, or to buy fruit or wine at the stores by the trolley stop.

Six months ago, in September, Shukumar was at an academic conference in Baltimore when Shoba went into labor, three weeks before her due date. He hadn't wanted to go to the conference, but she had insisted; it was important to make contacts, and he would be entering the job market next year. She told him that she had his number at the hotel, and a copy of his schedule and flight numbers, and she had arranged with her friend Gillian for a ride to the hospital in the event of an emergency. When the cab pulled away that morning for the airport, Shoba stood waving good-bye in her robe, with one arm resting on the mound of her belly as if it were a perfectly natural part of her body.

Each time he thought of that moment, the last moment he saw Shoba pregnant, it was the cab he remembered most, a station wagon, painted red with blue lettering. It was cavernous compared to their own car. Although Shukumar was six feet tall, with hands too big ever to rest comfortably in the pockets of his jeans, he felt dwarfed in the back seat. As the cab sped down Beacon Street, he imagined a day when he and Shoba might need to buy a station wagon of their own, to cart their children back and forth from music lessons and dentist appointments. He imagined himself gripping the wheel, as Shoba turned around to hand the children juice boxes. Once, these images of parenthood had troubled Shukumar, adding to his anxiety that he was still a student at thirty-five. But that early autumn morning, the trees still heavy with bronze leaves, he welcomed the image for the first time.

A member of the staff had found him somehow among the identical convention rooms and handed him a stiff square of stationery. It was only a telephone number, but Shukumar knew it was the hospital. When he returned to Boston it was over. The baby had been born dead. Shoba was lying on a bed, asleep, in a private room so small there was barely enough space to stand beside her, in a wing of the hospital they hadn't been to on the tour for expectant parents. Her placenta had weakened and she'd had a cesarean, though not quickly enough. The doctor explained that these things happen. He smiled in the kindest way it was possible to smile at people known only professionally. Shoba would be back on her feet in a few weeks. There was nothing to indicate that she would not be able to have children in the future.

These days Shoba was always gone by the time Shukumar woke up. He would open his eyes and see the long black hairs she shed on her pillow and think of her, dressed, sipping her third cup of coffee already, in her office downtown, where she searched for typographical errors in textbooks and marked them, in a code she had once explained to him, with an assortment of colored pencils. She would do the same for his dissertation, she promised, when it was ready. He envied her the specificity of her task, so unlike the elusive nature of his. He was a mediocre student who had a facility for absorbing details without curiosity. Until September he had been diligent if not dedicated, summarizing chapters, outlining arguments on pads of yellow lined paper. But now he would lie in their bed until he grew bored, gazing at his side of the closet which Shoba always left partly open, at the row of the tweed jackets and corduroy trousers he would not have to choose from to teach his classes that semester. After the baby died it was too late to withdraw from his teaching duties. But his adviser had arranged things so that he had the spring semester to himself. Shukumar was in his

sixth year of graduate school. "That and the summer should give you a good push," his adviser had said. "You should be able to wrap things up by next September."

But nothing was pushing Shukumar. Instead he thought of how he and Shoba had become experts at avoiding each other in their three-bedroom house, spending as much time on separate floors as possible. He thought of how he no longer looked forward to weekends, when she sat for hours on the sofa with her colored pencils and her files, so that he feared that putting on a record in his own house might be rude. He thought of how long it had been since she looked into his eyes and smiled, or whispered his name on those rare occasions they still reached for each other's bodies before sleeping.

In the beginning he had believed that it would pass, that he and Shoba would get through it all somehow. She was only thirty-three. She was strong, on her feet again. But it wasn't a consolation. It was often nearly lunchtime when Shukumar would finally pull himself out of bed and head downstairs to the coffeepot, pouring out the extra bit Shoba left for him, along with an empty mug, on the countertop.

Further Resources

BOOKS

Bala, Suman. *Jhumpa Lahiri, the Master Storyteller: A Critical Response to Interpreter of Maladies.* New Delhi: Khosla Publishers, 2002.

PERIODICALS

Crain, Caleb. "Subcontinental Drift." *The New York Times Book Review,* July 11, 1999, 11–12.

Lewis, Simon. "Lahiri's The Interpreter of Maladies." *The Explicator* 59, no. 4, Summer 2001, 219.

Noor, Ronny. "Interpreter of Maladies." *World Literature Today* 74, no. 2, Spring 2000, 365–366.

Shapiro, Laurie. "India Calling." *Newsweek,* July 19, 1999, 67.

WEBSITES

"Jhumpa Lahiri." SAWNET Bio. Available online at http://www.umiacs.umd.edu/users/sawweb/sawnet/books/jhumpa_lahiri.html; website home page: http://www.umiacs.umd.edu (accessed July 9, 2003).

Reader's Guide for *Interpreter of Maladies.* Available online at http://www.houghtonmifflinbooks.com/readers_guides/interpreter_maladies.shtml; website home page: http://www.houghtonmifflinbooks.com (accessed July 6, 2003).

Taylor, Charles. "Interpreter of Maladies." *Salon.com* July 27, 1999. Available online at http://archive.salon.com/books/review/1999/07/27/lahiri/; website home page: www.salon.com (accessed July 9, 2003).

2

BUSINESS AND
THE ECONOMY

PATRICK D. REAGAN

Entries are arranged in chronological order by date of primary source. For entries with one primary source, the entry title is the same as the primary source title. Entries with more than one primary source have an overall entry title, followed by the titles of the primary sources.

Important Events in Business and the Economy, 1990–1999

1990

- On January 1, 60 percent of U.S. women with children under age 6 work outside the home.

- On January 1, unions represented only 16 percent of 101 million U.S. workers.

- On January 2, the Dow Jones Industrial Average reaches a record high, closing at 2800.15.

- On January 10, Warner Communications and Time Inc. complete a $14.1 billion merger, establishing the world's largest media conglomerate.

- On January 31, McDonald's Corporation opens its first fast-food restaurant in Pushkin Square, Moscow.

- On February 13, Drexel Burnham Lambert declares bankruptcy in the largest securities company failure ever.

- In April, Congress raises the minimum wage to $3.80 per hour.

- On April 18, bankruptcy court forces Frank Lorenzo, who earned notoriety for slashing jobs, pay and benefits throughout the airline industry, to leave Eastern Airlines.

- On May 23, reports indicate that the cost to taxpayers of rescuing the savings and loan industry may be as high as $130 billion.

- On June 1, the Dow Jones Industrial Average hits a record high, closing at 2900.97.

- On June 4, bus company Greyhound Lines Inc. files for bankruptcy.

- On November 21, a federal court sentences junk-bond financier Michael R. Milken to ten years in jail for securities violations.

- On November 26, Japanese business giant Matsushita Electric Industrial Company agrees to buy MCA Inc. for $6.6 billion.

- On December 28, the U.S. Labor Department reports that its chief economic forecasting gauge, the Index of Leading Indicators, plunged 1.2 percent in November, the fifth consecutive month of decline.

1991

- On January 8, Pan American World Airways (Pan Am) files for bankruptcy.

- On January 17, the Dow Jones Industrial Average rises 114.60 points, the second largest one-day gain ever.

- In April, Congress raises the minimum wage to $4.25 per hour.

- On April 7, the Dow Jones Industrial Average closes above 3,000 for the first time.

- On July 3, Apple Computer and IBM combine in an effort to exchange technologies and develop new equipment.

1992

- On January 3, the Dow Jones Industrial Average closes above 3,200 for the first time, ending the day at 3201.48.

- On January 7, President George Herbert Walker Bush arrives in Japan for trade talks, determined to "increase access for American goods and services."

- On February 24, General Motors Corporation announces a record $4.5 billion loss in 1991 and says it will close twenty-one plants and lay off some 74,000 workers in the next four years.

- On April 13, American Airlines reduces its first-class fares 20 to 50 percent.

- On April 23, McDonald's opens its first fast-food restaurant in Beijing, China.

- On June 5, the U.S. Labor Department announces unemployment at 7.5 percent, the highest in nearly eight years.

- On July 2, Braniff Airlines goes out of business.

- On September 5, a strike that had idled nearly forty-three thousand General Motors workers ends as members of the United Auto Workers (UAW) in Lordstown, Ohio, approve a new contract.

- In December, the U.S. trade deficit reached $84.3 billion.

1993

- On January 1, unemployment is 7.2 percent, and the federal debt exceeds $4 trillion.

- In February, President Bill Clinton asks Congress to raise taxes on middle and high income Americans, including a 10 percent surtax on incomes over $250,000, on energy production and consumption, and on corporations.

- On February 4, a jury finds General Motors negligent. The company knew of a faulty fuel-tank design that caused the death of a teenager but did not correct it.

- On April 9, the U.S. Transportation Department asks General Motors to recall millions of trucks that may be hazardous.

- On June 8, the Equal Employment Opportunity Commission (EEOC) rules that employers cannot refuse to hire disabled employees because of high insurance costs.

- On June 25, the U.S. Supreme Court rules that employees must prove discrimination in bias cases.

- On July 27, IBM announces an $8.9 million program to revive the company, including the elimination of sixty thousand jobs and the closing of factories.

- On November 2, the Dow Jones Industrial Average records a high of 3,697.64.

- On November 9, Vice President Al Gore and businessman H. Ross Perot debate the North American Free Trade Agreement (NAFTA) on the CNN television program "Larry King Live."

- On December 14, the United Mine Workers (UMW) approve a five-year contract, ending a strike that had affected seven states and some of the biggest coal operators in the nation.

- On December 28, the Dow Jones Industrial Average hits a record high of 3,793.49.

1994

- Viacom Inc. completes an $8.4 billion merger with Blockbuster Entertainment Corporation.

- On January 1, NAFTA reduces tariffs among the U.S., Canada, and Mexico.

- On January 7, the U.S. Labor Department reports unemployment at a three-year low of 6.4 percent in December 1993.

- On January 24, the Dow Jones Industrial Average closes above 3,900 for the first time, ending the day at 3,914.48.

- On February 4, the Federal Reserve Board increases interest rates for the first time in five years in a surprise announcement, leading Wall Street investors to sell their stock.

- On April 1, the U.S. Labor Department reports March unemployment unchanged from February, at 6.5 percent.

- On April 4, Marc Andresson founds Netscape Communications.

- On May 24, the United States and Japan agree to revive negotiations to open Japanese markets to U.S. goods.

- On July 15, in a settlement with the Justice Department, Microsoft promises to end practices used to corner the personal computer software program market.

- In November, a flaw in its new Pentium processor costs Intel more than $475 million.

- On December 12, Princeton University economist John Nash receives the Nobel Prize in economics.

1995

- On February 14, a federal judge rejects the U.S. Justice Department's proposed antitrust settlement with Microsoft Corporation; the decision is overturned on appeal.

- On February 23, the Dow Jones Industrial Average closes above 4,000 for the first time, ending the day at 4,003.33.

- On February 26, the United States and China avert a trade war by signing an agreement.

- On March 10, the U.S. Labor Department reports that unemployment dropped to 5.4 percent in February, down 0.3 percent from January.

- On April 12, billionaire Kirk Kerkorian and former Chrysler chairman Lido Anthony "Lee" Iacocca offer to buy Chrysler for $22.8 billion, but Chrysler refuses.

- On May 15, Dow Corning Corporation declares bankruptcy, citing large expenses from liability lawsuits.

- On May 26, in the largest recall in tobacco-industry history, Philip Morris stops selling several cigarette brands, including the top-selling Marlboro, because some filters are reported to be contaminated.

- On June 18, the Dow Jones Industrial Average closes above 4,500 for the first time, ending the day at 4,510.79.

- On July 19, in the busiest trading day in its history, the Dow Jones Industrial Average ends at 4,628.87 after plunging more than 130 points earlier in the day.

- On August 21, the Philip Morris and R. J. Reynolds tobacco companies agree to drop libel suits against ABC News when it apologizes for an earlier report that cigarette companies add nicotine to addict smokers.

- On September 14, the Dow Jones Industrial Average closes above 4,800, ending the day at a record 4,801.80.

- On September 20, AT&T stuns Wall Street, announcing its intention to split into three companies: a long distance carrier, an Internet service provider, and a telephone equipment company.

- On September 22, Time Warner Inc. announces it will buy Turner Broadcasting System Inc for $7.5 billion.

- On November 21, the Dow Jones Industrial Average closes above 5,000 for the first time, rising 40.46 points to 5,023.55.

- On November 24, Westinghouse Electric Corporation buys CBS Inc. for $5.4 billion.

- On December 18, the Dow drops 101.52 points, its biggest one-day loss in four years.

1996

- For the first time, personal computers outsell televisions.

- On January 4, retailers report 1995 Christmas sales the worst since 1990.

- On April 1, SBC Communications buys Pacific Telesis for $17 billion.

- On April 22, Bell Atlantic and NYNEX agree to unite in one of the largest mergers in U.S. history, making the new company the second largest U.S. telephone company after AT&T.

- On May 2, 3M Media, in a move sure to hurt cigarette manufacturers, announces it will no longer accept tobacco contracts for its billboards after 1996.

- On July 17, the Federal Trade Commission (FTC) approves the Time-Warner merger with Turner Broadcasting System, creating the world's largest media company.

- On September 6, the U.S. Labor Department reports unemployment at 5.1 percent, the lowest in seven years.

- On October 7, the Dow Jones Industrial Average surpasses 6,000.

- In November, Archer Daniels Midland (ADM) announces it will pay a record $100 million fine for price fixing.

- On November 15, Texaco settles a racial discrimination lawsuit, agreeing to pay more than $140 million, a record for racial discrimination cases.

- On December 15, Boeing Company announces plans to buy McDonnell-Douglas Corporation for $13.3 billion, the largest business deal in the aerospace industry.

1997

- On January 9, Volkswagen agrees to pay $100 million to General Motors to settle an espionage lawsuit in which GM accused Volkswagen of stealing trade secrets.

- On January 23, the worst freeze in more than seven years damages more than $250 million of Florida crops.

- On January 24, supermarket chain Publix agrees to pay $81.5 million to settle a lawsuit accusing the chain of discrimination against one hundred thousand female employees.

- On January 31, the U.S. Labor Department reports the lowest inflation in thirty years.

- On February 5, Morgan Stanley and Dean Witter Discover agree to merge.

- On February 13, the Dow Jones Industrial Average surpasses 7,000.

- On May 20, General Motors announces it will begin making cars in China.

- On June 6, the U.S. Labor Department reports 4.8 percent unemployment, the lowest since 1973.

- On July 28, *Forbes* magazine lists the three richest people or families in the world: William Henry "Bill" Gates III of Microsoft ($36.4 billion); the Walton family of Wal-Mart retailers ($27.6 billion); and financier Warren Buffett ($25.2 billion).

- On August 3, a strike by 185,000 United Parcel Service (UPS) workers inconveniences many businesses.

- On August 6, Microsoft and Apple form a partnership.

- On August 30, NationsBank announces its acquisition of Florida franchise Barnett Banks for a record $15.5 billion in stock.

- On September 1, Congress raises the minimum wage from $4.75 to $5.15 an hour.

- On September 2, the Dow Jones Industrial Average gains 257.35 points, the largest single-day rise.

- On September 24, Travelers Group announces a $9 billion merger with Wall Street powerhouse Salomon Brothers.

- On November 7, the U.S. Department of Labor reports 4.7 percent unemployment, the lowest since 1973.

- On November 10, Worldcom Inc. buys MCI Communications, the second largest long-distance U.S. phone company, for $43 billion, the largest merger in U.S. history.

- On November 11, the Eastman Kodak Company announces it will lay off ten thousand workers, almost 10 percent of its workforce in the largest layoff of 1997.

- On December 5, the U.S. Labor Department reports that the economy gained more than four hundred thousand jobs in November, that unemployment is 4.8 percent, and that hourly wages increased by seven cents.

- On December 13, the United States and 101 other countries, meeting in Geneva, Switzerland, sign a global trade agreement that will open financial markets by permitting foreign ownership of banks and investment firms.

- On December 24, thirty brokerage firms, including some of the most respected and well known on Wall Street, agree to pay $900 million to end a suit accusing them of conspiring to fix prices on the Nasdaq stock exchange.

1998

- With a market value of $262 million, software maker Microsoft passes General Electric as the biggest company in the United States.

- On January 9, the stock market declines nearly 3 percent (222 points) with news that the financial crisis in Asia could diminish U.S. exports and the value of U.S. investments in Asia.

- On January 19, *The New York Times* reports that Compaq, Intel, and Microsoft, the big three in the computer industry, will announce a joint venture with the largest local telephone companies to improve Internet service over phone lines.

- On March 4, the U.S. Supreme Court rules unanimously that federal law protects employees from sexual harassment in the workplace by people of the same sex.

- On April 6, Citicorp and Travelers Group Inc. disclose that they have agreed to a merger, valued at more than $70 billion, that will create the world's largest financial services firm.

- On April 13, NationsBank and Bank America agree to merge, as do Banc One and First Chicago.

- On May 6, German automaker Daimler-Benz A.G., manufacturer of Mercedes-Benz automobiles, announces that it will buy Chrysler Corporation for $36 billion, the largest industrial takeover in history and the largest foreign purchase of a U.S. company.

- On May 8, the U.S. Department of Labor reports 4.3 percent unemployment in April, the lowest since 1970.

- On May 11, SBC Communications announces that it will buy Ameritech Corporation for $62 billion, creating the largest U.S. telephone company.

- On May 14 Microsoft Corporation agrees, hours before state and federal agencies are to file antitrust lawsuits against it, to postpone for 3 days the launch of its newest operating system, Windows '98.

- On June 8, the FTC files an antitrust lawsuit against Intel, the world's largest computer chip maker, alleging that the company had tried to coerce three computer manufacturers to sell Intel the rights to patented technologies.

- On June 10, Federal Reserve Chairman Alan Greenspan announces that the Fed will not raise interest rates.

- On June 15, Wall Street indexes plunge 207 points over persistent fears that Asian financial instability will stall U.S. economic growth.

- On June 24, AT&T announces it will purchase Tele-Communications Inc., the second-largest U.S. cable TV company, for $31.8 billion.

- On July 26, AT&T and British Telecom announce that they will merge most of their international operations into a jointly owned company.

- On July 28, Bell Atlantic announces it will buy GTE for $52.8 billion in stock.

- On July 31, the U.S. Commerce Department reports that the U.S. economy grew slowly during the second quarter.

- On August 9, nearly 73,000 telephone workers go on strike against Bell Atlantic because the company also uses nonunion workers.

- On August 11, British Petroleum (BP) announces it will buy U.S. oil giant Amoco for $48.2 billion in the largest oil merger to date.

- On August 27, the Dow plunges 4.19 percent (more than 357 points), causing international markets to fall as well in the worst trading day of 1998.

- On August 28, the Dow falls another 114 points, making this week the worst since 1989.

- On August 31, the Dow falls 512 points, almost 6.4 percent, as both large and small investors sell.

- On September 1, the Dow regains almost half of what it had lost as a record 1.21 billion shares trade hands.

- On September 29, the Federal Reserve cuts interest rates ¼ of 1 percent, in response to fluctuations in stock prices.

- On October 15, the Federal Reserve again cuts interest rates another ¼ percent.

- On November 24, America Online announces plans to buy Netscape Communications Corporation.

- On December 1, the largest U.S. oil company, Exxon, announces it will buy the second largest oil company, Mobil, for $80 billion to form the world's largest corporation.

1999

- On March 8, RJR Nabisco, facing lawsuits, announces it will split its food and tobacco businesses.

- On March 29, the Dow closes above 10,000 for the first time.

- On April 13, after meeting with twenty business executives, the White House announces it will resume trade negotiations with China.

- On May 3, the Dow closes above 11,000 only twenty-four trading days after breaking 10,000, the fastest rise in history.

- On September 7, Viacom Inc. announces it will buy the CBS Corporation for $37.3 billion in the largest media merger to date.

- On October 4, MCI Worldcom Inc., the second-largest long-distance U.S. phone carrier, agrees to purchase Sprint Corporation for $108 billion in stock.

- On October 15, the Dow plunges almost 267 points (2.59 percent), ending one of the worst weeks since October 1989.

- In December, the Dow again climbs to 10,000 points.

"Industry Employment and the 1990–91 Recession"

Journal article

By: Christopher J. Singleton

Date: July 1993

Source: Singleton, Christopher J. "Industry Employment and the Recession of 1990–91." *Monthly Labor Review* 116, July 1993, 15. Available online at http://www.bls.gov/opub /mlr/1993/07/art2exc.htm; website home page: http://www .bls.gov (accessed June 4, 2003).

About the Author: Christopher J. Singleton worked for the Office of Employment and Unemployment Statistics in the Bureau of Labor Statistics, the U.S. Department of Labor in Washington, D.C., which conducts research regarding numbers, cycles, and patterns in official employment and unemployment rates. ∎

Introduction

Ever since the Panic of 1819, a new pattern of ups and down in the national economy has emerged that was later called the business cycle. For the rest of the nineteenth and twentieth centuries, the American economy went through a series of cyclic changes, moving from a period of growth in product inventories, new investment, and more jobs through a peak period of prosperity followed by a slowing of growth that led to falling investment and rising unemployment. Some of the business cycles were short, averaging about eighteen months long. A second kind of cycle lasted longer for an average period of about twenty years. Economists have studied these cycles in an attempt to understand the factors that influence how they operates. Much remains to be learned about whether the ups and downs of the business cycle can be controlled or moderated through changes in the nation's economic policies by individual firms, entire industries, or the federal government. Politicians have tried to impose order of the turns in the business cycle to little avail. Republican and Democratic presidents have often announced the end or disappearance of the business cycle, only to see it come back to haunt their political fortunes.

After a short, sharp decline in 1981–1982, the U.S. economy experienced positive growth for the rest of the decade, in contrast to the stagnation of the 1970s. Yet at the end of the growth part of the long business cycle of the 1980s, the American economy turned downward in a number of key areas in the summer of 1990. This downturn led to the loss of many jobs and a significant rise in the unemployment rate. Statisticians conduct ongoing research to trace changes in the economic cycle. Their findings for the early 1990s are described here, pointing to the savings and loan scandal, the end of the cold war, and the crisis in the Persian Gulf in the wake of Iraq's invasion of Kuwait as key factors in bringing on this latest downturn in the economy.

Significance

Following the economic downturn of 1981–1982, the United States moved into a period of stronger economic growth than the previous decade. For most of the 1980s, business leaders and politicians reminded the public that America was now in the longest period of economic expansion in the country's history, one that was creating millions of jobs. While some economic indicators supported such claims, structural changes in the national and international economies had shifted the geographical location, skill levels, and pay for many jobs. Under an older industrial economy, working Americans had gotten used to stable, long-term employment. Working Americans began to take for granted benefits such as health insurance, paid holidays, and annual vacations for themselves and family members. They looked forward to a comfortable future based on financial returns from job-related retirement plans.

The recession of 1990–1991 brought an end to the growth of the 1980s, which in retrospect proved less healthy than advertised at the time. More importantly, this downturn resulted in the loss of many industrial jobs that would never come back—a pattern that had emerged in the 1980s but remained little noticed until it hit large numbers of middle- and upper-middle-class employees in this recession. Increasingly, more Americans discovered that they would have to take new jobs with no expectation of permanent employment. It was difficult to get used to lower wages or salaries that had allowed for a consumer economy to do well. Often centered in the retail sales, service, and finance sectors, these new jobs provided limited or no benefits. The recession of the early 1990s proved less severe and shorter than the recession of 1981–1982, yet many Americans entered the new decade with falling expectations about their economic future. While the 1990s did not appear to begin well, economic growth, including job growth, would turn out much stronger than many expected by the mid- and late 1990s.

Demonstrators march in a 1992 protest of massive layoffs and growing unemployment. As President Bush found himself presiding over an economic recession, he broke his campaign promise of "no new taxes" and angered many in the public struggling under the hard economy. © WALLY MCNAMEE/CORBIS. REPRODUCED BY PERMISSION.

Primary Source

"Industry Employment and the 1990–91 Recession" [excerpt]

> **SYNOPSIS:** Statistician Christopher J. Singleton describes the impact of the recession of 1990–1991 on the nation's labor market.

The Nation's longest peacetime expansion officially ended in July 1990 as the economy entered its first downturn since the 1981–82 period. Nonfarm employment had peaked a month earlier, in June 1990, and then fell in 10 consecutive months. Nearly 1.5 million jobs—1 1/2 percent of the work force—were lost through April 1991. The labor market subsequently improved in relative terms during mid-1991, as the job losses became smaller and less persistent. Employment finally reached a low point in February 1992, but the job recovery remained fairly modest through the remainder of the year.

Although generally milder than the typical postwar recession, the 1990–91 downturn was exacerbated by several external factors such as the Persian Gulf crisis, the savings and loan collapse, and continued job cutbacks as a result of lower defense spending. Furthermore, a renewed emphasis on efficiency and cost containment prompted firms, particularly large firms, to restructure their work forces. Reflecting the increased competitive environment confronting many companies, the phenomenon has tampered the recovery of lost jobs. Also, healthy growth in labor productivity, to some extent, has mitigated against the need to rapidly expand industry work forces.

Further Resources

BOOKS

Bartlett, Donald L., and James B. Steele. *America: What Went Wrong?* Kansas City, Mo.: Andrews and McMeel, 1992.

Bernstein, Michael A., and David E. Adler, eds. *Understanding American Economic Decline.* New York: Cambridge University Press, 1994.

Norton, Hugh S. *The Quest for Stability: From Roosevelt to Bush.* New York: Columbia University Press, 1990.

Phillips, Kevin. *Boiling Point: Democrats, Republicans, and the Decline of Middle-Class Prosperity.* New York: Random House, 1993.

Preamble to the North American Free Trade Agreement (NAFTA)
Treaty

By: Governments of the United States, Canada, and Mexico
Date: 1994
Source: Preamble to the North American Free Trade Agreement between U.S., Canada, and Mexico. Available online at http://www-tech.mit.edu/Bulletins/Nafta/00.preamble; website home page: http://www-tech.mit.edu (accessed June 5, 2003). ∎

Mexican president Carlos Salinas de Gortari, U.S. president George H.W. Bush, and Canadian prime minister Brian Mulroney (all standing, left to right) sign the 1994 North American Free Trade Agreement, creating the largest free trade area in the world at that time. © BETTMANN/CORBIS. REPRODUCED BY PERMISSION.

Introduction

Since the late nineteenth century, the United States had emerged as an economic world power. By 1914, the nation was the largest, most productive industrial power in the world. Most of America's economic growth in the first half of the twentieth century came from domestic production and consumption. Yet after the 1950s, trade with other nations became increasingly more important. Between 1960 and 1980, many of America's trading partners modernized their economies while the United States relied on an aging set of plants and industries. By the late 1980s, key political and economic leaders began making the case for the importance of creating a large free trade zone in North America that would include Canada, the United States, and Mexico. Economic projections suggested that this zone would have to compete with other large trade zones in Western Europe and Asia for investment dollars, new technologies, new products, new plants, and customers. Organizing in powerful interest groups, they pressured the U.S. government to negotiate a complex trade treaty with Canada and Mexico that would give U.S. businesses access to large markets and inexpensive labor.

Much of the negotiation took place under the administration of President George H.W. Bush (served

1989–1993), while it was formally signed by members of the administration of President Bill Clinton (served 1993–2001) in 1994. Labor union leaders, community activists, environmentalists, and some business leaders opposed the North American Free Trade Agreement (NAFTA). Implementing the NAFTA treaty, they argued, would destroy jobs, disrupt whole communities, shift environmental costs from the relatively wealthy United States and Canada to a relatively poorer Mexico, and force many businesses to move to new locations or go out of business. The language of the NAFTA treaty below provides a good example of how its supporters envisioned the potential impact of this important international trade alliance.

Significance

After ratification of the General Agreement on Tariffs and Trade (GATT) in the 1930s, American business leaders had argued for expanding the nation's trade relations with other countries. NAFTA negotiations proved the successor of these earlier efforts, which had resulted in numerous treaties with America's trading partners. As the world economy emerged from cold war limitations in the 1990s, many economists, policy analysts, and government officials joined with business leaders to envision a global economy based on large free trade zones that would dominate the economy of the twenty-first century. Advocates and supporters saw NAFTA as the first step in building the North American zone with the United States as the dominant member. During the 1990s, a number of U.S. firms moved plants and factories to the border regions between Texas and Mexico to establish maquiladoras (foreign-owned factories in Mexico where parts are assembled by cheap labor into products to be exported back to the United States) through a Mexican government agency. American workers saw their jobs and livelihood move away from their communities, leaving them to shift for new jobs at lower wages.

The debate over NAFTA appeared in many places in American life in the 1990s, including the presidential election of 1992, when independent candidate Ross Perot argued that NAFTA would create a "giant sucking sound" as it drained jobs away from Americans. New Democrats Bill Clinton and Al Gore supported ratification of NAFTA with minor modifications from the draft treaty inherited from the Bush administration. Organized labor, which had supported the Clinton–Gore ticket in 1992, were angry at what they saw as government support for exporting American jobs and income in the name of free trade. Economists debated the impact of NAFTA. While the treaty neither destroyed nor created large numbers of American jobs, it did seem to create a small, positive net growth in numbers of new jobs. Yet many of these jobs paid lower wages and were less secure than American workers had come to expect in the postwar years. Mexican workers obtained jobs and higher incomes than they were used to, but working conditions were harsh, while environmental damage followed in the wake of some of the maquiladoras.

Primary Source

Preamble to the North American Free Trade Agreement (NAFTA)

SYNOPSIS: The introductory section of the North American Free Trade Agreement of 1994 revealed the hopes of supporters of a free trade alliance among Canada, the United States, and Mexico.

Preamble

The Government of Canada, the Government of the United Mexican States and the Government of the United States of America, resolved to:

STRENGTHEN the special bonds of friendship and cooperation among their nations;

CONTRIBUTE to the harmonious development and expansion of world trade and provide a catalyst to broader international cooperation;

CREATE an expanded and secure market for the goods and services produced in their territories;

REDUCE distortions to trade;

ESTABLISH clear and mutually advantageous rules governing their trade;

ENSURE a predictable commercial framework for business planning and investment;

BUILD on their respective rights and obligations under the General Agreement on Tariffs and Trade and other multilateral and bilateral instruments of cooperation;

ENHANCE the competitiveness of their firms in global markets;

FOSTER creativity and innovation, and promote trade in goods and services that are the subject of intellectual property rights;

CREATE new employment opportunities and improve working conditions and living standards in their respective territories;

UNDERTAKE each of the preceding in a manner consistent with environmental protection and conservation;

PRESERVE their flexibility to safeguard the public welfare;

PROMOTE sustainable development;

STRENGTHEN the development and enforcement of environmental laws and regulations; and

PROTECT, enhance and enforce basic workers' rights.

Further Resources

BOOKS

Bertrab, Hermann von. *Negotiating NAFTA: A Mexican Envoy's Account.* Westport, Conn.: Praeger, 1997.

Buchanan, Patrick J. *The Great Betrayal: How American Sovereignty and Social Justice are Sacrificed to the Gods of the Global Economy.* Boston: Little, Brown, 1998.

Metz, Alan, ed. *A NAFTA Bibliography.* Westport, Conn.: Greenwood Press, 1996.

Rosenberg, Jerry M., ed. *Encyclopedia of the North American Free Trade Agreement, the New American Community, and Latin American Trade.* Westport, Conn.: Greenwood, 1995.

PERIODICALS

Becker, Thomas H. "Eyes South: The U.S. and Mexico Get Down to Business." *Management Review* 80, June 1991, 10–16.

Schlefer, Jonathan. "What Price Economic Growth?" *Atlantic Monthly,* December 1992, 113–118.

WEBSITES

Office of NAFTA and Inter-American Affairs, Government of Mexico. Available online at http://www.mac.doc.gov /NAFTA; website home page: http://www.mac.doc.gov (accessed June 5, 2003).

United States International Trade Commission website. Available online at http://www.usitc.gov (accessed June 5, 2003).

AUDIO AND VISUAL MEDIA

Challenge to America: Competing in the New Global Economy. Produced by Hedrick Smith (PBS). Films for the Humanities. Videocassette, 1994.

New Rules of the Game. WGBH Boston Video. Videocassette, 2002.

Wal-Mart: A History of Sam Walton's Retail Phenomenon

Nonfiction work

By: Sandra S. Vance and Roy V. Scott

Date: 1994

Source: Vance, Sandra S., and Roy V. Scott. *Wal-Mart: A History of Sam Walton's Retail Phenomenon.* New York: Twayne, 1994, 156–167.

About the Authors: Economic and business historian Sandra S. Vance (1946–) has written about retail businesses and teaches in the Social Science Department of Hinds Community College in Raymond, Mississippi. Historian Roy V. Scott (1927–), author of a number of books and articles on agricultural and railroad history, teaches at Mississippi State University.■

Introduction

Economists and business historians have often argued that small businesses oriented toward retail sales have served historically as the backbone of the American economy. Yet retailing in the 1990s continued its long-term trend toward combining elements of small business with the economies available to big businesses. Perhaps the best example of this came with the rapid growth of Bentonville, Arkansas-based Wal-Mart. Led by Sam Walton, who portrayed himself as the stereotypical small-town merchant looking after the needs and wants of his fellow citizens and customers, Wal-Mart exploded in growth by targeting small-town markets in the South, then moving into newer areas in the Midwest and Northeast in the 1990s. Similar to franchise businesses such as McDonald's in the fast-food industry, Wal-Mart used its high-volume, low-price operations to develop previously ignored markets in the rural and small-town South. Using sophisticated statistical tracking of inventories, pricing, and local demand, Wal-Mart managers brought low-priced, relatively high-quality goods to working and middle-class consumers. Tapping into the personal face-to-face hometown image of traditional small businesses, Wal-Mart became an advertising, sales, and purchasing giant. By the end of the decade, Sam Walton and members of his family were among the wealthiest Americans listed in *Fortune* magazine's annual Top 100 issue.

Yet economists, local businesses, and citizens who were ambiguous about rapid economic growth in their communities noted that the "Wal-Marting" of America was a double-edged phenomenon. While the firm's quick expansion and reliable transmission of low-priced goods to consumers brought growth and jobs to many small towns, they also brought fierce competition and labor market pressures to local businesses. In some communities, business leaders charged that Wal-Mart so thoroughly underpriced their local competitors that they were driven out of business.

Significance

The American economy of the 1990s achieved considerable increases in productivity and consumption. Millions of consumers and families shopped at low-cost retailers to purchase necessities and some name-brand products in their own communities. Consumer spending became the single most important factor driving the economy. Wal-Mart served as a representative leading example of how business, consumption, and employment interacted in an economy moving away from heavy industry toward knowledge and service. Like many other American firms in the 1990s, Wal-Mart drove down costs by dropping prices and not offering employees benefit packages, including health insurance, overtime pay, paid vacation days, and weekends off. Wal-Mart managers took to calling employees "associates" while fostering the image of the firm as a small family in advertising and employee training. Yet often employees were paid near or at minimum wage, had to work at fast speeds, and were allowed to work only thirty-six hours or less per week. By drawing on the historic anti-union tradition of the South, Wal-Mart could hire workers for low costs, then drop prices and sell in high volume to make huge profits.

Since the early 1970s, the key issue in American economic growth centered on how to increase productivity. In the 1990s, many American families found that both parents had to enter paid employment in order to afford food, housing, clothing, and transportation, whose costs seemed to rise faster than income. Scholars pointed to the emergence of a two-tiered labor market in which highly skilled workers made relatively high wages that allowed them to join the consumer culture, while low-skill workers engaged in low-paying work with few benefits and little chance for a better future. Driven by these kinds of pressures, many Americans turned to discount retailers such as Wal-Mart. Older retailers such as Sears and Kmart fell behind Wal-Mart, which found Sam's Clubs sales so successful that the firm also began opening Wal-Mart Supercenters throughout the South that served as social centers as well as sales outlets. While Franklin D. Roosevelt and New Deal Democrats had used the song "Happy Days Are Here Again" as their campaign music in the Depression of the 1930s, by the 1990s that same song was used on television ads for Wal-Mart. In one sense, Wal-Mart became a subculture of the larger post-war consumer culture. "Wal-Marting" became a way of life for millions of Americans.

Primary Source

Wal-Mart: A History of Sam Walton's Retail Phenomenon [excerpt]

SYNOPSIS: Business historians Sandra S. Vance and Roy V. Scott describe the phenomenal growth of re-tailing giant Wal-Mart in the 1990s.

The 1980s had been a decade of tremendous success for Wal-Mart, and as the 1990s dawned the firm continued its precedent-setting pace of growth. In fiscal 1991 Wal-Mart enlarged its trade territory to 34 states by entering 6 new states, opening 10 stores in California, 3 in Nevada, 5 in North Dakota, 3 in Pennsylvania, 7 in South Dakota, and 5 in Utah. This growth fulfilled the company's aim of expanding to the West Coast and the Northeast. . . .

While expansion to both coasts at last made Wal-Mart a national chain, these new regions presented special challenges for the firm. In the West Wal-Mart was entering a market dominated by a strong competitor, Dayton Hudson's successful Target discount chain. In the Northeast Wal-Mart faced higher real estate costs and a more competitive market, as well as the task of finding employees who exhibited as high a degree of dedication as those in the small towns of the South. The firm also confronted the prospect of a stronger union presence, which could create problems for Wal-Mart similar to the union-related difficulties encountered by the struggling Carrefour hypermarket in Philadelphia. The company believed a stronger union environment could threaten the familial relationship between corporate management and hourly associates that had characterized the company throughout its first 20 years of growth. Indeed, the overall appeal of Wal-Mart's homespun image, which had done so much to ingratiate the firm with shoppers throughout its

original market area, was uncertain with the North-east's more sophisticated consumers.

. . . The firm closed out this remarkable year of expansion by opening a record-breaking 36 stores on a single day, 30 January 1991. Wal-Mart's additions brought the total number of discount stores to 1,573, and they encompassed 111 million square feet of retail space, an increase of 19 percent over the preceding year. The stores continued to grow not only in number but also in size. By fiscal 1991 standard store sizes ranged from 30,000 to more than 110,000 square feet; 65,000 square feet was the average. During the same year, the firm embarked on another retail experiment by converting four surplus buildings into stores it called Bud's Warehouse Outlet. These 40,000-square-foot stores sold mainly closed out and refurbished goods, few of which came from Wal-Mart's discount stores.

. . . During fiscal 1991 Wal-Mart not only was the nation's fastest-growing retailer, but it was also the nation's most profitable. It had a net income of $1.3 billion on net sales of $32.6 billion, an increase over the previous year's net income of 20 percent and over the previous year's net sales of 26 percent overall and 10 percent for existing stores. Comparable gross sales per square foot in all retail divisions grew to $263, up from $250 the preceding year. This record of performance caused Wal-Mart to pass Kmart in November 1990 to become the nation's second largest retailer. Then, in early 1991, the long-anticipated moment arrived: Wal-Mart overtook Sears to become the nation's largest retailer. Behind Wal-Mart, K mart occupied the second spot with an increase in sales of 8.5 percent to $32.1 billion in its fiscal year, while Sears slipped to number three with an increase in sales of only 1.2 percent to $31.9 billion for the calendar year 1990. Wal-Mart had been steadily gaining on Sears throughout the 1980s. Just 10 years earlier, Wal-Mart's net sales of $2.4 billion had been less than 12 percent of Sears', but by the end of the decade Sears' North American sales (including those from 131 stores in Canada and Mexico) had increased from $28 billion in 1988 to $31.9 billion in 1990, a growth rate of only 14 percent. During the same period, Wal-Mart's sales had more than doubled, from $16 billion to $32.6 billion.

A number of factors contributed to Wal-Mart's triumph over Sears and K mart. One key element was the firm's small-town origins. By locating stores on the outskirts of small communities where local merchants were its only rivals, Wal-Mart absorbed

Wal-Mart became a nationwide force to be reckoned with during the 1990s, when it continued its expansion of the 1980s and gave similar stores such as Kmart and Target a formidable competitor in the marketplace. © JAMES MARSHALL/CORBIS. REPRODUCED BY PERMISSION.

business for miles around. Unfettered by competition from major retail chains, Wal-Mart refined the fundamental business practices that ultimately would enable it to reach the pinnacle of retail success. Wal-Mart's rural locations had compelled the firm to invest in its own inventory-replenishment system, which had evolved into an intricate network of distribution centers, an extensive fleet of trucks, and state-of-the-art computer and communications systems that enabled the firm to function with great efficiency.

In addition to efficient inventory replenishment, Wal-Mart's intricate distribution and technology systems contributed to the firm's low cost of sales. During fiscal 1991, for example, the company's overhead expenses of 15 percent of sales were significantly below K mart's 23 percent and Sears' 29 percent. Wal-Mart's ability to surpass Sears was due in part to these lower overhead expenses. Years of top-heavy bureaucratic management had caused Sears' operating costs to spiral. In 1990, for example, Sears' headquarters staff consisted of 6,000 employees, compared with Wal-Mart's 2,500. Sears, moreover, had proved unable to get its swollen expenses under control, despite cutbacks in its unwieldy catalog offerings and painful reductions in personnel.

Wal-Mart's lower overhead expenses allowed the company to maintain one of its greatest advantages over its rivals—prices that were uniformly and consistently attractive to consumers. The overwhelming appeal of Wal-Mart's prices generated a burgeoning sales volume that stimulated further economies for the firm, which, in turn, made Wal-Mart even more efficient than its competitors. In fiscal 1990, for example, Wal-Mart's sales per square foot of $250 were significantly better than K mart's $150. The productivity level of Wal-Mart's personnel also was superior to that of its competitors. In fiscal 1991, for example, Wal-Mart's 328,000 associates, whose ranks had grown from 41,000 in fiscal 1982, generated an average of more than $95,000 in sales per employee, compared with approximately $85,000 for Sears employees.

Wal-Mart's ability to keep its stores well stocked and its prices low were complemented by another asset, the high quality of its products. Beginning in the mid-1970s, the priorities of American consumers changed dramatically. Shoppers increasingly resented the business methods of traditional retailers, including declining customer service, too-frequent sales promotions, and higher markups, which translated into higher prices. At the same time consumers found their disposable income squeezed by such factors as inflation, recession, and the widening gap between rich and poor in America that was caused in part by declining union influence, increasingly rigorous education requirements for better-paying jobs, and the rise in the divorce rate. As a result, dollar-conscious consumers demanded greater value in their retail purchases—and to shoppers value meant paying affordable prices for nationally advertised, brand-name goods, because brand names implied higher quality and status. . . . [B]y expanding its emphasis on brand names as it grew, while at the same time keeping its prices low, Wal-Mart had acquired the image of offering greater value than its competitors.

Still another way in which Wal-Mart surpassed its rivals was in its ability to create an appealing retail environment. Surveys indicated, for example, that K mart trailed Wal-Mart in customer satisfaction. Beyond the obvious advantage of price, consumers who frequented Wal-Mart indicated that they found it a comfortable place to shop—clean, well organized, and friendly. Customers at K Mart, on the other hand, often expressed frustration at the dingy atmosphere and poor service they encountered there. The more appealing ambience of Wal-Mart's stores was attributable in part to the wide disparity between the age of Wal-Mart's and K mart's outlets. . . .

At Sears, as well, customer service had declined and stores looked dull and dated. In an effort to replace the bulky, outdated appearance of Sears' outlets with a more vibrant shopping environment, Sears chief executive officer Edward Brennan not only refurbished the stores but also reorganized some of them by introducing so-called power formats, which were boutique-like areas where shoppers could buy brand-name items in settings resembling specialty shops. Sears' most successful power format was its Brand Central showrooms for appliances and electronics. While Brennan's efforts to rejuvenate Sears were an improvement, the greatest impediment to their efficient execution companywide was Sears' cumbersome organizational structure. . . .

Wal-Mart's leadership proved more astute than K mart's or Sears' in the matter of diversification. While Wal-Mart diversified during the mid 1980s into the lucrative membership-warehouse business, both K mart and Sears diverted vital cash flow from their respective financial bases of retailing and discounting to pursue less successful ventures. About the

same time that Wal-Mart established its Sam's Clubs, Bernard Fauber, then K mart's chief executive officer, wrongly assumed that the chain's markets were becoming saturated and rejected the opportunity to enter the warehouse-club business, instead choosing to diversify into specialty retailing. Only belatedly did K mart enter the warehouse-club business by purchasing Pace Membership Warehouse, Inc., in 1989. While Sam's Clubs contributed significantly to Wal-Mart's corporate sales and profits, K mart's specialty businesses did not. . . . As for Sears' diversification, some analysts believe that Sears placed too much emphasis on nonretailing pursuits following its restructuring in 1980, and they partly attribute the decline in Sears' share of general-merchandise sales from 41 percent in 1980 to 13 percent 10 years later to the firm's preoccupation during those years with its real estate and financial services subsidiaries.

One of Wal-Mart's most unique advantages over its rivals was the dedication of its workforce. Reflecting the conservative, deeply religious examples of Sam and Helen Walton, Wal-Mart's employees readily exhibited the small-town virtues of hard work and friendliness, tempered with a certain vague suspicion of anyone not steeped in the firm's value system. Many of Wal-Mart's associates were not college graduates, which did not alarm the firm's senior executives, who stated flatly that they were not very interested in individuals who possessed a master of business administration or a similar advanced degree, since such specialists tended to devote more attention to "numbers" than to "people." Instead, the firm seemed to prefer high school graduates, whose ideals it could mold into utter loyalty to the company, primarily through intensive training seminars at Bentonville. One manifestation of the company's apparent perception of higher education as an impediment to the absorption of the Wal-Mart way of doing things was the firm's commitment to promoting mostly from within the company.

Nowhere was the high level of enthusiasm exhibited by Wal-Mart's employees more evident than at the general headquarters in Bentonville. Throughout the bustling facility employees were uniformly pleasant and at the same time highly protective of Wal-Mart's image. Their manner was one of crisp efficiency coupled with guarded courtesy. When asked about the cheerful industry that pervaded the facility, company spokespeople maintained that it was inspired largely by the self-effacing example of Sam Walton himself. Significant too, of course, was the handsome benefits package for employees, built around an enviable stock-option program and generous incentives for early retirement; this undoubtedly played no small role in the manifest goodwill that emanated from Bentonville. But whatever its source, a peculiarly religious atmosphere seemed to pervade Wal-Mart's headquarters. In fact, employee allegiance to the company's corporate culture, that almost mystical formula of success based on the zeal of Wal-Mart's associates and the company's willingness to treat them as partners and listen to their ideas, at times seemed to take on nearly cult-like proportions.

Undeniably, the prevailing reason for Wal-Mart's triumph over its competitors was Sam Walton. Having provided his firm with stable guidance for 30 years, Walton manifested a steadfast commitment to the business fundamentals of price, quality, efficiency, and customer service that stood in stark contrast to Sears and K mart, where changes in leadership sometimes took those firms in desultory directions, causing them to stray from the precepts on which their success had been built. Beyond his remarkable managerial skills, Walton possessed other talents that were invaluable to Wal-Mart's rise to retail preeminence. The quintessential merchant, he had the ability to anticipate what his customers would buy and to recognize and capitalize on nascent retail trends. His engaging personality, moreover, had a significant impact on Wal-Mart's growth, giving the company an image that was unique among retail firms. His charisma inspired a remarkable degree of loyalty and admiration from both his personnel and his customers. . . .

As the 1990s began, Wal-Mart's management was keenly aware that the decade would be characterized by intensive competition. In 1989 David Glass had caused a sensation when he forecast that 50 percent of the nation's existing retail operations would be out of business by the year 2000 (he later added that this projected rate of failure was too low). Analysts predicted that the heightened competition of the 1990s would be caused by such factors as a slow growth in the number of consumers, a reduction in disposable income, a saturated marketplace, and a demand for convenience, due to the continued decrease in the amount of time consumers would have to shop. Wal-Mart's executives realized, moreover, that since its inception, discount merchandising in particular had been a highly competitive industry. For example, of the top ten discounters in 1962—the year that Wal-Mart, K mart,

and Target had been founded—not one was still in business 30 years later.

During the early years of the decade, America's three leading discount firms, Wal-Mart, K mart, and Target (who collectively controlled 70 percent of the discount market in 1991) already were girding themselves for the competitive struggles that lay ahead. One way that Wal-Mart hoped to perpetuate its remarkable record of growth in this competitive environment was by enlarging its commitment to the $300 billion-a-year supermarket business through the expansion of its Supercenters. The firm operated 12 Supercenters in August 1992, and some analysts predicted that there would be 400 Supercenters by 1996. Another path of growth for the company was through the expansion of its Sam's Clubs, whose sales in fiscal 1992 rose 30 percent to $9.4 billion. Wal-Mart also hoped to maintain its rapid growth by expanding more deeply into the Northeast, California, and Mexico. In the pursuit of these goals, however, Wal-Mart would face aggressive competition from a revitalized K mart and an expanding Target, as well as from efficient category killers such as Toys "R" Us and Home Depot.

Wal-Mart's greatest challenge in the years ahead would lie not in its ability to compete with rival retail organizations but in its capacity to overcome irreplaceable loss. As his discount empire continued to grow, Sam Walton's physical strength ebbed. Early in 1990 Walton was diagnosed as having a form of bone cancer known as multiple myeloma. In the months that followed, declining health compelled him to diminish his involvement in corporate affairs, and he busied himself with writing his autobiography, *Sam Walton: Made in America, My Story.* In March 1992 President George [H.] Bush flew to Bentonville to present the Medal of Freedom, the nation's highest civilian honor, to a frail and wheelchair-bound Walton. Soon thereafter, on 5 April 1992, Sam Walton died at the age of 74. Following his father's death, Rob Walton took his place as chairman of Wal-Mart, and David Glass, as president and chief executive officer, continued to direct the company.

Sam Walton, one of the nation's leading twentieth-century entrepreneurs, built a business that transformed mass merchandising in America. Wal-Mart significantly altered the relationship between manufacturer and merchant by expanding the power and influence of the retailer in the marketing and distribution of products. By consistently offering consumers brand-name goods at discount prices, Wal-

Mart imposed rigorous price and quality standards on the retail industry as a whole and revolutionized the shopping habits and expectations of a generation of consumers. Yet Walton's accomplishments transcended the world of commerce. As he neared the end of his life his popularity grew, and the public lavished on him a measure of affection rarely accorded a businessman. Although widely respected and admired for his success, many Americans simply liked Sam Walton as a person, possibly because they looked beyond the magnate of wealth and achievement and found in the man a refreshing devotion to hard work, modesty, and simplicity that was worthy of acclaim.

Further Resources

BOOKS

Trimble, Vance H. *Sam Walton: The Inside Story of America's Richest Man.* New York: Dutton, 1990.

Walton, Sam, with John Huey. *Sam Walton: Made in America, My Story.* New York: Doubleday, 1992.

PERIODICALS

Vance, Sandra S., and Roy V. Scott. "Sam Walton and Wal-Mart Stores, Inc.: A Study in Modern Southern Entrepreneurship." *Journal of Southern History* 58, May 1992, 231–252.

President Clinton's State of the Union Address January 23, 1996

Speech

By: Bill Clinton

Date: January 23, 1996

Source: Clinton, Bill. State of the Union Address. January 23, 1996. Available online at http://clinton2.nara.gov/WH /New/other/sotu.html; website home page: http://clinton2 .nara.gov (accessed June 5, 2003).

About the Author: President William Jefferson "Bill" Clinton (1946–; served 1993–2001) rose to power in Arkansas serving as leader of the centrist Democratic Leadership Council, which provided research, leaders, and policy recommendations for his moderate Democratic administration of the 1990s. He served two terms as the forty-second president of the United States. ∎

Introduction

At the start of the 1990s, the U.S. economy faced serious short- and long-term challenges. Under the administrations of presidents Ronald W. Reagan (served 1981–1989) and George H.W. Bush (served 1989–1993),

new economic policies were implemented that led to massive annual government deficits and huge increases in the total federal debt. In the wake of the recession of 1990–1991, Bill Clinton and Al Gore teamed up with other veterans of the Democratic Leadership Council to pare down spending, balance the annual budget, and lay the groundwork to pay down the federal debt. Clinton declared himself a "New Democrat" who would not rely on ever increasing government spending, would work with American businesses, and would seek to restore prosperity for all Americans.

The first step Clinton took after assuming office in January 1993 was to call for an economic summit meeting of government officials, bankers, financiers, corporate managers, and small business people to discuss possible economic policies for the future. The Little Rock, Arkansas, summit was broadcast on national television, received wide press coverage, and later published verbatim transcripts of the meeting. Clinton and Gore sought to promote increased productivity, millions of new jobs, and prosperity for all Americans. Clinton used the occasion of his fourth State of the Union address before a joint session of Congress to showcase the economic revival of the 1990s before the American public. Attempting to combine traditional values of economic opportunity, hard work, and community, Clinton realized that as the leader of a new generation of centrist Democrats he would have to shrink the role of the federal government and rely more on individual and private-sector institutional activities to restore growth. Perhaps the most famous words of this January 1996 speech came when a Democratic president announced that "the era of big government is over"—moving away from the central point of Democratic policy making since the New Deal of the 1930s. His appeal to Americans of all social classes and both political parties reflected Clinton's moderate approach to economic policy making that left some role for the federal government but a much bigger role for working Americans and businesses.

Significance

Since the end of World War II in 1945, American economic policy had rested on the foundations of what came to be called a "mixed economy." The New Deal response to the Great Depression and massive spending for the wartime mobilization of 1941–1945 showed the role that federal spending could play in investing taxpayer money when individuals either could not or would not. Yet during and after the war, business leaders and conservative politicians had called for a restoration of free enterprise, private investment, lower taxes, and as small a role for the federal government as possible in promoting mass production and mass consumption. The postwar economy of abundance created historically high rates of

In his January 1996 State of the Union address, President Bill Clinton addressed the nation's economy and stated that "The era of big government is over." AP/WIDE WORLD PHOTOS. REPRODUCED BY PERMISSION.

productivity, employment, and consumption that led to a truly middle-class American way of life only glimpsed in the prewar years. Defense spending for the cold war in the 1950s and for the social programs of the Great Society and the anticommunist crusade in Vietnam in the 1960s maintained a high level of economic growth that Americans began to take for granted.

Yet after price inflation began in the late 1960s and the oil price shocks of the 1970s shattered Americans' confidence in the future, policy makers, politicians, and economic leaders began debating the need for new policies that could bring back the golden age of the postwar years. Some argued that a new age of limits was upon America and there was no going back. Others argued for increased investment by individuals and businesses that could become possible with tax cuts, lowered interest rates, speeded-up tax depreciation laws, and government loans and loan guarantees. These would spark new technologies, products, and consumer demand. In the 1990s, the United States followed economic policies that sparked renewed investment, productivity gains, and wage and salary gains for many American workers in the private sector. By the mid-1990s, the American economic renaissance had begun. In the late 1990s, some of those

gains began to trickle down to most American individuals and families whose standard of living had deteriorated considerably since the early 1970s. Clinton's 1996 speech reflected renewed hope and optimism among Americans who at the start of the decade had seen little to get excited about.

Primary Source

President Clinton's State of the Union Address January 23, 1996 [excerpt]

SYNOPSIS: President Bill Clinton describes the state of the U.S. economy in his 1996 State of the Union Address before a joint session of Congress.

The state of the Union is strong. Our economy is the healthiest it has been in three decades. We have the lowest combined rates of unemployment and inflation in 27 years. We have created nearly 8 million new jobs, over a million of them in basic industries, like construction and automobiles. America is selling more cars than Japan for the first time since the 1970s. And for three years in a row, we have had a record number of new businesses started in our country.

Our leadership in the world is also strong, bringing hope for new peace. And perhaps most important, we are gaining ground in restoring our fundamental values. The crime rate, the welfare and food stamp rolls, the poverty rate and the teen pregnancy rate are all down. And as they go down, prospects for America's future go up.

We live in an age of possibility. A hundred years ago we moved from farm to factory. Now we move to an age of technology, information, and global competition. These changes have opened vast new opportunities for our people, but they have also presented them with stiff challenges. While more Americans are living better, too many of our fellow citizens are working harder just to keep up, and they are rightly concerned about the security of their families.

We must answer here three fundamental questions: First, how do we make the American Dream of opportunity for all a reality for all Americans who are willing to work for it? Second, how do we preserve our old and enduring values as we move into the future? And, third, how do we meet these challenges together, as one America? We know big government does not have all the answers. We know there's not a program for every problem. We have worked to give the American people a smaller, less bureaucratic government in Washington. And we have to give the American people one that lives within its means.

The era of big government is over. But we cannot go back to the time when our citizens were left to fend for themselves. Instead, we must go forward as one America, one nation working together to meet the challenges we face together. Self-reliance and teamwork are not opposing virtues; we must have both.

I believe our new, smaller government must work in an old-fashioned American way, together with all of our citizens through state and local governments, in the workplace, in religious, charitable and civic associations. Our goal must be to enable all our people to make the most of their own lives—with stronger families, more educational opportunity, economic security, safer streets, a cleaner environment in a safer world.

To improve the state of our Union, we must ask more of ourselves, we must expect more of each other, and we must face our challenges together.

Here, in this place, our responsibility begins with balancing the budget in a way that is fair to all Americans. There is now broad bipartisan agreement that permanent deficit spending must come to an end.

I compliment the Republican leadership and the membership for the energy and determination you have brought to this task of balancing the budget. And I thank the Democrats for passing the largest deficit reduction plan in history in 1993, which has already cut the deficit nearly in half in three years.

Since 1993, we have all begun to see the benefits of deficit reduction. Lower interest rates have made it easier for businesses to borrow and to invest and to create new jobs. Lower interest rates have brought down the cost of home mortgages, car payments and credit card rates to ordinary citizens. Now, it is time to finish the job and balance the budget.

Though differences remain among us which are significant, the combined total of the proposed savings that are common to both plans is more than enough, using the numbers from your Congressional Budget Office to balance the budget in seven years and to provide a modest tax cut.

These cuts are real. They will require sacrifice from everyone. But these cuts do not undermine our fundamental obligations to our parents, our children, and our future, by endangering Medicare, or Medicaid, or education, or the environment, or by raising taxes on working families.

I have said before, and let me say again, many good ideas have come out of our negotiations. I have learned a lot about the way both Republicans and Democrats view the debate before us. I have learned a lot about the good ideas that we could all embrace.

We ought to resolve our remaining differences. I am willing to work to resolve them. I am ready to meet tomorrow. But I ask you to consider that we should at least enact these savings that both plans have in common and give the American people their balanced budget, a tax cut, lower interest rates, and a brighter future. We should do that now, and make permanent deficits yesterday's legacy.

Further Resources

BOOKS

Berman, William C. *From the Center to the Edge: The Politics and Policies of the Clinton Presidency.* Lanham, Md.: Rowman and Littlefield, 2001.

Blumenthal, Sidney. *The Clinton Wars.* New York: Farrar Straus and Giroux, 2003.

Levy, Peter B., ed. *Encyclopedia of the Clinton Presidency.* Westport, Conn.: Greenwood, 2002.

Metz, Allan. *Bill Clinton: A Bibliography.* Westport, Conn.: Greenwood, 2002.

PERIODICALS

Friedman, Benjamin M. "The Clinton Budget: Will It Do?" *New York Review of Books* 40, no. 13, July 15, 1993. Available online at http://www.nybooks.com/articles/2499; website home page: http://www.nybooks.com (accessed June 5, 2003).

———. "Clinton's Opportunity." *New York Review of Books* 39, no. 20, December 3, 1992. Available online at http://www.nybooks.com/articles/2726; website home page: http://www. nybooks.com (accessed June 5, 2003).

WEBSITES

Clinton Presidential Materials Project. National Archives and Records Administration. Available online at http://www .clinton.archives.gov (accessed June 5, 2003).

"The Clinton Years." Available online at http://www.pbs.org /wgbh/pages/frontline/shows/clinton; website home page: http://www.pbs.org (accessed June 5, 2003).

AUDIO AND VISUAL MEDIA

The Clinton Years. PBS Home Video. VHS, 2001.

"WorldCom Together"
Interview

By: Bernard Ebbers with Joshua Cooper Ramo
Date: November 10, 1997

Source: Ebbers, Bernard, with Joshua Cooper Ramo. "World-Com Together." Interview with Phil Ponce. *MacNeil/Lehrer News Hour.* November 10, 1997. Available online at http://www.pbs.org/newshour/bb/business/july-dec97/mci_11-10.html; website home page: http://www.pbs.org (accessed June 5, 2003).

About the Author: Bernard Ebbers, chief executive officer of WorldCom, led a small telecommunications company in Mississippi in the 1990s to merge with MCI, the second largest long-distance telephone company in the nation. On the day of the merger, Ebbers discusses the significance of the merger with PBS NewsHour reporter Phil Ponce and reporter Joshua Cooper Ramo of *Time* magazine. ∎

Introduction

The decade of the 1980s came to be called the "Decade of Greed" as a result of stock market speculation, insider trading, leveraged buyouts, and poor financial practices. Yet the explosion of corporate mergers and acquisitions in the 1990s made the dizzying sums of monies in the bull market of the previous decade pale in comparison. Some of the largest mergers in U.S. business history occurred in the course of the economic rebirth of the decade. In 1993, entertainment giant Viacom announced an $8.4 billion merger with Blockbuster. Two years later Time-Warner bought Turner Broadcasting System for $7.5 billion. After the Federal Trade Commission approved that deal in September 1996, aviation leader Boeing acquired competitor McDonnell-Douglas for $13.3 billion—the biggest deal in aerospace industry history, consolidating two major defense contractors in the wake of the end of the cold war. When WorldCom executive Bernard Ebbers led the press conference announcing the merger with MCI on November 10, 1997 for $43 billion, it was the largest corporate merger in American business history.

While few could imagine it at the time, the World-Com/MCI merger would not last long as the largest one in U.S. history. In April 1998, financial services firm Citicorp announced its merger with insurance giant Travelers Group for $70 billion, leading the Dow Jones Industrial Average to break the 9,000 mark. One month later, SBC Communications, one of the regional telephone companies left after the breakup of AT&T, acquired Ameritech Corporation for $62 billion to become the largest phone company in America. A month and a half after that merger, AT&T, longtime leader in the long-distance telephone market, bought Tele-Communications, Inc., the second largest cable television company in the nation, for $31.8 billion in a bid to become a full-service provider in the telecommunications industry, which seemed to be consolidating TV, cable, Internet, and videotape-on-demand services. Bell Atlantic followed suit in July 1998 when it purchased GTE for $52.8 billion in stock. Merger mania hit the United

States economy with a bang. A few years later, investment scandals involving some of these firms such as WorldCom and major Wall Street investment houses such as Salomon Smith Barney broke out on the front page of newspapers across the nation.

Significance

Over the broad sweep of modern U.S. business history, the American economy has gone through a series of merger-and-acquisitions waves such as those of 1895–1905, the 1920s, the 1950s, and the 1980s. The merger mania of the 1990s dwarfed these earlier waves in terms of the amounts of money or stock involved. News reports throughout the decade left viewers in shock as one merger after another set historic records. Many of the mergers took place in the telecommunications industries in the aftermath of the personal computer, knowledge, and mass entertainment revolutions that so thoroughly changed American life. At the time, many Americans, including financial and business leaders and journalists, joined the national chorus of praise for such record-setting transactions. Yet not all mergers brought positive results. On May 6, 1998, German automobile maker Daimler-Benz announced its purchase of Chrysler Corporation for $36 billion. One member of the American Big Three automakers—GM and Ford were the two leaders—Chrysler had come upon hard times in an overcrowded world car market. The merger was the largest industrial takeover in history and the largest foreign-owned corporate purchase of a U.S. firm in national history. Despite the decline of older industrial firms, merger mania continued at a frenzied pace throughout the 1990s. On December 1, 1998, Exxon, the largest oil firm in the United States, announced its purchase the second largest oil company in the country, Mobil Oil, to form the largest corporation in the world.

Primary Source

"WorldCom Together" [excerpt]

SYNOPSIS: NewsHour reporter Phil Ponce interviews Bernard Ebbers, CEO of WorldCom, and reporter Joshua Cooper Ramo of *Time* about the merger of WorldCom and MCI.

Phil Ponce: Last month when WorldCom, Inc. first made a $30 billion bid to buy phone giant MCI, WorldCom was not exactly a household name. But today it was announced WorldCom sweetened its offer to $37 billion and MCI had said yes. Now, the little-known Mississippi company could make history for causing the largest corporate merger in U.S. history. Headquartered in Jackson, Mississippi, WorldCom got its start in 1983, selling long distance service at a discount. WorldCom went public in 1989 and in the past five years has acquired more than 40 companies. The most recent additions relate to the Internet, including World-Com's acquisition of CompuServe. Some industry observers say the purchase of CompuServe put WorldCom on the map as a key player in telecommunications. WorldCom is already the nation's fourth largest long distance company and by far the largest phone company provider of Internet services. But MCI would be WorldCom's biggest catch. MCI's the second largest long distance carrier behind only AT&T. MCI had other corporate suitors, including British Telecom and GTE, but MCI said no to both. Is WorldCom's hunger for acquisitions now satisfied?

Bernard Ebbers, CEO, WorldCom, Inc.: Entrepreneurs are, by nature, people that look for opportunities. Both MCI's senior management and the WorldCom senior management. If there are opportunities out there that make sense, we certainly won't shy away from it.

Phil Ponce: If today's deal is approved by federal regulators, the new company will be called MCI/WorldCom. With us now is Joshua Cooper Ramo, a senior editor at *Time* magazine who covers technology and business. Mr. Ramo, welcome. And if this merger is approved, what kind of a company would this be in terms of the services that it offers to its customers?

Joshua Cooper Ramo, *Time* magazine: I think it's going to be a remarkable company that emerges. You can't really underestimate the amount of change that's going on in the telecommunications business. When World-Com got its start back in 1983, the idea of competing against a monopoly like AT&T just seemed ridiculous. They had dominant market share. They had 99 percent of the U.S. households connected for long distance service. The notion that you could move in that space and do something competitive was an idea that was really radical for its time. Here we are 15 years later and Ebbers has built a company which is going to be a very real competitor to AT&T.

Phil Ponce: You're talking about Mr. Ebbers, the head of WorldCom.

Joshua Cooper Ramo: Yes, that's right. What you're going to see, I think, from the com-

Bernard J. Ebbers holds a 1997 press conference about WorldCom's offer to buy MCI. © D. RENTAS/N.Y. POST/CORBIS SYGMA. REPRODUCED BY PERMISSION.

bined company is not only incredible strength in the long distance business but also aggressive moves into local telephony. They'll have about a hundred different cities that they're going to be able to start with but, most importantly, a recognition that data traffic is going to be the real revenue key in the future. In 1995, the amount of data traffic on the world's networks passed the amount of voice traffic. That's something that's never going to go back. And the companies that are going to profit from that are the companies that are well positioned technologically to take advantage of that. This merged company is a perfect example of the kind of organization you want.

Phil Ponce: So when one industry observer said that this is the—this is sort of the prototype of the telecommunications company in the future, that person was not overstating that.

Joshua Cooper Ramo: No, not at all. Prototypical, interestingly, in a variety of ways. Probably the first way is by having this ability to recognize these lightning fast changes in the business.

AT&T ran its business for 40 years without changing very much. What these new guys bring to the party is a recognition that change is an opportunity to really build empire. And so in that sound clip you just played from Ebbers he was saying entrepreneurs look for new opportunities. And phone companies of the future are not going to be big, staid, solid structures. They're going to be things which are changing over and over again. So that's the first important point; that change is a key element here. The second one is that the nature of that the kinds of services that phone companies are going to provide is changing very radically. Five years ago phone companies were mostly in the business of providing voice communications. Five years from now your telephone company is going to be providing everything from data communications to electronic commerce to movies on demand. And Ebbers is absolutely right in believing that this company's structure is the prototypical structure to make a lot of money in that world.

Phil Ponce: Right. Now, how many companies are out there that provide local service, long distance service, hookups to the Internet?

Joshua Cooper Ramo: Well, this is actually one of the fascinating things about this deal. One analyst down on Wall Street has estimated that there are roughly 150 times the amount of capacity in the year 2010 than is going to be necessary of all of these phone companies that are out there—and there are literally hundreds of them—continue to stay in business. What Ebbers has recognized and he recognized it since he started a small company called LDDS at the diner, the local diner in Jackson, Mississippi, in 1983, is that size is an important ingredient here, so though there are hundreds of companies that are competing in this space, they really believe that by creating something that's vertically integrated they're going to be able to move a lot more aggressively than some of these small players.

Phil Ponce: Both British Telecom and GTE wanted to buy MCI. Why did MCI say yes to WorldCom?

Joshua Cooper Ramo: I think that's a fascinating question. A year ago or so when the MCI-BT discussions began, you would talk to these guys from MCI. And what they were the most excited about was the possibility that this was going to give them this global reach. I remember talking to somebody who'd just come back from pitching the government of Paraguay, and they said Paraguay is going to buy all of its phone services from Concert, which was the name of the combined BT-MCI organization. What MCI's board apparently seems to have decided is that mastering the technology for a global communications company is more important than merging with a company that has a lot of global outposts. What WorldCom has is undisputed leadership in the business of providing end-to-end connectivity for data transmission. By merging that with MCI's very broad customer base they believe they'll be able to go global.

Phil Ponce: Mr. Ramo, you pointed out—you alluded to the fact that in 1983 Ebbers and his—the other people who started WorldCom were sitting in around in Day's Inn in Hattiesburg, Mississippi. Where do these guys come from in that relatively short period of time?

Joshua Cooper Ramo: Absolutely. It is really one of the great business stories of the age. I mean, one of the things we hear all the time is, you know, we're living in this—this period of warp speed change, and companies have got to learn to take advantage of it. What Ebbers was able to do was really focus very quickly on where exactly changes were occurring in the telecommunications business and then target his acquisitions very precisely to make sure that they were timed in such a way that the revenues they would get from those deals would be able to vault them to the next levels. Of course, the famous statistic you hear about WorldCom is that it's delivered 53 percent annual growth to shareholders. If you'd invested $10,000 in WorldCom five years ago, it would be worth $75,000 today. Where these guys came from was an implicit realization that they could grow the company by acquiring the right businesses at the right time. The joke on Wall Street is that WorldCom is the ultimate proof that you can build a company by starting with more investment bankers than customers.

Further Resources
BOOKS
Blair, Margaret M., ed. *The Deal Decade: What Takeovers and Leveraged Buyouts Mean for Corporate Governance.* Washington, D.C.: Brookings Institution, 1993.

Gaughan, Patrick A. *Mergers, Acquisitions, and Corporate Restructuring.* 3rd ed. New York: Wiley, 2002.

Gordon, John Steele. *The Great Game: The Emergence of Wall Street as a World Power, 1653–2000.* New York: Scribner, 1999.

Seligman, Joel. *The Transformation of Wall Street: A History of the Security and Exchange Commission and Modern Corporate Finance.* Boston: Houghton Mifflin, 1982.

Sobel, Robert. *Dangerous Dreamers: The Financial Innovators from Charles Merrill to Michael Milken.* New York: Wiley, 1993.

———. *The Rise and Fall of the Conglomerate Kings.* New York: Stein and Day, 1984.

Wasserstein, Bruce. *Big Deal: The Battle for Control of America's Leading Corporations.* New York: Warner Books, 1998.

"Life on the Internet: Timeline"

Website

By: Public Broadcasting System

Date: 1997

Source: "Life on the Internet: Timeline." PBS Online, 1997. Available online at http://www.pbs.org/internet/timeline /timeline-txt.html; website home page: http://www.pbs.org (accessed June 4, 2003).

About the Organization: Founded in 1969 the Public Broadcasting System is a non-profit corporation consisting of a network of public television stations across the United States which broadcasts quality educational and news programs. It maintains an extensive Internet site to accompany its programs and provide balanced information on significant events in American culture. ■

Introduction

In the late 1960s, the Defense Advanced Research Projects Agency (DARPA) created a small system of networked computers that would allow for continued communications among civilian and military leaders in the wake of a nuclear war. Over the next thirty years, that small project grew quickly to become part of many Americans' day-to-day lives. Initially intended to allow for communication among national leaders, the Internet soon received support from the National Science Foundation to allow scientists access to high-speed computers for research and data sharing with fellow scientists. By the mid-1990s, this rapidly expanding system of large mainframe and desktop personal computers was privatized and opened to civilian and commercial users. Technological limitations in the size, speed, and capacity of modems, computer chips, memory, and hard drives allowed for

sharing only of textual information. In 1989, scientist Tim Berners-Lee, working at the European Organization for Nuclear Research (CERN) in Geneva, Switzerland, developed a simple coding process called Hyper Text Markup Language (HTML). HTML coding allowed for the transfer of images and later sounds as well as text over the Internet through electronic mail (e-mail) and World Wide Web sites (websites). Americans took advantage of this new form of communication across the nation and the globe for work, home life, recreation, information gathering, and online shopping in ever-increasing numbers. Some economists predicted that large productivity gains would emerge from the use of personal computers, e-mail, and business-to-business commerce on the Internet. Others remained skeptical that this new technology could revolutionize the nature of American economic activity.

Significance

Over the broad sweep of American economic history, new technologies such as steamboats, the railroad, the telegraph, cameras, telephones, movie cameras, automobiles, radios, motion pictures, the transitor, televisions, solid state circuits, satellites, magnetic tape recording, VCRs, and cable television seemed to promise great economic potential. Each time a new technology emerged, advocates and entrepreneurs argued that it would dramatically transform—even revolutionize—some part of the nation's economy. Yet every time, the adoption and widespread use of the new technology took longer to occur than early promoters predicted. Often, competing versions of technology meant that early businesses producing and selling new products often fell behind later companies with superior design, manufacturing, marketing, or service. In the 1990s, American society and culture were deluged with similar kinds of predictions about the use of personal computers, modems, e-mail, and websites.

Yet as in the past, there were those who remained skeptical about the possibilities of new technology. Americans who had grown up writing letters by hand, using the typewriter, and making calls on the telephone often were reluctant to adopt or use the Internet. "Technophobia"—fear of new technology—entered American English as a new word. Younger Americans eager to engage and experiment with the new technology redefined the term "geek" to describe people who learned everything they could about computers and "the Net." What had served as a term of derision in earlier decades now became a badge of honor among young computer "hackers" who worked at learning how computer servers and security systems worked to "hack into" government and private computers and computer databases. Movies and television shows focusing on computers and the Net made the new technology appear to be everywhere in American life. By the end of the decade, younger Americans who had grown up with the Internet thought carbon paper, typewriters, eight-track tapes, and even prerecorded cassette tapes of popular music were relics of the past.

Primary Source

"Life on the Internet: Timeline"

SYNOPSIS: This PBS timeline history of the Internet captures the significant growth of e-mail, the Internet, and online commerce in the 1990s.

1960

There is no Internet. . . .

1961

Still no Internet. . . .

1962

The RAND Corporation begins research into robust, distributed communication networks for military command and control.

1962–1969

The Internet is first conceived in the early '60s. Under the leadership of the Department of Defense's Advanced Research Project Agency (ARPA), it grows from a paper architecture into a small network (ARPANET) intended to promote the sharing of supercomputers amongst researchers in the United States.

1963

Beatles play for the Queen of England.

1964

"Dr Strangelove" portrays nuclear holocaust which new network must survive.

1965

The DOD's Advanced Research Project Association begins work on "ARPANET."

1965

ARPA sponsors research into a "cooperative network of time-sharing computers."

1966

US *Surveyor* probe lands safely on moon.

1967

First ARPANET papers presented at Association for Computing Machinery Symposium

1967

Delegates at a symposium for the Association for Computing Machinery in Gatlinburg, TN discuss the first plans for the ARPANET.

1968

First generation of networking hardware and software designed.

1969

ARPANET connects first 4 universities in the United States. Researchers at four US campuses create the first hosts of the ARPANET, connecting Stanford Research Institute, UCLA, UC Santa Barbara, and the University of Utah.

1970

ALOHANET developed at the University of Hawaii.

1970–1973

The ARPANET is a success from the very beginning. Although originally designed to allow scientists to share data and access remote computers, email quickly becomes the most popular application. The ARPANET becomes a high-speed digital post office as people use it to collaborate on research projects and discuss topics of various interests.

1971

The ARPANET grows to 23 hosts connecting universities and government research centers around the country.

1972

The InterNetworking Working Group becomes the first of several standards–setting entities to govern the growing network. Vinton Cerf is elected the first chairman of the INWG, and later becomes known as a "Father of the Internet."

1973

The ARPANET goes international with connections to University College in London, England and the Royal Radar Establishment in Norway.

1974

Bolt, Beranek & Newman opens Telenet, the first commercial version of the ARPANET.

1974–1981

The general public gets its first vague hint of how networked computers can be used in daily life as the commercial version of the ARPANET goes online. The ARPANET starts to move away from its military/research roots.

1975

Internet operations transferred to the Defense Communications Agency.

1976

Queen Elizabeth goes online with the first royal email message.

1977

UUCP provides email on THEORYNET.

1978

TCP checksum design finalized.

1979

Tom Truscott and Jim Ellis, two grad students at Duke University, and Steve Bellovin at the University of North Carolina establish the first USENET newsgroups. Users from all over the world join these discussion groups to talk about the net, politics, religion and thousands of other subjects.

1980

Marc Andreesen turns 8. 14 more years till he revolutionizes the Web.

1981

ARPANET has 213 hosts. A new host is added approximately once every 20 days.

1982

The term "Internet" is used for the first time.

1982–1987

Bob Kahn and Vint Cerf are key members of a team which creates TCP/IP, the common language of all Internet computers. For the first time the loose collection of networks which made up the ARPANET is seen as an "internet," and the Internet as we know it today is born.

The mid-80s marks a boom in the personal computer and super-minicomputer industries. The combination of inexpensive desktop machines and powerful, network-ready servers allows many companies to join the Internet for the first time. Corporations begin to use the Internet to communicate with each other and with their customers.

1983

TCP/IP becomes the universal language of the Internet.

1984

William Gibson coins the term "cyberspace" in his novel "Neuromancer." The number of Internet hosts exceeds 1,000.

1985

Internet e-mail and newsgroups now part of life at many universities.

1986

Case Western Reserve University in Cleveland, Ohio creates the first "Freenet" for the Society for Public Access Computing.

1987

The number of Internet hosts exceeds 10,000.

1988

Internet worm unleashed.

1988–1990

By 1988 the Internet is an essential tool for communications, however it also begins to create concerns about privacy and security in the digital world. New words, such as "hacker," "cracker" and "electronic break-in," are created.

These new worries are dramatically demonstrated on Nov. 1, 1988 when a malicious program called the "Internet Worm" temporarily disables approximately 6,000 of the 60,000 Internet hosts.

1988

The Computer Emergency Response Team (CERT) is formed to address security concerns raised by the Worm.

1989

System administrator turned author, Clifford Stoll, catches a group of Cyberspies, and writes the

A significant development in the evolution of the Internet was the advent of high-speed Internet access service, for both commercial and residential use. **AP/WIDE WORLD PHOTOS. REPRODUCED BY PERMISSION.**

best-seller "The Cuckoo's Egg." The number of Internet hosts exceeds 100,000.

1990

A happy victim of its own unplanned, unexpected success, the ARPANET is decommissioned, leaving only the vast network-of-networks called the Internet. The number of hosts exceeds 300,000.

1991

The World Wide Web is born!

1991–1993

Corporations wishing to use the Internet face a serious problem: commercial network traffic is banned from the National Science Foundation's NSFNET, the backbone of the Internet. In 1991 the NSF lifts the restriction on commercial use, clearing the way for the age of electronic commerce.

At the University of Minnesota, a team led by computer programmer Mark MaCahill releases "gopher," the first point-and-click way of navigating the files of the Internet in 1991. Originally designed to ease campus communications, gopher is freely distributed on the Internet. MaCahill calls it "the first Internet application my mom can use." 1991 is also the year in which Tim Berners-Lee, working at CERN in Switzerland, posts the first computer code of the World Wide Web in a relatively innocuous newsgroup, "alt.hypertext." The ability to combine words, pictures, and sounds on Web pages excites many computer programmers who see the potential for publishing information on the Internet in a way that can be as easy as using a word processor.

Marc Andreesen and a group of student programmers at NCSA (the National Center for Supercomputing Applications located on the campus of University of Illinois at Urbana Champaign) will eventually develop a graphical browser for the World Wide Web called Mosaic.

1991

Traffic on the NSF backbone network exceeds 1 trillion bytes per month.

1992

One million hosts have multi-media access to the Internet over the MBONE.

1992

The first audio and video broadcasts take place over a portion of the Internet known as the "MBONE." More than 1,000,000 hosts are part of the Internet.

1993

Mosaic, the first graphics-based Web browser, becomes available. Traffic on the Internet expands at a 341,634% annual growth rate.

1994

The Rolling Stones broadcast the Voodoo Lounge tour over the M–Bone. Marc Andreesen and Jim Clark form Netscape Communications Corp. Pizza Hut accepts orders for a mushroom, pepperoni with extra cheese over the net, and Japan's Prime Minister goes online at www.kantei.go.jp. Backbone traffic exceeds 10 trillion bytes per month.

1995

NSFNET reverts back to a research project, leaving the Internet in commercial hands. The Web now comprises the bulk of Internet traffic. The Vatican launches www.vatican.va. James Gosling and a team of programmers at Sun Microsystems release an Internet programming language called Java, which radically alters the way applications and information can be retrieved, displayed, and used over the Internet.

1996

Nearly 10 million hosts online. The Internet covers the globe.

1996

As the Internet celebrates its 25th anniversary, the military strategies that influenced its birth become historical footnotes. Approximately 40 million people are connected to the Internet. More than $1 billion per year changes hands at Internet shopping malls, and Internet related companies like Netscape are the darlings of high-tech investors.

Users in almost 150 countries around the world are now connected to the Internet. The number of computer hosts approaches 10 million.

Within 30 years, the Internet has grown from a Cold War concept for controlling the tattered remains of a post-nuclear society to the Information Super-highway. Just as the railroads of the 19th century enabled the Machine Age, and revolutionized the society of the time, the Internet takes us into the Information Age, and profoundly affects the world in which we live.

The Age of the Internet has arrived.

1997

Today some people telecommute over the Internet, allowing them to choose where to live based on quality of life, not proximity to work. Many cities view the Internet as a solution to their clogged highways and fouled air. Schools use the Internet as a vast electronic library, with untold possibilities. Doctors use the Internet to consult with colleagues half a world away. And even as the Internet offers a single Global Village, it threatens to create a 2nd class citizenship among those without access. As a new generation grows up as accustomed to communicating through a keyboard as in person, life on the Internet will become an increasingly important part of life on Earth.

Further Resources

BOOKS

Akera, Atsushi, and Frederik Nebeker. *From 0 to 1: An Authoritative History of Modern Computing.* New York: Oxford University Press, 2002.

Campbell-Kelly, Martin, and Williams Aspray. *Computer: A History of the Information Machine.* New York: Basic Books, 1996.

———. *From Airline Reservations to Sonic the Hedgehog: A History of the Software Industry.* Cambridge, Mass.: MIT Press, 2003.

Reagan, Patrick D. *History and the Internet: A Guide.* New York: McGraw-Hill, 2002.

Reid, Robert H. *Architects of the Web: 1,000 Days that Built the Future of Business.* New York: Wiley, 1997.

Sunstein, Cass. *Republic.com.* Princeton, N.J.: Princeton University Press, 2001.

PERIODICALS

Drucker, Peter F. "The Age of Social Transformation." *Atlantic Monthly,* November 1994, 53–80.

Frazier, Ian. "The Typewriter Man." *Atlantic Monthly,* November 1997, 81–92.

John, Richard H., ed. "Special Issue: Computers and Communications Networks." *Business History Review* 75, Spring 2001, 1–176.

Usselman, Steven W. "Computer and Communications Technology." In *Encyclopedia of the United States in the Twentieth Century, Vol II,* ed. Stanley I. Kutler. New York: Simon & Schuster, 1996, 799–829.

WEBSITES

Charles Babbage Institute, Center for the History of Information Technology, University of Minnesota. Available online at http://www.cbi.umn.edu (accessed June 4, 2003).

Computer Museum History Center. Available online at http://www.computerhistory.org (accessed June 4, 2003).

Defense Advanced Research Projects Agency (DARPA). Available online at http://www.darpa.mil (accessed June 4, 2003).

History of Computing Information (U.S. Army Research Lab). Available online at http://ftp.arl.mil:80/~mike/comphist (accessed June 4, 2003).

"Is Cyberspace Destroying Society? An Online Conference with Sven Birkerts, May 30, 1995." *The Atlantic Online.* Available online at http://www.theatlantic.com/unbound /aandc/trnscrpt/birkerts.htm; website home page: http:// www.theatlantic.com (accessed June 4, 2003).

"Is the Internet Good for Democracy?" *Boston Review* 26, Summer 2001. Available online at http://bostonreview .net/BR26.3/contents.nclk; website home page: http:// bostonreview.net (accessed June 4, 2003).

U.S. Internet Council. Available online at http://www .usinternetcouncil.org (accessed June 4, 2003).

AUDIO AND VISUAL MEDIA

Nerds 2.0.1: A Brief History of the Internet. Produced and directed by Stephen Segaller. PBS Video. Videocassette, 1998.

Silicon Valley: Center of a Modern Renaissance, 1970's– 1990's. Produced and directed by John R. MacLaughlin. Films for the Humanities. Videocassette, 1999.

"The New Demon"

Book review

By: Benjamin M. Friedman

Date: October 8, 1998

Source: Friedman, Benjamin M. "The New Demon." *New York Review of Books* 45, no. 15, October 8, 1998.

About the Author: Economist Benjamin Friedman (1944–) has worked for the Federal Reserve Banks of New York and Boston, the Board of Governors of the Federal Reserve System, Morgan Stanley, and as program director in Financial Markets and Monetary Economics of the National Bureau of Economic Research. He has served as chair of the Economics Department at Harvard University, where he has held the William Joseph Maier Professorship in Political Economy since 1989. ∎

Introduction

A continuing paradox of the American economy in the 1990s was that even though productivity increased from that of the preceding decade, the wages and incomes of employees failed to increase at the same time. Since the early 1970s, wages and income for most Amer-

icans had stagnated due to a falling rate of productivity growth. Yet when the productivity rate went up in the 1990s, individual and family incomes did not rise as well. Some economists explained this by pointing to the explosive use of computers in the workplace, which led to increases in the amount of work done with the same or fewer employees.

In this review of conservative commentator Patrick Buchanan's *The Great Betrayal: How American Sovereignty and Social Justice Are Being Sacrificed to the Gods of the Global Economy* (1998), Harvard economist Benjamin Friedman points to a change in the structure of the American economy that led to the loss of millions of industrial jobs that had provided relatively good pay and benefits to several generations of American workers. Stagnant wages in turn, he argues, led to growing income inequality for the entire decade of the 1980s and most of the 1990s. Millions of Americans watched as corporate executives' pay and benefits exploded in growth while the buying power of their own wages or salaries seemed to buy less than in earlier years. Friedman rejects Buchanan's view that these trends were caused primarily by free trade and global competition to argue that the problem was created by a range of factors, including technological changes, organizational changes in some industries, lagging business investment, and weaknesses in American primary and secondary education.

Significance

American economic performance in the 1990s seemed to be considerably better than it had been in the 1980s. Evaluated in terms of productivity growth rates, this view was accurate. Yet the social costs of economic change as the economy shifted from an industrial structure to a service and knowledge economy left millions of employees with lower pay, fewer benefits, disappearing jobs, and few opportunities for the future. While working-class, lower-middle-class, middle-class, and even some upper-middle-class Americans experienced these problems in their daily lives, news coverage and political campaigning largely overlooked the matter. Democrats Bill Clinton and Al Gore tinkered around the edges of the problem by lowering annual federal deficits and paying off the debts run up in the 1980s, yet there were no resources to address the broad issues of lagging economic growth and growing inequality of income and wealth. Businesses invested money in new technologies such as word processing, databases, and personal computers. Yet there was a human cost of failing to create enough new jobs for young people entering the workforce or middle-aged Americans forced to find new jobs or careers as their old jobs were abolished.

In 1996 President Bill Clinton signed into law an increase in the minimum wage. U.S. wages have not kept up with inflation. AP/WIDE WORLD PHOTOS. REPRODUCED BY PERMISSION.

Economists such as Friedman and some public commentators carefully examined factual and statistical evidence to discover this problem, but journalists, politicians, and many business leaders did not pay much attention. Compared to the 1980s, the U.S. economy was better off. Yet compared with the long-term postwar period from 1945 to 1973, the economy experienced relatively low rates of growth in historical perspective. Later research indicated that after 1995, this wage and income gap began to shrink, but following the stock market collapse of 2000 and the terrorist attacks on New York City and Washington, D.C., on September 11, 2001, these limited gains stopped and began reversing.

Primary Source

"The New Demon" [excerpt]

SYNOPSIS: In this review of a book by Patrick Buchanan, Friedman offers his own view to explain the failure of wages and salaries to keep up with growth in the economy.

Over the past quarter-century most Americans' wages have failed to keep up with inflation, and most families' incomes have remained stagnant despite the increase in two-earner households. The average full-time worker in US business now makes $440 per week. Twenty-five years ago the average worker made $517 a week in today's dollars. In 1996 (the latest available data), the median family income in the United States was $42,300. A decade ago, in comparable dollars, it was $42,700. Even twenty-five years ago, it was already fully $40,100, just 5 percent less than in 1996. Little wonder that so many Americans have lost their sense of getting ahead, and that so many parents now fear for their children's financial future.

Such trends, and the human difficulties they create, have been especially acute among the industrial workers who are the particular object of Mr. Buchanan's concern. These men and women usually graduate from high school but not from college.

Many of them used to work on assembly lines and in foundries but no longer do so. For the first time since the Industrial Revolution, the number of jobs in US manufacturing is declining. Today only 18.8 million Americans (out of 126 million at work) have manufacturing jobs. Twenty-five years ago there were 20.2 million such jobs (out of just 77 million overall). Since manufacturing firms traditionally provided higher wages and more generous benefits, it is easy to understand all the talk about the absence of "good jobs" despite today's remarkably low unemployment rate.

Moreover, as Mr. Buchanan emphasizes, incomes in America have also become dramatically unequal. Families who scrimp to buy $12 bleacher seats at the ball park, and know they can't afford $30 each for "cheap" tickets for a basketball game, read daily about the players' seven- or even eight-figure salaries. Corporate employees who consider themselves lucky to have jobs that give increases of a percent or two beyond the cost of living know that their firms' top executives are making millions in salary and further tens of millions on stock options. Each new merger eliminates more of the jobs of people who earn $20,000 to $50,000 and leaves more CEOs worth $20 million to $50 million.

These and other recent developments in American society (for example, widespread drug addiction) that Mr. Buchanan laments are certainly disheartening—indeed, in some cases they are appalling and infuriating. But the question is whether free trade and global competition are their root cause. And the question that follows, for practical purposes, is not whether steps should be taken to deal with these problems but whether a return to protectionism is the right step to take.

The truth of the matter is that the stagnating wages and widening inequalities that now afflict much of the American work force have not one cause but many, and no one knows how much weight to give each of the diverse factors that, taken together, are plausibly responsible. Rapid changes in technology are eliminating some jobs but at the same time creating new ones, even whole new industries, and are also rendering some workers' skills and training obsolete while placing a premium on what others know how to do. Changes in the organization of already mature industries, typically through consolidation, as with banking and retailing, likewise create hardships for some but opportunities for others.

The inadequacy of US businesses' investment, which has only recently begun to revive now that the large government deficits of the Reagan-Bush era have dwindled and disappeared, has constrained increases in productivity and hence in wages. (If US investment in new factories and machinery had not shrunk so much as a share of our national income in the 1980s, the number of jobs in our manufacturing industries would not be so diminished today.) So too has productivity been limited by the widely discussed deficiencies of America's primary and secondary education systems. And especially for workers with little education, immigration policies that often favor unskilled over skilled new arrivals have held down already low wages.

No doubt the rising force of global competition belongs on this list too. But is such competition the main cause of America's stagnating wages and widening inequalities?

Further Resources

BOOKS

Buchanan, Patrick J. *The Great Betrayal: How American Sovereignty and Social Justice Are Being Sacrificed to the Gods of the Global Economy.* Boston: Little, Brown, 1998.

Frank, Robert H., and Philip J. Cook. *The Winner-Take-All Society: Why the Few at the Top Get So Much More Than the Rest of Us.* New York: Free Press, 1995.

Hacker, Andrew. *Money: Who Has How Much and Why.* New York: Simon and Schuster, 1997.

Levy, Frank. *Dollars and Dreams: The Changing American Income Distribution.* New York: W.W. Norton, 1988.

Phillips, Kevin. *Wealth and Democracy: A Political History of the American Rich.* New York: Broadway Books, 2002.

PERIODICALS

Kuttner, Robert, et al. "Homestead Security: Broadening America's Riches, A Special Report on Wealth in America." *The American Prospect* 14, May 2003, A1–A23.

WEBSITES

Steckel, Richard H. "A History of the Standard of Living in the United States." EH.Net Encyclopedia, edited by Robert Whaples, July 22 2002. Available online at http://www.eh.net/encyclopedia/steckel.standard.living.us.php; website home page: http://www.eh.net (accessed June 5, 2003).

The New Economy Index: Understanding America's Economic Transformation

Report

By: Robert D. Atkinson and Randolph H. Court

Date: 1998

Source: Atkinson, Robert D., and Randolph H. Court. "The New Economy Index: Understanding America's Economic Transformation." Progressive Policy Institute Report, November 18, 1998. Available online at http://www.ppionline.org /ndol/print.cfm?contentid=1270; website home page: http://www.ppionline.org (accessed June 5, 2003).

About the Authors: Robert D. Atkinson was one of the founders of the Progressive Policy Institute in Washington, D.C. Randolph H. Court was a researcher at this centrist think tank. ∎

Introduction

Over the course of the twentieth century, a series of independent research institutions in a variety of subject areas were founded. Eventually, they were called "think tanks." The first generation emerged during the Progressive era (1900–1917) and World War I (1914–1918) to deal with the growing complexity of American life. In the 1920s and 1930s, a second generation evolved into specialized research centers dealing with economic policy, national income and wealth, social policy, and the building of a national social science network. By the post-World War II (1939–1945) years, hundreds of think tanks dotted the American landscape from liberal, centrist, and conservative perspectives. During the 1960s, the Ford Foundation and the Brookings Institution provided the administrations of presidents John F. Kennedy (served 1961–1963) and Lyndon B. Johnson (served 1963–1969) with expert advisers, policy research and recommendations, and specialized reports. By the 1980s and 1990s, politicians commonly used the research and recommendations of think tanks to develop economic policies.

In this November 1998 report, economic analysts Robert D. Atkinson and Randolph H. Court from the centrist think tank Progressive Policy Institute describe the emergence of what they call "the New Economy" of the 1990s. As an arm of the New Democrats, this tank tank report argues for the need to create a new set of economic indicators that will accurately evaluate the new service and knowledge economy rather than relying on older industrial economy analysis. The authors address the key issues of structural economic change, the use of technological innovation, and the impact of the new economy of the 1990s on American work and society. They also point to the need for new national policies in government, economic growth, technological innovation, and education to prepare for future economic development in the twenty-first century.

Significance

At one level, U.S. economic activity in the 1990s seemed to grow faster and stronger than in the 1980s. Yet national economic policy still had not solved the problem of how to grow the economy at a faster rate in order to create more and better jobs that would pay good wages and salaries along with necessary benefits such as health insurance and retirement plans. Economists, business leaders, politicians, and policy advisers engaged in an important debate about whether the American and world economies in this decade had entered a new period based on a different set of rules of operation than in the industrial era since the nineteenth century. One side in this debate argued that traditional ways of evaluating the economy developed in the 1920s and 1930s no longer sufficed. The other side argued that most economic change occurs more gradually, so the industrial sector of the American economy should not be overlooked as a continuing important element. Advocates and supporters of the "New Economy" such as the authors of this 1998 report worked at coming up with new ways to collect, analyze, and make sense of the information-based economy.

Federal Reserve Board chairman Alan Greenspan did not appear to know how to come down in this debate. As head of the nation's key banking system responsible for making decisions about whether to raise or lower the interest rate the Federal Reserve charged its member banks, Greenspan had to walk a carefully balanced line in the debate. President Bill Clinton (served 1993–2001) came down on the side of proponents of the New Economy. He used the monetary policy of the Greenspan-led Federal Reserve Board, private investment, and relatively small amounts of government spending to promote economic growth throughout the decade. In terms of raising productivity, creating new jobs, and sparking consumption, the economy of the 1990s saw the longest period of economic growth in the country's history. Yet as the authors of this report noted in 1998, problems remained in matching education, skill, and people to the jobs of this new economy. When the stock market collapsed in March 2000, the celebration of the New Economy cooled down as the nation moved into the new century.

Primary Source

The New Economy Index: Understanding America's Economic Transformation [excerpt]

> **SYNOPSIS:** Economic analysts Robert D. Atkinson and Randolph H. Court describe attributes of the New Economy.

President Bill Clinton (center), Microsoft President Bill Gates (left), and World Bank President James Wolfensohn attend a session of the White House Conference on the New Economy, where economists and industry experts met to discuss global economic trends and future possibilities.
© AFP/CORBIS. REPRODUCED BY PERMISSION.

The U.S. economy is undergoing a fundamental transformation at the dawn of the new millennium. Some of the most obvious outward signs of change are in fact among the root causes of it: revolutionary technological advances, including powerful personal computers, high-speed telecommunications, and the Internet. The market environment facilitated by these and other developments in the last decade and a half has been variously labeled the "information economy," "network economy," "digital economy," "knowledge economy," and the "risk society." Together, the whole package is often simply referred to as the "New Economy."

The story of how businesses are changing in today's economy has been told and retold with such frequency in recent years that it has become something of a cliche: the new rules of the game require speed, flexibility, and innovation. New, rapidly growing companies are selling to global markets almost from their inception, and established companies are being forced to reinvent their operations to stay competitive in the new terrain. This is the part of the New Economy that was born in Steve Jobs' and Steve Wozniak's garage, at Bell Labs, Xerox PARC, and in the trunk of Michael Dell's car. It is Silicon Valley: Netscape, Yahoo!, and the next Big Thing. And of course it is Microsoft, with a market capitalization now second only to General Electric's.

But this New Economy is about more than high technology and the frenetic action at the cutting edge. Most firms, not just the ones actually producing technology, are organizing work around it. The New Economy is a metal casting firm in Pittsburgh that uses computer-aided manufacturing technology to cut costs, save energy, and reduce waste. It is a farmer in Nebraska who sows genetically altered seeds and drives a tractor with a global satellite positioning system. It is an insurance company in Iowa that uses software to flatten managerial hierarchies and give its workers broader responsibilities and autonomy. It is a textile firm in Georgia that uses the Internet to take orders from customers around the world.

It is also as much about new organizational models as it is about new technologies. The New Economy is the Miller brewery in Trenton, Ohio, which produces 50 percent more beer per worker than the company's next-most-productive facility, in part because a lean, 13-member crew has been trained to work in teams to handle the overnight shift with no oversight.

Yet while the social and political implications of this New Economy are clearly vast, our system for tracking economic progress—the set of indicators we use as a gauge—has not kept up with the pace of evolution. Our statistical system was essentially established to measure a stable economy with most of the output in agricultural and manufactured goods. Until the Great Depression, economic indicators were often measures of natural resources and commodity production: the number of bales of cotton produced, hogs raised, steel ingots melted. (Even today, the United States spends three times more on agricultural statistics than on national income statistics, according to MIT economist Lester Thurow.) After the New Deal and the creation of federal statistical agencies, our economic indicators began to focus on monetary measures related to managing the business cycle. For example, significant effort is made to track the gross domestic product (GDP), inflation and changes in the money supply, business inventories, and consumer purchases thought to affect the business cycle, such as housing and autos. (The first 15 pages of the Congressional Joint Economic Committee's monthly "Economic Indicators" are devoted to these sorts of indicators of the business cycle. It is not until the sixteenth page that the report gets to arguably the most important indicator of economic well-being: productivity.)

The purpose of this report is to draw on a new set of indicators, gathered from existing public and private data, to examine some of the key characteristics of the New Economy. We have divided these indicators into three groups. The first group tracks some of the elemental structural changes that collectively mark the transition to the New Economy: industrial and occupational change, globalization, the changing nature of competition and economic dynamism, and the progress of the information technology (IT) revolution. The second group examines the implications of this transition for working Americans: what is happening to incomes and economic growth, jobs, and employment dynamics. The third group assesses the nation's performance in terms of three main foundations for growth in the New Economy: the pace of transition to a digital economy, investment by business and government in technology and innovation, and progress on the development of education and skills.

Structural Transformation

Beyond the technological advances, what is actually new about the so-called New Economy? In one respect, nothing. We still work at jobs for a living, and we still buy, sell, and trade products and services, just like we always have. As Federal Reserve Chairman Alan Greenspan has noted, the heart of the economy is, as it always has been, grounded in human nature, not in any new technological reality. In Greenspan's analysis, *"The way we evaluate assets, and the way changes in those assets affect our economy, do not appear to be coming out of a set of rules that is different from the one that governed the actions of our forebears. . . . As in the past, our advanced economy is primarily driven by how human psychology molds the value system that drives a competitive market economy. And that process is inextricably linked to human nature, which appears essentially immutable and, thus, anchors the future to the past."* [Emphasis in original.] Nonetheless, Greenspan and other economists agree that some of the key rules of the game are changing, from the way we organize production, to our patterns of trade, to the way organizations deliver value to consumers.

The global economic crisis that began in Asia in 1997 has caused growing concern that one of the fundamental hallmarks of the New Economy, the increasingly complex state of global interconnectedness, may in fact be a harbinger of financial chaos. Many of the Asian economies that were touted as economic miracles for the better part of this decade are now in profound economic and social disarray. Slower growth and falling demand have plunged Russia into default, and now threaten Latin America. No one can precisely predict how these events will continue to unfold, but we believe that the worst-case scenario—a serious world-wide recession—would, at most, only slow the pace of the forces described in this report.

The trends at the heart of the New Economy are long-term structural trends. It is true that globalization is one of these new structural realities, and thus business cycles will increasingly tend to be world-wide in scale. But the current problems in Asia and elsewhere should not be seen as inherent features of the New Economy. The troubles are not simply a byproduct of the ability of capital to move instantaneously from market to market at the whims of international investors. Rather, one of the basic reasons for the Asian economic crisis is that Asian economies have not yet fully adapted their institutional structures (particularly their finance, investment, and banking systems), their business practices, or their policies to match the imperatives of the New Economy. In Japan, for example, slow growth in the service sector has hindered overall economic growth. Failure to dismantle barriers to imports and foreign direct investment, along with low levels of entrepreneurship, have limited competition. In turn, there have been insufficient pressures for corporate and financial restructuring. Moreover, low levels of investment in information technology have meant a slower transition to a more digital economy, and a slower overall pace of change.

The fallout of the economic crisis, while extremely destructive and painful in the short term, could eventually yield constructive developments. The turbulence puts pressure on governments to establish New Economy policy frameworks, on industries to embrace new business practices, and on societies to adopt new attitudes. One example of a constructive outcome would be the creation of modern, transparent banking and financial reporting systems which rely on the most realistic vehicle for both national governments and firms to deliver regular financial reports and other information to a worldwide audience in real time—the Internet. Such a system already exists in the United States; public companies must file their required documents and reports in electronic form with the Securities and Exchange Commission so the information can be archived and made immediately available to the public via Edgar, the agency's online database.

The United States is ahead of the curve in a number of areas. Here, one of the most noticeable structural changes in the New Economy is the degree to which dynamism, constant innovation, and adaptation have become the norm. One of the keys to the recent strong U.S. economic performance has been the country's ability to embrace these changes. Nearly three quarters of all net new jobs are being created by 350,000 new fast-growing "gazelle" firms (companies with sales growth of at least 20 percent per year for four straight years). Almost a third of all jobs are now in flux (either being born or dying, added or subtracted) every year. This churning of the economy is being spurred by new technology, but also by increasing competition, a trend that is in turn partly a product of increasing globalization. Between 1970 and 1997, U.S. imports and exports grew three and a half times faster than GDP in 1992 dollars.

Another striking structural characteristic of the New Economy is occupational change. Between 1969 and 1995, virtually all the jobs lost in the production or distribution of goods have been replaced by jobs in offices. Today, almost 93 million American workers (which amounts to 80 percent of all jobs) do not spend their days making things—instead, they move things, process or generate information, or provide services to people.

The Challenge Ahead

Is all of this turbulence, change, and complexity temporary, simply the byproduct of the transition from the Industrial Age to an information era? Or are these intrinsic and permanent aspects of the New Economy? The Progressive Policy Institute believes that the latter is true and that the challenge now is to learn how to manage and govern in an era of sustained and constant innovation and adaptation.

Some see the emergence of the New Economy as disruptive and threatening. Others celebrate it uncritically, ignoring the social strains created by its constant change and uneven distribution of costs and benefits, and rejecting any role for government. PPI subscribes to a third view, embracing the inherent new possibilities born of unleashed entrepreneurial energy for technological and economic progress, while supporting policies that foster growth and innovation, and equip all Americans with the tools they need to succeed. The New Economy is not an end in itself, but the means to advance larger progressive goals: new economic opportunities and higher living standards, more individual choice and freedom, greater dignity and autonomy for working Americans, stronger communities, and wider citizen participation in public life.

Today, though the foundations for the New Economy are in place, widespread benefits haven't yet been realized. Despite job growth, low unemployment, and other notable signs of economic progress—and despite gushing press accounts of fabulous new wealth and opportunities—a central paradox of the emerging New Economy is that the 1980s and 1990s have seen productivity and per capita GDP growth rates languish in the 1.25 percent range, while income inequality has grown. Our challenge is to create a progressive economic policy framework that will encourage a new era of higher growth, while promoting and enabling a broad-based prosperity that produces the widest possible winners' circle.

Old economic policy, shaped by the Great Depression, largely focused on creating jobs, controlling inflation, and managing the business cycle. The New Economy brings new concerns. Technology, as well as a highly competent Federal Reserve policy, may have lessened the importance and severity of the domestic business cycle. We have shown that we can create jobs—over nine million of them in the first five years of the Clinton Administration. And there is general agreement that in the new global economy, with increased competition and technology, the risk of inflation is reduced. The real challenge of economic policy now is to support and foster continued adaptation, including policies that lead to a fully digital economy characterized by continuous, high levels of innovation and a highly educated and skilled workforce.

The nascent transformation to a digital economy, where an increasing share of economic value is a product of electronic means, has the potential to usher in a new period of sustained higher productivity and wage growth in America. Most of the indicators of the transformation to a digital economy forecast steady progress. Computing and telecommunications costs have been falling dramatically, and the U.S. Internet economy is projected to be worth $350 billion by 2001 (when nearly 40 percent of U.S. households are projected to be online). But realizing the digital economy's potential will depend in part on regulatory, tax, and procurement policies—at all levels of government—aimed first at not hindering, and where possible at fostering this transformation. Government also clearly has a role to play in spurring the transformation by encouraging the electronic delivery of public services, though it has taken little more than baby steps in the right direction at this point.

New Economy economists like Paul Romer, Richard Nelson, and Rob Shapiro have focused on knowledge, technology, and learning as keys to economic growth and have begun to focus on how policy can actually affect innovation. A consensus has emerged that investments to develop and commercialize research and technology play a major role in increased standards of living for Americans. However, indicators of innovation and investment suggest cause for concern. In the last five years, federal support for both basic and applied research have fallen precipitously. Industry investment in basic research has also declined. Similarly, over the last decade the stock of machinery and equipment that American workers use to be productive has fallen as a share of GDP. Education is another economic foundation area showing a lack of sufficient progress. Corporate expenditures on employee training have fallen in the 1990s as a share of GDP. Meanwhile, K–12 performance has simply failed to keep up with the pressing need for a skilled workforce, in spite of continued increases in education spending. We need a set of policies to ensure that American companies have the skilled workers they need to be productive, and that American workers have the skills they need to navigate, adapt, and prosper in the New Economy.

The New Economy puts a premium on what Nobel Laureate economist Douglas North calls "adaptive efficiency"—the ability of institutions to innovate, continuously learn, and productively change. In the old economy, fixed assets, financing, and labor were principal sources of competitive advantage for firms. But now, as markets fragment, technology accelerates, and competition comes from unexpected places, learning, creativity, and adaptation are becoming the principal sources of competitive advantage in many industries. Enabling constant innovation has become the goal of any organization committed to prospering, and should also become the goal of public policy in the New Economy.

PPI believes that a progressive innovation-oriented policy framework for the New Economy should rest on four pillars:

1. Investment in new economic foundations, specifically education, training, and scientific and technological research.

2. Creation of an open and flexible regulatory and trade regime that supports growth and innovation, including policies that support the IT revolution.

3. Development of policies to enable American workers to have the tools they need to navigate, adapt, and prosper in a continually changing economic environment.

4. Reinvention—and digitization—of government to make it fast, responsive, and flexible.

In summary, if we are to ask workers to take the risks inherent in embracing the New Economy, we must equip them with the tools to allow them to prosper and cope with change and uncertainty. If we fail to invest in a knowledge infrastructure—world-class education, training, science, and technology—our enterprises will not have the skilled workers and cutting-edge tools they need to grow and create well-paying jobs. And if Industrial Age government does not transform itself into Information Age government, it will become an inefficient, anachronistic institution, impeding rather than advancing progress.

Further Resources
BOOKS

Greider, William. *One World, Ready or Not: The Manic Logic of Global Capitalism.* New York: Simon and Schuster, 1997.

Krugman, Paul K. *Peddling Prosperity: Economic Sense and Nonsense in the Age of Diminished Expectations.* New York: W.W. Norton, 1994.

McGann, James G., and R. Kent Weaver, eds. *Think Tanks and Civil Societies: Catalysts for Ideas and Action.* New Brunswick, N.J.: Transaction Publishers, 2000.

Reich, Robert B. *The Future of Success: Working and Living in the New Economy.* New York: Knopf, 2001.

Smith, James A. *The Idea Brokers: Think Tanks and the Rise of the New Policy Elite.* New York: Free Press, 1991.

Thurow, Lester C. *Building Wealth: The New Rules for Individuals, Companies and Nations in a Knowledge-Based Economy.* New York: HarperCollins, 1999.

PERIODICALS

Farrell, Chris. "The New Economy in Historic Perspective." *NBER Digest,* December 2000. Available online at http://www.nber.org/digest/dec00/w7833.html; website home page: http://www.nber.org (accessed June 5, 2003).

AUDIO AND VISUAL MEDIA

Silicon Valley: Center of a Modern Renaissance, 1970's–1990's. Produced and directed by John R. MacLaughlin. Films for the Humanities. VHS, 1999.

"Bull Market Keynesianism"

Journal article

By: Dean Baker

Date: 1999

Source: Baker, Dean. "Bull Market Keynesianism." *The American Prospect* 10, no. 42, January 1–February 1, 1999. Available online at http://www.prospect.org/print/V10/42/baker-d.html; website home page: http://www.prospect.org (accessed June 5, 2003).

About the Author: Dean Baker was the codirector of Center for Economic and Policy Research and authored the *Economic Reporting Review,* which reviews business and economic reporting done by *The New York Times* and the *Washington Post.* ∎

Introduction

Professional economists in the United States assumed in the years after 1945 that price inflation and the unemployment rate were tied together. When prices increased too much, that would lead to a higher rate of unemployment. When unemployment went down, prices would go up. Yet economic behavior since the stagnant 1970s suggested that this assumption may have been incorrect. In the wake of the simultaneous rise in prices (inflation) and unemployment during the 1970s, stagflation suggested that economic policies from the late 1930s to the late 1960s were obsolete. Keynesian economic policy (named after British economist John Maynard

Keynes) had argued that when an economy turned down, government needed to step in to pick up lagging private investment until growth returned. During the 1980s the supply-side economic policies of the Reagan and Bush administrations rejected Keynesian policies to advocate tax cuts that would boost private investment.

In the 1990s, the Clinton administration adopted the policy of reducing the huge budget deficits of the 1980s, arguing that this would drive down the cost of loans, allowing businesses to increase investment, create new jobs, and provide more money to employees and consumers. In this article from *The American Prospect,* Dean Baker of the Center for Economic and Policy Research argues that, ironically, the economy of the 1990s showed that Keynesian policies were not obsolete. By reducing the federal deficit while the Federal Reserve Board reduced interest rates, economic policies in the 1990s led to a stock market boom. Investors who saw their stock holdings rise in value fed a consumption-driven growth spurt that seemed to lead to dramatic growth. Baker shows that the average rates of growth, job creation, and productivity in the 1990s were no better, and in some cases worse, than in the three preceding decades.

Significance

Political rhetoric and media coverage of economic policies and performance in the 1990s, as in earlier decades, was often based more on short-term developments than on long-term realities. Economic analyst Dean Baker, writing at the end of the decade, argues that Bill Clinton's adoption of deficit reduction and the conservative monetary policy by Alan Greenspan at the Federal Reserve Board did not really promote economic prosperity defined in terms of growth, new jobs, or increased productivity. By the end of the century, consumption by millions of Americans drove the economy. Seeing stock portfolios increase in paper value, many Americans felt wealthier, so they spent more. Baker terms this "stock market Keynesianism." He notes that this behavior had a potentially negative side. Once the stock market began declining from its peak on January 14, 2000, consumption could fall as quickly as it had risen in the 1990s. More importantly, in failing to save a significant amount or percentage of their income, Americans failed to provide the economy with the investment monies needed to rebuild the nation's infrastructure—roads, bridges, airports, and highways.

In failing to provide for more attention to what former Secretary of Labor Robert Reich and others called "human capital," Americans were not constructing a strong foundation for the national economy in the early twenty-first century. Baker's key point is that investment in both private-sector technology, physical plant, and people and public-sector programs meant that the economic prosperity of the 1990s was more of a short-run phenomenon than a long-term development in increased productivity and growth. The great economic lesson of the twentieth century—that a mass-production, mass-consumption economy required constant attention to capital, labor, investment, private business, and government—seemed to have been forgotten. Once the stock market reversed course in January 2000, economic growth slowed, and the terrorist attacks of September 11, 2001, followed by the war in Iraq, caused the U.S. economy to stumble into the new century.

Primary Source

"Bull Market Keynesianism"

> **SYNOPSIS:** Dean Baker, codirector of Center for Economic and Policy Research, looks back on the economy of the 1990s to argue that the apparent prosperity of the decade was more of a short-term phenomenon than part of a long-term development.

As we wait for the dust to settle from the current global financial turmoil, it is a good time to assess the lessons to be learned from the nineties business cycle.

First, it is important to get the basic numbers right. Although the economy experienced robust growth in 1996 and 1997, on the whole this business cycle has had the slowest growth of any in the postwar period. [See Jeff Madrick, "The Treadmill Economy," *The American Prospect,* September–October 1998.] Growth rates are best judged from peak to peak, taking the entirety of the business cycle into account. The average growth rate since the last business-cycle peak in 1989 has been 2.3 percent. This compares with a growth rate of 2.7 percent in the eighties cycle, 3.2 percent in the seventies cycles, and 4.4 percent in the sixties cycle. The rate of job growth has also been slower than in previous cycles. The economy added jobs at the rate of 1.6 percent annually in the nineties. This compares with rates of 1.8 percent in the eighties, 2.5 percent in the seventies, and 2.8 percent in the sixties. Neither has there been a boom in productivity growth. The 1.2 percent annual rate of productivity growth in the current cycle is only slightly higher than the 1 percent rate during the eighties, and well below the 2.5 percent annual rate racked up during the economy's golden age from 1947 to 1973. The last two years have provided good economic news, but not nearly enough to justify talk of an economic boom, at least not by any historical measure.

But while this simple recounting of the numbers should be sufficient to dispel euphoria, the American economy has nonetheless experienced a respectable rate of growth over the last decade—one that looks quite good judged against the anemic growth rates of Japan, Germany, and many other industrialized nations. The unemployment rate in the United States has fallen to the lowest level in a quarter century and is now below that of every major industrialized nation except Japan, which has always had comparatively low rates of unemployment. Although wage and income inequality has increased over the cycle, income gains in the last two years have been broadly based. Workers at all points along the income distribution have experienced genuine wage gains. In other words, even if there has not been a boom, the recent economic record provides enough good news to make it worth asking just what went right.

Keynes Lives

The great irony of the nineties cycle is that while the major engineers of the nation's economic policy were determinedly anti-Keynesian, the outcome of their policies has largely vindicated traditional Keynesian economic precepts. Both the Clinton administration and the Federal Reserve Board adopted the view that the best way to promote long-run economic growth was through deficit reduction, which in turn would lead to more private investment and a higher rate of productivity growth. They also accepted the view that the economy had a non accelerating inflation rate of unemployment (NAIRU) in the range of 5.8–6.5 percent. This meant that they believed that if the unemployment rate were allowed to fall below the NAIRU, then the economy would experience accelerating inflation. And that inflation would continue to accelerate until the unemployment rate was pushed back up to at least the NAIRU.

But the nineties recovery has shown that both these assumptions were wrong. Lower deficits actually did not lead to any significant increase in private investment. The share of gross domestic product (GDP) going to investment is virtually unchanged from the last business-cycle peak in 1989, even though the budget deficit has been completely eliminated and the government is now running a surplus. The unemployment rate has now been below 6 percent for four full years, and below 5 percent for more than twelve months. And yet inflation has actually decelerated over this period. True, falling oil prices and the recent rise in the dollar have helped to lower the inflation rate. But it is hard to find any evidence for accelerating inflation anywhere in the data. We can only conclude that if the NAIRU exists at all, it must lie below 4.5 percent.

Dead Dogma

While the seeming nonexistence of the NAIRU in the nineties has been noted before, the collapse of this economic doctrine is important enough to merit further discussion. Prior to the current upturn, the existence of a NAIRU within a range between 5.8 and 6.5 percent was among the most deeply held articles of faith among macroeconomists. [See "Can't We Go Faster?" *The American Prospect,* September–October 1997.] Few seriously entertained the possibility that the NAIRU might not exist at all or that it might be significantly lower than the conventional wisdom implied. Consider the consequences of those attitudes. Had economic policy been guided by a dogmatic commitment to the NAIRU view, the unemployment rate never would have been allowed to fall below the bottom end of this range. The Federal Reserve Board would have raised interest rates enough to keep the unemployment rate above 5.8 percent, or its best guess of the NAIRU.

The costs of pursuing such a policy would have been enormous. Had the Federal Reserve prevented the unemployment rate from falling below 6 percent, 4.5 million fewer workers would have jobs than currently do. Allowing the unemployment rate to drop to its current level of 4.5 percent had a particularly dramatic impact on the job prospects for disadvantaged demographic groups. The unemployment rate for African-American adults, for example, was 10.1 percent back when the overall unemployment rate was 6 percent. At its low point in June, when the overall unemployment rate had fallen to 4.3 percent, the unemployment rate for African Americans hit 7.3 percent. Over this same period the unemployment rate for African-American teens dropped from 35.1 percent to 20.1 percent.

In general, the drop in the overall unemployment rate from the old supposed NAIRU level of 6 percent to the 4.3–4.5 percent range of recent months has disproportionately benefited the least-well-off segment of the population. Those with the least education and experience have seen the greatest increase in their employment rates. In addition, the low unemployment rate (along with the increases in the minimum wage) is one of the factors that have finally caused wages to start rising for those at the bottom end of the income distribution. There is no politically plausible government program that could have provided benefits as large for the poor and near

poor as this drop in the unemployment rate. And the hardships that welfare reform will impose on the poor would be far worse if the unemployment rate had not been allowed to fall below the NAIRU.

It is also important to recognize the magnitude of the economic gains derived from lower unemployment relative to the potential gains from other types of economic policy. The standard estimate of the relationship between unemployment and GDP holds that a one percentage point fall in the unemployment rate is associated with a 2 percent increase in GDP. This implies that the U.S. economy has produced more than $500 billion in additional output over the last four and a half years because the unemployment rate was allowed to fall below the accepted measures of the NAIRU. By comparison, the Congressional Budget Office's estimates of the cumulative economic gains from moving to a balanced budget over this period are under $50 billion. The gains that the Organization for Economic Cooperation and Development (OECD) estimated the United States would receive from the 1994 General Agreement on Tariffs and Trade (GATT) accord are even less. Balancing the budget and the latest GATT round were touted as important economic policies, but even by their proponents' reckoning the benefits associated with these policies do not even come close to those associated with significant reductions in the unemployment rate. If we err by allowing the unemployment rate to be higher than it could be, there is no feasible way of offsetting the enormous losses that the country thus needlessly incurs.

While the Federal Reserve deserves credit for allowing the unemployment rate to fall to its current level, it is not at all clear that this was really their intention. As the unemployment rate fell into the accepted NAIRU range in early 1994, Alan Greenspan testified that he thought that the labor markets were reaching their limits and that unemployment could not fall further. He also engineered a series of interest rate hikes, raising the federal funds rate by a full three percentage points (from 3 to 6 percent) between February 1994 and February 1995. His words and actions certainly indicated that he did not want the unemployment rate to fall below what he considered to be the NAIRU. However, the resilience of the economy surprised most forecasters (myself included), and the unemployment rate continued to edge down in spite of the increase in interest rates. To Greenspan's credit, he did not raise interest rates further once it became clear that lower unemployment was not leading to accelerating inflation. As a result, the nation's workers have enjoyed two years

The stock market was a powerful force in U.S. economic growth throughout the 1990s. © DAVID POLLACK/CORBIS. REPRODUCED BY PERMISSION.

of relative prosperity as tight labor markets have finally allowed them to benefit from the recovery.

Deficits Don't Hurt

The other Keynesian principle that seems to have been vindicated in this business cycle is the non-relationship between government deficits and private investment. The Clinton administration jettisoned its plans for promoting growth through public investment shortly after it took office, opting instead for a strategy of promoting private investment through deficit reduction. The standard economic rationale began with the assumption that lower deficits would lead to lower interest rates. Lower interest rates would in turn lead to both more private domestic investment and more net exports, and therefore more foreign investment.

But it hasn't quite turned out that way. Setting aside the recent decline in interest rates attributable to the flight to the dollar resulting from financial meltdowns around the world, the real interest rate—the nominal rate minus inflation—at the peak of this business cycle was virtually the same as it was at the peak of the last cycle, back in the big-deficit era. The real interest rate on 30-year government bonds averaged 4.9 percent in 1997. In 1989 the real interest rate on 30-year government bonds averaged 3.9 percent. There is not much of a case that lower deficits led to lower interest rates.

Nor was there much of an upturn in investment associated with deficit reduction. Much recent reporting on the economy speaks of an investment boom in this cycle. The most commonly noted measure of investment, the growth rate in "chained 1992 dollars," can give the impression that there has been an investment boom. But it turns out that most of the growth in this measure of investment is attributable to the way in which the Commerce Department measures the quality of computers. This measure shows the quality of computers improving at the rate of 40 percent a year. That means that a $2,000 computer purchased this year will be 40 percent more useful to an individual or corporation than the $2,000 computer they could have purchased in 1997. By the Commerce Department's reasoning, this quality adjustment means that the $2,000 that a firm spends on a computer this year counts as $2,800 of investment in 1992 chained dollars. In the last two years, this quality adjustment for computers has added approximately ten percentage points a year to the growth rate of investment.

A less questionable way to measure trends in investment is to compare the share of GDP that is attributable to investment at present with the peak of the last business cycle. By this measure, there is not much of a case for an investment boom. In the third quarter of 1998, nonresidential investment was 10.9 percent of GDP. This is an increase of 0.5 percent from its 10.4 percent share in 1989. However this increase was completely offset by a decline in net exports. The trade deficit rose from 1.5 percent of GDP in 1989 to 2.0 percent of GDP in the third quarter of 1998, implying a decline in net foreign investment of the same magnitude. If investment and net exports are added together (in effect the combined movement of domestic and foreign investment), the increase in the share of GDP going to investment did not change.

But if investment didn't pick up in response to deficit reduction, just what absorbed the gap in demand created by deficit reduction? The answer is consumption. The share of GDP that went to consumption rose by 2.4 percentage points from 1989 to the third quarter of 1998, almost completely offsetting the decline in the share of GDP that went to government spending. In other words, soaring consumption led this recovery, not soaring investment. That should be apparent from the sharp decline in the savings rate, which stood at less than 1 percent in the third quarter of 1998. From the perspective of national savings, this recovery saw a large increase in public savings (the shift from large budget deficits to budget surpluses) but a completely offsetting decline in private savings. National saving—the sum of public and private savings—was virtually unaffected. As it turns out, the effort to stimulate investment through deficit reduction was a failure, just as Keynes would have predicted.

The other part of the story is no less interesting. What spurred consumption and drove down savings was the enormous run-up in stock prices. The stock market rose by almost 160 percent in real terms from 1993 to its peak earlier this year. This created more than $8 trillion in new wealth. Not surprisingly, this new wealth caused stockholders to spend more and save less. It was this spending that kept the economy growing as the deficit shrank. This

effect was particularly strong in the last two years, as the stock market created more than $5 trillion of additional wealth in 1996 and 1997 alone.

It is ironic that the rising stock market has led to this consumption boom. The textbook theory holds that high stock prices should lead to more investment by effectively decreasing the cost to firms of borrowing on the stock market. But the stock market has not been a major source of capital for most corporations for decades. In fact, corporations have been net lenders, not borrowers, on the stock exchange. In 1997 they actually bought $41.2 billion more in stock shares than they issued, even as price to earnings ratios were at record highs. Stock prices clearly have very little impact on firms' investment decisions.

However, stock prices do have a significant impact on consumers' savings and consumption decisions. By creating $8 trillion in new wealth, the stock market provided a basis for a spending spree among the segment of the population that owns significant amounts of stock. (Unfortunately, this is still a very small share of the population. Less than half of households own any stock at all, including indirect ownership through 401 (k) plans. Of those that own stock, the median holding is under $20,000.) The run-up in stock prices had the same sort of stimulatory effect on consumption as if the Federal Reserve Board had printed $8 trillion and dispersed it among the population. However, in this case, the Fed didn't have to do anything; the private sector created the paper wealth. Call it stock market Keynesianism.

The Bubble Bursts

But there's a catch. If the booming stock market was the major force propelling consumption and growth, what happens when the market reverses course, as now seems to be happening? It's not a pretty picture. Unlike the case with conventional fiscal policy, there is no one at the controls when the market turns south. Consumption demand will likely fall sharply as stockholders realize that their portfolios are worth much less than they had thought. This decline in demand will be accentuated by the plunge in exports to developing nations, which are suffering from their own financial collapses. Government budget policy is likely to make matters worse, as the administration tries to run large budget surpluses to "save Social Security." (This is the same fiscal strategy recently pursued by Japan with such great success.)

With the major components of demand all moving downward, we will be fortunate to avoid a recession. If the Fed is slow to react to the downturn and the administration remains wedded to the pursuit of budget surpluses, the downturn could be quite severe. The most recent business cycle should provide renewed confidence in the power of simple Keynesian remedies to reverse a slump. But it remains to be seen whether Washington's policymakers are too dogmatic to absorb these lessons.

Further Resources

BOOKS

Phillips, Kevin. *Wealth and Democracy: A Political History of the American Rich.* New York: Broadway Books, 2002.

Reich, Robert B. *The Future of Success: Working and Living in the New Economy.* New York: Knopf, 2001.

Yergin, Daniel, and Joseph Stanislaw. *The Commanding Heights: The Battle for the World Economy.* New York: Simon and Schuster, 2002.

PERIODICALS

Farrell, Chris. "The New Economy in Historic Perspective." *NBER Digest,* December 2000. Available online at http://www.nber.org/digest/dec00/w7833.html; website home page: http://www.nber.org (accessed June 5, 2003).

"Job Growth in the 1990s: A Retrospect"

Journal article

By: Julie Hatch and Angela Clinton

Date: December 2000

Source: Hatch, Julie, and Angela Clinton. "Job Growth in the 1990s: A Retrospect." *Monthly Labor Review* 123, no. 12, December 2000, 13–14. Available online at http://www.bls.gov/opub/mlr/2000/12/art1full.pdf; website home page: http://www.bls.gov (accessed June 6, 2003). ∎

Introduction

As long as the postwar prosperity lasted, most Americans continued to think of employment in terms of industrial jobs. Yet already by the mid-1950s, the majority of the nation's workforce labored in white-collar rather than blue-collar jobs. In the 1990s, job growth exploded in the services industries, accounting for 70 percent of new jobs in the ten industries creating new employment. A number of employers began using what labor historians called a "two-tier" labor market. Permanent employees made real gains in the decade, while holding on to benefits. Yet part-time and temporary workers in various service jobs were recruited by firms specializing in find-

ing people with limited or no job skills. Businesses tried out these temporary workers without having to commit to full-time pay or benefits until they were sure these employees would work out for their firms. Americans who belonged to the upper tier saw upward mobility, better pay, and long-term employment. Those who were in the second tier often faced dead-end jobs, low pay, and ongoing uncertainty about keeping their jobs. Not surprisingly, the business press and mainstream news outlets tended to publish stories about the successful while overlooking the social costs born by the new service workers.

Millions of individuals began using personal computers with word processing and database software programs at work in the 1990s. Economists began debating whether computerization of American businesses would result in long-term productivity gains following a period of increased investment costs for the new technology and training time for employees to acquire or sharpen computer skills. Computer-literate college graduates found themselves in a seller's market. Employers seeking skilled workers paid premium salaries and bonuses to recruit these young employees. Information became a valuable tool that transformed the marketplace, leading companies to focus on data entry, storage, access, manipulation, and analysis as a growing part of their day-to-day operations. Commentators started talking about the new Knowledge Economy that made information as important to the new service economy as products and services had been to the older industrial economy. As agricultural employment continued to shrink, demand grew for engineers, managers, and health care and social service workers.

Significance

Although white-collar and service work already dominated the American labor force by the middle of the 1950s, the significance of service industries did not strike many Americans until the 1990s. With the structural shift of the national economy from industry to services and knowledge, the largest numbers of new jobs created to replace industrial-era employment were in the service areas. As the postwar baby boom generation hit middle age, their sons and daughters joined the labor force in entry-level service jobs that growing numbers called "McJobs." Seeing little room for advancement in pay, skill, or career opportunities, these younger workers reflected a widespread concern for a future unlike that of their parents and grandparents. The booming videogame and personal computer markets created the first generation of Americans that grew up using a wide variety of electronic devices without much conscious thought.

Scholars debated the broader impact of the new service and knowledge economy. Some argued that it was

The service industry, particularly in health care, experienced high growth in the 1990s. © R.W. JONES/CORBIS. REPRODUCED BY PERMISSION.

dramatically changing not only the nature of work but also the larger society and culture. Economists often remained skeptical about the productivity gains that were promised but that always seemed just over the horizon. The postwar consumer culture continued to expand into every corner of American life with homes, cars, public spaces, and businesses showing signs of the commercialization of everyday life. Older workers who had grown up assuming that good-paying, permanent jobs with benefits such as paid holidays and vacations, health insurance, and retirement plans would always be available saw thousands of such jobs disappear. At times, entire communities and industries shut down, as seen on the streets of steel and textile towns in the Northeast and Midwest. For those willing to move into the new economy with its uncertain future, it was an exciting time that promised a bright tomorrow.

Primary Source

"Job Growth in the 1990s: A Retrospect" [excerpt]

> **SYNOPSIS:** Economists Julie Hatch and Angela Clinton of the Bureau of Labor Statistics describe the importance of service industries jobs to economic growth in the 1990s.

Services Leads Job Growth

The services industry was the driving force behind job growth during the 1990s. Rapid technological transformation helped prolong the longest economic expansion on record and helped create a substantial number of employment opportunities in services. Of the 10 specific industries adding the most jobs during the decade, 7 were in services.

Business Services: The Real McCoy

Employment in business services grew more than any other industry group during the decade. . . . Business services accounted for approximately a third of all job growth in the services division. Topping the list of most jobs added and third in growth rate, personnel supply services, which includes both traditional employment agencies and help supply firms (primarily temporary help agencies), accounted for half the strength in business services. Employment opportunities exploded in the help supply industry as more firms relied on temporary help as a way to manage labor more effectively. Businesses adopted the concept of "just-in-time labor," similar to just-in-time production which is common in the automobile industry. Labor supplied by the help supply industry enabled firms to quickly adjust their labor forces to stay competitive.

Firms expanded demand for temporary workers, especially for more highly skilled ones. During the 1980s, firms typically used temporary workers for more repetitive clerical and menial-labor tasks. This practice transformed during the next decade as companies routinely purchased the services of highly skilled workers from temporary agencies to meet their diverse needs in areas such as financial services, health services, telecommunications, and information technology. Skilled workers were added to payrolls, and training was offered to expand the skills of all workers in areas such as word processing and computer-based applications. In addition to providing a wider range of workers, some help supply establishments began to take on the functions of traditional employment agencies, as client firms increasingly used temporary agencies to try out potential permanent employees. Some businesses even opted to have temp firms handle all of their staffing needs and provided on-site offices for a temporary agency.

Computer and data processing services mimicked help supply in its demand for more highly skilled computer professionals. Even though employment growth remained strong during the decade, recession included, there were signs of slowing very late in the decade. Colleges and universities could not produce graduates with computer degrees fast enough, as firms scrambled to cure the Y2K bug and design chips and software for computers and other consumer products.

Computer and data processing services added more than a million jobs during the decade. The computer market expanded during the 1990s as a response to the technological advancements made and the continual reduction of price. Parents began to purchase computers as educational tools for their children. Within computer and data processing services, employment grew especially in information retrieval services and the software industry. Computer game software became more sophisticated with the evolution of the computer chip, and helped employment in the software industry grow. More Americans increasingly integrated the Internet into their everyday routines, and as a result, employment blossomed in information retrieval services. Computer consulting services, which dominates the residual category, were greatly in demand during the decade. Demand for consulting services expanded as businesses set up local area networks, developed websites, and rewrote programs for the new millennium.

Although engineering and management services grew at half the pace of business services, it outpaced the rate of total nonfarm employment growth by one and a half times. Engineering and management services added 800,000 jobs during the decade. Much of this strength can be attributed to the value added to most industry sectors by engineering and management personnel. The construction industry in particular benefited greatly from the engineering and architectural industry. Finance, insurance, and real estate businesses frequently relied upon management and public relation services to improve productivity. Management and public relations accounted for more than half of all job growth in management and engineering services.

Huge Gains Arise from Serving People

Health services, while growing less than half as fast as business services during the 1990s, still contributed more than 2.5 million jobs to nonfarm payrolls. The growth rate slowed from that of the previous decade. The growing popularity of HMOs and the implementation of the perspective payment plan by Congress led to decreased health care expenditures. Not all health service industries experienced the slower growth phenomena. Home health care services grew the fastest of all the industries, and also made the list of the top 20 in terms of number of jobs gained. Several factors contributed to this above-average growth. First, medicare expanded benefits to make more people eligible for home health care coverage, the cost associated with care at home was relatively less costly compared to that at hospitals, and technological advancements provided people the option to receive medical treat-

ment in the comfort of their own home. Nevertheless, home health care also was affected by cutbacks in health expenditures, and ended the decade with employment 78,000 lower than its July 1997 peak. Offices and clinics of medical doctors added jobs at a considerably slower rate than in the 1980s, but still faster than average for services. Offices and clinics of medical doctors ranked 7th in the number of jobs added. Hospital employment also increased by more than a half a million jobs, but the rate of growth in this huge industry was anemic. This, in part, is due to the decreased average length of stay and the restructuring of hospital staffs to reduce costs.

Social services grew twice as rapidly as health services during the 1990s, increasing employment by 70 percent or more than a million employees. The growth was concentrated in three industries—residential care services, individual and family services, and child day care services. Each of these industries made the top-20 list for both the number of jobs gained and the growth rate. Job training, which benefited from the restructuring of the American workforce, also added jobs at a rapid pace. People needed skills that did not exist 10 years ago as a result of the rapidly changing technology.

In a lighter vein, two industries that serve up entertainment—motion picture services and amusement and recreation services experienced strong rates of job growth during the 1990s. The strong U.S. economy enabled these industries to prosper throughout the majority of the decade. As disposable income continued to increase, the public devoted more time and money to these luxury items.

Further Resources
BOOKS

Chandler, Alfred D., and James W. Cortada, eds. *A Nation Transformed by Information: How Information Has Shaped the United States from Colonial Times to the Present.* New York: Oxford University Press, 2000.

Coupland, Douglas. *Microserfs.* New York: Regan Books, 1995.

Dubofsky, Melvyn, and Foster Rhea Dulles. *Labor in America: A History.* 6th ed. Wheeling, Ill.: Harlan Davidson, 1999.

Ehrenreich, Barbara. *Nickel and Dimed: On (Not) Getting by in America.* New York: Metropolitan Books, 2001.

Krugman, Paul K. *Peddling Prosperity: Economic Sense and Nonsense in the Age of Diminished Expectations.* New York: W.W. Norton, 1994.

Thurow, Lester C. *Building Wealth: The New Rules for Individuals, Companies and Nations in a Knowledge-Based Economy.* New York: HarperCollins, 1999.

"A Fair Deal for the World"

Book review

By: Joseph E. Stiglitz

Date: May 23, 2002

Source: Stiglitz, Joseph E. "A Fair Deal for the World." *New York Review of Books* 49, no. 9, May 23, 2002.

About the Author: Joseph E. Stiglitz, an economist at Columbia University, received the 2001 Nobel Prize in Economics. He has served as chairman of the Council of Economic Advisers and vice president of the World Bank. He is the author of *Globalization and Its Discontents* (2002). ∎

Introduction

In his review of internationally known investor and philanthropist George Soros' *On Globalization,* economist Joseph Stiglitz discusses the complexities of the debate over globalization. Economists have long argued that the modern economic ideas and institutions of capitalism have expanded all over the world. In 1944, at the end of World War II (1939–1945), the victorious Allied powers established the Bretton Woods system, which includes the World Bank and the International Monetary Fund (IMF) to aid developing and underdeveloped countries in economic modernization through advice, loans, and other forms of assistance. For much of the postwar period, the World Bank, IMF, and other international economic development institutions (such as the World Trade Organization created in 1995) were widely respected and encountered little criticism. That changed in the 1990s.

As multinational corporations in the industrial world expanded overseas from home countries, the world balance of trade and distribution of economic resources became increasingly more and more unequal. In the 1990s, individuals, social movements, organizations, and nations began to reconsider the role of these international economic agencies in economic, social, political, and environmental terms. By the last half of the decade, meetings of the industrialized nations and economic development institutions sometimes occurred in the context of large protests in the streets around their meetings. Perhaps the most well known were protests that occurred at the 1999 meeting of the World Trade Organization in Seattle, Washington. Yet respected individuals also joined the growing debate over globalization. George Soros, author of the book under review here, is the chairman of Soros Fund Management. He is also an internationally recognized philanthropist who heads the Open Society Institute.

Significance

During the 1990s, the global impact of economic change in the wake of industrialization, wars, international trade, and modernization created both opportunities and challenges. In the United States, various news media used coverage of protests organized by community activists in the local, national, and international arenas to highlight violence in the streets. Yet serious reappraisal of globalization took place not only among dissidents but also mainstream economic leaders. Stiglitz and Soros both wrote well-received books that were critical of the World Bank, the IMF, and the World Trade Organization. Both works were widely and positively reviewed in a number of significant journals in the United States, giving millions of Americans the chance to learn about this vitally important international economic debate that could dominate much of their lives in the twenty-first century.

This post-September 11, 2001, review suggests that economic change, international instability after the end of the cold war, and the disruptions of religions, societies, and cultures by globalization were serious issues that would have to be addressed not only by economists, bankers, and business leaders but also by ordinary citizens, politicians, and labor and environmental activists. Both Stiglitz and Soros suggest that the United States could no longer afford to ignore such issues. In the twentieth-first century, Americans would have to learn not only what they opposed—terrorism, authoritarian governments, and backward economies—but also what they and the country stood for. The economic, social, political, and cultural challenges of the new century required new ways of thinking, acting, and cooperating with other peoples and other nations in a truly international global system.

Primary Source

"A Fair Deal for the World" [excerpt]

SYNOPSIS: In his review of George Soros' *On Globalization,* economist Joseph Stiglitz examines the complexities of the global economic system.

Seeking to explain what is wrong with globalization, and in particular with the international economic institutions, Soros, consistent with his non-utopian approach, looks in this new book for practical proposals, reforms that might reasonably be adopted. To be sure, he recognizes that there are forces that will work against these changes, that special interests in the United States benefit from the current arrangements. But he is a great believer in global civil society, and one of its strongest supporters. Global civil society has, at times, been able to overcome these established forces. In 2000 the Jubilee Movement, an international coalition of economic activists, called for, and succeeded in obtaining, debt

Opinions are split on the issue of economic globalization, as was illustrated in November 1999 when the World Trade Organization met in Seattle, Washington, and encountered massive demonstrations that later turned violent. **AP/WIDE WORLD PHOTOS. REPRODUCED BY PERMISSION.**

relief for more than twenty of the poorest countries of the world.

Previously, the IMF had imposed such high hurdles for poor countries to qualify for relief from debt that few could meet the standards it set. Anyone who has watched the change in attitudes, both inside the institutions and in the general public, over the past five years must recognize the power of global civil society. It is now a commonplace that the international trade agreements about which the United States spoke so proudly only a few years ago were grossly unfair to countries in the third world. As I go to meetings of businessmen, whether in the rarefied seminars of Davos or the financial circles of New York or the high-tech world of Silicon Valley, practically all the people I see recognize the inequities and hypocrisies of American government policies. They are, however, more critical of the abuses of others' special private interests, whether they involve steel, textiles, or agriculture; when it comes to their own interests they often claim that special treatment is either deserved or necessary.

Soros is one of the growing band of experts who, while recognizing the power of globalization to increase wealth, also recognize its adverse effects. His indictment is simple: globalization has hurt many people, especially the poor in the developing world. Globalization has distorted the allocation of resources in favor of private goods at the expense of public goods. And global financial markets are prone to crisis. No one who has looked dispassionately at the process of globalization over recent years could disagree with any of the elements of this indictment.

The inequities associated with globalization have long been evident to those concerned about global social justice. And, at least since the global financial crisis of 1997–1998, the instabilities of globalization have been a source of much anxiety. But the events of September 11 have added a new dimension to the globalization debate. It is not just goods and services that move easily across borders. Secret offshore bank accounts are used for a variety of illegitimate transfers and deserve special scrutiny. They are responsible for part of the lack of transparency that may have contributed to the Asian crisis but served the purpose of important financial interests well. They are used to launder money for the drug trade; they also provide a mechanism for corrupt officials to move money out of their countries, and enable the rich to avoid taxation, and, as we've recently been made aware, they also help provide the financing for terrorism.

Before September 11, the US Treasury vetoed the efforts of the OECD to limit the secrecy protecting such accounts—evidently it served Wall Street's interests too well, regardless of the costs imposed on others in the global system. After September 11, even the US Treasury had to change its position. Moreover, while the links between poverty and terrorism are complicated, few would deny that poverty, and especially high unemployment rates among young men, provide fertile ground on which terrorism can grow. Ensuring that globalization will be more helpful to the poor thus becomes not just a moral imperative but also something that should be viewed as a matter of self-interest.

Soros's book is written with a simplicity that makes it an excellent introduction to the international economic organizations, including the IMF, the WTO, and the World Bank. While these institutions are often blurred in the minds of the public, they are distinct institutions, with different missions, cultures, and governing authorities. All of them take an important part in the unfolding drama of globalization, and they accordingly bear much of the blame for its failures. As Soros says, "They are being operated for the benefit of the rich countries that are in control, often to the detriment of the poor ones. . . ."

Soros's book is about economics, but, like the rest of us, he has been touched by the events of September 11, and these have led him to a broader set of reflections—on both politics and human nature. He points out that "we cannot protect" ourselves against the new threats "by increasing our military superiority over other states."

Global leadership requires not only being against something; it requires being for something. We have an alliance against terrorism. We should also have an alliance for more global justice and a better global environment. Globalization has made us more interdependent, and this interdependence makes it necessary to undertake global collective action. The United States must take the lead to provide global public goods—including law and order. It should be working to bring about reforms in the world economic order, away from the "Washington consensus"—the

ideologically driven "model" of market fundamentalism. But as Soros also points out, for the US to be a leader will require some deep changes:

> We must abandon the unthinking pursuit of narrow self-interest and give some thought to the future of humanity. . . . [We need] a reassertion of morality amid our amoral preoccupations. It would be naive to expect a change in human nature, but humans are capable of transcending the pursuit of narrow self-interest. Indeed, they cannot live without some sense of morality. It is market fundamentalism, which holds that the social good is best served by allowing people to pursue their self-interest without any thought for the social good—the two being identical—that is a perversion of human nature.

In the same vein, Soros concludes by emphasizing a theme that runs throughout his book—that compassion is also a matter of pragmatic realism:

> The fight against terrorism cannot succeed unless we can also project the vision of a better world. The United States must lead the fight against poverty, ignorance, and repression with the same urgency, determination, and commitment of resources as the war on terrorism.

Further Resources

BOOKS

Chua, Amy. *World on Fire: How Exporting Free Market Democracy Breeds Ethnic Hatred and Global Instability.* New York: Doubleday, 2002.

Gray, John. *False Dawn: The Delusions of Global Capitalism.* New York: New Press, 1998.

Greider, William. *One World, Ready or Not: The Manic Logic of Global Capitalism.* New York: Simon and Schuster, 1997.

Lovett, William A., Alfred E. Eckes, Jr., and Richard L. Brinkman. *U.S. Trade Policy: History, Theory, and the WTO.* Armonk, N.Y.: M.E. Sharpe, 1999.

Soros, George. *Crisis of Global Capitalism: Open Society Endangered.* New York: Public Affairs, 1998.

Yergin, Daniel, and Joseph Stanislaw. *The Commanding Heights: The Battle for the World Economy.* New York: Simon and Schuster, 1998, 2002.

WEBSITES

The Office of International Programs of the U.S. Department of State website. Available online at http://usinfo.state.gov /topical/econ/group8/homepage.htm; website home page: http://usinfo.state.gov (accessed June 6, 2003).

World Bank website. Available online at http://www.worldbank .org (accessed June 6, 2003).

World Trade Organization website. Available online at http:// www.wto.org (accessed June 6, 2003).

"Dow Jones Industrial Average, 1990–1999"

Graph

By: Dow Jones

Date: August 2002

Source: "Dow Jones Industrial Average, 1990–1999." Available online at http://www.djindexes.com/downloads/DJIA _broch.pdf; website home page: http://www.djindexes.com (accessed June 6, 2003).

About the Author: The Dow Jones company provides investors with detailed information about the buying and selling of stocks and bonds, especially with its creation of the Dow Jones Industrial Average Index in 1896. ∎

Introduction

On May 26, 1896, the Dow Jones Industrial Average was first published by creator Charles Dow, one of the founders of *The Wall Street Journal* newspaper. Since then, the makeup of this well-known stock index (one of many, including the NASDAQ and the Russell 1000, 2000, and 3000 indices) has changed over time. The initial Dow Jones average included twelve industrial stocks, twenty in 1916, and thirty since 1928. The Dow Jones Index is a mathematical calculation of all thirty stock prices divided by an adjustment factor. That factor takes into account changes in the stocks included in the index, splits in individual stocks, mergers and acquisitions, and new stocks. The Dow Jones Index makes

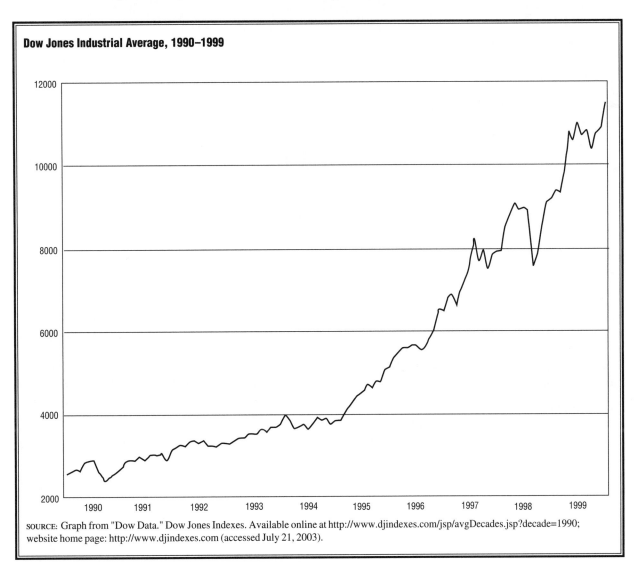

Dow Jones Industrial Average, 1990–1999

SOURCE: Graph from "Dow Data." Dow Jones Indexes. Available online at http://www.djindexes.com/jsp/avgDecades.jsp?decade=1990; website home page: http://www.djindexes.com (accessed July 21, 2003).

Primary Source

"Dow Jones Industrial Average, 1990–1999"

SYNOPSIS: This chart of the Dow Jones Industrial Average Index from 1990 to 1999 shows the advance of the great bull market during the 1990s.

A bull market dominated the U.S. economy throughout the early 1990s. AP/WIDE WORLD PHOTOS. REPRODUCED BY PERMISSION.

up roughly 25 to 30 percent of the total market values of all U.S. stocks. Financial advisers, brokerage houses, institutional investors, and individual investors use the index as a measure of changes in key stock prices over time, allowing them to make decisions about buying, holding, or selling.

During the 1920s and the 1980s, the American stock market experienced rapid growth in what came to be called a "bull market." Bull markets are often followed by "bear markets," when the prices of stock fall or stay stagnant over a period of time. During the 1990s, the United States experienced a tremendous bull market, shown by this graph, which includes fluctuations of the Dow Jones and the Standard & Poor 500 (another index, which includes the stock prices of 500 of the largest U.S. industrial stocks) from 1990 to 1999. Investment activity in the form of mergers, acquisitions, and sale of stocks and bonds became so heated in the decade that these two major stock indices achieved historically record-high levels, as represented graphically on this chart.

Significance

On March 29, 1999, the Dow Jones Index went over the 10,000 mark for the first time. Financially, this was not really significant, but it symbolized an important psychological barrier that media across the globe turned into an internationally covered story. In 1951 *Fortune* magazine had published *U.S.A.: The Permanent Revolution,* which argues that "people's capitalism" had arrived in America. While that was not true, it came closer to reality in the 1990s than at any other time in U.S. history. During the 1990s, almost half of all American households owned some kind of investment in the stock market in the form of stocks, bonds, or mutual funds (a collection of stocks and bonds intended to reduce investor risk and reward long-term investment).

Prior to the 1990s, most Americans who did invest followed stock prices in the financial sections of newspapers or magazines. With the emergence of cable television and widespread use of the Internet in the 1990s, millions of Americans began following the story of the stock market twenty-four hours a day, seven days a week on specialized financial news channels and websites. They often watched reporting of daily, weekly, monthly, and annual changes in stock prices in either numerical or graphical image formats to the point where the subject became commonly discussed in many workplaces and homes. While the impression was left that most Americans held stocks in a democratically arranged system, in fact, as had been true for all of American history, the value of most stocks and other investment devices was concentrated in the hands of a small number and percentage of individuals and institutions. Careful studies showed the rising inequality of income was matched by rising inequality of wealth in the years after 1973. The potential for continuous, explosive growth in stock prices related to computers, the Internet, and other high-technology markets led investors to spark a huge increase in stock prices reflected in graphs of major indices such at the Dow Jones Industrial Index and the Standard & Poor 500 Index. The bull market of the 1990s peaked on January 14, 2000, at 11,722.98, then declined in the wake of the bursting of the high-technology stock bubble, economic weaknesses, and the terrorist attacks of September 11, 2001.

Further Resources

BOOKS

Gordon, John Steele. *The Great Game: The Emergence of Wall Street as a World Power, 1653–2000.* New York: Scribner, 1999.

Seligman, Joel. *The Transformation of Wall Street: A History of the Security and Exchange Commission and Modern Corporate Finance.* Boston: Houghton Mifflin, 1982.

Sicilia, David B., and Jeffrey L. Cruikshank. *The Greenspan Effect: Words That Move the World's Markets.* New York: McGraw-Hill, 2000.

Sobel, Robert. *The Big Board: A History of the New York Stock Market.* Washington, D.C.: Beard Books, 2000.

WEBSITES

American Stock Exchange website. Available online at http://www.amex.com (accessed June 6, 2003).

New York Stock Exchange website. Available online at http://www.nyse.com (accessed June 6, 2003).

U.S. Securities and Exchange Commission website. Available online at http://www.sec.gov (accessed June 6, 2003).

"Economy in Perspective: Consumer Price Index, 1961–2002"

Graph

By: *Washington Post*
Date: 2003

Alan Greenspan, chairman of the Federal Reserve, attends a 1997 hearing of the House banking subcommittee. As Federal Reserve chairman, Greenspan is seen as a powerful force in the nation's economic performance. AP/WIDE WORLD PHOTOS. REPRODUCED BY PERMISSION.

Source: "Economy in Perspective: Consumer Price Index, 1961–2002." *Washington Post.* Available online at http://www.washingtonpost.com/wp-srv/flash/business/econ/economics.html; website home page: http://www.washingtonpost.com (accessed September 10, 2003). ■

Introduction

One of the problems with comparing prices and what wages and salaries will purchase over time is that the relative value of money and prices changes as economic conditions change. As a result, economists and statisticians in the private and public sectors have developed a yardstick measurement called the Consumer Price Index (CPI) that allows for adjustment of money, prices, and income over time based on statistical formulas. The U.S. government's official definition of the CPI is based on a shopping basket of necessary goods commonly purchased by consumers living in a typical American city. Use of CPI data allows for adjusting retail prices, hourly wages, and salaries to account for changes in the real, or actual, cost of living.

This graph from the *Washington Post* website shows annual percentage changes in the CPI between 1961 and 2002. It reveals long-term trends in the cost of living. In

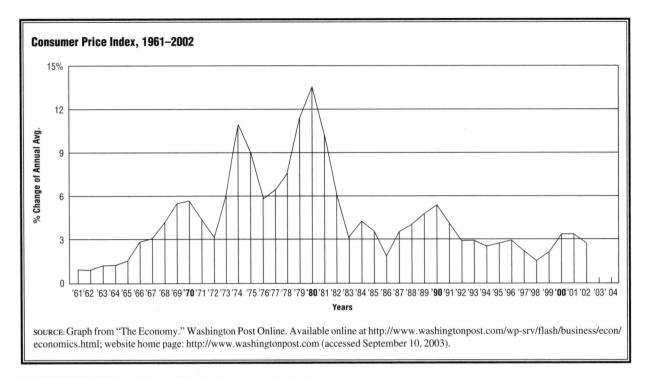

Consumer Price Index, 1961–2002

SOURCE: Graph from "The Economy." Washington Post Online. Available online at http://www.washingtonpost.com/wp-srv/flash/business/econ/ economics.html; website home page: http://www.washingtonpost.com (accessed September 10, 2003).

Primary Source

"Economy in Perspective: Consumer Price Index, 1961–2002"

SYNOPSIS: The Consumer Price Index (CPI) was at its lowest points throughout the 1990s. Though the earlier part of the decade saw a CPI of almost 6 percent, the later years held steady at or near 3 percent.

contemporary American economic history, prices began to show sizable increases after 1965; inflation accelerated in the 1970s, reached double-digit rates (above 10 percent) in 1979–1980, then declined dramatically in the first half of the 1980s. Price rises in the late 1980s reversed for most of the 1990s, returning to average rates of 3 percent or lower. After 1998, prices began climbing again, but not as quickly as most of the period in the decades of the 1970s and 1980s.

Significance

For most of the post-World War II (1939–1945) era, most Americans were not overly concerned about increases in the prices they had to pay for basic economic necessities. Then after 1965, after prices had gone up most years, stagnant hourly wages or salaries did not provide many individuals or families with enough money to pay bills. While small purchases remained affordable, larger purchases such as homes and consumer durables (household goods such as furniture, refrigerators, ovens, and other appliances) became noticeably more expensive. By the end of the 1970s, millions of Americans felt the impact of price inflation in the interest rates paid on car loans, home mortgages, small appliance loans, and business or education loans. During the 1980s and 1990s, the Federal Reserve Board un-

der chairmen Paul Volcker and Alan Greenspan implemented policies that resulted in bringing the rate of price inflation under control. Yet while the rate of price inflation decreased markedly, stagnant wages and income resulted in a relative increase in economic inequality of income and wealth for most of the period from 1973 through the mid-1990s. Only in the last half of the 1990s did wages and salaries go up enough to appear in statistical measurement like the CPI.

Throughout the twentieth century, more and more Americans participated in the emergence of a consumer culture based on mass production and mass consumption. By the end of the 1990s, consumer spending accounted for about two-thirds of annual economic growth. Buying goods and services had become a central feature not only of American economic activity but also of the broader society and culture.

Further Resources

BOOKS

Baker, Dean. *Getting Prices Right: The Debate over the Consumer Price Index.* Armonk, N.Y.: M.E. Sharpe, 1997.

Cohen, Lizabeth. *A Consumers' Republic: The Politics of Mass Consumption in Postwar America.* New York: Knopf, 2003.

Schor, Juliet B., and Douglas B. Holt, eds. *The Consumer Society Reader.* New York: The New Press, 2000.

WEBSITES

Bureau of Labor Statistics, U.S. Department of Labor. "Consumer Price Indexes." Available online at http://www.bls .gov/cpi (accessed June 4, 2003).

"The Inflation Calculator." Available online at http://www .westegg.com/inflation/ (accessed June 4, 2003).

Steckel, Richard H. "A History of the Standard of Living in the United States." EH.Net Encyclopedia. Available online at http://www.eh.net/encyclopedia/steckel.standard.living.us.php; website home page: http://www.eh.net (accessed June 4, 2003).

3

EDUCATION

MILLIE JACKSON

Entries are arranged in chronological order by date of primary source. For entries with one primary source, the entry title is the same as the primary source title. Entries with more than one primary source have an overall entry title, followed by the titles of the primary sources.

Important Events in Education, 1990–1999

1990

- The U.S. Department of Education reports that enrollment of African Americans at private colleges and universities in the United States rose by 7.1 percent between 1986 and 1988, while African American enrollment in public universities rose by only 0.2 percent in the same period.

- Scholastic Aptitude Test (SAT) scores show that the national average for mathematics remained constant at 476, while the average score on the verbal section fell from 427 to 424, the lowest in a decade.

- The College Board, in its annual report on college costs, reports that the average cost of a year of college increased by 5 to 8 percent for the 1990–1991 school year. The most expensive colleges are Bennington College in Vermont ($21,550 for tuition and room and board), Sarah Lawrence College in New York ($21,490), and New York University ($21,400).

- The National Assessment of Educational Progress releases a report on the first test of student geography skills. Although most students are able to locate major countries on a map and demonstrate knowledge of places and subjects recently in the news, they struggle with trade, environment, and population growth.

- The Teach for America program begins to recruit young liberal-arts graduates to teach for two years.

- On January 9, the U.S. Supreme Court rules unanimously that universities do not hold any special status that would protect them against disclosure of confidential peer review materials.

- In February, the Home School Legal Defense Association reports that 33 states permit home instruction as a substitute for attendance at a public or private school.

- On February 6, the Los Angeles Board of Education, in an effort to relieve overcrowding in its schools, votes to require all schools within the district to convert to a year-round schedule as of July 1991.

- On February 23, Bishop College in Dallas, once the largest African American college in the western United States, is sold at a bankruptcy auction, believed to be the first auction of an entire college in the nation.

- On March 5, "Channel One," a commercially sponsored television news program for high school classrooms, debuts in four hundred schools across the U.S.

- On March 7, West Virginia teachers strike for better pay and an upgrading of the state's education system in the first statewide teachers' strike in West Virginia. Teachers return to classes on March 19.

- On April 30, the Carnegie Foundation for the Advancement of Teaching releases the report "Campus Life: In Search of Community," which decries administrators' lack of concern over student crime, alcohol abuse, and growing racial and sexual intolerance.

- On May 18, the trustees of all-women Mills College in Oakland, California, vote to rescind a May 3 decision to admit men after two weeks of student protests and boycotts had shut down the 138-year-old school.

- In June, an Illinois court affirms that only the state may revoke a teacher's license. A school board does not have this authority.

- On June 4, the U.S. Supreme Court upholds a federal law that requires public high schools to give student political and religious groups the same access to facilities that is available for other extracurricular activities.

- On June 5, the New Jersey Supreme Court rules that the state's funding of public education with local property taxes is unconstitutional because it benefits wealthy schools at the expense of poor ones.

- On June 12, North Dakota voters reject a one-year increase in the state sales tax. The increase, from 5 to 6 percent, would have raised some $42 million for public education.

- On September 25, President George Herbert Walker Bush signs a $1.6 billion law to improve vocational education by urging states to integrate academic skills into vocational classes, to develop standards for measuring vocational-technical students' competencies in basic and advanced skills, as well as providing funding for "tech-prep" programs linking high schools with local community colleges.

- On November 9, President George H. W. Bush signs into law the Student Right-to-Know and Campus Security Act requiring all colleges and universities to publish annual statistics on their graduation and crime rates, and security procedures.

- On December 7, astronauts aboard the space shuttle *Columbia* beam a classroom lesson on star formation and celestial radiation from space to forty-one middle-school students gathered at National Aeronautics and Space Administration (NASA) centers in Huntsville, Alabama, and Greenbelt, Maryland.

1991

- A Gallup poll instituted by an insurance network reports that 6 percent of U.S. teenagers said they had tried to commit suicide. Another 15 percent said they had "come very close to trying."

- The U.S. Department of Education reports that Spanish-speaking students learned English at about the same rate regardless of whether they were in bilingual programs or in all-English programs.

- More than one hundred students in Duncan, South Carolina, are suspended for displaying the Confederate battle flag or protesting the school's decision to ban it. The suspensions lead to a debate about racism and freedom of expression at James F. Byrnes High School, where 23 percent of students are African American.

• On March 28, a U.S. District Court judge in New York City rules it illegal for a company to assemble photocopies of articles and book excerpts into anthologies for sale to college and university students.

• In April, the Centers for Disease Control and Prevention reports, based on its 1990 Youth Risk Behavior Survey, that almost one in five American high school students sometimes carried a gun, knife, or other weapon to school.

• On May 22, the U.S. Justice Department signs a consent decree with eight Ivy League colleges and universities. The schools agree not to share information on student financial aid and tuition or faculty salaries, thereby preventing action on charges of antitrust violations.

• On July 12, H. Joachim Maitre resigns as dean of Boston University's College of Communications after it was revealed that he had plagiarized an article by Public Broadcasting Service (PBS) film critic Michael Medved in a May commencement address.

• On October 21, trustees of the University of Bridgeport in Connecticut reject a takeover and aid offer from Reverend Sun Myung Moon's Unification Church. The Moon organization had offered $50 million in aid, plus a guarantee of at least one thousand additional students, in exchange for control of the university.

• On November 1, a physics graduate student, distraught over his failure to win an academic award, shoots and kills five people and injures another at the University of Iowa.

• On November 13, Doreen Kimura releases a study that found, like her previous study of the effect of female hormonal cycles, that men's standardized test results varied with the cycle of the hormone testosterone. In the fall, when testosterone levels rose, scores were highest, while in the spring, when levels fell, results were lowest.

• On November 26, the New York City Public School system begins to provide free condoms upon request as part of an AIDS education program. The plan sparks controversy since it does not require students to obtain parental permission to receive condoms.

1992

• The U.S. Department of Education reports that high school-dropout rates among sixteen to twenty-four-year-old Hispanics increased from 34.3 percent in 1972 to 35.3 percent in 1991. For those same years, the rate for African Americans ages sixteen to twenty-four declined from 21.3 percent to 13.6 percent, and the rate for whites in that age group dropped from 12.3 percent to 8.9 percent.

• The Association for the Evaluation of Educational Achievement finds that U.S. students rank second among nine-year-olds and ninth among fourteen-year-olds in a thirty-one nation study.

• A Gallup poll of 1,306 adults finds that 68 percent support the distribution of condoms without restriction in public schools, whereas 25 percent support the idea only with parental consent.

• A New York state judge, rejecting an argument by Educational Testing Service (ETS) that it is impossible to raise an SAT score from 620 to 1,030 in eight months, orders reinstatement of the score earned by Brian Dalton, who claims he was ill during the first examination and had since taken a coaching course.

• On January 18, a seventeen-year-old shoots and kills an English teacher and a janitor and holds classmates hostage at a Grayson, Kentucky, high school.

• On February 12, the report "How Schools Shortchange Girls," commissioned by the American Association of University Women Educational Foundation and prepared by the Wellesley College Center for Research on Women, states that girls face bias in classrooms across the United States.

• On February 26, a student kills two classmates in a hallway at Thomas Jefferson High School in Brooklyn, New York, less than two hours before Mayor David Dinkins was to visit the school to urge pupils to avoid drugs and violence.

• On February 26, the U.S. Supreme Court rules unanimously in *Franklin v. Gwinnett County Public Schools* that Title IX of a 1972 education law entitled students who were the victims of sexual harassment and other forms of sex discrimination at schools receiving federal funds to sue for monetary damages.

• On May 1, a twenty-year-old dropout kills four, wounds nine, and holds dozens of others hostage for more than eight hours at Lindhurst High School in Olivehurst, California.

• On June 24, the U.S. Supreme Court rules, 5-4, that nonsectarian prayers delivered at a public high school graduation violate the Establishment Clause of the First Amendment.

• On June 26, the U.S. Supreme Court decides, 8-1, that the state of Mississippi has not satisfied its obligation to eliminate segregation within its public universities by applying "race-neutral" admission policies at its five formerly "whites-only" campuses or its three historically African American campuses.

• On July 30, the U.S. Census Bureau reports that people in cities tend to be more educated than those living elsewhere. The proportion of people with at least a bachelor's degree was 22.5 percent in cities and 13 percent in other areas.

• In August, Glassboro State College changes its name to Rowan College of New Jersey after businessman Henry M. Rowan donates $100 million, the largest individual gift ever given to a public college or university.

• On September 1, the liberal constitutional rights group People for the American Way reports 376 attempts to censor public-school texts and other educational materials in 1991, a 50 percent increase over 1990. Forty-one percent of censorship attempts succeeded.

• On September 11, a seventeen-year-old runs through a crowded hallway shooting a revolver and injuring six students in Amarillo, Texas.

• On September 28, the U.S. Department of Education Office for Civil Rights announces, after two years of investigation, that the University of California at Berkeley's law school had violated federal civil rights laws by giving preference to minority applicants in an attempt to diversify the student body.

- On October 23, a student is sentenced to six months in jail for lying under oath about cheating on the SAT in what was believed to be the first criminal prosecution related to the college-entrance exam.

- On November 6, a thirteen-year-old boy shoots into a crowded playground, killing an eighteen-year-old student in Lancaster, Pennsylvania.

1993

- Tensions rise at the University of Pennsylvania when five African American sorority sisters charge a white student with racial harassment after he called them "water buffalo."

- On January 21, in Los Angeles, California, a fifteen-year-old who took a gun to school because he feared gang members accidentally fires the pistol in the classroom, killing one classmate and wounding another. The school district begins random screening of students with portable metal detectors.

- On February 22, a fifteen-year-old kills a seventeen-year-old in the hallway of San Fernando Valley, California, high school.

- From May 6 to May 10, South Boston High School closes following a racially-charged brawl outside the school when white students staged a walkout over safety issues during a visit by Boston mayor Raymond Flynn (D).

- In June, the American Federation of Teachers (AFT) reports that public school teachers across the nation earned an average salary of $35,104 during the 1992–1993 school year. The highest state average was Connecticut ($48,918), while South Dakota was lowest ($24,291).

- On August 3, the U.S. Senate confirms former University of Pennsylvania president and distinguished historian Sheldon Hackney chairman of the National Endowment for the Humanities.

- On September 2, a sixteen-year-old kills a fifteen-year-old in the hallway of Franklin D. Roosevelt High School in Dallas, Texas.

- On September 8, the Boston Teachers Union approves a new contract that ties teacher pay to improvements in student performance.

- On September 20, about 90 percent of New York City public schools open after emergency asbestos inspections caused an eleven-day delay. The mayor ordered the new inspections when it was revealed that many inspections were mishandled in the 1980s.

- On October 15, University of Massachusetts chancellor David Scott announces that the school will retain the Minuteman mascot that protestors charged with promoting racism, sexism, and violence in the form of a white man toting a musket.

- On November 1, school officials in Hempstead, Texas, reverse a ban on pregnant girls belonging to the cheerleading squad after threat of a lawsuit from the National Organization for Women (NOW) and the American Civil Liberties Union (ACLU). The school had removed four of

the fifteen-member squad under the policy and reinstated one after she had an abortion.

- On November 3, the school board in Minneapolis, Minnesota, votes unanimously to hire a consulting firm to run the city's schools.

1994

- Harvard University announces it will use the Common Application, a standard college application form used by more than 135 other private colleges and universities nationwide.

- The annual survey of college freshmen by the American Council on Education and the University of California, Los Angeles reveals that only 31.9 percent of freshmen, the lowest percentage in twenty-nine years, reported that "keeping up with political affairs" is an important goal.

- Eighty percent of Connecticut students take the SAT, the highest percentage in the U.S. Mississippi and Utah trail with 4 percent.

- On January 21, a seventeen-year-old Kennard, Texas, student shoots and kills himself during his first-period class.

- On March 19, the Scholastic Assessment Test replaces the Scholastic Aptitude Test as the most widely used college entrance exam. The College Board changes the test in response to criticisms of bias and unreliability.

- On April 12, a ten-year-old shoots and kills an eleven-year-old classmate on an elementary school playground in Butte, Montana.

- In May, the U.S. Naval Academy expels twenty-four midshipmen for their part in a cheating scandal involving an electrical engineering exam in December 1992.

- On June 5, ten-year-old Michael Kearney is the youngest American to graduate from college when he receives a bachelor's degree with a major in anthropology from the University of South Alabama in Mobile.

- On August 7, Harry Kloor, a graduate student at Purdue University, is the first person in the United States to receive two simultaneous Ph.D.s, in physics and chemistry.

- On September 7, a sixteen-year-old student is gunned down in front of his high school in an apparent gang-related incident in Hollywood, California.

1995

- The Education Resources Institute reports that federal college loans in 1994 totaled $23.1 billion, an increase over the 1984 figure of $7.9 billion. Analysts attribute the rise to the failure of federal grants to keep pace with rising costs.

- Stockbroker Anne Scheiber bequeaths $22 million to Yeshiva University in New York City. Yeshiva will use the money to endow scholarships for Jewish female students at the Stern College for Women and Albert Einstein College of Medicine.

- The Economic Policy Institute reports that increases in school spending during the past twenty-five years went largely to uses other than traditional classrooms.

- Retired investment banker John L. Loeb and his wife give $70.5 million to Harvard University in one of the ten largest private gifts ever made to a U.S. college or university.

- The National Assessment of Educational Progress rates only 34 percent of high school seniors proficient readers, down from 37 percent in 1992.

- The Harvard School of Public Health confirms that the rate of alcohol consumption among college students is higher for fraternity and sorority members than for students who do not belong to such organizations.

- The Consortium on Productivity in the Schools, a panel of productivity experts, reports that U.S. public schools did not use effectively the $285 billion received yearly from the federal government. The consortium recommends more autonomy for schools, teachers, and principals, financial rewards for schools that show the most progress, and national examinations for students to earn their diplomas.

- On March 3, a federal judge puts the Cleveland, Ohio, public school system, a 74,000-student district, under state control because of its $125 million debt.

- On April 5, the *Wall Street Journal* reports that many colleges and universities report false test scores and graduation rates to people compiling data for popular guides that rank schools. In a comparison of those guides with reports sent to debt-ratings agencies and investors, the study found inflated average SAT scores and graduation rates.

- On April 26, the U.S. Supreme Court votes, 5-4, to overturn the Gun-Free School Zones Act of 1990, which had made possession of a firearm within one thousand feet of a school a federal offense.

- On May 5, University of Washington officials announce a $10 million gift from Microsoft Corporation founder Bill Gates for the Mary Gates Endowment for Students in memory of his late mother. Gates had donated $12 million to the university in 1991 to establish a biotechnology department.

- On May 28, Ethiopian student Sinedu Tadesse stabs her roommate to death in their dormitory room at Harvard University, wounds an overnight guest, and then hangs herself in a dorm bathroom in an apparent reaction to a request to change roommates.

- On June 26, the U.S. Supreme Court votes, 6-3, to uphold a random drug-testing program for public school student athletes. The case, *Veronia School District v. Acton,* is the first ruling on a school-sponsored program and the first in which the court upheld a program that tested individuals at random.

- On June 29, the U.S. Supreme Court rules, 5-4, that the University of Virginia violated a student group's First Amendment right to publish a student-run Christian journal by denying it the same funding that was available to secular student-run magazines.

- On July 31, U.S. District Judge Frank Mays Hull upholds a Georgia law that required a minute of silent meditation at the beginning of each school day because it does not violate the U.S. Supreme Court's 1971 decision to allow prayer in school if it has a secular purpose, does not advance or promote religion, and does not excessively intertwine the government with religion.

- In September, the Edison Project, founded by media entrepreneur Christopher Whittle, opens at four public elementary schools across the United States. The new program operates by the philosophy that public schools would be more effective if they were privately run, cutting down government bureaucracy.

- On September 12, U.S. Justice Richard P. Matsch ends a court-supervised desegregation program from 1969, which included compulsory race-based busing for many students in Denver, Colorado, public schools.

- On October 1, Michael Bloomberg, the founder and owner of the Bloomberg L.P. news and information service, announces that he will donate $55 million to Johns Hopkins University.

- On October 25, seven high school students, ages fourteen to eighteen, die and more than two dozen others are injured when a commuter train crashes into a school bus in Fox River Grove, Illinois, a small town about forty miles northwest of Chicago.

- On November 9, Gordon Y.S. Wu, a prominent Hong Kong developer, gives $100 million to Princeton University's School of Engineering and Applied Science, the largest cash donation by a foreigner to a U.S. university.

- On November 9, Courtney and Chris Salthouse, fraternal twins from Chamblee, Georgia, become the first twins simultaneously to achieve the highest possible score (1600) on the SAT college entrance examination.

- In December, the AFT reports that public school teacher salaries in the 1994–1995 school year increased by an average of 2.7 percent nationwide from the previous school year, just below the 2.8 percent inflation.

- On December 5, an Arizona state court judge rules that a public school district has the right to require students to wear school uniforms. The ruling affirms that parents cannot overrule this requirement.

1996

- The College Board reports that the average cost of attending a U.S. college or university continues to outpace inflation. The average cost of tuition and fees for in-state students attending public four-year colleges and universities increases to $2,966 for the 1996–1997 academic year, up 5.5 percent from the previous year.

- The Education Trust, using figures from the National Assessment of Educational Progress, reports that the gap in achievement between white and minority students has widened in recent years.

- The U.S. Department of Education reported that the percentage of student borrowers who defaulted on their federal loans fell to 11.6 percent in the 1993 fiscal year.

- The U.S. Census Bureau report, "Educational Attainment in the United States: March 1995," reveals that for the first time the high school graduation rate for African Americans roughly equaled that of whites, although the rate for Hispanic Americans continued to trail the nation's overall graduation rate.

- A panel of teachers and historians revises the national standards for the teaching of history. The new standards established broad guidelines of what primary and secondary students should learn about U.S. and world history and omitted sample assignments.

- On January 23, the board of education in Hartford, Connecticut, cancels a contract that would have granted a private firm, Educational Alternatives, Inc., control of the district's thirty-two public schools.

- On February 2, a fourteen-year-old shoots two students and a teacher at Frontier Junior High School in Moses Lake, Washington.

- In March, the American Association of University Professors reports the average salary of college and university faculty at $50,980 for the 1995–1996 academic year. The 3 percent increase was slightly ahead of the 2.5 percent inflation.

- In April, the American Council on Education reports that the number of racial and ethnic minorities attending U.S. colleges and universities increased by 5 percent from 1993 to 1994, an increase twice that of the previous year.

- On April 11, a sixteen-year-old kills an eighteen-year-old with a shotgun in the parking lot of Talladega High School in Alabama.

- On May 8, a federal judge lifts a desegregation order that required the Cleveland, Ohio, school district to integrate its public schools through busing after the district said that ending the court-ordered busing would save the schools $10 million.

- On May 20, administrators at Muskogee High School in Oklahoma deny three students, one Native American and two African Americans, their high school diplomas because they wore cultural symbols on their clothing at commencement, violating the graduation dress code.

- On August 15, a graduate student opens fire with a handgun at the defense of his engineering thesis, killing three professors at San Diego State University. The faculty had rejected his thesis.

- On September 26, police arrest a sixteen-year-old student for killing an English teacher at his Dekalb County, Georgia, alternative school.

- On September 30, the Chicago school board places 109 of its 557 public schools on academic probation.

- On October 29, police arrest George Kobayashi, the head of a test-preparation center, for a scam that took advantage of time-zone differences to provide answers to students taking standardized tests in California to determine admission to graduate schools.

- On October 31, a student kills a seventeen-year-old classmate in the hallway of their St. Louis, Missouri, high school.

- On November 14, the federally appointed Washington, D.C., financial control board reports that Washington's public school system is unacceptable "by every important educational and management measure."

- On November 15, the public school system in Boston, Massachusetts, announces an end to racial preferences (35 percent of admissions are minorities) in response to a lawsuit from the father of a white girl who was denied admission to the elite Boston Latin School even though her entrance exam scores were higher than 103 African American and Hispanic students who were admitted.

- On December 20, delegates from the United States and 159 other nations meeting in Geneva, Switzerland, reach two treaties to extend international copyright protection to material distributed by electronic media such as the Internet. The treaties uphold the practice of "fair use" for copying excerpts for educational purposes.

1997

- Voters in Orange County, California, support a local school board's decision to abandon bilingual education.

- On February 8, President Bill Clinton announces the first $14.3 million out of $200 million in U.S. Department of Education grants to public schools to help them connect to the Internet.

- On February 13, eighteen of the nineteen trustees of Adelphi University, New York, resign to avoid a court battle over their dismissal. At issue is their lack of oversight in allowing the president to receive, without proper evaluations, compensation that exceeded the standard at similar institutions.

- On March 16, Georgetown University, a Catholic institution, accepts the resignation of Dr. Mark R. Hughes after he admitted performing research on human embryos for in vitro fertilization, a practice opposed by the church.

- On March 17, police charge three Detroit high school students with murder following the shooting death of a sixteen-year-old freshman at Pershing High School.

- On March 24, the Ohio Supreme Court orders the legislature to formulate a more equitable school-funding system. Annual spending per pupil in Ohio ranges from four thousand to twelve thousand dollars in the current property tax-based system.

- On April 2, an Epitope, Inc., executive resigns after his firm had imported tainted frozen Mexican strawberries that caused an outbreak of Hepatitis A in several Michigan schools. Federal law prohibits the serving of food grown outside the United States in federally-funded school lunch programs.

- On April 16, the Connecticut Senate and House of Representatives transfer control of the Hartford Public School system from local authorities to the state following allegations of mismanagement and poor student achievement.

- In May, Yale University rejects a multimillion dollar donation from homosexual playwright Larry Kramer to fund a permanent gay studies professorship at the school, saying that only the faculty may determine the curriculum and establish tenured professorships.

- From May 2 to May 4, fifteen hundred youths in Boulder, Colorado, throw stones and bricks at police when they arrive to put out a bonfire set by University of Colorado students celebrating the end of their classes. The following night some five hundred students gather in the same spot for a second confrontation with police.

- On May 6, the AFT elects Sandra Feldman, president of New York City's United Federation of Teachers, to succeed the late Albert Shanker as president.

- On June 4, President Bill Clinton signs a bill revising the 1975 Individuals with Disabilities Education Act. Major provisions change the funding formulas (relieving some of the local district burdens), require that most federal spending benefit the classroom (not administrators and attorneys), and grant flexibility in disciplining disabled students.

- On June 5, the F.W. Olin Foundation donates two hundred million dollars, the largest gift ever to a U.S. college or university, to build the Franklin W. Olin College of Engineering in Needham, Massachusetts.

- On June 23, the U.S. Supreme Court rules, 5-4, that the Constitution does not prohibit public school teachers from entering parochial schools to provide remedial education and guidance counseling to poor children who are struggling academically.

- On August 7, school officials in Washington, D.C., report, for the third time in four years, that schools will open late because of uncompleted repairs to buildings.

- On August 26, Louisiana State University student Benjamin Wynne dies of alcohol poisoning after downing more than twenty drinks while celebrating his fraternity's pledge week. Three others at the party are hospitalized.

- On August 26, the College Board reports the results of the SAT for 1997: the average math score rose from 508 to 511, the highest in twenty-six years, and the average verbal score remained at 505.

- On September 29, Scott Krueger, an eighteen-year-old pledge at the Phi Gamma Delta fraternity at the Massachusetts Institute of Technology, dies of alcohol poisoning following a drinking binge.

- On October 1, a sixteen-year-old student murders his mother and kills two fellow students in Pearl, Mississippi.

- On October 21, a National Assessment of Education Progress examination reveals that two out of three U.S. students have a basic understanding of science.

- On November 7, a fourteen-year-old student is killed and another wounded across the street from their Jacksonville, Florida, high school.

- On December 1, a fourteen-year-old boy opens fire on classmates at Heath High School in West Paducah, Kentucky, killing three girls and injuring five others.

- On December 11, Madlyn Abramson announces a $100 million gift from her family to the University of Pennsylvania for a cancer research center. The gift is the largest to a cancer center in the U.S. and one of the ten largest to a university.

1998

- Republicans block a plan by President Bill Clinton for a tax initiative to boost state spending on school construction.

- A group of business leaders, in an initiative called the Children's Scholarship Fund, pledges to raise $200 million for private-school tuition vouchers for poor students.

- The College Board commissions a study on grade inflation after a comparison of SAT scores of students with A averages shows an increase in the percentage of students with high grades and lower test scores.

- Results of the Third International Mathematics and Science Study indicate that 55 percent of U.S. twelfth graders—

more than any of the other twenty countries in the study—said they work at least three hours a day at a paid job.

- On February 4, police arrest Mary Kay Letourneau, a former Seattle teacher, after discovering her in a car with a former student whom she had confessed to having sex with since he was thirteen years old.

- On March 24, an eleven-year-old and a thirteen-year-old kill four students and a teacher and wound ten others at their junior high school in Jonesboro, Arkansas.

- On April 24, a fourteen-year-old middle-school student shoots and kills a teacher and wounds two students and a second teacher near Edinboro, Pennsylvania.

- On May 2, nearly three thousand students protest Michigan State University's ban on alcohol at a favorite tailgating locale in Lansing.

- On May 2, the *Chronicle of Higher Education* reports that the number of alcohol-related arrests has risen 10 percent at five hundred college campuses. Drug arrests have risen 5 percent.

- On May 19, an eighteen-year-old honor student opens fire in a parking lot at his Fayetteville, Tennessee, high school, killing a classmate.

- On May 21, a fifteen-year-old high school student in Springfield, Oregon, kills his parents and then opens fire in his school cafeteria, killing two students and wounding twenty-two others.

- On June 15, a fourteen-year-old boy wounds a teacher and a classroom aide in Richmond, Virginia, when he fires an automatic handgun in the hallway of Armstrong High School.

- On September 1, the College Board reports in its annual release of national average SAT scores that suburban students scored about thirty points higher than urban ones on each section of the test.

- On September 24, George Soros, a Hungarian-born financier, announces his donation of $1.2 million over four years to the Maryland State Department of Education's Correctional Educational Program to fund post-secondary courses for the state's inmates and to help released prisoners find jobs.

- On October 7, President Bill Clinton signs a bill reauthorizing the 1965 Higher Education Act for five years with provisions for lower interest rates for student loans and an increase in the total available through a Pell Grant.

- On October 21, police arrest two men in the beating death of a twenty-one-year-old homosexual University of Wyoming student.

- On October 22, President Bill Clinton signs a bill expanding federal aid to charter schools while setting stricter standards for schools to qualify for federal funding.

- On October 31, President Bill Clinton signs a bill overhauling the federal vocational programs. The bill increases the percentage of funds available to local authorities and schools from 75 percent to 85 percent.

- On November 30, Martha Ingram, chairwoman of Ingram Industries, Inc., a wholesale distributor based in Nashville, Tennessee, donates stock valued at $300 million to Vanderbilt University in what may be the largest private donation ever made to a college or university.

1999

- The Center for Education Information reports that teacher-candidates tend to be older (around thirty) and are more likely to be male, a change from the 1984 profile.

- Harvard University researchers report that 3.5 percent of college students have guns other than hunting weapons at school.

- Denver public school teachers begin a pilot study of merit pay increases linked to student performance.

- On January 20, Sylvan Learning Centers, Inc., a private education company that provides testing and tutoring services, announces its first step in developing a global network of for-profit colleges with the purchase of Universidad Europea de Madrid.

- On February 9, Dartmouth College president James Wright bans single-sex fraternities and sororities in an effort to promote healthier relations between men and women and to curb binge drinking.

- On March 3, the U.S. Supreme Court rules, 7-2, that disabled students in public schools may have individuals who are not physicians help them during the school day.

- On March 22, the U.S. Supreme Court rules, 8-1, that the state of Ohio does not need to apply a policy on time spent in the classroom during labor negotiations with public university professors.

- On April 20, Radcliffe College announces it will merge with Harvard University, a neighboring institution with which the college had been affiliated since its inception in 1879.

- On April 20, two boys, ages seventeen and eighteen, shoot and kill twelve students and a teacher, and wound more than twenty others at Columbine High School in Littleton, Colorado. Both perpetrators commit suicide.

- On April 21, Metro-Goldwyn-Mayer, Inc. recalls video copies of its 1995 movie, *The Basketball Diaries,* in the wake of the Columbine High School shootings because it depicts a character in a black coat shooting a teacher and students.

- On April 29, President Bill Clinton signs into law the "Ed-Flex" bill, granting states greater flexibility over federal funds for education.

- On May 5, ten state governors announce a cooperative effort to develop curricula and standardized tests for middle school mathematics through the nonprofit organization Achieve, Inc.

- On May 20, a fifteen-year-old boy opens fire on an indoor commons at Heritage High School in Conyers, Georgia, injuring six students.

- On June 5, the space shuttle *Discovery* releases a $1 million educational satellite, *Starshine,* into orbit so students around the world may track it.

- On August 10, a thirty-seven-year-old man opens fire in a Jewish day care center in Los Angeles, California, wounding five students and caretakers.

- On August 23, the Harrison County School Board exempts religious symbols from a ban against the wearing of gang symbols after a student displays a Star of David pendant at his Gulfport, Mississippi, high school.

- On September 6, ten-year-old Gregory Smith begins his freshman year at Randolph-Macon College in Ashland, Virginia, after completing high school in twenty-two months.

- On September 8, after a week-long strike, the Detroit Federation of Teachers ratifies a new three-year contract that reduces classes in kindergarten through third grade to seventeen students. Classes had averaged more than twice that before negotiations.

- On September 16, Microsoft Corporation chairman Bill Gates and his wife Melinda announce the creation of a $1 billion college scholarship fund, the largest donation ever in education, for minority students to be administered by the United Negro College Fund, the Hispanic Scholarship Fund, and the American Indian College Fund.

- On October 1, police arrest a forty-one-year-old white man on charges that he had planted two bombs at predominantly African American Florida A&M University.

- On November 8, Reverend Jesse Jackson leads a protest march in Decatur, Illinois, after seven students were expelled for two years from the school for their participation in a brawl at the September 17 Eisenhower High School football game.

Horace's School: Redesigning the American High School

Educational treatise

By: Theodore R. Sizer

Date: 1992

Source: Sizer, Theodore R. *Horace's School: Redesigning the American High School.* Boston: Houghton Mifflin, 1992, 120–132.

About the Author: Theodore R. Sizer (1932–), a leading educator who proposed reform of U.S. schools, served as dean of the Graduate School of Education at Harvard, was the headmaster at Phillips Academy in Andover, Massachusetts, and taught at Brown University prior to retiring. He was the founding director of the Annenberg Institute of School Reform and later founded the Coalition of Essential Schools. ■

Introduction

Theodore (Ted) Sizer was no stranger to issues in school reform when he wrote *Horace's School: Redesigning the American High School.* Sizer had been on the forefront of educational reform and the efforts to create truly effective schools. The second volume of a trilogy, *Horace's School* follows Horace Smith through the process of chairing a committee to restructure Franklin High School. The previous volume, *Horace's Compromise,* was published in 1984 and addressed how educational standards transfer into the reality of a day-to-day classroom. The final volume, *Horace's Hope,* published in 1996, revisits the typical high school.

The arguments about failing schools and the need for higher standards and restructuring were certainly not new when Sizer wrote his first book. *A Nation at Risk* informed Americans how far behind their schools were in the world. E.D. Hirsch and Allan Bloom had argued that too many people were culturally illiterate and did not share a common core of knowledge or values. Committees, studies, and research were all under way to improve the schools. By the time the second book appeared, President George H.W. Bush had hosted the summit on education in Charlottesville and Goals 2000 had been written.

Unlike some of these earlier reports, Sizer does not forget the teacher, who rallies his strength each day to go back into the classroom and teach the children of America. Sizer creates the fictionalized Horace Smith as his spokesperson, as well as a group of colleagues. There may be stereotypes in the group, but the trilogy endeavors to create a true picture of what schools and teachers face on a daily basis.

In *Horace's School,* the committee led by Horace is trying to reform a suburban public high school. While the school is a composite of many public high schools which Sizer and his colleagues studied, it shares problems that many schools face. The members of the committee represent teachers whom Sizer met and worked with over the years. His goal was to assist teachers "in shaping a new design, one that respects the best traditions of secondary schooling, yet acknowledges that we must do better in readying adolescents, for their sake and ours."

Significance

Horace Smith, a well-respected, veteran English teacher, was worried about his school. While the school enjoys a good reputation in the community, Horace knew that the goals of the school were vague, that the schedule did not truly reflect a unified and meaningful curriculum, and that overcrowded classes were not serving the needs of the students. He noted the lack of rigor in his students' work and was concerned about their future. He and his colleagues were frustrated by the control over testing and curriculum decisions exerted by outside entities. This was a typical picture of high school in America in the early 1990s. The focus of the school should be the student and intellect. Sizer believed that students needed to exhibit what they had learned in ways other than by standardized testing. The book includes examples of tasks created by the fictional committee for this purpose. Reviewers called the book required reading for educators.

Ted Sizer had studied many high schools. The Coalition of Essential Schools, which he founded, was trying to make a difference in teachers' and students' lives. The group attempted to get beyond the political and bureaucratic jargon that bogged down efforts at school reform and the discussion of standards. In *Horace's School,* Sizer presents the views of those who run the school and listens to what they say. The outcomes are from the studies conducted by the Coalition of Essential Schools, but these are by no means universally applicable. Schools, even in the same town, have different populations and needs. Criteria that is meaningful and represents the concerns of the school and community must be decided. Compromise and negotiation are essential skills in finding a common ground where standards can be established and measured.

Primary Source

Horace's School: Redesigning the American High School [excerpt]

SYNOPSIS: The physical environment of a school is just as important as the curriculum. Students and teachers need places where they are valued as individuals and as a group. Likewise, necessary supplies and tools can create a difference in attitude and in how easy it is to do the challenging job of educating the young.

"When we get to recommendations, Horace, be sure to insist on a copier machine for every department . . . or least for our department." Laughter. "And a fax." More laughter. "What about a coat-hook?" Groans.

"Let's not get into details yet." Horace tried to brake the discussion.

"This isn't a detail," Green demurred. "It stands for something, a symbol of something bigger."

A chorus of complaint suddenly rose. No phones for private calls. No place to lock up one's materials. No offices. Inadequate washrooms. Glacially slow responses to book orders. No access to the building except when students are there.

Gripes continued. The kids get away with murder. The parents don't care . . . just how many came to the last Parents' Night? Parents treat the staff like servants. Parents always complain. They never say thank you. We're cursed with the students' goddam cars, and with easing up on the kids so that they can earn the money they need to pay for their hotrods. The school is amoral: What about the sheepish reactions to teenage unmarried parents? What about our own hypocrisies, pretending not to talk with the kids about pregnancy and abortion while in fact we're doing so? Why is there so much cheating at Franklin High? Why do we tolerate, glorify, violence in athletics . . .

The two parent members listened, aghast. The two students smirked. The face of the school board member was hard. She spoke: "This is remarkable talk from professionals . . ." the last word spat out almost as an insult. She herself was startled at her reaction. So were the teachers.

Horace turned again to Green. "What did you mean when you said that the copier problem was bigger?"

"They don't respect us."

"Who's 'they'?"

Patches, scoffing: "We shouldn't respect ourselves." The school board member thought she had an ally, but she was quickly disappointed. "The school board," Patches continued, "simply doesn't understand what it takes to teach well. They starve us, and we just accept it. Professionals, indeed."

The school board member flared. "Money doesn't grow on trees in this town, you know. We do our best, and you know it. And your union's demands need some looking after too . . ." She paused. The room was tense. "How much respect is there in all those union demands for rules about what teachers can and can't do? The union tells teachers precisely what to do. Is that respect? Doesn't the union believe its members have minds of their own?"

The two students were fascinated by the confrontation. . . .

The mathematics teacher: "Treating students better. Treating us better. It's all of a piece. It starts with how we get along, with how we feel about each other and our work."

"Feeling takes time." It popped out of a student. People stopped at this observation, silly on the surface but provocative below.

The mathematics teacher: "Sure it takes time. But if we had a sense of what we want here, a sense of community about that, a goal that spoke of this school as a decent place as well as a producer of high test scores . . ."

"Yes," Green agreed. "It's what sort of community we are." She eyed Patches, knowing that any kind of "community" talk riled him. He didn't react. She went on: "It's not that complicated . . . it's just what we believe. If we could settle on that, we'd be able to get some ideas, some priorities."

Inwardly, Horace sagged. He knew that Green had the essence here, if it could be strained out. The kind of place Franklin could become was crucial, far more so than copiers or a new syllabus.

■ ■ ■

So much about what makes up a good school is simple, obvious, supported by common sense and often by research. The pity is that many schools, and the system as a whole, often seem to operate with different rules.

People tend to copy those whom they respect. People of all ages are likely to work harder when they feel they are valued and respected. The essence of respect is being known. Those who are mere numbers or whose identity is characterized solely on the basis of paper credentials or scores or race or gender or age are demeaned, their personhood belittled and their ambition denied. . . .

If people have the right tools and the appropriate amount of time to use them, they do their jobs better. People who are denied the tools and time they need quickly become discouraged; they believe that those responsible for their work do not respect it. Neglect breeds cynicism.

In jobs that require judgment and that by their nature cannot be subject to routine, time must be available both to arrive at judgments and to consult with informative colleagues. In jobs where the knowledge or technology required is in constant evolution, time must be available for workers to keep up with it.

Friends make better teammates than do strangers. Teams that share values are successful. Values for sharing cannot be summarily imposed from the outside.

People who are distracted work poorly. People who feel that their workplace is hostile or unsafe cannot be effective. People who are asked to do too much either cut corners, depreciating their own efforts, or give in, collapse.

People like to know why they are asked to do things. They value an enterprise whose purposes are clear. Most people like to care about the communities in which they work. Most appreciate symbolic rituals that affirm the collective enterprise. . . .

Respect means assuming that the file of a student—test scores, personal data—is a bare beginning in an understanding of that student, and that time has to be allocated regularly for his teachers to consult on how best to serve him. Respecting students means asking much of them and giving them the time to meet that standard. In most schools this means narrowing the tasks the student is asked to take on and raising the standard that the student is expected to meet.

Respect is modeled. Students who eat meals at school should help to prepare them. Students who make messes should clean them up. Respectful communities do not signal that the Good Life is a right to a free lunch, and they do not farm out their own scutwork to be done by others. No one is wholly another's servant.

There is nothing radical about such propositions, but they represent values rarely accommodated in typical high school programs. They are indeed *val-*

Education reform activist Theodore Sizer. SIZER, THEODORE R., PHOTOGRAPH. © 2003 THEODORE R. SIZER. REPRODUCED BY PERMISSION.

ues; they reflect fundamental moral—democratic—convictions, ones long embraced by Americans. Individuality means something, we believe. If so, then it must be addressed. If, on the other hand, we believe that students are the school's products-in-the-making, then we can treat them as if they were fenders awaiting installation on an automobile assembly line. Adolescents who sense this drop out of school, usually psychologically, sometimes physically.

Adults who themselves are accorded respect are likely to respect students. Put alternatively, teachers who are shabbily treated are likely to treat their students the same way. If your judgment is not respected—for example, if the performance and potential of a student are judged largely on the basis of brief examinations, with no heed paid to the considered opinions of teachers—it stings, and you readily begin not to care. *Why should I worry about this kid? Even if I did, I couldn't do anything about it. No one wants my opinion.*

It is hard to stay at the enervating business of helping a hostile kid learn to read when the system does not give you appropriate books to do the job.

It takes stubbornness to persist in making copies of recent and relevant articles for your students if the system denies you ready use of a copier machine.

It takes special loyalty to a student when you make the telephone call to her home on your quarter at an overused public telephone in the hallway. It requires doggedness to insist that your students come by for one-on-one chats when you have neither private place nor dependable hours.

It tests your sense of community when there are few faculty meetings, and those which are held deal only with administrative trivialities. It is impossible to build a team of teachers for any purpose when staff assignments to the school are made by administrators in a distant central office solely on the basis of technical certificates and seniority.

It requires the tolerance of a saint quietly to accept an overstuffed curriculum designed by strangers for students who are not like yours, and which is to be covered in too few days and by all students equally. It is difficult to retain a sense of your own scholarly and professional growth if the time formally allotted for that purpose is pre-empted by programs devised by strangers in a central office. It is insulting to be "in-serviced," particularly when nothing follows from it.

Respect for students starts with respect for teachers, for them as individuals, for their work, and for their workplace. Who could disagree? Yet the conditions that reflect disrespect, however unintended, persist. The rhetoric of a different school world is widely heard, but meaningful substance is rarely achieved. The practical implications of taking these commonsense matters seriously are daunting.

Behind this matter of respect lies the issue of purpose, of a common resolve around which the teachers and, all hope, the students can rally. The kind of school—its character—gives all a focus, a basis on which to make decisions of priority. This character arises less from a particular orientation, such as that commonly associated with magnet schools ("This is the High School of the Performing Arts"), than from its nature as a functioning community, a school infused with the practice of thoughtfulness. As is so often the case, the character is difficult to describe accurately; one has to sense it.

The school with more than a superficial mission has an air of collective assurance, an ease, pride. One sees it in the ability of many of its students to describe substantively what they are working on and why. One feels it in the interaction of adults; they are colleagues, not free-lance professionals sharing a building and students and functioning by the rules of an administrative hierarchy. A school's assurance arises from its knowledge about what its core values are—and from having the authority to act upon them. Given traditions of top-down bureaucracy, such schools are rare.

People of all ages learn best when they are not distracted, when they can engage with ideas long enough to grasp them, when the culture of their school reinforces careful, thorough work, when they are not physically and acoustically crowded together. This takes time, an intellectually coherent program, and widely understood standards. Such a culture requires agreements on what is more or less important. It is, in sum, the antithesis of the shopping mall high school, full of every sort of curricular, extracurricular, and social activity. The very richness of offerings confuses; the frenetic choosing sets bad habits. . . . It all too often devastatingly distracts, and, being much of many things, is little of any one thing.

High school, of course, absorbs but a fraction of an adolescent's time. Even for dutiful students, high school casts a shadow over but eight months of the year and attracts attention for about six hours a day for five days of the week. Few students do much more than an hour's worth of serious homework each night, if that; a student not physically at school is usually not engaging with the school's agenda. Further, the flat and lifeless nature of much of traditional school work makes distractions all the more potent. Lectures in chemistry have to compete with the soaps on TV and the cute girl across the classroom's laboratory table, mathematics problem sets vie with football games, the reading from a text about early Mesopotamia with a job. School's residual attraction for many kids is simple: it is where their friends are.

And so teachers have to struggle for their students' attention. The effort is made all the more difficult when the student's world beyond the school is not only unmindful of what a good education implies but, intentionally or unintentionally, is hostile to it. Media that mock schools and teachers, political leaders who blatantly lie ("I misspoke . . .") and engage in grotesque hypocrisy, employers who press kids to be on duty long hours, businesses that hawk anything that will sell, however tawdry or corrupt, parents who show no interest in their children's school work or who belittle it, communities that abuse and frighten children: the list is stunning and well documented.

Further, some Americans do not see the schools as engines both of information and of intellectual liberation. Indeed, they find the latter—especially when so described—to be intolerable. The schools, they insist, are to teach young people what is true, what is right, and what is wrong. Anything beyond that is anathema. Their argument is seductive but flawed, especially when one gets to schooling beyond the rudiments. There is too much information to purvey, and choices have to be made. And what is right and what is wrong are, however much we may regret it, uncertain in most important matters. Should schools teach a particular kind of certainty? Or should they attempt to teach the craft and habit of deciding for oneself, on the merits? The only "good" that they would teach (perhaps) is a respectful commitment to the facts, to the logic of an argument, and to an awareness of when one is working at a level of principle or opinion rather than of provable fact. They would encourage opinions to be freely expressed, particularly to those who want deeply to conform.

Some find this approach both wishy-washy and dangerous. They prefer that the schools teach *their* definition of truth, at the expense of that of (presumably misguided) others. They fear that teachers will use their authority to force students to adopt other opinions, or at the least to keep open the possibility of other ideas winning out. The bigger fear for all of us, though, is that students may have no opinion at all.

However, most communities rarely even debate these matters. Parents and teachers are all very busy. School is school. The kids should be there, "preparing for life," having enough of a good time to stay with it, and not rocking many boats. Indifference is school's major enemy.

. . . School reform does not start with schools. It starts with families, with their communities, with the culture. At the least we should start laughing at the ironies. Only a forlorn society could believe that it is helping education by running state lotteries ostensibly for the schools' benefit: lotteries absolutely depend either on a citizenry ignorant of simple mathematics and the laws of probability, or on desperate individuals addicted to gambling.

Good schools are thoughtful places. The people in them are known. The units are small enough to be coherent communities of friends. Amenities are observed. There are quiet places available as well as places for socializing. No one is ridiculed. No one is the servant of another. The work is shared. The entire place is thoughtful: everything in its routines meets a standard of common sense and civility. At such places do adolescents learn about the thoughtful life.

∎∎∎

"All this is so idealistic. It asks too much. We can't do this."

This came from a middle school teacher, one of the three who had joined the committee when it decided to start its plan earlier, with younger children. She was a practical sort, a highly skilled teacher of both mathematics and science. She had won the state's Teacher of the Year award. She had been touted as a "local heroine" in the city's newspaper. She let these accolades slide over her: her realism dominated. She was the veteran's veteran, an old pro.

"What can't we do?" Horace asked.

The veteran explained: "There's so much here, so much expected of so many people. We're asking for a change in the community's attitudes right down to how the budget is spent."

"That's right. Can we do otherwise?" Horace pushed back.

The veteran paused, eyeing Horace. Then: "I suppose we do have to be idealistic. But how can we expect so much of others if we can't get our own act together?"

"Who are 'we'?"

"Us. We teachers. Us people."

"What do you mean, 'us people'? What's wrong with us?" Some of the high school faculty were getting defensive.

The veteran paused again, looking steadily around at the others. They waited her out, and she knew they would. "Let's take the—your—English Department, for example." Horace tensed. "You can't get much done as a group. You are not a group, a thoughtful community. You get from day to day by avoiding one another. You don't meet much because you'd fight like cats and dogs. Each of you goes his own way. Everyone knows that. The students know that. And now we want to build some sort of collective commitment, a 'thoughtful community'?" She let that sink in. "Let's get some thoughtful communities within the departments for starters."

The committee seemed frozen. The two students, now joined by a terrified eighth-grader from the middle school, were rapt. No one argued with the veteran or asserted that she was wrong.

Horace finally broke the silence. "Our department doesn't get along not because we disagree about educational matters. It's about personalities." His language was unusually clumsy because of his emotion.

The veteran kept the pressure on. "If it's not educational matters, then what is it? You're all friends in that department."

Indeed they were. Most had joined the faculty together, several years after Horace had come. They were mostly now in their mid-forties, colleagues who had been in collective harness for almost twenty years.

Horace explained: "We know each other too well. I suppose that we compete, though I doubt whether any of us really wants to. I guess it's that we're bored with each other, bored with the kids and the routine. We love it, but we don't love it. Its familiarity is a joy and a pain. The only new thing we seem able to do is chafe each other. It's not happy."

The veteran continued to press. "So, what do you do about that? Your own lives are getting in the way of school."

"No, they're not," Horace flared, but he knew that they were, and he knew that every other teacher there sensed that the chippiness in the high school's English Department arose not from disagreements over the program but from abrasion among its members. He knew he was floundering. "What do we do with this?"

The veteran, now that her point was made, pushed further, constructively. "We've got to shake things up, get some newer, better things on people's agenda, something more important to worry about than the staleness of being forty-five years old at Franklin High School . . . Change for change's sake, almost. A new mountain to climb." The clichés multiplied but were apt.

"Something worthy of abrasion," said Green. "Getting on with the idealistic. We should go for it. The school needs something bold, for its own morale, its own soul even."

The veteran swung toward Horace. "Sorry for picking on the English Department. There's much that can be said about all of us, at both schools."

"We deserve it," said Horace, relieved.

"How are we going to get people off the dime, away from their old squabbles?" asked the visitor.

She admired the veteran; the committee had moved abruptly forward since the middle school teachers had joined in. Curiously, the tension the newly arrived teachers brought seemed to accelerate good thinking. The members surely knew that they were at points of importance because these were often points that hurt. The little wars within the departments, for example, had finally surfaced, to be recognized and addressed.

"The school itself can be a part of the curriculum." The principal spoke. Some thought she was trying to turn the discussion from the high school's faculty squabbles.

The principal pushed ahead. "That sounds mushy, but it doesn't have to be. What could be done to create a better environment here that also advances the academic goals we've agreed on?"

"You mean," said Patches, "what's curricular and what's extracurricular?"

"We don't have time for the truly extracurricular," said Green. "If it isn't important for the overall goals of the school, it shouldn't be here at all. Everything is curricular."

The gasps were audible. The second student: "What happens to Student Council? The yearbook? The band? Sports? Come on . . ."

"You misunderstand me," argued Green. "Everything we do, and that can include sports and the school newspaper, must tie in to the goal of making this a thoughtful school."

"Just my point," said the principal. The fact that she was arguing this way encouraged Horace. He had been skeptical of her since she joined the school the previous year. At first she seemed weak, but what she had been doing, wisely, was lying low, figuring out the place—or so many of the older teachers now believed. She had a pleasant but reserved style. She didn't feel that she had to be a Leader—Franklin's Joan of Arc. She led now; that much was sure. The kids knew who their principal was. But with the teachers, she played a more collegial game. When she suggested things, they came across as though they were from a colleague rather than from a superior. She seemed to trust the faculty, more so since she had served on this committee. She clearly was a "teacher"; she thought and reacted like one. She knew kids, and they liked her. Horace felt that this boded well for the group's work.

The school board member: "If it's important for the school's central program, you'll have to be able to see it when it happens. Are there Exhibitions here?" The suggestion jolted some: Exhibitions for matters not tied directly to courses?

This question appeared especially to galvanize Green. "That's just right . . . We always try to make important extracurricular things into courses, the newspaper into a journalism class as though it were like Biology One . . . It doesn't work . . . What we need are activities, not ones that meet as though they were formal courses, activities that help kids prepare for Exhibitions . . . general sorts of Exhibitions. This will give those activities importance, make them a real incentive for the kids." She paused. "So many of these extracurricular-curricular things that are just classes are taken by kids who want an easy time and credit for their college applications."

"It's not that way in sports," said Coach.

The school board member pressed her question again. "How can there be some Exhibitions that give the students a rigorous, serious, and academically useful target and at the same time strengthen this school in its effort to be a thoughtful place, a school that models what it hopes for the students?"

To which Horace added, "And give some new life to a school engrossed in its old little personal battles."

Further Resources

BOOKS

Angus, David L., and Jeffrey E. Mirel. *The Failed Promise of the American High School, 1890–1995*. New York: Teachers College Press, 1999.

Sizer, Theodore R. *Horace's Compromise: The Dilemma of the American High School*. Boston: Houghton Mifflin, 1984.

———. *Horace's Hope: What Works for the American High School*. Boston: Houghton Mifflin, 1996.

Wood, George H. *Schools That Work: America's Most Innovative Public Education Programs*. New York: Dutton, 1992.

PERIODICALS

Sizer, Theodore R. "The Substance of Schooling." *American School Board Journal* 77, no. 2, January 1992, 27–29.

Stoddart, Pat. "Sizer's Horace Returns to Redesign the American High School." *English Journal* 82, no. 2, February 1993, 88–89.

WEBSITES

Coalition of Essential Schools. Available online at http://www.essentialschools.org/ (accessed April 19, 2003).

"Standards and School Reform: Asking the Essential Questions." Available online at http://www.essentialschools.org/cs/resources/view/ces_res/106; website home page: http://www.essentialschools.org (accessed April 19, 2003).

How Schools Shortchange Girls—The AAUW Report

Report

By: American Association of University Women

Date: 1992

Source: American Association of University Women. *How Schools Shortchange Girls—The AAUW Report*. American Association of University Women Educational Foundation, 1992. Reprint, with updated foreword and index, New York: Marlowe, 1995, 148–154.

About the Organization: The American Association of University Women (AAUW) is an organization for all women who have college degrees. It was founded in 1881 by Marion Talbott and a group of the country's first female college alumnae. The association promotes educational opportunities for women and girls, provides funding for education and research on the education of women, promotes lifelong learning, and is active in social justice. AAUW is a national organization, with over 1,300 branch associations in cities around the United States. ■

Introduction

The American Association of University Women commissioned the Center for Research on Women at Wellesley College to research the experiences of girls and young women in America's schools. Title IX, part of the 1972 extension of the 1964 Civil Rights Act to education, had not brought about the equity in education that it had promised. The late 1980s and early 1990s presented yet another opportunity to fight for gender equity in education as governmental agencies concentrated on improving standards in education. The association and the authors sought to take advantage of a moment in history when gender equity could be achieved.

How Schools Shortchange Girls synthesized 1,300 studies on gender and schooling. Most of the studies examined, however, addressed the problems of teen pregnancy or school dropout rather than the more common problems of low self-esteem and confidence as girls enter middle school and high school. Scores in math and science became a particular concern in the AAUW study and in other studies in the 1990s. As the world was becoming more technologically advanced, it was recognized that girls had to have the same opportunities to pursue careers and education in the hard sciences as boys were given.

This was not the only report that the AAUW sponsored in the 1990s. *Growing Smart: What's Working for Girls in School* examined five hundred studies on schools with the goal of promoting achievement for both sexes. In a 1991 poll called *Shortchanging Girls, Shortchanging America* conducted by Greenberg-Lake, the Analysis Group, girls and boys between nine and fifteen were questioned about their career goals and aspirations, self-esteem, interest in math and science, and educational experiences. Taken together, this body of work was a valuable tool for assessing how boys and girls learn and are treated in the classroom.

Significance

The AAUW study showed that girls were not being treated equally in school. This study made the case for improving opportunities for girls in school. The studies did not say that boys did not deserve attention and opportunity to achieve, but rather that girls were being left behind.

The AAUW study showed, for example, that although women received more bachelor's degrees than men, they still faced gender barriers in science and technology. This gender gap did not begin in college but rather started in elementary school. According to some researchers, the root of these problems can be found in the elementary classroom, where boys often received more attention than girls. When boys "call out" in class, they received attention; when girls did the same, they were told to "raise their hand" or "wait their turn." In this way teachers were sending messages that boys and girls were not equal. This is not a new finding, but the body of research presented in the 1990s focused attention on it. Study after study showed that boys and girls learned differently and that the amount of attention they received in the classroom was important.

The AAUW study included a list of forty recommendations on how to achieve gender equity in education. The recommendations went beyond the school walls and extended into societal beliefs about girls and learning. As long as society maintained values that said girls should not be good at math or that girls should not hold certain jobs, inequity would remain in place. The AAUW study was a milestone in showing Americans how girls might be treated differently in school and how this treatment harmed society in the long run.

Primary Source

How Schools Shortchange Girls—The AAUW Report
[excerpt]

> **SYNOPSIS:** Role models are a significant part of improving school experiences and encouraging risk taking in areas that girls may not feel they can explore. Providing experiences for girls and boys to read about and meet people who have nontraditional jobs and roles would discourage stereotypes.

The Recommendations

Strengthened Reinforcement of Title IX Is Essential.

1. Require school districts to assess and report on a regular basis to the Office for Civil Rights in the U.S. Department of Education on their own Title IX compliance measures.

2. Fund the Office for Civil Rights at a level that permits increased compliance reviews and full and prompt investigation of Title IX complaints.

3. In assessing the status of Title IX compliance, school districts must include a review of the treatment of pregnant teens and teen parents. Evidence indicates that these students are still the victims of discriminatory treatment in many schools.

Teachers, Administrators, and Counselors Must be Prepared and Encouraged to Bring Gender Equity and Awareness to Every Aspect of Schooling.

4. State certification standards for teachers and administrators should require course work on gender issues, including new research on women, bias in classroom-interaction patterns, and the ways in which schools can develop and implement gender-fair multicultural curricula.

5. If a national teacher examination is developed, it should include items on methods for achieving gender equity in the classroom and in curricula.

6. Teachers, administrators, and counselors should be evaluated on the degree to which they promote and encourage gender-equitable and multicultural education.

7. Support and released time must be provided by school districts for teacher-initiated research on curricula and classroom variables that affect student learning. Gender equity should be a focus of this research and a criterion for awarding funds.

8. School-improvement efforts must include a focus on the ongoing professional development of teachers and administrators, including those working in specialized areas such as bilingual, compensatory, special, and vocational education.

9. Teacher-training courses must not perpetuate assumptions about the superiority of traits and activities traditionally ascribed to males in our society. Assertive and affiliative skills as well as verbal and mathematical skills must be fostered in both girls and boys.

10. Teachers must help girls develop positive views of themselves and their futures, as well as an understanding of the obstacles women must overcome in a society where their options and opportunities are still limited by gender stereotypes and assumptions.

The Formal School Curriculum Must Include the Experiences of Women and Men from All Walks of Life. Girls and Boys Must See Women and Girls Reflected and Valued in the Materials they Study.

11. Federal and state funding must be used to support research, development, and follow-up study of gender-fair multicultural curricular models.

12. The Women's Educational Equity Act Program (WEEAP) in the U.S. Department of Education must receive increased funding in order to continue the development of curricular materials and models, and to assist school districts in Title IX compliance.

13. School curricula should deal directly with issues of power, gender politics, and violence against women. Better-informed girls are better equipped to make decisions about their futures. Girls and young women who have a strong sense of themselves are better able to confront violence and abuse in their lives.

14. Educational organizations must support, via conferences, meetings, budget deliberations, and policy decisions, the development of gender-fair multicultural curricula in all areas of instruction.

15. Curricula for young children must not perpetuate gender stereotypes and should reflect sensitivity to different learning styles.

Girls Must Be Educated and Encouraged to Understand that Mathematics and the Sciences Are Important and Relevant to their Lives. Girls Must Be Actively Supported in Pursuing Education and Employment in These Areas.

16. Existing equity guidelines should be effectively implemented in all programs supported by local, state, and federal governments. Specific attention must be directed toward including women on planning committees and focusing on girls and women in the goals, instructional strategies, teacher training, and research components of these programs.

17. The federal government must fund and encourage research on the effect on girls and boys of new curricula in the sciences and mathematics. Research is needed particularly in science areas where boys appear to be improving their performance while girls are not.

18. Educational institutions, professional organizations, and the business community must work together to dispel myths about math and science as "inappropriate" fields for women.

19. Local schools and communities must encourage and support girls studying science and mathematics by showcasing women role models in scientific and technological fields, disseminating career information, and offering "hands-on" experiences and work groups in science and math classes.

20. Local schools should seek strong links with youth-serving organizations that have developed successful out-of-school programs for girls in mathematics and science and with those girls' schools that have developed effective programs in these areas.

Continued Attention to Gender Equity in Vocational Education Programs Must Be a High Priority at Every Level of Educational Governance and Administration.

21. Linkages must be developed with the private sector to help ensure that girls with training in nontraditional areas find appropriate employment.

22. The use of a discretionary process for awarding vocational-education funds should be encouraged to prompt innovative efforts.

23. All states should be required to make support services (such as child care and transportation) available to both vocational and prevocational students.

24. There must be continuing research on the effectiveness of vocational education for girls and the extent to which the 1990 Vocational Education Amendments benefit girls.

Testing and Assessment must Serve as Stepping Stones Not Stop Signs. New Tests and Testing Techniques Must Accurately Reflect the Abilities of Both Girls and Boys.

25. Test scores should not be the only factor considered in admissions or the awarding of scholarships.

26. General aptitude and achievement tests should balance sex differences in item types and contexts. Tests should favor neither females nor males.

27. Tests that relate to "real life situations" should reflect the experiences of both girls and boys.

Girls and Women Must Play a Central Role in Educational Reform. The Experiences, Strengths, and Needs of Girls from Every Race and Social Class Must be Considered in Order to Provide Excellence and Equity for All Our Nation's Students.

28. National, state, and local governing bodies should ensure that women of diverse backgrounds are equitably represented on committees and commissions on educational reform.

29. Receipt of government funding for in-service and professional development programs should be

conditioned upon evidence of efforts to increase the number of women in positions in which they are underrepresented. All levels of government have a role to play in increasing the numbers of women, especially women of color, in education-management and policy positions.

30. The U.S. Department of Education's Office of Educational Research and Improvement (OERI) should establish an advisory panel of gender-equity experts to work with OERI to develop a research and dissemination agenda to foster gender-equitable education in the nation's classrooms.

31. Federal and state agencies must collect, analyze, and report data broken down by race/ethnicity, sex, and some measure of socioeconomic status, such as parental income or education. National standards for use by all school districts should be developed so that data are comparable across district and state lines.

32. National standards for computing dropout rates should be developed for use by all school districts.

33. Professional organizations should ensure that women serve on education-focused committees. Organizations should utilize the expertise of their female membership when developing educational initiatives.

34. Local schools must call on the expertise of teachers, a majority of whom are women, in their restructuring efforts.

35. Women teachers must be encouraged and supported to seek administrative positions and elected office, where they can bring the insights gained in the classroom to the formulation of education policies.

A Critical Goal of Education Reform Must Be to Enable Students to Deal Effectively with the Realities of Their Lives, Particularly in Areas Such as Sexuality and Health.

36. Strong policies against sexual harassment must be developed. All school personnel must take responsibility for enforcing these policies.

37. Federal and state funding should be used to promote partnerships between schools and community groups, including social service agencies, youth-serving organizations, medical facilities, and local businesses. The needs of students, particularly as highlighted by pregnant teens and teen mothers, require a multi-institutional response.

38. Comprehensive school-based health- and sex-education programs must begin in the early grades and continue sequentially through twelfth grade. These courses must address the topics of reproduction and reproductive health, sexual abuse, drug and alcohol use, and general mental and physical health issues. There must be a special focus on the prevention of AIDS.

39. State and local school board policies should enable and encourage young mothers to complete school, without compromising the quality of education these students receive.

40. Child care for the children of teen mothers must be an integral part of all programs designed to encourage young women to pursue or complete educational programs.

Further Resources

BOOKS

American Association for University Women, Greenberg–Lake, the Analysis Group. *Shortchanging Girls, Shortchanging America.* Washington, D.C.: AAUW, 1991.

Hansen, Lorraine Sundal. *Growing Smart: What's Working for Girls in School.* Washington, D.C.: AAUW Foundation, 1995.

Orenstein, Peggy. *School Girls: Young Women, Self-esteem, and the Confidence Gap.* New York: Doubleday, 1994.

Sadker, Myra, and David Sadker. *Failing at Fairness: How Our Schools Cheat Girls.* New York: Touchstone Books, 1994.

PERIODICALS

Bailey, Susan McGee. "Shortchanging Girls and Boys." *Educational Leadership* 53, no. 8, May 1996, 75–79.

Weinman, Janice. "Why Schoolgirls Aren't Getting What They Need." *Educational Record* 78, no. 2, Spring 1997, 19–20.

WEBSITES

American Association of University Women. Executive Summary of *How Schools Shortchange Girls—The AAUW Report.* Available online at http://www.aauw.org/research /hssg.pdf; website home page: http://www.aauw.org/ (accessed April 19, 2003).

Statement of Secretary of Education Richard W. Riley Regarding the Goals 2000: Educate America Act

Statement

By: Richard W. Riley

Date: September 12, 1995

Source: Riley, Richard W. Statement of Secretary of Education Richard W. Riley before the Senate Appropriations Subcommittee on Labor, Health and Human Services and Education and Related Agencies Regarding the Goals 2000: Educate America Act. Available online at www.ed.gov /Speeches/09-1995/913-g2k.html; website home page: www .ed.gov (accessed April 19, 2003).

About the Author: Richard W. Riley (1933–) was born in South Carolina, where he attended Furman University and South Carolina School of Law. He served in the U.S. Navy from 1954 to 1956, then returned to South Carolina to pursue a career in law and state government. He served as governor of South Carolina from 1978 to 1986. Riley became U.S. secretary of education in 1993. ∎

Introduction

Goals 2000, much like *A Nation at Risk,* grew out of the concern for better education. President George H.W. Bush called the program "America 2000," but President Bill Clinton changed the name to "Goals 2000." The goals expanded from six to eight before a law finally passed Congress in 1994. In April 1996, Congress amended the act, deleting the commissions and other regulatory aspects of the act. Funding for the National Education Goals program ended June 30, 2001.

The program began in the first Bush administration and was carried on by President Clinton. President George Bush convened the National Education Summit at Charlottesville, Virginia, in September 1989. This meeting, which forty-nine governors attended, is remembered as a historic occasion in educational reform. A committee called the National Education Goals Panel formed and began work. In March 1994, President Clinton signed Goals 2000: Educate America Act (H.R. 1804), reinforcing the eight goals that the committee concluded were important.

When Richard Riley was named U.S. secretary of education in 1993, he became part of the effort to formulate the goals and to advocate for their implementation. His statements on September 12, 1995, emphasized that reform would not occur overnight and that steady progress was being made. He cited higher test scores and tougher classes as prime examples. Goals 2000 was meant to be flexible and to allow for creativity in the schools. States could apply for grants to fund programs in schools and districts. States were also allowed to decide if they would participate in the program or not. Riley and his staff worked to gain support for Goals 2000 by traveling across the country, speaking in communities and to teachers about the future of children.

Significance

Like most of the governmental reform programs, Goals 2000 was purposefully vague. The goals included school readiness, lifelong learning, an increase in high

Richard Riley, Secretary of Education to President Clinton. **GETTY IMAGES. REPRODUCED BY PERMISSION.**

school graduation rates, and demonstrations of competency in "challenging" subjects. Increased parental involvement, professional opportunities for teachers, and drug- and violence-free schools rounded out the goals. These are not significantly different from previous proposals to reform schools in America.

Riley was a proponent of improving schools while maintaining state and local control. This was the primary selling point to communities and educators. Because local and state control would be retained, the program appeared to be promising. Some educators were not convinced, however. Some argued that standards failed to address problems of hunger and homelessness many children faced and would not by themselves lead to excellence. Others objected to the bureaucratic programs that the act created. The nature of the educational assessment that Goals 2000 advocated was the focus of a special issue of *The Clearing House* in March/April 1995. Authors in the volume reviewed research and questioned if national tests were really the answer to reform.

As secretary of education, Riley frequently spoke and wrote about the educational goals of the act. Funding, of course, is at the heart of making any program a success. The occasion of Riley's speech cited here was to convince listeners that money would go to local schools and not be lost to bureaucratic functions. Despite the examples that Riley provides, the goals of the grant and demonstration programs appear vague. Funding for the program stopped in the early twenty-first century, and educators and reformers moved on to discover yet other answers to what were perceived as failing schools.

Primary Source

Statement of Secretary of Education Richard W. Riley Regarding the Goals 2000: Education America Act [excerpt]

SYNOPSIS: Goals 2000 required $700 million in funding. In the budget, grants to individual states and local schools had to be provided. This was a critical issue for Congress to tackle. Riley's job, in part, was to advocate for the funding and to explain misconceptions about the educational goals of the country.

Goals 2000 provides support to States, local communities and schools to help design and implement the school improvements most needed in that particular State or community—it is grassroots, bottom-up reform.

Goals 2000 creates a partnership between the Federal Government and States and communities working to improve their schools. Goals 2000 asks States to (1) set challenging academic standards; (2) develop their own comprehensive education reforms; and (3) do this with broad-based grass roots parental involvement. In return, the Federal Government provides funds and flexibility. Ninety percent of the dollars that this Subcommittee appropriates for Goals 2000 flows to *local* school districts and schools.

The Department has issued no regulations for Goals 2000. Under Goals 2000, States can receive waivers from other Federal laws if these regulations are limiting a State or local community's own approach to improving their schools. In addition, the historic "Ed-Flex" Demonstration Program gives six States the power to waive certain federal education regulations themselves. Oregon and Kansas have already been given this authority. We are fully committed to reducing federal education regulations. That is why one-third of all Federal education regulations that were on the books when I was sworn in no longer exist.

Goals 2000 Is Already Having an Impact

Forty-seven States are participating in Goals 2000 and have received their first-year grants. In ad-

dition, 24 States have received their second year funds already.

The response to Goals 2000 has been enthusiastic, and States have found Goals 2000 to be a "user-friendly" program, both because of the flexibility and our streamlined application process. Local interest in participating in Goals 2000 is also very strong. Initial evidence is that local applications for State Goals 2000 funds have exceeded available funds by between 200 and 600 percent, depending on the State.

I want to give you a few examples of how Goals 2000 funds are supporting school improvement:

- Michigan is using Goals 2000 funds to help local school districts adopt standards and core curricula in the academic subjects.

- In Burlington, Vermont, students at the Wheeler Elementary School receive daily intensive instruction from university student tutors, student teachers, parent volunteers and foster grandparents.

- In Kentucky, Goals 2000 is helping Harrison County to strengthen parental involvement in education by training teachers to recruit parents as volunteer instructional aides and by reaching out to parents through cable television programs and homework hotlines.

- In Philadelphia, Pennsylvania, Goals 2000 funds are helping to implement a new management structure—reorganizing six large regions into 22 smaller ones to provide school leaders maximum flexibility to implement school improvements.

- Massachusetts is using Goals 2000 funds to pay the start-up costs of 14 charter schools.

These examples demonstrate clearly the wide range of activities that Goals 2000 funding supports.

For fiscal year 1996, President Clinton has proposed to expand this partnership by providing $750 million for Goals 2000. This level of funding could help as many as 17,000 schools. The House did not provide any FY 1996 funding for Goals 2000. I believe the House action, unless reversed by the Senate, threatens to deal a tremendous setback to education reform in America, one from which we might not recover for a good many years.

Myths and Misconceptions about Goals 2000

Unfortunately the current debate over Goals 2000 rests largely on misconceptions about what the program actually does. The attacks on Goals 2000 are one part myth, one part misinformation and one part the politics of pandering. At the extreme, as *The Wall Street Journal* recently pointed out in a front page story, Goals 2000 is depicted as a United Nations cabal, mind control, and even a plot to take guns out of the homes of gun owners. All this is a little much. Here we are in the middle of an extraordinary era of new knowledge and information, and public leaders—who should know better—are listening to people who would lead us backwards.

Whatever the source, the false assertions are easily refuted. Perhaps the most common statement is that Goals 2000 will lead to a Federal takeover of local education. As a former Governor of South Carolina, I am very sensitive to concerns about Federal intrusion in local affairs, and I am a strong believer in the long American tradition of local control of education. I would not have supported Goals 2000 if I thought it remotely threatened to undermine that tradition. You don't have to take my word for that, however. Just look at the statute itself. Section 318 makes it absolutely clear that there are no mandates, and there will be no Federal takeover; and Section 319 specifically reaffirms that control of education is reserved to States and local school systems. Clearly, those who warn of a Federal takeover are raising fears without a shred of justification.

Further Resources

BOOKS

Carleton, David. *Landmark Congressional Laws on Education.* Westport, Conn.: Greenwood, 2002.

Goals 2000: A Progress Report. Washington, D.C.: U.S. Department of Education, 1995.

Jennings, John F. *Why National Standards and Tests?: Politics and the Quest for Better Schools.* Thousand Oaks, Calif.: Sage, 1998.

PERIODICALS

Cookson, Peter, Jr. "Goals 2000: Framework for the New Educational Federalism." *Teachers College Record* 96, no. 3, Spring 1995, 405–417.

"Educational Assessment: Local and National Changes." *The Clearing House* 68, no. 4, March/April 1995.

Ohanian, Susan. "Goals 2000: What's in a Name?" *Phi Delta Kappan* 81, no. 5, January 2000, 344–355.

Riley, Richard W. "Reflections on Goals 2000." *Teachers College Record* 96, no. 3, Spring 1995, 380–388.

WEBSITES

National Education Goals Panel. Available online at http://www.negp.gov/datasystemlinks.html; website home page: www.negp.gov (accessed April 19, 2003).

"A Public Policy Perspective on Televised Violence and Youth: From a Conversation with Peggy Charren"

Interview

By: Peggy Charren

Date: 1995

Source: Charren, Peggy. "A Public Policy Perspective on Televised Violence and Youth: From a Conversation with Peggy Charren." *Harvard Educational Review* 65, no. 2, Summer 1995, 282–291.

About the Author: Peggy Charren (1928–) was a director of film syndication and distribution for a TV station in New York before founding Action for Children's Television, Inc. (ACT) in 1968. She said of herself: "My interest in children's television grew out of an involvement with children's literature, theater, and film. I have tried to increase the diversity of television programming available to young audiences, and to fight efforts to censor television and other media. I believe that concern for the needs of children should not be used as an excuse to eat away at the concept of free speech." Her further involvement with various commissions, committees and boards continued to reflect her dedication to the best interests of children. ■

Introduction

Action for Children's Television (ACT) began out of concern over the gratuitous violence in children's television. In the 1960s, this violence appeared in cartoons, where a roadrunner blew up a coyote on a regular basis, a character hit another with a hammer, or a rabbit dodged a gun one more time. Violence also appeared during prime-time television, but not to the extent that it did in the twenty-first century. Peggy Charren took her concerns as a call to action and, along with other concerned parents, formed ACT in 1968. The organization was successful in getting federal legislation regarding children's television passed.

ACT continued as a national voice for educational programming until 1992, and although the organization ceased to exist, Peggy Charren remained active in advocating for better television for children. The group researched the effects of television on children, consulting educators, lawyers, and other experts before taking their case to the Federal Communications Commission (FCC).

Studies backed up what ACT thought about violence. Leonard Eron, a researcher at the University of Michigan, studied a group of eight-year-olds in 1960 to determine how violent television affected learned behavior. They followed up the initial study in 1971 and 1981 with many of the original subjects. What they found was a

Peggy Charren, a prominent and successful lobbyist for quality television programing for children, sits in the control room of TV's *Sesame Street* in 1992. © ROBERT MAASS/CORBIS. REPRODUCED BY PERMISSION.

distinct correlation between television violence and aggressive behavior.

In the early twenty-first century, the mass media was a strong presence in American life. In the interview, Peggy Charren discusses her views, her successes, and her continuing concerns regarding children's television programming. The issues are not limited to violence but also include television shows that have become extended commercials for products aimed at the children's market.

Significance

Charren's and ACT's work had a significant impact on prime-time programming. In 1990, legislation was passed regarding children's television programming, requiring an increase in educational shows. The 1993 Children's Protection from Violent Programming Act regulated what broadcasters are allowed to air during the prime hours when children are viewing television. Charren was concerned over how violence was shown in programming. Including a violent act for the sake of entertainment was not productive. Yet not showing a violent act that is part of a story line was not productive either because it diminished the severity of the act.

One of the most important aspects of Charren's group was that it was a grassroots organization. ACT proved that with the right approach, a small group of citizens could be heard and could advocate for change in what had become a major influence on Americans' lives. The group understood the dynamics involved in dealing

with the press and politicians. They knew that they faced obstacles to gain what they desired, but they persisted.

Charren and her group were not just concerned with violence, however. Commercial influences through advertising and the amount of television that children watched were also concerns. In addressing these issues, Charren stressed the need for regulation of advertising. Children (and adults) associated what they saw on television with what they wanted or perceived that they needed. The abuse of advertisers in targeting young children was a hot topic in the early 1990s. To alleviate the influence that television had on children, parents needed to be educated. They needed to know what was on television, what their children watched, and how the children might interpret the programming. Quality children's television remained a topic of national importance and debate.

Primary Source

"A Public Policy Perspective on Televised Violence and Youth: From a Conversation with Peggy Charren" [excerpt]

> **SYNOPSIS:** Peggy Charren discusses her reasons for beginning the Action for Children's Television. Her desire to see quality television for children is clear in her remarks. Her work resulted in significant changes in children's programming.

In fact, the Children's Television Act of 1990 resulted from a belief in presenting other options to censorship. Tell us about the legislation and why and how it was developed.

The Communications Act of 1934 enabled ACT to make the case for children's constitutional entitlement to quality programming, and allowed ACT to petition the Federal Communications Commission, saying, "It's time for broadcasters to take care of kids, and they are not doing it." That hook in the Communications Act served as a basis for the Children's Television Act of 1990. The 1990 Act requires broadcasters to air "educational and informational programming for children" as a condition for their license renewals. Through this legislation, ACT has tried to say that children are part of the public that broadcasters must serve, yet haven't.

Broadcasters have not been successful in meeting the demands for children's television programs because of the tension between the reality of the commercial marketplace and children's differing needs. In the commercial marketplace, the higher a program's ratings, the larger its audience, and the more money a television station is paid by its advertisers. But this system has not created the kind of environment that supports educational choices for children. As anyone who has ever tried to bring up a child knows, two-to fifteen-year-old children are the most diverse group in human development. As children move from preschool to school-age to preteen and teenage, they seem like three or four different species, with different interests and different languages. If commercial broadcasters attempt to target programs that will meet the specific interests and languages of these separate groups, they will not attract the largest share of the overall "child market," (two-to fifteen-year-olds) and will not generate the kind of money that comes from mass appeal, toy-based programs.

In a nutshell, the intention of the Children's Television Act is to offer a First Amendment-sensitive approach to television programs, calling for alternatives to violent, merchandise-based children's series, while working within the framework of the commercial television marketplace.

But has the Children's Television Act, by explicitly demanding that the "educational needs of children" be met, actually offered a new menu of choice and reduced the amount of violence on children's television? Some critics maintain that there is still little choice and that violence is as present as it ever was. How would you respond to those criticisms?

It is unrealistic to think that the minute a law passes, the problem the law set out to redress gets solved. After the passage of the Children's Television Act in 1990, broadcasters were given a year to initiate change because the FCC realized that broadcasters could not all of a sudden alter what they were doing, since they had contracts and commitments to fulfill. But the broadcasters' first license renewal filings under the new mandate indicated that the industry was not taking the law seriously. A 1992 report of industry compliance with the Children's Television Act pointed out that television stations claimed shows like The Jetsons, Super Mario Brothers, G.I. Joe, and many similar programs were "specifically designed" to educate children. Front-page stories in newspapers across the country pointed out that something is the matter with broadcasters if they think that The Jetsons was specifically designed to teach children about life in the twenty-first century.

The FCC is presently debating how to strengthen the guidelines of the new mandate. The best way the FCC can do this is by including a clearer definition of educational programming in their policy to avoid the problems of broadcasters' ambiguous interpretations of what is "educational," and by re-

quiring each station to air a specific number of hours per week of this programming.

Why do you think we need legislation like the Children's Television Act that deals with children's programming today, as opposed to any other time in television's history?

Basically, it is because the movers and shakers in the broadcast industry have changed over the years, and so have their attitudes. Keep in mind how networks and stations differ. The networks themselves have no legal obligation to serve the public, including children. Local stations do. Networks are delivery systems. When the FCC sends out a message that, "Hey, you broadcasters have to do better," the station affiliates put pressure on their network to create programming that helps them fulfill that public responsibility, including programs that serve as alternatives to violent ones.

Unlike today, in years past, the industry's leadership did not respond by saying, "How little can we get away with?" In the 1970s, the leaders were the same people who started electronic communications in this country. They were the people who invented the television set, the radio. They were the people who cared about communicating. They had a sense of what their mission was, even though they were going to make money. At least some of the time they wanted to do well by doing good. As the industry got involved in "mega-deals" and as the stations started selling out to big conglomerates and refrigerator salesmen, the commitment to serve the public changed. The pioneers of the field may have opposed what was going on in the marketplace, but all of a sudden there was nobody left to resist.

During the 1980s, children's television turned into thirty-minute toy commercials. There was a synergy among the toy manufacturers, toy promoters, and program producers. There was no sense that children were entitled to anything except comic book sales pitches. This destroyed anything that was happening for the good of children in the commercial broadcasting market.

Do you see other legislative avenues for dealing with television violence beyond the Children's Television Act?

One avenue is to increase funding for public broadcasting. Some powerful new members of Congress want to eliminate federal support for public broadcasting, a proposal that would undermine any efforts to provide quality programs as an alternative to violent television content. Given its limited resources, public broadcasting's record in serving young audiences is remarkable for the array of choices it has offered children of various ages, and for its willingness to tackle hard-to-handle topics and make them understandable to children.

In addition, the FCC could assert more influence on the industry with strong processing guidelines that require broadcasters to provide one hour of programs designed specifically for children to qualify for their license renewal. These programs should be a minimum of thirty minutes in length, air between 7 a.m. and 9 p.m., and serve a diverse age group—preschool, elementary, and teenage. If broadcasters do not meet these guidelines, the Commission could then initiate the necessary steps to relieve television licensees of their public service obligation to children. Then, the FCC could charge each television station a very small percentage—a reasonable amount is $100 million annually, which is less than one-half of one percent of the revenues of the television broadcast industry—and allocate the money as an add-on for the public broadcast service.

Further Resources

BOOKS

Bender, David L., ed. *Media Violence: Opposing Viewpoints.* San Diego, Calif.: Greenhaven, 1999.

Minow, Newton N. *Abandonment in the Wasteland: Children, Television, and the First Amendment.* New York: Hill and Wang, 1995.

United States Congress. Senate Committee on Commerce, Science, and Transportation. *S. 1383. Children's Protection from Violent Programming Act of 1993.* Washington, D.C.: U.S. G.P.O., 1994.

PERIODICALS

"How TV Violence Hits Kids." *Education Digest* 60, no. 2, October 1994, 16.

Tulloch, Marian I. "Evaluating Aggression: School Students' Responses to Television Portrays of Institutionalized Violence." *Journal of Youth and Adolescence* 24, no. 1, 1995, 95–115.

"When It Comes to Technology . . . the Postman Always Thinks Twice"

Interview

By: Neil Postman; Renee Olson
Date: May 1996

Source: Postman, Neil, with Renee Olson. "When It Comes to Technology . . . the Postman Always Thinks Twice." *School Library Journal* 42, no. 5, May 1996, 18–22.

About the Authors: Neil Postman, a social critic, joined the movement towards radical education reform in 1969 when he co-authored *Teaching as a Subversive Activity.* Later he changed his stance when he published *Teaching as a Conserving Activity* in 1979. Postman defends his newfound conservatism by arguing that in times of social stagnation, schools must direct change; in times of rapid social change, schools must conserve. Postman was applauded for his ability to adapt to the changing needs of education.

Renee Olson (1962–) is a news and features editor for the *School Library Journal,* which serves the needs of school and public librarians who work with children. It features articles, reviews, and columns that address the changes in libraries and the needs of children. ∎

Introduction

In the 1990s, there was a rush to implement technology in the classroom and in the library. Neil Postman, university professor and Paulette Goddard Chair of Media and Technology at New York University, cautioned educators and librarians to slow down and look at what they are doing.

Postman did not use a computer, but, ironically, he taught technology and communications courses at New York University. Postman approached technological change from the impact it had on society. Once an advocate of using television and other media that was developing in the 1960s, he changed his point of view. He came to see technology in terms of the social consequences it had. Television's ills are well known—there is too much violence, children watch too much television, there is nothing worthwhile to watch. He feared that computers would have the same consequences and that the rush toward technology would have a similar downside.

Postman's most important point might be that there was an information glut. While computer proponents glory in the access to information made available by the Internet and the increasing availability of computers, Postman despaired in it. He did not believe that more is better. Postman valued books and reading as a way to learn. He saw libraries as critical for providing information for local communities and schools.

Postman was not alone in his criticism of computers and the Internet. Clifford Stoll, once an advocate of technology, pointed out his doubts in *Silicon Snake Oil* published the same year as Postman's *The End of Education.*

Significance

Postman's views from the mid-1990s to the early twenty-first century did not change; if anything, they become more pronounced. In an interview with Jay Walljasper in *Utne Reader* (January 2000), Postman said, "I think the single most important lesson we should have learned in the past twenty years is that technological progress is not the same things as human progress. Technology always comes at a price. This is not to say that one should be, in a blanket way, against technological change. But it is time for us to be grownups, to understand if technology gives us something, it will take away something. It is not an unmixed blessing. We have to go into the future with our eyes wide open." Postman saw the importance of retaining what he called "older technologies," that is, books and reading, in order for society to function and for people to have a life rather than just to make a living.

In his 1996 interview with Renee Olson, Postman stressed the importance of public libraries. Libraries need to build collections of books, documents, and primary sources that children could touch while they learn about history. He saw these kinds of sources as vital for exciting children and making them want to read and learn.

Postman was not impressed by the digital projects that were in their infancy in the mid-1990s. In a short time, projects like the American Memory Project through the Library of Congress scanned and made available millions of images of primary documents and books. Although Postman would likely not agree, these documents have become an important source for researchers and educators as they tried to expose children to historical materials.

Computer technology was part of life in the twenty-first century and showed signs that it would remain so. Postman's views about thinking before automatically turning to technology for solutions were critical for educators. There were print sources that would turn a child into a reader and cause curiosity to grow.

Professor Neil Postman. © NAJLAH FEANNY/CORBIS SABA. REPRODUCED BY PERMISSION.

Primary Source

"When It Comes to Technology . . . the Postman Always Thinks Twice" [excerpt]

SYNOPSIS: Neil Postman had spent his life in education. His concerns about the use of technology went beyond the classroom walls into the library. He believed that librarians should think carefully before adding new technology.

In Technopoly, *you define a "technopoly" as a society whose central preoccupation is technology. Would you say that education is preoccupied with technology?*

Postman: Well, in my most recent book, *The End of Education,* I do make the claim that the god of technology has invaded the minds of many educators. Most educators, when they talk about reform-

ing education, put their hopes on technology. I do believe that it is a mistake, a distraction. I'm old enough to remember when people thought that 16mm film was the panacea. I also remember when they thought 8mm film would do it, when they thought structured teacher-proof textbooks would do it. Now, of course, it's computers. In America, we're always looking for a technological fix. I think that while computers will play a role in the future of education as libraries will, I don't think that there's any substitute for the interaction of teacher and student face-to-face.

What, then, should education's central preoccupation be?

Postman: In *The End of Education,* I wrote that, at its best, schooling can be about how to make a life, which is quite different from how to make a living. To help educators avoid being consumed by how education should be done, I tried my hand at offering five narratives in the book. Each narrative would be a story around which to organize education. One of them looks at America as a great experiment, and another is what I call "The Fallen Angel." I think [the latter] is the most promising one because the most common and persistent behavior of human beings is to make mistakes, as Steven [Postman points to the photographer setting up his equipment for SLJ's photo shoot] is demonstrating right now.

He is making some mistakes, but he will also demonstrate the angel part—that although we make mistakes the angel is capable of correcting our mistakes. The idea of curriculum built around this is very promising.

How do you think computers have changed the way teachers teach?

Postman: I don't know the answer to that. Alan Kay, a very good friend of mine at Apple Computer and one of the inventors of the personal computer, is famous for making the statement that, "Any problem schools cannot solve without the computer, they can't solve with the computer." He has led a research team working with schools in Los Angeles on this very question. So far I don't think the results have been that good. Alan believes they will discover ways of using computers [in education]. His view, however, is that most teachers are not using computers to maximize or even come close to maximizing what computers can do best.

To me, the benefit of computers is that they make resources available regardless of your location. If the Library of Congress puts, say, a historical document on the Web, you can get it in your classroom in Arizona.

Postman: But if your school in Arizona has a library. . . .

Libraries have limits in terms of space and money.

Postman: How many resources do you need, how much do you need to know? I have written a lot on how information has become a form of garbage. We no longer live in an age of information scarcity, but instead information glut. Human beings have never really had to face that problem.

We've heard from school librarians whose administrators want to replace their libraries with computer labs that have access to the Internet. What would you say to those administrators?

Postman: I would make a citizen's arrest on the spot. The invention of the library is one of the great achievements of humanity, and the idea that a school would not have a special place where book knowledge and the wisdom of humanity is collected

and preserved and promoted seems to me to be a world I wouldn't like to live in.

I would think that school administrators—as people who make their living in the field of education—would find libraries essential.

Postman: Well, it may be that one's attitude toward libraries and toward books is correlated with his or her life experience. The administrators that you're talking about might be under 40 or 45, meaning they grew up with television and perhaps were not themselves readers. Words probably did not make a deep emotional or intellectual connection with them. They may think, "Well, all sources of information are equal."

In 1970, you wrote, somewhat disparagingly, in the Harvard Educational Review *that, "The schools are still promoting the idea that the main source of wisdom is to be found in libraries." Do you think schools do this now?*

Postman: Well, actually, I hope they do. I suspect that in many schools the role of libraries and books generally is not stressed as much as it should be. When I wrote that article, I was rather more concerned with the schools acknowledging that knowledge and information could come from media other than books. But I must say that I didn't understand then the extent to which new media, especially television, were going to wreck American culture. I think if I had seen that more clearly, I wouldn't have written that article. I remember in those years I thought that there was too much emphasis on reading and not enough attention being given to other ways through which the young could learn.

But then about 13 or 14 years after that article I wrote *Teaching as a Conserving Activity* in which I took the measure as best I could of what was happening in American culture. I took the position that the visual media that were now dominating the culture were a very serious threat to literacy and to a language-oriented education. I advocated that the schools had a special responsibility to counter the kind of orientation that was being promoted in the culture at-large and one of the best ways to do that would be to emphasize reading.

What would someone find in a library that you created? I'll give you an unlimited budget.

Postman: An unlimited budget. . . . Well, the first thought that comes to mind is that I would have more older books than most school libraries do. I don't know how wise that is because many librarians would take the view, and it's a pretty sensible one, that the principal purpose here is just to get kids to love to read. Then they can eventually get to the wisdom of the past once they like to read. So, maybe, they do have a point. But I would make sure nonetheless that there were plenty of books in the library whose authors had a different orientation from what we have today. I think one of the great things about reading is that it's a consciousness raiser— it raises consciousness by revealing to us a point of view, even a world view, that is different from what we know about in Brooklyn, NY, for example.

I would definitely have everything that Jefferson wrote and everything that Lincoln wrote, since I think they're the two smartest Americans we've ever had. I would love to have in any library, school or otherwise, newspapers from the 19th century and documents from another time. Have you ever been to the British Museum? Well, what I like best is to look at Charles Darwin's laundry list and his wife's note to him to make sure he gets some milk. I think children love that stuff.

It's a wonderful way to get kids interested in history because history is very abstract to most kids. It's something that really didn't happen to people— it just existed in textbooks. There is something terrific about reading a newspaper account of the Battle of Gettysburg. Of course, I would not neglect having audio- and videotapes in the library—most libraries do.

Further Resources

BOOKS

Postman, Neil. *The End of Education: Redefining the Value of School.* New York: Knopf, 1995.

Stoll, Clifford. *Silicon Snake Oil: Second Thoughts on the Information Highway.* New York: Doubleday, 1995.

Tuman, Myron C. *Word Perfect: Literacy in the Computer Age.* Pittsburgh: University of Pittsburgh Press, 1992.

PERIODICALS

Silver, Daniel J. "Computers and Their Discontents."*Commentary* 100, July 1995, 31–35.

Walljasper, Jay. "Neil Postman Is No Progressive." *Utne Reader,* January 2000. Available online at http://www .consciouschoice.com/citizen/citizen1301.html; website home page: http://www.consciouschoice.com (accessed May 1, 2003).

WEBSITES

Neil Postman at edtechnot.com. Available online at http:// www.edtechnot.com/notpostman.html; website home page: http://www.edtechnot.com (accessed May 1, 2003).

"Neil Postman Ponders High Tech." Available online at http:// www.pbs.org/newshour/forum/january96/postman_1-17 .html; website home page: http://www.pbs.org (accessed May 1, 2003).

"Sex Segregation and the War Between the States"
Editorial

By: Cynthia Fuchs Epstein

Date: 1996

Source: Epstein, Cynthia Fuchs. "Sex Segregation and the War Between the States." *Dissent* 43, no. 4, Fall 1996, 12–13.

About the Author: Cynthia Fuchs Epstein is a distinguished professor in the sociology department at the City University of New York. She earned her Ph.D. from Columbia University in 1968. Epstein's major research interests include the sociology of gender and issues regarding time and work. ■

Introduction

The furor over admissions to the last two single-sex military academies erupted in 1989 when a female high school student in Virginia sought admission to Virginia Military Institute (VMI). This began a prolonged legal battle that also involved the all-male Citadel in South Carolina.

VMI did not admit women willingly. The Supreme Court reversed a lower court order on June 26, 1996, forcing VMI to allow women in the school. The first female students entered the Institute in 1997. The woman who sued VMI for admission was not identified.

Media attention intensified when Shannon Faulkner attempted to enroll at the Citadel in 1994. Her case began the year before. Faulkner was admitted to the Corps of Cadets under court order but left after only one week. On the first day of "hell week," Faulkner was taken to the infirmary, where she remained for the rest of the week. The scrutiny of the media and the intense disdain for women at the Citadel were contributing factors for her decision to leave. However, she became the pioneer who opened the door of the Citadel for other women. In 1999, Nancy Mace became the first female to graduate from this institution.

Cynthia Fuchs Epstein has written extensively on gender issues in education and on the VMI and Citadel cases. Her opinions in the commentary reprinted here liken the battle to a twentieth-century version of the Civil War. The institutions and their alumni viewed admitting women as a call to arms that would end traditions that had been in place for well over a century. However, the law was on the side of the women—they attend both schools.

Significance

Both VMI and the Citadel created leadership programs for women at female colleges—Mary Baldwin College (VMI) and Converse College (the Citadel). Neither

Women march in protest against the Virginia Military Institute's all-male admissions policy on January 17, 1996. Behind them is the U.S. Supreme Court, where the Justices are hearing arguments in the legal challenge to VMI's policies. **AP/WIDE WORLD PHOTOS. REPRODUCED BY PERMISSION.**

program met the criteria or the reputation of the programs in place for men. In a battle to provide separate but equal educational opportunities, the leadership academies paled in comparison to the facilities, opportunities, and faculty available to men. With traditional arguments, both schools fought against allowing women. Alumni and current members of the faculty and administration stated that women were not up to the challenge of the institutions either physically or mentally. They defended the traditions of the schools to produce male leaders. VMI defended the long-standing preparation of "citizen/soldiers" and one called women a "virus" that would plague the campus.

Epstein notes that the federal service academies began admitting women in 1976. Epstein's comparison to the Civil War reflected an attitude held by some who thought VMI was right. In this case Northern lawyers, under orders from Congress, were invading the elite Southern bastions of male military training over a century after the war had ended. VMI and the Citadel were state-supported institutions and, thus, had to be fair to all under the law. Title IX (an extension of the 1964 Civil

Rights Act passed in 1972) mandated educational equity, and previous cases had argued for equal opportunities based on race. The Court determined that the discrimination must end.

Forced equality is never easy, but both schools did admit female cadets. In 1998, VMI had 52 female students and 1,276 male students. In 1999, the Citadel's enrollment included 69 women and 1,702 men. The female numbers continued to rise and, like the federal military academies, it is expected that women on campus will become routine.

Primary Source

"Sex Segregation and the War Between the States"

SYNOPSIS: Cynthia Fuchs Epstein discusses the Supreme Court decision forcing the Virginia Military Institute and the Citadel to admit women. The Court ruling was only a beginning. Both cases resulted in a frenzy of media attention and focus on the young women who sought admission to the schools.

Women were admitted to the Virginia Military Institute for the first time in 1997. Here, a group of those freshmen smile for the camera in front of their dormitories on March 16, 1998. © ALONSO ANDERS R/CORBIS. REPRODUCED BY PERMISSION.

For many alumni of the Virginia Military Institute (VMI) and the Citadel, the last two state supported schools that hoped to continue their pattern of discrimination against women, the Civil War has been lost again. The suit by the Department of Justice against VMI was heard by the Supreme Court (litigation against the Citadel was deferred pending the decision on VMI) and VMI was found to be in violation of the Constitution's equal protection guarantee. These two military-style institutions, which give their sons handsome educations in engineering, the sciences, and liberal arts and a lifetime "oldboy" network of contacts, now have to admit women— and thus expose themselves to the "virus" women will bring, as one administrator at VMI put it.

Many wars were fought on the battlefields of these two cases. Alumni and administrators at both institutions did not appreciate the "northern" lawyers who came down from the Justice Department (in an action that was actually started during the Bush administration). Indeed, the schools posed the issue in terms of states' rights, of the war between the North and the South, and then used the language of the left to argue that they were offering programs to guarantee "diversity" and to benefit disadvantaged boys and girls (in their separate institutions). Debates on "difference" and "similarity" between the sexes brought forth arguments long familiar in feminist and popular literature. For example, VMI's expert witnesses argued that women were physically weaker and could not take stress as well as men, and that more than a hundred physiological differences contribute to a "natural hierarchy" in which women cannot compete with men. The fact that the federal service academies—West Point, Annapolis, and the Air Force Academy—have admitted women since 1976 was not taken into account in the lower court's ruling, which permitted segregated programs.

But in a seven-to-one decision handed down by Justice Ruth Bader Ginsburg (who as a lawyer had argued pivotal sex discrimination cases before the Court), the lower court ruling was overturned.

Ginsburg noted that VMI's separate but "comparable" program at the all-female Mary Baldwin College was far inferior to VMI's own program in every way, including its absence of tradition and prestige. This ruling also affected the Citadel, which had also instituted a "comparable" "leadership" program for women at Converse College, one that offered ROTC (Reserve Officer Training Corps), but hardly any of the other opportunities that the Citadel offers to men.

I had the opportunity to visit the Citadel and Converse College in preparation for my testimony as an expert witness for the plaintiff (I refuted the spurious "social science" evidence offered by the school that women required education based on different "methodologies" than men because of their presumed cognitive and psychological differences). At Converse, cordially escorted to classes and dormitories (but introduced as "the enemy") I found few computers, a dismal library, and low tech labs. At the Citadel, I saw lavish laboratories for computer science and engineering and a fabulous gym. And surprisingly, at the Citadel, so fiercely antagonistic to women, there was a real female presence—women faculty and day students (though not in the Corps of Cadets).

It was clearly the principle of the thing. Both schools fought hard, and their alumni came up with millions of dollars to keep their barracks (if not their campuses) free of women. Justice Antonin Scalia, the one voice of dissent in the Supreme Court (Justice Clarence Thomas recused himself from this case because his son is a student at VMI), decried the move from tradition ("the history of our people"). He argued that the court was making law, not interpreting it, by narrowing the standard of "intermediate scrutiny" (applied to cases of gender discrimination and considerably more lax than the "strict scrutiny" standard applied to cases of racial discrimination). The decision would also, he predicted, be the end of single-sex education (another sensitive debate among feminist and conservative educators today).

The traditions referred to by Scalia, honored at both schools, are to produce officers and gentlemen. Only about 15 percent of their graduates join the military. Their traditions, which range from close haircuts to abuse that would not pass scrutiny by Amnesty International, are a questionable educational benefit. And as for being gentlemen. . . . As a visiting woman educator from the North I found it pleasant to encounter the polished manners (many "Yes, ma'ams") of administrators and students, but

since then I have heard about their misogynistic attitudes. As Susan Faludi reported in the *New Yorker,* locker room talk at these schools characterizes women as whores and sluts.

Of course, there is the whole question of why, in this day and age, the notion that women will pollute the environment and undermine the opportunity to become "real men" still generates the kind of passions that made male students isolate and ridicule Shannon Faulkner (the lone woman who attempted to join the Citadel's Corps of Cadets under a court order) so badly that she withdrew from the school after a week.

United in their fight to exclude women at first, the Citadel appeared to be the good sport and VMI the sore loser after the battle. The Citadel announced that it would now welcome women "enthusiastically" because it has always obeyed the law, and has admitted four women. VMI dragged its heels, but faced with losing lavish state aid and having to buy the grounds and buildings from the state, it agreed to admit women in 1997. The war between the states and the war between the sexes are no longer "hot." But battles are still to be fought between those who would like to reinstitute sex segregation and those who understand the insidious consequences that would follow.

Further Resources
BOOKS
Brodie, Laura Fairchild. *Breaking Out: VMI and the Coming of Women.* New York: Pantheon, 2000.

Manegold, Catherine S. *In Glory's Shadow: Shannon Faulkner, the Citadel, and a Changing America.* New York: Knopf, 2000.

Stum, Philippa. *Women in the Barracks: The VMI Case and Equal Rights.* Lawrence, Kan.: University of Kansas, 2002.

PERIODICALS
McClay, Wilfred M. "Of 'Rats' and Women." *Commentary* 102, no. 3, September 1996, 46–49.

Salomone, Rosemary C. "The VMI Case: Affirmation of Equal Educational Opportunity for Women." *Trial* 32, no. 10, October 1996, 67–70.

WEBSITES
The Citadel. Available online at www.citadel.edu (accessed April 22, 2003).

"The Myths and Justifications of Sex Segregation in Higher Education: VMI and the Citadel." Available online at http://www.law.duke.edu/journals/djglp/articles/gen4p101.htm; website home page: http://www.law.duke.edu (accessed April 19, 2003).

Virginia Military Institute. Available online at www.vmi.edu (accessed April 22, 2003).

"The Controversy over Ebonics"

Journal article

By: Steven Fox

Date: November 1997

Source: Fox, Steven. "The Controversy over Ebonics." *Phi Delta Kappan* 79, no. 3, November 1997, 237–240.

About the Author: Steven Fox, an English teacher, taught at Shaker Heights High School in Ohio at the time this article was published. ∎

Introduction

On December 18, 1996, the school board in Oakland, California, adopted a policy to teach Ebonics, also referred to as Black English. The term was coined in 1973 by Dr. Robert L. Williams and encompassed the study of the language of African Americans as a culturally unique phenomenon. A debate ensued throughout the country about whether Ebonics was a language or a dialect. Related issues included whether English should be treated as a foreign language for children who spoke Ebonics, whether the schools should teach children Standard American English (SAE), the advantages and disadvantages of speaking SAE, and the number of people who actually spoke in Ebonics. Critics saw the Oakland school board as vying for federal funds through the proposal by declaring the children bilingual. They also thought that the proposal was racist, insulted the intelligence of African American children's ability to learn SAE, and counterproductive. Supporters said that the children had a right to speak their own language and that critics were ignoring the African roots of Ebonics. The issue was hotly debated in the press by linguists, and by the public in general. The Oakland school board appointed a task force to study the issue and wrote a new proposal that did not specifically mention Ebonics.

Steven Fox attempts to find the middle ground in the debate. He defends "Ebonics" as a dialect of English rather than a separate language. He points out that despite the criticism, the Oakland resolution caused the country to discuss an important issue. He also points out that how, when, and where children learn language is often taken for granted. Children are influenced by the language they hear and are exposed to in their daily lives. This fact is often forgotten by both parents and educators.

Significance

In the original resolution, the Oakland school board stated that Ebonics was related to genetics, a comment they would later withdraw. They cited the fact that children whose first language was Ebonics had trouble with standardized tests, had lower grades, and in general did not excel in school. The resolution encouraged teachers

and administrators to remedy the situation and to improve the educational opportunities for African American children in the Oakland Unified School District. These are the issues that were debated and that Steven Fox discusses in his article reviewing the controversy.

Fox's article adds to the discussion of Ebonics as a dialect rather than a separate language. He sees Ebonics as a legitimate dialect that has highly structured rules. The appropriateness for the classroom of Ebonics versus SAE is one of the points that Fox and authors such as Earl Ofari Hutchinson and Joseph N. Boyce, senior editor at *The Wall Street Journal,* question. Fox, a teacher who had tried to teach students SAE, discusses the complexities of this endeavor. He points out that children "need to know that, if they use a language different from that of the crowd, they may experience rejection." This debate was about far more than rejection, however. It was about the education of children and the successes or failures many experienced because of prejudices about the way they spoke.

Primary Source

"The Controversy over Ebonics" [excerpt]

SYNOPSIS: Steven Fox differentiates between language and dialect in his summary of the controversial Oakland Board of Education policy regarding Ebonics. Debates over the controversial issue appeared in academic journals and editorial pages of national newspapers. The revised resolution and recommendations sought respect and recognition for the language the students spoke at home, and, therefore, brought with them to the classroom.

The members of the school board in Oakland, California, probably had no idea that their actions regarding Ebonics would receive national attention. Nor did they expect that the nation's reaction would be so strong and so negative. They were, after all, just trying to find a way to solve a problem that has plagued their school system for a long time. Yet, as a result of their policy pronouncement, they have been hit with a barrage of criticism ranging from ridicule to hostility.

It may appear that nothing good can come from raising this issue, but I disagree. The entire nation has engaged in a conversation about the importance of language proficiency in a way that it has never done before, and there is general agreement that without language proficiency a person cannot expect to succeed in the adult world. The Oakland school board deserves credit for raising the consciousness of America about a persistent and bedeviling problem.

Oakland School Superintendent Carolyn Getridge during a media conference concerning the "Ebonics" controversy on January 12, 1997. AP/WIDE WORLD PHOTOS. REPRODUCED BY PERMISSION.

Unfortunately, the loudest noise often comes from people who don't know much about the subject. Some call Ebonics—what has generally been called Black English or Black English Vernacular—a language, some call it slang, some call it a dialect. Some say it is just bad English, some say it is sloppy, some say it is illegitimate, some say it is wrong. At one point the Oakland board unwisely used the word genetic to describe the origin of Ebonics (the board has since retracted that statement, claiming that it did not mean the word in its biological sense but in its linguistic sense). Others have said explicitly that Ebonics is a descendant of the language that was forced upon slaves, who were prevented from learning to speak as their white masters did. One thing is clear: many people are confused.

Perhaps I can help clear up some of the confusion. Ebonics is a dialect of American English. It is not a separate language, and it is not in itself slang, though it, like all languages and their dialects, employs slang to some degree. A language is a pattern of words and of rules governing the use of those words, spoken or written, that is mutually understandable by a group of people and not understand-

able by persons outside that group. Some languages are spoken by hundreds of millions of people. English, for example, has some 400,000,000 primary speakers—those who use it as their first language—and who knows how many secondary and tertiary speakers. According to linguist Paul Newman, Hausa—a language in the AfroAsiatic phylum of the Chadic family (which itself contains about 135 distinct languages)—claims around 25,000,000 speakers. But Hausa is no less and no more a language than English. And Sanskrit, the ancestor of many languages spoken widely on the Indian subcontinent, is the mother tongue of only a few thousand speakers. We do not judge one language or another to be superior because it is spoken by a greater number of people.

While all of us in America might agree that we share the English language, we also recognize that we hear among ourselves many different dialects. Our friends from Boston and Dallas do not sound alike, and that is because they speak different dialects. A dialect is a subgroup within a language, one dialect differing from another in three particular ways: vocabulary, pronunciation, and grammar. Speakers of two different dialects of the same language should be able to understand one another, while speakers of two different languages most often cannot.

For example, a man speaking the dialect we generally call Standard American English (SAE) might say that "my friends and I went to a movie," while his Australian acquaintance would say that "my mates and I took in a cinema." In addition to carrying different meanings, the word *mates* is pronounced differently by the American and the Australian, the Australian pronouncing the vowel less like long A and closer to long I. Such differences in vocabulary, pronunciation, and usage will not prevent communication between the two English speakers. But when their German friend says, *"Ich bin mit meiner Freunden ins Kino gegangen,"* neither one knows what he means.

Regional dialects in America employ slight differences in grammar as well. "That's as far as I can go," according to speakers of SAE, but speakers of the dialect heard in the Appalachians might say, "That's all the further I can go." Such differences are not altogether a matter of education, either. I know a couple from Texas, both with doctorates and professorships in English literature, one of whom said, when analyzing a bridge hand after it had been played, "I might should have led the spade."

Concern over dialect is not exclusively an American problem. In fact, I would say from my own experience that we care much less about it than do people in other countries who speak other languages. Parisians are notoriously snobbish about their pronunciation and consider theirs superior to that of native French speakers from Nice, Toulouse, and—à Dieu ne plaise—Montreal. Germans learn Hochdeutsch in their schools and speak Plattdeutsch in their villages. When I spent some time abroad during college, living with a Belgian family in Antwerp, the major city of the region known as Flanders, the local dialect was Flemish, but the national language was Dutch. We American students were taught Dutch, but if we asked local people what language they spoke, they would answer vlaams, Flemish. Though the spirit of nationalism was very strong, it was clear that their dialect had its place, and education was not that place. I recall the mama of the family I stayed with, on hearing her daughter Marie-Rose speaking with some of her friends, saying to her "geen dialekt in onze huis"—no dialect in our house.

The English also recognize a status dialect, the dialect of the British Broadcasting Company—what we call the Queen's English and what they call the "Received Pronunciation" or the RP. Those who have not "received" it cannot expect to advance in public life beyond their own local areas. Regional television announcers speak in their local dialects, but no one on the national telly does. Margaret Thatcher, who was prime minister during the time I taught in Lincolnshire, grew up in Grantham, the town where many of my pupils lived. Though Mrs. Thatcher was admired by many for her political acumen, she was criticized on a personal level by those from Lincolnshire, who saw that she had adopted the classier dialect of Kent and forsaken the local pronunciation (which, by the way, shares with Ebonics the characteristic of substituting "f" or "v" for "th," so that one of my pupils told me he could "wiggow [wiggle] 'is toof wiv 'is foomb"). The Kentish dialect is the RP, without which Thatcher could never have risen from local politics to the national and international prominence she enjoyed. The dialect of her Lincolnshire background was an impediment. In a way that no English person would see as hypocritical, her neighbors both required her to elevate her language and chastised her for distancing herself from her humble beginnings.

What is now being called Ebonics is a dialect of American English, and, as such, it differs from SAE, which is also a dialect, in matters of vocabulary, pronunciation, and grammar. Speakers of SAE cannot truly say that they find Ebonics unintelligeble; neither can speakers of Ebonics claim that they cannot understand SAE. Some grammatical features of Ebonics contradict the rules we learn in the standard dialect, so that the expression, "He don't got none" causes some purists to say that Ebonics is wrong, but in the Ebonics dialect the double negative is used for emphasis, and the third person singular form of the verb drops the "-s" ending. The fact that many listeners unfamiliar with Ebonics have not sorted out its regularities does not mean that it has none. The media have stressed that Ebonics is a highly rule-based dialect, and speakers of Ebonics do not carelessly drop the verb "to be" or word endings or any of the features we associate with SAE.

Further Resources

BOOKS

Baugh, John. Beyond Ebonics: Linguistic Pride and Racial Prejudice. New York: Oxford University Press, 2000.

Perry, Theresa, and Lisa Delpit, eds. The Real Ebonics Debate: Power, Language, and the Education of African-American Children. Boston: Beacon Press, 1998.

Smitherman, Geneva. Talking That Talk: Language, Culture and Education in America. New York: Routledge, 2000.

PERIODICALS

Boyce, Joseph N. "Oakland's Insult to Blacks and Equality." The Wall Street Journal, Eastern Ed., December 26, 1996, 6.

Hutchinson, Earl Ofari. "The Fallacy of Ebonics." The Black Scholar 27, no. 1, Spring 1997, 36–37.

Oakland School Board. "Text of the Oakland School Board Resolution on Ebonics." The Black Scholar 27, no. 1, Spring 1997, 4.

Smitherman, Geneva. "Black Language and the Education of Black Children: One Mo Once." The Black Scholar 27, no. 1, Spring 1997, 28–35.

WEBSITES

The Ebonics Issue. Available online at http://www.ntu.edu.au /education/csle/issues/ebonics.html; website home page: http://www.ntu.edu.au (accessed April 27, 2003).

"English Lesson, January 23, 1997." Online Newshour. Available online at http://www.pbs.org/newshour/bb/congress /january97/ebonics_1-23.html; website home page: http:// www.pbs.org/ (accessed April 27, 2003).

"As the Bell Curves: Is *The Bell Curve* the Stealth Public Policy Book of the 1990s?"

Magazine article

By: Dan Seligman and Charles Murray

Date: December 8, 1997

Source: Seligman, Dan, and Charles Murray. "As the Bell Curves: Is the Bell Curve the Stealth Public Policy Book of the 1990s?" *National Review,* December 8, 1997, 42–44, 60.

About the Authors: Dan Seligman, author of *A Question of Intelligence: The IQ Debate in America,* has been a contributing editor to *Forbes* magazine.

Charles Murray (1943–), social scientist and influential critic of the modern welfare state and its social consequences, co-authored the 1994 book *The Bell Curve.* Murray, a graduate of Harvard and the Massachusetts Institute of Technology, is a senior fellow at the American Enterprise Institute. ∎

Introduction

The debates over IQ testing and links between IQ and heredity were renewed in 1994 when Charles Murray and Richard J. Herrnstein published *The Bell Curve: Intelligence and Class Structure in American Life.* A bell curve is a graph used to plot standard distributions or deviations. Theoretically, the normal range, which is the highest number, is in the middle. The upper and lower ranges are on either end and indicate lower numbers and the extremes. Such a curve is shaped like a bell, giving it its name. Bell curves have been used to plot test scores and IQ ranges.

This debate over IQ and heredity became heated because many readers of the book concluded that Murray and Herrnstein were arguing that certain races were inferior and had lower IQs. The authors dismissed the arguments about the "average child," or the theory that any child could learn with the right education. Educators, politicians, and the general public reacted strongly to this text and the authors' presumptions.

Richard Herrnstein, who had been the Charles Sanders Pierce Professor of Psychology at Harvard, died in 1994, leaving Murray to defend their thesis, as he did in this interview with Dan Seligman and in many other interviews. Issues of affirmative action and the right to an education, particularly a higher education, are part of the discussion. There was no sound proof that *The Bell Curve* influenced the shift in public opinion away from supporting affirmative action programs, but the debates which swirled around the book coincided with a change of attitude in America. Murray claims that most culturally elite people never really encounter those who do not have the intelligence they

possess. He does not believe that even those with high IQs have the capacity to learn everything at the highest level possible. Murray points out the way that statistics can be skewed to represent what a person wants to show.

Significance

The controversy which appeared in the major newspapers and magazines across the country as well as in the pages of many academic journals only served to boost sales of the *The Bell Curve.* At the center of the debate were issues of race, genetics, IQ, and heredity.

Reviewers from all fields discussed the book because the suggestions of the authors, if taken seriously, would have a broad impact on American society. Some critics dismissed the book as pseudoscience which reflected a political agenda that would undermine social work to help the disadvantaged. They believed that if the authors were taken seriously, affirmative action would be a thing of the past, children of welfare mothers would be taken from them and placed with adoptive parents, and social programs that assisted disenfranchised people would be eliminated. Funding would be used for those with higher IQs, and the rest of the population would be left to their own devices. Other critics argued that the book provided answers to pressing social problems that were too easy and that failed to reflect the complexities teachers face in the classroom.

Others, however, supported Herrnstein and Murray. Chester E. Finn Jr., who had written several books documenting the failures of schools, agreed with them, asserting that many people held conflicting views of intelligence and secretly agreed with the book's thesis. He focused on the societal taboos which the authors exposed and that caused such hot debates. He did not think the conclusions for change were as comprehensive as they could be, but he believed that the book was an important contribution to the debate.

Primary Source

"As the Bell Curves: Is *The Bell Curve* the Stealth Public Policy Book of the 1990s?" [excerpt]

SYNOPSIS: Interviews and editorials became the common venue for Charles Murray to defend his views on intelligence and the suggestions that he and Richard Herrnstein make in their 1994 book. Murray's remarks appeared in both conservative and liberal press. In this article, Murray emphasizes that the focus of *The Bell Curve* was culture, not genetics, and contends that shapers of public policy agree with his book, even if they do so in secret.

DS: Three years after publication of *The Bell Curve,* I find myself endlessly reading news stories about great national controversies in which all the participants do their best to ignore the data you and Dick Herrnstein laid on the table. Three recent examples:

1. the row over school vouchers, whose advocates (e.g., Bill Bennett in the *Wall Street Journal*) endlessly take it for granted that poor performance by students reflects only inadequacies by the teaching profession— inadequacies among the learners being a huge unmentionable;

2. the President's astounding proposal (never characterized as such) that all American youngsters, including those with IQs at the left tail, should have at least two years of college;

3. the expressions of surprise and rage when it turned out that, in the absence of affirmative action, prestigious law schools would be admitting hardly any black students. The participants in these controversies were in no sense talking back to *The Bell Curve.* They were pretending its data do not exist.

What's your perspective?

CM: I read the same stories you do and ask the same question: Do these guys know but pretend not to? Or are they still truly oblivious? In the case of education vouchers, there is a sensible reason to ignore *The Bell Curve:* innercity schools are overwhelmingly lousy. Bill Bennett has read the book, understands it, and (rare indeed) has defended it on national television. But his battle cry is, and should be, "These kids are getting a raw deal"—not a lot of qualifications about the difficulties in raising IQ.

Bill Clinton and his pandering on college education is another story altogether. Vouchers for elementary school can be a good policy idea, no matter what our book says about IQ. But universal college education cannot be. Most people are not smart enough to profit from an authentic college education. But who among Republicans has had the courage to call Clinton on this one? A lot of silence about *The Bell Curve* can be put down to political cowardice.

Affirmative action was still politically sacrosanct when *The Bell Curve* came out in October 1994. Within a year, the tide had swung decisively. Did the book play any role? Damned if I know. Dick and I were the first to publish a comprehensive account of the huge gaps in SAT scores at elite colleges, but I have found not a single citation of the book during the affirmative-action debate.

Richard J. Herrnstein, co-author of *The Bell Curve.* **REPRODUCED BY PERMISSION OF SUSAN HERRNSTEIN.**

My best guess—and the broad answer to your question—is that *The Bell Curve* is the stealth public-policy book of the 1990s. It has created a subtext on a range of issues. Everybody knows what the subtext is. Nobody says it out loud.

DS: I am reading with fascination your "afterword" in the paperback edition, and I have an argumentative question about the passage where you speculate on long-term responses to the book. You postulate a three-stage process. In stage one, the book and its authors take endless rounds of invective from critics who simply want to suppress the message that human beings differ in mental ability. These critics turn to thought control because they look at your findings and conclude, in Michael Novak's words, that "they destroy hope"—a hope which Novak sees as a this-worldly eschatological phenomenon. In stage two, the invective attracts the interest of scholars not previously involved in these disputes. They look over the empirical record, deciding in the end that your case is supportable and may indeed have been understated in some areas. In stage three, these scholars build on your work, and in the end do more than *The Bell Curve* itself to demolish those eschatological hopes. In the long run, the thought control shoots itself in the foot.

Scientist Charles Murray, co-author of *The Bell Curve.* © FICARA JOHN/CORBIS SYGMA. REPRODUCED BY PERMISSION.

This process seems entirely plausible. But I wonder: Will the truth ever break out of the academic world? Remember, the basic message (including even a genetic factor in the black—white gap) was already pretty well accepted by scholars in the mid Eighties as the Snyderman-Rothman book documented. What I never see is acceptance of any part of this message in the public-policy world, where the term "IQ" is seldom uttered without the speaker's sensing a need to dissociate himself from it.

Among many horror stories is the current row over Lino Graglia, the University of Texas law professor now in trouble for having stated an obvious truth: that black and Mexican-American students are "not academically competitive" with white students.

Graglia gave the most benign possible explanation for this educational gap: minority students were not genetically or intellectually inferior but were suffering from a cultural background in which scholarship was not exalted. But that explanation got him nowhere. He has been attacked by every editorial page in Nexis that has weighed in on the matter. (He did better in the letters columns.)

Now, I can see the process you envision going forward—with some scholars and maybe even some journalists looking at actual academic performance at Texas and other universities. What I cannot imagine is defenders of Graglia surfacing in any institutional setting—at least not in the realms of politics and education, nor in major media. Meanwhile, what with Texas campus demonstrations and Jesse Jackson's call for Graglia to be made a social pariah (cheered at the demonstrations), scholars have got the crucial message: Stay under cover if you hold beliefs challenging to those eschatological hopes.

CM: Graglia said "culture." What everybody heard was "genes." As soon as anyone argues that racial differences in intelligence are authentic, not an artifact of biased tests, everyone decodes that as saying the differences are grounded in genes. It is a non-sequitur, but an invariable one in my experience. America's intellectual elites are hysterical about the possibility of black-white genetic differences in IQ.

As you know, *The Bell Curve* actually took a mild, agnostic stand on the subject. Dick Herrnstein and I said that nobody yet knows what the mix between environmental and genetic causes might be, and it makes no practical difference anyway. The only policy implication of the black-white difference, whatever its sources, is that the U.S. should return forthwith to its old ideal of treating people as individuals.

But how many people know this? No one who hasn't read the book. Everyone went nuts about genes, so much so that most people now believe that race and genes is the main topic of our book.

Why? The topic of race and genes is like the topic of sex in Victorian England. The intellectual elites are horrified if anyone talks about it, but behind the scenes they are fascinated. I will say it more baldly than Dick and I did in the book: In their heart of hearts, intellectual elites, especially liberal ones, have two nasty secrets regarding IQ. First, they really believe that IQ is the be-all and end-all of human excellence and that someone with a low IQ is inferior. Second, they are already sure that the black-white IQ difference is predominantly genetic and that this is a calamity—such a calamity indeed that it must not be spoken about, even to oneself. To raise these issues holds a mirror up to the elites' most desperately denied inner thoughts. The result is the kind of reaction we saw to Lino Graglia.

But when people say one thing and believe another, as intellectual elites have been doing about race, sooner or later the cognitive dissonance must be resolved. It usually happens with a bang. When the wall of denial gives way, not only will the received wisdom on race and IQ change, the change will happen very rapidly and probably go much too far. The fervor of the newly converted is going to be a problem. I fully expect, if I live another twenty years, to be in a situation where I am standing on the ram-

parts shouting: "Genetic differences weren't a big deal when we wrote *The Bell Curve* and they still aren't a big deal."

Further Resources

BOOKS

Fraser, Steven, ed. *The Bell Curve Wars: Race, Intelligence, and the Future of America.* New York: Basic Books, 1995.

Herrnstein, Richard J., and Charles Murray. *The Bell Curve: Intelligence and Class Structure in American Life.* New York: Free Press, 1994.

Jacoby, Russell, and Naomi Glauberman, eds. *The Bell Curve Debate: History, Documents, Opinions.* New York: Times Books, 1996.

PERIODICALS

Finn, Chester E., Jr. "For Whom It Tolls." *Commentary,* January 1995, 76–80.

Kardon, Sidney. "The Bell Curve: Intelligence and Class Structure in American Life." *Social Work* 41, no. 1, January 1996, 116–117.

Sternberg, Robert J. "The School Bell and *The Bell Curve:* Why They Don't Mix." *NASSP Bulletin,* February 1996, 46–56.

WEBSITES

"Two Views of *The Bell Curve.*" Available online at http://www.apa.org/journals/bell.html (accessed April 27, 2003).

"Life After Proposition 209: Affirmative Action May Be Dying, But the Dream Lives On"

Journal article

By: Terry Jones

Date: July 1998

Source: Jones, Terry. "Life After Proposition 209: Affirmative Action May Be Dying, But the Dream Lives On." *Academe,* July/August 1998, 22–28. Available online at http://www.proquest.umi.com.pqdweb?TS=104586; website home page: http://www.proquest.umi.com (accessed February 21, 2003).

About the Author: Terry Jones, a professor of sociology at California State University, Hayward, was recognized as an Outstanding Professor in 1989–1990. Jones served as the president of the California Faculty Association and as a member of the American Association of University Professors committee on Historically Black Institutions and the Status of Minorities in the Profession. ∎

Introduction

In 1991, Glynn Custred and Thomas Wood began a drive for a ballot initiative in California that would eliminate preferences based on race, sex, color, ethnicity, or national origin for purposes of public education, employment, or contracting—in other words, ending affirmative action programs. Their efforts culminated on November 5, 1996, when Proposition 209, or the California Civil Rights Initiative, passed by a 54 to 46 percent margin. Proposition 209 is a state law and does not end federal regulations concerning affirmative action.

The area of highest visibility was education, particularly admissions to state universities. Battles over admission of students based on race or gender turned into political battles at the University of California, one of the country's most prestigious university systems. In the article below, Terry Jones argues that education is about more than grades and test scores. In his view, in order to provide a diverse campus with rich opportunities for learning, a range of factors should be considered. Proposition 209 eliminated the factor of race from the equation of admission.

The impact of Proposition 209 and the end of affirmative action extends beyond numbers of minority students admitted to programs in California. It indicates a shift in the cultural climate on those campuses. Other factors are considered for some programs, which subvert Proposition 209. In the medical schools, for example, zip codes are used to guarantee that the student population represents communities that are underserved by medical professionals. This tactic reaches a varying level of socioeconomic classes and populations. The battle of Proposition 209 and its aftereffects continue into the twenty-first century as schools become more competitive and funding for educational programs decreases.

Significance

The supporters of Proposition 209 argued that they wanted to create a system that was fair to everyone. Their opponents argued that affirmative action and other measures to ensure representation of minorities, including women, in education and the workplace had been put in place to create equality for those who had always been overlooked. In their view, the effect of Proposition 209 was to reinforce racism. Further, they contended that the proposition left faculty at the colleges and universities in California feeling vulnerable and abandoned by those who had supported them in the past.

The University of California system felt the impact of Proposition 209 more than the California State University system did because of the differences in structure between them. The University of California system revised its admissions policies for the class of 2002 to include "hardship" as a factor. This policy does not mention race but accounts for family difficulties, caring for brothers and sisters, or other factors that may have made life difficult. The problem with this policy is the definition of "hardship."

Proposition 209 was only the beginning of altering laws and policies regarding affirmative action. Views vary about how to provide educational opportunities for all and be fair to the majority. The only certain thing is that the battle is far from over.

Primary Source

"Life After Proposition 209: Affirmative Action May Be Dying, But the Dream Lives On" [excerpt]

SYNOPSIS: In the following article, Terry Jones describes his view of the effects of the passage of Proposition 209 on colleges and universities in California and the response of various constituencies to it.

On November 5, 1996, the voters of California dealt affirmative action a damaging blow. Many of them thought that they were voting to protect civil rights when they approved Proposition 209, which was cleverly packaged as the California Civil Rights Initiative. In actuality, however, they voted to dismantle affirmative action and the support for civil rights it secured. The proposition read as follows: "The state shall not discriminate against, or grant preferential treatment to, any individual or group on the basis of race, sex, color, ethnicity, or national origin in the operation of public employment, public education, or public contracting." By eliminating affirmative action at the state level, California's voters discarded a conservative and incremental strategy designed to deal with overwhelmingly complex phenomena—racism, sexism, and inequality—in our society.

The overall effects of Proposition 209 vary. In higher education, early statistical evidence shows an impact ranging from the minimal to the catastrophic. It would be a mistake, however, to measure the influence of the amendment in statistical terms alone. Proposition 209 has put a chill on race relations in California, provided a road map to groups in other states with similar agendas, and challenged us to find alternative paths to justice for women and people of color in our society.

This article focuses on the impact of Proposition 209 on student admissions to California's public institutions of higher learning, but the measure affects faculty, administrators, and support staff as well. It is important to note also that the passage of Proposition 209 did not kill affirmative action in

California. Some federal affirmative action programs remain in place for school districts and colleges receiving funds from the U.S. Department of Education. In March 1997, U.S. Secretary of Education Richard W. Riley wrote:

> I want to confirm that the passage of Proposition 209, which would generally prohibit affirmative action under state law for women and racial minorities, has not changed the obligation of school districts and colleges to abide by federal civil rights statutes in order to remain eligible to receive department funding, nor has it changed the obligations of schools participating in a small number of federal programs administered by the department to consider race, as appropriate, under the terms of those programs.

Riley went on to explain that the department's Office for Civil Rights will investigate any complaints of violations of federal statutes as state officials carry out the terms and conditions of Proposition 209. One such complaint has already been filed with regard to the University of California's admissions process.

Higher Education in California

The University of California has become the battleground for affirmative action in higher education, and the battle lines have been drawn: because racial and gender preferences are "wrong," students given a place in the system's undergraduate, graduate, or professional schools on the basis of affirmative action take away a place that should have been awarded by more "legitimate and traditional means." Because of the value of admission to this elite system, the struggle has become politicized, and as the battle has intensified, considerations of sound educational policy have fallen by the wayside. With only a few exceptions, educators have been frozen out of the discussions, allowing political appointees of the governor to make the main decisions about affirmative action admissions to the UC system. With this development, shared governance has been pushed to the side, threatening an important element of academic culture.

The University of California is the jewel of California's three-tiered public higher education system. When the California Master Plan for Higher Education was enacted in 1960, it was seen as a management tool to guard against unwarranted competition between the different tiers. An attendant function was to guarantee anyone who wanted a higher education the opportunity to get one.

In theory, the master plan gave people from the most humble beginnings access to the University of California and its graduate and professional schools. It was argued that ambitious students could advance to these schools from the community colleges. In reality, however, the master plan was flawed. While it was easy for people of color and the poor to obtain entry to community colleges, it was only after the inception of affirmative action efforts in 1964 that the doors were opened at the elite University of California system. Even so, the doors have been pushed only slightly ajar.

The issue of access to the university is not academic. In a stratified society, income, power, and prestige are scarce resources, and the scarcer the resource, the more valuable it becomes. Nowhere is this more true than in higher education, the most important route to wealth, power, and prestige. The University of California is arguably the most prestigious higher education institution in California, if not the country. If admission to higher education is a ticket to ride, then entry into the UC system is the ticket to ride first class. Graduation from one of the University of California campuses opens doors to California politics, economics, and beyond. The California legislature is full of graduates from the UC system, and a look at any list of California attorneys is reminiscent of a UC roll call. Among the system's prominent graduates are people as diverse as Timothy Leary, the 1960s LSD guru and flower-child leader; Steve Wozniak, cofounder of Apple Computer Systems; and Ralph Bunche, a winner of the Nobel Peace Prize. A Berkeley degree is particularly coveted, as is one from the system's professional schools, especially in law or medicine, because such degrees often guarantee a slot in the upper-middle or upper class. People of color want and need access to these same opportunities, and for the time being, elite universities are the main vehicle for obtaining them.

But access to such opportunities is hard to get. During the debates about affirmative action, little, if any, attention was paid to availability of seat space in the UC system. The California Master Plan for Higher Education says that all California residents in the top eighth of their graduating classes are eligible for admission to the University of California. But there are more students qualified for admission than slots available. This year, for example, UC Berkeley received 30,000 applications from exceptional students. As in previous years, and as is customary at elite institutions, most of those who applied were turned away. Among the 22,000 applicants denied admission were 7,200 students who had 4.0 grade-point averages and median scores of 1,170 on the Scholastic Assessment Test (SAT). Among those 7,200 were 800 students from underrepresented minority groups. Competition has been so fierce over the past few years that the high school grade-point average of admitted students increased from 3.96 in 1996 to 3.99 this year.

Before passage of Proposition 209, many of the minority students with 4.0 grade-point averages and SAT scores of 1,170 would have been admitted. Now they find themselves on the outside looking in while students, both white and minority, with lesser grades but other kinds of qualifying attributes get into Berkeley. More than 4,000 white and Asian American students with 4.0 grade-point averages also failed to gain entry.

While grades and SAT scores are important for admission to the UC system, it obviously takes more. Right now, however, that "more" just cannot be race. Historically, admissions professionals have considered factors such as individual talent, economic background, regional diversity, physical disability, and even the quality of written essays. From an educational point of view, it was believed that exposure to diverse experiences and people added to the quality and depth of education. It is rather ironic that politicians have now determined that the only characteristic that cannot be considered is race.

A Chill on Race Relations

The numbers do not tell the whole story when it comes to the impact of Proposition 209 on higher education. It has affected the climate and culture of almost every campus in California. Most faculty members, administrators, and students still support affirmative action. Students continue to protest, and some faculty members have incorporated deliberations about affirmative action and Proposition 209 into class discussions or have questioned its effects on students and higher education. One student at UC Santa Barbara has filed a legal challenge to Proposition 209, while a student coalition is attempting to qualify an equal-educational-opportunity initiative for the November 1998 ballot. The student coalition has been joined by Berkeley Faculty for Educational Opportunity, a group of professors outraged over the projected drops in minority enrollment.

Even those resigned to the legality of Proposition 209 have not given up on increasing minority participation in higher education. They focus their efforts

on breaking the dominance of grades and SAT scores and push for a greater reliance on other criteria such as socioeconomic status, work experience, regional representation, and potential for growth. While this tactic is not a guarantee, its supporters argue that stressing factors other than grades could increase the percentage of students from underrepresented minority groups in higher education, especially in the elite UC system. They realize, however, that many whites and Asian Americans would also benefit from reliance on these categories.

Some minority students, faculty members, and student service personnel are telling minority students that the UC system is a hostile environment that does not welcome students of color, especially African Americans. This response is met by yet another, from those minority students and faculty who believe that students should not run from the battle. This group argues that staying at the heart of the struggle within the UC system has benefits, both educational and political. "UC belongs to us also and we should not cooperate with the forces of evil and just fade into the sunset," one activist student leader proclaimed. Proposition 209 is also beginning to affect the relationships between European American professors and their minority colleagues. While affirmative action has had minimal results in increasing the numbers of American-born faculty of color in California (especially in the UC and the CSU systems), those who are present report a change in climate and attitude since the measure passed. At least in the past, they point out, lip service was given to the need for affirmative action. But now the subject is seldom mentioned, and some of its opponents have even become bold enough to belittle "those affirmative action appointments that we will not have to make anymore."

It seems as if a new form of "political correctness" has arisen. Faculty of color and discussions of affirmative action are being driven from the radar screen of higher education. When affirmative action is mentioned, it is talked about as something that no longer requires attention. People will say, for example, "We don't have to be concerned with affirmative action; it is illegal," or "We don't have to say we are an affirmative action employer anymore. And we certainly do not have to insert language in job descriptions that favors minorities, do we?" By refusing to use language inviting minority candidates to apply for positions, search committee chairs decline to cooperate with university officials pushing for more diversity in faculty hiring.

A protest against Proposition 209 at the University of California at Berkeley, in 1996. © ED KASHI/CORBIS. REPRODUCED BY PERMISSION.

Faculty of color have responded to this new climate in several ways. Some report anger, while others say they feel abandoned by their European American colleagues. Still others are uncertain as to how to continue the fight for affirmative action and diversity. Most report a definite chill in the air since the passage of Proposition 209, arguing that it is now more difficult to discuss affirmative action and diversity. They feel that the silence around these issues is both deafening and telling. Deep beneath the surface, faculty of color are distressed that former allies appear to have abandoned the cause of affirmative action. For example, a recent faculty search came down to two highly qualified candidates, one African American and female, the other European American and male. In a reference to the television talk show host Oprah Winfrey, some members of the search committee argued against the African American female on the grounds that she would "Oprahize" the department. Several professors who voted for the European American male had previously made big shows of "if we could find a qualified minority, we would surely hire that person." They nonetheless chose to ignore the highly quali-

fied black female and champion the cause of the European American male. Will this be the rule of the day under Proposition 209? Many minority faculty in the UC and CSU systems are bracing themselves for more confrontations of this kind in the future.

For some people of color, Proposition 209 looks suspiciously like legislative vigilantism or an attempt to impose ethnic cleansing in higher education. Despite the claims of the proposition's advocates that it seeks only to treat everyone equally, progressive European Americans and people of color see it as a meanspirited and cleverly directed attempt to put affirmative action in blackface and scapegoat nonwhite minorities. Chanting their mantra of "we want a color-blind society," the proponents of Proposition 209 are trying to sell the absurd notion that racism does not exist. This is absolutely infuriating to people of color who have to live with the consequences of racism every day.

How are our youth of all races responding to the adult battles over affirmative action? Do we really want young European Americans to believe that racism is a thing of the past? Do we want young people of color to believe that they are being abandoned by politically motivated European Americans? In the past ten years, California has built more prisons (ten) than colleges (three), and none of these colleges are in the UC system. The message is that California will make enough room in prison for people of color but not in higher education. If the elimination of affirmative action denies opportunity and hope to young people of color, the consequences may be disastrous. Today, there are more young African American males in prisons in California than in colleges or universities. While the prisoners' futures may be in jeopardy, it certainly is not too late for their brothers and sisters of color. Do we really want to send a message that they are expendable and that society does not care? Do we want to deprive the European American students in our elite institutions of the opportunity to interact with people of color? People know when they are being toyed with, and our youth are no exception. When they see and hear proponents of Proposition 209 playing games with words and changing the meaning of sacred concepts like justice, equity, and equality, they take it in and make judgments and decisions that affect their future participation in society. They know that affirmative action was introduced in higher education because access to the educational system is not equal. Now that affirmative action is being taken away in California, little remains in its place, especially at elite institutions. Are we sure we are sending the right message with the passage of Proposition 209?

Further Resources

BOOKS

Chavez, Lydia. *The Color Bind: California's Battle to End Affirmative Action*. Berkeley, Calif.: University of California Press, 1998.

Ong, Paul M. *Impacts of Affirmative Action: Policies and Consequences in California*. Walnut Creek, Calif.: AltaMira Press, 1999.

Raza, M. Ali. *The Ups and Downs of Affirmative Action Preferences*. Westport, Conn.: Praeger, 1999.

PERIODICALS

Barkan, Joanne. "Affirmative Action: Second Thoughts." *Dissent* 45, no. 3, Summer 1998, 5–10.

Burgan, Mary. "Access: A Matter of Justice." *Academe* 84, no. 4, July/August 1998, 72.

Mortenson, Thomas G., Deborah J. Carter, and Michael A. Olivas. "A Conversation About Access and Diversity." *Academe* 84, no. 4, July/August 1998, 41–44.

WEBSITES

"AAD Project Proposition 209." Available online at http://aad.english.ucsb.edu/pages/Prop-209.html; website home page: http://www./aad.english.ucsb.edu (accessed April 27, 2003).

CADAP Home Page. Available online at http://www.cadap.org/ (accessed April 27, 2003).

NASULGC: Kellogg Commission on the Future of State and Land-Grant Universities. Available online at http://www.nasulgc.org/Kellogg/kellogg.htm; website home page: http://www.nasulgc.org (accessed April 29, 2003).

"Bill Gates on Education, Philanthropy, and Track Balls"

Interview

By: Bill Gates

Date: March 3, 1999

Source: Gates, Bill. "Bill Gates on Education, Philanthropy, and Track Balls." *Education Week* 18, no. 25, March 3, 1999.

About the Author: Bill Gates (1955–) is the co-founder and chairman of Microsoft, which produces more computer software than any other company in the world. Its trademark Windows system alone is used by more than three-fourths of the world's computer users. Gates built Microsoft from the ground up, beginning in 1975, when he and co-founder Paul Allen offered to write software for MIT's Altair 8800, a do-it-yourself computer for hobbyists. In 1979, Microsoft moved to Seattle, and a year later it acquired the precursor to MS-DOS from another company, which it licensed to IBM for use on the first personal computers, introduced in 1981. When the company went public five years later, Gates was made the youngest billionaire ever. ■

Introduction

During the 1990s, phrases like the "digital divide" and "digital nervous system" became common. The digital divide was discussed in relation to those who had access to technology and knew how to use it and those who did not. The "digital nervous system" is the connection between systems, applications, and information in computing environments.

Bill Gates, the founder of Microsoft, was part of the effort to bridge the digital divide and build the digital nervous system. In 1999, he announced the Schools Interoperability Framework (SIF), a system to define technical standards. Several companies, including Jostens Learning Corporation and Chancery Software, joined the project when Gates made his announcement. The standards were meant to allow a number of different software applications to become compatible. When schools changed software or upgraded to new machines, information was often lost because of incompatibility issues.

By 2003, pilot projects were running to demonstrate how the SIF was working.

Gates also played a critical role in increasing access to technology in educational institutions and public libraries. Through the Bill and Melinda Gates Foundation, grants allowed for the purchase of hardware and software and for training people, particularly those living in low-income areas, to use technology.

Significance

Standards for technology were developed across the industry, not just at Microsoft. The involvement of many companies across operating platforms was critical for any standards that were developed to succeed. The SIF website stated that the Schools Interoperability Framework is an industry initiative to develop an open specification for ensuring that K-12 instructional and administrative software applications worked together more effectively. SIF was not a product but rather an industry-supported technical blueprint for K-12 software that enabled diverse applications to interact and share data seamlessly. Schools used various software packages to track student grades, attendance, and other records. Compatibility within a district and across districts saved time and effort for school employees. Software could also make communication easier between teachers and parents.

In addition to the record-keeping functions, schools used computers for student learning. The ability to create educational tools for and with students changed the opportunities for learning. As Gates noted in his interview, authoring software would provide tools for students and teachers to work together on projects and presentations for greater learning. Hands-on involvement in learning was often more successful than watching or listening to presentations. Students who were actively engaged in their own learning would develop skills and retain information more than if they were passive learners.

Providing access to information in an organized fashion was vital for the Internet to be truly useful in education and other areas. Learning how to access, search for, and evaluate sources on the Internet was a crucial skill for students to learn. By providing access to technology through the classroom and in public libraries, students and adults had the opportunity to learn how to navigate information and could become comfortable with the digital nervous system.

Primary Source

"Bill Gates on Education, Philanthropy, and Track Balls"

SYNOPSIS: Bill Gates supported education and libraries through philanthropic giving. The Bill and Melinda Gates Foundation helped correct inequities that had occurred in schools. The foundation also partnered with public libraries to provide greater access to technology.

How do you think the "digital nervous system" will make an impact in the classroom? Will classroom teachers actually be better teachers, and learners better learners?

The digital-nervous-system vision is about access to information, that if you really empower people, get all the information out there and make it easy to find, it will enhance their curiosity and improve their ability to do analysis and make decisions.

Students are the ultimate example of that—where their job, if you call it that, is to learn. And the school wants to reinforce their general learning skills and their confidence so that they can solve tough problems. So if you're bringing the Internet into it, where they can browse, find the latest things, and as a group share what they find on the Internet and talk about those things, I think the impact is pretty dramatic, because the amount of sharing that's going to go on, and the amount of authoring that's going to go on by teachers and students, will be incredible.

In the past, students and teachers couldn't write textbooks. If they found a way of explaining something or making something fun to learn, they could contribute at their single classroom, but there was no leverage for any of the great ideas they had.

Well, in this Internet environment, they're not just users, they're contributors as well. So getting the authoring software, things like [Microsoft] Office and Front Page, into the mix has been part of our initiative.

Will the Schools Interoperability Framework have Windows as an essential requirement?

No. The Schools Interoperability Framework is a way of describing data, and so it can work with software that runs on any computer system. It's not at all Windows-specific, in the same way that we created the whole PC era by defining the standards of the PCs. PCs can run many different kinds of software. It's something we did to grow the industry—you know, achieve the potential.

In the case of the Schools Interoperability Framework, it's not biased towards any Microsoft software.

We ourselves don't write the application software. We're a great neutral party to pull this together and define it in a way that doesn't favor one

Bill Gates visits the Martin Luther King Library in Washington, D.C., on June 4, 1997. He had recently donated $1 million in cash and computer equipment to the library system. **AP/WIDE WORLD PHOTOS. REPRODUCED BY PERMISSION.**

school registration system over another. It works very, very well with all the different educational software packages.

You've given a great deal of your own money to libraries and to universities. What are your philanthropic plans for schools?

I've given a lot to private schools; for the school I went to, Lakeside [School in Seattle], I've done quite a bit.

The libraries was a clear thing where there was an opportunity to just go from a small percentage of libraries having the Internet and PCs to making sure that they all had them. And the contribution—although the financial part was a big part of it, buying the hardware and everything—actually the biggest impact has been the support people, the training people, the standard configurations.

With [public] schools, I have made contributions, but it's a more complex area in terms of where philanthropy comes in.

Schools often have combinations of Macintosh and Windows computers that make it difficult to purchase software. Is it an impossible dream for software applications to work across both platforms seamlessly, and do educators need to abandon that idea?

Well, there's no magic in the world. You're never going to have software made for one machine automatically run on the other [platform] and take advantage of what it does. People who use Macintoshes don't want Windows; they want the Macintosh user interface. They don't even want the same software that runs on the other machine. The idea that they'd have something that wouldn't exploit the

Mac is a very negative thing, if that's what you've bought.

So, the idea that software needs to be tailored to a particular machine, that's just a fact, and nothing's going to change that. We write as much software for the Macintosh as anyone except for Apple itself. We have some software we've chosen just to do on Windows because of the volume that's there.

What do you think policymakers should do to address the "digital divide," especially when homes are so different in the resources they have, and schools are trying to mediate between high-tech homes and homes that don't have anything but a phone?

The price of the PC is coming down, and the penetration has gone up pretty radically. I do think that if kids in their after-school hours, through community centers and libraries, can go in and have access to a PC, that's another leveling factor. That's why I gave a gift to make that possible in every library in the country.

Things like the [Microsoft] laptop program, where the parents get involved in paying a monthly fee [to lease a laptop computer], we've been impressed at how many parents have been interested in signing up to that. The program is in over 500 schools today, and we're going to see if we can spread it further, faster.

Could you tell me something you have learned about learning and computing in schools from watching your daughter in a technologically rich environment?

My daughter's not quite 3 yet, so I wouldn't say there's some grand learning. She loves using the computer software. She's learned her numbers and her letters, and she probably uses it about 50 minutes a day. She's playing around with it, and we're always sitting there with her, doing it together. She has that big track ball. You know kids at that age, maybe some use the mouse, but the track ball works because their hands are so small, and it just stays wherever they put it.

And you know, she's very lucky to have access at that age with those tools. When you see her fascination and how much she gets out of it, you think, "Boy, wouldn't it be nice if everybody's kids could have the same thing?" Certainly, when I grew up, there was nothing like it.

Further Resources

BOOKS

Andrews, Paul. *How the Web Was Won: Microsoft from Windows to the Web.* New York: Broadway Books, 1999.

Burge, Elizabeth, ed. *The Strategic Use of Learning Technologies.* San Francisco: Jossey-Bass, 2000.

Gates, Bill. *Business @ the Speed of Thought: Using a Digital Nervous System.* New York: Warner, 1999.

PERIODICALS

Cradler, John. "Research on E-Learning." *Learning and Leading with Technology* 30, no. 5, February 2003, 54–57.

Krasprowicz, Tim. "Managing the Classroom with Technology: On Progress Reports and Online Communications, and How to Manage the Two Different Communication Techniques." *Tech Directions* 61, no. 10, May 2002, 26–28.

WEBSITES

Bill and Melinda Gates Foundation. Available online at http://www.gatesfoundation.org/default.htm (accessed April 30, 2003).

Schools Interoperability Framework. Available online at http://www.sifinfo.org (accessed April 30, 2003).

"Analysis: What the Two Young Colorado Gunmen Were Really Like"

Radio broadcast

By: National Public Radio

Date: April 24, 1999

Source: National Public Radio. "Analysis: What the Two Young Colorado Gunmen Were Really Like." NPR News Weekend Edition, April 24, 1999. Available online at http://www.npr.org/transcripts/index.html; website home page: http://www.npr.org (accessed February 21, 2003). ∎

Introduction

On April 20, 1999, Dylan Klebold and Eric Harris began their day in an ordinary way—at the bowling alley. Later that morning, they carried two duffel bags into Columbine High School, each containing a twenty-pound propane bomb. The bags were placed in the cafeteria and set to go off at 11:17 A.M. When they did not detonate as planned, Klebold and Harris entered the suburban Denver school with explosives and semiautomatic weapons and began shooting students in what would be the deadliest instance of high school violence to date. After about forty-five minutes, twelve students and one teacher were dead and the two shooters had committed suicide. Twenty-three other students were wounded, some seriously.

This was only one incident in a wave of school violence that swept across the country in the 1990s. From small towns in Tennessee and Arkansas to suburbs in Oregon and Georgia, students were taking weapons to

Eric Harris. AP/WIDE WORLD PHOTOS. REPRODUCED BY PERMISSION.

school and shooting classmates. The question of why these troubling incidents took place was debated in schools, communities, and the halls of Congress. Television, video games, music, and the Internet were all pointed to as causes, along with a deterioration of family in America. The boys in Littleton, Colorado, were honor students from affluent families. Other boys in towns across the country fit a similar profile. Why would these children become killers? The answer seemed to rest in the isolation that teens experienced when others taunted and excluded those viewed as being different from the "normal" crowd.

The media sought answers from classmates and parents in the days following the shootings. Klebold and Harris were described as boys who had become progressively aggressive. Other students, who remained anonymous, described the "pure hell" of high school and blamed the treatment by "jocks" who taunted and tormented a group of students who were perceived as outcasts.

Significance

The Columbine shootings focused the nation on violence in the schools. Congress held hearings in which students, who had survived the incidents in Colorado as well as other places around the country, were asked to

testify. Students told members of Congress that laws would not help. Teenagers needed to be listened to and paid attention to in order to end the violence that was taking place. The target of the shootings seemed to be athletes whom Klebold and Harris thought mistreated them. An anonymous columnist in *The North American Review* wondered about the glorification of high school athletes. While he did not wish to disparage athletes, he pointed out that all students' interests and talents must be recognized and rewarded, not just those of a select group of students.

The governor of Colorado formed a commission to review the incident and issued a report outlining Klebold and Harris's actions and the results of their violence. The boys had spent a year planning the destructive day. Teachers and others had noted signs of their growing violence and aggression. Along with the governor's commission, the federal government created programs to examine youth violence and debated stronger gun legislation.

Schools responded to Columbine by enforcing tighter security. Police officers or security guards, metal detectors, and surveillance cameras were commonplace in many schools across the country in the early twenty-first century. Bomb threats were taken more seriously than they were in earlier decades. The best prevention seemed to be awareness of students' actions and listening when other teens said something might be wrong. Signs were present that Klebold and Harris both felt like outcasts. They had presented videotapes portraying shootings of jocks. The neighbors heard the sounds of their bomb-making efforts coming from the garage. If the signs had been taken seriously, perhaps the tragedy that changed the lives of the students on April 20, 1999, would have been averted.

Primary Source

"Analysis: What the Two Young Columbine Gunmen Were Really Like"

> **SYNOPSIS:** In the days following the massacre at Columbine High School, the media interviewed the victims' friends and classmates and members of the community about the tragedy. Everyone was seeking an answer to why two high school seniors would walk into their school with semiautomatic weapons and gun down other students. The interviews yielded speculation but no concrete answers.

Daniel Zwerdling, host: Of course, investigators are still trying to gather pieces of evidence to complete that puzzle. What were the two suspects in the massacre really like? What were their motives? NPR's Barbara Bradley reports from Littleton.

Barbara Bradley reporting: The home of Eric Harris is dark and shuttered. No cars in the driveway; no sign of life. Neighbors say it has been this way ever since the Harrises moved to this new, affluent cul-de-sac less than two years ago. Karen Good, who lives next door, says nobody in the neighborhood really knows the family.

Ms. Karen Good (Neighbor): We never really saw them much together as a family, like outside, doing things together or going places together or that kind of stuff. Like my one son said— he made the comment once he saw the father and the son out one time in the front yard together, and they didn't even speak to each other, hardly.

Bradley: After Tuesday's massacre at Columbine High School, these small details have taken on deeper significance. So, too, have the confrontations between other students in the school and the so-called Trench Coat Mafia, the group to which Eric Harris and Dylan Klebold belonged. Sophomore Chris Duven is an athlete and self-described "jock." He remembers a confrontation last year when the leader of the Trench Coat Mafia approached his table in the high school commons, where Duven was talking with other jocks on the wrestling team.

Chris Duven (Student, Columbine High School): He said, "Whoever's a real man stand up." And so me and three of my—or two of my friends stood up. So we went outside and they got all their little clan. There was, like, 12—no, 10 of them, and we were going to fight. And then all of a sudden the door opens behind us and, like, the whole commons just, like, came out and were backing us up, like—and I think that could have been, like, a big point in their life where they had a beef with the jocks.

Bradley: Whether a turning point or not, it symbolizes the isolation the Trench Coat kids felt. One member of the group, who wouldn't give his name, told The Denver Post that school life for him and his friends was, quote, "pure hell." He said athletes often threw rocks at them, slammed them against lockers, pelted them with mashed potatoes and other food at lunchtime. The group of outcasts banded together out of misery, this boy said, and they began to hone their image: black trench coats, a taste for German techno music, the dark

Dylan Klebold. AP/WIDE WORLD PHOTOS. REPRODUCED BY PERMISSION.

video games like the one called Doom. Sophomore Joshua Lapp says people steered clear of the group's members as they became increasingly aggressive.

Joshua Lapp (Student, Columbine High School): They weren't part of any group except for their own. They didn't associate with people. I mean, you could walk down the hall, you know, and see people, say hi to them, and they'd just get up in their face and say, "What do you mean, 'Hi'?" You know, "What's your problem?" You know, "What do you mean, 'Hi'?" I just thought that that was strange.

Bradley: Lapp and others say the students in the Trench Coat Mafia appeared to adopt Adolf Hitler as their hero. They were heard speaking German to each other, and some painted swastikas on their coats with Wite-Out. Alex Panneo(ph), a psychiatrist who works with troubled youth at the Adolescent and Family Institute of Colorado, notes there's an irony to the fact that the gunmen targeted athletes during the shootout. They were destroying the kinds of people Hitler wanted to reproduce his master race. But, he says, the apparent

On April 29, 1999, a mourner reaches out to touch a cross, part of a memorial to the fifteen people killed in the Columbine High School. © STEVE STARR/CORBIS. REPRODUCED BY PERMISSION.

contradiction only shows how alienated and confused they were.

Dr. Alex Panneo (Adolescent and Family Institute of Colorado): They really don't value anyone else that doesn't 100 percent agree, identify and enjoin them. And if you just think about the absurdity of that, you become a very small, very select, probably very paranoid little group. More than likely they will become violent, because the more they sense that they're right by virtue of being rejected by others, the more they have to redeem their inner sense of loss and become very powerful and aggressive.

Bradley: Panneo says the gunmen also targeted those they perceived as weak. For example, they shot a boy with cerebral palsy, and they appeared to single out racial minorities and Christians. Friends believe the gunmen knew 17-year-old Cassie Bernall because she had once been in a fringe group, then she became a born-again Christian, moving into the main-

stream of church and school life. Her friend Kevin Kerniger(ph) notes that with automatic weapons, the shooters could have easily gunned down everyone in the library that day, but chose to speak only to Cassie.

Kevin Kerniger (Friend of Shooting Victim): They went up to her and said, "Do you believe in Jesus?" And she paused for a long time, and then she said, "Yes, I love Jesus." And they said, "Why?" And then they shot her. And then they proceeded over to, I believe his name is Isaac, and the man said, "There's a nigger over here" and then they shot him.

Bradley: The boy, Isaiah Shoels, was one of only a handful of African-Americans at Columbine. There's still speculation about what exactly went on inside the minds of the gunmen, and the writings of suspect Eric Harris create a complex picture. In a posting on his Web site last year, he wrote, quote, "You know what I hate? Racism. Don't let me catch you making fun of someone just because they're a different color." People who knew Harris and Klebold but were not themselves in the Trench Coat Mafia described the pair as weird, but funny. Even the juvenile court officer who met with the boys after they broke into a car last year was taken with them. In his report, the so-called diversion officer described Harris and Klebold as "bright young men with a great deal of potential." Psychiatrist Alex Panneo isn't surprised by people's positive impressions.

Dr. Panneo: One of the components of a good sociopath is that the naïve person experiences them as charming and intelligent and bright and articulate, and, you know, those are all red flags as far as I'm concerned. At the same time that they were presenting all of these wonderful, endearing characteristics to, you know, this diversion officer, they were making bombs and plotting this destruction.

Bradley: Barbara Bradley, NPR News, Littleton, Colorado.

Further Resources

BOOKS

Hasday, Judy L. *Columbine High School Shooting: Student Violence.* Berkeley Heights, N.J.: Enslow, 2002.

PERIODICALS

"The Monsters Next Door: A Special Report on the Colorado School Massacre." *Time,* May 3, 1999.

"Special Report: Massacre in Colorado. Why? Portraits of the Killers, The Science of Teen Violence." *Newsweek,* May 3, 1999.

"Values: Will Columbine High Teach Us Anything?" *North American Review,* May/August 1999, 1, 6.

WEBSITES

Columbine High School. Available online at http://jeffcoweb .jeffco.k12.co.us/profiles/high/columbine.html; website home page: http://jeffcoweb.jeffco.k12.co.us (accessed April 27, 2003).

Governor's Columbine Review Commission Report. Available online at http://www.state.co.us/columbine/ (accessed April 27, 2003).

AUDIO AND VISUAL MEDIA

Glasser, William. *The Lessons of Littleton.* Quality Educational Media. VHS. 1999.

Evolution and the Kansas State School System

Kansas State Board of Education Meeting Minutes

Meeting minutes

By: Kansas Board of Education
Date: August 11, 1999
Source: Kansas State Department of Education. Kansas State Board of Education Meeting Minutes, August 11, 1999. Available online at http://www.ksbe.state.ks.us/Welcome.html (accessed April 29, 2003).
About the Organization: The Kansas State Board of Education oversaw public educational standards in the state of Kansas. The board met periodically to discuss issues in education and to approve changes to the curriculum. The board was charged with providing leadership for the state educational institutions while still acknowledging the importance of local control.

"Evolution Is Science"

Letter

By: Dr. Douglas Ruden; Dr. Paulyn Cartwright; and Dr. Bruce Lieberman
Date: July 1, 1999
Source: Ruden, Dr. Douglas, Dr. Paulyn Cartwright, and Dr. Bruce Lieberman. "Evolution Is Science." *Topeka Capital Journal,* July 1, 1999. Available online at http://www .cjonline.com/stories/070199/opi_letters30.shtml; website home page: http://www.cjonline.com (accessed May 5, 2003).

"Room for All Science"

Letter

By: Larry Bowden
Date: August 30, 1999
Source: Bowden, Larry. "Room for All Science." *Topeka Capital Journal,* August 30, 1999. Available online at http://www.cjonline.com/stories/083099/opi_letters30.shtml; website home page: http://www.cjonline.com (accessed May 5, 2003). ■

Introduction

In 1998 the Kansas State Board of Education formed a committee to revise the Kansas Science Education Standards. This committee consisted of teachers, science educators, and scientists. Open forums were held and the draft curriculum update, which had gained approval from national science organizations, was forwarded to the board for examination. The plan that was presented to the board was not significantly different from the one in place at the time. The draft was based on the standards published by the National Research Council, the American Association for the Advancement of Science, and the National Science Teachers Association, according to Dr. Loren Lutes, the co-chair of the Kansas Board of Education's Science Standards.

At the board's August 11, 1999, meeting, the opposition was prepared with an alternative plan. Three members of the board—Celtie Johnson, Linda Hollaway, and Steve Abrams—composed the alternative plan, which included fifty changes to the draft plan. Among them was the removal of macroevolution from the state's science standards in favor of a literal interpretation of the biblical story of creation.

A nationwide debate resulted after the board voted 6 to 4 to remove references to evolution from the state standards. The board minutes reflect the discussion that took place in which some of the board members asked for further discussion but others wanted an immediate vote. The *Topeka Capital Journal* printed a number of letters from both sides of the argument, reflecting that the citizens of the state were divided on the issue.

Significance

The debate over teaching evolution versus teaching creationism was not new. The Scopes Monkey Trial in the 1920s was a political battle as well as one of religion and First Amendment rights. The Kansas decision sparked debate over the role of religion in the schools and fueled opponents of the teaching of evolution across the country to seek similar actions in their states. Despite national movements, such as Project 2061, to strengthen the science curriculum and assure that all students reached a level of scientific literacy to provide knowledge for the twenty-first century, Kansas seemed to be taking a step backwards and similar controversies arose in Oklahoma, Illinois, Ohio, Arizona, and New Mexico. Essays and letters to the editor appeared not only in Kansas newspapers but also in the major daily U.S. papers and in science and education journals.

Eugenie C. Scott, executive director of the National Center for Science Education, wrote that "even though the Supreme Court has ruled that teaching creationism and creation 'science' are unconstitutional, we still get calls from parents, teachers, or school board members asking whether some impending resolution in their district requiring 'equal time' for creationism is appropriate." She goes on to explain that many districts violate the Constitution by teaching creationism and that the sentiment of the public seems to approve of this move.

The conservative school board members in Kansas overruled the moderate members, and what followed for Kansas was more than a year of negative publicity na-

tionally and even internationally. Two of the board members, including Linda Hollaway, the board chair, were defeated in primaries held in August 2000. The third member who supported the alternative plan resigned. With a new board in place, the Kansas State Board of Education restored evolution to the standards on February 14, 2001.

Primary Source

Kansas State Board of Education Meeting Minutes [excerpt]

SYNOPSIS: The decision about removing the teaching of evolution from the public school curriculum in Kansas ignited debate over values, teaching, and science. The Kansas State Board of Education faced national scrutiny following the decision to delete evolution from the curriculum.

Science Education Standards

Dr. John Staver, Co-Chair of the Science Standards writing committee, recognized committee members who were present and asked Dr. Loren Lutes, Co-Chair of the Committee, to report on the latest update of the Kansas science education standards. Dr. Lutes indicated the committee had met in May and June in open public session and the result was the Fifth Draft of the Kansas Science Standards which the committee recommended be adopted. He indicated the standards in their current form had the support of the Kansas Association of Teachers of Science, Kansas Association of School Superintendents, Unified School Administrators, KNEA, the Governor and the Regents presidents and had been reviewed and supported by outside evaluators and national science organizations. He indicated the high level of support was due to the fact the standards were based on national standards and the 1992 and 1995 Kansas standards. He indicated they had been scrutinized in every school building across the state and by citizens in a series of public hearings and that every oral or written comment had been considered. He further indicated that the standards had 100% support of the science standards writing committee and that no minority report had been proposed. He added that the committee was ready to provide leadership for inservice training, workshops and conferences for teachers and to assist in the development of testing strategies and writing assessment items. Dr. Lutes also stated the committee could not support the compromise standards being proposed which had made fifty significant changes to the committee's work, indicating that it was incomplete in its treatment of science

A Shawnee Mission West High School science teacher reviews an upcoming test with his Biology II honors students in October 1999. The Shawnee Mission school district opted out of the Kansas guidelines omitting the theory of evolution from state science standards. **AP/WIDE WORLD PHOTOS. REPRODUCED BY PERMISSION.**

and unacceptable with the near deletion of standards relating to the theory of origins and the removal of many assessment items. Dr. Staver handed out a chart of the changes that the writing committee had made in light of comments from the public and Board members. He indicated that the writing committee's standards were strongly based on and text was used from standards published by the National Research Council, the American Association for the Advancement of Science, and the National Science Teachers Association, and those organizations would need to review the whole text of whatever document was approved before allowing text from their standards to be incorporated. He recommended that whichever set of standards were adopted be examined very carefully by the Attorney General and the Board attorney in light of any potential legal problem. He also stated that of the members of the committee who had responded to communication from him, a little more than 50%, all asked that their names be removed from the document if the compromise standards were adopted. He

indicated the committee also wished to have the dedication replaced with one of the Board's own if the alternative standards were adopted. Dr. Staver closed his presentation by reading the Roman Catholic Church's official position statement on evolution, written by Pope John Paul II.

Mr. Hill offered a substitute motion, that the State Board approve Kansas Curricular Standards for Science as recommended by the State Board Subcommittee with the following changes:

Page 6, paragraph 1, sentence 2: change shall to should;

Page 6, paragraph 2, sentence 3: change shall to should;

Page 6, paragraph 2, sentence 3: change censured to censored;

Page 8 and 9: change items starting at Science as Inquiry through the History and Nature of Science to bulleted items under the heading Standards on page 8;

Page 36, Indicator 4: change to read "Suggest alternative scientific hypotheses or theories to current scientific hypotheses or theories;

Page 90: eliminate paragraphs 2, 3 and 4;

Page 91: eliminate paragraphs 1-4

Page 90 & 91-92: move the remaining language to Appendix 1 under Falsification on page 87; Remove all assessment flags throughout the document and refer to staff for recommendations on assessment items.

Dr. Abrams seconded the motion. Discussion followed.

Dr. Wagnon stated he could not support the substitute motion. He stated for individual board members to arrogate to themselves the responsibility of rewriting the proposal of the field committee appeared to do a great disservice to the relationship the Board should have with the field across the state. He noted that the Board depends heavily on volunteers from the field to spend countless hours on research at the Board's request to bring to the Board recommendations for a wide variety of issues. He stated his belief that when reports from the field do not conform to predetermined expectations it undermines the credibility of the Board's request to the field. He indicated that it was important in fulfilling its duty of general supervision for the Board to maintain a working relationship with the field and that to rewrite the standards based on a particular agenda reflecting the personal beliefs of a few members of the Board was doing a great disservice to that relationship. He further stated his concern about the changes the subcommittee had made to the standards and their effect on the quality of the holistic document. He indicated that to pick and choose certain items in life science and earth science to remove from the standards and to change the nature of science, left the students of the state with academic expectations that had been dumbed down. He stated that the result was a document that was fatally flawed and he could not support the substitute motion. Mrs. DeFever, reading from a prepared statement, stated that though she had been able to follow the changes made in the writing committee's Fifth Draft, she had been unable to clearly follow all the changes that had been made by the subcommittee. She indicated that if another committee had submitted a set of standards in a similar form, Board members would require a final cleaned-up draft before considering taking a final vote. Mrs. DeFever questioned the qualifications of

the three-Board-member subcommittee to do an adequate job of rewriting the science standards and stated she was skeptical how the alterations done by them had affected the standards. She indicated she was not sure what the implications of the changes had in the realm of real science and she was unable to support the subcommittee's document.

Chairman Holloway stated her firm support of the subcommittee's proposal. She then called for a vote on the substitute motion, with six Board members voting in favor and the subcommittee's proposal was adopted. Those who did not vote in favor were Mrs. DeFever, Mr. Rundell, Dr. Wagnon and Mrs. Waugh.

Primary Source

"Evolution Is Science"

SYNOPSIS: Opinions in Kansas on the teaching of evolution in the schools were divided. In this letter to the editor of the *Topeka Capital Journal*, three scientists at the University of Kansas defend evolutionary theory.

We would like to respond to some of the lies that creationists such as Klint Kegel, in his June 11 letter to the editor, have been recycling in their attack on evolution. In his letter, Mr. Kegel claims that "Since Darwin presented his theory 160 years ago, scientists have been trying to find any shred of evidence to support the theory (of macroevolution) and in all this time they have not found even one example."

"Macroevolution" means that a species of animal is split into two populations of animals which cannot form fertile offspring. It has been known for over 50 years that species often come into existence when their chromosome number changes. In fact, scientists, including one of us (Douglas Ruden), have generated hundreds of new species of the fruit fly by such means. This is evidence that speciation, or "macroevolution" as Mr. Kegel refers to it, is continuing to this day.

The second lie that we will correct is Mr. Kegel's claim that "ontogeny recapitulates phylogeny" has no scientific basis. This was an idea developed by Ernst Haeckel in the 19th century that means "the development of an organism resembles the evolution of that organism." One of us (Paulyn Cartwright) is an evolutionary developmental biologist. While Haeckel's theory, that human development can be seen to pass through stages like those of adult stages of more primitive species, is not generally accepted by modern biologists, it is still discussed because of the important principles it implies.

Haeckel realized that clues about evolution can be found by studying the development of organisms. Even today, studies of development play an important role in evolutionary biology. For instance, in the past decade many genes that control development have been found in different organisms. Across animals as different as humans and flies, such genes function in the same way.

Finally, Mr. Kegel argued that although microevolution has been amply demonstrated, macroevolution has no factual basis. One of us (Bruce Lieberman) is a paleontologist in the Department of Geology at the University of Kansas who studies macroevolution in the fossil record, and can explain that nothing is further from the truth. There are several scientific journals and books devoted to the study of macroevolution in the fossil record, and it is an active area of research. Over the past 140 years paleontologists studying the fossil record have uncovered numerous examples of evolution in action. Among the most famous of these examples was the 19th century discovery of the fossil Archaeopteryx from 180 million-year-old rocks in Germany. It represents a perfect transitional link between large land animals and birds.

However, there are numerous examples of more recent research that have shown how macroevolution occurs in the fossil record. One involves the Cambrian Explosion. This is an important episode in the history of life when the first animals appeared in the fossil record and started to diversify. Some creationists have suggested that the explosion occurred instantaneously.

It is being actively studied by several paleontologists at KU and elsewhere. These scientists have shown that the different major animal groups evolved over a 20 million year period beginning roughly 550 million years ago.

Regardless of what they can tell us about rates of macroevolution, studies of the Cambrian Explosion do not challenge the existence of God. Many of the scientists who study evolution have strong religious convictions, yet they accept the evidence, as we do, that macroevolution is a confirmed fact, as well documented as the fact that the Earth revolves around the sun.

■ ■ ■

Primary Source

"Room for All Science"

SYNOPSIS: In this letter to the editor of the *Topeka Capital Journal* from Minister Larry Bowden defends Creation science.

In a land whose people have fought and died for the freedom of speech and thought, the issue over creation science and evolution has brought out the worst in human beings. I am a Christian and a pastor (who is educated with a master's degree). I have also been a part-time substitute teacher in New York State. My wife and I fully support our public schools, administrators and teachers. We are directly involved in our children's education by being involved in positive, constructive ways.

But according to many of your readers who have written, because I believe in creationism, I am extreme and narrow-minded. I am a religious zealot. Creation science is not a religion or a superstition or a mindless extreme viewpoint. It is another explanation of how the universe and the Earth were formed. Creation science and evolution are both theories, because the beginning of the universe and the Earth cannot be duplicated in a laboratory. Science, therefore, is the search for evidence and then the drawing of conclusions.

The same evidence that evolution gives for its theories is strong evidence that our universe was formed out of the mind of a master designer. Both sides of this issue have to accept their beliefs on faith.

Christians look at the universe and marvel at all the complexity and harmony that exists. We encourage the study of science because we see the handiwork of a master designer. There is not a single Christian who wants to go back to the dark ages of medicine based on hocus pocus and scientific superstitions. We believe in an ongoing search for scientific truth.

Christians are not looking to overtake the world and force people to accept our beliefs. We believe that God has given us free will and the ability to think. That seems to be the goal of those who hold dearly to evolution. So what is the problem? Are science teachers and professors so intimidated by creation science that they cannot open their minds to another possibility? Yes, the religious world during Galileo's day condemn his theories. They were wrong. But how many times have scientists believed "facts" and realized they were wrong or condemned theories and they have had to recant?

Further Resources

BOOKS

Ackerman, Paul D., and Bob Williams. *Kansas Tornado: The 1999 Science Curriculum Standards Battle.* El Cajon, Calif.: Institute for Creation Research, 1999.

Eldredge, Niles. *The Triumph of Evolution and the Failure of Creationism.* New York: W. H. Freeman, 2000.

Webb, George Ernest. *The Evolution Controversy in America.* Lexington, Ky.: University Press of Kentucky, 1994.

PERIODICALS

"Evolution Returns to Kansas: Board Supports Science Standards." *Skeptical Inquirer,* May/June 2001, 6–7.

Fehrenbach, Carolyn R. "A Kansan Reflects on the 1999 Creationism/Evolution Controversy." *The Educational Forum* 66, Winter 2002, 166–169.

Scott, Eugenia C. "Not (Just) in Kansas Anymore." *Science,* May 5, 2000, 813, 815.

Stewart, Douglas E., Jr. "Going Back in Time: How the Kansas Board of Education's Removal of Evolution from the State Curriculum Violates the First Amendment's Establishment Clause." *Review of Litigation* 20, no. 2, Spring 2001, 549–588.

WEBSITES

Exploring Constitutional Conflicts: The Evolution Controversy. Available online at http://www.law.umkc.edu/faculty/projects/ftrials/conlaw/evolution.htm; website home page: http://www.umkc.edu (accessed April 30, 2003).

Rozen, Laura. "Trouble in the Holy City." *Salon.* Available online at http://www.salon.com/news/feature/1999/09/03/kansas/; website home page: http://www.salon.com (accessed April 30, 2003).

"The 2061 Challenge"

Interview

By: George Nelson; Lin Hundt

Date: 1999

Source: Nelson, George, with Lin Hundt. "The 2061 Challenge: An Interview with Dr. George "Pinky" Nelson, director of Project 2061 of the American Association for the Advancement of Science. *SACNAS News* 3, no. 3, Fall 1999, 33–35.

About the Authors: George Nelson (1950–) was an astronaut for NASA from 1978 to 1989 and a mission specialist on the Space Shuttle flights in 1984, 1986, and 1988. Later he was an associate professor for astronomy at the University of Washington and the director of science, mathematics, and technological education at Western Washington University.

Lin Hundt was associate director and K-12 education manager for the Society for the Advancement of Chicanos and Native Americans in Science (SACNAS), a national organization that encourages Chicano and Native American students to pursue graduate education in the sciences so that they may become researchers or science educators. ■

Introduction

Project 2061, named for the year that Halley's comet was projected to approach the sun, was founded in 1985 by the American Association for the Advancement of Science. The project stressed the importance of mathematical and scientific literacy for all Americans.

Project 2061 published *Science for All Americans* in 1990. It laid the groundwork for changing citizens' thinking about science literacy, which was essential for survival in the twenty-first century. This report talks about "habits of the mind" that develop from studying mathematical and scientific principles. These habits help the normal citizen solve complex problems they face in the world.

Benchmarks for Science Literacy, published in 1993, provides details about what all students should know before they graduate from high school. The guide was written by a team of educators and scientists from around the country. Designed to promote curriculum reform in the sciences, the benchmarks promoted "literacy in science, mathematics, and technology in order to help people live interesting, responsible, and productive lives." The curricular reforms predicted the skills that students would need in an increasingly technological world.

Dr. George D. Nelson, a former astronaut, served as the director of Project 2061 from 1998 to 2002. He moved on to become director of Science, Mathematics and Technology Education at Western Washington University. In his interview with Lin Hundt, Nelson highlights the importance of science for all people because of advances in the field which are changing society and the world. Nelson does not place blame on schools for not teaching science; rather, he seeks solutions for improving the teaching of science and math and preparing future teachers.

Significance

Nelson stresses four points about scientific literacy in his interview: development of the curriculum, lack of qualified teachers, integration of science into the curriculum, and community support. These issues must be addressed in order for scientific literacy to become a normal and expected part of the curriculum.

Changes in the school curriculum cannot begin in college. Science and math must be taught from kindergarten through high school. In an article on science literacy which appeared in *Educational Leadership,* Nelson noted that "more than half of the U.S. population doesn't know that the earth orbits the sun or how scientists figured out that it does." This indicated that American students and adults did not possess even basic science literacy. Students in other countries consistently scored ahead of American students in the math and science arenas.

Lack of science literacy was tied to the lack of qualified teachers. If schools could not hire teachers who had the necessary skills to teach science and math, students would not learn the skills. Project 2061 focused not only on improving the training of teachers but also on updating the textbooks used to learn about science and math. The studies on learning done by Project 2061 revealed that students needed time to explore and ask questions before true learning takes place. Single lessons on topics or concepts did not provide for significant learning.

Integration of scientific literacy into the entire curriculum was also necessary. This did not mean that math and science should be part of every subject but that the curriculum should make sense and progress logically. Being able to measure what students learned had to be accomplished easily.

Finally, without community and parental support, efforts to achieve science literacy, like any educational endeavor, would fail. Support included believing that science and math are important, as well as funding programs which taught these subjects. Project 2061 has been supported by governmental and private funding, but the guidelines it has provided could not solve the problem. Action and interest from the larger community was necessary in order to change attitudes toward the sciences and to stress the importance of scientific knowledge for all Americans.

Primary Source

"The 2061 Challenge" [excerpt]

SYNOPSIS: Dr. George "Pinky" Nelson discusses the importance of drawing students into the field of science. Organizations such as SACNAS help to encourage minority students to pursue careers in the sciences. This fills a gap not only for teachers and researchers but also for role models to encourage younger students to pursue the same path.

SACNAS: I wonder about your sensation of seeing the planet from outside and how that has impacted you.

GN: Well, I would say if there's one common experience that everybody who flies in space has, whether they're Marine test pilots or U.S. Senators or cosmonauts or whatever, is the changed perspective of the planet. I think everyone comes back an environmentalist.

It's not so much that the earth looks fragile—the earth looks like the earth, you know. But it's the overwhelming evidence of the impact that human beings have had on the planet in lots of ways—fires and roads and electric lights and big plumes out in the lakes and rivers. Everywhere you look, it's really obvious that human beings have had a tremendous impact on the planet. And that combined with the perspective of looking sideways through the atmosphere, you get a real impression of just how thin the atmosphere is. So if there's one aspect of the Earth that looks fragile it's just that there's so little air. So you can understand easily why pumping refrigerants or CO^2 into the air can have such a big impact. Because it just doesn't take very much in order to fill up the volume.

I think everyone who flies in space comes back feeling like we need to be better stewards of the planet. And since we're mostly technical people we come back with the notion that technology is not the evil that's caused all of this, but we are a technical species and that technology is probably going be one of the tools we have to employ to overcome the damage we are doing to the planet.

SACNAS: How does that play out in your work at Project 2061? Is there a stewardship or an environmental aspect to the Project?

GN: Well it's certainly one of the core ideas of science literacy that are in Project 2061. And for us, science includes science and mathematics, social science and engineering and technology, too. But in those core ideas are the ideas that we have to consider the impacts of technology. That what we do can have unforeseen consequences, and that technology is necessary for not only understanding more about the world, but for being able to do something about it. So, yeah, those ideas are very core to Project 2061.

SACNAS: How would you define math and science literacy?

GN: Well, we've done that. You have to read our little book, Science for All Americans. It's not an easy thing to say, you can't say it in a sentence. There are certain core ideas about science and math and technology that we think everyone should know to be a literate citizen. And those ideas involve not only understanding and knowing some of the content. It's important to know some of the facts and some of the mechanical manipulations and operations and all that, but it's also important also to understand the nature of the enterprise. How science works, and how engineering and mathematics work. And how groups work. So, it's [acquiring] certain habits of mind to understand the kind of thinking that goes on that makes something scientific. The necessity of evidence and things like that. Those ideas are all expressed in a pretty concise form in

Science for All Americans. Just what knowledge and skills an adult should have to be considered science literate.

SACNAS: What kinds of challenges face Project 2061, or the nation as a whole, in achieving the vision that you are talking about?

GN: Now, there's an easy one! There are tremendous challenges and they vary across the board. In the most general terms, I see the challenges as: one, we don't have good curriculum materials. We're getting pretty good materials in mathematics now, but in science there just aren't good textbooks or good curriculum materials on the web that are going to be useful for having kids learn the important ideas.

Second, there's a tremendous shortage of teachers who are qualified to teach good science and math. And those teachers aren't being produced in the colleges and universities today. And not blaming the colleges of education, because teachers learn their math and their science in the college of arts and sciences. Students, especially students who are going to be elementary and middle teachers, just are not graduating science literate from college, much less from high school. So producing the teachers we need is another huge challenge.

Third is this idea that if you have good curriculum materials and if you have good assessments that can measure students' performance, they still have to be integrated together to make a coherent package that runs K to 13, K to 12. So that you really have some idea of what students are learning all along, the way [we've] targeted the adult literacy goals.

Probably the biggest challenge of all is the policy one. To have the community on board. To really understand that to be successful in the 20th century, 21st century, as both individuals and as cities and regions and as a nation and world, science illiteracy isn't an option. Reform is a very scary word for almost everybody, so we need to get the business community, the parents, the education community, the political community all on board with the idea that change is necessary. Real change, not deck chair stuff, not just changing the number of hours in the day, or teaching physics first or doing one thing or another but really substantially, fundamentally changing the system. And we don't know how to do that yet. They have to stick with it and understand that they aren't going to do it in a year or two years, that this a generation that's got to be involved in improving the system; and when that generation's done, it'll be the next generation's turn. You know, we're never gonna be finished. We can always do better.

SACNAS: How do you ensure that scientists, educators and parents from minority communities take part in that discussion in a really full way?

GN: That's another of the big challenges. I think today that the minority community is, in a large part, left out of this discussion and this is one of the reasons we purposefully called our description of literacy *Science for All Americans.* In the next century, we can't afford to have just a white male elite that's running the scientific community. Our notion is that by promoting literacy, universal literacy, for all students, that if everyone graduates from high school science literate, you're already increasing the pool for those who are actually going to go on and become scientists and engineers by an enormous amount.

SACNAS: What is Project 2061 specifically doing to address that issue within the organization?

GN: Our goal is mostly focused on everybody, so we tend not to work specifically. We don't have a program, say, that's focused on Hispanic kids, but we try to work with those areas where the biggest need is. We're working with a lot of urban areas. And when you do that you're naturally getting those kids. So, we work in Philadelphia and San Antonio, San Francisco and San Diego.

SACNAS: What advice would you give to students who are involved in SACNAS, who are planning to enter science or science education?

GN: My standard advice is, number one, follow your interest.

You will be most successful if you do what really turns you on. Even though it may not seem like the best future career path—you know all the jobs may be in one area, but you're interested in something else. Well, you ought to pursue what you're most interested in because you'll be most successful, you will excel more and you will make your own niche. So that's my first bit of advice.

The second is that there's always another chance, that you will fail at some point in your career and you can always start over. You can always change direction, you can always change careers—the important part is that whatever you are doing, do it one hundred percent.

Don't give up. There's a lot of help out there. Don't be afraid to ask for help, to seek a mentor and hang onto 'em and learn from others. You know, you don't have to do this on your own . . . learn from your peers, from your teachers, from your family. There's a lot of support you can draw on.

Further Resources

BOOKS

Project 2061. *Benchmarks for Science Literacy.* New York: Oxford University Press, 1993.

———. *Blueprints for Reform.* New York: Oxford University Press, 1998.

PERIODICALS

Craven, John. "Science Literacy Through Inquiry, Reading, and Writing in Nature." *Science Scope* 25, no. 3, November/December 2001, 14–19.

Nelson, George D. "Science Literacy for All in the 21st Century." *Educational Leadership* 57, no. 2, October 1999, 14–17.

WEBSITES

Project 2061. Available online at http://www.project2061.org/ (accessed April 29, 2003).

SACNAS. Available online at http://www.sacnas.org/ (accessed April 29, 2003).

4

FASHION AND DESIGN

EUGENIA F. BELL

Entries are arranged in chronological order by date of primary source. For entries with one primary source, the entry title is the same as the primary source title. Entries with more than one primary source have an overall entry title, followed by the titles of the primary sources.

Important Events in Fashion and Design, 1990–1999

1990

- Hot pants and mini skirts are back; tent dresses and pants suits are in.

- New car brands Infiniti, Saturn, and Lexus are introduced.

- Clothing fads include pre-ripped jeans, Ninja Turtle stuff, wide head bands, and sneakers ranging in price from $125 to $175 a pair. The Reebok pump is a new item.

- In February, men's bolo ties are popular items. Designer Ralph Lauren shows them with his Polo line, while rock star Bruce Springsteen is photographed sporting one. These Western-influenced string-thin ties are fastened at the neck with decorative clasps that come in everything from silver to stone, with costs ranging from ten dollars to three hundred dollars.

- In March, *Vogue* declares: "Pretty Makes A Comeback." Designers show softer suits, jackets with softer shoulders, curvy tailoring, and fluid skirts and pants for women. The "power dressing" of the 1980s, with its sharply tailored suits and distinct shoulder pads, is over.

- In April, real estate tycoon Donald John Trump opens his Taj Mahal in Atlantic City, N.J. Architect Francis Xavier Dumont designed the 420-million-square-foot, $1 billion structure. Not everyone is impressed. Nancy Gibbs writes in *Time* that "the façade looks edible, the work of a candy-maker gone mad."

- In July, French designer Claude Montana's fall collection for men features the monochromatic look: black trousers and a black sports coat over a black mock turtleneck.

- In August, French designers such as Hermes, Christian Dior, Ungaro, Yohji Yamamoto, and Pierre Balmain all show generously cut overcoats for men that emphasize a comfortable, relaxed look.

- In September, men's designers, led by Italian designer Giorgio Armani, abandon the stiff tailoring of 1980s "power dressing" and instead turn out suits with more comfortable cuts. Colors remain traditional, with suits turning up in grays and browns.

1991

- Lingerie becomes outerwear. Singer/actress Cher is featured in a black lace bra paired with a black mesh top and blue jeans. Cindy Crawford dons a black lace bodysuit; singer Barbara Streisand wears a cream-colored bustier under a cream blazer; the fall Paris couture shows by Gianni Versace, Chanel, Christian Dior, Christian Lacroix, and Thierry Mugler feature versions of the corseted evening gown.

- In January, American firm I.M. Pei & Partners' new seventy-story tower for the Bank of China in Hong Kong becomes the tallest building in Asia and fifth-highest structure in the world.

- In February, with a nod to 1960s styles, women part their bobbed tresses on the side. Actress Laura Dern and models Linda Evangelista and Claudia Schiffer sport styles with parts—sometimes on the left, other times on the right.

- Psychedelic prints add a splash of color to the otherwise staid world of men's fashion. These colorful designs show up on shirts, jackets, pants, and accessories—but only among a select, and daring, set of men.

- In April, a sour economy inspires high-end designers to cast a creative eye toward frugality. Michael Kors, for example, shows summer suits from his KORS line that are suitable through the fall, while the design team Alphabeta sells a four-in-one reversible coat in silk taffeta.

- Fitness-inspired clothes such as bodysuits, maillots, unitards, and leggings are used as a base for clothes worn outside the gym; designers, such as Paris-based Karl Lagerfeld, show them as part of their ready-to-wear collections. Unlike the items worn in gyms, however, these body-hugging fashions come in fabrics that shimmer and shine.

- In June, sheer tops, worn over bras, are used by women for both day and evening wear. Bras-turned-tops come in everything from leather to lace.

- In July, sport sandals, particularly the popular Teva brand, make a splash. These must-have footwear feature sturdy soles with treads that will not slip on the trail, materials that dry quickly, and strong straps that do not give when being used for hiking or biking.

- Anna Sui has her first show with a fall collection that combines hip and classic lines, such as bright peacoat-style jackets over kilts. Nothing in the show costs more than four hundred dollars.

- Designers abandon the straight and narrow as they show skirts that allow for movement, with features such as pleats, slits, and asymmetric hems. Donna Karan, for example, offers a wool twill sarong for $470.

- In August, the European men's collections feature relaxed, roomy blazers that blur the line between formal office wear and casual dress. These sport coats come in hues of gray, brown, tan, and green.

- In September, long hair makes a comeback, as models Cindy Crawford, Elaine Irwin, and Karen Mulder show off their lengthy locks.

- Donna Karan introduces her first line of men's clothing with a fall collection that includes a navy wool crepe suit, a gray cashmere suit, and a black suit, as well as ties and vests in gold hues.

- In October, as part of the dressing-down trend, American and European design houses, such as Emporio Armani, Basile, Joseph Abboud, and Hugo Boss, feature sport jackets in chenille—a soft, lush fabric—in colors such as cranberry, brown, and blue.

- In November, the Guggenheim Museum taps California-based architect Frank O. Gehry to design a museum of modern art in Bilbao, Spain.

- Coach, started in 1941 with six employees working in a New York City loft, celebrates fifty years in business. Coach bags earned a loyal following, among both men and women, because of their classic look, trademark untreated leather, and brass fittings inspired by saddlery from the eighteenth and nineteenth centuries. To mark the occasion, Coach reissues limited-edition originals such as the "dinky shopping bag," releases new designs, and updates traditional bags in colors such as golden yellow and deep pink.

- In December, Giorgio Armani launches his first A/X: Armani Exchange in New York. The store carries the Armani Jeans label as well as a complete collection of casual clothes.

1992

- In January, renovations are under way on the Boston Public Library, a National Landmark designed by McKim, Mead & White and built between 1888 and 1894.

- In February, spring runway shows feature classic twin sets—lightweight knit shells worn under matching cardigans. Designer Michael Kors's version is a sleeveless silk turtleneck paired with the cardigan in winter white. TSE Cashmere shows its classic version with a crewneck collar in red, while Isaac Mizrahi unveils similar classic styles in black and purple.

- American and European designers exhibit warm-weather suits for men in less-than-traditional hues. Dolce & Gabbana shows suits in white, Andrew Fezza features a single-breasted linen sports jacket and trousers in burnt orange, and Byblos comes out with a double-breasted silk suit in pale orange.

- Frank O. Gehry unveils his collection of furniture, with four chairs, two tables, and one ottoman.

- Designers feature pantsuits in their spring shows, but they present them in unconventional ways. Vests stand in for jackets, while pants come in all sorts of styles, from pegged to fluid. Bra tops replace blouses—at least on the catwalk.

- In March, two-tone loafers for women are a hot commodity. Shoemakers turn them out in a variety of color combinations; Gucci, for instance, pairs lemon and white.

- Navy and khaki dominate men's spring fashions.

- Platform shoes, with their inches-high soles and even higher heels, enjoy a revival, particularly among younger women and teenagers. Rhinestone-covered shoes, wedge sandals, and foot-high vinyl sneakers are worn by women.

- In May, designers take scissors to their creations, adding ragged edges and tattered hems for a "sophisticated destruction," as Paris-based designer Karl Lagerfeld calls it. His designs for Chanel feature a dress with its hem ripped, a taffeta gown that appears to be losing its lining, and a jacket with its collar unraveling. Lagerfeld is not alone; Rei Kawakubo, for her spring line for the French design house of Comme des Garçons, features unfinished clothes and a trench coat hacked off at the waist.

- In August, camel is the cool color for women. Designers turn out dresses, suits, and coats in the hue, often mixing the shade with cream and brown.

- Boots are back in a variety of shapes and sizes. Among the choices are Nine West's colorful cowboy boots at $125 a pair. The September 1992 issue of *Vogue* calls them "perfect for any up-to-date urban cowgirl."

- In September, Joseph Abboud introduces a lower-priced second line, J.O.E. Calvin Klein also launches a second line, cK.

- In October, the Guggenheim Museum in New York City reopens after a $50 million expansion and renovation.

- In November, Spike Lee's movie *Malcolm X* debuts in theaters, helping to create a market for T-shirts and baseball caps bearing a simple "X" for Malcolm X, the slain 1960s leader of the Nation of Islam.

1993

- The Ford Taurus is the top selling car, beating the Honda Accord.

- In February, in a nod to 1970s nostalgia, designers start piecing patchwork into their collections. Designer Todd Oldham says, "I love patchwork because it's a way to paint with fabric—and one can work in the most obscure colors and patterns."

- In July, fall collections for women lack a unifying theme. In the *Vogue* "Runway Report," Katherine Betts says, "Rags? Romance? Rubber bands? Religion? Like a broken compass spinning aimlessly, the fall collections failed to indicate one strong direction. Never have fashion's camps been so splintered and the choices so plentiful."

- In August, as part of an overall trend to pare down, designers such as Calvin Klein bring a utilitarian approach to men's fashion, with stark, simple lines that echo Amish values. Suit jackets are single-breasted and worn with white cotton shirts; colors are staid—black, charcoal, and white.

- Native American jewelry enjoys a revival. Earrings, rings, pins, and tie clips feature motifs taken from the Southwest, such as jumping men, running animals, and charging warriors. Pieces come in silver, stone, and bone.

- In September, peacoats push past the traditional long coat as the hot choice for women. European couture houses such as Chanel and Gianni Versace, as well as American companies such as Guess and Calvin Klein, turn out peacoats, although designers update this classic by using unexpected colors and unusual fabrics, such as leather and cableknit.

- Donna Karan launches a second line for men, DKNY, adopting the same name as her women's second line, which was started in 1989.

- Men return to boots for fashion footwear.

- Vests in fabrics such as knit, leather, suede, and corduroy become a must-have accessory for men.

1994

- Popular fads include Lion King stuff from the Broadway musical, tattoos, and the thirty-fifth Anniversary Barbie doll, as well as bun firmers and ab exercisers.

- In January, designers point to a new direction in men's suits as they show leaner, longer shapes that create a close-to-the-body silhouette. Some of the American and European designers tapping into this new look are Joseph Abboud, Canali, Ermenegildo Zegna, and Donna Karan.

- In March, American and European designers add bold splashes of color to their collections for men with shirts and ties in vivid colors (yellows, reds, and blues) and patterns (stripes, checks, and plaids).

- In June, *Vogue* declares "the bold red lip" as the cosmetic style for the fall.

- Slick hair slides back into popularity; woman's hair, long or short, is worn off the face.

- In July, hemlines for skirts become more moderate. Designers tried to push long lines earlier in the decade, but they flopped; so did microminis. The new length is closer to the knee.

- Men turn to authentic, old-style denim jeans, spurred in part by collectors who pay five thousand dollars for a never-worn Levi's jacket from the 1940s and fifteen thousand dollars for a Lee cowboy jacket from the 1920s.

- In August, knitwear becomes a staple in the fall fashion menswear collections. Calvin Klein shows V-neck sweaters with his suits, Giorgio Armani designs three-piece suits in knit fabrics, and Donna Karan turns out a cardigan-style coat.

- The latest in women's hairstyles is the classic, unfussy, above-the-shoulder bob. Famous women sharing the style include actresses Sharon Stone, Jodie Foster, and Jennifer Jason Leigh, as well as models Linda Evangelista and Naomi Campbell.

- Sportswear designer Tommy Hilfiger unveils his first complete line of tailored men's clothing, showing classic styles in suits, sport jackets, and coats.

- In December, the Wonderbra becomes an instant hit in the United States, as women flock to stores to get the latest in push-up bra technology. Some stores even set a one-per-customer limit as Wonderbras fly off the shelves.

- *Time* names the Chrysler Neon as one of the best products of 1994, declaring: "Detroit's new subcompacts are stylish, drivable and affordable, too, none more so than this remarkably popular little Chrysler. Most striking are its aggressive lines, responsive handling and tops-in-class acceleration."

1995

- Ford sells more trucks than cars as sports utility vehicles become popular.

- Actress Jennifer Aniston, from the TV show Friends, influences women's hair styles.

- On January 18, the San Francisco Museum of Modern Art, designed by Swiss native Mario Botta, opens.

- Retro influences show up in clothes. British designer Vivienne Westwood shows duchess satin corsets and bustles; Richard Tyler features a white stretch-stain sheath as a nod to the 1930s; Anna Sui touts floral-print dresses reminiscent of the 1940s; and John Galliano, based in France, features 1950s-style peplumed suits.

- In February, nude-colored hosiery, for a bare-looking leg, is a key item to be worn with skirts.

- In April, Nautica, known for its sailing-inspired line of men's sportswear, introduces a complete collection of tailored clothing with items such as navy blazers, silk sport jackets, and seersucker suits.

- In July, the Korean War Veterans Memorial is unveiled and dedicated in Washington, D.C. It was originally designed by a team of architects from state College, PA. A revised design submitted by Cooper-Lechy Associates was approved; Frank Gaylord sculpted the figures and Louis Nelson created the wall of etched faces.

- Refinement returns after several seasons of a slumping economy and the accompanying trend toward modest and casual dressing. Women's clothes are elegant and tasteful; suits, sheath dresses, and classic camel coats all make comebacks.

- In August, slim-cut pants for women are back in style. Calvin Klein, Anne Klein, Marc Jacobs, DKNY, and Richard Tyler all feature them in their fall runway shows.

- The Rock and Roll Hall of Fame and Museum, designed by I. M. Pei, opens on the shores of Lake Erie in Cleveland, Ohio.

- In October, menswear takes on a slimming effect as designers use strict tailoring to create jackets that are close to the body and trousers that are narrow with plain fronts. While the clothes are far from tight-fitting, designers sometimes use stretch fabrics to ensure a comfortable fit.

- In November, men catch up with women this fall and turn to classic camel as the color of choice for jackets, pants, and overcoats.

- In December, Chanel's Vamp nail polishes, in dark blood-red colors, develop a following after first appearing on the Paris runways a year earlier.

1996

- Electric cars become available commercially.

- In January, the one-button single-breasted suit is the hot look for men, with designers such as Giorgio Armani, Calvin Klein, and Richard Tyler producing such outfits.

- In April, the Council on Tall Buildings and Urban Habitat, based in Bethlehem, Pennsylvania, names the 1,483-foot-tall Petronas Twin Towers, under construction in Kuala Lampur, Malaysia, as the world's tallest building. The structure, by Cesar Pelli & Associates, supercedes the record held by the Sears Tower in Chicago, which enjoyed a twenty-three-year run at the top spot.

- In May, the hit Broadway musical *Rent* inspires a line of clothing, as Bloomingdale's opens a *Rent* boutique in Manhattan. The look is colorful and youthful, with spandex pants, miniskirts, and halter tops in prices that range from thirty to sixty dollars.

- In June, following the comeback of classic-style clothes, the "updo" hairstyle returns. Some of the most stylish looks for summer are the French twist, chignon, and simple ponytail.

- Donna Karan's company goes public with a stock offering on Wall Street.

- In October, the period movie *Emma* inspires designers such as Christian Dior, John Galliano, and Chanel, who all show empire-waist dresses as part of their couture collections in Paris.

- The Mary Jane shoe, with schoolgirl styling, a rounded toe, a simple strap across the arch that buckles, and a modest heel that is fat and flared, becomes a hit.

1997

- Designer Tommy Hilfiger's clothes are popular.

- Beanie babies, small stuffed animals, become the newest fad.

- The newest trendy products are DVD players, digital cameras, and flavored vodka.

- In February, simple chic is the key term in fashion. The look is minimal, but not monastic. It's a no-frills, no-ruffles approach to dressing.

- In March, Men's suit jackets get a little longer, completely covering the trouser seat when the arms rest at the sides.

- In April, slides, a sandal-like shoe that features a simple stretch of material—often leather—across the top of the toot, becomes a popular look for summer.

- Men's footwear for spring features elegant square-toed loafers and lace-up shoes, as well as sturdy sandals and classic desert boots.

- In June, a pair of century-old Levi's found in a mineshaft sell for twenty-five thousand dollars.

- On October 19, the $100 million Guggenheim Museum in Bilbao, Spain, designed by Frank O. Gehry, opens. Shrouded in titanium, it looks like a spaceship, while providing gracious space within.

- On December 16, the J. Paul Getty Center in California, a collection of hilltop buildings on 710 acres, designed by Richard Meier, opens.

1998

- Fads include the television characters Rugrats and Teletubbies, items related to the luxury liner *Titanic*, health food supplement ginkgo biloba, and ballroom dancing.

- In January, the Spice Girls appear on the cover of *Vogue*. The original five members of this British pop group reflect the teen street style of the 1990s.

- The new length in skirts is just below the knee.

- In March, the minimalism seen in fashion during the early part of the decade slips away, as opulence—diamonds, pearls, designer suits, luxurious fabrics, furs, and ball gowns—becomes more acceptable and visible.

- Popular colors for women's clothing are fire-engine red, canary yellow, and sapphire blue.

- The sheath dress, a fitted A-line-style dress made popular by actress Audrey Hepburn in the 1960s, becomes a key look.

- On May 5, President Bill Clinton dedicates the Ronald Reagan Building and International Trade Center in Washington, D.C.

- In July, men turn away from the sculpted suit, returning to the more relaxed look of the sack suit. Despite its name, the garment has the classic lines of a formal suit in a more comfortable cut.

- Monona Terrace, a plaza first conceived by Frank Lloyd Wright, opens in Madison, Wisconsin, thirty-eight years after Wright's death.

- In October, in step with a revival of swing and ballroom music, women are wearing pretty, full skirts.

- In December, khakis are everywhere, seemingly replacing denim jeans as the first choice in casual dressing for both men and women.

1999

- Children's fads include Pokémon cards and characters, and the Harry Potter books.

- On February 17, Calvin Klein pulls his ads for children's underwear after critics charge that they are pornographic. The ads feature young boys and girls in their underwear jumping on a sofa.

- In May, designers pick up the popularity of khaki for their men's suits. Calvin Klein turns out one in linen and cotton for $1,195.

- In November, the tankini, a bathing suit with bikini bottoms paired with a tank top, rides a wave of popularity.

The Grunge Look: Alice in Chains

Clothing style

By: Karen Mason Blair

Date: 1990

Source: Mason Blair, Karen. "Alice in Chains." 1990. Corbis. Image no. KB001123. Available online at http://pro.corbis.com (accessed July 11, 2003). ∎

Introduction

In the late 1980s and early 1990s, the city of Seattle was the center for a growing high-tech industry second in size only to California's Silicon Valley. The city became home for the thousands of young, upwardly mobile professionals ("yuppies") who worked for gigantic companies such as Microsoft and Amazon. So-called "grunge" fashion developed as a reaction to their chic, dressed-up style by the city's anti-establishment youth. In deliberate antithesis to the corporate look, Seattle's young people began to favor the torn jeans, clunky boots, and plaid flannel shirts of Washington State's lumber country.

A second influence on the popularity of the grunge style came from the burgeoning popular music scene. Seattle became almost a Nashville West during this time, as rock bands such as Alice in Chains, Pearl Jam, Mother Love Bone, Mudhoney, and the perhaps best known, Nirvana, moved from their home towns to create a new music scene there. Many of the musicians were the children of families who made their livings in fishing, logging, and manufacturing. The style these musicians favored was what prevailed at home: practical, comfortable, well-worn clothing that was suitable for a wet, cold Northwest environment, typically jeans, broken-in work boots, and flannel shirts. As the bands became popular and the hybrid rock-heavy metal music took hold across the United States, the musicians' style of dress also found favor.

The grunge style served to set the Seattle bands and their music apart from other musical groups and styles. Grunge musicians and their fans grew their hair long, and their relaxed, work-style clothing distinguished the grungers from rock and heavy-metal musicians sporting expensive leather and elaborate costumes.

Trademarks of the grunge fashion included chain wallets, torn cardigan sweaters reminiscent of Mr. Rogers, baseball hats worn backwards, and heavy boots. The key to the look was that nothing matched, nothing was coordinated, and the old and worn were preferred to the new and neat. The point was to look tousled and unkempt, as though no conscious attention had been paid to one's appearance.

Significance

As the Seattle bands became popular, the members' fashion sense (or lack thereof) also acquired cachet. Young people discovered that they could achieve the "grunge" look by shopping in thrift stores and shops that specialized in work clothing. Soon, a pair of low-cost Dickies work pants or a pair of Caterpillar boots became the height of fashion.

Ironically, what was never considered a style inspired the fashion industry to promote the sloppy, laid-back look as a new fashion trend. "Grunge" became the vogue as retailers and designers began to offer clothing inspired by the style. Calvin Klein led the way by incorporating the grunge look in his collections of clothing and perfume. His spring 2000 jeans line shocked the fashion world and consumers alike by featuring dirty denim. The once-cheap, unself-conscious look became both expensive and deliberate. Calvin Klein's dirty denim jeans sold for as much as $78, while designer Donna Karan sold grunge tank tops for $80, denim jackets at $95, and sloppy cut-offs for $65.

As grunge became popular, a new niche opened in the fashion industry: processing garments to make them look worn, stained, and abused before they are put on the market. One especially enterprising U.S. company, Sights Denim Systems, Inc., was founded in 1987. Sights Denim specializes in the "finished wash" business, processing about 150,000 garments (mainly jeans) every week for the "dirty denim" market.

Despite its trendiness, many consumers found the grunge look ridiculous and criticized those who adopted it. Grunge fell out of favor within a year or two, but the fashion term remains to describe a deliberately careless and eminently comfortable way of dressing.

Further Resources

BOOKS

Austin, Joe. *Generations of Youth: Youth Cultures and History in Twentieth-Century America.* New York: New York University Press, 1998.

Primary Source

The Grunge Look: Alice in Chains

SYNOPSIS: Members of the grunge band Alice in Chains pose for a 1990 photo in Seattle, Washington. The grunge style sprang from the Pacific Northwest after bands such as Pearl Jam and Nirvana achieved national reputations. The widespread popularity of the sloppy, laid-back style was inspired by the fascination with musicians such as Eddie Vedder and Kurt Cobain. © KAREN MASON BLAIR/CORBIS. REPRODUCED BY PERMISSION.

Costantino, Maria. *Men's Fashion in the Twentieth Century: From Frock Coats to Intelligent Fibres.* New York: Costume & Fashion Press, 1997.

Hoffmann, Frank W. *Fashion and Merchandising Fads.* New York: Haworth Press, 1994.

PERIODICALS

"Grunging Acceptance." *Harper's Bazaar,* January 1993, 116.

Poneman, Jonathan. "Grunge and Glory." *Vogue,* December 1992, 254.

Tilsner, Julie. "From Trash Can Straight to Seventh Avenue." *Business Week,* March 22 1993, 39.

The End of Print: The Graphic Design of David Carson

Interview, Magazine article; Magazine cover

By: David Carson and Lewis Blackwell

Date: 1993

Source: Blackwell, Lewis, ed. *The End of Print: The Graphic Design Of David Carson.* San Francisco: Chronicle Books, 1998.

Primary Source

The End of Print: The Graphic Design of David Carson: Magazine article

SYNOPSIS: Former surfer and high school teacher David Carson followed an unusual career to success in the field of graphic design. Although often criticized for his chaotic designs, his iconoclastic approach has led to a revolution in contemporary typography and layout. This layout for an article and interview with the rock band Manic Street Preachers is an example of his innovative style. FROM AN ILLUSTRATION IN *THE END OF PRINT: THE GRAPHIC DESIGN OF DAVID CARSON.* "MANIC STREET PREACH-ERS," 1993. DESIGNED BY DAVID CARSON. REPRODUCED BY PERMISSION OF DAVID CARSON.

About the Author: David Carson (1956–) was born in Texas and earned a degree in sociology at San Diego State University. Early influences on his graphic design style included childhood travels in the United States, Puerto Rico, and the West Indies, and a three-week graphic design workshop in Switzerland. After teaching high school sociology for a time, Carson, who was also a top-ranked competitive surfer, became a graphic designer for *Transworld Skateboarding* magazine in 1983. He later worked for surf magazines *Surf* and *Beach Culture*. In 1992, he became the art director for the music magazine *Ray Gun*. It was here that Carson made a name for himself with his iconoclastic approaches to typography and visual design. He subsequently established his own design firm in New York City. ■

Introduction

Many reviewers hailed David Carson in the 1980s for the experimental typography and bold layouts he introduced in *Transworld Skateboarding* and *Surf* magazines. Yet the design community was mainly shocked in 1990 by the first issue of the surf magazine, *Beach Culture*. In that issue, Carson and a team of illustrators, including the legendary Milton Glaser, set out to challenge the reader with chaotic page layouts. The magazine featured such unexpected elements as folio numbers that were larger than the headlines, dozens of different type styles on a page, overlapping photographs scattered with text, and other violations of traditional graphic design principles.

In the uncertainty about whether *Beach Culture* was a surf magazine or an art and culture magazine, many advertisers withdrew their business, and only six issues were ever published. Although short-lived, the magazine won more than 150 design awards and initiated a change in the direction of magazine design. *Beach Culture* and the other publications it inspired attracted a new generation of mainly youthful readers who were willing to navigate the seemingly indecipherable text and intriguing visuals that characterized Carson's designs.

Carson later expanded from magazines to design for other, more mainstream clients, such as MCI, Ray-Ban sunglasses, and Jaguar automobiles. More recently, Carson designed graphics and advertisements for Pepsi, Levi's, and Nike, and has even made a Budweiser Superbowl commercial. Carson also makes experimental films and is an avid photographer. He continues to generate controversy. One critic has noted that Carson fractured "the Modernist grid [that] subverts the personality of the designer to the primacy of the corporate." That meant eliminating clean legibility in favor of a visually challenging layout of text and images. Carson explains: "Overall, people are reading less. I'm just trying to visually entice them to read."

Significance

It was especially Carson's creative direction at *Ray Gun Magazine,* launched in 1992, that secured him a reputation as an innovative designer. The alternative music magazine abandoned conventional design elements such as headlines, columns, and page numbers and made use of jarring juxtapositions of images and typographical innovations. Though controversial, the magazine's abstract style contributed to a new set of graphic design rules within the industry. His audacious designs set the stage for a number of new magazines outside the mainsteam that devoted as much space to visuals as to editorial content.

Carson's work in *Ray Gun* led to his first book, *The End of Print,* in 1998. The book compiles over a decade of Carson's graphic design work and is among the best-selling books on graphic design ever published. Carson is seen as part of a movement with roots in such schools as Cranbrook Institute of Art and the California Institute for the Arts, which were already promoting experimental and iconoclastic explorations by their students. He has attracted both fans and detractors. Carson is credited with revolutionizing magazine design through his work for *Ray Gun.* However, some reviewers disparage Carson for sacrificing legibility for scattered and incongruous layouts of text and photographs. Carson's critics (mainly among the older generation) claim that his lack of formal training led to the untidy style he has championed and which has proliferated in the design community.

On reviewing old issues of *Ray Gun* and *Beach Culture,* the magazines which featured Carson's first daring designs, the designer has said, "I was struck with how many bad pages there were." This professional modesty has made him popular with young designers, many of whom regard him as a role model. Of his book *The End of Print,* Carson said: "If I had any idea it was going to sell, I would have made a much better book."

Primary Source

The End of Print: The Graphic Design of David Carson: Interview [excerpt]

> **SYNOPSIS:** David Carson's innovative designs in *Ray Gun* and other publications garnered much attention and won him many fans, as well as many detractors. In this interview with editor Lewis Blackwell, David Carson responds to criticism of his work and explains his approach to graphic design.

Primary Source

The End of Print: The Graphic Design of David Carson: Magazine cover
The cover of this 1993 issue of *Ray Gun* features the upside-down portrait of J. Mascis of the band Dinosaur Jr.
FROM A COVER ILLUSTRATION IN *THE END OF PRINT: THE GRAPHIC DESIGN OF DAVID CARSON.* "RAY GUN," ISSUE # 3, 1993. DESIGNED BY DAVID CARSON. REPRODUCED BY PERMISSION OF DAVID CARSON.

You have come out with a line that "we shouldn't confuse legibility with communication." Is that a common problem? Have people become hung up on irrelevant rules of what they think governs legibility?

Just because something is legible doesn't mean it communicates: it could be communicating completely the wrong thing. Some traditional book titles, encyclopedias, or many books that young people wouldn't want to pick up, could be made more appealing. It is mostly a problem of publications sending the wrong message or not a strong enough message. You may be legible, but what is the emotion contained in the message? That is important to me.

You are unlikely to refer to the past in your work and you seem hooked in to the idea of the contemporary. Are you a populist, just seeking to lock into what makes people turn on to something?

I am not sitting down wondering what Generation X wants to see next. I am doing what makes the most sense to me for a particular project.

You are trying to bring into the communication something that is in you, something you care about. It is more like the approach you might get from an artist: it is not a straight response to the job. That suggests you are breaking with ideas of design being some kind of almost scientific process, and instead makes it a little mystical. So what are you bringing in?

It is a very personal, interpretative approach. That makes the end product more interesting—there is no other way you could arrive at it, there are no formal rules you could bring to something I work on and end up with the same solution. This way I think you end up at a more interesting and a more valid point. I am using my intuition, trying to express things I am reading in the way that makes the most sense to me. It is an important distinction to make that I am not trying to find "what it is they want."

So you are revealing what you want instead?

Yes. It can be deadly and boring if you don't put yourself in it. The fact that many designers don't is why there are a lot of bored designers and boring design out there. Somebody said everything I designed was self-indulgent, meaning it as an insult, but I would say "I hope it is self-indulgent." That is when you are going to get the best work. People use the idea of self-indulgence in a negative sense, but I wouldn't want someone working for me that wasn't passionate and very much trying to do the best possible thing they can. They have to bring some of themselves in, otherwise I might as well hire a technician who can flow in text and so on.

So what are you—a graphic designer or something else?

Yes. I consider myself a graphic designer, but I also consider myself an artist. I think the same of the photographers, illustrators, other designers who work with me. There are all types of art. Plenty of graphic design is art, but some people would say to that "graphic design is meant to communicate" as if art doesn't communicate as well. Some of the success of projects I have worked on is that what has come out of them has been right for the audience, although I hate to turn that into the most important aspect of graphic design. But you have to keep in mind your audience: what I am doing is very personal work that at some point feels right to me, but at the same time I have to keep in mind an audience.

Further Resources

BOOKS

Carson, David. *Second Sight: Grafik Design after the End of Print.* New York: St. Martin's Press, 1997.

Kuipers, Dean. *"Raygun": Out of Control.* New York: Simon and Schuster, 1997.

PERIODICALS

Plagens, Peter. "The Font of Youth." *Newsweek,* February 26, 1996, 64–65.

Charter of the New Urbanism
Charter

By: Congress for New Urbanism

Date: 1993

Source: Congress for New Urbanism. *Charter of the New Urbanism.* 1993. Available online at http://www.cnu.org /cnu_reports/Charter.pdf; website home page: http://www.cnu .org/ (accessed May 1, 2003).

About the Organization: The Congress for the New Urbanism (CNU) was started in 1993 by a group of architects. The organization brings architects together with planners, economists, real estate developers, government officials, citizen activists, and others who share a concern about the effects of urban and suburban sprawl on people and the environment. They promote the creation of a built environment that best serves its occupants while preserving the health of the natural world. ∎

Introduction

Before World War II (1939–1945), towns and town planning in the United States tended to integrate houses, shops, offices, and civic buildings into cohesive, self-sufficient communities. Many Americans lived in small or medium-sized towns and spent most of their time close to home. Because people moved around on foot or by public transportation, towns tended to be convenient and accessible for pedestrians. Most people had considerable pride in their communities and were ready to invest in them.

When the war ended, city and town populations swelled as returning G.I.s and rural migrants sought the jobs that were becoming available in and around the major cities. The demand for affordable housing sparked the building of Levittown and the proliferation of entire ready-made neighborhoods of identical houses and ordered street plans. Expediency and later zoning laws separated these look-alike "bedroom communities" from increasingly crowded and inconvenient commercial areas. As the economy and the population expanded, people's homes, jobs, and shopping moved farther apart. The explosion of private cars and the massive highway systems they demand all brought decisive changes in how Americans live and caused significant damage to the natural environment.

As suburbs grew larger and more distant from civic and regional centers, the sense of community tended to diminish for millions of Americans who spent more and more time in their cars and less and less time interacting near home with friends, neighbors, and local merchants. The vast growth of huge shopping centers, "big-box" chain stores, and fast-food outlets worsened the alienation of Americans from one another and from their sense of place. Traffic jams, air and water pollution, increased noise levels, and a general degradation of the natural landscape undermined the quality of life. Although a few cities (New York City and San Francisco, for example) still retain thriving, diverse, and proud neighborhoods, the "walkable," self-reliant community was almost non-existent by 1990.

Significance

The architects who established the Congress for the New Urbanism (CNU) in 1993 advocate a restoration of the pre-war ideals of community and style of life. According to the standards set forth by the CNU in its "Charter of the New Urbanism," New Urbanist developments and neighborhoods combine housing types and styles that attract a diverse population of income levels and age groups. The New Urbanist community is designed to promote and support local business and local civic action in order to facilitate and reward local investment. Such a community is built to minimize the need for cars, to encourage pedestrians, and to preserve and accommodate the landscape and ecosystem.

The CNU promotes the regeneration of existing urban and town centers and neighborhoods. They endorse the reconfiguration of sprawling suburbs into diverse, accessible, and environmentally friendly communities. They actively propose and support changes in public policy and zoning laws that are necessary. Yet many New Urbanist projects are newly created communities, the so-called "new towns" that are being built from the ground up all over the country. These towns are designed, planned, and built with a view to restoring the pre-war community life in accessible, livable surroundings. Critics claim that these new towns, often well removed from urban centers and hardly self-sufficient, are little different from the impersonal, homogeneous suburban communities they purportedly replace.

Although the movement has drawn criticism from some architects, the ideas behind CNU's charter have inspired changes in planning and architecture curricula at a number of architecture schools. By 2003, the CNU had 2,300 members around the world and was involved in over two hundred development projects.

Primary Source

Charter of the New Urbanism [excerpt]

SYNOPSIS: Developed by the Congress for the New Urbanism in 1993, this charter outlines the principles that CNU members promote in order to make American towns more self-reliant, pedestrian-friendly, and environmentally conscientious.

The Congress for the New Urbanism views disinvestment in central cities, the spread of placeless sprawl, increasing separation by race and income, environmental deterioration, loss of agricultural lands and wilderness, and the erosion of society's built heritage as one interrelated community-building challenge.

We stand for the restoration of existing urban centers and towns within coherent metropolitan regions, the reconfiguration of sprawling suburbs into communities of real neighborhoods and diverse districts, the conservation of natural environments, and the preservation of our built legacy.

We recognize that physical solutions by themselves will not solve social and economic problems, but neither can economic vitality, community stability, and environmental health be sustained without a coherent and supportive physical framework.

We advocate the restructuring of public policy and development practices to support the following principles: neighborhoods should be diverse in use and population; communities should be designed for the pedestrian and transit as well as the car; cities and towns should be shaped by physically defined and universally accessible public spaces and community institutions; urban places should be framed by architecture and landscape design that celebrate local history, climate, ecology, and building practice.

We represent a broad-based citizenry, composed of public and private sector leaders, community activists, and multidisciplinary professionals. We are committed to reestablishing the relationship between the art of building and the making of community, through citizen-based participatory planning and design.

We dedicate ourselves to reclaiming our homes, blocks, streets, parks, neighborhoods, districts, towns, cities, regions, and environment.

We assert the following principles to guide public policy, development practice, urban planning, and design:

The region. Metropolis, city, and town

1. Metropolitan regions are finite places with geographic boundaries derived from topography, watersheds, coastlines, farmlands, regional parks, and river basins. The metropolis is

made of multiple centers that are cities, towns, and villages, each with its own identifiable center and edges.

2. The metropolitan region is a fundamental economic unit of the contemporary world. Governmental cooperation, public policy, physical planning, and economic strategies must reflect this new reality.

3. The metropolis has a necessary and fragile relationship to its agrarian hinterland and natural landscapes. The relationship is environmental, economic, and cultural. Farmland and nature are as important to the metropolis as the garden is to the house.

4. Development patterns should not blur or eradicate the edges of the metropolis. Infill development within existing urban areas conserves environmental resources, economic investment, and social fabric, while reclaiming marginal and abandoned areas. Metropolitan regions should develop strategies to encourage such infill development over peripheral expansion.

5. Where appropriate, new development contiguous to urban boundaries should be organized as neighborhoods and districts, and be integrated with the existing urban pattern. Noncontiguous development should be organized as towns and villages with their own urban edges, and planned for a jobs/housing balance, not as bedroom suburbs.

6. The development and redevelopment of towns and cities should respect historical patterns, precedents, and boundaries.

7. Cities and towns should bring into proximity a broad spectrum of public and private uses to support a regional economy that benefits people of all incomes. Affordable housing should be distributed throughout the region to match job opportunities and to avoid concentrations of poverty.

8 The physical organization of the region should be supported by a framework of transportation alternatives. Transit, pedestrian, and bicycle systems should maximize access and mobility throughout the region while reducing dependence upon the automobile.

9. Revenues and resources can be shared more cooperatively among the municipalities and centers within regions to avoid destructive competition for tax base and to promote rational

coordination of transportation, recreation, public services, housing, and community institutions.

The neighborhood, the district, and the corridor

1. The neighborhood, the district, and the corridor are the essential elements of development and redevelopment in the metropolis. They form identifiable areas that encourage citizens to take responsibility for their maintenance and evolution.

2. Neighborhoods should be compact, pedestrian-friendly, and mixed-use. Districts generally emphasize a special single use, and should follow the principles of neighborhood design when possible. Corridors are regional connectors of neighborhoods and districts; they range from boulevards and rail lines to rivers and parkways.

3. Many activities of daily living should occur within walking distance, allowing independence to those who do not drive, especially the elderly and the young. Interconnected networks of streets should be designed to encourage walking, reduce the number and length of automobile trips, and conserve energy.

4. Within neighborhoods, a broad range of housing types and price levels can bring people of diverse ages, races, and incomes into daily interaction, strengthening the personal and civic bonds essential to an authentic community.

5. Transit corridors, when properly planned and coordinated, can help organize metropolitan structure and revitalize urban centers. In contrast, highway corridors should not displace investment from existing centers.

6. Appropriate building densities and land uses should be within walking distance of transit stops, permitting public transit to become a viable alternative to the automobile.

7. Concentrations of civic, institutional, and commercial activity should be embedded in neighborhoods and districts, not isolated in remote, single-use complexes. Schools should be sized and located to enable children to walk or bicycle to them.

8. The economic health and harmonious evolution of neighborhoods, districts, and corridors can be improved through graphic urban design codes that serve as predictable guides for change.

9. A range of parks, from tot-lots and village greens to ballfields and community gardens, should be distributed within neighborhoods. Conservation areas and open lands should be used to define and connect different neighborhoods and districts.

The block, the street, and the building

1. A primary task of all urban architecture and landscape design is the physical definition of streets and public spaces as places of shared use.

2. Individual architectural projects should be seamlessly linked to their surroundings. This issue transcends style.

3. The revitalization of urban places depends on safety and security. The design of streets and buildings should reinforce safe environments, but not at the expense of accessibility and openness.

4. In the contemporary metropolis, development must adequately accommodate automobiles. It should do so in ways that respect the pedestrian and the form of public space.

5. Streets and squares should be safe, comfortable, and interesting to the pedestrian. Properly configured, they encourage walking and enable neighbors to know each other and protect their communities.

6. Architecture and landscape design should grow from local climate, topography, history, and building practice.

7. Civic buildings and public gathering places require important sites to reinforce community identity and the culture of democracy. They deserve distinctive form, because their role is different from that of other buildings and places that constitute the fabric of the city.

8. All buildings should provide their inhabitants with a clear sense of location, weather and time. Natural methods of heating and cooling can be more resource-efficient than mechanical systems.

9. Preservation and renewal of historic buildings, districts, and landscapes affirm the continuity and evolution of urban society.

Further Resources

BOOKS

Garvin, Alexander. *The American City: What Works, What Doesn't.* New York: McGraw-Hill, 2002.

Jackson, Kenneth T. *The Crabgrass Frontier: The Suburbanization of the United States.* New York: Oxford University Press, 1987.

Kelbaugh, Doug. *Common Place: Toward Neighborhood and Regional Design.* Seattle: University of Washington Press, 2002.

PERIODICALS

Carey, John. "New Neighborhoods Can Combat Urban Sprawl." *Business Week,* August 23–30, 1999, 110.

Musser, George. "Between Burb and Burg." *Scientific American,* March, 2000, 28, 30.

WEBSITES

"New Urbanism." *Online NewsHour.* Available online at http://www.pbs.org/newshour/newurbanism/; website home page: http://www.pbs.org/newshour/ (accessed April 30, 2003).

AUDIO AND VISUAL MEDIA

Straight Talk About New Urbanism. Congress for the New Urbanism., 1999, VHS.

Dockers Advertisement
Advertisement

By: Levi Strauss & Co.

Date: 1997

Source: Dockers Advertisement. The Advertising Archive Ltd. Image no. F147 121.

About the Organization: Levi Strauss & Co. was started in San Francisco in 1853 as a small dry-goods business. The company began making denim jeans in its factories in 1873. The business grew rapidly, and the name "Levi's" soon became synonymous with denim jeans. ∎

Introduction

In the mid-1980s, Levi Strauss & Co. responded to a fashion trend away from jeans by developing a line of men's casual pants called "Dockers." The company started out slowly with a small line of pants that were modeled after the first khakis (also called chinos), that were originally introduced to the public in 1958. A new version of the tan cotton pants, originally part of a military uniform, were offered as a dressier option for men who normally wore jeans after work or on the weekends. The company also hoped that the Dockers line would help the clothier to expand its customer base by appealing to consumers who did not favor denim but nonetheless were seeking a casual look. Launching the Dockers brand was enormously risky for a company which had cultivated its reputation based on denim jeans.

The Dockers were not an instant success, but they eventually contributed to the increasing popularity of casual dressing at the American office. Dockers ultimately

Primary Source

Dockers Advertisement

SYNOPSIS: Levi Strauss & Co., known primarily for their denim jeans, was a pioneer in the business casual clothing trend. The company introduced the Dockers brand in the 1980s, and the brand burgeoned in the 1990s, due largely to the increased popularity of casual dressing in the workplace. THE ADVERTISING ARCHIVE LTD. REPRODUCED BY PERMISSION.

became almost a uniform among professional men who favored the pants for "casual Fridays." In 1992, Levi Strauss & Co. launched its "Dockers Style at Work" campaign to capitalize on the popularity of casual business wear. The company created a booklet entitled "Guide to Casual Business Wear" and sent it to 30,000 human resources managers. The company also mounted a touring fashion show that visited ten cities. The campaign promoted Dockers pants as the perfect compromise—dressy enough for the office, but casual and comfortable enough for your day off. The company used videos, fashion shows, and print and media campaigns in a vigorous promotion of the casual work attire.

Significance

Levi Strauss & Co. contributed significantly to the rise of "business casual" dressing at the office. The company used its Dockers line and a compelling marketing program to exercise a powerful influence on how Americans dress for work. Men (and later women) were happy to exchange the restrictions of conservative suits, uncomfortable ties, and dressy work outfits for the comfort and ease of Dockers. However, many employers became concerned about the broad interpretations of "business casual," giving rise to much sociological speculation about the effects of appearance on coworkers and customers and to a proliferation of professional business fashion consultants. Opinions differ as to the effect of casual dress on employee morale and productivity, and most employers—and their fashion advisers—insisted that "business casual" did not imply careless or haphazard dressing at work. Indeed, one Levi's representative claimed: "Levi Strauss never intended to promote sloppy, casual dress, with people wearing blue jeans with holes and sandals to work." Instead, the new look has become almost as standardized as the conventional business attire it has so largely replaced. In an intriguing reaction to this trend, some companies have instituted "dress-up Thursdays," one day in the week when employees are required to assume a more conventional business attire.

By the turn of the century, over eighty percent of all employers offered some form of "business casual" dress policy, and about one third allowed casual dress every day. The Dockers line of casual wear accounted for about one quarter of Levi Strauss's overall business in 2003.

Further Resources

BOOKS

Martin, Richard. *Khakis: Cut from the Original Cloth.* New York: Tondo Books, 1999.

PERIODICALS

Applegate, Jane. "Backlash Against Casual Friday." *Los Angeles Business Journal,* October 2, 2000.

The Getty Center
Architectural design

By: Richard Meier

Date: 1997

Source: The Getty Center. AP/Wide World Photos. Image no. LA104 2340848.

About the Architect: Richard Meier (1930–) was born in Newark, New Jersey. He graduated from Cornell University and worked with several architectural firms before establishing his own practice in 1963. Meier first won national acclaim in 1965 for his design of the Smith House in Darien, Connecticut. He added to his reputation in 1979, with the opening of his Visitors' Center at the utopian community of New Harmony, Indiana. In 1984, Meier became the youngest architect ever to be awarded the prestigious Pritzker Prize. He won the AIA Gold Medal in 1997. ∎

Introduction

One of the "New York Five," a group of architects who gained public attention in 1975, Richard Meier creates designs informed by neo-modern beliefs. His school represents a reaction to the impersonal, mechanistic modernist style and a return to the more organic, human-centered style of Swiss architect Le Corbusier. In 1965, one of Meier's early residential designs, the Smith House in Darien, Connecticut, brought him national attention. His trademark white, highly sculptural structures contributed to a new language of building design in the 1980s. In 1983, after he completed the High Museum of Art in Atlanta, a critic wrote that Meier was "becoming one of the preeminent architects of museums."

J. Paul Getty (1892–1976), oil baron, billionaire, and philanthropist, was also an avid art collector who was committed to making art available to the public. In 1953, Getty founded the J. Paul Getty Museum on his ranch in Malibu, California and opened it to the public. The museum displayed Greek and Roman antiquities, eighteenth-century French furniture, and European painting. In 1982, the trustees set out to expand the Getty in response to the rising numbers of visitors, the need for better acccommodation of the Getty collections, and to provide space for a range of new arts programs and more extensive research and conservation. They chose architect Richard Meier and his partners to design a completely new Getty Center complex in the Brentwood section of Los Angeles.

The goal of the project was to create a campus for the display, conservation, and study of high art within an architecture that was as significant as the museum's mission was ambitious. Built at a cost of a billion dollars, the new Getty Center took fourteen years to complete and opened in 1997. The years of construction were marked by on-going disputes among architect Richard Meier,

Primary Source

The Getty Center

SYNOPSIS: The Getty Center, a billion-dollar complex perched in the foothills above Los Angeles, opened in 1997. Within the center, the J. Paul Getty Museum of Art houses Greek and Roman antiquities, European paintings, manuscripts, decorative arts, and photography. The Center and the museum itself exemplify architect Richard Meier's neo-modernist interests, while the open, light-filled plan also reflects Meier's sensitivity to the importance of setting for the effective display and rewarding viewing of art. Since the Getty Center opened, over twice the expected number of people have visited the complex. AP/WIDE WORLD PHOTOS. REPRODUCED BY PERMISSION.

project artist Robert Irwin, museum executives, and the community. The completed complex has nevertheless won enormous acclaim.

Significance

The six buildings of the Getty Center, clad in gleaming Italian travertine, are set on a rocky crest in the foothills of the Santa Monica Mountains. The complex is designed to harmonize with the local topography and to offer as much open space and natural light as possible. Set among numerous gardens, terraces, and courtyards, two five-story pavilions house the Getty Museum

of Art, with galleries devoted to painting, furnishings, photography, manuscripts, sculpture, and decorative arts. The Center also accommodates the Getty Trust offices, the Getty Conservation Institution, the Getty Center for Education, and the Getty Grant Program. The buildings contain laboratories, libraries, an auditorium, and restaurants.

The Getty Center's dazzling acropolis exemplifies Meier's "big white box" style while it also accommodates the environmental and ecological demands of neo-modernism. Visitors park in a vast underground garage just off the San Diego Freeway and reach the Center itself by a special tram. Striking features of the project include the placement of buildings in relation to the landscape; the brilliant white cladding; the open, multi-leveled spaces; the use of gardens and flowers; the framing of stunning views; and the elaborate systems for providing and filtering natural light into the interior. When it opened in 1997, the billion-dollar project was the most expensive museum construction in U.S. history. The Getty Center is considered one of the world's best places to display and view art.

Further Resources

BOOKS

Getty, J. Paul. *As I See It: The Autobiography of J. Paul Getty*. Los Angeles: J. Paul Getty Museum, 2003.

Gribbon, Deborah. *The J. Paul Getty Museum and Its Collections: A Museum for the New Century*. Los Angeles: J. Paul Getty Museum, 1997.

Williams, Harold. *The Getty Center: Design Process*. Los Angeles: J. Paul Getty Trust, 1991.

PERIODICALS

Goldberger, Paul. "The People's Getty." *The New Yorker,* February 23, 1998, 178–181.

Rosenbaum, Lee. "View from the Getty: What Its Billions Bought." *Art in America,* May 1998, 92–97.

AUDIO AND VISUAL MEDIA

Artful Architecture: The Getty Center and the Guggenheim Museum Bilbao. Films for the Humanities and Sciences, 1999, VHS.

Concert of Wills: Making of the Getty Center. Maysles Films, Inc. Directed by Albert Maysles, Susan Froemke, and Bob Eisenhardt. 1997, VHS.

Monona Terrace

Architectural design

By: Frank Lloyd Wright

Date: 1997

Source: Grehan, Farrell. "The Monona Terrace Convention Center by Frank Lloyd Wright." 1997. Corbis. Image no. FG002643. Available online at http://pro.corbis.com (accessed July 10, 2003).

About the Architect: Frank Lloyd Wright (1867–1959) was born in Richland Center, Wisconsin. After studying engineering at the University of Wisconsin, Wright moved to Illinois in 1893 and worked for architect Louis Sullivan. Wright opened his own practice in Chicago in 1893 and went on to became one of the most celebrated architects of the twentieth century. He is especially known for his theory of "organic architecture," which emphasizes a harmonious integration between a structure and its site. He was also a proponent of the Prairie School of architecture, which produced low, horizontal buildings with fluid interior spaces. Wright died in 1959

at Taliesin West, a winter retreat and studio he had built in Phoenix, Arizona. ∎

Introduction

In 1907, a legislative commission in Madison, Wisconsin, designated a six-block area of the city as the site for a mall with large government buildings. The mall would follow Monona Avenue to link the new State Capitol building with the shore of Lake Monona. In 1910, John Nolen, a landscape architect from Boston, expanded the original plan to incorporate a lakefront esplanade. Although Nolen's complex was not built, the vision of a mall and esplanade with a series of waterfront buildings inspired the architect Frank Lloyd Wright, who had lived in Madison between the ages of eleven and nineteen. Wright began putting his ideas on paper in 1938.

During his career, Wright planned and designed thirty-two buildings in Madison. Nine of them were built, and eight still stand. Wright's best known Madison structures include the signature Prairie-style house, the Unitarian church, and the first Usonian house, Wright's prototype middle-class housing scheme. But Wright's plans for a Madison civic auditorium combined with a capital mall were on a completely different scale than the other projects, and were both ambitious and controversial. The design for Monona Terrace, as Wright called it, was unveiled in 1938. As described by *The New York Times,* Monona Terrace "was a grand vision of towers, fountains and terraces rising from the shores of Lake Monona in the shadow of the Capitol."

The city of Madison balked at the estimated cost of the project: some $17 million. Thereupon Wright, who was well known for his arrogance, insisted, "Madison could dig into its pocket and pay something for the charm nature has given it." He told a civic group, "You should have an eye to the future, instead of planning something that will be a dump as soon as it's built. . . . This building will take character, and courage, and vision and intelligence, yes, and sympathy with the beautiful."

In 1941, Madison voters approved funding for a municipal auditorium, and Wright's plan re-emerged into consideration. However, the plan was again put on hold when the United States entered World War II, and it was only in 1948 that the idea of a new administrative building in Madison came up again. Wright reworked his design several times, signing off on the final plans just weeks before his death in 1959. It was more than thirty years later, in 1992, that Madison voters finally approved financing for a community and convention center.

Significance

The Monona Terrace Community and Convention Center opened in July, 1997, 59 years after it was first proposed by Frank Lloyd Wright. The final plans blended

Primary Source

Monona Terrace

SYNOPSIS: In 1997, almost sixty years after Frank Lloyd Wright conceived his first plans, the city of Madison, Wisconsin, unveiled Monona Terrace, a new civic, convention, and recreational complex on Lake Monona near the City center. A modified version of Wright's 1938 design, Monona Terrace cost over $60 million to build. It offers state-of-the-art space for exhibitions, meetings, and public enjoyment. © FARRELL GREHAN/CORBIS. REPRODUCED BY PERMISSION.

The original drawing of Monona Terrace as presented by Frank Lloyd Wright in 1938. The completed building differs greatly from Wright's original vision. **THE DRAWINGS OF FRANK LLOYD WRIGHT ARE COPYRIGHT © 1962, 1990, 2003 THE FRANK LLOYD WRIGHT FOUNDATION, SCOTTSDALE, AZ.**

Wright's design for the exterior with an interior redesigned by Tony Puttnam, a Wright apprentice and a partner in the Taliesin Group established by Wright. The final project departed significantly from Wright's plan, which, had it been built, would probably have been an aesthetic masterpiece and a functional failure, as many of his buildings were. Nevertheless, Monona Terrace is the Frank Lloyd Wright building the city of Madison yearned for and fought over for many years.

The building Wright designed in 1938 was a five-deck structure covering seven and a half acres on the edge of Madison's Lake Monona. The top deck was to accommodate gardens and fountains, while the lower decks would house cocktail lounges, restaurants, art galleries, state and county offices, a jail, parking facilities, and a marina. The actual Monona Terrace is primarily a convention center and hotel and is about half as large as Wright intended. The semicircular structure links Lake Monona with the domed State Capitol building.

Although it is less ambitious than the building Wright envisioned, Monona Terrace Community and Convention Center is both impressive and remarkable. Pulitzer Prize-winning journalist and Madison native David Maraniss remarked on the splendor of Monona Terrace, adding how "stunningly stupid" it was that it took nearly sixty years to build.

Further Resources

BOOKS

Mollenhoff, David, and Mary Jane Hamilton. *Frank Lloyd Wright's Monona Terrace: The Enduring Power of a Civic Vision.* Oak Park, Ill.: Frank Lloyd Wright Preservation Trust, 1999.

Monona Terrace: Frank Lloyd Wright's Vision on the Lake. Madison, Wisc.: Madison Newspapers, Inc., 1997.

PERIODICALS

Elson, John. "The Wrong Wright?" *Time,* June 12 1995, 70.

"Wright Again—Sort Of." *The New Yorker,* March 13, 1995, 36–37.

WEBSITES

Frank Lloyd Wright Foundation. Available online at http://www.franklloydwright.org/ (accessed April 28, 2003).

Guggenheim Bilbao

Gehry Talks: Architecture + Process

Nonfiction work

By: Frank Gehry
Date: 1997

Source: Friedman, Mildred, ed. *Gehry Talks: Architecture + Process.* New York: Rizzoli International, 1999, 176–177.

Guggenheim Museum

Architectural design

By: Frank Gehry
Date: 1998
Source: Arthus-Bertrand, Yann. "Aerial View of Guggenheim Museum." Corbis. Image no. YA021122. Available online at http://pro.corbis.com (accessed July 10, 2003).
About the Architect: Frank O. Gehry (1929–) was born in Toronto, Canada. He studied architecture at the University of Southern California and Harvard University. He founded his first architectural firm in 1963. Gehry's best known designs include the Hollywood Bowl, the Walt Disney Concert Hall in Los Angeles, The American Center in Paris, the Frederick R. Weisman Museum in Minneapolis, the Bard College Center for the Performing Arts in Annandale-on-Hudson, NY, and the Guggenheim Museum in Bilbao, Spain. ■

Introduction

Frank Gehry's unique, highly sculptural architectural style emerged in the late 1970s when he began exploring non-traditional forms and using found objects to create collage-like models. In his earlier years, Gehry favored plywood, corrugated metal, and other mundane materials, which served to communicate his deconstructivist ideas. Gehry eventually developed a distinctive personal style unrestricted by allegiance to any particular school or theory.

Gehry's designs more nearly resemble a functional sculpture than conventional architectural structures. Indeed, the designer professes to seek the freedom from restraint that is associated with sculpture. His work reveals a debt to contemporary collage and assemblage, as in the work of Robert Rauschenberg. Many of Gehry's built projects, which include private houses, museums, concert halls, corporate headquarters, and educational buildings, characteristically appear unfinished or fractured, as they combine formal composition with an unusual disjointed aesthetic. The abstract, free-form components of this style were present in the early house (1979, 1987) he built for himself in Santa Monica, California, and most notably, at the Weisman Center in Minneapolis (1990), a precursor of the Guggenheim Museum Bilbao.

Many of Gehry's major architectural projects exhibit what have become his signature colliding and curvaceous forms. The building exteriors are often sheathed in metal "skins," especially titanium, in which Gehry is a master craftsman. This expressionist modern style is perhaps best represented in Gehry's striking design for the Guggenheim Museum Bilbao, which opened in 1998 in the industrial Basque city of Bilbao, Spain.

Dubbed by *Time* magazine as "the building of the century," the Guggenheim Museum Bilbao attracted more at-

A design process model by Frank Gehry for the Bilbao Guggenheim museum. Wood and cardboard were used. **REPRODUCED BY PERMISSION OF FRANK O. GEHRY & ASSOCIATES.**

tention in the media than any other new building during the year it opened (1998). Designed as part of a plan to revitalize the sagging economy of the Bilbao area and to enhance the city as a center of culture, the museum is generally regarded as an unmatched achievement of contemporary architecture.

Significance

Situated in the center of Bilbao, above the Nervión River and punctured by a major highway, the Guggenheim Museum Bilbao resembles a huge sculpture. The composition is a spectacular collision of shapes and forms. Orthogonal limestone blocks present a vivid contrast to curvaceous metal-skinned forms. Glass walls provide light and transparency to the interiors and are designed to illuminate the works of art while also protecting them from the effects of heat and radiation. Sections of the building's steel skeleton are visible in some places, but most of the curving, free-form surfaces are wrapped in an intricately worked titanium that gives the exteriors a fluid appearance. The half-millimeter thick "fish-scale" titanium panels are guaranteed to last a hundred years. Warm limestone and glass punctuate the structure here and there. Panels of irregular shapes and sizes, generated by a com-

puter program, were created for the building from the three main materials: stone, glass, and titanium.

The museum's nineteen exhibition galleries are located on three levels surrounding the central atrium. They are connected by curving suspended walkways, glass-walled elevators, and stairways. The collections feature mainly contemporary painting and sculpture from Europe and North America.

The museum, which received over thirteen million visitors during the first year, functions both as a superlative art museum and as a symbol of civic pride for a provincial city in the heart of Spain's politically troubled Basque region. The innovative design has helped to make Bilbao a place of pilgrimage for architecture aficionados and art lovers from around the world. In April 2002, it was reported that tourism in Bilbao had increased five-fold and that over eighty percent of visitors came purposely to visit the new museum.

Primary Source

Gehry Talks: Architecture + Process [excerpt]

SYNOPSIS: In this book, architect Frank Gehry comments on the design process for thirty-six of his most well-known structures, including the Guggenheim Museum in Bilbao, Spain. In this excerpt, he explains the origin of his concept for the museum.

Tom Krens talked about the Wright atrium a lot. I realized Frank Lloyd Wright wasn't interested in the kind of art I'm interested in, and he ignored it. So he created a building that was antithetical to the art. I said to Krens, I don't think the building has to be that antagonistic to the art. But he thought the atrium should be a contentious piece, and should provoke artists. So that's what I picked up on. If you look at the first iterations, it's boxy and square, like a quarry, and I saw the walls as shelves where you could hang the work. Tom said, "Do something else. Take it on. Make it better than Wright. Make a great space, and we'll deal with it, and then let's review it."

Primary Source

Guggenheim Museum

SYNOPSIS: The Guggenheim Museum in Bilbao has become the symbol of the once-depressed Spanish fishing village and at the same time has cemented Frank Gehry's reputation as a visionary architect. It has become Gehry's trademark building.

There are gestures in my sketches. How do you get them built? I was able to build them with the computer, with material I would never have tried before. You'll see the relationship to my sketches in Bilbao. This is the first time I've gotten it. And once you taste blood, you're not going to give up. I don't know where it can go. How wiggly can you get and still make a building?

I used to be a symmetrical freak and a grid freak. I used to follow grids and then I started to think and I realized that those were chains, that Frank Lloyd Wright was chained to the 30–60 grid, and there was no freedom in it for him, and that grids are an obsession, a crutch. You don't need that if you can create spaces and forms and shapes. That's what artists do, and they don't have grids and crutches, they just do it.

The Winton house plan is a kind of pinwheel form. It came into focus again on the Lewis house, when I started plunking down forms, and then I realized that the plan of the Lewis house was very unusual. When you drew the plan, it was weird. I had never seen anything like it. Then I carried those ideas into Bilbao, and when I drew the plan of Bilbao I was so happy, because I realized that it was a beautiful thing. I'd never seen anything like it except in those buildings. It just evolved. I didn't consciously do it, but it intuitively evolved.

It's a very long way from one room, what I used to call the "white canvas," to Bilbao. I enjoy the complexity of a big project, trying to organize it. It's different from one room, but I think the one-room idea gave me the beginning of a way to break down the scale of big things. Scale is a struggle. How do you make a big monolithic building that's humane? I try to fit into the city. In Bilbao I took on the bridge, the river, the road, and then tried to make a building that was scaled to the nineteenth-century city.

Then I said to myself, "Artists have trouble with scale in the city because the city is such a large scale. No one ever commissions artists to make sixty-story sculptures, and until one of them makes a sixty-story sculpture, their works will not stand beside the Empire State Building and mean anything." I thought, if you could metaphorically create a city that would allow them to play, that might work. Then I realized that this was an opportunity to make something in the tradition of the great metaphorical cities. And that's what led to what's there, using the ramps and the stairs as a kind of metaphorical city—a metropolis.

Further Resources

BOOKS

Dal Co, Francesco. *Frank O. Gehry: The Complete Works.* New York: Monacelli Press, 1998.

Frank Gehry, Architect. New York: Guggenheim Museum Publications, 2001.

Isenberg, Barbara. *State of the Arts: California Artists Talk About Their Work.* New York: Morrow, 2000.

PERIODICALS

McGuigan, Cathleen. "The Man Who Designed Bilbao." *Newsweek,* November 22, 1999, 92.

Stephens, Suzanne. "The Bilbao Effect." *Architectural Record,* May 1999, 168–173.

AUDIO AND VISUAL MEDIA

Frank Gehry: Bilbao and Before. Insight Media. 1998, VHS.

Guggenheim Museum Bilbao. Films for the Humanities. 1999, VHS.

"Making the Planet a Better Place"

Journal article

By: Diane Pilgrim

Date: 1997

Source: Pilgrim, Diane. "Making the Planet a Better Place." *ARTnews,* October 1997, 192.

About the Author: Diane H. Pilgrim (1942–) received her education at Pennsylvania State University and New York University's Institute of Fine Arts. She held research positions at the Metropolitan Museum of Art and then served as curator of decorative arts at the Brooklyn Museum. In 1988, Pilgrim was appointed as director of the Cooper-Hewitt, National Design Museum of the Smithsonian Institution. Pilgrim writes frequently for various art journals and also has contributed to several books on design. ■

Introduction

Diane Pilgrim became interested in art history while she was a student at Penn State. She entered the masters' degree program at New York University's Institute of Fine Arts, where she wrote her thesis on John Cotton Dana, the founder of the Newark Museum in New Jersey. Her career as a museum curator has been greatly influenced by the spirit of Dana's work, which stressed making art both visually and intellectually more accessible.

Pilgrim, who has had multiple sclerosis since 1978 and is confined to a wheelchair, contends that design is largely misunderstood. While most people think of design with respect to fashion or automobiles, Pilgrim points out, "Anything human-made is design. Our mission is to make people aware that design has a major impact on our lives every second of the day. People are out there making decisions that affect our lives in wholly profound ways."

Pilgrim has combined her beliefs about design and her own experiences as a physically challenged person to give radical direction to the Cooper-Hewitt, National Design Museum, in Washington, D.C. Before the museum was remodeled, Pilgrim could enter the building only through a back entrance, and she had to be carried to some places in the museum. In 1996, the Cooper-Hewitt completed the first phase of an ambitious $20 million renovation when it re-opened its first-floor galleries. In addition to providing better protection to the collections through state-of-the-art temperature and heating systems, the project added ramps and lifts to the multi-level historic structure, thus making the museum accessible to all visitors, including the disabled, the elderly, and parents with baby strollers. Pilgrim became a spokesperson for a new approach to industrial design known as "universal design."

The Center for Universal Design was formed in 1989 as the Center for Accessible Housing under a grant from the National Institute on Disability and Rehabilitation Research. Its initial mission was to improve the quality and availability of housing for the disabled and elderly. The name was changed in 1996 to reflect the expanded scope of the center to embrace universal design in the built environment.

Significance

The Center for Universal Design describes its approach as follows: "The intent of universal design is to simplify life for everyone by making products, communications, and the built environment more usable by as many people as possible at little or no extra cost. Universal design benefits people of all ages and abilities." Universal design dictates that anything conceived or made by humans should be both eminently functional and aesthetically pleasing. The underlying principle is accessibility—both to people with disabilities and to the fully able. Universal design seeks to redesign products and structures to make them easier to use. Universal design also turns it attention to the built environment and strives to make buildings, parks, and sports facilities more accessible and navigable.

Many of the objects that have been deliberately "universally designed" intrigue the viewer, prompting questions about what is so new and unusual about them and why they look so familiar. One of the goals of universal design is to remove the stigma of accessibility, that is, the assumption that places or items designed for accessibility are necessarily ugly, awkward, or expensive. Eating utensils and kitchen implements are colorful if clunky (making them easy to grasp). An office desk may look sleek and curvaceous, a design that also makes it ergonomically correct.

Universal design is not intended to be "experimental" or to be meaningful only to a narrow segment of the population. Universally designed products and environments can be used by most people, regardless of their level of ability, state of health, gender, ethnicity, or cultural outlook. Examples of universally designed solutions range from simple handheld implements such as scissors to public transportation systems to entire landscapes and cities. The scale at which universal design attempts to change the physical environment requires the support of individual designers and clients as well as the recognition by the public, the government, and the corporate world that universal design can be used to benefit individuals, communities, and the economy.

Primary Source

"Making the Planet a Better Place" [excerpt]

SYNOPSIS: Diane Pilgrim, curator of the Cooper-Hewitt, National Design Museum, is confined to a wheelchair. In this essay, published in the October 1997 issue of *ARTnews*, she writes about her experiences as a person with disabilities and explains how universal design can make public and private spaces more accessible to both the disabled and the fully abled.

Life has a way of coming around full circle. Over 30 years ago I wrote a master's thesis on John Cotton Dana at the Institute of Fine Arts of New York University. Dana, the founder and director of the Newark Museum, believed that public institutions were intended for the public—and that meant everyone. In 1909, the year he established the museum, this wasn't a common idea. For the next 20 years Dana initiated exhibitions and programs that were in every sense aimed at the general public and made the Newark Museum the most progressive in the United States.

When I applied for the position of director of Cooper-Hewitt, National Design Museum, in 1988, I realized that I would be able to put into practice the beliefs held so strongly by Dana that had influenced my own. During my 15 years as curator of decorative arts at the Brooklyn Museum, I oversaw projects in which art and design were put into a context that everyone could understand and enjoy. At Brooklyn, relationships between curators and educators were close and rewarding. I hoped to give the benefits of this experience to another institution.

A designer explains the innovations in the kitchen of a "Universal Design" home to a group from the American Association of Retired Persons. The kitchen is designed to accommodate the needs of tenants of any age or ability. AP/WIDE WORLD PHOTOS. REPRODUCED BY PERMISSION.

But before I could decide to take on the Cooper-Hewitt, I had to consider whether I would have the necessary stamina. In 1978 I was diagnosed with multiple sclerosis. Since that time, design and the word "accessibility" have taken on new meanings for me, as I moved from walking with a cane to a single crutch to two crutches to—ten years ago—a wheelchair. I knew that the directorship would require not just my physical strength but my mental and emotional stamina as well. In the end, I couldn't refuse the opportunity of leading the National Design Museum into its second decade.

I have a second, hidden, disability that helps explain why I believe that museums have such an essential educational role to play and why it is critical to make them accessible to everyone. I am dyslexic. I did poorly in school. I read very little. Writing has always been a difficult and dreaded task for me. I have always believed that if I could understand a museum label, anyone could. The visual arts have been my words, my way of learning, while music and dance were my ways of expressing my emotions. So

I know from my own experience that people think and learn in different ways. I know that museum exhibitions don't just reinforce what is already being taught in schools—they offer an alternative way to learn. I believe now, as I always have, that it is every museum's responsibility to reach as many people as possible and to enrich as many lives as possible. So I think a great deal about how museums can dismantle the barriers—intellectual, social, cultural, and physical—that prevent them from fulfilling their potential as educational and cultural forces. . . .

Whatever our occupations, we are all in a sense designers. Everything conceived or made by humans is designed. The modern concept of universal design suggests that all human-made things, from the most seemingly insignificant object to the complex urban plan, must be functional and esthetically enhancing, democratic, humane, adaptable, cost-effective, and inclusive. This applies to museums and museum programs as well.

Design involves both functional and esthetic problem solving: it is based on respect and a sense of responsibility for all people, as well as an appreciation of cultural and national differences. The nation and the world face many social, economic, and environmental problems. Designers are in a unique position to contribute to their solutions because they are trained to bridge the gaps between technology, science, art, and humanities. Why aren't their energies being put, for instance, into decent low-cost housing, better transportation systems, and responsible garbage-disposal systems?

Consumers and users of the designed world must also be active participants in design by demanding what they need and want. The built environment in far too many cases doesn't work for us. We have learned to adapt to it. But shouldn't it be the other way around? Why should it be so difficult to program a VCR or set a digital watch?

If you can't come up with a good example of what doesn't work, just ask me. I'm one of the 48 million "officially" disabled people in America. I'm still the same person I was before I got sick, the only real difference being that my wheels have become my legs and my arms are the engine that propel my movement. However, when I'm confronted with a flight of stairs or a bathroom without a solid "grab bar" or a sidewalk without a curb cut, I understand the power of design in a profound way. In the end, I'm handicapped in only one way—by the designed, built environment. In addition, I'm handicapped by attitudes about people with disabilities.

The term "universal design" that we're hearing all the time now sounds ironic to me. It seems that designing for the widest possible audience should be inherent in the process. After all, it makes good business sense: why produce products for a narrow segment of the population when, with a little thought and creativity, they can be designed for a broader range of users? The more people who can use a product, the more who will buy it; just as the more who have access to our museum programs, the more who will use them.

Design that works is important to everyone, disabled or not. Consider the "typical" consumer for many designers—young, in good physical condition, of a certain height and weight, right-handed, with good hearing and eyesight. He or she does not require cane, wheelchair, or hearing aid. Nor does this person push a baby stroller or have any infirmity, such as arthritis, that complicates movement.

Doesn't it seem that very few people fit this narrow range designated as "the norm?" The world is a giant obstacle course for more and more people. "Typical consumers" are the minority. Recognizing this fact, designers and educational institutions such as museums, design schools, and universities have begun to explore and advocate the idea of universal design as a way to reach the widest audience possible.

Design excellence is a cultural, social, and economic imperative. I hope that the design and museum professions, working with and for consumers, will recognize the audiences as they really are and will look at and listen to their needs. I hope that the term "universal design" will become redundant as our new design ethic—to create a world that works for and respects the majority of people rather than the minority—spreads.

I believe that we all have a responsibility in the effort—since, in a larger sense, we are all designers—to try to make this planet, our only home, a better place for everyone.

Further Resources

BOOKS
Dobkin, Irma. *Gracious Spaces.* New York: McGraw-Hill, 1999.

Preiser, Wolfgang. *Universal Design Handbook.* New York: McGraw-Hill, 2001.

Winter, Steven. *Accessible Housing by Design: Universal Design Principles in Practice.* New York: McGraw-Hill, 1997.

PERIODICALS
Lovelace, Joyce. "Design for Living." *American Craft,* August/September, 1996, 6.

Pryor, Kelli. "Pilgrim's Progress." *ARTnews,* April, 1989, 87–88.

Smith, Dinitia. "Renovation of Museum Opens Door for Director." *The New York Times,* August 22, 1996, C11.

WEBSITES
The Center for Universal Design. Available online at http://www.design.ncsu.edu/cud/ (accessed April 30, 2003).

"Fleeced"
Magazine article

By: Hal Espen

Date: February 15, 1998

Source: Espen, Hal. "Fleeced." *The New York Times Magazine,* February 15, 1998, 20–23.

About the Author: Hal Espen was the features editor of *Outside* magazine when he wrote this article for *The New York Times Magazine.* ■

Introduction

Until the middle of the twentieth century, mountaineers, hikers, and other outdoor enthusiasts typically wore wool for maximum protection from cold temperatures. Wool is very warm, but it has many disadvantages: woolen garments are usually heavy and can be irritating to the skin. Wool tends to get soggy in wet conditions and is very slow to dry. The development of synthetic substitutes began after World War II (1939–1945) and was spurred by the growing popularity of outdoor winter sports and the increasing demand for high-tech alternatives to the cumbersome wool.

Malden Mills of Massachusetts was one of the first firms to respond to the growing demand. Originally established as a manufacturer of wool and cotton textiles, Malden Mills began to produce synthetic materials, including the fake fur used in faux fur garments. The family-owned business was fairly successful in moving from natural to synthetic fibers, but in the early 1980s it filed for bankruptcy protection after overproducing a synthetic fur that proved unpopular.

Malden Mills became a pioneer in the manufacture of remarkably warm and lightweight outdoor clothing with the introduction of a synthetic fleece fabric called PolarPlus. The fabric was made from polyester, a derivative of crude oil. In 1984, the distinguished mountaineer Yvon Chouinard asked Malden Mills to create a lightweight, warm, and reliable fabric for his outdoor clothing company, Patagonia. Malden Mills improved and revised PolarPlus to produce a "synthetic chinchilla," or "synchilla," as Patagonia marketed the fabric. Thanks to Synchilla, Patagonia's sales almost doubled over the next couple of years.

Significance

In early 1991, Malden Mills relaunched its high-performance fleece as Polartec, and it soon began manufacturing fabrics that were suitable for every layer of clothing, from underwear to outerwear. A lightweight synthetic knit fiber, Polartec is celebrated for many virtues: It can warm and cool, it can insulate and breathe, and it can block wind and rain. Polartec is quick-drying. The fabric is perhaps is best known for its ability to "wick" moisture and sweat away from the skin and for its high warmth-to-weight ratio, vital advantages in clothing that is worn during heavy outdoor exertions. In 1999, *Time* named Polartec fleece one of the most important inventions of the twentieth century.

By the end of the twentieth century, fleece had almost replaced the heavier wool as the favored fabric for cold-weather jackets and vests. People of all ages began to wear fleece, and it quickly became popular for casual wear as well as for outdoor sports clothing. The success of Patagonia's Synchilla and Malden Mills' Polartec fabrics also inspired imitations of dubious quality by other manufacturers who were eager to capitalize on the fashion trend. Fleece clothing in a range of qualities has became widely available in high-end clothing emporia, discount stores, and specialty outdoor retailers.

In 1994, Malden Mills opened a plant in Göritz, Germany, to take greater advantage of an international market. The factory expanded its offerings into a wide array of colors, patterns, and weights. Its retail store offers fleece fabrics and garments for outdoor wear, competitive sports, hunting and fishing, fitness, workwear, and military use. Eventually the company moved beyond clothing and developed an upholstery line of pillows, blankets, place mats, and napkins. Malden Mills supplies their fabrics and products to over 600 "brand partners" in more than fifty countries. In 1998, the company claimed ninety percent of the "technical" outdoor clothing market and sold $500 million worth of fleece and other fabrics.

Primary Source

"Fleeced" [excerpt]

SYNOPSIS: In this article, published in the February 15, 1998, issue of *The New York Times Magazine*, outdoor journalist Hal Espen traces the fascinating story of the development of synthetic fleece, the wonder fabric of the 1990s.

Just one word: fleece.

In this American winter of our anxious contentment, fleece is, as style scouts like to say, everywhere. Unlike "plastics," that singular specter of conformity and inauthenticity that Dustin Hoffman was confronted with three decades ago in "The Graduate," fleece in our time enjoys a fuzzy, warm, unironic kind of ubiquity. Yet like plastic, fleece is a wholly synthetic product, derived from the Uberstaple of late-20th-century life: crude oil. It is, in fact, pure polyester, the stuff of hideous 70's shirts and disco tailoring—but polyester technologically refined and reconfigured so that its organic-seeming secondary characteristics and narrative connotations have become dominant. The art historian Anne Hollander has written that fashion mutates to match "the shifty character of what looks right" at a given moment; in these first chilly months of 1998, the right uniform for both comfort and violent change in the weather is fleece.

A longtime fundamental of outdoor-sports product lines, fleece has lately proliferated on the streets, in department stores, in Old Navy television commercials, in baby carriages and in beds. Vogue assures us that models can't live without Patagonia's fleece vest. In L.L. Bean's Christmas catalogue this year, fleece was the unrivaled star attraction, featured on the front and back covers and highlighted in the first 14 pages; more than 170 fleece items were available. Over on Seventh Avenue, Tommy Hilfiger and Polo by Ralph Lauren offer fleece designs; Donna Karan is selling a $300 fleece robe and a $170 fleece unitard, while Nicole Miller has made dresses and skirts of fleece. . . .

By far the most culturally resonant version of fleece is the nonspecialized "technical" sportswear that ranges from L.L. Bean's and Lands' End's high-volume lines to more hard-core outdoor-endeavor brands like the North Face, Marmot and Mountain Hardwear. The aura of these premium lines has benefited both from constant innovation in fleece design and from waves of marketing that extols the fabric's empowering qualities. Like jungle khaki before it, fleece has become associated with athleticism and risk-taking in exotic and remote wilderness areas, and in the process, an androgynous fashionable archetype has emerged: the trekker. . . .

Of course, earlier generations of explorers and adventurers had somehow managed to conquer mountains and survive the back-of-beyond without space-age clothing, but as the recreation boom took off, the stoical tolerance of discomfort began to seem a little stupid—and an obsessive attention to gear became half the fun. By the mid-80's, improved versions of Gore-Tex became tremendously popular, inspiring endless debate over the art and science of wicking moisture away from the skin.

A few years earlier, Patagonia, based in Ventura, Calif., had introduced what it would later describe as its "infamously homely yet unforgettable" pile jacket—a synthetic fleece garment that, it insisted in one of its patented authenticity-by-association gambits, was modeled on jackets used by North Sea fishermen. Its successor, called a bunting jacket, became the company's first runaway best seller in the early 80's. But the fateful date for fleece came in the spring of 1985, when Patagonia launched its Synchilla-fabric line of jackets, the first recognizably modern, fuzzy-smooth fleece outerwear. . . .

Backed by Yvon Chouinard's reputation for insisting on fanatical quality control and for possessing an exquisite, almost tortured corporate conscience, technical fleece was accepted as the real thing. For polyester, which had so ignominiously

A model sports a fleece pullover at a 1996 fashion show. Synthetic fleece, a now ubiquitous fabric, was developed by the Malden Mills textile company for use in outdoor clothing. The fabric proved remarkably successful, and by the mid-1990s fleece was commonly used not just for high-performance outdoor clothing, but for a whole range of casual garments as well. © MITCHELL GERBER/CORBIS. REPRODUCED BY PERMISSION.

fallen from favor at the end of the preceding decade, being embraced by the environmental purists and gnarly role models who bought Patagonia was the beginning of a triumphant comeback.

In Lawrence, Mass., the executives at Malden Mills watched the spread of Synchilla with growing intentness. After all, Malden and Patagonia had collaborated on the design of Synchilla, and Malden manufactured Synchilla and virtually all of the high-end fleece being sold through outdoor specialty catalogues and stores across the country. The company also made "lots of crummy fleece," as one Malden executive admits now, but it began to see that its fortune lay not in remaining merely a faithful supplier to brands like Patagonia but also in establishing its own brand as the quality standard.

Malden Mills Industries, which is privately held, was founded in 1906 by Henry Feuerstein, an Orthodox Jew from Hungary who had won and lost a fortune in the New York City garment business before trying his luck in Massachusetts. Malden became a leading manufacturer of furniture upholstery, fake fur and commodity fleece for the bunting trade. . . .

After first establishing its fleece in the 80's under the brand name Polarfleece, among others, Malden relaunched its high-performance fabric as Polartec in early 1991. The new name explicitly echoed the notion of technical clothing, and its new mountain-range logo seemed to be a conscious homage to Patagonia's. Malden's ambitions had grown far beyond the idea of providing only insulation. It began manufacturing fleece suitable for every layer of clothing, from underwear, socks, hats and gloves to sweaters, jackets and pants, both as inner layers and outerwear. It added four-way stretch and laminated breathable windproof and water-resistant membranes inside its two-layer fleece.

The range of garments reflects Malden's obsessiveness about fleece, as do its patents and trade secrets. Close attention is paid to variations in the polyester filament yarns it uses: tenacity, lubricity and colorfastness are crucial characteristics. Next, in order for polyester to become fleece, its knit design must incorporate a surface covered with tiny loops. The truly cunning stage of making fleece is the final one—the finishing—in which thousands of tiny needles grab and pull out the loops before shearing trims the fleece to a velourlike smoothness or a peltlike pile. The resulting products range from lightweight next-to-the-skin fleece ($4.50 a yard wholesale) to warm-water wet suits ($25 a yard). Basic Polartec 200 midweight fleece wholesales for $7 to $8 a yard; the price will increase four times or more by the time the material reaches the consumer in a finished garment. . . .

Malden is targeting anyone who works and plays outdoors. Talks are under way with the U.S. military (the Green Berets are already using a very technical version of Polartec's Power Stretch line, and Polartec is standard-issue wear for American troops stationed in Bosnia), with the Postal Service and with utility companies around the country. The company is going after the golf-apparel business in a big way. And more and more, fleece is making its way to the indigenous people whose way of life contributed so much tribal mystique to fleece: Sherpa guides are well stocked with Polartec hats and sweaters; so are Indians in the Andes and natives in the Arctic regions. . . .

Fleece, then, is on the verge of taking over the entire world; Aaron Feuerstein's eyes light up when he talks about the potential of fleece catching on in China. The only question that remains, as Malden races toward a future in which it becomes a billion-dollar company and as everyone you know eventually turns up wrapped in a colorful, nappy cocoon, is this: What is to become of that precious, perishable nimbus of authenticity that still hovers around fleece?

Probably something akin to the dilution of meaning that has befallen other formerly potent fashion sheaths in the aftermath of relentless exposure—coverings like denim for the counterculture, leather for various demimondes and even shamelessly unveiled human skin itself. Eventual obsolescence is the inescapable and melancholy fate of the authenticity that mass marketers have attached to fleece. To be sure, fleece is an ingenious and beneficial technological invention, but one day soon we'll recognize it as fake in every way and we'll be a little bit ashamed of what we once felt about it, if we think about it at all.

Further Resources

PERIODICALS

Connare, Carol. "Getting Fleeced at Malden Mills." *Yankee,* January 2000, 48–51.

"Tibor Kalman"

Interview

By: Tibor Kalman and Allan Casey

Date: Autumn, 1998

Source: Allan Casey. "Tibor Kalman."*Adbusters,* Autumn, 1998, 5. Available online at http://adbusters.org/campaigns/first/toolbox/tiborkalman/1.html; website home page: http://adbusters.org (accessed July 10, 2003).

About the Author: Tibor Kalman (1949–1999) was born in Budapest and lived most of his adult life in New York City. He was the principal of the design firm M&Co. When he died in 1999, his wife, Maira Kalman, who is a designer and illustrator, took over the firm. ■

Introduction

Tibor Kalman was born in Hungary and fled with his family to the United States in 1956 during the Soviet invasion of his country. The family settled in Poughkeepsie, New York, where Kalman was mocked as the class "geek" and isolated because of his poor English. His childhood loneliness and his love for all things American helped to steer him into a career in graphic design via journalism. A design magazine editor and close friend of Kalman's once explained, "He was keenly passionate about things of the American vernacular because he wasn't American. In that sense, he taught the whole profession to look at things that they may not have seen as closely or taken as seriously."

After earning a degree in journalism at New York University, Kalman took a job in the New York offices of Barnes and Noble Booksellers. One day he impressed his employer by his redesign of a window display. Kalman received other similar assignments, and he eventually became the store's art director, producing a series of corporate identity programs for the company.

Kalman opened his own design firm, M&Co, in 1979. The firm served a broad spectrum of clients, including corporations such as IBM and The Limited and bands such as The Talking Heads, for whom Kalman designed record album covers.

Between 1991 and 1997, Kalman lived and worked in Rome as editor of Benetton's magazine, *Colors*. He returned to New York in 1997 and until his death in 1999, he produced a wide range of works, including books of his work, newspaper editorials, music album covers, and public art (e.g, in New York City's Times Square). Some of Kalman's work is now part of the permanent design collections of the Museum of Modern Art in New York and the Cooper-Hewitt Museum. It has been observed that Kalman brought an insatiable curiosity and radical sense of humor to every project he undertook.

Significance

Kalman closed the offices of M&Co in New York and moved to Rome in 1991 to found the magazine *Colors,* a new publication for the Italian knitwear company Benetton. In *Colors* Kalman found the perfect vehicle for both his visual and his philosophical ideas. Significant examples of Kalman's thought-provoking and humorous style appeared in the magazine, where he took an inventive approach to both editorial content and design. He made innovative use of what was ostensibly a fashion magazine by presenting a popular forum for airing a range of human rights issues from a radical viewpoint, and he achieved this within a revolutionary design context. The

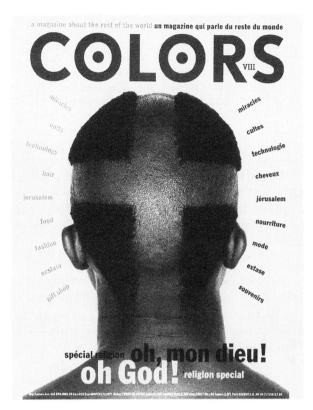

Each issue of *Colors* magazine focused on a different universal topic, such as religion, food, death, and war. Bold photographs depicting slices of life around the world, accompanied by brief text, sought to encourage readers to be more globally conscious. Each issue had text in two languages. KALMAN, TIBOR, GRAPHIC DESIGNER. FROM AN ILLUSTRATION IN *COLORS* MAGAZINE, VOL. 8, SEPTEMBER, 1994. REPRODUCED BY PERMISSION.

magazine was a unique house organ for a fashion company, offering a striking, graphics-heavy layout and featuring bilingual articles on topics such as race and AIDS.

The magazine Kalman created thus simultaneously promoted Benetton's sophisticated, multinational brand identity and advocated an all-embracing multiethnic philosophy. Kalman's *Colors* was unique in the world of magazine publishing and was both controversial and wildly successful.

Kalman's design sensibility has been characterized as optimistic, universally appealing, and instructive without being didactic. He once said, "My quandary is that designers have been taught to be liars. They have been taught to use their skills—just like lawyers and accountants—to distort information."

Primary Source

"Tibor Kalman" [excerpt]

SYNOPSIS: Tibor Kalman's intelligent and provocative design work ranged from album covers to opinion pieces to corporate identity programs. He is perhaps best remembered as the editor and art director of *Colors* magazine, the Benetton house publication, where he combined strong-minded political views with equally forthright visuals. In this interview he discusses his controversial work in *Colors* and explains his design and political philosophies.

What is it about you that makes people think you have all the answers?

Yeah, I have all the answers. I am just a person who is willing to speak out. I don't have any answers at all, but I am just willing to mouth off. A lot of people are much more cautious. I'm not, I've never been. . . .

What is your job, anyway . . .

These days I say "designer-slash-editor" just so people can have some sort of word. But I move from project to project. Today, I'm moving between another children's book that my wife is doing about Grand Central Station to designing a section of a book that is coming out about my work, to a new series of film documentaries about art, to helping promote something called The Robin Hood Foundation. They take money from rich people and give it to poor people in a kind of very straightforward way.

Doing a magazine piece on you is a bit of irony. You are on record as saying that magazines are all boring.

I mean that the magazine—as a medium of culture or social importance or of art, or of defining new ideas—is dead. The selection of magazines is vast, but they are all the same. There are a lot of different brands in North America, but they are all the same. There are a lot of different cars, but they have all been in the same wind tunnel. There are a lot of different CDs, but they all sound the same. And as you get further away from intellectually based property, stuff becomes even more identical. There are three or four brands of baked beans, and they all taste identical. The only difference is packaging and positioning.

If the product being created is market-driven, then it is going to be a piece of shit. A magazine is a very expensive object to create, and unless there is an angel with five or 10 million bucks, a magazine can't be any good, because it has to pander to advertisers, to the bland, average sphere.

And yet, you met such an angel in Luciano Benetton and the Benetton clothing company. They gave you the money and the freedom to create a different kind of magazine. You once said that you didn't

think Colors *was a magazine at all because it shattered so many conventions of the genre and had no advertisers to please.*

Colors broke all the rules because Benetton could afford to make a magazine that broke all the rules.

But in another sense, Colors *was an advertisement from cover to cover because it was (and is) published to help sell Benetton clothes.* Colors *was part of a marketing strategy.*

Anyone who gets paid is part of a strategy. There are not that many ways of keeping yourself pure, though that is not a defense of what I did. There were two truths about that project. The magazine represented and advocated things that I believed in—that was Truth Number One. Truth Number Two is: the things I believed in were part of their strategy.

The pages of Colors *you put out from New York and Rome were, depending whom you talked to, troubling, shocking, racially provocative, sacrilegious, staunchly humanist, virulently anti-corporate, leftist. It added up to one weird marketing strategy.*

Benetton's strategy, in my opinion, was to accomplish marketing by getting press. And I think they have done a masterful job in creating loyalty among sort of semi-hip, semi-young 15 to 35-year-olds who are sympathetic to the ideas in their advertising. But if you look at the clothing, it is designed for 35 to 55-year-old yuppies. It's a brilliant strategy, because the parents do the shopping and the kids like the brand, even if they don't like the clothes that much. . . .

And yet within the world of corporate advertising, you have found a lot of freedom to express yourself. The design writer Rick Poyner argues that you create what he calls "temporary autonomous zones" within corporations, from which you can express radical ideas. Are corporations themselves your medium?

I think corporations are very convenient media with which some work can get done. Benetton was an extremely convenient medium for me to be able to put out the ideas that were contained in *Colors* magazine. . . .

Does that mean there is hope for corporate America, that the system has a conscience buried somewhere?

There is no salvation for corporate America if a company's only intention is to manipulate its stock price upwards, or for the principals to make more money. There is nothing in that. . . . What you need is to go in there and create a corporate conscience,

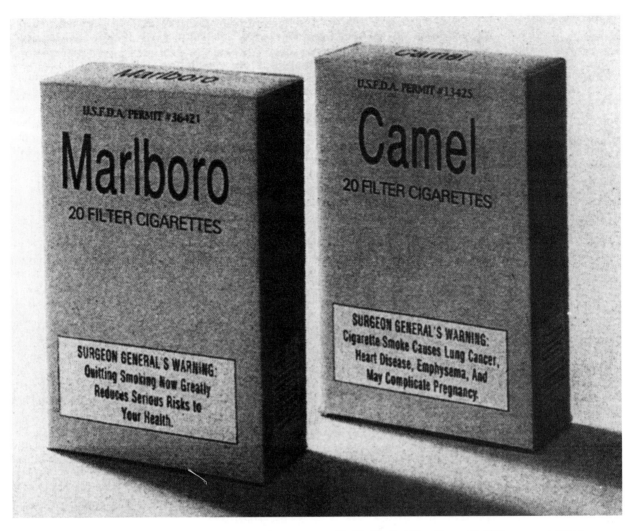

This image from a column by Tibor Kalman on marketing and cigarettes appeared in *The New York Times* January 15, 1997. **KALMAN, TIBOR, GRAPHIC DESIGNER. PRODUCTION BY ALAN HILL. PHOTOGRAPH BY NAUM KAZHDAM. COPYRIGHT © 1997,** *THE NEW YORK TIMES.* **REPRODUCED BY PERMISSION.**

to make corporations feel like they ought to spend money on things that make their workers' environments nicer, or make the world nicer, or help people outside their corporation. The only thing you can do is try to trick corporations into doing the nice things.

So who is going to infiltrate corporations for the common good? Ad agencies?

I have met more corporations with consciences than ad agencies. Agencies are just like accounting firms and law firms. They take the position of their client and try to make the most money for them.

What about you? You're an ad guy, and you have a conscience.

Well, I once did a project for RJ Reynolds . . . but I think what happened to me is that, as I succeeded, I ran into my own conscience. I had my choice of jobs and choices about which way to work

that a lot of designers don't have. Most designers are making a living, a few are winning awards. But there's few who are feeling comfortable enough to think maybe there's a better way. It all comes from privilege. I think that even generosity comes from privilege. Socialism comes from capitalism, not instead of it. It's a more highly evolved way of organizing the way we work.

Without formal design training, you've shaken up that whole industry. You proved that magazines could be global media. You've played Robin Hood with corporate profits, and tried to turn advertising to good purposes. You've given the world a Black Queen Elizabeth and a white Spike Lee. What compels you to turn things upside down?

I am an extremely privileged person, but I think it comes from the pursuit of work, as opposed to other things. People seem to pursue money, most commonly. Some pursue a political agenda, some pursue fame. I pursue the blissful moment of coming up with an idea. That makes me very, very happy.

Further Resources

BOOKS

Kalman, Tibor. *Tibor Kalman: Perverse Optimist.* New York: Princeton Architectural Press, 1999.

Peltason, Ruth A., ed. *(un)Fashion.* New York: Abrams, 2000.

PERIODICALS

"The Man With the Glass Half Full." *Interview,* August 1999, 112–117.

Wieners, Brad. "Color Him a Provocateur." *Wired Magazine,* December, 1996.

"Getting Involved in 'Green' Design: A Primer on the Important Issues and the Options Available to Architects"

Journal article

By: Sandy Mendler

Date: April 1999

Source: Mendler, Sandy. "Getting Involved in 'Green' Design: A Primer on the Important Issues and the Options Available to Architects." *Architectural Record,* April 1999, 24.

About the Author: Sandy Mendler is a senior designer at Hellmuth, Obata and Kassenbaum, an architectural firm in Washington, D.C. The firm, known especially for its sports-facility commissions, is also a leader in using sustainable, or "green," design in large-scale projects. Mendler leads the firm's sustainable-design team, and she is on the board of directors of the United States Green Building Council. ∎

Introduction

Over the past century, technological development, urban sprawl, and the exploitation of natural resources have combined to change the world in dramatic ways. On the one hand, the standard of living has improved for millions of people worldwide. On the other hand, ecosystem destruction and pollution have created serious problems. As the huge financial and other costs of these problems have become more obvious, people have grown more aware of the need for a proactive approach to preserving the natural environment through the wise management and enlightened design of the man-made environment. There is a growing conviction that we can deliberately

shape human environments and simultaneously promote a greater sensitivity to and respect for the integrity of our natural world.

From initial design to final use, architectural and industrial structures and the systems that support them necessarily draw upon natural resources for materials and energy. Construction makes an enormous demand on resources and raw materials. It is also the single largest contributor to the stream of waste and environmental contamination. Design professionals, who shape our information, our tools, and our built environment, are regarded as an indispensable source of solutions that can prevent further degrading of the environment, if not correct the damage that has already been done.

In the middle of the twentieth century, many buildings were designed and built without energy efficiency or environmental "friendliness." Houses, office buildings, and factories were often made of materials that were unstable or even dangerous (asbestos insulation, for example). Similarly, some of the most popular architectural styles—for example, the "glass-box" office buildings representative of the International Style—were very inefficient in their energy consumption. These buildings are expensive to operate and are over-reliant on natural resources.

Significance

Before the 1980s, "sustainable" or "green" was applied to an iconoclastic, fringe approach to building. It was associated with eco-fanatics who wanted to live in the backcountry in naturalistic structures. However, toward the end of the century, in large part facilitated by the development of new technologies, the idea took hold that "sustainable" or "green" design was the only responsible way to build. Practitioners of the approach began creating designs that promoted efficient use of resources and materials. They also began to concern themselves with such issues as the affordability and durability of their structures, and to pay serious attention to the health, safety, and comfort of the occupants.

Since the 1990s, "green" architecture has revolutionized the design, construction, and maintenance of structures. Prompted by new laws, rising energy costs, workplace health concerns, and diminishing natural resources, American architects increasingly make the protection and preservation of the environment a central motive in their design work. Green architecture combines ancient principles of construction (for example, the use of rammed earth and the employment of natural light and ventilation) with sophisticated technology and maintenance systems to create environments that are decidedly more healthy and conducive to the greater well being and productivity among their occupants.

Architect Mike Reynolds stands on the steps of an "earthship," a house he designed to be self-sustaining. The walls are made of beer cans, mud, and cement. Water used in the home is caught on its roof. © ROGER RUSSMEYER/CORBIS. REPRODUCED BY PERMISSION.

Consumer preferences and a growing awareness of the benefits of green design are helping to turn sustainable building into a mainstream idea. Architecture publications have begun to highlight green buildings. Books on the topic have proliferated. The techniques have been applied both to home construction and to institutional building. Distinguished architects, such as Pritzker Prize-winners Renzo Piano and Norman Foster, are becoming known for their integrated green solutions, thus helping to improve the status of "sustainable design" in the world of architecture and in the public eye.

Primary Source

"Getting Involved in 'Green' Design: A Primer on the Important Issues and the Options Available to Architects"

> **SYNOPSIS:** In this article, published in *Architectural Record* in April 1999, Sandy Mendler, an architect and a leader in the green design movement, encourages others in her profession to set forth a re-

alistic set of plans and goals in building "green." Mendler outlines an overall strategy for designers of sustainable projects.

You have just been given a terrific opportunity to design a "green" building. What next? What to think about first? There are many critical issues to address at each stage of the design process—and due to their complexity, it would take a long time to address each of them fully. But to get started, this overview can be used as a framework.

Initiating the project

Select team members who share an interest in sustainable design and look for allies to supplement your efforts, such as local green building organizations and university resources. Build a common vocabulary and understanding of the issue involved. Invest time in sustainable design goal setting. Develop an energy budget and quantitative performance goals wherever possible. Consider using the U.S. Green Building Council's rating system to identify performance targets (see www.USGBC.org).

Considering the context

Look at possible reuse of existing structures and redevelopment of urban areas to reduce sprawl. Develop links to public transit and strategies to create pedestrian-friendly, livable communities. Respond to the cultural and historic context and protect sensitive natural areas.

Siting the building

Consider how the massing and orientation will affect energy performance, opportunities for daylighting, and natural ventilation. Look at how design options will influence water features such as flood plains, wetlands, and stream corridors. To preserve natural amenities, minimize the need for cut-and-fill and control the location of site utilities.

Shaping the design solution

Consider passive heating, cooling, and ventilating strategies and daylighting opportunities. Integrate renewable energy systems and water-reuse strategies. Evaluate heating and cooling loads of proposed building configurations, heat-recovery opportunities, and locations of intake and exhaust air.

Developing the planning concept

Create planning strategies and flexible infrastructures to enhance long-term flexibility and avoid premature building obsolescence. Provide effective ventilation and isolate potential sources of contamination. Develop strategies to accommodate recycling, including collection facilities at the point of use on each floor and staging areas at the loading dock.

Developing specifications: Clearly identify environmental performance goals in specifications, such as maximum allowable volatile organic compounds (VOC) content, minimum recycled content, nonpermissible toxic materials, and energy and/or water efficiency of appliances, fixtures, and equipment. Develop specifications for construction-waste recycling, reuse of on-site materials, tree protection, and erosion control.

Optimizing the design

Use the building envelop to reduce heating and cooling loads while maximizing the use of daylighting. Use energy and daylight modeling to determine optimal glazing performance, insulation values, and interior and exterior sunshading. Develop daylight strategies in tandem with electric lighting. Consider ceiling height, reflectivity of interior finishes and furniture, fixture efficiency, and lamp longevity.

Investigating materials

Search for materials that are durable and low-maintenance and will have low environmental impact throughout their life cycle. This includes raw materials, production processes, packaging and shipping, installation and use, and disposal and reuse. Explore opportunities to use smaller quantities of materials, reclaim existing, salvaged, or refurbished ones, and incorporate locally manufactured materials.

Getting it built

Communicate the project's environmental goals to the construction team. Carefully review submittals, shop drawings, and proposed materials substitutions, and document the lessons you have learned for future projects.

Further Resources

BOOKS

Gissen, David. *Big and Green: Toward Sustainable Architecture in the 21st Century.* New York: Princeton Architectural Press, 2002.

Hawken, Paul, Amory Lovins, and Hunter Lovins. *Natural Capitalism.* New York: Little, Brown, and Co., 1999.

Spiegel, Ross, and Dru Meadows. *Green Building Materials: A Guide to Product Selection and Specification.* New York: John Wiley and Sons, 1999.

PERIODICALS

Talarico, Wendy. "The Nature of Green Architecture." *Architectural Record,* April 1998, 149.

Wagner, Michael. "Green Design." *Interiors,* January 1995, 124–125.

WEBSITES

"Green Design/Sustainable Architecture: Information Sources." Environmental Design Library, University of California, Berkeley. Available online at http://www.lib.berkeley.edu /ENVI/GreenAll.html; website home page http://www.lib .berkeley.edu (accessed April 30, 2003).

Michael Graves Toaster
Work of art

By: Michael Graves

Date: 1999

Source: Michael Graves Toaster. Designed for Target Stores and manufactured by Black & Decker. 1999. Photograph

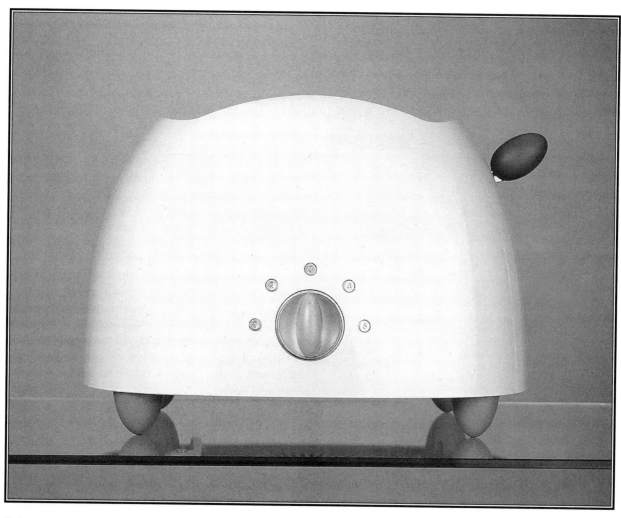

Primary Source

Michael Graves Toaster

SYNOPSIS: Architect Michael Graves moved into the spotlight and radically revised discount-store merchandise in the 1990s when Target Stores retained him to design a line of household items, including this award-winning toaster. The collaboration was a huge success and made pioneering design, at affordable prices, available to the average American chain-store shopper. **PHOTO COURTESY OF MICHAEL GRAVES & ASSOCIATES. AWARD WINNING TOASTER DESIGNED IN 1999 FOR TARGET STORES AND MANUFACTURED BY BLACK & DECKER.**

available online at www.michaelgraves.com (accessed April 29, 2003).

About the Designer: Michael Graves (1934–) was born in Indianapolis. He studied architecture at the University of Cincinnati and Harvard University. After a two-year fellowship at the American Academy in Rome, he started his own architectural firm in Princeton, New Jersey, in 1964. Graves has distinguished himself in the world of architecture both as a designer and as a theorist, and he has received some of the profession's most prestigious awards. He is also professor emeritus at Princeton University, where he taught architecture for forty years. ■

Introduction

In the late 1960s and early 1970s, Michael Graves was a member of the "New York Five." This group of architects explores design ideas that are grounded in the modernist theories of Swiss architect Le Corbusier. By the mid-1970s, however, Graves had moved away from this legacy to develop a broad eclecticism involving the use of modernized classical forms and emphatic uses of color. Although the mass and sense of order in Graves' buildings evoke classical ideals, his vision of classicism has a sardonic character, often incorporating, even seeming to celebrate, elements of pastiche and kitsch.

During the 1980s, Graves secured an international reputation for such imposing and sometimes playful commissions as the U.S. Courthouse in Washington, D.C.; the Hyatt Hotel in Fukuoka, Japan; the Portland Building in Washington State; and two Disneyworld

An aisle at a Target store in Manhattan Beach, California, stocked with Michael Graves-designed houseware products. © DAVID BUTOW/ CORBIS SABA. REPRODUCED BY PERMISSION.

theme hotels in Orlando, Florida. As a professor of architecture at Princeton University, Graves has inspired countless students and practitioners of postmodernist architecture through his methodologies and aesthetic vision. He has been credited with leading American architectural thought into postmodernism. One of the principal figures of twentieth-century architecture, Graves has had a profound influence, directly or indirectly, on American aesthetic taste.

Graves was interested early on in product design as well as architecture, carrying his fascination with textures, colors, and shape into ideas for home furnishings and appliances. He secured his reputation in that arena with his 1985 teapot, featuring a playful bird spout, for the Italian design firm Alessi. Over half a million were sold, and the teapot has achieved the status of a collector's item.

From the outset, Graves' firm often designed both the interiors and the appointments—furnishings, textiles, lighting, hardware, and fixtures—for its structures. In the mid 1990s, a merchandising director for Target Stores approached Graves to ask if Graves Design, the firm's consumer products division, would create housewares and small appliances for the discount chain. Graves toured a Target Store, putting yellow stickers on the hundreds of products he thought he could improve. Ultimately he agreed to create 350 original product designs for Target.

Significance

The Graves collection for Target stores has been very successful. There are now 500 Graves-designed products being sold in Target Stores in the United States— ranging from toilet brushes to teakettles. The products are practical and playful, and they have proved extremely popular to Target's new, more upscale customers. Prices vary widely and suit every budget: At the low end are $13 wooden picture frames with cast-iron bases evocative of ancient Pompeiian artifacts; an award-winning $40 toaster; and a $35 teakettle with a red whistle that has become a Graves trademark. The high end features an Indonesian hardwood patio set, with umbrella, for $580, and other costly items of furniture. Graves objects to skimping on design details just because Target is a discount chain. "Design has nothing to do with economic class. If I were designing for Cartier or Tiffany, I would expend the same energy," he says.

Graves created products that are both aesthetically appealing and ergonomically designed for comfortable use. He also insisted on controlling the packaging of his products in order to elevate their status among Target's other merchandise and to attract buyers by their distinctive look. Gradually, this "Graves effect" moved to other areas of the Target stores. For the first time, American consumers could buy trendy, well-designed products at reasonable prices at large, discount chain stores.

Within three years, the Target deal amounted to about a quarter of Graves' business and helped to reinforce his architecture practice. When the Target chain and its vendors decided to help fund the restoration of the Washington Monument, they recruited Graves to design the scaffolding.

Further Resources

BOOKS
Bertsch, Georg C. *The Water Kettle by Michael Graves.* Frankfurt am Main: Verlag Form, 1997.

Iovine, Julie V. *Michael Graves.* San Francisco: Chronicle Books, 2002.

PERIODICALS
Freund, Charles Paul. "Downmarket Deluxe." *Reason,* January, 2001, 58.

Goldberger, Paul. "A Postmodernist Goes Shopping." *The New Yorker,* February 1, 1999, 23–24.

WEBSITES
Napoli, Lisa. "Target Hits Bull's-eye with 'Guests.'" MSNBC News, January 23, 2003. Available online at http://www .msnbc.com/news/692938.asp?0bl=-0; website home page: http://www.msnbc.com (accessed April 29, 2003).

The Celebration Chronicles

Nonfiction work

By: Andrew Ross

Date: 1999

Source: Ross, Andrew. *The Celebration Chronicles.* New York: Ballantine, 1999, 4–6, 9–10, 14, 17–19.

About the Author: Andrew Ross (1956–), born in Scotland, is a cultural critic and professor of American Studies at New York University. In 1997, he lived in Disney's New Urbanist town, Celebration, Florida, and wrote a frank and ambivalent account of his experience. ■

Introduction

Located just south of Orlando, Celebration is an old-fashioned small town that was built from the ground up in the mid-1990s by the Walt Disney Company. Situated on about 5,000 acres of recovered swamp and farmland, the planned community cost some $2.5 billion dollars to build. The town plan and the design of its structures are Disney's interpretation of New Urbanism ideals, which, in broad terms, oppose the spread of suburbs and seek to diminish the ill effects of suburban sprawl.

Disney recruited celebrated architects to design individual buildings, including Cesar Pelli for the Art Deco movie theater, Michael Graves for the post office, and Philip Johnson for the imposing town hall. Critics call Celebration an "architectural jumble" characterized by a melange of styles without a unifying style. Developers defend the town by arguing that the mixture of styles more closely reflects how a "real town" evolves over time.

Celebration was intended to foster a courtesy and calm reminiscent of the old American South. The town's houses are based on six styles and are situated close to the street in attractive neighborhoods. Prices of the homes range from $199,000 for a small townhouse to as much as $1.7 million for a luxurious custom home. Although real estate prices are on average twenty percent higher than for comparable homes in the area, demand for the houses has been high. An anticipated 20,000 residents will inhabit the projected 8,000 apartments and houses when the construction is complete in about 2010.

Significance

Cultural critic Andrew Ross decided to live for a year in Celebration, "the town that Disney built," in order to find out how "real" a city created by the masters of make-believe could be. An inveterate urban New Yorker, Ross was prepared to hone and exercise his Disney-bashing skills during his year of residence. He was therefore surprised to discover that his neighbors were not Disney-theme fanatics, but people who simply wanted to live somewhere clean, dependable, and safe. Ross immersed himself in the community, volunteered at the controversial local school, and became an honorary Celebrationite. His book, *The Celebration Chronicles,* was published in 1999 with the subtitle: "Life, Liberty, and the Pursuit of Property Value in Disney's New Town."

Andrew Ross's first reactions to Celebration were decidedly cynical: Disney wasn't content to decide how people should relax on vacation, what they should watch at movie theaters, and what they should hear on the radio. Now, with the creation of Celebration, the company famous for theme parks and cartoon characters seemed to be dictating how people should live. Ross tended to agree with critics who saw Celebration as an exercise in corporate social engineering. He observed that the town is really just another Orlando suburb—if a more attractive one than most. The irony is that Celebration is a characteristically American place, in both its utopian ideal and its commercial reality.

Celebration is the latest in a long line of utopian American communities. Many wealthy and eager romantics were enticed to the town by their belief that Disney magic would make for a perfect community. Many residents soon found their dreams being pitted against Disney's financial goals and restrictive rules for what residents could do with their homes. They engaged in a grass-roots activism that did more to bring their community together than any of the schemes of the Disney "imagineers." In this effort, Ross considers that the town residents discovered the true benefits of the New Urbanism.

Primary Source

The Celebration Chronicles [excerpt]

SYNOPSIS: Cultural critic and historian Andrew Ross spent the year 1997 living in Celebration, Florida, a planned community developed by the Walt Disney Corporation in the New Urbanist spirit. Ross's book about his experiences challenged the expectation that Celebration would be a real-world version of a Disney theme park. In these excerpts, he discusses the reasons the town was built and his early days as a resident.

Like most new blueprints for the pursuit of happiness, the reason for Celebration was rooted in repulsion for the existing order of things. In the early 1950s, Walt Disney's disgust for the postwar urban sprawl of Los Angeles (and his distaste for the lack of hygiene in other popular entertainment facilities) fueled his idea to build a theme park in Anaheim. Disneyland sprang up as a quarantine zone, artificially purged of the urban ills, design tragedies, and traffic atrocities that plagued its California area

Housing developers converse in a new suburb of Celebration, a community planned by Disney. © **MARK PETERSON/CORBIS SYGMA.**
REPRODUCED BY PERMISSION.

surroundings. Almost overnight, however, the park spawned a commercial tourist sprawl directly outside its gates. . . .

So what was I doing here? Unlike most of the new residents streaming into town in the late summer of 1997, neither attraction nor repulsion had drawn me to Celebration. I was on a year's sabbatical from New York City. The dense turbulence, multicultural throngs, and ultra-liberal lifestyles of downtown Manhattan, where I live and work, seem to repel more Americans than they attract. For people like myself, it is a step closer to utopia than just about anywhere else (and about as far from a master-planned community as you could imagine). But Manhattanites are chronically insular and loath to recognize other signs of terrestrial life, especially the quality and purpose of suburban Middle America. If we are ever to be good neighbors in the larger landscape, there is much to learn about places and people that do not feature on Saul Steinberg's famous cartoon map of the "New Yorker's View of the World." It was partly in this spirit that I accepted my

publisher's assignment to live and work in Celebration. Friends, colleagues, and familiars of my past writings were dubious of my motive. Disney-bashing is a favored sport in New York City, and has taken on a fresh vigor with the company's new presence on 42nd Street. I left behind a town frothing with offense at the Disneyfication of Times Square. But if Disney-bashing had been my chief goal, I could have written this book from a safe distance, in common with most armchair practitioners of that ballooning genre. Conversely, once in Celebration, it would take some energy on my part to dispel the suspicion, inside and outside of town, that I was somehow in cahoots with the Walt Disney Company. . . .

First Day

On my first day in Celebration . . . Kennedy Donofrio, Celebration's rental property manager, is eager to help out. It is a relief to see a real personality emerge from the phone voice through which I have gotten to know her. The Disney hospitality voice is a formidable thing; the unstoppable friendliness of its tender pitch, and intonation is designed to disarm the skepticism of everyone it encounters. Finely calibrated at Disney University, where all new employees (or "cast members") are trained, this voice is the official greeting of consumer capitalist America, as distinctively authoritative a form of English speech as the pukka curtness of a British colonial administrator might have been for an earlier time. Things are not always what they seem in Celebration, however, and it turns out that Kennedy and his assistant Dawn Thomas, whose Trinidadian lilt has been flattened if not vanquished, are not Disney employees at all. Their management company, ZOM, is one of the many subcontractors in town, delicately buffering relations between residents and the world-famous underwriter of this new community.

Kennedy had found me a downtown apartment at the foot of Market Street, with a balcony view of the central lake. If nearby Kissimmee had not snagged the name over a century ago (Osceola County forbids the repetition of street names), I would be living on Main Street, as Walt once did in his Disneyland apartment, ostensibly to take delight in the first reactions of visitors to the idealized town square setting. Everyone who visits or takes a stroll in downtown Celebration will pass beneath my perch along the petite, palm-lined promenade. In no time, I would become familiar with the traffic in and out of the stores across the street: Max's Café, the bakery Bread Alone, M Fashion's fragrant boutique, the more casual Soft as a Grape, Dunn's antique furniture, and Goodings' grocery store. I would soon get used to street conversation drifting up from the sidewalk bench outside Village Mercantile, mecca for youth gear, and would even learn to endure the Muzak piped into the street from speakers buried in the bases of the palm trees. As I make a debut appearance on my balcony, the first of many pictures is snapped by tourists below, as eager to document a native resident of this town as they would be to snap an Amazon rain-forest dweller, a kilted Highlander, or a Bedouin on a camel. . . .

Just across from my balcony, three solid wooden rocking chairs are set out on the lakeside promenade. Unoccupied, they still look like three elderly citizens holding a leisurely conversation. The rockers are placed there for public use and they command the best downtown vantage point. From there, the view up Market Street is unimpeded, and you can see the entire sweep of Front Street and Bloom Street as they hug the northern portion of the lake. Their facades all glowing brightly in the sun, the downtown buildings draw on regional styles and borrow liberally from much-admired southern townscapes. There are balconies from New Orleans on Market Street, and Charleston sideyard porches on Front Street. According to the Architectural Walking Tour pamphlet, which you can pick up from the sales Preview Center, the garden apartment buildings on Campus Street, to the west, with their green clapboard upper stories, steep gabled roofs, and shallow eaves are "inspired by the traditional houses of St. Augustine." On Bloom Street, the model is the Low Country houses found in the coastal areas of the Carolinas. Many of the background buildings on Market and Front draw on Anglo-Caribbean "crossbred" styles that mix colonial and classical architecture. . . .

The Big Draw

Less than two years before, on Founders Day (November 18, 1995), almost five thousand people thronged around the marquees on an open field between route 192 and Celebration Place, the town's 100-acre business park (opened six months earlier). Three hundred and fifty home sites were up for lottery, and prospective buyers waited, checkbooks in hand, to lay down a deposit if they drew a respectable number. A good deal more orderly than the Oklahoma land rush, it was still a scene from the storyboards—a heady stir of Disney fever, America fever, and property fever. A brass band played, and the county-fair ambience included balloons, hot dogs, and puppet shows. The assembled were from far and wide, but mostly from Florida, the eastern seaboard, and the Midwest. Few of the people standing in line had seen anything like a detailed rendering of a house, let alone a floor plan. They had been drawn there by gilded rumor and a boffo advertising campaign that often read like scenes from a Ray Bradbury story stripped of all the stuff that makes your scalp stiffen:

> There once was a place where neighbors greeted neighbors in the quiet of summer twilight. Where children chased fireflies. And porch swings provided easy refuge from the care of the day. The movie house showed cartoons on Saturday. The grocery store delivered. And there was one teacher who always knew you who had that "special something." Remember that place? Perhaps from your childhood. Or maybe just from stories. It held a magic all its own. The special magic of an American home town. Now, the people at Disney—itself an American family tradition—are creating a place that celebrates this legacy. A place that recalls the timeless traditions and

boundless spirit that are the best parts of who we are.

Or

There is a place that takes you back to that time of innocence. A place where the biggest decision is whether to play Kick the Can or King of the Hill. A place of caramel apples and cotton candy, secret forts, and hopscotch on the streets. That place is here again, in a new town called Celebration. . . . A new American town of block parties and Fourth of July parades. Of spaghetti dinners and school bake sales, lollipops, and fireflies in a jar. And while we can't return to these times we can arrive at a place that embraces all of these things. Someday, 20,000 people will live in Celebration, and for each and every one of them, it will be home.

The brochures also promised them a state-of-the-art package of progressive education, high technology, unequaled health facilities, and quality homes, but the fantasy glue that sealed the package was a story about going home again. Traditionally, this country's luckier migrants have always been promised something new, somewhere different, some place in the future they had never been before—whether in a little house on the prairie, a brownstone apartment in the city, a bungalow in a canyon, or a Cape Cod in the suburbs. This was a different kind of promise. It seemed to be channeling the sharp rush of baby-boomers' hunger to be homeward bound to a place that lies well off the century's main drag—behind the fast curve of modernity, where their grandparents had once lived. At prices ranging from $150,000 for a townhouse all the way to a cool million for a mansion, it would not be a cheap detour.

Further Resources

BOOKS

Frantz, Douglas. *Celebration, U.S.A.: Living in Disney's Brave New Town.* New York: Henry Holt, 1999.

PERIODICALS

Phillips, Andrew. "The Disney Dream." *Maclean's,* July 21 1997, 24–25.

Pollan, Michael. "Mickey for Mayor?" *House & Garden,* October, 1996, 62–64.

"Office Culture: Banana Republicans"

Magazine article

By: Laurie Sandell and Jessica Lustig

Date: October 23, 2000

Source: Sandell, Laurie, and Jessica Lustig. "Office Culture: Banana Republicans." *New York Magazine,* October 23, 2000, 20. ■

Introduction

Before the 1990s, every American worker, from veteran professional to entry-level office employee, knew how to dress for office work. Appropriate business attire meant one thing: a business suit. Both men and women typically dressed up for interviews and on the job. Some companies even required a prospective employee to wear a business suit when coming in to pick up a job application.

Business attire began to change in the 1990s in response to other changes in work and the workplace. Telecommuting became common, work schedules grew more flexible, corporate structures changed, and a less formal, more relaxed office atmosphere began to prevail. Gradually, company dress codes also began to change. First, some employers instituted "casual Fridays," one day a week when employees were allowed to dress informally. In time, casual attire became standard for everyday wear in many offices. Retailers like the Gap and Banana Republic capitalized on this trend toward a "khaki culture" by energetically promoting an entirely new category of clothing known as "business casual." A 1999 survey of about 750 corporate executives by the Society for Human Resource Management, revealed that 42 percent of employers allowed casual attire every day, an increase from 36 percent reported in 1998.

Sociologists who study workplace dynamics agree that creating a casual dress code can help to improve company morale. It can also serve to reflect a greater concern on the part of employers for the comfort and well being of their employees. Dressing casually at work was supposed to make life easier. But it also led to confusion across corporate America. At the turn of the century, there was still no general consensus as to what constitutes "business casual"—some people think it means taking off your suit jacket, while others show up to the office in T-shirts and shorts.

Significance

Many employers were concerned that casual dressing had a detrimental effect on productivity and could harm a company's image with customers and clients.

When they realized that the rules for the new attire were open to very broad interpretation, they responded by working with the clothiers to establish a standard for the new style. One New York law firm, Cadwalader, Wickersham and Taft, turned to Polo Ralph Lauren for help in counseling its staff and defining "business casual." When the firm instituted an every-day casual dress code in 1999, it offered its workers a one-night seminar at Polo's flagship store in New York City.

Other New York corporations followed the law firm's example. The October 23, 2000, issue of *New York Magazine* reported that the banking giant Credit Suisse First Boston had gone one step further: the firm sponsored a "business casual" fashion extravaganza at its New York headquarters that ended in the sale of the clothing that was being modeled as a new office "uniform" of sorts. Today a proliferation of "image consultants" and fashion advisers offer their services to professionals and companies alike.

By standardizing "the new suit" for the new millennium, the shrewd Banana Republic clothing chain and its parent company, The Gap, not only sold clothes and a look, but they secured a profitable brand loyalty from the bankers and corporate executives that were its new customers. In 1998, Banana Republic sales exceeded one billion dollars in what one observer called "the casualization, the Banana Republic-ization of men's wear."

Robert Park sits in the boardroom of Ernst and Young in San Jose, California, in 1998. Like many others, the company began allowing casual wear every day. **AP/WIDE WORLD PHOTOS. REPRODUCED BY PERMISSION.**

Primary Source

"Office Culture: Banana Republicans" [excerpt]

SYNOPSIS: In 1999, Banana Republic capitalized on the growing popularity of casual dressing in corporate workplaces by attempting to create casual dress "uniforms." They staged fashion shows at the offices of major companies in an attempt to sell wardrobe packages to employees.

"Putting on a suit was like putting on a uniform; it got you in the right mind frame," sighs a trader at Credit Suisse First Boston. "I mean, they wouldn't let the guys in the NBA run around in their own shorts." As it happens, some of the companies issuing casual-Friday-every-day mandates have no intention of letting employees run around in their own shorts, either. They've gratefully seized a proposal by Banana Republic to standardize the khakis and pullovers of the new dress code—to create, in effect, the suit of the new millennium—and invited the canny clothier into their offices to do it." A lot of companies are doing things to address the confusion in the workplace," says a Banana Republic spokeswoman. "But we've taken it to the next level."

To kick off its in-house "stores," Banana Republic treated CSFB troops to a twelve-piece Cuban orchestra and sushi bar, Scient staff was served green-apple martinis "deskside" at 6 p.m., and HBO was treated to a coffee-and-cake spread ("HBO is an 'earlier' crowd," a Banana Republic rep tactfully explained). The highlight of each party was a runway fashion show featuring employees who strutted the catwalk while their co-workers jeered them on.

Soon, conference rooms were transformed into sample sales: tables piled with V-necks, racks full of purple shirts. The CSFB "store" filled with traders fondling sweaters while a techno beat thumped in the background. Some consulted with the on-site tailor; others scheduled fittings with perky, headset-wearing Banana Republic employees. Sure, stock was low ("There were thirteen other people my size trying on the same shirt," one guy grumbled), and one style of pants were available only in "short," so everyone emerged from the fitting rooms in high-waters. But at least it was all 20 percent off. Which wasn't enough for one enterprising CSFB trader: "Maybe I'll just take them off the mannequins at night," he schemed, "when no one's around."

Further Resources

BOOKS

Amiel, Ilene. *Business Casual Made Easy: The Complete Guide to Business Casual Dress for Men and Women.* New York: Business Casual Publications, 1999.

Molloy, John. *The New Woman's Dress for Success.* New York: Warner, 1996.

PERIODICALS

Bragg, Rick. "Nowadays Workers Enjoy Dressing Down for the Job." *The New York Times,* July 15, 1994, A1.

Mannix, Margaret. "Casual Friday, Five Days a Week." *US News and World Report,* August 4, 1997, 60.

Sloan, Paul. "Is That Gordon Gekko at the Gap?" *US News and World Report,* April 24, 2000, 46.

5

GOVERNMENT AND POLITICS

PAUL G. CONNORS

Entries are arranged in chronological order by date of primary source. For entries with one primary source, the entry title is the same as the primary source title. Entries with more than one primary source have an overall entry title, followed by the titles of the primary sources.

Important Events in Government and Politics, 1990–1999

1990

- On June 26, President Bush reverses his campaign pledge "Read My Lips, No New Taxes" by agreeing to raise taxes in order to lower the federal deficit.

- On July 26, President Bush signs the landmark Americans With Disabilities Act.

- On August 7, following Iraq's invasion of Kuwait on August 2, President Bush orders the deployment of American troops to the Middle East.

- On August 22, President Bush calls up United States military reserves.

- On November 8, President Bush orders further military deployments to give "offensive options" to American forces in the Middle East.

- On November 20, a suit is filed by forty-five liberal Democratic legislators demanding that President Bush seek Congressional approval for military operations, but the suit is thrown out of court.

- On November 22, President Bush, his wife, Barbara Bush, and several cabinet officials visit servicemen in the Middle East for Thanksgiving.

1991

- On January 12, the 102nd Congress passes Senate Joint Resolution 2, authorizing the President to use United States Armed Forces against Iraq pursuant to U.N. Security Council Resolution 678.

- On July 1, President Bush nominates the conservative jurist Clarence Thomas to replace the retiring liberal jurist Thurgood Marshall on the United States Supreme Court.

- On October 6, Oklahoma University law professor Anita Hill accuses Clarence Thomas of sexually harassing her in the 1980s.

- On October 11, the United States Senate Judiciary Committee delays its confirmation vote on Judge Thomas for five days in order to hold hearings on the merits of Professor Hill's charges.

- On October 15, Thomas is confirmed as an associate justice of the Supreme Court by a Senate vote of 52-48. He takes the judicial oath on October 23.

- From December 2 to December 4, three remaining American hostages are freed in Lebanon by Syrian intervention. All Western hostages will be released by June 17, 1992.

1992

- On January 26, Arkansas Governor Bill Clinton, a candidate for the Democratic nomination for president, and his wife, Hillary Rodham Clinton, appear on CBS's *60 Minutes* to discuss rumors about their marriage.

- On February 1, President Bush and Russian President Boris Yeltsin proclaim a formal end to the Cold War.

- On February 21, the United States lifts trade sanctions against China.

- On June 16, former Secretary of Defense Caspar W. Weinberger (1981–1987) is indicted for his actions in the Iran-Contra affair (1985–1986), a scandal that arose out of a secret deal by the Reagan administration to sell $30 million in arms to Iran in order to use the profits to fund covert activities in Nicaragua.

- On July 13, the Democratic National Convention, meeting in New York City, nominates Governor Clinton for president and Senator Al Gore of Tennessee as vice president.

- On August 20, the Republican National Convention, meeting in Houston, nominates President Bush for reelection and Dan Quayle of Indiana for vice president.

- On November 3, the Clinton-Gore ticket receives 43 percent of the vote to defeat the Bush-Quayle ticket.

- On December 24, as his term in office nears an end, President Bush pardons all former Reagan officials who were involved in the Iran-Contra affair.

1993

- On January 20, Bill Clinton is inaugurated as the forty-second President of the United States.

- On January 25, President Clinton appoints First Lady Hillary Clinton to head a task force on National Health Care Reform.

- On January 29, President Clinton back tracks on his campaign promise to lift the ban on gays in the military by announcing a six-month "Don't Ask Don't Tell" policy that prohibits the military from asking recruits about their sexual orientation. In July, the policy becomes permanent.

- On February 1, President Clinton signs into law the Family Medical Leave Act, which enables millions of Americans to take up to twelve weeks unpaid leave to care for sick family members.

- On February 26, a bomb explodes in the basement garage of the World Trade Center in New York City. Six people are killed and more than one thousand injured, many by smoke inhalation during the course of the evacuation.

- On April 19, a fifty-one-day siege by the Federal Bureau of Investigation (FBI) and Bureau of Alcohol, Tobacco, and Firearms (ATF) of the Branch Davidian compound near Waco, Texas, ends in a fiery inferno, killing approximately eighty men, women, and children. Despite a federal hearing and a criminal trial, the cause of the conflagration is not determined.

- On August 10, Ruth Bader Ginsburg becomes the second woman to serve on the Untied States Supreme Court.

- In October, the Resolution Trust Corporation, which was authorized to investigate failed savings and loan institutions, makes nine criminal referrals involving Madison Guarantee Savings and Loan including. One of the criminal referrals charges the savings and loan with paying off Bill Clinton's 1985 gubernatorial campaign debt.

- On November 17, the House of Representatives approves the North American Free Trade Agreement (NAFTA).

- On November 30, President Clinton signs the Brady Handgun Violence Prevention Act, which regulated firearm sales by requiring background checks for purchasers.

- On December 8, Congress ratifies the North American Free Trade Agreement creating the world's largest free trade zone.

1994

- On January 12, under tremendous political pressure President Clinton requests a special prosecutor be appointed to investigate the Whitewater affair.

- On February 3, Attorney General Janet Reno appoints Robert B. Fiske as independent Whitewater counsel.

- On February 3, President Clinton ends the trade embargo against the Republic of Vietnam, which had been put into effect in 1975.

- On March 24, President Clinton goes on national television to defend his Whitewater business dealings.

- On April 22, former president Richard Nixon dies in a New York City hospital.

- On May 6, Paula Corbin Jones files suit in federal court charging President Clinton with having committed sexual harassment against her while he was governor of Arkansas.

- On June 26, the House of Representatives Banking Committee begins hearings on Whitewater.

- On August 5, Kenneth Starr, former solicitor general for President Bush, is appointed independent counsel, replacing Robert Fiske.

- On September 13, President Clinton signs into law the assault weapons act.

- On September 27, three hundred Republican candidates for the House of Representatives sign the "Contract With America" on the steps of the United States Capitol.

- On November 6, the Republicans sweep the midterm elections; on January 4 they take control of both houses of the U.S. Congress.

- On December 5, Newton Leroy "Newt" Gingrich (R-Georgia) is chosen as Speaker of the House.

1995

- On February 14, the alleged mastermind of the World Trade Center bombing, Ramzi Ahmed Yousef, is arrested in Pakistan and returned to the United States for trial.

- On February 21, the United States approves a $20 billion aid package to help the ailing Mexican economy.

- On April 19, a bomb hidden in a rental truck explodes outside the Alfred P. Murrah Federal Building in Oklahoma City and kills 168 people, including children at a daycare center in the structure.

- In summer, Monica S. Lewinsky serves as an intern at the White House.

- On July 18, the United States Senate Whitewater Hearings begin.

- On August 7, before the House Banking Committee an Resolution Trust Corporation investigator testifies that the White House pressured her superiors to thwart the Whitewater investigation.

- On September 8, Senator Robert William "Bob" Packwood (R-Oreg.) resigns under pressure because of charges of sexual harassment, obstructing an investigation, and conflict of interest for soliciting employment for his wife from influential constituents.

- In December, the White House and Congressional Republicans joust over the national budget, resulting in the longest federal shutdown in United States history, twenty-two days, ending on January 6, 1996.

1996

- On March 5, Senator Robert Joseph Dole (R-Kans.) wins the Super Tuesday Republican primaries.

- On April 3, United States Secretary of Commerce Ronald H. Brown and thirty-four others, including several CEOs of U.S. firms, are killed while on a trade mission when their plane crashes in Croatia.

- On April 6, Lewinsky obtains a $33,000-a-year job in public relations at the Pentagon.

- On April 9, President Clinton signs the Line-Item Veto bill.

- On May 17, President Clinton signs "Megan's law," which requires states to notify communities when sexual predators move into a community.

- On May 28, President Clinton's former Whitewater business partners Jim and Susan McDougal are convicted of fraud.

- On June 18, the United States Senate Whitewater probe concludes. Republican members criticize Hillary Clinton and Democratic aids of obstructing the investigation.

- On August 14, the Republican National Convention, meeting in San Diego, nominates Senator Dole for president and Representative Jack Kemp of New York for vice president.

- On August 20, President Clinton signs into a law a bill increasing the minimum wage $.90 an hour to $5.15. This is the first increase in six years.

- On August 22, Congressional Republicans pressure President Clinton to sign into law the monumental Welfare Reform Act.

- On August 26, the Democratic National Convention, meeting in Chicago, renominates President Clinton and Vice President Gore.

- On November 5, the Clinton-Gore ticket is reelected with 49 percent of the vote, but the Republicans retain control of Congress.

1997

- On January 17, Gingrich is found guilty of ethics violations ten days after being reelected as House Speaker.

- On January 20, President Clinton is inaugurated for his second term in office.

- On July 28, the Clinton administration and Republicans agree on a balanced budget.

- On December 2, Attorney General Janet Reno decides that telephone calls made from the White House, allegedly for political purposes, by President Clinton and Vice President Gore do not warrant an independent investigation.

1998

- On January 21, President Clinton denies an alleged affair with former White House intern Lewinsky.

- On February 3, President Clinton proposes first balanced budget since 1973.

- On February 12, the line-item veto is found unconstitutional by the United States Supreme Court.

- On July 25, Independent Counsel Kenneth W. Starr subpoenas President Clinton to testify in a grand jury investigation.

- On August 6, Lewinsky testifies before the grand jury.

- On August 17, President Clinton testifies before the grand jury and admits his affair with Lewinsky.

- On September 11, Starr submits his report to Congress, outlining the basis for Articles of Impeachment against the President.

- On November 3, the Democrats unexpectedly gain seats in Congress during the midterm elections.

- On November 9, Gingrich resigns his office and seat in Congress.

- On December 9, the House Judiciary Committee begins discussion on four articles of impeachment.

- On December 18, amid the impeachment debate, United States planes drop bombs over Baghdad, Iraq in retaliation for violations of the U.N.-sanctioned no-fly zone.

- The House of Representatives begins debate on the four articles of impeachment.

- On December 19, the House of Representatives approves two articles of impeachment against President Clinton.

- On December 28, House Speaker-elect Robert L. Livingston, Jr. (R-La.), resigns from Congress after revelations of marital infidelity.

1999

- On January 6, the House of Representatives elects John Dennis Hastert (R-Ill.) as Speaker of the House.

- On January 7, the United States Senate impeachment trial of President Clinton begins with Chief Justice William Rehnquist presiding.

- On January 13, President Clinton's legal team presents his defense.

- On February 12, the Senate fails to convict President Clinton on the two articles of impeachment.

The Americans with Disabilities Act Becomes Law

Bill Summary and Status for the 101st Congress, S.933

Report

By: U.S. Congress

Date: July 26, 1990

Source: Bill Summary and Status for the 101st Congress. S.933, sponsored by Sen. Tom Harkin. U.S. Congress, July 26, 1990.

About the Author: The U.S. Congress is the legislative arm of the government and consists of both the Senate and the House of Representatives. Tom Harkin (1939–) sponsored the Americans with Disabilities Act. He was born in Cummings, Iowa. After earning a degree at Iowa State University in government and economics, Harkin entered the Navy, where he served as a jet pilot from 1962 to 1967. In 1972, after earning a law degree from Catholic University, Harkin moved back to Iowa. Two years later, Harkin, a Democrat, returned to the nation's capital as a member of the House of Representatives. In 1984, he was elected to the United States Senate.

The Americans with Disabilities Act of 1990

Law

By: U.S. Congress

Date: 1990

Source: *The Americans with Disabilities Act of 1990.* U.S. Congress. Available online at http://www.dol.gov/esa/regs /statues/ofccp/ada.htm; website home page: http://www.dol .gov (accessed August 4, 2003). ■

Introduction

The disability movement was pioneered in the mid-nineteenth century by Dr. Samuel Gridley Howe of Boston, Massachusetts. At the time, anyone unable to attain the minimum education level—equivalent to a third-grade education by contemporary standards—was classified (and stigmatized) as "feebleminded." This term covered a variety of disabilities, including mental impairment, vision and hearing loss, speech impediments, or any ailment hindering the ability to socialize with peers, making it difficult to attend school.

In 1846, the Massachusetts legislature appointed Dr. Howe to head a commission to examine the problem. Based on Howe's recommendation, the legislature appropriated revenue to create the Massachusetts School for Idiotic Children and Youth in 1849. Initially, the school emphasized teaching students basic skills that would allow them to be integrated back into their families and communities. However, by 1874, against Howe's wishes, students were institutionalized permanently. Families either did not want to resume their disabled children's care, or they assumed that their child was better off in an institution.

In the early twentieth century, the "feebleminded" were threatened by the eugenics movement. Viewed as a burden and a menace on society, disabled women were involuntarily sterilized. From 1922 to 1938, thirty-three states passed laws that required the sterilization of feebleminded, insane, epileptic, blind, deaf, and crippled individuals. From 1921 to 1964, over 63,000 persons were involuntarily sterilized. Further, in 1927, the United States Supreme Court, in *Buck v. Bell* (274 US 200), upheld a Virginia statute that prohibited the disabled to marry or become parents. This law was not repealed until 1972.

After World War I (1914–1918), returning blind veterans, who refused to spend the rest of their lives making brooms and cane chairs, spearheaded the disability movement. Founding the American Foundation for the Blind, they sought to educate the public that the blind can lead independent, fruitful lives. Next, World War II (1939–1945) veterans organized the Paralyzed Veterans of America, asserting their right to live independently. In 1950, parents who insisted that their mentally retarded children be mainstreamed into the public school system formed the National Association for Retarded Citizens. By the 1960s, the disabled had gained valuable organizing experience through involvement in the Civil Rights Movement, the Vietnam (1964–1975) anti-war movement, the women's movement, and grassroots Democratic and Republican Party politics.

After decades of hard work, the disability movement reached a milestone during the 1988 presidential election. According to polling conducted before the Democratic convention, Michael Dukakis held a three percent point lead over George H.W. Bush (served 1989–1993). Voters who identified themselves as being disabled provided much of this lead. That summer, Bush announced

President George H.W. Bush signs the Americans with Disabilities Act of 1990 during a ceremony on the White House's South Lawn, July 26, 1990. AP/WIDE WORLD PHOTOS. REPRODUCED BY PERMISSION.

his commitment to legislation mainstreaming persons with disabilities. In November 1988, he beat Dukakis by seven percentage points. Polling data suggests that almost half of his margin of victory consisted of disabled voters who had switched their vote to Bush.

Significance

On the morning of July 26, 1990, on the south lawn of the White House, with 3,000 disability rights advocates in attendance, President Bush signed into law the Americans with Disabilities Act (P.L. 101-336), commonly known as the Persons with Disabilities Civil Rights Act. Afterward, he said, "Let the shameful wall of exclusion finally come tumbling down." Modeled after the Civil Rights Act of 1964, the act was the world's first comprehensive law that promoted equal opportunities by outlawing discrimination against people with disabilities. At the time of its passage, it provided an estimated forty-three million disabled Americans with the same civil rights protections provided to women and minorities in the areas of employment, transportation, public accommodations, and telecommunications. In ad-

dition, the law required every state to pass enabling legislation.

Primary Source

Bill Summary and Status for the 101st Congress, S.933

> **SYNOPSIS:** In May 1989, when Senator Harkin introduced S.933, it had overwhelming bipartisan support. Nevertheless, even popular bills take a seemingly long time to navigate the unwieldy legislative process. In the Senate, members tried to amend the legislation sixteen times. The measure then stalled in the House, before being submitted to conference committee. Almost fifteen months after its introduction, the House passed the bill 377 to 28, and the Senate 91 to 6.

5/9/1989

- Read twice and referred to the Committee on Labor and Human Resources.
- Committee on Labor and Human Resources. Hearings held. Hearings printed: S.Hrg. 101-156.

5/10/1989

- Subcommittee on Handicapped (Labor and Human Res.). Hearings held.

5/16/1989

- Subcommittee on Handicapped (Labor and Human Res.). Hearings held.

6/22/1989

- Committee on Labor and Human Resources. Hearings held.

8/1/1989

- S.AMDT.541 Referred to the Committee on Labor and Human Resources.
- To amend the Communications Act of 1934 to require telecommunications services for hearing-impaired and speech-impaired individuals.

8/2/1989

- Committee on Labor and Human Resources. Ordered to be reported with an amendment in the nature of a substitute favorably.

8/30/1989

- Committee on Labor and Human Resources. Reported to Senate by Senator Kennedy under the authority of the order of Aug 2, 89 with an amendment in the nature of a substitute. With written report No. 101-116. Additional views filed.

- Placed on Senate Legislative Calendar under General Orders. Calendar No. 216.

9/7/1989

- Measure laid before Senate by unanimous consent.

9/7/1989

- S.AMDT.708 Proposed by Senator Hatch. To end discrimination on the basis of disability in Federal wilderness areas.

9/7/1989

- S.AMDT.708 Amendment SP 708 agreed to in Senate by Voice Vote.
- S.AMDT.711 Proposed by Senator Harkin. To provide a technical amendment.
- S.AMDT.712 Proposed by Senator Harkin. To provide for a technical amendment.
- S.AMDT.711 Amendment SP 711 agreed to in Senate by Voice Vote.
- S.AMDT.712 Amendment SP 712 agreed to in Senate by Voice Vote.
- S.AMDT.709 Proposed by Senator Hatch. To provide a refundable tax credit for the costs of small businesses complying with the public accommodations requirement.
- S.AMDT.709 Point of order raised in Senate with respect to SP 709.
- S.AMDT.709 Motion to waive the Budget Act with respect to rejected in Senate by Yea-Nay Vote. 48-44. Record Vote No: 170.
- S.AMDT.709 SP 709 ruled out of order by the chair.
- S.AMDT.713 Proposed by Senator Boschwitz. To require a judge to consider if a defendant who is accused of discrimination on the basis of disability has acted in good faith.
- S.AMDT.713 Amendment SP 713 agreed to in Senate by Yea-Nay Vote. 90-0. Record Vote No: 171.
- S.AMDT.714 Proposed by Senator Hollings. To amend sections 304 and 305 relating to the accessibility of over-the-road buses to individuals with disabilities.

- S.AMDT.714 Amendment SP 714 agreed to in Senate by Voice Vote.
- S.AMDT.715 Proposed by Senator Helms. To clarify the definition of handicapped under the Rehabilitation Act of 1973 relating to the uses of illegal drugs.
- S.AMDT.715 Amendment SP 715 agreed to in Senate by Voice Vote.
- S.AMDT.716 Proposed by Senator Helms. Providing that the term "disabled" or "disability" shall not apply to an individual solely because that individual is a transvestite.
- S.AMDT.716 Amendment SP 716 agreed to in Senate by Voice Vote.
- S.AMDT.717 Proposed by Senator Harkin. To make technical corrections.
- S.AMDT.717 Amendment SP 717 agreed to in Senate by Voice Vote.
- S.AMDT.718 Proposed by Senator Harkin. To exclude an employee or applicant who is a current user of illegal drugs from the definition of "qualified individual with a disability."
- S.AMDT.719 Proposed by Senator Dole. To provide a plan to provide entities with technical assistance.
- S.AMDT.719 Amendment SP 719 agreed to in Senate by Voice Vote.
- S.AMDT.720 Proposed by Senator Grassley. To include Congress as a beneficiary of this Act.
- S.AMDT.720 Amendment SP 720 agreed to in Senate by Division Vote.
- S.AMDT.718 Amendment SP 718 agreed to in Senate by Voice Vote.
- S.AMDT.721 Proposed by Senator Humphrey. To provide that an individual with a "disability" shall not include any individual who uses illegal drugs.
- S.AMDT.721 Amendment SP 721 agreed to in Senate by Voice Vote.
- S.AMDT.722 Proposed by Senator Armstrong. To more clearly define the term "disability."
- S.AMDT.722 Amendment SP 722 agreed to in Senate by Voice Vote.
- S.AMDT.723 Proposed by Senator Dole. To allow certain capital expenditures of small businesses for auxiliary aids and services and reasonable accommodations to be treated as expense items, and for other purposes.

- S.AMDT.723 Proposed amendment SP 723 withdrawn in Senate.

- S.AMDT.724 Proposed by Senator Harkin. To establish that should any provision in the Act be found to be unconstitutional by a court of law, such provision shall be severed from the remainder of the Act, and such action shall not affect the enforceability of the remaining provisions of the Act.

- S.AMDT.724 Amendment SP 724 agreed to in Senate by Voice Vote.

- The committee substitute as amended agreed to by Voice Vote.

- Passed Senate with an amendment by Yea-Nay Vote. 76-8. Record Vote No: 173.

9/12/1989

- Message on Senate action sent to the House.

9/12/1989 2:41pm

- Received in the House.

9/12/1989 2:42pm

- Held at the desk.

10/16/1989

- Senate ordered measure printed as passed with amendments of the Senate numbered.

5/22/1990 3:04pm

- Considered under the provisions of rule H. Res. 394.

- The House struck all after the enacting clause and inserted in lieu thereof the provisions of a similar measure H.R. 2273. Agreed to without objection.

5/22/1990 3:05pm

- On passage Passed without objection.

- Motion to reconsider laid on the table Agreed to without objection.

- A similar measure H.R. 2273 was laid on the table without objection.

5/24/1990 9:33pm

- Mr. Hoyer asked unanimous consent that the House insist upon its amendment, and request a conference.

5/24/1990 9:34pm

- On motion that the House insist upon its amendment, and request a conference Agreed to without objection.

- Motion to reconsider laid on the table Agreed to without objection.

- Mr. Fish moved that the House instruct conferees.

5/24/1990 9:36pm

- On motion that the House instruct conferees Agreed to by voice vote.

5/24/1990 9:37pm

- Motion to reconsider laid on the table Agreed to without objection.

5/24/1990 9:38pm

- The chair appointed conferees—from the Committee on Education and Labor for consideration of the Senate bill, and the House amendment, and modifications committed to conference: Hawkins, Owens (NY), Martinez, Bartlett, and Fawell.

- The chair appointed conferees—from the Committee on Energy and Commerce for consideration of the Senate bill, and the House amendment, and modifications committed to conference.: Dingell, Markey, Thomas Luken, Lent, and Whittaker.

5/24/1990 9:38pm

- The chair appointed conferees Except that, for consideration of title IV of the Senate bill, and title IV of the House amendment, Mr. Rinaldo is appointed in lieu of Mr. Whittaker.

- The chair appointed conferees—from the Committee on Public Works and Transportation for consideration of the Senate bill, and the House amendment, and modifications committed to conference: Anderson, Roe, Mineta, Hammerschmidt, and Shuster.

- The chair appointed conferees—from the Committee on the Judiciary for consideration of the Senate bill, and the House amendment, and modifications committed to conference: Brooks, Edwards (CA), Kastenmeier, Fish, and Sensenbrenner.

5/24/1990 9:39pm

- The chair appointed an additional conferee on the Senate bill, and the House amendment, and modifications committed to conference: Hoyer.

- The chair appointed an additional conferee for consideration of section 103(d) of the House amendment, and modifications committed to conference: Chapman.

- Message on House action received in Senate and held at desk: House amendments to Senate bill and House requests a conference.

6/6/1990

- Measure laid before Senate by unanimous consent.

- Senate disagreed to the House amendments by Voice Vote.

- Senate agreed to request for conference by Unanimous Consent.

- Motion to table the motion to instruct the conferees rejected in Senate by Yea-Nay Vote. 40-53. Record Vote No: 110.

- Senate Conferees instructed.

- Motion by Senator Grassley to instruct conferees made in Senate.

- Motion to instruct conferees withdrawn in Senate.

- Senate appointed conferees Kennedy; Harkin; Metzenbaum; Simon; Hatch; Durenberger; Jeffords.

- Senate appointed conferees Hollings; Inouye; Danforth from the Committee on Commerce, Science and Transportation, solely for consideration of issues within that Committee's jurisdication (telecommunications, commuter transit, and drug testing of transportation employees).

6/7/1990

- Message on Senate action sent to the House.

6/25/1990

- Conferees agreed to file conference report.

6/26/1990 6:12pm

- Conference report H. Rept. 101-558 filed.

- Conference papers: Senate report and managers' statement and official papers held at the desk in Senate.

7/11/1990

- Conference report considered in Senate. By Unanimous Consent.

- Motion to recommit conference report with instructions entered in Senate.

- S.AMDT.2118 Proposed by Senator Hatch. To permit the reassignment of food handlers with infectious and communicable diseases and to grant State and local food handling laws pre-eminence over Federal laws in this area.

- S.AMDT.2119 Proposed by Senator Helms. To include the human immunodeficiency virus (HIV) on the list of infectious diseases that may be transmitted through food supply, and to grant employers the right to reassign food handlers with HIV or AIDS.

- S.AMDT.2119 Amendment SP 2119 not agreed to in Senate by Yea-Nay Vote. 39-61. Record Vote No: 148.

- S.AMDT.2118 Amendment SP 2118 agreed to in Senate by Yea-Nay Vote. 99-1. Record Vote No: 149.

- Conference report recommitted by Senate. Voice Vote.

7/12/1990 5:00pm

- Conference report H. Rept. 101-596 filed.

7/12/1990 5:49pm

- Mr. Hawkins brought up conference report H.Rept. 101-596 for consideration as a privileged matter.

7/12/1990 6:53pm

- The previous question was ordered without objection.

7/12/1990 6:54pm

- Mr. Dannemeyer moved to recommit with instructions to the conference committee.

7/12/1990 7:18pm

- On motion to recommit with instructions to conference committee Failed by the Yeas and Nays: 180-224 (Roll no. 227).

7/12/1990 7:25pm

- On agreeing to the conference report Agreed to by recorded vote: 377-28 (Roll no. 228).

- Conference papers: message on House action held at the desk in Senate.

7/13/1990

- Conference report considered in Senate.
- Senate agreed to conference report by Yea-Nay Vote. 91-6. Record Vote No: 152.
- Cleared for White House.

7/16/1990

- Message on Senate action sent to the House.

7/17/1990

- Measure Signed in Senate.
- Presented to President.

7/26/1990

- Signed by President.
- Became Public Law No: 101-336.

Primary Source

The Americans with Disabilities Act of 1990 [excerpt]

SYNOPSIS: The Americans with Disabilities Act stated the findings and purposes of Congress in formulating the bill, defined discrimination, and established a number of regulations to ensure that people with disabilities are afforded the same opportunities and treatment as others.

SEC. 2. FINDINGS AND PURPOSES.

(a) Findings.—The Congress finds that—

(1) some 43,000,000 Americans have one or more physical or mental disabilities, and this number is increasing as the population as a whole is growing older;

(2) historically, society has tended to isolate and segregate individuals with disabilities, and, despite some improvements, such forms of discrimination against individuals with disabilities continue to be a serious and pervasive social problem;

(3) discrimination against individuals with disabilities persists in such critical areas as employment, housing, public accommodations, education, transportation, communication, recreation, institutionalization, health services, voting, and access to public services;

(4) unlike individuals who have experienced discrimination on the basis of race, color, sex, national origin, religion, or age, individuals who have experienced discrimination on the basis of disability have often had no legal recourse to redress such discrimination;

(5) individuals with disabilities continually encounter various forms of discrimination, including outright intentional exclusion, the discriminatory effects of architectural, transportation, and communication barriers, overprotective rules and policies, failure to make modifications to existing facilities and practices, exclusionary qualification standards and criteria, segregation, and relegation to lesser services, programs, activities, benefits, jobs, or other opportunities;

(6) census data, national polls, and other studies have documented that people with disabilities, as a group, occupy an inferior status in our society, and are severely disadvantaged socially, vocationally, economically, and educationally; . . .

SEC. 3 DEFINITIONS

(2) Disability.—The term "disability" means, with respect to an individual—

(A) a physical or mental impairment that substantially limits one or more of the major life activities of such individual;

(B) a record of such an impairment; or

(C) being regarded as having such an impairment.

■ ■ ■

SEC. 102. DISCRIMINATION.

(a) General Rule.—No covered entity shall discriminate against a qualified individual with a disability because of hte disability of such individual in regard to job application procedures, the hiring, advancement, or discharge of employees, employee compensation, job training, and other terms, conditions, and privileges of employment.

■ ■ ■

SEC. 222. PUBLIC ENTITIES OPERATING FIXED ROUTE SYSTEMS.

(a) Purchase and Lease of New Vehicles.—It shall be considered discrimination for purposes of section 202 of this Act and section 504 of the Rehabilitation Act of 1973 (29 U.S.C. 794) for a public entity which operates a fixed route system to purchase or lease a new bus, a new rapid rail vehicle, a new light rail vehicle, or any other new vehicle to be used on such system, if the solicitation for such purchase or lease is made after the 30th day following the effective date of this subsection and if such bus, rail vehicle, or other vehicle is not readily accessible to and usable by individuals with disabilities, including individuals who use wheelchairs.

■■■

SEC. 302. PROHIBITION OF DISCRIMINATION BY PUBLIC ACCOMODATIONS.

(a) General Rule.—No individual shall be discriminated against on the basis of disability in the full and equal enjoyment of the goods, services, facilities, privileges, advantages, or accommodations of any place of public accommodation by any person who owns, leases (or leases to), or operates a place of public accommodation.

■■■

SEC. 308. ENFORCEMENT

(B) Potential violation.—If the Attorney General has reasonable cause to believe that—

(i) any person or group of persons is engaged in a patteron or practice of discrimination under this title; or

(ii) any person or group of persons has been discriminated against under this title and such discrimination raises an issue of general public importance, the Attorney General may commence a civil action in any appropriate United States district court.

■■■

"SEC. 225. TELECOMMUNICATIONS SERVICES FOR HEARING-IMPAIRED AND SPEECH-IMPAIRED INDIVIDUALS.

"(b) Availability of Telecommunications Relay Services.—

"(1) In general.—In order to carry out the purposes established under section 1, to make available to all indivduals in the United States a rapid, efficient nationwide communication service, and to increase the utility of the telephone system of the Nation, the Commission shall ensure that interstate and intrastate telecommunications relay services are available, to the extent possible and in the most efficient manner, to hearing-impaired and speech-impaired individuals in the United States.

■■■

SEC. 502. STATE IMMUNITY

A State shall not be immune under the eleventh amendment to the Constitution of the United States from an action in Federal or State court of competent jurisdiction for a violation of this Act. In any action against a State for a violation of the requirements of this Act, remedies (including remedies both a law and in equity) are available for such a violation to the same extent as such remedies are available for such violation in an action against any public or private entity other than a State.

■■■

SEC. 503. PROHIBITION AGAINST RETALTIATION AND COERCION

(a) Retaliation.—No person shall discriminate against any individual because such individual has opposed any act or practice made unlawful by this Act or because such individual made a charge, testified, assisted, or participated in any manner in an investigation, proceeding, or hearing under this Act.

(b) Interference, Coercion, or Intimidation.—It shall be unlawful to coerce, intimidate, threaten, or interfere with any individual in the exercise or enjoyment of, or on account of his or her having exercised or enjoyed, or on account of his or her having aided or encourage any individual in the exercise or enjoyment of, any right granted or protected by this Act.

Further Resources

BOOKS

Bogdan, Robert. *Freak Show: Presenting Human Oddities for Amusement and Profit.* Chicago: University of Chicago Press, 1988.

Gallagher, Hugh Gregory. *FDR's Splendid Deception.* New York: Dodd, Mead & Company, 1985.

Shapiro, Joseph P. *No Pity. People with Disabilities Forging a New Civil Rights Movement.* New York: Random House, 1993.

PERIODICALS

"The Americans with Disabilities Act: Washington Prevails." *Wall Street Journal,* August 5, 1992.

Rovner, Julie. "Rights Bill Linkage, Turf Spats Slow ADA Progress in House." *Congressional Quarterly Weekly Report,* February 24, 1990, 600.

WEBSITES

"ADA Home Page." United States Department of Justice. Available online at http://www.usdoj.gov/crt/ada/adahom1 .htm; website home page http://www.usdoj.gov (accessed April 4, 2003).

"New Freedom Initiative." The President of the United States. The White House. President George W. Bush. Available online at http://www.whitehouse.gov/infocus/newfreedom/; website home page http://www.whitehouse.gov (accessed April 4, 2003).

National Security Directive 45: U.S. Policy in Response to the Iraqi Invasion of Kuwait

Memo

By: George H.W. Bush

Date: August 20, 1990

Source: Bush, George H.W. *National Security Directive 45: U.S. Policy in Response to the Iraqi Invasion of Kuwait.* August 20, 1990. Reproduced in the National Security Archive. Available online at http://www.gwu.edu/~nsarchiv/NSAEBB /NSAEBB39; website home page: http://www.gwu.edu (accessed April 4, 2003).

About the Author: George H.W. Bush (1924–) was born in Milton, Massachusetts. On his eighteenth birthday, Bush enlisted in the U.S. Navy. During World War II (1939–1945), he flew fifty-eight combat missions and received the Distinguished Flying Cross. After graduating from Yale University in 1948, Bush entered the Texas oil business. Later, he served as the U.S. ambassador to the United Nations, a U.S. envoy to China, director of the Central Intelligence Agency (CIA), and vice president and president of the United States (served 1989–1993). ∎

Introduction

In 1990, Saddam Hussein, president of Iraq, ordered the invasion of Kuwait, a country bordering southern Iraq. The order was given at the tail end of a series of strategic and diplomatic miscalculations. First, Kuwait had been nominally a part of the Ottoman Empire before Britain granted it independence in 1961. For years, Iraq claimed that Kuwait, an Ottoman province in southern Iraq, was legally part of Iraq. Second, Kuwait made a series of costly loans to Iraq during the post-Iran-Iraq War period. By invading Kuwait, Iraq might have pressured the Kuwaiti government into forgiving the bulk of this debt. Third, by annexing a number of rich Kuwaiti oil fields, Iraq would have been able to pay back debts to the United States and neighboring countries through petroleum sales. Finally, a week prior to the invasion of Kuwait, the U.S. ambassador to Iraq assured Hussein that the United States would not intervene.

At the time, this assurance was consistent with U.S. foreign policy. Since 1980, the United States had viewed Iraq as a balancing power in the region, a counter-weight to Muslim radicals in neighboring Iran. During the Iran-Iraq War (1980-1988), for example, the United States sold $60 billion in arms to the Iraqi military, and the CIA shared classified information with Hussein's intelligence agency concerning Iranian military capabilities. In addition, the United States sold Iraq $2 billion worth of sophisticated weapons technology, which the Iraqi government used to bolster its fledgling nuclear, biological, and chemical (NBC) weapons programs.

Previous to the invasion, Hussein declared that Kuwait had illegally siphoned oil from the Rumalia oil field, a significant reservoir located mostly in Iraq, but whose southern tip is located beneath the sands of Kuwait. Iraq also accused Kuwait of producing more oil than allowed under quotas set by the Organization of Petroleum Exporting Countries (OPEC), thereby depressing the price of oil, Iraq's main export. In fact, no such infraction had taken place. Kuwait channeled most of the profits it earned from explorations in Rumalia to Iraq during the Iran-Iraq War. Additionally, around this time, Iraq revived its historical claim to Kuwaiti territory. Iraq would later attempt to justify its invasion as an act of territorial reunification. A number of diplomatic meetings were organized by neighboring Arab states, in hopes that Kuwait and Iraq would peacefully resolve their disputes. Each of these, however, ended in increasingly harsher accusations and charges by each side that the other was acting as aggressor.

Iraq's motivations for occupying Kuwait were a mixture of economic incentives and historical territorial claims. The Iran-Iraq war had cost Iraq one-third of its gross domestic product. After the war, Baghdad continued to expand and enlarge its military, spending billions on the development of NBC weapons. Consequently, Iraq's foreign debt had risen to between $80 and $100 billion. To make matters worse, the price of oil exports, the country's chief source of wealth, had declined. As a result, Iraq could neither meet its foreign debt payments, nor continue its military buildup. By invading Kuwait, whose oil investments were worth more than $100 billion, Hussein's regime hoped to improve Iraq's overall financial situation and increase its status in the region.

Significance

In all, a coalition of thirty-eight nations agreed to participate in Operation Desert Storm. Under the authority of the United Nations Security Council, a coalition force of 700,000—the majority of which made up of American forces—moved into the region with the objective of liberating Kuwait. After five weeks of intense surgical bombing of Iraqi targets, coalition forces began driving the Iraqi military from Kuwait. This ground war lasted almost one hundred hours.

The war was significant for several reasons. First, nearly two decades after the United States withdrew from Vietnam (and nearly a decade after its retreat from Lebanon), the U.S. military had spent a number of years untested overseas. Additionally the matter of its reputation was in question, as U.S. forces had departed in defeat from both of the above conflicts. A quick, decisive victory in Iraq restored some level of prestige to U.S. military prowess. Second, the Kuwaiti oil fields, part of the lifeline of an increasingly global (and petroleum-fueled) economy, were returned to the legal ownership of the Kuwaiti government. Third, the first Gulf War marked the first time that a military force under the mandate of the United Nations had achieved a decisive military victory. This would set a precedent for future UN military actions throughout the 1990s and up to the present. Fourth, Saddam Hussein remained in power in Iraq, and the Iraqi Republican Guard forces remained intact. Due to the restrictions of the UN mandate authorizing military action, coalition forces were prohibited from invading Iraqi territory. A number of neighboring states wanted the Hussein regime to remain in power to counterbalance Iran in the region. The Iraqi regime, therefore, continued to be a destabilizing force in the region and a serious threat to the national security of the United States. Iraqi attempts to expand NBC weapons programs-in violation of UN sanctions and arms embargoes-would later lead the United States to invade Iraq a second time in 2003, with the stated objective of removing Saddam Hussein and the Ba'ath party from power.

Primary Source

National Security Directive 45: U.S. Policy in Response to the Iraqi Invasion of Kuwait

SYNOPSIS: President Bush signed National Security Directive 45, outlining American interests in the Middle East. It articulated four principles that would guide U.S. foreign policy throughout the crisis. In short, U.S. objectives included Iraq's complete withdrawal from Kuwait and the restoration of Kuwait's government as it was prior to the invasion.

Memorandum For

The Vice President
The Secretary of State
The Secretary of the Treasury
The Secretary of Defense
The Attorney General
The Secretary of Energy
The Director of the Office of Management and Budget
The Assistant to the President for National Security Affairs
The Director of Central Intelligence
The Chairman of the Joint Chiefs of Staff
The Director, United States Arms Control and Disarmament Agency
The Director, United States Information Agency
SUBJECT: U.S. Policy in Response to the Iraqi Invasion of Kuwait

President George H.W. Bush waves after a briefing at the Pentagon regarding the situation between Kuwait and Iraq. **AP/WIDE WORLD PHOTOS. REPRODUCED BY PERMISSION.**

U.S. Interests

U.S. interests in the Persian Gulf are vital to the national security. These interests include access to oil and the security and stability of key friendly states in the region. The United States will defend its vital interests in the area, through the use of U.S. military force if necessary and appropriate, against any power with interests inimical to our own. The United States also will support the individual and collective self-defense of friendly countries in the area to enable them to play a more active role in their own defense. The United States will encourage the effective expressions of support and the participation of our allies and other friendly states to promote our mutual interests in the Persian Gulf region.

On Thursday, August 2, 1990 the government of Iraq, without provocation or warning, invaded and occupied the State of Kuwait, thereby placing these vital U.S. interests at risk. Four principles will guide U.S. policy during this crisis:

• the immediate, complete, and unconditional withdrawal of all Iraqi forces from Kuwait;

• the restoration of Kuwait's legitimate government to replace the puppet regime installed by Iraq;

• a commitment to the security and stability of the Persian Gulf; and,

• the protection of the lives of American citizens abroad.

U.S. troops from the 1st Calvary Division deploy across the Saudi desert on November 4, 1990, as part of the United States' response to Iraq's invasion of Kuwait. AP/WIDE WORLD PHOTOS. REPRODUCED BY PERMISSION.

To meet these principles and to bring the crisis to an immediate, peaceful, and just end, I hereby direct that the following diplomatic, economic, energy and military measures be undertaken.

Diplomatic

The United States will continue to support the precepts of UNSC resolution 660 and 662 condemning Iraq's invasion and subsequent annexation of Kuwait and calling for the immediate and unconditional withdrawal of Iraqi forces from Kuwait. The Secretary of State should continue to work bilaterally with our allies and friends, and in concert with the international community through the United Nations and other fora, to find a peaceful solution to end the Iraqi occupation of Kuwait and to restore Kuwait's legitimate government.

Economic

Consistent with my authority under the International Emergency Economic Powers Act, the National Emergencies Act, the United Nations Participation Act, and section 301 of title 3 of the United States Code, the Executive Orders signed on August 2 and August 9, 1990 freezing Kuwaiti and Iraqi assets in this country and prohibiting transactions with Iraq and Kuwait remain in force. The Secretary of the Treasury, in consultation with the Secretary of State, should continue to take such actions, including the promulgation of rules and regulations, as may be necessary to carry out the purposes of these Orders. Furthermore, the United States will continue to support UNSC Resolution 661 imposing mandatory economic sanctions against Iraq and Kuwait under Chapter VII of the United Nations Charter. We will emphasize individual and collective compliance with these sanctions, but are prepared, if necessary, to enforce them in the exercise of our inherent right of individual and collective self-defense under Article 51 of the UN Charter.

Energy

The United States now imports nearly half the oil it consumes and, as a result of the current crisis, could face a major threat to its economy. Much of the world is even more dependent on imported oil and more vulnerable to Iraqi threats. To minimize any impact that oil flow reductions from Iraq and Kuwait will have on the world's economies, it will be our policy to ask oil-producing nations to do what they can to increase production to offset these losses. I also direct the Secretaries of State and Energy to explore with the member countries of the International Energy Agency (IEA) a coordinated drawdown of strategic petroleum reserves, and implementation of complementary measures. I will continue to ask the American public to exercise restraint in their own consumption of oil products. The Secretary of Energy should work with various sectors of the U.S. economy to encourage energy conservation and fuel switching to non-oil sources, where appropriate and economic. Finally, I will continue to appeal to oil companies to show restraint in their pricing of crude oil and products. The Secretary of Energy, as appropriate, should work with oil companies in this regard.

Military

To protect U.S. interests in the Gulf and in response to requests from the King of Saudi Arabia and the Amir of Kuwait, I have ordered U.S. military forces deployed to the region for two purposes: to deter and, if necessary, defend Saudi Arabia and other friendly states in the Gulf region from further Iraqi aggression; and to enforce the mandatory Chapter 7 sanctions under Article 51 of the UN Charter and UNSC Resolutions 660 and 661. U.S. forces will work together with those of Saudi Arabia and other Gulf countries to preserve their national integrity and to deter further Iraqi aggression. Through their presence, as well as through training and exercises, these multinational forces will enhance the overall capability of Saudi Arabia and other regional states to defend themselves.

I also approve U.S. participation, in conjunction with the forces of other friendly governments, in two separate multinational forces that would provide for the defense of Saudi Arabia and enforce the UN mandated sanctions. These two groups will be called the Multinational Force for Saudi Arabia (MNFSA) and the Multinational Force to enforce sanctions (MNFES) against Iraq and Kuwait. The United States should coordinate closely with the Saudis, the Kuwaitis and others on the composition and organization of these forces.

The MNFSA:

The MNFSA is to deter aggression by Iraq against Saudi Arabia and other friendly Arab states in the Gulf, to ensure the territorial integrity and political independence of Saudi Arabia and other members of the GCC, and to conduct exercises and training to enhance the proficiency of Saudi forces in the defense of the Kingdom.

Adequate legal basis exists under the UN Charter and UNSC resolutions for the implementation of multinational efforts. I do not believe it is necessary now for the United States to seek additional UN endorsement for the MNFSA. If I subsequently determined that further UN endorsement is required, we should ensure that any UN-led effort is acceptable to U.S. military commanders and an adequate command structure is established and operating beforehand.

In concert with the other UNSC Permanent members, I authorize U.S. participation in discussions of the UN Military Staff Committee on the MNF operation for Saudi Arabia. If such talks are initiated, they should be of lower priority than talks concerning the MNFES.

Soviet participation in the MNFSA is warranted only if the Saudis request it. If so, we should work with the Saudis to insure that the Soviet mission is acceptable to us and that Soviet forces are deployed at a distance from U.S. operations in these countries. Soviet assistance in providing lift support to others providing forces inside Saudi Arabia should be encouraged.

The MNFES:

The MNF to enforce economic sanctions against Iraq and Kuwait is designed to bring about the withdrawal of Iraqi forces from Kuwait, and to restore Kuwait's sovereignty, independence and territorial integrity. Participating countries would seek to prevent the export of all commodities and products originating in Iraq or Kuwait, regardless of port of embarkation or transshipment point, and prevent the shipment to Iraq or Kuwait, regardless of declared port of destination or transshipment point, of any commodities or supplies whose provision to Iraq or Kuwait is contrary to UNSC Resolutions 660 and 661. These efforts should complement individual and collective compliance measures already in force.

In accordance with Article 51 of the UN Charter and UNSC resolutions 660 and 661, I hereby direct that all imports and exports, except medicines and food for humanitarian purposes (i.e., natural disasters) bound to and from Iraq and Kuwait be intercepted immediately. I direct the Secretary of Defense to immediately organize and coordinate a multinational force as requested by the Government of Kuwait. U.S. forces, in coordination with other cooperating national forces, should take necessary action to intercept vessels on a case-by-case basis until sufficient U.S. and other forces are available for more comprehensive enforcement. I also approve the submission to Congress of a separate letter informing it of the character and basis for our intercept operations in keeping with my commitment to congressional consultations on matters of national importance. The GCC states and potential contributors to the MNFES should be notified of the implementation of the intercept operation. I also agree to Soviet participation in the MNFES.

Since the UN Charter provides the legal basis for the conduct of this operation, I do not believe it is necessary now to obtain additional UN endorsement for the MNFES. Subject to the consent of the UNSC Permanent members, I agree to allow U.S. participation in discussions of the MNFES operation for enforcing sanctions against Iraq and Kuwait by the UN Military Staff Committee.

Further Resources

BOOKS

Atkinson, Rick. *Crusade: The Untold Story of the Persian Gulf War.* Boston: Houghton Mifflin Company, 1993.

Scales, Brig. Gen. Robert H. *Certain Victory: The U.S. Army in the Gulf War.* Washington, D.C.: Brassey's, 1994.

Schubert, Frank, and Theresa L. Kraus. *The Whirlwind War: The United States Army in Operations Desert Shield and Desert Storm.* Washington, D.C.: Center of Military History, United States Army, 1994. Available online at http://www.army.mil/cmh-pg/books/www/Wwindx.htm; website home page http://www.army.mil (accessed April 4, 2003).

PERIODICALS

Lewis, David A. and Roger P. Rose. "The President, the Press, and the War-Making Power: An Analysis of Media Coverage prior to the Persian Gulf War." *Presidential Studies Quarterly,* 32, 2002, 559–571

Weller, Sheila. "When Mommy Came Marching Home: What Happened to the Women Who Served in the Gulf War." *Redbook,* January 1996, 68–75.

WEBSITES

"Frontline: The Gulf War." Available online at http://www.pbs.org/wgbh/pages/frontline/gulf; website home page http://www.pbs.org (accessed April 4, 2003).

"Operation Desert Storm Ten Years After." The National Security Archives at George Washington University. Available online at http://www.gwu.edu/~nsarchiv/NSAEBB/NSAEBB80/; website home page http://www.gwu.edu (accessed April 4, 2003).

Joint Declaration at U.S.–Russian Summit

Statement

By: George H.W. Bush and Boris Yeltsin

Date: February 1, 1992

Source: Bush, George H.W., and Boris Yeltsin. Joint Declaration at U.S.–Russian Summit. February 1, 1992. Reprinted in the NATO-Russia Archive: U.S.-Russia Relations. Available online at http://www.bits.de/NRANEU/US-Russia.htm#A (accessed July 18, 2003).

About the Authors: George H.W. Bush (1924–) was born in Milton, Massachusetts. On his eighteenth birthday, Bush enlisted in the U.S. Navy. During World War II (1939–1945), he flew fifty-eight combat missions and received the Distinguished Flying Cross. After graduating from Yale University in 1948, Bush entered the Texas oil business. Later, he served as U.S. ambassador to the United Nations, U.S. envoy to China, director of the Central Intelligence Agency (CIA), and vice president and then president of the United States (served 1989–1993).

Boris Yeltsin (1931–) was born in Bukta, Russia. At age thirty, he joined the Communist Party of the Soviet Union, working his way up the ranks until he was appointed Moscow party chief in 1985. Yeltsin was a strong supporter of political and economic reform in the early days of Mikhail Gorbachev's *perestroika.* When the Cold War ended, Yeltsin became the new, democratically-elected president. He continued to press for reforms and a new constitution. By 1995, faced with an unpopular war in the breakaway republic of Chechnya and growing economic problems, Yeltsin's popularity was dwindling. He resigned at the end of 1999. ∎

Introduction

In 1991 the Cold War came to a symbolic end with the collapse of the Soviet Union. The Cold War was more of a conflict over two competing political ideologies—democracy and communism—than a military conflict in the conventional sense. After World War II (1939–1945) Western democracies led by the United States competed with a bloc of Eastern communist nations for international influence. The nations involved tried to promote their system of government in the international arena. Although there was no single, direct, and definitive military conflict that characterized the Cold War, the ideological war dominated international affairs for decades and ignited moments of intense international crisis.

During World War II the United States and the Soviet Union allied to defeat a common enemy to rid the world of Nazi fascism. Tensions, however, emerged between the two shortly after the war over how to divide conquered Germany. This marked the beginning of the Cold War. The nations decided to divide Germany into Eastern and Western halves, and the country later became officially divided into two nations, while a wall was erected to separate the city of Berlin into Eastern and Western zones. In 1949 the United States created a military alliance among Western democracies called the North Atlantic Treaty Organization (NATO) whose purpose was to defend Europe against the spread of communism. The Soviet Union responded in 1955 by forming a military alliance of its own with Eastern European countries, called the Warsaw Pact.

One of the most notable events of the Cold War came in 1962 when the Soviet Union attempted to erect a nuclear missile launch site in Cuba, a mere ninety miles from U.S. soil. The ensuing standoff between U.S. president John F. Kennedy (served 1961–1963) and Soviet prime minister Nikita Khrushchev, known as the Cuban Missile Crisis, brought the world the closest it had ever been to nuclear war. President Kennedy delivered a chilling speech to the American public and explained that his response was to order a military blockade to prevent the Soviets from delivering further supplies to Cuba. Khrushchev eventually ordered the dismantling of the missile base but not before receiving assurances from the United Sates that it would not invade Cuba.

From the end of World War II until the collapse of the Soviet Union in 1991 the Cold War was the central issue around which U.S. foreign policy was drafted. The Korean and Vietnam wars were, in large part, extensions of the Cold War. The United States became involved in these conflicts in an effort to stop the spread of communism in Asia. Under the administration of Jimmy Carter (served 1977–1981), efforts were made to ease Cold War tensions. Carter formally recognized communist China and, although it ultimately failed in Congress, he proposed an arms-limitation agreement with the Soviet Union.

Under the administration of Ronald Reagan (served 1981–1989) the United States and Soviet Union accelerated defense spending, building enormous nuclear arsenals. The notion of "mutually assured destruction" which described each country's ability to destroy the other in the event of a nuclear attack, ironically reduced the chances of war. It was not until the latter part of Reagan's second term in office that the United States and Soviet Union began thawing Cold War tensions. Ronald Reagan and Soviet leader Mikhail Gorbachev began Strategic Arms Limitation Talks (SALT), designed to reduce both nation's reserve of nuclear weapons. In addition, Gorbachev began introducing democratic institutions into society, a clear signal that the Cold War was coming to an end. He began to restructure the economy *(perestroika)* and promote political openness *(glasnost)*. Gorbachev's reforms, however, were not enough for his increasingly discontent public and in 1991 he was replaced by Boris Yeltsin in Russia's first direct presidential election. Later that year, Yeltsin announced the end

Four months after a February 1992 U.S.–Russian summit at Camp David, U.S. president George Bush and Russian president Boris Yeltsin signed a landmark agreement to destroy thousands of nuclear weapons. AP/WIDE WORLD PHOTOS. REPRODUCED BY PERMISSION.

of the Soviet Union and drafted a constitution for the new Commonwealth of Independent States.

Significance

The sudden collapse of the Soviet Union marked the end of the Cold War. For more than forty years, the United States fought an ideological battle with the Soviet Union that resulted in many indirect conflicts as both sides fought to have the greater number of countries on their side. For generations, Americans endured fear of nuclear annihilation, and taxpayers spent approximately $4 trillion on developing nuclear weapons. In June 1992, in an historical agreement, Yeltsin pledged to give up all Russian land-based MIRV missiles and to deactivate all missiles aimed at the United States. Members of NATO returned the gesture of goodwill by announcing a 50 percent troop reduction and signing non-aggression pacts with former communist nations of Eastern Europe. Measures like these helped solidify the symbolic end of the Cold War—the tearing down of the Berlin Wall—and resulted in an official declaration of the end of the adversarial relationship between the United States and former Soviet Union, signed by U.S. president George H.W. Bush (served 1989–1993) and Russian president Boris Yeltsin.

Primary Source

Joint Declaration at U.S.-Russian Summit

SYNOPSIS: In February 1992, U.S. president George H.W. Bush and Russian president Boris Yeltsin met at Camp David at a U.S.–Russian Summit and issued a Joint Declaration. In this historic declaration, Russia and the United States agreed to not regard each other as potential adversaries. Further, the two agreed that their future relationship would be based on "mutual trust and a respect and a common commitment to democracy and economic freedom."

At the conclusion of this meeting between an American president and the president of a new and democratic Russia, we, the leaders of two great peoples and nations, are agreed that a number of principles should guide relations between Russia and America.

1. Russia and the United States do not regard each other as potential adversaries. From now on the relationship will be characterized by friendship and partnership founded on mutual trust and respect and a common commitment to democracy and economic freedom.

2. We will work to remove any remnants of cold war hostility, including taking steps to reduce our strategic arsenals.

3. We will do all we can to promote a mutual well-being of our peoples and to expand as widely as possible the ties that now bind our peoples. Openness and tolerance should be the hallmark of relations between our peoples and governments.

4. We will actively promote free trade, investment and economic cooperation between our two countries.

5. We will make every effort to support the promotion of our shared values for democracy, the rule of law, respect for human rights, including minority rights, respect for borders and peaceful change around the globe.

6. We will work actively together to:

• Prevent the proliferation of weapons of mass destruction and associated technology, and curb the spread of advanced conventional arms on the basis of principles to be agreed upon.

• Settle regional conflicts peacefully.

• Counter terrorism, halt drug trafficking and forestall environmental degradation.

In adopting these principles, the United States and Russia today launch a new era in our relationship. In this new era, we seek a peace, and enduring peace that rests on lasting common values. This can be an era of peace and friendship that offers hope not only to our peoples, but to the peoples of the world.

For a while our conflicts helped divide the world for a generation. Now, working with others and with each other, we can help unite the globe through our friendship—a new alliance of partners working against the common dangers we face.

Further Resources

BOOKS

Beschloss, Michael, and Strobe Talbott. *At the Highest Levels: The Inside Story of the End of the Cold War.* Boston: Little, Brown, 1993

Odom, William E. *The Collapse of the Soviet Military.* New Haven, Conn.: Yale University Press, 1998.

Schweizer, Peter. *Reagan's War: The Epic Story of His Forty-Year Struggle and Final Triumph Over Communism.* New York: Doubleday, 2002.

PERIODICALS

D'Souza, Dinesh. "How Reagan Won the Cold War: Ronald Reagan Came to the Presidency Without Foreign-Policy Credentials, but his Victory in the Cold War was not a Lucky Accident." *National Review,* November 24, 1997, 35–41.

"The Last Cold War President." *The New York Times,* December 15, 1992, A22.

WEBSITES

"Cold War." *CNN Interactive.* Available online at http://www.cnn.com/SPECIALS/cold.war; website home page http://www.cnn.com (accessed April 4, 2003).

"Cold War International History Project." The National Security Archive at George Washington University. Available online at http://cwihp.si.edu (accessed April 4, 2003).

"The Whisper of AIDS"

Speech

By: Mary Fisher

Date: August 19, 1992

Source: Fisher, Mary. "The Whisper of AIDS." Speech delivered at the Republican National Convention, 19 August 1992. Reprinted in Great American Speeches. Available online at http://www.pbs.org/greatspeeches/timeline/m_fisher_s1.html; website homepage: http://www.pbs.org/greatspeeches/ (accessesd October 15, 2002).

About the Author: Mary Fisher (1948–) is the daughter of the multi-millionaire philanthropist and financier, Max Fisher. Born in Louisville, Kentucky, she grew up in an affluent suburb of Detroit, Michigan. After dropping out of the University of Michigan, Fisher became a television producer. In the mid-1970s, she worked as a staff assistant to President Gerald Ford (served 1974–1977). Afterwards, she designed a signature line of boutique items; she also became an accomplished painter and creator of handmade paper works. ∎

Introduction

In 1981, medical doctors in the United States encountered one of the most serious diseases ever to be diagnosed in this country. Initially, the mysterious viral disease seemed to affect otherwise young, healthy gay men, destroying their natural defenses against a debilitating succession of infections, as well as rare types of pneumonia and cancer. The United States Department of Health and Human Services' Centers for Disease Control and Prevention (CDC) called the disease "GRID" (gay-related immune deficiency). Gay political activists, however, vigorously complained that the name further stigmatized the group. Beginning in 1982, the CDC referred to the disease as "AIDS" (Acquired Immune Deficiency Syndrome). That year, 422 cases were reported in twenty-four states, and 184 people died.

The appearance of AIDS coincided with the political rise of the conservative movement, long dormant at the federal level. This movement consisted of several powerful coalitions. Of particular importance were the evangelical Christian organizations, the Moral Majority and the Christian Coalition. These religious fundamentalist groups—who had long railed against the counterculture of the 1970s gay liberation movement—identified AIDS as a logical consequence of gay behavior. Another important coalition was the "New Right." Heavily influenced by economist Milton Friedman and writer William F. Buckley, this coalition called for smaller government. It advocated slashing federal social programs, devolving federal power to the states, fiscal austerity, and tax reductions. Together, evangelical Christians and the New Right helped elect President Ronald Reagan (served 1981–1989) twice.

The Reagan administration did not aggressively support AIDS prevention, research, and treatment efforts—in part, to satisfy its religious and New Right constituencies. The latter saw the growing epidemic not as a national problem, but primarily as a San Francisco and New York City crisis to be solved by the affected states. Moreover, there were very few trained clinicians and researchers at the CDC familiar with the diseases associated with the AIDS virus. It was not until 1985 that President Reagan realized the seriousness of the epidemic. That year, his old friend Rock Hudson, a well-known actor, died of AIDS. Despite Hudson's death and 12,591 others AIDS-related deaths that year, the administration proposed to reduce AIDS spending by ten percent. In 1986, Dr. C. Everett Koop, the U.S. Surgeon General, released a very controversial report on AIDS. The report was significant because it was the first time that the federal government addressed the epidemic in terms of public health, and not as a moral issue. In 1987, Reagan, after six years of silence, used the word AIDS in public for the first time. Three years later, he apolo-

gized for not doing more to eradicate the disease. By 1990, the AIDS epidemic had spread beyond gay men, to include intravenous drug users, their sex partners, and their babies. Unlike his predecessor, President George H.W. Bush (served 1989–1993) took a more aggressive stance against the disease. In 1990, he signed the Comprehensive AIDS Resources Emergency Act, which appropriated $2.6 billion annually to combat the disease.

Significance

From 1981 to 1994, the annual number of deaths among persons with AIDS increased steadily. Due to highly active antiretroviral therapies (HAART), however, there has been a significant decline in AIDS-related deaths from 1995 to 2002. As of 2002, the cumulative number of reported AIDS cases was 816,149, and the total number of deaths was 467,910. In 2003, President George W. Bush declared that AIDS was not a partisan issue. Amid a stubborn economic recession, he proposed to increase the HIV/AIDS budget $905 million to a total of $12.9 billion annually. The budget would also include $144 million to fight AIDS across the globe.

Primary Source

"The Whisper of AIDS"

SYNOPSIS: At the Republican National Convention in 1992, Mary Fisher addressed the nation. Two years prior, she had contracted HIV (Human Immunodeficiency Virus) from her husband, an intravenous drug user. Her message to the country was that AIDS does not discriminate in choosing its victims—everyone is at risk.

Less than three months ago, at the platform hearings in Salt Lake City, I asked the Republican party to lift the shroud of silence which has been draped over the issue of HIV/AIDS. I have come tonight to bring our silence to an end.

I bear a message of challenge, not self-congratulation. I want your attention, not your applause. I would never have asked to be HIV positive. But I believe that in all things there is a good purpose, and so I stand before you, and before the nation, gladly.

The reality of AIDS is brutally clear. Two hundred thousand Americans are dead or dying; a million more are infected. Worldwide, forty million, sixty million, or a hundred million infections will be counted in the coming few years. But despite science and research, White House meetings and congressional hearings; despite good intentions and bold initiatives, campaign slogans and hopeful

Mary Fisher gives a speech before the Republican National Convention in Houston, Texas, August 19, 1992. Fisher founded the Family AIDS Network and is herself HIV positive. **AP/WIDE WORLD PHOTOS. REPRODUCED BY PERMISSION.**

promises—despite it all, it's the epidemic which is winning tonight.

In the context of an election year, I ask you—here, in this great hall, or listening in the quiet of your home—to recognize that the AIDS virus is not a political creature. It does not care whether you are Democrat or Republican. It does not ask whether you are black or white, male or female, gay or straight, young or old. [Applause.]

Tonight, I represent an AIDS community whose members have been reluctantly drafted from every segment of American society. Though I am white, and a mother, I am one with a black infant struggling with tubes in a Philadelphia hospital. Though I am female, and contracted this disease in marriage, and enjoy the warm support of my family, I am one with the lonely gay man sheltering a flickering candle from the cold wind of his family's rejection. [Applause.]

This is not a distant threat; it is a present danger. The rate of infection is increasing fastest among women and children. Largely unknown a decade ago, AIDS is the third leading killer of young-adult Ameri-

cans today—but it won't be third for long. Because, unlike other diseases, this one travels. Adolescents don't give each other cancer or heart disease because they believe they are in love. But HIV is different. And we have helped it along—we have killed each other—with our ignorance, our prejudice, and our silence.

We may take refuge in our stereotypes, but we cannot hide there long. Because HIV asks only one thing of those it attacks: Are you human? And this is the right question: Are *you* human? Because people with HIV have not entered some alien state of being. They are human. They have not earned cruelty and they do not deserve meanness. They don't benefit from being isolated or treated as outcasts. Each of them is exactly what God made: a person. Not evil, deserving of our judgment; not victims, longing for our pity. People. Ready for support and worthy of compassion. [Applause.]

My call to you, my Party, is to take a public stand no less compassionate than that of the President and Mrs. Bush. They have embraced me and my family in memorable ways. In the place of judgment, they have shown affection. In difficult moments, they have raised our spirits. In the darkest hours, I have seen them reaching not only to me, but also to my parents, armed with that stunning grief and special grace that comes only to parents who have themselves leaned too long over the bedside of a dying child.

With the President's leadership, much good has been done; much of the good has gone unheralded; and as the President has insisted, "Much remains to be done."

But we do the President's cause no good if we praise the American family but ignore a virus that destroys it. [Applause.] We must be consistent if we are to be believed. We cannot love justice and ignore prejudice, love our children and fear to teach them. Whatever our role, as parent or policy maker, we must act as eloquently as we speak—else we have no integrity.

My call to the nation is a plea for awareness. If you believe you are safe, you are in danger. Because I was not a hemophiliac, I was not at risk. Because I was not gay, I was not at risk. Because I did not inject drugs, I was not at risk.

My father has devoted much of his lifetime to guarding against another holocaust. He is part of the generation who heard Pastor Niemoeller come out of the Nazi death camps to say, "They came after the Jews, and I was not a Jew, so I did not protest. They came after the Trade Unionists, and I was not a Trade Unionist, so I did not protest. They came after the Roman Catholics, and I was not a Roman Catholic, so I did not protest. Then they came after me, and there was no one left to protest." [Applause.]

The lesson history teaches is this: If you believe you are safe, you are at risk. If you do not see this killer stalking your children, look again. There is no family or community, no race or religion, no place left in America that is safe. Until we genuinely embrace this message, we are a nation at risk.

Tonight, HIV marches resolutely toward AIDS in more than a million American homes, littering its pathway with the bodies of the young. Young men. Young women. Young parents, and young children. One of the families is mine. If it is true that HIV inevitably turns to AIDS, then my children will inevitably turn to orphans.

My family has been a rock of support. My eighty-four-year-old father, who has pursued the healing of the nations, will not accept the premise that he cannot heal his daughter. My mother has refused to be broken; she still calls at midnight to tell wonderful jokes that make me laugh. Sisters and friends, and my brother Phillip, whose birthday is today—all have helped carry me over the hardest places. I am blessed, richly and deeply blessed, to have such a family.

But not all of you [Applause], but not all of you have been so blessed. You are HIV-positive but dare not say it. You have lost loved ones, but you dared not whisper the word AIDS. You weep silently; you grieve alone.

I have a message for you: It is not you who should feel shame, it is we. We who tolerate ignorance and practice prejudice, we who have taught you to fear. We must lift our shroud of silence, making it safe for you to reach out for compassion. It is our task to seek safety for our children, not in quiet denial but in effective action.

Someday our children will be grown. My son Max, now four, will take the measure of his mother; my son Zachary, now two, will sort through his memories. I may not be here to hear their judgments, but I know already what I hope they are.

I want my children to know that their mother was not a victim. She was a messenger. I do not want them to think, as I once did, that courage is the absence of fear; I want them to know that courage is the strength to act wisely when most we are afraid. I want them to have the courage to step

forward when called by their nation, or their Party, and give leadership—no matter what the personal cost. I ask no more of you than I ask of myself, or of my children.

To the millions of you who are grieving, who are frightened, who have suffered the ravages of AIDS firsthand: Have courage and you will find support.

To the millions who are strong I issue the plea: Set aside prejudice and politics to make room for compassion and sound policy. [Applause.]

To my children, I make this pledge:

I will not give in, Zachary, because I draw my courage from you. Your silly giggle gives me hope. Your gentle prayers give me strength. And you, my child, give me the reason to say to America, "You are at risk."

And I will not rest, Max, until I have done all I can to make your world safe. I will seek a place where intimacy is not the prelude to suffering. I will not hurry to leave you, my children. But when I go, I pray that you will not suffer shame on my account.

To all within the sound of my voice, I appeal: Learn with me the lessons of history and of grace, so my children will not be afraid to say the word AIDS when I am gone. Then their children, and yours, may not need to whisper it at all.

God bless the children, and bless us all—good night.

Further Resources

BOOKS

Foment, Michael. *The Myth of Heterosexual AIDS.* New York: Basic Books, 1990.

Moen, Matthew C. *The Christian Right and Congress.* Tuscaloosa, Ala.: University of Alabama Press, 1989.

Shilts, Randy. *And the Band Played On: Politics, People, and the AIDS Epidemic.* New York: St. Martin's Press, 1987.

PERIODICALS

Colby, David, and Timothy Cook. "Epidemics and Agendas: The Politics of Nightly News Coverage of AIDS." *Journal of Health Politics, Policy and Law,* 16, no. 2, Summer 1991, 215–249.

Eberstadt, Nicholas. "The Future of AIDS." *Foreign Affairs,* 81, November-December 2002, 22.

WEBSITES

"AIDS: Twenty Years of an Epidemic." *CNN.* Available online at http://www.cnn.com/SPECIALS/2001/aids/; website main page http://www.cnn.com (accessed April 4, 2003).

National Center for HIV, STD and TB Prevention, Divisions of HIV/AIDS Prevention. Centers for Disease Control & Prevention. Available online at http://www.cdc.gov/hiv/pubs /facts.htm; website home page http://www.cdc.gov (accessed April 4, 2003).

Presidential Debate, October 11, 1992

Debate

By: George H.W. Bush, Bill Clinton, and H. Ross Perot

Date: October 11, 1992

Source: *Presidential Debate, October 11, 1992*. Transcripts from The Commission on Presidential Debates. Available online at http://www.debates.org/pages/trans92a1.html; website home page http://www.debates.org (accessed April 4, 2003).

About the Authors: George H.W. Bush (1924–) was born in Milton, Massachusetts. On his eighteenth birthday, Bush enlisted in the U.S. Navy. During World War II (1939–1945), he flew fifty-eight combat missions and received the Distinguished Flying Cross. After graduating from Yale University in 1948, Bush entered the Texas oil business. Later, he served as the U.S. ambassador to the United Nations, a U.S. envoy to China, director of the Central Intelligence Agency (CIA), and vice president and president of the United States (served 1989–1993).

Bill Clinton (1946–) was born in Hope, Arkansas. After earning an international relations degree from Georgetown University, Clinton received a Yale law degree. In 1978, at the age of thirty-two, Clinton was elected governor of Arkansas. After losing his reelection bid, he was elected again and maintained the position until becoming president (served 1993–2001) of the United States. He was the first Democrat since Franklin D. Roosevelt (served 1933–1945) to be reelected to a second presidential term.

H. Ross Perot (1930–) was born in Texarkana, Texas, the son of a cotton broker and horse dealer. In 1953, after graduating from the United States Naval Academy, Perot spent four years on active duty. Later, Perot, with no specialized computer or electronic training, founded Electronic Data Systems (EDS). In 1984, he sold EDS to General Motors, receiving $1 billion in cash and 5.5 million shares in new stock, while remaining the president of the company. ∎

Introduction

Following the nation's impressive victory in the Gulf War in 1991, conventional wisdom held that President George H.W. Bush (served 1989–1993) would win reelection easily. Bush's poll approval rating reached an unprecedented 91 percent in February 1991. However, by late spring 1992, his approval rating had plummeted to fifty percent, and it fell to 34 percent that summer. There were a variety of reasons for Bush's political free fall. First, he reneged on his 1988 campaign promise not to raise taxes. Faced with a $220 billion budget deficit, Bush compromised with the Democrat-controlled Congress to trade a tax hike for budget cuts. Consequently, Bush alienated many fiscal conservatives, who, in turn, sat out the 1992 election. Bush also undercut his support with Republican and Independent women when his Supreme Court nominee, Clarence Thomas, was accused of sexual harassment. The biggest reason for Bush's declining poll numbers, however, was the poor economy. During his presidency, the gross national product, the total annual output of the nation's goods and services, increased at .07 percent annually, the slowest rate of growth since the Great Depression. As a result, Bush had the lowest poll ratings of any first term president in his fourth year in office since Herbert Hoover in 1932.

Due to Bush's high approval ratings early in 1991, few big-name Democrats were eager to challenge the president. The political void allowed Bill Clinton (served 1993–2001), governor of Arkansas, to enter the presidential campaign. Heading into the New Hampshire primary, Clinton was the frontrunner. Allegations of past womanizing, however, dogged his bid for the presidency. With two politically damaged candidates, H. Ross Perot announced on the *Larry King Live* cable talk show in February 1992 that he would run for president as an independent, if voters in all fifty states put him on the ballot. Initially, Perot was a formidable contender, because, as a billionaire, he was willing to bankroll the campaign himself. Perot also captured the public's attention with his blunt, humorous personality. He had a knack of simplifying complicated economic issues for the American people. Bush and Clinton both viewed Perot as a serious contender.

In June 1992, Perot's poll ratings reached 39 percent—compared to 31 percent for Bush and 25 percent for Clinton. Fearing a potential political crisis, a Senate committee began hearings to change the Electoral College by constitutional amendment. Oddly enough, Perot unexpectedly bowed out of the race at the height of his popularity. A couple of months later, however, he reentered the race. Perot's indecision ultimately cost him any chance of winning the presidency. Yet, he remained a dangerous challenger because he could draw just enough support from Bush or Clinton to propel the eventual winner into the White House. On October 1, Perot relaunched his presidential efforts with a thirty-three-day campaign that included his participation in three nationwide televised debates.

Significance

After the first debate, polling data showed that Perot had been the clear winner. Although he stood little chance of winning, he forced Bush and Clinton to publicly confront the spiraling national debt, commercial trade imbalance, and other important economic issues during the debate. Later that fall, Perot hosted two thirty-minute nationally televised infomercials. Sitting at a desk, armed with a silver pointer and numerous pie charts, he gave the nation a crash course on economics. On November 3, 1992, Bill Clinton received more than twice the num-

Presidential candidates (from left) H. Ross Perot, Bill Clinton, and President George H.W. Bush meet in St. Louis, Missouri, for their first debate in October 1992. **AP/WIDE WORLD PHOTOS. REPRODUCED BY PERMISSION.**

ber of Electoral College votes than George H.W. Bush, but defeated Bush by less than six percentage points (43.3 percent to 37.7 percent, respectively). Perot received 19.1 percent, faring better than any third party presidential candidate since Teddy Roosevelt in 1912. Though Perot drew support from both candidates, he drew more votes from Bush, perhaps costing Bush reelection.

Primary Source

Presidential Debate, October 11, 1992 [excerpt]

SYNOPSIS: The first presidential debate was October 11, 1992, in St. Louis, Missouri. The Bush campaign had insisted that Perot be included in the contest, reasoning that Clinton would best the president in a one-on-one showdown. From the beginning of the debate, Perot put his opponents on the defensive with his folksy, quirky demeanor and ability to speak honestly about the nation's economic ills.

Perot: I think the principal that separates me is that 5 and a half million people came together on their own and put me on the ballot. I was not put on the ballot by either of the 2 parties; I was not put on the ballot by any PAC money, by any foreign lobbyist money, by any special interest money. This is a movement that came from the people. This is the way the framers of the Constitution intended our government to be, a government that comes from the people. Over time we have developed a government that comes at the people, that comes from the top down, where the people are more or less treated as objects to be programmed during the campaign with commercials and media events and fear messages and personal attacks and things of that nature. The thing that separates my candidacy and makes it unique is that this came from millions of people in 50 states all over this country who wanted a candidate that worked and belonged to nobody but them. I go into this race as their servant, and I belong to them. So this comes from the people.

Lehrer: Governor Clinton, a one minute response.

Clinton: The most important distinction in this campaign is that I represent real hope for change, a departure from trickle-down economics, a departure from tax and spend economics, to invest in growth. But before I can do that, I must challenge the American people to change, and they must decide. Tonight I have to say to the President: Mr. Bush, for 12 years you've had it your way. You've had your chance and it didn't work. It's time to change. I want to bring that change to the American people. But we must all decide first we have the courage to change for hope and a better tomorrow.

Lehrer: President Bush, one minute response, sir.

President Bush: Well, I think one thing that distinguishes is experience. I think we've dramatically changed the world. I'll talk about that a little bit later, but the changes are mind-boggling for world peace. Kids go to bed at night without the same fear of nuclear war. And change for change sake isn't enough. We saw that message in the late 70s when heard a lot about change, and what happened, that misery index went right through the roof. But my economic program is the kind of change we want. And the way we're going to get it done is we're going to have a brand new Congress. A lot of them are thrown out because of all the scandals. I'll sit down with them, Democrats and Republicans alike, and work for my agenda for American renewal, which represents real change. But I'd say, if you had to separate out, I think it's experience at this level.

Lehrer: Governor Clinton, how do you respond to the President on the—you have two minutes—on the question of experience? He says that is what distinguishes him from the other two of you.

Clinton: I believe experience counts, but it's not everything. Values, judgment, and the record that I have amassed in my state also should count for something. I've worked hard to create good jobs and to educate people. My state now ranks first in the country in job growth this year, fourth in income growth, fourth in reduction of poverty, third in overall economic performance, according to a major news magazine. That's because we believe in investing in education and in jobs. And we have to change in this country. You know, my wife, Hillary, gave me a book about a year ago in which the author defined insanity as just doing the same old thing over and over again and expecting a different result. We have got to have the courage to change. Experience is important, yes. I've gotten a lot of good experience in dealing with ordinary people over the last year and month. I've touched more people's lives and seen more heartbreak and hope, more pain and more promise, than anybody else who's run for president this year. I think the American people deserve better than they're getting. We have gone from first to thirteenth in the world in the last twelve years, since Mr. Bush and Mr. Reagan have been in. Personal income has dropped while people have worked harder. In the last four years, there have been twice as many bankruptcies as new jobs created. We need a new approach. The same old experience is not relevant. We're living in a new world after the Cold War, and what works in this new world is not trickle down, not government for the benefit of the privileged few, not tax and spend, but a commitment to invest in American jobs and American education, controlling American health care costs, and bringing the American people together. That is what works. And you can have the right kind of experience and the wrong kind of experience. Mine is rooted in the real lives of real people, and it will bring real results if we have the courage to change.

Lehrer: President Bush, one minute to respond.

Bush: I just thought of another—another big difference here between me. I don't believe Mr. Perot feels this way, but I know Governor Clinton did because I want to accurately quote him. He thinks, I think he said, that the country is coming apart at the seams. Now, I know that the only way he can win is to make everybody believe the economy's worse than it is. But this country is not coming apart at the seams, for heaven's sakes. We're the United States of America. In spite of the economic problems, we're the most respected economy around the world. Many would trade for it. We've been caught up in a global slowdown. We can do much, much better, but we ought not try to convince the American people that America is a country that's coming apart at the seams. I would hate to be running for president and think that the only way I could win would be to convince everybody how horrible things are. Yes, there are big problems, and yes, people are hurting. But I believe that this Agenda for American renewal I have is the answer to do it, and I believe we can get it done now, whereas we didn't in the past, because you're going to have a whole brand new bunch of people in the Congress that are going to have to listen to the same American people I'm listening to.

Lehrer: Mr. Perot, a minute response, sir.

Perot: Well, they've got a point. I don't have any experience in running up a $4 trillion debt. (Laughter.) I don't have any experience in gridlock government where nobody takes responsibility for anything and everybody blames everybody else. I don't have any experience in creating the worst public school system in the industrialized world, but I do have a lot of experience in getting things done. So, if we're at a point in history where we want to stop talking about it and do it, I've got a lot of experience in figuring out how to solve problems, making the solutions work, and then moving on to the next one. I've got a lot of experience in not taking 10 years to solve a 10-minute problem. So, if it's time for action, I think I have experience that counts. If there's more time for gridlock and talk and finger pointing, I'm the wrong man.

Lehrer: President Bush, the question goes to you. you have two minutes. And the question is this: Are there important issues of character separating you from these other two men?

Bush: I think the American people should be the judge of that. I think character is a very important question. I said something the other day where I was accused of being like Joe McCarthy because I questioned—I put it this way; I think it's wrong to demonstrate against your own country or organize demonstrations against your own country in foreign soil. I just think it's wrong. I—well, maybe they say, "Well, it was a youthful indiscretion." I was 19 or 20 flying off an aircraft carrier and that shaped me to be Commander-in-Chief of the armed forces and I'm sorry, but demonstrating—it's not a question of patriotism. It's a question of character and judgment. They get on me—Bill's gotten on me about, "read my lips." When I make a mistake I'll admit it. But he has made—not admitted a mistake and I

just find it impossible to understand how an American can demonstrate against his own country in a foreign land—organizing demonstrations against it when young men are held prisoner in Hanoi or kids out of the ghetto were drafted. Some say, "well, you're a little old fashioned." Maybe I am, but I just don't think that's right. Now, whether it's character or judgment—whatever it is—I have a big difference here on this issue and so we'll just have to see how it plays out. But I—I couldn't do that. And I don't think most Americans could do that. And they all say, "Well, it was a long time ago." Well, let's admit it then. Say, "I made a terrible mistake." How could you be Commander-in-Chief of the armed forces and have some kid say—when you have to make a tough decision, as I did in Panama or Kuwait and then have some kid jump up and say, "Well, I'm not going to go. The Commander-in-Chief was organizing demonstrations halfway around the world during another era. So there are differences but that's about the main area where I think we have a difference. I don't know about—we'll talk about that a little with Ross here in a bit.

Lehrer: Mr. Perot, you have one minute.

Perot: I think the American people will make their own decisions on character and at a time when we have work to do and we need action I think they need to clearly understand the backgrounds of each person. I think the press can play a huge roll in making sure that the backgrounds are clearly presented in an objective way. Then, make a decision. Certainly anyone in the White House should have the character to be there. But, I think it's very important to measure when and where things occurred. Did they occur when you were a young person, in your formative years? Or did they occur while you were a senior official in the federal government? If you make it as a young man, time passes. So I would say just, you know, look at all three of us. Decide who you think will do the job. Pick that person in November because believe me, as I've said before, "The party's over and it's time for the clean-up crew." And we do have to have change and people who never take responsibility for anything when it happens on their watch and people who are in charge—

Lehrer: Your time is up.

Perot: The time is up. (Laughter).

Lehrer: The time is up.

Perot: More later.

Further Resources

BOOKS

Follett, Ken. *On Wings of Eagles.* New York: W. Morrow, 1983

Levin, Doron P. *Irreconcilable Differences: Ross Perot versus General Motors.* Boston: Little, Brown, 1989.

Posner, Gerald L. *Citizen Perot: His Life and Times.* New York: Random House, 1996.

PERIODICALS

Rothenberg, Stuart, "Where Have You Gone, Ross Perot?" *Roll Call,* April 12, 2001.

Stone, Walter J. "It's Perot Stupid! The Legacy of the 1992 Perot Movement in the Majority-Party System, 1994-2000." *Political Science & Politics,* March 2001, 49–59.

WEBSITES

"Directory of U.S. Political Parties." Politics1. Available online at http://www.politics1.com/parties.htm; website home page http://www.politicsl.com (accessed April 4, 2003).

"Reform Party Official Website." Reform Party of the United States of America. Available online at http://www.reform party.org (accessed April 4, 2003).

"The Coming White Underclass"

Newspaper article

By: Charles Murray

Date: October 29, 1993

Source: Murray, Charles. "The Coming White Underclass." *The Wall Street Journal,* October 29, 1993.

About the Author: Charles Murray (1943–) was born in Newton, Iowa. After graduating from Harvard University in 1965, Murray joined the Peace Corps, serving in Thailand for five years. In 1974, he earned a Ph.D. in political science at the Massachusetts Institute of Technology. He has become one of the United States' most prominent social scientists, libertarians, and influential conservative thinkers. ∎

Introduction

During the Great Depression, the nation faced the near collapse of public and private resources to assist the poor. In 1935, Congress passed the Social Security Act, which included the program Aid to Families with Dependent Children (AFDC). Originally, the act provided federal funds through dollar-matching arrangements with state governments for children of destitute widows. In 1961, the federal government extended AFDC to include children of an unemployed parent and that parent. Con-

sequently, AFDC caseloads exploded from three million in 1960 to ten million in 1971. Over the same period, federal and state expenditures rose from $1 billion to $6.2 billion. Moreover, the percentage of persons eligible for benefits who actually received them climbed from thirty-three percent to ninety percent. By the early 1970s, AFDC was the largest expenditure for direct public assistance.

In 1965, Daniel Patrick Moynihan wrote a controversial report that examined how culture and economics were interrelated. Not surprisingly, the report revealed that during the 1950s increasing welfare caseloads mirrored high unemployment rates. Moynihan, however, also demonstrated that in 1963, although unemployment among blacks decreased, more blacks went on welfare. According to Moynihan, many of these new welfare recipients were fatherless, as out-of-wedlock births had increased from seventeen percent in 1950 to twenty-six percent in 1965. Moynihan concluded that the black family was deteriorating.

From the late 1960s to the early 1990s, the federal government failed to comprehensively reform welfare. Richard Nixon's (served 1969–1974) Family Assistance Plan (1969-1972) passed the House, but died in the Senate. Jimmy Carter's (served 1977–1981) Program for Better Jobs and Incomes (1977) failed to pass the House. Ronald Reagan's (served 1981–1989) 1981 Omnibus Budget Reconciliation Act did not slash welfare rolls over the long run, and his New Federalism (1982) was never introduced in Congress. Further, the incremental reforms of George H. Bush's (served 1989–1993) Family Support Act (1988) were not bold enough to have a lasting impact. As a result, between August 1989 and October 1992, the number of AFDC cases increased thirty percent. Moreover, federal and state AFDC benefits topped $20 billion in 1992.

Significance

Throughout the 1980s, the general public and policymakers increasingly viewed AFDC policy as anti-work and anti-family. The traditional rationale that a generous welfare program fostered stability among poor families was undermined. Instead, welfare dependence was seen as the main cause of out-of-wedlock births and child poverty. In 1992, President Bill Clinton (served 1993–2001) campaigned on the issue of "ending welfare as we know it."

In 1996, a Republican Congress passed the Personal Responsibility and Work Opportunity Act. The act was the most extraordinary, conservative shift in social policy in sixty years. It replaced AFDC with the Temporary Assistance for Needy Families (TANF). TANF ended the benefit entitlement of individual families, mandated work requirements, and provided states with fixed block grants and significant discretion in administering benefits. In return, states were prohibited from extending TANF to un-wed parents under eighteen years of age—unless they lived under adult supervision, and, if high school dropouts, attended school.

To avoid loss of TANF funds, states were required to engage fifty percent of adult recipients in "work activities" for a general average of thirty hours weekly (twenty hours for single parents of preschool children). From 1994 to 2002, the number of families on welfare dropped from a record high of five million to two million. This decrease occurred despite twenty-eight states experiencing increases in the number of families on welfare between June 2001 and June 2002. Moreover, from 1994 to 2002, the poverty rate among children in single families headed by a female dropped from fifty-three percent to thirty-nine percent.

Primary Source

"The Coming White Underclass"

SYNOPSIS: In this essay, author Charles Murray revealed that the white illegitimacy rate had risen to 22 percent in 1991, creating a white underclass. This percentage was very close to that of blacks in 1965, a rate that had convinced Daniel Patrick Moynihan that the black family was in crisis. Murray further states, "In raw numbers, European-American whites are the ethnic group with the most people in poverty, most illegitimate children, most women on welfare, most unemployed men, and most arrests for serious crimes."

Every once in a while the sky really is falling, and this seems to be the case with the latest national figures on illegitimacy. The unadorned statistic is that, in 1991, 1.2 million children were born to unmarried mothers, within a hair of 30% of all live births. How high is 30%? About four percentage points higher than the black illegitimacy rate in the early 1960s that motivated Daniel Patrick Moynihan to write his famous memorandum on the breakdown of the black family.

The 1991 story for blacks is that illegitimacy has now reached 68% of births to black women. In inner cities, the figure is typically in excess of 80%. Many of us have heard these numbers so often that we are inured. It is time to think about them as if we were back in the mid-1960s with the young Moynihan and asked to predict what would happen if the black illegitimacy rate were 68%.

Impossible, we would have said. But if the proportion of fatherless boys in a given community were to reach such levels, surely the culture must be 'Lord of the Files' writ large, the values of unsocialized

male adolescents made norms—physical violence, immediate gratification and predatory sex. That is the culture now taking over the black inner city.

But the black story, however dismaying, is old news. The new trend that threatens the U.S. is white illegitimacy. Matters have not yet quite gotten out of hand, but they are on the brink. If we want to act, now is the time.

In 1991, 707,502 babies were born to single white women, representing 22% of white births. The elite wisdom holds that this phenomenon cuts across social classes, as if the increase in Murphy Browns were pushing the trendline. Thus, a few months ago, a Census Bureau study of fertility among all American women got headlines for a few days because it showed that births to single women with college degrees doubled in the last decade to 6% from 3%. This is an interesting trend, but of minor social importance. The real news of that study is that the proportion of single mothers with less than a high school education jumped to 48% from 35% in a single decade.

These numbers are dominated by whites. Breaking down the numbers by race (using data not available in the published version), women with college degrees contribute only 4% of white illegitimate babies, while women with a high school education or less contribute 82%. Women with family incomes of $75,000 or more contribute 1% of white illegitimate babies, while women with family incomes under $20,000 contribute 69%.

The National Longitudinal Study of Youth, a Labor Department study that has tracked more than 10,000 youths since 1979, shows an even more dramatic picture. For white women below the poverty line in the year prior to giving birth, 44% of births have been illegitimate, compared with only 6% for women above the poverty line. White illegitimacy is overwhelmingly a lower-class phenomenon.

This brings us to the emergence of a white underclass. In raw numbers, European-American whites are the ethnic group with the most people in poverty, most illegitimate children, most women on welfare, most unemployed men, and most arrests for serious crimes. And yet whites have not had an 'underclass' as such, because the whites who might qualify have been scattered among the working class. Instead, whites have had 'white trash' concentrated in a few streets on the outskirts of town, sometimes a Skid Row of unattached white men in the large cities. But these scatterings have seldom been large enough to make up a neighborhood. An

A pilot program in Portland, Oregon, for single mothers under age 18 and on public assistance includes classes in birth control, motherhood, and job skills, 1995. © SHEPARD SHERBELL/CORBIS SABA. REPRODUCED BY PERMISSION.

underclass needs a critical mass, and white America has not had one.

But now the overall white illegitimacy rate is 22%. The figure in low-income, working-class communities may be twice that. How much illegitimacy can a community tolerate? Nobody knows, but the historical fact is that the trendlines on black crime, dropout from the labor force, and illegitimacy all shifted sharply upward as the overall black illegitimacy rate passed 25%.

The causal connection is murky—I blame the revolution in social policy during that period, while others blame the sexual revolution, broad shifts in cultural norms, or structural changes in the economy. But the white illegitimacy rate is approaching that same problematic 25% region at a time when social policy is more comprehensively wrongheaded than it was in the mid-1960s, and the cultural and sexual norms are still more degraded.

The white underclass will begin to show its face in isolated ways. Look for certain schools in white neighborhoods to get a reputation as being unteachable, with large numbers of disruptive students and indifferent parents. Talk to the police; listen for stories about white neighborhoods where the incidence of domestic disputes and casual violence has been shooting up. Look for white neighborhoods with high concentrations of drug activity and large numbers of men who have dropped out of the labor force. Some readers will recall reading the occasional news story about such places already.

As the spatial concentration of illegitimacy reaches critical mass, we should expect the deterioration to be as fast among low-income whites in the 1990s as it was among low-income blacks in the 1960s. My proposition is that illegitimacy is the single most important social problem of our time—more important than crime, drugs, poverty, illiteracy, welfare or homelessness because it drives everything else. Doing something about it is not just one more item on the American policy agenda, but should be at the top. Here is what to do:

In the calculus of illegitimacy, the constants are that boys like to sleep with girls and that girls think babies are endearing. Human societies have historically channeled these elemental forces of human behavior via thick walls of rewards and penalties that constrained the overwhelming majority of births to take place within marriage. The past 30 years have seen those walls cave in. It is time to rebuild them.

The ethical underpinning for the policies I am about to describe is this: Bringing a child into the world is the most important thing that most human beings ever do. Bringing a child into the world when one is not emotionally or financially prepared to be a parent is wrong. The child deserves society's support. The parent does not.

The social justification is this: A society with broad legal freedoms depends crucially on strong nongovernmental institutions to temper and restrain behavior. Of these, marriage is paramount. Either we reverse the current trends in illegitimacy—especially white illegitimacy—or America must, willy-nilly, become an unrecognizably authoritarian, socially segregated, centralized state.

To restore the rewards and penalties of marriage does not require social engineering. Rather, it requires that the state stop interfering with the natural forces that have done the job quite effectively for millennia. Some of the changes I will describe can occur at the federal level; others would involve state laws. For now, the important thing is to agree on what should be done.

I begin with the penalties, of which the most obvious are economic. Throughout human history, a single woman with a small child has not been a viable economic unit. Not being a viable economic unit, neither have the single woman and child been a legitimate social unit. In small numbers, they must be a net drain on the community's resources. In large numbers, they must destroy the community's capacity to sustain itself. Mirabile dictu, communities everywhere have augmented the economic penalties of single parenthood with severe social stigma.

Restoring economic penalties translates into the first and central policy prescription: to end all economic support for single mothers. The AFDC (Aid to Families With Dependent Children) payment goes to zero. Single mothers are not eligible for subsidized housing or for food stamps. An assortment of other subsidies and in-kind benefits disappear. Since universal medical coverage appears to be an idea whose time has come, I will stipulate that all children have medical coverage. But with that exception, the signal is loud and unmistakable: From society's perspective, to have a baby that you cannot care for yourself is profoundly irresponsible, and the government will no longer subsidize it.

How does a poor young mother survive without government support? The same way she has since time immemorial. If she wants to keep a child, she must enlist support from her parents, boyfriend, siblings, neighbors, church or philanthropies. She must get support from somewhere, anywhere, other than the government. The objectives are threefold.

First, enlisting the support of others raises the probability that other mature adults are going to be involved with the upbringing of the child, and this is a great good in itself.

Second, the need to find support forces a self-selection process. One of the most short-sighted excuses made for current behavior is that an adolescent who is utterly unprepared to be a mother 'needs someone to love.' Childish yearning isn't a good enough selection device. We need to raise the probability that a young single woman who keeps her child is doing so volitionally and thoughtfully. Forcing her to find a way of supporting the child does this. It will lead many young women who shouldn't be mothers to place their babies for adoption. This is good. It will lead others, watching what happens to their sisters, to take steps not to get pregnant. This is also good. Many others will get abortions. Whether this is good depends on what one thinks of abortion.

Third, stigma will regenerate. The pressure on relatives and communities to pay for the folly of their children will make an illegitimate birth the socially horrific act it used to be, and getting a girl pregnant something boys do at the risk of facing a shotgun. Stigma and shotgun marriages may or may not be good for those on the receiving end, but their deterrent effect on others is wonderful—and indispensable.

What about women who can find no support but keep the baby anyway? There are laws already on the books about the right of the state to take a child from a neglectful parent. We have some 360,000 children in foster care because of them. Those laws would still apply. Society's main response, however, should be to make it as easy as possible for those mothers to place their children for adoption at infancy. To that end, state governments must strip adoption of the nonsense that has encumbered it in recent decades.

The first step is to make adoption easy for any married couple who can show reasonable evidence of having the resources and stability to raise a child. Lift all restrictions on interracial adoption. Ease age limitations for adoptive parents.

The second step is to restore the traditional legal principle that placing a child for adoption means irrevocably relinquishing all legal rights to the child. The adoptive parents are parents without qualification. Records are sealed until the child reaches adulthood, at which time they may be unsealed only with the consent of biological child and parent.

Given these straightforward changes—going back to the old way, which worked—there is reason to believe that some extremely large proportion of infants given up by their mothers will be adopted into good homes. This is true not just for flawless blue-eyed blond infants but for babies of all colors and conditions. The demand for infants to adopt is huge.

Some small proportion of infants and larger proportion of older children will not be adopted. For them, the government should spend lavishly on orphanages. I am not recommending Dickensian barracks. In 1993, we know a lot about how to provide a warm, nurturing environment for children, and getting rid of the welfare system frees up lots of money to do it. Those who find the word 'orphanages' objectionable may think of them as 24-hour-a-day preschools. Those who prattle about the importance of keeping children with their biological mothers may wish to spend some time in a patrol car or with a social worker seeing what the reality of life with welfare-dependent biological mothers can be like.

Finally, there is the matter of restoring the rewards of marriage. Here, I am pessimistic about how much government can do and optimistic about how little it needs to do. The rewards of raising children within marriage are real and deep. The main task is to shepherd children through adolescence so that they can reach adulthood—when they are likely to recognize the value of those rewards—free to take on marriage and family. The main purpose of the penalties for single parenthood is to make that task easier.

One of the few concrete things that the government can do to increase the rewards of marriage is make the tax code favor marriage and children. Those of us who are nervous about using the tax code for social purposes can advocate making the tax code at least neutral.

A more abstract but ultimately crucial step in raising the rewards of marriage is to make marriage once again the sole legal institution through which parental rights and responsibilities are defined and exercised.

Little boys should grow up knowing from their earliest memories that if they want to have any rights whatsoever regarding a child that they sire—more vividly, if they want to grow up to be a daddy—they must marry. Little girls should grow up knowing from their earliest memories that if they want to have any legal claims whatsoever on the father of their children, they must marry. A marriage certificate should establish that a man and a woman have entered into a unique legal relationship. The changes in recent years that have blurred the distinctiveness of marriage are subtly but importantly destructive.

Together, these measures add up to set of signals, some with immediate and tangible consequences, others with long-term consequences, still others symbolic. They should be supplemented by others based on a re-examination of divorce law and its consequences.

That these policy changes seem drastic and unrealistic is a peculiarity of our age, not of the policies themselves. With embellishments, I have endorsed the policies that were the uncontroversial law of the land as recently as John Kennedy's presidency. Then, America's elites accepted as a matter of course that a free society such as America's can sustain itself only through virtue and temperance in the people, that virtue and temperance depend centrally on the socialization of each new generation, and that the socialization of each generation depends on the matrix of care and resources fostered by marriage.

Three decades after that consensus disappeared, we face an emerging crisis. The long, steep climb in black illegitimacy has been calamitous for black communities and painful for the nation. The reforms I have described will work for blacks as for whites, and have been needed for years. But the brutal truth is that American society as a whole could survive when illegitimacy became epidemic within a comparatively small ethnic minority. It cannot survive the same epidemic among whites.

Further Resources

BOOKS

Moynihan, Daniel Patrick. *The Negro Family—the Case for National Action.* Washington, D.C.: United States Department of Labor, 1965.

Murray, Charles. *Losing Ground: American Social Policy, 1950—1980.* New York: BasicBooks, 1984.

Weaver, R. Kent. *Ending Welfare As We Know It.* Washington, D.C.: Brookings Institution Press, 2000.

PERIODICALS

Kristol, Irving. "The Best of Intentions, the Worst of Results." *The Atlantic Monthly,* August 1971. Available online at http://www.theatlantic.com/unbound/flashbks/welfare/kristolf.htm; website home page www.theatlantic.com (accessed April 4, 2003).

WEBSITES

The Brookings Institution. "Welfare Reform and Beyond." Available online at http://www.brook.edu/dybdocroot/wrb/wrb_hp.htm; website home page http://www.brook.edu (accessed April 4, 2003).

Burke, Vee. "Welfare Reform: An Issue Overview." Issue Brief for Congress. Congressional Research Service, Library of Congress. Available online at http://www.house.gov/htbin/crsprodget?/ib/IB93034; website home page http://www.house.gov (accessed April 4, 2003).

The United States Department of Health and Human Services, The Administration for Children and Families. "Welfare Reform." Available online at http://www.house.gov/htbin/crsprodget?/ib/IB93034; website home page http://www.house.gov (accessed April 4, 2003).

"Press Conference of the President on North Korea"

Press conference

By: Bill Clinton

Date: June 22, 1994

Source: Clinton, Bill. "Press Conference of the President on North Korea, June 22, 1994." Reprinted in the Federation of American Scientists Space Policy Project. Available online at http://www.fas.org/spp/starwars/offdocs/w940622.htm; website home page http://www.fas.org (accessed April 4, 2003).

About the Author: Bill Clinton (1946–) was born in Hope, Arkansas. After earning an international relations degree from Georgetown University, Clinton received a Yale law degree. In 1978, at the age of thirty-two, Clinton was elected governor of Arkansas. After losing his reelection bid, he was elected again and maintained the position until becoming president (served 1993–2001) of the United States. He was the first Democrat since Franklin D. Roosevelt (served 1933–1945) to be reelected to a second presidential term. ∎

Introduction

In June 1950, northern Korea, along with its communist ally the People's Republic of China, launched a full-scale invasion of the southern part of Korea. In order to contain what was perceived as the communist menace, President Harry S. Truman (served 1945–1953), under the auspices of the United Nations (UN), sent Americans into battle. Although the Korean War (1950–1953) was fought under the blue banner of the UN, more than ninety percent of its forces were American. The war ended with both sides signing an armistice, creating a truce, but not a permanent resolution ending hostilities. The Korean nation was divided at the thirty-eighth parallel, creating North Korea, also known as the Democratic People's Republic of Korea (DPRK), and South Korea, also known as the Republic of Korea. During the war, the United States suffered 33,652 deaths, 103,284 wounded, with 8,177 unaccounted for. In 1954, the United States and South Korea entered into a Mutual Defense Treaty. Early in the twenty-first century, with a renewed threat perceived from North Korea, the United States deployed 37,000 troops along the Demilitarized Zone (DMZ) to support South Korea's army of 650,000. Across the DMZ, North Korea amassed its 1.2 million of its soldiers, resulting in a tense standoff between both sides.

An important emphasis of U.S. foreign policy has been preventing rogue nations–those that operate outside accepted international laws and practices—such as North Korea, from acquiring nuclear weapons. In 1970, under the Nuclear Nonproliferation Treaty (NPT), the United States, Great Britain, the Soviet Union, France, and China agreed not to provide other nations with nuclear weapons or nuclear technology. The non-nuclear states agreed to allow the International Atomic Energy Agency (IAEA) to inspect their nuclear facilities to ensure that peaceful nuclear technology was not diverted for military purposes. Since the end of the Cold War in 1991, only India, Pakistan, Israel, and Cuba have refused to sign the NPT.

In 1985, North Korea joined the NPT, but refused to allow the IAEA to inspect its nuclear facilities. Two years later, two North Korean agents blew up Korean Air Lines Flight 007 in mid-air and the United States subsequently placed North Korea on its list of countries supporting international terrorism. This event was just the first in a number of high profile occurrences that raised U.S. and international concern over the country frequently referred to as "the Hermit Kingdom." In 1992, with its economy collapsing, its factories operating at less than thirty percent of capacity, a famine ravaging the countryside, and a regime nearly completely isolated from world affairs, North Korea turned to nuclear brinkmanship. It threatened to withdraw from the NPT, continue its nuclear activities, and turn Seoul, the capital of South Korea, into a "sea of fire." To avoid these consequences without resorting to the use of force, the United States promised to provide the economic assistance needed to keep the isolated country from total collapse.

Significance

In October 1994, the Clinton administration settled the nuclear crisis on the Korean Peninsula when it entered into the Agreed Framework with North Korea. The United States agreed to export 500,000 tons of oil annually to compensate for the electricity-generating capacity lost by North Korea in freezing its nuclear reactors, as well as to facilitate the construction and financing of two light-water reactors costing $5 billion, to move toward full normalization of political and economic relations, and to provide formal assurances that the United States would not threaten or use nuclear weapons against North Korea. In return, North Korea agreed to freeze operation of its plutonium-reprocessing plant and construction of a nuclear reactor at Yongbyon. These facilities were to be dismantled prior to the completion of the second light-water reactor. Additionally, IAEA inspections would be resumed, and North Korea would remain in the NTP.

In October 2002, North Korea announced that it had violated the 1994 agreement by operating a secret, uranium-enriched nuclear weapons program. In response, President George W. Bush (served 2001–) stated that North Korea must suspend its nuclear program before the United States would resume direct negotiations with it. North Korea, however, did not comply. In 2003, it withdrew from the NPT, expelled IAEA inspectors, restarted a plutonium reactor, and threatened to export missile technology to other terrorist nations if the Bush administration did not enter into a new agreement. As of July 2003, the situation remained at an impasse, with the United States unwilling to compromise and North Korea unwilling to back down. The Agreed Framework developed by the Clinton administration lay in shambles.

Primary Source

"Press Conference of the President on North Korea"

SYNOPSIS: In 1994, President Bill Clinton held a press conference thanking former President Jimmy Carter (served 1977–1981) for brokering an initial agreement with North Korean dictator Kim Il Song. Kim promised to freeze its nuclear program while the two nations negotiated a new long-term agreement. In rejecting his critics' claims that North Korea would secretly pursue its nuclear ambitions, Clinton stated he was convinced that confirmation could be made.

The President: Good afternoon. Today I want to announce an important step forward in the situation in North Korea. This afternoon we have received formal confirmation from Noth Korea that it will freeze the major elements of its nuclear program while a new round of talks between our nations proceeds.

In response, we are informing the North Koreans that we are ready to go forward with a new round of talks in Geneva early next month. North Korea has assured us that while we go forward with these talks it will not reload its five-megawatt reactor with new fuel, or reprocess spent fuel. We have also been assured that the Iaea will be allowed to keep its inspectors and monitoring equipment in place at the Yongbyon nuclear facilty, thus allowing verification of North Korea's agreement.

We welcome this very positive development which restores the basis for talks between North Korea and the United States.

In addition to addressing the nuclear issue, we are prepared to discuss the full range of security, political and economic issues, that affects North Korea's relationship with the international community. During these discussions we will suspend our efforts to pursue a sanctions resolution in the United Nations Security Council. We also welcome the agreement between South Korea and North Korea to pursue a meeting between their Presidents.

I would like to thank President Carter for the important role he played in helping to achieve this step. These developments mark not a solution to the problem, but they do mark a new opportunity to find a solution. It is the beginning of a new stage in our efforts to pursue a nonnuclear Korean Peninsula. We hope this will lead to the resolution of all the issues that divide Korea from the international community.

In close consultation with our allies, we will continue as we have over the past year and more to pursue our interests and our goals with steadiness, realism and resolve. This approach is paying off, and we will continue it. This is good news. Our task now is to transform this news into a lasting agreement.

Mr. President, are you going to try to insist on finding out whether or not they have already built a bomb and getting the facts on any past violations as part of these talks?

Well, let me say that, first of all, we have been in touch with the North Koreans in New York almost at this moment. We will set up these talks and we will have ample opportunity to discuss the range of issues that will be discussed in the talks. And we expect to discuss, obviously, all the issues that have divided us.

Spent nuclear fuel rods rest in a cooling pond at North Korea's nuclear facilities in Yongbyon in 1996. AP/WIDE WORLD PHOTOS. REPRODUCED BY PERMISSION.

Mr. President, what concessions did we make to bring this about? And why is it that you did not meet with President Carter face to face? Here's a man who actually met Kim Il Sung, one of the few—our profiles may not jive and so forth. You would have had a great chance to debrief him, and instead, you talked to him on the telephone.

We talked to him for a long time on the telephone. The only reason we didn't is because I didn't want to ask him to come all the way up to Camp David, and we had planned to go up there for the weekend. And he decided and I decided that—we know each other very well, we've known each other for 20 years—we decided we didn't need to do it; we could just have a long talk on the phone, and that's what we did.

Did we make any concessions—

No.

—to the North Koreans to bring this about?

No. The only thing that we said was that we would suspend our efforts to pursue sanctions if there was a verifiable freeze on the nuclear program while the talks continued, which included no refueling of the reactor and no reprocessing.

When President Carter came back he said—this was the cautionary note I raised in Chicago last Friday when I was asked to comment on this statement—he said that he believed that Kim Il Sung had made that statement to him. We said that we would wait for official confirmation. We received it today. That confirmation gives us the basis for resuming the talks.

President Clinton, some of your aides are saying, we got everything we want here. Is this one of those cases where the other guy blinked?

I don't think it's useful for me to characterize it in that way. We know what the facts are. If you look at what we've done over the last year and a half,

President Bill Clinton greets Jo Myong Rok, the first vice chairman of North Korea's National Defense Commission. AP/WIDE WORLD PHOTOS. REPRODUCED BY PERMISSION.

we have followed basically a two-pronged policy. We have worked as hard as we could to be firm, to be resolute, to bring our allies closer and closer together. And when I say our allies on this issue, I consider not just South Korea and Japan, but Russia and China to be our allies. All of us have the same interests and the same desires.

We also always kept the door open. We always said—I always said I did not seek a confrontation, I sought to give North Korea a way to become a part of the international community.

When President Carter was invited and expressed a willingness to go to North Korea, I thought it gave us one opportunity that we would not otherwise have with a private citizen, but a distinguished American private citizen, to communicate the position of our administration and to do it—the very fact that he went, I think, was a gesture of the importance that we placed on resolving this matter, and not just for ourselves but for the world.

And so I think that we know what the facts are. We know we pursued a firm course. We know that President Carter went and made a very persuasive case, and we know what the North Koreans did. I don't think it's useful to characterize this in terms of winners and losers. I think the world will be the winner if we can resolve this. But we've not done it yet.

Brit.

Mr. President, it would appear that President Carter may have either seen something that perhaps you and others may not have seen as clearly as he did, or that perhaps this was a more closely coordinated effort between you and Mr. Carter than it may have appeared at the time. Is either of those things correct?

Well, I don't know that I would characterize it in that way. He called me; we talked about it. I wanted to make sure he had adequate briefings. I have always—I have, as you probably know, I have—and I've said this I believe publicly—I have sought other means of personally communicating to Kim Il Sung that the desires of the United States and the interests of the United States and the policy of the United States was to pursue a nonnuclear Korean Peninsula and to give North Korea a way of moving with dignity into the international community and away from an isolated path, which we found quite disturbing for all the reasons that I've already said.

It seemed to me that when President Carter expressed a willingness to go and they had given him an invitation of some longstanding to come, that that gave us the opportunity to give North Korea a direct message to their leader from a distinguished American citizen, without in any way undermining the necessary and correct government-to-government contacts that we had going on at other levels.

President Carter, I think, was very faithful in articulating the policy of our government. And I think that that provided a forum in which the North Korean leader, Kim Il Sung, could respond as he did. And I'm very pleased about it.

When we were called last Thursday and this whole issue was discussed, and we said what we said about we hope that their message meant that they were willing to freeze their nuclear program, then they said they were. Then we got formal confirmation today of the definition of freeze. Their definition was the same as ours. We had the basis to go forward. I'm very happy about it.

Yes, Wolf.

Could I—there will be critics, as you well know, who will argue that once again the North Koreans have succeeded in stalling and, clandestinely, this will give them an opportunity while their negotiators talk to U.S. negotiators in Geneva to pursue their nuclear ambitions, which they're not about to give up. How do you verify that they are sincere in this effort?

Well, that was a big part of the statement, of course, of the letter that we got—not just that there would be an agreement to freeze the program, but that the agreement be verifiable. The Iaea inspectors and the monitoring equipment on the ground can be and will be used to verify the commitment not to reprocess and not to refuel.

If we didn't have some way of verifying it, you and I wouldn't be having this conversation at this moment.

Yes—one last question.

Mr. President, could you tell us, beyond just the focus of the talks, could you tell us what your longer-range view is? Do you see the Koreas being reunified? What do you see happening, coming out of all this?

Well, I think, first of all, that is a decision for the peoples and their leaders in South and North Korea to resolve. What the United States wants is for the agreement that the Koreas made in 1991 to make the Peninsula nonnuclear to be carried through.

The United States wants the Npt to be a success with regard to North Korea. The United States wants North Korea, in whatever relationship it pursues with South Korea—that is up to them—to move toward becoming an integral and responsible member of the international community. That will auger well for the peace and prosperity of the peoples of north Asia as well as for the security interest of the United States. That is what we have pursued with great diligence, and I'm very hopeful that these talks will bring us closer to that.

As I said, this does not solve the problem, but it certainly gives us the basis for seeking a solution. And I'm quite pleased.

Thank you very much.

Have you called Jimmy Carter?

Oh, I have. I called him, talked to him about the letter. We had a very good talk; told him again I was glad he went and I thought it was a trip worth taking, a risk worth taking, and I was very pleased.

You didn't mind his criticism of your sanctions policy? He was pretty blunt, wasn't he?

No. No, as long as the agreement—like I said, we've been friends a long time. The agreement was that he would faithfully communicate our position. I am absolutely convinced he did it, and I'm absolutely convinced now that they have met the agreement. And I feel good about it.

Further Resources

BOOKS

Gilbert, Bill. *Ship of Miracles: 14,000 Lives and One Miraculous Voyage.* Chicago: Triumph Books, 2000.

Oberdorfer, Don. *The Two Koreas: A Contemporary History.* New York: Basic Books, 2001.

Owen, Joseph R. *Colder Than Hell: A Marine Rifle Company at Chosin Reservoir.* Annapolis: Naval Institute Press, 1996.

PERIODICALS

Laney, James T. and Jason T. Shaplen. "How to Deal With North Korea." *Foreign Affairs,* 82, March-April 2003, 16.

Roskey, William. "The Second Korean Conflict." *Military History,* October 16, 1999, 38.

WEBSITES

"Korean News." News From Korean Central News Agency of DPRK (Democratic People's Republic of Korea). Available online at http://www.kcna.co.jp/index-e.htm; website home page http://www.kcna.co.jp (accessed April 4, 2003).

"North Korea: A Country Study." Library of Congress. Available online at http://memory.loc.gov/frd/cs/kptoc.html; website home page http://memory.loc.gov (accessed April 4, 2003).

"Republican Contract with America"

Political platform

By: Newt Gingrich

Date: September 24, 1994

Source: Gingrich, Newt. "Republican Contract With America." September 27, 1994. Available online at http://www.house.gov/house/Contract/CONTRACT.html; website homepage: http://www.house.gov (accessed October 15, 20020.

About the Author: Newton "Newt" Gingrich (1943–) was born in Harrisburg, Pennsylvania. In 1971, he earned a Ph.D. in American history from Tulane University. After serving briefly as a professor at West Georgia College, he was elected to the United States House of Representatives in 1978. After leading the Republican Party to capturing the majority of the House in 1994, his colleagues elected him to the powerful position of Speaker. After some ethical lapses, Gingrich resigned his congressional seat in 1998. ∎

Introduction

In 1933, President Franklin D. Roosevelt's (served 1933–1945) New Deal radically changed the role and the scope of the federal government. Though his legislative program did not end the Great Depression or its attending massive unemployment, it nevertheless permanently expanded the power of the federal government. Under President Lyndon B. Johnson's (served 1963–1969) Great Society programs of the 1960s, the federal government continued to grow—assuming additional responsibility over the environment, education, and the arts.

Since the 1950s, conservative Republicans harshly criticized the Democratic Party's big government policies. Conservatives argued that these policies not only failed to solve pressing economic and social problems, but also sacrificed individual liberties in the process. Instead, they maintained that the power of the federal government should be scaled back, and responsibility given back to state and local governments, the private sector, families and individuals. During the 1980s, conservatives were encouraged when Ronald Reagan (served 1981–1989) won the White House. However, the Democrats, who continued to control Congress, thwarted much of President Reagan's conservative agenda. Republicans realized that in order to transform the nature of government, they would have to wrestle control of Congress away from the Democrats. This would be a formidable task. By 1994, the federal government's budget, with over 20,000 permanent employees, exceeded $1.6 trillion annually.

As the 1994 congressional elections neared, Republicans recognized a golden opportunity to win a clear, conservative majority in the House. In his first two years in office, President Bill Clinton's (served 1993–2001) popularity waned. Clinton experienced bitter battles over gays in the military, tax increases, ethical charges, and health care reform during his first two years in office. Although Democrats had controlled Congress and the presidency for two years, they had failed to effect substantive policy changes. The United States was in an anti-incumbent mood.

Republicans, however, realized that Clinton's unpopularity alone was not enough for them to win control of the House. To achieve this, Republicans crafted a positive, detailed ten-point political agenda. It sought to capitalize on widespread voter disillusionment, portraying Republicans as forward thinkers—in stark contrast to the old, tired Democratic policies of the past. In September 1994, 367 Republican candidates for congressional office staged a mass signing of the "Contract With America" on the steps of the U.S. Capitol. The candidates promised to roll back federal power by passing all ten items within the first one hundred days of the 1995–1996 session, echoing the famous "First Hundred Days" of Roosevelt's New Deal. "If we break this Contract, throw us out," they pledged.

Significance

In November 1994, the Republicans regained control of both branches of Congress for the first time in forty years. House Republicans won control of the House (235 to 197), including twenty-two seats formerly held by Democrats. Senate Republicans gained a 54 to 47 majority, picking up seven seats—including two incumbent Democratic senators who switched to the GOP. Further, Gingrich became Speaker of the House. As the Contract with America's signatories promised, the entire platform was acted upon within the first hundred days. Nine out of the ten items passed the House. Only an attempt to draft a proposed constitutional amendment involving term limits was defeated. In the end, the House set an example by cutting one-third of House committees, along with one-third of committee staffs. Only two of the ten items, however, were passed into law. First, Congress would no longer be exempt itself from the laws, mandates, and regulations it imposed on the rest of the nation. Moreover, the federal government was prohibited from imposing unfunded mandates on state and local governments.

The Republican "revolution" soon stalled. After announcing "he had gotten the message," Clinton moderated his legislative agenda and cleverly depicted congressional Republicans as ideological extremists. In 1996, Clinton won reelection in a landslide victory.

Primary Source

"Republican Contract with America"

SYNOPSIS: In a stroke of political genius, Gingrich advertises the Contract with America in an October 1994 issue of the *TV Guide,* which had actress Suzanne Somers on the cover. Although the magazine does not normally carry political ads, Republicans realized that it had a tremendous circulation, particularly among independent voters whom the GOP desperately needed to win the election.

As Republican Members of the House of Representatives and as citizens seeking to join that body we propose not just to change its policies, but even more important, to restore the bonds of trust between the people and their elected representatives.

That is why, in this era of official evasion and posturing, we offer instead a detailed agenda for national renewal, a written commitment with no fine print.

This year's election offers the chance, after four decades of one-party control, to bring to the House a new majority that will transform the way Congress works. That historic change would be the end of government that is too big, too intrusive, and too easy with the public's money. It can be the beginning of a Congress that respects the values and shares the faith of the American family.

Like Lincoln, our first Republican president, we intend to act "with firmness in the right, as God gives us to see the right." To restore accountability to Con-

Newt Gingrinch, the House Minority Whip, addresses Republican congressional candidates during a 1994 rally where Republicans pledged a "Contract with America," calling for tax cuts, term limits, and a balanced budget amendment. **AP/WIDE WORLD PHOTOS. REPRODUCED BY PERMISSION.**

gress. To end its cycle of scandal and disgrace. To make us all proud again of the way free people govern themselves.

On the first day of the 104th Congress, the new Republican majority will immediately pass the following major reforms, aimed at restoring the faith and trust of the American people in their government:

- FIRST, require all laws that apply to the rest of the country also apply equally to the Congress;

- SECOND, select a major, independent auditing firm to conduct a comprehensive audit of Congress for waste, fraud or abuse;

- THIRD, cut the number of House committees, and cut committee staff by one-third;

- FOURTH, limit the terms of all committee chairs;

- FIFTH, ban the casting of proxy votes in committee;

- SIXTH, require committee meetings to be open to the public;

- SEVENTH, require a three-fifths majority vote to pass a tax increase;

- EIGHTH, guarantee an honest accounting of our Federal Budget by implementing zero baseline budgeting.

Thereafter, within the first 100 days of the 104th Congress, we shall bring to the House Floor the following bills, each to be given full and open debate, each to be given a clear and fair vote and each to be immediately available this day for public inspection and scrutiny.

1. The Fiscal Responsibility Act: A balanced budget/ tax limitation amendment and a legislative line-item veto to restore fiscal responsibility to an out-of-control Congress, requiring them to live under the same budget constraints as families and businesses.

2. The Taking Back of Our Streets Act: An anti-crime package including stronger truth-in-sentencing, "good faith" exclusionary rule exemptions, effective death penalty provisions, and cuts in social spending from this summer's

"crime" bill to fund prison construction and additional law enforcement to keep people secure in their neighborhoods and kids safe in their schools.

3. The Personal Responsibility Act: Discourage illegitimacy and teen pregnancy by prohibiting welfare to minor mothers and denying increased AFDC for additional children while on welfare, cut spending for welfare programs, and enact a tough two-years-and-out provision with work requirements to promote individual responsibility.

4. The Family Reinforcement Act: Child support enforcement, tax incentives for adoption, strengthening rights of parents in their children's education, stronger child pornography laws, and an elderly dependent care tax credit to reinforce the central role of families in American society.

5. The American Dream Restoration Act: A $500 per child tax credit, begin repeal of the marriage tax penalty, and creation of American Dream Savings Accounts to provide middle class tax relief.

6. The National Security Restoration Act: No U.S. troops under U.N. command and restoration of the essential parts of our national security funding to strengthen our national defense and maintain our credibility around the world.

7. The Senior Citizens Fairness Act: Raise the Social Security earnings limit which currently forces seniors out of the work force, repeal the 1993 tax hikes on Social Security benefits and provide tax incentives for private long-term care insurance to let Older Americans keep more of what they have earned over the years.

8. The Job Creation and Wage Enhancement Act: Small business incentives, capital gains cut and indexation, neutral cost recovery, risk assessment/cost-benefit analysis, strengthening the Regulatory Flexibility Act and unfunded mandate reform to create jobs and raise worker wages.

9. The Common Sense Legal Reform Act: "Loser pays" laws, reasonable limits on punitive damages and reform of product liability laws to stem the endless tide of litigation.

10. The Citizen Legislature Act: A first-ever vote on term limits to replace career politicians with citizen legislators.

Further, we will instruct the House Budget Committee to report to the floor and we will work to enact additional budget savings, beyond the budget cuts specifically included in the legislation described above, to ensure that the Federal budget deficit will be less than it would have been without the enactment of these bills.

Respecting the judgment of our fellow citizens as we seek their mandate for reform, we hereby pledge our names to this Contract with America.

Further Resources

BOOKS

Carter, Dan T. *From George Wallace to Newt Gingrich: Race in the Conservative Counterrevolution 1963–1994.* Baton Rouge: Louisiana State University Press, 1996.

Drew, Elizabeth. *On the Edge: The Clinton Presidency.* New York: Simon and Schuster, 1994.

Gingrich, Newt. *To Renew America.* New York: HarperCollins, 1995.

PERIODICALS

Gayner, Jeffrey B. "The Contract With America: Implementing New Ideas In the U.S." *The Heritage Foundation,* 1995. Available online at http://www.heritage.org/Research /PoliticalPhilosophy/HL549.cfm; website home page http:// www.heritage.org (accessed April 4, 2003).

Saletan, William. "What I Saw at the Decline of the Revolution." *Mother Jones,* July-August 1996, 47.

Richard Peterson to All Staff Judge Advocates and Military Judges November 3, 1994

Memo

By: Richard A. Peterson

Date: November 3, 1994

Source: United States Air Force, Judge Advocate General. "Memorandum for All Staff Judge Advocates and Military Judges." November 3, 1994. Reproduced as "Don't Ask, Don't Tell, Don't Pursue." Available online at http://dont .stanford.edu/regulations/AFmemo.pdf; website home page: http://dont.stanford.edu (accessed July 19, 2003).

Introduction

Traditionally, the United States armed services have relied on two provisions for removing gays and lesbians from military services. In 1920, the Articles of War were amended, making sodomy a court martial offense. This regulation did not change until it was recodified as Article 125 of the Uniform Code of Military Justice (UCMJ) in 1951. The armed forces, in the past, have also removed gays and lesbians from the service through personnel regulations. Between the two world wars, the military attempted to exclude gays from entering the service by denying those deemed too feminine—those lacking sufficient facial and body hair. During World War II (1941–1945), the military devised psychological procedures to attempt to identify overt homosexual behavior at induction.

In 1981, the military issued Directive 1332.14, which, for the first time, bluntly stated that homosexuality was incompatible with military service. The directive provided mandatory discharge for any person who "engaged in, has attempted to engage in, or has solicited another to engage in a homosexual act." Between 1981 and 1990, the military discharged 16,919 personnel for sexual orientation and behavior issues. These discharges involved 1.7 percent of all involuntary discharges in the Department of Defense during this period. Although most of these discharges were honorable, the discharge papers clearly stated to future employers the basis for the discharge. In 1991, the issue of gays in the military became politicized when returning Gulf War (1991) veterans publicly announced their homosexuality and criticized military policy.

That October, presidential candidate Bill Clinton (served 1993–2001), speaking before Harvard University's Kennedy School of Government, stated that if elected he would issue an Executive Order ending discrimination in the military on the basis of sexual orientation. In December 1992, following Clinton's political victory, Colin Powell, chairman of the Joint Chiefs of Staff (JCS), warned the incoming administration that the JCS would resign en masse if the order were issued. The JCS was willing to scrap Directive 1332.14, but refused to change Article 125 of the UCMJ. The military argued that avowed gays would undermine unit cohesion. Opponents countered that the military policy was clearly discriminatory.

The high profile controversy was a difficult problem for President Clinton. His liberal supporters demanded that he keep his campaign promise. Conversely, Congress, the body with the sole authority to amend the UCMJ, would have overwhelmingly refused to codify the order—handing the new administration an early, high-profile defeat. In January 1993, to avoid the pending political defeat, Clinton ordered Secretary of Defense Les Aspin to consult with the military and develop a compromise proposal. Six months later, Aspin announced the administration's "Don't Ask, Don't Tell" policy, which allows gays and lesbians to serve as long as they do not proclaim their sexual orientation or violate Article 125. Further, the policy stipulates that military commanders may not initiate an investigation into an individual's sexual orientation without credible evidence. Because the policy did not have the force of law and could be repealed in 1993, Congress codified the policy with the passage of P.L. 103–160 by a veto-proof margin of 273–135 in the House, and 77–22 in the Senate, respectively.

Significance

Like all good compromises, the "Don't Ask Don't Tell" policy pleased no one. Conservatives condemned the policy because it eased the absolute ban on homosexuals in the military. Liberals criticized the policy because gays and lesbians were prohibited from revealing their sexual orientations. Unable to amend the law in Congress, liberals turned to the courts for legal redress. However, federal courts generally have been hesitant to become involved in this issue. Deferring to legislative and military experience and expertise, federal courts maintain that they "lack the competence" to overrule military decision in such matters. From 1994 to 2001, 7,800 gay service members were discharged from the military.

Primary Source

Richard Peterson to All Staff Judge Advocates and Military Judges November 3, 1994

SYNOPSIS: In 1994, the Department of the Air Force issued this memorandum to all military judges to ensure that commanders comply with the "new" homosexual policy, codified by Congress in 1994. It also provides "tips" and "sample questions" for inquiry to determine whether credible evidence exists to initiate removal from the service.

FROM: HQ USAF/JAG
1420 Air Force Pentagon
Washington, DC 20330–1420

SUBJECT: Commander Inquiries on Members Stating They Are Homosexual

This is in response to the questions we have received about the impact of the U.S. Court of Appeals for the Ninth Circuit decision in *Meinhold v. Department of Defense* on the "new" homosexual policy. At the outset we stress that *Meinhold* is an "old" policy case. Neither the "new" DoD policy nor the Air Force implementation of the "new" DoD policy have been changed in response to the *Meinhold* decision. Nevertheless, the decision in *Meinhold* cannot be totally ignored. We need to make an effort to make

Colin Powell, chairman of the Joint Chiefs of Staff, shakes hands with a graduating student of Harvard University who's wearing a "Lift the Ban" sign, referring to the ban against gays and lesbians in the military. Powell gave the commencement speech to Harvard's 1993 graduating class. AP/WIDE WORLD PHOTOS. REPRODUCED BY PERMISSION.

each administrative discharge case for homosexual conduct as legally unassailable as possible.

In spite of weaknesses in the court's reasoning, the decision has been made not to request reconsideration *en banc* from the Ninth Circuit or seek *certiorari* from the U.S. Supreme Court in *Meinhold*. We thus are left with a precedent in the Ninth Circuit that specifically recognizes that it is constitutionally permissible to discharge members for homosexual conduct. At the same time, the precedent essentially allows a court to retroactively reinterpret military regulations under the guise of making them conform to the constitution. Using this technique, the Ninth Circuit added to the "old" policy a new requirement that discharges solely based upon statements be supported by evidence reasonably demonstrating that an individual has a "concrete,"

"fixed," or "expressed" desire to commit homosexual acts.

Because the "new" policy has the added weight of Congressional hearings and is based on federal statute, it remains to be seen whether the Ninth Circuit can apply the reasoning of *Meinhold* to the "new" policy. Consequently, commanders should continue to apply the "new" policy as written. To the extent possible, consistent with the facts, separations should be initiated based upon acts or marriages; even *Meinhold* supports discharge based upon acts. When evidence or acts or marriages is not available, commanders should continue to initiate separations based upon statements alone.

Air Force policy requires a commander to have credible information that a basis for discharge exists prior to initiating an inquiry. We stress that the policy on homosexual conduct does *not* prohibit commanders from initiating inquiries on a member who states that he is a homosexual. In these cases, the inquiry establishes the facts and circumstances surrounding the statement, because statements of homosexuality have been used in an attempt to avoid military service or to avoid specific assignments or deployments. Factors of concern may include the timing of the statement in relation to an imminent PCS or receipt of education.

The most compelling cases for an inquiry are those in which the member has received substantial benefits from the government, such as advanced education or training, and then, just prior to entering on active duty, announce that they are homosexual. We have had five such cases since the implementation of the "new" policy, three involving medical school, one involving law school, and one involving graduate school. Four of the five cases have been processed within the Air Education and Training Command (AETC).

HQ AETC policy is that in cases in which a member states that he is a homosexual after receiving substantial government benefits, but before fulfilling his military obligations, a judge advocate normally will be appointed to conduct an inquiry. The purpose of the inquiry is to determine the truthfulness of the statement. The inquiry is conducted in accordance with DoD and Air Force policy. We recommend the practice of appointing judge advocates for these high profile cases, which usually involve physicians, because a judge advocate is much more likely to be able to perform a thorough inquiry within the parameters of the policy. A judge advocate need not be appointed as inquiry officer, however, in cases other than these high profile cases.

If after investigation, it is found that the statement is true and separation action is initiated against the member, the member may still be subject to recoupment action under 10 U.S.C. 2005. (See IMC 94–4 to AFR 39–10, AFI 36–3206, paragraph 4.37). A member, who is separated for the homosexual conduct of stating he is homosexual, is subject to recoupment if a finding is made that the member made the statement for the purpose of seeking separation. The fact that the statement is true does not protect the member from recoupment.

Whether a commander initiates an inquiry into a member who states he is homosexual is dependent upon the facts and circumstances of the case. For example, if the facts and circumstances raise concern that the member is making a false official statement to avoid military service, the commander may initiate an inquiry. The purpose of the inquiry is to determine if the commander possesses credible information upon which to initiate separation action or if other action should be taken because the member has made a false statement to avoid service; the intent of the member in making the statement also should be examined as being highly probative to recoupment. The purpose of the inquiry is *not* to discover evidence of homosexual acts or to ferret out other homosexuals in the military. If acts or other military members are discovered during the *proper* course of the investigation, however, appropriate action may be taken.

If your commander wants to initiate an inquiry into a member who has received substantial government benefits, we recommend you discuss the proposed inquiry with your MAJCOM. A judge advocate inquiry officer is not always necessary, but may be prudent in cases involving substantial government benefits because advocacy organizations or outside counsel may be involved. Two of our current cases are represented by the same civilian attorney, who we are advised also represents several other similarly-situated members in the other services. If an officer other than a judge advocate conducts an inquiry in this type of case, we strongly recommend a judge advocate serve as a very close advisor to the IO.

Attached are tips for officers appointed to inquire into this type of case and some sample pattern questions. Our POC is Major Mike Gilbert at DSN 224–4075.

Richard A. Peterson
Deputy Chief, General Law Division
Officer of the Judge Advocate General

Tips for Inquiry Officers of Cases Involving Members Who State They Are Homosexuals

You have been appointed to serve as an inquiry officer in a case involving a member stating he or she is homosexual or bisexual. Making such a statement is homosexual conduct that subjects the member to involuntary separation action because the statement creates a rebuttable presumption that the member engages in, attempts to engage in, has a propensity to engage in, or intends to engage in homosexual acts. Moreover, if the member has received educational assistance, special pay, or bonuses, the member may be subject to recoupment of an amount of government benefits proportional to the amount of the member's military service that has not been fulfilled.

The purpose of the inquiry is to determine if the commander possesses credible information upon which to initiate separation action or if other action should be taken because the member has made a false statement to avoid service. The intent of the member in making the statement also must be examined because it is highly probative to the issue of recoupment. The purpose of the inquiry is not to discover evidence of homosexual acts or to ferret out other homosexuals in the military. As an inquiry officer (IO), you must look at all relevant evidence to enable you to make a finding on the truth of the statement by the member that he or she is homosexual. You also should make a finding on the member's purpose for stating he or she is homosexual or bisexual.

You initially should interview the subject member. Ensure you notify counsel if the member already has retained counsel. You also should interview the following persons:

a. Parents and siblings. If the member does not provide this information, DD Form 398 should have this data.

b. Look at the DD Form 398 for any other possible leads for interview subjects.

c. School counselor and advisor.

d. Any other knowledgeable school officials.

e. School career development office; did the member interview for civilian jobs? Did the student apply for fellowships, internships, etc., that would have been displaced by military service?

f. Roommates and close friends, including people the subject dated.

g. Mental health medical records.

h. AFIT program manager. Did the member apply for deferment of military service? If the member is in medical school, was the member assigned to intern in an area of medicine he or she did not want?

i. Air Force career manager.

You should prepare a list of anticipated questions and forward them to your MAJCOM staff judge advocate for review and comment. Attached is a list of suggested questions for interviewing the subject member; many also can be used for other witnesses.

Sample Question for Inquiry Concerning Member Who States He Is Homosexual After Receiving Advanced Education Benefits

Review AFI 90–301, Attachment 5, which contains the script for introduction of an inquiry officer. (Also review Attachment 6 to AFI 90–301, which is an inquiry officer guide.) Tell the witness/subject member if you are recording the interview.

1. Read the member the Air Force policy on homosexual conduct. (See 10 U.S.C. 654 and the attached.) Remember that a member must be given a rights advisement under Article 31, UCMJ, if the discussion begins to involve acts or conduct that violate the UCMJ. (As an inquiry officer in a statement-only case, you should not ask questions concerning homosexual acts unless you have credible information of such acts, such as if the member raised the topic.)

2. Verify the member's full name and social security number. Also verify his address and phone number.

3. Swear the member in by oath or attestation.

4. If a written statement is in question, ask if he recognizes the statement.

a. Is the signature on the statement that of the member?

b. Did the member write the statement himself or did he have assistance, such as an attorney?

c. Did the member understand the policy on homosexual conduct at the time he made the statement?

5. If the statement in question is not written, ask the member if he made the statement.

a. If so, when did he make it? To whom? Where?

b. Under what circumstances?

6. Had the member ever been briefed on the policy on homosexual conduct? If so, by whom and where?

7. When did the member enter the education program, such as HPSP or FLEP?

8. What status is the member, e.g., Reserves?

9. What was the member obligated to do in return for education assistance?

10. If currently in the education program, what school is the member attending, what year of studies, when will the member graduate?

11. Who is the member's academic and/or faculty advisor? Advisor for thesis, dissertation, etc.?

12. If HPSP, what area of medicine does the member intend to pursue?

a. Has the member applied for any intern or residency programs?

b. If so, where and for when?

c. Has the Air Force directed the member to choose from specified specialties? If so, which ones?

13. Why did the member make the statement? If written, why did the member choose to send the letter where he did?

14. Why did the member choose this particular time to make the statement?

15. If the member used certain terms, such as "homosexual orientation" or "propensity," ask the following questions: What did the member mean by "homosexual orientation" or "propensity?" (Note: If the member states he means what the regulation says, ask him to explain what he means in his own words.)

16. Does the member have a "propensity to engage in homosexual acts?" If so, can he explain what he means?

17. How does he know he has a "homosexual orientation" and/or "propensity?"

18. When did he realize he has a "homosexual orientation" and/or "propensity?"

19. Whom has he told he is a homosexual or that he has a "homosexual orientation" and/or "propensity?" When did he tell them? Why did he tell them?

20. Has the member been dating anybody (opposite or same sex)?

a. How frequently has the member dated?

b. How recently?

c. How can these persons be contacted?

21. Did the member belong to any homosexual student organizations at school?

a. If so, which?

b. How can other members of the organization, who knew of his membership, be contacted?

22. Has the member told any of his family members? If so, whom? How can they be contacted?

23. Who are close friends of the member and how can they be contacted?

24. How does the member feel about the Air Force?

25. Does the member prefer to remain in the Air Force, or would he rather be discharged?

26. What is the member's understanding of the possibility of the Air Force recouping the costs of his educational assistance?

27. What, if any, influence did the recoupment policy have on making the statement?

28. Are there any other witnesses or documents that could verify the member's statement that he is homosexual?

29. Is there any further information, statements, or evidence concerning the matters discussed?

Further Resources

BOOKS

Berube, Alan. *Coming Out Under Fire: The History of Gay Men and Women in World War Two.* New York: The Free Press, 1990.

Scott, Wilbur and Sandra Carson Stanley, eds. *Gays and Lesbians in the Military: Issues, Concerns, and Contrasts.* New York: Walter de Gruyter, 1994.

Shilts, Randy. *Conduct Unbecoming: Gays and Lesbians in the U.S. Military.* New York: St. Martin's Press, 1993

PERIODICALS

Hackworth, David. "The Case for a Military Gay Ban." *The Washington Post,* June 28, 1992.

Service Members Legal Defense Network. Conduct Unbecoming. The Eight Annual Report on "Don't Ask, Don't Tell, Don't Pursue, Don't Harass," (2002) available online at http://www.sldn.org/binary-data/SLDN_ARTICLES/pdf_file/496.pdf; website home page http://www.sldn.org (accessed April 4, 2003).

WEBSITES

Department of Defense. "Washington Headquarters Services." Available online at http://www.whs.pentagon.mil (accessed April 4, 2003).

Remarks by Representative Henry Hyde on Prohibition of Partial Birth Abortions

Speech

By: Henry Hyde

Date: September 19, 1996

Source: U.S. House of Representatives. Remarks by Representative Henry Hyde on Prohibition of Partial Birth Abortions. H.R. 1833, 104th Cong., 2nd sess. *Congressional Record,* September 19, 1996, vol. 142.

About the Author: Henry Hyde (1924–) was born in Chicago, Illinois. In 1942, he enlisted in the United States

Navy, and he saw combat in the Philippines during World War II (1941–1945). In 1949, Hyde earned a law degree from Loyola University–Chicago. He was elected to the U.S. House of Representatives from Illinois in 1974, and he chaired the powerful House Judiciary Committee from 1995–2001. During the Clinton impeachment trial in the Senate, he was the lead House manager. ∎

Introduction

Prior to 1973, the vast majority of states in the United States classified abortion as a felony offense. This criminalization was a relatively recent phenomenon. Under colonial common law, abortions performed before "quickening," the first recognizable fetus movements in utero appearing around the seventeenth week of pregnancy, were not a crime because the fetus was regarded as a part of the mother. Moreover, abortions were considered misdemeanors when performed after quickening. In the early 1800s, scientists discovered that human life did not begin at quickening, but rather at fertilization during conception. By the mid-nineteenth century, a powerful anti-abortion movement, led by the American Medical Association (AMA), successfully lobbied many states to prohibit all abortions. By 1860, eighty-five percent of the nation's population resided in states that prohibited abortions. Nearly one hundred years later, all fifty states had banned abortion.

Since the 1950s, however, an abortion reform movement gained momentum. Advocates were alarmed at the significant number of women who were forced to undergo the dangerous procedure in unsanitary back allies or garrets by poorly trained abortionists. By 1967, following the complete reversal on the issue by the AMA, Colorado and California legalized some abortions. In 1970, New York, which had passed the country's first abortion law in 1828, became the sixteenth state to legalize the procedure.

In 1973, in the landmark cases *Roe v. Wade* and *Doe v. Bolton,* the United States Supreme Court for the first time recognized that the constitutional right to privacy allowed a woman to abort her fetus at any point in the pregnancy, as long as the mother's "health" was in danger. The court broadly defined the word "health" to include a number of social and economic problems, as judged by the mother herself. After the *Roe* decision, abortion became a bitterly divisive political issue. Abortion advocates believed that each woman has the right to make reproductive decisions for herself; anti-abortion forces believed in the right to life of the unborn.

In 1992, anti-abortion advocates devised a "modest, first step" strategy they hoped would lead to the total prohibition of late-term abortions. By seeking to ban partial-birth abortion, anti-abortion advocates forced abortion rights supporters (many of whom advocate for no limitations on the availability of abortion) defend the procedure. That year, anti-abortion advocates publicized a doctor who had performed 700 "D&X" (dilation and extraction) procedures. The vast majority of these abortions were elective procedures, occurring in late-term pregnancies. Even the AMA opposed this surgical procedure, which destroyed a living fetus, whose kicking feet were out of the birth canal during the procedure. In 1995, U.S. Representative Charles T. Canady introduced H.R. 1833, the Partial-Birth Abortion Ban. The measure passed the House on a vote of 288-139 and the Senate 54-44. However, in April 1996, President Bill Clinton (served 1993–2001) vetoed the bill. On September 19, 1996, the House debated whether to override the veto.

Significance

The House overrode the veto by more than the required two-thirds vote. However, in the Senate, the measure failed to override the veto. Abortion advocates supported President Clinton's veto because, if enacted, it would have constituted the first federal ban on a form of abortion. It also would have been the first step in the prohibition of all late-term abortions. Because the veto was sustained, thirty-one states enacted laws banning partial-birth abortion between 1995 and 2002. However, in 2000 the U.S. Supreme Court, in *Stenberg v. Carhart,* invalidated a Nebraska statute that prohibited the procedure, as the law lacked an exception to protect the mother's health. Similar bills were introduced in Congress in 1999 and 2002, but died.

Primary Source

Remarks by Representative Henry Hyde on Prohibition of Partial Birth Abortions [excerpt]

SYNOPSIS: In this speech, Representative Hyde spoke out in defense of the Partial-Birth Abortion Act, describing the procedure and stating his belief that it went beyond what was an acceptable medical procedure.

Mr. Speaker, I beg the indulgence of my colleagues not to ask me to yield because I cannot and will not and I would appreciate their courtesy. I also want to say briefly that those who have charged us with politics, invidious politics, for delaying this debate ought to understand that Americans cannot believe this practice exists and it has taken months to educate the American people and it will take many more months to educate them as to the nature and extent of this horrible practice. That is one reason it has taken so long.

Supporters of the pro-life movement rally around Dallas City Hall on January 22, 1996, the 23rd anniversary of the Supreme Court's *Roe v. Wade* decision legalizing abortion. **AP/WIDE WORLD PHOTOS. REPRODUCED BY PERMISSION.**

The law exists to protect the weak from the strong. That is why we are here.

Mr. Speaker, in his classic novel *Crime and Punishment,* Dostoyevsky has his murderous protagonist Raskolnikov complain that "Man can get used to anything, the beast!"

That we are even debating this issue, that we have to argue about the legality of an abortionist plunging a pair of scissors into the back of the tiny neck of a little child whose trunk, arms and legs have already been delivered, and then suctioning out his brains only confirms Dostoyevsky's harsh truth.

We were told in committee by an attending nurse that the little arms and legs stop flailing and suddenly stiffen as the scissors is plunged in. People who say "I feel your pain" are not referring to that little infant.

What kind of people have we become that this procedure is even a matter for debate? Can we not draw the line at torture, and baby torture at that? If

we cannot, what has become of us? We are all incensed about ethnic cleansing. What about infant cleansing? There is no argument here about when human life begins. The child who is destroyed is unmistakably alive, unmistakably human and unmistakably brutally destroyed.

The justification for abortion has always been the claim that a women can do with her own body what she will. If you still believe that this four-fifths delivered little baby is a part of the woman's body, then I am afraid your ignorance is invincible.

I finally figured out why supporters of abortion on demand fight this infanticide ban tooth and claw, because for the first time since *Roe v. Wade* the focus is on the baby, not the mother, not the woman, but the baby, and the harm that abortion inflicts on an unborn child, or in this instance a four-fifths born child. That child whom the advocates of abortion on demand have done everything in their power to make us ignore, to dehumanize, is as much a bearer of human rights as any Member of this House. To deny those rights is more than the betrayal of a powerless individual. It betrays the central promise of America, that there is, in this land, justice for all.

The supporters of abortion on demand have exercised an amazing capacity for detaching themselves from any sympathy whatsoever for the unborn child, and in doing so they separate themselves from the instinct for justice that gave birth to this country.

The President, reacting angrily to this challenge to his veto, claims not to understand why the morality of those who support a ban on partial birth abortions is superior to the morality of "compassion" that he insists informed his decision to reject Congress' ban on what Senator Moynihan has said is "too close to infanticide."

Let me explain, Mr. President. There is no moral nor, for that matter, medical justification for this barbaric assault on a partially born infant. Dr. Pamela Smith, director of medical education in the Department of Obstetrics and Gynecology at Chicago's Mount Sinai Hospital, testified to that, as have many other doctors.

Dr. C. Everett Koop, the last credible Surgeon General we had, was interviewed by the American Medical Association on August 19, and he was asked:

Question: "President Clinton just vetoed a bill on partial birth abortions. In so doing, he cited several cases in which women were told these procedures were necessary to preserve their health and their ability to have future pregnancies. How would you characterize the claims being made in favor of the medical need for this procedure?"

Answer: Quoting Dr. Koop, "I believe that Mr. Clinton was misled by his medical advisors on what is fact and what is fiction in reference to late term abortions."

Question: "In your practice as a pediatric surgeon, have you ever treated children with any of the disabilities cited in this debate? Have you operated on children born with organs outside of their bodies?"

Answer: "Oh, yes, indeed. I've done that many times. The prognosis usually is good. There are two common ways that children are born with organs outside of their body. One is an omphalocele, where the organs are out but still contained in the sac composed of the tissues of the umbilical cord. I have been repairing those since 1946. The other is when the sac has ruptured. That makes it a little

more difficult. I don't know what the national mortality would be, but certainly more than half of those babies survive after surgery.

"Now every once in a while, you have other peculiar things, such as the chest being wide open and the heart being outside the body. And I have even replaced hearts back in the body and had children grow to adulthood."

Question: And live normal lives?

Answer: Living normal lives. In fact, the first child I ever did with a huge omphalocele much bigger than her head went on to develop well and become the head nurse in my intensive care unit many years later.

The abortionist who is a principal perpetrator of these atrocities, Dr. Martin Haskell, has conceded that at least 80 percent of the partial-birth abortions he performs are entirely elective; 80 percent are elective. And he admits to over a thousands of these abortions, and that is some years ago.

We are told about some extreme cases of malformed babies as though life is only for the privileged, the planned and the perfect. Dr. James McMahon, the late Dr. James McMahon, listed nine such abortions he performed because the baby had a cleft lip.

Many other physicians who care both about the mother and the unborn child have made it clear this is never a medical necessity, but it is a convenience for the abortionist. It is a convenience for those who choose to abort late in pregnancy when it becomes difficult to dismember the unborn child in the womb.

Well, the President claims he wants to solve a problem by adding a health exception to the partial-birth abortion ban. That is spurious, as anyone who has spent 10 minutes studying the Federal law, understands. Health exceptions are so broadly construed by the court, as to make any ban utterly meaningless.

If there is no consistent commitment that has survived the twists and the turns in policy during this administration, it is an unshakable commitment to a legal regime of abortion on demand. Nothing is or will be done to make abortion rare. No legislative or regulatory act will be allowed to impede the most permissive abortion license in the democratic world.

The President would do us all a favor and make a modest contribution to the health of our democratic process if he would simply concede this obvious fact.

In his memoirs Dwight Eisenhower wrote about the loss of 1.2 million lives in World War II, and he said: "The loss of lives that might have otherwise been creatively lived scars the mind of the civilized world."

Mr. Speaker, our souls have been scarred by one and a half million abortions every year in this country. Our souls have so much scar tissue there is not room for any more.

And say, what do we mean by human dignity if we subject innocent children to brutal execution when they are almost born? We all hope and pray for death with dignity. Tell me what is dignified about a death caused by having a scissors stabbed into your neck so your brains can be sucked out.

We have had long and bitter debate in this House about assault weapons. Those scissors and that suction machine are assault weapons worse than any AK-47. One might miss with an AK-47: the doctor never misses with his assault weapon, I can assure my colleagues.

It is not just the babies that are dying for the lethal sin of being unwanted or being handicapped or malformed. We are dying, and not from the darkness, but from the cold, the coldness of self-brutalization that chills our sensibilities, deadens our conscience and allows us to think of this unspeakable act as an act of compassion.

If my colleagues vote to uphold this veto, if they vote to maintain the legality of a procedure that is revolting even to the most hardened heart, then please do not ever use the word compassion again.

A word about anesthesia. Advocates of partial-birth abortions tried to tell us the baby does not feel pain; the mother's anesthesia is transmitted to the baby. We took testimony from five of the country's top anesthesiologists, and they said it is impossible, that result will take so much anesthesia it would kill the mother.

By upholding this tragic veto, those colleagues join the network of complicity in supporting what is essentially a crime against humanity, for that little, almost born infant struggling to live is a member of the human family, and partial-birth abortion is a lethal assault against the very idea of human rights and destroys, along with a defenseless little baby, the moral foundation of our democracy because democracy is not, after all, a mere process. It assigns fundamental rights and values to each human being, the first of which is the inalienable right to life.

One of the great errors of modern politics is our foolish attempt to separate our private consciences from our public acts, and it cannot be done. At the end of the 20th century, is the crowning achievement of our democracy to treat the weak, the powerless, the unwanted as things? To be disposed of? If so, we have not elevated justice; we have disgraced it.

This is not a debate about sectarian religious doctrine nor about policy options. This is a debate about our understanding of human dignity, what does it mean to be human? Our moment in history is marked by a mortal conflict between culture of death and a culture of life, and today, here and now, we must choose sides.

I am not the least embarrassed to say that I believe one day each of us will be called upon to render an account for what we have done, and maybe more importantly, what we fail to do in our lifetime, and while I believe in a merciful God, I believe in a just God, and I would be terrified at the thought of having to explain at the final judgment why I stood unmoved while Herod's slaughter of the innocents was being reenacted here in my own country.

This debate has been about an unspeakable horror. While the details are graphic and grisly, it has been helpful for all of us to recognize the full brutality of what goes on in America's aborturaries day in and day out, week after week, year after year. We are not talking about abstractions here. We are talking about life and death at their most elemental, and we ought to face the truth of what we oppose or support stripped of all euphemisms, and the queen of all euphemisms is "choice" as though one is choosing vanilla and chocolate instead of a dead baby or a live baby.

Now, we have talked so much about the grotesque; permit me a word about beauty. We all have our own images of the beautiful; the face of a loved one, a dawn, a sunset, the evening star. I believe nothing in this world of wonders is more beautiful than the innocence of a child.

Do my colleagues know what a child is? She is an opportunity for love, and a handicapped child is an even greater opportunity for love.

Mr. Speaker, we risk our souls, we risk our humanity when we trifle with that innocence or demean it or brutalize it. We need more caring and less killing.

Let the innocence of the unborn have the last word in this debate. Let their innocence appeal to what President Lincoln called the better angels of our nature. Let our votes prove Raskolnikov is wrong. There is something we will never get use to. Make it clear once again there is justice for all, even for the tiniest, most defenseless in this, our land.

Further Resources

BOOKS

Gold, Rebecca Benson. *Abortion and Women's Health: A Turning Point for America?* New York: The Alan Guttmacher Institute, 1990.

Olasky, Marvin. *Abortion Rights: A Social History of Abortion in America.* Washington, D.C.: Regnery Publishing, 1995.

Tribe, Laurence H. *Abortion: The Clash of Absolutes.* New York: W. W. Norton & Company, 1990

PERIODICALS

Arkes, Hadley. "Slouching Towards Infanticide: Why a Ban on Partial-Birth Abortion Is Not Enough." *The Weekly Standard,* May 25, 1998, 26–29.

Wolfe, Naomi. "Our Bodies, Our Souls: Rethinking Pro-Choice Rhetoric." *The New Republic,* October 16, 1995, 26–35.

WEBSITES

National Right to Life. Available online at http://www.nrlc.org /abortion/pba/index.html; website home page at http://www .nrlc.org/ (accessed April 4, 2003).

Planned Parenthood Federation of America. Available online at http://www.plannedparenthood.org (accessed April 4, 2003).

Usama bin Ladin: Islamic Extremist Financier

Report

By: Central Intelligence Agency

Date: 1996

Source: Central Intelligence Agency. *Usama bin Ladin: Islamic Extremist Financier.* Available online at http://www .gwu.edu/~nsarchiv/NSAEBB/NSAEBB55/index1.html; website home page http://www.gwu.edu (accessed April 4, 2003).

About the Organization: In 1947, President Harry S. Truman signed the National Security Act creating the Central Intelligence Agency (CIA). The CIA is an independent, federal agency that reports directly to the president of the United States through the Director of Central Intelligence. It is part of the executive branch of the U.S. government, whereas the majority of other intelligence organizations belong to the Defense Department. The CIA's primary mission is to collect, evaluate, and distribute foreign intelligence to assist the president and congressional intelligence oversight committees in making decisions affecting national security. The CIA is prohibited by law from collecting intelligence relating to the domestic activities of United States citizens. ∎

Introduction

On September 11, 2001, the largest terrorist attack in modern history took place in New York City, Washington, D.C., and Pennsylvania. Nineteen terrorists hijacked four fuel-laden passenger jetliners with the intent to crash them and kill as many people as possible. Two of the planes hit the World Trade Center in New York City, resulting in the collapse of the two towers. One plane struck the Pentagon in Arlington, Virginia, near Washington, D.C. The fourth plane crashed in a Pennsylvania field before it could reach its intended target. More than three thousand people were killed in the coordinated attack.

Responsibility for the assault was quickly found to lie with the al-Qaeda terrorist organization. Its leader, Osama bin Laden (also spelled Usama bin Ladin), was not new to the U.S. intelligence community. The Central Intelligence Agency had released a document in 1996 entitled "Usama bin Ladin: Islamic Extremist Financier," which reported that bin Laden was one of the most significant financial sponsors of "Islamic extremist activities" in the world. It was intended to provide the media with information about bin Ladin, whose name had been hitting the headlines in relation to various terrorist incidents and activities around the world in recent years, many of which were believed to be sponsored or supported by bin Laden himself.

A series of terrorist attacks during the early and mid-1990s drew increasing attention to Osama bin Laden and his group of militants, the Islamic Salvation Foundation, which came to be known popularly as al-Qaeda (also spelled al-Qaida, Arabic for "the base"). The combination of attacks on U.S. military personnel and assets in Somalia in 1992—killing 19 U.S. Marines—was the first time some connection was made between bin Laden and individuals attacking the United States. Terrorists linked to bin Ladin were also believed responsible for the February 26, 1993, bombing of the World Trade Center in New York City; the unsuccessful attack against New York City's Lincoln-Holland Tunnels and George Washington Bridge in July 1993; the planned assassination of President Bill Clinton (served 1993–2001) in the Philippines in 1995; the planned bombing of eleven American jumbo jets over the Pacific Ocean in 1995; the car bombing of the U.S. military mission in Riyadh, Saudi Arabia, in 1995; and the truck bombing of the Khobar Towers housing complex in Dhahran, Saudi Arabia, in 1996—killing nineteen American military personnel and wounding 240 others.

Later, after the publication of the CIA's 1996 report, other events would also be attributed to the group: the simultaneous truck bombings of the U.S. embassies in Kenya and Tanzania in 1998; the plan to bomb the Los Angeles International Airport on New Year's 2000; the suicide dinghy attack on the USS *Cole* while in port at Aden, Yemen—killing seventeen American

Police and injured workers exit the World Trade Center after an explosion on February 26, 1993. The blast killed two people and injured 150.
© REUTERS NEWMEDIA INC./CORBIS. REPRODUCED BY PERMISSION.

The 1993 bombing of the World Trade Center was linked to Osama bin Laden's al-Qaeda terrorist network, where bomber Ramzi Yousef received training and funding. **AP/WIDE WORLD PHOTOS. REPRODUCED BY PERMISSION.**

sailors and injuring thirty-nine others in October 2000; and the September 11 attack that resulted in the deaths of more than three thousand people from over eighty nations.

Significance

The CIA's 1996 report is one of the first public U.S. government documentations of Osama bin Laden's activities, especially with regard to his financial dealings, which spanned across the region from Saudi Arabia and Sudan, to Pakistan and Afghanistan. It was not until 1998, after the U.S. embassy bombings in Kenya and Tanzania, however, that bin Laden was actually dubbed a "Specially Designated Terrorist" (SDT), and his organization, al-Qaeda, was designated a "Foreign Terrorist Organization" under U.S. Executive Order 12947. Moreover, it was not until this 1998 order that U.S. financial transactions with bin Laden and al-Qaeda were effectively banned and law enforcement could freeze their assets in the United States. This may indicate that the true threat posed to the United States by bin Laden and al-Qaeda—and their financial prowess—was not fully realized until that time, even though the 1996 document

begins to outline bin Laden's vast financial network and sophistication.

After the events of September 11, 2001, U.S. president George W. Bush (served 2001–) declared a "war on terror," specifically targeting bin Laden and al-Qaeda and stating that he wanted bin Laden "dead or alive." Law enforcement was granted greater powers to freeze terrorist assets and the Departments of Justice and Treasury carefully examined *hawalas*, or Islamic charities, some of which were known or suspected to have helped funnel money to support terrorist groups.

Primary Source

Usama Bin Ladin: Islamic Extremist Financier

SYNOPSIS: The following document provides some detail about Osama bin Laden's financial activities from 1985 to 1996, when it was published. It is not an exhaustive intelligence study, but rather summarizes for public consumption the most important developments regarding bin Laden's financial dealings in support of extremist activities up to 1996. It also addresses bin Ladin's activities in Afghanistan during the Afghan resistance to the Soviet occupation of that country during the 1980s. Bin Laden played an integral role in bringing foreign fighters from other Muslim countries to assist the Afghans, and it was during this period that he personally became increasingly radicalized. After the Afghans defeated the Soviets in 1989, bin Laden worked to maintain the network of foreign fighters, many of whom had also become radicalized and more militant. This informal network would, later in the 1990s, form the basis of the terrorist group that came to be known as al-Qaeda.

Usama bin Muhammad bin Awad Bin Ladin is one of the most significant financial sponsors of Islamic extremist activities in the world today. One of some 20 sons of wealthy Saudi construction magnate Muhammad Bin Ladin—founder of the Kingdom's Bin Ladin Group business empire—Usama joined the Afghan resistance movement following the 26 December 1979 Soviet invasion of Afghanistan. "I was enraged and went there at once," he claimed in a 1993 interview. "I arrived within days, before the end of 1979."

Bin Ladin gained prominence during the Afghan war for his role in financing the recruitment, transportation, and training of Arab nationals who volunteered to fight alongside the Afghan mujahedin. By 1985, Bin Ladin had drawn on his family's wealth, plus donations received from sympathetic merchant families in the Gulf region, to organize the Islamic Salvation Foundation, or al-Qaida, for this purpose.

The 1993 World Trade Center Bombing

On September 1, 1992, Ramzi Yousef, a naturalized Pakistani citizen, landed at John F. Kennedy Airport in New York City. At customs, Yousef presented immigration officials with an Iraqi passport, but no visa documents. Arriving illegally, officials therefore briefly detained and fingerprinted him. Yousef was granted asylum, pending a formal hearing. On the morning of February 26, 1993, Yousef met others at a New Jersey gas station. After filling up a rented van, the men headed to lower Manhattan in New York City. They parked the van in the basement garage of the World Trade Center (WTC) and left. In the back of the van was a 1,500-pound, urea-nitrate bomb, set to explode at noon. Yousef was a key organizer of the terrorist attack.

The WTC was a sixteen-acre complex, containing seven buildings, including the 110-story twin towers. On a typical day, the complex housed nearly 20,000 people and had 80,000 visitors. At the prescribed time, an enormous blast wrought a 200-foot long by 100-foot wide cavity extending seven stories deep into the building's garage. It caused smoke to spiral up to the forty-sixth floor. The twin towers, designed to endure the shock of a Boeing 707 jet crash, remained standing. The detonation, however, resulted in 6,000 tons of debris and caused $300 million in property damage. Six innocents were killed, and more than one thousand were injured. As terrible as the event was, it could have been much worse. The terrorists laced the bomb with sodium cyanide, hoping to kill everyone in the structure. Fortunately, the toxic substance incinerated instead of vaporizing.

Yousef's connections to Osama bin Laden and al-Qaeda were established prior to the 1993 bombing. They include his attendance at a terrorist training camp in Afghanistan, which was run by al-Qaeda. It was there that he became an explosives expert. Yousef later joined the Egyptian Islamic Jihad, a militant group with ties to al-Qaeda. After the WTC bombing, Yousef slipped out of the country, traveling to the Philippines. In January 1995, he started to implement a plot to simultaneously blow up twelve United and Delta airplanes en route between the United States and Asia. While mixing the needed chemical explosives, his Manila apartment caught fire, forcing him to evacuate the premises. The subsequent police investigation turned up Yousef's laptop computer, containing coded files detailing the WTC conspiracy. The next month, the Federal Bureau of Investigation arrested him in Islamabad, Pakistan, and he was extradited to the United States. In a high profile trial, Yousef was convicted of masterminding the WTC bombing and sentenced to life in prison.

- A network of al-Qaida recruitment centers and guesthouses in Egypt, Saudi Arabia, and Pakistan has enlisted and sheltered thousands of Arab recruits. This network remains active.

- Working in conjunction with extremist groups like the Egyptian al-Gama'at al-Islamiyyah, also know as the Islamic Group, al-Qaida organized and funded camps in Afghanistan and Pakistan that provided new recruits paramilitary training in preparation for the fighting in Afghanistan.

- Under al-Qaida auspices, Bin Ladin imported bulldozers and other heavy equipment to cut roads, tunnels, hospitals, and storage depots through Afghanistan's mountainous terrain to move and shelter fighters and supplies.

After the Soviets withdrew from Afghanistan in 1989, Bin Ladin returned to work in the family's Jeddah-based construction business. However, he continued to support militant Islamic groups that had begun targeting moderate Islamic governments in the region. Saudi officials held Bin Ladin's passport during 1989–1991 in a bid to prevent him from solidifying contacts with extremists whom he had befriended during the Afghan war.

Bin Ladin relocated to Sudan in 1991, where he was welcomed by National Islamic Front (NIF) leader Hasan al-Turabi. In a 1994 interview, Bin Ladin claimed to have surveyed business and agricultural investment opportunities in Sudan as early as 1983. He embarked on several business ventures in Sudan in 1990, which began to thrive following his move to Khartoum. Bin Ladin also formed symbiotic business relationships with wealthy NIF members by undertaking civil infrastructure development projects on the regime's behalf:

- Bin Ladin's company, Al-Hijrah for Construction and Development, Ltd., built the Tahaddi (challenge) road linking Khartoum with Port Sudan, as well as a modern international airport near Port Sudan.

- Bin Ladin's import-export firm, Wadi al-Aqiq Company, Ltd., in conjunction with his Taba Investment Company, Ltd., secured a near monopoly over Sudan's major agricultural exports of gum, corn, sunflower, and sesame products in cooperation with prominent NIF members. At the same time, Bin Ladin's Al-Themar al-Mubarakah Agriculture Company, Ltd. grew to encompass large tracts of land near Khartoum and in eastern Sudan.

- Bin Ladin and wealthy NIF members capitalized Al-Shamal Islamic Bank in Khartoum. Bin Ladin invested $50 million in the bank.

Bin Ladin's work force grew to include militant Afghan war veterans seeking to avoid a return to their own countries, where many stood accused of subversive and terrorist activities. In May 1993, for example, Bin Ladin financed the travel of 300 to 480 Afghan war veterans to Sudan after Islamabad launched a crackdown against extremists lingering in Pakistan. In addition to safehaven in Sudan, Bin Ladin has provided financial support to militants actively opposed to moderate Islamic governments and the West:

- Islamic extremists who perpetrated the December 1992 attempted bombings against some 100 U.S. servicemen in Aden (billeted there to support U.N. relief operations in Somalia) claimed that Bin Ladin financed their group.

- A joint Egyptian-Saudi investigation revealed in May 1993 that Bin Ladin business interests helped funnel money to Egyptian extremists, who used the cash to buy unspecified equipment, printing presses, and weapons.

- By January 1994, Bin Ladin had begun financing at least three terrorist training camps in northern Sudan (camp residents included Egyptian, Algerian, Tunisian and Palestinian extremists) in cooperation with the NIF. Bin Ladin's Al-Hijrah for Construction and Development works directly with Sudanese military officials to transport and provision terrorists training in such camps.

- Pakistani investigators have said that Ramzi Ahmed Yousef, the alleged mastermind of the February 1993 World Trade Center bombing, resided at the Bin Ladin-funded Bayt Ashuhada (house of martyrs) guesthouse in Peshawar during most of the three years before his apprehension in February 1995.

- A leading member of the Egyptian extremist group al-Jihad claimed in a July 1995 interview that Bin Ladin helped fund the group and was at times witting of specific terrorist operations mounted by the group against Egyptian interests.

- Bin Ladin remains the key financier behind the "Kunar" camp in Afghanistan, which pro-

vides terrorist training to al-Jihad and al-Gama'at al-Islamiyyah members, according to suspect terrorists captured recently by Egyptian authorities.

Bin Ladin's support for extremist causes continues despite criticisms from regional governments and his family. Algeria, Egypt, and Yemen have accused Bin Ladin of financing militant Islamic groups on their soil (Yemen reportedly sought INTERPOL's assistance to apprehend Bin Ladin during 1994). In February 1994, Riyadh revoked Bin Ladin's Saudi citizenship for behavior that "contradicts the Kingdom's interests and risks harming its relations with fraternal countries." The move prompted Bin Ladin to form the Advisory and Reformation Committee, a London-based dissident organization that by July 1995 had issued over 350 pamphlets critical of the Saudi Government. Bin Ladin has not responded to condemnation leveled against him in March 1994 by his eldest brother, Bakr Bin Ladin, who expressed, through the Saudi media, his family's "regret, denunciation, and condemnation" of Bin Ladin's extremist activities.

Further Resources

BOOKS

Bodansky, Yossef. *Bin Ladin: The Man Who Declared War on America.* New York: Prima, 1999.

Dwyer, Jim et al. *Two Seconds Under the World: Terror Comes to America—The Conspiracy Behind the World Trade Center Bombing.* New York: Crown Publishers, 1994.

Malkin, Michelle. *Invasion: How America Still Welcomes Terrorists, Criminals, & Other Foreign Menaces to Our Shores.* New York: Regnery, 2002.

PERIODICALS

Lewis, Bernard. "License to Kill: Usama bin Ladin's Declaration of Jihad." *Foreign Affairs,* November/December, 1998.

Myroie, Laurie. "The World Trade Center Bomb: Who is Ramzi Yousef? And Why it Matters." *The National Interest,* 42, Winter 1995/96, 3–15.

WEBSITES

"Analysis: Al-Qaeda's Origins and Links." *BBC News,* May 16, 2003. Available online at http://news.bbc.co.uk/1/hi/world/south_asia/1670089.stm; website home page http://news.bbc.co.uk (accessed April 4, 2003).

"Hunting Bin Ladin." PBS *Frontline,* April 1999, updated September 2001. Available online at http://www.pbs.org/wgbh/pages/frontline/shows/binladen; website home page http://www.pbs.org (accessed April 4, 2003).

Referral to the United States House of Representatives (The Starr Report)

Report

By: Kenneth Starr

Date: September 9, 1998

Source: Office of the Independent Counsel. *Referral to the United States House of Representatives* (The Starr Report). September 9, 1998. Available online at http://thomas.loc.gov /icreport/2toc.htm; website home page http://thomas.loc.gov (accessed April 4, 2003).

About the Author: Kenneth Starr (1946–) was born in Vernon, Texas. In 1973, he earned a law degree from Duke University. After clerking for two years for Supreme Court Chief Justice Warren Burger, he later was appointed to the U.S. Circuit Court of Appeals. In 1989, President George H. Bush (served 1989–1993) appointed him Solicitor General, where he argued numerous cases before the Supreme Court. In 1993, he became a partner in a prestigious Washington, D.C. law firm. ∎

Introduction

President Bill Clinton (served 1993–2001) is likely the most investigated president in American history. The most serious of these probes initially looked into the president's conduct in Whitewater, an Arkansas real estate venture. In 1978, the Clintons, along with two Arkansas associates, borrowed $203,000 to purchase riverfront acreage in the Ozark Mountains. The two couples formed the development corporation with the intention of building and selling vacation homes.

In 1985, James McDougal, one of Clinton's Whitewater partners, held a fundraising event helping then-Governor Clinton to eliminate a $50,000 campaign debt. It was alleged that this revenue was improperly withdrawn from the accounts of depositors from McDougal's Madison Guaranty, a savings and loan that McDougal owned. In 1989, Madison financially collapsed, and the federal government spent $60 million to bail it out.

In 1992, the Federal Resolution Trust Corporation, which investigated the causes for Madison's failure, named the Clintons as "potential beneficiaries" of alleged illegal activities at Madison. The referral was sent to the U.S. Justice Department. In 1993, Vince Foster, Deputy White House Counsel (who had also acted as personal counsel for the Clintons), committed suicide. A month prior to his death, Foster had filed three years of delinquent Whitewater Development Corporation tax returns. Immediately after Foster's death, the White House denied federal investigators access to Foster's office. However, Clinton's associates were allowed to enter his

President Bill Clinton gives testimony before the grand jury that will determine whether to take the charges of impeachment against the president to trial. © **WALLY MCNAMEE/CORBIS. REPRODUCED BY PERMISSION.**

office. It was widely speculated that Clinton's aides had removed relevant Whitewater records, and records from Foster's office were discovered eventually in the private living quarters of the Clintons.

In January 1994, Attorney General Janet Reno appointed Robert Fiske as Independent Counsel to investigate Bill and Hillary Clinton's involvement in Whitewater. That August, at the insistence of Congressional Republicans, Kenneth Starr replaced Fiske. At this point, the focus of the investigation shifted from Whitewater to Clinton's personal life. The sudden change resulted from a civil lawsuit filed by Paula Jones, an Arkansas clerical worker. Jones charged that when Clinton was Governor, he had sexually harassed her in a Little Rock hotel room.

Remarkably, during the Jones controversy, Clinton began an eighteen-month illicit affair with a twenty-two year old White House intern, Monica Lewinsky. Lewinsky confided intimate details of the affair to a friend, Linda Tripp, who secretly tape-recorded twenty hours of their telephone conversations. Tripp then gave the recordings to Starr. On January 17, 1998, when President Clinton gave a pretrial deposition in the Jones suit, he denied having "sexual relations" with Lewinsky and did not remember ever being alone with her in the White House. This denial would become grounds for an article of impeachment. That July, Starr granted Lewinsky full immunity in return for her assistance. In September 1998, Starr delivered a 453-page report and thirty-six boxes of evidence to the House, enumerating eleven impeachable offenses allegedly committed by Clinton.

Significance

On December 18, 1998, the House of Representatives, for the first time since 1867, debated whether to impeach a president. For thirteen hours, over two hundred Representatives delivered impassioned speeches attacking and defending the president. Contributing to the almost surreal atmosphere was President Clinton's simultaneous order to begin bombing Iraq. After being impeached by the House on two counts, Clinton was tried in the Senate. On February 12, the Senate overwhelmingly acquitted the President on both articles of impeachment. At the end of the trial, to the lasting frustration of House Republicans, Clinton's approval ratings ranged between 65 and 70 percent. Most Americans believed that he had lied to the country, but wanted him censured, not impeached.

Primary Source

Referral to the United States House of Representatives (The Starr Report) [excerpt]

SYNOPSIS: On September 11, 1998, the Republicans on the House Judiciary Committee posted the Starr report on the Internet, allowing thousands of Americans to download it. The most controversial portion of the report was its detailed description of the President's relationship with Lewinsky. Although later Clinton admitted to having "inappropriate intimate contact" with her, he denied having "sexual relations" with her during the Jones deposition and in his immediately following public disclosure of the relationship.

B. Evidence Establishing Nature of Relationship

1. Physical Evidence

Physical evidence conclusively establishes that the President and Ms. Lewinsky had a sexual relationship. After reaching an immunity and cooperation agreement with the Office of the Independent Counsel on July 28, 1998, Ms. Lewinsky turned over a navy blue dress that she said she had worn during a sexual encounter with the President on February 28, 1997. According to Ms. Lewinsky, she noticed stains on the garment the next time she took it from her closet. From their location, she surmised that the stains were the President's semen.

Initial tests revealed that the stains are in fact semen. Based on that result, the OIC asked the President for a blood sample. After requesting and being given assurances that the OIC had an evidentiary basis for making the request, the President agreed. In the White House Map Room on August 3, 1998, the White House Physician drew a vial of blood from the President in the presence of an FBI agent and an OIC attorney. By conducting the two standard DNA comparison tests, the FBI Laboratory concluded that the President was the source of the DNA obtained

from the dress. According to the more sensitive RFLP test, the genetic markers on the semen, which match the President's DNA, are characteristic of one out of 7.87 trillion Caucasians.

In addition to the dress, Ms. Lewinsky provided what she said were answering machine tapes containing brief messages from the President, as well as several gifts that the President had given her.

2. Ms. Lewinsky's Statements

Ms. Lewinsky was extensively debriefed about her relationship with the President. For the initial evaluation of her credibility, she submitted to a detailed "proffer" interview on July 27, 1998. After entering into a cooperation agreement, she was questioned over the course of approximately 15 days. She also provided testimony under oath on three occasions: twice before the grand jury, and, because of the personal and sensitive nature of particular topics, once in a deposition. In addition, Ms. Lewinsky worked with prosecutors and investigators to create an 11-page chart that chronologically lists her contacts with President Clinton, including meetings, phone calls, gifts, and messages. Ms. Lewinsky twice verified the accuracy of the chart under oath.

In the evaluation of experienced prosecutors and investigators, Ms. Lewinsky has provided truthful information. She has not falsely inculpated the President. Harming him, she has testified, is "the last thing in the world I want to do."

Moreover, the OIC's immunity and cooperation agreement with Ms. Lewinsky includes safeguards crafted to ensure that she tells the truth. Court-ordered immunity and written immunity agreements often provide that the witness can be prosecuted only for false statements made during the period of cooperation, and not for the underlying offense. The OIC's agreement goes further, providing that Ms. Lewinsky will lose her immunity altogether if the government can prove to a federal district judge—by a preponderance of the evidence, not the higher standard of beyond a reasonable doubt—that she lied. Moreover, the agreement provides that, in the course of such a prosecution, the United States could introduce into evidence the statements made by Ms. Lewinsky during her cooperation. Since Ms. Lewinsky acknowledged in her proffer interview and in debriefings that she violated the law, she has a strong incentive to tell the truth: If she did not, it would be relatively straightforward to void the immunity agreement and prosecute her, using her own admissions against her. . . .

5. Consistency and Corroboration

The details of Ms. Lewinsky's many statements have been checked, cross-checked, and corroborated. When negotiations with Ms. Lewinsky in January and February 1998 did not culminate in an agreement, the OIC proceeded with a comprehensive investigation, which generated a great deal of probative evidence.

In July and August 1998, circumstances brought more direct and compelling evidence to the investigation. After the courts rejected a novel privilege claim, Secret Service officers and agents testified about their observations of the President and Ms. Lewinsky in the White House. Ms. Lewinsky agreed to submit to a proffer interview (previous negotiations had deadlocked over her refusal to do so), and, after assessing her credibility in that session, the OIC entered into a cooperation agreement with her. Pursuant to the cooperation agreement, Ms. Lewinsky turned over the dress that proved to bear traces of the President's semen. And the President, who had spurned six invitations to testify, finally agreed to provide his account to the grand jury. In that sworn testimony, he acknowledged "inappropriate intimate contact" with Ms. Lewinsky.

Because of the fashion in which the investigation had unfolded, in sum, a massive quantity of evidence was available to test and verify Ms. Lewinsky's statements during her proffer interview and her later cooperation. Consequently, Ms. Lewinsky's statements have been corroborated to a remarkable degree. Her detailed statements to the grand jury and the OIC in 1998 are consistent with statements to her confidants dating back to 1995, documents that she created, and physical evidence. Moreover, her accounts generally match the testimony of White House staff members; the testimony of Secret Service agents and officers; and White House records showing Ms. Lewinsky's entries and exits, the President's whereabouts, and the President's telephone calls.

C. Sexual Contacts

1. The President's Accounts

a. Jones Testimony

In the Jones deposition on January 17, 1998, the President denied having had "a sexual affair," "sexual relations," or "a sexual relationship" with Ms. Lewinsky. He noted that "[t]here are no curtains on the Oval Office, there are no curtains on my private office, there are no curtains or blinds that can

close [on] the windows in my private dining room," and added: "I have done everything I could to avoid the kind of questions you are asking me here today. . . ." . . .

b. Grand Jury Testimony

Testifying before the grand jury on August 17, 1998, seven months after his Jones deposition, the President acknowledged "inappropriate intimate contact" with Ms. Lewinsky but maintained that his January deposition testimony was accurate. In his account, "what began as a friendship [with Ms. Lewinsky] came to include this conduct." He said he remembered "meeting her, or having my first real conversation with her during the government shutdown in November of '95." According to the President, the inappropriate contact occurred later (after Ms. Lewinsky's internship had ended), "in early 1996 and once in early 1997."

The President refused to answer questions about the precise nature of his intimate contacts with Ms. Lewinsky, but he did explain his earlier denials. As to his denial in the Jones deposition that he and Ms. Lewinsky had had a "sexual relationship," the President maintained that there can be no sexual relationship without sexual intercourse, regardless of what other sexual activities may transpire. He stated that "most ordinary Americans" would embrace this distinction.

The President also maintained that none of his sexual contacts with Ms. Lewinsky constituted "sexual relations" within a specific definition used in the Jones deposition. . . .

H. Secrecy

1. Mutual Understanding

Both Ms. Lewinsky and the President testified that they took steps to maintain the secrecy of the relationship. According to Ms. Lewinsky, the President from the outset stressed the importance of keeping the relationship secret. In her handwritten statement to this Office, Ms. Lewinsky wrote that "the President told Ms. L to deny a relationship, if ever asked about it. He also said something to the effect of if the two people who are involved say it didn't happen—it didn't happen." According to Ms. Lewinsky, the President sometimes asked if she had told anyone about their sexual relationship or about the gifts they had exchanged; she (falsely) assured him that she had not. She told him that "I would always deny it, I would always protect him," and he responded approvingly. The two of them had, in her

Kenneth Starr served as independent counsel investigating President Clinton on charges of impeachment. He holds a copy of his report in a session before the House Judiciary Committee, November 19, 1998. **AP/WIDE WORLD PHOTOS. REPRODUCED BY PERMISSION.**

words, "a mutual understanding" that they would "keep this private, so that meant deny it and . . . take whatever appropriate steps needed to be taken." When she and the President both were subpoenaed to testify in the Jones case, Ms. Lewinsky anticipated that "as we had on every other occasion and every other instance of this relationship, we would deny it."

In his grand jury testimony, the President confirmed his efforts to keep their liaisons secret. He said he did not want the facts of their relationship to be disclosed "in any context," and added: "I certainly didn't want this to come out, if I could help it. And I was concerned about that. I was embarrassed about it. I knew it was wrong." Asked if he wanted to avoid having the facts come out through Ms. Lewinsky's testimony in *Jones,* he said: "Well, I did not want her to have to testify and go through that. And, of course, I didn't want her to do that, of course not."

2. Cover Stories

For her visits to see the President, according to Ms. Lewinsky, "[T]here was always some sort of a cover." When visiting the President while she worked at the White House, she generally planned to tell anyone who asked (including Secret Service officers and agents) that she was delivering papers to the President. Ms. Lewinsky explained that this artifice may have originated when "I got there kind of saying, 'Oh, gee, here are your letters,' wink, wink, wink, and him saying, 'Okay, that's good.'" To back up her stories, she generally carried a folder on these vis-

its. (In truth, according to Ms. Lewinsky, her job never required her to deliver papers to the President.) On a few occasions during her White House employment, Ms. Lewinsky and the President arranged to bump into each other in the hallway; he then would invite her to accompany him to the Oval Office. Later, after she left the White House and started working at the Pentagon, Ms. Lewinsky relied on Ms. Currie to arrange times when she could see the President. The cover story for those visits was that Ms. Lewinsky was coming to see Ms. Currie, not the President.

While the President did not expressly instruct her to lie, according to Ms. Lewinsky, he did suggest misleading cover stories. And, when she assured him that she planned to lie about the relationship, he responded approvingly. On the frequent occasions when Ms. Lewinsky promised that she would "always deny" the relationship and "always protect him," for example, the President responded, in her recollection, "'That's good,' or—something affirmative. . . . [N]ot—'Don't deny it.'"

Once she was named as a possible witness in the *Jones* case, according to Ms. Lewinsky, the President reminded her of the cover stories. After telling her that she was a potential witness, the President suggested that, if she were subpoenaed, she could file an affidavit to avoid being deposed. He also told her she could say that, when working at the White House, she had sometimes delivered letters to him, and, after leaving her White House job, she had sometimes returned to visit Ms. Currie. (The President's own testimony in the Jones case mirrors the recommendations he made to Ms. Lewinsky for her testimony. In his deposition, the President testified that he saw Ms. Lewinsky "on two or three occasions" during the November 1995 government furlough, "one or two other times when she brought some documents to me," and "sometime before Christmas" when Ms. Lewinsky "came by to see Betty.")

In his grand jury testimony, the President acknowledged that he and Ms. Lewinsky "might have talked about what to do in a nonlegal context" to hide their relationship, and that he "might well have said" that Ms. Lewinsky should tell people that she was bringing letters to him or coming to visit Ms. Currie. But he also stated that "I never asked Ms. Lewinsky to lie."

3. Steps to Avoid Being Seen or Heard

After their first two sexual encounters during the November 1995 government shutdown, according to

Ms. Lewinsky, her encounters with the President generally occurred on weekends, when fewer people were in the West Wing. Ms. Lewinsky testified:

> He had told me . . . that he was usually around on the weekends and that it was okay to come see him on the weekends. So he would call and we would arrange either to bump into each other in the hall or that I would bring papers to the office.

From some of the President's comments, Ms. Lewinsky gathered that she should try to avoid being seen by several White House employees, including Nancy Hernreich, Deputy Assistant to the President and Director of Oval Office Operations, and Stephen Goodin, the President's personal aide.

Out of concern about being seen, the sexual encounters most often occurred in the windowless hallway outside the study. According to Ms. Lewinsky, the President was concerned that the two of them might be spotted through a White House window. When they were in the study together in the evenings, he sometimes turned out the light. Once, when she spotted a gardener outside the study window, they left the room. Ms. Lewinsky testified that, on December 28, 1997, "when I was getting my Christmas kiss" in the doorway to the study, the President was "looking out the window with his eyes wide open while he was kissing me and then I got mad because it wasn't very romantic." He responded, "Well, I was just looking to see to make sure no one was out there."

Fear of discovery constrained their sexual encounters in several respects, according to Ms. Lewinsky. The President ordinarily kept the door between the private hallway and the Oval Office several inches ajar during their encounters, both so that he could hear if anyone approached and so that anyone who did approach would be less likely to suspect impropriety. During their sexual encounters, Ms. Lewinsky testified, "[W]e were both aware of the volume and sometimes . . . I bit my hand—so that I wouldn't make any noise." On one occasion, according to Ms. Lewinsky, the President put his hand over her mouth during a sexual encounter to keep her quiet. Concerned that they might be interrupted abruptly, according to Ms. Lewinsky, the two of them never fully undressed.

While noting that "the door to the hallway was always somewhat open," the President testified that he did try to keep the intimate relationship secret: "I did what people do when they do the wrong thing. I tried to do it where nobody else was looking at it."

4. Ms. Lewinsky's Notes and Letters

The President expressed concern about documents that might hint at an improper relationship between them, according to Ms. Lewinsky. He cautioned her about messages she sent:

> There were . . . some occasions when I sent him cards or notes that I wrote things that he deemed too personal to put on paper just in case something ever happened, if it got lost getting there or someone else opened it. So there were several times when he remarked to me, you know, you shouldn't put that on paper.

She said that the President made this point to her in their last conversation, on January 5, 1998, in reference to what she characterized as "[a]n embarrassing mushy note" she had sent him. In addition, according to Ms. Lewinsky, the President expressed concerns about official records that could establish aspects of their relationship. She said that on two occasions she asked the President if she could go upstairs to the Residence with him. No, he said, because a record is kept of everyone who accompanies him there.

The President testified before the grand jury: "I remember telling her she should be careful what she wrote, because a lot of it was clearly inappropriate and would be embarrassing if somebody else read it."

5. Ms. Lewinsky's Evaluation of Their Secrecy Efforts

In two conversations recorded after she was subpoenaed in the *Jones* case, Ms. Lewinsky expressed confidence that her relationship with the President would never be discovered. She believed that no records showed her and the President alone in the area of the study. Regardless of the evidence, in any event, she would continue denying the relationship. "If someone looked in the study window, it's not me," she said. If someone produced tapes of her telephone calls with the President, she would say they were fakes.

In another recorded conversation, Ms. Lewinsky said she was especially comforted by the fact that the President, like her, would be swearing under oath that "nothing happened." She said:

> [T]o tell you the truth, I'm not concerned all that much anymore because I know I'm not going to get in trouble. I will not get in trouble because you know what? The story I've signed under—under oath is what someone else is saying under oath. . . .

Further Resources

BOOKS

Dumas, Ernest. *The Clintons of Arkansas.* Fayetteville, Ark.: University of Arkansas Press, 1993.

Maraniss, David. *First in His Class: A Biography of Bill Clinton.* New York: Simon and Schuster, 1995.

Posner, Richard A. *An Affair of the State. The Investigation, Impeachment, and Trial of President Clinton.* Cambridge, Mass.: Harvard University Press, 1999.

PERIODICALS

Moore, David W. "Good Times For Clinton As President: But Personal Reputation Hits New Low." *The Gallop Poll Monthly,* January 1999, 3.

Sullivan, Andrew. "The Death of Overkill." *The New Republic.* March 8, 1998, 18.

WEBSITES

"The Clinton Years." British Broadcasting Company. Available online at http://news.bbc.co.uk/1/hi/world/americas/1113811.stm; website home page http://news.bbc.co.uk (accessed April 4, 2003).

"The New Democrat President." The American President. Available online at http://www.americanpresident.org/kotrain/courses/BC/BC_In_Brief.htm; website home page (accessed April 4, 2003).

The Impeachment Trial of President Clinton

Henry Hyde's Statement During the Trial of President Clinton, January 16, 1999

Speech

By: Henry Hyde

Date: January 16, 1999

Source: U.S. Senate. Representative Henry Hyde of Ohio. Statement During the Trial of President Clinton, *Congressional Record.* January 16, 1999. 106th Cong., 1st sess., vol. 145, no. 7.

About the Author: Henry Hyde (1924–) was born in Chicago, Illinois. In 1942, he enlisted in the United States Navy and he saw combat in the Philippines during World War II (1941–1945). In 1949, he earned a law degree from Loyola University–Chicago. He was elected to the U.S. House of Representatives in 1974, and he chaired the powerful House Judiciary Committee from 1995 to 2001. During the Clinton impeachment trial in the Senate, he was the lead House manager.

Joseph Lieberman's Statement During the Trial of President Clinton, February 12, 1999

Speech

By: Joseph Lieberman

Date: February 12, 1999

Source: U.S. Senate. Senator Joseph Lieberman of Connecticut. Statement During the Trial of President Clinton, *Congressional Record.* February 12, 1999. 106th Cong., 1st sess., vol. 145, no. 7.

About the Author: Joseph Lieberman (1942–) was born in Stamford, Connecticut. In 1967, he earned a law degree from Yale Law School. For the next ten years, he served in the Connecticut State Senate. From 1982 to 1988, Lieberman was Connecticut's Attorney General. Afterwards, he was elected to the United States Senate. In 2000, he was elected to his third term. During that same election cycle, Vice President Al Gore chose Lieberman to run as his vice presidential running mate in the 2000 Presidential election. ∎

Introduction

Article I, sections 2 and 3 of the United States Constitution define the process by which federal officials may be removed by impeachment from office. First, the House of Representatives issues a formal accusation of misconduct, otherwise known as the "articles of impeachment." Second, the impeached official is tried in the Senate and a two-thirds vote is needed for conviction. If convicted, the official is removed from office and prohibited from holding that office again. The impeachment process is controversial and arguably subjective, as the Constitution does not define what constitutes an impeachable offense.

Article I, section 4 specifies that only "treason, bribery, or other high Crimes and Misdemeanors" are impeachable offenses. The Constitution explicitly defines treason and statutory law clearly defines bribery. The meaning of "high Crimes and Misdemeanors," however, is not self-evident. Further, Congress has never passed a statute defining and cataloguing impeachable behaviors. Consequently, there are two schools of thought on the matter. First, some constitutional scholars argue that "high Crimes and Misdemeanors" include only those offenses for which one can be charged under federal and state law. Conversely, other scholars have a broader interpretation, which include violations of the basic principles of the Constitution and the rule of law—including political acts that violate the public trust, but are not against federal or state law. Ultimately, Congress must determine the meaning of this ambiguous phrase. In 1970, Representative (later president) Gerald Ford (served as president from 1974–1977) perhaps stated it best when he said: "An impeachable offense is whatever a majority of the House of Representatives considers it to be at a given moment of history."

Since 1789, the House of Representatives had impeached only sixteen officials. The Senate had convicted and removed seven, all federal judges. Prior to 1999, only one president had been impeached. In December 1867, the House of Representatives brought eleven articles of impeachment against President Andrew Johnson (served 1865–1869). Following the assassination of Abraham Lincoln, Vice President Johnson became the seventeenth president of the United States. Johnson's impeachment was an overtly political process. Characterized as a southern sympathizer, he promoted a lenient Reconstruction policy toward the South after the Civil War (1861–1865). His accusers in the House were Radical Republicans, who demanded that Reconstruction, in part, include black suffrage and political and physical protection of the freed slaves. In the Senate, Johnson escaped removal from office by one vote.

The only other president to face impeachment, other than the brief and ineffectual political moves against presidents Herbert Hoover (served 1929–1933) and Harry S. Truman (served 1945–1953), was President Richard Nixon (served 1969–1974). In 1973 and 1974, Nixon's participation in the Watergate cover-up forced the House to accuse him of obstruction of justice, abuse of power, and contempt of Congress. He resigned from office when the House was preparing to vote on the articles of impeachment.

Significance

The impeachment and trial of President Bill Clinton (served 1993–2001) is significant, because it may prove to be a pivotal event in the evolution of the presidency. The impeachment involved vastly different issues than those surrounding the Johnson and Nixon impeachment efforts. Unlike Johnson's impeachment, the Clinton controversy was not about opposing political ideologies or important constitutional questions concerning the separation of powers. Unlike the Nixon affair, the articles of impeachment against Clinton did not accuse him of subverting the Constitution. Instead, it may be argued that the Clinton impeachment pertained to issues of personal integrity.

The Clinton impeachment focused on his sexual relationship with a young White House intern, Monica Lewinsky. Clinton committed adultery with Lewinsky, and then lied about it while testifying under oath. When Clinton's actions became known, a scandal ensued. The House of Representatives voted to impeach Clinton, accusing him of committing perjury and obstructing justice. Though clearly reprehensible behavior, Clinton's actions were not directly related to his constitutional duties as president. Many questioned if the president should be stripped of his office over what was essentially a private matter, while others responded that through his ac-

tions Clinton had lost the public trust. The Senate ultimately decided that Clinton's behavior did not constitute "high Crimes and Misdemeanors." Thus the Senate acquited President Clinton, and he served out the remainder of his term.

Primary Source

Henry Hyde's Statement During the Trial of President Clinton, January 16, 1999

> **SYNOPSIS:** During an impeachment trial in the U.S. Senate a team of U.S. Representatives presents the case for why the Senate should act on the House's recommendations and remove someone from office. Representative Henry Hyde was the manager of the House team during the trial of President Clinton. In this speech, Hyde presents the basic argument for removing President Clinton from office: Clinton lied under oath, thereby betraying the public trust.

Mr. Manager Hyde: Mr. Chief Justice, counsel for the President, distinguished Members of the Senate, 136 years ago, at a small military cemetery in Pennsylvania, one of Illinois' most illustrious sons asked a haunting question—whether a nation conceived in liberty and dedicated to the proposition that all men are created equal can long endure. America is an experiment never finished. It is a work in progress. And so that question has to be answered by each generation for itself, just as we will have to answer whether this Nation can long endure.

This controversy began with the fact that the President of the United States took an oath to tell the truth in his testimony before the grand jury, just as he had on two prior occasions sworn a solemn oath to preserve, protect, and defend the Constitution and to faithfully execute the laws of the United States.

One of the most memorable aspects of this proceeding was the solemn occasion wherein every Senator in this Chamber took an oath to do impartial justice under the Constitution.

But I must say, despite massive and relentless efforts to change the subject, the case before you Senators is not about sexual misconduct, infidelity or adultery—those are private acts and none of our business. It is not even a question of lying about sex. The matter before this body is a question of lying under oath. This is a public act.

The matter before you is a question of the willful, premeditated deliberate corruption of the Nation's system of justice, through perjury and obstruction of justice. These are public acts, and when committed by the chief law enforcement officer of the land, the one who appoints every United States district attorney, every Federal judge, every member of the Supreme Court, the Attorney General—they do become the concern of Congress.

That is why your judgment, respectfully, should rise above politics, above partisanship, above polling data. This case is a test of whether what the Founding Fathers described as "sacred honor" still has meaning in our time: two hundred twenty-two years after those two words—sacred honor—were inscribed in our country's birth certificate, our national charter of freedom, our Declaration of Independence.

Every school child in the United States has an intuitive sense of the "sacred honor" that is one of the foundation stones of the American house of freedom. For every day, in every classroom in America, our children and grandchildren pledge allegiance to a nation, "under God." That statement, is not a prideful or arrogant claim. It is a statement of humility: all of us, as individuals, stand under the judgment of God, or the transcendent truths by which we hope, finally, to be judged.

So does our country.

The Presidency is an office of trust. Every public office is a public trust, but the Office of President is a very special public trust. The President is the trustee of the national conscience. No one owns the Office of President, the people do. The President is elected by the people and their representatives in the electoral college. And in accepting the burdens of that great office, the President, in his inaugural oath, enters into a covenant—a binding agreement of mutual trust and obligation—with the American people.

Shortly after his election and during his first months in office, President Clinton spoke with some frequency about a "new covenant" in America. In this instance, let us take the President at his word: that his office is a covenant—a solemn pact of mutual trust and obligation—with the American people. Let us take the President seriously when he speaks of covenants: because a covenant is about promise-making and promise-keeping. For it is because the President has defaulted on the promises he made—it is because he has violated the oaths he has sworn—that he has been impeached. . . .

In recent months, it has often been asked—so what? What is the harm done by this lying under oath, by this perjury? Well, what is an oath? An oath is an asking almighty God to witness to the truth of

what you are saying. Truth telling—truth telling is the heart and soul of our justice system.

I think the answer would have been clear to those who once pledged their sacred honor to the cause of liberty. The answer would have been clear to those who crafted the world's most enduring written constitution.

No greater harm can be done than breaking the covenant of trust between the President and the people; among the three branches of our government; and between the country and the world.

For to break that covenant of trust is to dissolve the mortar that binds the foundation stones of our freedom into a secure and solid edifice. And to break that covenant of trust by violating one's oath is to do grave damage to the rule of law among us.

That none of us is above the law is a bedrock principle of democracy. To erode that bedrock is to risk even further injustice. To erode that bedrock is to subscribe, to a "divine right of kings" theory of governance, in which those who govern are absolved from adhering to the basic moral standards to which the governed are accountable. We must never tolerate one law for the ruler, and another for the ruled. If we do, we break faith with our ancestors from Bunker Hill, Lexington and Concord to Flanders Field, Normandy, Iwo Jima, Panmunjom, Saigon and Desert Storm.

Let us be clear: The vote that you are asked to cast is, in the final analysis, a vote about the rule of law. . . .

Primary Source

Joseph Lieberman's Statement During the Trial of President Clinton, February 12, 1999

SYNOPSIS: In this speech Senator Joseph Lieberman argues against removing President Clinton from office. While he does not dispute that Clinton did the things he is accused of, Lieberman maintains that the offenses do not meet the standard of "high Crimes and Misdemeanors."

Mr. Lieberman: Mr. Chief Justice, throughout the history of this great country, we have endured trials that have strained the sinews of our democracy and sometimes even threatened to tear apart our unparalleled experiment in self-government. Each time the nation has returned to the Constitution as our common lodestar, trusting in its vision, its values and its ultimate verity. Each time we have emerged from these tests stronger, more resilient, more certain of Daniel Webster's claim of "one country, one constitution, one destiny." (Speech to a Whig Party rally in New York City, March 15, 1837.) And each time our awe of the Founders' genius has been renewed, as has our reverence for the brilliantly-calibrated instrument they crafted to guide their political progeny in the unending challenge of governing as a free people.

At this moment, we face a test that, although not as grave or perilous as some before, is nevertheless unlike anything this nation has ever experienced. As my colleagues well know, the impeachment trial of William Jefferson Clinton marks the first time in our history that the United States Senate has convened as a court of impeachment to consider removing an elected President from office. But what also makes this trial unprecedented are the underlying charges against President Clinton, which stem directly from his private sexual behavior. The facts of this case are complicated, embarrassing, demoralizing, and infuriating. They raise questions that Madison, Hamilton, and their brethren could never have anticipated that the Senate would have to address in the solemn context of impeachment.

The public examination of these difficult questions—about private and public morality, about the role of the Independent Counsel, and about our expectations of Presidential conduct—has been a wrenching, dispiriting and at times unseemly process for the nation. It has divided us as parties and as a people, reaching its nadir in the partisan bickering and badgering that unfortunately defined the impeachment vote in the House of Representatives and compromised the legitimacy of this process in the eyes of many Americans. It has set off a frenzy in the news media that has degraded and devalued our public discourse and badly eroded the traditional boundaries between public and private life, leaving a pornographer to assume the role or arbiter of our political mores. And it has so alienated the American people that many of them are hardly paying attention to a trial that could result in the most radical disruption of the presidency—excepting assassination—in our nation's history.

Yet despite the significant pain this trauma has caused for the country, I take heart from the fact that we have once again reaffirmed our commitment to the Constitution and the fundamental principles underpinning it. The conduct of the trial here in the Senate has been passionate at times, but never uncivil, and while some votes have broken along party

Senator Joseph Lieberman meets with reporters on Capitol Hill prior to the start of the Senate impeachment trial in January 1999. **AP/WIDE WORLD PHOTOS. REPRODUCED BY PERMISSION.**

lines, they have never broken the spirit of common purpose we share. Indeed, throughout the past several weeks we as a body have grown closer as we have continually measured our actions with the same constitutional yardstick, and each of us has sought to remain faithful to the Founders' vision as we understand it in fulfilling our responsibilities as triers of the President. This, I believe, is in the end a remarkable testament to the foresight of our forefathers, that even in this most unusual of crises, we could and would rely on the Constitution as our compass to find a peaceable and just resolution.

We are about to achieve that resolution and complete our constitutional responsibilities by rendering a judgment, a profound judgment, about the conduct of President Clinton and the call of the House of Representatives to remove him from office. This is the duty we accepted when we swore to do "impartial justice," and it is a duty that I, as each of you, have pondered night and day since this trial began.

As I have stated previously on this Senate floor, I have been deeply disappointed and angered by this President's conduct—that which is covered in the Articles, and the more personal misbehavior that is not—and like all of us here, I have struggled uncomfortably for more than a year with how to respond to it. President Clinton engaged in an extramarital sexual relationship with a young White House employee in the Oval Office, which, though consensual, was irresponsible and immoral, and thus raised serious questions about his judgment and his respect for the high office he holds. He then made false or misleading statements about that relationship to the American people, to a Federal district court judge in a civil deposition, and to a Federal grand jury; in so doing, he betrayed not only his family but the public's trust, and undermined his moral authority and public credibility.

But the judgment we must now make is not about the rightness or wrongness of the President's relationship with Monica Lewinsky and his efforts to conceal it. Nor is that judgment about whether the President is guilty of committing a specific crime. That may be determined by a criminal court, which the Senate clearly is not, after he leaves office.

No, the question before us now is whether the President's conduct—as alleged in the two articles of impeachment—makes his continuance in office a threat to our government, our people, and the national interest. That, I conclude, is the extraordinarily high bar the Framers set for removal of a duly-elected President, and it is that standard we must apply to the facts to determine whether the President is guilty of "high Crimes and Misdemeanors."

Each side has had ample opportunity to present its case, illuminating the voluminous record from the House, and we Senators have been able to ask wide-ranging questions of both parties. The House was also authorized to conduct depositions of the three witnesses it deemed most important to its case. I have listened intently throughout, watched the videotaped depositions, and been very impressed by both the House Managers and the counsel for the President. The House Managers, for their part, have presented the facts and argued the Constitution so effectively that they impelled me more than once to seriously consider voting for removal.

But after much reflection and review of the extensive evidence before us, of the meaning of the term "high Crimes and Misdemeanors," and, most importantly, of the best interests of the nation, I have concluded that the facts do not meet the high standard the Founders established for conviction and removal. No matter how deeply disappointed I am that our President, who has worked so suc-

cessfully to lift up the lives of so many people, so lowered himself and his office, I conclude that his wrongdoing in this sordid saga does not justify making him the first President to be ousted from office in our history. I will therefore vote against both Articles of Impeachment.

Further Resources

BOOKS

Beschloss, Michael. *The Impeachment and Trial of President Clinton.* New York: Random House, 1999.

Van Tassel, Emily Field and Paul Finkleman. *Impeachable Offenses: A Documentary History from 1787 to the Present.* Washington, D.C.: Congressional Quarterly, 1999.

Woodward, Bob. *Shadow: Five Presidents and the Legacy of Watergate.* New York: Simon and Schuster, 1999.

PERIODICALS

Bennett, William J. "Why He Must Go." *The Wall Street Journal,* August 19, 1998.

Katyal, Neal Kumar. "The Public and Private Lives of Presidents." *The William and Mary Bill of Rights Journal,* 8, April 2000, 677–692.

WEBSITES

"Clinton Accused." *The Washington Post.* Available online at http://www.washingtonpost.com/wp-srv/politics/special/clinton/clinton.htm; website home page http://www.washingtonpost.com (accessed April 4, 2003).

"The Impeachment Trial." Online NewsHouse, The Democracy Project, PBS. Available online at http://www.pbs.org/newshour/impeachment; website home page http://www.pbs.org (accessed April 4, 2003).

"You Are a NATO Bombing Target"

Flyer

By: 4th Psychological Operations Group

Date: 1999

Source: 4th Psychological Operations Group. "You Are a NATO Bombing Target." AP/Wide World Photos.

About the Author: The 4th Psychological Operations Group (PSYOP) is headquartered at Fort Bragg, North Carolina. It is the only active duty U.S. Army Psychological Operations Group. It consists of about 1,100 soldiers and 50 civilian analysts. The purpose of PSYOP is to demoralize the enemy by causing chaos among its ranks—while at the same time convince the local population to support American troops. ∎

Introduction

The Balkan Peninsula is the southernmost peninsula of Europe. It is the size of Texas and Oklahoma combined;

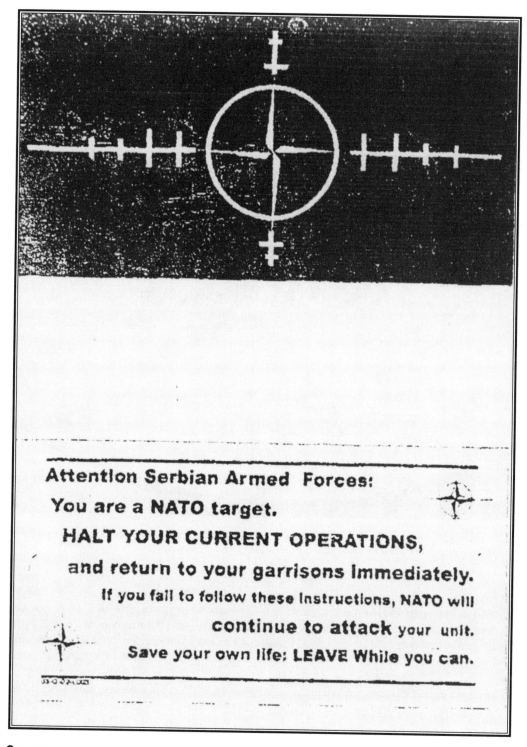

Primary Source

"You Are a NATO Bombing Target"

SYNOPSIS: During the Kosovo air campaign, PSYOP developed a multimedia campaign, including leaflets, handbills, posters, and radio and television broadcasts aimed at intimidating Serbian forces and countering the distorted news reports coming out of Belgrade. MC-130H Combat Talon aircraft from the 7th Special Operations Squadron dropped over 100 million leaflets over Serbia. AP/WIDE WORLD PHOTOS. REPRODUCED BY PERMISSION.

A U.S. Air Force A-10A Warthog drops away from a refueling tanker during NATO Operation Allied Force, April 22, 1999. **AP/WIDE WORLD PHOTOS. U.S. AIR FORCE, SENIOR AIRMAN GREG L. DAVIS. REPRODUCED BY PERMISSION.**

the Black, the Aegean, the Mediterranean, and the Adriatic seas surround it. The peninsula has a stormy past, as it lies at the crossroads of European and Asian civilizations. For hundreds of years, dozens of ethnic groups with distinct religious identities lived autonomously among the mountain gorges and valleys—geography that impeded regional, political, economic, or cultural integration.

One of the more troubled of the Balkan provinces is Serbia. After World War I (1914–1918), one cause of which was Serbian nationalism, Serbia became part of Yugoslavia, a mixture of Serbs, Slovenes, Croats, Bulgarians, Macedonians, Montenegrins, Bosnians, and Albanians. In 1945, Yugoslavia turned to communism. Through ruthless means, its communist leaders were able to suppress ethnic hostilities. However, in 1989, when the communists were swept out of power and non-Serbian regions seceded from Belgrade's (the capital of Serbia) control, the country plunged into civil war.

In 1989, Serbian nationalist, Slobadan Milosevic, visited the southern province of Kosovo. Unlike the Slavic Serbians, the Kosovars were eighty percent ethnic Albanians. At a rally commemorating the six hundredth anniversary of the Battle of Kosovo, where the Ottoman Turks defeated the Serbs, Milosevic called on his countrymen to "Avenge Kosovo." Envisioning a Greater Serbia, Milosevic revoked Kosovar autonomy and committed extensive human rights abuses. Milosevic's actions in Kosovo precipitated a greater crisis when the Serbs launched a crusade of "ethnic cleansing" against neighboring Croats and Bosnians, killing 250,000.

In 1995, President Bill Clinton (served 1993–2001), after ordering U.S.-led air strikes against Bosnian Serbs, forced Milosevic to sign a peace treaty with the Croats and Bosnians in Dayton, Ohio. In 1998, ethnic Albanians, calling themselves the Kosovo Liberation Army, began to fight back, attacking Serbian police stations and

Yugoslav army troops. In response, the Serbians escalated their policy of ethnic cleansing. Between February 1998 and May 1999, Serbian forces drove 1.5 million people, or 90 percent of the population of Kosovo, from their homes. Over 10,000 ethnic Albanians were killed, and thousands were abused, tortured, and raped. Further, 225,000 Kosovar men were believed missing. As the refugees flowed into Western Europe, the war threatened to destabilize the entire region.

Significance

Despite that Milosevic's genocidal crusade was occurring in Europe's "backyard," both the European Union and the United Nations hesitated over how to respond to the crisis. Consequently, the United States and the North Atlantic Treaty Organization (NATO) got involved. In a risky decision, President Clinton opted not to deploy ground forces. NATO had estimated that 150,000 to 200,000 troops would be required to drive Serbian forces from Kosovo with minimum casualties. Instead, Clinton authorized an air campaign on March 24, 1999. This was a risky strategy because, if the campaign failed and the massacres continued, the credibility of the NATO alliance would have been severely damaged. Moreover, a failed air campaign would have undermined American global leadership in the post–Cold War world and further embolden North Korea, China, Iraq, Iran, as well as Islamic terrorists.

NATO aircraft inflicted tremendous damage on Serbian heavy machine plants, fuel storage areas, roads, and bridges to pressure Milosevic to withdraw from Kosovo. After 37,000 sorties and seventy-eight days of heavy bombing, Milosevic accepted a NATO peace plan. The plan called for Serbian withdrawal from Kosovo; the deployment of international peacekeepers; an international administration to govern the province until elections were held; and widespread autonomy of Kosovo within Yugoslavia. In March 2002, Kosovo formed an elected government, an important step in continued stability in the province. In March 2003, Milosevic was charged with crimes against humanity before the UN International Criminal Tribunal.

Further Resources

BOOKS

Daalder, Ivo H., and Michael E. O'Hanlon. *Winning Ugly: NATO's War to Save Kosovo*. Washington, D.C.: Brookings Institution, 2000. Available online at http://brookings.nap.edu/books/0815716966/html/; website home page http://brookings.nap.edu (accessed April 4, 2003).

Kaplan, Robert D. *Balkan Ghosts: A Journey Through History*. New York: St. Martin's Press, 1993.

Vickers, Miranda. *Between Serb and Albanian: A History of Kosovo*. New York: Columbia University Press, 1998.

PERIODICALS

Pryce-Jones, David. "The Meaning of Kosovo." *National Review*, April 19, 1999, 18–19.

Schork, Kurt. "Province of Doom." *The New Republic*, February 22, 1999, 20–23.

WEBSITES

"NATO's Role in Kosovo." NATO, May 28, 2003. Available online at http://www.nato.int/kosovo/kosovo.htm; website home page http://www.nato.int (accessed April 4, 2003).

"Related Sites on the Kosovo Crisis." CNN. Available online at http://www.cnn.com/SPECIALS/1998/10/kosovo/related.sites/; website home page http://www.cnn.com (accessed April 4, 2003).

6

LAW AND JUSTICE

SCOTT A. MERRIMAN

Entries are arranged in chronological order by date of primary source. For entries with one primary source, the entry title is the same as the primary source title. Entries with more than one primary source have an overall entry title, followed by the titles of the primary sources.

Important Events in Law and Justice, 1990–1999

1990

- On January 3, Manuel Antonio Noriega Moreno, dictator of Panama (1983–1989), is arrested on drug smuggling, racketeering, and money-laundering charges. He is sentenced to forty years in prison on July 10, 1992.

- On January 9, in *University of Pennsylvania* and *E.E.O.C.* the Supreme Court ruled that requiring a university to disclose confidential peer review materials in a racial discrimination investigation does not violate the First Amendment.

- On January 17, in *Swaggart Ministries* and *California Board of Equalization,* the Supreme Court rules that California's imposition of a sales and use tax on the sale of religious materials does not violate the Free Exercise or Establishment Clauses of the First Amendment.

- On January 18, Raymond Buckey and Peggy McMartin Buckey, former preschool operators in California, are acquitted of fifty-two child molestation charges.

- On January 18, Washington, D.C. mayor Marion Barry is arrested on drug charges.

- On January 19, former Supreme Court Justice Arthur J. Goldberg dies.

- On March 12, Clarence Thomas, who was nominated by President George Bush, takes the oath of office as a judge on the U.S. Court of Appeals for the District of Columbia Circuit.

- On March 23, a judge in Alaska sentences former Exxon Valdez captain Joseph Hazelwood to help clean up Prince William Sound and to pay fifty thousand dollars for his part in the 1989 oil spill. Hazelwood was convicted by a jury on March 22 of the negligent discharge of oil, but acquitted on three other more serious charges.

- On April 18, the Supreme Court rules in *Osborne v. Ohio* that banning the possession of child pornography did not violate the First Amendment.

- On June 4, the Supreme Court rules in *Westside Community Schools v. Mergens* that a school board violated the Establishment Clause of the First Amendment when it denied permission to a group of students wishing to form an after-school student Christian club. The proposed club was to have the same privileges and meeting terms as other Westside clubs.

- On June 11, the Supreme Court rules in *U.S. v. Eichman* that the Federal Flag Protection Act of 1989 violated the First Amendment. The challenge to the statute arose when Eichman burned a flag on the steps of the U.S. Capitol.

- On June 14, the Supreme Court rules in *Michigan Department of State Police v. Sitz* that drunk driving roadblocks, which are publicized in advance, do not violate motorists' Fourth Amendment privacy rights.

- On June 25, the Supreme Court rules in *Cruzan v. Missouri Department of Health* that absent "clear and convincing" evidence that an incompetent person would have desired to have life-sustaining treatments withdrawn, parents or other relatives lacked the authority to make that decision on behalf of the patient.

- On June 27, the Supreme Court rules, in *Maryland v. Craig,* that permitting a child to testify via closed circuit television in a sexual abuse case does not violate the Confrontation Clause of the Sixth Amendment.

- On July 20, Justice Brennan retires from the Supreme Court.

- On August 10, Marion S. Barry, Jr., mayor of Washington, D.C., is found guilty on one misdemeanor charge of cocaine possession.

- On October 5, a gallery and its director are acquitted of obscenity charges by an Ohio jury for displaying sexually graphic photographs by Robert Mapplethorpe.

- On October 9, David Hackett Souter is sworn in as an associate justice of the Supreme Court.

1991

- On March 3, Rodney King is beaten by Los Angeles police officers following a high-speed automobile chase. The beating is caught on videotape.

- On March 20, the Supreme Court rules, in *Automobile Workers v. Johnson Controls,* that a policy barring all women, except those whose infertility was medically documented, from jobs involving actual or potential lead exposure violates Title VII of the 1964 Civil Rights Act.

- On March 22, a New Hampshire jury convicts Pamela Smart, a high school instructor, of murder and conspiracy for persuading her high school-aged lover to kill her husband.

- On June 21, the Supreme Court rules, in *Barnes v. Glen Theatre Inc.,* that a state may prohibit complete nudity in public places without violating the First Amendment.

- On July 22, serial killer Jeffrey L. Dahmer is arrested in Milwaukee, Wisconsin. Convicted in 1992, he is killed by a fellow prisoner on November 28, 1994.

- On October 1, after twenty-four years on the Supreme Court, Thurgood Marshall retires.

- On October 16, in Killeen, Texas, a man crashes his vehicle into a restaurant, kills twenty-three, and finally himself.

- On October 23, Clarence Thomas takes a seat on the Supreme Court.

- On December 10, in *Simon and Schuster v. New York Crime Victims Board,* the Supreme Court rules that New York's "Son of Sam" law, which was intended to prevent criminals from profiting from their crimes by selling their stories, violates the First Amendment.

- On December 11, William Kennedy Smith is acquitted in Florida of sexual assault and battery.

1992

- On March 26, boxing champion Mike Tyson receives six years in prison for raping a Miss Black America contestant.

- On April 2, mob boss John Gotti is convicted in New York on murder and racketeering charges.

- On April 10, Charles Keating, Jr., receives a nine-year prison sentence for swindling investors when his Lincoln Savings and Loan collapsed. His convictions were later overturned.

- On April 21, Robert Alton Harris becomes the first person to be executed in twenty-five years in California. The execution stemmed from the 1978 murder of two teenage boys.

- On April 29, rioting and looting claims fifty-four lives and causes $1 billion in damages in Los Angeles, after a jury acquits four police officers of most charges in the videotaped beating of Rodney King.

- On June 22, the Supreme Court invalidates a bias-motivated criminal ordinance in *R.A.V. v. St. Paul.* The case stemmed from the conviction of several teenagers who engaged in a cross-burning.

- On June 24, the Supreme Court rules that warnings about the dangers of cigarette smoking did not necessarily preclude lawsuits by injured smokers, in *Cippolone v. Liggett Group.*

- On June 26, the Secretary of the Navy H. Lawrence Garrett III resigns because of the Tailhook sex abuse scandal.

- On June 29, the Supreme Court upholds a woman's right to an abortion in *Planned Parenthood v. Casey,* but upholds restrictions imposed by the Pennsylvania legislature.

- On August 21, Samuel Weaver, the fourteen-year-old son of Randy Weaver, is shot and killed by a U.S. Marshal during a standoff between Weaver and federal agents at Ruby Ridge, Idaho. The following day, Weaver's wife, Vicki, is shot and killed by federal agents.

- On September 25, Gregory Kingsley, a minor at the time, is legally emancipated from his biological mother by a Florida judge on the grounds she neglected and abused him.

- On December 1, Amy Fisher is sentenced for shooting and seriously wounding Mary Jo Buttafuoco, the wife of her boyfriend, on May 19.

- On December 24, President Bush pardons six persons involved in the Iran-Contra affair, including former Defense Secretary Caspar Weinberger.

1993

- On January 12, President Clinton asks Attorney General Janet Reno to appoint a special counsel to investigate the Whitewater real estate dealings.

- On January 13, in *Nixon and U.S.,* the Supreme Court refuses to interfere in the impeachment of federal district judge Walter Nixon.

- On January 24, former Justice Thurgood Marshall dies.

- On January 25, a gunman kills two CIA employees outside agency headquarters in Virginia.

- On February 5, Kimba Wood, a federal judge and President Clinton's appointee for attorney general, withdraws her name from nomination because she had employed an illegal alien babysitter for years.

- On February 8, General Motors sues NBC, alleging that "Dateline NBC" rigged crashes showing that GM pickups were prone to fires. NBC quickly settled the lawsuit.

- On February 26, the World Trade Center in New York City is bombed, killing six and injuring more than a thousand people. Several Islamic extremists are later arrested and convicted for the attack.

- On February 28, the standoff between federal agents and the Branch Davidians begins when ninety heavily-armed Bureau of Alcohol, Tobacco, and Firearms (ATF) agents attempt to serve a search and arrest warrant at the Mt. Carmel compound near Waco, Texas. Four agents and six Davidians are killed.

- On March 10, Dr. David Gunn is shot to death outside the Pensacola, Florida, abortion clinic where he worked.

- On March 13, Janet Reno becomes the first female attorney general of the U.S., after having been unanimously confirmed by the Senate the day before.

- On April 19, the standoff at Mt. Carmel ends in a massive conflagration of the Branch Davidian compound. David Koresh, leader of the group, and dozens of his followers are killed.

- On June 18, the Supreme Court rules in *Zobrest v. Catalina Foothills School District* that a school district may not refuse to provide an interpreter for a deaf child who attends a parochial school.

- On June 28, Byron White, associate justice of the Supreme Court, retires, after thirty-one years on the bench.

- On July 8, Randy Weaver and Kevin Harris are found not guilty of the death of a federal agent during the 1992 standoff at Ruby Ridge. Weaver is also acquitted on weapons trafficking charges.

- On July 20, White House Deputy Counsel Vincent W. Foster, Jr., is found dead in Fort Marcy Park, Virginia. The death was determined to be a suicide.

- On August 10, Ruth Bader Ginsburg takes the oath as associate justice of the U.S. Supreme Court.

- On November 15, Joey Buttafuoco receives six months in jail for the statutory rape of Amy Fisher, his teenage girlfriend who shot and injured Buttafuoco's wife.

- On November 30, Richard Allen Davis is arrested in California. Davis confesses to abducting twelve-year-old Polly Klaas from her bedroom in Petaluma and killing her. Davis is sentenced to death.

1994

- On January 21, Lorena (Gallo) Bobbitt, charged with malicious wounding for cutting off the penis of her husband, John Wayne Bobbitt, is found not guilty by reason of insanity and is committed to a mental health facility for observation.

- On February 1, Jeff Gillooly enters a guilty plea for his part in the January 6, 1994 attack on skater Nancy Kerrigan.

- On February 4, Byron De La Beckwith is convicted in Mississippi of the 1963 murder of civil rights leader Medgar Evers. De La Beckwith receives a life sentence.

- On March 14, Webster Hubbell, associate attorney general and longtime friend of President and Mrs. Clinton, resigns over a billing controversy stemming from his earlier private law practice in Arkansas. On June 28, 1995, he receives a prison sentence of twenty-one months.

- On March 16, Olympic skater Tonya Harding pleads guilty and is fined one hundred thousand dollars by an Oregon judge for her role in covering up the attack on ice skating rival Nancy Kerrigan.

- On April 19, Rodney King is awarded $3.8 million in damages for his 1991 beating by four Los Angeles police officers.

- On April 28, Aldrich Ames, former CIA official, pleads guilty to espionage and tax evasion charges stemming from years of spying for the Soviet Union and Russia. Ames receives life in prison.

- On May 10, convicted serial killer John Wayne Gacy, Jr., is executed by lethal injection in Illinois. During the 1970s he killed thirty-three young men and boys.

- On May 24, four men convicted in the World Trade Center bombing are each sentenced to 240 years in prison.

- On June 12, Nicole Brown Simpson and Ronald Goldman are brutally murdered outside her Los Angeles home; Simpson's ex-husband and former football star, O.J. Simpson, is arrested days later following a slow-motion police chase.

- On August 3, Stephen Gerald Breyer is sworn in as an Associate Justice of the U.S. Supreme Court of the United States. He was nominated by President Clinton.

- On August 11, a federal jury awards $286.8 million to about ten thousand commercial fishermen for losses resulting from the 1989 Exxon Valdez oil spill.

- On November 3, Susan Smith is arrested for drowning her two young sons, nine days after she claimed the boys had been kidnapped by a carjacker. A jury rejects the death penalty for Smith on July 28, 1995; instead she is sentenced to life in prison.

1995

- On February 7, Ramzi Yousef is arrested in Pakistan for his role in the 1993 bombing of the World Trade Center.

- On March 22, Colin Ferguson receives life in prison for the 1993 killings of six people on the Long Island Rail Road commuter train.

- On March 31, singer Selena is shot and killed in Texas by Yolanda Saldivar, the woman who founded her fan club. Salvidar is convicted of the murder on October 23.

- On April 19, a bomb explodes at the Alfred P. Murrah Federal Building in Oklahoma City, Oklahoma, killing 168 people and injuring more than 500, in the most deadly do-

mestic terrorist attack in U.S. history. Timothy McVeigh is later convicted and executed for masterminding the explosion.

- On May 24, Heidi Fleiss is sentenced to three years in prison for her Hollywood call girl ring.

- On May 22, in *Wilson v. Arkansas,* the Supreme Court rules that the Fourth Amendment requires police officers to knock and announce their presence before entering a private residence.

- On June 19, in *Hurley v. Irish American Gay Group of Boston,* the Supreme Court rules that it is a violation of the First and Fourteenth Amendments to require a private group of citizens organizing a parade to include in the parade others desiring to express a message that the organizers do not wish to convey.

- On June 25, Warren E. Burger, retired chief justice of the Supreme Court, dies. Warren was appointed by President Richard Nixon in 1969 and retired in 1986.

- On June 26, in *Veronia School District v. Acton,* the Supreme Court rules that random drug testing of student athletes does not violate the Fourth Amendment.

- On June 29, in *Rosenberger v. University of Virginia,* the Supreme Court rules that the First Amendment requires the University of Virginia to subsidize student religious publication on the same basis as other student publications.

- On September 19, with the approval of the Federal Bureau of Investigation (FBI), *The New York Times* and *The Washington Post* publish the Unabomber Manifesto, which rails against modern technology and environmental destruction, two areas in which the bombing attacks had been targeted.

- On October 3, O.J. Simpson is acquitted of the murders of his former wife, Nicole Brown Simpson, and Ronald Goldman.

- On November 7, three U.S. servicemen admit in a Japanese courtroom that they ambushed and raped a twelve-year-old Okinawa schoolgirl.

- On November 22, in *U.S. v. National Treasury Employees Union,* the Supreme Court rules that an across-the-board ban on federal employees' acceptance of honoraria violates the First Amendment's free speech provisions.

1996

- On January 26, First Lady Hillary Rodham Clinton testifies before a grand jury in connection with the Whitewater investigation.

- On March 25, a standoff begins between federal law enforcement officials and antigovernment Freeman at a ranch near Jordan, Montana. After eighty-one days, sixteen members of the group surrender to the FBI.

- On April 3, Theodore John "Ted" Kaczynski is arrested by FBI agents at his Montana cabin in connection with the Unabomber case. The FBI was tipped off to the identity and whereabouts of the alleged bomber by his brother David.

- On April 9, Dan Rostenkowski, former chairman of the House Ways and Means Committee, pleads guilty to two counts of mail fraud. He is sentenced to seventeen months in prison.

• On April 28, President Clinton provides more than four hours of videotaped testimony as a defense witness in the criminal trial of Whitewater defendants.

• On March 20, a jury rejects the death penalty for Lyle and Erik Menendez. Instead the brothers receive life in prison without parole in the shotgun murders of their parents, Kitty and Jose Menendez.

• On May 20, the Supreme Court found that an amendment to Colorado's constitution violated the Fourteenth Amendment's Equal Protection Clause. In *Romer v. Evans,* the high court invalidated the amendment, which precluded any governmental action intended to protect persons from discrimination based on their sexual orientation.

• On June 26, in *U.S. v. Virginia,* the Supreme Court finds that Virginia's Military Institute's plan to establish a separate military school for females violates the Equal Protection Clause of the Fourteenth Amendment.

• On July 27, a pipe bomb explodes at a park in Atlanta during the Olympics. One person is killed and more than one hundred are injured.

• On August 20, Susan McDougal is sentenced to two years in prison for her role in obtaining an illegal loan for the Whitewater land deal. Less than a month later, before beginning this sentence, she is jailed for contempt of court for refusing to testify before a grand jury about President Clinton's possible involvement in Whitewater.

• On September 7, rapper Tupac Shakur is shot in Las Vegas. He dies six days later.

• On October 2, former detective Mark Fuhrman, known for his role in investigating the O.J. Simpson case, pleads no contest to perjury charges.

• On October 26, federal officials clear former security guard Richard Jewell of involvement in the Atlanta Olympic Park bombing.

• On November 12, Jonathan Schmitz is convicted of second-degree murder for shooting Scott Amedure. Amedure was a gay man who had revealed a crush on Schmitz during a taping of the "The Jenny Jones Show." In 1999 a Michigan jury orders the show to pay Amedure's family $25 million.

• On December 26, six-year-old JonBenet Ramsey, a child beauty queen, is found dead in her Boulder, Colorado, home. No arrest is made.

1997

• On January 16, two bombs explode just an hour apart and injure six people at an Atlanta abortion clinic.

• On January 23, Mir Aimal Kasi is sentenced to death for the 1993 killings at CIA headquarters.

• On February 4, a California jury finds O.J. Simpson civilly liable for the deaths of his ex-wife, Nicole Brown Simpson, and Ronald Goldman.

• On February 19, in *Schenck* and *Pro-Choice Network of Western New York,* the Supreme Court rules that fixed buffer zones which prohibited demonstrations within fifteen feet of entrances to abortion clinics, parking lots, or driveways, are permitted under the First Amendment, but floating buffer zones around people or moving vehicles are not.

• On February 19, in *Regents of the University of California* and *Doe,* the Supreme Court rules that the Eleventh Amendment protects state-run schools from being sued unwillingly in federal court, even where any award of monetary damages would come from a third party, rather than the state.

• On February 23, a Palestinian male kills one person and wounds six before killing himself when he opens fire on the observation deck of the Empire State Building.

• On February 25, a Pennsylvania jury convicts multimillionaire John E. du Pont of third-degree murder, but finds he was mentally ill when he killed world-class wrestler David Schultz.

• On March 9, Christopher Wallace, better known as gangsta rapper The Notorious B.I.G., is killed in a drive-by shooting in Los Angeles.

• On March 20, cigarette maker Ligget Group settles twenty-two state lawsuits. The company agrees to include a warning on every pack that smoking is addictive. It also admits that the industry markets cigarettes to teenagers.

• On March 27, Dexter King, the son of Martin Luther King, Jr., meets with his father's convicted assassin, James Earl Ray. Ray denies involvement in the shooting, and Dexter King announces he believes him.

• On April 14, James B. McDougal is sentenced to three years in prison for his conviction on eighteen fraud and conspiracy charges in the Whitewater land deal.

• On April 29, a military drill instructor, Delmar Simpson, is convicted of raping six female trainees. Simpson is dishonorably discharged and given a twenty-five-year sentence.

• On May 22, Kelly Flinn, the Air Force's first female bomber pilot certified for combat, accepts a general discharge. By doing so she avoids court-martial for adultery, lying, and disobeying an order.

• On May 27, the U.S. Supreme Court rules unanimously in *Clinton v. Jones* that President Clinton could not delay the civil suit brought against him by Paula Corbin Jones. He wanted to delay the proceedings until he left office.

• On May 30, Jesse K. Timmendequas is convicted in Trenton, New Jersey, of raping and strangling Megan Kanka, a seven-year-old neighbor, in 1994. He is later sentenced to death. Megan's murder inspired "Megan's Law," requiring that communities be notified when sex offenders move in.

• On June 2, Timothy James McVeigh is convicted on murder, conspiracy to commit murder, use of weapons of mass destruction, and conspiracy to use weapons of mass destruction charges in connection with the Murrah Federal Building bombing in Oklahoma City. On August 14, 1997 he is sentenced to death by lethal injection.

• On June 20, the tobacco industry agrees to a massive settlement.

• On June 23, the U.S. Supreme Court rules, in *Idaho v. Coeur D'alene Tribe of Idaho,* that the Eleventh Amendment bars suits by Indian tribes against state governments.

• On June 23, the U.S. Supreme Court rules, in *Agostini v. Felton,* that the Establishment Clause of the First Amendment is not violated when public school teachers instruct in a parochial school. The decision overruled the 1985 case of *Aguilar v. Felton.*

• On June 23, Betty Shabazz, civil rights activist and widow of Malcolm X, dies in New York of burns sustained in a fire set by her twelve-year-old grandson on June 1.

• On June 24, the U.S. Supreme Court refuses to hear President Clinton's appeal regarding his claim to lawyer-client privilege regarding subpoenaed notes dealing with Whitewater.

• On June 24, Melissa Drexler is charged with murder in the death of her newborn son. Drexler gave birth at her high school prom. She eventually served three years for aggravated manslaughter.

• On June 26, the Supreme Court holds unconstitutional parts of the 1996 Communications Decency Act. In *Reno v. ACLU,* the high court invalidated portions of the law on the basis of the First and Fifth Amendments, holding that the law was overly broad and vague in defining what types of internet activity were to be criminalized.

• On June 26, the Supreme Court rules in *Washington v. Glucksberg,* that Washington's ban on physician-assisted suicide did not violate the constitutional rights of competent terminally ill adults. The high court reaches the same conclusion regarding a New York law in *Vacco v. Quill.*

• On June 26, the Supreme Court held unconstitutional part of the Brady Handgun Violence Protection in *Printz v. U.S.*

• On July 15, Gianni Versace is shot outside his Miami home. Suspected killer Andrew Cunanan apparently kills himself eight days later.

• On July 24, former associate justice William J. Brennan, Jr., dies.

• On September 3, Arizona Governor Fyfe Symington is convicted on charges that he illegally obtained loans for his real estate business. His conviction is overturned in 1999, and in 2001 President Clinton pardons him.

• On September 25, sportscaster Marv Albert pleads guilty on assault and battery charges for biting a girlfriend.

• On November 3, Attorney General Janet Reno determines that President Clinton did not violate the law by holding White House coffees and permitting big contributors to spend the night at the White House.

• On November 10, a Massachusetts judge reduces English au pair Louise Woodward's murder conviction to manslaughter and reduces her sentence to time served (279 days) for the death of eight-month-old Matthew Eappen.

• On November 12, Ramzi Yousef is found guilty of planning the 1993 bombing of the World Trade Center.

• On December 1, a fourteen-year-old student opens fire on a morning prayer group at a high school in West Paducah, Kentucky. Three are killed and five wounded. In October 1998 Michael Carneal pleads guilty by reason of mental illness and receives life in prison, without the possibility of parole for twenty-five years.

• On December 23, Terry Lynn Nichols is convicted of conspiracy to use weapons of mass destruction and manslaughter in connection with the bombing of the Murrah Federal Building in Oklahoma City. He is sentenced to life in prison without the possibility of parole.

1998

• On January 29, a bomb explodes at a Birmingham, Alabama, abortion clinic and kills an off-duty policeman and severely wounds a nurse.

• On February 3, Karla Faye Tucker Brown, convicted of two brutal murders in 1983, is executed in Texas. She is the first woman to be executed in the United States in the decade and the first in Texas since 1863. On March 30, Judias V. Buenoano, who poisoned her husband, is electrocuted in Florida; she is the first female put to death in the state in 150 years.

• On February 26, Oprah Winfrey is vindicated by a Texas jury when it rejects an $11 million lawsuit brought by Texas cattlemen who blamed Winfrey for a price fall after she aired a segment on mad-cow disease on her talk show.

• On March 23, the Supreme Court upholds term limits for state lawmakers.

• On March 24, two young boys open fire outside their Jonesboro, Arkansas, school, killing four students, one teacher, and injuring ten others.

• On April 1, U.S. District Judge Susan Webber Wright dismisses Paula Jones' sexual harassment lawsuit against President William Clinton.

• On May 4, Unabomber Kaczynski receives a life sentence without parole in exchange for a guilty plea.

• On May 26, the Supreme Court decides, in *New Jersey v. New York,* that New Jersey has sovereign authority under lands on Ellis Island that had previously been submerged, despite an 1834 pact giving New York over Ellis Island.

• On May 27, Michael Fortier receives twelve years for not warning anyone about the plan to bomb the Murrah building in Oklahoma City.

• On May 28, actor Phil Hartman is shot in his Encino home by his wife, Brynn, who then kills herself.

• On May 28, Arkansas Governor Jim Guy Tucker and James and Susan McDougal, are convicted of fraud. They were President Clinton's business partners in the Whitewater land deal.

• On June 7, African American James Byrd, Jr., is dragged to his death behind a pickup truck. On February 25, 1999, a Texas jury sentences white supremacist John William King to death for the murder. Another defendant, Shawn Allen Berry, is convicted on November 18, 1999, but the jury does not impose the death penalty.

• On June 12, a Mississippi jury convicts Luke Woodham, seventeen, of killing two students and wounding seven others at Pearl High School.

• On June 26, the Supreme Court rules in *Burlington Industries v. Ellerth* that employers may be liable for their supervisors' misconduct in sexual harassment cases, even if the company knew nothing about the behavior.

• On July 24, a man kills two police officers in the U.S. Capitol. The gunman is wounded and arrested.

- On August 6, in Philadelphia, Marie Noe is charged with first-degree murder for the smothering deaths of eight of her children between 1949 and 1968.

- On August 6, Monica Lewinsky testifies before a grand jury concerning her relationship with President Clinton. She was given immunity from prosecution on July 28.

- On August 17, President Clinton answers questions before a grand jury about the Monica Lewinsky affair.

- On August 25, Lewis F. Powell, Jr., dies. Powell served as an associate justice from 1972 to 1987.

- On August 26, Attorney General Janet Reno reopens the investigation into the assassination of Martin Luther King, Jr.

- On September 21, the video recording of President Clinton's grand jury testimony regarding his relationship with former White House intern Monica S. Lewinsky is televised.

- On October 12, Matthew Shepard, a gay college student, dies from injuries suffered five days earlier when he was beaten, robbed and tied to a wooden fence post outside of Laramie, Wyoming.

- On October 14, federal authorities charge Eric Robert Rudolph with the bombing at the 1996 Summer Olympics in Atlanta. Rudolph's whereabouts are unknown.

- On October 23, Dr. Bernard Slepian is shot in his home in Buffalo, New York, by an anti-abortion sniper.

- On November 13, President Clinton settles his sexual harassment lawsuit with Paula Jones, agreeing to pay her $850,000, but neither admitting guilt nor apologizing.

- On December 1, in *Minnesota v. Carter,* the Supreme Court rules that household visitors do not enjoy the same Fourth Amendment search and seizure protections in a home as do residents or overnight guests.

- On December 2, a federal jury acquits former Clinton administration Agriculture Department secretary Albert Michael "Mike" Espy of corruption. He had been charged on August 27, 1998.

1999

- On March 3, in *Cedar Rapids Community School District v. Garret F. and Charlene F.,* the Supreme Court ruled that schools receiving federal funding under the Individuals with Disabilities Education Act must pay for one-on-one nursing assistance for certain disabled students.

- On March 4, retired associate justice Harry A. Blackmun dies.

- On March 22, Dr. Jack Kevorkian goes on trial in Michigan for assisting in a suicide that was videotaped and shown on the television show "60 Minutes." Kevorkian acts as his own lawyer.

- On March 30, an Oregon jury awards $81 million from the Philip Morris Company to a deceased man's family. The man died from lung cancer after smoking Marlboros for decades.

- On March 31, four New York police officers are charged in the February 4 killing of Amadou Diallo, an immigrant from Africa.

- On April 5, in *Mitchell v. U.S.,* the Supreme Court rules that entering a guilty plea in federal court does not waive a defendant's Fifth Amendment privilege against self-incrimination during sentencing.

- On April 12, for the first time in U.S. history, a sitting president is held in contempt of civil court. U.S. District Court Judge Susan Webber Wright holds Clinton in contempt for "giving false, misleading and evasive answers that were designed to obstruct the judicial process" when he was asked about his relationship with Lewinsky. Clinton is required to pay the Court twelve hundred dollars.

- On April 13, Dr. Jack Kevorkian received a sentence of ten to twenty-five years for assisting the suicide of Thomas Youk. The 1998 assisted suicide was videotaped and shown on the television show, "60 Minutes."

- On April 20, Dylan Klebold and Eric Harris go on a rampage at Columbine High School in Littleton, Colorado, killing twelve students, one teacher, and finally themselves.

- On May 24, in the case of *Wilson v. Layne,* the Supreme Court holds that an accused's Fourth Amendment guarantees against unreasonable search and seizure are violated when police allow media personnel to accompany them when executing a search warrant.

- On May 24, in the case of *Davis v. Monroe County Board of Education,* the Supreme Court holds that a school board can be held liable under Title IX of the Education Amendments of 1972 for the harassment of one student by another.

- On June 10, in the case of *Chicago v. Morales,* the Supreme Court invalidates a Chicago ordinance making it unlawful for "criminal street gang members" to loiter in public places.

- On July 7, a jury in Miami holds cigarette makers liable for making a defective product that causes emphysema, lung cancer and other illnesses.

- On July 29, a day trader in Atlanta opens fire in two brokerage offices. He kills nine people and wounds thirteen, then turns the gun on himself. In addition, he kills his wife and two children.

- On July 30, Linda Tripp is charged in Maryland with illegally wiretapping phone conversations with Monica Lewinsky. The charges are later dropped.

- On September 15, Larry Ashbrook opens fire in a Fort Worth, Texas, church, killing seven and himself.

- On September 24, seventeen-year-old Kip Kinkel pleads guilty to killing his parents and two classmates in Springfield, Oregon on May 23, 1998.

- On October 7, American Home Products Corporation agrees to a settlement of up to $4.83 billion regarding allegations that the fen-phen diet drug combination caused dangerous heart valve problems.

- On November 4, one day after his conviction, Aaron McKinney, the murderer of gay college student Matthew Shepard, agrees never to appeal his conviction and accepts life in prison in exchange for escaping the death penalty.

- On November 5, a U.S. District Judge rules that computer software giant Microsoft Corporation is a monopoly.

• On December 6, SabreTech, an aircraft maintenance company, is convicted for mishandling oxygen canisters aboard a ValuJet plane that crashed in the Everglades and killed 110 people in 1996.

• On December 10, Wen Ho Lee is arrested on charges that he removed secrets from secure computers at the Los Alamos weapons lab, where he worked as a computer scientist.

Arizona v. Fulminante

Supreme Court decision

By: Byron White and William H. Rehnquist

Date: March 26, 1991

Source: White, Byron, and William H. Rehnquist. *Arizona v. Fulminante,* 499 U.S. 279 (1991). Available online at http://laws.findlaw.com/us/499/279.html; website home page http://laws.findlaw.com (accessed May 4, 2003).

About the Authors: Byron White (1917–2002) was a Rhodes Scholar and talented athlete in college. He got his law degree from Yale University and played for a short time in the NFL. President John F. Kennedy (served 1961–1963) appointed White to the United States Supreme Court in 1962, and White served as an associate justice until 1993.

William H. Rehnquist (1924–), after military service in World War II (1939–1945), received degrees from Stanford and Harvard, before graduating from Stanford Law School. President Richard Nixon (served 1969–1974) appointed Rehnquist to the Supreme Court in 1971. In 1986, President Ronald Reagan (served 1981–1989) appointed Rehnquist Chief Justice, and Rehnquist has generally led the court in a more conservative direction. ■

Introduction

The Bill of Rights amended the United States Constitution in 1791, stating certain rights held by all Americans. However, the meaning and proper application of these rights were (and are) not self-evident, especially in the context of the criminal justice system. An established principle of American law is that coerced confessions may not be used in a court of law against a defendant accused of a crime. Until the 1960s, different criminal procedures and constitutional protections very often applied at the state and federal level. The police also often had, especially after police forces were institutionalized, incentives for discouraging people to pursue their constitutional rights—as those policemen with higher confession rates and cleared cases were likely to be promoted faster. It was also unclear under the Constitution whether individuals had to be informed of their rights.

In the 1960s, the Warren Court began increasing the constitutional protections for criminal defendants and applying the same level of constitutional protections to de-

fendants in both state and federal courts. In 1963, the Warren Court, at the urging of twenty-three states uncertain as to when indigent defendants had to receive appointed counsel, held that the right to counsel was fundamental to a fair trial. In 1964, the Court held that a confession obtained when a defendant was not able to consult his lawyer, and was not informed of his right to remain silent, was inadmissible in state courts. Finally, in 1966, in *Miranda v. Arizona,* the Supreme Court held that the police were required to inform defendants of their constitutional rights.

Miranda was in some ways the high point of defendants' rights, because since that time, the Burger and Rehnquist courts generally have moved to limit them. The courts have generally held that any counsel fulfills one's constitutional right to counsel—a lawyer falling asleep in a death penalty case was not enough to overturn a conviction. In 1991, the Supreme Court heard a case dealing with the introduction of a coerced confession in *Arizona v. Fulminante.* Fulminante was suspected of the murder of his stepdaughter, but had not been tried. He was convicted and imprisoned on an unrelated felony in New York, where he encountered an FBI informant. Fulminante was being threatened due to other prisoners' beliefs that Fulminante had killed his stepdaughter. The informant, posing as a mob boss, offered Fulminante protection in prison if Fulminante told him the truth about his kids. Fulminante then confessed. He also provided a second, more detailed confession six months later. Fulminante returned to Arizona and was convicted of murdering his stepdaughter, based in part on the confessions.

Significance

The Supreme Court overturned the conviction of Fulminante, because it had been obtained in part through the use of a coerced confession. The important thing, though, was the standard used by Chief Justice Rehnquist in determining when the use of a coerced confession must cause the verdict to be overturned. Rehnquist and the majority of the court held that if the introduction of a coerced confession was merely a "harmless error" (the appellate court would need to review the remainder of the record to determine whether the admission of the confession was harmless beyond a reasonable doubt) then the conviction could still stand; and if it was not, then the conviction must be overturned and a new trial ordered. Previously, any use of a coerced confession in court generally caused the conviction to be overturned. This battle was won—another coerced confession was excluded—but the war to protect defendants' rights may have been lost because coerced confessions may be allowed in the future. It might not seem very important to protect Fulminante, as he confessed twice to brutally murdering his stepdaughter, but it is important to consider what crimes people might confess to, even if they have not done them, in order to be protected in a prison.

Primary Source

Arizona v. Fulminante [excerpt]

SYNOPSIS: White first holds that there was a credible threat of violence. He and three other dissenting judges stated that the admission of a coerced confession can never be harmless error; that the conviction must be overturned, and the case remanded for a new trial to exclude the first confession. Rehnquist holds, for the court, that the admission of a confession can be a harmless error, but, in dissent, argues that there was no coerced confession here.

Justice White delivered the opinion Parts I, II, and IV of which are the opinion of the Court, and Part III of which is a dissenting opinion. . . .

We deal first with the State's contention that the court below erred in holding Fulminante's confession to have been coerced. The State argues that it is the totality of the circumstances that determines whether Fulminante's confession was coerced, . . . but contends that, rather than apply this standard, the Arizona court applied a "but for" test, under which the court found that but for the promise given by Sarivola, Fulminante would not have confessed. . . . Indeed, the Arizona Supreme Court stated that a "determination regarding the voluntariness of a confession . . . must be viewed in a totality of the circumstances," . . . and under that standard plainly found that Fulminante's statement to Sarivola had been coerced.

. . . The Arizona Court declared: "[T]he confession was obtained as a direct result of extreme coercion, and was tendered in the belief that the defendant's life was in jeopardy if he did not confess. This is a true coerced confession in every sense of the word." . . .

We normally give great deference to the factual findings of the state court. . . . Nevertheless, "the ultimate issue of 'voluntariness' is a legal question requiring independent federal determination." . . .

Although the question is a close one, we agree with the Arizona Supreme Court's conclusion that Fulminante's confession was coerced. The Arizona Supreme Court found a credible threat of physical violence unless Fulminante confessed. Our cases have made clear that a finding of coercion need not depend upon actual violence by a government agent; a credible threat is sufficient. . . . Accepting the Arizona court's finding, permissible on this record, that there was a credible threat of physical violence, we agree with its conclusion that Fulminante's will was overborne in such a way as to render his confession the product of coercion.

Four of us, Justices Marshall, Blackmun, Stevens, and myself, would affirm the judgment of the Arizona Supreme Court on the ground that the harmless error rule is inapplicable to erroneously admitted coerced confessions. We thus disagree with the Justices who have contrary views.

The majority today abandons what until now the Court has regarded as the "axiomatic [proposition] that a defendant in a criminal case is deprived of due process of law if his conviction is founded, in whole or in part, upon an involuntary confession, without regard for the truth or falsity of the confession . . . The Court has repeatedly stressed that the view that the admission of a coerced confession can be harmless error because of the other evidence to support the verdict is "an impermissible doctrine," . . . for "the admission in evidence, over objection, of the coerced confession vitiates the judgment because it violates the Due Process Clause of the Fourteenth Amendment." . . . Today, a majority of the Court, without any justification, . . . overrules this vast body of precedent without a word, and, in so doing, dislodges one of the fundamental tenets of our criminal justice system.

In extending to coerced confessions the harmless error rule of *Chapman v. California,* . . . the majority declares that because the Court has applied that analysis to numerous other "trial errors," there is no reason that it should not apply to an error of this nature as well. The four of us remain convinced, however, that we should abide by our cases that have refused to apply the harmless error rule to coerced confessions, for a coerced confession is fundamentally different from other types of erroneously admitted evidence to which the rule has been applied. Indeed, as the majority concedes, *Chapman* itself recognized that prior cases "have indicated that there are some constitutional rights so basic to a fair trial that their infraction can never be treated as harmless error," and it placed in that category the constitutional rule against using a defendant's coerced confession against him at his criminal trial. . . .

The inability to assess its effect on a conviction causes the admission at trial of a coerced confession to "defy analysis by 'harmless error' standards," cf. post, at 309 (opinion of Rehnquist, C.J.), just as certainly as do deprivation of counsel and trial before a biased judge.

. . . [O]mission of a reasonable doubt instruction, though a "trial error," distorts the very structure of the trial, because it creates the risk that the jury will convict the defendant even if the State has not met its required burden of proof. . . .

These same concerns counsel against applying harmless error analysis to the admission of a coerced confession. A defendant's confession is "probably the most probative and damaging evidence that can be admitted against him," . . . so damaging that a jury should not be expected to ignore it even if told to do so, . . . and because, in any event, it is impossible to know what credit and weight the jury gave to the confession.

. . . The search for truth is indeed central to our system of justice, but "certain constitutional rights are not, and should not be, subject to harmless error analysis, because those rights protect important values that are unrelated to the truthseeking function of the trial." . . . The right of a defendant not to have his coerced confession used against him is among those rights, for using a coerced confession "abort[s] the basic trial process" and "render[s] a trial fundamentally unfair." . . .

For the foregoing reasons, the four of us would adhere to the consistent line of authority that has recognized as a basic tenet of our criminal justice system, before and after both *Miranda* and *Chapman,* the prohibition against using a defendant's coerced confession against him at his criminal trial. Stare decisis is "of fundamental importance to the rule of law," . . . the majority offers no convincing reason for overturning our long line of decisions requiring the exclusion of coerced confessions.

Since five Justices have determined that harmless error analysis applies to coerced confessions, it becomes necessary to evaluate under that ruling the admissibility of Fulminante's confession to Sarivola. . . . In so doing, it must be determined whether the State has met its burden of demonstrating that the admission of the confession to Sarivola did not contribute to Fulminante's conviction. . . . Five of us are of the view that the State has not carried its burden, and accordingly affirm the judgment of the court below reversing petitioner's conviction.

A confession is like no other evidence. . . . In the case of a coerced confession such as that given by Fulminante to Sarivola, the risk that the confes-

sion is unreliable, coupled with the profound impact that the confession has upon the jury, requires a reviewing court to exercise extreme caution before determining that the admission of the confession at trial was harmless. . . .

We have a quite different evaluation of the evidence. Our review of the record leads us to conclude that the State has failed to meet its burden of establishing, beyond a reasonable doubt, that the admission of Fulminante's confession to Anthony Sarivola was harmless error. . . . Because a majority of the Court has determined that Fulminante's confession to Anthony Sarivola was coerced, and because a majority has determined that admitting this confession was not harmless beyond a reasonable doubt, we agree with the Arizona Supreme Court's conclusion that Fulminante is entitled to a new trial at which the confession is not admitted. Accordingly the judgment of the Arizona Supreme Court is

Affirmed. . . .

Chief Justice Rehnquist, with whom Justice O'Connor joins, Justice Kennedy and Justice Souter join as to Parts I and II, and Justice Scalia joins as to Parts II and III, delivering the opinion of the Court as to Part II, and dissenting as to Parts I and III.

The Court today properly concludes that the admission of an "involuntary" confession at trial is subject to harmless error analysis. Nonetheless, the independent review of the record which we are required to make shows that respondent Fulminante's confession was not, in fact, involuntary. And even if the confession were deemed to be involuntary, the evidence offered at trial, including a second, untainted confession by Fulminante, supports the conclusion that any error here was certainly harmless. . . .

The admissibility of a confession such as that made by respondent Fulminante depends upon whether it was voluntarily made. . . .

I am at a loss to see how the Supreme Court of Arizona reached the conclusion that it did. Fulminante offered no evidence that he believed that his life was in danger or that he, in fact, confessed to Sarivola in order to obtain the proffered protection. . . . The decision of the Supreme Court of Arizona rests on an assumption that is squarely contrary to this stipulation, and one that is not supported by any testimony of Fulminante. . . .

Fulminante was an experienced habitue of prisons, and presumably able to fend for himself. In concluding on these facts that Fulminante's confession was involuntary, the Court today embraces a more expansive definition of that term than is warranted by any of our decided cases.

Since this Court's landmark decision in *Chapman v. California,,* in which we adopted the general rule that a constitutional error does not automatically require reversal of a conviction, the Court has applied harmless error analysis to a wide range of errors, and has recognized that most constitutional errors can be harmless. . . .

The common thread connecting these cases is that each involved "trial error"—error which occurred during the presentation of the case to the jury, and which may therefore be quantitatively assessed in the context of other evidence presented in order to determine whether its admission was harmless beyond a reasonable doubt. . . .

It is on the basis of this language in *Chapman* that Justice White, in dissent, concludes that the principle of stare decisis requires us to hold that an involuntary confession is not subject to harmless error analysis. I believe that there are several reasons which lead to a contrary conclusion. In the first place, the quoted language from *Chapman* does not, by its terms, adopt any such rule in that case. . . .

The admission of an involuntary confession—a classic "trial error"—is markedly different from the other two constitutional violations referred to in the *Chapman* footnote as not being subject to harmless error analysis. . . . Each of these constitutional deprivations is a similar structural defect affecting the framework within which the trial proceeds, rather than simply an error in the trial process itself. . . .

It is evident from a comparison of the constitutional violations which we have held subject to harmless error, and those which we have held not, that involuntary statements or confessions belong in the former category. The admission of an involuntary confession is a "trial error," similar in both degree and kind to the erroneous admission of other types of evidence. The evidentiary impact of an involuntary confession, and its effect upon the composition of the record, is indistinguishable from that of a confession obtained in violation of the Sixth Amendment—of evidence seized in violation of the Fourth Amendment—or of a prosecutor's improper comment on a defendant's silence at trial in violation of the Fifth Amendment. When reviewing the erroneous admission of an involuntary confession, the appellate court, as it does with the admission of other forms of improperly admitted evidence, simply reviews the remainder of the evidence against the defendant to determine whether the admission of the confession was harmless beyond a reasonable doubt.

Nor can it be said that the admission of an involuntary confession is the type of error which "transcends the criminal process." This Court has applied harmless error analysis to the violation of other constitutional rights similar in magnitude and importance, and involving the same level of police misconduct. . . .

Of course an involuntary confession may have a more dramatic effect on the course of a trial than do other trial errors—in particular cases, it may be devastating to a defendant—but this simply means that a reviewing court will conclude in such a case that its admission was not harmless error; it is not a reason for eschewing the harmless error test entirely. The Supreme Court of Arizona, in its first opinion in the present case, concluded that the admission of Fulminante's confession was harmless error. That court concluded that a second and more explicit confession of the crime made by Fulminante after he was released from prison was not tainted by the first confession, and that the second confession, together with physical evidence from the wounds (the victim had been shot twice in the head with a large calibre weapon at close range and a ligature was found around her neck) and other evidence introduced at trial rendered the admission of the first confession harmless beyond a reasonable doubt. . . .

I would agree with the finding of the Supreme Court of Arizona in its initial opinion—in which it believed harmless error analysis was applicable to the admission of involuntary confessions—that the admission of Fulminante's confession was harmless. Indeed, this seems to me to be a classic case of harmless error: a second confession giving more details of the crime than the first was admitted in evidence and found to be free of any constitutional objection. Accordingly, I would affirm the holding of the Supreme Court of Arizona in its initial opinion, and reverse the judgment which it ultimately rendered in this case.

Further Resources

BOOKS

Bosmajian, Haig A. *The Freedom Not to Speak.* New York: New York University Press, 1999.

Davis, Sue Justice. *Rehnquist and the Constitution.* Princeton, N.J.: Princeton University Press, 1989.

Dudley, William. *The Bill of Rights: Opposing Viewpoints.* San Diego, Calif.: Greenhaven Press, 1994.

Hutchinson, Dennis J. *The Man Who Once was Whizzer White: a Portrait of Justice Byron R. White.* New York: Free Press, 1998.

Levy, Leonard Williams. *Origins of the Fifth Amendment: The Right Against Self-Incrimination.* New York: Oxford University Press, 1968.

PERIODICALS

Gangi, William. "The Supreme Court and Coerced Confessions: *Arizona v. Fulminante* in Perspective." *Harvard Journal of Law & Public Policy* 16, no. 2, Spring 1993, 493.

McAuley, Daniel G. Jr. "Rehnquist Loses Battle but Wins War of Harmless Error: *Arizona v. Fulminante.*" *New England Journal on Criminal and Civil Confinement* 19, no. 1, Winter 1993, 175.

A Season For Justice: The Life and Times of Civil Rights Lawyer Morris Dees

Autobiography

By: Morris Dees and Steve Fiffer

Date: 1991

Source: Dees, Morris, and Steve Fiffer. *A Season For Justice: The Life and Times of Civil Rights Lawyer Morris Dees.* New York: Charles Scribner's Sons, 1991, 332–336, 337.

About the Author: Morris Dees (1936–) founded the Southern Poverty Law Center in the early 1970s to defend poor black clients. In 1981, Dees founded Klanwatch, whose goal was to keep an eye on the KKK. In the mid-1980s, Dees sued the United Klan of America, claiming that this group was civilly responsible for promoting the murder of a young black man. Dees won a seven million dollar judgment that essentially closed down the Klan. Dees also has written three books. ∎

Introduction

Racism unfortunately has long been a part of American history. Thomas Jefferson, author of the Declaration of Independence with its famous line "all men are created equal," himself owned slaves. The whole of American culture supported slavery, and many in the North profited from "the peculiar institution" as well. Many Northern-owned shipping companies carried the products of slavery, and much of the cheap clothing produced by Northern factories was sold to semi-clothe the slaves. The laws of the period throughout the United States discriminated against blacks, both slaves and free. The Civil War (1861–1865) brought the end of slavery, and a promise of equality in the Fourteenth Amendment, but that promise went long ignored.

The nation slowly shifted its thinking on race relations, with the strong prodding of civil rights groups.

President Lyndon Johnson (served 1963–1969) in his Great Society speech came out strongly in favor of civil rights legislation and managed to pass the 1964 and 1968 Civil Rights Acts—which promised equal treatment in employment and accommodations and equal treatment in housing. Johnson also pushed through the 1965 Voting Rights Act that enfranchised million of blacks. This forever changed the political climate, and the power of the government supported equality. Those who committed racist murders were prosecuted much more frequently, and the federal government, to varying degrees, kept trying to move the nation forward in civil rights.

For some, however, this was not enough. They believed that these changes did not reach to the core of the problem. Many people who committed racist murders did not simply wake up one day and have that idea pop, fully formed, into their minds; instead racist groups, such as the Ku Klux Klan (KKK), had encouraged them. The KKK had originally been formed after the Civil War, but died out after reconstruction left the South. It formed again in the 1920s, and reformed in the 1950s to fight against integration. The KKK, unfortunately, was still a healthy organization in the 1980s. Morris Dees, an attorney who had formed the Southern Poverty Law Center to defend poor African Americans, sued the Klan, claiming that it was civilly liable for financial damages to the mother of a man killed in a racist murder. Dees won, and he discusses what it was like to collect on that settlement, and his success in this strategy.

Significance

Dees' strategy bankrupted one branch of the Klan, paving the way for the prosecution of other groups who promote dangerous agendas, but who might escape conviction in a criminal court. Some suggest, however, that once a group is bankrupt, it can be more dangerous, because it has nothing left to lose. Dees, though, clearly believes that his suit was a success.

It is not just civil rights groups who have turned to the civil courts for relief when the criminal courts prove unsatisfactory or unavailable. The estate of Nicole Brown Simpson sued O.J. Simpson in civil court after he was acquitted in the criminal case, winning a large monetary judgment. Some individuals who argue that the descendants of former slaves are owed reparations for their ancestors' treatment have turned to civil court and sued companies who profited from slavery. Civil courts are favored by most of these groups because those injured can receive monetary judgments, and because the burden of proof is lower. Usually parties need only establish a "preponderance of the evidence," rather than guilt "beyond a reasonable doubt." Also, criminal procedure protections, designed to safeguard the rights of the accused, are not applicable in the civil courts.

Primary Source

A Season For Justice: The Life and Times of Civil Rights Lawyer Morris Dees [excerpt]

SYNOPSIS: Dees first argues that many people in the present lack an understanding of the civil rights movement. He then discusses the building of the Civil Rights Memorial in Montgomery, Alabama, and details how his work helped to imprison many Klan members, including those who tried to murder him. The piece also discusses Dees' ongoing lawsuits to close down the Klan. He closes by noting that a change of heart in the Klan is needed, even as he acknowledges that he cannot keep the fight up forever.

Beulah Mae Donald lived less than a year after moving into her new home. The pain of losing her Michael was too much for her heart to bear.

Before Mrs. Donald died, she and I were honored at the annual Alabama NAACP convention. I repeated to those gathered the portion of my closing argument about the roll call in heaven for fallen civil rights leaders. After my speech, a group of teenagers came forward for autographs. One young man asked me about some of the people I had named. "Who were Medgar Evers, Viola Liuzzo, and Emmett Till?" he asked.

During the drive home that night, I was troubled that today's young people, black and white, have no real sense of civil rights history. These teenagers, not even born when Dr. King marched to Montgomery in 1965, enjoy the movement's benefits yet have little knowledge of the necessary past sacrifices.

Data gathered by Klanwatch showed a rising tide of racial violence, more in the North than the South, and much of it coming from young people. Black demagogues, as well as white, were spreading racial hatred. Candidate George Bush, sensing fertile political ground, had shamelessly played on white America's fear and prejudice by running commercials about Willie Horton, a black convict on furlough who assaulted a white woman. Bush's flimsy excuse for this commercial was that it proved his opponent was soft on crime. In the previous campaign, candidate Jesse Jackson had referred to New York as "hymie town." Our nation needed to be reminded of the horrible price we paid so few years earlier in the civil rights movement.

I proposed to the Center's board that we build a Civil Rights Memorial honoring those slain in the movement. On November 5, 1989, more than ten thousand people gathered in Montgomery to dedicate this monument, designed by Maya Lin, the architect who also designed the Vietnam Memorial in Washington, D.C. At the dedication, Myrlie Evers spoke of seeing her husband Medgar drag his bullet-ridden body to their door. Chris McNair recalled the painful loss of his eleven-year-old daughter Denise in the Sixteenth Street Baptist Church bombing. Marie Till Mobley talked of her son Emmett as if he was sharing the podium with her; she tried to explain the inexplicable, then closed by saying, "Now the world will remember." Rosa Parks, the graying mother of the movement, said, "We must learn to love more than we hate."

This striking monument, with its curved black granite wall and unique granite table listing the names of the fallen, graces the plaza in front of the Southern Poverty Law Center. Water flows down the wall and across the table. On the wall are carved the words from Amos used by Dr. King: UNTIL JUSTICE ROLLS DOWN LIKE WATERS AND RIGHTEOUSNESS LIKE A MIGHTY STREAM. Each week hundreds of people come by and read and touch the forty names etched into the table. I watch them from my office window as they ponder the inscriptions describing how and why each man, woman, and child died.

The night before the memorial was dedicated, I received a phone call from former Governor George Wallace, my onetime hero who had lost my allegiance when he vowed never to be "out-segged" by a political opponent. He received the black vote in his third and last term as governor after publicly admitting he was wrong to support segregation. The governor, himself the victim of senseless violence, is seriously ill now. I had invited him to the ceremonies. "Morris," he said in his weak but unforgettable voice, "I'm not going to be able to come. I have to go into the hospital tomorrow. But tell everybody I wish I could be there and that I'm with you all in spirit. I think the memorial is a wonderful thing."

At a dinner for the families of those named on the memorial, I retold the story of Tiger Knowles's plea to Mrs. Donald for understanding and of her forgiveness. This, I said, is the most dramatic and memorable moment of my thirty years of jury trials. This was a higher justice, a love we speak so much of but know so little about. I thanked Beulah Mae Donald, present in spirit if not in body, for giving me the rare chance to experience it.

Justice of a more earthly kind befell Frank Cox and Bennie Hays. Using evidence we supplied, Mobile District Attorney Chris Galanos indicted the

The Ku Klux Klan was still a healthy organization in the 1980s, but a successful lawsuit brought against them in 1991 bankrupted one of its branches.
© BETTMANN/CORBIS. REPRODUCED BY PERMISSION.

pair for Michael Donald's murder. Cox was convicted and given a life sentence. Hays had a heart seizure during his trial. Another trial is pending. Convicted or not, Hays, the architect of Michael Donald's lynching, is a broken man, and UKA Unit 900 is no more.

Opal Hays died as Mrs. Donald did, grieving over the tragedy that befell her family. In a sense, she, too, was a victim of Bennie's racism and hate. Before her death, Mrs. Hays became a leader of a group of mothers of death row inmates. These mothers, mostly black, joined hands with Opal, caring little about skin color. If Henry Hays, who still sits on death row, loses his appeals, I intend to ask our governor to spare his life. Mrs. Donald, I believe, would approve.

Steve Miller and his cohorts also sit in prison, convicted of the Pizza Hut robbery and conspiracy to murder me. Steve received a ten-year sentence.

Glenn Miller's whereabouts are unknown. In 1987, he went underground while on bond awaiting the appeal of his criminal contempt conviction, taking along Doug Sheets and Robert Jackson, the munitions experts fingered by Robert Jones. Miller had planned to kill me and others he targeted as enemies of the people. He mailed me a death threat and sent a letter to his followers saying I was worth 888 points dead.

Miller and his men were eventually flushed out of a rented mobile home near Springfield, Missouri, at dawn by an FBI swat team. The FBI found an arsenal of illegal weapons and explosives rivaling those described by Jones. Sheets and Jackson received long prison terms, Miller pled guilty to threatening me by mail and received a five-year sentence.

This light sentence was partial payoff by federal prosecutors for Miller's agreement to testify against Louis Beam and twelve other high-level white supremacist leaders charged with sedition. At this trial Miller admitted receiving two hundred thousand dollars of stolen armored-car receipts from Order founder Robert Mathews. He also testified that he had heard Mathews discuss killing me. Unfortunately, a white Fort Smith, Arkansas, jury acquitted all defendants, apparently not seeing them as a threat to overthrow the United States government and possibly agreeing with much of the men's philosophy. One female juror later married a defendant.

Morris Dees, an attorney defending poor African Americans, sued the Ku Klux Klan, claiming that it was civilly liable for financial damages to the mother of a man killed in a racist murder. **GETTY IMAGES. REPRODUCED BY PERMISSION.**

Glenn Miller is hiding somewhere today in the government's witness protection program—a once proud savior of the white race turned informant to save his own white hide.

The Decatur case, filed in 1981, ended in January 1989 with a happier result than the sedition trial. The civil case was finally settled with a most unusual agreement that resulted in Klan leaders attending a course on race relations. The defendants also agreed to pay damages to the black marchers and refrain from participating in white supremacy activity.

The evidence we delivered to federal prosecutors in 1983, less than twelve hours before our building burned, resulted in the indictment and conviction of ten Invisible Empire officials in Alabama for violating the marchers' civil rights. All served jail terms.

I felt the Decatur case, our first attempt to use the civil court to stop Klan violence, had served its purpose. What more fitting conclusion to nearly ten years of painstaking investigation and arduous litigation than to have Klan leaders sit down with the black leaders whom they had assaulted. This novel remedy reminded me of Dr. King's words in his 1963

speech on the Washington Mall: "I have a dream that someday in the red clay hills of Georgia, the sons of slaves and the sons of former slaveholders will sit down around the table of brotherhood."

Dr. Joseph Lowery, Jr., the Decatur march leader and head of King's SCLC, conducted the class. His wife Evelyn, who was almost killed by a Klansman's bullet that day in 1979, also attended. When the private meeting ended, Klansman Terry Joe Tucker told the press that he had learned a lot about brotherhood. "We should have been talking more," he said.

Sometimes I think a great deal has been accomplished by our suits and the Justice Department's diligent prosecutions. Traditional Klan groups have been severely damaged. Recruits are scarce. But new extremist groups are emerging with the same message, only their uniforms are different. Their victims are still blacks, Jews, and other minorities. Their numbers are limited, and if we move quickly, we may be able to eliminate them also.

As I write, we are in the midst of a suit against Tom Metzger and his White Aryan Resistance (WAR) organization based in Fallbrook, California, as well as two skinhead members of Portland's East Side White Pride gang. These skinheads beat a black man's brains out with a baseball bat in November 1988. On behalf of the victim's family, we claim agents of Metzger and WAR encouraged these skinheads. The legal theory is similar to the one we used against Shelton's United Klans. A victory could destroy Metzger's group before he spreads his hate-filled message to other embittered young people confused and fearful of our complicated racial climate.

Portland is twenty-seven hundred miles from Montgomery. Gathering evidence for the skinhead case has taken more than one year, and I have traveled more than fifty thousand miles. I long to be home with my family rather than in strange motels whose names I can't remember. Some nights I am so tired that sleep will not come. As I settle back into my Delta seat somewhere in the air between Oregon and Alabama, I wonder how long I can keep up this pace and fight these battles.

It seems like only yesterday when Little Buddy and I were carefree, running barefoot down cotton rows. Or when I could quickly climb a hundred-foot oak while hunting with T.J. Hendricks. I'd scale the tallest tree in the swamp or even cut it down to keep from losing a raccoon.

In August I spoke at T.J.'s funeral. More than fifteen years ago we had gone to court to get the gravel road that ran in front of his house and the houses of other blacks paved, and we had won. As I took that road to the little church where he lay in state, I wished for those simpler times—times when Daddy and T.J. and their sons walked the hardwood forest, hunting game for the table. This hunting party never gave race a thought. Thomas Jefferson Hendricks and my father were friends, and when T.J. died, a piece of my past left forever.

I know the feeling of tracking a big buck, matching survival skills, and then, at the moment when I have the advantage, feeling a kinship—not wanting to triumph because he will lose. When I had Glenn Miller, Louis Beam, and Robert Shelton in my sights, I wanted to say, "Hey, fellows, let's go somewhere, sit down and talk." I'd tell them that if they knew T.J. or Clarence or Mrs. Donald or the Smith sisters as people, as I did, they could not hate them.

These men and others like them are bright and completely dedicated. With a change of heart, they could build bonds between the races. Sadly, they hate so deeply that their words and deeds destroy all they touch. I cannot give up hope that they may someday change.

Clients like Beulah Mae Donald keep my hope alive and refresh me, giving me strength to fight another day, or maybe a few more years. But I know there won't be that many more years because no one, not even Ellie's guardian angel, can slow the clock. My three grandchildren remind me that others, not just the victims of injustice, need to share my time. . . .

I'll always be a trial lawyer. No higher calling has come my way. I do not know when the next case will come or if I will be able to resist.

Clarence Darrow, the lawyer whose life spurred my decision to enter the arena, wrote words of wisdom I failed to notice two decades ago: "Nature treats all her children as she does the fields and forest; in late autumn, as the cold blasts are coming on, she strips us for the ordeal that is waiting. Our steps grow slower, our efforts briefer, our journeys shorter; our ambitions are not so irresistible, and our hopes no longer wear wings."

Further Resources

BOOKS

Dees, Morris, and James Corcoran. *Gathering Storm: America's Militia Threat.* New York: HarperCollins Publishers, 1996.

Dees, Morris, and Steve Fiffer. *Hate on Trial: the Case Against America's Most Dangerous Neo-Nazi.* New York: Villard Books, 1993.

MacLean, Nancy. *Behind the Mask of Chivalry: the Making of the Second Ku Klux Klan.* New York: Oxford University Press, 1994.

Rose, Douglas D. *The Emergence of David Duke and the Politics of Race.* Chapel Hill, N.C.: University of North Carolina Press, 1992.

Stanton, Bill. *Klanwatch: Bringing the Ku Klux Klan to Justice.* New York: Weidenfeld, 1991.

WEBSITES

Southern Poverty Law Center. Available online at http://www .splcenter.org/splc.html; website home page: http://www.spl center.org (accessed May 2, 2003).

AUDIO AND VISUAL MEDIA

Line of Fire: the Morris Dees Story. Directed by John Korty. New York: NBC, Videocassette, 1991.

4 Little Girls. Directed by Spike Lee. New York: HBO Home Video, Videocassette, 1998.

Planned Parenthood of Southeastern Pennsylvania v. Casey

Supreme Court decision

By: Sandra Day O'Connor and William H. Rehnquist

Date: June 29, 1992

Source: O'Connor, Sandra Day and William H. Rehnquist. *Planned Parenthood of Southeastern Pennsylvania v. Casey* 505 U.S. 833 (1992). Available online at http://laws.findlaw.com /us/505/833.html; website home page: http://laws.findlaw.com (accessed May 2, 2003).

About the Authors: Sandra Day O'Connor (1930–) attended Stanford Law School, graduating third in her class. Because of gender bias, though, no firm would hire her, so she went to work for the government. In 1981, she was nominated by President Ronald Reagan (served 1981–1989) and became the first woman appointed to the United States Supreme Court.

William H. Rehnquist (1924–), after military service in World War II (1939–1945), received degrees from Stanford and Harvard, before graduating from Stanford Law School. President Richard Nixon (served 1969–1974) appointed Rehnquist to the Supreme Court in 1971. In 1986, President Ronald Reagan (served 1981–1989) appointed Rehnquist Chief Justice, and Rehnquist has generally led the court in a more conservative direction. ■

Introduction

Abortion was decried by some ancient medical texts, but most midwives were knowledgeable as to which herbs and roots generally promoted abortion. The common law put much emphasis upon the whole idea of "quickening" or the time when "viability" occurred. Quickening is when fetal movement is first detected in the mother, whereas viability is generally recognized as the point when the fetus might live outside the woman's body. Before the middle of the nineteenth century, abortion was generally criminalized after quickening, but not before. States began to take more of an interest in the matter in the nineteenth century, partly due to the risks of abortion, and partly because abortion was attempted more often through surgical intervention rather than herbs. During the first three-quarters of the twentieth century, abortion became a much safer procedure when performed in a hospital and by registered medical personnel. When abortion was not legally available, many women died from illegal or self-induced abortions.

During this time as well, the legal system became much more interested in the individual. The Supreme Court shifted its focus from economic regulations to individual rights. Louis Brandeis argued for the "right to be let alone" as part of a right to privacy as early as 1928. The later Supreme Court built upon this right to overturn a Connecticut ban on the use of contraceptives. In 1973 this right was used to strike down a Texas law banning abortions in *Roe v. Wade*. In that case, Justice Blackmun balanced the privacy interest of the mother against the state's interest in potential life. Blackmun devised an approach based on the trimesters of a pregnancy: prior to the end of the first trimester, the abortion decision was left to the woman and her attending physician; in the second trimester, the state could regulate the abortion procedure in ways reasonably related to maternal health; in the third trimester, after viability, the state could promote its interest in the potentiality of human life, and ban abortion except for the preservation of the life or health of the mother.

This decision provoked a firestorm of controversy, and many candidates for public office argued for a constitutional amendment overturning *Roe*. Ronald Reagan, while running for the presidency, promised to appoint Supreme Court justices who would oppose *Roe*. In 1983, the Supreme Court, in *Akron v. Akron Center for Reproductive Health* struck down Akron's abortion regulations. However, Justice O'Connor, Reagan's first appointment, indicated a desire in *Akron* to see *Roe* overturned. In 1989, the Supreme Court upheld a ban on public facilities being used in elective abortions in *Webster v. Reproductive Health Services*. The next major case on abortion was *Casey* in 1992. By that point, Presidents Reagan and Bush (served 1989–1993) had appointed five justices, and many thought that *Roe* might be overruled.

Significance

In *Casey*, the justices in the "ideological center" of the court determined that *Roe* not be overturned. O'Connor, in an apparent change from her earlier position, makes a cogent plea for *Roe*, arguing that in order for the rule of law to survive, *stare decisis* (the idea that decisions should stand unless there is a reason for overturning them) must generally control the law on abortion, unless there is a fundamental reason to overrule the prior decision. This indicates a shift in O'Connor's thinking, and her creation of a "center" on the court identifies her as a major force. The Supreme Court, though, did allow most of Pennsylvania's restrictions to stand—including informed consent, parental consent for minors seeking abortions, and a twenty-four-hour waiting period after informed consent was given. The court replaced the trimester framework of *Roe* with the standard of viability being the point at which the state could begin to interfere generally; before viability, the state could not place an "undue burden" on the woman seeking an abortion. The dissent strongly argued for the upholding of *Webster*, and a further move away from *Roe*. Few major abortion decisions have come since, but with the possible appointment of new justices, as several on the court approach retirement, the fate of *Roe v. Wade* still hangs in the balance.

Primary Source

Planned Parenthood of Southeastern Pennsylvania v. Casey [excerpt]

SYNOPSIS: Justice O'Connor, joined by Justices Kennedy and Souter, first reaffirms *Roe*'s central holding that abortion is legal and notes that previous constitutional rulings should not be overturned unless constitutional thought greatly changes; and it has not. The authors then note that the trimester system of *Roe* is unworkable, and hold that the state's interest becomes compelling at the point of viability. Chief Justice Rehnquist dissents, arguing explicitly that *Roe* only stands because of *stare decisis,* and implicitly, that it should be overruled. Furthermore, he states that the approach in *Webster,* not that of the plurality in this case, provides the sounder basis for the law in this area.

Justice O'Connor, Justice Kennedy, and Justice Souter announced the judgment of the Court and delivered the opinion of the Court with respect to Parts I, II, III, V-A, V-C, and VI, an opinion with respect to Part V-E, in which Justice Stevens joins, and an opinion with respect to Parts IV, V-B, and V-D.

I.

Liberty finds no refuge in a jurisprudence of doubt. Yet, 19 years after our holding that the Constitution protects a woman's right to terminate her pregnancy in its early stages, . . . that definition of liberty is still questioned. Joining the respondents

A case brought before the Supreme Court by Planned Parenthood reaffirmed the *Roe v. Wade* central holding that abortion is legal and should not be abolished, but allowed most of Pennsylvania's abortion restrictions to stand. **AP/WIDE WORLD PHOTOS. REPRODUCED BY PERMISSION.**

as amicus curiae, the United States, as it has done in five other cases in the last decade, again asks us to overrule *Roe*. . . .

At issue in these cases are five provisions of the Pennsylvania Abortion Control Act of 1982, as amended in 1988 and 1989. . . .

It must be stated at the outset and with clarity that *Roe*'s essential holding, the holding we reaffirm, has three parts. First is a recognition of the right of the woman to choose to have an abortion before viability and to obtain it without undue interference from the State. Before viability, the State's interests are not strong enough to support a prohibition of abortion or the imposition of a substantial obstacle to the woman's effective right to elect the procedure. Second is a confirmation of the State's

power to restrict abortions after fetal viability if the law contains exceptions for pregnancies which endanger the woman's life or health. And third is the principle that the State has legitimate interests from the outset of the pregnancy in protecting the health of the woman and the life of the fetus that may become a child. These principles do not contradict one another; and we adhere to each.

II.

Constitutional protection of the woman's decision to terminate her pregnancy derives from the Due Process Clause of the Fourteenth Amendment. It declares that no State shall "deprive any person of life, liberty, or property, without due process of law." The controlling word in the cases before us is "liberty." Although a literal reading of the Clause might suggest that it governs only the procedures by which a State may deprive persons of liberty, for at least 105 years, the Clause has been understood to contain a substantive component as well, one "barring certain government actions regardless of the fairness of the procedures used to implement them." . . . Thus all fundamental rights comprised within the term liberty are protected by the Federal Constitution from invasion by the States. . . . [T]he guaranties of due process, though having their roots in Magna Carta's "per legem terrae" and considered as procedural safeguards "against executive usurpation and tyranny," have in this country "become bulwarks also against arbitrary legislation." . . .

The most familiar of the substantive liberties protected by the Fourteenth Amendment are those recognized by the Bill of Rights. We have held that the Due Process Clause of the Fourteenth Amendment incorporates most of the Bill of Rights against the States. . . . It is tempting, as a means of curbing the discretion of federal judges, to suppose that liberty encompasses no more than those rights already guaranteed to the individual against federal interference by the express provisions of the first eight amendments to the Constitution. . . . But of course this Court has never accepted that view. . . .

Neither the Bill of Rights nor the specific practices of States at the time of the adoption of the Fourteenth Amendment marks the outer limits of the substantive sphere of liberty which the Fourteenth Amendment protects. . . .

The inescapable fact is that adjudication of substantive due process claims may call upon the Court in interpreting the Constitution to exercise that same capacity which, by tradition, courts always have exercised: reasoned judgment. Its boundaries are not susceptible of expression as a simple rule. That does not mean we are free to invalidate state policy choices with which we disagree; yet neither does it permit us to shrink from the duties of our office. . . .

Men and women of good conscience can disagree, and we suppose some always shall disagree, about the profound moral and spiritual implications of terminating a pregnancy, even in its earliest stage. Some of us as individuals find abortion offensive to our most basic principles of morality, but that cannot control our decision. Our obligation is to define the liberty of all, not to mandate our own moral code. The underlying constitutional issue is whether the State can resolve these philosophic questions in such a definitive way that a woman lacks all choice in the matter, except perhaps in those rare circumstances in which the pregnancy is itself a danger to her own life or health, or is the result of rape or incest.

It is conventional constitutional doctrine that, where reasonable people disagree, the government can adopt one position or the other. . . . That theorem, however, assumes a state of affairs in which the choice does not intrude upon a protected liberty. Thus, while some people might disagree about whether or not the flag should be saluted, or disagree about the proposition that it may not be defiled, we have ruled that a State may not compel or enforce one view or the other. . . .

Our law affords constitutional protection to personal decisions relating to marriage, procreation, contraception, family relationships, child rearing, and education. . . . Our cases recognize the right of the individual, married or single, to be free from unwarranted governmental intrusion into matters so fundamentally affecting a person as the decision whether to bear or beget a child. . . . Our precedents "have respected the private realm of family life which the state cannot enter." . . . These matters, involving the most intimate and personal choices a person may make in a lifetime, choices central to personal dignity and autonomy, are central to the liberty protected by the Fourteenth Amendment. At the heart of liberty is the right to define one's own concept of existence, of meaning, of the universe, and of the mystery of human life. Beliefs about these matters could not define the attributes of personhood were they formed under compulsion of the State.

These considerations begin our analysis of the woman's interest in terminating her pregnancy, but cannot end it, for this reason: though the abortion decision may originate within the zone of conscience and belief, it is more than a philosophic exercise. Abortion is a unique act. It is an act fraught with consequences for others: for the woman who must live with the implications of her decision; for the persons who perform and assist in the procedure; for the spouse, family, and society which must confront the knowledge that these procedures exist, procedures some deem nothing short of an act of violence against innocent human life; and, depending on one's beliefs, for the life or potential life that is aborted. Though abortion is conduct, it does not follow that the State is entitled to proscribe it in all instances. That is because the liberty of the woman is at stake in a sense unique to the human condition, and so, unique to the law. The mother who carries a child to full term is subject to anxieties, to physical constraints, to pain that only she must bear. That these sacrifices have from the beginning of the human race been endured by woman with a pride that ennobles her in the eyes of others and gives to the infant a bond of love cannot alone be grounds for the State to insist she make the sacrifice. Her suffering is too intimate and personal for the State to insist, without more, upon its own vision of the woman's role, however dominant that vision has been in the course of our history and our culture. The destiny of the woman must be shaped to a large extent on her own conception of her spiritual imperatives and her place in society. . . .

While we appreciate the weight of the arguments made on behalf of the State in the cases before us, arguments which in their ultimate formulation conclude that *Roe* should be overruled, the reservations any of us may have in reaffirming the central holding of *Roe* are outweighed by the explication of individual liberty we have given, combined with the force of stare decisis. We turn now to that doctrine.

III.

. . . The Court's duty in the present case is clear. In 1973, it confronted the already-divisive issue of governmental power to limit personal choice to undergo abortion, for which it provided a new resolution based on the due process guaranteed by the Fourteenth Amendment. Whether or not a new social consensus is developing on that issue, its divisiveness is no less today than in 1973, and pressure to overrule the decision, like pressure to retain it, has grown only more intense. A decision to overrule *Roe*'s essential holding under the existing circumstances would address error, if error there was, at the cost of both profound and unnecessary damage to the Court's legitimacy, and to the Nation's commitment to the rule of law. It is therefore imperative to adhere to the essence of *Roe*'s original decision, and we do so today.

IV.

From what we have said so far, it follows that it is a constitutional liberty of the woman to have some freedom to terminate her pregnancy. We conclude that the basic decision in *Roe* was based on a constitutional analysis which we cannot now repudiate. The woman's liberty is not so unlimited, however, that, from the outset, the State cannot show its concern for the life of the unborn and, at a later point in fetal development, the State's interest in life has

sufficient force so that the right of the woman to terminate the pregnancy can be restricted.

That brings us, of course, to the point where much criticism has been directed at *Roe,* a criticism that always inheres when the Court draws a specific rule from what in the Constitution is but a general standard. We conclude, however, that the urgent claims of the woman to retain the ultimate control over her destiny and her body, claims implicit in the meaning of liberty, require us to perform that function. Liberty must not be extinguished for want of a line that is clear. And it falls to us to give some real substance to the woman's liberty to determine whether to carry her pregnancy to full term.

We conclude the line should be drawn at viability, so that, before that time, the woman has a right to choose to terminate her pregnancy. . . .

The woman's right to terminate her pregnancy before viability is the most central principle of *Roe v. Wade.* It is a rule of law and a component of liberty we cannot renounce. . . .

We give this summary:

a. To protect the central right recognized by *Roe v. Wade* while at the same time accommodating the State's profound interest in potential life, we will employ the undue burden analysis as explained in this opinion. An undue burden exists, and therefore a provision of law is invalid, if its purpose or effect is to place a substantial obstacle in the path of a woman seeking an abortion before the fetus attains viability.

b. We reject the rigid trimester framework of *Roe v. Wade.* To promote the State's profound interest in potential life, throughout pregnancy, the State may take measures to ensure that the woman's choice is informed, and measures designed to advance this interest will not be invalidated as long as their purpose is to persuade the woman to choose childbirth over abortion. These measures must not be an undue burden on the right.

c. As with any medical procedure, the State may enact regulations to further the health or safety of a woman seeking an abortion. Unnecessary health regulations that have the purpose or effect of presenting a substantial obstacle to a woman seeking an abortion impose an undue burden on the right.

d. Our adoption of the undue burden analysis does not disturb the central holding of *Roe v.*

Wade, and we reaffirm that holding. Regardless of whether exceptions are made for particular circumstances, a State may not prohibit any woman from making the ultimate decision to terminate her pregnancy before viability.

e. We also reaffirm *Roe*'s holding that, subsequent to viability, the State, in promoting its interest in the potentiality of human life, may, if it chooses, regulate, and even proscribe, abortion except where it is necessary, in appropriate medical judgment, for the preservation of the life or health of the mother. . . .

Chief Justice Rehnquist, with whom Justice White, Justice Scalia, and Justice Thomas join, concurring in the judgment in part and dissenting in part.

The sum of the joint opinion's labors in the name of stare decisis and "legitimacy" is this: *Roe v. Wade* stands as a sort of judicial Potemkin Village, which may be pointed out to passers-by as a monument to the importance of adhering to precedent. But behind the facade, an entirely new method of analysis, without any roots in constitutional law, is imported to decide the constitutionality of state laws regulating abortion. Neither stare decisis nor "legitimacy" are truly served by such an effort.

We have stated above our belief that the Constitution does not subject state abortion regulations to heightened scrutiny. Accordingly, we think that the correct analysis is that set forth by the plurality opinion in Webster. A woman's interest in having an abortion is a form of liberty protected by the Due Process Clause, but States may regulate abortion procedures in ways rationally related to a legitimate state interest.

Further Resources

BOOKS

Baird, Robert M., and Stuart E. Rosenbaum. *The Ethics of Abortion: Pro-Life vs. Pro-Choice.* Buffalo: Prometheus Books, 1993.

Craig, Barbara Hinkson, and David M. O'Brien. *Abortion and American Politics.* Chatham, N.J.: Chatham House, 1993.

Davis, Sue Justice. *Rehnquist and the Constitution.* Princeton, N.J.: Princeton University Press, 1989.

Harrison, Maureen, and Steve Gilbert. *Abortion Decisions of the United States Supreme Court: the 1990's.* Beverly Hills, Calif.: Excellent Books, 1993.

Riddle, John M. *Eve's Herbs: a History of Contraception and Abortion in the West.* Cambridge, Mass.: Harvard University Press, 1997.

Tucker, D.F.B. *The Rehnquist Court and Civil Rights.* Aldershot, N.H.: Dartmouth, 1995.

Van Sickel, Robert W. *Not a Particularly Different Voice: the Jurisprudence of Sandra Day O'Connor.* New York: P. Lang, 1998.

WEBSITES

Abortion and Reproduction Law. http://biotech.law.lsu.edu /cases/reproduction/index.htm; website home page: http:// biotech.law.lsu.edu (accessed May 2, 2003).

Lucas v. South Carolina Coastal Council

Supreme Court decision

By: Antonin Scalia and Harry A. Blackmun

Date: June 29, 1992

Source: Scalia, Antonin and Harry A. Blackmun *Lucas v. South Carolina Coastal Council,* 505 U.S. 1003 (1992). Available online at http://laws.findlaw.com/us/505/1003.html; website home page: http://laws.findlaw.com (accessed May 4, 2003).

About the Authors: Antonin Scalia (1936–) graduated from Harvard Law School in 1961. In 1986, President Ronald Reagan (served 1981–1989) nominated Scalia to the Supreme Court. On the Court, he has been an advocate of "textualism," or holding the Constitution to its literal meaning in the text.

Harry A. Blackmun (1908–1999) was on the Eighth Circuit Court of Appeals from 1959 to 1970. President Richard Nixon (served 1969–1974) nominated Blackmun to the Supreme Court in 1970, and he remained there until 1994. Blackmun is most famous as the author of *Roe v. Wade.* ∎

Introduction

The Bill of Rights was adopted to limit the federal government and to settle the apprehensions of many Anti-Federalists who worried that the federal government might become too powerful. The Fifth Amendment states, in part, that "nor shall private property be taken for public use without just compensation," frequently called the "takings" clause. For the first century of the Bill of Rights's existence, though, this limitation only applied against the federal government. Some constraints were imposed against the states in 1868 with the passage of the Fourteenth Amendment.

In the twentieth century, the Supreme Court began to apply constitutional protections from the Bill of Rights against the states. This served to limit what the states could do in restricting civil liberties, and also expanded a defendant's rights relating to criminal procedure. The takings clause, however, was not often used to limit action either by the state or federal government.

In the 1960s, concerns began to grow about the misuse of the environment. Rachel Carson's book, *Silent*

Spring, documenting the effects of the deadly pesticide, DDT, led to a movement in the United States to ban that chemical's use in this country. Carson's book, along with other scientific information and a growing concern for the environment, launched the modern environmentalist movement. This led to events like Earth Day, which started in 1970. The federal government founded the Environmental Protection Agency (EPA) that same year; the EPA has served, in varying degrees, to protect the environment and to manage modern America's use of it. Nearly every state has established a state equivalent of the EPA.

Governmental agencies, influenced by the environmentalist movement, began to prevent some uses of land and reinforced the regulation of zoning codes to regulate how land was to be used. South Carolina prohibited the building of new homes on certain parts of the coast. David Lucas owned coastal property affected by this South Carolina restriction. Lucas sued, claiming that this constituted a "taking," and that he was owed compensation. The case reached the U.S. Supreme Court.

Significance

The Supreme Court, in a decision written by Justice Antonin Scalia, held for Lucas, reversing the South Carolina Supreme Court, and remanding the case. In order to restrict the usage without compensation under the takings clause, the state would need to demonstrate that Lucas's intended use constituted a public nuisance. This was a major restriction on the power of the government, as Lucas's land was not taken under eminent domain. Lucas retained ownership of the property, but was prohibited from building on the land to prevent further environmental damage. The dissenting opinion points out that the shifting coastline and unstable seashore was a factor in the government's decision to ban the use. This decision was a major setback for the environmentalist movement, since it means that any time a use is banned for the good of the environment—such as the building of homes in unstable areas—the property owner may be able to sue for compensation.

This decision also points out an interesting fact about Justice Scalia's textualism—the theory limiting the constitution to only what is textually specified. However, the Fifth Amendment (and state equivalents) does not prohibit a government from banning certain uses of the land, but only from taking private property to be used by the public, such as for a public road. Scalia is interpreting the Constitution here to add a limitation on government, something contrary to his own theory of textualism. The Lucas decision is a major impediment to government's efforts to prevent abuses of the land and protect the environment, and a major victory for property owners.

Primary Source

Lucas v. South Carolina Coastal Council [excerpt]

SYNOPSIS: Scalia defines a "taking" and notes that while the government can ban "noxious" uses of property, those uses cannot be banned without compensation unless they were not part of the title when the property was bought. Thus, the regulation here constitutes a taking. Blackmun bitingly dissents, arguing that the lower court's ruling, reversed here, was correct, and that the majority has retreated to the overly complex common law, and that the ruling is not supported by history.

Justice Scalia delivered the opinion of the Court.

In 1986, petitioner David H. Lucas paid $975,000 for two residential lots on the Isle of Palms in Charleston County, South Carolina, on which he intended to build single-family homes. In 1988, however, the South Carolina Legislature enacted the Beachfront Management Act, . . . which had the direct effect of barring petitioner from erecting any permanent habitable structures on his two parcels. . . . A state trial court found that this prohibition rendered Lucas' parcels "valueless." . . . This case requires us to decide whether the Act's dramatic effect on the economic value of Lucas' lots accomplished a taking of private property under the Fifth and Fourteenth Amendments requiring the payment of "just compensation." . . .

Justice Holmes recognized in Mahon, however, that, if the protection against physical appropriations of private property was to be meaningfully enforced, the government's power to redefine the range of interests included in the ownership of property was necessarily constrained by constitutional limits. . . . These considerations gave birth in that case to the oft-cited maxim that, "while property may be regulated to a certain extent, if regulation goes too far, it will be recognized as a taking." . . .

We have never set forth the justification for this rule. Perhaps it is simply, . . . that total deprivation of beneficial use is, from the landowner's point of view, the equivalent of a physical appropriation. . . . On the other side of the balance, affirmatively supporting a compensation requirement, is the fact that regulations that leave the owner of land without economically beneficial or productive options for its use—typically, as here, by requiring land to be left substantially in its natural state—carry with them a heightened risk that private property is being pressed into some form of public service under the guise of mitigating serious public harm. . . . The many statutes on the books, both state and federal, that provide for the use of eminent domain to impose servitudes on private scenic lands preventing developmental uses, or to acquire such lands altogether, suggest the practical equivalent in this setting of negative regulation and appropriation.

We think, in short, that there are good reasons for our frequently expressed belief that, when the owner of real property has been called upon to sacrifice all economically beneficial uses in the name of the common good, that is, to leave his property economically idle, he has suffered a taking. . . .

It is correct that many of our prior opinions have suggested that "harmful or noxious uses" of property may be proscribed by government regulation without the requirement of compensation. For a number of reasons, however, we think the South Carolina Supreme Court was too quick to conclude that that principle decides the present case. The "harmful or noxious uses" principle was the Court's early attempt to describe in theoretical terms why government may, consistent with the Takings Clause, affect property values by regulation without incurring an obligation to compensate—a reality we nowadays acknowledge explicitly with respect to the full scope of the State's police power. . . .

The transition from our early focus on control of "noxious" uses to our contemporary understanding of the broad realm within which government may regulate without compensation was an easy one, since the distinction between "harm-preventing" and "benefit-conferring" regulation is often in the eye of the beholder. It is quite possible, for example, to describe in either fashion the ecological, economic, and esthetic concerns that inspired the South Carolina Legislature in the present case. . . . Whether Lucas' construction of single-family residences on his parcels should be described as bringing "harm" to South Carolina's adjacent ecological resources thus depends principally upon whether the describer believes that the State's use interest in nurturing those resources is so important that any competing adjacent use must yield.

When it is understood that "prevention of harmful use" was merely our early formulation of the police power justification necessary to sustain (without compensation) any regulatory diminution in value; and that the distinction between regulation that "prevents harmful use" and that which "confers benefits" is difficult, if not impossible, to discern on an objective, value-free basis; it becomes self-evident that noxious-use logic cannot serve as a touchstone to distinguish regulatory "takings"—which require

compensation—from regulatory deprivations that do not require compensation. A fortiori, the legislature's recitation of a noxious-use justification cannot be the basis for departing from our categorical rule that total regulatory takings must be compensated. If it were, departure would virtually always be allowed. . . .

Where the State seeks to sustain regulation that deprives land of all economically beneficial use, we think it may resist compensation only if the logically antecedent inquiry into the nature of the owner's estate shows that the proscribed use interests were not part of his title to begin with. . . .

The "total taking" inquiry we require today will ordinarily entail (as the application of state nuisance law ordinarily entails) analysis of, among other things, the degree of harm to public lands and resources, or adjacent private property, posed by the claimant's proposed activities, . . . the social value of the claimant's activities and their suitability to the locality in question, see, . . . and the relative ease with which the alleged harm can be avoided through measures taken by the claimant and the government (or adjacent private landowners) alike . . . The fact that a particular use has long been engaged in by similarly situated owners ordinarily imports a lack of any common law prohibition (though changed circumstances or new knowledge may make what was previously permissible no longer so . . .). So also does the fact that other landowners, similarly situated, are permitted to continue the use denied to the claimant.

It seems unlikely that common law principles would have prevented the erection of any habitable or productive improvements on petitioner's land; they rarely support prohibition of the "essential use" of land . . . The question, however, is one of state law to be dealt with on remand. We emphasize that, to win its case, South Carolina must do more than proffer the legislature's declaration that the uses Lucas desires are inconsistent with the public interest, or the conclusory assertion that they violate a common law maxim such as *sic utere tuo ut alienum non laedas*. . . . Instead, as it would be required to do if it sought to restrain Lucas in a common law action for public nuisance, South Carolina must identify background principles of nuisance and property law that prohibit the uses he now intends in the circumstances in which the property is presently found. Only on this showing can the State fairly claim that, in proscribing all such beneficial uses, the Beachfront Management Act is taking nothing. . . .

The judgment is reversed, and the case is remanded for proceedings not inconsistent with this opinion.

So ordered.

Justice Blackmun, H., dissenting.

Today the Court launches a missile to kill a mouse. . . .

My fear is that the Court's new policies will spread beyond the narrow confines of the present case. For that reason, I, like the Court, will give far greater attention to this case than its narrow scope suggests—not because I can intercept the Court's missile, or save the targeted mouse, but because I hope perhaps to limit the collateral damage. . . .

Petitioner Lucas is a contractor, manager, and part owner of the Wild Dune development on the Isle of Palms. He has lived there since 1978. In December 1986, he purchased two of the last four pieces of vacant property in the development. The area is notoriously unstable. In roughly half of the last 40 years, all or part of petitioner's property was part of the beach or flooded twice daily by the ebb and flow of the tide. . . . Determining that local habitable structures were in imminent danger of collapse, the Council issued permits for two rock revetments to protect condominium developments near petitioner's property from erosion; one of the revetments extends more than half-way onto one of his lots. . . .

If the state legislature is correct that the prohibition on building in front of the setback line prevents serious harm, then, under this Court's prior cases, the Act is constitutional. Long ago it was recognized that all property in this country is held under the implied obligation that the owner's use of it shall not be injurious to the community, and the Takings Clause did not transform that principle to one that requires compensation whenever the State asserts its power to enforce it. . . . The Court consistently has upheld regulations imposed to arrest a significant threat to the common welfare, whatever their economic effect on the owner. . . .

Because that legislative determination cannot be disregarded in the absence of such evidence, . . . and because its determination of harm to life and property from building is sufficient to prohibit that use under this Court's cases, the South Carolina Supreme Court correctly found no taking. . . .

Clearly, the Court was eager to decide this case. But eagerness, in the absence of proper jurisdiction,

must—and in this case should have been—met with restraint. . . .

The Court does not reject the South Carolina Supreme Court's decision simply on the basis of its disbelief and distrust of the legislature's findings. It also takes the opportunity to create a new scheme for regulations that eliminate all economic value. From now on, there is a categorical rule finding these regulations to be a taking unless the use they prohibit is a background common law nuisance or property principle. . . .

This Court repeatedly has recognized the ability of government, in certain circumstances, to regulate property without compensation, no matter how adverse the financial effect on the owner may be. . . .

Until today, the Court explicitly had rejected the contention that the government's power to act without paying compensation turns on whether the prohibited activity is a common law nuisance. . . . Instead the Court has relied in the past, as the South Carolina court has done here, on legislative judgments of what constitutes a harm.

The Court rejects the notion that the State always can prohibit uses it deems a harm to the public without granting compensation because "the distinction between 'harm-preventing' and 'benefit-conferring' regulation is often in the eye of the beholder." . . . Since the characterization will depend "primarily upon one's evaluation of the worth of competing uses of real estate," . . . the Court decides a legislative judgment of this kind no longer can provide the desired "objective, value-free basis" for upholding a regulation. . . . The Court, however, fails to explain how its proposed common-law alternative escapes the same trap.

The threshold inquiry for imposition of the Court's new rule, "deprivation of all economically valuable use," itself cannot be determined objectively. As the Court admits, whether the owner has been deprived of all economic value of his property will depend on how "property" is defined. . . .

Even more perplexing, however, is the Court's reliance on common law principles of nuisance in its quest for a value-free takings jurisprudence. In determining what is a nuisance at common law, state courts make exactly the decision that the Court finds so troubling when made by the South Carolina General Assembly today: They determine whether the use is harmful. Common law public and private nuisance law is simply a determination whether a particular use causes harm. . . . There is nothing magical in the reasoning of judges long dead. They determined a harm in the same way as state judges and legislatures do today. If judges in the 18th and 19th centuries can distinguish a harm from a benefit, why not judges in the 20th century, and if judges can, why not legislators? There simply is no reason to believe that new interpretations of the hoary common law nuisance doctrine will be particularly "objective" or "valuefree." Once one abandons the level of generality of sic utere tuo ut alienum non laedas, . . . one searches in vain, I think, for anything resembling a principle in the common law of nuisance.

Finally, the Court justifies its new rule that the legislature may not deprive a property owner of the only economically valuable use of his land, even if the legislature finds it to be a harmful use, because such action is not part of the 'long recognized' "understandings of our citizens." . . . It is not clear from the Court's opinion where our "historical compact" or "citizens' understanding" comes from, but it does not appear to be history. . . .

Even into the 19th century, state governments often felt free to take property for roads and other public projects without paying compensation to the owners. . . .

Although, prior to the adoption of the Bill of Rights, America was replete with land-use regulations describing which activities were considered noxious and forbidden . . . the Fifth Amendment's Takings Clause originally did not extend to regulations of property, whatever the effect. . . .

In short, I find no clear and accepted "historical compact" or "understanding of our citizens" justifying the Court's new takings doctrine. Instead, the Court seems to treat history as a grab bag of principles, to be adopted where they support the Court's theory and ignored where they do not. If the Court decided that the early common law provides the background principles for interpreting the Takings Clause, then regulation, as opposed to physical confiscation, would not be compensable. If the Court decided that the law of a later period provides the background principles, then regulation might be compensable, but the Court would have to confront the fact that legislatures regularly determined which uses were prohibited, independent of the common law, and independent of whether the uses were lawful when the owner purchased. What makes the Court's analysis unworkable is its attempt to package the law of two incompatible eras and peddle it as historical fact.

The Court makes sweeping and, in my view, misguided and unsupported changes in our takings doctrine. While it limits these changes to the most narrow subset of government regulation—those that eliminate all economic value from land—these changes go far beyond what is necessary to secure petitioner Lucas' private benefit. One hopes they do not go beyond the narrow confines the Court assigns them to today.

Further Resources

BOOKS

Bagley, Constance E., and Christy A. Haubegger. *Cutting Edge Cases in the Legal Environment of Business.* Minneapolis/St. Paul: West Pub. Co., 1993.

Brisbin, Richard A. *Justice Antonin Scalia and the Conservative Revival.* Baltimore, Md.: Johns Hopkins University Press, 1997.

Echeverria, John D., and Raymond Booth Eby. *Let the People Judge: Wise Use and the Private Property Rights Movement.* Washington, D.C.: Island Press, 1995.

Garcia, Alfredo. *The Fifth Amendment: a Comprehensive Approach.* Westport, Conn.: Greenwood Press, 2002.

Levy, Leonard. *Origins of the Bill of Rights.* New Haven, Conn.: Yale University Press, 1999.

United States Senate Committee on the Judiciary. *The Right to Own Property.* Washington, D.C.: U.S. G.P.O. 1996.

PERIODICALS

"Symposium, the Jurisprudence of Justice Harry A. Blackmun." *Hastings Constitutional Law Quarterly* 26, no. 1, Fall 1998.

WEBSITES

A Photographic Essay on the Lucas Property.. Available online at http://www.dartmouth.edu/~wfischel/lucasessay.html; website home page: http://dartmouth.edu (accessed May 4, 2003).

AUDIO AND VISUAL MEDIA

The Debate: Resolved: Lucas Should be Overruled. Millersville, Md.: Recorded Resources Corp., 1997.

Beyond the Burning Cross
Memoir

By: Edward J. Cleary

Date: 1994

Source: Cleary, Edward J. *Beyond the Burning Cross: A Landmark Case of Race, Censorship, and the First Amendment.* New York: Vintage Books, 1994, 219–224.

About the Author: Edward J. Cleary (1952–) graduated from the University of Minnesota Law School. He worked for the Ramsey County Public Defender's Office and defended a wide variety of clients from different racial and ethnic groups. In 1990, Cleary was assigned to defend R.A.V., who was named by his initials because he was a juvenile, and who had been accused of burning a cross for racial or ethnic reasons. ■

Introduction

Free speech was not a frequently litigated issue in the eighteenth and nineteenth centuries. This was due to a number of reasons, including the fact that there were few laws clearly affecting free speech. Another reason limiting discussion of free speech during this time was that the First Amendment, creating freedom of speech, was held to limit only the federal government, not state governments. However, around the turn of the twentieth century, this issue began to be discussed more often. In the 1920s, the Supreme Court expanded the protection of freedom of speech by applying the First Amendment against the states. In the 1930s, the Supreme Court continued this expansion by overruling legislation that prohibited the use of a red flag as infringing on the freedom of speech. Previously, the red flag had been banned because it was supposed to represent anarchism.

In the 1950s, the Supreme Court for a time was shaped by the Red Scare, generally allowing governmental repression of free speech. During the 1960s, the Warren Court increased many of the freedoms in the Bill of Rights. In 1969, the Supreme Court held that speech could only be banned if it advocated the use of force, *and* that advocacy was directed towards producing "imminent lawless action," *and* that advocacy was likely to succeed in producing that lawless action.

Such a standard, however, did not clearly cover actions, and one must wonder if these actions were to be considered part of free speech. For instance, the Warren Court in the 1960s held that wearing a shirt with an obscene message was protected free speech. In the late 1980s, there were several instances of flag burnings as political protests, and the Supreme Court held that flag burning was protected under the First Amendment. Racist groups such as the KKK had long used a burning cross as a symbol, and frequently had burned crosses in front of the homes of those the KKK disliked. Whether such an act was protected under the First Amendment was tested in *R.A.V. v. St. Paul.* Edward Cleary was the attorney challenging a Minnesota law, prohibiting cross burning as a sign of hatred. After winning his case, he returned to hear the oral arguments of a challenge of a similar law the next year.

Significance

Cleary won because the law targeted a specific viewpoint of speech, making those viewpoints illegal. The Supreme Court has long held that a law cannot discriminate against speech based upon its viewpoint. Since the Supreme Court had extended the freedom of speech to

acts such as flag burning, the next step was to protect cross burning, as five justices did. All nine justices, though, struck down the law, as it was overbroad. Cleary was not arguing that cross burning not be criminalized, but that a law singling out one viewpoint to be criminalized, should be unconstitutional. Cleary would have had the cross burners charged, if he were prosecuting the case, under trespass statutes, among other things. While this may have worked, it is obviously of little comfort to those who had crosses burned in their front yards. In the case which increased the penalty for assault if that assault was based on race or gender hatred, the law was upheld. The court concluded that the First Amendment did not protect assaults. The First Amendment continues to be debated in our courts and our homes as America struggles with what limits, if any, should be placed on the freedom of speech.

Primary Source

Beyond the Burning Cross [excerpt]

> **SYNOPSIS:** After Edward Cleary challenged a Minnesota law prohibiting cross burning and won the case, he returned to Washington to hear arguments challenging a similar law. Cleary argues for absolute freedom of expression.

The Lessons of History

The men were dressed in dark uniforms with concealed automatic weapons. As they patrolled from the top of the building, they looked down below at the fenced-in group of mostly Jewish observers. Several towers stood starkly outlined against the threatening clouds above. Frigid gusts of wind and rain pelted the crowd below, who sat or stood in a sea of mud.

This was not Germany or Poland in 1943. The date was April 22, 1993, as I sat with others and awaited the beginning of the dedication ceremony for the United States Holocaust Memorial Museum in Washington, D.C. The armed guards were there to protect visiting dignitaries as well as the president, the vice president, and their wives. The towers were part of the museum, purposely designed to re-create the appearance of a concentration camp. The mostly Jewish crowd was confined voluntarily. On this day and in this place, the effect was chilling.

For the first time since the United States Supreme Court decided *R.A.V.,* I had returned the previous day to Washington, D.C., to observe the oral arguments before the Court in the case of *Wisconsin v. Mitchell.* As I entered the Court chamber, I was seated near the area of the room reserved for members of the media. In discussing the case with several members of the press, it became clear that they were divided regarding the probable outcome.

R.A.V. had been charged under both the ill-fated St. Paul ordinance and an "enhancement" hate-crime law similar to the Wisconsin law challenged by Mitchell. The St. Paul ordinance had been directed solely at expression. Speech or symbolic speech that aroused "anger, alarm or resentment in others" on the basis of certain subject matter could lead to prosecution. Although the allegations in *R.A.V.* had constituted criminal conduct (i.e., trespass, terroristic threats), the St. Paul ordinance had addressed not that criminal conduct but the offensive viewpoint. Consequently, we had challenged only the ordinance and not the enhancement law, believing that the Court would give much greater latitude to lawmakers to punish conduct motivated by bias, rather than allowing them to prohibit the expression of the viewpoint itself. We were a little surprised that the Wisconsin Supreme Court threw out the state's hate-crime law the day after the *R.A.V.* decision, based in part on the reasoning of the Court in *R.A.V.* The St. Paul ordinance was clearly directed at expression and more closely mirrored the speech codes prevalent on campuses throughout the nation; enhancement laws were easily distinguishable in principle, if not in spirit.

As the oral argument in *Wisconsin v. Mitchell* began on the morning of April 21, it was immediately apparent that the members of the Court saw a very clear distinction between laws aimed at expression and laws initially directed at criminal conduct.

The case had split many of the same traditional allies who had opposed each other in the *R.A.V.* case. Although we had not challenged the enhancement provision in *R.A.V.*, I was not in favor of such laws. I believed that it was a mistake to confuse the meeting of minimal constitutional standards with the formulating of wise public policy. I was disappointed to learn that the ACLU had filed a brief on behalf of the government; I could not understand how a civil liberties organization could argue for lengthening the incarceration period for defendants while minimizing the danger of governmental regulation of individual beliefs. The issue was never one of public safety; a severe sentence for one convicted of criminal conduct is not necessarily objectionable. The same sentence becomes dangerous only when it is attributed in part to the actor's beliefs, opinions, and even hatreds.

Mitchell involved a repugnant act (an assault on a defenseless individual) initiated as a result of a despicable underlying impetus—hatred based on racial identity. Yet the penalty-enhancement approach to punishment of such conduct is not limited to such egregious circumstances. By separately punishing motive, such laws open the door to increased incarceration for other unpopular opinions. Significantly, sentences for crimes against property (trespass) are enhanced in many states, as well as crimes against the person (assault). It does not take a great deal of insight to see how this practice could go awry. Increased sentences could be levied against those who "trespassed" while expressing other unpopular beliefs (e.g., abortion protesters, abortion-rights advocates, civil rights marchers, antiwar demonstrators). Selective prosecution based on majoritarian beliefs would remain a danger; the fragmentation of society would continue in the name of public safety.

As is often the case with First Amendment principles, those who argue the potential danger of such laws are accused of being First Amendment "absolutists." Yet as I sat and listened to the argument in *Wisconsin v. Mitchell,* unintended applications of such laws seemed inevitable. Consider this exchange between a member of the Court and Attorney General James Doyle arguing on behalf of the state of Wisconsin:

> Question: What if in the draft card case the statute said that your penalty would be enhanced if you did it because of disagreement with the person's views about the Vietnam war, whether they were pro or con?

> Answer: In my view . . . that would be constitutional.

Those who believed that the Court would extend the *R.A.V.* doctrine to laws that primarily punish criminal conduct failed to consider that this was a "law and order" Court. Having acknowledged a year earlier the risk in allowing a law to endanger the First Amendment right of free expression, the Court now seemed to minimize the potential peril when a law focuses initially on criminal conduct. Chief Justice Rehnquist and Justices Scalia and Kennedy, the core of the majority in *R.A.V.,* clearly indicated by their questions to Lynn Adelman (the state senator from Milwaukee who was arguing in behalf of Mitchell) that they saw a sharp distinction between the St. Paul ordinance and the Wisconsin statute. A principled and dedicated man politically left of center, Adelman believed passionately in his cause. Since

I thought the laws were probably constitutional though ill conceived, it was difficult to hear the Court sympathize with the government's argument.

Learning that Lynn Adelman's parents had tickets to the dedication ceremony the next day but would be unable to attend, I asked for and received a ticket to the museum's dedication events. The cherry blossoms had mostly faded and the weather turned ugly as the morning of April 22 dawned. As I sat in the rain waiting for the ceremony to begin I observed a large video screen showing scenes from Germany and Poland during World War II, and watched intently as the screen flashed a photograph of a Nazi book-burning rally from the 1930s; it was a stark, three-story black-and-white image of a nation sliding into the abyss six decades earlier.

The lesson seemed clear, though it has often been disregarded because of the passions of the moment. When government officials, well-meaning or evil, attempt to dictate acceptable thought, word, or opinion, a nation is in grave peril. It can happen anywhere, but it is less likely to occur when the members of a society are willing to allow all viewpoints, even discredited and unpopular ones, to be expressed. The Framers had understood this; the Court in *R.A.V.* had reaffirmed the necessity of eternal vigilance against the imposition of orthodoxy.

As each speaker reminded the audience of the necessity never to forget the horror of state-sanctioned genocide, the audience sat silently in the rain and the wind. Elie Wiesel reminded President Clinton of the horrors in Bosnia, and I recalled once again that man's inhumanity to man knows no ethnic or religious boundaries; the killing fields of Cambodia, the deserts of Iraq, and the mountains of Bosnia all serve as significant reminders of the end result of collective hatred. Yet hatred cannot be outlawed; the solution is much more complex.

As in *R.A.V. v. St. Paul,* the United States Supreme Court reached a unanimous decision in the case of *Wisconsin v. Mitchell.* That is where the similarity ended. The Court had taken over six months to reach a decision in *R.A.V.; Mitchell* was decided in less than two. The *R.A.V.* decision included a majority opinion and three concurring opinions; *Mitchell* consisted of one brief, unanimous opinion less than a quarter of the length of *R.A.V.* The collective energy of the Court appeared to have been spent on *R.A.V.; Mitchell* appeared simply to delineate the parameters of the *R.A.V.* doctrine. . . .

R.A.V. stands for the proposition that every citizen has a right to think what he wants and to say

Edward Cleary challenged a Minnesota law, prohibiting cross burning as a sign of hatred, like that used by the Ku Klux Klan, and won the case.
© GREG SMITH/CORBIS SYGMA. REPRODUCED BY PERMISSION.

what he thinks. *Mitchell* further defines that doctrine; laws are permissible that focus on criminal conduct as a prerequisite to punishing beliefs. If convicted of criminal conduct, one is now subject to additional punishment for one's motivation, even if that motivation is a strongly held belief.

A year earlier, a conservative Court had stood up for the First Amendment in an emotionally charged case. Believing that they were not retreating from this position, the Court now stated that where government could justify its actions (maintaining the public safety) without favoring one side of the debate (targeting those who violate the criminal code motivated by a belief on either side of an issue), the First Amendment was not at risk.

Yet there is a thin line between punishing motivation and penalizing dissenting opinion. The Court's focus on the governmental interest asserted allows officials to use the broad justification of law and order as a subterfuge to suppress the expression of unpopular beliefs. Too many criminal laws (against trespass, disorderly conduct, etc.) lend themselves to this type of misapplication. *R.A.V.*

prohibits the direct suppression of dissenting opinion; *Mitchell* must not be allowed to indirectly undermine that critical holding. Presumably the Court will view other laws much differently if there is, in Justice Scalia's words from *R.A.V.*, a "realistic possibility that official suppression of ideas is afoot." The Court did not feel the Wisconsin law constituted such a threat; it remains to be seen whether other such laws do.

As I left the dedication ceremony for the Holocaust museum, I was confronted by several angry protesters holding signs and screaming anti-Semitic epithets at me. As police officers on horseback moved to protect the crowd, I stared back at the demonstrators. Looming behind their placards stood the familiar outline of the Jefferson Memorial. Jefferson understood that beliefs—any beliefs—will never be genuine if held under the threat of force, and that our nation must always tolerate the dissenting voice. Over two centuries later, the struggle for individual liberty continues, and as I turned away from the demonstrators and started down the street, I recalled the inscription encircling Thomas Jefferson in his Memorial:

> I have sworn upon the altar of God eternal hostility against every form of tyranny over the mind of man.

Further Resources

BOOKS

Baird, Robert M., and Stuart E. Rosenbaum. *Hatred, Bigotry, and Prejudice: Definitions, Causes & Solutions.* Amherst, N.Y.: Prometheus Books, 1999.

Bezanson, Randall P. *Speech Stories: How Free Can Speech Be?* New York: New York University Press, 1998.

Brisbin, Richard A. *Justice Antonin Scalia and the Conservative Revival.* Baltimore. Md.: Johns Hopkins University Press, 1997.

Eastland, Terry. *Freedom of Expression in the Supreme Court: the Defining Cases.* Lanham, Md.: Rowman & Littlefield Publishers, 2000.

Harrison, Maureen, and Steve Gilbert. *Landmark Decisions of the United States Supreme Court IV.* La Jolla, Calif.: Excellent Books, 1994.

Heumann, Milton, et. al. *Hate Speech on Campus: Cases, Case Studies, and Commentary.* Boston: Northeastern University Press, 1997.

Schultz, David A., and Christopher E. Smith. *The Jurisprudential Vision of Justice Antonin Scalia.* Lanham, Md.: Rowman & Littlefield Publishers, 1996.

WEBSITES

First Amendment Center—R.A.V. Available online at http://www.freedomforum.org/fac/91-92/rav92.htm; website home page: http://www.freedomforum.org (accessed May 5, 2003).

U.S. v. Virginia

Supreme Court decision

By: Ruth Bader Ginsburg, William H. Rehnquist, Antonin Scalia

Date: June 26, 1996

Source: Ginsburg, Ruth Bader, William H. Rehnquist, Antonin Scalia. *U.S. v. Virginia*, 518 U.S. 515 (1996). Available online at http://laws.findlaw.com/us/518/515.html; website home page: http://laws.findlaw.com (accessed May 5, 2003).

About the Authors: This case featured decisions by three justices of the United States Supreme Court. Ruth Bader Ginsburg (1933–) is credited with great contributions to the women's rights movement. She was appointed to the federal bench in the early 1980s and to the Supreme Court in 1993. William H. Rehnquist (1924–) was named to the Supreme Court in 1971 and in 1986, he was appointed Chief Justice. Antonin Scalia (1936–) was appointed to the U.S. Court of Appeals in 1982. In 1986, he was nominated to the Supreme Court. ∎

Introduction

Gender discrimination has unfortunately long been a part of America, especially between individuals. Until the late-nineteenth and early-twentieth centuries, few people questioned the literal interpretation most gave to the clause in the Declaration of Independence: "All men are created equal." Only New Jersey allowed women to vote after the American Revolution (1775–1783), and it soon reversed its policy. In 1868, Congress passed the Fourteenth Amendment that reaffirmed the whole idea of equality, as requiring "equal protection of the laws." It did not, however, extend to gender. Many individuals, colleges and states, still denied equal treatment to women in the twentieth century, with many law and medical schools excluding women. Most Ivy League schools only admitted men, and had sister schools ("the Seven Sisters") to educate the daughters of America's elite. Those individuals who did become doctors and lawyers, but happened to be female, were denied jobs.

Although Ruth Bader Ginsburg graduated at the top of her class from Columbia in the early 1960s, she could not find a job in corporate America because law firms refused to hire women. Justice Felix Frankfurter refused to hire her as a law clerk for the same reason. In 1964, Congress greatly helped out women by banning sexual discrimination in hiring in the 1964 Civil Rights Act. However, individuals did not necessarily always follow these acts, nor did businesses. Women also continued to suffer because they did not have the advantages created by attending top schools.

The service academies, for instance, only admitted women in the 1970s, and graduation from a service academy was long seen as an important factor in military pro-

Kendra Russell and Amanda Harris are among the first group of women ever to attend the Virginia Military Institute in its 158-year history. **AP/WIDE WORLD PHOTOS. REPRODUCED BY PERMISSION.**

motions. A few schools, even as late as the 1980s and 1990s, continued to deny admission to women. The federal government sometimes brought lawsuits to force these schools to sexually integrate. Two of the schools that continued to deny women admission were The Citadel, in South Carolina, and Virginia Military Institute (VMI). These schools did not prepare many to go into the military, despite the names, but did give graduates the connections to prosper in business and government in those states—as there was a huge connection of alumni. When VMI proposed the creation of a separate

but equal program at a nearby women's college, the admission of women came in front of the Court. In *U.S. v. Virginia,* the U.S. Supreme Court addressed the constitutionality of denying women access to these institutions.

Significance

Ginsburg, in her opinion, makes it clear that Virginia's proposed solution is not equality, and nothing short of admitting women will bring about full equality. It is one of Ginsburg's better-known opinions and demonstrates how she is becoming a force on the court, despite her short tenure. This decision is also one of the few women's rights victories in the 1990s. Scalia's dissent indicates that he does not think VMI's tradition should be destroyed, and the main reason VMI is being attacked is because it is traditional and defends honor.

Since the decision, women have been admitted to the Virginia Military Institute and The Citadel, both of which maintain a harsh system of discipline. At VMI and at The Citadel, several males have been expelled for harassing female cadets. In 1999, the first female graduated from both VMI and the Citadel, and in 2001, the first class of female students at VMI who had entered as first year students graduated. Thirteen graduated out of the twenty-five who had entered. The number of female VMI and Citadel students continues to increase.

Primary Source

U.S. v. Virginia [excerpt]

> **SYNOPSIS:** Ginsburg first notes the "unique" system employed at VMI. She then holds that women can be admitted into VMI without destroying its mission and that a companion program, established by VMI at a nearby women's college, cannot be made equal to the VMI experience. Rehnquist concurs, holding that equality in all things does not need to be offered, and that the similar program cannot be made similar enough. Scalia dissents, holding that VMI is not banned by the Constitution and that VMI's honor is the reason it is being attacked and destroyed.

Justice Ginsburg delivered the opinion of the Court. . . .

VMI's distinctive mission is to produce "citizen-soldiers," men prepared for leadership in civilian life and in military service. VMI pursues this mission through pervasive training of a kind not available anywhere else in Virginia. Assigning prime place to character development, VMI uses an "adversative method" modeled on English public schools and once characteristic of military instruction. VMI constantly endeavors to instill physical and mental discipline in its cadets and impart to them a strong moral code. The school's graduates leave VMI with heightened comprehension of their capacity to deal with duress and stress, and a large sense of accomplishment for completing the hazardous course. . . .

VMI's "adversative model" is further characterized by a hierarchical "class system" of privileges and responsibilities, a "dyke system" for assigning a senior class mentor to each entering class "rat," and a stringently enforced "honor code," which prescribes that a cadet " 'does not lie, cheat, steal nor tolerate those who do.' " . . .

VMI attracts some applicants because of its reputation as an extraordinarily challenging military school, and "because its alumni are exceptionally close to the school." . . . "[W]omen have no opportunity anywhere to gain the benefits of [the system of education at VMI]." . . .

Virginia proposed a parallel program for women: Virginia Women's Institute for Leadership (VWIL). The 4-year, state-sponsored undergraduate program would be located at Mary Baldwin College, a private liberal arts school for women, and would be open, initially, to about 25 to 30 students. Although VWIL would share VMI's mission—to produce "citizen-soldiers"—the VWIL program would differ, as does Mary Baldwin College, from VMI in academic offerings, methods of education, and financial resources. . . .

We note, once again, the core instruction of this Court's pathmarking decisions. . . . Parties who seek to defend gender-based government action must demonstrate an "exceedingly persuasive justification" for that action. . . .

The State must show "at least that the [challenged] classification serves 'important governmental objectives and that the discriminatory means employed' are 'substantially related to the achievement of those objectives.' " . . . The justification must be genuine, not hypothesized or invented post hoc in response to litigation. And it must not rely on overbroad generalizations about the different talents, capacities, or preferences of males and females. . . .

Measuring the record in this case against the review standard just described, we conclude that Virginia has shown no "exceedingly persuasive justification" for excluding all women from the citizen-soldier training afforded by VMI. . . .

Single-sex education affords pedagogical benefits to at least some students, Virginia emphasizes, and that reality is uncontested in this litigation. Similarly, it is not disputed that diversity among public educational institutions can serve the public good. But Virginia has not shown that VMI was established, or has been maintained, with a view to diversifying, by its categorical exclusion of women, educational opportunities within the State. . . .

Neither recent nor distant history bears out Virginia's alleged pursuit of diversity through single-sex educational options. . . .

In sum, we find no persuasive evidence in this record that VMI's male-only admission policy "is in furtherance of a state policy of 'diversity.' " . . . However "liberally" this plan serves the State's sons, it makes no provision whatever for her daughters. That is not equal protection.

Virginia next argues that VMI's adversative method of training provides educational benefits that cannot be made available, unmodified, to women. Alterations to accommodate women would necessarily be "radical," so "drastic," Virginia asserts, as to transform, indeed "destroy," VMI's program. . . .

The notion that admission of women would downgrade VMI's stature, destroy the adversative system and, with it, even the school, is a judgment hardly proved, a prediction hardly different from other "self-fulfilling prophec[ies]," once routinely used to deny rights or opportunities. . . .

Women's successful entry into the federal military academies, and their participation in the Nation's military forces, indicate that Virginia's fears for the future of VMI may not be solidly grounded. The State's justification for excluding all women from "citizen-soldier" training for which some are qualified, in any event, cannot rank as "exceedingly persuasive," as we have explained and applied that standard. . . .

In the second phase of the litigation, Virginia presented its remedial plan—maintain VMI as a male-only college and create VWIL as a separate program for women. . . .

VWIL affords women no opportunity to experience the rigorous military training for which VMI is famed. . . .

Virginia, in sum, while maintaining VMI for men only, has failed to provide any "comparable single-gender women's institution." . . . Instead, the Commonwealth has created a VWIL program fairly appraised as a "pale shadow" of VMI in terms of the range of curricular choices and faculty stature, funding, prestige, alumni support and influence. . . .

[W]e rule here that Virginia has not shown substantial equality in the separate educational opportunities the State supports at VWIL and VMI. . . . VMI, too, offers an educational opportunity no other Virginia institution provides, and the school's "prestige"—associated with its success in developing "citizen soldiers"—is unequaled.

VMI, beyond question, "possesses to a far greater degree" than the VWIL program "those qualities which are incapable of objective measurement but which make for greatness in a . . . school," including "position and influence of the alumni, standing in the community, traditions and prestige." . . . Women seeking and fit for a VMI-quality education

cannot be offered anything less, under the State's obligation to afford them genuinely equal protection.

A prime part of the history of our Constitution, historian Richard Morris recounted, is the story of the extension of constitutional rights and protections to people once ignored or excluded. VMI's story continued as our comprehension of "We the People" expanded. . . . There is no reason to believe that the admission of women capable of all the activities required of VMI cadets would destroy the Institute rather than enhance its capacity to serve the "more perfect Union." . . .

Chief Justice Rehnquist, concurring in judgment. . . .

Accordingly, the remedy should not necessarily require either the admission of women to VMI, or the creation of a VMI clone for women. An adequate remedy in my opinion might be a demonstration by Virginia that its interest in educating men in a single-sex environment is matched by its interest in educating women in a single-sex institution. . . . It would be a sufficient remedy, I think, if the two institutions offered the same quality of education and were of the same overall calibre. In the end, the women's institution Virginia proposes, VWIL, fails as a remedy, because it is distinctly inferior to the existing men's institution and will continue to be for the foreseeable future.

VWIL simply is not, in any sense, the institution that VMI is. In particular, VWIL is a program appended to a private college, not a self-standing institution; and VWIL is substantially underfunded as compared to VMI. I therefore ultimately agree with the Court that Virginia has not provided an adequate remedy.

Justice Scalia, dissenting.

Today the Court shuts down an institution that has served the people of the Commonwealth of Virginia with pride and distinction for over a century and a half. To achieve that desired result, it rejects (contrary to our established practice) the factual findings of two courts below, sweeps aside the precedents of this Court, and ignores the history of our people. . . .

But in my view the function of this Court is to preserve our society's values regarding (among other things) equal protection, not to revise them; to prevent backsliding from the degree of restriction the Constitution imposed upon democratic government, not to prescribe, on our own authority, progressively higher degrees. For that reason it is my view that, whatever abstract tests we may choose to devise, they cannot supersede—and indeed ought to be crafted so as to reflect—those constant and unbroken national traditions that embody the people's understanding of ambiguous constitutional texts. More specifically, it is my view that "when a practice not expressly prohibited by the text of the Bill of Rights bears the endorsement of a long tradition of open, widespread, and unchallenged use that dates back to the beginning of the Republic, we have no proper basis for striking it down." . . .

The all-male constitution of VMI comes squarely within such a governing tradition. . . .

And the same applies, more broadly, to single-sex education in general, which, as I shall discuss, is threatened by today's decision with the cut-off of all state and federal support. Government-run non-military educational institutions for the two sexes have until very recently also been part of our national tradition. . . .

Today, however, change is forced upon Virginia, and reversion to single-sex education is prohibited nationwide, not by democratic processes but by order of this Court. Even while bemoaning the sorry, bygone days of "fixed notions" concerning women's education, . . . the Court favors current notions so fixedly that it is willing to write them into the Constitution of the United States by application of custom-built "tests." This is not the interpretation of a Constitution, but the creation of one. But besides its single-sex constitution, VMI is different from other colleges in another way. It employs a "distinctive educational method," sometimes referred to as the "adversarial, or doubting, model of education."

. . . There can be no serious dispute that, as the District Court found, single-sex education and a distinctive educational method "represent legitimate contributions to diversity in the Virginia higher education system." . . .

The Court contends that "[a] purpose genuinely to advance an array of educational options . . . is not served" by VMI. . . . It relies on the fact that all of Virginia's other public colleges have become co-educational. . . . The apparent theory of this argument is that unless Virginia pursues a great deal of diversity, its pursuit of some diversity must be a sham. This fails to take account of the fact that Virginia's resources cannot support all possible permutations of schools, . . . and of the fact that Virginia coordinates its public educational offerings with the offerings of in-state private educational institutions

that the Commonwealth provides money for its residents to attend and otherwise assists—which include four women's colleges. . . .

The Court simply dispenses with the evidence submitted at trial—it never says that a single finding of the District Court is clearly erroneous—in favor of the Justices' own view of the world, which the Court proceeds to support with (1) references to observations of someone who is not a witness, nor even an educational expert, nor even a judge who reviewed the record or participated in the judgment below, but rather a judge who merely dissented from the Court of Appeals' decision not to rehear this case en banc, . . . (2) citations of nonevidentiary materials such as amicus curiae briefs filed in this Court, . . . and (3) various historical anecdotes designed to demonstrate that Virginia's support for VMI as currently constituted reminds the Justices of the "bad old days." . . . It is not too much to say that this approach to the case has rendered the trial a sham. But treating the evidence as irrelevant is absolutely necessary for the Court to reach its conclusion. . . .

Court argues that VMI would not have to change very much if it were to admit women. . . . The principal response to that argument is that it is irrelevant: If VMI's single-sex status is substantially related to the government's important educational objectives, as I have demonstrated above and as the Court refuses to discuss, that concludes the inquiry. There should be no debate in the federal judiciary over "how much" VMI would be required to change if it admitted women and whether that would constitute "too much" change. . . .

It is worth noting that none of the United States' own experts in the remedial phase of this case was willing to testify that VMI's adversarial method was an appropriate methodology for educating women. This Court, however, does not care. Even though VWIL was carefully designed by professional educators who have tremendous experience in the area, and survived the test of adversarial litigation, the Court simply declares, with no basis in the evidence, that these professionals acted on "'overbroad' generalizations," . . .

As is frequently true, the Court's decision today will have consequences that extend far beyond the parties to the case. What I take to be the Court's unease with these consequences, and its resulting unwillingness to acknowledge them, cannot alter the reality.

Under the constitutional principles announced and applied today, single-sex public education is unconstitutional. . . .

The only hope for state-assisted single-sex private schools is that the Court will not apply in the future the principles of law it has applied today. That is a substantial hope, I am happy and ashamed to say. After all, did not the Court today abandon the principles of law it has applied in our earlier sex-classification cases? And does not the Court positively invite private colleges to rely upon our ad-hocery by assuring them this case is "unique"? . . .

Justice Brandeis said it is "one of the happy incidents of the federal system that a single courageous State may, if its citizens choose, serve as a laboratory; and try novel social and economic experiments without risk to the rest of the country." . . . But it is one of the unhappy incidents of the federal system that a self-righteous Supreme Court, acting on its Members' personal view of what would make a "more perfect Union," . . . can impose its own favored social and economic dispositions nationwide. As today's disposition, and others this single Term, show, this places it beyond the power of a "single courageous State," not only to introduce novel dispositions that the Court frowns upon, but to reintroduce, or indeed even adhere to, disfavored dispositions that are centuries old. . . . The sphere of self-government reserved to the people of the Republic is progressively narrowed. . . .

In an odd sort of way, it is precisely VMI's attachment to such old-fashioned concepts as manly "honor" that has made it, and the system it represents, the target of those who today succeed in abolishing public single-sex education. The record contains a booklet that all first-year VMI students (the so-called "rats") were required to keep in their possession at all times. Near the end there appears the following period-piece, entitled "The Code of a Gentleman":

> . . . The honor of a gentleman demands the inviolability of his word, and the incorruptibility of his principles. He is the descendant of the knight, the crusader; he is the defender of the defenseless and the champion of justice . . . or he is not a Gentleman. . . .

I do not know whether the men of VMI lived by this Code; perhaps not. But it is powerfully impressive that a public institution of higher education still in existence sought to have them do so. I do not think any of us, women included, will be better off for its destruction.

Further Resources

BOOKS

Bayer, Linda N. *Ruth Bader Ginsburg.* Philadelphia: Chelsea House Publishers, 2000.

Brisbin, Richard A. *Justice Antonin Scalia and the Conservative Revival.* Baltimore, Md.: Johns Hopkins University Press, 1997.

Brodie, Laura Fairchild. *Breaking Out: VMI and the Coming of Women.* New York: Pantheon Books, 2000.

Davis, Sue. *Justice Rehnquist and the Constitution.* Princeton, N.J.: Princeton University Press, 1989.

Jones, Brenn. *Learning About Equal Rights from the Life of Ruth Bader Ginsburg.* New York: Rosen Publishing Group, 2002.

Manegold, Catherine S. *In Glory's Shadow: Shannon Faulkner, the Citadel, and a Changing America.* New York: A.A. Knopf, 2000.

Strum, Philippa. *Women in the Barracks: the VMI Case and Equal Rights.* Lawrence: University Press of Kansas, 2002.

WEBSITES

Equal Opportunity at VMI: United States v. Virginia. Available online at http://www.law.siu.edu/lawjour/22_2/dawes.htm; website home page: http://www.law.siu.edu (accessed May 5, 2003).

Ninia Baehr, Genora Dancel et al. v. John C. Lewin
Court case

By: Stephen H. Levinson

Date: 1993

Source: Levinson, Stephen H. *Ninia Baehr, Genora Dancel et al. v. John C. Lewin.* Reprinted in Hall, Kermit L., et. al. *American Legal History: Cases and Materials.* 2nd ed. New York: Oxford University Press, 1996, 572–574.

About the Author: Steven H. Levinson was born in Cincinnati, Ohio, attended Stanford University for his bachelor's degree, and received his law degree from the University of Michigan. While at Michigan Law School, Levinson wrote an article in the *Michigan Journal of Law Reform.* He worked for a law firm, and served on the Circuit Court of the First Judicial Circuit for three years before joining the Hawaii Supreme Court in 1992. ∎

Introduction

United States laws have generally criminalized homosexual behavior, although current thought (beginning with the Kinsey Reports in the 1940s and 1950s) suggests there is nothing aberrant about it. Indeed, gay and lesbian tradition has a long history in the United States, as do laws prohibiting sexual encounters between people of the same sex. For example, sodomy was criminalized by all thirteen states at the time of the Constitution's adoption. In the nineteenth century, many single women lived together in what were termed "Boston marriages," and many of the people living in such "marriages" were lesbians. Culturally, Americans held strong biases against gays and lesbians. Newspapers danced around terms to use when referring to them—"homosexual" becoming the politically correct alternative. *The New York Times* used the term very infrequently in the first half of the twentieth century—first in 1926, and not again until 1943. Homosexual communities did arise, however, especially in larger cities.

Marriage is something which was (and is) generally governed by state law. Each state establishes its own marriage requirements, such as residency and blood tests. Every other state, generally is obliged to respect the marriage (and divorce) decrees due to the "full faith and credit" clause of the U.S. Constitution, and because of a legal doctrine called comity. This has not always been the case, however. In the late 1800s, a famous divorce case occurred where a man paid for a married woman to move to Indiana from New York. The woman moved, waited and divorced her husband in Indiana. When she returned to New York and married the other man, New York refused to recognize Indiana's divorce. In general, however, marriage and divorce decrees have usually been accepted by all.

But what constitutes a marriage? Most states, implicitly or explicitly, defined marriage as being between one man and one woman. When homosexuality became a more public lifestyle after the late 1960s, gays and lesbians argued in favor of same sex marriages. No favorable court ruling for gays and lesbians came until the Supreme Court of Hawaii heard *Baehr v. Lewin* in 1993.

Significance

The three couples involved in this same-sex marriage case in Hawaii, won the battle, but in many ways lost the war. Hawaii soon acted to ban gay and lesbian marriages, passing legislation to that effect. The federal government got into the act, passing the "Defense of Marriage Act." This act held that no state was required to recognize any marriage from another state, unless that marriage was between one man and one woman. This "defense" of course, is from a heterosexual perspective.

Gays and lesbians did better in Vermont though. Vermont, which has recently been much more progressive than most other states (they elected an independent congressman with socialist views recently), acted to help gays and lesbians. That state created a "civil union,"

which gays and lesbians could enter into with their partners, and this civil union gave all the benefits of marriage in Vermont. Of course, if another state does not recognize the civil union there, the benefit only really exists within Vermont. As gay and lesbian issues receive more attention, the issue of gay and lesbian marriages will continue to simmer.

Primary Source

Ninia Baehr, Genora Dancel et al. v. John C. Lewin
[excerpt]

SYNOPSIS: Levinson holds that the only reason these couples have been denied the right to marry is that they are homosexual, and this makes the law presumably unconstitutional under the Hawaii Constitution. Levinson then notes the benefits denied these couples because they are not married and reviews the case of *Loving v. Virginia,* which struck down an interracial marriage ban. The court then holds the marriage ban to be a sex-based classification, and therefore unconstitutional.

In addition to the alleged violation of their constitutional rights to privacy and due process of law, the applicant couples contend that they have been denied the equal protection of the laws as guaranteed by . . . the Hawaii Constitution. . . . [W]e agree . . . that: homosexuals . . . constitute a "suspect class" for purposes of equal protection analysis under . . . the Hawaii Constitution. . . .

The applicant couples correctly contend that the DOH's [Department of Health's] refusal to allow them to marry on the basis that they are members of the same sex deprives them of access to a multiplicity of rights and benefits that are contingent upon that status. Although it is unnecessary in this opinion to engage in an encyclopedic recitation of all of them, a number of the most salient marital rights and benefits are worthy of note. They include: (1) a variety of state income tax advantages, including deductions, credits, rates, exemptions, and estimates. . . . (2) public assistance from and exemptions relating to the Department of Human Services. . . . (3) control, division, acquisition, and disposition of community property. . . . (4) rights relating to dower, curtesy, and inheritance. . . . (5) rights to notice, protection, benefits, and inheritance. . . . (6) award of child custody and support payments in divorce proceedings. . . . (7) the right to spousal support. . . . (8) the right to enter into premarital agreements. . . . (9) the right to change of name. . . . (10) the right to file a nonsupport action. . . . (11) post-divorce rights relating to support

A Hawaii Supreme Court struck down a ban on same-sex marriage, stating that a sex-based classification for marriage was unconstitutional. AP/WIDE WORLD PHOTOS. REPRODUCED BY PERMISSION.

and property division. . . . (12) the benefit of the spousal privilege and confidential marital communications. . . . (13) the benefit of the exemption of real property from attachment or execution. . . . and (14) the right to bring a wrongful death action. . . . For present purposes, it is not disputed that the applicant couples would be entitled to all of these marital rights and benefits, but for the fact that they are denied access to the state-conferred legal status of marriage.

[The law] on its face, discriminates based on sex against the applicant couples in the exercise of the civil right of marriage, thereby implicating the equal protection clause . . . of the Hawaii Constitution.

. . . [T]he extent of permissible state regulation of the right of access to the marital relationship is subject to constitutional limitations or constraints. [Here the court cited *Loving v. Virginia* (1967).] It has been held that a state may deny the right to marry only for compelling reasons. [In a footnote the Court gave such examples of "'compelling' reasons as consanguinity (to prevent incest), immature age (to protect the welfare of children), presence of venereal disease (to foster public health), and to prevent bigamy."]

The equal protection clauses of the United States and Hawaii Constitutions are not mirror images of one another. The fourteenth amendment to the United States Constitution somewhat concisely provides, in relevant part, that a state may not "deny to any person within its jurisdiction the equal protection of the laws." Hawaii's counterpart is more elaborate . . . provid[ing] in relevant part that "no person shall . . . be denied the equal protection of the laws, nor be denied the enjoyment of the person's civil rights or be discriminated against in the exercise thereof because of race, religion, sex, or ancestry." Thus, by its plain language, the Hawaii Constitution prohibits state-sanctioned discrimination against any person in the exercise of his or her civil rights on the basis of sex.

"The freedom to marry has long been recognized as one of the vital personal rights essential to the orderly pursuit of happiness by free [people]" [quoting *Loving v. Virginia*]. So "fundamental" does the United States Supreme Court consider the institution of marriage that it has deemed marriage to be "one of the 'basic civil rights of [men and women].'"

. . . [O]n its face and (as Lewin admits) as applied, [the law] denies same-sex couples access to the marital status and its concomitant rights and benefits. It is the state's regulation of access to the status of married persons, on the basis of the applicants' sex, that gives rise to the question whether the applicant couples have been denied the equal protection of the laws in violation of . . . the Hawaii Constitution.

Relying primarily on four [state] decisions construing the law of other jurisdictions, Lewin contends that "the fact that homosexual (sic—actually, same-sex) partners cannot form a state-licensed marriage is not the product of impermissible discrimination" implicating equal protection considerations, but rather "a function of their biologic inability as a couple to satisfy the definition of the status to which they aspire." Put differently, Lewin proposes that "the right of persons of the same sex to marry one another does not exist because marriage, by definition and usage, means a special relationship between a man and a woman." We believe Lewin's argument to be circular and unpersuasive.

Significantly, the appellants' equal protection rights—federal or state—were not asserted in [the state cases cited by Lewin and thus the state courts were] relieved of the necessity of addressing and attempting to distinguish the decision of the United States Supreme Court in *Loving*. *Loving* involved the appeal of a black woman and a caucasian man (the Lovings) who were married in the District of Columbia and thereafter returned to their home state of Virginia to establish their marital abode. The Lovings were duly indicted for and convicted of violating Virginia's miscegenation laws, which banned interracial marriages. In his sentencing decision, the trial judge stated, in substance, that Divine Providence had not intended that the marriage state extend to interracial unions:

> Almighty God created the races white, black, yellow, malay and red, and he placed them on separate continents. And but for the interference with his arrangement there would be no cause for such marriages. The fact that he separated the races shows that he did not intend for the races to mix.

In a landmark decision, the United States Supreme Court, through Chief Justice Warren, struck down the Virginia miscegenation laws on both equal protection and due process grounds. . . .

The facts in *Loving* and the respective reasoning of the Virginia courts, on the one hand, and the United States Supreme Court, on the other, both discredit the reasoning . . . and unmask the tautologi-

cal and circular nature of Lewin's argument that [the law] does not implicate . . . the Hawaii Constitution because same sex marriage is an innate impossibility. Analogously to Lewin's argument . . . the Virginia courts declared that interracial marriage simply could not exist because the Deity had deemed such a union intrinsically unnatural, and, in effect, because it had therefore never been the "custom" of the state to recognize mixed marriages, marriage "always" having been construed to presuppose a different configuration. With all due respect to the Virginia courts of a bygone era, we do not believe that trial judges are the ultimate authorities on the subject of Divine Will, and, as *Loving* amply demonstrates, constitutional law may mandate, like it or not, that customs change with an evolving social order.

As we have indicated, [Hawaii's marriage law] on its face and as applied, regulates access to the marital status and its concomitant rights and benefits on the basis of the applicants' sex. As such, [the law] establishes a sex-based classification.

[In a previous decision] we clearly and unequivocally established, for purposes of equal protection analysis under the Hawaii Constitution, that sex-based classifications are subject, as a per se matter, to some form of "heightened" scrutiny, be it "strict" or "intermediate," rather than mere "rational basis" analysis. Second, we assumed, arguendo, that such sex-based classifications were subject to "strict scrutiny." Third, we reaffirmed the longstanding principle that this court is free to accord greater protections to Hawaii's citizens under the state constitution than are recognized under the United States Constitution. . . .

Accordingly, we hold that sex is a "suspect category" for purposes of equal protection analysis under . . . the Hawaii Constitution and that [Hawaii's marriage law] . . . is presumed to be unconstitutional. . . .

Further Resources

BOOKS

Baird, Robert M., and Stuart E. Rosenbaum. *Same-Sex Marriage: the Moral and Legal Debate.* Amherst, N.Y.: Prometheus Books, 1997.

Curry, Hayden. *A Legal Guide for Lesbian and Gay Couples.* Berkeley, Calif.: Nolo Press, 1998.

Eskridge, William N. *Equality Practice: Civil Unions and the Future of Gay Rights.* New York: Routledge, 2002.

McKenna, George, and Stanley Feingold. *Taking Sides: Clashing Views on Controversial Political Issues.* Guilford, Conn.: Dushkin Pub. Group, 1997.

Merin, Yuval. *Equality For Same-Sex Couples: the Legal Recognition of Gay Partnerships in Europe and the United States.* Chicago: University of Chicago Press, 2002.

Strasser, Mark Philip. *On Same-Sex Marriage, Civil Unions, and the Rule of Law: Constitutional Interpretation at the Crossroads.* Westport, Conn.: Praeger, 2002.

PERIODICALS

Fajer, Marc A. "Toward Respectful Representation: Some Thoughts on Selling Same-Sex Marriage." *Yale Law & Policy Review* 15, no. 2, 599–627.

WEBSITES

Lesbian and Gay Marriage through History and Culture http://www.gay-bible.org/other/halsall.htm; website home page: http://www.gay-bible.org (accessed May 4, 2003).

"The Rodney King Videotape: Why the Case Was Not Black and White"

Journal article

By: Elizabeth F. Loftus and Laura A. Rosenwald

Date: 1996

Source: Loftus, Elizabeth F., and Laura A. Rosenwald. "The Rodney King Videotape: Why the Case Was Not Black and White." Reprinted in Hall, Kermit L., et al. *American Legal History: Cases and Materials.* 2nd ed. New York: Oxford University Press, 1996, 575–578.

About the Authors: Elizabeth F. Loftus (1944–) received her Ph.D. from Stanford. She has taught for the University of Washington at Seattle since 1970. She has received grants from the National Institute of Mental Health, and she has been named a fellow of the American Council on Education.

Laura A. Rosenwald, a former editor of the *Washington Law Review,* has published several books and articles, including "Buried Memories, Shattered Lives" and *Law and Mental Health Professionals.* ∎

Introduction

Rioting has a long history in American culture. There were many riots in colonial times, and patriots used rioting to express their dissatisfaction with the British government. In fact, Boston in colonial times had riots every few years. After the Revolutionary War (1775–1783), riots tended to lessen, but they still occurred. During the Civil War (1861–1865), anti-draft riots flared up all over America—the most notable being, in 1863, in New York City, where over 100 people were killed.

Riots continued for the next century. In the 1960s, many of the urban riots were race riots—those trapped in the city expressed their rage against a racially-biased system. Among the most famous of the 1960s race riots were in the Watts neighborhood of Los Angeles (where thirty-four people died) and Detroit (where forty-three died). After the assassination of Martin Luther King Jr., more rioting broke out, and some sixty cities were affected. After the 1960s, race riots diminished, and most cities experienced a relative calm.

However, many minorities were not being treated well, even though the cities were somewhat peaceful. Since their creation in the late 1800s, professional police forces have historically hired relatively few minorities. Particularly in the South, the police often abused minorities and harshly enforced the laws. In Mississippi, Andrew Goodman, Michael Schwerner, and James Chaney, three civil rights workers, were killed by the police in 1964. Such brutality seldom brought criminal charges, or even disciplinary action. When complaints were made, they were either dismissed—or were "investigated." Once the police who were involved denied the charges, the matter was dropped. As a result, minorities came to distrust the police.

A clear-cut case of police brutality seemed to come in front of the nation in 1991. After an auto chase, the Los Angeles police captured Rodney King. During the arrest, the police repeatedly beat King, and, unlike most previous incidents, a bystander captured this on videotape. Part of the tape (after editing) was shown repeatedly on television, and many in the nation were outraged. However, an all-white jury acquitted the officers, sparking a riot. In the following piece, a law student and a psychology professor discuss why the videotape seen on television was not enough to convict the police officers.

Significance

Loftus and Rosenwald are correct in noting that the whole tape was rarely shown on the news, and that fact played a role in the acquittal. That the acquittal might have been the right verdict, legally, did not change public perception or help stop the rioting. The riots of the 1960s often led to the rebuilding of destroyed areas, but in the case of the 1992 Los Angeles riot, the city had no funds to rebuild. Similar to the O.J. Simpson trial, reaction to the Rodney King verdict is very polarized by race. Those who are white and have watched the whole videotape and carefully considered the evidence, are much more likely to agree with the jury verdict, than are blacks. Nationwide, little was changed by the Rodney King trial and subsequent riot—America in the 1990s was generally not interested in discussing race. But in Los Angeles, police training and procedures were altered, and a black police chief was hired. Studies demonstrate that the LA Police Department did somewhat improve its racial treatment. During the riot Rodney King pleaded, "Can't we just all get along?" The answer to that plea has yet to be given by America.

Riots broke out in the streets of Los Angeles after several police officers were acquitted of the charges in the beating of Rodney King. © PETER TURNLEY/CORBIS. REPRODUCED BY PERMISSION.

Primary Source

"The Rodney King Videotape: Why the Case Was Not Black and White"

SYNOPSIS: The two authors note that many people assume racism was the underlying cause of the King verdict. They then comment on the increasing use of videotaping and its growing power. However, the authors also argue that the video was not conclusive since it was shaped by both the camera operator and the editor, and they note these effects in the King case.

I. Introduction

In 1960, a *New York Times* reporter traveled to Mississippi to write about the lynching of a black man who had been dragged by a white mob from a jail where he was serving a sentence for raping a white woman. Perhaps not surprisingly, the local grand jury later failed to indict anyone for the murder. A local official told the *Times* reporter, "You couldn't convict the guilty parties if you had a sound film of the lynching."

More than thirty years later, many Americans reached a similar conclusion when they learned of the verdicts in the trial of four white Los Angeles police officers accused of beating Rodney King, a black man. This time, there was sound film: an explosive eighty-one second videotape of the beating that shocked most Americans when it aired on nationwide television news in March 1991. Yet a jury drawn from a mostly white Los Angeles suburb acquitted the officers on all but one charge, on which the jury split. To many, the only explanation was racism.

The *Wall Street Journal* recently compared the King beating to another incident of brutality captured on film a decade ago at an upstate New York prison. The tape shows a group of white guards attacking an 18-year-old Chinese inmate. The inmate yells, "Kill me, kill me," and a guard replies, "Give me an excuse, give me one." A microphone recorded the sounds of officers' batons cracking the inmate's skull, like baseballs colliding with bats. The Clinton County prosecutor handed the case over to federal prosecutors because he believed that they would provide a more impartial investigation. Despite the clear evidence, the 1982 trial before a federal jury in Albany ended in a mistrial.

Underlying the public response to incidents like these is a belief that videotape is powerful and conclusive. When it fails to persuade a jury, as in the Los Angeles and Clinton County trials, the only possible explanation is racism. But in the rush to judgment, people may overlook important truths about videotape and how it can be successfully used—or combated—in the criminal justice system. While videotape may be the most potent evidentiary tool since wiretapping, the Rodney King trial proved that a skillful defense attorney can overcome its impact.

The lessons of the Rodney King trial are worth learning. With the recent proliferation of video cameras in American homes, we can expect to see a proliferation of video evidence. For instance, prosecutors preparing charges resulting from the Los Angeles riots that followed the King verdict studied 329 videotapes made by amateurs and television news crews. "There has never been anything like this," FBI spokesman John Hoos told the New York Times. "The new technology has created a wealth of vital information that is revolutionizing our ability to do investigations like this."

Video is being used in many other ways in the criminal justice system. Police officers use it to protect themselves against brutality charges. By one estimate, police departments have purchased 20,000 cameras for installation in patrol cars.

During the 1992 Republican National Convention in Houston, the American Civil Liberties Union distributed video cameras to monitor demonstrators and police abuses. . . .

Video is also showing up increasingly in civil litigation. A New York state judge recently allowed videotaped depositions of witnesses even though the witnesses were available to testify in person at trial. The plaintiff's attorney had argued that videotape would preserve the nuances of the deposition, and would cost about half as much as the cost of a stenographer. "Video depositions are here to stay for, surer than death or taxes, lawyers like to play with new toys," said Judge Bernard F. McCaffrey.

The media is contributing to the craze. . . . News organizations give amateurs strong economic incentives to record crimes. Los Angeles resident Timothy Goldman, along with his brother and a friend, filmed the beating of white truck driver Reginald Denny in the rioting that followed the King verdict. After hearing reports of the rioting on their police scanner, each grabbed a camera and began filming on a corner near Goldman's home. Goldman has earned tens of thousands of dollars from selling the broadcast rights to his tapes.

Average citizens have always played an important role as witnesses in trials. But with a video camera in hand, a person has a chance at an even larger role. By recording a crime in progress, he or she may enable, or even force, an otherwise unlikely prosecution. While police brutality is considered common in some American cities, prosecutions such as the one that took place in Los Angeles are rare. Had plumbing salesman George Holliday merely watched the King beating and not videotaped it, prosecutors might have rejected the case as too difficult to win. But Holliday's graphic tape was impossible to ignore.

While the proliferation of video cameras may be a boon to prosecutors, the King verdict demonstrated that a video's force can be successfully countered by a skillful advocate.

II. The Power of Video

Video's power to influence people is unquestioned. During the civil rights movement, television reports of southern racial clashes stirred northerners in a way that words could not. As Yale Law School Professor Alexander M. Bickel wrote, "Compulsory segregation, like states' rights and like 'The Southern Way of Life,' is an abstraction and, to a good many people, a neutral or sympathetic one. These riots, which were brought instantly, dramatically, and literally home to the American people, showed what it means concretely."

IV. Explaining the Post-Watergate Era

Videotaped evidence has figured prominently in criminal proceedings ever since Abscam introduced the public to video crime; arguably, it established the enduring image of congressmen as crooks. One explanation for the force of video evidence is that it is significantly more detailed and vivid than written words. . . .

V. The Shaping of Tape

If vivid verbal descriptions are persuasive, videotape is even more so. Unlike humans, tape does not lie or forget. This may explain the public's outrage over the Rodney King tape and its disbelief of the verdict. Although videotape is extremely effective as evidence, it is not conclusive.

To begin with, the camera operator exercises a substantial control by initially deciding whether to tape at all, how long to tape, what to focus on, and from what perspective to film. Later, the filmmaker

After an auto chase, the Los Angeles police arrested Rodney King and repeatedly beat him. A bystander captured this beating on videotape. **AP/WIDE WORLD PHOTOS. REPRODUCED BY PERMISSION.**

can remove or enhance certain parts by splicing and juxtaposing. The circumstances under which viewers watch the tape, including context and presentation, can also affect their reactions. Televised violence, like the King beating, suddenly transports the unprepared viewer to the scene of a crime. Exposure to violence in a courtroom, on the other hand, may be less jarring because it is more expected. These facts should be kept in mind when evaluating the King videotape.

First, television viewers saw only a snipped segment of the eighty-one second tape played for the jury. Roger Parloff, a lawyer and senior reporter for the American Lawyer, watched the trial on television. He reported what occurred on the parts of the tape that were edited out for network television news because they were blurred. In the unedited version, King refused the officers' command to lie prone and be handcuffed and searched. He knelt on all fours, but then shook off four officers and stood up. After issuing a warning, one officer stunned King twice with electric current from a Taser gun. At that point, with King finally lying on the ground, the shortened television version of the tape begins. Neither the long nor the short television versions of the tape showed the car chase at up to 100 mph that preceded the beating, or conveyed the chaotic atmosphere of the arrest scene, with milling officers,

wailing sirens, and a helicopter buzzing overhead. There were details that a tape could not reveal, such as the fact that the officers' Taser gun had run out of electricity, or that several officers believed, mistakenly, that King was on the drug PCP. Because the trial judge put a gag order on the attorneys, these facts did not come to light until the trial was underway. But this had little effect on public opinion, which solidified against the police immediately after the tape aired.

Second, the defense chose to show the tape over and over again to the jury as a way of lessening its impact. The goal was to make the beating as familiar—and about as stimulating—as a cereal advertisement. Some attorneys might have rejected this strategy, fearing that multiple viewings would merely imprint the beatings on jurors' minds. However, research has shown that repeated exposure to visual information does not necessarily have that effect. . . . The converse is also true: an event seen just once can have a profound impact. This explains why those who saw the King beating on television could have experienced a stronger reaction than a juror who watched it repeatedly.

Finally, while the tape dominated the public's exposure to the case, one juror described it as "just another piece of evidence." The trial featured fifty-five witnesses during twenty-nine days of testimony.

One reporter who covered the trial likened the silent tape played again and again on a big-screen television, often in slow motion, to "a disembodied video in a department store."

VI. Conclusion

The King case has enormous implications for the judicial system. It both illustrated the power of videotape evidence and stimulated its production. But attorneys should recognize that the camera is not simply a neutral eye that keeps an objective record. Video, like any kind of evidence, is part of a mosaic. It needs context, and is subject to widely varying interpretations and manipulations.

Further Resources

BOOKS

Cannon, Lou. *Official Negligence: How Rodney King and the Riots Changed Los Angeles and the LAPD.* New York: Times Books, 1997.

Deitz, Robert. *Willful Injustice: a Post-O.J. Look at Rodney King, American Justice, and Trial by Race.* Washington, D.C.: Regnery Pub, 1996.

Gibbs, Jewelle Taylor. *Race and Justice: Rodney King and O.J. Simpson in a House Divided.* San Francisco: Jossey-Bass, 1996.

Khalifah, H. Khalif. *Rodney King and the L.A. Rebellion: A 1992 Black Rebellion in the United States: Analysis & Commentary.* Hampton, Va.: U.B. & U.S. Communications Systems, 1992.

AUDIO AND VISUAL MEDIA

The "Rodney King" Case: What the Jury Saw in CA v. Powell. Directed by Dominic Palumbo. Oak Forest, Ill.: MPI Home Video, Videocassette, 1991.

The Rodney King Incident: Race and Justice in America. Directed by Michael Pack. Princeton, N.J.: Films for the Humanities & Sciences, Videocassette, 1998.

Reasonable Doubts: The Criminal Justice System and the O.J. Simpson Case

Memoir

By: Alan M. Dershowitz

Date: 1996

Source: Dershowitz, Alan M. *Reasonable Doubts: The Criminal Justice System and the O.J. Simpson Case.* New York: Touchstone Books, 1996, 161–162, 165–167, 180–181.

About the Author: Alan Dershowitz (1938–) attended Yale Law School and clerked for Supreme Court Justice Arthur Goldberg. At twenty-eight, he was appointed full professor at Harvard Law School, the youngest full professor in school history. In addition to his teaching, in 1972, Dershowitz began to represent clients—many of whom were well known—including Leona Helmsley, Patricia Hearst, Claus von Bulow, F. Lee Bailey, and, of course, O.J. Simpson. He has written over a dozen books. ■

Introduction

The "trial of the century" has occurred many times in American history, and many more times in world history. As early as 1806, with the Aaron Burr treason trial, a criminal court proceeding took center stage in this country. President Thomas Jefferson (served 1801–1809) himself was behind the efforts to have Burr convicted of treason. Trials continued to interest the American public throughout the rest of the century, including those of individuals such as Lizzie Borden, alleged to have murdered her mother and father with an ax. Borden was acquitted of the criminal charges, but the public continued to believe her guilty.

As the twentieth century opened, radio, and ultimately television, turned trials that held wide interest into spectacles. Several factors had to converge for a case to be considered a "trial of the century:" the crime was very interesting or a burning question, and a well-known person was involved, either as defendant or lawyer. Also, the media had to cover the events. The first "trial of the 20th century" might well have been in 1924 with the (Nathan) Leopold and (Richard) Loeb case, where two affluent youths were charged with the senseless killing of a young boy. Clarence Darrow, a well-known attorney, pled the two defendants guilty, but then convinced a jury that their mental capacities were diminished, saving them from the death penalty. In the 1930s, the baby of Charles A. Lindbergh Jr., one of America's heroes and the first person to fly solo across the Atlantic, was kidnapped, and that case became a "trial of the century." Throughout the rest of the 1900s—with the Rosenbergs, the Chicago 7, Patty Hearst, and the Rodney King beating trial—the "trials of the century" continued. One of the latest to claim this dubious honor was the O.J. Simpson trial, a case in which Simpson, a former football star and actor, was accused of murdering his former wife and a man who was visiting her. Alan Dershowitz served on Simpson's defense team.

Significance

O.J. Simpson was acquitted, without much help from Dershowitz—Dershowitz himself admits that he was mostly working on an appeals brief had there been a conviction. Dershowitz claims that any trial tactics necessary on the part of the defense team are legal, because they are representing a client; whereas the prosecutor represents justice. That claim may cause concern for readers who think that the whole process of a trial is to produce justice.

In the O.J. Simpson case, racial polarization was also a factor. Some blacks believe that the Los Angeles Police Department tried to frame Simpson—making the acquittal just; and some whites think that Simpson got away with murder. Simpson continues to claim that he is searching for the "real killer." Dershowitz is back teaching at Harvard and America waits for its next "trial of the century."

Primary Source

Reasonable Doubts: The Criminal Justice System and the O.J. Simpson Case [excerpt]

SYNOPSIS: Dershowitz defines himself as "one of the few" true civil libertarians. He discusses varying reactions people had to his defense of O.J. Simpson and the hate mail he received. He also talks about the people who thought his motivation was financial, and the people who hated him for working with Johnnie Cochran. He closes by arguing that a defense lawyer's only obligation is to his client, while a prosecutor must pursue justice.

The role of defense lawyers and prosecutors in criminal cases is misunderstood by much of the public, including the well-informed public. Even many lawyers have little real understanding of what advocates are expected to do in a hotly contested criminal trial.

Several weeks after the Simpson verdict, my wife and I were walking down Madison Avenue in New York when a well-dressed woman approached us and said, "I used to love you so much, and now I'm so disappointed in you—and my husband would use even stronger words." She explained, "You used to defend Jews like Scharansky and Pollard. Now you defend Jew-killers like O.J." I replied that she was wrong ever to have loved me because she probably didn't understand what I do. A few blocks farther along, a black man hugged me and said, "Great job. I love what you do." I told him not to love what I do or else he would soon be disappointed.

These two encounters—and the hundreds like them I have experienced over the years, especially since the Simpson verdict—underline the public reaction to defense lawyers. When we represent defendants they like, the public loves us. When we represent defendants they dislike, the public hates us. For some criminal lawyers, this poses no problem, since they choose clients on the basis of their popularity. These lawyers would never dream of rep-

resenting any client who is disliked by the public. I know several such lawyers, some of whom consult with public relations experts before they take on a controversial client.

Other criminal lawyers select their clients on the basis of causes or constituencies. They will represent defendants who may be disliked by the *general* public, as long as their *particular* constituents approve of the defendant. Many feminist lawyers will defend any woman who has killed or maimed a man, regardless of the circumstances, because they know they can count on support from certain feminist groups. William Kunstler, a political lawyer, often represented clients who were unpopular with the general public; but they were always popular with Kunstler's particular left-wing constituency. There are right-wing analogues to Kunstler.

Criminal lawyers who are true civil libertarians have no constituency. Many lawyers who claim to be civil libertarians are merely *using* principles of civil liberties to further their political ends. During the period when the left was persecuted by anti-labor forces, McCarthyites and anti-immigration zealots, many on the left became civil libertarians. More recently, when civil liberties were employed against some of the left's own agendas—such as racial quotas, university speech codes, and "political correctness"—some began to see civil libertarians as the enemies of the left. At about the same time, a few conservatives took on the mantle of civil liberties to challenge these same agendas. Many African-Americans who champion free speech when Louis Farrakhan is censored by some university call for censorship of white racist speakers. Many Jews who supported freedom of speech for Meir Kahane were appalled when the ACLU defended the right of neo-Nazis to march in Skokie. Fair-weather civil libertarians are often "disappointed" by civil libertarians who defend the rights of the individual without regard to politics, gender, race, or other agenda concerns.

The verdict in the Simpson case resulted in an outpouring of "disappointment" unlike that in any other case during my thirty-two-year career as a lawyer. Many people took the acquittal personally, as if they themselves had been denied justice by what they perceived as an illegitimate result. My hate mail, which used to be limited to crackpot anti-Semites railing against my Jewishness, suddenly became more mainstream, although certainly no less vitriolic. Indeed, some of the most virulent, hateful and bigoted letters came from Jews who said they

Acquitted for the murder of his former wife, O.J. Simpson sits in court with members of his defense team (from left to right): Barry Scheck, Peter Neufeld, O.J., Johnnie Cochran, and Robert Shapiro. **AP/WIDE WORLD PHOTOS. REPRODUCED BY PERMISSION.**

used to love me, but now hate me. Most of them focused on one of three themes. The first is typical of all my hate mail: How can you represent someone who I think is guilty? . . .

The second theme is particularly disturbing, coming as it does predominantly from Jewish letter-writers. It articulates a stereotype about Jews that usually comes from bigoted non-Jews: that all Jews care about is money. The word "greed" appeared over and over again, but this time from the mouths of Jews. . . .

I never take cases because of the fee, and half of my cases are pro bono. In fact, my fee in the Simpson case was relatively small, but when critics don't like which side a lawyer is on, they often focus on the fee.

The third—and most disturbing—theme revolved around the actions of my co-counsel Johnnie Cochran in "comparing" Detective Mark Fuhrman to Adolf Hitler, in surrounding himself with Nation of Is-

lam bodyguards after receiving death threats in the courtroom, and in "playing the race card." . . .

Finally, there was vehement criticism of the defense for "playing the race card." The term itself—as Henry Louis Gates, Jr., tells us—is "a barrier to inter-racial comprehension" which "infuriates many blacks." Race was irretrievably introduced into the trial when Marcia Clark embraced Mark Fuhrman *after* being told of his racism. She had to know that Fuhrman was lying when he denied using racist epithets. So did dozens of other prosecutors, police, and friends of Fuhrman, who all sat silently by and allowed the lie to go uncorrected until the tapes were discovered. The so-called race card was dealt by the prosecution and trumped by the defense, as the defense was obliged to do.

As the respected judge Leon Higginbotham put it: "If the defendant had been Jewish and the police officer had a long history of expressed anti-Semitism and having planted evidence against innocent persons

Alan Dershowitz, a member of O.J. Simpson's defense team, wrote a book about this famous trial. **AP/WIDE WORLD PHOTOS. REPRODUCED BY PERMISSION.**

who were Jewish, I can't believe that anyone would have been saying that defense counsel was playing the anti-Semitism card." Would anyone feel that the Jewish defendant had been adequately defended if the bias of that anti-Semitic witness had not been exposed? . . .

The most common complaint about lawyers—especially criminal defense lawyers—is that they distort the truth, and there is some sense in that accusation. But as I explained in Chapter II, a criminal trial is anything but a pure search for truth. When defense attorneys represent guilty clients—as most do, most of the time—their responsibility is to try, by all fair and ethical means, to *prevent* the truth about their client's guilt from emerging. Failure to do so—failure or unwillingness to object to the truth on the ground that it was improperly obtained—is malpractice, which could get a defense lawyer disbarred and earn his client a new trial, at which he would be represented by a zealous defense lawyer willing and able to try to stop the truth from being proved.

Like it or not—and I like it—that is what our Constitution and our legal system require of defense counsel. Our legal system also permits the prosecutor to try to prevent certain truths from being

proved, if the defense tries to prove them through hearsay or other improper evidence. But our legal system insists that the truth be suppressed exclusively by lawful and ethical means. A "sleazy" lawyer—at least according to the Code of Professional Responsibility—is one who tries to prevent the truth from emerging by unethical or illegal means. A sleazy lawyer is also one who generally behaves in a manner inconsistent with the proper role of the professional advocate.

In the Simpson case, as in any long and hotly contested case, neither side behaved perfectly. (Nor did any of the other participants, ranging from the judge to the media.) The prosecution and the defense worked long hours, under the pressure of unprecedented publicity and scrutiny. It is fair to say that both sides made mistakes, lost tempers, indulged in pettiness, and went right up to—and perhaps, in some instances, over—various legal and ethical lines. It is tempting to Monday morning quarterback, as many commentators did. It is easy to focus on the mistakes and ignore the good lawyering. Each of the major lawyers had their great moments, and many of them had some very bad moments. I certainly miscalculated the effect that my statement about police perjury would have, and if I could do it over again, I would have waited until the trial was over to say what I did about the pervasiveness of this problem. Virtually every defense lawyer I have spoken to regrets at least one statement, question, argument, or decision he or she made during the case. I am certain the same is true of the prosecutors. . . .

A good defense attorney, especially one with a civil liberties perspective, could never win elective office because he or she must occasionally represent very unpopular defendants—and sometimes even win. In Florida, public defenders must run for office. I can only imagine what the campaign must be like. One candidate says: "Vote for me as your public defender and I'll win more cases than my opponent. I'm such a good defense lawyer that the streets will be filled with murderers, rapists, and robbers." His opponent counters: "No, vote for me. I'm the world's worst lawyer. If I'm elected, no defendant will ever win. The streets will be safe with me in office."

Prosecutors, on the other hand, are supposed to be good citizens. It is no surprise, therefore, that being a prosecutor is a stepping-stone to elective office. The job of the prosecutor is to please the public. The job of the defense attorney—whether he's a private lawyer or a public defender—is to win for his client, without regard to what the public thinks. A defense attorney must represent his client zealously within the bounds of law, whether the client is guilty or innocent, popular or unpopular, rich or poor, male or female, black or white. Since most defendants are guilty, and since an even larger percentage are *assumed* to be guilty, defense attorneys will continue to disappoint most of the public most of the time. Prosecutors, on the other hand, will continue to be heroes to most of the public—whether they win or lose, whether they do a good professional job or a mediocre one, as the prosecutors in the Simpson case most assuredly did.

Recently my wife, who holds a doctorate in psychology, had a minor legal dispute, which was submitted to mediation and resolved favorably. The other side was represented by a decent lawyer who tried very hard to settle the matter amicably, which is what happened. This lawyer was unfailingly polite, soft-spoken, and low-key. As we left the mediation, settlement in hand, my wife—who is also amicable, soft-spoken, and low-key—started to tell me how she couldn't stand the opposing lawyer and thought he was a "terrible person" for representing her oppo-

nent. She realized, of course, that this is exactly how other people react to me. But even after we joked about her reaction, she quickly returned to disliking everything about the other side, especially its lawyer. She found it difficult to separate the lawyer from his client in a case in which she was so personally involved. This small incident gave me a much deeper insight into the reaction so many people have to defense attorneys, especially in cases where they *feel*—not just think—that an injustice has been done, and that the injustice was abetted by the advocacy of the defense lawyer.

So the answer to the question posed by the title of this chapter is that both prosecutors and defense attorneys are supposed to be advocates for their clients. But prosecutors are also supposed to be advocates for justice, while defense attorneys are not even permitted to try to achieve justice, if by doing so they would disserve the legitimate interests of their clients. Again, since most criminal defendants are, as a statistical matter, guilty, defense attorneys are not usually engaged in the business of serving justice—at least not in the short run. But by zealously defending their clients, guilty or innocent, they help preserve a system of justice that only rarely convicts the innocent.

Further Resources

BOOKS

Bugliosi, Vincent. *Outrage: the Five Reasons Why O.J. Simpson Got Away With Murder.* New York: W.W. Norton & Co., 1996.

Clark, Marcia, and Teresa Carpenter. *Without a Doubt.* New York: Viking, 1997.

Darden, Christopher A., and Jess Walter. *In Contempt.* New York: ReganBooks, 1996.

Gibbs, Jewelle Taylor. *Race and Justice: Rodney King and O.J. Simpson in a House Divided.* San Francisco: Jossey-Bass, 1996.

Lee, Henry C., and Jerry Labriola. *Famous Crimes Revisited: from Sacco-Vanzetti to O.J. Simpson, including Lindbergh Kidnapping, Sam Sheppard, John F. Kennedy, Vincent Foster, JonBenet Ramsey.* Southington, Conn.: Strong Books, 2001.

Schuetz, Janice E., and Lin S. Lilley. *The O.J. Simpson Trials: Rhetoric, Media, and the Law.* Carbondale: Southern Illinois University Press, 1999.

WEBSITES

The O.J. Simpson Trial. Available online at http://www.law.umkc.edu/faculty/projects/ftrials/Simpson/simpson.htm; website home page: http://www.umkc.edu (accessed May 5, 2003).

Vacco v. Quill

Supreme Court decision

By: William H. Rehnquist

Date: June 26, 1997

Source: Rehnquist, William H. *Vacco v. Quill* 521 U.S. 793 (1997). Available online at http://laws.findlaw.com/us/521 /793.html; website home page: http://laws.findlaw.com (accessed May 4, 2003).

About the Author: William H. Rehnquist (1924–), after military service in World War II (1939–1945), received degrees from Stanford and Harvard, before graduating from Stanford Law School. President Richard Nixon (served 1969–1974) appointed Rehnquist to the Supreme Court in 1971. In 1986, President Ronald Reagan (served 1981–1989) appointed Rehnquist Chief Justice. He has generally led the Court in a more conservative direction. ∎

Introduction

The right to privacy and to be left alone is implied in many amendments of the Bill of Rights. Perhaps the most direct place is the Fourth Amendment, which states that one's property cannot be seized without a search warrant, and search warrants cannot be issued except for probable cause. As early as 1928, Justice Louis D. Brandeis expanded upon the Fourth Amendment, arguing that one has "a right to be left alone." In the criminal arena, the whole issue of search warrants was a murky one, but the waters became much muddier when a person's body was the object of this search warrant.

In the 1970s, the laws concerning the beginnings of life, and the choice of giving birth to a new life were changing based on the right to privacy. This right was officially recognized in *Griswold v. Connecticut,* which held that a state could not ban the use of contraceptives. The right to privacy was further expanded in 1973 in *Roe v. Wade,* which held that a woman had a right to an abortion in the first trimester.

Around the same time, there was a great deal of controversy and discussion about the ending of life. Dr. Kubler-Ross and others began to write more about death and coming to terms with death, urging people to accept death as just another stage of life. Many different cultures have different ways of celebrating one's passing, but death was seldom discussed in America as a whole. In 1990, a very public court case came in front of the Supreme Court dealing with a "right to die." Nancy Cruzan, a young woman, had been in a car accident and had slipped into an irreversible coma. Her parents wished to remove her feeding tube and let her die. The state, however, did not think that her parents had the legal right to make this decision. The Supreme Court decided against the parents, citing that the parents had not proven Nancy's wish not to be kept alive. The parents were able to prove the daughter's wishes clearly on remand, and the feeding tube was removed. (Nancy died twelve days later.)

In the 1990s, the whole issue of death remained in the media. Jack Kevorkian, an unlicensed pathologist, began arguing for a right to die, saying that terminally ill people should be able to get help in dying. He gave lethal injections to several individuals, and was convicted of homicide. Most states banned this "assisted suicide." Whether such a ban was legal reached the Supreme Court in *Vacco v. Quill.*

Significance

The Supreme Court upheld the ban on assisted suicide, distinguishing assisted suicide from the right to die issues in *Cruzan.* The Court found that while an individual can make the decision not to be resuscitated, and can make the decision to die with dignity, the intervention of another person in an assisted suicide moves the decision enough beyond a privacy issue—and a state can ban assisted suicide. Since *Vacco,* the whole issue of assisted suicide has somewhat passed from the national radar screen, although there have been several state referendums on the issue. While *Vacco* allows a state to ban assisted suicide, it does not force a state to do so—leaving open to the question of how individuals want to die, and what assistance they may obtain to do so.

Primary Source

Vacco v. Quill [excerpt]

> **SYNOPSIS:** Rehnquist first notes that it is a crime in New York to assist in a suicide. He then discusses that the refusal to accept medical treatment is permitted because of the equal protection clause, banning assisted suicide does not violate this principle. Rehnquist clearly differentiates these two paths. He notes how the Supreme Court has agreed with this distinction as well, and then upholds the law.

Chief Justice Rehnquist delivered the opinion of the Court.

In New York, as in most States, it is a crime to aid another to commit or attempt suicide, but patients may refuse even lifesaving medical treatment. The question presented by this case is whether New York's prohibition on assisting suicide therefore violates the Equal Protection Clause of the Fourteenth Amendment. We hold that it does not. . . .

The Equal Protection Clause commands that no State shall "deny to any person within its jurisdiction the equal protection of the laws." This provision creates no substantive rights. . . . Instead, it embodies a general rule that States must treat like cases alike but may treat unlike cases accordingly. . . . If a legislative classification or distinction "neither burdens a fundamental right nor targets a suspect class, we will uphold [it] so long as it bears a rational relation to some legitimate end." . . .

New York's statutes outlawing assisting suicide affect and address matters of profound significance to all New Yorkers alike. They neither infringe fundamental rights nor involve suspect classifications. . . . These laws are therefore entitled to a "strong presumption of validity." . . .

On their faces, neither New York's ban on assisting suicide nor its statutes permitting patients to refuse medical treatment treat anyone differently than anyone else or draw any distinctions between persons. Everyone, regardless of physical condition, is entitled, if competent, to refuse unwanted lifesaving medical treatment; no one is permitted to assist a suicide. Generally speaking, laws that apply evenhandedly to all "unquestionably comply" with the Equal Protection Clause.

. . . We think the distinction between assisting suicide and withdrawing life sustaining treatment, a distinction widely recognized and endorsed in the medical profession and in our legal traditions, is both important and logical; it is certainly rational. . . .

The distinction comports with fundamental legal principles of causation and intent. First, when a patient refuses life sustaining medical treatment, he dies from an underlying fatal disease or pathology; but if a patient ingests lethal medication prescribed by a physician, he is killed by that medication. . . .

Furthermore, a physician who withdraws, or honors a patient's refusal to begin, life sustaining medical treatment purposefully intends, or may so intend, only to respect his patient's wishes and "to cease doing useless and futile or degrading things to the patient when [the patient] no longer stands to benefit from them." . . .

The law has long used actors' intent or purpose to distinguish between two acts that may have the same result. . . .

Given these general principles, it is not surprising that many courts, including New York courts, have carefully distinguished refusing life sustaining treatment from suicide. . . . In fact, the first state court decision explicitly to authorize withdrawing lifesaving treatment noted the "real distinction between the self infliction of deadly harm and a self determination against artificial life support." . . . And re-

The Supreme Court decision in *Vacco v. Quill* allows a state to ban assisted suicide, but does not force a state to do so. Here Timothy Quill testifies before the House subcommittee on the Constitution. AP/WIDE WORLD PHOTOS. REPRODUCED BY PERMISSION.

cently, the Michigan Supreme Court also rejected the argument that the distinction "between acts that artificially sustain life and acts that artificially curtail life" is merely a "distinction without constitutional significance—a meaningless exercise in semantic gymnastics," insisting that "the Cruzan majority disagreed and so do we." . . .

Similarly, the overwhelming majority of state legislatures have drawn a clear line between assisting suicide and withdrawing or permitting the refusal of unwanted lifesaving medical treatment by prohibiting the former and permitting the latter. . . . And "nearly all states expressly disapprove of suicide and assisted suicide either in statutes dealing with durable powers of attorney in health care situations, or in 'living will' statutes." . . . Thus, even as the States move to protect and promote patients' dignity at the end of life, they remain opposed to physician assisted suicide.

New York is a case in point. The State enacted its current assisted suicide statutes in 1965. Since then, New York has acted several times to protect patients' common law right to refuse treatment. . . .

Attorney General of New York, Dennis Vacco, defended his state's ban on physician-assisted suicide before the Supreme Court. AP/WIDE WORLD PHOTOS. REPRODUCED BY PERMISSION.

In so doing, however, the State has neither endorsed a general right to "hasten death" nor approved physician assisted suicide. Quite the opposite: The State has reaffirmed the line between "killing" and "letting die." . . . More recently, the New York State Task Force on Life and the Law studied assisted suicide and euthanasia and, in 1994, unanimously recommended against legalization. . . . In the Task Force's view, "allowing decisions to forego life sustaining treatment and allowing assisted suicide or euthanasia have radically different consequences and meanings for public policy." . . .

This Court has also recognized, at least implicitly, the distinction between letting a patient die and making that patient die. In *Cruzan* . . . we concluded that "[t]he principle that a competent person has a constitutionally protected liberty interest in refusing unwanted medical treatment may be inferred from our prior decisions," and we assumed the existence of such a right for purposes of that case. . . . But our assumption of a right to refuse treatment was grounded not, as the Court of Appeals supposed, on the proposition that patients have a general and abstract "right to hasten death," . . . but on well es-

tablished, traditional rights to bodily integrity and freedom from unwanted touching. . . . In fact, we observed that "the majority of States in this country have laws imposing criminal penalties on one who assists another to commit suicide." . . . *Cruzan* therefore provides no support for the notion that refusing life sustaining medical treatment is "nothing more nor less than suicide."

For all these reasons, we disagree with respondents' claim that the distinction between refusing lifesaving medical treatment and assisted suicide is "arbitrary" and "irrational." . . . Granted, in some cases, the line between the two may not be clear, but certainty is not required, even were it possible. Logic and contemporary practice support New York's judgment that the two acts are different, and New York may therefore, consistent with the Constitution, treat them differently. By permitting everyone to refuse unwanted medical treatment while prohibiting anyone from assisting a suicide, New York law follows a longstanding and rational distinction.

New York's reasons for recognizing and acting on this distinction—including prohibiting intentional killing and preserving life; preventing suicide; maintaining physicians' role as their patients' healers; protecting vulnerable people from indifference, prejudice, and psychological and financial pressure to end their lives; and avoiding a possible slide towards euthanasia—are discussed in greater detail in our opinion in Glucksberg. . . . These valid and important public interests easily satisfy the constitutional requirement that a legislative classification bear a rational relation to some legitimate end.

The judgment of the Court of Appeals is reversed.

It is so ordered.

Further Resources

BOOKS

Battin, M. Pabst, et. al. *Physician Assisted Suicide: Expanding the Debate.* New York: Routledge, 1998.

Davis, Sue Justice. *Rehnquist and the Constitution.* Princeton, N.J.: Princeton University Press, 1989.

Demy, Timothy J., and Gary Stewart. *Suicide: A Christian Response: Crucial Considerations for Choosing Life.* Grand Rapids, Mich.: Kregel Publications, 1998.

Loving, Carol. *My Son, My Sorrow: The Tragic Tale of Dr. Kevorkian's Youngest Patient.* Far Hills, N.J.: New Horizon Press, 1998.

Uhlmann, Michael M. *Last Rights?: Assisted Suicide and Euthanasia Debated.* Washington, D.C.: Ethics and Public Policy Center, 1998.

Waymack, Mark H., and George Taler. *Medical Ethics and the Elderly: A Case Book.* Chicago: Pluribus Press, 1988.

AUDIO AND VISUAL MEDIA

Physician-assisted Suicide after Vacco v. Quill & Washington v. Glucksberg Millersville, Md: Recorded Resources Corp., Videocassette, 1998.

Reno v. American Civil Liberties Union

Supreme Court decision

By: John Paul Stevens

Date: June 26, 1997

Source: Stevens, John Paul. *Reno v. American Civil Liberties Union.* 521 U.S. 844 (1997). Available online at http://laws .findlaw.com/us/521/844.html; website home page: http:// laws.findlaw.com (accessed May 5, 2003).

About the Author: John Paul Stevens (1920–) graduated from the University of Chicago and Northwestern Law School, and clerked for Supreme Court Justice Rutledge in 1947-1948. Before serving on the Court, he worked in private practice and taught at Northwestern and the University of Chicago. From 1970 to 1975, he served on the Seventh Circuit Court of Appeals. He was considered to be a moderate when appointed to the Court. However, he has more often than not aligned himself with the Court's liberal wing. ∎

Introduction

In the early American republic, control of obscenity was always done at the local level. Local and state laws defined obscenity, and federal courts, and the Constitution, were not involved. The federal government had to observe the First Amendment in its actions, but the states did not—as the Bill of Rights was not held to apply against the states. The federal government first became involved in regulating obscenity with the 1873 Comstock Act, which prohibited "obscene" materials from the interstate mails. This act was named after Anthony Comstock, an anti-vice crusader who pushed the law through because he believed that the current state laws were inadequate. The Comstock Act was enforced against the distributors of birth control information, as well as against a number of different books and magazines. None of these prosecutions violated the First Amendment, because the First Amendment did not protect obscenity or its publication. Freedom of the press was also repressed during World War I (1914–1919), as courts upheld the power of government to censor the press.

In 1925, the landscape of the freedom of the press began to change. In light of the Fourteenth Amendment, the Supreme Court stated that the First Amendment free-

doms of speech and the press applied against the states, as well as the federal government. The question then became whether the First Amendment protected "obscenity." In 1942, in *Chaplinsky v. New Hampshire,* the court held again that obscenity was not protected. In 1955, another conviction under the Comstock Act reached the Supreme Court. The Court defined obscenity as material which lacked the "slightest redeeming social importance," and upheld the convictions. The Court also declared that "contemporary community standards" would be applied to test whether something had "redeeming social importance." This standard continued into the 1960s and 1970s, and was held to apply to radio programs, film, and television. In the 1980s and 1990s, the "community standard" continued, except that material which claimed literary or artistic value would be decided based upon a nationwide standard, rather than a community standard. By the end of the century the "community standard" rule for obscenity seemed to be firmly entrenched.

With the rise of the Internet, however, the whole issue of the "contemporary community standard" lacked relevance—people who posted materials on the Internet often had no idea where the documents would be downloaded. The rise of the Internet and the World Wide Web prompted several attempts to regulate it. One of the first was the Communications Decency Act (CDA), the issue before the court in *Reno v. American Civil Liberties Union.*

Significance

Reno delineated the difficulties of keeping potentially "obscene" material from youths—while noting the problems with the "contemporary community standards" doctrine used for interpreting what is obscene. The Court struck down the CDA because the act was overbroad, prohibiting both material that is not obscene, as well as prohibiting material to adults simply because it might be obscene if viewed by minors. This setback did not stop the Congress, however—"protecting the innocent children" is a favorite and well-worn political issue. Several other attempts to regulate the Internet have also been considered, and at least two have been passed. The Courts, however, have struck both, and no workable solution has been found to regulating a worldwide medium by local community standards. Politicians, though, will surely try again.

Primary Source

Reno v. American Civil Liberties Union [excerpt]

SYNOPSIS: Stevens opens by holding that one cannot verify a viewer's age on the Internet, making age-based restrictions, established by the Communications Decency Act (CDA), unworkable. He then holds that the CDA is ambiguous and vague, thus violating the First Amendment. There is no way to restrict content to minors, while not censoring it for adults. Stevens closes by noting that the CDA overly censors the Internet, destroying free expression, and is therefore, unconstitutional.

Justice Stevens delivered the opinion of the Court.

At issue is the constitutionality of two statutory provisions enacted to protect minors from "indecent" and "patently offensive" communications on the Internet. Notwithstanding the legitimacy and importance of the congressional goal of protecting children from harmful materials, we agree with the three judge District Court that the statute abridges "the freedom of speech" protected by the First Amendment. . . .

The problem of age verification differs for different uses of the Internet. The District Court categorically determined that there "is no effective way to determine the identity or the age of a user who is accessing material through e-mail, mail exploders, newsgroups or chat rooms." The Government offered no evidence that there was a reliable way to screen recipients and participants in such fora for age. Moreover, even if it were technologically feasible to block minors' access to newsgroups and chat rooms containing discussions of art, politics or other subjects that potentially elicit "indecent" or "patently offensive" contributions, it would not be possible to block their access to that material and "still allow them access to the remaining content, even if the overwhelming majority of that content was not indecent." . . .

Neither before nor after the enactment of the CDA have the vast democratic fora of the Internet been subject to the type of government supervision and regulation that has attended the broadcast industry. Moreover, the Internet is not as "invasive" as radio or television. The District Court specifically found that "[c]ommunications over the Internet do not 'invade' an individual's home or appear on one's computer screen unbidden. Users seldom encounter content 'by accident.'" . . . It also found that "[a]lmost all sexually explicit images are preceded by warnings as to the content," and cited testimony that "'odds are slim' that a user would come across a sexually explicit sight by accident." . . . We agree with its conclusion that our cases provide no basis for qualifying the level of First Amendment scrutiny that should be applied to this medium.

Regardless of whether the CDA is so vague that it violates the Fifth Amendment, the many ambigu-

ities concerning the scope of its coverage render it problematic for purposes of the First Amendment. For instance, each of the two parts of the CDA uses a different linguistic form. The first uses the word "indecent," . . . while the second speaks of material that "in context, depicts or describes, in terms patently offensive as measured by contemporary community standards, sexual or excretory activities or organs." . . . Given the absence of a definition of either term, this difference in language will provoke uncertainty among speakers about how the two standards relate to each other and just what they mean. Could a speaker confidently assume that a serious discussion about birth control practices, homosexuality, the First Amendment issues raised by the Appendix to our Pacifica opinion, or the consequences of prison rape would not violate the CDA? This uncertainty undermines the likelihood that the CDA has been carefully tailored to the congressional goal of protecting minors from potentially harmful materials.

The vagueness of the CDA is a matter of special concern for two reasons. First, the CDA is a content based regulation of speech. The vagueness of such a regulation raises special First Amendment concerns because of its obvious chilling effect on free speech. . . . Second, the CDA is a criminal statute. In addition to the opprobrium and stigma of a criminal conviction, the CDA threatens violators with penalties including up to two years in prison for each act of violation. The severity of criminal sanctions may well cause speakers to remain silent rather than communicate even arguably unlawful words, ideas, and images. . . . As a practical matter, this increased deterrent effect, coupled with the "risk of discriminatory enforcement" of vague regulations, poses greater First Amendment concerns than those implicated by the civil regulation reviewed in Denver Area Ed. . . .

The Government argues that the statute is no more vague than the obscenity standard this Court established in *Miller v. California*. . . .

Because the CDA's "patently offensive" standard (and, we assume arguendo, its synonymous "indecent" standard) is one part of the three prong Miller test, the Government reasons, it cannot be unconstitutionally vague.

The Government's assertion is incorrect as a matter of fact. The second prong of the Miller test—the purportedly analogous standard—contains a critical requirement that is omitted from the CDA: that the proscribed material be "specifically defined by

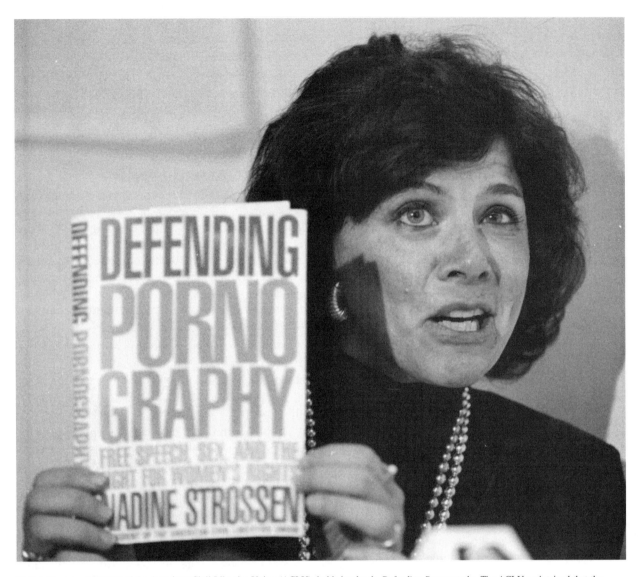

Nadine Strossen, president of the American Civil Liberties Union (ACLU), holds her book, *Defending Pornography*. The ACLU maintained that the Communications Decency Act (CDA) would lead to censorship of speech in the medium of cyberspace and violate the First Amendment. **AP/WIDE WORLD PHOTOS. REPRODUCED BY PERMISSION.**

the applicable state law." This requirement reduces the vagueness inherent in the open ended term "patently offensive" as used in the CDA. Moreover, the Miller definition is limited to "sexual conduct," whereas the CDA extends also to include (1) "excretory activities" as well as (2) "organs" of both a sexual and excretory nature.

The Government's reasoning is also flawed. Just because a definition including three limitations is not vague, it does not follow that one of those limitations, standing by itself, is not vague. Each of *Miller*'s additional two prongs—(1) that, taken as a whole, the material appeal to the "prurient" interest, and (2) that it "lac[k] serious literary, artistic, political, or scientific value"—critically limits the uncer-

tain sweep of the obscenity definition. The second requirement is particularly important because, unlike the "patently offensive" and "prurient interest" criteria, it is not judged by contemporary community standards. . . . This "societal value" requirement, absent in the CDA, allows appellate courts to impose some limitations and regularity on the definition by setting, as a matter of law, a national floor for socially redeeming value. The Government's contention that courts will be able to give such legal limitations to the CDA's standards is belied by *Miller*'s own rationale for having juries determine whether material is "patently offensive" according to community standards: that such questions are essentially ones of fact.

The rise of the Internet and the World Wide Web prompted attempts to regulate pornography, led by Attorney General Janet Reno. © CORBIS. REPRODUCED BY PERMISSION.

In contrast to *Miller* and our other previous cases, the CDA thus presents a greater threat of censoring speech that, in fact, falls outside the statute's scope. Given the vague contours of the coverage of the statute, it unquestionably silences some speakers whose messages would be entitled to constitutional protection. That danger provides further reason for insisting that the statute not be overly broad. The CDA's burden on protected speech cannot be justified if it could be avoided by a more carefully drafted statute.

We are persuaded that the CDA lacks the precision that the First Amendment requires when a statute regulates the content of speech. In order to deny minors access to potentially harmful speech, the CDA effectively suppresses a large amount of speech that adults have a constitutional right to receive and to address to one another. That burden on adult speech is unacceptable if less restrictive alternatives would be at least as effective in achieving the legitimate purpose that the statute was enacted to serve. . . .

It is true that we have repeatedly recognized the governmental interest in protecting children from harmful materials. . . . But that interest does not justify an unnecessarily broad suppression of speech addressed to adults. . . .

In arguing that the CDA does not so diminish adult communication, the Government relies on the incorrect factual premise that prohibiting a transmission whenever it is known that one of its recipients is a minor would not interfere with adult to adult communication. The findings of the District Court make clear that this premise is untenable.

Given the size of the potential audience for most messages, in the absence of a viable age verification process, the sender must be charged with knowing that one or more minors will likely view it. Knowledge that, for instance, one or more members of a 100 person chat group will be minor—and therefore that it would be a crime to send the group an indecent message—would surely burden communication among adults.

The District Court found that at the time of trial existing technology did not include any effective method for a sender to prevent minors from obtaining access to its communications on the Internet without also denying access to adults. . . .

The breadth of the CDA's coverage is wholly unprecedented. Unlike the regulations upheld in Ginsberg and Pacifica, the scope of the CDA is not limited to commercial speech or commercial entities. Its open ended prohibitions embrace all nonprofit entities and individuals posting indecent messages or displaying them on their own computers in the presence of minors. The general, undefined terms "indecent" and "patently offensive" cover large amounts of nonpornographic material with serious educational or other value. Moreover, the "community standards" criterion as applied to the Internet means that any communication available to a nation wide audience will be judged by the standards of the community most likely to be offended by the message. The regulated subject matter includes any of the seven "dirty words" used in the Pacifica monologue, the use of which the Government's expert acknowledged could constitute a felony. . . . It may also extend to discussions about prison rape or safe sexual practices, artistic images that include nude subjects, and arguably the card catalogue of the Carnegie Library. . . .

The breadth of this content based restriction of speech imposes an especially heavy burden on the Government to explain why a less restrictive provision would not be as effective as the CDA. It has not done so. The arguments in this Court have referred to possible alternatives such as requiring that indecent material be "tagged" in a way that facilitates parental control of material coming into their homes, making exceptions for messages with artistic or educational value, providing some tolerance for parental choice, and regulating some portions of the Internet—such as commercial web sites—differently than others, such as chat rooms. Particularly in the light of the absence of any detailed findings by the Congress, or even hearings addressing the special problems of the CDA, we are persuaded that the CDA is not narrowly tailored if that requirement has any meaning at all.

In an attempt to curtail the CDA's facial overbreadth, the Government advances three additional arguments for sustaining the Act's affirmative prohibitions: (1) that the CDA is constitutional because it leaves open ample "alternative channels" of communication; (2) that the plain meaning of the Act's "knowledge" and "specific person" requirement significantly restricts its permissible applications; and (3) that the Act's prohibitions are "almost always" limited to material lacking redeeming social value.

The Government first contends that, even though the CDA effectively censors discourse on many of the Internet's modalities—such as chat groups, newsgroups, and mail exploders—it is nonetheless constitutional because it provides a "reasonable opportunity" for speakers to engage in the restricted speech on the World Wide Web. . . . This argument is unpersuasive because the CDA regulates speech on the basis of its content. A "time, place, and manner" analysis is therefore inapplicable. . . . It is thus immaterial whether such speech would be feasible on the Web (which, as the Government's own expert acknowledged, would cost up to $10,000 if the speaker's interests were not accommodated by an existing Web site, not including costs for database management and age verification). The Government's position is equivalent to arguing that a statute could ban leaflets on certain subjects as long as individuals are free to publish books. In invalidating a number of laws that banned leafletting on the streets regardless of their content—we explained that "one is not to have the exercise of his liberty of expression in appropriate places abridged on the plea that it may be exercised in some other place." . . .

The Government also asserts that the "knowledge" requirement . . . especially when coupled with the "specific child" element . . . saves the CDA from overbreadth. . . . Even the strongest reading of the "specific person" requirement of §223(d) cannot save the statute. It would confer broad powers of censorship, in the form of a "heckler's veto," upon any opponent of indecent speech who might simply log on and inform the would be discoursers that his 17 year old child—a "specific person . . . under 18 years of age . . ."—would be present.

Finally, we find no textual support for the Government's submission that material having scientific, educational, or other redeeming social value will necessarily fall outside the CDA's "patently offensive" and "indecent" prohibitions. . . .

We agree with the District Court's conclusion that the CDA places an unacceptably heavy burden on protected speech, and that the defenses do not constitute the sort of "narrow tailoring" that will save an otherwise patently invalid unconstitutional provision. In *Sable*, . . . we remarked that the speech restriction at issue there amounted to "'burn[ing] the house to roast the pig.'" The CDA, casting a far darker shadow over free speech, threatens to torch a large segment of the Internet community. . . .

In this Court, though not in the District Court, the Government asserts that—in addition to its interest in protecting children—its "[e]qually significant" interest in fostering the growth of the Internet provides an independent basis for upholding the constitutionality of the CDA. . . . The Government apparently assumes that the unregulated availability of "indecent" and "patently offensive" material on the Internet is driving countless citizens away from the medium because of the risk of exposing themselves or their children to harmful material.

We find this argument singularly unpersuasive. The dramatic expansion of this new marketplace of ideas contradicts the factual basis of this contention. The record demonstrates that the growth of the Internet has been and continues to be phenomenal. As a matter of constitutional tradition, in the absence of evidence to the contrary, we presume that governmental regulation of the content of speech is more likely to interfere with the free exchange of ideas than to encourage it. The interest in encouraging freedom of expression in a democratic society outweighs any theoretical but unproven benefit of censorship.

Further Resources

BOOKS

American Civil Liberties Union. *Censorship in a Box: why Blocking Software is Wrong for Public Libraries.* Wye Mills, Md.: ACLU Publications, 1998.

Heins, Marjorie. *Not in Front of the Children: "Indecency," Censorship and the Innocence of Youth.* New York: Hill and Wang, 2001.

Italia, Bob, and Paul J. Deegan. *John Paul Stevens.* Edina, Minn.: Abdo & Daughters, 1992.

Lipschultz, Jeremy Harris. *Free Expression in the Age of the Internet: Social and Legal Boundaries.* Boulder, Colo.: Westview Press, 2000.

Parker, Richard A. *Free Speech on Trial: Communication Perspectives on Landmark Supreme Court Decisions.* Tuscaloosa: The University of Alabama Press, 2003.

Sickels, Robert J. *John Paul Stevens and the Constitution: A Search for Balance.* University Park: Pennsylvania State University Press, 1988.

Strauch, A. Bruce. *Publishing and the Law: Current Legal Issues.* New York: Haworth Information Press, 2001.

WEBSITES

Clarence Thomas Confirmation Hearings

Testimony

By: Clarence Thomas and Anita Hill

Date: 1998

Source: Thomas, Clarence, and Anita Hill. Clarence Thomas Confirmation Hearings. Reprinted in Marcus, Robert, and Anthony Marcus, eds. *On Trial: American History Through Court Proceedings and Hearings.* St. James, N.Y.: Brandywine, 1998, 205, 210–212, 217, 219–220.

About the Authors: Clarence Thomas (1948–) graduated from Yale Law School, worked for John Danforth, the attorney general of Missouri, and then was head of the Equal Employment Opportunity Commission (EEOC). He was nominated to the federal appeals court in 1990, and to the Supreme Court in 1991.

Anita Hill (1956–) graduated from Yale Law School and worked as Thomas's assistant at the EEOC. She taught at Oral Roberts University, the University of Oklahoma College of Law, and Brandeis University. ∎

Introduction

The United States Senate, under the Constitution, is given the power to grant or refuse consent on appointments to the Supreme Court. This approval historically has been generally a rubberstamp, as most Supreme Court nominations have been approved with little controversy. One of the first Supreme Court nominees to run into publicized confirmation difficulties was Louis D. Brandeis, who was opposed solely because he was Jewish and a Progressive. Brandeis, though, was approved. As the twentieth century progressed, most presidential nominees for the Supreme Court were approved.

Presidents Lyndon B. Johnson (served 1963–1969) and Richard Nixon (served 1969–1974), however, did not have the same good fortune as their predecessors. Johnson's nominee for Chief Justice, Abe Fortas, was found to have some questionable financial dealings and not only failed to become chief justice, but also was forced to resign his seat as an associate justice. Nixon nominated two Southerners to be Supreme Court Justices, Clement Haynesworth and G. Harrold Carswell, who also happened to agree with his desire for "law and order." They were defeated because both were seen as defenders of segregation. Additionally, Carswell was viewed as unqualified. After that, the nominations for the Supreme Court for the following fifteen years were relatively uncontroversial.

Ronald Reagan (served 1981–1989), however, ran into difficulties with his nomination of Robert Bork in 1986. Bork was viewed as being intellectually gifted—but far too conservative—and was defeated. Douglas Ginsburg, the next nominee, withdrew his name after allegations of prior marijuana use surfaced. Ginsburg was among the first nominees since Brandeis where personal issues had played a role in the process. Reagan then settled on Anthony Kennedy, who was approved. George H.W. Bush's (served 1989–1993) first appointment, David Souter, presented no difficulties in the consent process, but his second did. Thurgood Marshall, the first African American Supreme Court Justice, resigned, and Bush picked Clarence Thomas to replace him.

During the hearings, Thomas's lack of qualifications and lack of appellate experience bothered many, but it appeared that he would be confirmed. Then Anita Hill, a law professor at the University of Oklahoma—and prior subordinate to Thomas—accused him of sexual harassment. During the 1980s, sexual harassment gained visibility, as many women refused to tolerate it in the workplace. What had been commonplace in many working environments—men sexually harassing women—was no longer going to be accepted. Hill's accusations against Thomas for harassment provided a highly publicized forum for the issue.

Significance

Many in the Senate who favored Thomas's appointment appeared to ignore the serious nature of Hill's comments. This is reflected in the remark of Senator Specter, who noted casually that the Senate discussed breasts all the time, implying that Hill should not have been offended by Thomas's discussion of them. Thomas was confirmed by a 52-48 vote.

Many women were outraged by the seeming dismissal of Hill's complaints. And in 1992, forty-nine women were elected to Congress, including three to the Senate. Several senators were forced to resign due to sexual harassment complaints. Sexual harassment complaints in front of the Equal Employment Opportunity Commission, the federal agency (formerly run by Thomas) that oversees these issues, greatly increased; and sexual harassment judgments more than quadrupled during the 1990s. Nearly every company instituted "sexual harassment policies" to prevent sexual harassment, and these worked to varying degrees. Hill remains in academia. In Thomas's twelve years on the Supreme Court, he has voted with the conservative block, but has written few memorable opinions.

Primary Source

Clarence Thomas Confirmation Hearings [excerpt]

SYNOPSIS: The excerpt opens with a cast of characters. Anita Hill testifies first, describing Thomas's sexual harassment. Several senators question her, including some who question her veracity, and suggest that she should not have been embarrassed by the harassment. Thomas then testifies, arguing that the hearing is "a high-tech lynching for uppity blacks," that none of Hill's testimony is true, even though he had not listened to it, and denying that he had ever harassed Hill.

Committee on the Judiciary

Joseph R. Biden, Jr., Delaware, *Chairman*

Edward M. Kennedy, Massachusetts

Howard M. Metzenbaum, Ohio

Dennis Deconcini, Arizona

Patrick J. Leahy, Vermont

Howell Heflin, Alabama

Paul Simon, Illinois

Herbert Kohl, Wisconsin

Strom Thurmond, South Carolina

Orrin G. Hatch, Utah

Alan K. Simpson, Wyoming

Charles E. Grassley, Iowa

Arlen Specter, Pennsylvania

Hank Brown, Colorado

Dates of hearings:

Friday, October 11, 1991

Saturday, October 12, 1991

Sunday, October 13, 1991

Witnesses

Hill, Anita F., professor of law, University of Oklahoma, Norman, OK

Thomas, Judge Clarence, of Georgia, to be Associate Justice of the U.S. Supreme Court

Testimony of Anita F. Hill, Professor of Law, University of Oklahoma, Norman, Oklahoma

The Chairman: Can you tell the committee what was the most embarrassing of all the incidents that you have alleged?

Ms. Hill: I think the one that was the most embarrassing was this discussion of pornography involving women with large breasts and engaged in a variety of sex with different people, or animals. That was the thing that embarrassed me the most and made me feel the most humiliated.

The Chairman: If you can, in his words—not yours—in his words, can you tell us what, on that occasion, he said to you? You have described the essence of the conversation. In order for us to determine—well, can you tell us, in his words, what he said?

Ms. Hill: I really cannot quote him verbatim. I can remember something like, you really ought to see these films that I have seen or this material that I have seen. This woman has this kind of breasts or breasts that measure this size, and they got her in there with all kinds of things, she is doing all kinds of different sex acts. And, you know, that kind of, those were the kinds of words. Where he expressed his enjoyment of it, and seemed to try to encourage me to enjoy that kind of material, as well.

The Chairman: Did he indicate why he thought you should see this material?

Ms. Hill: No.

The Chairman: Why do you think, what was your reaction, why do you think he was saying these things to you?

Ms. Hill: Well, coupled with the pressures about going out with him, I felt that implicit in this discussion about sex was the offer to have sex with him, not just to go out with him. There was never any explicit thing about going out to dinner or going to a particular concert or movie, it was, "we ought to go out" and given his other conversations I took that to mean, we ought to have sex or we ought to look at these pornographic movies together.

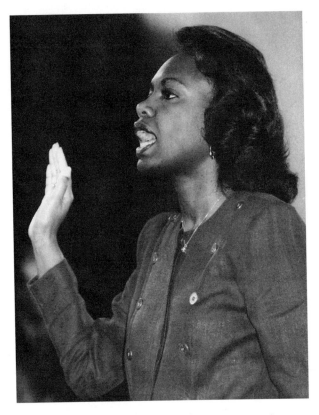

During the Senate confirmation hearing of Clarence Thomas to the Supreme Court, Anita Hill accuses Thomas of sexual harrassment. AP/WIDE WORLD PHOTOS. REPRODUCED BY PERMISSION.

The Chairman: Professor, at your press conference, one of your press conferences, you said that the issue that you raised about Judge Thomas was "an ugly issue." Is that how you viewed these conversations?

Ms. Hill: Yes. They were very ugly. They were very dirty. They were disgusting.

The Chairman: Were any one of these conversations—this will be my last question, my time is up—were any one of these conversations, other than being asked repeatedly to go out, were any one of them repeated more than once? The same conversation, the reference to—

Ms. Hill: The reference to his own physical attributes was repeated more than once, yes.

The Chairman: Now, again, for the record, did he just say I have great physical attributes or was he more graphic?

Ms. Hill: He was much more graphic.

The Chairman: Can you tell us what he said?

Ms. Hill: Well, I can tell you that he compared his penis size, he measured his penis in terms of length, those kinds of comments.

The Chairman: Thank you. . . .

Sen. Specter: We have a statement from former dean of Oral Roberts Law School who quotes you as making laudatory comments about Judge Thomas, that he "is a fine man and an excellent legal scholar." In the course of three years when Dean Tuttle knew you at the law school, that you had always praised him and had never made any derogatory comments. Is Dean Tuttle correct?

Ms. Hill: During the time that I was at Oral Roberts University I realized that Charles Kothe, who was a founding dean of that school, had very high regard for Clarence Thomas. I did not risk talking in disparaging ways about Clarence Thomas at that time.

I don't recall any specific conversations about Clarence Thomas in which I said anything about his legal scholarship. I did not really know of his legal scholarship, certainly at that time.

Sen. Specter: Well, I can understand it if you did not say anything, but Dean Tuttle makes the specific statement. His words are, that you said, "the most laudatory comments."

Ms. Hill: I have no response to that because I do not know exactly what he is saying.

Sen. Specter: There is a question about Phyllis Berry who was quoted in *The New York Times* on October 7, "In an interview Ms. Barry [*sic*] suggested that the allegations," referring to your allegations, "were the result of Ms. Hill's disappointment and frustration that Mr. Thomas did not show any sexual interest in her."

You were asked about Ms. Berry at the interview on October 9 and were reported to have said, "Well, I don't know Phyllis Berry and she doesn't know me." And there are quite a few people who have come forward to say that they saw you and Ms. Berry together and that you knew each other very well.

Ms. Hill: I would disagree with that. Ms. Berry worked at the EEOC. She did attend some staff meetings at the EEOC. We were not close friends. We did not socialize together and she has no basis for making a comment about my social interests, with regard to Clarence Thomas or anyone else.

I might add, that at the time that I had an active social life and that I was involved with other people.

Sen. Specter: Did Ms. Anna Jenkins and Ms. J.C. Alvarez, who both have provided statements attesting to the relationship between you and Ms. Berry, a friendly one. Where Ms. Berry would have known you [sic], were both Ms. Jenkins and Ms. Alvarez co-workers in a position to observe your relationship with Ms. Berry?

Ms. Hill: They were both workers at the EEOC. I can only say that they were commenting on our relationship in the office. It was cordial and friendly. We were not unfriendly with each other, but we were not social acquaintances. We were professional acquaintances.

Sen. Specter: So that when you said, Ms. Berry doesn't know me and I don't know her, you weren't referring to just that, but some intensity of knowledge?

Ms. Hill: Well, this is a specific remark about my sexual interest. And I think one has to know another person very well to make those kinds of remarks unless they are very openly expressed.

Sen. Specter: Well, did Ms. Berry observe you and Judge Thomas together in the EEOC office?

Ms. Hill: Yes, at staff meetings where she attended and at the office, yes.

Sen. Specter: Let me pick up on Senator Biden's line of questioning. You referred to the "oddest episode I remember," then talked about the Coke incident. When you made your statement to the FBI, why was it that that was omitted if it were so strong in your mind and such an odd incident.

Ms. Hill: I spoke to the FBI agents and I told them the nature of comments, and did not tell them more specifics. I referred to the specific comments that were in my statement.

Sen. Specter: Well, when you talked to the FBI agents, you did make specific allegations about specific sexual statements made by Judge Thomas.

Ms. Hill: Yes.

Sen. Specter: So that your statement to the FBI did have specifics.

Ms. Hill: Yes.

Sen. Specter: And my question to you, why, if this was such an odd episode, was it not included when you talked to the FBI?

Ms. Hill: I do not know. . . .

Sen. Specter: You testified this morning, in response to Senator Biden, that the most embarrassing question involved—this is not too bad—women's large breasts. That is a word we use all the time. That was the most embarrassing aspect of what Judge Thomas had said to you?

Ms. Hill: No. The most embarrassing aspect was his description of the acts of these individuals, these women, the acts that those particular people would engage in. It wasn't just the breasts; it was the continuation of his story about what happened in those films with the people with this characteristic, physical characteristic.

Sen. Specter: With the physical characteristic of—

Ms. Hill: The large breasts.

Sen. Specter: Well, in your statement to the FBI you did refer to the films but there is no reference to the physical characteristic you describe. I don't want to attach too much weight to it, but I had thought you said that the aspect of large breasts was the aspect that concerned you, and that was missing from the statement to the FBI.

Ms. Hill: I have been misunderstood. It wasn't the physical characteristic of having large breasts. It was the description of the acts that this person with this characteristic would do, the acts that they would engage in, group acts with animals, things of that nature involving women.
. . .

Testimony of Hon. Clarence Thomas of Georgia, to be Associate Justice of the U.S. Supreme Court

The Chairman: Do you have anything you would like to say?

Judge Thomas: Senator, I would like to start by saying unequivocally, uncategorically that I deny each and every single allegation against me today that suggested in any way that I had conversations of a sexual nature or about pornographic material with Anita Hill, that I ever attempted to date her, that I ever had any personal sexual interest in her, or that I in any way ever harassed her.

Despite the accusations of Anita Hill, the nomination of Clarence Thomas to the Supreme Court was confirmed by the Senate in a 52-48 vote. **AP/WIDE WORLD PHOTOS. REPRODUCED BY PERMISSION.**

Second, and I think a more important point, I think that this today is a travesty. I think that it is disgusting. I think that this hearing should never occur in America. This is a case in which this sleaze, this dirt, was searched for by staffers of members of this committee, was then leaked to the media, and this committee and this body validated it and displayed it in prime time over our entire nation.

How would any member on this committee or any person in this room or any person in this country would like sleaze said about him or her in this fashion or this dirt dredged up and this gossip and these lies displayed in this manner? How would any person like it?

The Supreme Court is not worth it. No job is worth it. I am not here for that. I am here for my name, my family, my life and my integrity. I think something is dreadfully wrong with this country, when any person, any person in this free country would be subjected to this. This is not a closed room.

There was an FBI investigation. This is not an opportunity to talk about difficult matters privately or in a closed environment. This is a cir-

cus. It is a national disgrace. And from my standpoint, as a black American, as far as I am concerned, it is a high-tech lynching for uppity blacks who in any way deign to think for themselves, to do for themselves, to have different ideas, and it is a message that, unless you kow-tow to an old order, this is what will happen to you, you will be lynched, destroyed, caricatured by a committee of the U.S. Senate, rather than hung from a tree. . . .

Sen. Heflin: Now, I suppose you have heard Professor Hill, Ms. Hill, Anita F. Hill testify today.

Judge Thomas: No, I haven't.

Sen. Heflin: You didn't listen?

Judge Thomas: No, I didn't. I have heard enough lies.

Sen. Heflin: You didn't listen to her testimony?

Judge Thomas: No, I didn't.

Sen. Heflin: On television?

Judge Thomas: No, I didn't. I've heard enough lies. Today is not a day that, in my opinion, is high among the days in our country. This is a travesty. You spent the entire day destroying what it has taken me forty-three years to build and providing a forum for that.

Sen. Heflin: Judge Thomas, you know we have a responsibility too, and as far as I am involved, I had nothing to do with Anita Hill coming here and testifying. We are trying to get to the bottom of this. And, if she is lying, then I think you can help us prove that she was lying.

Judge Thomas: Senator, I am incapable of proving the negative that did not occur.

Sen. Heflin: Well, if it did not occur, I think you are in a position, with certainly your ability to testify, in effect, to try to eliminate it from people's minds.

Judge Thomas: Senator, I didn't create it in people's minds. This matter was investigated by the Federal Bureau of Investigation in a confidential way. It was then leaked last weekend to the media. I did not do that. And how many members of this committee would like to have the same scurrilous, uncorroborated allegations made about him and then leaked to national newspapers and then be drawn and dragged before a national forum of this nature to discuss those allegations that should have been resolved in a confidential way?

Sen. Heflin: Well, I certainly appreciate your attitude towards leaks. I happen to serve on the Senate Ethics Committee and it has been a sieve.

Judge Thomas: But it didn't leak on me. This leaked on me and it is drowning my life, my career and my integrity, and you can't give it back to me, and this committee can't give it back to me, and this Senate can't give it back to me. You have robbed me of something that can never be restored.

Sen. DeConcini: I know exactly how you feel.

Sen. Heflin: Judge Thomas, one of the aspects of this is that she could be living in a fantasy world. I don't know. We are just trying to get to the bottom of all of these facts.

But if you didn't listen and didn't see her testify, I think you put yourself in an unusual position. You are, in effect, defending yourself, and basically some of us want to be fair to you, fair to her, but if you didn't listen to what she said today, then that puts it somewhat in a more difficult task to find out what the actual facts are relative to this matter.

Judge Thomas: The facts keep changing, Senator. When the FBI visited me, the statements to this committee and the questions were one thing. The FBI's subsequent questions were another thing. And the statements today, as I received summaries of them, are another thing.

I am not—it is not my fault that the facts change. What I have said to you is categorical that any allegations that I engaged in any conduct involving sexual activity, pornographic movies, attempted to date her, any allegations, I deny. It is not true.

So the facts can change but my denial does not. Ms. Hill was treated in a way that all my special assistants were treated, cordial, professional, respectful.

Sen. Heflin: Judge, if you are on the bench and you approach a case where you appear to have a closed mind and that you are only right, doesn't it raise issues of judicial temperament?

Judge Thomas: Senator? Senator, there is a difference between approaching a case objectively and watching yourself being lynched. There is no comparison whatsoever.

Sen. Hatch: I might add, he has personal knowledge of this as well, and personal justification for anger.

Sen. Heflin: Judge, I don't want to go over this stuff but, of course, there are many instances in which she has stated, but—and, in effect, since you didn't see her testify I think it is somewhat unfair to ask you specifically about it.

I would reserve my time and go ahead and let Senator Hatch ask you, and then come back.

Further Resources

BOOKS

Danforth, John C. *Resurrection: the Confirmation of Clarence Thomas.* New York: Viking, 1994.

Gerber, Scott Douglas. *First Principles: the Jurisprudence of Clarence Thomas.* New York: New York University Press, 1999.

Hill, Anita, and Emma Coleman Jordan. *Race, Gender, and Power in America: the Legacy of the Hill-Thomas Hearings.* New York: Oxford University Press, 1995.

Levy, Anne, and Michele Antoinette Paludi. *Workplace Sexual Harassment.* 2nd ed. Upper Saddle River, N.J.: Prentice Hall, 2002.

Morrison, Toni. *Race-ing Justice, En-gendering Power: Essays on Anita Hill, Clarence Thomas, and the Construction of Social Reality.* New York: Pantheon Books, 1992.

Phelps, Timothy M., and Helen Winternitz. *Capitol Games: Clarence Thomas, Anita Hill, and the Story of a Supreme Court Nomination.* New York: Hyperion, 1991.

WEBSITES

An Outline of the Clarence Thomas/Anita Hill Debate. Available online at http://chnm.gmu.edu/courses/122/hill/hillframe .htm; website home page http://chnm.gmu.edu (accessed May 2, 2003).

AUDIO AND VISUAL MEDIA

Sexual Harassment? You Decide: Real Situations for Discussion. Des Moines, Iowa: VisionPoint, 2002.

The Starr Report: The Findings of Independent Counsel Kenneth W. Starr on President Clinton and the Lewinsky Affair

Report

By: Kenneth Starr

Date: 1998

Source: Starr, Kenneth. *The Starr Report: The Findings of Independent Counsel Kenneth W. Starr on President Clinton and the Lewinsky Affair.* New York: PublicAffairs, 1998, 19–20, 150–151, 153–155. Available online at http://www .access.gpo.gov/congress/icreport/; website home page: http:// www.access.gpo.gov (accessed May 5, 2003).

About the Author: Kenneth Starr (1946–) attended George Washington University for his bachelor's degree, Brown University for a master's degree, and Duke University for his law degree. He clerked for Chief Justice Warren Burger, and then joined a corporate law firm. In 1983, he was named to the Circuit Court of Appeals for the District of Columbia; in 1989, he became solicitor general. Starr gained national prominence for his five-year investigation as special prosecutor into various matters concerning President Bill Clinton (served 1993–2001). ■

Introduction

The Articles of Confederation, America's first government, was too weak, and the U.S. Constitution was created to form a more effective federal government. For the most part, the Constitution's three-branch system worked fairly well for the first century and a half of America's existence. The federal government was limited in size, but with the rise of the modern bureaucracy in the twentieth century, the executive branch ballooned. The larger size was supported by the public for a time, but in the 1960s doubts began to grow about government.

The Watergate scandal, under President Richard Nixon (served 1969–1974), shocked America. In that scandal, funds from Nixon's campaign were used to pay for a break-in into the Democratic Headquarters in the Watergate building. Nixon then authorized a cover-up of the break-in. Congress wanted to make sure that future presidents would and could not abuse justice, and so passed the 1978 Ethics in Government Act. This act created an appointment process for a special prosecutor, who could only be fired for "good cause." In several court cases, the Supreme Court upheld this act.

Sexual "misconduct" in political officials is nothing new. In the elections of 1796 and 1800, the Thomas Jefferson-Sally Hemmings affair was the subject of gossip. In the election of 1884, among others, Grover Cleveland's (served 1885–1889 and 1893–1897) illegitimate child became a campaign issue. Cleveland's opponents chanted "Ma, Ma, where's my pa?" (Cleveland's supporters answered "Off to the White House, Ha, Ha, Ha.") Cleveland may have had the best answer when he allegedly said, "I support my bastards, what about you?"

Throughout the twentieth century, many presidents and presidential hopefuls had extramarital affairs. In the middle of the twentieth century (1933–1968), the only president without a rumored affair was Harry S. Truman (served 1945–1953). Until the 1970s, though, the private affairs of presidents were not generally covered in the press. In the 1980s, Gary Hart, a candidate for the Democratic nomination, was caught in an affair, on the boat *Monkey Business,* and was forced out of the presidential race. None of this became subject to a referral to an independent counsel, however.

In the 1990s, all this changed. Kenneth Starr was appointed independent counsel in 1994 to investigate President Clinton's land dealings in the Whitewater case. It eventually expanded into an investigation of several matters, including aspects of Clinton's sexual relationship with white house intern, Monica Lewinsky. Five years later, in 1999, Starr produced a report arguing for the impeachment of Clinton for lying about his sexual relations with Lewinsky during sworn deposition testimony in the lawsuit filed against him by Paula Jones for sexual harassment, among other allegations.

Significance

Clinton was eventually impeached by the House of Representatives, but was not removed by the Senate. Throughout this period, Clinton's presidential popularity ratings remained high. It seems clear that much of the public did not think that Clinton's affair and subsequent perjury should bring about his impeachment, and did not want him to resign. Part of this, of course, was due to the relative prosperity America enjoyed in the 1990s.

It remains to be seen if future sexual "misconduct" will bring about more investigations. The Independent

Counsel Act lapsed, and is no longer in effect—there being little public support for reviving the statute at the present time. Whether future opposition parties will use investigations to harass the president remains to be seen. History, however, would suggest that many past presidents would have been removed if a similar standard of purity had been used. One might argue that cheating on one's wife could lead to cheating on one's country, but history suggests otherwise. President Nixon (served 1969–1974), as best we know, did not cheat on his wife. However, President Clinton was the first to lie about the relationship under oath in a civil deposition, as well as in testimony before a grand jury. Thus, the impact of "Monica-gate" remains to be seen. Politics will play a part in future investigations, and an open eye to history should be retained when evaluating them.

Primary Source

The Starr Report: The Findings of Independent Counsel Kenneth W. Starr on President Clinton and the Lewinsky Affair [excerpt]

SYNOPSIS: Starr introduces the report by stating the various grounds upon which then-President Clinton could be impeached. He discusses Clinton's various denials, both to the press and to his own Cabinet. The report lists the background to this investigation and outlines why Starr finds a basis for the impeachment. In laying out the details for the impeachment proceedings, Starr defends the use of the explicit sexual testimony in his report.

As required by Section 595(c) of Title 28 of the United States Code, the Office of the Independent Counsel ("OIC" or "Office") hereby submits substantial and credible information that President William Jefferson Clinton committed acts that may constitute grounds for an impeachment.

The information reveals that President Clinton:

- lied under oath at a civil deposition while he was a defendant in a sexual harassment lawsuit;

- lied under oath to a grand jury;

- attempted to influence the testimony of a potential witness who had direct knowledge of facts that would reveal the falsity of his deposition testimony;

- attempted to obstruct justice by facilitating a witness's plan to refuse to comply with a subpoena;

- attempted to obstruct justice by encouraging a witness to file an affidavit that the President

Kenneth Starr was appointed independent counsel in 1994 to investigate President Clinton's land dealings in the Whitewater case. Five years later, he produced a report arguing for the impeachment of Clinton. © AFP/ CORBIS. REPRODUCED BY PERMISSION.

knew would be false, and then by making use of that false affidavit at his own deposition;

- lied to potential grand jury witnesses, knowing that they would repeat those lies before the grand jury; and

- engaged in a pattern of conduct that was inconsistent with his constitutional duty to faithfully execute the laws.

The evidence shows that these acts, and others, were part of a pattern that began as an effort to prevent the disclosure of information about the President's relationship with a former White House intern and employee, Monica S. Lewinsky, and continued as an effort to prevent the information from being disclosed in an ongoing criminal investigation. . . .

In the ensuing days, the President, through his Cabinet, issued a number of firm denials. On January 23, 1998, the President started a Cabinet meeting by saying the allegations were untrue. Afterward, several Cabinet members appeared outside the White House; Madeline Albright, Secretary of State, said: "I believe that the allegations are completely untrue." The others agreed. "I'll second that, definitely," Commerce Secretary William Daley said. Secretary of Education Richard Riley and Secretary of Health and Human Services Donna Shalala concurred.

An investigation of President Bill Clinton's sexual relationship with White House intern, Monica Lewinsky, led to his impeachment for lying about it during sworn deposition testimony. **AP/WIDE WORLD PHOTOS. REPRODUCED BY PERMISSION.**

The next day, Ann Lewis, White House Communications Director, publicly announced that "those of us who have wanted to go out and speak on behalf of the president" had been given the green light by the President's legal team. She reported that the President answered the allegations "directly" by denying any improper relationship. She believed that, in issuing his public denials, the President was not "splitting hairs, defining what is a sexual relationship, talking about 'is' rather than was. You know, I always thought, perhaps I was naive, since I've come to Washington when you said a sexual relationship, everybody knew what that meant." Ms. Lewis expressly said that the term includes "oral sex."

On Monday, January 26, 1998, in remarks in the Roosevelt Room in the White House, President Clinton gave his last public statement for several months on the Lewinsky matter. At an event promoting after-school health care, the President denied the allegations in the strongest terms: "I want to say one thing to the American people. I want you to listen to me. I'm going to say this again: I did not have sexual relations with that woman, Miss Lewinsky. I never told anybody to lie, not a single time. Never. These allegations are false." . . .

Introduction

Pursuant to Section 595(c) of Title 28, the Office of Independent Counsel (OIC) hereby submits substantial and credible information that President Clinton obstructed justice during the Jones v. Clinton sexual harassment lawsuit by lying under oath and concealing evidence of his relationship with a young White House intern and federal employee, Monica Lewinsky. After a federal criminal investigation of the President's actions began in January 1998, the President lied under oath to the grand jury and obstructed justice during the grand jury investigation. There also is substantial and credible information that the President's actions with respect to Monica Lewinsky constitute an abuse of authority inconsistent with the President's constitutional duty to faithfully execute the laws.

There is substantial and credible information supporting the following eleven possible grounds for impeachment:

1. President Clinton lied under oath in his civil case when he denied a sexual affair, a sexual relationship, or sexual relations with Monica Lewinsky.

2. President Clinton lied under oath to the grand jury about his sexual relationship with Ms. Lewinsky.

3. In his civil deposition, to support his false statement about the sexual relationship, President Clinton also lied under oath about being alone with Ms. Lewinsky and about the many gifts exchanged between Ms. Lewinsky and him.

4. President Clinton lied under oath in his civil deposition about his discussions with Ms. Lewinsky concerning her involvement in the Jones case.

5. During the Jones case, the President obstructed justice and had an understanding with Ms. Lewinsky to jointly conceal the truth about their relationship by concealing gifts subpoenaed by Ms. Jones's attorneys.

6. During the Jones case, the President obstructed justice and had an understanding with Ms. Lewinsky to jointly conceal the truth of their relationship from the judicial process by a scheme that included the following means: (i) Both the President and Ms. Lewinsky understood that they would lie under oath in the Jones case about their sexual relationship; (ii) the President suggested to Ms. Lewinsky that she prepare an affidavit that, for the President's purposes, would memorialize her testimony under oath and could be used to prevent questioning of both of them about their relationship; (iii) Ms. Lewinsky signed and filed the false affidavit; (iv) the President used Ms. Lewinsky's false affidavit at his deposition in an attempt to head off questions about Ms. Lewinsky; and (v) when that failed, the President lied under oath at his civil deposition about the relationship with Ms. Lewinsky.

7. President Clinton endeavored to obstruct justice by helping Ms. Lewinsky obtain a job in New York at a time when she would have been a witness harmful to him were she to tell the truth in the Jones case.

8. President Clinton lied under oath in his civil deposition about his discussions with Vernon Jordan concerning Ms. Lewinsky's involvement in the Jones case.

9. The President improperly tampered with a potential witness by attempting to corruptly influence the testimony of his personal secretary, Betty Currie, in the days after his civil deposition.

10. President Clinton endeavored to obstruct justice during the grand jury investigation by refusing to testify for seven months and lying to senior White House aides with knowledge that they would relay the President's false statements to the grand jury—and did thereby deceive, obstruct, and impede the grand jury.

11. President Clinton abused his constitutional authority by (i) lying to the public and the Congress in January 1998 about his relationship with Ms. Lewinsky; (ii) promising at that time to cooperate fully with the grand jury investigation; (iii) later refusing six invitations to testify voluntarily to the grand jury; (iv) invoking Executive Privilege; (v) lying to the grand jury in August 1998; and (vi) lying again to the public and Congress on August 17, 1998—all as part of an effort to hinder, impede, and deflect possible inquiry by the Congress of the United States.

The first two possible grounds for impeachment concern the President's lying under oath about the nature of his relationship with Ms. Lewinsky. The details associated with those grounds are, by their nature, explicit. The President's testimony unfortunately has rendered the details essential with respect to those two grounds, as will be explained in those grounds.

Further Resources

BOOKS

Dershowitz, Alan M. *Sexual McCarthyism: Clinton, Starr, and the Emerging Constitutional Crisis.* New York: Basic Books, 1998.

Posner, Richard A. *An Affair of State: the Investigation, Impeachment, and Trial of President Clinton.* Cambridge: Harvard University Press, 1999.

Starr, Kenneth. *First Among Equals: the Supreme Court in American Life.* New York: Warner Books, 2002.

Tassel, Van, Emily Field, and Paul Finkelman. *Impeachable Offenses: a Documentary History from 1787 to the Present.* Washington: Congressional Quarterly, 1999.

PERIODICALS

"Scandal and Government: Current and Future Implications of the Clinton Presidency." *PS* 32, no. 3, September 1999, 538–561.

WEBSITES

Impeachment Inquiry of Bill Clinton. Available online at http://www.npr.org/news/national/hearings.html; website home page: http://npr.org (accessed May 5, 2003).

AUDIO AND VISUAL MEDIA

Grand Jury Testimony of William Jefferson Clinton, August 17, 1998. MPI Home Video, 1998, VHS.

Rhetorical Highlights From the Impeachment of Bill Clinton. Directed by Roger A. Cook. Educational Video Group, 2000, VHS.

7

LIFESTYLES AND SOCIAL TRENDS

TIMOTHY G. BORDEN

Entries are arranged in chronological order by date of primary source. For entries with one primary source, the entry title is the same as the primary source title. Entries with more than one primary source have an overall entry title, followed by the titles of the primary sources.

Important Events in Lifestyles and Social Trends, 1990–1999

1990

• A poll shows that football is the nation's favorite sport, with 35 percent of Americans counting themselves as fans. Baseball remains a distant second at 16 percent.

• "Politically correct," or "PC," gains wide usage in an effort to rid the English language of racism and sexism. For example, "enslaved person" becomes PC for "slave" because it emphasizes the personhood of the oppressed. "Differently abled" becomes the politically correct term for "disabled." "Humankind" replaces "mankind" and "longer-living" is the PC term for "old."

• On January 1, Maryland becomes the first state to ban the sale of cheap handguns known as "Saturday night specials."

• On March 22, the first edition of Microsoft Windows 3.0 is shipped to consumers.

• On March 27, a government report states that Americans spend more than $30 billion each year on weight loss products and programs that officials consider to be dangerous or ineffective.

• In April, the minimum wage is raised to $3.80 an hour.

• On June 6, Greyhound Bus Lines files for bankruptcy.

• On June 30, the National Academy of Science announces that the AIDS epidemic is spreading to new groups in society, most specifically to African American and Hispanic women.

• On July 26, President George Bush signs a landmark law protecting the rights of some 43 million disabled Americans. The new law forbids discrimination in transportation, public accommodations, and employment.

• On September 8, Illinois law student Marjorie Judith Vincent becomes the fourth African American woman to be crowned Miss America.

• On November 1, under pressure from environmental groups, McDonald's agrees to replace styrofoam containers with paper wrappers.

• On November 29, immigration policies are given their most extensive revision in sixty-six years. A total of 700,000 immigrants will be admitted each year, but most of these places are reserved for skilled workers or relatives of American citizens.

• On December 10, the Food and Drug Administration (FDA) approves the first new contraceptive device in twenty-five years. The set of small tubes implanted under a woman's skin gradually release a hormone than prevents conception. The device can remain effective for up to five years.

1991

• The number of Asian Americans has more than doubled since 1980, and the nation's Hispanic population has increased by 53 percent. In addition, three times as many Americans identify themselves as American Indian than did in 1960.

• Nearly one of every four babies in the United States is born to a single woman.

• The number of African American/white interracial marriages has more than tripled since 1970.

• The Census Bureau reports that the income of the top 20 percent of nation's households rose by 14 percent between 1984 and 1988, but that the average income for the rest of the population actually declined during that period.

• A poll reveals that 61 percent of women have experienced some form of sexual harassment at work, but that only 4 percent have reported the incidents.

• On January 25, federal officials report that 161 thousand cases of AIDS have been reported in the United States since 1981, and that the death toll has now passed one hundred thousand. More than 215,000 others are expected to die from AIDS in the next three years.

• On February 3, the price of a first-class postage stamp is raised from 25¢ to 29¢ cents.

• On February 14, homosexual and unmarried heterosexual couples begin registering under a new law in San Francisco to be recognized as "domestic partners."

• On March 16, members of the Irish Gay and Lesbian Organization march in the annual New York City St. Patrick's Day Parade.

• On April 1, the minimum wage is raised to $4.25 an hour.

• On April 22, Intel releases the 486SX computer chip.

• On May 20, the Red Cross announces stricter procedures for screening blood for the AIDS virus.

• On August 22, calm returns after tensions between African American and Jewish residents in Brooklyn's Crown Heights neighborhood erupt into four days of rioting. Eighty-four police officers and at least twenty-five civilians were injured during the unrest.

• From September 5 to September 7, Naval and Marine aviators attending the thirty-fifth annual Tailhook convention (named after an aircraft-carrier landing device) assault dozens of women, including fourteen fellow officers, in a drunken ritual called "the gauntlet."

• On November 6, the FDA announces sweeping changes in food labeling practices, which will require a more detailed listing of contents.

• On November 26, condoms are handed out to thousands of New York City high-school students.

1992

- In the first six months of the year, 4.1 billion "cents-off" coupons are redeemed, an increase of 10 percent over 1991. Experts see this an indicator that bad economic times are ahead.

- With 445 inmates per 100,000 Americans, the United States has a higher percentage of its population in prison than does any other nation, and double the rate of incarceration in 1980.

- A survey shows that 80 percent of Americans hold a single-family dwelling as their ideal home, but that increasing numbers do not have the money to purchase one.

- A study finds that the average American is working more and has less leisure time than 20 years ago. Workers are putting in 140 hours more per year than in 1962—in part because, in terms of buying power, their wages have declined over that period.

- On January 7, AT&T releases a videotelephone.

- On February 24, General Motors Corporation announces a record $4.5 billion loss in 1991 and that it will close twenty-one plants; 74,000 workers will lose their jobs over the next four years.

- On March 6, computer users brace themselves for the computer virus "Michelangelo"; only scattered cases of missing files are reported.

- On April 5, some 500,000 demonstrators march in Washington, D.C., to support abortion rights, as the Supreme Court hears case involving a Pennsylvania law that limits those rights. On June 29, the Court reaffirms a woman's right to an abortion, but at the same time allows states to place some restrictions on it.

- On April 29, three days of widespread rioting begin in south central Los Angeles after four police officers are acquitted in the beating of an African American man, even though the incident was videotaped. Over sixty-three hundred people are arrested and more than thirty-seven buildings are burned in the unrest. Fifty-one persons are killed and nearly eighteen hundred injured before federal troops and the National Guard finally restore order.

- On June 5, the unemployment rate jumps to 7.5 percent—the highest level in eight years.

- On June 23, pilot Jessica Hearns is reinstated by Continental Airlines after having a sex-change operation.

- On August 11, the Mall of America, the biggest shopping complex built in the United States, opens in Bloomington, Minnesota.

- On October 1, the United States goes "metric" with the official adoption of the International Unit of Measure.

- On October 3, Microsoft founder William Henry "Bill" Gates III heads the list in *Forbes* of "400 Richest Americans" with an estimated net worth of $6.3 billion.

- On November 8, to commemorate the tenth anniversary of the Vietnam Memorial, volunteers begin reading aloud the 58,183 names that are inscribed on the monument.

- On November 23, ten thousand cellular phones have been sold in the United States.

1993

- AIDS is now the leading killer of American men between the ages of fifteen and forty-four. Also, a twenty-five-year decline in smoking seems to be coming to an end.

- A Gallup poll reveals that more teenagers than adults go to church, and that young people attend 10 percent more often than their parents.

- On January 18, the Martin Luther King, Jr., national holiday is observed for the first time in all fifty states.

- On January 25, Sears and Roebuck announces it will close its catalogue-sales department after ninety-seven years of operation.

- On January 30, the city of Los Angeles officially opens the "Red Line," its first modern subway.

- On February 2, smoking is officially prohibited at the White House.

- In March, the Intel Pentium computer chip makes its debut.

- On March 11, a doctor who performed abortions is shot and killed outside a Pensacola, Florida, clinic by an anti-abortion activist.

- From March 12 to March 14, the "storm of the century," with record snowfalls and high winds, paralyzes the eastern seaboard, killing approximately 270 people.

- On April 19, after a fifty-one-day stalemate, eighty members of the Branch Davidian cult, including at least seventeen children, die in a fire as the result of a botched assault by federal agents on their compound in Waco, Texas.

- On April 20, the FDA approves the French abortion pill RU-486, popularly known as the "morning after pill," for manufacture and sale in the United States.

- On April 22, the United States Holocaust Memorial Museum in Washington, D.C., is dedicated.

- On April 25, gay-rights activists and supporters march on Washington demanding equal rights and freedom from discrimination.

- On April 28, the first "Take Our Daughters to Work Day," organized by the Ms. Foundation to boost young girls' self-esteem by visiting their parents' workplaces, takes place.

- On April 28, the Defense Department approves the use of female pilots in air combat. Women will also be allowed to serve in combat positions on Navy ships for the first time.

- On July 14, in a move toward a more healthy product, Kentucky Fried Chicken (KFC) removes the word *fried* from its logo and unveils "Rotisserie Gold Roasted Chicken."

- On July 29, ground is broken for the Vietnam Women's Memorial in Washington, D.C.

- On November 11, the Walt Disney Company announces plans to build a U.S. history theme park in northern Virginia; however, in the face of local opposition, the company later backs down.

1994

- The Census Bureau reports that the number of full-time workers whose income falls below the poverty level has increased 50 percent since 1980.

- Sixty-five percent of women their fifties are in the work-force. The number has been increasing steadily for the past ten years.

- Tatoos, long the label of sailors and outlaw bikers, become the fad among young mainstream American men and women.

- One third of all adults are at least 20 lbs. overweight.

- More than thirty thousand Cubans flee to the United States, but most are intercepted and settled in camps in Panama or at Guantanamo Bay. In September U.S. and Cuban officials agree that Cuba will prevent its citizens from fleeing and, in return, the United States will accept twenty thousand legal Cuban immigrants per year

- On February 5, white separatist Byron De La Beckwith is convicted of the 1963 murder of civil-rights leader Medgar Evers in Jackson, Mississippi, and is sentenced to life in prison.

- On April 8, smoking is banned at the Pentagon and all U.S. military bases. Five states—California, Maryland, Michigan, Vermont, and Washington—also take action to discourage smoking during the year.

- On May 12, Congress passes a law to prohibit blockades, threats, and violence against abortion clinics.

- On June 26, thousands of homosexuals gather in New York City for the twenty-fifth anniversary of the Stonewall Inn Riot, the birthplace of the gay-rights movement.

- On July 22, a federal judge orders the all-male military school The Citadel, a state-financed college in South Carolina, to admit women.

- On September 12, the Netscape Navigator web browser is introduced.

- On October 11, the Colorado Supreme Court strikes down an anti-gay-rights measure as unconstitutional.

- On December 6, Orange County, California, one of the wealthiest municipalities in the country, becomes the largest municipality to file for bankruptcy protection; because of risky and poor investments the county was $2 billion in the red.

1995

- The Census Bureau reports that 8.7 percent of the American population was born outside the United States, highest percentage since World War II.

- The Zenith Electronics Corporation, the last American manufacturer of television sets, is purchased by a South Korean company.

- Teenage smoking has increased by 30 percent since 1990, and a poll shows that a large majority of Americans favor government action to prevent it. Teen sex is decreasing, however. Of teenagers, 53 percent are sexually active. The bad news is that only half of them are using condoms.

- About 55 percent of American women provide at least half of the household income.

- Over 7 million people subscribe to computer on-line services. America Online, CompuServe, and Prodigy are the largest.

- On February 3, IBM relaxes its dress code and allows employees to wear whatever they think appropriate to the office. The company's action reflects a general trend toward less formal dress in the workplace. Slacks and even jeans are replacing business suits in many offices.

- On February 18, the National Association for the Advancement of Colored People (NAACP) ousts Dr. William F. Gibson as president; Myrlie Evers-Williams, widow of Medgar Evers, is elected to the office.

- On April 13, Coretta Scott King, widow of slain civil-rights leader Martin Luther King, Jr., loses a court battle in which she tries to regain possession of her husband's papers from Boston University.

- On April 19, in an act of domestic terrorism, a tremendous blast from a truck bomb destroys the Alfred P. Murrah Federal Building in Oklahoma City, killing 168 people.

- On June 27, Philip Morris tobacco company launches "Action Against Access," a program to prevent children from smoking. The company also will remove advertising from stadiums and sports arenas that might be seen on television.

- On August 15, in an out-of-court settlement, the U.S. government pays $3.1 million to the family of white separatist Randall C. Weaver, whose wife and son were killed by government agents in 1992.

- On October 16, more than four hundred thousand African American men gather in Washington, D.C., in the Million Man March. The rally was called by Nation of Islam leader Louis Farrakhan to promote African American male solidarity and to encourage African American males to take greater leadership roles in their communities.

1996

- The volume of e-mail exceeds the volume of surface mail for the first time. Also for the first time, more money is spent to purchase computers than to purchase TVs.

- The Census Bureau reports that the gap between the richest and poorest Americans is the widest it has been since World War II. However, most Americans are enjoying their highest standard of living yet. At the same time, they are filing for bankruptcy at a record rate—and the number of bankruptcies for 1996 is expected to be 25 percent higher than in 1995.

- Americans are not only living longer than ever before, they also are developing fewer chronic diseases and other disabling conditions.

- The use of tobacco, marijuana, and other drugs by teens continues to rise. More than a third of teens under age seventeen say they have smoked tobacco, about a 10 percent increase since 1993. Marijuana use has jumped 141 percent over about the same time period.

- The "traditional" family of two parents and children under the same roof is making a comeback. The divorce rate has dropped by more than 10 percent since 1980.

- On February 16, a U.S. District Judge bans government from enforcing a new law that would punish anyone making "indecent" material available to minors through computers.

- On March 14, AT&T introduces Internet access service.

- On March 25, a new one hundred dollar bill, redesigned to inhibit counterfeiting, goes into circulation.

- On April 23, Sotheby's begins a four-day auction of possessions belonging to Jacqueline Kennedy Onassis; the auction will bring in $34.5 million.

- On May 2, the U.S. Senate passes an immigration bill making it more difficult for aliens to get jobs and access to social services.

- On May 5, the Federal Bureau of Investigation (FBI) releases figures showing that the number of serious crimes reported in the United States has dropped for the fourth straight year.

- On July 4, HotMail, a new free Internet e-mail service, begins operation.

- On July 12, the U.S. House of Representatives votes overwhelmingly to define marriage in federal laws as the legal union of men and women only, regardless of what individual states recognize.

- On August 13, Microsoft releases Internet Explorer 3.0 to compete with Netscape Navigator.

- On September 19, IBM announces it will extend health benefits to partners of gay and lesbian employees.

- On September 21, President Bill Clinton signs a bill into law that enables states to refuse to recognize same-sex marriages performed in other states that permit them.

- On September 29, the Nintendo 64 video game debuts in the United States.

- On October 1, the minimum wage is raised to $4.75 an hour.

- On October 12, thousands of Hispanic Americans march in Washington, D.C., to show support for a simplified citizenship process and a higher minimum wage.

- On November 27, a federal judge blocks enforcement of California initiative that would dismantle state affirmative-action programs.

- On December 3, a judge in Hawaii rules that the state must issue marriage licenses to same-sex couples.

1997

- The Mattel Company, manufacturer of the Barbie doll, announces that there are more Barbie dolls in existence (250 million) than the entire population of the United States.

- Four major tobacco companies agree to pay several state governments a total of $368.5 billion as compensation for the costs the states have incurred over the decades in providing services to citizens whose health has been damaged by smoking.

- In a *Time*/CNN poll, 22 percent of Americans believe that aliens from outer space have been in contact with humans; another 13 percent believe that aliens have abducted human beings in order to observe them or perform experiments on them.

- On March 27, members of a religious cult called Heaven's Gate commit mass suicide in California. They believe they will be joining space aliens who are traveling with the

Hale-Bopp comet, which is passing near Earth for the first time in forty-two hundred years.

- On August 9, the city of Memphis declares August 9 to August 17 "Elvis Presley Week" in honor of the twentieth anniversary of the singer-entertainer's death.

- On September 1, the federal minimum wage increases form $4.75 to $5.15 per hour.

- On November 4, voters in Houston, Texas, approve the retention of affirmative-action programs in the city.

- On December 3, President Clinton holds a "town meeting" in Akron, Ohio, to open a "national conversation" about race.

- On December 5, the U.S. government reports that 404,000 new jobs were created, that unemployment is now at 4.6 percent, the lowest since 1973, and that hourly earnings have climbed seven cents in the last year.

- On December 15, a special investigative panel urges the Pentagon to "roll back" the integration of men and women in basic- and advanced-training programs.

1998

- Betty Crocker, the homemaker icon created by General Mills, starts a website.

- The four major tobacco companies agree to pay $200 billion to forty-six states and five U.S. territories. The settlement also prohibits the use of cartoon in cigarette advertising.

- On January 1, the Census Bureau estimates that the current population of the United States is 268,921,733 persons.

- On January 14, the first woman to enroll at the Virginia Military Institute (VMI) withdraws.

- On January 22, the states of New York and New Jersey argue before the Supreme Court to determine which state owns Ellis Island, the national historic gateway for more than sixteen million immigrants. The court will split ownership, with New Jersey being given approximately twenty-two acres, while New York retains five acres.

- On January 23, Netscape begins giving its browsers away free on the Internet in an attempt to compete with Microsoft's Internet Explorer, which Netscape charges has gained an unfair and possibly unlawful trade advantage over its competitors.

- On February 10, a college dropout who had e-mailed threats to Asian students is convicted of committing the first "hate crimes in cyberspace."

- On March 27, the FDA approves the male impotence drug Viagra. Sales of the new drug instantly explode.

- On June 7, James Byrd, Jr., an African American man, is dragged to death by three white supremacists in a pickup truck near Jasper, Texas. The horrific murder attracts national attention and causes Americans of all races to question how much the nation's racial divisions have truly healed over recent decades.

- On August 17, after months of denial, President Clinton admits to a sexual affair with a young White House intern in a televised address to the nation.

• On August 21, a former Ku Klux Klan wizard, Sam H. Bower, is convicted for the 1966 fire-bombing death of Vernon Dahmer, Sr., who had registered African Americans to vote at his store outside Hattiesburg, Mississippi.

• On October 6, Matthew Shepard, a gay student at the University of Wyoming, is beaten to death by two men because of his sexual orientation. The murder is classified as a hate crime.

1999

• Summer along the eastern United States brings serious rainfall shortages, with many states experiencing the worst drought on record.

• Online auction site eBay receives some 1.5 million bids each day on a wide variety of items that merchants and individuals have posted for sale there.

• As the millennium approaches, apprehension grows about the Y2K bug. This is a programming glitch that may cause older computer chips to be unable to recognize dates after 1999, and thereby render the devices they control inoperable. Doomsayers warn that at 12:01 AM in January 1, 2000, many computer-dependent operations, from medical equipment to financial networks to building elevators, will shut down across the nation. When the New Year arrives, however, these fears prove unfounded.

• On January 10, the cost of a postage stamp is raised from thirty-two to thirty-three cents.

• On February 9, in an article published in his *National Liberty Journal*, Rev. Jerry Falwell warns parents that the purple, purse-toting "Tinky-Winky" of the popular Public Broadcasting Service (PBS) children's program "Teletubbies" is a role model for homosexuality.

• On February 11, a federal jury in Brooklyn finds that gun manufacturers, in the first case of its kind, are liable for shootings done by illegally obtained handguns.

• On February 23, John William King is convicted and sentenced to death in the dragging murder of James Byrd, Jr., in June 1998. King is the first white to be so sentenced for the murder of an African American since Texas reinstated the death penalty in 1970.

• On March 27, a New Jersey man initiates a nationwide panic when he attaches a computer virus he has created to some e-mails that he sends. The so-called Melissa virus is designed to spread by forwarding itself to the addresses in the e-mail address book of each person who receives it. Many businesses and other organizations worry about their computer networks as the virus rapidly spreads across the Internet.

• On April 11, a report from *The New York Times* states that tax returns from Americans earning more than one hundred thousand dollars a year and from the larger corporations are escaping the scrutiny of the Internal Revenue Service (IRS).

• On April 20, two teenage boys storm Columbine High School in Littleton, Colorado, and kill thirteen before committing suicide. Investigation later reveals their plot to kill five hundred students and blow up the school. The two had been persistently harassed and taunted by other students and had decided to get revenge.

• On July 8, President Clinton ends a four-day tour of "poverty in America," which receives minimal coverage from the press.

The Turner Diaries

Fictional work

By: Andrew MacDonald

Date: 1978

Source: MacDonald, Andrew. *The Turner Diaries.* Washington, D.C.: National Vanguard Press, 1978. Reprint, New York: Barricade Books, 1996, 1–2, 4–7.

About the Author: Andrew MacDonald was a pseudonym adopted by William L. Pierce (1933–2002) for his 1978 novel *The Turner Diaries,* which became infamous for its racist, anti-Semitic call to violence. With a doctorate in physics, Pierce pursued a career as a professor and scientist before founding the National Alliance in 1974. With its message of white supremacy, the National Alliance was considered one of the most dangerous organizations in America and was blamed for encouraging hate crimes against minorities. ■

Introduction

The 1990s witnessed a series of confrontations that pitted the government against right-wing extremist groups. In August 1992, a shoot-out between U.S. marshals and white supremacist Randy Weaver at Ruby Ridge, Idaho, left one marshal and two members of Weaver's family dead, and the violence fueled conspiracy theories among other separatist groups about the government's motives. The following year, when eighty Bureau of Alcohol, Tobacco, and Firearms (ATF) agents stormed the compound of the Branch Davidians, led by self-styled prophet David Koresh, in Waco, Texas, four ATF agents and possibly six Branch Davidians died after a fifty-one-day standoff. Outraged by the government's actions, Gulf War veteran Timothy McVeigh focused his anger through the Michigan Militia, one of many such organizations that had sprung up during the decade. Often espousing neo-Nazi, separatist, or survivalist platforms, the various militia groups fed upon fears of government repression. By the mid-1990s, there were an estimated eight hundred militia groups throughout the United States—most of them small in number and short-lived—with as many as 100,000 members.

McVeigh became the most infamous militia member by undertaking the bombing of the Alfred P. Mur-

David Duke's Senate Campaign

In his bid for political legitimacy, David Duke toned down the worst excesses of his racist rhetoric in his campaigns for political office. In his 1996 run for the U.S. Senate, Duke claimed that a liberal conspiracy was plotting his defeat. Outlining his outrage against a "New World Order," Duke calls for an end to affirmative action, immigration, welfare programs, and free-trade agreements.

"David Duke for Senate" [excerpt]

I'm David Duke, the man who the liberal media FEARS the most. I'm running for the U.S. Senate and I need your support. . . .

My victory will be YOUR victory. I will be the only U.S. Senator who dares to stand up against the New World Order, speak openly about the preservation of our White, Christian heritage and rights. . . .

My last earthshaking races caused Republicans and some populist Democrats all across America to take up parts of my program, including opposition to affirmative action as well as welfare and immigration reform, and even the "flat tax." . . .

In this campaign, I'll make the survival of our heritage a primary issue. We have a right—indeed, we must—preserve the heritage of the United States of America and NOT let it become another Mexico or Haiti. Immigration and welfare-financed birth rates will make traditional Americans a minority in our own country! . . .

Is that the America you want to live in, or have your children live in? We CAN save America, but only if we act TODAY. . . .

Help me to stand up and speak for YOU, fight for YOU, . . . to win this Senate race for YOU! Please give me a helping hand today!

SOURCE: "David Duke for Senate." Formerly available online at http://web.archive.org/eb/19961103172812/www.duke.org/intro1.htm.

rah Federal Office Building in Oklahoma City on April 19, 1995, killing 168 people—up to that time, the deadliest terrorist attack on American soil. The following year, during the 1996 Atlanta Summer Olympic Games, a bomb went off in Centennial Park that killed one spectator and injured 111 others. In 1998, Eric Robert Rudolph, an anti-abortion extremist already under indictment for two other bombings, was indicted for the Centennial Park attack as well as another Atlanta bombing at a gay nightclub. Rudolph, claiming to represent the "Army of God," had already gone into hiding before the indictments came down. Rudolph was added to the FBI's Ten Most Wanted Fugitives list, but he eluded capture until he was discovered at a shopping center in Murphy, North Carolina, in 2003.

Significance

Right-wing extremism took on a politically mainstream face in the person of David Duke, a former grand wizard of the Louisiana Ku Klux Klan and founder of the National Association for the Advancement of White People. He moderated the worst excesses of his racist and antigovernment rhetoric and ran on a conservative platform of lower taxes and less government regulation in 1988 to win a seat in the Louisiana State Legislature. Duke's electoral success made international headlines and embarrassed the Republican Party. Undeterred, Duke ran for the U.S. Senate in 1990 and 1996 as a Republican and raised the biggest controversy of his career with his 1991 bid for the Louisiana governor's office. Duke made it through the primary to challenge former governor Edwin Edwards, who had faced ongoing criminal investigations into his administration, in the final election. A popular bumper sticker advised Louisianans, "Vote for the crook. It's important," and Duke lost the election with 39 percent of the vote.

The revulsion over the militia movement's agenda and increased surveillance by the government gradually led to a drop in the number of right-wing extremist organizations. By the end of the decade, only about two hundred such groups remained active. Duke, as the nation's leading white supremacist, also lost most of his mainstream credibility after he was indicted on tax evasion and mail fraud charges related to fraudulent fundraising activities in 1999. After fleeing the United States to avoid jail, Duke returned to Louisiana in late 2002 to begin serving his fifteen-month sentence.

McVeigh, who was quickly captured after the Oklahoma City bombing, received a death sentence for his actions and was executed on June 11, 2001.

Primary Source

The Turner Diaries [excerpt]

SYNOPSIS: Considered by many to be the most dangerous book in America, and a blueprint for violent overthrow of the government, *The Turner Diaries* sold about 200,000 copies and fueled the extremist right-wing movement. The book consists of the diary of a fictional character, white supremacist leader Earl Turner, as published after his death by a fictional narrator. The book details a militia uprising against the government, which is denounced for being controlled by Jewish leaders working in conjunction with African Americans to oppress whites.

I'll never forget that terrible day: November 9, 1989. They knocked on my door at five in the morning. I was completely unsuspecting as I got up to see who it was.

I opened the door, and four Negroes came pushing into the apartment before I could stop them. One was carrying a baseball bat, and two had long kitchen knives thrust into their belts. The one with the bat shoved me back into a corner and stood guard over me with his bat raised in a threatening position while the other three began ransacking my apartment.

My first thought was that they were robbers. Robberies of this sort had become all too common since the Cohen Act, with groups of Blacks forcing their way into White homes to rob and rape, knowing that even if their victims had guns they probably would not dare use them.

Then the one who was guarding me flashed some kind of card and informed me that he and his accomplices were "special deputies" for the Northern Virginia Human Relations Council. They were searching for firearms, he said.

I couldn't believe it. It just couldn't be happening. Then I saw that they were wearing strips of green cloth tied around their left arms. As they dumped the contents of drawers on the floor and pulled luggage from the closet, they were ignoring things that robbers wouldn't have passed up: my brand-new electric razor, a valuable gold pocket watch, a milk bottle full of dimes. They *were* looking for firearms!

Right after the Cohen Act was passed, all of us in the Organization had cached our guns and ammunition where they weren't likely to be found. Those in my unit had carefully greased our weapons, sealed them in an oil drum, and spent all of one tedious weekend burying the drum in an eight-foot-deep pit 200 miles away in the woods of western Pennsylvania.

But I had kept one gun out of the cache. I had hidden my .357 magnum revolver and 50 rounds of ammunition inside the door frame between the kitchen and the living room. By pulling out two loosened nails and removing one board from the door frame I could get to my revolver in about two minutes flat if I ever needed it. I had timed myself.

But a police search would never uncover it. And these inexperienced Blacks couldn't find it in a million years.

After the three who were conducting the search had looked in all the obvious places, they began slit-

The Branch Davidian compound in Waco, Texas, burns on April 19, 1993, after a botched raid by the federal government following a 51-day stand-off. **AP/WIDE WORLD PHOTOS. REPRODUCED BY PERMISSION.**

ting open my mattress and the sofa cushions. I protested vigorously at this and briefly considered trying to put up a fight.

About that time there was a commotion out in the hallway. Another group of searchers had found a rifle hidden under a bed in the apartment of the young couple down the hall. They had both been handcuffed and were being forcibly escorted toward the stairs. Both were clad only in their underwear, and the young woman was complaining loudly about the fact that her baby was being left alone in the apartment. . . .

The list of persons to be raided, it turned out, had been compiled primarily from firearms sales records which all gun dealers had been required to keep. If a person had turned a gun in to the police after the Cohen Act was passed, his name was marked off the list. If he hadn't it stayed on, and he was raided on November 9—unless he lived in a Black neighborhood.

In addition, certain categories of people were raided whether they had ever purchased a firearm from a dealer or not. All the members of the Organization were raided.

The government's list of suspects was so large that a number of "responsible" civilian groups were deputized to assist in the raids. I guess the planners in the System thought that most of the people on their list had either sold their guns privately before the Cohen Act, or had disposed of them in some other way. Probably they were expecting only about a quarter as many people to be arrested as actually were.

Anyway, the whole thing soon became so embarrassing and so unwieldy that most of the arrestees were turned loose again within a week. The group I was with—some 600 of us—was held for three days in a high school gymnasium in Alexandria before being released. During those three days we were fed only four times, and we got virtually no sleep.

But the police did get mug shots, fingerprints, and personal data from everyone. When we were released we were told that we were still technically under arrest and could expect to be picked up again for prosecution at any time.

The media kept yelling for prosecutions for awhile, but the issue was gradually allowed to die.

Actually, the System had bungled the affair rather badly. . . .

As soon as the public had been reassured by the media that *they* were in no danger, that the government was cracking down only on the "racists, fascists, and other anti-social elements" who had kept illegal weapons, most relaxed again and went back to their TV and funny papers.

As we began to realize this, we were more discouraged than ever. We had based all our plans—in fact, the whole rationale of the Organization—on the assumption that Americans were inherently opposed to tyranny, and that when the System became oppressive enough they could be led to overthrow it. We had badly underestimated the degree to which materialism had corrupted our fellow citizens, as well as the extent to which their feelings could be manipulated by the mass media.

As long as the government is able to keep the economy somehow gasping and wheezing along, the people can be conditioned to accept any outrage. Despite the continuing inflation and the gradually declining standard of living, most Americans are still able to keep their bellies full today, and we must simply face the fact that that's the only thing which counts with most of them.

Discouraged and uncertain as we were, though, we began laying new plans for the future. First, we decided to maintain our program of public recruiting. In fact, we intensified it and deliberately made our propaganda as provocative as possible. The purpose was not only to attract new members with a militant disposition, but at the same time to purge the Organization of the fainthearts and hobbyists—the "talkers."

We also tightened up on discipline. Anyone who missed a scheduled meeting twice in a row was expelled. Anyone who failed to carry out a work assignment was expelled. Anyone who violated our rule against loose talk about Organizational matters was expelled.

We had made up our minds to have an Organization that would be *ready* the next time the System provided an opportunity to strike. The shame of our failure to act, indeed, our inability to act, in 1989 tormented us and drove us without mercy. It was probably the single most important factor in steeling our wills to whip the Organization into fighting trim, despite all obstacles. . . .

It is ironic that while the Organization has always warned the public against the dangers of racial in-

tegration of our police, this has now turned out to be a blessing in disguise for us. The "equal opportunity" boys have really done a wonderful wrecking job on the FBI and other investigative agencies, and their efficiency is way down as a result. Still, we'd better not get over-confident or careless.

Further Resources

BOOKS

Bridges, Tyler. *The Rise of David Duke.* Jackson, Miss.: University of Mississippi Press, 1994.

Crothers, Lane. *Rage on the Right: The American Militia Movement from Ruby Ridge to Homeland Security: People, Passions, and Power.* Lanham, Md.: Rowan and Littlefield, 2003.

Heymann, Philip B. *Terrorism and America: A Commonsense Strategy for a Democratic Society.* Cambridge: MIT Press, 1998.

Rose, Douglas, ed. *The Emergence of David Duke and the Politics of Race.* Chapel Hill, N.C.: University of North Carolina Press, 1992.

Williams, Rhys H. "Breaching the 'Wall of Separation': The Balance Religious Freedom and Social Order." In *Armageddon in Waco: Critical Perspectives on the Branch Davidian Conflict,* edited by Stuart A. Wright, 299–322. Chicago: University of Chicago Press, 1995.

Periodicals

"'Turner Diaries' Introduced in McVeigh Trial." *CNN Interactive,* April 28, 1997. Available online at http://www.cnn.com /US/9704/28/okc; website home page: http://www.cnn.com (accessed July 11, 2003).

WEBSITES

"Southern Poverty Law Center Intelligence Report." Available online at http://www.splcenter.org/intelligenceproject/ip-index.html (accessed March 2, 2003).

"The Turner Diaries." Anti-Defamation League. Available online at http://www.adl.org/learn/Ext_US/Turner_Diaries.asp; website home page: http://www.adl.org (accessed July 11, 2003).

Generation X: Tales for an Accelerated Culture
Novel

By: Douglas Coupland

Date: 1991

Source: Coupland, Douglas. *Generation X: Tales for an Accelerated Culture.* New York: St. Martin's Press, 1991, 105–106.

About the Author: Canadian Douglas Coupland (1961–) grew up in Vancouver, British Columbia, and studied art and design and business before turning to writing. In 1991, he published *Generation X: Tales for an Accelerated Culture,* which instantly turned him into the voice of the post-baby-boom cohort. Coupland followed it with a series of witty novels that explored the themes of technology, alienation, and popular culture, including *Microserfs* (1995) and *Miss Wyoming* (2000), and nonfiction works such as *Souvenir of Canada* (2002), a photo essay of what it means to be Canadian. ■

Introduction

In 1990, the last members of the baby-boom generation, roughly defined as those born between 1946 and 1960, turned thirty years old. Now that they were officially middle age, the differences between the country's largest demographic cohort and those who followed in its wake—soon to be dubbed "Generation X"—became clear. Baby boomers had freely experimented with marijuana and LSD in the 1960s and cocaine in the 1970s; Generation Xers were plagued by a crack cocaine epidemic that devastated inner-city America. Free love, open relationships, and widespread sexual experimentation were rites of passage for many baby boomers; Generation X was left with AIDS, herpes, and a host of other sexually transmitted diseases that were debilitating and even fatal. The boomers, it was said, even ruined rock and roll, as MTV stifled truly original music from getting on the airwaves.

To the under-thirty crowd in the 1990s, the idealism and optimism of the 1960s seemed a long way off. With the skyrocketing divorce rate, many Generation Xers had grown up in single-parent or "blended" families with step-siblings; with the divorce rate stubbornly persisting at one out of every two marriages, many had given up on the idea of having a nuclear family themselves. Nor did they share in the boomers' experience of growing up during a nearly uninterrupted economic expansion. Instead of sharing in the golden age of the American economy, Generation Xers had to contend with the energy crisis and deindustrialization of the 1970s and the Wall Street scandals of the 1980s. By their sheer numbers, the baby boomers also prevented Generation Xers from upward career mobility; all the good jobs, it seemed, were already taken.

Significance

It was not until Douglas Coupland published *Generation X* in 1991 that the post-baby-boom generation had a name. The book traced the seemingly disconnected and at times alienated lives of three twenty-something friends, Andy, Claire, and Dag. Not only did the novel name the generation it portrayed, it popularized many of their catch phrases as well, from "McJob"—a dead-end, low-paying career position that was the fate of many Generation Xers—to "Boomer envy"—resentment over the greed

Douglas Coupland, author of *Generation X: Tales for an Accelerated Culture.* PHOTOGRAPH BY RICHARD DREW. AP/WIDE WORLD PHOTOS. REPRODUCED BY PERMISSION.

and consumerism of those who had once attended Woodstock, generationally speaking.

Although *Generation X* was not a blockbuster bestseller, its influence far outweighed its actual sales. Suddenly, the media pounced on the term to explain all sorts of sociological phenomena, from falling educational standards to political disengagement to an apparent crisis in faith over America's future greatness. Others invoked the novel to criticize Generation X as a group of whiners who wrongly blamed society for their lack of economic opportunities and alienation instead of taking responsibility for their lives. To those who actually read the book, however, a more positive impression of Generation X emerged. Having grown up in so-called broken homes, they formed their own families out of their friends and colleagues with similar interests. Coming of age after the civil rights and women's and gay rights movements, they were comfortable with racial diversity, feminism, and homosexuality. In an era of economic uncertainty, the independence and self-reliance of Generation Xers were also admirable qualities.

Coinciding with the rise of the grunge music scene in Seattle, Generation X soon had its symbolic leader in Nirvana lead singer Kurt Cobain. As the media hype

Generation X Lexicon

MCJOB: A low-pay, low-prestige, low-dignity, low-benefit, no-future job in the service sector. Frequently considered a satisfying career choice by people who have never held one.

HISTORICAL UNDERDOSING: To live in a period of time when nothing seems to happen. Major symptoms include addiction to newspapers, magazines, and TV news broadcasts.

HISTORICAL OVERDOSING: To live in a period of time when too much seems to happen. Major symptoms include addiction to newspapers, magazines, and TV news broadcasts.

EMOTIONAL KETCHUP BURST: The bottling up of opinions and emotions inside oneself so that they explosively burst forth all at once, shocking and confusing employers and friends—most of whom thought things were fine.

BLEEDING PONYTAIL: An elderly sold-out baby boomer who pines for hippie or presellout days.

BOOMER ENVY: Envy of material wealth and long-range material security accrued by older members of the baby boom generation by virtue of fortunate births.

CLIQUE MAINTENANCE: The need of one generation to see the generation following it as deficient so as to bolster its own collective ego: *"Kids today do nothing. They're so apathetic. We used to go out and protest. All they do is shop and complain."*

CONSENSUS TERRORISM: The process that decides in-office attitudes and behavior.

BREAD AND CIRCUITS: The electronic era tendency to view party politics as corny—no longer relevant or meaningful or useful to modern societal issues, and in many cases dangerous.

VOTER'S BLOCK: The attempt, however futile, to register dissent with the current political system by simply not voting.

REBELLION POSTPONEMENT: The tendency in one's youth to avoid traditionally youthful activities and artistic experiences in order to obtain serious career experience. Sometimes results in the mourning for lost youth at about age thirty, followed by silly haircuts and expensive joke-inducing wardrobes.

RECREATIONAL SLUMMING: The practice of participating in recreational activities of a class one perceives as lower than one's own: *"Karen! Donald! Let's go bowling tonight! And don't worry about shoes . . . apparently you can rent them."*

CONVERSATIONAL SLUMMING: The self-conscious enjoyment of a given conversation precisely for its lack of intellectual rigor. A major spin-off activity of *Recreational Slumming.*

OCCUPATIONAL SLUMMING: Taking a job well beneath one's skill or education level as a means of retreat from adult responsibilities and/or avoiding possible failure in one's true occupation.

DOWN-NESTING: The tendency of parents to move to smaller, guest-room-free houses after the children have moved away so as to avoid children aged 20 to 30 who have boomeranged home.

HOMEOWNER ENVY: Feelings of jealousy generated in the young and the disenfranchised when facing gruesome housing statistics.

SOURCE: Coupland, Douglas. *Generation X: Tales for an Accelerated Culture.* New York: St. Martin's, 1991, 5, 7, 8, 21, 80, 106, 113, 144.

rolled on, Hollywood got in on the act with several movies aimed squarely at the Generation X audience, including *Singles* (1992) and *Reality Bites* (1994). Both movies failed to make much impact at the box office, demonstrating one of the defining characteristics of Generation X: media-savvy and skeptical, they were rarely persuaded by traditional marketing campaigns.

Primary Source

Generation X: Tales for an Accelerated Culture
[excerpt]

> **SYNOPSIS:** In this excerpt, Coupland contrasts the alienation felt by Generation Xers with their younger siblings, the "Global Teens," who are much more materialistic, corporate-loving, and just plain spoiled. Marketers would later turn youngsters such as Coupland's "Global Teens" into "Generation Y." As the first generation born to the original baby boomers, Generation Y kids indeed exhibited many of the traits that Coupland outlines in this passage, from their love of technology to unfettered, and perhaps unreasonable, ambition and expectations.

[Editor's note: ¶ symbol in text below appears as in original document.]

Why am I Poor?

It's Prince Tyler of Portland on the phone, my baby brother by some five years; our family's autumn crocus; the buzz-cut love child; spoiled little monster who hands a microwaved dish of macaroni back to Mom and commands, "There's a patch in the middle that's still cold. Reheat it." (Me, my two other brothers, or my three sisters would be *thwocked* on the head for such insolence, but such baronial dictums from *Tyler* merely reinforce his princely powers.) ¶"Hi, Andy. Bagging some rays?" ¶"Hi, Tyler. Actually I *am*." ¶"Too cool, too cool. Listen: Bill-cubed, the World Trade Center, Lori, Joanna, and me are coming down to stay in your spare bungalow on January 8 for five days. That's Elvis's birthday. We're going to have a KingFest. Any problem with that?" ¶"Not that I can think of, but you'll be packed like hamsters in there. Hope you don't mind. Let me check." (Bill-cubed, actually Bill[3], is three of Tyler's friends, all named Bill; the World Trade Center is the Morrissey twins, each standing six feet six inches.) ¶I rummage through my bungalow, hunting for my reservations book (the landlord places me in charge of rentals). I muse all the while about Tyler and his clique—Global Teens, as he labels them, though most are in their twenties. It seems amusing and confusing—unnatural—to me the way Global Teens, or Tyler's friends, at least, live their lives so *together* with each other: shopping, traveling, squabbling, thinking, and breathing, just like the Baxter family. (Tyler, not surprisingly, has ended up becoming fast friends, via me, with Claire's brother Allan.)

How cliquish *are* these Global Teens? It really boggles. Not *one* of them can go to Waikiki for a simple one-week holiday, for example, without several enormous gift laden send off parties in one of three classic sophomoric themes: Tacky Tourist, Favorite Dead Celebrity, or Toga. And once they arrive there, nostalgic phone calls soon start: sentimental and complicated volleys of elaborately structured trans-Pacific conference calls flowing every other day, as though the jolly vacationer had just hurtled toward Jupiter on a three-year mission rather than six days of overpriced Mai Tais on Kuhio Street.

"The Tyler Set" can be really sucky, too—no drugs, no irony, and only moderate booze, popcorn, cocoa, and videos on Friday nights. And elaborate wardrobes—*such wardrobes!* Stunning and costly, coordinated with subtle sophistication, composed of only the finest labels. Slick. And they can afford them because, like most Global Teen princes and princesses, they all live at home, unable to afford what few ludicrously overpriced apartments exist in the city. So their money all goes on their backs.

Tyler is like that old character from TV, Danny Partridge, who didn't want to work as a grocery store box boy but instead wanted to start out owning the whole store. Tyler's friends have nebulous, unsalable but *fun* talents—like being able to make really great

coffee or owning a really *good* head of hair (oh, to see Tyler's shampoo, gel, and mousse collection!).

They're nice kids. None of their folks can complain. They're *perky*. They embrace and believe the pseudo-globalism and ersatz racial harmony of ad campaigns engineered by the makers of soft drinks and computer-inventoried sweaters. Many want to work for IBM when their lives end at the age of twenty-five *("Excuse me, but can you tell me more about your pension plan?")*. But in some dark and undefinable way, these kids are also Dow, Union Carbide, General Dynamics, and the military. And I suspect that unlike Tobias, were their AirBus to crash on a frosty Andean plateau, they would have little, if any, compunction about eating dead fellow passengers. Only a theory. . . .

Further Resources

BOOKS

Bagby, Meredith. *We've Got Issues: The Get Real, No B.S., Guilt-free Guide to What Really Matters.* New York: PublicAffairs, 2000.

Gaslin, Glenn, and Rick Porter. *The Complete, Cross-Referenced Guide to the Baby Buster Generation's Collective Unconscious.* New York: Boulevard Books, 1998.

Lancaster, Lynne C., and David Stillman. *When Generations Collide: Who They Are. Why They Clash. How to Solve the Generational Puzzle at Work.* New York: HarperBusiness, 2002.

Mitchell, Susan. *Generation X: Americans Ages 18 to 34.* Ithaca, N.Y.: New Strategist, 2001.

Tulgan, Bruce. *Managing Generation X: How to Bring Out the Best in Young Talent.* New York: Norton, 1996.

Wesson, Vann. *Generation X Field Guide and Lexicon.* San Diego, Calif.: Orion Media, 1997.

PERIODICALS

Beck, Melinda. "The New Middle Age." *Newsweek,* December 7, 1992, 50–56.

WEBSITES

"Douglas Coupland Official Web Site." Available online at http://www.coupland.com (accessed February 20, 2003).

AUDIO AND VISUAL MEDIA

Reality Bites. Directed by Ben Stiller. Universal Studios, 1994, VHS.

Singles. Directed by Cameron Crowe. Warner Studios, 1992, VHS.

Talk Radio and the Republican Revolution

The Way Things Ought to Be

Nonfiction work

By: Rush H. Limbaugh III

Date: 1992

Source: Limbaugh, III, Rush H. *The Way Things Ought to Be.* New York: Pocket Books, 1992, 204–207.

See, I Told You So

Nonfiction work

By: Rush H. Limbaugh III

Date: 1993

Source: Limbaugh, III, Rush H. *See, I Told You So.* New York: Pocket Books, 1993, 266–267.

About the Author: H. Rush Limbaugh III (1951–) grew up in a wealthy, conservative family in Missouri. After flunking out of college, he pursued his long-held ambition of becoming a radio disk jockey in 1971. He worked at various stations throughout the 1970s, and after a stint as a salesman for the Kansas City Royals, he returned to the airwaves in 1984 as the host of a call-in show in Sacramento. In 1988, Limbaugh syndicated his show to fifty-six radio stations and expanded it to a weekday, three-hour slot from noon to 3:00 P.M. By 1993, his show had expanded to six hundred AM radio stations and claimed a weekly audience of eighteen million listeners. ∎

Introduction

One of the most important deregulatory actions by the Reagan administration in the 1980s was the nullification of the Fairness Doctrine in radio broadcasting. In the past, radio stations were held to strict standards requiring them to give airtime to opposing viewpoints and to correct any factual misstatements they broadcasted. Intended to free broadcasters from federal supervision, the end of the Fairness Doctrine meant that political commentaries could air uninterrupted and without rebuttal—and without obligation to ensure that their content was factually accurate and refrained from personal attacks.

The radio program of Rush Limbaugh, which went into national syndication in 1988, was an example of the changes in broadcasting after the Fairness Doctrine was struck down. Limbaugh, who called himself "the most dangerous man in America," was unabashedly conservative in his political and social commentary. Although he faced criticism for alleged misstatements he made on the air and for what some saw as the harsh tone of some of his skits against homosexuals, feminists, environmental-

ists, and civil rights leaders, Limbaugh's audience grew to an estimated eighteen million listeners each week by 1993. Two books that reiterated his beliefs, *The Way Things Ought to Be* (1992) and *See, I Told You So* (1993) both became best-sellers.

As a champion of Republican leader Newt Gingrich, Limbaugh took much of the credit for helping foster the Republican Revolution of 1994, when the party took control of both houses of Congress. Although Limbaugh's television career failed to take off, he seemed comfortably ensconced as the nation's leading radio talk-show host throughout the mid-1990s and served as one of the leading critics of the Clinton administration.

Significance

Limbaugh remained on the air with a loyal audience of "Dittoheads," as his listeners were nicknamed, throughout the 1990s. Although the conservative talk-show field became crowded with new programs by Sean Hannity, Laura Schlesinger, and others, Limbaugh remained the most popular figure in the genre. He was not, however, without his detractors. In the aftermath of the domestic terrorist attack on the Alfred P. Murrah Federal Office Building by Timothy McVeigh in Oklahoma City in 1995, some pointed to Limbaugh's antigovernment rhetoric as a contributing factor to the rise of the extremist militia movement. Limbaugh flatly rejected such claims and did little to moderate his critiques. Limbaugh was also mocked by humorist Al Franken's 1995 book *Rush Limbaugh Is a Big, Fat Idiot,* which topped the best-seller list just as Limbaugh's own books had done some years earlier.

Limbaugh's crowning achievement of helping the Republicans take control of Congress also dimmed. As the Clinton administration rebounded from some awkward moments in its early days, Republicans lost their legislative momentum and Clinton cruised to an easy victory in the presidential race in 1996. Limbaugh gave considerable airtime to reports of the president's affair with White House intern Monica Lewinsky, which surfaced early in 1998, and demanded his ousting. In their effort to impeach the president, however, Limbaugh and the Republicans crucially misgauged the temperament of the American public, for Clinton survived the scandal and remained in office.

Primary Source

The Way Things Ought to Be [excerpt]

> **SYNOPSIS:** In print and on the air, Limbaugh returned often to his critiques of women's and gay rights activists and other groups. He often grouped the movements together as supporters of "multiculturalism," which in Limbaugh's opinion was responsible for weakening the moral fiber of the nation. In

the second excerpt, Limbaugh outlines his support for the individualistic nature of America's capitalist system and argues that the government should not intervene to correct the natural outcome of market forces.

Multiculturalism

A few years ago, radical students at Stanford University protested against a required course in the great texts of Western civilization. They organized a march, led by the Reverend Jesse Jackson, with a chant, "Hey, hey, ho, ho, Western culture's gotta go." And Stanford capitulated and abolished the Western civilization requirement. It was replaced with watered-down courses in which books were supposed to be examined from the perspective of "race, class, and gender," and readings from St. Augustine and John Locke were interspersed with such works as the autobiography of Guatemalan Marxist guerrilla fighter Rigoberta Menchu and a documentary on Navajo Indians entitled "Our Cosmos, Our Sheep, Our Bodies, Ourselves."

Multiculturalism is billed as a way to make Americans more sensitive to the diverse cultural backgrounds of people in this country. It's time we blew the whistle on that. What is being taught under the guise of multiculturalism is worse than historical revisionism; it's more than a distortion of facts; it's an elimination of facts. In some schools, kids are being taught that the ideas of the Constitution were really borrowed from the Iroquois Indians, and that Africans discovered America by crossing the Atlantic on rafts hundreds of years before Columbus and made all sorts of other scientific discoveries and inventions that were later stolen from them. They are told that the ancient Greeks and Romans stole all of their ideas from the Egyptians and that the Egyptians were black Africans.

In fact, most historians and anthropologists will tell you that while there was a lot of cultural exchange in the ancient world and the Greeks and Romans absorbed some of the Egyptian ideas, it was only one of many influences. And the ancient Egyptians were dark-skinned but not black, even though many scholars have been so intimidated that they will only say this off the record. My purpose here is not to be critical of Africans or African culture, but simply to point out that not one syllable of any of our founding documents can be traced to the roots of tribal Africa—and that neither I nor anyone else is going to improve racial relations by pretending otherwise.

Radio talk-show host Rush Limbaugh took much of the credit for helping foster the Republican Revolution of 1994, when the party took control of both houses of Congress. **AP/WIDE WORLD PHOTOS. REPRODUCED BY PERMISSION.**

There is a fallacious premise out there that black kids have low self-esteem because they don't have any roots. They don't have anything to relate to in their past except slavery and degradation, and to elevate their self-esteem we must teach them about the great cultures of their ancestors. I think the multiculturalists are perpetrating a tremendous and harmful fraud when they take young black kids in public schools and teach them things that are irrelevant or even counterproductive to their future as Americans. They teach that street slang is just as good as grammatical English, that whites are cold and logical but blacks are warm and intuitive, and that Africans have a different approach to numbers that doesn't emphasize precision. Well, if you want to get a job with IBM you've got to have the skills that will help you get that job. And that involves a lot of things. Not just the skills, such as logical thinking and mathematics, but language, appearance, showing up on time. And if the kids have been taught that learning these things means compromising themselves and conforming to white values, how on earth can they be expected to succeed? If you want to prosper in America, if you want access to opportunity in America, you must be able to assimilate: to become part of the American culture. Just as in any other country of the world—if an American moved there, he would have to adapt to its culture if he wanted to succeed. The so-called minorities in this country are not being done any favors when the multiculturalist crowd forces their attitudinal segregation from mainstream society. The politics of cultural pride are actually the politics of alienation, in a different uniform. . . .

What is this American culture toward which we should all aspire? American culture is defined primarily by the idea of self-reliance. That's how this country was built: people of every background fending for themselves and for their families. And it's something we are losing. If you tell someone to get a job, you are using dirty words now; you are being insensitive. Now you are told to define yourself by your place within a tribe or a group. People have accused me of racism or insensitivity when I challenge the multiculturalist view on history and education. But far from being a racist, far from being a bigot, I have a great deal of compassion and love for people of all backgrounds, and I also love my country. I want this to be a great country, and a great country needs as many great individuals as there can be. These young black kids in public schools in America are Americans. Not Africans, not Jamaicans, but Americans. And we have to treat them as such. It is in our nation's best interest, and in their best interest too, for them to grow up as good Americans, to know American culture, to learn to prosper in America. And I have that hope. I want everyone to be taught the things that are necessary for them to prosper as Americans, not black something or brown something or red something, but as Americans.

Of course there are people in the multiculturalist movement who have the best of intentions, who think the movement is dedicated to helping members of minority cultures become more well rounded. And I don't want to castigate all advocates of multiculturalism. In fact, if people want to teach ancient African history, or Third World cultures, or women's studies, that's fine—as long as it doesn't become the primary perspective and doesn't supplant the things that all American kids need to know—and as long as it is not coupled with the fraudulent message that the minorities' best opportunity of succeeding in this society is to jealously cling to their past.

Primary Source

See, I Told You So [excerpt]

> **SYNOPSIS:** Limbaugh supported conservative economic causes as well as social causes. In this excerpt, Limbaugh outlines his support for the individualistic nature of America's capitalist system and argues that the government should not intervene to correct the natural outcome of market forces.

It is utopian, and therefore unrealistic, to expect that every citizen will eat equally every day of the year. It is utopian to expect that every citizen will be provided the exact health care that citizens want every day of the year. It is utopian to believe that suffering of any kind can be eliminated through government intervention and action. As I have told you, there will always be poor people, however earnestly we try to eradicate poverty.

Certainly, it's honorable to attempt to reduce hunger, suffering, and poverty. But it is not realistic to expect that every citizen can be provided the same amounts of good food, comfortable housing, and fine health care. That is what communism and socialism tried to accomplish. Instead of producing utopia, instead of narrowing the gap between the haves and have-nots, the bourgeoisie and proletariat, they created a more rigid class structure. The ruling class arrogates all the power and riches to itself, while the rest of the people remain servants of the state. Just look around the world. Examine the societies that have attempted to make life more prosperous for people by relying on centralized authorities. You won't find much prosperity, and you won't find anything remotely resembling an equitable distribution of resources.

Equality of outcome or result is impossible because no two individuals are alike. We all have different abilities, talents, desires, ambitions, capabilities, and other characteristics. There is no way these differences can be equalized—even by force. Today, in the name of fairness and equality, the U.S. government is coercing greater and greater amounts of wealth transfers and redistribution. The utopians believe it is unfair that some have so much and others have so little. They see themselves as glorified Robin Hoods.

Once again, it doesn't work. If you penalize achievement and punish success, there is less wealth produced for everyone. This is the fatal flaw of utopianism. Also, the value to someone of something that is given to him is always less than the value of something he earned with his own blood, sweat, and tears. This is the lesson that countless socialist governments have learned in just the last five years. Why aren't we learning it here in the United States?

Further Resources

BOOKS

Colford, Paul D. *The Rush Limbaugh Story: Talent on Loan from God: An Unauthorized Biography.* New York: St. Martin's Press, 1993.

Gingrich, Newt, ed. *Contract with America: The Bold Plan by Rep. Newt Gingrich, Rep. Dick Armey and the House Republicans to Change the Nation.* New York: Times Books, 1994.

Rendall, Steven, Jim Naureckas, and Jeff Cohen. *The Way Things Aren't: Rush Limbaugh's Reign of Error.* New York: New Press, 1995.

Seib, Philip. *Rush Hour: Talk Radio, Politics, and the Rise of Rush Limbaugh.* Fort Worth, Tex.: Summit Group, 1993.

PERIODICALS

Corrigan, Don. "Limbaugh Program Demonstrates Need for the Return of the Fairness Doctrine." *St. Louis Journalism Review,* December 2000, 16.

WEBSITES

"The Rush Limbaugh Show." Available online at http://www.rushlimbaugh.com (accessed February 20, 2003).

My Life

Autobiography

By: Earvin "Magic" Johnson with William Novak

Date: 1992

Source: Johnson, Earvin "Magic," with William Novak. *My Life.* New York: Random House, 1992, 224–225, 249–252, 265–267.

About the Author: Earvin Johnson Jr. (1959–) grew up in a family of ten children in Lansing, Michigan, where his standout basketball playing on his high school team earned him the nickname "Magic." Johnson led Michigan State University to a National Collegiate Athletic Association basketball title in 1979. The first draft pick of the Los Angeles Lakers in 1979, Johnson led the team to five championships in the 1980s and was the highest-paid player in the NBA. On November 7, 1991, he announced that he had contracted the HIV virus, which precipitated his retirement as an NBA player. After playing for the gold-medal-winning U.S. men's basketball team at the 1992 Barcelona Summer Olympic Games, he became a successful entrepreneur and AIDS educator. ■

Introduction

With about two-thirds of AIDS cases occurring among gay men in the 1980s, the gay community led protests to demand more research, testing, and treatment to meet the health-care crisis. Yet the leadership of activist groups such as the Gay Men's Health Crisis and ACT-UP reinforced the notion among many heterosexual Americans that AIDS was a "gay disease," with little impact on their own lives. By 1991, a decade after reports of AIDS first surfaced in medical journals, that perception was slowly changing.

Although the death of movie actor Rock Hudson from AIDS in 1985 brought enormous attention to the disease, most Americans still knew little about it. That year, Kokomo, Indiana, teenager Ryan White, a hemophilic who had contracted AIDS from a blood transfusion, was barred from attending his high school out of fears that he might inadvertently pass the human immunodeficiency virus (HIV) or AIDS to the other students. The local resistance to White's school attendance forced his family to move to another town, but a national outcry arose over his plight. Until his death in 1990, White appeared frequently on talk shows to educate the public about the disease. Given his small-town, Hoosier identity, White's story showed the country that AIDS afflicted more than just urban, gay men and intravenous drug users.

Despite the headlines, ad campaigns, and federal expenditures of about $1.6 billion on AIDS research through 1990, the announcement by Los Angeles Lakers basketball star Earvin "Magic" Johnson in November 1991 that he had contracted HIV from one of his many heterosexual encounters stunned the nation. In the previous ten years, Johnson had led his team to five NBA championships and he had just married his longtime girlfriend, Earleatha "Cookie" Kelly. At the time of his announcement, the Johnsons were expecting their first child, a son; fortunately, both mother and Earvin Johnson III had not contracted the disease.

Significance

As one of the most popular sports stars of his generation, Johnson's announcement profoundly changed the public's perception of HIV and AIDS. The realization that anyone could contract the disease was reinforced on April 8, 1992, when tennis star Arthur Ashe disclosed that he had contracted HIV from a blood transfusion several years earlier. He died from AIDS-related pneumonia on February 6, 1993. Johnson, who followed an aggressive regime of daily medication to prevent his HIV from developing into AIDS, remained free from AIDS over a decade after his initial announcement. As a movie theater developer, talk-show host, sports commentator, and AIDS educator, Johnson was possibly more popular than he had been during his NBA days. He was now a hero to more than just sports fans.

The frank public discussion fostered by Johnson's HIV status, accompanied by a wave of safe-sex campaigns aimed at a broad spectrum of Americans, helped to stem the tide of a disease that had reached epidemic proportions in some cities. Yet some Americans were displeased by the candor that accompanied safe-sex ads. Some were also outraged at safe-sex programs that distributed condoms to high school students, which they viewed as an endorsement of sexual activity. Finally, a small group of religious conservatives continued to promote their belief that AIDS was exclusively a "gay" disease that had spread through morally objectionable activities. Other, more mainstream religious leaders refrained from condemning AIDS sufferers but insisted that abstinence from sexual activities outside of marriage was the only way to avoid AIDS.

Most Americans, however, rejected abstinence as a lifestyle choice and welcomed the information on AIDS and safe sex. One sign of their awareness of the issue was the steady increase in condom sales: No longer displayed behind pharmacy counters, the item was now widely available alongside cash register checkouts, in public bathrooms, and in grocery store aisles.

Primary Source

My Life [excerpt]

SYNOPSIS: In his memoir, Johnson admits that, like many professional athletes, he conducted a sexually promiscuous lifestyle without thinking about the consequences of his behavior. He was stunned when a routine insurance physical in late 1991 revealed that he had contracted HIV, the virus that causes AIDS. In this excerpt, Johnson takes us through the days leading up to his public announcement that he was HIV-positive. The announcement commenced Johnson's new career as an HIV and AIDS educator and broadened the public's understanding that the diseases could strike anyone.

Women and Me

The truth is, I wouldn't be writing this chapter at all if I hadn't contracted HIV somewhere along the way. That's why I have a responsibility to deal with this subject, although I'd be a lot happier not to. This is my private life we're talking about.

I'm not writing about the women in my life in order to brag; I'm no Wilt Chamberlain. But I have to acknowledge that the virus in my body, which came from a casual encounter, has created tremendous curiosity about the role sex has played in my life. So I owe it to the reader to be candid. At the same time, I owe it to the women I've known, and also to Cookie

and to myself, to be discreet. So there are no names here, no numbers, no graphic descriptions.

And no apologies. In the age of AIDS, unprotected sex is reckless. I know that now, of course. But the truth is, I knew it then, too. I just didn't pay attention. As often as I had heard about the importance of being careful, I never took it seriously. I couldn't believe that anything like this could happen to me. . . .

Bad News

Friday, October 25, 1991

The phone call came at 2:15 P.M. The Lakers had just checked into our hotel in Salt Lake City. That night, we were to play a preseason exhibition game against the Utah Jazz. Dr. Michael Mellman, the team physician, was on the line from Los Angeles.

"Earvin," he said, "I'd like you to fly back here and see me right away."

"Why?"

"I've just learned that you failed your insurance physical."

As part of a complicated deal, my latest contract with the Lakers had included a low-interest loan. Because of it, I had taken a routine life-insurance physical a few weeks earlier. It was so simple that I barely remembered it. During my annual Laker checkup, somebody from the insurance company had come in to take a blood test.

"Can't this wait until tomorrow?" I said, "We just got here." He must have known we had a game that night.

"It really can't."

I didn't ask any questions. Whatever this was about, something in Mickey's voice told me we'd have to discuss it in person.

I dialed Lon at his office. "Mickey just called," I told him. "He wants me to come right back. Do you know anything about this?"

"Yeah, he called me, too," said Lon. "But he wouldn't say what this was about. He needs to talk to you first. Do you want me to get him on the phone?"

"Sure."

Lon put me on hold as he set up a conference call. As I sat on the bed, listening to that dumb "hold" music, I wondered what the hell this could be. And why couldn't it wait?

Mickey came on the line. "Does it really have to be today?" Lon asked him. "There's a game tonight. Can't he come back tomorrow?"

Mickey was grim. "Lon it's my medical opinion that Earvin should come back immediately."

"Okay. Earvin, is there anything you want to ask Mickey?"

Nothing that he would answer on the phone. "No," I said. Mickey signed off.

"I'll book you a seat on the next flight out," Lon said. "Stay right there. I'll call you back."

Five minutes later: "It's all set," Lon said. "There's a prepaid ticket waiting for you at Delta. It leaves at four twenty-eight and gets in at five-fifteen. Don't worry about checking out. Just leave the hotel and take a cab to the airport I'll pick you up, usual spot."

It wasn't until I was on the plane that I had a chance to really think about this. For the past five days, ever since we'd returned from a week of exhibition games over in Paris, I had been feeling rundown. Then, just after we returned, there had been back-to-back games at the Forum. But Mickey had mentioned the insurance physical. That had been about a month ago. So what could it be? High blood pressure? My father had that. Cancer? I hoped not AIDS? Not likely. Didn't you have to be gay to get that? Or a drug user?

Whatever it was, I had to pay attention. You don't get called back from Utah for a pulled hamstring. . . .

Mickey led us into his office. He pointed to an empty chair, and cleared some papers from a second chair so Lon could sit down, too.

Mickey sat facing me. He's about seven years older than I am, and he'd looked after me for most of my career with the Lakers. He had always talked straight to me. We weren't just doctor and patient—we were friends, too. Mickey had watched me grow up. We had shared a lot of laughs together, and a few championship trophies.

But today he looked drawn and pale. I could see by his eyes that this was difficult for him. Whatever it was, the news was going to be bad. Maybe very bad.

He turned toward the desk and opened a Federal Express envelope. Inside it was a smaller envelope.

He looked straight at me. "Earvin, I have the test results from your life-insurance physical. It says

Earvin "Magic" Johnson speaks during a 1992 press conference.
BETTMANN NEWSPHOTOS. REPRODUCED BY PERMISSION.

here that you tested positive to HIV, the virus that causes AIDS." He went on to explain exactly what that meant.

Lon and I looked at each other without speaking. Then Mickey explained the test results, and what they showed.

I didn't want to believe him. But this was Mickey talking, and I could see that he didn't want to believe it, either. Inside, I knew, he was crying for me.

I was in shock, too stunned to react.

"These tests are rarely wrong," he said. "But just in case, I'd like to run them again. You never know."

"What about Cookie?" I asked. "She's pregnant." Mickey didn't know that. We had found out for sure only that week, and we weren't telling people yet.

"I don't know about Cookie," he replied. "We'll have to test her anyway, as soon as possible."

"And the baby?"

"If Cookie is negative, the baby will be fine." . . .

■ ■ ■

At one-thirty, an hour and a half before the press conference was to begin, I walked into the locker room to tell my teammates. Until then, I hadn't cried—not when I heard the news, or even when I told Cookie. But when I told my teammates what was going on, they were in tears. And when they embraced me, one by one, I felt that power rush through my body. And I cried with them.

The press conference was held in the back of the Forum Club. As Lon and I walked through the suite of offices to get there, he pulled me aside into a tiny room.

"Are you okay?"

"I'm fine."

"You know what you're going to say?"

"I know."

"But don't say you have AIDS."

"What?"

"I just spoke to one of the doctors. Remember, you don't have AIDS. You tested positive for HIV."

"Okay, HIV. Look, I think I'll make it through this press conference. But if I don't, I want you to get up there and take over."

But we both knew that wouldn't happen.

The last time I'd been at a press conference in that room was in 1990, when I won the MVP for the third time. Some of the same people were there then, too: David Stern, Jerry West, Jerry Buss. It was the identical setup: the same podium, the same microphones, the same blue backdrop.

But now there were more reporters and cameramen than I had ever seen before. There were so many that some of them couldn't even get in—they had to watch it on television from the next room. Meanwhile, hundreds of fans had gathered outside the building.

By now the news was out. On my way to the Forum, I had turned on the radio and heard it myself: "According to still-unconfirmed reports, Magic Johnson has AIDS and will be retiring from basketball. The Lakers have called a press conference for three o'clock today, where Johnson is scheduled to make an announcement."

As our little group walked in, a hush fell over the room. I led the way, followed by Cookie, Jerry West, Kareem, Mickey, and Lon. Practically the only thing you could hear was the clicking of automatic cameras, like little machine guns going off. Some of the

reporters were live on the air. You could hear them whispering, like at a golf tournament.

I walked straight to the podium and started talking.

"Good afternoon. Because of the HIV virus that I have attained, I will have to retire from the Lakers today. I just want to make clear, first of all, that I do not have the AIDS disease. I know a lot of you want to know that. I have the HIV virus. My wife is fine. She's negative, so no problem with her.

"I plan on going on living for a long time, bugging you guys like I always have. So you'll see me around. I plan on being with the Lakers and the league, and going on with my life. I guess now I get to enjoy some of the other sides of living that I've missed because of the season and the long practices and so on. I'm going to miss playing.

"I will now become a spokesman for the HIV virus. I want people, young people, to realize that they can practice safe sex. Sometimes you're a little naïve about it and you think it could never happen to you. You only thought it could happen to other people. It *has* happened. But I'm going to deal with it. Life is going to go on for me, and I'm going to be a happy man . . .

"Sometimes we think only gay people can get it, or it's not going to happen to me. Here I am, saying it can happen to everybody.

"Even me, Magic Johnson."

Looking back now, what I did that day was right. There were just too many questions—about my stamina, the effects of the medicine, and what the virus would do to my body. But deep down inside, I now realize, I still wanted to get back on the court as soon as I could.

Further Resources

BOOKS

Burkett, Elinor. *The Gravest Show on Earth: America in the Age of AIDS.* Boston: Houghton Mifflin, 1995.

Crimp, Douglas, with Adam Rolston. *AIDS Demographics.* Seattle: Bay Press, 1990.

Johnson, Earvin "Magic," with Richard Levin. *Magic.* New York: Viking, 1983.

Johnson, Eavin "Magic." *What You Can Do to Avoid AIDS.* New York: Times Books, 1992.

PERIODICALS

Cowley, Geoffrey. "AIDS: The Next Ten Years." *Newsweek,* June 25, 1990, 20–27.

Kantrowitz, Barbara. "Teenagers and AIDS." *Newsweek,* August 3, 1992, 44–49.

————. *Newsweek,* July 1, 1991, 48–57.

WEBSITES

"The Magic Johnson Foundation." Available online at http://www.magicjohnson.org (accessed February 20, 2003).

Thinking Inside and Outside the Box

Reengineering the Corporation: A Manifesto for Business Revolution

Nonfiction work

By: Michael Hammer and James Champy

Date: 1993

Source: Hammer, Michael, and James Champy. *Reengineering the Corporation: A Manifesto for Business Revolution.* New York: HarperCollins, 1993, 1–3.

About the Author: Dr. Michael Hammer (1948–) was the leader of the "reengineering" movement in the 1990s. A former engineer and professor of computer science at the Massachusetts Institute of Technology, Hammer emphasized efficiency, planning, and a focus on "process-centered" management in his works, which included the 1993 best-seller *Reengineering the Corporation,* written with James Champy (1942–).

The Dilbert Principle

Nonfiction work, Cartoon

By: Scott Adams

Date: 1996

Source: Adams, Scott. *The Dilbert Principle.* New York: HarperBusiness, 1996, 274–279.

About the Author: Using his seventeen years of experience as a computer programmer at the Crocker Bank and engineer at the Pacific Bell telecommunications company, Scott Adams (1957–) struck a nerve with his irreverent *Dilbert* cartoon strip. Adams began drawing small-scale sagas of the corporate world featuring Dilbert to relieve the tedium and express the absurdities he sometimes encountered during his career. His favorite targets included the endless staff meetings, reorganizations, and management fads that gripped the workplace in the 1990s. Dilbert became a hero to many white-collar workers. ∎

Introduction

On any given day in the 1990s, a person could be convinced that it was either the best of times or worst of times in corporate America. Pessimistic pundits were convinced that America lagged behind other nations in the global marketplace, particularly Japan, and that the nation's economic future looked bleak. Indeed, ample evidence bore this out. Just as blue-collar workers suffered under deindustrialization in the 1980s, many white-collar professionals were "downsized" in the early 1990s, when 5 percent of men and 4 percent of women in the workforce were laid off or fired each year from 1991 to 1993. Although the large-scale downsizings took place during the initial stage of the longest economic expansion in the country's history, it was the wave of white-collar layoffs that captured the headlines.

More optimistic observers at the beginning of the decade predicted that the massive investment in new technology would soon pay off in increased productivity and efficiency in the workplace. Their prediction proved to be correct, as productivity gains in the United States far surpassed those in Europe and Japan in the latter half of the 1990s. Despite the rosier picture of corporate health, however, many professionals were still worried about keeping their technological skills current, maintaining customer satisfaction, and somehow finding enough free time for a personal life. With unemployment hitting record lows in many regions, human resource managers also scrambled to retain their most valuable employees, particularly in the tech sector.

Capitalizing on the ongoing insecurities, a large number of books by such management gurus as Tom Peters, Edward de Bono, and Michael Hammer encouraged aspiring corporate leaders to "think outside the box" of traditional management strategies. Those who staffed the cubicles of the corporate workplace, however, often viewed the prescriptions for change as little more than old rhetoric repackaged with new terms like "reengineering" and "multitasking," which invariably ended up with them doing more work in less time and with fewer resources.

Significance

By the end of the decade it was clear that America had retained its competitive edge in the global marketplace. Yet it was difficult to determine whether the new workplace was more like the one imagined by Michael Hammer in his 1993 book *Reengineering the Corporation,* where employees were creative, empowered, and enthusiastic, or more like the office-cubicle hell rendered by Scott Adams in his *Dilbert* comic strip and books. If best-seller lists were any indication, the public identified more with Adams' vision, as two of the top-selling nonfiction books of 1996 were *Dilbert* titles.

Another round of white-collar downsizing related to the tech-stock downturn on Wall Street at the end of the decade renewed fears of layoffs and economic insecurity among many middle-class Americans. With consumer debt—often related to high housing prices, larger and more expensive cars, and massive credit-card spending—at an all-time high, the ominous economic news threatened to undermine the affluent lifestyle that many Americans enjoyed in the 1990s.

Primary Source

Reengineering the Corporation: A Manifesto for Business Revolution [excerpt]

SYNOPSIS: In their provocative introduction, the authors issue a call for nothing less than a complete overhaul of the way American companies do business. In the high-tech, competitive global marketplace, managers must lead the way in restructuring their businesses for total customer satisfaction—or face extinction.

A set of principles laid down more than two centuries ago has shaped the structure, management, and performance of American businesses throughout the nineteenth and twentieth centuries. In this book, we say that the time has come to retire those principles and to adopt a new set. The alternative is for corporate America to close its doors and go out of business.

The choice is that simple and that stark.

American entrepreneurs, executives, and managers created and operated companies that for more than one hundred years met the expanding demand for mass market products and services. American managers and the companies they ran set the performance standard for the rest of the business world. Sadly, that is no longer the case.

The book you are holding describes a conceptually new business model and an associated set of techniques that American executives and managers will have to use to reinvent their companies for competition in a new world.

To reinvent their companies, American managers must throw out their old notions about how businesses should be organized and run. They must abandon the organizational and operational principles and procedures they are now using and create entirely new ones.

The new organizations won't look much like today's corporations, and the ways in which they buy, make, sell, and deliver products and services will be very different. They will be companies designed specifically to operate in today's world and tomorrow's, not institutions carried over from an earlier, glorious, but no longer relevant age.

For two hundred years people have founded and built companies around Adam Smith's brilliant discovery that industrial work should be broken down into its simplest and most basic *tasks.* In the post-industrial business age we are now entering, corporations will be founded and built around the idea of reunifying those tasks into coherent business *processes.*

In this book we demonstrate how existing corporations *can* reinvent themselves. We call the techniques they can use to accomplish this *business reengineering,* and it is to the next revolution of business what the specialization of labor was to the last. America's largest corporations—even the most successful and promising among them—must embrace and apply the principles of business reengineering, or they will be eclipsed by the greater success of those companies that do.

Reengineering isn't another idea imported from Japan. It isn't another quick fix that American managers can apply to their organizations. It isn't a new trick that promises to boost the quality of a company's product or service or shave a percentage off costs. Business reengineering isn't a program to hike worker morale or to motivate the sales force. It won't push an old computer system to work faster. Business reengineering isn't about *fixing* anything.

Business reengineering means starting all over, starting from scratch.

Business reengineering means putting aside much of the received wisdom of two hundred years of industrial management. It means forgetting how work was done in the age of the mass market and deciding how it can best be done now. In business reengineering, old job titles and old organizational arrangements—departments, divisions, groups, and so on—cease to matter. They are artifacts of another age. What matters in reengineering is how we want to organize work today, given the demands of today's markets and the power of today's technologies. How people and companies did things yesterday doesn't matter to the business reengineer.

Reengineering capitalizes on the same characteristics that have traditionally made Americans such great business innovators: individualism, self-reliance, a willingness to accept risk, and a propensity for change. Business reengineering, unlike management philosophies that would have "us" become more like "them," doesn't try to change the behavior of American workers and managers. Instead, it takes advantage of American talents and unleashes American ingenuity.

Primary Source

The Dilbert Principle: Cartoon

SYNOPSIS: "Reengineering with Help from the Devil." This short Dilbert cartoon humorously captures workers' experiences in business. This panel deals with the common business practice of reengineering processes. DILBERT. REPRINTED BY PERMISSION OF UNITED FEATURE SYNDICATE, INC.

At the heart of business reengineering lies the notion of *discontinuous thinking*—identifying and abandoning the outdated rules and fundamental assumptions that underlie current business operations. Every company is replete with implicit rules left over from earlier decades: "Customers don't repair their own equipment." "Local warehouses are necessary for good service." "Merchandising decisions are made at headquarters." These rules are based on assumptions about technology, people, and organizational goals that no longer hold. Unless companies change these rules, any superficial reorganizations they perform will be no more effective than dusting the furniture in Pompeii.

Primary Source

The Dilbert Principle: Nonfiction work [excerpt]

> **SYNOPSIS:** The Dilbertian view of reengineering is decidedly more cynical. Instead of unleashing the creativity and productivity of employees, the process leads to job uncertainty, workplace confusion, and ultimately calls for a new wave of reengineering.

Reengineering

Reengineering was invented by Dr. Jonas Salk as a cure for Quality programs.

Just kidding.

The acknowledged parents of reengineering are Michael Hammer and James Champy. When I say they're the "parents" I don't mean they had sex—and I apologize for making you think about it. I mean

they wrote the best-selling business book *Reengineering the Corporation*, which was published in 1993.

Businesses flocked to reengineering like frat boys to a drunken cheerleader. (This analogy wasn't necessary, but I'm trying to get my mind off that Hammer and Champy thing.)

Reengineering involves finding radical new approaches to your current business processes. On paper, this compares favorably with the "Quality" approach, which involves becoming more efficient at the things you shouldn't be doing.

But there is a dark side to reengineering. There's a risk that whatever natural incompetence is present in the company can be unleashed in epic scale instead of doled out in puny "Quality" portions. This can be dangerous if—as I've often stated—we're all a bunch of idiots.

Hammer noted this risk and cleverly followed up with another book in 1995, *The Reengineering Revolution.* It describes all the boneheaded things that managers did to screw up his recipe for reengineering. . . .

Reengineering has a tendency to reduce the number of employees needed to perform a function. That unfortunate side effect causes fear and mistrust in the employees whose participation is vital to making reengineering a success. You might think fear and mistrust would sabotage the effort, but that doesn't have to be the case. There are many examples of processes that work just fine even when there's plenty of fear and mistrust. Examples:

- Capital punishment
- Presidential elections
- Multilevel marketing. . . .

Camouflage Defense

Mid-level managers who are threatened by reengineering will make clever defensive adjustments. They quickly redefine whatever they're already doing as reengineering. Suddenly your "Customer Service Project" gets renamed to "Customer Service Reengineering Project." You're not getting a haircut, you're "reengineering your head." You're not going to lunch, you're "reengineering your intestines." Pretty soon there's so much reengineering going on that it's hard to find anything that *isn't* reengineering, at least in name.

Then comes budget time.

Senior executives know they should be funding something called "reengineering" or else they'll look like troglodytes. Reengineering is "in" and it's happening. The cheapest way to fund reengineering is by calling the stuff you're already funding "reengineering." (Senior managers were once middle managers; they know how to manage a budget.)

The executives might throw a bone to the one "real" reengineering project by giving it some money to do a small trial.

Reengineering Trial

A reengineering trial is a small-scale test of a proposed new "reengineered" process. Typically, none of the technology or resources that are proposed for the large-scale reengineering project is available for the trial. So planning for the trial goes like this:

Team Member #1: "We'll need distributed workstations, all connected by a worldwide satellite network system."

Team Member #2: "All we have is this pot of decaf coffee that was left here from the meeting before ours."

Team Member #3: "Let's use it. We can interpolate the results."

Team Member #1: "Are you nuts? That's *decaf*."

Conclusion

Reengineering a company is a bit like performing an appendectomy on yourself. It hurts quite a bit, you might not know exactly how to do it, and there's a good chance you won't survive it. But if it does work, you'll gain enough confidence to go after some of the more vital organs, such as that big red pumping thing.

Further Resources

BOOKS

Adams, Scott. *The Dilbert Future: Thriving on Stupidity in the Twenty-First Century.* New York: HarperBusiness, 1997.

———. *Dogbert's Top Secret Management Handbook.* New York: HarperBusiness, 1996.

———. *The Joy of Work: Dilbert's Guide to Finding Happiness at the Expense of Your Co-Workers.* New York: HarperBusiness, 1998.

Boisnert, Bill. "Apostles of the New Entrepreneur: Business Books and the Management Crisis." In *Commodify Your Dissent: Salvos from 'The Baffler,'* edited by Thomas Frank and Matt Weiland, 81–111. New York: Norton, 1997.

Hammer, Michael. *Beyond Reengineering: How the Process-Centered Organization Is Changing Our Work and Our Lives.* New York: HarperBusiness, 1996.

Hammer, Michael, and Steven A. Stanton. *The Reengineering Revolution: A Handbook.* New York: HarperBusiness, 1995.

Harmon, Roy L. *Reinventing the Business: Preparing Today's Enterprise for Tomorrow's Technology.* New York: Free Press, 1996.

PERIODICALS

Conelly, Julie. "Have We Become Mad Dogs in the Office?" *Fortune,* November 28, 1994, 197.

WEBSITES

"The Official Dilbert Website." Available online at http://www.unitedmedia.com/comics/dilbert; website home page: http://www.unitedmedia.com (accessed March 1, 2003).

Closing Arguments in the O.J. Simpson Trial

Speech

By: Johnnie Cochran

Date: September 28, 1995

Source: Cochran, Johnnie. Closing Arguments in the O.J. Simpson Trial. September 28, 1995. Available online at http://simpson.walraven.org/sep28.html; website home page: http://simpson.walraven.org (accessed July 10, 2003).

About the Author: Johnnie L. Cochran, Jr. (1937–) earned his law degree from Loyola University in 1962. He worked for the Los Angeles City Attorney's Office from 1962 to 1965 before establishing his own practice. Specializing in police-brutality lawsuits, Cochran eventually won over $45 million in judgments against the Los Angeles Police Department

(LAPD). He also became a sought-after lawyer by celebrities facing criminal prosecution and civil lawsuits, including football player Jim Brown, actor Todd Bridges, and entertainer Michael Jackson. Cochran became a national celebrity himself as part of the "Dream Team" of defense lawyers representing O.J. Simpson in his double-murder trial in 1994–1995. ■

Introduction

On June 12, 1994, Nicole Brown Simpson, the ex-wife of former professional football star O.J. Simpson, and her friend, Ronald Goldman, were found murdered on the steps of her Los Angeles home. Suspicion immediately fell on Simpson as the primary suspect in the murders: he had a history of domestic violence against his ex-wife, his temper was known to be explosive, and there were no other obvious suspects for the brutal attack. Five days later Simpson and his friend, Al Cowlings, led police on a low-speed, sixty-mile chase on the Los Angeles highways before surrendering. An estimated two-thirds of American homes—ninety-five million viewers—were tuned into the event, which was televised in its entirety.

Simpson, who was jailed while he awaited trial for the murders, assembled an impressive "Dream Team" for his legal defense. Led by legendary Los Angeles attorney Johnnie Cochran, the team also included F. Lee Bailey, Barry Scheck, and Robert Shapiro. Despite the DNA and other physical evidence linking Simpson to the murders, Cochran and his colleagues cast doubt on the validity of the forensic evidence. Not only was the lab work unreliable, they claimed, but the LAPD was so infested by racist cops that it was not farfetched to imagine that the cops had concocted a conspiracy to frame Simpson for murder. The defense case bolstered its claim of racism by proving that detective Mark Fuhrman, who had denied ever using the word *nigger*, had in fact used it repeatedly in taped conversations. Constantly raising accusations of racism and sloppy police work, the defense was able to convince jurors that there was reasonable doubt that Simpson had committed the murders. On October 3, 1995, the jury found Simpson not guilty. An estimated 91 percent of televisions that were turned on at the time of the verdict were tuned in to hear the outcome.

Significance

Just as the not-guilty verdicts in the trial of four LAPD officers accused of savagely beating Rodney King had outraged many Americans in 1992, the verdict in the Simpson case proved equally controversial. Predictably, the reaction broke down along racial lines. Many African Americans focused on the history of police brutality against minorities and concluded that it was likely that Simpson had been caught up in a racist conspiracy engineered by the LAPD. In response, some commentators suggested that the Simpson verdict was a payback for the King verdict. In setting Simpson free, it was suggested, the predominantly African American jury had tried to even the score.

In contrast, most white Americans were convinced that Simpson had committed the murders. Cochran's blatant playing of the "race card" throughout the trial was dismissed as an emotional tactic that should not have been allowed in a court of law. Many feminists were also bewildered that the jury seemed to dismiss the history of domestic violence by Simpson against his former wife, which they viewed as persuasive evidence that he had killed her.

In a later civil trial for the wrongful deaths of Brown-Simpson and Goldman brought by their survivors, Simpson was ordered to pay $33.5 million in compensatory and punitive damages. He retained custody of his two children by his late wife and moved to Florida, where he faced numerous legal problems throughout the 1990s. The Goldman and Brown families remained active in promoting victims' rights in legal cases and publicizing the danger and prevalence of domestic violence. No one was ever convicted at criminal trial for the deaths of Nicole Brown Simpson and Ronald Goldman.

Primary Source

Closing Arguments in the O.J. Simpson Trial [excerpt]

SYNOPSIS: A specialist in police-brutality lawsuits, Cochran throughout the trial raised the issue of sloppy detective work and a possible conspiracy on the part of the LAPD. His most effective tactic, however, was suggesting that the racism of the LAPD destroyed its credibility. Building on this theme, he peppered his closing argument with references to the civil rights movement and concluded by telling the jurors that he knew they would "do the right thing"—the title of a Spike Lee movie about race relations—and set Simpson free.

When we concluded last night, ladies and gentlemen, we had discussed a number of things, and I'm sure you have them very much in mind. To summarize some of the things that we talked about and put it in perspective, we talked about a police department who from the very beginning was more interested in themselves and their image, and that carried through. We talked about socks that appeared all of a sudden that weren't there, socks where evidence was planted on them. We talked about police officers who lie with immunity, where the oath doesn't mean anything to them. We talked

A crowd of pedestrians watches the large television screen in New York's Times Square as the news announces that O.J. Simpson was found not guilty of killing his ex-wife and her boyfriend, October 3, 1995. Public response to the verdict varied between outrage and satisfaction. **AP/WIDE WORLD PHOTOS. REPRODUCED BY PERMISSION.**

about messengers where you couldn't trust the message. We talked about gloves that didn't fit, a knit cap that wouldn't make any difference, a prosecution scenario that is unbelievable and unreasonable. In short, we talked about reasonable doubt. We talked about something that has made this country great, that you can be accused in this country for crime, but that is just an accusation, and when you enter a not guilty plea, since the beginning of the time of this country, since the time of the Magna Carta, that sets the forces in motion and you have a trial. This is what this is about. That is why we love what we do, an opportunity to come before people from the community, the consciences of the community. You are the consciences of the community. You set the standards. You tell us what is right and wrong. You set the standards. You use your common sense to do that. Your verdict goes far beyond these doors of this courtroom. As Mr. Darden said, the whole world is watching and waiting for your decision in this case. That is not to put any pressure on you, just to tell you what is really happening out there. So we talked about all of those things, hopefully in a logical way. Hopefully something I said made some sense to you. Hopefully as a advocate, you know my zeal, you know the passion I feel for this. We've all got time invested in this case. But it

is not just about winning, it is about what is right. It is about a man's life that is at stake here. So in voir dire you promised to take the time that was necessary, and you have more than done that. Remember I asked you, though, that when you got down to the end of the case, when you kept all your promises about coming here everyday and taking these notes and paying attention, and you know, listening to us drone on and on and on, that pretty soon it would be in your hands and then you couldn't just rush through that, could you? And we tried to make it a little more simple with regard to the issues, but still we are going to have twelve minds coming together, twelve open minds, twelve unbiased minds to come together on these issues. And you will give it, I'm sure, the importance to which it is entitled. Please don't compromise your principles or your consciences in rendering this decision. Don't rush to judgment. Don't compound what they've already done in this case. Don't rush to judgment. Have a judgment that is well thought out, one that you can believe in the morning after this verdict. I want you to place yourself the day after you render the verdict, when you get up and you look in the mirror and you are free, you are no longer sequestered, you will probably look for each other but you will be happy to be home again. But what is important, look in that mirror and say, have I been true to my oath? Did I do the right thing? Was I naive? Was I timid? Or was I courageous? Did I believe in the constitution. Did I believe in justice? Did I do my part for integrity and honesty? That is the mission you are on in this journey toward justice. . . .

We live in a society where many people are apathetic, they don't want to get involved, and that is why all of us, to a person, in this courtroom, have thanked you from the bottom of our hearts. Because you know what? You haven't been apathetic. You are the ones who made a commitment, a commitment toward justice, and it is a painful commitment, but you've got to see it through. Your commitment, your courage, is much greater than these police officers. This man could have been off the force long ago if they had done their job, but they didn't do their job. People looked the other way. People didn't have the courage. One of the things that has made this country so great is people's willingness to stand up and say that is wrong. I'm not going to be part of it. I'm not going to be part of the cover-up. That is what I'm asking you to do. Stop this cover-up. Stop this cover-up. If you don't stop it, then who? Do you think the police department is going to stop it? Do you think the D.A.'s office is going to stop it? Do you think we can stop it by ourselves? It has to be stopped by you. And you know, they talked about Fuhrman, they talked about him in derisive tones now, and that is very fashionable now, isn't it? Everybody wants to beat up on Fuhrman, the favored whipping boy in America. I told you I don't take any delight in that because you know before this trial started, if you grow up in this country, you know there are Fuhrmans out there. You learn early on in your life that you are not going to be naive, that you love your country, but you know it is not perfect, so you understand that, so it is no surprise to me, but I don't take any pride in it. But for some of you, you are finding out the other side of life. You are finding out—that is why this case is so instructive. You are finding out about the other side of life, but things aren't always as they seem. It is not just rhetoric, it is the actions of people, it is the lack of courage and it is a lack of integrity at high places. That is what we are talking about here. Credibility doesn't attach to a title or position; it attaches to the person, so the person who may have a job where he makes two dollars an hour can have more integrity than the highest person. It is something from within. It is in your

heart. It is what the lord has put there. That is what we are talking about in this case. . . .

And so as great as America is, we have not yet reached the point where there is equality in rights or equality of opportunity. I started off talking to you a little bit about Frederick Douglas and what he said more than a hundred years ago, for there are still the Mark Fuhrmans in this world, in this country, who hate and are yet embraced by people in power. But you and I, fighting for freedom and ideals and for justice for all, must continue to fight to expose hate and genocidal racism and these tendencies. We then become the guardians of the constitution, as I told you yesterday, for if we as the People don't continue to hold a mirror up to the face of America and say this is what you promised, this is what you delivered, if you don't speak out, if you don't stand up, if you don't do what's right, this kind of conduct will continue on forever and we will never have an ideal society, one that lives out the true meaning of the creed of the constitution or of life, liberty and justice for all. I'm going to take my seat, but I get one last time to address you, as I said before. This is a case about an innocent man wrongfully accused. You have seen him now for a year and two days. You observed him during good times and the bad times. Soon it will be your turn. You have the keys to his future. You have the evidence by which you can acquit this man. You have not only the patience, but the integrity and the courage to do the right thing. We believe you will do the right thing, and the right thing is to find this man not guilty on both of these charges. . . .

It is now up to you. We are going to pass this baton to you soon. You will do the right thing. You have made a commitment for justice. You will do the right thing. I will some day go on to other cases, no doubt as will Miss Clark and Mr. Darden. Judge Ito will try another case some day, I hope, but this is O.J. Simpson's one day in court. By your decision you control his very life your hands. Treat it carefully. Treat it fairly. Be fair. Don't be part of this continuing cover-up. Do the right thing remembering that if it doesn't fit, you must acquit, that if these messengers have lied to you, you can't trust their message, that this has been a search for truth. That no matter how bad it looks, if truth is out there on a scaffold and wrong is in here on the throne, when that scaffold sways the future and beyond the dim unknown standeth the same God for all people keeping watch above his own. He watches all of us and he will watch you in your decision. Thank you for your attention. God bless you.

Further Resources

BOOKS

Clark, Marcia, with Teresa Carpenter. *Without a Doubt.* New York: Viking, 1997.

Darden, Christopher, with Jess Walter. *In Contempt.* New York: HarperCollins, 1996.

Fuhrman, Mark. *Murder in Brentwood.* Washington, D.C.: Regnery Publishing, 1997.

Goldman, Ron, the family of, with William and Marilyn Hoffer. *His Name Is Ron.* New York: William Morrow, 1997.

Hixon, Walter L. *Murder, Culture, and Injustice: Four Sensational Cases in American History.* Akron, Ohio: The University of Akron Press, 2001.

Schmalleger, Frank M., ed. *The Trial of the Century: The People of the State of California v. Orenthal James Simpson.* Upper Saddle River, N.J.: Pearson Education, 1996.

Simpson, O.J. *I Want to Tell You: My Response to Your Letters, Your Messages, Your Questions.* Boston: Little, Brown, 1995.

Toobin, Jeffrey. *The Run of His Life: The People v. O.J. Simpson.* New York: Random House, 1996.

"Women's Rights Are Human Rights"

Speech

By: Hillary Rodham Clinton

Date: 1995

Source: Rodham Clinton, Hillary. "Women's Rights Are Human Rights: Remarks to the United Nations Fourth World Conference on Women." September 5, 1995.

About the Author: Hillary Rodham Clinton (1947–) grew up in the Chicago area. She earned her bachelor's degree in political science at Wellesley College in 1969 and in 1973 completed a law degree at Yale University, where she began a relationship with fellow law student Bill Clinton. The two married in 1975 and lived in Clinton's native Arkansas, where he pursued a political career as she taught and practiced law. She served on several state boards related to health care, educational reform, and children's welfare. When her husband was elected president in 1992, she took on a policy role on health care and children's issues. In 2000, she became the only former First Lady to win office when she was elected to the U.S. Senate from New York. ■

Introduction

Like most of her predecessors, Hillary Rodham Clinton, who served as the nation's First Lady from 1993 to 2001, was a lightning rod for criticism and commendation. A Yale-educated lawyer and public policy expert in her own right, she had continued to pursue her own legal career during her husband's terms as attorney general and governor of Arkansas. Although she made concessions to the conservative culture of her adopted home state—finally using her husband's surname of Clinton instead of her own in public appearances—she remained as driven to succeed as a lawyer as her husband was as a politician. As presidential candidate Bill Clinton boasted on the campaign trail in 1992, the voters would get a "two-fer" deal if they elected him, as he would rely on his wife's expertise on health care and education issues in the White House as he had in Arkansas.

As a wife, mother, and professional woman, Rodham's image contrasted greatly with then-First Lady Barbara Bush, who had dropped out of college to get married and had not worked outside of the home. "I suppose I could have stayed home and baked cookies and had teas, but what I decided to do was pursue my profession," Rodham said in one interview, a comment that riled some traditional homemakers. Rodham quickly reassured the public that she would indeed fulfill the duties of First Lady without major changes, but that she also intended to serve in an advisory role on issues that were important to her.

Significance

After Bill Clinton's election to the presidency, Rodham started to work on the Task Force on National Health Care Reform, which sought to keep health-care costs down while providing coverage to the uninsured and underinsured. Her visibility on the highly politicized issue resulted in a backlash against her role as a nonelected policy advisor. Some commentators took to calling the president and his wife "Billary," implying that she was too involved in his administration's decision making. In the end, health-care-industry lobbyists killed the proposed reforms and the First Lady withdrew from such an open role as a policy maker, although she gave forceful speeches on behalf of women's and children's rights to education, health care, and economic opportunities.

Although her unapologetic feminism was sometimes perceived as a political liability for her husband's administration, Clinton was reelected in 1996. When another round of allegations about Clinton's infidelities surfaced in early 1998, however, Rodham was crucial in helping her husband survive the political fallout. As it became clear that the president had engaged in a sexual affair with White House intern Monica Lewinsky, Rodham mostly refrained from comment aside from claiming that a "right-wing conspiracy" drove the media frenzy to oust her husband from office. By the end of the Lewinsky scandal, not only had Clinton survived impeachment hearings, but some of his chief adversaries in the Republican Party had been forced to resign after their own infidelities were revealed. For her part, Rodham benefited from an outpouring of public sympathy for her role as the wronged wife. At the end of her husband's second term as president, Rodham once again made history by announcing her candidacy for the U.S. Senate from New York, where the Clintons had bought a home. Showing her political skills on the campaign trail, Rodham was elected with 55 percent of the vote.

Primary Source

"Women's Rights Are Human Rights" [excerpt]

SYNOPSIS: Hillary Rodham Clinton had been active on family issues long before she assumed her role as First Lady. In 1995 she traveled to Beijing, China, to address the United Nations Conference on Women and delivered a speech that highlighted her interest in the welfare of the world's women and their families and children. Aware of the attention she commanded as the First Lady, Clinton acknowledges in her remarks, "The great challenge . . . is to give voice to women everywhere whose experiences go unnoticed, whose words go unheard."

Remarks to the United Nations Fourth World Conference on Women

Mrs. Mongella, Under Secretary Kittani, distinguished delegates and guests:

I would like to thank the Secretary General of the United Nations for inviting me to be part of the United Nations Fourth World Conference on Women. This is truly a celebration—a celebration of the contributions women make in every aspect of life: in the home, on the job, in their communities, as mothers, wives, sisters, daughters, learners, workers, citizens and leaders.

It is also a coming together, much the way women come together every day in every country.

We come together in fields and in factories. In village markets and supermarkets. In living rooms and board rooms.

Whether it is while playing with our children in the park, or washing clothes in a river, or taking a break at the office water cooler, we come together and talk about our aspirations and concerns. And time and again, our talk turns to our children and our families. However different we may be, there is far more that unites us than divides us. We share a common future. And we are here to find common ground so that we may help bring new dignity and respect to women and girls all over the world—and in so doing, bring new strength and stability to families as well.

Hillary Rodham Clinton, pictured with her daughter Chelsea, was a prominent supporter of women's rights in the 1990s during her husband Bill Clinton's years as U.S. president. **REUTERS/BETTMANN. REPRODUCED BY PERMISSION.**

By gathering in Beijing, we are focusing world attention on issues that matter most in the lives of women and their families: access to education, health care, jobs and credit, the chance to enjoy basic legal and human rights and participate fully in the political life of their countries. . . .

What we are learning around the world is that if women are healthy and educated, their families will flourish. If women are free from violence, their families will flourish. If women have a chance to work and earn as full and equal partners in society, their families will flourish.

And when families flourish, communities and nations will flourish.

That is why every woman, every man, every child, every family, and every nation on our planet has a stake in the discussion that takes place here.

Over the past 25 years, I have worked persistently on issues relating to women, children and families. Over the past two-and-a-half years, I have had the opportunity to learn more about the challenges facing women in my own country and around the world.

I have met new mothers in Jojakarta, Indonesia, who come together regularly in their village to discuss nutrition, family planning, and baby care.

I have met working parents in Denmark who talk about the comfort they feel in knowing that their children can be cared for in creative, safe, and nurturing after-school centers.

I have met women in South Africa who helped lead the struggle to end apartheid and are now helping build a new democracy.

I have met with the leading women of the Western Hemisphere who are working every day to promote literacy and better health care for the children of their countries.

I have met women in India and Bangladesh who are taking out small loans to buy milk cows, rickshaws, thread and other materials to create a livelihood for themselves and their families.

I have met doctors and nurses in Belarus and Ukraine who are trying to keep children alive in the aftermath of Chernobyl.

The great challenge of this Conference is to give voice to women everywhere whose experiences go unnoticed, whose words go unheard. . . .

As an American, I want to speak up for women in my own country—women who are raising children on the minimum wage, women who can't afford health care or child care, women whose lives are threatened by violence, including violence in their own homes.

I want to speak up for mothers who are fighting for good schools, safe neighborhoods, clean air and clean airwaves; for older women, some of them widows, who have raised their families and now find that their skills and life experiences are not valued in the workplace; for women who are working all night as nurses, hotel clerks, and fast food cooks so that they can be at home during the day with their kids; and for women everywhere who simply don't have time to do everything they are called upon to do each day.

Speaking to you today, I speak for them, just as each of us speaks for women around the world who are denied the chance to go to school, or see a doctor, or own property, or have a say about the direction of their lives, simply because they are women. The truth is that most women around the world work both inside and outside the home, usually by necessity.

We need to understand that there is no formula for how women should lead their lives. That is why we must respect the choices that each woman makes for herself and her family. Every woman deserves the chance to realize her God-given potential.

We also must recognize that women will never gain full dignity until their human rights are respected and protected. . . .

Now it is time to act on behalf of women everywhere. If we take bold steps to better the lives of women, we will be taking bold steps to better the lives of children and families too.

Families rely on mothers and wives for emotional support and care; families rely on women for labor in the home; and increasingly, families rely on women for income needed to raise healthy children and care for other relatives.

As long as discrimination and inequities remain so commonplace around the world—as long as girls and women are valued less, fed less, fed last, overworked, underpaid, not schooled and subjected to violence in and out of their homes—the potential of the human family to create a peaceful, prosperous world will not be realized.

Let this Conference be our—and the world's—call to action.

And let us heed the call so that we can create a world in which every woman is treated with respect and dignity, every boy and girl is loved and cared for equally, and every family has the hope of a strong and stable future.

Thank you very much.

God's blessings on you, your work and all who will benefit from it.

Further Resources

BOOKS

Clinton, Hillary Rodham, with Carl Sferrazza Anthony. *An Invitation to the White House.* New York: Simon and Schuster, 2000.

Clinton, Hillary Rodham. *It Takes a Village and Other Lessons Children Teach Us.* New York: Simon and Schuster, 1996.

Drew, Elizabeth. *On the Edge.* New York: Simon and Schuster, 1995.

Milton, Joyce. *The First Partner: Hillary Rodham Clinton.* New York: William Morrow, 1999.

Sheehy, Gail. *Hillary's Choice.* New York: Random House, 1999.

Stephanopoulos, George. *All Too Human.* Boston: Little, Brown, 1999.

Stewart, James B. *Blood Sport: The President and His Adversaries.* New York: Simon and Schuster, 1996.

WEBSITES

Clinton Presidential Center. Available online at http://www .clintonpresidentialcenter.com (accessed February 25, 2003).

Senator Hillary Rodham Clinton. Available online at http://clinton.senate.gov/ (accessed February 25, 2003).

Microsoft Network Home Page

Website

By: Microsoft Corporation

Date: 1996

Source: Microsoft Network home page, 1996. Available online at http://web.archive.org/web/19961022175327/http://msn .com (accessed March 11, 2003).

About the Author: The Microsoft Corporation (originally "Micro-Soft") was founded in 1975 by childhood friends Bill Gates (1955–) and Paul G. Allen (1953–). Both had a long-standing interest in building their own computers and left college to develop software for the new personal-computer market. Developing programs for computer manufacturers, Microsoft had annual revenues of $1 million by 1978. In 1980, Microsoft entered into an agreement with IBM for the Microsoft Disk Operating System (MS-DOS), which became one of the standard software programs in the industry. The phenomenal growth of the personal computer industry and Microsoft's dominance of its field made Gates a billionaire by the end of the 1980s, and both partners were consistently ranked on the list of the richest people in the world throughout the 1990s. ∎

Introduction

In the 1990s, personal computers and the Internet transformed American society in ways that rivaled the changes brought by the automobile earlier in the century. Personal computers had been on the market since the 1970s, and by 1989 fifteen percent of American homes had at least one "PC." Used primarily for word processing and other basic computer functions, the PC expanded its usefulness and influence with the increasing availability of the Internet in the early 1990s. Like the PC, which had sprung from military research to calculate weapons trajectories in World War II, the Internet also had its origins in the defense sector. The Advanced Research Project Agency (ARPA), a sector of the Department of Defense, constructed the ARAPNET in the 1960s as a way of sharing information among its supercomputers to avoid data destruction in case of a nuclear attack.

In 1969, four universities in California and Utah were linked to ARAPNET, which quickly showed its usefulness as a means of electronic communication among researchers. Later, the use of electronic messages, or "e-mail," would become one of the most popular uses of the system.

As ARAPNET spread to dozens of universities in the 1970s, the first commercial web system, Telenet, appeared in 1974. In 1982, users of the various webs started to use the term "Internet" to describe the collection of online networks. By the mid-1980s, there were over 1,000 Internet sites, and e-mail started to be used more frequently for corporate and personal use. In 1990, when APAPNET was decommissioned, there were over 300,000 Internet hosts. The following year, after the government decided to allow commercial traffic to be carried through its net, a new era of electronic commerce had begun. With technology that made it possible to transmit moving pictures and sound through the World Wide Web, Internet sites increasingly became multimedia, interactive attractions.

Significance

The rapid technological development of the Internet led to a surge in its popularity as it became more widely available and easier to use. By 1996 e-commerce amounted to over $1 billion in sales and traditional, "bricks-and-mortar" retail operations felt considerable pressure to maintain an online presence in the face of competition by sites such as Amazon.com. In the workplace, the use of the Internet and personal computers led to significant increases in productivity, which fueled the country's longest economic expansion in the 1990s. The stock market also witnessed an economic boom with new Internet companies leading the market through much of the decade. Many educators also hailed the new technology as a way of offering courses online to attract nontraditional students. With more government agencies putting their records online, the public also benefited from having greater access to forms, databases, and other important information. As the use of online bulletin boards and chat rooms became commonplace, many Americans discovered new "virtual" communities of people with shared interests.

The popularity of the Internet in the 1990s was not without criticism. From 1988 onward there were many well-publicized cases of malicious Internet "worms" and "viruses" that attacked the net and damaged PCs. Many Americans were also disturbed at the ease with which violent, sexually explicit, and other potentially objectionable material was made so easily available on the Internet. Some psychologists began to diagnose "Internet addiction" among users who spent more and more time on the World Wide Web. The recording industry also voiced

simplify your online life
Create a free custom start page.

 msn.

Now it's easy to find your way around the

Web. With MSN's Custom Start Page

stock quotes, sports scores, news, weather,

comics, movies, music, Web sites, and lots

more are just a click away.

m s n ● c o m
made fresh daily

oh...
and if you are new to the Internet...
click here for our internet tutorial

Welcome!

Start your travel here—with Microsoft Expedia travel services! Try Microsoft Investor—the easiest way to follow your investments. Visit our sponsors. See Slate for an original take on politics and culture. Go to Baseball Postseason Extra for game reports, analysis, and commentary on the playoffs and World Series. Sneak a peek at the new msn.com beta!

customize my page

MSNBC News   Services   Search   Preview
Tutorial   Links   Sitemap   Try MSN   Feedback
Sponsors   FAQ   Free Software

© 1996 Microsoft and/or its suppliers. All rights reserved.

Primary Source

Microsoft Network Home Page

SYNOPSIS: This Internet home page is one of the earliest posted by the Microsoft Network. The MSN page, from 1996, is tailored for individual, home-based users and offers entertainment clips, news items, and shopping opportunities. It also has a special "Internet tutorial" for new users. **COURTESY OF MICROSOFT CORPORATION. REPRODUCED BY PERMISSION.**

strong objections to music-sharing services on the net such as Napster, which they argued were infringing on their copyrights. Some stock market investors were also dismayed when the "tech-stock" bubble burst near the

Children gather around a computer to study, 1999. © ROYALTY-FREE/CORBIS. REPRODUCED BY PERMISSION.

WEBSITES

"Bill Gates." Available online at http://www.microsoft.com/bill gates/bio.asp (accessed February 5, 2003).

"The Internet Archive." http://www.archive.org/ (accessed March 1, 2003).

AUDIO AND VISUAL MEDIA

Nerds 2.0.1: A Brief History of the Internet. PBS Home Video, 1998.

end of the decade. Most Internet start-ups had never generated profits despite their high stock prices, which led to the sudden extinction of many well-known Internet ventures in 1999–2000.

The grandest and lengthiest Internet controversy, however, related to efforts by the U.S. government against alleged unfair business practices by pioneering software giant Microsoft. The two parties first clashed in June 1990 when the Federal Trade Commission began looking into deals between Microsoft and IBM to dominate the PC software market. Microsoft later came under fire for bundling its Internet Explorer browser into its software package, which forced PC manufacturers to load it onto their products instead of the rival Navigator browser. Microsoft defended its actions as being beneficial to consumers and enhancing competition in the software marketplace. After more than ten years of legal battles in the United States and Europe, the antitrust suits against Microsoft continued to drag on, but the company had managed to corner an 80 percent share of the world's software market.

Further Resources

BOOKS

Andrews, Paul. *How the Web Was Won: The Inside Story of How Bill Gates and His Band of Internet Idealists Transformed a Software Empire.* New York: Broadway Books, 1999.

Auletta, Ken. *World War 3.0: Microsoft and Its Enemies.* New York: Random House, 2001.

Tsang, Cheryl. *Microsoft First Generation: The Success Secrets of the Visionaries Who Launched a Technology Empire.* New York: Wiley, 2000.

PERIODICALS

"In Search of Google." *Time,* August 21, 2000, 66.

Levy, Steven. "The World According to Google." *Newsweek,* December 16, 2002, 46.

"The Manifest Destiny of Anna Nicole Smith"

Essay

By: Lisa Carver

Date: 1996

Source: Carver, Lisa. "The Manifest Destiny of Anna Nicole Smith." In *Dancing Queen: The Lusty Adventures of Lisa Crystal Carver.* New York: Henry Holt, 1996, 133–137.

About the Author: Lisa Carver (1969–) grew up in Dover, New Hampshire, and worked as a performance artist in the 1980s. Her self-published *Rollerderby* was one of the most popular "zines" of the 1990s, with essays on popular culture, class relations, and sex. Carver's work also appeared on the Internet website Nerve.com. The subject of Carver's essay, Anna Nicole Smith, was born Vickie Lynn Hogan in Mexia, Texas, in 1967. After a brief teenage marriage, Smith worked as a stripper in Houston and appeared in *Playboy* magazine in 1992. The following year she was named Playmate of the Year, modeled for Guess? jeans, and began a film career. Her 1994 marriage to eighty-nine-year-old oil billionaire J. Howard Marshall II left her widowed in 1995. While Smith went through a lengthy court battle with one of Marshall's sons over his estate, she appeared on the *E! Entertainment Television* network in a reality show of her daily life beginning in 2002. The show became the network's highest-rated program. ■

Introduction

In the 1990s, many media and social critics noted a growing vulgarity in American society. Television news items were more graphically violent and sexually explicit, talk shows focused on the most bizarre personal-interest stories they could find, and talk radio programs broadcasted coarse and confrontational rhetoric, often personally attacking public figures. Some deemed this trend a "tabloidization" of American culture, a reference to the enduring popularity of the gossip-fueled celebrity-oriented tabloids for sale at supermarket checkout stands.

The tabloids indeed defined many of the biggest news stories of the 1990s with their bold investigative approach to scandals that major news outlets were hesitant to follow. Although the *Enquirer, Globe, Star,* and

Anna Nicole Smith poses at a publicity event, February 8, 1993.
© STEVE STARR/CORBIS. REPRODUCED BY PERMISSION.

other major tabloids were criticized for practicing "checkbook journalism" by paying for interviews—which some said compromised the objectivity of the resulting reports—it was the tabloid press that exhibited some of the best investigative journalism of the decade, including stories about the criminal investigation of O.J. Simpson in 1995 and 1996 and the investigation of President Clinton's sexual indiscretions with White House intern Monica Lewinsky.

The sensationalism of the tabloids, however, could not compete with the direct impact of exploitative daytime talk shows hosted by Jerry Springer, Jenny Jones, Sally Jesse Raphael, and Ricki Lake, all of which were immensely popular throughout the decade. Deliberately shocking and low-brow, the shows could rarely attract celebrity guests but instead offered bizarre human-interest stories, often with explicit sexual topics.

Significance

Although some pundits condemned the ongoing fascination with celebrities, sex, and scandal, the popularity of such topics, reflected by Carver's *Dancing Queen*, meant that the tabloids also influenced the way more circumspect, mainstream media outlets handled news coverage. Throughout the decade, morning and nightly

network news shows devoted less time to covering international affairs and politics and more time covering entertainment news, gossip, and other social trends and lifestyle topics. Some politicians adapted to the new media format, dubbed "infotainment," and devoted more of their time to offering simple "soundbites" to fit into the shorter news segments.

As tabloid circulation ebbed near the end of the decade, some media experts predicted that the tabloid era was over. A backlash had indeed set in after the 1997 death of Britain's Princess Diana in a Paris car crash as she was being chased by tabloid photographers. Talkshow host Jenny Jones also lost a $25 million lawsuit brought by the family of one of her former guests, who had been killed after appearing on her show in 1995 as part of a same-sex "secret crush" segment. *The Jenny Jones Show* quickly went off the air, and other shows, including the daytime ratings leader hosted by Oprah Winfrey, pledged that they would steer clear of such extreme topics in the future.

Did the tabloidization of American culture further coarsen the public airwaves in the 1990s, or did the trend merely reflect American society more accurately, if at times explicitly? As Lisa Carver wrote in her 1996 book *Dancing Queen,* "We seem ashamed of our talk shows for their emotional explosions, their leaps from topic to topic, their rowdiness, their excess—but *that's* what's so great about America! Let other countries be patient. Let other countries be refined. Let other countries think all the time. They do it better anyway."

Primary Source

"The Manifest Destiny of Anna Nicole Smith" [excerpt]

SYNOPSIS: In this essay, Lisa Carver focuses on one of her favorite celebrities, Anna Nicole Smith, who constantly made tabloid headlines with her over-the-top appearance, tumultuous personal life, and ostentatious lifestyle. Far from being critical of the former *Playboy* Playmate of the Year, Smith's lust for life—and just plain lust—impress Carver as quintessentially American traits.

When seven-year-old Jessica Dubrof died trying to be the youngest pilot to fly across the country, all these self-righteous men and disapproving women called up the radio stations to say how awful it was she was flying. I guess they think she should've stayed in her room. They feel seven-year-olds should be humble, and it's the parents' responsibility to strong-arm them into that humility. *U.S. News and World Report* censoriously suggests that Jessica's father somehow forced, or at least encouraged, her to act cheerful and brave, as if that was the epitome of evil parenting. The radio callers say she didn't get a chance to live her life. I got so mad I called up the radio and told them she *was* living her life, which is more than most people can say. There are some people who are born risk takers, willful and extravagant, and even their failures are greater than the greatest accomplishments of the people who stay in their room and never die in a plane crash. Our country was made great by having so many of those types, but now their existence just seems to make people mad.

America is divided today into offended citizens and citizens paralyzed with the fear of offending. Some unhappy souls are both at once. I hope this blight is temporary, because it just isn't natural. We're not that way! I wonder when it happened that offending someone became so terrible and special. Getting offended is part of life, like falling out of love or having to go to the bathroom really bad on a long car trip with no exits in sight. There's no cure for being offended, any more than there's a cure for life. All of a sudden, feeling offense is the surest guarantee to get what you want. This landlady was offended by those living in sin, and refused to rent to any. One rejected renter got on the news and said. "I was so offended!" So she sued the old lady right up to the Supreme Court, so they could decide who had the bigger right to feel offended. She was supposedly suing to force the landlady to rent to her and her boyfriend, but they didn't even want to live there anymore! She was just driven by offendedness.

I wish these people would get a grip. I don't even think of them as Americans—they're nothing like the wild ones who carved out this big country. Fear of offending—sometimes called "sensitivity"—has stopped the American from letting his or her naturally odd, lusty, lively personality flower. The biggest offense of all today seems to be being different. People take it as a personal attack. Anna Nicole Smith's breasts, being different from the average breasts, are taken as an open and deliberate insult. They're not the type of breasts to stay in their room and be humble. The way people treat those breasts in conversation, you'd think they were twin marauders breaking into houses and stealing the family jewels.

Anna Nicole is my hero. Her personality matches her larger-than-life figure. She's a real take-charge type of person; she wasn't born an heiress, so she made herself one. No one marries eighty-nine-year-olds anymore . . . no one but A.N.S. Anna Nicole

is the only role model available to Dover youth too antsy to do data processing at the navy yard and too lacking in social skills to be a cosmetician. Stripper, heiress, addict, mother—most people can only manage one or two, or at most three, of those in their lifetime. Not our Anna—she can do all that at once, and more!

She has flair. She spent one million dollars a day on her husband's credit card until he died. I couldn't even spend a million dollars in my whole life! I get tired just walking around the mall trying to spend $200 on Christmas presents. Where does she get all her energy? She is so spectacularly American that Europeans are knocked senseless by her charms. Billboards of Anna Nicole had to be taken down in Germany because they were causing too many traffic accidents. See how powerful it can be when you let your national character really flower?

Like her home state of Texas (where she worked in a fried-chicken shop), which is on the bottom of the map. A.N.S. started out on the bottom of life. Everyone told her she was too fat to be a model, but she didn't care—she bleached her hair white-blonde, put on tight dresses, and became *Playboy* Pet of the Year and modeled Guess jeans. Then she landed a juicy role in *Naked Gun 33⅓*. She did very well at acting, I felt. She lit up the screen! The rest of the theater audience—a gaggle of eleven-year-old boys—felt the same way. I'm tired of every single woman in entertainment being "smart" and talking in interviews such in a smart and humble way. "How will you feel if you win the Golden Globe Award?" "Oh, I don't think about that, just to be nominated is such an honor. There are so many other talented actresses nominated, they all deserve the award." They think they're going to fool everyone into thinking they're sweet and down to earth, but actually it is very poor manners not to get excited about a gift. Sandra Bullock *refused* her nomination, claiming it should go to an actress with "a larger body of work." I think Miss Smith has quite a large body of work, and she should get nominated. Voracious Anna would say, "I want it! Give it to me! Give me that statue!"

I believe she and her husband loved each other. She claimed she liked his personality, and who am I to doubt her word? She also said he was "frisky." People thought Anna Nicole's lowcut funeral dress and the gold glitter and teddy bears with which she decorated the funeral parlor proved that she didn't really care about her husband and was using his death as a publicity event. (I did think wearing lipstick the color of caked blood was a little morbid, but then all the greatest glamour contains a touch of morbidity.) But gold glitter, teddy bears and lowcut dresses were exactly what made Howard (the husband) call Anna Nicole "the light of my life." There had been a lot of sadness in Howard's life—shortly after his first wife died of Alzheimer's, his girlfriend, "Jewel" the stripper, died while having cosmetic surgery. Anna Nicole, gaudy, cutesy, sexeee and nuts—what a bright creature to enter a sad man's life! . . .

I admire Anna Nicole because she is living out the American dream: making the most of her God-given talents without a shred of guilt. Plus, she takes good care of her young son. She's tops!

Further Resources

BOOKS

Alterman, Eric. *Sound and Fury: The Making of the Punditocracy.* Ithaca, N.Y.: Cornell University Press, 1999.

Fox, Richard L. *Tabloid Justice: Criminal Justice in an Age of Media Frenzy.* Boulder, Colo.: Lynne Rienner, 2001.

Gamson, Joshua. *Claims to Fame: Celebrity in Contemporary America.* Berkeley, Calif.: University of California Press, 1994.

————. *Freaks Talk Back: Tabloid Talk Shows and Sexual Nonconformity.* Chicago: University of Chicago Press, 1998.

Sloan, Bill. *"I Watched a Wild Hog Eat My Baby": A Colorful History of the Tabloids and Their Cultural Impact.* Amherst, N.Y.: Prometheus, 2001.

WEBSITES

"The Anna Nicole Show." Available online at http://www.eon line.com/On/AnnaNicole2/index.html (accessed March 2, 2003).

"Rollerderby Online." Available online at http://slick.org/Roller derby/ (accessed March 2, 2003.)

"Worker Rights for Temps!"

Essay

By: Jeff Kelly

Date: 1997

Source: Kelly, Jeff. "Worker Rights for Temps!" *The Best of Temp Slave!* Madison, Wisc.: Garrett County Press, 1997, 139–140.

About the Author: Born around 1960 in Pennsylvania, Jeff Kelly eventually relocated to Madison, Wisconsin. When a job as a temporary worker failed to materialize into a promised permanent position in 1993, Kelly produced his first issue of *Temp Slave!* in his last days at work. Kelly went on to publish the iconoclastic "zine" through 1999 "as an attempt to analyze the changing face of work in America," as

he told the *Zine Book* website. "It's also geared toward bringing humor into the political scene." After Kelly secured a permanent job as a press operator, he stopped publishing *Temp Slave!* but remained a frequently quoted commentator on the plight of working Americans. ∎

Introduction

In 1992, Bill Clinton won the presidency on a platform that highlighted voters' concerns with the country's economy. Noting the rising hours and falling wages of the average worker, Clinton often noted that Americans were working more for less than in previous years. The statistics bore out Clinton's claim. As measured in inflation-adjusted dollars, weekly wages had peaked at $469.44 in 1973 and had steadily fallen to $395.37 by 1995. Economists pointed to an array of factors to explain the drop, including decreasing levels of unionization and global competition for manufacturing jobs. Most agreed, however, that the spread of lower-wage service-sector jobs, many of which were part-time and offered no benefits, were a primary cause of the national decline in wages. The average hourly wage for service-sector jobs in 1995 was $9.23 for men and $6.94 for women. With an hourly wage of $7.28 needed to live above the poverty line, almost 30 percent of the men and 36 percent of the women in the American workforce failed to meet that threshold.

The nation's largest service-sector employer—in fact, the largest private employer in the world by the end of the 1990s—was Wal-Mart, a chain of retail stores that began with one store in Rogers, Arkansas, in 1962. Founder Sam Walton followed a policy of selling goods at high volume, with a small profit on each sale, and pioneered the concept of creating "superstores," where people could buy everything from tractors to shampoo to dog food. To live up to the company's slogan of "Always Low Prices," Walton was also stringent with his employees' hourly wages and benefits, which were significant costs to the company. After the company went public in 1970 (meaning that the public could buy stock in the company), Walton's retailing empire grew to fifty-five stores by 1973, most of them located in small towns. A decade after Walton's death in 1992, Wal-Mart had 3,244 discount, supercenter, Sam's Club warehouse, and other stores in the United States and another 4,414 outlets around the world.

Significance

Walton's folksy image—he often appeared wearing a tattered baseball cap with his company's logo on it—was widely recognized in the 1990s. The company also wielded considerable political clout as one of the major contributors to Bill Clinton's presidential campaigns. Clinton's wife, Hillary Rodham Clinton, had also served on Wal-Mart's board of directors during her husband's terms as governor of Arkansas.

Despite the chain's influence and power, however, Wal-Mart increasingly came under fire for its corporate practices and long-range plans. A series of complaints to the National Labor Relations Board alleging illegal, antiunion practices and a number of lawsuits alleging unfair labor practices and gender discrimination tarnished the company's reputation. One lawsuit, which Wal-Mart lost in an Oregon federal court in 2002, revealed that the company routinely forced its managers to work overtime without paying them; thirty-nine similar lawsuits were pending at the time of the jury's decision. The revelation in 1996 that the company stocked clothing under its Kathie Lee Gifford line that was made in sweatshops in Central America also focused attention on its corporate practices.

The company, which had built its success on serving rural markets that other retailers ignored, also faced accusations of destroying the commercial life of the small towns where it was located. Small retailers, who did not have the advantage of Wal-Mart's high volume and discount prices, often closed their doors after Wal-Mart opened, leaving empty storefronts on many downtown streets. By the late 1990s, many local groups had formed to prevent Wal-Mart from opening in their neighborhoods, and the company was still under constant scrutiny for its labor practices and the origins of its merchandise.

Primary Source

Worker Rights for Temps! [excerpt]

SYNOPSIS: *Temp Slave!* was one of many popular, self-published "zines" that attracted more than just an underground audience in the 1990s. With the rise of the Internet, many print zines reappeared as web logs (or "blogs") or as full-fledged websites. In this rant, *Temp Slave!* founder Jeff Kelly lays out the rules for a less exploitative temp experience. The first rule: Don't Speed Up! Slow Down!

A temp worker has little or no rights in the workplace. In essence, a temp worker is close to being a nonentity. Sadly, not much can be done to alleviate the situation. A temp worker can be moved from job to job within a workplace, even though the temp may have been told they would do only one kind of job. As for job security, obviously there is none.

The normal avenues of channeling discontent about a job are not open to temps. For example, the normal course of unionizing a workplace is out of the question. Most companies set up Human Resource departments to act as a buffer between their

---

Wal-Mart's Fundamental Principles

Even after his death in 1992, the company Sam Walton founded thirty years earlier continued to highlight his folksy image and traditional values of hard work, customer service, and teamwork—all reflected in the company's website page about working at the company.

"Careers at Wal-Mart" [excerpt]

. . . Wal-Mart has remained No. 1 by staying true to our basic values and beliefs. The roots of our success remain firmly grounded in three fundamental principles:

Respect for the Individual

Service for our Customers

Striving for Excellence

SOURCE: "Careers @ Wal.Mart." Internet Archive. Available online at http://web.archive.org/web/19990210083608/wal-mart.com/careers (accessed March 8, 2003).

---

workers and management. If a problem arises, the Human Resource managers are summoned to sort out the mess. But, this does nothing for temps since any overt complaints about a job by a temp will more than likely result in termination. Finally, getting unemployment benefits off a temp agency is like pulling teeth. Most of the time, requests for benefits are denied.

So a temp is forced to put up and shut up or get out. However, there are a few things a temp can do to gain a semblance of power in the workplace.

First, DON'T SPEED UP! SLOW DOWN! Most of the time a temp is expected to work at the rate that a full-time worker does or faster. At first a temp may want to impress upon the fact that they are capable of doing the job. But, once this is accomplished there is no reason for a temp to continue the pace. If you are working with a group of temps, band together and SLOW DOWN your rate of work. Slowing down your work allows your assignment to linger on longer. After all, why put yourself out of work? Plus, a group of temps working together cohesively puts the company notice that people cannot be treated like slaves.

Second, NEVER rat on another temp to the bossman! Trying to put yourself above other temps is a silly and ultimately a hopeless thing to do. The per-

A Wal-Mart employee wears a vest with the inspirational slogan "Our People Make the Difference," 1996. Maintaining morale among workers in the new economy, many of whom were temporary workers, was a problem businesses sought to surmount in the 1990s. © JAMES LEYNSE/CORBIS SABA. REPRODUCED BY PERMISSION.

son doing the ratting may think they are getting ahead, or think that the bossman will grant special favors, or think it will lead to a full-time job. But it seldom ever does. What it does do is divide the workforce and keep people in place. To get rid of a rat, a few simple things can be done—"lose" their paperwork (make them look bad in the eyes of the bossman), chill out the rat (do not associate with the person on break time). And never volunteer to work with a rat if two people are needed for a job. In other words, make it known that they are not wanted within your work area.

Third, GET BACK AT THE BASTARDS! If you are being treated like shit by a company give it right back. Many companies entrust you with sensitive information. Use this info, "lose" it, sabotage it. Learn your job well and take every advantage possible with it.

Finally, if you are ending an assignment and really want to mess up the works legally, there is a fun thing you can do. Start talking union to everyone in the workplace. This gives you the opportunity to file charges with the National Labor Relations Board (NLRB). The NLRB is a national governmental agency set up to broker labor disputes. Under law, a worker is allowed to organize unions in the workplace. But, even with the law, workers are still fired. However, filing charges with the NLRB is a kick in the ass to a company because it forces them to deal with investigations and endless paperwork. In the best case scenario you may win your case and receive back pay sometimes amounting to thousands of dollars. But, even if you lose you can go away happy knowing that you were an incredible pain in the ass to the corporate hacks.

In closing, a workforce divided by petty jealousies, fear and self loathing is a workforce that plays into the hands of the bosses.

DON'T MAKE IT EASY FOR THEM! THEY DON'T DESERVE IT!

Further Resources

BOOKS

Ehrenreich, Barbara. *Nickel and Dimed: On (Not) Getting By in America.* New York: Metropolitan Books, 2001.

Mishel, Lawrence, with Jared Bernstein and John Schmitt. *The State of Working America, 1996–1997.* Armonk, N.Y.: M.E. Sharpe, 1997.

Ortega, Bob. *In Sam We Trust: The Untold Story of Sam Walton and How Wal-Mart Is Devouring America.* New York: Times Business, 1998.

Parker, Robert E. *Flesh Peddlers and Warm Bodies: The Temporary Help Industry and Its Workers.* New Brunswick, N.J.: Rutgers University Press, 1994.

Schor, Juliet B. *The Overworked American: The Unexpected Decline of Leisure.* New York: Basic Books, 1991.

Trimble, Vance H. *Sam Walton: The Inside Story of America's Richest Man.* New York: Dutton, 1990.

Walton, Sam, with John Huey. *Sam Walton: Made in America: My Story.* New York: Doubleday, 1992.

Yates, Michael D. *Longer Hours, Fewer Jobs: Employment and Unemployment in the United States.* New York: Monthly Review Press, 1994.

WEBSITES

"An Interview with the Creator of Temp Slave!" Available online at http://www.zinebook.com/interv/temp.html (accessed March 2, 2003).

The Immigration Debate

"To Reunite a Nation"

Speech

By: Patrick J. Buchanan
Date: January 18, 2000
Source: Buchanan, Patrick J. "To Reunite a Nation." Delivered at the Richard M. Nixon Library, January 18, 2000. Available online at http://www.buchanan.org/pa-00-0118-immigration.html (accessed March 8, 2003).
About the Author: Patrick J. Buchanan (1938–) was raised in a Catholic family in Washington, D.C., where he learned the argumentative style that would later serve him well. After studying at Georgetown University and the Columbia University School of Law, he began a career as a journalist before joining the New York City law firm where Richard Nixon practiced. When Nixon was elected president in 1968, Buchanan joined his administration as a speechwriter. He returned to journalism as a columnist in the 1970s and began a television broadcast career. Aligning himself with the Republican Party, Buchanan launched unsuccessful presidential bids in 1992, 1996, and 2000 on a conservative platform that opposed abortion and free trade and called for a reduction in immigration.

"Will It Come to This?"

Advertisement

By: U.S. English, Inc.
Source: U.S. English, Inc. Available online at http://www.us-english.org/inc/printad4.htm (accessed March 8, 2003).
About the Organization: U.S. English, Inc. was founded in 1983 to support efforts to make English the official language of the United States. The organization believed that federal expenditures on bilingualism were better spent on efforts to teach immigrants English, which would help to unite the country by serving as the nation's common language. ∎

Introduction

As the United States enjoyed the longest economic expansion in its history in the 1990s, it remained the destination for the majority of the world's immigrants. Although people came to the United States seeking political and religious freedom, most came for the higher wages, better job opportunities, and an improved standard of living. The economic lure of life in the United States was so strong that many immigrants entered the country illegally, particularly from nearby Latin American countries. Critics of the government's lackluster efforts to stem the tide of illegal immigration noted that some employers took advantage of their uncertain legal status to pay them less than the minimum wage while forcing them to work in unsafe conditions. Some anti-immigration groups even argued that the United States should build a high, concrete wall along the border with Mexico to make it more difficult for people to enter the country illegally.

In California, the state most affected by immigration from Latin America, demographers predicted that a majority of residents would be Latino by 2010. In response, immigration opponents put Proposition 187 on the ballot in 1996; the measure to eliminate public services, including education and health care, for illegal aliens passed with 75 percent of the vote. Voters in California also passed Proposition 227 to eliminate public funding for bilingual education. The 1998 referendum passed with 61 percent of the vote, although it, like Proposition 187, was struck down by a court decision. Supporters of the measures argued that public services such as bilingual education allowed immigrants to stay insulated in their own ethnic communities, which in turn threatened the nation's unity. Opponents of the measures portrayed them as blatant attempts to prevent Latino residents from gaining full access to the educational, health-care, and political systems.

Significance

Anti-immigration sentiment simmered throughout the 1990s and became the basis for Republican Patrick J. Buchanan's 1992, 1996, and 2000 presidential runs.

Most voters rejected Buchanan's suggestions that immigration was ruining the country's social fabric and economic future, and his candidacy petered out each time. With the robust economy of the 1990s, it was indeed difficult for the average American to understand how immigration had hurt the country at all. Most experts agreed that the addition of immigrants to the workforce had actually been a boon to economic growth, contrary to anti-immigrant arguments.

With the growth in Hispanic populations from immigration and higher birth rates in key states such as Florida, Texas, and California, both the Democratic and Republican parties put more effort into attracting their votes. Like other ethnic groups before them, Latino Americans seemed poised to become an effective political bloc not only in cities where they were now the majority but on the national stage as well. With Latinos poised to become the nation's largest minority group well before the 2010 census, experts predicted that a Hispanic candidate would almost certainly gain a Supreme Court or presidential administration appointment, and perhaps even be named to the national ticket of one of the major parties.

Primary Source

"To Reunite a Nation" [excerpt]

SYNOPSIS: A commanding public orator, Buchanan uses this speech, delivered at the Richard M. Nixon Presidential Library, to raise awareness of the "troubling signs of a nation turning away from the idea that we are one people." As he concludes from the threat of a multicultural, multilingual nation, "we have no choice if we are to remain one nation—we must slow down the pace of immigration."

Like all of you, I am awed by the achievements of many recent immigrants. Their contributions to Silicon Valley are extraordinary. The over-representation of Asian-born kids in advanced high school math and science classes is awesome, and, to the extent that it is achieved by a superior work ethic, these kids are setting an example for all of us. The contributions that immigrants make in small businesses and hard work in tough jobs that don't pay well merits our admiration and deepest respect. And, many new immigrants show a visible love of this country and an appreciation of freedom that makes you proud to be an American.

Northern Virginia, where I live, has experienced a huge and sudden surge in immigration. It has become a better place, in some ways, but nearly unrecognizable in others, and no doubt worse in some

realms, a complicated picture over all. But it is clear to anyone living in a state like California or Virginia that the great immigration wave, set in motion by the Immigration Act of 1965, has put an indelible mark upon America.

We are no longer a biracial society; we are now a multi-racial society. We no longer struggle simply to end the divisions and close the gaps between black and white Americans; we now grapple, often awkwardly, with an unprecedented ethnic diversity. We also see the troubling signs of a national turning away from the idea that we are one people, and the emergence of a radically different idea, that we are separate ethnic nations within a nation. . . .

Concerns of this sort are even older than the Republic itself. In 1751, Ben Franklin asked: "Why should Pennsylvania, founded by the English, become a Colony of Aliens, who will shortly be so numerous as to Germanize us instead of our Anglifying them?" Franklin would never find out if his fears were justified. German immigration was halted by the Seven Years War; then slowed by the Great Lull in immigration that followed the American Revolution. A century and half later, during what is called the Great Wave, the same worries were in the air.

In 1915 Theodore Roosevelt told the Knights of Columbus: "There is no room in this country for hyphenated Americanism. . . . The one absolutely certain way of bringing this nation to ruin, of preventing all possibility of its continuing to be a nation at all, would be to permit it to become a tangle of squabbling nationalities." Congress soon responded by enacting an immigration law that brought about a virtual forty-year pause to digest, assimilate, and Americanize the diverse immigrant wave that had rolled in between 1890 and 1920.

Today, once again, it is impossible not to notice the conflicts generated by a new "hyphenated Americanism." In Los Angeles, two years ago, there was an anguishing afternoon in the Coliseum where the U.S. soccer team was playing Mexico. The Mexican-American crowd showered the U.S. team with water bombs, beer bottles and trash. The Star Spangled Banner was hooted and jeered. A small contingent of fans of the American team had garbage hurled at them. The American players later said that they were better received in Mexico City than in their own country.

Last summer, El Cenizo, a small town in south Texas, adopted Spanish as its official language. All town documents are now to be written, and all town

I pledge allegiance to the bandera de los Estados Unidos de Amerika und der Republik...

Will it come to this?

We hope not. But it doesn't look good. Because the language that unites our country—English—is under attack in our schools, in our courts, and by bureaucrats and self-appointed leaders for immigrant groups.

The whole notion of a melting pot society is threatened if new immigrants aren't encouraged to learn the language of the majority.

With nearly 700,000 members, we're the largest organization fighting to make English the official language of government at all levels.

We're not suggesting that people shouldn't hold onto their native languages. We just don't believe that the government should spend money providing services in multiple languages,

when money could be better used teaching new immigrants English. Join us. Support us. Fight with us. While we can still understand each other.

Speak up for America. Call 1-800-U.S.ENGLISH

U.S.ENGLISH

1747 Pennsylvania Avenue, NW, Suite 1100
Washington, DC 20006

Primary Source

"Will It Come to This?"

SYNOPSIS: This ad from U.S. English, Inc., asks the public to "fight with us" and demand that English be adopted as the sole, official language of the United States. It claims that the history and culture of the nation are threatened and that various parties are attacking the country's social fabric by asking for public services in languages other than English. © U.S. ENG-LISH, INC. ALL RIGHTS RESERVED. REPRODUCED BY PERMISSION.

A corrugated metal fence stands on the border between the United States and Mexico, decorated with crosses laid in memory of those who died trying to cross into the United States. LATINFOCUS.COM. REPRODUCED BY PERMISSION.

business conducted, in Spanish. Any official who cooperates with U.S. immigration authorities was warned he or she would be fired. To this day, Governor Bush is reluctant to speak out on this de facto secession of a tiny Texas town to Mexico.

Voting in referendums that play a growing part in the politics of California is now breaking down sharply on ethnic lines. Hispanic voters opposed Proposition 187 to cut off welfare to illegal aliens, and they rallied against it under Mexican flags. They voted heavily in favor of quotas and ethnic preferences in the 1996 California Civil Rights Initiative, and, again, to keep bilingual education in 1998. These votes suggest that in the California of the future, when Mexican-American voting power catches up with Mexican-American population, any bid to end racial quotas by referendum will fail. A majority of the state's most populous immigrant group now appears to favor set-asides and separate language programs, rather than to be assimilated into the American mainstream. . . .

I don't want to overstate the negatives. But in too many cases the American Melting Pot has been reduced to a simmer. At present rates, mass immi-

gration reinforces ethnic subcultures, reduces the incentives of newcomers to learn English; and extends the life of linguistic ghettos that might otherwise be melded into the great American mainstream. If we want to assimilate new immigrants—and we have no choice if we are remain one nation—we must slow down the pace of immigration.

Whatever its shortcomings, the United States has done far better at alleviating poverty than most countries. But an America that begins to think of itself as made up of disparate peoples will find social progress far more difficult. It is far easier to look the other way when the person who needs help does not speak the same language, or share a common culture or common history.

Americans who feel it natural and right that their taxes support the generation that fought World War II—will they feel the same way about those from Fukien Province or Zanzibar? If America continues on its present course, it could rapidly become a country with no common language, no common culture, no common memory and no common identity. And that country will find itself very short of the social cohesion that makes compassion possible.

Further Resources

BOOKS

Brimelow, Peter. *Alien Nation: Common Sense About America's Immigration Disaster*. New York: Random House, 1995.

Buchanan, Patrick J. *The Death of the West: How Dying Populations and Immigrant Invasions Imperil Our Country and Civilization*. New York: Thomas Dunne, 2002.

——. *The Great Betrayal: How American Sovereignty and Social Justice Are Being Sacrificed to the Gods of Global Economics*. Boston: Little, Brown, 1998.

Ramos, Jorge. *The Other Face of America: Chronicles of the Immigrants Shaping Our Future*. New York: Rayo Books, 2002.

WEBSITES

"Immigration and Naturalization Service." Available online at http://www.ins.gov (accessed February 24, 2003).

"Pat Buchanan for President 2000 Official Web Site." Available online at http://www.buchanan.org (accessed March 8, 2003).

Kurt Cobain Journals

Personal journal

By: Kurt Cobain

Date: 2002

Source: Cobain, Kurt. *Kurt Cobain Journals*. New York: Riverhead, 2002, 44, 167–170.

About the Author: Kurt Cobain (1967–1994) grew up in the logging town of Aberdeen, Washington. Scarred by his parents' divorce, Cobain dropped out of high school and began singing and playing guitar with several local punk bands. He formed Nirvana with bassist Krist Novoselic around 1986; the band was completed with the addition of drummer Dave Grohl in 1990. After the release of *Bleach* on the Seattle-based Sub Pop label in 1989, Nirvana signed with Geffen Records in 1990 and released its major-label debut, *Nevermind*, in 1991. The band released just one more original studio album, *In Utero* (1993) before Cobain's death from suicide, which was discovered on the morning of April 8, 1994. Cobain was survived by his wife, singer and actress Courtney Love, and their daughter. ∎

Introduction

The domination of MTV over the music and culture of young Americans in the 1980s sparked numerous complaints about the direction that the nation was headed. Parents, educators, and law-enforcement groups were disturbed by videos that glamorized sex and violence, and they were far from alone in their concerns. Conservatives and feminists alike were appalled by the routine vulgarities that cropped up in popular culture aimed at young people. Not only were the lyrics offensive to many people, but the video images, typically featuring scantily clad models in suggestive poses, were accused of objectifying women for the sake of selling records.

Many young people were also disturbed at the influence of MTV, not only for the macho sexism that it reinforced but for the corporate stranglehold on music that it represented. With musicians more dependent on record-company contracts to pay for their expensive videos and record companies wanting a sure return on their investment, creativity seemed to have lost out to commercialism. In the late 1980s, however, the grunge music movement of Seattle offered an alternative vision. Bands with grassroots followings—Nirvana, Mudhoney, and Soundgarden among them—released low-budget, independent albums with lots of guitars, screaming vocals, and riotous drums. Far from the superficial romantic lyrics that dominated pop music, grunge musicians sang about surviving child abuse and broken homes, drug addiction, obsessive love, and occasionally, just having a good time.

By the time Nirvana's major-label debut, *Nevermind*, was released late in 1991, lead singer and guitarist Kurt Cobain had become the poster boy for grunge rock. Never fully comfortable with his fame, Cobain nevertheless used his new celebrity to rail against sexism and homophobia in music and society; he reserved some of his most passionate criticism, however, for corporate America and the values of capitalism. When Nirvana appeared on the cover of *Rolling Stone* in 1992 as its album reached the top of the charts, Cobain defiantly wore a shirt with a slogan he had scrawled across it: "Corporate Magazines Still Suck."

Significance

Nirvana's first hit single, "Smells Like Teen Spirit," regularly topped critics' polls as the most influential song of the 1990s from possibly the leading group of the decade. Yet the song reached only number six on *Billboard*'s pop chart in early 1992, showing the hesitation that many radio stations had in playing the song. In terms of sales, the single for "Smells Like Teen Spirit" in fact *did* reach number one, but it never cracked the top forty in terms of radio airplay. The album *Nevermind* had no such problem, hitting number one and selling ten million copies. All of the group's subsequent albums were both critical and commercial successes.

The dazzling achievements of Nirvana—critical acclaim, best-selling albums, and sold-out tours—made Cobain's rapid decline from stomach problems and drug use all the more shocking. After leaving a drug rehabilitation center in late March 1994, Cobain returned to his home in Seattle and committed suicide with a shotgun blast to his head. After his body was discovered by a repairman on the morning of April 8, 1994, the announcement stunned Nirvana fans worldwide. For the young generation, the moment they heard about Cobain's death served as a unifying event, much like President Kennedy's shooting in Dallas in 1963 or the *Challenger* space shuttle explosion in 1986. The generational impact of twenty-seven-year-old Cobain's death was reinforced just days later when *60 Minutes* commentator and senior citizen Andy Rooney dismissed his suicide as another example of self-pitying whining among young Americans.

In the decade after Cobain's death, a steady release of Nirvana compilations and the publication of his *Journals* added to his legacy. They also served as a reminder that no other figure had taken his place as a critic of corporate America and traditional values.

Primary Source

Kurt Cobain Journals [excerpt]

SYNOPSIS: This excerpt from Kurt Cobain's *Journals* is taken from a letter Cobain wrote to then-girlfriend Tobi Vail, drummer for Bikini Kill, in 1991. Outlining a critique of corporate America, he describes the making of the video for "Smells Like Teen Spirit." Despite his hesitation to deal with the mass-media conglomerates that dominated the record industry, Cobain had come to terms with the band's future: "Suck 'em in with quality entertainment," he writes about Nirvana's game plan, "and hit 'em with reality." [Editor's note: spelling and usage errors present in the original.]

Hi,

Yeah, all Isms feed off one another, but at the top of the food chain is still the white, corporate, macho, strong ox male. Not redeemable as far as I'm concerned. I mean, classism is determined by sexism because the male decides whether all other isms still exists. It's up to men. I'm just saying that people can't deny any ism or think that some are more or less subordinate. Except for sexism. He's in charge, He decides. I still think that in order to expand on all other isms, sexism has to be blown wide open. It's almost impossible to de-program the incestually-established, male oppressor, especially the one's who've been weaned on it thru their family's generations like die hard N.R.A. freaks and inherited, corporate, power mongrels, the ones who were born into no choice but to keep the torch and only let sparks fall for the rest of us to gather at their feet. But there are thousands of green minds. Young gullible 15 year old boys out there just starting to fall into the grain of what they've been told of what a man is supposed to be, and there are plenty of tools to use. The most effective tool is enter-

tainment. The entertainment industry is just now starting to accept us. (Mainly because of trendy falseness on environmentally, socially concience hype) i.e. the new 90s attitude, which is at a total stand still because of the patriotic aftermath of the war and all its numbery rally-parades) but they're using Media!! Media. Major labels. (The evil corporate Oppressors, (god I need a new word!) the ones who are in kahoots with the government, the ones the underground movement went into retaliation against in the early 80s.) The corporations are finally allowing supposedly subversive, alternative thinking bands to have a loan of money to expose their crusade, obviously they aren't forking out loans for this reason, but more because it looks to be a money making, comodity. But we can use them! We can pose as the enemy to infiltrate the mechanics of the system to start its rot from the inside. Sabotage the empire by pretending to play their game. Compromise just enough to call their bluff. And the hairy, sweaty, macho, sexist dickheads will soon drown in a pool of razor blades and semen, stemmed from the uprising of their children, the armed and deprogrammed crusade, littering the floors of wallstreet with revolutionary debris.

Assasinating both the lesser and greater of two evils, bringing an everlasting, sterile and bacterial herbacious and botanical and corporate cleansing for our ancestors to gaze in wonderment and Awe. AWE! Geezus Christ. (repeat): Posing as the enemy to infiltrate the mechanics of the empire and slowly start its rot from the inside, it's an inside job—it starts with the custodians and the cheerleaders, and ends with the entertainers.

The youth are waiting, impatiently. Homophobe Vaccectomy.

It's like what Kathleen said about how in school there was this class that you went to and they were teaching the girls how to prepare themselves for rape and when you looked outside and saw the rapers outside playing football and you said "They are the ones who should be in here being taught not to rape."

How true. Suck em in with quality entertainment and hit em with reality.

The revolution will be televised.

Theres this new 24 hour channel on cable called the 90s, which is available only in a few states so far and its magazine version can be seen on PBS (Public Broadcasting System) once a week, it's pretty damn informative and it exposes injustices in a kind

my lyrics are a big pile of contradictions.
they're split down the middle between
very sincere opinions and feelings that I have
and sarcastic and hopefully - humorous
rebuttles towards cliché - bohemian ideals
that have been exhausted for years.
    I mean it seems like there are only two
options for personalities of songwriters either
they're SAd, tragic visionaries like morrisey
or michael Stipe or Robert smith. or theres
the goofy, nutty white boy, Hey, lets party
and forget every thing people like Van Halen
or All that other Heavy metal crap

· I mean I like to be passionate and
Sincere, but I also like to have
fun and act like a dork.
        Geeks unite.

Primary Source

Kurt Cobain Journals [excerpt]

SYNOPSIS: In the excerpt presented here, Cobain muses in his journal about song writing. The tension between writing meaningful songs and simple pop tunes remained central in Nirvana's work and fueled some of Cobain's best songs, including "Smells Like Teen Spirit," the group's sole top-ten hit. FROM *KURT COBAIN JOURNALS*: RIVERHEAD BOOKS, 2002. COPYRIGHT © 2002 BY THE END OF MUSIC, LLC. ALL RIGHTS RESERVED. REPRODUCED BY PERMISSION.

Kurt Cobain, vocalist of the grunge rock group Nirvana, 1990.
© S.I.N./CORBIS. REPRODUCED BY PERMISSION.

of conservative–liberal format, but its new so it has to be that way. I've seen it a few times and really liked it. Also Night Flight is back. You know, the show that used to play New Wave Theatre?

We plan to use these shows and others if given the chance. Yeah I know, I'm a confused, uneducated, walking cliché, but I don't need to be inspired any longer, just supported.

Oh yeah, Gluttony, I almost forgot Gluttony. The band now has an image: the anti-gluttony, materialism and consumerism image that we plan to incorporate into all of our videos. The first one: Smells Like Teen Spirit, will have us walking through a mall throwing thousands of dollars into the air as mall goers scramble like vulchers to collect as much as they can get their hands on, then we walk into a jewelry store and smash it up in anti-materialist fueled, punk rock violence. Then we go to a pep assembly at a high school and the cheerleaders have Anarchy As on their sweaters and the custodian-militant-

revolutionarys hand out guns with flowers in the barrels to all the cheering students who file down to the center court and throw their money and jewelry and Andrew Dice Clay tapes into a big pile then we set it on fire and run out of the building screaming. Oh, didn't twisted Sister already do this?

Things that have been taken from me within the past 2 months: 1 wallet, drivers license, etc., $400.00, three guitars (including the Moserite) all my neato 70s effect boxes, apartment and phone. But I got a really neato left handed 67 fender Jaguar which is in my opinion, almost as cool as a Mustang. So I consider it a fair trade for the Moserite.

While staying in L.A. we almost got killed by gang members. Well, sort of. Dave Franz and I were in the parking lot of a famous, female-mudwrestler-night club scoring lewds, when all of a sudden two gas guzzling cars pulled up next to us and five Cho-los with knives and guns walked over to the car closest to ours and started yelling and cursing in gang lingo at each other. But then by the motto of "To Protect and Serve" the cops show up, which insighted the gang bangers to flee away in their cars, resulting in a hot pursuit-car chase. There were even helicopters with searchlights. Needless to say we scored our lewds and split. We played a really fun show with Fits of Depression at a really small coffee house called the Jabberjaw. We were indescribably fucked up on booze and drugs, out of tune and rather uh, sloppy. It took me about fifteen minutes to change my guitar string while people heckled and called me drunk. Robyn Zander (cheap trick lead singer?). After the show I ran outside and vomited, then I came back in to find Iggy Pop there so I gave him a sloppy-puke breath kiss and hug. He's a really friendly and cool and nice and interesting person. It was probably the most flattering moment of my life.

As you may have guessed by now I've been taking a lot of drugs lately. It might be time for the Betty Ford Clinic or the Richard Nixon Library to save me from abusing my anemic, rodent–like body any longer. I can't wait to be back at home (wherever that is) in bed, neurotic and malnourished and complaining how the weather sucks, and its the whole reason for my misery. I miss you, Bikini Kill. I totally love you.

Kurt

Further Resources

BOOKS

Arnold, Gina. *Route 666: On the Road to Nirvana*. New York: St. Martin's Press, 1993.

Azerrad, Michael. *Come as You Are: The Story of Nirvana.* New York: Doubleday, 1993.

Borzillo, Carrie. *Nirvana: The Day-by-Day Eyewitness Chronicle.* New York: Thunder Mouth's Press, 2000.

Kitts, Jeff, Brad Tolinski, and Harold Steinblatt, eds. *Nirvana and the Grunge Revolution.* Milwaukee, Wisc.: Hal Leonard, 1998.

PERIODICALS

Ali, Lorraine. "Cries from the Heart." *Newsweek,* October 28, 2002, 60–68.

"Nirvana: Life After Death." *Q,* October 2002, 65–90.

AUDIO AND VISUAL MEDIA

Nirvana. *Bleach.* Sub Pop Records, 1989.

———. *From the Muddy Banks of the Wishkah.* Geffen Records, 1996.

———. *In Utero.* Geffen Records, 1993.

———. *Insecticide.* Geffen Records, 1992.

———. *Nevermind.* Geffen Records, 1991.

———. *Nirvana.* Geffen Records, 2002.

———. *Unplugged in New York.* Geffen Records, 1994.

8

THE MEDIA

MILLIE JACKSON

Entries are arranged in chronological order by date of primary source. For entries with one primary source, the entry title is the same as the primary source title. Entries with more than one primary source have an overall entry title, followed by the titles of the primary sources.

Important Events in the Media, 1990–1999

1990

- Large city newspaper readership continues to decline. More than nine million New Yorkers bought Sunday papers in 1950. In 1990 that figure is 3.2 million.

- More than five hundred of the nation's 3,100 magazines begin publication this year. Most of the new mags fall into the categories of lifestyle, sex, and service.

- The police/courtroom *Law and Order, Twin Peaks,* and *America's Funniest Home Videos* all premiere. The sitcoms *In Living Color* and *Fresh Prince of Bel Air,* starring Damon Wayans and Will Smith respectively, also debut, as do the highly successful cartoon series *The Simpsons.* and a sitcom about "nothing" called simply *Seinfeld.*

- On February 22, Hughes Communications, News Corp, National Broadcasting Company (NBC), and Cablevision Systems Corporation create Sky Cable, a joint effort to launch direct-broadcast satellite TV program service with as many as 108 channels.

- On March 6, Whittle Communications LP airs its first installment of *Channel One,* a daily news program for high school students.

- On March 29, the major music producers agree to place warning labels on recordings that might offend some people. Some companies have already been warning of lyrics that are explicit about sex or violence. However, the new labels will have a uniform design and wording.

- On April 4, Columbia Broadcasting System (CBS), NBC, and American Broadcasting Company (ABC) announce the formation of Network Television Association, designed to promote network television to advertisers and agencies.

- On May 18, *The Forward,* a new national English-language Jewish newspaper, based on the Yiddish *Forverts* (starting 1897), begins publication.

- On July 12, the quirky television series *Northern Exposure* premieres.

- On September 25, the three hundredth anniversary of *Publick Occurrences,* the first newspaper published in what is now the United States (Boston), is observed.

- On September 26, the movie rating system is revised to replace the "X" rating with "NC-17," meaning that no one under 17 years of age will be admitted. The change is in response to moviemakers' complaints that the "X" symbol has long been used by pornographers.

- On November 9, the Cable News Network (CNN) defies a federal judge's orders and airs taped phone conversations between former Panama dictator Manuel Antonio Noriega Moreno and members of his legal defense team. The network argues no court has the right to decide what the news media may broadcast.

1991

- After sixty years, cartoon character Blondie, wife of Dagwood and namesake of the comic strip, announces her need for a career.

- On April 16, NBC News identifies the alleged victim of the William Kennedy Smith case, ending the traditional media practice of withholding the names of victims of alleged rapes. The next day *The New York Times* also publishes her name.

- In October, liberal magazine the *New Republic* appoints conservative and gay Andrew Sullivan as editor.

- On October 6, National Public Radio (NPR) and *Newsday* announce Anita F. Hill's allegations of sexual harassment against Supreme Court nominee Clarence Thomas.

- On December 4, Associated Press correspondent Terry Anderson is freed after seven years as a hostage in Beirut.

- On December 21, media mogul Robert Edward "Ted" Turner III marries actress Jane Fonda.

1992

- The sitcom *Mad About You* with Helen Hunt and Paul Reiser premieres.

- On April 30, the final episode of *The Cosby Show* airs. TV's most popular sitcom since 1984, it once spent a record sixty-nine consecutive weeks atop the ratings charts.

- On May 19, Vice President Dan Quayle attacks sitcom character Murphy Brown during a campaign speech, saying that the character is fostering lax family values.

- On May 22, Johnny Carson ends his thirty-year run as host of the *Tonight Show.* With tears in his eyes, he tells millions of television viewers, "It has been an honor and a privilege to come into your home all these years and entertain you." As the highest-paid TV performer in history, Carson made about $2,380 per minute on the air.

- On October 5, Congress passes over President Bush's veto, a bill to regulate cable TV companies. The new law authorizes the Federal Communications Commission (FCC) to write guidelines from which local governments can set "reasonable" prices for cable service in their communities. It also allows traditional broadcasters to charge cable companies for the right to carry their programs.

1993

- Sales of country music recordings have more than tripled since 1988, and more than twenty-two hundred radio stations now have country-music formats.

• *NYPD Blue; Walker, Texas Ranger; Homicide, Life on the Street; The X-Files;* and *Frasier,* a spinoff of the highly popular comedy series *Cheers,* all premiere on network television.

• On May 30, the final episode of *Cheers* is aired. Advertisers pay $650,000 for a thirty-second spot on the last show.

• On June 1, Dan Rather and Connie Chung co-anchor the *CBS Evening News* for the first time.

• On June 30, the TV networks head off threatened federal-government action by agreeing to post warning notices at the start of shows that contain sex, vulgar language, or graphic violence.

• On September 24, *60 Minutes* celebrates its twenty-fifth anniversary.

• On September 28, *The New York Times* acquires *The Boston Globe,* New England's largest-circulation newspaper.

1994

• The comedy series *Friends,* the drama series *ER,* and *Touched by an Angel* debut on TV.

• In January, *Women's Wire,* a San Francisco-based on-line service for women, is launched. Beset by financial woes, the formerly feminist service was taken over in 1995 and relaunched as a cyberspace version of a traditional women's magazine.

• On April 3, Charles Kuralt, TV journalist and *CBS News Sunday Morning* commentator, retires at age 59.

• On May 23, the Fox Network establishes itself as a major player in television entertainment when it lures eight important CBS affiliates, as well as three stations from ABC and one from NBC, to switch to its network.

• On May 27, TV talk show host Arsenio Hall calls it quits after five years on the air in the late-night wars.

• On June 17, former football star and sometime movie actor O.J. Simpson is charged with the murder of his ex-wife Nicole Brown Simpson and her friend Ronald Goldman. Media helicopters televise Simpson's flight from the police in a white Ford Bronco along a Los Angeles freeway.

• In September, *She TV,* a breakthrough sketch comedy show focusing on and creatively developed by women, premieres.

• In September, Ken Burns's eighteen-hour documentary on baseball airs on Public Broadcasting Service (PBS).

• On December 31, *Far Side* creator Gary Larson retires from his daily cartoons, which ran in nearly nineteen hundred newspapers.

1995

• On July 31, the Walt Disney Company purchases Capital Cities/ABC TV for $19 billion. With $17 billion in annual income, the combined firm will be the most powerful entertainment and media company in the world.

• On August 1, Westinghouse Electric Corp. buys CBS for $5.4 billion. With this purchase, all of the formerly independent TV networks are now subsidiaries of other companies.

• On August 21, ABC News apologizes to tobacco giant Philip Morris for a story it ran on *Day One* claiming the industry spiked cigarettes with nicotine.

• On September 20, communications giant AT&T, which is valued at more than $101 billion, announces that it will split into three separate companies. The split will be the largest corporate breakup in U.S. history.

• On November 9, CBS pulls a *60 Minutes* segment critical of the tobacco industry from that week's show.

• On December 7, *The New York Times* refuses to run an ad placed by a right-wing Japanese group wanting to rewrite Japan's war record.

1996

• A study finds that the amount of violence depicted on TV programs declined in the 1995–1996 season. Only five shows raised concerns, compared to nine the previous season.

• The drama series *Murder She Wrote* ends a highly successful twelve-year run on TV.

• On January 17, daytime talk show host Phil Donahue announces his retirement after thirty years on television. His audience participation show was the model for *Oprah, Jenny Jones,* and other such shows that by 1996 fill daytime programming.

• On February 1, Congress votes to rewrite the sixty-one-year-old Communications Act, opening the way for television, phone, and computer companies to offer products in each other's fields.

• On February 7, President Bill Clinton signs the Communications Decency Act, part of the Telecommunications Reform Act of 1996.

• On March 1, researchers transmit one trillion bits of information a second over an optical fiber network. This accomplishment is equal to transmitting the contents of three hundred years of daily newspapers in just one second.

• On March 17, the Museum of Television and Radio opens in Beverly Hills, California. It is a companion to the East Coast museum that opened in New York in 1975. The new museum provides access to more than 750,000 radio and TV programs broadcast over seven decades.

• On June 20, the nation's two largest radio broadcasting companies merge when Westinghouse Electric buys Infinity Broadcasting. The deal is made possible by a new federal law lifting the limit on how many radio stations one company may own. The combined company will operate eighty-three.

• On June 20, the Museum of Modern Art opens a film storage center at Hamlin, Pennsylvania. The facility will safely keep and preserve more than thirteen thousand films from the earliest kintoscopes of the 1890s to modern popular movies.

• On July 29, pressured by the Federal Communications Commission (FCC), television broadcasters agree to include three hours of educational children's programming in their weekly schedules.

• On November 26, Penguin Group announces plans to acquire the Putnum Berkley Group in a merger that will represent 12 percent of the nation's book sales.

1997

• Two TV series about Boston law firms, *The Practice,* a drama, and *Ally McBeal,* a quirky comedy-drama, premiere.

• Sitcom star Ellen DeGeneres "outs" herself and thereby becomes the first openly lesbian woman to have her own TV series.

• On January 23, a North Carolina jury orders ABC to pay Food Lion supermarkets $5.5 million for a story on unsanitary conditions in food preparation areas. The case did not attack the truthfulness of the report, but charged fraud in the manner in which the reporters obtained their information. The judgment was later reduced to $315,000.

• On May 20, After a nine-year run on ABC, the successful sitcom *Roseanne,* starring "domestic goddess" Roseanne Barr, ends.

• On July 9, a new ratings system for TV programs is launched, revising and expanding the system already in use. A rating of the program's age-appropriateness must appear onscreen for fifteen seconds at the beginning of all broadcast network and cable programs, except for news and sports programs.

• On August 11, *The View,* a critically acclaimed talk show on ABC featuring Barbara Walters and four other high-powered women discussing the most important topics of the day, premieres.

• On November 10, MCI Communications, the second-largest long-distance phone company, agrees to merge with Worldcom for $43 billion, making the deal the largest merger in U.S. business history.

• On December 1, a U.S. District Judge rules that New York City Mayor Rudolph Giuliani must put ads mocking the mayor back on city buses. The ads had been yanked in November.

• On December 16, President Clinton signs the No Electronic Theft Act, which imposes criminal penalties on copyright violators who do not profit from their actions, into law.

1998

• Tina Brown resigns as editor of *The New Yorker,* in an unexpected event that shocks the publishing world.

• NBC agrees to pay $13 million per episode for the next three years for broadcast rights to the top-rated television series *ER.* The $850 million total payout is the highest price ever paid for a TV show.

• On January 5, Pope John Paul II honors media mogul Rupert Murdoch with a papal knighthood.

• On January 9, *People* owner Time Inc. launches *Teen People,* a new monthly aimed at teenagers.

• On January 17, Internet reporter Matt Drudge publishes the story of Clinton's alleged affair with White House intern Monica S. Lewinsky on-line in his infamous *Drudge Report,* scooping the traditional media.

• On January 21, broadcast and cable networks televise the Pope's visit to Cuba.

• On January 26, an African-American-owned weekly newspaper, the *Jackson* (Miss.) *Advocate,* is firebombed. The *Advocate* is known for its investigations and battles with local officials.

• On February 2, two paparazzi, Giles Harrison and Andrew O'Brien, are found guilty of misdemeanor false imprisonment stemming from a May run-in with Arnold Schwarzenegger and Maria Shriver.

• On February 20, the *Nashville Banner* ceases publication after 122 years.

• On February 27, the Virginia Supreme Court upholds the dismissal of a Virginia Tech administrator's defamation lawsuit against the school newspaper, the *Collegiate Times.*

• On March 3, *Time* magazine celebrates its 75th anniversary.

• On April 20, Associated Press celebrates its 150th anniversary.

• On November 2, twenty-four hundred unionized ABC employees walk off the job in New York, San Francisco, Los Angeles, Chicago, and Washington, D.C., in a dispute over health benefits.

1999

• On November 9, members of the Feminist Coalition on Public Broadcasting meet with PBS representatives to discuss the network's airing of an antifeminist series, particularly in the context of a PBS lineup that underrepresents women and people of color.

• On November 12, CBS resolves the contempt case of producer Mary Mapes, who was cited for contempt for failing to turn over unaired video of a Dan Rather interview with murder defendant Shawn Allen Berry. The interview aired on *60 Minutes II* on September 28.

• On December 20, *Time* magazine runs an exclusive story based on the content of homemade video tapes recorded by Eric Harris and Dylan Klebold in the weeks before they killed twelve Columbine High students, a teacher, and themselves.

Mr. Rogers' Neighborhood

Dear Mister Rogers, Does It Ever Rain in Your Neighborhood?

Letters

By: Fred Rogers

Date: 1996

Source: Rogers, Fred. *Dear Mister Rogers, Does It Ever Rain in Your Neighborhood?* New York: Penguin, 1996, 3–4, 38, 39–40.

Mister Rogers Talks With Parents

Nonfiction work

By: Fred Rogers and Barry Head

Date: 1983

Source: Rogers, Fred, and Barry Head. *Mister Rogers Talks With Parents.* New York: Berkley, 1983, 9, 10–11.

About the Author: Fred McFeely Rogers (1928–2002) grew up in Latrobe, Pennsylvania, and completed his bachelor's degree in music composition at Rollins College. While working at the NBC network in the early 1950s, Rogers was inspired to create a children's television show, which he produced at Pittsburgh's WQED public television station from 1953 to 1962. After earning a divinity degree from the Pittsburgh Theological Seminary and being ordained as a Presbyterian minister, Rogers returned to WQED with *Mr. Rogers' Neighborhood* in 1967. The longest-running children's show on television, over 700 episodes were aired to great critical acclaim over the next thirty-five years. ■

Introduction

In many respects the 1990s were a wonderful time in which to grow up. With the economy experiencing its longest-ever expansion and violent crime going down, most of the nation's children enjoyed more material goods as well as safer streets and schools. Yet the decade was marked by continuing anxiety over issues of parenthood and child-rearing. Parents worked longer hours in the 1990s than ever before, sometimes to pay for a larger home, extra minivan, or expensive after-school activities for their children, but other times simply to make ends meet. Although violent crime and drug use by young Americans were declining, a series of fatal school shootings in Jonesboro, Arkansas, Springfield, Oregon, and Columbine, Colorado made headlines throughout the decade.

Attempting to explain why many Americans were so anxious about their children's future in an age of plenty, many social critics blamed the media for the seemingly random acts of violence committed by younger Americans in the 1990s. In one fatal instance, a five-year-old Ohio boy set his trailer home on fire after seeing a similar act performed by the title characters of MTV's *Beavis and Butthead* cartoon show. The fire killed his two-year-old sister. Defenders of the show insisted that poor parental supervision was the primary cause of the accident, as the network only aired the program after 10:00 P.M. They also questioned the direct link between witnessing violence on a cartoon program and subsequently imitating the act in real life. The debate intensified after MTV began airing the *Jackass* program in 2000, which showed a series of health- and even death-defying stunts performed by its cast. The media immediately began reporting a rash of injuries due to adolescents and teenagers imitating the stunts they saw on the program, including lighting themselves on fire, jumping from moving vehicles, and running into walls.

Significance

In a decade of contentious discussions about the media's impact on childhood and parenting, one of the more reassuring voices came from Fred Rogers, who had been appearing on public television stations in episodes of *Mr. Rogers' Neighborhood* since 1967. Dressed in a cardigan sweater and speaking in deliberate, reassuring tones, Rogers addressed topics that included feeling sad over the loss of a pet, being afraid of the dark, and experiencing jealousy over the arrival of a new sibling or stepparent. Rogers also welcomed viewers into his "Neighborhood of Make Believe," where he played out sketches with puppet characters, all teaching something about friendship, good manners, respect, or other life lessons. In contrast to the bombardment of vivid images and sharp dialogue that predominated on most children's television shows on the commercial networks, *Mr. Rogers' Neighborhood* was an oasis of civility, reassurance, and character-building. At the time of Rogers' death in 2002, his show was the longest-running children's program on television.

Although the commercial networks failed to follow Rogers' approach, another public-television character, a giant purple dinosaur who appeared on *Barney and Friends,* became equally popular in the 1990s. Just as Mr. Rogers' sang his theme song, "Won't You Be My Neighbor?" at the beginning of every show, Barney's sing-along "I Love You, You Love Me" song became well

Mister Rogers poses on the set of his television show *Mister Rogers' Neighborhood* in 1996. AP/WIDE WORLD PHOTOS. REPRODUCED BY PERMISSION.

known to children and parents. The resurgence of traditional child-rearing values also propelled two of former Secretary of Education William J. Bennett's books onto the bestseller lists. In *The Book of Virtues* (1993) and *The Children's Book of Virtues* (1995) the conservative pundit called for a return to such enduring values as compassion, integrity, and respect. At the other end of the political spectrum, First Lady Hilary Rodham Clinton also had a best seller with *It Takes a Village, and Other Lessons Children Teach Us* (1996), which explored the importance of community-wide participation and support in raising America's next generation.

Primary Source

Dear Mr. Rogers, Does It Ever Rain in Your Neighborhood? [excerpt]

> **SYNOPSIS:** Fred Rogers published some of the letters he received from viewers, along with his responses, in 1996's *Dear Mr. Rogers, Does It Ever Rain in Your Neighborhood?* Careful to distinguish between the make-believe world of his show and the real-life concerns of his audience, Rogers used many of the exchanges to impart life lessons on topics ranging from friendship to responsibility to managing one's fears.

Dear Mister Rogers,

Are you for real? Are you under a mask or costume like Big Bird? Are you for real? Are you for real or not? My birthday wish is I want to know if you are for real.

Timmy, age 5

Dear Timmy,

. . . That's a good question. It's hard for children to understand what they see on television. I'm glad that you are a person who wonders about things and that you ask questions about what you're wondering. Asking questions is a good way to grow and learn!

You asked if I am a real person. I am a real person, just the way you are a real person. There are some things on television that aren't real—the cartoons and the monsters and scary things like that, but I'm a real person. Your television set is a special way that you can see the picture of me and hear my voice. I can't look out through the television set to see or hear my television friends, but I think about them whenever we make our television visits. . . .

Dear Mister Rogers,

Does it ever rain in your neighborhood?

Rebecca, age 4

Dear Rebecca,

Our television Neighborhood is set up inside, in a big room called a television studio. Of course, it doesn't rain inside, but we sometimes make it look like it's raining. It takes a lot of work to make it look like it's raining in the studio, and we don't do that very often. But once in a while we do. I like to talk with my television friends about different kinds of weather. I know it's not always a "beautiful day" outside, but I like to think we can make it a "beautiful day" inside because we enjoy having a television visit together. . . .

Dear Mister Rogers,

What is the purpose of feeding the fish every day? To demonstrate responsibility?

Meaghan, age 10

Dear Meaghan,

There are a few reasons why we feed the fish every day. First of all, when we feed the fish, we're showing that we "take care of" other living things, and being taken care of is something very important to children. They know they need grown-ups to provide them with food, like the fish in our tank need us to feed them. It does have a lot to do with responsibility, as you mentioned. I also like to watch anything that swims!

Primary Source

Mr. Rogers Talks With Parents [excerpt]

SYNOPSIS: In *Mister Rogers Talks With Parents,* published in 1983, Rogers uses his trademark non-threatening style to encourage parents to embrace parenthood despite all of their anxieties and doubts.

When I was starting out in television, that grand old character actor, Gabby Hayes, was hosting an afternoon film program at NBC in New York, where I had my first job. One day I asked him how he felt when he sat there talking to a huge audience of children. "Freddy," he told me, "I just think of one little buckaroo."

That's what I've been doing ever since on *Mister Rogers' Neighborhood*—imagining that I'm talking with one "television friend." And that's how I want to write this book—imagining that I'm writing it for one fellow parent.

By "parent" I don't mean just a biological parent, but rather anyone who has primary responsibility for the care of a young child or young children. One definition of parent is "a source from which other things are derived," and that's how I'd like to think of you—as a source from which a young child is deriving nourishment, shelter, character, and love. To provide all that is an enormous job. "You are special" is something I often say to my young television friend on *Mister Rogers' Neighborhood,* but parents are special, too. . . .

When young people tell me that they're going to "settle down and raise a family," as though it were the most natural thing in the world, I always feel some anxiety. Of course, in some ways it *is* the most natural thing in the world, but I long to be able to give them at least an inkling of what lies ahead—not so much to warn them of difficulties, but to prepare them a little for the new growth tasks they are undertaking for themselves. I'd like them to be able, at least, to sense the depth and intensity of parenting. But even that doesn't seem possible to get across, any more than conveying our complex feelings when we catch our aging reflections in a store window. It's only if you've "been there" that you'll know what I mean. *Essentially parenthood is not learned: Parenthood is an inner change.*

Often we may be tempted to say to our children, "You're just too young to understand!" as though there were something deficient about being young. We might do better to say, "You just see it differently at your age than I do at mine." We have all been chil-

"Won't You Be My Neighbor?"

It's a beautiful day in this neighborhood,
A beautiful day for a neighbor.
Would you be mine?
Could you be mine?

It's a neighborly day in this beauty wood,
A neighborly day for a beauty.
Would you be mine?
Could you be mine?

I've always wanted to have a neighbor just like
you.
I've always wanted to live in a neighborhood
with you.

So, let's make the most of this beautiful day.
Since we're together we might as well say:
Would you be mine?
Could you be mine?
Won't you be my neighbor?
Won't you please,
Won't you please?
Please won't you be my neighbor?

SOURCE: Fred M. Rogers. "Won't You Be My Neighbor?" Family Communications, Inc., 1967. Available online at http://www.mister-rogers.org/mister_rogers_neighborhood/be_my_neighbhor.asp (accessed March 12, 2003).

dren and have had children's feelings . . . but many of us have forgotten. It's not our fault, but we *have* forgotten. We've forgotten what it's like not to be able to reach the light switch. We've forgotten a lot of the monsters that seemed to live in our room at night. Nevertheless, those memories are still there, somewhere inside us, and can sometimes be brought to the surface by events, sights, sounds, or smells. Children, though, can never have grown-up feelings until they've been allowed to do the growing.

Feelings *are* closely tied to age, and that's one reason for the so-called generation gap. The best and surest bridge across the gap is trust. In fact, sometimes trust may be the only possible bridge. We need to trust that our children's feelings are honest and true for their particular age, and we need to help them learn that ours are honest and true, too.

Further Resources

BOOKS

Collins, Mark and Margaret Mary Kimmel, eds. *Mister Rogers' Neighborhood: Children, Television, and Fred Rogers.* Pittsburgh: University of Pittsburgh Press, 1996.

Gunter, Barrie and Jill McAleer. *Children and Television.* New York: Routledge, 1997.

Hollis, Tim. *Hi There, Boys and Girls!: America's Local Children's TV Programs.* Jackson: University of Mississippi Press, 2001.

Rogers, Fred. *You Are Special: Words of Wisdom for All Ages from a Beloved Neighbor.* Reprint, New York: Penguin Books, 1995.

PERIODICALS

McCormick, John. "Where Are the Parents?" *Newsweek,* Fall/Winter 1990: 54–58.

WEBSITES

"Brilliant Careers: Fred Rogers." Available online at http://www.salon.com/people/bc/1999/08/10/rogers/; website home page: http://www.salon.com (accessed March 11, 2003).

"Fred Rogers' Biography." Available online at http://www.misterrogers.org/mister_rogers_neighborhood/biography.asp; website home page: http://www.mistrerrogers.org (accessed March 12, 2003).

"Mister Rogers' Neighborhood." Available online at http://pbskids.org/rogers/ (accessed March 11, 2003).

"The Real 'Mister Rogers'." Available online at http://www.pcusa.org/pcusa/today/features/feat9803a.htm (accessed March 11, 2003).

"The Art World & I Go On Line"

Magazine article

By: Robert Atkins

Date: December 1995

Source: Atkins, Robert. "The Art World & I Go On Line." *Art in America* 83, no. 12, December 1995, 58–59, 63.

About the Author: Robert Atkins is the author of *ArtSpoke: A Guide to Modern Ideas, Movements and Buzzwords (1848–1944)* and *ArtSpeak: A Guide to Contemporary Ideas, Movements and Buzzwords 1945 to the Present.* He is an art historian, curator, writer, and editor. Atkins created the first online journal about online art, *TalkBack! A Forum for Critical Inquiry,* in 1995. He has also written widely about AIDS. ■

Introduction

The increasing use and availability of the Internet and the World Wide Web changed the way people communicated and accessed information. In the early 1990s, browsers and websites that would seem primitive even a few years later began to proliferate. The Web became a relatively easy and inexpensive medium for displaying information. As technology improved, so did the websites.

In the pre–1990 world, art could often only be viewed in galleries or museums. Seeing a painting or a sculpture required going to the gallery or museum. Pho-tographs in catalogs or art books provided some access points, but unknown or beginning artists often did not appear in these works. With the Internet's growth, online art became available for viewers. While the experience is not the same, the Internet provides exposure to artists and works that may have gone unnoticed in the traditional world of art.

As an art historian and critic, Robert Atkins provides an insider's view of the quality of art and the accessibility of art on the Internet. His observations center on what was online as well as who was online. In an update to the article evaluating the 1994–1995 season, when he claims the "art world & I" went online, he discusses the commercial aspects of the online art world in 1997–1998. Taken together, the fluid nature of the Internet could be seen. Changes in language and in how we talk about art online are other important aspects of Atkins' work and of the work that appeared on the Internet.

Significance

Robert Atkins surveys the 1994–1995 season of artistic works on the Internet. His exploration, as a personal journal, provides an overview of what was online and how easy it was to locate.

Online artwork presented different pros and cons than online text. The quality of the reproduction was one issue that those displaying artwork through an Internet site had to bear in mind. Quality of the image or of the browser could change the way the artwork looked. There were several positive factors for displaying artwork online, and Atkins highlights them in his journal discussions. One of the significant factors in the growth of the World Wide Web was the exposure that an unknown artist could get through a website. Creating a website was relatively easy, as was scanning artwork into a site or creating artwork that was a digital medium. There was also a downside to Internet exhibitions of art. The experience of viewing art often depended upon the materials used and the details of a painting or other art form. On the Internet, the tactile and visual aspects of art were not always as clear as they could be in person. The technology of 1994–1995, however, was much more primitive than it was even a few years later. With the advances in technology, art could be viewed as a three-dimensional object. Sound and animation could be added to a website. And details could be viewed in a painting in ways that they could not be viewed in an art museum or gallery, because Internet illustrations could focus on certain sections of a painting.

In the early twenty-first century, frustrations remained with art on the World Wide Web. Searching for information on the Internet remained a problem. Key words in online search engines did not always yield expected results. Museum sites had carved out a presence on the Internet, however. These sites were often more than directories and information, providing guides to artists' works, online exhibitions that were valuable educational tools, and links to other sources. As the Internet continued to grow, the art world continued to develop its place in cyberspace.

Primary Source

"The Art World & I Go On Line" [excerpt]

SYNOPSIS: Through a series of journal entries, Robert Atkins relays how he has discovered the growing world of art, galleries, and museums online. The advent of the Internet has caused communities to change and has allowed artists who may have barely been known to exhibit their work for wider audiences.

Future art historians will mark the 1994–95 season as the year the art world went on line. Art buffs with the requisite computer-and-modem hardware and Internet access could discuss the Whitney Biennial and Lacanian theory, inspect an international array of museum schedules search the *International Repertory of the Literature of Art* (RILA), and peruse auction prices from Sotheby's and Christie's. They could also view art works—some for sale and others designed for electronic, interactive formats—by artists ranging from paleolithic daubers to Laurie Anderson.

The advent of this brave new electronic art world coincided, of course, with the emergence of a vast and rapidly expanding electronic communication network in society at large. By last summer, some eight percent of American households were on line, most via commercial services such as America Online, Prodigy and CompuServe. Computer-equipped consumers could preview Sony's current film offerings, read—and discuss—Noam Chomsky's articles and monitor Congress, Socks (the White House cat), the Cannes Film Festival or the O.J. Simpson trial through transcripts updated daily on Time-Warner's *Pathfinder* site. Corporations, institutions and individuals have established approximately 300,000 Internet outposts since mid-1993. (Although the Defense Department-initiated Internet has been on line since 1969, until recently it has been used mostly by researchers.) The majority of the new sites are on the World Wide Web (WWW), a portion of the Internet built on hypertext technology and the closest thing yet to that ill-defined "Information Superhighway." The astonishing rapidity of this information explosion has been matched only by the media-driven hype surrounding it.

During the past year, hardly a day has gone by without the major dailies running breathless coverage of some aspect of the Internet. In the midst of a flood of books on the subject, *Being Digital,* Nicholas Negroponte's stimulating collection of columns from *Wired* magazine, turned out to be a huge best-seller. The enthusiasm of the *Wired* crowd was carried to a hyperbolic extreme by the magazine's founder and publisher, Louis Rossetto. "I thought there was a revolution going on more powerful than any political revolution," he recalled in an Apr. 11 lecture at the New York Public Library. Is it any wonder that such hype has spawned a backlash? This perhaps inevitable phenomenon came in the form of recent books like Clifford Stoll's *Silicon Snake Oil* and Kirkpatrick Sale's *Rebels Against the Future: The Luddites and Their War on the Industrial Revolution.* On Apr. 26, the FBI released a letter by the "Unabomber," the mail-bomb terrorist(s), that dramatically underscored such criticism: "If you had any brains," he wrote, "you would have realized that there are a lot of people out there who resent bitterly the way techno-nerds like you are changing the world." As Sale observed, the apt connection here is not to information-age haves and have-nots, but to the early-19th-century Luddites who mounted attacks on English factories and machines because they feared that industrialization would impair their livelihoods and culture.

The new communications technology has already significantly affected museums and libraries. Will it also revolutionize the *production* of art? As software mogul and art collector Peter Norton observed at a packed gathering of the American Section of the International Association of Art Critics at the Museum of Modern Art on Apr. 10. "We're at a crossroads. It's our job as critical thinkers to assess what's good and bad . . . in the new kinds of speech like multimedia and e-mail."

My notes from that meeting bear two scrawled comments: "Remind S never to let anyone publish my e-mail" and "Weren't we all going to become TV producers—rather than consumers—after Nam June Paik introduced us to affordable video cameras?" Some anthropologists would argue that the history of technology *is* the history of humankind and that the essential questions about technology simply recur, rather than change. The appropriate art analogy may be that much of the most effective electronic art can, in fact, only be understood within the *tradition*

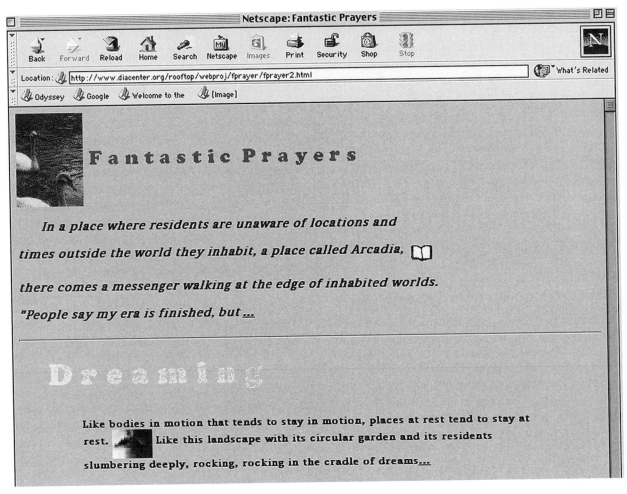

Fantastic Prayers, website by Constance De Jong, Tony Oursler, and Stephen Vitiello, 1995. The artists created the web project for the Dia Art Foundation's then brand new web site which launched March 31, 1995. CONSTANCE DE JONG, TONY OURSLER, AND STEPHEN VITIELLO, FANTASTIC PRAYERS. HTTP://WWW.DIAART.ORG/ROOFTOP/WEBPROJ/FPRAYER/FPRAYER.HTML, 1995. PUBLISHED AND PRODUCED BY DIA ART FOUNDATION. © DIA ART FOUNDATION.

of information-oriented conceptual, media and video art that emerged during the 1960s and '70s. Even in these ahistorical times, we all know that the Renaissance did not spring full-blown from Giotto's head.

The 1994–95 season was also the season I went on line. What follows is an account, partly in diary form, of my experiences from my first extended exposure to bulletin boards and on-line art works last fall to my decision at the end of the season to order the (expensive) hardware necessary to upgrade my system for Net "surfing" at home. I also stress the subjectivity of this report because no single individual could partake of more than a tiny percentage of the available on-line art and art discourse. In this article, I will discuss only a fraction of what I've seen on line this year.

According to Timothy Druckrey, co-editor of the invaluable anthology *Culture on the Brink: Ideologies*

of Technology, more than 5,000 artists have staked out sites on the Internet. Likewise, every large city offers several local electronic bulletin boards that compete with the corporate giants' services. Some of them host art conferences; most provide access to newsgroups—noncommercial forums on the Internet, some of them art-related. To call this array of choices staggering is a gross understatement—even if, as with the cornucopia of programming offered by cable television, most of it warrants only a passing glance.

Consider this article my preliminary notes for a guide to the exploding online art world. I also discuss some of the social and political forces—such as the increasing tendency to censor electronic communication—that are shaping the emerging media. A note about the article's format: The diary entries that follow are in italic type, while commentary that chronologically extends those entries to include related developments throughout the 1994–95 season is printed in roman type. . . .

Oct. 20: Bulletin Board Chat Fest

Today I went on line with Echo—the self-styled hip, arts-oriented New York bulletin board and on-line service provider—and began to monitor the conferences run by sponsors like the Village Voice *and the Whitney Museum of American Art. (Echo can be reached at (212) 292–0900; for those with a computer and modem, Echo's log-on number is (212) 292–0910—type "newuser." Echo's Web site is: http://www.echonyc.com.) The Whitney is the second museum to host an ongoing conference on a bulletin board. (The Smithsonian's conference on America Online has been around longer.) Museum curators and guests occasionally log on for real-time chat events, but the conference mostly provides ongoing bulletin-board style discussions on such topics as "Artspeak from Hell," "My Favorite Works of Art" and "The Biennial."*

I discovered that one can initially read months of old postings and then decide whether or not to add to the "conversation." Unfortunately, the discussion is almost invariably pretty unfocused, and too reminiscent of all-night, college bull sessions. The Whitney's "Art Critics" discussion-topic, for instance, began in mid-1994 with these posted comments:

Tetsuwan Nemo: Why isn't everyone a critic?

KZ: I thought everyone was.

Neandergal: I usually like reading any kind of criticism more than experiencing the actual "thing" whether it's a book, movie, painting etc. That's why I spend all my time on Echo instead of reading books. . . . It's all commentary and you never have to feel anything.

Ironically, of the entire 15-or-so months of postings I perused, these first comments seem most representative—and salient.

■ ■ ■

One problem with the BBS (bulletin board service) format—which allows users to post messages and conduct on-line "discussions"—derives from its unnuanced quality vis-à-vis spoken conversation. (Just how much irony *did* Neandergal intend to communicate?) Another difficulty is anonymity. Vast numbers of bulletin board and Internet users employ "tags" or "handles." Many users find this elective role-play liberating and have referred to the intimacy-

inducing quality of such exchanges. But I remain dubious about the state of intimacy in our televison- and radio-talk-show-ridden culture. What can intimacy mean when it's cloaked in anonymity?

This week I also started to monitor The Thing, which may be the oldest visual-art bulletin board in the country and certainly provides the most challenging level of posted art discourse—or on-line chat—of any I've encountered. (The Thing can be reached at 212–604–0698; its log-on number is 212–366–1199.) The Thing's several hundred subscribers sometimes passionately debate cultural and critical theory. (Users from branches—or nodes—in London, Geneva, Düsseldorf, Cologne and Vienna can also join the conversation.) Its conferencing areas are augmented with files of images and essays, access to such publications as the Journal of Contemporary Art, *and frequently changing exhibitions and artworks.*

During the 1994–95 season, the range of The Thing's on-line art extended from James Nares's swirl-art-evoking prints to David Platzker's quicktime movies of artist's books by John Baldessari, which were simultaneously on view under glass at Printed Matter. I found the former seductively eye-popping; the latter—though crudely produced—provided a welcome look at the artist's classic, two-decade-old works. Thing projects are also exhibited on its Web site at http://www.thing.net/thingnye.

Two years ago, I asked artist Wolfgang Staehle—one of the founders of the nonprofit bulletin board—whether or not the four-year-old enterprise constituted his art. He adamantly denied it. Now it's the New York resident's full-time creative work and another "social sculpture"; it also brings to mind the salon-style talk-fests that Tom Maroni has been hosting for two decades at his Museum of Conceptual Art in San Francisco. In the face of mounting competition from corporate on-line services, boutique boards like The Thing are the Mom-and-Pop-store Davids battling the chain-store Goliaths. Staehle is currently scrambling to broaden his audience by providing subscribers with full on-line services and Internet access.

Nov. 8: The World's First Collaborative Sentence

Douglas Davis opened his exhibition InterActions 1967–1981 *at the Lehman College Art Gallery in the Bronx. (He co-directs the college's Center for Long Distance Art and Culture with gallery director Susan Hoeltzel.) Davis has long pioneered the creation of interactive performances and installations that humanize technology by revealing the desire embodied in cold steel and cathode rays. He's exhorted viewers* to reach up and press their hands (and other body parts) against video monitors, and he produced the first global satellite performance in 1977. In the exhibition, the documentation of such activities, and the presentation of related art works, demonstrated the continuity of his output.

At the opening of his show, he presented an on-line performance called Discours Amoureux, *which was a scripted dialogue with Russian artist Nathalie Novarina, who responded on a computer in Galerie St. Gervais in Geneva. Their elliptical, bilingual discussion of the nature of love was carried live on Echo.*

■■■

In December, Davis inaugurated a Web site through the center's server or host computer (http://math240.lehman.cuny.edu/art). The title says it all: *The World's First (and probably longest) Collaborative Sentence.* As of September, more than 50,000 collaborators had left their mark on this text. Thirty or so lines into it some one wrote: "who do we think we are James Joyce's great grandchildren" and someone else responded "or some kind of gertrude"; *The Sentence* is a surprising, often amusing work that makes ingeniously simple (and cheap) use of the hypertext medium Davis recently presented the piece in gallery format a Korea's Kwangju Biennale. A first: in the spring of 1995, shortly before his untimely death, New York mega-collector Eugene Schwartz purchased *The Sentence* for "what dinner for eight would cost at decent restaurant."

Jan. 9, 1995: Virtual Museums . . .

Unfortunately, most museums seem to regard their Internet outposts mainly as vehicles for the dissemination of publicity and programming information, rather than education or viewer interaction. At the critics' panel at MOMA on Apr. 10, Dia Center for the Arts director Michael Govan noted that Dia's primary motive for establishing its site (http://www.diacenter.org) was to more efficiently spread the word about Dia programs to an international audience. This should probably come as no surprise in an era when nearly every museum's publicity director has been renamed "director of communications." (The Dia site features Tony Oursler's and Constance de Jong's *Fantastic Prayers* performance, but its fragmented video clips and performance stills don't add up to much.)

Even the Whitney, under the direction of new-media aficionado David Ross, offers little innovative programming on its Web branch (http://www.echo

nyc.com/∼whitney). At its best, it presents an irresistible artist's project by Conceptualist and former California gubernatorial candidate Lowell Darling culled from his Hollywood Archaeology archive of enigmatic found photos. (The text-and-image amalgams of photo-conceptualism are perfectly suited to digital reproduction.) At its worst, the museum succumbs to the prevailing lust for visibility by soliciting users to click onto the Whitney's Web site from *The File Room*'s guestbook—normally a place for comments. (No permissions are required for creating this sort of interactivity.) Instead of confronting its own record on censorship—every museum has one—the Whitney simply offered a side trip to its site.

The most stimulating exception to the U.S. museum world's lack of imagination in Internet programming is the interactive examination in text form of the ethics of bioengineering (http://www.exploratorium.edu/) which complemented the "Diving Into the Gene Pool" exhibition (it closed on Sept. 4) at the Exploratorium—San Francisco's museum of hands-on science and art.

If an on-line model for American museums exists, it is the program at the state-supported French museums. These well-financed institutions have collectively staked out a more sophisticated Internet presence than any of their counterparts throughout the world. The constantly expanding Louvre site (http://www.louvre.fr/louvre/francais/musee) offers images of works from the collection, floor plans of the museum and historical information, as well as a list of current exhibitions. Even so, the most conceptually and visually rewarding World Wide Web site to appear this year is the French Ministry of Culture's showcase for the Paleolithic cave paintings found in the Ardèche. The caves were discovered last Christmas and the Web site—with four gorgeous reproductions from the closed-to-the-public caves—was up less than two months later (http://dmf.culture.fr/culture/gvpda-en.html).

Ironically, while American museums' education, publication, conservation and communications departments have already, in many cases, gone digital, few contemporary-art curators have shown electronic—much less on-line—art works. Interested individuals like former New Museum curator Laura Trippi or the San Francisco Museum of Modern Art's Robert Riley have already presented digital-format works with on-line components, but they seem wary of placing computer terminals in museum galleries. By contrast, Karlsruhe, Germany, is completing an art and media-technology center (Zentrum für Kunst und Medientechnologie) that will include a museum devoted primarily to video- and electronic art of the past 25 years. (Its Web site is located at http://www.uni-karlsruhe.de/zkm/).

Further Resources

BOOKS

Bender, Gretchen, and Timothy Druckrey. *Culture on the Brink: Ideologies of Technology.* Seattle: Bay Press, 1994.

Jones, Lois Swan. *Art Information and the Internet: How to Find It, How to Use It.* Phoenix: Oryx Press, 1999.

Negroponte. Nicholas. *Being Digital.* New York: Knopf, 1995.

PERIODICALS

Atkins, Robert. "State of the (on–line) art." *Art in America* 87, no.4, April 1999, 89–95.

Sarraf, Suzanne. "A Survey of Museums on the Web: Who Uses Museum Websites?" *Curator* 42, no. 3, July 1999, 231–243.

WEBSITES

artnet. Available online at http://www.artnet.com/index.asp ?N=1 (accessed June 17, 2003).

"Hypocrisy Rules the Airwaves"

Newspaper article

By: Joe Saltzman

Date: March 1996

Source: Saltzman, Joe. "Hypocrisy Rules the Airwaves." *USA Today* 124, March 1996, 77.

About the Author: Joe Saltzman (1939–) is a professor of journalism at the University of Southern California's Annenberg School for Communications. Saltzman was also an award-winning broadcast journalist. His main research interest is the image of journalists in the media and how these images influence the American public. ■

Introduction

Talk radio shows originated in the 1930s. The shows of the 1930s through the 1950s were very different from those of the early twenty-first century, however. The talk radio shows of the first half of the twentieth century were scripted. The producers and the hosts knew what was going to be said. In the 1960s this began to change. The first true talk radio station was KABC in Los Angeles, followed by KGO in San Francisco. The number of talk radio stations grew to roughly 860 stations by 1994. Talk radio had become more improvisational in nature, and the format included interviews.

Larry King's overnight radio show was one of the most popular of the new breed. King interviewed guests and then opened the lines for callers to chat with him during the overnight hours. Rush Limbaugh joined the ranks of radio talk shows in 1988. He was credited "with the universal acceptance by the audience of the term host to describe a radio talk jockey." This is an important fact in talk radio, because ultra-conservative Limbaugh's views were seen as entertainment.

Another part of the radio talk mix was Howard Stern. Stern, and hosts like him, were known as "shock jocks." They would say anything that came to mind on the air. Unlike King and Limbaugh, Stern's radio show aired on rock music stations. Stern was conversational, uninhibited, and controversial.

Significance

Howard Stern's troubles centered around his use of language. Joe Saltzman compared the way Jerry Seinfeld and Stern used language to discuss similar topics. The same words that viewers thought were funny coming out of Seinfeld's mouth were offensive from Stern. There was more to consider than just the word that was used, however. The context and the intent behind the language were what incited ire over Howard Stern's language and may have prevented listeners from defending him. Also, while they may have talked about the same topics, Seinfeld usually used a euphemism rather than being blatantly honest, as Stern was.

It was difficult to explain what attracted people to Howard Stern's raunchy, rude remarks. Saltzman claimed that Stern's excellent interviewing skills and his brutal honesty were the keys to his success. Stern "refuses to take responsibility for his influence on the audience," saying that they could change the channel if they didn't like his views. *Time* magazine wrote that "Stern's national success is an entirely new phenomenon in radio. . . . Stern is the first to dominate morning drive time from coast to coast with what is essentially a transplanted local program." The time of day may have been a factor in the battles over Stern's radio program. Complaints waged that children were in the audience and that the remarks were inappropriate for them to hear. Stern and his company, Infinity Broadcasting, disagreed. The target audience for Stern's show was the 25- to 54-year-old male listener.

Howard Stern's indecent remarks on the nation's radio stations resulted in a number of complaints being filed with the Federal Communications Commission (FCC), the governmental agency overseeing broadcasting. Stern and his employer claimed that he never used the "seven dirty words" prohibited by the FCC. Nonetheless, Infinity Broadcasting paid $1.7 million in fines in 1995 over Stern's on-air remarks. An analyst said, "Stern brings in many times over what he might cost in attorneys' fees."

Radio jockey Howard Stern was fined for using language deemed indecent by the Federal Communications Commission (FCC). AP/WIDE WORLD PHOTOS. REPRODUCED BY PERMISSION.

Primary Source

"Hypocrisy Rules the Airwaves"

> **SYNOPSIS:** Saltzman compared the topics that Jerry Seinfeld and Howard Stern used in their programs. Seinfeld, the comic who played himself on a successful television show, and Stern, the shock jock radio personality, talked about similar things. Seinfeld got away with his antics, while Stern was fined by the FCC for indecency. The difference was in the language they used.

Television comic Jerry Seinfeld can do nothing wrong. He and his cohorts can discuss sexual intercourse, masturbation, bodily functions, male and female sex organs, impotence, homosexuality, birth control methods, and the like. Yet, America and its media love him and millions watch his program.

Radio comic Howard Stern can do nothing right. He and his cohorts discuss sexual intercourse, masturbation, bodily functions, male and female sex organs, impotence, homosexuality, birth control methods, and the like. Yet, America and its media hate him even though millions listen to his program.

What's going on here? One explanation might be that Seinfeld comes up with cute euphemisms

such as "master of your domain" (for masturbation) and Stern simply uses street language familiar to almost every American. But older people consider this kind of everyday language impolite and even dangerous when broadcast on the airwaves because it might influence children. Using such language is not a proper way to behave.

Another explanation might be that Seinfeld and friends look safe. They are the kinds of people most white Americans wouldn't mind meeting at a party. They are not only funny, but also nice. Stern is everyone's nightmare. He and his cohorts are the kind of people most Americans try to avoid. They may be funny, but they are likely to be naughty, even "dangerous."

Most of those who rave about Seinfeld watch his program. Most people who rant about Stern haven't actually listened to his radio show.

The perception of Stern changes if you are familiar with his work. Those who listen to him regularly know that he may be the best interviewer, especially of celebrities, in the history of the medium. He asks the sort of questions most listeners would ask if they had the opportunity and the guts to do so. Stern also can be very funny. When on a successful riff, his improvised comments are hilarious.

It is true that Stern is overly preoccupied with scatological material, that he can be especially cruel when berating his staff or complaining about his station's facilities, and that occasionally he is unbearably crude and offensive, but so are many Americans when they get together informally. The language Stern uses as well as the offensive bodily sounds he casually refers to on the air are not alien to the majority of men and women, especially teenagers and college students.

The real reason so many Americans may be worried about Stern is his brutal honesty. No one is so blunt, so uncompromising, and so candid with his audience, whether it involves a freedom of speech issue, a political controversy, or his daily toilet habits. Whatever floats into Stern's mind goes onto the airwaves.

Stern also is paired with Robin Quivers, whose infectious laugh is one of the best reasons for getting a daily dose of Stern. Many Americans are still frightened when confronted with a sharp-tongued African-American woman who is not afraid to say in strong language what is on her mind. Quivers, like Stern and many of his other on-air pals, is quite unlike the usual Seinfeld "Friends" clones who populate the airwaves. And different is scary to many Americans.

Comedian Lenny Bruce also was different, brutally honest, and scary. When he was alive, he was hounded by members of the media, law enforcement agencies, and the courts. After he died, he was lionized by many in the entertainment business and politics who were silent during the many years he was harassed off the stage. One of the saddest moments in show-biz history was when Bruce took to the nightclub stage to read from transcripts of his legal battles, and few bothered to stay around to listen.

Stern now is being persecuted by the same kind of minds who hounded Bruce, but since his venue is radio, it is the Federal Communications Commission that is doing the dirty work. Again, most of those in the entertainment and political communities are looking the other way. Just for talking about nothing more than what Seinfeld and friends discuss weekly, Stern was cited for more than 100 claims of indecency by a vengeful FCC.

Stern vowed to fight forever, but Infinity Broadcasting Corp. of New York, Stern's employer, recently caved in and paid the startling sum of $1,700,000 to resolve all pending FCC actions against the company. It was the largest settlement of its kind. More than that, it proved that the government could pursue an individual selectively. It could pick and choose a specific media personality and try to force him off the air. If Stern weren't as popular as he is, the FCC would have been successful in hounding him off radio. It's all a matter of money. One reason Infinity finally settled was that the government was dragging its feet in approving Infinity's past purchases of radio stations and Infinity wanted the government off its back. An angry Stern can console himself by looking at his bulging bank account. It's the rest of us who should be worried.

Stern is immodest and indelicate, bawdy and crude, but he speaks to something important in the American experience and, like Bruce, he reveals much about us that is important. Yet, few have defended Stern or attacked the FCC action. Many affluent and influential Americans who listen to Stern daily refuse to get involved. Instead of a collective shout over this injustice, the nation goes about its business as if nothing much has happened.

If the FCC had gone after NBC and Seinfeld instead, the hue and cry would have been deafening. Because Howard Stern is offensive to some, however, everyone caves in and lets it pass. But like Howard Stern or not, his battle with the FCC has repercussions for all Americans. Selective persecution by the government in any area of life is odious. It is especially frightening when it happens to someone who simply says on the airwaves, albeit in a much more amusing manner, what most Americans routinely say and do in their homes every day.

Further Resources

BOOKS

Allen, Steve. *Vulgarians at the Gate: Trash TV and Rauch Radio, Raising the Standards of Popular Culture.* Amherst, N.Y.: Prometheus Books, 2001.

Hilliard, Robert L., and Michael C. Keith. *Waves of Rancor: Tuning in the Radical Right.* Armonk, N.Y.: M.E. Sharpe, 1999.

Laufer, Peter. *Inside Talk Radio: America's Voice or Just Hot Air?* New York: Birch Lane Press, 1995.

PERIODICALS

Kim, Jeanhee. "You Can't Shut Up Howard Stern, but You Can Profit From Him." *Money,* August 1995, 52.

McConnell, Chris. "Radio Indecency Complaints on Front Burner at FCC." *Broadcasting & Cable.* October 7, 1996, 62–63.

"Shock Jock." *Time,* November 30, 1992, 72.

WEBSITES

Federal Communications Commission. Available online at http://www.fcc.gov/ (accessed June 17, 2003).

"The Next Big Thing: A Bookstore?"

Magazine article

By: Michael H. Martin
Date: December 9, 1996
Source: Martin, Michael H. "The Next Big Thing: A Bookstore?" *Fortune* 134, December 9, 1996, 168–170. ■

Introduction

Most people bought books in traditional, brick-and-mortar stores before the growth of the Internet. Prior to the 1990s there were chain bookstores; however, most bookstores were small and locally owned. Many publishers were also small or independently owned prior to the 1990s. As the Internet grew and as business practices changed, the world of bookselling also changed.

Publishing changed during the 1990s with mergers of smaller independents and with large companies. For example, the German company Bertelsmann bought the larger publisher Random House. As the publishers began being purchased, the competition of bookselling narrowed.

Bookstores were slow to join the e-commerce and dot.com movement at first. Customers retained loyalty to their independent stores. As the Internet grew and as technology developed, many predicted the book would become a thing of the past. This has not happened, however. Bookstore chains Barnes & Noble and Borders have built megastores throughout the country that draw customers. Online bookstores and publishers have attracted customers, but the draw of reading books on the Web has not grown as quickly as predicted.

This was all changed by Amazon.com in 1995. With deep discounts and fast service, Jeff Bezos created not only an online bookstore, but also a revolution in the way people buy and search for books. Bezos's company was able to offer a broad selection because of agreements with book distributors and because of low overhead costs. These factors drew customers and sales.

Significance

In 1994 Jeff Bezos changed the world of bookselling forever. He created the first, and at the time the largest, online bookseller in the world. Amazon.com sold its first book in July 1995. Bezos's business sense was the key to Amazon.com's success. He began with deep discounts, a few employees in a garage, no overhead, and no large warehouses to pay for. The most important thing Bezos did was build brand loyalty, however. Amazon encouraged users to write reviews of the books and participate in the site, building a community. By making the customer part of the site and the product, Bezos began attracting return business. This began to make the bricks-and-mortar bookstores nervous and, thus, brought more booksellers online.

Bezos told Bernhard Warner, "Amazon has come to represent service and selection." The business grew into more than a bookseller after it began in 1995. Amazon.com later sold music, videos, toys, and household goods. The company expanded to include auctions and used books and goods as well.

As significant as Amazon.com's success was, their success at drawing other booksellers onto the Web to gain a piece of the e-commerce was just as important. Borders, Barnes & Noble, and Portland, Oregon-based Powell's Books all joined the electronic market, as did many other startup companies. Many independent bookstores also maintained a presence online with ordering capabilities through larger sites like Booksense. The competition caused the various booksellers, including Amazon.com, to carve out a niche. For example, Powell's specialized in hard-to-find books and delivered them at lower shipping costs than some other booksellers.

The way that consumers purchased items and the way that companies delivered goods changed with the growth of the Internet. Jeff Bezos and Amazon.com were part of this change.

Primary Source

"The Next Big Thing: A Bookstore?"

SYNOPSIS: Amazon.com grew from a garage-based business in 1995 to a multimillion-dollar international company by the early twenty-first century. The company, which was a dream of Jeff Bezos in 1994, drew attention as it grew and forced traditional booksellers to rethink book marketing. While Amazon.com was not always popular with people in the book business, it became a success.

Amazon.com is leading a wave of digital shops out to invade established industries. They need no bricks and mortar, and they speak directly to their customers—these upstarts have a shot.

Back in 1994, Jeff Bezos was a young senior vice president on the rise at a thriving Wall Street hedge fund. But when the explosive growth of the World Wide Web caught his eye, he saw an even bigger opportunity: online commerce. Two years later Bezos, CEO of the Internet bookstore Amazon.com, is one of a crew of young entrepreneurs using cyberspace technology to steal real-world customers from traditional businesses with strong consumer and industrial franchises.

How can a small player establish a beachhead in industries as entrenched as publishing, insurance, stock trading, and Yellow Pages advertising? Start with the fact that digital businesses need little real estate. Add the power of interactive Web pages and E-mail, which provide direct links with customers. The combination is potent: In recent years, BigBook, in San Francisco, has started taking a slice of the $11-billion-a-year yellow-pages market that's dominated by the Baby Bells; PCOrder, in Austin, Texas, offers a way to buy custom-designed computers over the Web; E*Trade, in Palo Alto, California, provides online stock-trading at discounts that undercut even Olde and Schwab. None of these outfits are profitable yet. But as they win loyal customers, they are creating models of how to use the Web to challenge much larger rivals.

Of all the Web upstarts, Bezos's is the one the others are watching. Back in 1994, he considered getting into some of those other businesses. He drew up a list of 20 products that he figured could be sold online—including books, music, magazines, and PC hardware and software. After narrowing the list to books and music, Bezos settled on books for two reasons. First, there are more to sell (about 1.3 million books in print, vs. 300,000 music titles). Second, the goliaths of publishing seemed less imposing. While six major record companies dominate music, Bezos says, "there are no 800-pound gorillas in book publishing or distribution." The biggest chain—Barnes & Noble—accounts for under 12% of the industry's $25 billion in annual sales.

Carpe diem! Bezos quit his job, packed his belongings, and informed the movers that he'd call when he'd chosen among Colorado, Oregon, or Washington. His wife, MacKenzie, handled the driving westward while Jeff rode shotgun, pounding out a business plan on a laptop and rounding up seed capital via his cellular phone. He chose the Seattle area because of its proximity to both high-tech talent and a major book distributor, Ingram's warehouse in Roseburg, Oregon. He and MacKenzie rented a suburban house; even before their furniture caught up with them, Bezos and his first four employees had set up computers in the garage, where they started writing the software that would make Amazon.com work.

He decided to call the company Cadabra, but friends thought it sounded like "cadaver." So he opted for Amazon, after the world's largest river—the idea being that the company would carry many times more books than conventional stores. Bezos sold his first book in July 1995.

Amazon.com is truly virtual. Though it has become a multimillion-dollar business that employs 110, there's still no storefront and little inventory. Customers connect via Amazon's Website, where they can search a database of 1.1 million books by title, author, subject, or keyword. If they find a book they want to buy, they use online forms to specify hardcover or paperback, gift wrapping, and mode of shipment. Payment is by credit card, submitted via telephone or via the Web—the transaction is safeguarded by encryption.

Orders in hand, Amazon requests books from a distributor or publisher, which delivers them to the company's Seattle warehouse. The order is then packed and shipped. On average, customers get books five days after ordering—pay extra, and they speed the process by a day or two.

Employees at Amazon.com prepare orders in 1999. Since selling its first book in 1995, the company has greatly expanded its services. In addition to books, it sells products ranging from appliances to cars. © DAVID SAMUEL/CORBIS SYGMA. REPRODUCED BY PERMISSION.

Other online bookstores operate in a similar way—but none are as successful as Amazon. Bezos says the keys to success are simple: comprehensive selection ("Our goal is that if it's in print, it's in stock") and 10% to 30% discounts on most books. "It's a huge mistake not to offer discounts," he says. "Most online businesses fail because they misestimate the value proposition."

In other words, even in cyberspace, customers want bargains. Bezos declines to disclose revenues, but analyst estimates for 1996 reach well over $10 million. He does say that orders have been increasing this year by 34% a month. And 44% of Amazon's sales are to repeat customers, who can sign up to be notified by E-mail when, say, the next Stephen King novel comes out.

A cyber storefront opens all kinds of marketing possibilities. Amazon is one of the first sites to cash in on the Web's so-called communities of interest. Say you're fascinated by vintage cars, and you create a Website to share information with like-minded folks. Link your site to Amazon, and you'll get a 3% to 8% commission on each purchase made by anyone who follows that link and buys a book. Amazon has enlisted over 1,800 such "associates" in the past three months. In the works are customized storefronts—a regular customer who tends to buy computer books will automatically be presented with the latest Microsoft programming manual when he logs in, while a mystery fan might see a tout for the latest Patricia Cornwell thriller.

Amazon.com is digging into an industry with a historically flawed way of conducting business. In traditional book publishing, suppliers and retailers work at cross purposes. Publishers have to decide months in advance how many copies of a book to print. But they can't accurately gauge demand until they pitch the book to the retailers. To encourage retailers to accept lots of copies and display them prominently, publishers give stores the right to return unsold books for credit. Big chains like Barnes & Noble or Borders get the best deals. Retailers often over-order, since they want to be sure they have adequate stock on hand, and since loading up poses little risk. Says Bezos: "It's not a rational business. The publisher takes all the return risk and the retailer makes the demand predictions."

Amazon gives publishers a lot to like. Most important, since the company orders books that customers have agreed to buy, its return rate is less than 0.25%, vs. 30% for the industry overall. Publishers also are greedy for Amazon's ability to track customer preferences and ordering patterns, the kind of data that they would love to use to forecast demand. So far Bezos has resisted sharing such information. He explains: "This is the Web. People are concerned about privacy. And if someone feels mistreated by us, they don't tell five people—they tell 5,000."

Like most Web retailers, Bezos says that the race is for market share first, profits later. "If we're profitable within the next two years," he says, "it'll be by accident." Early investors were told not to expect profits for five years. But that hasn't stopped some of the sharpest Internet investors from betting big on Amazon. Venture capital firm Kleiner Perkins Caufield & Byer recently put up $10 million, its biggest single placement ever—more than its original investment in Netscape. In return, the firm received under 15% of the company and a board seat for Kleiner partner John Doerr.

Bezos is spending some of the money on staff—instead of clerks and managers, he is hiring programmers who can make his service even more efficient. He's not laying out much for office furniture—many Amazonians' desks consist of unfinished doors laid across sawhorses. The bulk of the company's capital goes to increasing Amazon's visibility, with low-cost ads on popular Websites, and more expensive spots in traditional media like the New York Times Book Review. The challenge is to create a brand as recognizable as Barnes & Noble, which is expected to go online next year. Says Bezos: "Frankly, I'm more concerned about two guys in a garage." All the same, he's taken precautions, including using the lure of stock options to cherry-pick book-industry managers. "By the year 2000," he says, "there will be two or three big online bookstores. We need to be sure we're one."

Further Resources

BOOKS

Daisey, Mike. *21 Dog Years: Doing Time @ Amazon.com.* New York: Free Press, 2002.

Goolsbee, Austan and Judith A. Chevalier. *Measuring Prices and Price Competition Online: Amazon, and Barnes and Noble.* Cambridge, Mass.: National Bureau of Economic Research, 2002.

Spector, Robert. *Amazon.com: Get Big Fast.* New York: HarperBusiness, 2000.

PERIODICALS

Bannan, Karen J. "Bookbattle." *Brandweek* 41, no. 9, February 28, 2000, 80–84.

"Playing the Amazon Game." *Internet Business Advantage* 2, no. 23, November 23, 1998, 3–4.

Warner, Bernhard. "Jeff Bezos: Volume Discounter." *Brandweek* 39, no. 38, S18–S22.

Walt Handelsman Editorial Cartoons

Political cartoons

By: Walt Handelsman

Date: 1996

Source: Handelsman, Walt. Editorial Cartoons. (New Orleans) *Times-Picayune.* 1996. Available online at http://www.pulitzer.org/year/1997/editorial-cartooning/; http://www.pulitzer.org/ (accessed June 4, 2003).

About the Artist: Walt Handelsman is an award-winning editorial cartoonist. He has been on the staff of *Newsday* in New York and was the editorial cartoonist for *The Times-Picayune* (New Orleans) and *The Scranton Times* (Pennsylvania). Handelsman earned his bachelor's degree from the University of Cincinnati. ∎

Introduction

Editorial cartoonists provide interpretations of social and political events through their humorous drawings. Patrick Oliphant, an editorial cartoonist who began in the 1960s, influenced the style and content of the editorial cartoon for years. Satire and caricature dominate editorial cartoons, rather than crayon-like drawings that were popular earlier.

Primary Source

Walt Handelsman Editorial Cartoons

SYNOPSIS: Examples of Walt Handelsman's cartoons show his typical style and flair for capturing the hot issue of the day. Handelsman said that he tried to "draw a cartoon that you don't have to be a news junkie to understand." His "targets" came from national and local politics and could draw positive and negative reactions from readers. © 2003 TRIBUNE MEDIA SERVICES, INC. ALL RIGHTS RESERVED. REPRINT WITH PERMISSION.

Like other creators of regular features in newspapers, most editorial cartoonists fall into either liberal or conservative camps and have their work syndicated to many newspapers across the country. Syndication, which increased in popularity in the 1980s, provided larger audiences for cartoonists' work and for their opinions. Paul Somers quoted William A. Henry, who believed "syndication tends to soften the most acerbic cartoonist." Rather than thinking of just a small audience for a local newspaper, the cartoonist must gauge the climate of the country as he creates for syndication. A cartoonist may use a particularly volatile local issue in a cartoon to draw attention to a problem that others across the country would be unaware of otherwise. Gary Trudeau, creator of *Doonesbury,* highlighted Palm

Beach and "their law requiring nonresidents to carry an identification card" in 1985, bringing national attention to the issue.

Politics and politicians have always been a favorite target for the editorial cartoonist. Bill Clinton, George Bush, and the tensions in the Middle East were all subjects of political cartoons during the 1990s. No matter what they believe politically, "cartoonists are primarily critics. We're looking for the flaw in the argument, the fly in the ointment," according to Kevin Siers. Walt Handelsman is no different. His sense of humor and observations about politicians and about social issues in America earned him the 1997 Pulitzer Prize for editorial cartooning over Jeff MacNelly of the *Chicago Tribune* and Chip Bok of the *Akron Beacon* (Ohio).

Primary Source

Walt Handelsman Editorial Cartoons
Bill Clinton mimics statements given by Bob Dole in this Walt Handelsman cartoon. © 2003 TRIBUNE MEDIA SERVICES, INC. ALL
RIGHTS RESERVED. REPRINT WITH PERMISSION.

Significance

Walt Handelsman's Pulitzer Prize was significant for many reasons. It was his first Pulitzer, and unexpected. It was also among the first Pulitzer Prizes for *The Times-Picayune* of New Orleans. When he learned he had won, Handelsman laughed, "I can stop worrying about winning it now. . ." On a more serious note, he said, "It gives me more confidence—and confidence is the key to doing good, creative work."

Walt Handelsman is known for his wry humor and thought-provoking commentary. He began working as a cartoonist as a hobby and then moved into paid work. Handelsman, like other editorial cartoonists, had to look for his topics in the issues of the day. He said that he "peruses the *Times–Picayune, The New York Times,* and *USA Today*" for subjects. The examples of his editorial cartoons for the Pulitzer Prize show his edge and under-

standing of not only politics, but also of social issues. One titled "Children's Chalk Drawings" shows "then" and "now." The difference is a happy child with sunshine versus a drawing of a body on the pavement. With a few strokes of his pen, Handelsman communicated how the world of the 1990s had changed for children. Like his contemporaries, Handelsman has fun with caricaturing politicians. Ross Perot has huge ears. Bob Dole scowls. Bill Clinton has a slightly off-center face. Unlike editorial columnists or other newspaper writers, the editorial cartoonist does not need much text to tell the viewer how he perceives an issue or a person. In the cartoon "FBI Seeks New Suspects in Olympic Bombing" and in one with "Richard Jewell" hanging from the ceiling, Handelsman's opinion of the bungled search for the person whose bomb killed and injured several people at Centennial Park is clear.

Primary Source

Walt Handelsman Editorial Cartoons

Walt Handelsman pokes fun at Bob Dole and the 1996 Republican National Convention. © 2003 TRIBUNE MEDIA SERVICES, INC. ALL RIGHTS RESERVED. REPRINT WITH PERMISSION.

Walt Handelsman's colleagues in the editorial cartooning field have had high praise for his work. Dick Locher, of the *Chicago Tribune,* noted that "his work can be very serious and very funny. It goes both ways. Walt surprises you—I like that a lot. He's really clever and knows political issues." Ben Sargent called him "clever and real consistent." Overall, Walt Handelsman's work, like that of other great editorial cartoonists, drew reactions for his readers.

Further Resources

BOOKS

Colldeweih, Jack, and Kalman Goldstein. *Graphic Opinions: Editorial Cartoonists and Their Art.* Bowling Green, Ohio: Bowling Green State University Popular Press, 1998.

Somers, Paul P. Jr. *Editorial Cartooning and Caricature: A Reference Guide.* Westport, Conn.: Greenwood Press, 1998.

PERIODICALS

Astor, David. "Back to Work After Post-Pulitzer Frenzy." *Editor & Publisher* 130, no. 17, April 26, 1997, 94–95.

———. "Former Pulitzer Recipients Discuss the Newest Winner." *Editor & Publisher* 130, no. 17, April 26, 1997, 95.

Bender, Steve, James T. Black, and Dianne Young. "Crusader Cartoonists." *Southern Living* 32, no. 4, April 1997, 150–154.

Jones, Stacy. "81st Annual Pulitzer Prizes." *Editor & Publisher* 130, no. 16, April 12, 1997, 7–11, 38–40.

WEBSITES

The Association of American Editorial Cartoonists. Available online at http://pc99.detnews.com/aaec/ (accessed June 17, 2003).

Walt Handelsman. Available online at http://www.comicspage .com/handelsman/ (accessed June 17, 2003).

"What Level of Protection for Internet Speech?"

Newspaper article

By: Linda Greenhouse
Date: March 24, 1997

Source: Greenhouse, Linda. "What Level of Protection for Internet Speech?" *The New York Times,* March 24, 1997, D5.

About the Author: Linda Greenhouse (1947–) joined the staff of *The New York Times* in 1968. She earned degrees from both Radcliffe and Yale Law School. Greenhouse has covered the Supreme Court for the Washington bureau of *The New York Times* since 1978. Greenhouse is also a panelist on PBS's *Washington Week.* ∎

Introduction

President Bill Clinton signed Title V of the Telecommunications Act of 1996 into law on February 8, 1996. The common title for this law, an update of the Telecommunications Act of 1934, was the Communications Decency Act. The law was meant to protect children and families from indecent speech on the Internet, but found challengers immediately. Those opposing the act thought that it would restrict access, force scrutiny from the government and Internet providers, and prohibit free speech under the First Amendment. The ACLU, with a broad coalition of business and other concerned entities, fought all the way to the United States Supreme Court. The Supreme Court then had to determine what falls under the First Amendment regarding free speech and what may violate rights of the public with access to broadcast or radio. Different levels of protection have been assigned to various kinds of media in the twentieth century. While some language is prohibited from network television, the same language can appear in print in a daily newspaper. The distinctions are fine and decided case by case. In this case, *Reno v. American Civil Liberties Union,* the courts decided that the Internet is protected by the First Amendment. Justice Stevens succinctly articulated the exigency: "The record demonstrates that the growth of the Internet has been and continues to be phenomenal. . . . [but] The interest in encouraging freedom of expression in a democratic society outweighs any theoretical but unproven benefit of censorship."

The Supreme Court's ruling did not end debate on the proper use and content of the Internet. In the years since 1996, the question of censorship and the Internet has come up time and time again. Filters, parental rights, the responsibilities of libraries, and the role of Internet service providers have been only a few of the issues under discussion. As the Internet continues to expand as a communications tool, the debate over its use will also continue.

Significance

What kind of speech does the Internet represent? Is it like a television because a computer resembles a television? Or is communicating over the Internet like a telephone conversation? These were the thorny questions that faced the Supreme Court and had already been argued in the lower courts by early 1997. The decisions made by the courts would affect Internet service providers (ISPs), Web users, and Web site creators. Linda Greenhouse, the Pulitzer Prize-winning *New York Times* reporter, covers the Supreme Courts debates on this issue in her article "What Level of Protection for Internet Speech?"

The Clinton Administration fought to keep the provisions regarding indecent speech in the Communications Decency Act of 1996. Senator Patrick Leahy, of Vermont, fought as one the strongest voices on the Senate floor for this section of the act to be rescinded. The ramifications for the inclusion of the indecency provisions affected businesses and community networks. While there was software to identify and block some incidences of indecent language, there was not software to identify graphic images and some other forms of communication being sent over the Internet. Yet the ISP would also be responsible for the transmissions under this law. The enforcement of the section of the CDA would be costly and, as the civil libertarians suggested, limit free speech. The amendments to the CDA included prohibiting harassment and included a broad range of telecommunication media that were not removed. These were the key questions that were in the beginning stages as Greenhouse reported on the March 1997 discussions in the Supreme Court. The decision and Greenhouse's article point out the importance of definitions for free speech and the interpretation of the Constitution when use of new media and communications devices become widespread. Part of the questions were answered when the Court aligned the Internet with the rights of print media; however, there are still other questions about the use of the Internet that will be discussed.

Primary Source

"What Level of Protection for Internet Speech?"

SYNOPSIS: Linda Greenhouse summarizes problems facing the Supreme Court as they decided upon issues surrounding the rights of individuals to send information over the Internet. The decisions were broader than e-mail communications; they included what could be displayed on websites and monitoring systems.

Underlying last week's Supreme Court argument on free speech on the Internet was a premise so fundamental and obvious to all the participants, lawyers and Justices alike, that it did not even need to be articulated in the courtroom: not all speech is created equal.

Rather, there is a hierarchy of speech, under Supreme Court precedents dating back many decades

Protestors demonstrate against pornography on the Internet in front of the Supreme Court, March 19, 1997. The Court that day heard arguments in the case of *Reno v. American Civil Liberties Union,* which had struck down part of Communications Decency Act that restricted "indecent" material, such as graphic pornography, from the Internet. © **WALLY MCNAMEE/CORBIS. REPRODUCED BY PERMISSION.**

that calibrate the degree of First Amendment protection with the particular medium of expression.

A decision from nearly 50 years ago, holding that speech that would be perfectly acceptable if uttered in a public park could constitutionally be banned when broadcast from a sound truck, offers a vivid example of the Court's approach. "The moving picture screen, the radio, the newspaper, the handbill, the sound truck and the street corner orator have differing natures, values, abuses and dangers," Justice Robert H. Jackson wrote in a concurring opinion in that 1949 case, *Kovacs v. Cooper.* Each means of expression, he said, "is a law unto itself."

So only by deciding for themselves what the Internet is can the Justices decide where to place it on the hierarchy of First Amendment values. That placement, in turn, is likely to determine whether the challenge to the Communications Decency Act, which makes it a Federal crime to display "patently offensive," sexually explicit material over the Internet in a manner available to children, succeeds or fails.

Not surprisingly, there was a subtext to last week's argument, one not always audible through the convoluted discussion of the technology of shielding children from indecent content that took up much of the 70 minutes in the courtroom. The subtext was the struggle by the lawyers for both sides to present, and by the Justices to select, the most apt analogy for the Internet.

Analogy is the only real road map for courts when technological change leaves them in unknown legal territory. Thirty years ago, for example, the Court was confronted with finding a constitutional framework for electronic eavesdropping, a technology that did not fit neatly into existing categories. Without the physical intrusion that usually constitutes a "search," is eavesdropping covered by the Fourth Amendment's prohibition against unreasonable searches?

Yes, the Court ruled in a 1967 landmark, *Katz v. United States,* holding that Federal agents had conducted an unconstitutional search when they

Anti-Defamation League director Abraham Foxman displays the site of a neo-Nazi hate group. Efforts by groups interested in restricting hate group and pornography sites from the Internet have been largely unsuccessful. **AP/WIDE WORLD PHOTOS. REPRODUCED BY PERMISSION.**

used an eavesdropping device, placed without a warrant on the outside of a public telephone booth, to listen to a gambler's calls. The Justices reasoned by analogy. When the gambler shut the phone booth's door, the Court said, he intended to shut out "the uninvited ear" no less than someone in another line of work who closed the door of his office.

For the Internet, the most obvious physical analogy is television. A computer monitor, after all, looks most like a television screen; turn the computer on, and the blank screen fills with images. But a physical analogy is imperfect at best, particularly when the old technology functions entirely differently from the new. Television, after all, has tended to be a one-way medium sending images and sound to many viewers; the Internet allows many people to communicate simultaneously with many others.

The coalition of Internet providers and users challenging the Communications Decency Act has always known that it could not succeed in its First Amendment challenge unless it persuaded the Court to look beyond the physical analogy and see the Internet as something new and unfettered by the long line of precedents upholding broad Federal regula-

tion of the broadcast medium. By the same token, the Clinton Administration knew that its best chance of defending the law successfully was to anchor the Internet firmly in the world of broadcast.

The Government's briefs rely heavily on the Supreme Court's broadcast precedents, particularly a 1978 case, *Federal Communications Commission v. Pacifica Foundation,* that upheld the Government's daytime ban on the broadcast of sexually explicit speech—the "seven dirty words" of the comedian George Carlin's well-known monologue.

An effort by any level of government to censure a newspaper for printing the same words would be a flagrant violation of the First Amendment. Nor can a government tell a newspaper what to print; a 1974 Supreme Court decision, *Miami Herald v. Tornillo,* struck down a Florida law giving political candidates a "right of reply" to criticism in the state's newspapers. But the Court has upheld similar compelled-access rules for broadcasters.

The Court has offered various rationales for relegating first radio and then television to a low rung of the First Amendment hierarchy: the finite size of the broadcast spectrum, justifying Federal regulation in the public interest; their "uniquely pervasive presence in the lives of all Americans," as the Court said in the *Pacifica* case, and the ease with which children too young to read can turn a dial and be exposed to unsuitable material.

The Court is somewhat more protective of speech on cable television, where the capacity to offer dozens of channels negates the spectrum-scarcity rationale. But the Justices have been strikingly skittish about pinning themselves down to a legal standard for regulation of cable, citing evolving technology and the absence of a "definitive choice among competing analogies," as Justice Stephen G. Breyer put it in a splintered decision last June on regulating indecency on cable television.

Can a Court that is nervous about cable television even begin to tackle the Internet, surely as dramatic a departure from the old means of communication as eavesdropping was from an old-fashioned police search?

During the argument, the Justices appeared surprisingly uninterested in pursuing the television analogy. There was more discussion, in fact, about telephones. Justice Breyer asked several questions comparing conversation over the Internet to telephone conversations—not good news for the Government, given that the Court in a 1989 decision declared a Federal ban on dial-a-porn prerecorded sex messages to be unconstitutional. In that case, *Sable Communications v. F.C.C.,* the Court said that private telephone conversations did not share the "uniquely pervasive" dangers of radio and televisions broadcasts that can turn unwilling listeners into a captive audience.

"The Internet is rather like the telephone," Justice Breyer said. Deputy Solicitor General Seth P. Waxman was quick to object. A telephone conversation is a "discrete communication," he said, while material "placed on a computer by anybody, anywhere, is available to everybody everywhere."

Another vision beckons, although it was not clear from the argument how much appeal it has for the Court. The three-judge Federal District Court panel in Philadelphia, which declared the Communications Decency Act unconstitutional last June in the case now before the Court, depicted the Internet as a never-ending global conversation that deserves the highest level of protection the First Amendment has to offer.

"The most participatory marketplace of mass speech that this country—and indeed the world—has yet seen," is how Judge Stewart R. Dalzell described it in his separate opinion. An analogy to end all analogies, if the Justices are ready for it.

Further Resources

BOOKS

Grossman, Wendy M. *From Anarchy to Power: The Net Comes of Age.* New York: New York University Press, 2001.

Hunter, Richard. *World Without Secrets: Business, Crime, and Privacy in the Age of Ubiquitous Computing.* New York: John Wiley, Inc., 2002.

Shields, Rob. *Cultures of Internet: Virtual Spaces, Real Histories, Living Bodies.* Thousand Oaks, Calif.: Sage, 1996.

PERIODICALS

Cole, Terry W. "ACLU v. Reno: An Exigency for Cyberethics." *The Southern Communication Journal* 64, no. 3, Spring 1999, 251–260.

Whitman, Michael E., Anthony M. Townsend, and Robert J. Alberts. "The Communications Decency Act is Not as Dead as You Think." *Communications of the ACM* 41, no. 1, January 1999, 15–17.

WEBSITES

Speech Issues in the High-Tech Context. Available online at http://www.usdoj.gov/criminal/cybercrime/speech.html; website home page: http://www.usdoj.gov (accessed June 17, 2003).

The Telecommunications Act of 1996. Available online at http://www.ntia.doc.gov/otiahome/TOP/publicationmedia/newsltr/telcom_act.htm; website home page: http://www.ntia.doc.gov/ (accessed June 5, 2003).

"Roll Over, Ward Cleaver"

Magazine article

By: Bruce Handy

Date: April 14, 1997

Source: Handy, Bruce. "Roll Over, Ward Cleaver." *Time* 149, April 14, 1997, 78–82. ∎

Introduction

Over the decades, television sitcoms have dealt with social issues of their eras. In 1953, the word "pregnant" wasn't allowed on *I Love Lucy,* even though Lucille Ball and Desi Arnaz were also married in real life. Bea Arthur's character in *Maude* decided to have an abortion in 1972, an issue that later became forbidden. Candice Bergen's character drew comments from Vice President Dan Quayle in 1992 when she had a child out of wedlock. Controversy was no stranger to television. All of these episodes preceded Ellen DeGeneres coming out in 1997. Though other gay and lesbian characters were part of regular television shows, none were main characters.

Until Ellen's coming-out episode, the sitcom lacked a focus and point of view. Ellen DeGeneres felt the show needed a spark and that she needed to come out to audiences, both herself and as her character on the show. The episode was followed by two more that focused on coming out to her family and friends. In the final season of the show, *Ellen* was gay-themed. This change of focus was blamed for the cancellation of the show as well as the loss of advertising revenue.

Significance

Ellen broke new ground with an episode featuring the main character's coming out. As the first main character to be openly gay, Ellen Morgan, played by Ellen DeGeneres, was not necessarily comfortable with her sexuality. Growing more comfortable with herself would be part of the next season's plot. For Ellen DeGeneres herself, the decision to come out was personal, even though several groups tried to make it political.

The episode, titled "The Puppy Episode," aired in April 1997 near the end of the season, but not as the final episode. There had been a running joke that Ellen's problems would be solved if she got a puppy. There were more serious' issues at stake, however. The writers allowed time for the story to develop over the next two episodes before ending the season. DeGeneres, who did not necessarily want to return to the show after that season, only had one more season. ABC replaced the show midseason.

DeGeneres received praise and hate for her coming-out episode. Significantly, teens wrote to her, thanking her for portraying an openly gay character on national television. The letters signaled support and the importance of dealing with the issue in an honest, if comic, manner.

ABC, owned by Disney, was supportive but not overly so of DeGeneres's move. In the final season, a parental warning was added to the show, labeling the show as having adult content. DeGeneres felt the warnings were unfair, and this turned out to be the breaking point between the network and the star.

Although her show did not survive, DeGeneres paved the way for other openly gay and lesbian characters on television. By 1999 there were as many as thirty gay or lesbian characters on prime time television. In the early twenty-first century these were no longer small parts for actors and actresses, but often major roles. Like Ellen, however, the characters were still often the only gay or lesbian characters or were not in serious relationships. Shows like *Will & Grace* dealt openly with gay issues in prime time. The comfort level and acceptance of the viewing public seemed to have gone up in just a few seasons.

Primary Source

"Roll Over, Ward Cleaver" [excerpt]

SYNOPSIS: Sitcoms in the early twenty-first century had risky subject matter and topics that Ward Cleaver, the father in *Leave it to Beaver,* never could have imagined. In the 1990s, comedies like *Ellen* and *Seinfeld* took on issues that were not necessarily popular with the country and the networks.

Different media have different thresholds for scandal. Controversy in the movies might mean making a film that glorifies one of the nation's most repugnant pornographers. Controversy in literature might mean writing a memoir about the affair you had with your father when you were in your 20s. In television, which functions not just as a business and debased art form but also as an increasingly fractured nation's de facto mirror of itself, the threshold is much lower. Controversy could mean starring in a sitcom as a gently scatterbrained former bookstore owner who, after years of adult floundering, reluctantly comes to a realization about her homosexuality and begins to take a few hesitant baby steps out of the closet and toward getting a life.

"I hate that term 'in the closet,'" says Ellen DeGeneres, the aforementioned sitcom star whose all-pants wardrobe and sometimes awkward chemistry with male ingenues was provoking curiosity from fans and reporters long before her sexuality became a minor national obsession. "Until recently I hated the word lesbian too," she continues. "I've said it enough now that it doesn't bother me. But lesbian sounded like somebody with some kind of disease. I didn't like that, so I used the word gay more often."

What she hasn't been able to bring herself to do, until now, is use the word gay along with "I am" in public. Indeed, for a lot of men and women whose livelihood depends on the goodwill of millions, those may be the three scariest words in the English language. "I always thought I could keep my personal life separate from my professional life," says DeGeneres while sitting in a patio at her home in Beverly Hills. "In every interview I ever did"—she's squinting, too polite to interrupt this one even though the sun is clearly in her eyes—"everyone tried to trap me into saying I was gay. And I learned every way to dodge that. Or if they just blatantly asked me, I would say I don't talk about my personal life. I mean, I really tried to figure out every way to avoid answering that question for as long as I could."

That became a lot harder last September when the news leaked, unintentionally by all accounts, that DeGeneres wanted to have the character she plays on *Ellen,* her three-year-old ABC sitcom, discover that she—the character, that is—is a lesbian. For De-Generes, 39, the decision was the culmination of a long process of struggling with feelings about her own sexuality, her fears about being rejected for it, her wish to lead a more honest and open life in public, her weariness at the effort it took her not to. For the public, the news was a sensation: a gay lead on TV—that would be a first, and to those who attach importance to these sorts of things, either a long time coming or another way station on the road to moral abandon.

Or maybe it was just something to gossip about. In a series of TV interviews last fall, previously scheduled to promote a new CD but suddenly subjected to intense scrutiny because of the coming-out rumors, DeGeneres joked awkwardly that she was Lebanese, or that the real news was that a character named Les Bian would be joining *Ellen*'s cast. She even kidded her own teasing reticence on an episode of *The Larry Sanders Show* that had her hopping into bed for man-woman sex with the fictional male talk-show host.

Finally, after things dragged on all winter, ABC announced last month that the character of Ellen Morgan would indeed be coming out in a special one-hour episode on the last day of April, just in time for sweeps. That resolved, DeGeneres, who had felt constrained from speaking frankly about the issue while her sitcom's fate was still in the balance, is coming out too. "For me," she says, "this has been the most freeing experience because people can't hurt me anymore. I don't have to worry about somebody saying something about me, or a reporter trying to find out information. Literally, as soon as I made this decision, I lost weight. My skin has cleared up. I don't have anything to be scared of, which I think outweighs whatever else happens in my career."

In a sense, the burden lifted from DeGeneres' shoulders has landed on those of her bosses at ABC and Touchstone Television, which co-produces *Ellen* (both, of course, are part of the Walt Disney Co.). Dealing with controversy isn't usually a TV executive's strongest suit. It's not that there aren't already gay characters on television. There are—so many, in fact (22 as of February, according to the *Advocate,* a national gay-and-lesbian magazine, from the lovelorn Smithers on *The Simpsons* to the lovelorn

Ellen DeGeneres at the VH1 Fashion Awards in 1998. DeGeneres created controversy when her sitcom character came out as a lesbian in a 1997 episode. © MITCHELL GERBER/CORBIS. REPRODUCED BY PERMISSION.

Matt on *Melrose Place*), that one of *Ellen*'s producers offers the half-joking observation that homosexuals "have become the new stock character, like the African-American pal at the workplace."

But all those characters are either peripheral or part of an ensemble. Like Mary Richards before her, Ellen Morgan functions as her show's center, around whom the rest of the cast revolves—structurally, Ellen Morgan is Mary Richards, except she likes girls. She provides the window into the show's comedic world; she is the character we are asked to identify with, the person to whom we are asked to give tacit approval. That's why, in a country that still has a lot of conflicts about homosexuality, this formerly innocuous, intermittently funny series is now pushing buttons in a way that other shows with gay characters haven't. It's also why, after a telephone threat, the soundstage on the neat and tidy Disney lot in Burbank where Ellen is filmed had to be cleared before the final segment of the coming-out episode was shot and bomb-sniffing dogs brought in.

All this comes at a time when television is subject to greater scrutiny than ever before—dating back, at least, to then Vice President Dan Quayle's famous 1992 speech in which he lambasted the character Murphy Brown for choosing to have a child out of wedlock. One can endlessly debate the question of whether television influences society or reflects it: Does Ellen Morgan's coming out in what is still our massest medium legitimize homosexuality, or does the sponsorship of a bottom-line business like ABC merely reflect its acceptance by a significant portion of the population? Clearly, the answer is both, that TV and culture play off each other in ways that are hard to codify. Any attempt to reduce these complex reverberations to a black-or-white issue is, well, the kind of thing you'd expect from television.

Ironically, this ongoing obsession with TV's responsibility comes at a time when the networks' hold on the viewing public continues to erode—just this past February the networks' share of the total viewing audience dropped 4.6% from a year ago, continuing a two-decades-long decline. But whatever *Ellen*'s fate with the Nielsens, television's treatment of sexuality is likely to continue becoming increasingly frank, vulgar or immoral, depending on one's vantage point and what, of course, one is viewing (*Chicago Hope*? *Married . . . With Children*? A made-for-TV movie starring Tori Spelling as a hooker?) The medium—and America—has patently come a long way from the 1952-53 season, when the cast of *I Love Lucy* couldn't utter the word pregnant during Little Ricky's gestation period, or 1965 when, a year after network TV got its first double marital bed on *Bewitched*, Barbara Eden was forbidden by NBC to show her belly button on *I Dream of Jeannie*.

It would be a mistake, however, to think of TV history as one long, uninterrupted drift toward untrammeled license. Moral values are, of course, relative. *Party of Five* features yards of premarital sex, yet is also a warmer celebration of family bonds than, say, *Leave It to Beaver* or *The Donna Reed Show*. Today there are new taboos. "Nobody's going to do abortion on a sitcom today, but *Maude* did it back in 1972," says Bruce Helford, co-creator and executive producer of *The Drew Carey Show*. He's referring to the famous episodes of *Maude* in which Bea Arthur's title character not only considered having an abortion, as a number of TV characters have in years since, but actually went out and got one. "Abortion," Helford believes, "is way too hot a subject now. Stuff that shows like *All in the Family* did—I don't think they'd let you get away with the kind of show with humor about racism, like the episode

where Archie Bunker met Sammy Davis Jr. We've really gone backward in a big way." Marta Kauffman, co-creator and executive producer of *Friends,* complains that her series wasn't allowed to show an actual condom, whereas just a few seasons earlier, *Seinfeld* was. "Things have changed over the past few years," she grumbles. "You couldn't do the masturbation episode of *Seinfeld* today."

In the big *Ellen* episode—filmed over two consecutive Fridays last month amid an atmosphere that seemed half party, half support group—an old college friend (male) comes on to Ellen, who slowly realizes that she is attracted to the friend's female colleague, played by Laura Dern, a close friend of DeGeneres' in real life (a description that should not be read into). Oprah Winfrey, in a surprisingly droll and low-key performance, plays Ellen's therapist. A whole flock of other celebrities—also friends of DeGeneres', including Demi Moore, Melissa Etheridge, k.d. lang and Billy Bob Thornton—showed their support by doing cameos on the episode.

Both ABC and Touchstone seem to be genuinely pleased with the results. "We're very proud. We think *Ellen* and the show's staff have executed it beautifully," says Jamie Tarses, president of ABC Entertainment. At the same time, she adds, "obviously this is an experiment. We're not sociologists. We don't know how this is going to be received."

Well, they could have wagered a few easy guesses. The news that Ellen Morgan would come out brought predictable applause from the Gay & Lesbian Alliance Against Defamation, which is building a national "Come Out with Ellen" day around the episode; and predictable denunciations from the Rev. Jerry Falwell, who referred to the star in gentlemanly fashion as "Ellen DeGenerate," and from the Rev. Donald E. Wildmon, whose American Family Association has issued barely veiled threats to boycott *Ellen*'s advertisers. A stalwart ABC says it nevertheless expects that *Ellen* will be fully sponsored, although two occasional advertisers on *Ellen,* J.C. Penney and Chrysler, have announced they won't continue to sponsor the show. This can't have made ABC happy. But even for controversial shows there are usually enough advertisers to go around if the ratings promise to be high enough, which controversy often ensures. The network remains optimistic.

Further Resources

BOOKS

DeGeneres, Ellen. *My Point—And I Do Have One.* New York: Bantam Books, 1995.

Tropiano, Stephen. *The Prime Time Closet: A History of Gays and Lesbians on TV* New York: Applause Theater & Cinema Books, 2002.

Walters, Suzanna Danuta. *All the Rage: The Story of Gay Visibility in America.* Chicago: University of Chicago Press, 2001.

PERIODICALS

Cagle, Jess. "As Gay As It Gets?" *Entertainment Weekly* 431, May 8, 1998, 26–32.

Poniewozik, James. "TV's Coming Out Party." *Time,* October 25, 1999, 116–118.

"Comparing Net Directories"

Journal article

By: Greg R. Notess

Date: 1997

Source: Notess, Greg R. "Comparing Net Directories." *Database* 20, February/March 1997, 61–64.

About the Author: Greg R. Notess (1962–) is a reference librarian at Montana State University, a consultant, a writer, and a speaker. ∎

Introduction

The World Wide Web has been called the "greatest organized catastrophe ever seen." With the proliferation of Web sites being added to the Internet daily in the early twenty-first century, it was difficult to keep up with what was current as well as what was accurate. As the technology improved and the Web grew, there was a growing need for software and websites that would "organize" all of the information available.

Early versions of databases that attempted to organize websites did not always yield favorable results. While some used traditional Boolean searching, familiar to librarians, other sites used key word searches that picked up results only from a title or throughout an entire document. The sites, like other Internet businesses, were fluid. If the site was good, it lasted. Otherwise, the site disappeared or another company bought it.

There were distinctions between commercial sites, available to anyone with Internet access, and those that were produced by companies who possibly also produced print versions. Academic institutions also joined in the quest to organize the Web. The sites like Yahoo!, available with Internet access, provided subject directories and keyword searching. The commercial sites also featured advertisements to pay for the content and production costs. Databases created by vendors, such as Gale, evaluated and indexed content that appeared in the product. Academic projects, such as the Internet Scout Project at the University of Wisconsin, Madison, provided weekly reviews of selected websites. Websites, as well as Web directories, were constructed for different purposes and audiences.

Significance

Comparing the directories and search tools available on the Internet was a necessary part of learning how to find information. The distinction between the kind of websites and tools available was equally important. Web directories were collections of links from the Internet. For marketing purposes, each site looked slightly different, though they may have worked similarly. The quality and ease of use was what was important and was what made articles like Notess's important.

Web directories could contain millions of links, but this was still only a small part of the Web. The comparison between the popular directories of 1997, Yahoo!, Excite, Magellan, and Lycos, pointed out some of the factors used in creating the sites and in the results. One had advantages over another, however. The creators of the site were important. For example, Excite was created by journalists and therefore had a certain point of view about included information . Yahoo! included subject directories and was hierarchical in its structure. The frequency of updates was another factor that was significant for directories.

The greatest factor in examining Web directories was change. Some of the directories that were popular in 1997 remained popular. Others either ceased to exist or changed in character. The technology grew to include more "mega" and "meta" sites, which could search over many databases or directories at once. The advanced techniques and software improved many sites' searching capabilities. Web directories continued to be one of the best ways to locate information on the World Wide Web.

Primary Source

"Comparing Net Directories" [excerpt]

> **SYNOPSIS:** Directories were a popular and convenient way to locate information on the Internet. They differed in quality and in currency, however, and could disappear with a company merger. Commercial websites, like Yahoo! and Excite, emerged and became popular search engines whereby Internet users could locate material

Finding appropriate and relevant information resources on the World Wide Web is often a hit or miss endeavor. The large search engines routinely find an amazing number of irrelevant sites sprinkled

Jerry Yang (right) and Jeff Filo, co-founders of Yahoo!, hold a prop in their Santa Clara office. Yang and Filo met at Stanford University where they were both electrical engineering doctoral candidates. **PHOTOGRAPH BY PAUL SAKUMA. AP/WIDE WORLD PHOTOS. REPRODUCED BY PERMISSION.**

with a few gems. Bookmark lists of your favorite sites become dated in a few months with dead ends resulting from site reorganizations, resources moving to different hosts, or the demise of entire sites. Frequently updated, well-organized, subject-oriented directories of Internet resources may come as close as anything in providing the most useful starting points for actual information retrieval on the Net.

With the surprising commercial success of Yahoo! and other directory companies, many directory efforts have been spawned. Excite offers Excite Reviews, Lycos bought out Point and a2z, McKinley launched Magellan, and other competitors are waiting in the wings. Let us see how some of these compare to each other and how well they describe, rate, and cover sites in specific subject areas.

Excite Reviews

Excite has been expanding its search offerings to include a variety of special search features beyond its Web search engines. One of these is called Excite Reviews, covering about 60,000 sites with ratings on a scale of one to four and brief descriptions of a few sentences in length. The Excite Reviews are

classified by subject, and are accessible by subject terms as well as by keyword search. Reviews are written by a team of editors. Each of the 16 subject areas of the Excite Reviews begins with an introductory paragraph by the section editor that highlights a few of the sites.

Excite's team of editors consists of journalists. Their writing style is typically at a popular level, which often emphasizes evaluation based on how intriguing the content is rather than an objective evaluation of the information content. For example, under Patents and Intellectual Property Reviews, the entry for Cornell's U.S. Patent Law site reads "This site reads like an encyclopedia entry (yawn!) but does provide lots of info on the law. Mostly in legalese, Cornell Law School describes the law and its constitutional origin and implications." While rating a yawn and a score of two, this is a site that provides substantial content on patent law, including links to relevant sections from the U.S. Code, the Patent Cooperation Treaty, the Paris Convention, and recent patent decisions from the Supreme Court.

It is usually easy to criticize a directory for entries that are not included. Since the directories are selective, there are bound to be sites that were not selected. Even so, it is disappointing that the Patents category in the Excite Reviews lists neither the U.S. Patent and Trademark Office's patents databases (http://patents.cnidr.org:4242/) nor Questel Orbit's QPAT US service with its patent database and full-text patents (http://www.qpat.com/).

Excite uses the same search engine for Excite Reviews as for the full Excite Web search. This search engine uses a process called Intelligent Concept Extraction (ICE). In a technical paper on ICE (http://www.excite.com/ice/tech.html), Excite presents an intriguing overview of information search technology, beginning by describing Boolean searching as "the earliest, most primitive technology" and finishing with a claim of increased precision and recall when using ICE. Try out their Intelligent Concept Extraction and judge for yourself if it is more precise than basic Boolean searching.

Magellan

With Excite's recent purchase of Magellan, the two services will be merging their databases, but for now Magellan has both a general Web search engine and a subject directory of sites that have been reviewed and rated. The directory is arranged by subject in 26 categories and can be searched by keyword. Each entry includes a one paragraph description, keywords, audience, producer, and information on cost. Like Excite, a team of editors and writers review and rate sites in Magellan. The ratings, which range from one to four, are based on a numeric scoring system that evaluates sites on criteria such as ease of use, "Net appeal," currency, and comprehensiveness.

The descriptions in Magellan are a bit less breezy than the Excite Reviews. Since they are typically about twice as long, there is more room to include mention of the actual content of a site. For the Patent Law site at Cornell, Magellan does list some of the documents available on the site, although it still ends the description with an inane, "You'll have to stay up late if you open this box, chums." Again, Cornell gets only a score of two. Given the criteria used for ranking, anyone looking primarily for information content can safely ignore the ranking and try to evaluate potential usefulness of a site based on the description.

Magellan also fails to include an entry for either the CNIDR or QPAT US patent databases, although it does include a Questel Orbit Patent page that links directly to QPAT US. One useful feature in Magellan

is that on the top of a search, Magellan suggests related topics. These are subject categories that are suggested for finding related sites, and the links can be quite useful if the first search does not turn up relevant sites.

Lycos Top 5% and a2Z

Another well-known source for ranking of Web sites is Lycos' Top 5% Sites, formerly known as Point. Going along with the trend among Web search engines to add subject directories to their search offerings, Lycos acquired both Point and a2z. Prior to acquisition, Point made a name for itself on the Internet by designating sites as being in the top 5% of Web sites and making a graphic available to sites included in the listing. The honored sites then added the graphic and a link back to Point, providing very effective advertising for Point. Lycos continues the practice with its renamed Top 5% Sites section. Unfortunately, the criteria for inclusion in the Top 5% are not clearly identified. Ratings within the Top 5% Sites are on a scale of zero to 50 in three categories: content, presentation, and experience. However, like the other ratings directories, the ratings are not very useful in determining the quality or even the quantity of actual information content on specific sites.

The descriptions of sites in the Top 5% are typically a paragraph long, about the same as Magellan. The tone is similar as well. Rather than a concise description of the significant information content on a site, it too lapses in its commentary. For example, the European Patent Office is considered "useful, but not really too, ah, inventive." After reading a few of these reviews, it is easy to wonder what criteria cause a site to be included in the roughly 5% of Web sites considered "Top." Access to the Top 5% Sites ratings and reviews is via the 16 main subject categories and their subcategories and is keyword searchable.

The former a2z directory, another Lycos acquisition, is now listed on Lycos' site as Sites by Subject. It is both searchable and browsable by subject category. The criterion for inclusion in Lycos' a2z is that the site is one of the 10% of Web sites in Lycos that is most linked-to by users. Although some sites link to a Top 5% review, the others include no rating. The brief, one or two sentence descriptions are much more concise and informative than any of the other directories mentioned so far.

Both of the Lycos databases seem to have missed the patent databases in their collections. It

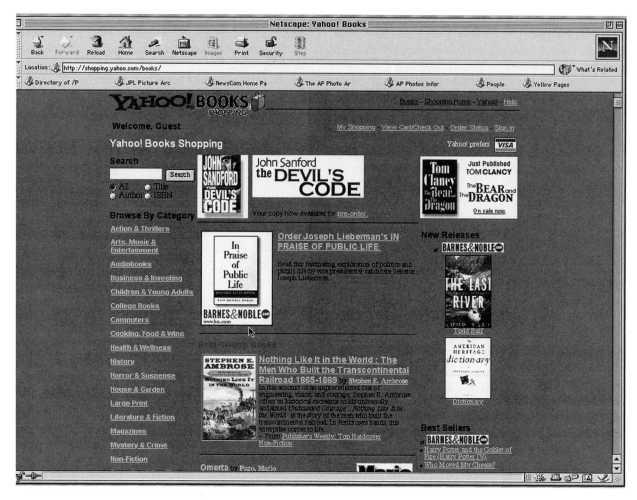

Screenshot of one of Yahoo!'s online shopping pages. AP/WIDE WORLD PHOTOS. REPRODUCED BY PERMISSION.

is less surprising here since the closest category available is the general Law category. Their absence also can be surmised to be due to a lack of links to these sites, since the Lycos directories base inclusion on a measure of the number of links to a site or an appearance of being in the top 5%.

Another feature on both Lycos databases, which is rare among other Internet search engines, is the ability to sort. Within the subject categories (which are quite similar between the two databases), sort options are given near the top. The default sort is alphabetical, but the a2z sections can also be sorted by listing the most popular first or in random order. The Top 5% categories can be sorted by any of the three rating criteria.

Yahoo!

The best-known and most popular of the subject directories is Yahoo!. While the others provide reviews, ratings, and descriptions, Yahoo! concen-

trates on the indexing and arrangement of sites into hierarchical subject categories. Access is through the 14 top-level categories, and then subcategories, or through a keyword search. For each category, a number in parentheses designates how many entries are in that category. This is helpful information when navigating through Yahoo! and can be used to gauge how large a category is.

Yahoo! consists of sites submitted by users, so it is not a very selective directory. Many sites are submitted by the companies themselves, but anyone can submit a site. Due to Yahoo!'s prominence on the Web, its coverage of commercial Web sites is especially good. Formerly, after running a keyword search, all the individual sites found would just display alphabetically by category. Thus, the extensive Business listings would appear first, even if the user was looking for a scientific site. Search results now display matching categories first, before the individual listings. Note that keyword searching defaults to automatic truncation and that multiple word searches default to an AND operator. Choose the Options link to change those defaults or to change the number of results to display per page.

Many entries contain no description, while others may have a descriptive phrase or sentence after the listing. Recently, Yahoo! has begun to add reviews for a few sites. In general, there is little rating of sites, except for an occasional "Cool" graphic (looks like a pair of sunglasses), which denotes those sites that the Yahoo! team considers to have good presentation or content for their respective topic area.

In terms of Yahoo!'s coverage of patents and the patents databases, it fares better than its competitors, but still has room for improvement. The Cornell Patent site is listed, although with no descriptive statement. QPAT US is listed under Business and Economy:Companies:Law: Intellectual Property:Patents: Services. There are many other links to patent sites and multiple categories. The other patents database, housed at CNIDR, is not listed directly, although it can be found from the Patent and Trademark Office site, which is listed.

A Comparative Case Study

Unlike the larger Web search engines, a straight across-the-board comparison of these directories is more complex than just trying to gauge the number of entries in each database. The ideal directory will list just those sites that provide quality information content for every topic that a user will need. No directory is likely to ever live up to the ideal of high precision and recall for all searches. As one quick measure of the usefulness and accuracy of the various directories, reviews, and rating services, I compared the treatment of a known Internet resource: the Code of Federal Regulations (CFR), available on the U.S. House of Representatives' Law Library site (http://law.house.gov/cfr/) and searchable with software from Personal Library Software, Inc. (PLS).

A number of features of this version of the CFR make this a useful case study. The CFR is a major resource for federal regulations, and it would seem a logical item to include in any directory that includes a law section. Secondly, when PLS first made the CFR available, it was set up as a demonstration project and used an older version of the CFR. The page itself notes that some of the sections are quite dated. A statement noting that this source contains out-of-date regulations should be included by any responsible directory. Third, the URL for this resource

changed in mid-1996. While the old URL (http://www.pls.com:8001/ his/cfr.html) still exists, it now states that the site has moved and points to the current URL (http://law.house.gov/cfr.htm). Thus, noting which URL is listed can give a sense of how frequently entries are verified.

The results of this experiment proved disappointing. None of the directories that included a description for the CFR site mention that this version of the CFR is dated and does not contain up-to-date regulations. While the Excite Reviews and Yahoo! point to the current URL, both of the Lycos sites point to the old one. Magellan does not include an entry for the CFR, although it does have an entry for the whole Internet Law Library site. That entry has the current URL, but again, no comment on the date of resources available with the Internet Law Library.

Yahoo! includes entries for both the dated version of the CFR and an entry for a CFR version from Counterpoint. The latter shows up under two categories: Business and Economy: Companies:Publishing: Counterpoint Publishing and Government: Documents. The dated version appears under Government:Law:Federal. Entries for the full House Internet Law Library appear under two other categories: Government:Law:General Information and Government: Legislative Branch:House of Representatives. This demonstrates more entries for CFR sources than the other directories, but it also points out inconsistency in the use of the Yahoo! categories. Multiple subject headings makes sense, but both versions of the CFR should appear under the same subjects headings, and they do not.

These subject directories are very useful resources. While a critical look turns up many defects, deficiencies, and inaccuracies, these directories remain one of the most effective ways to begin a search for specific information on the Internet. Due to its size, search features, and organization, Yahoo! remains one of the best initial approaches for a search. There are plenty of other directories, such as Elnet's Galaxy and subject specific directories. See Yahoo! under Computers and Internet:Internet: World Wide Web:Searching the Web: Directories for many more options.

Further Resources
BOOKS

Mintz, Anne P., ed. *Web of Deception: Misinformation on the Internet.* Medford, N.J.: CyberAge Books, 2002.

Morville, Peter. *The Internet Searcher's Handbook: Locating Information, People & Software.* New York: Neal-Schuman Publishers, 1999.

Sherman, Chris. *The Invisible Web: Uncovering Information Sources Search Engines Can't See.* Medford, N.J.: Cyber-Age Books, 2001.

PERIODICALS

Balas, Janet L. "It's the Little Things that Count." *Computers in Libraries* 18, no. 10, November/December 1998, 35–39.

"The Great Portal Race." *Fortune,* Winter 1999, 232–236.

WEBSITES

Internet Scout Project. Available online at http://scout.wisc.edu/ (accessed June 17, 2003).

Internet Search Engines. University at Albany Libraries. Available online at http://library.albany.edu/internet/engines.html (accessed June 17, 2003).

"Assignment: The Cable News Battle"

Journal article

By: James Snyder

Date: 1997

Source: Snyder, James. "Assignment: The Cable News Battle." *Television Quarterly* 28, no. 4, 1997, 49–53.

About the Author: James Snyder has been a news writer, reporter, CBS News producer, and radio and TV news director. He contributes to *Television Quarterly* regularly. Snyder was the vice president of news for the Post Newsweek Stations for 22 years. ■

Introduction

Network news traditionally covered the nation and the world, leaving local news for the affiliate newsrooms to handle. The networks also relied on the personality and style of one or two anchors to define their broadcast and to be identified with the news program. These factors changed when the cable news channels began to enter the market.

In the early years of cable news, CNN did not affect the format or the choice of anchors on the networks. CNN's philosophy was to hire newscasters who could deliver the news. The channel did not care about big names and expensive salaries. CNN became known for hard, timely news. The channel's reports were accurate and frequently longer than those of the major networks or local stations.

The entry of other cable news channels changed the philosophies of news broadcasting. Other factors also had an impact on news shows. The audiences who watched the news were getting older. To draw a younger audience that was attractive to advertisers, the news had to become more "hip." A survey commissioned by PBS's *NewsHour*

found that Fox News, who already had made a name for entertainment and sports on its Fox Television station, knew how to attract the younger audiences. It also discovered that MSNBC had worked to provide talk show formats during the daytime hours to attract a younger demographic.

The competition of new channels in the market caused a renewed energy in providing and producing the news on cable. Formats, sets, and what comprised news all become more significant than they were when the stakes were lower.

Significance

By 1997 the cable news wars were in full swing. Fox News and MSNBC both challenged rival CNN for a share of the audience. There were differences in the styles and ideologies of each cable channel, just as there were differences in the three network news broadcasts. Each cable channel had its strengths and weaknesses and was learning from its competitors.

Anchors were an important part of any newscast. On the networks, the anchors defined the news with their personalities and style. CNN's tradition of not hiring big-name news anchors had to change as MSNBC and Fox entered the market. MSNBC was able to draw from veteran reporters at NBC and a well-established newsroom to staff its news and talk shows. Fox News lured big-name talent from major networks and from other cable stations to fill out its staff. Anchors with name recognition and that viewers trusted proved to be an important part of the flagship newscasts on each cable channel.

The style of each channel defined who the audience would be and when they would tune in. CNN was traditionally known for its in-depth and quick-acting reporters. The network also established relationships with television stations throughout the country so CNN could be first on the scene when a story broke. Fox News tried to imitate this style with its Fox Television affiliates but by the early twenty-first century, it had not yet established the edge that CNN had. MSNBC relied on its NBC affiliates to provide local coverage when needed. The other difference in style came in programming. Fox News was far more contentious in its interviewing style than the other two cable news stations were. The conservative ideology of Fox News and its executives promoted a debate style of interviewing, rather than a milder approach to the news.

The news wars had just started to heat up in 1997 when James Snyder provided his analysis of the three cable news channels. The wars continued after that, with each station trying to find its way to the top of the ratings. As they carved out their niche in the news market, CNN, Fox News, and MSNBC continued to change and develop further.

Primary Source

"Assignment: The Cable News Battle" [excerpt]

SYNOPSIS: Three cable news channels began competing for news audiences in the fall of 1996 when Fox Cable News appeared. CNN, the founded in 1981 and the oldest of the cable news channels, had to change its style to compete. MSNBC, which appeared in the summer of 1996, was affiliated with both NBC and Microsoft and drew upon their resources to compile its news and programming.

I have spent many more hours than most viewers the past seven months watching the 24-hour cable news channel combat between CNN and its two new competitors, MSNBC and Fox Cable News. I liked seeing all that energy and journalistic thought displayed daily by so many talented people on and off camera. It all prompted two big questions, "Is this news glut?" and "Can all three survive?"

As MSNBC debuted in July and Fox Cable News in October, CNN, although profitable, was still struggling with its dilemma of many years. When there's no Gulf War or O.J. Simpson criminal trial CNN's ratings take a big dip to surprisingly low levels. That had happened in the spring of 1996; not encouraging for CNN and a message for MSNBC and Fox Cable News that they had to appeal to more than just the loyal CNN viewers.

At this point in its short history MSNBC, when it is reporting the news—as opposed to talking it to death or deviating into broadcasting the Imus 6-to-9 a.m. radio show or the part-infomercial The Site at 10 p.m.—is a worthy cousin of NBC News. It figures since its top brass are all creatures of the big three network news world. MSNBC covers the news the way NBC does but is free to devote much more airtime to breaking stories.

So too with Fox Cable News which has, at times, a more newsy format with less reliance on talk during the day than MSNBC. From 6 to 9 a.m. it does 15-minute "wheels" of the top stories which may appeal more to viewers who can't abide watching one camera staring at Imus and a couple other guys doing a radio show on MSNBC. It fills its afternoon hours in part by reaching out for live interviews with correspondents and newsmakers around the country. Fox Cable News, owned by Rupert Murdoch and directed by Roger Ailes, who is not a creature of the network news world, wants to be more feisty and is more likely to provoke critics into labeling it "tabloidy."

Political conservatives Murdoch and Ailes are on record against "bias and lack of balance" in the mainstream media. The Murdoch/Ailes view could make their cable news product different, and controversial to some. For example, Fox Cable producers were recently reported to be working on a segment which would examine the "lack of creativity" in the big three network nightly newscasts.

CNN after 18 years of being the only cable news service was ripe for some competition. Critics complained of bureaucracy, "robotic anchors," unimaginative production and downright dullness when there was no blockbuster story to cover. CNN's greatest strength in the new competitive climate is what it has done best for years: gathering the news quickly from anywhere. When a major story breaks at home or abroad, it is difficult to outdo CNN.

In January, when the House Ethics Committee was about to hold its first public hearing on the Newt Gingrich affair, everyone had pool video of people milling around the hearing room. MSNBC had its anchor talking to a correspondent who was ad-libbing as he stood in front of a marble column outside the Capitol Building. CNN was better prepared with their congressional correspondent in a studio voicing over the pool video and doing split screen interviews with two impressive veterans of work in and around the Congress. CNN has spent years building up its Washington savvy, and it shows.

One afternoon in December, fires had broken out in a residential area of Orange County, California. By 1 p.m. CNN had live helicopter coverage and correspondent reports from an area near the burning houses. Fox's coverage was dismal for a couple of hours. They did not have a correspondent report from the scene until about 3:30 and that was poorly done. Fox anchorwoman's ad-libs clanked on my ear when she said "Orange County, that's Los Angeles."

Another CNN strength is its working relationship with scores of local stations, including network affiliates, which buy its news service. This has been going on for about 15 years and gives CNN a powerful news gathering tool.

I remember taking a tour of CNN facilities in Atlanta when it was just starting. After the tour, I talked with Reese Schoenfeld, who ran CNN in its early years. I gave him my mostly favorable impressions. CNN was the first network to produce news programs from an open control room setup a few feet from the anchor desk. And they were using satellite technology in a way no one else had done to gather news from around the nation and the world.

My only negative impression was prompted by the absence of any well-known news anchors. Ted Turner was opposed to spending large sums on such

NBC Anchor Brian Williams speaks at the announcement of the new MSNBC network in 1996. © NAJLAH FEANNY/CORBIS SABA. REPRODUCED BY PERMISSION.

people. He was critical of what he called "the god-like network anchors." So Schoenfeld hired people who did not have any large market success on their resumes and could not command large salaries.

Things have improved in the last ten years but it is obvious MSNBC and Fox feel there are anchor weaknesses at CNN that they can exploit. Enter Tom Brokaw, Bob Costas, Katie Couric, Jane Pauley and Brian Williams at MSNBC; and Catherine Crier, Bill O'Reilly, Mike Schneider, John Scott, and Washington correspondent Brit Hume at Fox Cable. CNN labels news programs as *The World Tonight* or *Inside Politics.* At its competitors, the shows are named for the star anchor—*The Brian Williams Show* or *Time and Again with Jane Pauley* on MSNBC, *The Mike Schneider Show* and *The Catherine Crier Show* on Fox Cable.

MSNBC, unlike Fox, went on the air offering a striking difference in their on-air look from CNN,

which hadn't changed its look in years. I like MSNBC's sets, lighting, graphics and production style. The Brian Williams hour-long news show at 9 p.m. will never be accused of copying CNN.

Williams' easygoing style and sly humor is a welcome break with tradition. The departure from the straight-ahead-shot-of-the-anchor approach makes the newscast distinctive and more enjoyable. CNN has long honored the practice of having the anchors bolted to their chairs to be seen only from the waist up no matter what the design of the desk. Walter Cronkite once remarked that a lot of people thought he had no legs because they had seen him only on TV behind an anchor desk.

I also give extra points to MSNBC for not insisting that there be two anchors on the program. Williams and his producers appear to be free to try things on the air. CNN anchors could use a little of that.

The MSNBC set is the largest departure from the news set norm any network has made in my memory. Parts of it do look like the walls of a loft somewhere that is in various stages of renovation and decoration with electronic devices. Roger Ailes, Chairman of Fox Cable News and a veteran generator of barbed comment, said of this set, "They have brought back the coffee basements of the 1960s." The Fox Cable News sets break no new ground.

I like the MSNBC set because of its bright lighting and the camera angles available to a show director. *The Brian Williams Show* displays Williams as a whole human being, legs and all, and varies the shots to include, of all things, Brian from the side and back.

I also applaud the practice of making NBC News and Fox network news correspondents available for live shots on the cable news services. It enriches the news shows and reduces the traditional frustration of network reporters having to fight to get painfully brief stories on the nightly news programs. I remember a CBS correspondent who complained to the executive producer in New York that I, as Washington producer for the *Cronkite News,* was trying to destroy his career by preventing him from appearing on Walter's show more than twice a week.

One recent afternoon, I watched NBC correspondent Andrea Mitchell do a strong live report for MSNBC from its Washington Bureau. Andrea, one of the hardest charging reporters I have ever known, obviously enjoyed the assignment, all 10 minutes of it. It was therapy for her years of fashioning *NBC Nightly News* reports that could not be a few seconds more than a minute. An appearance a few minutes later by the NBC Pentagon correspondent, Ed Rabel, was another reminder of how the pool of seasoned NBC reporters is invaluable to MSNBC.

For years, as the three major networks became more reluctant to interrupt regular programming for extended live coverage of breaking stories (even Presidential news conferences are routinely passed over by the big three), CNN and sometimes C-SPAN have reaped much audience praise by filling the gap. Now MSNBC and Fox also are happy to provide extensive live coverage whenever possible. That means viewers also have more variety in the analysis included with the live coverage.

The conventional nightly network half-hour news programs deplore the long sound-bite. No one makes extended remarks on the nightly news. But they do on MSNBC and Fox, especially in live interviews. This can be a curse as well as a blessing for the people who must decide how to fill up all that time on a cable news service. The staffers who book the many guests cable news organizations need are as important as their bosses. There is nothing more painful than a booker mistake, putting someone on the air who is boring and incapable of holding anyone's attention past the first 10 seconds.

I give all three cable news services high marks for covering the news, staying on top of the daily news flow and reacting quickly when live coverage or interviews anywhere in the country can be used to advance the story. CNN after all these years is best at this. MSNBC, with all the help it gets from NBC News staff, is not far behind CNN now. Fox Cable News managers have the right instincts, but they do not yet have the news organization the other two services have and so are sometimes limited in where they can quickly go for live coverage. And Fox is also limited because some of its affiliate stations do not have strong news departments to call. MSNBC, however, has many excellent NBC affiliate news operations to turn to.

Whatever their differences in style, formats or talent, all three cable services deserve praise for bringing fast coverage of important, interesting stories that CBS, NBC and ABC prefer to hold till their next scheduled newscast rather than interrupt regular programming. Of course, there are things I don't like about the three cable news services. CNN loses me with its afternoon show *Talk Back Live*. I am allergic to too much interactivity. If I never hear another ludicrous or ill-informed telephone call from a viewer, I'll be happy. Expecting profundities from a studio audience is a hazardous business too. The hour-long *Talk Back Live* was aptly called a "channel changer" by a *Newsweek* critic.

Further Resources

BOOKS

Johnston, Carla B. *Winning the Global TV News Game.* Boston: Focal Press, 1995.

Silvia, Tony, ed. *Global News: Perspectives on the Information Age.* Ames, Iowa: Iowa State University Press, 2001.

PERIODICALS

Cooper, Jim. "News War." *Mediaweek,* May 31, 1999, 34–35.

McAvoy, Kim. "The News Junkies." *Broadcasting & Cable,* August 16, 1999, 24–28.

WEBSITES

Cable News Wars, Online NewsHour. Available online at http://www.pbs.org/newshour/media/cablenews/analysis_high lights.html (accessed June 17, 2003).

"Who Won the Mosaic War?"

Journal article

By: Hal Berghel

Date: October 1998

Source: Berghel, Hal. "Who Won the Mosaic War?" *Communications of the ACM* 41, no. 10, October 1998, 13–16.

About the Author: Hal Berghel (1946–) is a professor and chair of computer science at the University of Nevada at Las Vegas. Berghel has published widely on computing; his research interests include electronic communities, electronic information management, and software and information architectures. Berghel received the Association for Computing Machinery (ACM) Outstanding Lecturer of the Year award in 1996, 1997, and 1998. ∎

Introduction

In the 1990s boom of the technology industry, dot.coms and companies that developed and sold software sprang up by the hundreds. On paper these companies could make millions of dollars in a short time. The quickly moving technology market and the economy could not support all of the companies that developed, however. The dot.com industry fell off by the end of the 1990s.

Along with the development of Web browsers and software, language to discuss computing developed. UNIX, Mosaic, and FTP became more common terms for the public. Cello was not just a musical instrument; it was also an early Web browser. Further terms became common in the language as e-mail and Web surfing became more popular.

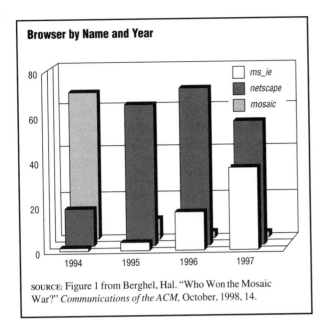

Browser by Name and Year

SOURCE: Figure 1 from Berghel, Hal. "Who Won the Mosaic War?" *Communications of the ACM,* October, 1998, 14.

Competition was a key part of the computing industry. Netscape started as the Mosaic Communications Corporation until the University of Illinois' National Center for Supercomputing Applications claimed the rights to the name "Mosaic," since they had developed the browser by the same name. Nevertheless, in 1995, Netscape became the browser of choice as it knocked out Mosaic and gave away its product for free with a radical kind of marketing plan. The founders of Netscape relied on corporate clients to pay for services and to help make the company a success.

Hal Berghel writes about the wars over browsers and the competition between companies catering to the Internet. He hones in on the short history of Internet browsers and predicts the future, with some accuracy. Embedded technologies continued to be a challenge for computer and software developers in the early twenty-first century.

Significance

Life continued to be interesting for the Web and for development of computing. Hal Berghel highlights some of the significant developments of the mid- to late-1990s in his article. He identifies the competition that resulted over browsers and the issues of desktop computing, and predicts that the embedded technologies will change computing further. He could not have predicted the impact of the Microsoft antitrust case on the industry, though he did identify the issue.

Berghel condenses the history of Web browsers up to 1998. Mosaic, the first major browser, was the forerunner of Netscape. In Web and computing history, Mosaic and Netscape were winners in the war for a brief time. The development of Netscape from Mosaic seemed

inevitable. Developments in browsers passed quickly in the 1990s. Competitors took over once-popular and freely available browsers. Netscape was sold to AOL, one of Microsoft's competitors for e-mail and other Web services. Microsoft began bundling Internet Explorer with all of its operating software. This was the central issue of the lawsuit just beginning when Berghel's article was published.

The key question in computing was how to keep up with new technology. By the time one Microsoft lawsuit was settled, others had started over altering Java, Web authoring, and allowing other browser and Internet providers to be bundled with software. In the early twenty-first century, the development of computing and software continued to speed ahead. Changes kept it an interesting industry to watch.

Primary Source

"Who Won the Mosaic War?" [excerpt]

SYNOPSIS: The metaphor of war was an apropos one. The competition between browsers, software companies, and computer manufacturers became intense during the 1990s. Lawsuits against companies, especially Microsoft, became the norm and made headlines across the nation.

Remember the Mosaic War? It was the hot topic of techie conversation a few years ago. The term hearkens back to the kinder and simpler era of Web antiquity (circa, 1994!). Like "navigator/browser," "helper app" and "X-windows," the term signifies a bygone era—the Web-gilded age every software developer believed they had a chance at market dominance and Web surfing was a favorite pastime. It might be useful at this point to see if we can identify winners and losers in this Mosaic War of old, especially if we could then anticipate the outcome of remaining hostilities. But first we wander down memory lane.

The Web was conceived by Tim Berners-Lee and his colleagues at CERN (now called the European Laboratory for Particle Physics) in 1989 as a shared information space supporting collaborative work. Berners-Lee defined HTTP and HTML at that time. As a proof of concept prototype, he developed the first Web client navigator-browser in 1990 for the NeXTStep platform. Nicola Pellow developed the first cross-platform Web browser in 1991 while Berners-Lee and Bernd Pollerman developed the first server application—a phone book database. By 1992, the interest in the Web was sufficient to produce four additional browsers—Erwise, Midas, and Viola for X Windows, and Cello for Windows.

The following year, Marc Andreessen of the National Center for Supercomputer Application (NCSA) wrote Mosaic for X Windows which soon became the browser standard against which all others would be compared. Andreessen went on to cofound Netscape Communications in 1994 whose current browser, Netscape Navigator, succeeded Mosaic as the next de facto standard Web browser. That's when the Mosaic War started; aggressive and imaginative developers were trying to out-Mosaic Mosaic. The feverish pace of development was something to behold. Within months, literally dozens of new start-up companies appeared. By 1994 it appeared as if browser vendors would proliferate like wire coat hangers.

Fast forward to 1995 . . . a turning point in the Mosaic War. By year's end, Mosaic is basically out of the picture as a navigator/browser [as shown in Figure: Browser by Name and Year]. It went from over 90% of the browser market to under 5% in just over two years. So the first major fatality in the Mosaic War was, ironically enough, Mosaic itself. Meanwhile, Netscape displaced Mosaic as the de facto standard within the same time frame and became the new de facto browser standard. By the end of 1995, spirited developers worldwide attempted to capture the half of the browser market that wasn't already Netscape's. By this time the Mosaic War became known as the "browser war" for obvious reasons.

So, in the end, Mosaic went the same way as Cello, Viola, Erwise, and Midas before it. These Web fatalities confirmed that the Web was highly unforgiving of technology deficiencies. On the other hand, the big winner of the Mosaic War was clearly

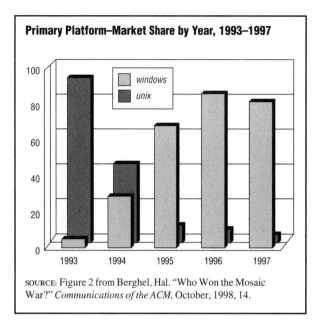

Primary Platform–Market Share by Year, 1993–1997

SOURCE: Figure 2 from Berghel, Hal. "Who Won the Mosaic War?" *Communications of the ACM,* October, 1998, 14.

Netscape. Netscape's dominance was the result of a constant stream of innovations—much to the chagrin of the World Wide Web Consortium (www.w3c .org) and the Internet Engineering Task Force (www .ietf.org) which preferred to introduce innovations in an orderly and deliberative manner through their RFC's and standards committees. In any event, some of Netscape's more popular innovations appear in [Table: Netscape Extensions to Browserdom, 1994–1998].

Armed with imposing innovations from 1995–1997, Netscape appeared to be the clear victor in the browser war as well. However, two external factors changed Netscape's future. First, the dominance of Windows as the OS of choice for the overwhelming majority of Web users provided a strong disincentive to developers of client-side software for other OS environments [as shown in Figure: Primary Platform-Market Share by Year, 1993–1997]. As Windows rapidly became the dominant OS, Netscape's commitment to multiplatform development (approximately 20 platforms) became increasingly uneconomical. While the expenses of Web client development are basically constant across platforms, the potential revenue streams vary with the size of the customer bases (that is, the Windows market is approximately 20 times the size of the Mac and Unix markets, and hence potentially 20 times the revenue). The commitment to multiplatform development really hurt Netscape's overall competitiveness, since their main rival, Microsoft's Internet Explorer,

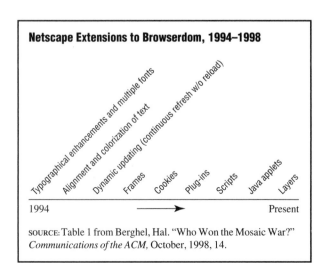

Netscape Extensions to Browserdom, 1994–1998

SOURCE: Table 1 from Berghel, Hal. "Who Won the Mosaic War?" *Communications of the ACM,* October, 1998, 14.

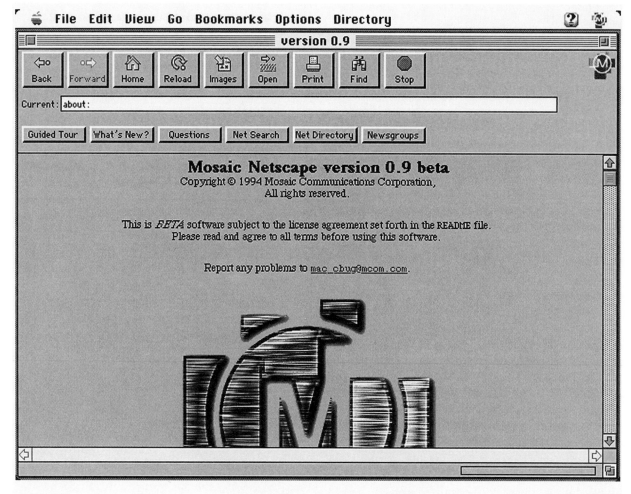

Screen capture, Mosaic Netscape 0.9

Screenshot of the NCSA Mosaic 0.9 browser. A now familiar feature not yet added to the browser is the address bar. Users of this version of Mosaic had to select "Open" from the File menu to go to a new web page. © 2002 NETSCAPE COMMUNICATIONS CORPORATION. SCREENSHOT USED WITH PERMISSION.

chose to focus their development effort primarily on a single-platform.

The second major event that challenged Netscape's hegemony in the browser arena was Microsoft's combined marketing strategy to both provide Internet Explorer without charge, and bundle it with Windows OS. Not surprisingly, Netscape found that it is difficult to compete with products both seamlessly integrated into the OS and also free. This situation was not overlooked by the Department of Justice who recently brought an antitrust case to the U.S. Court of Appeals claiming Microsoft has used its OS dominance to achieve a monopoly in the browser market. Netscape has since unbundled its browser, Navigator 5.x, from its group-ware suite, Communicator, and has agreed to release and license the

source code of Navigator to interested developers in a disparate attempt to keep their code alive.

Figures, [Browser by Name and Year and Primary Platform-Market Share by Year, 1993–1997], taken together, show that Internet Explorer is doing to Netscape what Netscape did to Mosaic. There is an important difference, however. Netscape unseated Mosaic primarily through innovation, whereas Microsoft's successes are primarily due to its dominance of the OS market and its unrivaled marketing prowess (I assume few would claim marquis, background sound, table colors and stationary backgrounds are strong representatives of IE innovation.). Failing intervention by the Federal Trade Commission, or successful antitrust litigation against Microsoft from the Department of Justice, it appears that history will repeat itself in the most recent incarnation of the browser war. It seems all but inevitable.

So what's next? The end of the browser war coincides with the beginning of the "desktop war." The stage is set: Goliath Microsoft will do battle with the Davids of client-side software development over compatibility with the full range of Windows applications. The war is heating up as I write, the major players trying to outflank each other on choices between Windows API vs. Swing Set interfaces, Visual Basic vs. Java scripting languages, dynamic HTML vs. pure HTML with Java document standards, Secure Sockets Layer vs. Java security model, ActiveX vs. CORBA middleware, and so forth. This fight is going to get nasty before its over (sometime around the turn of the millennium, I suspect). We're talking trench warfare here with digital nerve gas.

But the previous wars will pale in comparison to the ultimate bloodbath, over "embedded applications" in which the forces of good and evil will fight for supremacy over our thin Web clients: PDA's, televisions, appliances, automobiles, phones, games, smart cards and digital jewelry (that's right, Sun has already created a prototype of a Java ring (see www.javasoft.com). The embedded apps war will be the true test of mastery over all things digital, because it will extend dominion beyond the general-purpose computing desktops to the special-purpose embedded applications around which our life is based. This topic is so new that developers are just now beginning to define their positions. By the time the winners of the desktop war are identified, the embedded applications war will be in full swing.

So, let's return to our original question: "Who Won the Mosaic War?" The answer is Netscape. However, as we've seen, this is a shallow victory for Netscape as it struggles to hang onto its leadership position in the client-side browser area. As the dust settles on the browser war, the apparent victor is Microsoft's Internet Explorer. However, like the Mosaic War, the outcome of the browser war may not have much strategic impact, because of its narrow scope. In terms of impact, the effect of the desktop war will be far more important. While Microsoft remains in the leadership position, the absence of widely accepted standards makes it possible for real innovation to surface. Smart money will probably bet on Microsoft to emerge victorious.

But even the desktop war won't by itself have the most effect on the world of networking. That honor will go to the big war, the no holds barred,

winner-take-all embedded applications war which will be fought over our televisions, air conditioners, and security systems. The embedded applications war will be the Bosnia of the Internet software development community and could easily lead to digital "ethnic cleansing" as developers scramble among chaos for survivability. Unlike previous wars, the embedded applications war will be about lifestyle computing—control over the digital appliances we take for granted. I'll repeat what I said in 1995. These are exciting times!

Further Resources

BOOKS
Grossman, Wendy M. *From Anarchy to Power: The Net Comes of Age.* New York: New York University Press, 2001.

Rawlins, Gregory J.E. *Moths to the Flame: The Seductions of Computer Technology.* Cambridge: MIT Press, 1996.

PERIODICALS
Bottoms, David. "Jim Clark: The Shooting Star @ Netscape." *Industry Week* 244, no. 23, December 18, 1995, 12–16.

Nath, Manju. "Low-cost Techniques Bring Internet Connectivity in Embedded Devices." *EDN* 44, no. 23, November 11, 1999, 159–166.

Reichard, Kevin. "Web Browsers and Internet Access Tools." *Accounting Technology* 11, no. 11, December 1995, 49.

WEBSITES
National Center for Supercomputing Applications (NCSA). Available online at http://www.ncsa.uiuc.edu/ (accessed June 17, 2003).

"Much Ado About Nothing: Some Final Thoughts on *Seinfeld*"
Journal article

By: Albert Auster

Date: 1998

Source: Auster, Albert. "Much Ado About Nothing: Some Final Thoughts on *Seinfeld*." *Television Quarterly* 29, no. 4, 1998, 24–33.

About the Author: Albert Auster (1940–) teaches in the Communications & Media Studies Department of the Graduate School at Fordham University. As a media critic, Auster has published widely in journals and books. He received his Ph.D. from SUNY Stonybrook in 1981. ∎

Introduction

During the 1970s, sitcoms were a popular staple of television lineups. *The Mary Tyler Moore Show, Taxi, All in the Family,* and *Barney Miller* provided laughter. After a few years of no new sitcoms, they enjoyed a renaissance in the 1980s with the creation of shows like *Cheers* and *The Cosby Show.* The NBC Thursday night lineup was home to many of the humorous and award-winning comedies that were popular with audiences. All of the shows mentioned above had plots. They followed characters through situations and often referred to previous episodes as part of an ongoing story. Sam and Diane's relationship on *Cheers* carried over several seasons. The Huxtable children of *The Cosby Show* grew up and learned from each other.

It was not until the 1990s that comedy was ready for a show about nothing. Some viewers never adjusted to Jerry Seinfeld's wacky brand of humor, but others watched every week. *Seinfeld* took over the *Cheers* Thursday night spot when the show went off the air. The series revolved around the minutiae of four friends' lives. Jerry, a stand-up comic; George, his high school friend; Elaine, Jerry's ex-girlfriend, and Kramer, the crazy neighbor, made up the main cast of the show. The friends served as a pseudo family for one another, though both Jerry's and George's parents were also regulars on the show.

Not everyone loved *Seinfeld.* Critics such as James Collins pointed out that although *Seinfeld* was number one for the 1994–1995 season and consistently second after *E.R.* in other seasons, its audience share was really smaller than other popular sitcoms. Enough people did like *Seinfeld*'s humor to create an almost hysteric response to its finale.

Significance

Seinfeld left its mark on America through its weird sense of humor. Episodes became well known and topics of conversation. The coffee shop was a place to gather and to discuss the daily complications of life.

The unorthodox characters were politically incorrect in their points of view and in their comments. According to Nicholaus Mills, "What lay at the center of *Seinfeld* and made it the leading sitcom of the nineties was the delight it took in attacking political correctness. *Seinfeld*'s writers were fearless in a way that few in academic life have been. There was no way to predict, as there had been with the political right over the last decade, the manners or values they would target." Episodes made fun of a "bubble boy" who was obnoxious, criticized others for minor imperfections, and had Kramer assaulted when he refused to wear a ribbon in an AIDS walk. These were not the subjects of the previous generation's sitcoms.

Rob Owen noted that "*Seinfeld* had a knack for winding all the elements of an episode together." The plots were a "mess of coincidences." This is true of the final episode, which draws together characters from pre-

vious episodes. The four friends set off for Paris on a free plane trip, but wind up being charged with a crime under the "Good Samaritan" law. At the end of the show, the four are in jail, where they will presumably remain for the rest of their days because there is no one to rescue them this time.

Seinfeld contrasted generations, made fun of the things we are not supposed to laugh at, and featured humor about urban society. It concentrated on the daily annoyances of life instead of big issues. *Seinfeld* didn't try to be more than it was—a show about four people trying to muddle through life in a big city.

Primary Source

"Much Ado About Nothing: Some Final Thoughts on *Seinfeld*." [excerpt]

SYNOPSIS: The show about nothing's final episode aired on May 14, 1998. *Seinfeld* became the most popular syndicated television show in history, drawing larger audiences than some currently running programs. In 2002, *TV Guide* named the comedy the number one program in its "50 Greatest TV Shows of All Time" list.

Seinfeld was unique in that it examined the not so discreet churlish charm of the bourgeoisie. In contrast to the generations of family- and friends-style sitcoms, whose characters, despite frequent misunderstandings, were ultimately generous and mutually supportive of one another. Jerry, George, Kramer and Elaine never missed an opportunity to compete with, lie, and back stab one another.

Not only did the fearsome foursome wreak havoc on each other, it usually extended to anyone in their wake. Heading the long list of Seinfeld's victims—which included the likes of Jerry's friend Babu, who was deported back to Pakistan because Jerry forgot to file his visa application—was George's Job-like fiancee, Susan Ross (Heidi Swedeborg). Even before their fatal engagement, she had to endure Kramer's misplaced Cuban cigar burning down her parents' cabin as well as the later embarrassment of the discovery of love letters from novelist John Cheever to her father found in the cabin's ashes; losing her job at NBC; and the breakup of a lesbian relationship—all because of George.

This cycle of devastation even extended to their own families. For example, when Jerry's parents heard that the dreaded Costanzas were about to move to their condominium in Florida, they moved in with Jerry, thus putting an end to his precious "buffer zone." Similarly, when Jerry bought his father a new Cadillac it resulted in the condo's board, of which he was president, voting to impeach him à la "Watergate"—they thought he must be embezzling funds, because they didn't believe a mere comedian could afford to buy his father such an expensive car. Indeed, though Jerry Seinfeld himself claimed Abbott and Costello as another of his comic muses (and the series use of dialogue and language confirmed this), the main characters' stick in the eye approach to one another, and everyone else, seemed more akin to the Three Stooges.

Nothing, however, rivaled *Seinfeld* for its version of post-modern etiquette. There was for instance the *Seinfeld* guide to dating that included how many dates you had to have before it was still proper to break up a relationship over the phone rather than in person (only two); how long after sleeping with a woman you had to keep dating her (three weeks). And for those needing guidance on the subject, the information that the longer you knew someone, the shorter you have to wait for them in the street; that you only have to keep a thank-you card for two days after you receive it (unless you have a mantle); and you should never degift (take back something you gave) or regift (give away something you received).

Less frequently acknowledged but nonetheless an essential ingredient of quite a few *Seinfeld* episodes, was their mild satiric jabs at political correctness (especially ironic in a show supposedly about nothing). For example, Kramer was beaten up at an AIDS walkathon for refusing to wear an AIDS ribbon; George's father's car was vandalized when he parked in a disabled parking spot; and in an episode that prompted a network apology, Kramer was attacked when he stomped on a burning Puerto Rican flag during the Puerto Rican Day Parade. The inspiration for these incidents was neither conservative nor liberal politically; instead they seemed inspired by the series' radical individualism, or put in a showbiz idiom, "Screw 'em, if they can't take a joke!"

Unfortunately, this indifference to politics and society did have its downside. For example, black characters in their infrequent appearances on the series rarely rose above the level of caricature. Thus, lawyer Jackie Chiles, the series parody of Johnnie Cochran, seemed an Amos 'n Andy lineal descendant of George "Kingfish" Stevens and Algonquin J. Calhoun.

If the series did have one strong point in its dealings with race, it was with the embarrassment and uneasyness that middle class whites often feel about the issue. As a result in one episode, Elaine,

In an episode of *Seinfeld*, Kramer, played by actor Michael Richards, has an encounter with a chimpanzee. THE KOBAL COLLECTION/NBC TV/CARIN RICHARDS. REPRODUCED BY PERMISSION.

because she's afraid of being considered a bigot, goes through all sorts of contortions in order to find out if the somewhat swarthy man she's been dating, who Jerry thinks is black, is indeed a black man.

Of course, Elaine's racial guessing game is mild in comparison to the larger question that often plagued the series—the extent to which the series often went to hide not only its cultural Jewishness but any sort of religiosity. Though the series, apropos of Tartikoff's caveat, is replete with Jewish body language and syntax (George's head slappings and comments like, "again with the keys"); references (Bar Mitzvahs, the Holocaust, Florida condos and Elaine being referred to as having shiksappeal).

Nevertheless, *Seinfeld* was always the artful dodger in explicitly acknowledging its Judaism. As a result, throughout the series you had funerals of relatives from Krakow without a yarmulke in sight, a bris (circumcision) without even a hint of Rabbi, and when George wants to convert to "Latvian Orthodox" in order to impress a woman, it's never really made clear what religion he wants to convert from.

All of these elements, both positive and negative, came together in the series' intellectually consistent, but generally less than hilarious final episode. It was a conclusion which some finale mavens rated as inferior to *Mary Tyler Moore*'s sign off, but better than *M*A*S*H*'s, and undoubtedly the equal of *Cheers* curtain calls. Nevertheless, the hoopla that surrounded the show paid off in Superbowl type ratings that almost equalled *Cheers*' final episode (which to be fair is quite good, given the fact that the champion *M*A*S*H*'s and *The Fugitive*'s finales never had to contend with the inroads of cable).

There was, in addition, one other record set by the passing of *Seinfeld*. Some sort of Guinness mark must have been achieved for shortest post-TV-finale attention span by the modern media hype machine. In less time than it took to say "get out," that colossus had made a one-hundred-and-eighty-degree turn, and was in overdrive about another story—the death of Frank Sinatra. In the heat of the coverage of the death of the man, whose voice had become the soundtrack for millions of lives worldwide, the ballyhoo over *Seinfeld* faded like a snowstorm in July.

As a matter of fact, in what seemed like less than a nanosecond, the Upper West Side had been exorcised by images of Hoboken on the television landscape—memories of the antics of Jerry, George, Kramer and Elaine replaced by nostalgia about the hijinks of Rat Packers Frank, Dino, Sammy, Peter, Joey, and Shirley, and ring-a-ding-ding substituted for yada, yada, yada.

The hype meltdown aside, *Seinfeld*'s finale's most solid achievement was to manage to conclude without violating the consistency of the series' major characters or its major themes. This was perhaps a bit more difficult for *Seinfeld* than either *M*A*S*H*, *Mary Tyler Moore*, and *Cheers*. In those earlier finales, there was the end of the Korean War, the purchase of the TV station by a media conglomerate, and the closing of the bar to serve as justifications for these programs' bittersweet conclusions. For *Seinfeld*, there was no such easy rationale.

Also in comparison to *MTM*, *M*A*S*H*, and *Cheers*, where fans and critics cited certain episodes such as "Chuckles the Clown Bites the Dust," "Abbysinia, Henry," etc., as highlights of the series, but left it for latter generations to decide which of them were "classics," *Seinfeld*'s fans, along with a number of entertainment periodicals and critics, had already constructed an elaborate pantheon of the series' most inspired episodes and anointed them as the *Seinfeld* canon. As a result, there was hardly much room for additions, which made the task of any final episode much more difficult.

The final episode, however, if not fall-on-the-floor funny, was still amusing, and, in this most self-referential of all series, must have set a record for self-references. Concocted under a cloak of secrecy that the media claimed rivaled the Manhattan Project, former co-executive producer and head writer Larry David created a virtual concordance of some of the series' major moments, characters, and themes. Receiving curtain calls were story lines such as "The Jerry Show," George and Jerry's self-reflexive show about nothing, which they had tried unsuccessfully to peddle to the network in the series' fourth season. Characters included lawyer Jackie Chiles, the Bubble Boy, Susan Ross's parents, and others, all of whose appearances, as character witnesses, were occasioned by the trial of the foursome for violating the Lowell, Massachusetts, "Good Samaritan" Law.

In addition, David, in a bow to the show's most ardent fans, even included moments that alluded to their dreams of how the series should end. Thus, to those who believed that the show's rightful consummation should have been Jerry and Elaine's wedding, there was a moment when the corporate jet on which they are flying seemed about to crash and Elaine appeared about to confess her abiding love for Jerry, only to squelch it moments later when they were saved.

Finally, in a homage to the only love affair the show really ever had—its passion for symmetry—the finale's concluding moments made a bow to the series origins with Jerry in a jailhouse jumpsuit (George and Kramer in attendance, but Elaine nowhere in sight) doing his standup routine for the cons, spouting trademark insouciant lines such as "So, what's the story about the 'yard'?."

This final allusion to the fictional and the real Jerry's beginnings in standup, may be to some extent a suggestion about his immediate future. However, one might not go wrong in predicting another sitcom in the not-too-distant Seinfeld future. As a matter of fact, after the show's finale a very sober, almost solemn Jerry (in contrast to the *Cheers* cast which was boisterously and blissfully drunk in its curtain call on *The Tonight Show* after its finale) appeared with Jay Leno to talk about his future. Upon his entrance, the studio audience's standing ovation was so intense and so prolonged that it prompted him to wave and seem to head off stage teasingly shouting, "O.K., Come on, let's do another season."

Whether Jerry Seinfeld can resist the future siren call of the sitcom better than the likes of equally talented standups, who starred in hit sitcoms, such as Bill Cosby and Bob Newhart, remains to be seen. What is not moot is that in a sitcom world where there is so much unrelieved similarity, *Seinfeld* stood out because of its originality and steadfast insistence on being true to itself. This makes it especially noteworthy in a medium where we've become so inured to the sameness of sitcoms that some teenagers can even shout story lines back to the screen à la *The Rocky Horror Show.*

Seinfeld was also special because it continued and kept alive a tradition inherent in *The Mary Tyler Moore Show, M*A*S*H* and *Cheers*: that at its very best the sitcom has the potential to become an authentic American comedy of manners. In this, *Seinfeld* succeeded by becoming the television comedy that pointed out the imprecision of our contemporary relationships and gave a name to the sources of our modern urban anxiety.

As a result of these efforts, *Seinfeld* achieved something that not even *MTM, M*A*S*H,* and *Cheers* ever accomplished, which was to create adjectives akin to the literary-inspired Dickensian and Kafkaesque. Therefore, something is Seinfeldian— or in its more common usage an event or character, is "just like a *Seinfeld* episode," means that it breaks the fourth wall of conventional expectations to reveal the potential of the everyday as a source of both art and philosophy. So, despite its best efforts at adhering (even onto the very last) to its rule of "no hugging, no learning," *Seinfeld* left us with a very rich legacy after all.

Further Resources

BOOKS

Hibbs, Thomas S. *Shows about Nothing: Nihilism in Popular Culture from The Exorcist to Seinfeld.* Dallas: Spence Publishers, 1999.

Seinfeld, Jerry. *Seinlanguage.* New York: Bantam, 1995.

Seinfeld, Jerry and Larry David. *The Seinfeld Scripts: The First and Second Seasons.* New York: Perennial, 1998.

PERIODICALS

Collins, James. "Goodbye Already." *Time,* May 18, 1998, 82–86.

Mills, Nicolaus. "So Long, Jerry Seinfeld." *Dissent* 45, no. 3, Summer 1998, 89–92.

WEBSITES

Seinfeld: The Last Yada. Available online at http://www.cnn.com/SHOWBIZ/seinfeld/ (accessed June 17, 2003).

"Ken Burns Makes History Happen Now"
Interview

By: Martin C. Pedersen

Date: 1998

Source: Pedersen, Martin C. "Ken Burns Makes History Happen Now." *Graphis* no. 315, May/June 1998, 99–100.

About the Author: Martin Pedersen purchased *Graphis,* an internationally recognized magazine concentrating on design and visual communications. In 1986 he moved it from Switzerland to New York City and expanded the magazine's presence in the United States. *Graphis* also published books on visual and design communications. ∎

Introduction

History is traditionally taught as a top-down process. First we are taught about the great men and events, and then, if time allows, about other figures and events. There never seems to be time for the other stories, however. Methods for teaching history changed in the last decades of the twentieth century. Curriculum in women's history, as well as in the history of blacks and other minority groups, have been added to history courses. Primary documents such as photographs, diaries, and letters make history come alive.

Documentary film is one way to teach historical events. These, too, have depended on the "important" figures and events in history. Films have also traditionally relied upon the third-person narration and on film clips from earlier eras. Single shots of photographs may appear in a documentary film.

Ken Burns changed these traditional methods of teaching history and filming history. He began his career as a documentary filmmaker in 1975 after graduating from Hampshire College in Amherst, Massachusetts. Along with a couple of friends, Burns began Florentine Films, an independent film company. Burns's first successful film was *Brooklyn Bridge,* a 1982 film based on David McCullough's *The Great Bridge.* The film was the first of his award-winning documentaries.

In his *Graphis* interview, Burns talks about his multipart series, *The Civil War, Baseball,* and *Jazz.* Each one explored a subject from American history in a way to make history alive. Each series, shown on prime-time television, drew record-setting audiences and were rebroadcast in encore presentations.

Significance

In 1975, Ken Burns set out on a journey to redefine the historical documentary film. In his 1991 Lowell Lecture at Harvard University, Burns notes the importance of story connected to history. He says that "these emotional connections become a kind of glue which makes the most complex of past events stick in our minds and our hearts, permanently, a part of who each of us is now." History can be successfully told from the point of view of the ordinary citizen or of the important figures of history.

Burns and his creative teams assemble the script for a film or series from extensive research. Unlike the traditional documentary, research is not a separate phase of the process completed by a person not responsible for writing the film's script. This is a vital difference because the history, the reading, and the information become part of the process and continue as the work goes on and the editing is completed. The creative team realizes where gaps may be or when interesting characters may appear who will add another dimension to the film. Two additional vital aspects of Burns's films are the photographs and use of music. Burns finds stories within still photographs, which has changed the way that audiences view historical documentaries and the interpretation of historical photographs. Burns's affinity for looking beyond the obvious uncovers details that many have overlooked.

Finally, Ken Burns's retelling of the Civil War, as well as the history of baseball, jazz, and historical figures' lives, is popular because he finds the story within the events. Through the use of diaries, letters, personal papers, paintings, and photographs, Burns finds the voices for making history relevant to this generation. His use of professional historians, television personalities, and actors add to the vibrancy of the historical moments he uncovers and brings to life.

Primary Source

"Ken Burns Makes History Happen Now" [excerpt]

SYNOPSIS: Ken Burns creates history through stories he finds in old photographs and quotes. Burns and his colleagues at Florentine Films compile thousands of images and recordings before the editing process starts. The process may take a number of years to complete, depending on the subject and the available material.

Graphis: What is your feeling about the use of still photographs? Are they somehow limiting in a way that the moving image isn't?

Burns: No. I believe that a still photograph is liberating. Many of my contemporaries only choose subjects once the newsreel era has entered, once film was invented. Because they feel much more comfortable illustrating with film images. I feel almost exactly the opposite. There *is* something wonderful about newsreel footage. But imagine you had newsreel footage of Babe Ruth rounding the bases. Ba-

sically, you could only talk about Babe Ruth hitting home runs at that moment. But if you had a *portrait* of Babe Ruth, you could talk, as you looked at that still photograph, about him running around the bases, but you could also talk about his unhappy childhood in Baltimore, you could talk about his controversial and scandalous off-field behavior, you could talk about his failed relationships with women, you could talk about his death. That still photograph—seemingly limited, seemingly static—allows for a wide variety of choices and options. It's a tabula rasa. Now I don't wish to take away from the wonderful image of this spindly-legged man with this huge torso, mincing along as he ran around the bases—a priceless image—but I do believe that we are not at a deficit when we have only still images with which to deal with our subject.

Graphis: Let's talk about the use of music. Why is it always such a powerful element in your films?

Burns: Film music is called a score. And that is essentially a mathematical term. When a film is finished, it is locked. That means the timing of that film will not change. And then someone with a great musical ability is brought in to essentially amplify or isolate and point out certain dramatic moments in the film. It's a completely mathematical process, in which the music is timed to something that's already been done. It's hardly organic.

But what if you treated the music as you treated your historical photograph? Or the first-person diary entries that you were assembling? You would then, as we do, have to begin the collecting of music at the very beginning of the process. Unconcerned with its length. You would look for authentic, historically accurate music, arranged as it was back then. And then, as we do, take a group of musicians into the studio well before we begin editing, and get fifteen or twenty versions of fifteen or twenty different songs. We lay down what we call "musical beds."

Graphis: How many different versions of "Take Me out to the Ballgame" did you record for Baseball?

Burns: I recorded well over 250 different versions. And they ranged from the simplest, single-notes on the piano to the most lounge-lizardy cocktail music. All of which variations we used. But it allows us to have an inventory. Then a very interesting thing happens. The music helps to direct the editing, and you have a much more organic use of music, which is why music always stands out in these films. And why, against all conceivable odds, I own a gold record for a soundtrack to a film. Of a documentary, no less.

Graphis: Now will this pose a special challenge to Jazz, where the subject matter is the music itself?

Burns: In almost every film, there are always benefits and deficits. *Jazz* of course is all about music. So that's a wonderful possibility to constantly hear music being made. At the same time this is not a performance film. This is not a concert film. This is a history of jazz, in which we see in the study of this particular subject much larger social, political, and human themes. So how do you balance the impulse to stop and do mini music videos, with the concerns and the exigencies of a narrative that wishes to go forward? That will be a great challenge, for which at this moment I do not have an answer. Because we just started editing last Wednesday.

Graphis: As the editing process continues, do you reshoot and reinterview subjects as you see holes in the script?

Burns: Not so much holes in the script . . . yes, I guess that's a fair thing to say. For *Jazz* we've done 80, if not 90, percent of our interviews. We've probably shot 70 percent of our old photographs. And we've collected and identified and isolated–if we haven't re-photographed into our format–say 50 percent of the motion pictures. And as the script evolves, and as the editing progresses, we will fill in holes by finding new images. For example, when I say that research never ends, it might suggest that we need to follow the threads of a new person's life. We just did an interview a few weeks ago with Artie Shaw. We're pleased enough with it that we want to enlarge the already significant mention of Shaw, into a much larger character. So that suggests going out and finding more historical photographs of Shaw and other footage of him.

Graphis: Let's say you have this great photograph of Louis Armstrong. How do you actually go about shooting it, making it come alive?

Burns: Our archival setup is quite primitive. It's essentially a table with a two-by-four with a groove in it. Into this groove I set a piece of metal. On the metal I place the photograph of Louis Armstrong, held in place by four industrial magnets. It's now fastened there. I've got my movie camera on a tripod. I'm already lighting it with two small, thousand-watt umbrella lights. For the film that I'm using, which is rated at 100 ASA, I've got an exposure of around 5.6, or 5.6 1/2. This is going to give me a little bit of cheating in depth of field in case, in my panning or tilting, I've gone out of focus range. That way I don't have to spend all that much time pulling focus. So once I've set that up I don't change my

Filmmaker Ken Burns holds a movie camera in front of Monticello, the home of Thomas Jefferson. Burns's 1996 documentary on Jefferson was widely acclaimed for its accuracy and insight. **AP/WIDE WORLD PHOTOS. REPRODUCED BY PERMISSION.**

lighting at all. I just remove and put up, remove and put up these photographs for days on end.

So I pick up that Louis Armstrong photograph. I say, "That's great," but I don't really look at it that long. And then I go into the camera, through the viewfinder, and start searching out the parts.

Graphis: So you want to really look at the photograph for the first time through the lens of your camera?

Burns: That's correct. I'm not saying that I haven't stolen a peek at it. I've probably chosen it, or someone very close to me has chosen it. Then they hand it to me. I'm going to look at it for a millisecond, put it up on the easel without looking at it, but then *fully* look at it through the viewfinder. And then it comes alive. Then it yields up its potential secrets. For instance, there might be a nice dark area off the face. So if I put on my close-up attachment and move in, I can pan from this out-of-focus, completely indecipherable gray area, and reveal the face in an intensity that creates a drama that I think is fantastic. I've also done a wide shot. Maybe it turns out there's something interesting in it. Louis

Armstrong, we've been told, wore a Star of David in honor of a Russian-Jewish immigrant family in New Orleans who fed him and clothed him for a number of years. Perhaps that photograph has that Star of David and I might put on my most extreme close-up attachment to pull that off his neckline. Something that might have even gone unnoticed by the original photographer. Some people I know think I'm crazy, but I don't know a more exciting thing than finding these new stories in these photographs.

Graphis: You do something unique in your films. Most feature filmmakers cast actors, you cast voices. How do you do that?

Burns: I realized 25 years ago that the past spoke for itself better than anything I could do. It's very important to have a poetic and evocative third person narration, but at the same time I felt that if someone in the past said it, in a letter, in a diary, in a newspaper, they ought to be allowed to express it. I felt that the style and the ways of articulation of the people in the past was itself an access to the truth of that past. So I people my films with first-person voices. You know, we've all seen it when it's been done so poorly. It's not just enough to get that voice, we need to have those people, those professionals, who understand about meaning. So who better to go to than the best actors, and men and women in arts and letters, who know how to wrap themselves around words. Who know how to inhabit the meaning of a piece. Which is what I do. In the case of *Civil War,* I researched and found maybe 2500 quotes. I then recorded about 500 of them. And I recorded most of them by five different people, and each one of those people did it five different ways. You can do the math yourself, It's incredible three-dimensional chess. But it allows you a certain variation. Just like those old variations of "Take Me Out to the Ballgame" in the *Baseball* series. You've got options to work with.

Graphis: How do you keep all those straight? How do you keep track of them?

Burns: It's just about time. You can't know everything, but you can know what you need to know at that moment. You listen. You're at this place and go, "Gee, didn't Gregory Peck do two or three voices already this episode? Aren't people going to be fatigued or wonder what's he doing playing this other voice?" Yes. "Well, don't we have Eli Wallach reading this too?" Yes, let's listen to it. "Yes, he did a great job there." Or, "No, this other person didn't do a great job, why don't we look and see if we can find Arthur Miller doing it." Or, as the film emerges,

what you thought was a great job on Tuesday, the following Tuesday is now a little bit over the top.

Graphis: You're such a strong storyteller. Do you have any interest in directing feature films?

Burns: I always have. When I was in high school, I wanted to be John Ford. Or Alfred Hitchcock or Howard Hawks. But I went to Hampshire College in Amherst, Massachusetts, which was then beginning its second year of existence. I was one of the guinea pigs. It was a school that stressed self-initiated study. And it was a school that focused its film and photography department almost entirely on social documentary photography. And my professors there—Jerome Liebling and Elaine Mayes—were social documentary still-photographers. Not really filmmakers, though they had made films. And that's where I was inculcated with the notion that there is much more drama and, obviously, more truth in things that are and were, than in anything that the human imagination can think of.

Graphis: I'm curious—as someone who looks at literally thousands of photographs, do you follow contemporary photography?

Burns: Not as much as I should. Over the past several months I've been getting *DoubleTake* magazine, which has helped to re-inject me into that. But I'm disappointed the major flow of things in photography and aesthetics seems to be moving into computers and into manipulation. For me, I find that all meaning accrues in duration. That is to say, in an MTV generation, where images just hurtle by, we accept that the human eye is capable of receiving images in a fraction of a second. But that doesn't necessarily translate into enduring meaning. For me, to look at a photograph, and then to hold it, and then hold it again, is to sustain and develop meaning. And I want to cut away from that image the moment you've reached the apogee of that particular photograph's power and service. That is a much more difficult art, than the superficial, sexual, political (with a small "p") use of imagery that I see today. I'm not trying to suggest that I'm a Luddite, but I do find, in traditional discipline, salvation.

Further Resources
BOOKS

Edgerton, Gary R. *Ken Burns's America.* New York: Palgrave, 2001.

Foner, Eric. *Who Owns History?: Rethinking the Past in a Changing World.* New York: Hill and Wang, 2002.

Toplin, Robert Brent, ed. *Ken Burns's The Civil War: Historians Respond.* New York: Oxford University Press, 1996.

PERIODICALS

Edgerton, Gary R. "Ken Burns's America: Style, Authorship, and Cultural Memory." *Journal of Popular Film and Television* 21, no.2, 1993, 50–62.

Heller, Steven. "Ken Burns, Documentary Filmmaker." *Print* 55, no. 5, September/October 2001, 52–56, 342–343.

WEBSITES

Burns, Ken. "The Documentary Film: Its Role in the Study of History." Lowell Lecture, Harvard. May 2, 1991. Available online at www.dce.harvard.edu/pubs/lowell/kburns.html (accessed September 20, 2002).

Ken Burns on PBS. Available online at http://www.pbs.org /kenburns/ (accessed June 2, 2003).

"Is Fox News Fair?"

Journal article

By: Neil Hickey

Date: 1998

Source: Hickey, Neil. "Is Fox News Fair?" *Columbia Journalism Review,* March/April 1998, 30–32, 35.

About the Author: Neil Hickey is an editor for the *Columbia Journalism Review. CJR* covers day-to-day media in America. It includes reports on economic, political, technological, social, and legal issues in the media. ∎

Introduction

When Fox News began broadcasting in October 1996, it did not seem that there was a need for one more news channel. Yet Fox News helped to define what a news network could be in an already-crowded market; it also carved out its own place.

The "big three" news networks, ABC, CBS, and NBC, all provided versions of themselves to the public. In broadcasts of 30 minutes, the news of the nation and the globe was dispensed to the audience. In the competitive market, news had to become more entertaining, however. Therefore, public interest features also became a part of the news. This left little time for in-depth reporting. The major networks added an assortment of news programs to prime time in the late 1980s and the 1990s. Many of these programs (*Dateline, 48 Hours,* and *Prime Time*) also covered more feature stories than hard news. ABC's *Nightline* and CBS's *60 Minutes,* both long-running programs, might have been the exceptions.

CNN, started by Ted Turner in 1980, was the oldest cable contender to network news. Established as a 24-hour news channel, CNN challenged the networks and drew audiences with its ability to gather news quickly. As upstarts, MSNBC and Fox News both tried to gain audience share from CNN. Fox aimed to be different from the start.

Fox News could draw on Rupert Murdoch's large network of publications and on the already-established Fox Television. Murdoch owned newspapers throughout the world. Ironically, many of them were tabloid journalism, while Fox News was trying to be a station that viewers could trust for fair and balanced reporting of the news.

Significance

Rupert Murdoch began Fox News in October 1996 to complete his media empire in the United States. In 1985, Murdoch, an Australian, established the Fox Television Network as an alternative to the other big three channels. He also purchased exclusive rights to the National Football League broadcasts. These moves did not make him a popular figure. Murdoch's business practices were challenged by the FCC and resulted in some litigation.

Despite the controversy, Rupert Murdoch's Fox Television and Fox News became contenders in the media wars. Fox News began to challenge the other cable news outlets, CNN and MSNBC. CNN was an established station at the time that Fox News began in 1996, and MSNBC was only a few months old. The major arguments about Fox News dealt with its conservative bent on the news. When Roger Ailes was made CEO of the News Division, it was a clear signal to others in the industry that Fox would follow his political lead: Republican. Fox was able to draw major talent away from other news programs and build a strong conservative voice on the air. They found nothing wrong with this and claimed that "we report, you decide." While Fox News was filled with mainly conservative-minded reporters, there were some liberal minds on staff as well. And the news was only one part of the Fox News mix. Programming included several hours of chat and entertainment news programs. Hickey makes the important distinction between the types of programming on Fox, which helped to make the channel a success.

Fox News carved out its place in the news world by providing more detailed coverage of news events. During the Clinton years, the channel was often accused of making too much of the scandals and negative news stories. Fox News added its voice to the increasingly controversial world of news broadcasting.

Primary Source

"Is Fox News Fair?" [excerpt]

> **SYNOPSIS:** In a short time, Fox News grew into a major player in the news broadcasting world. According to Alex Jones, "Fox News reported that its prime time viewership had grown 17 percent for the month [of November], compared with November 2001." Programs like *The O'Reilly Factor,* the

top-rated cable news show in 2002, drew viewers because topics were controversial. Brit Hume's *Special Report,* a show that combined news and talk, was another popular alternative to network news shows.

"I don't think there's ever been anything like it," Brit Hume declares with undisguised enthusiasm. He's talking about the Fox News Channel, Rupert Murdoch's fledgling, all-news cable network, a competitor to CNN and MSNBC launched October 6, 1996 with an estimated sticker price of $475 million and now available in 25 million U.S. homes. As the network's managing editor and chief Washington correspondent, Hume is FNC's highest profile figure—twenty-three years a reporter for ABC News, eight years as its chief White House correspondent, an Emmy winner in 1991 for his gulf war coverage. In a promotional announcement aired often on FNC. Hume tells viewers: "The intention here is to do a broadcast people can trust."

"Trust." "Fairness and balance." "We report, you decide." Those terms punctuate FNC's broadcast day like a drumbeat, along with viewer mail flashed on the screen: "We are thrilled with the unbiased and fair coverage." "Thank you for finally providing a TV home for me." "Until Fox News Channel, I was about to 2 give up on news." "It's nice to have a newsperson say, 'You can draw your own conclusions.'" "TV news magazines have fluff. Fox has facts." "Fox News Channel has boldly earned the right to declare they are fair and balanced." "Finally, objective journalism. . . . You're long overdue." "Thank you for putting together a team that tells the whole story."

For Murdoch, playing the FNC chip is a huge gamble. CNN, in its eighteenth year, is a pillar on the international news scene, and a cash cow for its owner, Time Warner—the world's biggest media conglomerate. MSNBC is the privileged offspring of behemoth parents, GE and Microsoft. Those two cable networks were duking it out vigorously for a share of the relatively small all-news audience—with CNN comfortably the world champ—when FNC entered the ring as a brash challenger. It's looking at losses for the two years 1997 and 1998 of $150 million, and won't be operationally solvent (say its proprietors) until sometime in 2000, with years to go beyond that before News Corp. recoups its investment.

Nonetheless, it's a briar patch that Murdoch, 68, was eager to leap into. He needed news as the final piece of his three-legged stool to be truly a ma-

jor player in American television, like ABC, CBS, and NBC. Although hugely successful in entertainment (*The X-Files, The Simpsons*) and sports (National Football League games) via his Fox broadcasting network, the Australian-born magnate never was a presence in national TV news in the U.S., and his affiliated stations were a rag-tag crew of mostly UHF outlets with little history of local news coverage. Now, the recently-forged Fox News division, under Murdoch's chosen instrument for progress, Roger Ailes, 56, is busily trying to change all that by building a national TV news organization and a chain of news-conscious local stations that can play on the same ball field with the big kids.

Having thus committed to a cable news network, the question for Murdoch became: What kind of network? What would be its taste and texture? How would it differ from the entrenched dynamic duo, CNN and MSNBC? The answer emerged from Murdoch's conviction that most TV journalists are far more liberal than the population as a whole.

There is some evidence that he is correct. In a 1996 Freedom Forum/Roper Center survey of 139 Washington-based newspeople, 61 percent of the sample professed to being either "liberal" or "liberal to moderate," and a paltry 9 percent "conservative" or "moderate to conservative." In 1992, Bill Clinton got 89 percent of their votes, George Bush 7 percent. In a famous Wall Street Journal op-ed piece in February 1996, CBS newsman Bernard Goldberg hurled a hand grenade at his colleagues, saying: "The old argument that the networks and other 'media elites' have a liberal bias is so blatantly true that it's hardly worth discussing anymore." Even Walter Cronkite declared last year that most journalists "are probably tilted toward the liberal side."

Enter Murdoch, stage right. In February 1996, he installed as chairman and c.e.o. of the Fox News division the tough, profane political consultant and TV producer, Ailes, who'd advised a string of Republican office-seekers: Nixon, Reagan, Bush, New York Senator Alfonse D'Amato, and New York Mayor Rudolph Giuliani. Ailes had been a central figure in Joe McGinniss's celebrated book about the 1968 Nixon campaign, *The Selling of the President,* which depicted Ailes as a ranting, blustery partisan whose showbiz talents cut to the core of Nixon's image problems. (Famous Ailes quote from the book: " . . . a lot of people think Nixon is dull . . . a bore, a pain in the ass. . . . He's a funny looking guy. He looks like somebody hung him in a closet overnight and he jumps out in the morning with his suit all bunched up and starts running around saying 'I want to be President.'")

Ailes went on to help create syndicated entertainments like *A Current Affair, The Maury Povich Show, The Leeza Show, Tom Snyder's Tomorrow: Coast to Coast,* and Rush Limbaugh's TV chat program. He was president of CNBC, which he turned into a profitable business news channel, but was less successful with America's Talking, NBCs attempt to build an all-talk cable network.

The questions persist: Can a news network with executives and onscreen talent so conspicuously and so heavily right of center fulfill a promise of delivering "fair and balanced" news, information, and opinion? Does the oft-repeated slogan "We report. You decide" accurately describe how the network delivers news'? In FNC's round-the-clock format—unlike those of its competitors at CNN and MSNBC—hard news, except for breaking stories, is mostly confined to a few minutes on the hour and half-hour, plus an hour-long newscast at 7 P.M. Most of the rest is chat shows, interviews—discussions of trends, technology, health, entertainment, education, pets, as well as some old newsreels from the Fox Movietone archives.

A close monitoring of the channel over several weeks indicates that the news segments tend to be straightforward, with little hint of political subtext except for stories the news editors feel the "mainstream" press has either down-played or ignored. Nobody, least of all FNC, downplayed the allegations surrounding President Clinton's relationship with Monica Lewinsky.

Quick off the mark on January 21, the day the story broke, FNC had the first photo of Lewinsky on the air at 9 A.M., and, that same day, the first interview with Gennifer Flowers. It began devoting all of its daytime schedule to the crisis, except for brief segments on other news, along with weekend specials attracting hundreds of viewer phone calls. The network even inaugurated a whole new early-evening series, *Special Report with Brit Hume,* to keep daily tabs on the evolving story "for the duration of the developments." Staffers from bureaus around the country were rushed in to reinforce the Washington team. "I've been proudest of our restraint," says FNC v.p. John Moody.

Another Clinton story—unrelated to the alleged sex scandal—got the full FNC treatment because, according to Brit Hume, nobody else was doing it. On January 7, the FNC dinner hour news program introduced a report saying: "Hillary Clinton and the

Media mogul Rupert Murdoch gives a press conference in 1996.
AP/WIDE WORLD PHOTOS. REPRODUCED BY PERMISSION.

White House broke the rules. But the taxpayer may end up paying the bill." The story described a $286,000 sanction imposed by a federal judge against the administration for a "coverup" (in the judge's words) of efforts to keep the proceedings of Hillary Clinton's 1993 health care task force a secret. The White House had been shifty in responding to a legal request for the records, the FNC story suggested; interviewees were adamant that taxpayers ought not get stuck with paying the fine.

If Fox's collective news hole—small for an all-news cable channel—offers largely untilted coverage, its discussion programs regularly and unabashedly convey a right-of-center sensibility, sometimes subtle, at other times overt. In a promo for the *Hannity & Colmes* show, Sean Hannity declared his view that "a liberal is somebody who thinks he has a right to my hard-earned money." Bill McCuddy, the entertainment reporter, once announced: "Janet Reno—if you dressed her in drag, how could you tell?"

A talk show guest, Tim Graham of the Washington-based Media Research Center, declared it "outrageous" that the indictments of two Clinton cabinet members received only "eight or nine seconds of network airtime," and that "so many Clinton scandals don't get sufficiently covered." The host, Eric Burns, wondered if that was because "the media are so liberally biased." Graham answered that if one compares Clinton's coverage to Ronald Reagan's, it's "hard to conclude that there isn't a liberal bias here." He added: "Clearly you can say there's a liberal bias when you've got CNN's president staying in the Lincoln bedroom and nobody seems to care at CNN."

But nobody can object to a "fair and balanced" news service, nor one that simply "reports" and lets you "decide." Those terms have become a marketing device and a fig leaf for Fox staffers who are other-wise perfectly candid (as they were in interviews for this article) about their right-of-center convictions. But the same yardstick must apply to them as they demand from their competitors: keeping the hard news pristinely free of ideology.

Is the output of Fox News Channel, in its totality, truly "fair" and "balanced"? The answer is a qualified no. It's no more fair and balanced than the *National Review* or *The Nation,* which flaunt no such claims. In its patchwork quilt of talk shows, FNC is, inevitably, the product of its creators, interlocutors, and guests. That makes it unmistakably a bully pulpit for conservative sentiment in America—and, consequently, robustly controversial, which, for better or worse, expands the boundaries of our national discourse. It's one more stone in what's becoming an avalanche of news and opinion hurtling at the public. But the antidote to controversial speech, as is regularly pointed out in journalistic circles, is more controversial speech—not less.

Further Resources

BOOKS

Chenoweth, Neil. *Rupert Murdoch: The Untold Story of the World's Greatest Media Wizard.* New York: Crown Business, 2001.

Rohm, Wendy Goldman. *The Murdoch Mission: The Digital Transformation of a Media Empire.* New York: John Wiley, 2002.

PERIODICALS

Grover, Ronald. "Murdoch vs. Everyone." *Business Week,* December 9, 1996, 75.

Jones, Alex S. "Fox News Moves From the Margins to the Mainstream." *The New York Times,* December 1, 2002. D4.

"It's a Wonderful Life"

Journal article

By: Marc Fisher

Date: 1999

Source: Fisher, Marc. "It's a Wonderful Life." *American Journalism Review* 21, no. 6, July/ August 1999, 40–45.

About the Author: Marc Fisher (1958–) is a columnist for the *Washington Post.* He has worked for the *Washington Post* since 1986 and has also served as the Special Reports Editor. Fisher's book, *After the Wall: Germany, The Germans and the Burdens of History,* was published in 1995 and examines the reunification of Germany from a journalist's point of view. ∎

Introduction

National Public Radio (NPR) and Public Radio International (PRI) provided a different kind of programming than the usual talk shows on many commercial radio stations. Programming such as like *All Things Considered,* the humor of Garrison Keillor, and the information and interviews from *Talk of the Nation* or *Fresh Air* host Terry Gross were popular.

This American Life host Ira Glass began working for National Public Radio at the age of 19. Over the years he worked on *All Things Considered* and *Morning Edition.* Glass learned his documentary techniques when he covered a year in a Chicago high school. When he asked Joe DeMott, a documentary filmmaker, for advice, he was told, "Act like you are at a cocktail party. You'll be talking to some people: one will interest you more than others and you'll follow him around, then you'll be drawn to someone else, so stick with them awhile. Sooner or later you'll be led to something that intrigues you."

Public radio provided a niche for shows like Glass's *This American Life.* Glass was part of the trend in new journalism. Instead of just presenting the news or stories as fact-laden, traditional manner, the new journalist looked for the heart of the story.

Significance

This American Life began in 1995 at WBEZ in Chicago. It later became a popular among public radio listeners. *Busineek Week* columnist Thane Peterson wrote that "it gives you a glimmer of what American journalism might be like if you deported all the weak-kneed, homogenizing editors and TV producers, the lazy, tin-eared reporters, and then let the best, funniest, and most imaginative writers do the stories they really want to do."

Unlike other interview programs on the radio, *This American Life* found stories "that are not about the news." The commentators and the people they interviewed might have had definite political opinions, or opinions in general, but they did not accost the listener like many other radio personalities who became popular in the late twentieth and early twenty-first century. *This American Life* explored a new kind of journalism. The show may have appeared to be casual talk, but programs were carefully edited and researched.

The program was a documentary of people's lives. The first-person narrative style was not common on radio when Glass launched his program in 1995. In a short time, the style became very popular. Glass said that every story should be "irresistible . . . If a story is not surprising, it is dead." What happened to the people? How did they react and feel? The format and the revolutionary idea that Glass invented drew well-known writers and celebrities to the show. David Sedaris, a humorist, was a regular part of *This American Life,* sharing his offbeat adventures with the listeners.

This American Life provided a venue for stories that were interesting and quirky. For 30 minutes each week, the listener could meet unique people.

Primary Source

"It's a Wonderful Life"

> **SYNOPSIS:** Ira Glass looked for the unusual story for his show, *This American Life.* The eccentric tales of people across America drew thousands of listeners to their public radio stations each week to hear what Glass and his staff had uncovered. The show was described as one with a "mission to document everyday life in this country."

This is a story about a radio show that is helping to spark a new approach to American journalism. A program on the radio. A program run out of three tiny rooms at a Chicago public station located in the shadow of an enormous Ferris wheel at the edge of a pier on Lake Michigan. A program that is, like most endeavors that inspire and challenge, something of a cult, a frenzied pursuit bursting out of a single, fertile mind.

This American Life is Ira Glass and his stories. Glass is a journalist who works on deadline—very, very close to deadline—but his stories are almost never about anything that happened yesterday or even this week. They are news stories, but they are not about the news. They are stories that are changing what we think stories are.

More than 800,000 people listen to *This American Life* each weekend on 332 public radio stations. Each show presents two, three, four or five stories vaguely related to a theme, such as Do-Gooders or Pray or Fiascoes or Poultry. There are performance

Host of the radio show *This American Life,* Ira Glass. **PHOTOGRAPH BY RICHARD FRANK. © 2001 RICHARD FRANK. REPRODUCED BY PERMISSION.**

pieces by comedians and essayists, memoirs by unknown voices and reported pieces by Glass, his three producers, several regular contributors and, most remarkably, by some of the country's top magazine and book writers.

The New Yorker's Malcolm Gladwell on middle-class blacks in New York City and Toronto, *Esquire's* Michael Paterniti on a man who disappeared from the regular crowd at his local dog run, and other big-name writers, reading their own work or trying their hand at creating a reported piece for radio: authors Gay Talese and Tobias Wolff, *The Atlantic*'s Ian Frazier. People who regularly command $10,000 to $20,000 for a magazine piece, working for public radio at a day rate of $200—just to be edited by, just to be closer to, Ira.

At a moment when the definition of news is up for grabs, *This American Life* is probing the boundaries: In Washington, when WAMU, one of the most listened-to public radio stations in the country, decided to add *This American Life* to its schedule, it put the show on at 6 p.m. Sundays, replacing NPR's *All Things Considered.*

On a news-talk station, the new news was in, the old news silenced.

■ ■ ■

Glass is in hour No. 3 of editing Paterniti's script for a reported piece on the dog run near his house.

Glass sits in a dark studio, the script splayed out before him. Across the table sits producer Alix Spiegel, one of the three young women who commission, edit, write and report pieces for the show. For this conference call with Paterniti, who is at his parents' home in Connecticut, Glass and Spiegel wear headphones and speak into microphones, which means that in their conversation, they hear themselves as if they were on the radio, which means that they speak in that warm and affected and intimate and knowing and curious manner that is *This American Life.*

Moments before this editing session began, Spiegel hurried into Glass' tiny, windowless office to announce, "It's worse," meaning that the rewrite Paterniti has e-mailed after an initial chat with Spiegel is not nearly the quality of his original draft.

Glass: "Worse?"

Spiegel: "It's much worse."

Glass: "We can put some of the old stuff back; let me see."

He closes the door, sits down with the script, props his feet up on the desk. In nine minutes, he makes four tiny jots in the margins. Suddenly, he jumps from his chair, steps over to Spiegel's cubicle, and says, "OK, I see the path."

Together, they bound down the hall to the studio. Glass says, "He should go back to putting the Jeff stuff where it was. He needs to actually make a point. OK, fire up the Batmobile."

Spiegel patches Paterniti into the conversation and the three of them begin a word-by-word dissection. Between sips of Diet Pepsi, Glass approaches the writer gingerly. "I think you should go back to the wording the way it was. Do you feel that, too?"

"Totally," Paterniti says. "Suddenly, it got sort of aimless."

As the conversation wends its way toward a new version, Glass occasionally speaks directly ("Make it feel like something's going to happen"), but more often edits elliptically ("What he's saying here is, this is, you know, this is, in fact, like, you know, he's saying, you could go right there").

Glass listens intently. Very intently. "Is that a dot-matrix printer there?"

"Huh?" Paterniti replies.

"It sounds like a dot-matrix printer in the room where you are."

It is.

Three hours after the edit began, the script is a tad longer, yet much tighter, and in places considerably more artful. The story now has a bit more foreshadowing, a better sense of movement, a clearer statement of meaning. And the script now sounds much more like, well, like Ira Glass.

All of which Paterniti resents not one bit. He has loved every minute of it.

"It's just the most original thing going on," the writer says, "this amazing exercise in aural storytelling, especially for people who grew up in the 'Brady Bunch' times." Because of *This American Life,* Paterniti says, "writing has become more vernacular. There's an attempt in a lot of what I'm reading now to be more conversational. There's this license now to show more abandon. NPR has loosened up. Even *Time* magazine is much more conversational, much more willing to be hip and cool."

The theory behind this story is that Glass, the spike-haired, baby-faced, adenoidal 40-year-old at the center of the *This American Life* cult, is a revolutionary. The radio part of the story is well told, well accepted: Glass is the boy wonder, a rumpled genius in the minuscule world of radio documentaries, a quizzical character who hides behind trademark oversized black plastic eyeglass frames and takes radio journalism to places it has not traveled before.

This American Life has been on the air for more than three-and-a-half years. It won a Peabody Award in its first year. In its second year it snared a $350,000, three-year grant from the Corporation for Public Broadcasting—more than double the money Glass had applied for. But while Glass quickly conquered the small world of public radio, persuading about 120 stations to pick up the program in its first year, what's happening now is even more remarkable: In ways small but clear, as inspiration if not direct model, TAL is at the vanguard of a shift in American journalism.

Further Resources

BOOKS

McCourt, Tom. *Conflicting Communication Interests in America: The Case of National Public Radio.* Westport, Conn.: Praeger, 1999.

PERIODICALS

Hovey, Kendra. "State of the Art." *Dialogue* 21, no. 4, September/October 1998, 5–6.

Sella, Marshall. "The Glow at the End of the Dial." *The New York Times Magazine,* April 11, 1999, 68–74.

WEBSITES

Peterson, Thane. "Tuning In to the Voices of America." *BusinessWeek Online,* April 3, 2001. Available online at http://www.businessweek.com/bwdaily/dnflash/apr2001/nf20010

43_560.htm; website home page: http://www.businessweek .com/ (accessed June 17, 2003).

Snyder, Rachel Louise. "Salon Interview: Ira Glass." July 1999. Available online at http://www.salon.com/people/lunch/1999 /07/16/glass/; website home page: http://www.salon.com /people/ (accessed June 17, 2003).

This American Life. Available online at http://www.thislife.org/ (accessed June 17, 2003).

9

MEDICINE AND HEALTH

JACQUELINE LESKEVICH

Entries are arranged in chronological order by date of primary source. For entries with one primary source, the entry title is the same as the primary source title. Entries with more than one primary source have an overall entry title, followed by the titles of the primary sources.

Important Events in Medicine and Health, 1990–1999

1990

- On January 1, the National Practitioner Data Bank (NPDB), established by the Health Care Quality Improvement Act of 1986 to record malpractice data on physicians, dentists, and other health care providers, goes into operation.

- On January 3, First Lady Barbara Bush receives radiation to relieve double vision caused by Graves' disease (hyperthyroidism).

- On January 15, the Food and Drug Administration (FDA) rescinds its approval of the Jarvik-7 artificial heart.

- On January 22, Dr. Charles S. Lieber of the Mt. Sinai School of Medicine reports greater susceptibility of women than men to alcohol intoxication.

- On February 5, a report estimates that the Shanghai flu infected fifty to sixty million Americans in forty states.

- On February 25, smoking is banned on all U.S. domestic flights fewer than six hours.

- On March 4, Hank Gathers collapses and dies of heart failure while playing in a basketball game for Loyola Marymount University, raising questions of why his medication for heart arrhythmia had been reduced and why he was allowed to continue competing.

- On March 9, Dr. Antonia Novello becomes the first female and first Hispanic U.S. Surgeon General.

- On March 16, Dr. Jonathan Mann, director of the United Nations Global Program on AIDS, resigns over policy disputes with his boss, Dr. Hiroshi Nakajima of the World Health Organization (WHO).

- On April 29, Representative Morris King Udall (D-Arizona) resigns because of Parkinson's disease; he dies on December 12, 1998.

- On August 13, the FDA approves the production and sale of Exosurf Intratracheal Suspension, a synthetic surfactant for the treatment of premature babies with respiratory distress, manufactured by Burroughs Wellcome.

- On September 14, U.S. geneticist W. French Anderson performs the first gene therapy on a human, injecting engineered genes into a four-year-old child to repair her immune system, at the National Institutes of Health (NIH) in Bethesda, Maryland.

- On December 10, the FDA approves Norplant, an implantable contraceptive device for women.

- On December 14, a Jasper County, Missouri, judge rules that the feeding tube keeping alive Nancy Beth Cruzan, age thirty-three, may be removed.

1991

- On April 19, President George H. Bush is hospitalized overnight with atrial fibrillation (abnormal heartbeat).

- On July 15, former National Football League player Lyle Martin Alzado announces he has brain cancer, which his physicians attribute to steroid use. He dies on May 14, 1992.

- On October 23, Marjorie Lee Wantz and Sherry Ann Miller commit suicide in Michigan with the aid of Dr. Jack Kevorkian.

- On November 7, Los Angeles Laker guard Earvin "Magic" Johnson announces he has the human immunodeficiency virus (HIV) and retires from professional basketball.

- On November 20, Michigan revokes Dr. Jack Kevorkian's medical license for helping terminally ill patients kill themselves.

- On December 30, Senate Minority Leader Robert "Bob" Dole (R-Kans.) has surgery for prostate cancer.

1992

- The American Academy of Pediatrics recommends that babies be placed on their backs to sleep, leading to a decrease in Sudden Infant Death Syndrome (SIDS).

- On June 15, Earvin Johnson III, son of Magic and Cookie Johnson, is born. Mother and child are HIV negative.

- On October 6, President George H. W. Bush signs the 1993 appropriations bill for the Department of Health and Human Services (HHS), including millions of dollars for the Agency for Health Care Policy and Research.

1993

- On January 20, President Bill Clinton appoints Donna E. Shalala, former chancellor of the University of Wisconsin, Secretary of HHS.

- In March, HHS allows Oregon to expand Medicaid enrollment to all residents whose income is at or below 100 percent of the federal poverty level.

- On June 30, Dr. Antonia Novello completes her term as U.S. Surgeon General.

- In July, HHS allows Hawaii to integrate Medicaid with two state programs for uninsured residents and to create a large purchasing pool that will allow the indigent to purchase healthcare coverage through a process in which managed-care plans will compete for the lowest bid.

- On July 19, President Bill Clinton nominates African American pediatrician Joycelyn Elders, who advocates the distribution of condoms in schools and is pro-choice, as U.S. Surgeon General.

- On September 8, the U.S. Senate confirms Dr. Joycelyn Elders as Surgeon General.

- On October 27, embryologist Jerry Hall of George Washington University reports the first cloning of a human embryo.

• On October 27, President Bill Clinton delivers his 1,342-page Health Plan to Congress.

1994

• On February 21, Jacqueline Kennedy Onassis announces that she has non-Hodgkin's lymphoma; she dies on May 19.

• On May 2, a jury acquits Dr. Jack Kevorkian of charges stemming from the assisted suicide of Thomas Hyde, in Detroit, Michigan.

• On August 29, Vice President Albert Gore is hospitalized after rupturing his Achilles tendon during a basketball game with former Senate colleagues.

• In November, former president Ronald Reagan announces in an open letter to the American public that he has Alzheimer's disease.

• On December 15, the FDA permits the first U.S. test of RU-486, an abortion pill, in Des Moines, Iowa.

• On December 19, Paul Jennings Hill, a former minister and antiabortion activist, is sentenced for the July 29 murder of Dr. John Bayard Britton and his bodyguard, James H. Barnett, outside of a Pensacola, Florida, abortion clinic.

• On December 31, Dr. Elders resigns as Surgeon General, following controversial remarks about sex education, abortion, and drugs; she returns to the University of Arkansas Medical Center as professor of pediatrics.

1995

• In March, the FDA approves the first U.S. vaccine against chicken pox, a childhood disease afflicting 3.7 million each year.

• On March 6, Olympic gold-medal diver Greg Louganis announces he is HIV positive in his autobiography, *Breaking the Surface*.

• On June 12, Christopher Reeve, the actor known for his role as *Superman* in four movies, is hospitalized with a neck fracture, spinal injury, and paralysis after falling from a horse. He becomes an advocate of spinal-injury research.

• On August 12, U.S. cigarette companies Philip Morris and R.J. Reynolds drop libel suits against ABC News after it apologizes for accusing them of adding nicotine to cigarettes to addict smokers.

1996

• From April 11 to April 13, macaque monkeys shipped from the Philippines to labs in Texas are found to have Ebola Reston virus, resulting in the destruction of forty-nine animals. The Centers for Disease Control and Prevention (CDC) states that this strain of Ebola does not kill humans as do Ebola Zaire and Ebola Sudan.

• On May 13, the FDA approves the first new antiobesity drug in twenty-three years, Redux (dexfenfluramine), manufactured by Wyeth-Ayerst. In August 1997 the FDA will rescind approval after several dieters die.

• On May 14, a jury acquits Dr. Jack Kevorkian of assisted suicide for the third time, in Pontiac, Michigan.

• In November, Massachusetts legislators pass the first state law to permit consumers access to background information about physicians, including malpractice data.

1997

• Driver and passenger side airbags are required to be installed in all new cars.

• On January 1, *Time* magazine names Dr. David Da-i Ho "Man of the Year" for his AIDS research.

• On August 18, ABS Global Inc. announces the birth of Gene, the first bull calf cloned from fetal stem cells, in De-Forest, Wisconsin.

• On August 19, the American Medical Association (AMA) endorses Sunbeam Corporation products in an effort to raise money. Pressure from the public and physicians forces the AMA to retract its endorsement.

• On October 20, a $300-million settlement is reached between the tobacco industry and Norma Brown, the lead plaintiff in a $5-billion lawsuit filed on behalf of sixty thousand flight attendants seeking damages for illness from secondhand smoke.

• On December 15, the FDA approves nuclear irradiation to rid beef of *E. coli* and other bacteria that can harm humans.

1998

• On August 19, Nushawn Williams, a twenty-year-old New York man, is indicted on charges of felony reckless endangerment and attempted assault for knowingly exposing a fifteen-year-old girl to HIV while having sex. He pleads guilty on February 19, 1999, and is suspected of having exposed dozens of other women to HIV.

• On September 2, the FDA approves the Preven Emergency Contraceptive Kit, which includes birth control pills that prevent pregnancy when taken up to seventy-two hours after intercourse.

• On October 21, President Bill Clinton signs the 1999 Omnibus Appropriations Bill, requiring health plans to cover postmastectomy breast reconstruction.

1999

• On February 15, Former Chicago Bears running back Walter Payton announces he has a rare liver ailment, *primary sclerosing cholangitis*. He dies on November 1, 1999.

• On March 26, a Michigan jury convicts Dr. Jack Kevorkian of second-degree murder and the delivery of a controlled substance and sentences him on April 13 to ten to twenty-five years in prison.

• On July 25, U.S. cyclist Lance Armstrong, a survivor of metastatic testicular cancer, wins the world's most famous bicycle race, the Tour de France.

• On September 22, the U.S. Department of Justice files suit against tobacco companies to recover the costs of medical care that result from the use of tobacco.

• On September 24, the U.S. Court of Appeals for the Eighth Circuit strikes down as unconstitutional "partial birth" abortion statutes in Nebraska, Arkansas, and Iowa.

- On October 7, the U.S. House of Representatives passes "Patient's Rights" that would give patients the right to sue their Health Maintenance Organization (HMO).
- On October 12, the FDA orders Schering-Plough Corporation to cease gene therapy studies after the death of Jesse Gelsinger on September 17.
- On October 15, the Swedish Royal Academy awards the 1999 Nobel Peace Prize to Doctors Without Borders, the rapid-reaction group of medical volunteers who have led humanitarian interventions around the world.
- On October 18, ABC News announces the closing of the Ryan White AIDS Charity Foundation. Donations had dropped because many people erroneously believed that AIDS was no longer a crisis in the United States.

- On December 1, scientists from the United States, Japan, and England announce the first mapping of the human genome, a goal of the Human Genome Project.
- On December 12, ophthalmologists at Johns Hopkins University announce the use of a computerized miniature video camera and a chip imbedded in the eye to restore sight.
- On December 28, surgeons remove a benign lump from the thyroid of Mary Elizabeth "Tipper" Gore, wife of Vice President Albert Gore.
- On December 28, Rhode Island becomes the last state to approve the use of prescription drugs, including mifepristone (RU-486), as an alternative to surgical abortion.

Estrogen and Hormone Therapy

"Estrogen: Dangerous Drug or Fountain of Youth?"

Magazine article

Date: December 1990

Source: "Estrogen: Dangerous Drug or Fountain of Youth?" *The Women's Letter* 3, no. 12, December 1990, 1–3; Available online at http://web2.infotrac.galegroup.com/itw/infomark /533/604/32167241w2/purl=rcl_HRCA; website home page: http://web2.infotrac.galegroup.com (accessed January 19, 2003).

"A Woman's View of Hormone Therapy"

Magazine article

By: Phyllis Kernoff Mansfield

Date: April 1990

Source: Mansfield, Phyllis Kernoff. "A Woman's View of Hormone Therapy." *The Women's Letter* 3, no. 4, April 1990, 8. Available online at http://web2.infotrac.galegroup.com/itw /infomark/603/411/31883549w6/purl=rcl_HRCA; website home page: http://web2.infotrac.galegroup.com (accessed January 19, 2003). ∎

Introduction

In animals, hormones are chemical messengers that are excreted into the blood stream by glands and carry messages to cells, tissues, and organs throughout the body. Estrogen refers to a group of animal hormones. In females, estrogens are produced in the ovaries and affect the uterus, breasts, brain, bones, and heart. Estrogens are called steroids because they are derived from cholesterol. Estrogens and other steroids have a distinctive chemical structure, denoted by 17 carbon atoms connected together in a series of rings and containing at least one oxygen atom. Estradiol, the most important estrogen hormone, contains two oxygen atoms.

Estrogen's most important role is in the development of the breasts and the regulation of menstrual cycles dur-

ing a woman's reproductive years. Each month, female estrogen levels cycle. When estrogen is abundant, it (along with progesterone) causes the lining of the uterus to thicken in preparation for providing sustenance to a fertilized egg. If fertilization does not take place, estrogen levels drop and the uterus sheds its nourishing lining. Because of its role in the menstrual cycle, estrogen, in the form of oral contraceptives (birth control pills), have been prescribed for a variety of reasons to women of reproductive age. In addition to preventing pregnancy, birth control pills are prescribed to treat severe menstrual cramps, ovarian cysts, pelvic inflammatory disease, and ectopic pregnancy.

Estrogen also affects bone, heart, and brain tissue. It helps build bones and prevent bone loss and may contribute to a healthy heart by preventing a buildup of atheriosclerotic plaque in blood vessels. Finally, it may also have positive effects on brain function, including the prevention of dementia and stroke.

As women age and approach menopause, the levels of estrogen begin to drop. After menopause a woman's ovaries no longer produce estrogen. The lack of estrogen is associated with hot flashes and moodiness, osteoporosis (bone loss), and coronary artery disease. To counteract these symptoms, doctors in the 1990s prescribed estrogen to replace the estrogen the body no longer produced.

Significance

Hormone replacement therapy (HRT) was often in the headlines during the 1990s. At first, HRT was prescribed to treat the many uncomfortable symptoms of menopause and decrease the risk of osteoporosis in older women. When studies indicated that estrogen may increase the risk of developing uterine cancer, the treatment was modified to add progesterone, another important female reproductive hormone. Progesterone was thought to counteract the risk of uterine cancer.

HRT was also prescribed to prevent coronary artery disease in postmenopausal women. Early studies showed that estrogen helped to raise the levels of high-density lipoproteins (HDLs—so-called good cholesterol) and lowered the levels of low-density lipoproteins (LDLs—so-called bad cholesterol), therefore preventing the buildup of atheriosclerotic plaque. As a result, doctors began to prescribe HRT to prevent coronary artery disease in postmenopausal women.

As more studies were completed, the benefits and risks of HRT became confusing. Some reports said estrogen increased a woman's risk for certain cancers, while other reports said it lowered her risk for heart disease. Some results were questioned, especially estrogen's contributions towards alleviating coronary artery disease. By the end of the 1990s it was becoming clear that estrogen was linked to breast cancer. Cancer results when cells divide uncontrollably. One of estrogen's normal functions in a young woman is to stimulate cell division in breast tissue. Studies showed that women who developed breast cancer tended to have higher levels of estrogen circulating in their bodies than women without breast cancer.

In 2002, a national study on the effects of HRT on postmenopausal women was discontinued. While researchers involved in the study were examining some preliminary data, they found a statistically significant increase in the number of women on HRT who developed breast cancer. They discontinued the study since they felt the risks to women outweighed the benefits.

Primary Source

"Estrogen: Dangerous Drug or Fountain of Youth?"

SYNOPSIS: This article points out the confusing and sometimes conflicting reports about the risks and benefits of estrogen and hormone replacement therapy.

Estrogen replacement therapy is one of the most ardently debated topics in contemporary medicine. Some recent studies indicate that women who take estrogen postmenopausally are statistically at greater risk of developing breast cancer, uterine cancer, or osteoporosis than those who don't. Now two new studies, published in the *Archives of Internal Medicine* (Vol. 150, December 1990), furnish additional evidence that estrogen therapy may significantly increase the life expectancy of older women.

In one study a team of epidemiologists who surveyed nearly 9,000 postmenopausal women in southern California concluded that taking estrogen increased the women's survival rate by 20% to 40%. In the second study, researchers who examined 2,268 Tennessee women over age 55 with suspected coronary artery disease found that estrogen use had "a significant, independent effect on survival."

In the first study, Brian E. Henderson, MD, et al. of the Kenneth Norris Jr. Comprehensive Cancer Center in Los Angeles, California, spent seven and a half years analyzing the records of 8,881 female residents of Leisure World, a mostly white retirement community in Laguna Hills, California, to determine the relationship of estrogen use to mortality. These residents were provided with "a largely centralized medical care system, with good documentation of medical care and disease diagnosis."

Lower Risk of Dying

Beginning in 1981, and continuing through 1985, the researchers mailed questionnaires to all female residents in the Laguna Beach community. Of the 8,881 who ultimately participated in the study, more than half (4,988) had used estrogen for periods ranging from one to 40 years, with a mean duration of nine years. At the end of the study, 31% were still on estrogen replacement therapy. Some 1,147 of the original subjects had died. After the researchers validated the information gleaned from the respondents' questionnaires by comparing them with medical and pharmacy records, they concluded that all women who had ever used estrogen had at least a 20% reduction in their mortality rates.

Furthermore, the researchers stated, "mortality decreased with increasing duration of estrogen use and was lower among current users than among women who used estrogen only in the distant past. Current users with more than 15 years of estrogen use had a 40% reduction in their overall mortality."

The researchers also found that women using estrogen significantly reduced their risk of dying from "all categories of acute and chronic arteriosclerotic disease and cerebrovascular disease." The most likely explanation for this, they said, was "a favorable alteration in lipoprotein cholesterol levels" caused by estrogen—as has been demonstrated by other studies. However, they said, lipid changes alone may not account for this improvement. "Estrogens may affect the prostaglandin-thromboxane system, causing vascular dilatation and reduced platelet aggregation.

Breast Cancer Not a Factor

One "unexpected" finding of the study was the absence of any evidence of increased mortality due to breast cancer among the Leisure World estrogen users. (Other studies have strongly suggested that there is a link between longterm estrogen replacement therapy use and breast cancer.) The researchers hypothesize that because of the "enhanced medical surveillance," breast cancer may be diagnosed earlier at Leisure World than in the general population. Also, the researchers speculate, there could be "a fundamental difference in the behavior of estrogen-associated breast cancer versus that occurring in nonestrogen users."

In the second study, conducted in Memphis, Tennessee, from 1972 to 1985, Jay M. Sullivan, MD, et al. retrospectively examined the records of 2,268 older women who were heart patients and undergoing coronary angiography. The researchers' purpose was to determine the relationship between estrogen use, coronary stenosis, and survival.

About one-fifth (466) of the women showed no evidence of coronary disease of these, 377 had never used estrogen and 69 were users. After 10 years the difference in survival rates of these two groups was statistically insignificant, the authors say.

However, among 644 women suffering mild to moderate coronary disease (lesions up to 69% of the vessel diameter) the 10-year rate of survival was 96% for estrogen users versus 85% for nonusers—a "statistically significant" result.

And among the 1,178 women with serious coronary disease (lesions occluding 70% or more of the coronary artery) the rate of survival in estrogen users was 97%, but a mere 60% for nonusers—a difference the researchers term "highly significant."

"We found all-cause mortality over a 10-year period to be significantly lower in women with coronary artery disease who used estrogen replacement than in those who never used estrogen," Sullivan et al. conclude.

While asserting that estrogen use after menopause "prolongs life when coronary disease is present," the authors warn that it also increases the risk of other diseases, notably uterine cancer and some types of gall bladder problems.

Nonetheless, the researchers conclude, in postmenopausal women with coronary artery problems "the risk of dying from coronary disease is greater than the risk of dying from endometrial carcinoma or disease of the gall bladder."

In a recent interview Henderson asserted that most women would appear to benefit from estrogen. He recommends estrogen therapy for all postmenopausal women except those with a risk of breast cancer—who might be candidates for preventive therapy with tamoxifen.

However, other specialists, including Elizabeth Barrett-Connor, MD, from the University of California at San Diego, say that more work needs to be done on the longterm effects of tamoxifen before this antiestrogen drug can be safely recommended for preventive therapy against cancer.

Henderson's study concludes on a note of caution: "Given the complexity of issues surrounding the risk-benefit equation for hormone replacement therapy, it is especially important that the postmenopausal patient be fully informed . . . regarding

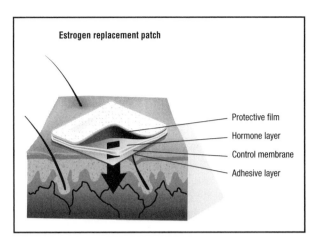

Estrogen replacement therapy was commonly practiced during the 1990s for women in menopause. ILLUSTRATION. THE GALE GROUP.

these risks . . . and fully participate with her doctor in decisions regarding choice of therapy.

"Despite the substantial overall mortality benefit afforded estrogen users, if the decision is to begin therapy, it is imperative that both physician and patient place high priority on surveillance of unexplained uterine bleeding and breast lumps."

Primary Source

"A Woman's View of Hormone Therapy"

SYNOPSIS: This article provides one woman's view of estrogen replacement therapy for menopausal women.

Imagine thinking of premenarcheal girls as "estrogen deficient" because their hormone levels fall below those of women in their childbearing years. Nonsense, you say; these preteens have the correct levels of hormones for their developmental stage.

Now imagine all healthy middle-aged men agreeing to ingest, for the rest of their lives, a potent medication known to cause cancer and other health problems, to possibly prevent a disease they don't have and may never get. Never happen, you declare: The men would never agree to such a dangerous course of action.

Yet hormone replacement therapy is promoted on just these grounds. Older women are judged "deficient" because their hormone levels are lower than those of younger women. And the discovery that lifetime dosages of estrogen (alone—not with progestogen, as in the newer combination therapies) could reduce bone loss and heart disease provided pharmaceutical companies with a new tactic for promotion.

What's needed is a woman-centered approach to hormone replacement therapy. The decision to take or refuse estrogen must be a personal one, and certain fundamental practices must be adopted by the medical profession.

First, young women must be informed of strategies (e.g., nutrition, exercise) so they won't need potentially dangerous hormones later in life. Second, women deserve full and accurate information about hormone therapy and contraception.

Further Resources

BOOKS

Coney, Sandra. *The Menopause Industry: How the Medical Establishment Exploits Women.* Alameda, Calif.: Hunter House, 1994.

Nachtigall, Lila, E., and Joan Rattner Heilman. *Estrogen.* New York: Harper Resource, 2000.

Romoff, Adam, and Ina L. Yalof. *Estrogen: How and Why It Can Save Your Life.* New York: Golden Books, 1999.

PERIODICALS

Friedrich, M.J. "Teasing Out Effects of Estrogen on the Brain." *Journal of the American Medical Association* 287, January 2, 2002, 29–31.

Fuchs, Nan Kathryn. "Understanding Estrogens." *Women's Health Letter* 8, March 2002, 3–6.

Rogers, June. "Estrogen Forever?" *Chatelaine* 69, no. 2, February 1996, 51–57.

WEBSITES

Cornell University. "Estrogen and Breast Cancer Risk: What Is the Relationship?" Available online at http://www.cfe.cornell .edu/bcerf/FactSheet/General/fs9.estrogen.cfm; website home page: http://www.cfe.cornell.edu (accessed March 16, 2003).

"Hormone Replacement Therapy During Menopause: What to Do." Available online at http://www.mayoclinic.com/invoke .cfm?id=WO00037; website home page: http://www.mayo clinic.com (accessed March 16, 2003).

Prescription: Medicide—The Goodness of Planned Death

Nonfiction work

By: Jack Kevorkian

Date: 1991

Source: Kevorkian, Jack. *Prescription: Medicide—The Goodness of Planned Death.* Buffalo, N.Y.: Prometheus Books, 1991, 221–230.

About the Author: Jack Kevorkian (1928–) was born in Pontiac, Michigan. He attended the University of Michigan School of Medicine and was granted his M.D. in 1952. After completing his internship at Pontiac General Hospital, he worked under the auspices of the Pacific Hospital in Long Beach, California for some twenty-five years. On November 25, 1998, Kevorkian was charged with murder, assisted suicide, and delivery of a controlled substance in the death of Thomas Youk. On March 26, 1999, he was convicted of second-degree murder and delivery of a controlled substance and was given a ten- to twenty-five-year sentence. ■

Introduction

Before Jack Kevorkian decided to assist terminally ill patients, he was the founder and ardent proponent of the radical concept of allowing prisoners on death row to donate their bodies to medicine and science. He traveled around the country making a case for allowing condemned criminals to choose death by irreversible general anesthesia. This would allow the harvesting of their organs for donation and/or the use of their entire bodies for medical experimentation. He spoke to legislators from several states about his idea but received little support.

Kevorkian coined the term "medicide" to indicate mercy killing performed by a doctor, nurse, paramedic, physician's assistant, or medical technician. In the late 1980s, after abandoning his organ donation idea, Kevorkian decided to pursue what he termed a new medical specialty. As a cardiac doctor is concerned with a patient's heart, a brain surgeon with the brain, Kevorkian's medical specialty focused on what he called "medicide," or mercy killing.

Janet Adkins was the first person to ask Kevorkian to assist at her death. With Kevorkian's help, she took her life on June 4, 1990, at the age of fifty-four. The "Mercitron" was the machine Kevorkian developed to aid in the assisted suicide. When Janet flicked the switch, her body began to receive a large infusion of the barbiturate thiopental. Within twenty to thirty seconds, she was in a deep coma. She was not aware when the Mercitron stopped pumping thiopental into her body and began administering a strong solution of potassium chloride, triggering her heart muscle to freeze. A few minutes later Janet was dead.

Significance

Jack Kevorkian became known as "Dr. Death." According to his own estimates, he helped at least 130 people commit suicide up to 1998, when he assisted at the death of Thomas Youk. The television show *60 Minutes* aired a videotape of Kevorkian injecting potassium chloride into Thomas Youk, who suffered from amyotrophic lateral sclerosis (Lou Gehrig's disease). Michigan, along with virtually all other states, has laws specifically forbidding assisting in a suicide, so Kevorkian was charged with murder, assisted suicide, and delivery of a controlled substance for his role in Youk's death. He was later con-

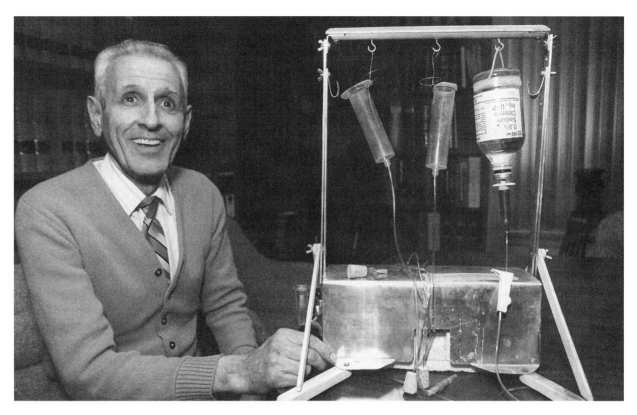

Jack Kevorkian, a proponent of physician-assisted suicide, continued to help patients to their death in the 1990s despite laws forbidding such action. AP/WIDE WORLD PHOTOS. REPRODUCED BY PERMISSION.

victed of second-degree murder and delivery of a controlled substance. Dr. Kevorkian brought national attention to the "right to die" movement and the debate over whether physicians should have any role in hastening death for terminally ill patients.

Euthanasia is from the Greek meaning "good death." The right-to-die movement advocates for the personal *right* to have control over the time and manner of one's death. Many people believe that the right to die is inherent in the laws and mores of the American system. They believe Americans have a "common law" right to self-determination and a "constitutional" right of privacy that allows them to choose the manner of their death. The right-to-die movement believes that the quality of life is more important than the sanctity of life. On the other side of the debate, others believe that the acceptance of mercy killing will lead society down a slippery slope from voluntary euthanasia, to directed euthanasia, and finally to involuntary euthanasia.

Doctors are represented on both sides of the issue. Some doctors believe hastening a patient's death violates the Hippocratic Oath to "do no harm;" while other doctors believe that some patients do not want to be kept alive by high-tech medical interventions. Because terminally ill patients are asking doctors to assist with their death, doctors are at the center of the right-to-die debate.

Primary Source

Prescription: Medicide—The Goodness of Planned Death [excerpt]

SYNOPSIS: In this excerpt from his book, Jack Kevorkian describes the circumstances surrounding the suicide of Janet Adkins, the first patient he helped to die.

The Birth of Medicide

Amid the flurry of telephone calls in the fall of 1989 was one from a man in Portland, Oregon, who learned of my campaign from an item in *Newsweek* (November 13, 1989). Ron Adkins's rich, baritone, matter-of-fact voice was tinged with a bit of expectant anxiety as he calmly explained the tragic situation of his beloved wife. Janet Adkins was a remarkable, accomplished, active woman—wife, mother, grandmother, revered friend, teacher, musician, mountain climber, and outdoorsperson—who, for some time, had noticed (as did her husband) subtle and gradually progressive impairment of her memory. The shock of hearing the diagnosis of Alzheimer's disease four months earlier was magnified by the abrupt and somewhat callous way her doctor announced it. The intelligent woman knew what the diagnosis portended, and at that instant decided she would not live to experience the horror of such a death.

Knowing that Janet was a courageous fighter, Ron and their three sons pleaded with her to reconsider and at least give a promising new therapy regimen a try. Ron explained to me that Janet was eligible to take part in an experimental trial using the newly developed drug Tacrine® or THA [1, 2, 3, 4—Tetrahydro—9—acridinamine] at the University of Washington in Seattle. I concurred that Janet should enroll in the program because any candidate for the Mercitron must have exhausted every potentially beneficial medical intervention, no matter how remotely promising.

I heard nothing more from the Adkinses until April 1990. Ron called again, after Janet and he saw me and my device on a nationally televised talk show. Janet had entered the experimental program in January, but it had been stopped early because the new drug was ineffective. In fact, her condition got worse; and she was more determined than ever to end her life. Even though from a physical standpoint Janet was not imminently terminal, there seemed little doubt that mentally she was—and, after all, it is one's mental status that determines the essence of one's existence. I asked Ron to forward to me copies of Janet's clinical records, and they corroborated what Ron had said.

I then telephoned Janet's doctor in Seattle. He opposed her planned action and the concept of assisted suicide in general. It was his firm opinion that Janet would remain mentally competent for at least a year (but from Ron's narrative I concluded that her doctor's opinion was wrong and that time was of the essence). Because Janet's condition was deteriorating and there was nothing else that might help arrest it, I decided to accept her as the first candidate—a qualified, justifiable candidate if not "ideal"—and well aware of the vulnerability to criticism of picayune and overly emotional critics.

A major obstacle was finding a place to do it. Because I consider medicide to be necessary, ethical, and legal, there should be nothing furtive about it. Another reason to pursue the practice aboveboard is to avert the harrassment or vindictiveness of litigation. Consequently, when searching for a suitable site I always explained that I planned to assist a suffering patient to commit suicide. That posed no problem for helping a Michigan resident in his or her own residence. But it was a different matter for an out-of-state guest who must rent temporary quarters.

And I soon found out how difficult a matter it could be. My own apartment could not be used because of lease constraints, and the same was true of my sister's apartment. I inquired at countless motels, funeral homes, churches of various denominations, rental office buildings, clinics, doctors' offices for lease, and even considered the futile hope of renting an emergency life-support ambulance. Many owners, proprietors, and landlords were quite sympathetic but fearful and envisioned the negative public reaction that could seriously damage and even destroy their business enterprises. In short, they deemed it bad for public relations. More dismaying yet was the refusal of people who are known supporters and active campaigners for euthanasia to allow Janet and me the use of their homes.

Finally, a friend agreed to avail us of his modest home in Detroit; I immediately contacted Ron to finalize plans. My initial proposal was to carry out the procedure at the end of May 1990, but Ron and Janet preferred to avoid the surge of travel associated with the Memorial Day weekend. The date was postponed to Monday, June 4th.

In the meantime, my friend was warned by a doctor, in whom he confided, not to make his home available for such a purpose. Soon thereafter the offer was quickly withdrawn. With the date set and airline tickets having been purchased by Janet, Ron, and a close friend of Janet's, I had to scamper to find another site. The device required an electrical outlet, which limited the possibilities.

I had made a Herculean effort to provide a desirable, clinical setting. Literally and sadly, there was "no room at the inn." Now, having been refused everywhere I applied, the *only alternative* remaining was my 1968 camper and a suitable campground.

As expected, the owners of a commercial site refused permission, even though they were sympathetic to the proposed scheme. They then suggested the solution by recommending that I rent space at a public camping site not too far away. The setting was pleasant and idyllic.

As with many other aspects of this extraordinary event, I was aware of the harsh criticism that would be leveled at the use of a "rusty old van." In the first place, the twenty-two-year-old body may have been rusting on the outside, but its interior was very clean, orderly, and comfortable. I have slept in it often and not felt degraded. But carping critics missed the point: the essence and significance of the event are far more important than the splendor of the site where it takes place. If critics are thus deluded into denouncing the exit from existence under these circumstances, then why not the same delusional denunciation of entrance into existence when a baby is, of necessity, born in an old taxicab? On the contrary, the latter identical scenario seems to arouse only feelings of sentimental reverence and quaint joy.

But the dishonesty doesn't stop there. I have been repeatedly criticized for having assisted a patient after a short personal acquaintance of two days. Overlooked or ignored is my open avowal to be the first practitioner in this country of a new and as yet officially unrecognized specialty. Because of shameful stonewalling by her own doctors, Janet was forced to refer herself to me. And acting as a unique specialist, of necessity self-proclaimed, solitary, and independent, I was obligated to scrutinize Janet's clinical records and to consult with her personal doctor. The latter's uncooperative attitude (tacitly excused by otherwise harsh critics) impaired but did not thwart fulfillment of my duties to a suffering patient and to my profession.

It is absurd even to imply, let alone to protest outright, that a medical specialist's competence and ethical behavior are contingent upon some sort of time interval, imposed arbitrarily or by fiat. When a doctor refers a patient for surgery, in many cases the surgical specialist performs his *ultimate* duty after personal acquaintance with the patient from a mere hour or two of prior consultation (in contrast to my having spent at least twelve hours in personal contact with Janet). In a few instances the surgeon operates on a patient seen for the first time on the operating table—and anesthetized to unconsciousness.

Moreover, in sharp contrast to the timorous, secretive, and even deceitful intention and actions of other medical euthanasists on whom our so-called bioethicists now shower praise, I acted openly, ethically, legally, with complete and uncompromising honesty, and—even more important—I remained in personal attendance during the second most meaningful medical event in a patient's earthly existence. Were he alive today, it's not hard to guess what Hippocrates would say about all this.

My two sisters, Margo and Flora, and I met with Ron, Janet, and Janet's close friend Carroll Rehmke in their motel room on Saturday afternoon, 2 June 1990. After getting acquainted through a few minutes of conversation, the purpose of the trip was thoroughly discussed. I had already prepared authorization forms signifying Janet's intent, determi-

Figure 3. My classified newspaper ads, placed in June 1987

These three classified newspaper advertisements were placed by Jack Kevorkian in June 1987. FROM AN ILLUSTRATION IN *PRESCRIPTION: MEDICIDE—THE GOODNESS OF PLANNED DEATH.* PROMETHEUS BOOKS, 1991. COPYRIGHT © 1991 BY JACK KEVORKIAN. REPRODUCED BY PERMISSION.

nation, and freedom of choice, which she readily agreed to sign. Here again, while she was resolute in her decision, and absolutely mentally competent, her impaired memory was apparent when she needed her husband's assistance in forming the cursive letter "A." She could print the letter but not write it, and the consent forms required that her signature be written. So her husband showed her on another piece of paper how to form the cursive "A," and Janet complied. At this time, Ron and Carroll also signed a statement attesting to Janet's mental competence. Following this signing session, I had Flora videotape my interview with Janet and Ron. The forty-five-minute taping reinforced my own conviction that Janet was mentally competent but that her memory had failed badly. However, the degree of memory failure led me to surmise that within four to six months she would be too incompetent to qualify as a candidate. It should be pointed out that in medical terms loss of memory does not automatically signify mental incompetence. Any rational critic would concede that a mentally sound individual can be afflicted with even total amnesia.

Around 5:30 P.M. that same day all six of us had dinner at a well-known local restaurant. Seated around the same table for many hours, our conversation covered many subjects, including the telling of jokes. Without appearing too obvious, I constantly observed Janet's behavior and assessed her moods as well as the content and quality of her thoughts. There was absolutely no doubt that her mentality was intact and that she was not the least depressed over her impending death. On the contrary, the only detectable anxiety or disquieting demeanor was among the rest of us to a greater or lesser degree. Even in response to jokes, Janet's appropriately timed and modulated laughter indicated clear and coherent comprehension. The only uneasiness or distress she exhibited was due to her embarrassment at being unable to recall aspects of the topic under discussion at the time. And that is to be expected of intelligent, sensitive, and diligent individuals.

We left the restaurant at 12:30 A.M. Sunday. Janet and Ron enjoyed their last full day by themselves.

At 8:30 A.M. the next day, Monday, 4 June 1990, I drove into a rented space at Groveland Park in north Oakland County, Michigan. At the same time, my sisters drove to the motel to fetch Janet, who had composed (and submitted to my sister) a brief and clear note reiterating her genuine desire to end her life and exonerating all others in this desire and the actual event. For the last time, Janet took tearful leave of her grieving husband and Carroll, both of whom were inconsolable. It was Janet's wish that they not accompany her to the park.

The day began cold, damp, and overcast. I took a lot of time in setting up the Mercitron and giving it a few test runs. In turning to get a pair of pliers in the cramped space within the van, I accidentally knocked over the container of thiopental solution, losing a little over half of it. I was fairly sure that the remainder was enough to induce and maintain adequate unconsciousness, but I chose not to take the risk. I drove the forty-five miles home and got some more.

In the meantime, at about 9:30 A.M. my sisters and Janet had arrived at the park. They were dismayed to learn of the accidental spill and opted to accompany me on the extra round trip, which required two and one-half hours. We reentered the park at approximately noontime. Janet remained in the car with Margo while Flora helped me with minor tasks in the van as I very carefully prepared and tested the Mercitron. Everything was ready by about 2:00 P.M., and Janet was summoned.

She entered the van alone through the open sliding side door and lay fully clothed on the built-in bed covered with freshly laundered sheets. Her head rested comfortably on a clean pillow. The windows were covered with new draperies. With Janet's permission I cut small holes in her nylon stockings at the ankles, attached ECG electrodes to her ankles and wrists, and covered her body with a light blanket. Our conversation was minimal. In accordance with Janet's wish, Flora read to her a brief note from her friend Carroll, followed by a reading of the Lord's prayer. I then repeated my earlier instructions to Janet about how the device was to be activated, and asked her to go through the motions. In contrast to my sister and me, Janet was calm and outwardly relaxed.

I used a syringe with attached needle to pierce a vein near the frontal elbow area of her left arm. Unfortunately, her veins were delicate and fragile; even slight movement of the restrained arm caused the needle to penetrate through the wall of the vein resulting in leakage. Two more attempts also failed, as did a fourth attempt on the right side. Finally an adequate puncture was obtained on the right arm. (It was reassuring to me to learn later that doctors in Seattle had had similar difficulty with her veins.)

The moment had come. With a nod from Janet I turned on the ECG and said, "Now." Janet hit the Mercitron's switch with the outer edge of her palm. In about ten seconds her eyelids began to flicker and droop. She looked up at me and said, "Thank you, thank you." I replied at once as her eyelids closed, "Have a nice trip." She was unconscious and perfectly still except for two widely spaced and mild coughs several minutes later. Agonal complexes in the ECG tracing indicated death due to complete cessation of blood circulation in six minutes.

It was 2:30 P.M. Suddenly—for the first time that cold, dank day—warm sunshine bathed the park.

Further Resources

BOOKS

Smith, Wesley, J. *Culture of Death: The Assault on Medical Ethics in America.* San Francisco, Calif.: Encounter Books, 2000.

Urofsky, Melvin, I. *Letting Go: Death, Dying, and the Law.* New York: Scribner's, 1993.

Yount, Lisa. *Physician-Assisted Suicide and Euthanasia.* New York: Facts on File, 2000.

PERIODICALS

Bascom, Paul B., and Susan W. Tolle. "Responding to Requests for Physician-Assisted Suicide." *Journal of the American Medical Association* 288, July 3, 2002, 91–99.

Bostrom, Barry, A. "In the Michigan Court of Appeals: People vs. Jack Kevorkian." *Issues in Law and Medicine* 18, Summer 2002, 57–65.

WEBSITES
"The Kevorkian Verdict. The Life and Legacy of the Suicide Doctor." Available online at http://www.pbs.org/wgbh/pages /frontline/kevorkian/; website home page: http://www.pbs .org (accessed March 15, 2003).

Presidential Debate, October 15, 1992

Debate

By: Bill Clinton

Date: October 15, 1992

Source: *Presidential Debate. October 15, 1992.* Transcripts from the Commission on Presidential Debates. Available online at http://www.debates.org /pages/mission.html (accessed February 2, 2003).

About the Author: Bill Clinton (1946–) was born in Hope, Arkansas. After earning an international relations degree from Georgetown University, Clinton received a Yale law degree. In 1978, at the age of thirty-two, Clinton was elected governor of Arkansas. After losing his reelection bid, he was elected again and maintained the position until becoming president (served 1993–2001) of the United States. He was the first Democrat since Franklin D. Roosevelt (served 1933–1945) to be reelected to a second presidential term. ∎

Introduction

In the 1992 presidential campaign, Democratic candidate Bill Clinton, then governor of Arkansas, and independent candidate H. Ross Perot challenged Republican incumbent George H. W. Bush. All three candidates addressed the health care issue. Ensuring that all Americans have access to adequate health care has been an issue for U.S. presidents for decades. But in the early 1990s, health care in the United States was in crisis. Tens of millions of Americans had no health insurance, prices for medical procedures, doctor visits, medical accessories, and pharmaceuticals were exorbitant, "unnecessary" treatments and procedures were performed at alarming rates, and malpractice claims were rising.

President Bush's solutions to the health care crisis included capping malpractice awards, providing insurance vouchers for low-income persons, and pooling individual insurance policies to bring the costs of insurance down. Bush firmly believed in keeping the government out of the industry as much as possible. Perot did not have a clearly defined plan. He blamed the influence of insurance, pharmaceutical, and health care lobbyists on the government for keeping health care costs high.

Clinton made health care reform a centerpiece of his campaign. He promised that if elected he would give the nation a health care plan within his first hundred days in office. Clinton identified six problems with the health care system. First, the entire system was *insecure.* More Americans than ever were uninsured, and millions more were one catastrophe away from financial ruin. Second, the system was *too complex.* Administrative costs were high, and there was too much paperwork and bureaucracy. Third, *costs were steadily rising.* Each year from 1980 to 1992, the proportion of American dollars spent on health care was getting larger and larger. Fourth, the *quality of health care was decreasing.* Americans were getting less and less for their health care dollars. Fifth, *choices were eroding.* Health care plans continually restricted which doctors and what kinds of doctors its members could visit. Sixth, *insurance and pharmaceutical companies were acting irresponsibly.* Insurance companies only insured "healthy individuals," and pharmaceutical companies charged Americans outrageous prices for their products. Clinton's reform plan intended to counteract these problems by offering security, simplicity, savings, quality, choice, and responsibility.

Significance

As president, Bill Clinton had the opportunity to put his plan to work. He immediately appointed his wife, Hillary Rodham Clinton, to head a special task force to address the health care crisis. The two presented the *Health Security Plan* to the nation nine months later.

With the details of the plan worked out, the president needed to gain the support of Congress before the plan could become law. Congressional members were lobbied hard by groups that opposed the Clinton plan. They were particularly averse to the plan's complexity (ironically, because simplicity was one of the six principles upon which the plan was supposed to have been based), its reliance on government administration, and employer mandates. Additionally, the plan was too complicated for the public to understand. As a result, congressional support for Clinton's plan collapsed and it never became law.

Clinton's plan promoted the concept of "universal coverage," meaning health insurance for everyone. It declared health care to be a right, not a privilege. The concept is not new. In 1976, Jimmy Carter also promised to offer universal and mandatory health coverage for all Americans. The concept returned in the speeches of presidential hopefuls in 2003 and policy statements from such groups as the American Public Health Association and the American College of Physicians.

Primary Source

Presidential Debate, October 15, 1992 [excerpt]

> **SYNOPSIS:** Democratic presidential candidate Bill Clinton responds to a question about the rising costs of health care.

Presidential candidate Bill Clinton (right) revealed his plans for the nation's health care in a 1992 debate with President George H.W. Bush (left) and independent candidate H. Ross Perot (center). AP/WIDE WORLD PHOTOS. REPRODUCED BY PERMISSION.

Simpson: Thank you very much. We have a question over here.

Audience Member: I'd like to ask Governor Clinton, do you attribute the rising costs of health care to the medical profession itself, or do you think the problem lies elsewhere? And what specific proposals do you have to tackle this problem?

Clinton: I've had more people talk to me about their health care problems I guess than anything else, all across America—you know, people who've lost their jobs, lost their businesses, had to give up their jobs because of sick children. So let me try to answer you in this way. Let's start with a premise. We spend 30% more of our income than any nation on earth on health care, and yet we insure fewer people. We have 35 million people without any insurance at all—and I see them all the time. A hundred thousand Americans a month have lost their health insurance just in the last 4 years.

So if you analyze where we're out of line with other countries, you come up with the following conclusions. Number one, we spend at least $60 billion a year on insurance, administrative cost, bureaucracy, and government regulation that wouldn't be spent in any other nation. So we have to have, in my judgment, a drastic simplification of the basic health insur-

ance policies of this country, be very comprehensive for everybody.

Employers would cover their employees, government would cover the unemployed.

Number 2, I think you have to take on specifically the insurance companies and require them to make some significant change in the way they rate people in the big community pools. I think you have to tell the pharmaceutical companies they can't keep raising drug prices at three times the rate of inflation. I think you have to take on medical fraud. I think you have to help doctors stop practicing defensive medicine. I've recommended that our doctors be given a set of national practice guidelines and that if they follow those guidelines that raises the presumption that they didn't do anything wrong.

I think you have to have a system of primary and preventive clinics in our inner cities and our rural areas so people can have access to health care.

The key is to control the cost and maintain the quality. To do that you need a system of managed competition where all of us are covered in big groups and we can choose our doctors and our hospitals, a wide range, but there is an incentive to control costs. And I think there has to be—I think Mr. Perot and I agree on this, there has to be a national commission of health care providers and health care consumers that set ceilings to keep health costs in line with inflation, plus population growth.

Now, let me say, some people say we can't do this but Hawaii does it. They cover 98% of their people and their insurance premiums are much cheaper than the rest of America, and so does Rochester, New York. They now have a plan to cover everybody and their premiums are two-thirds of the rest of the country.

This is very important. It's a big human problem and a devastating economic problem for America, and I'm going to send a plan to do this within the first 100 days of my presidency. It's terribly important.

Further Resources

BOOKS

Johnson, Haynes, and David S. Broder. *The System: The American Way of Politics at the Breaking Point.* Boston, New York: Little, Brown, 1996.

Konner, Melvin. *Medicine at the Crossroads.* New York: Pantheon, 1993.

White House Domestic Policy Council. The President's Health Security Plan. New York: Times Books, Random House, 1992.

PERIODICALS

Bovbjerg, Randell, R., Charles C. Griffin, and Caitlin E. Carroll. "U.S. Health Care Coverage and Costs: Historical Development and Choices for the 1990s." *Journal of Law, Medicine and Ethics* 21, no. 2, Summer 1993, 141–162.

Harrison, Bridget. "A Historical Survey of National Health Movements and Public Opinion in the United States." *Medical Student Journal of American Medical Association* 289, March 5, 2003, 1163–1164.

Longo, Daniel, R., and Ryan R. Cox. "How to Reform the Health Care System Given the Experience of Past Failures." *Journal of Health Care Finance* 29, Winter 2002, 1–4.

Lowes, Robert. "Take the Money and Grumble." *Medical Economics* 75, no. 20, October 19, 1998, 25–33.

WEBSITES

Center for Health Care Strategies. Available online at http://www.chcs.org/ (accessed March 14, 2003).

National Coalition on Health Care. Available online at http://www.nchc.org/ (accessed March 14, 2003).

William J. Clinton to the Secretary of Health and Human Services, January 22, 1993

Memo

By: Bill Clinton

Date: January 22, 1993

Source: Clinton, Bill. William J. Clinton to the Secretary of Health and Human Services, January 22, 1993 *1993 Public Papers of the Presidents of the United States,* vol. 1, January 22, 1993. Available online at http://frwebgate5.access.gpo.gov (accessed March 24, 2003).

About the Author: William Jefferson Clinton (1946–) was born William Jefferson Blythe IV in Hope, Arkansas. His father had died three months previously in a traffic accident. When Bill was four years old, his mother married Roger Clinton, and in high school, Bill took the Clinton name. Clinton received a bachelor's degree from Georgetown University in 1968. He attended Oxford University in England as a Rhodes scholar and upon his return to the United States entered Yale Law School, receiving his law degree in 1973. He served as the governor of Arkansas and the forty-second president of the United States (served 1993–2001). ∎

Introduction

Within the first weeks of taking office in 1993, Bill Clinton reversed a number of policies that had been established under Republican presidents Reagan and Bush. One of the first directives Clinton issued was to end the federal moratorium on the use of fetal tissue for federally funded medical research. Presidents Reagan and Bush had contended that the use of fetal tissue for research could lead to more abortions. The moratorium prevented the National Institutes of Health (NIH) grant money from being given to projects using aborted tissue, though privately funded research was being done. Many groups welcomed the lifting of the moratorium, believing federal oversight of fetal tissue research is crucial and that this oversight is lost when federal funds are not used.

Fetal tissue has been used to treat various medical conditions since the 1920s. In 1928, researchers transplanted fetal tissue into patients suffering with diabetes, and later it was used to help develop the polio and rubella vaccines. Fetal tissue is desirable to scientists for many reasons. Unlike adult tissue, it is very adaptable—it has not yet undergone complete differentiation into specialized cells (like heart, liver, brain). It has an excellent capacity to rapidly divide and grow in many different environments. Researchers have used fetal tissue to investigate fetal development, learn more about birth defects, and treat diseases. Patients with a wide range of diseases may benefit from the use of fetal tissue research, such as those with Parkinson's disease, strokes, Alzheimer's disease, spinal cord injuries, and others. Fetal tissue is most promising as a replacement and stimulation for the regrowth of damaged tissue in the brain, spinal cord, and heart.

Significance

The use of fetal tissue in medical research is at the center of a political, legal, and moral controversy. The scientific research community maintains that fetal tissue is critical to, and extremely promising for, the treatment of many diseases, especially those involving the brain and spinal cord. Anti-abortion groups, in contrast, insist that using aborted fetuses is morally wrong and exploits a fetus as a means for another person's gain. Additionally, people from both sides of the issue have concerns about the potential commercialization and payment for aborted fetuses.

In 1998 researchers at the University of Wisconsin attained a scientific breakthrough when they isolated and cultured human embryonic stem cells in the laboratory. Cells that can turn into different types of cells are called *stem cells.* Even adults have some stem cells in tissues that regenerate, such as bone and muscle. But adult stem

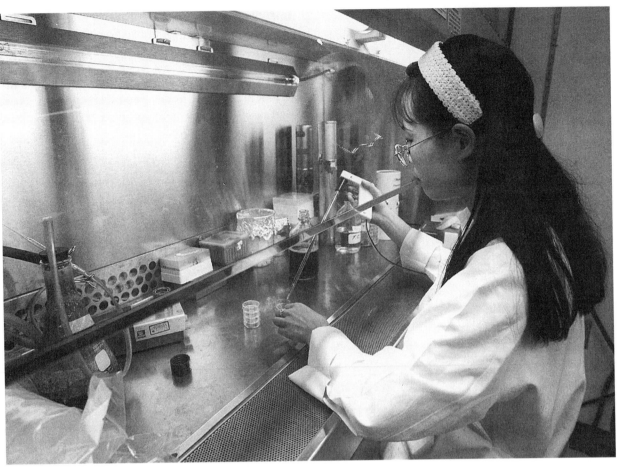

In 1993 President Bill Clinton authorized the lifting of a moratorium on fetal tissue research, allowing medical researchers to renew tests of tissue cell cultures to develop treatments for serious diseases such as Alzheimer's and diabetes. **AP/WIDE WORLD PHOTOS. REPRODUCED BY PERMISSION.**

cells can only turn into a limited number of cells. As embryos develop and cells begin to differentiate into specialized cells, those cells lose their flexibility to be any type of cell. Cells from embryo tissue, however, are even more immature and adaptable than fetal cells and have the ability to develop into any kind of cell.

The isolation of embryonic stem cells fueled the controversy. Embryos represent the period up until about the eighth week after conception, while a fetus is represented by the period from nine weeks until birth. Embryo tissue and fetal tissue are distinct under the law. However, the use of both fetal tissue and embryonic tissue raises many of the same moral, ethical, and scientific issues.

Fetal and embryonic tissue research will remain a part of the political agenda for some time to come. Each U.S. president since Ronald Reagan, along with Congress and federal regulatory agencies such as the National Institutes of Health, have debated the research use of any type of tissue from undeveloped humans, embryonic or fetal. When the tissue is obtained from an abortion, the debate becomes even more heated. Yet research on hu-man embryos and fetal tissue transplantation may provide important insights into human development and hold great benefits for the treatment of many devastating injuries and diseases.

Primary Source

William J. Clinton to the Secretary of Health and Human Services, January 22, 1993

SYNOPSIS: On January 22, 1993, within weeks of taking office, President Bill Clinton issued the following memorandum ending the federal moratorium on fetal tissue research to the Secretary of the Department of Health and Human Services.

Monday, January 25, 1993
Volume 29—Number 3
Pages 57–91
Administration of William J. Clinton
Memorandum on Fetal Tissue Transplantation
Research

January 22, 1993
Memorandum for the Secretary of Health and Human Services
Subject: Federal Funding of Fetal Tissue Transplantation Research

On March 22, 1988, the Assistant Secretary for Health of Health and Human Services ("HHS") imposed a temporary moratorium on Federal funding of research involving transplantation of fetal tissue from induced abortions. Contrary to the recommendations of a National Institutes of Health advisory panel, on November 2, 1989, the Secretary of Health and Human Services extended the moratorium indefinitely. This moratorium has significantly hampered the development of possible treatments for individuals afflicted with serious diseases and disorders, such as Parkinson's disease, Alzheimer's disease, diabetes, and leukemia. Accordingly, I hereby direct that you immediately lift the moratorium.

You are hereby authorized and directed to publish this memorandum in the Federal Register.

William J. Clinton

Further Resources

BOOKS

Langston, J.W., and Jon Palfreman. *The Case of the Frozen Addicts*. New York: Pantheon, 1995.

Maynard-Moody, Steven. *The Dilemma of the Fetus: Fetal Research, Medical Progress, and Moral Politics*. New York: St. Martin's Press, 1995.

Moore, Keith L., and T.V.N. Persaud. *The Developing Human: Clinically Oriented Embryology*. Philadelphia: Saunders, 1998.

PERIODICALS

Beardsley, Tim. "Aborting Research: Fetal Cell Transplants." *Scientific American,* August 1992, 17–18.

Trefil, James. "Brave New World." *Smithsonian,* December 2001, 38–46.

WEBSITES

"Human Embryo and Stem Cell Research." Available online at http://www.religioustolerance.org/emb_rese.htm; website home page: http://www.religioustolerance.org (accessed March 24, 2003).

National Institutes of Health. "Stem Cells: A Primer." Available online at http://www.nih.gov/news/stemcell/primer.htm; website home page: http://www.nih.gov (accessed February 27, 2003).

National Library of Medicine. "Fetal Development." Available online at http://www.nlm.nih.gov/medlineplus/ency/article/002398.htm; website home page: http://www.nlm.nih.gov (accessed March 24, 2003).

"Experimental Cloning of Human Polyploid Embryos Using an Artificial Zona Pellucida"

Conference proceedings

By: Jerry L. Hall and Robert J. Stillman, et al.

Date: October 13, 1993

Source: Hall, Jerry L. and Robert J. Stillman, et al. "Experimental Cloning of Human Polyploid Embryos Using an Artificial Zona Pellucida." Abstract of paper presented at the Conjoint meeting of the American Fertility Society and the Canadian Fertility and Andrology Society. Montreal, Quebec, Canada, October 11–14, 1993, Abstract 001, S1.

About the Authors: Jerry L. Hall (1946–) received his Ph.D. in 1974 from the University of Mississippi, then completed a three-year postdoctoral fellowship at the University of Pennsylvania, School of Medicine, Department of Obstetrics and Gynecology. Hall is the laboratory director of the Institute for Reproductive Medicine and Genetic Testing, an affiliate of the Tyler Medical Clinic.

Dr. Robert Stillman earned his medical degree at Georgetown University. He completed a residency in obstetrics and gynecology at Duke University and a two-year fellowship in reproductive endocrinology at Harvard University. Dr. Stillman is a clinical professor at Georgetown medical school's Department of Obstetrics and Gynecology and is on staff at the Shady Grove Fertility Clinic. ∎

Introduction

Cloning is a scientific term that means "making an exact copy." DNA, genes, and single cells have been routinely cloned in recombinant DNA procedures. It has also been fairly easy to clone entire plant organisms, such as trees, herbs, and flowers for a number of years. However, the cloning of an entire animal has been accomplished only fairly recently with Dolly the sheep.

Cloning an animal is much different from cloning DNA, genes, single cells, and even plants. There are only a few ways to do it. Somatic cell nuclear transfer (SCNT) is the most practical technique and the one most used to clone nonhuman animals like Dolly. In SCNT, the nucleus of an egg is removed and replaced with the nucleus from an adult cell of the individual to be cloned. The developing embryo now has the exact DNA of that individual.

There are essentially two outcomes of human cloning: embryonic stem cells or a pregnancy. Therapeutic cloning produces embryonic stem cells that are used for medical research to treat or reverse diseases such as Parkinson's, diabetes, Alzheimer's, and spinal cord injuries. Reproductive cloning produces an embryo to be implanted in a surrogate womb for pregnancy.

A technician works with frozen embryos. An initial study concluded that the cloning or twinning of human embryos is scientifically feasible. © FIREFLY PRODUCTIONS/CORBIS. REPRODUCED BY PERMISSION.

The procedure that Jerry Hall and Robert Stillman carried out can be called cloning in the sense that an exact copy was made. However, it is more properly called artificial human twinning, or embryo splitting. The process of artificial twinning involves dividing a human embryo, when it is only a few days old and consists of just a few cells, into two *separate* embryos. When this happens spontaneously inside a woman's womb, she will conceive identical twins. The reason twinning can occur is that at this extremely early stage in development, the embryo is *toti-potent.* This means that each of its cells has the ability to develop into any kind of cell or even a *whole organism.* As embryos develop and cells begin to differentiate into specialized cells, like heart, lung, liver, or brain cells, they lose their toti-potency.

Hall and Stillman performed the first artificial twinning of a human embryo in the following manner. First, a sperm and an egg were joined in a Petri dish (just as in an in vitro fertilization procedure). After the resulting embryo reached the stage of just two cells, a chemical was added to the Petri dish to remove the *zona pellucida,* which is a jellylike coating that forms around the embryo to protect it between the time of conception and the time of implantation (when the embryo settles into the nutrient-rich womb). Once the zona pellucida was removed,

the researchers had access to and could split the embryo. After the embryo was split, each of the two embryos was coated with an *artificial zona pellucida* and allowed to continue developing.

For ethical reasons, Hall and Stillman selected embryos with no possibility of ever becoming newborn babies. The embryos they used were *aneuploid* embryos, meaning that they either lacked chromosomes or had too many chromosomes. Hall and Stillman used embryos with an extra set of chromosomes with no chance to develop for any extended length of time.

Significance

Hall and Stillman demonstrated for the first time that it was technically possible to carry out twinning of human embryos in the laboratory. They used seventeen genetically flawed human embryos, which would have died in a few days. They were derived from an egg that had been fertilized by two sperm, resulting in an extra set of chromosomes—essentially dooming them. Hall and Stillman reported their results at a special meeting of the American Fertility Society (AFS) in Montreal on October 13, 1993. The American and international news media picked up on the information and reported "the first human cloning." In large part, Hall and Stillman's experiment was condemned around the world. They never officially published the methods used or their results in a scientific journal. The only technical report of their experiment was published as an abstract of their presentation at the AFS Montreal meeting.

Human cloning is one of the most controversial issues in biomedicine today. Most people think of a human clone as a human grown from a single body cell of one person (its parent) which is genetically identical to it. Twinning results in two separate individuals with the same genetic makeup derived from a single egg. Identical twins are the result of spontaneous or natural twinning. Hall and Stillman showed that it was technically feasible to induce twinning artificially.

Two types of cloning are being discussed in relation to humans: therapeutic cloning and reproductive cloning. Therapeutic cloning is supported by many scientists and advocates for sufferers of spinal cord injuries, Parkinson's, and other diseases. Anti-abortion groups represent a large portion of the people who oppose therapeutic cloning. They claim that using embryos in this manner may encourage abortions. Reproductive cloning has far more opposition than therapeutic cloning. Most scientists claim that the science is not yet available for cloned human embryos to develop into viable human beings. Experiments in sheep, cows, goats, and pigs show many problems in actually producing a healthy baby animal from a cloned embryo. In general, except for some fringe groups, most people do not support human reproductive cloning.

Primary Source

"Experimental Cloning of Human Polyploid Embryos Using an Artificial Zona Pellucida"

SYNOPSIS: The only published account of Hall and Stillman's demonstration of human artificial twinning is the following abstract published in the meeting abstracts from the joint meeting of the American Fertility Society and the Canadian Fertility and Andrology Society in Montreal, Quebec, Canada, on October 11–14, 1993.

Wednesday, October 13, 1993

8:00 A.M.

General Program Prize Paper

O-001

Experimental Cloning of Human Polyploid Embryos Using an Artificial Zona Pellucida. J. L. Hall, D. Engel, P. R. Gindoff, G. L. Mottla, R. J. Stillman, Division of Reproductive Endocrinology and Fertility, Department of Obstetrics and Gynecology, The George Washington University Medical Center, Washington, D.C.; The Center for Reproductive Research and Testing, Rockville, MD.

Objectives: We sought to evaluate the potential of forming multiple embryos from one, as has been shown in the animal industry (Willadsen, 1979). This technique could be useful to patients who have difficulty producing sufficient number of embryos for transfer. Twinning or cloning studies could provide important information on the developmental potential of single blastomeres from different stages of early human preimplantation embryos.

Design: Two-cell through eight-cell embryos, created as a result of polyspermic penetration and therefore not clinically useable, were separated into individual blastomeres. They were coated with an artificial zonal [sic] pellucida (AZP) (Hall and Yee, 1991) and cultured in vitro through their maximum number of cleavages. This work with polyploid embryos may serve as a model for study of normal diploid embryo development for if this technique becomes clinically acceptable.

Materials and Methods: From IVF patients, we obtained 22 polyploid embryos that were made zona free with 0.9% pronase and placed into calcium-free medium for dissociation of the blastomeres. Each blastomere from 17 of the embryos was coated with 1% sodium alginate and cultured at 37°C in 5% CO_2 and Human Oviduct Fluid Medium. Blastomeres from the five remaining embryos were cultured without an artificial zona. Blastomere development in both groups was recorded daily until there was no further cleavage.

Results: From 17 intact embryos (eight 2-cell, two 3-cell, five 4-cell and two eight-cell), 48 blastomeres, or theoretically 48 new totipotent embryos, were obtained after separation and addition of the AZP. The percentage of individual blastomeres that cleaved was similar for each stage (87, 80, 88, 73%, respectively). Although these new embryos were aneuploid and typically cease development earlier than normal embryos, morulas were achieved when blastomeres from two-cell embryos were cultured in the AZP. Blastomeres from four-cell embryos, however, developed only to the 16-cell state and no blastomeres derived from the eight cell stage went past eight cells, possibly due to insufficient cytoplasmic volume. Blastomeres from the five embryos not coated with the AZP exhibited linear division and fused with blastomeres of other embryos when cultured together implying that chimeras could result when a natural or artificial zona is absent.

Conclusion: This initial study utilizing aneuploid embryos confirms that experimental cloning or twinning of human embryos is feasible. Splitting at the two-cell stage appears to be more conducive to further development than does separation at the four-cell or eight-cell stage. The maximum stage from which a single blastomere can be reprogrammed to exhibit totipotency by itself or with addition of cytoplasmic mass by fusion with enucleated oocytes is unknown. Extending these studies would require obtaining permission to clone and cryopreserve blastomeres from supernumerary diploid embryos remaining after a transfer of fresh embryos. Data on the implantation potential of these embryos would then require transfer in subsequent cryo-thaw cycles.

Further Resources

BOOKS

Andrews, Lori B. *The Clone Age: Adventures in the New World of Reproductive Technology.* New York: Henry Holt, 1999.

Kass, Leon, and James Q. Wilson. *The Ethics of Human Cloning.* Washington, D.C., AEI Press, 1998.

Nussbaum, Martha Craven, and Cass R. Sunstein. *Clones and Clones: Facts and Fantasies about Human Cloning.* New York: Norton, 1998.

PERIODICALS

Cibelli, Jose B., Robert P. Lanza, and Michael D. West. "The First Human Cloned Embryo." *Scientific American,* January 2002, 44–51.

Wilmut, Ian. "Cloning for Medicine." *Scientific American* December 1998, 58–63.

WEBSITES

Association of Reproductive Health Professionals. "Human Cloning and Genetic Modification: The Basic Science You Need to Know." Available online at http://www.arhp.org /patienteducation/onlinebrochures/cloning/index.cfm?ID=2 82; website home page: http://www.arhp.org (accessed March 23, 2003).

"Cloning: A Webliography." Available online at http://www.lib .msu.edu/skendall/cloning/; website home page: http://www .lib.msu.edu (accessed February 27, 2003).

Counterbalance Meta Library. "Genetics, Ethics, and Theology." Available online at http://www.meta-library.net/media /gene-frame.html; website home page: http://www.meta library.net (accessed March 24, 2003).

Cancer and Genetics

"A Strong Candidate for the Breast and Ovarian Cancer Susceptibility Gene *BRCA1*"

Journal article

By: Mark Skolnick

Date: October 7, 1994

Source: Skolnick, Mark H., et al. "A Strong Candidate for the Breast Cancer Susceptibility Gene *BRCA1*." *Science,* October 7, 1994, 66–71.

About the Author: Mark H. Skolnick (1946–) received a bachelor's degree in economics from the University of California at Berkeley in 1968 and a Ph.D. in genetics from Stanford University in 1975. In 1991, he founded the biotechnology company, Myriad Genetics. ∎

"The Hottest Race in Cancer Genetics"

Journal article

By: *Science*

Date: September 23, 1994

Source: "The Hottest Race in Cancer Genetics." *Science,* September 23, 1994, 1997. ∎

Introduction

Like all cancers, breast cancer is caused by uncontrollable cell division. Cells keep dividing and eventually lead to conglomerations of cells, or tumors. As the tumors grow, they disrupt normal bodily functions, and if they are not removed or prevented from growing, they can lead to death. Among women, breast cancer is the second most commonly diagnosed cancer and the second leading cause of cancer deaths. A National Cancer Institute (NCI) report estimates that about one in eight women in the United States will develop breast cancer during her lifetime. Doctors have known for quite some time that some breast cancer is hereditary. Women whose mother or grandmother had breast cancer are several times more likely to develop it themselves.

When the general location of the first ever breast cancer gene was discovered, many researchers rushed to zoom in on it. Mary-Claire King from the University of California at Berkeley mapped the approximate location of a potential breast cancer gene in 1990. Believing there had to be some factor that increased a woman's breast cancer risk, she studied 1,600 women with breast cancer and identified 326 high-risk families. She made headlines around the world when she announced that a stretch of some one thousand genes on the long arm of chromosome 17 contained a gene that predisposed women to breast cancer. She named the gene *BRCA1* (she claims the *B* and *C* stand for Berkeley, California, not breast cancer). While King was among the list of researchers in the race to find the exact location and sequence of *BRCA1*, it was ultimately found by Mark Skolnick's team of some forty researchers from government, academia, and private industry.

BRCA1 is a very large and complex gene—about ten times the size of most of our genes. The larger the gene, the higher the odds that it can mutate. Skolnick's team identified eight different mutations of the *BRCA1* gene.

Significance

Mutations in two genes seem to play important roles in breast cancer. A year after *BRCA1* was discovered, a sister gene, *BRCA2*, was discovered. Unlike *BRCA1*, which is located on chromosome 17, the *BRCA2* gene is located on chromosome 13. Both *BRCA1* and *BRCA2* are helping to identify women at an especially high risk for breast cancer.

BRCA1 is not the key to all breast cancer, but it provides a big piece of the breast cancer puzzle. A defective *BRCA1* is responsible for the majority of inherited breast and ovarian cancers. In inherited breast cancers, the *BRCA1* gene clearly makes a defective protein. In some breast cancers that do not appear to be inherited, however, a differently mutated *BRCA1* appears to make a protein that looks normal but does not function properly. Even though *BRCA1* is not directly responsible for all breast cancer, its discovery has helped to shed light on how tumors grow.

The real gold mine to understanding a disease caused by a defective gene is to identify the *protein product* of the gene. In 1995, a research team from the University of Texas found that *BRCA1*'s protein product is a transcription factor. Transcription factors are proteins that bind to DNA and play a role in turning specific genes on or off. The *BRCA1* transcription factor seems to turn tumor-suppressing genes off. When the protein is present and active in cells, it somehow prevents cells from dividing inappropriately, as they do in cancer.

Primary Source

"A Strong Candidate for the Breast and Ovarian Cancer Susceptibility Gene *BRCA1*" [excerpt]

SYNOPSIS: The excerpt below is from an article in the journal *Science* detailing the discovery of the exact location of *BRCA1*, a gene that predisposes women to breast cancer.

Yoshio Miki, Jeff Swensen, Donna Shattuck-Eidens, P. Andrew Futreal, Keith Harshman, Sean Tavtigian, Qingyun Liu, Charles Cochran, L. Michelle Bennett, Wei Ding, Russell Bell, Judith Rosenthal, Charles Hussey, Thanh Tran, Melody McClure, Cheryl Frye, Tom Hattier, Robert Phelps, Astrid Haugen-Strano, Harold Katcher, Kazuko Yakumo, Zahra Gholami, Daniel Shaffer, Steven Stone, Steven Bayer, Christian Wray, Robert Bogden, Priya Dayananth, John Ward, Patricia Tonin, Steven Narod, Pam K. Bristow, Frank H. Norris, Leah Helvering, Paul Morrison, Paul Rosteck, Mei Lai, J. Carl Barrett, Cathryn Lewis, Susan Neuhausen, Lisa Cannon-Albright, David Goldgar, Roger Wiseman, Alexander Kamb, Mark H. Skolnick

A strong candidate for the 17q-linked *BRCA1* gene, which influences susceptibility to breast and ovarian cancer, has been identified by positional cloning methods. Probable predisposing mutations have been detected in five of eight kindreds presumed to segregate *BRCA1* susceptibility alleles. The mutations include an 11–base pair deletion, a 1–base pair insertion, a stop codon, a missense substitution, and an inferred regulatory mutation. The *BRCA1* gene is expressed in numerous tissues, including breast and ovary, and encodes a predicted protein of 1863 amino acids. This protein contains a zinc finger domain in its amino-terminal region, but is otherwise unrelated to previously described proteins. Identification of *BRCA1* should facilitate early diagnosis of breast and ovarian cancer susceptibility in some individuals as well as a better understanding of breast cancer biology.

■ ■ ■

Breast cancer is one of the most common and important diseases affecting women. Current estimates indicate that one in eight American women who reach age 95 will develop breast cancer. Treatment of advanced breast cancer is often futile and disfiguring, making early detection a high priority in medical management of the disease. Ovarian cancer, although less frequent than breast cancer, is often rapidly fatal and is the fourth most common cause of cancer mortality in American women.

Genetic factors contribute to an ill-defined proportion of breast cancer incidence, estimated to be about 5% of all cases but approximately 25% of cases diagnosed before age 30. Breast cancer has been subdivided into two types, early-onset and late-onset, a division that is based on an inflection in the age-specific incidence curve around age 50. Mutation of one gene, *BRCA1,* is thought to account for approximately 45% of families with significantly high breast cancer incidence and at least 80% of families

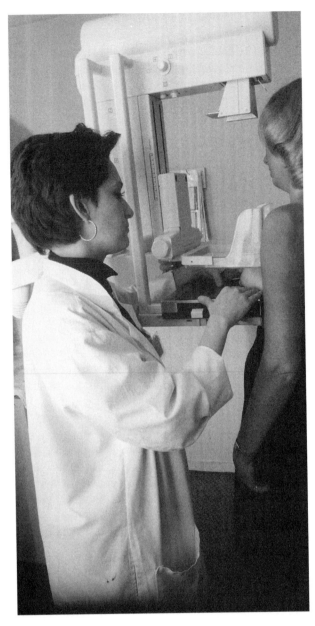

The gene BRCA1, which appears in numerous tissues, may help the medical community identify women at greater risk for breast and ovarian cancer. CUSTOM MEDICAL STOCK PHOTO, INC. REPRODUCED BY PERMISSION.

attributable to unmapped genes for familial cancer and rare germline mutations in genes such as *TP53,* which encodes the tumor suppressor protein p53. It has also been suggested that heterozygote carriers of defective forms of the gene predisposing to ataxia telangiectasia are at higher risk for breast cancer. Late-onset breast cancer is often familial in origin, although the risks in relatives are not as high as those for early-onset breast cancer. The percentage of such cases that are due to genetic susceptibility is unknown.

Like many other genes involved in familial cancer, *BRCA1* appears to encode a tumor suppressor, a protein that acts as a negative regulator of tumor growth. Cancer-predisposing alleles typically carry mutations that cause loss or reduction of gene function. Predisposition to cancer is inherited as a dominant genetic trait, whereas the predisposing allele generally behaves as a recessive allele in somatic cells. Thus, a single inherited copy of the mutant allele causes predisposition, and loss or inactivation of the wild-type allele completes one of the steps in progression toward malignancy. When chromosome loss is observed in breast and ovarian tumors from patients who carry *BRCA1* predisposing alleles, the wild-type copy of *BRCA1* is invariably lost while the presumptive mutant allele is retained. This finding supports the hypothesis that *BRCA1* is a tumor suppressor gene and suggests that the functional *BRCA1* protein is present in normal breast and ovarian epithelium tissue and is altered, reduced, or absent in some breast and ovarian tumors.

Genetic analysis of recombinant chromosomes in members of large kindreds allowed localization of *BRCA1* initially to a region of 1 to 2 megabases on chromosome 17 and, subsequently, to a region of about 600 kilobase pairs (kb) between markers *D17S1321* and *D17S1325.* A physical map comprised of overlapping yeast artificial chromosomes (YACs), P1; bacterial artificial chromosomes (BACs), and cosmid clones was generated for this region.

with increased incidence of both early-onset breast cancer and ovarian cancer. Intense efforts to isolate the *BRCA1* gene have proceeded since it was first mapped to chromosome arm 17q in 1990. A second locus, *BRCA2,* recently mapped to chromosome arm 13q, appears to account for a proportion of early-onset breast cancer roughly equal to that resulting from *BRCA1.* Unlike *BRCA1,* however, *BRCA2* may not influence ovarian cancer risk. The remaining susceptibility to early-onset breast cancer is likely

Primary Source

"The Hottest Race in Cancer Genetics"

> **SYNOPSIS:** This article discusses Mary-Claire King and her pursuit of the breast cancer susceptibility gene BRCA1—how she and her team narrowed their hunt for the gene and its ultimate discovery.

In October 1990, University of California, Berkeley, geneticist Mary-Claire King completed a feat that many had deemed unachievable. She mapped a breast cancer susceptibility gene to a region of the long arm of chromosome 17. It was only a rough location—the stretch of DNA probably contains well over 1000 genes—but King's work transformed the gene, which she called *BRCA1* from the genetic equivalent of the unicorn into a potentially trappable trophy.

"It galvanized research," recalls Mark Skolnick of the University of Utah Medical Center in Salt Lake City, who had turned his back on *BRCA1* in 1979 after having made his own "not-too-fruitful" attempts to localize the gene. Following King's discovery, hundreds of researchers—including Skolnick—jumped into the fray, melding and dissolving international alliances according to conflicting desires to pool resources, avoid work-style clashes, and capture the glory of snaring *BRCA1*.

All the competitors employed the same basic strategy: First, they narrowed the search using linkage analysis, the technique King used to map the gene in the first place. This involves monitoring the inheritance of genetic markers—easily identifiable stretches of genomic DNA—in families with a high incidence of breast cancer. If a marker is consistently inherited along with the disease, but is not inherited by unaffected family members, that indicates the marker lies close to the culprit gene. By studying hundreds of markers, the gene hunters homed in on a smaller and smaller region of chromosome 17. Next, they pulled out candidate genes from that region and searched them for crippling mutations that occur in family members who have the disease. The fact that Skolnick and his many colleagues managed to nab the gene first was due, in part, to their expertise in these latter techniques, Skolnick's competitors say.

Once they had the gene in the bag, the Skolnick team rushed off a paper to *Science,* but they purposely omitted an important piece of information from the draft version of the manuscript: the DNA sequence (or GenBank accession numbers) of the *BRCA1* gene itself, and of the PCR primers used to detect and amplify its segments. The reason, says Skolnick, is that they feared the information would get into the hands of their competitors before the paper had been accepted for publication. "Even though it should never happen, papers circulate even during the review process," he says. The sequences have since been deposited in GenBank, however, and as of 7 October—the paper's publication date—can be obtained using GenBank accession number UI4680.

The unpublished manuscript was indeed faxed to rival teams around world—but only after *Science* lifted the embargo on the manuscript last week. "It's hard not to be disappointed," says Jeff Boyd of the University of Pennsylvania, a member of the *BRCA1* team that includes King and Francis Collins, director of the National Center for Human Genome Research in Bethesda, Maryland. But, he adds, when he met with Collins to discuss *BRCA1*'s discovery, "the bottom line was that we were happy that some progress had been made." Mary-Claire King shared that sentiment. "I keep asking myself am I suddenly going to feel terrible about this. But I don't. I think it's great."

Further Resources

BOOKS

Love, Susan. *Dr. Susan Love's Breast Book.* Cambridge, Mass.: Perseus, 2000.

Plant, Jane A. *Your Life in Your Hands: Understanding, Preventing and Overcoming Breast Cancer.* New York: St. Martin's Press, 2001.

Stabiner, Karen. *To Dance with the Devil: The New War on Breast Cancer: Politics, Power, People.* New York: Delacorte, 1997.

PERIODICALS

Biéche, I., and Lidereau, R. "Genetic Alternations in Breast Cancer." *Genes, Chromosomes, and Cancer* 14, 1995, 227–251.

Chen, Y., et al. "BRCA1 is a 220-kDa Nuclear Phosphoprotein That Is Expressed and Phosphorylated in a Cell Cycle-Dependent Manner." *Cancer Research* 56, no. 14, July 15, 1996, 3168–3172.

Fearon, E.R. "Human Cancer Syndromes: Clues to the Origin and Nature of Cancer." *Science* 278, 1997, 1043–1050.

WEBSITES

American Cancer Society. "Cancer Reference Information." Available online at http://www.cancer.org/docroot/CRI/CRI_2_1x.asp?dt=5; website home page: http://www.cancer.org (accessed March 23, 2003).

Hoffman, Michelle. "Desperately Seeking BRCA1." *Science Observer,* November–December 1996. Available online at http://www.americanscientist.org/Issues/Sciobs96/Sciobs96-11Brca1.html; website home page: http://www.americanscientist.org (accessed March 23, 2003).

"First Total Synthesis of Taxol"

Journal article

By: Robert A. Holton

Date: 1994

Source: Holton, Robert A., et al. "First Total Synthesis of Taxol." *Journal of American Chemical Society* 116, no. 4, 1994, 1597–1598.

About the Author: Robert A. Holton received a bachelor's degree from the University of North Carolina. He was a faculty member at Virginia Tech, Purdue, and Stanford Universities and has been on the faculty at Florida State University since 1985. Dr. Holton's research since 1973 has been in the area of organic synthesis of complex molecules. ■

Introduction

Plants have metabolic pathways that are not found in humans or other animals. Photosynthesis is an obvious example. Another is plant secondary metabolism, the process by which plants churn out an incredible array of unique compounds evolved to protect them from insects, animals, and even other plants. Some products of plant secondary metabolism are flavonoids, lignans, and coumarins.

Humans have exploited plant secondary metabolites for thousands of years. The first chemicals isolated from plants in the 1800s were morphine and strychnine. Beginning in the mid-1950s, many scientists began looking to plants for anticancer (also called antitumor or chemotherapy) chemicals. Some of the most effective anticancer agents are found naturally in plants, bacteria, and fungi.

Probably the most famous plant anticancer chemical is paclitaxel, best known as Taxol. In the 1960s, the National Cancer Institute screened tens of thousands of plants to check for chemicals with anticancer activity. One of the plant species they screened was the Pacific yew tree. Monroe Wall, a chemist from North Carolina, discovered that Taxol, a large and complex polycyclic organic molecule isolated from the bark of the Pacific yew dramatically reduced the growth of tumor cells. During cell division, Taxol interferes with the development of the microtubules needed for cell duplication, thus inhibiting the faster growing tumor cells. This is different from other anticancer agents that work by interfering with the DNA of tumor cells.

Taxol's effective anticancer activity generated a great deal of interest in the Pacific yew, a small shrublike evergreen tree found in the Pacific Northwest region of the United States and Canada. Once Taxol's excellent anticancer properties were discovered, yew trees were coveted. But the Pacific yew is a scarce understory tree, and Taxol's popularity threatened it and the old-growth forests in the Pacific Northwest.

The environmental impact surrounding extinction of the Pacific yew and the realization that yew trees would probably never be able to meet the need for Taxol spurred researchers around the world to synthesize Taxol in the laboratory. Dr. Robert Holton's group at Florida State University made the most progress. In 1984 and 1988,

The chemical synthesis of taxol was announced in 1994. Taxol is a derivative of the Pacific yew tree and is used in treating cancer.
© KEVIN SCHAFER/CORBIS. REPRODUCED BY PERMISSION.

he synthesized molecules that were "close" to Taxol. Finally, in early 1994, Holton published an article in the *Journal of the American Chemical Society* that described the total synthesis of Taxol.

Significance

Before the laboratory synthesis of Taxol, only a limited supply was available. As a result, only a few experimental clinical trials of the drug could be conducted between 1971, when it was first found to have antitumor properties, and the early 1990s. Taxol is found in yew bark only in small quantities; it took at least three and sometimes as many as ten trees to get enough Taxol to treat just one cancer patient. To obtain yew bark, the tree had to be harvested. A large Pacific yew two feet in diameter would be approximately two hundred years old. It was clear that isolating enough Taxol would eventually mean the elimination of the yew. Several environmental groups united in an effort to preserve the yew. This became the subject of a considerable controversy, one which also involved the U.S. Congress.

The American pharmaceutical company Bristol Myers Squibb (BMS) and cancer patients were ecstatic when Holton published his group's findings in the *Journal of the American Chemical Society*. Holton patented the process—one requiring more than forty steps—and licensed it to BMS. The vast majority of Taxol is now made based on Holton's method, and BMS announced that it would no longer harvest yew bark. Taxol is mass-produced on a scale that the yew tree could never have supplied.

Taxol is the most prescribed chemotherapy drug in the world and generates billions of dollars in sales. It was approved by the FDA for the treatment of advanced ovarian cancer in 1992 and for the treatment of advanced breast cancer in 1994. It is also approved for early-stage breast cancer and lung cancer and is being investigated for its potential to treat leukemia, lymphoma, and other cancers.

Primary Source

"First Total Synthesis of Taxol"

SYNOPSIS: Holton and his researchers describe the technical details of the complete synthesis of Taxol, a chemotherapy drug used to treat breast, ovarian, and lung cancer.

First Total Synthesis of Taxol. 1. Functionalization of the B Ring

Robert A. Holton,* Carmen Somoza, Hyeong-Baik Kim, Feng Liang, Ronald J. Biediger, P. Douglas Boatman, Mitsuru Shindo, Chase C. Smith, Soekchan Kim, Hossain Nadizadeh, Yukio Suzuki, Chunlin Tao, Phong Vu, Suhan Tang, Pingsheng Zhang, Krishna K. Murthi, Lisa N. Gentile, and Jyanwei H. Liu

Dittmer Laboratory of Chemistry
Florida State University, Tallahassee, Florida 32306

Received December 21, 1993

The total synthesis of the potent antitumor agent taxol (**1**), isolated by Wall and Wani in 1971, has stood for over 20 years as a major challenge for organic chemists. Taxol has been the subject of extensive chemical and biological studies, which have recently been summarized in several reviews, and many synthetic approaches have been described.

Until now, our taxane research program has produced a synthesis of the taxane ring system, a total synthesis of taxusin, and a (now commercialized) semisynthesis of taxol. Here and in the following communication we describe the first total synthesis of taxol.

The facile epimerization of taxol at C-7 is well documented, and we chose to pursue a synthetic strategy in which this stereocenter would be introduced at an early stage and carried throughout most of the synthesis in the absence of a C-9 carbonyl group. Thus, our route to taxol proceeds retrosynthetically through C-7 protected baccatin III (**2**) to the tricyclic ketone **3**, which arises from C ring closure of a precursor **4**, properly functionalized at C-1, C-2, C-3, C-7, and C-8. Synthesis of this precursor, made possible by conformational control of the

eight-membered B ring, via the aldol product **5**, is described herein.

The fragmentation of bicyclic epoxy alcohols pioneered in our laboratory nine years ago, known as the "epoxy alcohol fragmentation" and the cornerstone of our syntheses of the taxane skeleton, taxusin, and now taxol, has enabled the synthesis of a variety of molecules having the bicyclo [5.3.1] skeleton. Spectroscopic studies of these compounds have demonstrated that there are *four distinct conformations of this eight-membered ring,* as shown in Scheme 1.

For a given compound the equilibrium will shift to favor conformations which orient substituents toward the periphery of the B ring to minimize nonbonded interactions.

Although the natural taxanes have a C-10β hydroxy or acyloxy substituent, the combination of a C-10β alkoxy group, a C-8β methyl group, and a C-3 ketone in this ring system shifts the equilibrium to strongly favor the chair-boat conformation. Our studies have shown that a C-3 ketone in the chair-boat conformation does not undergo deprotonation at C-8α. Therefore, to enable C-8α deprotonation (and subsequent aldol condensation), we chose to utilize a C-10α silyloxy substituent as a conformational control element. Silylation (TESCl, pyridine) of **5a**, a taxusin intermediate readily available from camphor in either enantiomeric form, gave **5b**, which then underwent epoxy alcohol fragmentation and protection at C-13 to give **6** in 93% overall yield. Although **6** was found to be in the chair-boat conformation, calculations indicate that, while the chair-boat con-

Scheme I

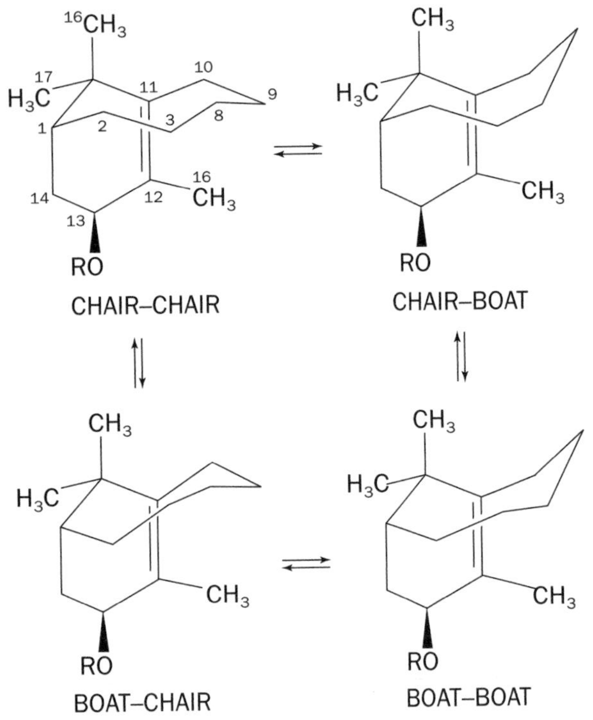

CHAIR–CHAIR

CHAIR–BOAT

BOAT–CHAIR

BOAT–BOAT

former is lowest in energy, the chair-chair and boat-chair conformers are only ca. 2.5 kcal/mol less stable. Presumably deprotonation of one of these other conformers at C-8 is facile.

In the event, the magnesium enolate of ketone **6** (HN(iPr)$_2$, THF, MeMgBr, 25 °C, 3 h, then **6**, 1.5 h) underwent aldol condensation with 4-pentenal (THF, -23 °C, 1.5 h), and the crude product was directly protected (Cl$_2$ CO, pyridine, CH$_2$ Cl$_2$, -10 °C, 0.5 h, then ethanol, 0.5 h) to give ethyl carbonate **7**, a ca. 6:1 mixture of chair-chair and boat-chair conformers (CDCl3), in 75% yield. Hydroxylation at C-2 (**7**, LDA, THF, -35 °C, 0.5 h, then -78 °C, 1.0 molar equiv of (plus)-camphorsulfonyl oxaziridine (for the enantiomer leading to taxol; (minus)-camphorsulfonyl oxaziridine for the enantiomer leading to *ent* - taxol), 0.5 h) gave hydroxy carbonate **8** (chair-chair conformation) in 85% yield. Reduction of **8** from the periphery of the molecule (20 molar equiv of Red-Al, toluene, -78 °C, 6 h, then warm to 25 °C over 6 h) gave a triol which, without isolation, was converted to carbonate **9** (Cl$_2$ CO, pyridine, CH$_2$ Cl$_2$, -78 to 25 °C, 1 h, 97%). Carbonate **9** could be obtained directly from Red-Al reduction of **8**, but complete reduction followed by regeneration of the cyclic carbonate was operationally easier and more efficient.

Synthesis of the C-1 through C-3 portion of taxol required introduction of a second conformational control element, a sufficiently large epimerizable substituent at C-3α, to shift the equilibrium in favor of the boat-chair conformation. This conformation was expected to permit generation of the C-1, C-2 enolate of a C-2 ketone, which would undergo hydroxylation at C-1 followed by hydride reduction of the C-2 carbonyl from the periphery to generate the C-2α alcohol. Finally, epimerization at C-3 would return the B ring to the chair-chair conformation.

Thus, **9** underwent Swern oxidation to give C-2 ketone **10** in 95% yield. That **10** was still in the chair-chair conformation (apparently the C-3α oxygen substituent is not bulky enough) was a matter of some concern. Treatment of **10** with 1.05 molar equiv of LTMP from -25 to -10 °C gave hydroxy lactone **11** in 90% yield. This remarkable result is analogous to the Chan rearrangement, which, to our knowledge, has been used but once in synthesis. The formation of 11 is the first example of this reaction in a cyclic system, and this is also the first indication that this can be a very stereoselective process.

The chair-chair conformation of **11** aligns the C-3α hydroxyl for facile reductive removal, and its samarium diiodide reduction led to the stable enol **12**, which, upon treatment with silica gel, was converted to a 6:1 mixture of cis- and trans-fused lactones **13**, from which the cis-fused lactone **13c** (boat-chair conformation) could be obtained by crystallization. Treatment of the transfused lactone **13t** with KOtBu in THF followed by quenching with acetic acid gave back **12**, and through this recycling **13c** was obtained in 91% yield from **11**. Attempts to gen-

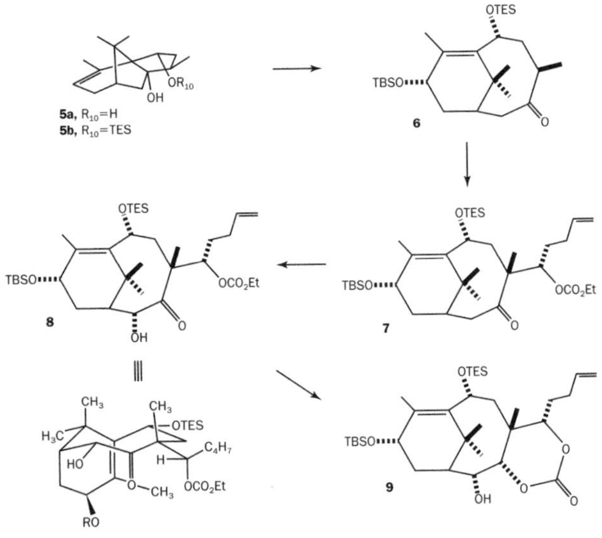

5a, R$_{10}$=H
5b, R$_{10}$=TES

6

7

8

9

erate and hydroxylate a dienolate from **12** were unsuccessful. Lactone **13t** was not deprotonated by LTMP at temperatures up to -10 °C and was recovered unchanged. However, treatment of **13c** with 4 molar equiv of LTMP at -10 °C followed by addition of (±)-camphorsulfonyl oxaziridine (5 molar equiv) to the enolate at -40 °C gave 88% of **14c** along with 8% of its trans-fused isomer **14t**, which was formed upon chromatographic separation of the small amount (3%) of unreacted **13c**. It is remarkable that *deprotonation of 13c with LTMP apparently occurs first, and perhaps only, at C-1,* even though the C-3 proton would normally be expected to be more acidic. Reduction of **14c** with Red-Al (THF, -78 °C, 1.5 h) followed by a basic workup gave C-2α-hydroxy trans-fused lactone (88%) and 4% of **14t**, which could be converted to the C-2α-hydroxy trans-fused lactone almost quantitatively by samarium diiodide reduction. The C-2α-hydroxy trans-fused lactone was quantitatively converted to carbonate **15** by treatment with phosgene (10 molar equiv, pyridine, CH_2Cl_2, -23 °C, 0.5 h).

Therefore, as outlined here, **5a** can be transformed to lactone carbonate **15** in 12 steps and 40% overall yield. This series of reactions provides functionality at C-1, C-2, C-3, C-7, and C-8 as needed for a synthesis of taxol through careful conformational control of the bicyclo [5.3.1] eight-membered ring.

Conversion of **15** to taxol requires completion of the C ring, introduction of the D ring, and oxidation at C-9 along with adjustment of the C-9, C-10 regio- and stereochemistry. . . . These efforts are the subject of the following communication.

Acknowledgment: We thank the National Cancer Institute (CA 42031, CA 55131) and private donors to the Taxol Research Fund for financial support of this work.

Supplementary Material Available: Experimental procedures and spectral data for compounds **5b**

through **15** (20 pages). This material is contained in many libraries on microfiche, immediately follows this article in the microfilm version of the journal, and can be ordered from the ACS; see any current masthead page for ordering information.

Further Resources

BOOKS

Goodman, Jordan, and Vivien Walsh. *The Story of Taxol: Nature and Politics in the Pursuit of an Anti-cancer Drug.* New York: Cambridge University Press, 2001.

National Cancer Institute. *Proceedings of the Second National Cancer Institute Workshop on Taxol and Taxus: Held at Alexandria, Virginia, September 23–24, 1992.* Washington D.C.: U.S. Department of Health and Human Services, 1994.

Ojima, Iwao, Gregory D. Vite, and Karl-Heinz Altman. *Anticancer Agents: Frontiers in Cancer Chemotherapy.* Washington, D.C.: American Chemical Society, 2001.

PERIODICALS

Nicolaou, K.C., Rodney K. Guy, and Pierre Potier. "Taxoids: New Weapons Against Cancer." *Scientific American,* June 1996, 94–98.

Wani, M.C., et al. "Plant Antitumor Agents. VI. The Isolation and Structure of Taxol, A Novel Antileukemic and Antitumor Agent from Taxus Brevifolia." *Journal of American Chemical Society* 93, no. 9, May 5, 1971, 2325–2327.

WEBSITES

"The Taxol Story." Available online at http://www.taxol.com /timeli.html (accessed March 23, 2003).

"The Taxol Story: An Overview." Available online at http:// www.pfc.forestry.ca/ecology/yew/taxol_e.html; website home page: http://www.pfc.forestry.ca (accessed March 23, 2003).

Taxolog Incorporated. Available online at http://www.taxolog .com/taxol.html (accessed March 23, 2003).

"Interview with Dr. David Ho"

Interview

By: David Ho

Date: December 1996

Source: Ho, David with Judy Woodruff. "Interview with Dr. David Ho." *Time,* December 30, 1996, and January 6, 1997. Available online at http://www.time.com/time/special/moy/ho/ho.html (accessed March 22, 2003).

About the Author: David Ho (1952–) was born in Taichung, Taiwan. At the age of twelve, David's family moved to Los Angeles, California. Ho earned a bachelor's degree in physics from the California Institute of Technology and attended medical school at Harvard University. He began studying the human immunodeficiency virus (HIV) at Massachusetts General Hospital and the UCLA School of Medicine. Ho was named *Time*'s 1996 Man of the Year. In 2003, Ho continued his work at the Aaron Diamond AIDS Research Center. ∎

Introduction

Dr. Ho was a leader in the American scientific contingent that battled the human immunodeficiency virus (HIV—the virus that causes AIDS) in the 1980s and 1990s. His research revealed fundamental information about how HIV mounts its initial infectious attack and then completely overwhelms the immune system. His work set the stage for a monumental shift in AIDS treatment.

At first in the 1980s, doctors felt completely helpless against HIV and the dreadful opportunistic infections that plagued AIDS sufferers. But this began to change with the advent of new anti-AIDS drugs and treatment strategies. In 1987, Zidovudine (AZT) became the first drug approved by the Federal Drug Administration to fight AIDS, but it merely slowed the virus. Protease inhibitors, introduced later, were much more effective. Proteases are proteins that act by chopping up other proteins. Since a protease is necessary for HIV to infect cells, blocking the protease disabled HIV. During this time, doctors also made progress in preventing opportunistic infections from taking hold in AIDS patients. Overall, the care and quality of life of AIDS patients improved in the 1990s.

Scientists knew that there was a long delay between infection with HIV and the onset of AIDS. The conventional wisdom at the time was that HIV was inactive or dormant during this time. However, Dr. Ho and his colleagues found that there is no dormant stage of infection; HIV begins rapidly multiplying right from the beginning. People with AIDS were asymptomatic for several years not because the virus was not actively replicating but be-

cause the immune system was keeping the virus in check. For every billion viruses that were made, the immune system made a billion T-4 cells (infection fighting proteins). Eventually, however, the immune system crashed; this is when full-blown AIDS developed.

Dr. Ho's research led to a new AIDS treatment strategy based on attacking HIV early and aggressively. As soon as HIV was detected, AIDS patients were given a mixture of the strongest protease inhibitors and other anti-AIDS drugs called reverse transcriptase inhibitors, the so-called antiretroviral cocktail. The treatment was a resounding success. Tests on AIDS patients showed that levels of infection-fighting T-4 cells shot up dramatically after an early dose of the antiretroviral cocktail. With continued administration, the cocktail helped AIDS patients' immune systems keep HIV in check. For the first time, doctors and scientists had rendered a mighty blow to HIV. More importantly, people with AIDS were given a new lease on life. Rather than a death sentence, AIDS was something they could live with.

Significance

The concept of AIDS treatment based on Dr. Ho's research represented a major victory over HIV and contributed a basic understanding of how HIV mounts its attack. He combined his own research with that of others, especially on protease inhibitors, to devise an AIDS treatment that for the first time enabled AIDS sufferers to actually get better.

The success of the antiretroviral cocktail shifted the focus of AIDS treatment research from the later stages of the disease to the early stages. Doctors had been conserving their forces and delaying treatment until they thought that the virus was coming out of its supposed hibernation. However, by then the immune system was already overwhelmed and exhausted from trying to match HIV's frenetic replication. Dr. Ho's strategy was to give the patient an antiretroviral cocktail as soon as HIV was detected in their blood. The strong protease inhibitors in the cocktail killed enough HIV to enable the immune system to beat the virus back to a small percentage of its previous numbers. Once their immune systems were restored, AIDS patients were able to fight insidious opportunistic infections, such as Kaposi's sarcoma, *Pneumocystis carinii* pneumonia (PCP), toxoplasmosis, *cryptococcus,* and cryptosporidiosis.

Primary Source

"Interview with Dr. David Ho" [excerpt]

> **SYNOPSIS:** In this excerpt, Judy Woodruff interviews David Ho about the ground-breaking research that led to the development of an antiviral cocktail, given early and aggressively, to treat AIDS.

Dr. Ho, let me begin by asking you what does it mean to you to be considered for Time*'s Man of the Year?*

It obviously is a great honor, and I'm quite overwhelmed by this honor. But I do want to emphasize that this honor should be shared with a lot of people in AIDS research: my colleagues, my collaborators, and many other researchers who laid the foundation for the success of the last couple of years. So I am honored, but I want to make sure that the credit is properly given to a lot of people. I'd also like to say that this honor, I think, reflects the new optimism in AIDS research, the new understanding, the better treatment, particularly in the form of combination of treatment, that is now available to some patients in our society. And obviously these patients are benefitting more than previously. But we also don't want to convey to everybody that the AIDS problem is over. In fact, the odyssey is far from over. A lot remains to be done. So I do want to emphasize those points while being honored in this way. . . .

So then talk about how your own more recent research—you were interested in measuring the amount of the virus, and what's interesting, I think, to some people, and you've commented on this yourself, is that . . . —typically that might have been done sooner. You might have expected—one might have expected that it would be done sooner, but it hadn't been. How did all that come about, and what did you think needed to be done in that area?

I think that when HIV was discovered and began to be characterized, a lot of people went on to do a lot of experiments as I just outlined, but a lot of it involved new biology, go and characterize the genes and solve the structure of the proteins of this virus. Something that is rather fundamental to a classical virologist, such quantifying it in various specimens from patients, quantifying the virus in blood, in urine and in other bodily samples, is a common practice in virology. We do that for other viruses. But that wasn't done for HIV at the beginning and wasn't done for a few years. So in the late 1980s when my colleagues and I had the opportunity to conduct a trial involving a new therapeutic called soluble CD4, we wanted to come up with a test that would monitor the antiviral effect of that new drug. And so we asked the question, "Well, how do we do that and how come that wasn't done earlier?" So we, from that point on, began to do quantitation experiments, to look at the amount of virus in blood of infected individual. And what we found surprised us, and we did not believe in those initial results for a while. This would be late 1988, early 1989.

Pathologist and AIDS researcher David Ho was named the 1996 Man of the Year by *Time.* © JEFF ALBERTSON/CORBIS. REPRODUCED BY PERMISSION.

Why didn't you believe them?

Because we were finding that in the blood of infected people there was quite a bit of virus. In fact, we could inoculate tiny amounts of plasma into a culture and still recover virus. That suggests there has to be a fair amount per cc of blood—per cc of plasma, for example. And we didn't have to use too many cells from the patient to turn a culture positive. That implied there has to be a fair amount of virus per million cells from the blood, for example. We had questioned our initial findings because the notion from the mid '80s on was that we were dealing with an infection that was largely quiescent. And perhaps that impression was due to the fact that patients could be infected with HIV and be clinically latent for a while; that is, they don't have symptoms for periods of years and sometimes 10 years. And so that began to create a notion that this virus wasn't doing very much for a while. And our findings during the late '80s suggested that wasn't the case and, in fact, we're looking—even though the patient may be asymptomatic, feeling great, and even when CD4 cell count could be reasonably high, there was a fair amount of virus. And I would still view the technologies that we used in 1988, '89 to be rather crude, but we were still picking up a fair amount of virus. So that began to—for me—to paint a different picture. Even in some of the early cases of HIV infection, we were finding a reasonable amount of virus, and that began to suggest maybe this virus is more active than we had previously thought. And so our research direction was altered quite a bit by those initial findings. And subsequently we've been pursuing these viral measurement studies in a very serious way. And so I would say we continued that research effort through the early '90s to show that more and more virus is associated with more and more advanced disease, and then the opportunity really came in 1994 when some of the better drugs became available and we actually had a tool to figure out how active the virus replication really is. And let me give you an analogy. We know that certain individuals have a certain amount of virus in their circulation, but if we ask, "Well, how much—how many viral particles are produced each day?" you cannot get the information just by taking the level of the virus, because that level could be kept fairly constant because of high production and high clearance. And so you reach that equilibrium. Or very low production and very low clearance, and yet you could still maintain that same level. So you have to use something to perturb the system, and we used the new drugs that became available in 1994 to perturb this balance between the virus and the host. And by doing so, we could then throw in this drug and the virus falls. And by tracking it and in quantifying that and analyzing that, we could get at the kinetics of what's going on, and the subsequent realization after analyzing the result is that we're looking at an enormously active process. This virus is constantly churning, producing more progeny virus which go on to produce new infections. And this goes on relentlessly. So we came to this realization in mid 1994, and unbeknownst to us, another group had been pursuing the same, and that's the group of George Shaw and his colleagues at the University of Alabama, Birmingham. And they came to the same realization completely independently, and in casual conversations we actually came to know about the other's findings. And so we decided to publish our results back to back, which came out in 1995.

And what implications did that have for a philosophy of treatment, then, of AIDS?

If one then utilized the information generated from these initial studies to understand how active the virus is, then—and we know this virus is quite error prone when it tries to copy its genes, because this reverse transcriptase that HIV carries makes

mistakes at a high frequency. So that, if you have virus replication and high frequency, then you could see that the virus is going to make a lot of mutant viruses. And some of those mutant viruses could escape from the drug one uses, from AZT for example. So the numerology here predicted that we would have a great deal of difficulty treating the virus with a single drug, and it essentially predicted the doom of mono therapy as was being administered to most patients at the time. And the numbers allow us to make certain predictions about combining drugs, cornering the virus simultaneously with multiple drugs, forcing the virus to mutate in many different positions at the same time. And that—the numbers suggested it would be difficult—not impossible, but more difficult—for HIV to do so. And so that led us to the conclusion that, if we began now to treat much more aggressively with a combination of anti-HIV drugs, we should begin to see better results. And, fortunately, along with these new understandings of what's going on, came the better agents against—to use against HIV. Drugs such as 3TC was developed as another reverse transcriptase inhibitor. And the new family of drugs that targeted a different side of the virus, and that is the protease side, were being developed, and several of them show great potency; in fact, much more potent than the prior drugs.

Let's see, you brought us up to, I think, 1995, and then at that point you wanted to apply this information to real patients. What happened at that stage?

Well, with the new information and the advent of the new potent drugs, we wanted to test the principle for whether we could indeed control the virus well with combination therapy. So in 1995 we initiated several different programs to treat patients, some at the very early stage of HIV infection and some at later stages of HIV infection, and treated them with what we thought was the best combination therapy. So that involved two inhibitors of reverse transcriptase and an inhibitor of the protease. And by administering these, we were very happy to see that the virus indeed responded dramatically to the treatment by dropping precipitously in the first few weeks so one could measure, for example, a hundred-fold decrease in the amount of virus in the bloodstream of a person in the first few weeks, and then this continues to decrease, although much more slowly thereafter. And then it was quite common for most of the patients who could tolerate the regimen and be compliant with the regimen that the virus eventually, after eight, 10 weeks, would dip below detection. So we then went after better and better detection techniques in collaboration with some scientists in industry who are developing such assays to measure virus. We were able to show that, even with the better techniques, the amount of virus was not detectable in the bloodstream, and that is an outcome that we had not seen previously. And this was being achieved consistently in the patients. And concurrently as the virus went down, there is some immunological improvement so the CD4 T-cells typically went up by 100 or 150 cells per cubic millimeter, and this is a significant increase. And, most importantly, associated with these changes in the laboratory values, the patients felt better, and some dramatically better. We realize that this is just the first step. This is not a cure. We, basically, have, for the first time, staggered the virus, and the new optimism comes from the fact that we now realize maybe, just maybe, this virus is not as invincible as we have previously thought. So that's, in my view, the reason for the new optimism. But, as I said, at the outset, this is just a beginning of this battle, and I think we have taken the first step successfully.

Further Resources

BOOKS

Pantaleo, G., and Bruce D. Walker. *Retroviral Immunology: Immune Response and Restoration.* Totowa, N.J.: Humana Press, 2001.

Rabkin, Judith G., Robert H. Remien, and Christopher R. Wilson. *Good Doctors, Good Patients: Partners in HIV Treatment.* New York: NCM, 1994.

Ugen, Kenneth E., and Mauro Bendinelli. *Human Retroviral Infections: Immunological and Therapeutic Control.* New York: Kluwer Academic/Plenum, 2000.

PERIODICALS

Ho, David. "Time to Hit HIV, Early and Hard." *New England Journal of Medicine* 333, no. 7, August 17, 1995, 450–451.

Ho, D.D., et al. "Rapid Turnover of Plasma Virions and CD4 Lymphocytes in HIV-1 Infection." *Nature,* January 12, 1995, 123–129.

Wei, X., et al. "Viral Dynamics in Human Immunodeficiency Virus Type 1 Infection." *Nature,* January 12, 1995, 117–122.

WEBSITES

Hall of Science and Exploration. "David Ho, M.D., AIDS Research Interview, May 23, 1998, Jackson Hole, Wyoming. Available online at http://www.achievement.org/autodoc /page/hoa0int-1; website home page: http://www.achieve ment.org (accessed March 22, 2003).

Time Man of the Year. "Dr. David Ho. Turning the Tide Against Aids." Available online at http://www.time.com/time/special /moy/ho/index.html; website home page: http://www.time .com (accessed March 22, 2003).

S.148 To Amend the Public Health Service Act to Provide a Comprehensive Program for the Prevention of Fetal Alcohol Syndrome

Legislation

By: Thomas A. Daschle

Date: January 21, 1997

Source: Daschle, Thomas A. *S.148 To Amend the Public Health Service Act to Provide a Comprehensive Program for the Prevention of Fetal Alcohol Syndrome.* 105th Congress, 1st sess. Washington, D.C.: U.S. Government Printing Office, 1997.

About the Author: Thomas A. Daschle (1947–) was born in Aberdeen, South Dakota. He earned a political science degree from South Dakota State University in 1969 and served three years as an intelligence officer in the U.S. Air Force Strategic Air Command. He has represented South Dakota as a U.S. Congressman since 1978. ■

Introduction

S.148 was one of several Fetal Alcohol Syndrome (FAS) bills introduced in Congress in the late 1990s. The bill would have directed the U.S. Centers for Disease Control (CDC) to establish a program to prevent fetal alcohol syndrome. *S.148* was introduced in 1997, but it was not enacted by Congress. However, Daschle guided a similar bill, *S.1875,* through Congress a year later. *S.1875,* which became Public Law 105-392, directs the CDC to create a program to prevent FAS, to educate women about FAS, and to coordinate medical research into the effects of FAS.

FAS and a related disease, Fetal Alcohol Effects (FAE), refer to birth defects that occur to infants while still in their mother's womb. FAS is more devastating than FAE. Babies born with FAS have an array of physical abnormalities. Most have microencephaly (abnormally small heads) and subtle but recognizable facial abnormalities. FAS also includes damage to the baby's developing brain, leading to a wide range of mental health and developmental disabilities. FAE is a milder form of FAS.

The effects of drinking alcohol during pregnancy have been noted throughout history. It was not until 1973, however, that specific physical and mental defects were clearly linked to doing so. The term fetal alcohol syndrome was coined in 1973 by two pediatric doctors, David Smith and Ken Jones, at Harborview Hospital in Seattle, Washington. Dr. Smith and Dr. Jones noticed "an unusual pattern of physical anomalies" in six infants with a "failure to thrive who all had alcoholic mothers." They

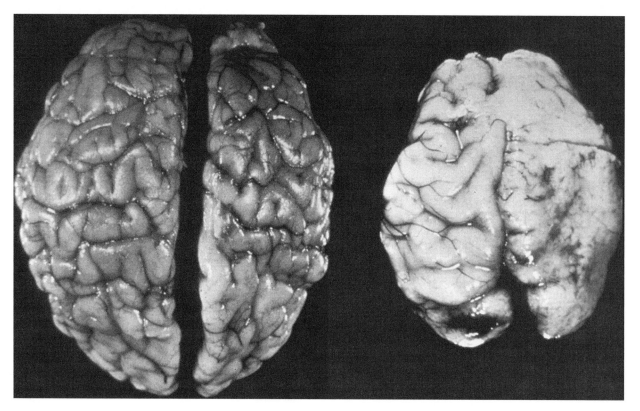

The brain of an infant with fetal alcohol syndrome (right) is contrasted with that of a normal infant. **STERLING K. CLARREN. REPRODUCED BY PERMISSION.**

published their initial findings in 1973 in the medical journal *Lancet.* A second *Lancet* article that same year gave this pattern of physical and mental characteristics a name—fetal alcohol syndrome. FAS and FAE were recognized as part of a spectrum of disabilities that result from prenatal alcohol exposure.

Significance

Drinking alcohol during pregnancy can cause serious birth defects, of which fetal alcohol syndrome (FAS) is the most devastating. FAS children have identifiable head and facial abnormalities; reduced intellectual functioning; difficulties in learning, memory, problem solving, and attention; and difficulties with mental health and social interactions. Fetal alcohol effects (FAE) is a related syndrome, which often goes undiagnosed. FAE children lack the characteristic physical defects of FAS but still experience alcohol-induced mental impairments.

Senator Tom Daschle, who introduced several FAS-related bills in Congress in the late 1990s, is from South Dakota, home to many Sioux tribes. The rate of FAS is highest in the Native American population. Some reports have said that alcoholism affects nearly every family in some Indian reservations. Social workers at the Pine Ridge Indian reservation in South Dakota have estimated that between 60 and 80 percent of babies on the reservation are born with FAS.

Legislation like *S.148* and *S.1875* provided for the creation of a nationwide FAS program focusing on education, prevention, and treatment. *S.1875* was eventually enacted and became a federal law. In response, the CDC established a National Task Force on FAS and FAE. The CDC's National Center on Birth Defects and Developmental Disabilities (NCBDDD) is carrying out many of the task force's recommendations and taking various steps to alleviate the problem of FAS. They have developed several programs to reach out to women and prevent drinking during pregnancy. They are also collecting data to monitor the incidence of fetal alcohol syndrome nationwide. Finally, they are funding research into ways to help individuals and families affected by FAS.

Primary Source

S.148 To Amend the Public Health Service Act to Provide a Comprehensive Program for the Prevention of Fetal Alcohol Syndrome [excerpt]

> **SYNOPSIS:** This excerpt from Senator Tom Daschle's bill lists the reasons behind the need for a national program to prevent fetal alcohol syndrome.

Mr. Daschle (for himself, Mr. Chafee, Mr. Bingaman, Mr. Inouye, Mrs. Murray, Mr. Johnson, Mr. Campbell, and Mr. Reid) introduced the following bill; which was read twice and referred to the Committee on Labor and Human Resources

A Bill

To amend the Public Health Service Act to provide a comprehensive program for the prevention of Fetal Alcohol Syndrome.

Be it enacted by the Senate and House of Representatives of the United States of America in Congress assembled,

Section 1. Short Title

This Act may be cited as the "Comprehensive Fetal Alcohol Syndrome Prevention Act."

Sec. 2. Findings

Congress finds that—

1. Fetal Alcohol Syndrome is the leading known cause of mental retardation, and it is 100 percent preventable;

2. each year, up to 12,000 infants are born in the United States with Fetal Alcohol Syndrome, suffering irreversible physical and mental damage;

3. thousands more infants are born each year with Fetal Alcohol Effects, which are lesser, though still serious, alcohol-related birth defects;

4. children of women who use alcohol while pregnant have a significantly higher infant mortality rate (13.3 per 1000) than children of those women who do not use alcohol (8.6 per 1000);

5. Fetal Alcohol Syndrome and Fetal Alcohol Effects are national problems which can impact any child, family, or community, but their threat to American Indians and Alaska Natives is especially alarming;

6. in some American Indian communities, where alcohol dependency rates reach 50 percent and above, the chances of a newborn suffering Fetal Alcohol Syndrome or Fetal Alcohol Effects are up to 30 times greater than national averages;

7. in addition to the immeasurable toll on children and their families, Fetal Alcohol Syndrome and Fetal Alcohol Effects pose extraordinary financial costs to the Nation, including the costs of health care, education,

A 1997 Senate bill noted that, each year, 12,000 children in the United States are born with fetal alcohol syndrome, which results in physical and mental damage. © **DAVID H. WELLS/CORBIS. REPRODUCED BY PERMISSION.**

foster care, job training, and general support services for affected individuals.

8. the total cost to the economy of Fetal Alcohol Syndrome was approximately $2,500,000,000 in 1995, and over a lifetime, health care costs for one Fetal Alcohol Syndrome child are estimated to be at least $1,400,000;

9. researchers have determined that the possibility of giving birth to a baby with Fetal Alcohol Syndrome or Fetal Alcohol Effects increases in proportion to the amount and frequency of alcohol consumed by a pregnant woman, and that stopping alcohol consumption at any point in the pregnancy reduces the emotional, physical, and mental consequences of alcohol exposure to the baby; and

10. though approximately 1 out of every 5 pregnant women drink alcohol during their pregnancy, we know of no safe dose of alcohol during pregnancy, or of any safe time to drink during pregnancy, thus, it is in the best interest of the Nation for the Federal Government to take an active role in encouraging all

women to abstain from alcohol consumption during pregnancy.

Sec. 3. Purpose

It is the purpose of this Act to establish, within the Department of Health and Human Services, a comprehensive program to help prevent Fetal Alcohol Syndrome and Fetal Alcohol Effects nationwide.

Further Resources

BOOKS

Dorris, Michael, and Louise Erdrich. *The Broken Cord: A Family's Ongoing Struggle with Fetal Alcohol Syndrome.* New York: HarperCollins, 1989.

McNeer, M. *American Indian Story.* New York: Farrar Straus and Giroux, 1963.

Stratton, Kathleen, Cynthia Howe, and Frederick Battaglia, eds. *Fetal Alcohol Syndrome Diagnosis, Epidemiology, Prevention, and Treatment.* Washington, D.C.: National Academy Press, 1996.

Streissguth, Ann, Jonathan Kanter, and Mike Lowry. *The Challenge of Fetal Alcohol Syndrome: Overcoming Secondary Disabilities.* Seattle, Wash.: University of Washington Press, 1997.

PERIODICALS

Golden, J. "A Tempest in a Cocktail Glass: Mothers, Alcohol, and Television, 1977–1996." *Journal of Health Politics, Policy and Law* 25, 2000, 473–498.

Hankin, J.R. "Fetal Alcohol Syndrome Prevention Research." *Alcohol Research and Health* 26, 2002, 58–65.

Vallee, B.L. "Alcohol in the Western World." *Scientific American* June 1998, 80–85.

Jones, Kenneth L., and David W. Smith. "Recognition of the Fetal Alcohol Syndrome in Early Infancy." *Lancet* 2, 1973, 999–1001.

WEBSITES

National Center on Birth Defects and Developmental Disabilities. "Fetal Alcohol Syndrome." Available online at http://www.cdc.gov/ncbddd/fas/; website home page: http://www.cdc.gov (accessed March 18, 2003).

National Institute on Alcohol Abuse and Alcoholism Graphics Gallery. "Areas of the Brain That Can Be Damaged in Utero by Maternal Alcohol Consumption." Available online at http://www.niaaa.nih.gov/gallery/fetal/mattson.htm; website home page: http://www.niaaa.nih.gov (accessed March 18, 2003).

"Bloodsafety Resolution—August 1997"

Statement

By: Advisory Committee on Blood Safety and Availability
Date: August 1997

Source: Advisory Committee on Blood Safety and Availability. "Bloodsafety Resolution—August 1997." Available online at http://www.hhs.gov/bloodsafety/resolutions/resaug97.html; website home page: http://www.hhs.gov (accessed March 21, 2003).

About the Organization: The Blood Safety and Availability Advisory Committee was established in the early 1990s to prevent a reoccurrence of the tragedy of the 1980s in which HIV (human immunodeficiency virus) was transmitted to many people through the national blood supply. The committee is made up of consumer advocates, bioethics experts, public health lawyers, health educators, transfusion experts, and hematology (blood) experts. Their task is to advise the Secretary of Health and Human Services on a wide range of issues related to the national blood supply. The committee met for the first time on April 24, 1997. ■

Introduction

The blood supply plays a vital role in the American health system. About three to four million Americans receive transfusions of whole blood or blood products, such as platelets or plasma. The safety of the blood supply is of national importance. Several government and private organizations work to ensure the safety of the blood supply. It is primarily the responsibility of the Food and Drug Administration (FDA) to regulate the blood industry.

During the 1990s, the overseers of the national blood supply were diligent in trying to ensure its safety. The AIDS epidemic of the 1980s fostered a mind-set of proactiveness toward blood supply safety. The Blood Safety and Availability Advisory Committee met several times during 1997 to discuss the hepatitis C virus and the safety of the blood supply.

The word *hepatitis* means inflammation of the liver. Hepatitis can be caused by many things, such as excessive alcohol consumption, drugs, or viruses. The five major viruses that cause inflammation of the liver are hepatitis A, B, C, D, and E. Each of these viruses causes a different type of liver disease. An important characteristic of hepatitis viruses is whether they cause acute or chronic disease. Hepatitis viruses A and E cause only acute disease. These illnesses can be severe, even fatal, but once the disease runs its course, the virus is eliminated from the body.

In contrast, chronic hepatitis usually never goes away. The virus persists in the blood of infected individuals indefinitely. Infection with the hepatitis C virus causes chronic hepatitis. The actual disease progression varies widely from person to person, but typically the virus slowly causes damage to liver cells over a period of ten to fifteen years. During this time, most people are completely unaware they are infected, but the hepatitis C virus has ravaged the liver of so many people that it is the leading cause of liver transplants today. Tens of thousands of Americans die each year from complications arising from hepatitis C.

Significance

During the late 1970s and throughout the 1980s, hepatitis viruses were common blood contaminants. At this time, scientists were only able to identify the hepatitis A and B viruses, but another hepatitis virus was showing up in the blood supply as well. In fact, this hepatitis was the most prevalent viral contaminant in blood at the time. Based on testing, they knew it was related to hepatitis, but it was neither hepatitis A nor B.

The identification of hepatitis C and the development of blood-screening tests led many Americans to learn they had a serious disease. In 1987, Chiron Corporation researchers discovered the hepatitis C virus. This allowed for the development of an enzyme-linked immunosorbent assay (ELISA) test for hepatitis C around 1990. ELISA is the most widely used and most effective method to detect antibodies (immune-fighting proteins the body makes to fight specific pathogens, like viruses). One of the recommendations of the Blood Safety and Advisory Committee was to do a "lookback" at all the blood that tested positive for non-A and non-B hepatitis in the 1980s and early 1990s and notify both donors and recipients, who received letters in the mail informing them that they may harbor a potentially deadly virus.

Historically, viral infections have been very hard to treat, but a new antiviral treatment using interferon A has been successful in eliminating hepatitis C in some patients. Until interferons were purified and produced on a large scale, there were few antiviral medications. However, interferon A combined with another antiviral medication called Ribavirin has been very effective against hepatitis C. Many patients are virus free after undergoing the combination treatment. These people can actually say they have been cured of hepatitis C, something unheard of previously.

Primary Source

"Bloodsafety Resolution—August 1997" [excerpt]

SYNOPSIS: The Blood Safety and Availability Advisory Committee met several times in 1997 to discuss the ramifications of the hepatitis C virus for the safety of the national blood supply. In August that year, the committee issued the following resolution.

DATE: August 18, 1997
TO: Interested Parties
FROM: Stephen D. Nightingale, MD, Executive Secretary
Advisory Committee on Blood Safety and Availability
SNIGHTIN@OSOPHS.DHHS.GOV
SUBJECT: Committee Resolution of August 12, 1997 . . .

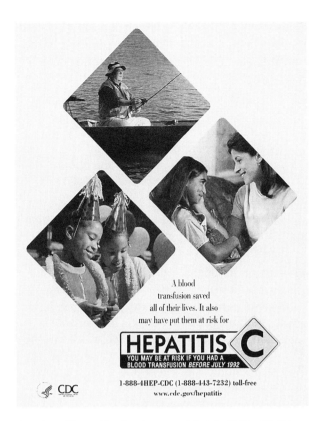

An estimated four million Americans were infected with Hepatitis C in the mid- to late 1990s. Since 1992, the availability of Hepatitis C testing has made it easier to identify people in need of treatment. **COURTESY OF THE CDC. REPRODUCED BY PERMISSION.**

Resolution

Hepatitis C virus (HCV) is a major cause of chronic liver disease which can progress to cirrhosis and liver failure in some infected persons, usually over the course of 20 or more years. An estimated 4 million Americans have been infected with HCV, of whom about 7% may have acquired their infection from blood transfusion, most before 1992. The first donor screening test for HCV infection was introduced in 1990, and an improved second generation screening test was introduced in 1992. Since 1992, the availability of a confirmatory test has made possible the more precise identification of persons who may have been infected with HCV, and it has become apparent that

1. Many HCV-infected persons are unaware of their infection because it may remain silent for many years;

2. Persons with HCV infection may benefit from treatment or behavioral interventions.

In view of these considerations and the Committee's belief that persons who may have received blood or blood components from an HCV-infectious donor should be notified of the risks associated with transfusion of the blood or blood components they received, we recommend to the Secretary of Health and Human Services the following:

1. a program to educate providers of medical care regarding the importance of identification of persons at risk for HCV infection, including those who received blood or blood components prior to 1992, and the appropriate measures for prevention, counseling, diagnosis, and treatment;

2. an aggressive and sensitive public education campaign to notify and test recipients transfused prior to 1992;

3. a targeted lookback program triggered by donors detected as HCV-confirmed positive by second generation screening and supplemental testing (1992 and after). This lookback should extend to January 1987 or 12 months prior to the donor's most recent negative second generation HCV test and should include tracing

   a. recipients of blood or blood components from HCV-confirmed positive donors who had previously tested negative by a second generation test for HCV infection between 1992 and the present;

   b. recipients of blood or blood components from HCV-confirmed positive donors who had previously tested negative by a first generation test for HCV infection between 1990 and 1992; and

   c. recipients of blood or blood components from HCV-confirmed positive donors who had no prior HCV test.

Further Resources

BOOKS

Berkman, Alan, and Nicholas Bakalar. *Hepatitis A to G: The Facts You Need to Know About All the Forms of this Dangerous Disease.* New York: Warner, 2000.

Clendinnen, Inga. *Tiger's Eye: A Memoir.* New York: Scribner, 2001.

Turkington, Carol. *Hepatitis C: The Silent Epidemic.* Lincolnwood, Ill.: Contemporary Books, 1998.

PERIODICALS

Bren, Linda. "Hepatitis C. Disease Development and Treatment Side-effects." *FDA Consumer* 35, July 2001, 24.

Shelton, Deborah, L. "Quiet Epidemic Coming to Light." *American Medical News,* September 28, 1998, 26.

Tong, Myron J., Neveen S. El-Farra, Andrew R. Reikes, and Ruth L. Co. "Clinical Outcomes After Transfusion-

Associated Hepatitis C." *New England Journal of Medicine* 332, no. 22, June 1, 1995, 1463–1467.

WEBSITES

Koop, C. Everett. "Hepatitis C: An Epidemic for Anyone." Available online at http://www.epidemic.org/index2.html; website home page: http://www.epidemic.org (accessed March 21, 2003).

National Center for Infectious Diseases. "Viral Hepatitis C." Available online at http://www.cdc.gov/ncidod/diseases /hepatitis/c/; website home page: http://www.cdc.gov (accessed March 21, 2003).

"Statement on First Federal Obesity Clinical Guidelines"

Press release

By: National Heart, Lung, and Blood Institute

Date: June 3, 1998

Source: National Heart, Lung, and Blood Institute of the National Institutes of Health. "Statement on First Federal Obesity Clinical Guidelines." June 3, 1998. Available online at http://www.nih.gov/news/pr/jun98/nhlbi-03.html; website home page: http://www.nih.gov (accessed April 22, 2003).

About the Organization: The origins of the National Heart, Lung, and Blood Institute extend back to June 16, 1948, when President Harry S. Truman signed the National Heart Act. Later, Surgeon General Leonard Scheele established the National Heart Institute (NHI). Twenty-four years later, through section 413 of the National Heart, Blood Vessel, Lung, and Blood Act (P.L. 92-423), Congress required the NHI to expand. The NHI was renamed the National Heart, Lung, and Blood Institute (NHLBI). The NHLBI is a part of the National Institutes of Health (NIH). ∎

Introduction

Obesity was a major health story in the 1990s. Worldwide, the numbers of obese people increased beginning in 1980 and continuing through the 1990s. In some countries, including the United States, over half the adult population was estimated to be overweight or obese. Certain women and ethnic groups are particularly disposed to become overweight. Eastern Europeans, people from the Mediterranean region, American Indians, Hispanic Americans, Pacific Islanders, and African American women have some of the highest rates of obesity in the world.

The 1998 obesity guidelines issued by the National Heart, Lung, and Blood Institute (NHLBI) were the first such guidelines on obesity issued for doctors. In the past, doctors, along with the rest of society, tended to view obesity as a cosmetic problem or a failure of self-discipline.

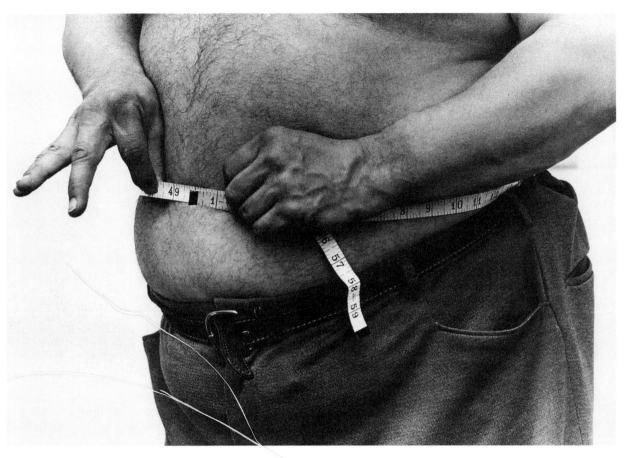

The National Institutes of Health released the first federal guidelines regarding obesity in 1998. Obesity is an increasing health concern in the United States. © DAN LAMONT/CORBIS. REPRODUCED BY PERMISSION.

Doctors would treat the symptoms of obesity, such as diabetes, stroke, or coronary artery disease, but obesity itself was not considered a disease. The NHLBI guidelines changed this view by directing and guiding physicians to treat obesity as a disease itself.

The guidelines included a method that doctors should use to determine whether or not a patient was obese—the Body Mass Index (BMI), the best and most widely used measure of obesity. At a meeting in 1997, the World Health Organization (WHO) agreed that BMI would be used as the worldwide standard for obesity. A BMI of 30 or greater indicates obesity.

Doctor intervention was determined to be a key factor in effective treatment of obesity. In a vacuum of medical advice, many overweight and obese people turned to commercial weight-loss programs, but they were also vulnerable to "lose weight quick schemes" and treatments. It was found that obese patients who received advice from a doctor or other medical professional were more apt to lose weight.

Since obesity was deemed a disease, doctors were advised in ways to treat it. The recommended treatment included an individualized program of physical activity, moderate food intake, counseling, and prescription medications when necessary. Obesity medications generally are appetite-suppressant drugs, which act by increasing the levels of serotonin, one of the chemical messengers in the brain. Another type of anti-obesity medication was approved by the Food and Drug Administration (FDA) in 1999. The new drug works by reducing the body's ability to absorb dietary fat.

Significance

Many public health officials and organizations have tried to warn the public about the dangers of obesity. One of the strongest warnings came from the surgeon general, who stated that a failure to address overweight and obese Americans "could wipe out some of the gains we've made in areas such as heart disease, several forms of cancer, and other chronic health problems." The public health community has launched informational campaigns focusing on the medical consequences of extreme weight gain. All of this seems to have had little effect; obesity rates in the United States have continued to rise. In 2000,

How to Determine Your BMI

Multiply your weight in pounds by 703, then divide the answer by your height in inches squared. For example, a 5 foot 6 inch woman who weighs 135 pounds would compute her BMI as follows: $(135 \times 703) / (66^2)$; has a BMI of 21.7.

30.5 percent of adults were considered obese, compared to 22.9 percent in 1994.

Medical professionals are worried about obese children. Childhood obesity is blamed on eating frequent meals away from home, a sedentary lifestyle, and high-fat and high-calorie diets. Childhood obesity produces a special set of problems for the health field. Weight patterns for children more often than not are carried into adulthood, where it is even harder to lose weight. But diabetes is a bigger concern. Obesity induces type 2 diabetes mellitus, a metabolic disorder leading to high blood sugar levels and an inability to properly metabolize carbohydrates, proteins, and fats. Obese children who develop diabetes may lose weight, but they will never be able to lose diabetes once they have it. Additionally, obese children are at a greater risk for psychological problems. Obesity and its complications threaten to overwhelm the health care system in the near future.

The National Heart, Lung, and Blood Institute guidelines classified obesity as *a metabolic disease*. Research into the molecular causes of obesity have provided some insights into the disease. So far five different genes, ten hormones, and imbalances in the neurotransmitter serotonin have been implicated in causing people to eat excessively. Many scientists are looking at evolution to provide clues as to why humans are becoming increasingly overweight. They theorize that a survival mechanism that benefited humans millions of years ago may be causing more people to be overweight now. Ancient humans who survived through periods of food shortages were those who were able to use calories more efficiently and store fat for future use. In addition, humans have strong biological signals to consume food and weak signals for when to stop.

Primary Source

"Statement on First Federal Obesity Clinical Guidelines"

SYNOPSIS: The following guidelines issued by the National Heart, Lung, and Blood Institute alerted the medical community to the need to treat obesity as

a medical condition and described the Body Mass Index.

The first Federal guidelines on the identification, evaluation, and treatment of overweight and obesity in adults are scheduled to be released on June 17 by the National Heart, Lung, and Blood Institute (NHLBI), in cooperation with the National Institute of Diabetes and Digestive and Kidney Diseases (NIDDK). Due to a premature release in the news media of erroneous information about the guidelines, some of the key recommendations of the report are being released now. The intent is to ensure that accurate information about the guidelines is available to the public.

The guidelines were developed by a 24-member expert panel chaired by Dr. F. Xavier Pi-Sunyer, director of the Obesity Research Center, St.Luke's/Roosevelt Hospital Center in New York City. They are currently being reviewed by 115 health experts at major medical and professional societies. The NHLBI is in the process of receiving comments and endorsements from these experts.

Based on the most extensive review of the scientific evidence on overweight and obesity conducted to date, these clinical practice guidelines for physicians present a new approach for the assessment of overweight and obesity and establish principles of safe and effective weight loss.

According to the guidelines, assessment of overweight involves evaluation of three key measures—body mass index (BMI), waist circumference, and a patient's risk factors for diseases and conditions associated with obesity.

The guidelines' definition of overweight is based on research which relates body mass index to risk of death and illness. The expert panel that developed the guidelines defined overweight as a BMI of 25 to 29.9 and obesity as a BMI of 30 and above, which is consistent with the definitions used in many other countries. BMI describes body weight relative to height and is strongly correlated with total body fat content in adults. According to the guidelines, a BMI of 30 is about 30 pounds overweight and is equivalent to 221 pounds in a 6' person and to 186 pounds in someone who is 5'6'.

The panel recommends that BMI be determined in all adults. People of normal weight should have their BMI reassessed in 2 years.

According to a new analysis of the National Health and Nutrition Examination Survey (NHANES

III), as BMI levels rise, average blood pressure and total cholesterol levels increase and average HDL or good cholesterol levels decrease. Men and women in the highest obesity category have five times the risk of hypertension, high blood cholesterol, or both compared to individuals of normal weight.

The guidelines recommend weight loss to lower high blood pressure, to lower high total cholesterol and to raise low levels of HDL or good cholesterol, and to lower elevated blood glucose in overweight persons with two or more risk factors and in obese persons who are at increased risk. They recommend that overweight patients without risk factors work on maintaining current weight or preventing further weight gain.

According to the guidelines, 97 million American adults—55 percent of the population—are now considered overweight or obese. These individuals are at increased risk of illness from hypertension, lipid disorders, type 2 diabetes, coronary heart disease, stroke, gallbladder disease, osteoarthritis, sleep apnea and respiratory problems, and certain cancers. The report of the guidelines also notes that obesity is associated with higher death rates and, after smoking, is the second leading cause of preventable death in the U.S. today. The total costs attributable to obesity-related disease approaches $100 billion annually.

In addition to measuring BMI, health care professionals can assess an individual patient's risk status through evaluating risk factors for obesity, such as elevations in blood pressure or family history of obesity-related disease. At a given level of overweight or obesity, patients with additional risk factors are considered to be at higher risk for health problems, requiring more intensive therapy and modification of any risk factors.

Physicians are also advised to determine waist circumference, which is strongly associated with abdominal fat. Excess abdominal fat is an independent predictor of disease risk. The panel concluded that waist circumference is a better marker of abdominal fat and a better predictor of disease risk than the current method of calculating the waist-to-hip ratio. A waist circumference of over 40 inches in men and over 35 inches in women signifies increased risk in those who have a BMI of 25 to 34.9.

The new guidelines stress that there are no new or magic cures for weight loss. The most successful strategies for weight loss include calorie reduction, increased physical activity, and behavior

therapy designed to improve eating and physical activity habits. The guidelines advise physicians to have their patients try lifestyle therapy for at least 6 months before embarking on physician-prescribed drug therapy. Weight loss drugs approved by the FDA for long-term use may be tried as part of a comprehensive weight loss program that includes dietary therapy and physical activity in carefully selected patients (BMI ≥ 30 without additional risk factors, BMI ≥ 27 with two or more of the following risk factors— diabetes, high blood pressure, high blood cholesterol, and sleep apnea) who have been unable to lose weight or maintain weight loss with conventional nondrug therapies. Drug therapy can also be used during the weight maintenance phase of treatment. However, drug safety and effectiveness beyond one year of total treatment have not been established.

When published, *Clinical Guidelines on the Identification, Evaluation, and Treatment of Overweight and Obesity in Adults* will be distributed to primary care physicians in the U.S. as well as to other interested health care practitioners. It will also be available on the NHLBI website—http://www.nhlbi.nih.gov/nhlbi/ on June 17.

Further Resources

BOOKS

Fumento, Michael. *The Fat of the Land: The Obesity Epidemic and How Americans Can Help Themselves.* New York: Viking, 1997.

Shell, Ellen Ruppel. *The Hungry Gene: The Science of Fat and the Future of Thin.* New York: Atlantic Monthly Press, 2002.

PERIODICALS

Allison, David, B. "The Direct Health Care Costs of Obesity in the United States." *American Journal of Public Health* 89, no. 8, August 1999, 1194–1199.

Nestle, Marion, and Michael F. Jacobson. "Halting the Obesity Epidemic: A Public Health Policy Approach." *Public Health Reports* 115, January–February 2000, 12–24.

Shelton, Deborah, L. "Heavyweight Danger." *American Medical News,* March 3, 1997, 10–16.

Willi, Denise. "Couch Potato Crisis: Diabetes, Obesity, Little Physical Exercise . . . The News Is Bleak for the Health of America's Children." *Instructor,* March 2003, 20–22.

WEBSITES

American Obesity Association Fact Sheets. Available online at http://www.obesity.org/subs/fastfacts/aoafactsheets.shtml; website home page: http://www.obesity.org (accessed March 15, 2003).

"Overweight and Obesity: The Surgeon General's Call to Action to Prevent and Decrease Overweight and Obesity." Available online at http://www.surgeongeneral.gov/topics/obesity/; website home page: http://www.surgeongeneral.gov (accessed March 15, 2003).

"The Biotech Death of Jesse Gelsinger"

Newspaper article

By: Sheryl Gay Stohlberg

Date: November 28, 1999

Source: Stohlberg, Sheryl Gay. "The Biotech Death of Jesse Gelsinger." *The New York Times,* November 28, 1999. Reprinted in Cohen, Jesse, ed. *The Best American Science Writing 2000.* New York: HarperCollins, 2000, 45–56. ∎

Introduction

After the first gene therapy treatment occurred in 1990, there was immense hope that it could miraculously cure hundreds of inherited metabolic disorders. It seemed so simple: replace the defective gene with a functional gene—the disorder is cured. Gene therapy had given many people suffering from such metabolic diseases as ornithine transcarbamylase (OTC) the best reason to hope for a cure than they had ever had. In the late 1990s, when Jesse Gelsinger volunteered, several gene therapy trials were occurring across the country. However, no one had yet been cured by gene therapy.

Inherited metabolic disorders, such as OTC deficiency, are natural candidates for gene therapy treatment. OTC is a metabolic disease caused by a mutated gene located on the X chromosome. The defective gene is responsible for making the enzyme ornithine transcarbamylase, or OTC, which plays an important role in breaking down dietary proteins. The relationship between the gene defect and the disease is straightforward and simple: one defective gene causes one defective enzyme (enzymes are proteins), which leads to disease. If somehow an undamaged OTC gene could be incorporated into the genome of someone with the disorder, the new gene would make a properly functioning OTC enzyme.

The most challenging part of gene therapy is getting the new gene into the patient's genome. In Jesse's case, adenovirus, a human cold virus, was used. A virus is a logical choice; viruses are simple, consisting only of protein and DNA. Human viruses function by inserting "virus DNA" into the human cell's genome, thereby causing human cells to make viral proteins. In gene therapy, doctors use the virus's machinery for getting DNA into the cell, but they replace the viral DNA with human DNA, that is, the gene therapy gene. One challenge is finding the right amount of virus to send into the patient. A large amount of virus gets more of the gene into the cell's nucleus and genome, but too much increases the risk of side effects.

Researchers used a deactivated adenovirus to bring the OTC gene into Jesse's liver cells, hoping his liver would then make the properly functioning enzyme. However, the tradeoff between dosage and effectiveness worked against Jesse. He received too much virus, and his body responded by mounting a fierce immune response, which inflamed and damaged Jesse's organs one by one until he died.

Significance

Federal regulators quickly reacted to Jesse's death. The Food and Drug Administration (FDA) temporarily halted all gene therapy trials until the reasons for Jesse's death could be determined. Later, the FDA charged those involved in the trial with disobeying various FDA protocols. The charges included not adequately informing Jesse of the risks involved in the experimental therapy and using Jesse in the trial when he should have been rejected because of preexisting liver problems.

After an investigation, the National Institutes of Health (NIH) issued a report on Jesse's death. They concluded that Jesse probably died from the effects of a high dose of the adenovirus. The report also said that administering the adenovirus directly to Jesse's liver probably played a major role in his death. The NIH also discovered that many incidents of severe side effects and deaths had already occurred in gene therapy studies that used adenoviruses. Only a small percentage of these incidents, however, were reported to the NIH or the FDA.

Jesse's death brought to a head the ethical issues regarding the use of human subjects in experimental trials. In general, risky, unproven experiments use desperately ill people who have exhausted more traditional treatments so have little to lose. Jesse, though, was not gravely ill and would not have benefited from the therapy. Many wondered why he was allowed to participate. Recently, the NIH and the FDA toughened the rules about the way patients are recruited into medical trials. Additionally, the medical profession appeals to scientists to act ethically in using human subjects in research.

Adenoviruses are still used to deliver genes in gene therapy trials. The NIH report concluded that the adenovirus can be used to safely deliver genes, but caution must be exercised. Gene therapy is still in the experimental phase and has not yet produced any significant successes.

Primary Source

"The Biotech Death of Jesse Gelsinger"

> **SYNOPSIS:** *New York Times* journalist Sheryl Gay Stohlberg tells the story of Jesse Gelsinger and his death in an experimental gene therapy trial.

The jagged peak of Mount Wrightson towers 9,450 feet above Tucson, overlooking a deep gorge where the prickly pear cactus that dots the desert floor gives way to a lush forest of ponderosa pine. It is said that this is as close to heaven as you can get in southern Arizona. Jesse Gelsinger loved this place. So it was here, on a clear Sunday afternoon in early November, that Paul Gelsinger laid his eighteen-year-old son to rest, seven weeks after a gene-therapy experiment cost him his life.

The ceremony was simple and impromptu. Two dozen mourners—Jesse's father; his mother, Pattie; his stepmother, Mickie; and two sisters, a brother, three doctors and a smattering of friends—trudged five miles along a steep trail to reach the rocky outcropping at the top. There, Paul Gelsinger shared stories of his son, who loved motorcycles and professional wrestling and was, to his father's irritation, distinctly lacking in ambition. Jesse was the kind of kid who kept $10.10 in his bank account. "You need $10 to keep it open," Gelsinger explained but those assembled on the mountaintop agreed that he had a sharp wit and a sensitive heart.

At Gelsinger's request, the hikers had carried Jesse's medicine bottles filled with his ashes, and now they were gathered at the edge of the peak. Steve Raper, the surgeon who gave Jesse what turned out to be a lethal injection of new genes, pulled a small blue book of poetry from his pocket. "Here rests his head upon the lap of Earth," Raper read, reciting a passage from an elegy by Thomas Gray, "a youth to Fortune and Fame unknown. / Fair Science frowned not on his humble birth." Then the surgeon, the grieving father and the rest scattered Jesse's ashes into the canyon, where they rose on a gust of wind and fell again in a powerful cloud of fine gray dust. "I will look to you here often, Jess," Paul Gelsinger said sadly.

Jesse Gelsinger was not sick before he died. He suffered from ornithine transcarbamylase (OTC) deficiency, a rare metabolic disorder, but it was controlled with a low-protein diet and drugs, thirty-two pills a day. He knew when he signed up for the experiment at the University of Pennsylvania that he would not benefit; the study was to test the safety of a treatment for babies with a fatal form of his disorder. Still, it offered hope, the promise that someday Jesse might be rid of the cumbersome medications and diet so restrictive that half a hot dog was a treat. "What's the worst that can happen to me?" he told a friend shortly before he left for the Penn hospital, in Philadelphia. "I die, and it's for the babies."

As far as government officials know Jesse's death on September 17 was the first directly related to gene therapy. The official cause, as listed on the death certificate filed by Raper, was adult respiratory distress syndrome: his lungs shut down. The truth is more complicated. Jesse's therapy consisted of an infusion of corrective genes, encased in a dose of weakened cold virus, adenovirus, which functioned as what scientists call a vector. Vectors are like taxicabs that drive healthy DNA into cells; viruses, whose sole purpose is to get inside cells and infect them, make useful vectors. The Penn researchers had tested their vector, at the same dose Jesse got, in mice, monkeys, baboons and one human patient, and had seen expected, flulike side effects, along with some mild liver inflammation, which disappeared on its own. When Jesse got the vector, he suffered a chain reaction that the testing had not predicted—jaundice, a blood-clotting disorder, kidney failure, lung failure and brain death: in Raper's words, "multiple-organ-system failure." The doctors are still investigating; their current hypothesis is that the adenovirus triggered an overwhelming inflammatory reaction—in essence, an immune-system revolt. What they do not understand yet is why.

Every realm of medicine has its defining moment, often with a human face attached. Polio had Jonas Salk. In vitro fertilization had Louise Brown, the world's first test-tube baby. Transplant surgery had Barney Clark, the Seattle dentist with the artificial heart. AIDS had Magic Johnson. Now gene therapy has Jesse Gelsinger.

Until Jesse died, gene therapy was a promising idea that had so far failed to deliver. As scientists map the human genome, they are literally tripping over mutations that cause rare genetic disorders, including OTC deficiency, Jesse's disease. The initial goal was simple: to cure, or prevent, these illnesses by replacing defective genes with healthy ones. Biotech companies have poured millions into research—not for rare hereditary disorders but for big-profit illnesses like cancer, heart disease and AIDS. As of August, the government had reviewed 331 gene-therapy protocols involving more than 4,000 patients. Just 41 were for the "monogeneic," or single-gene, defect diseases whose patients so desperately hoped gene therapy would be their salvation.

At the same time, the science has progressed slowly; researchers have had trouble devising vectors that can carry genes to the right cells and get them to work once they are there. Four years ago, Dr. Harold Varmus, the director of the National Institutes of Health, commissioned a highly critical re-

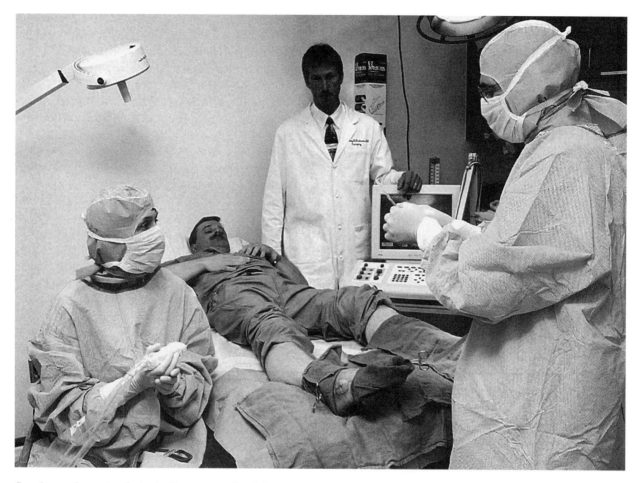

Gene therapy, the practice of using healthy genes to replace faulty ones, was a promising and growing medical field in the 1990s and can assist patients coping with a variety of diseases, such as muscular dystrophy. **AP/WIDE WORLD PHOTOS. REPRODUCED BY PERMISSION.**

port about gene therapy chiding investigators for creating "the mistaken and widespread perception of success." Since then, there have been some accomplishments: a team at Tufts University has used gene therapy to grow new blood vessels for heart disease patients, for instance. But so far, gene therapy has not cured anyone. As Ruth Macklin, a bioethicist and member of the Recombinant DNA Advisory Committee, the National Institutes of Health panel that oversees gene-therapy research, says, bluntly, "Gene therapy is not yet therapy."

On December 8, the "RAC," as the committee is called, will begin a public inquiry into Jesse's death, as well as the safety of adenovirus, which has been used in roughly one-quarter of all gene-therapy clinical trials. The Penn scientists will report on their preliminary results, and investigators, who at the RAC's request have submitted thousands of pages of patient safety data to the committee, will discuss the side effects of adenovirus. Among them will be researchers from the Schering-Plough Corpo-

ration, which was running two experiments in advanced liver cancer patients that used methods similar to Penn's. Enrollment in those trials was suspended by the Food and Drug Administration after Jesse's death. The company, under pressure from the RAC, has since released information showing that some patients experienced serious side effects, including changes in liver function and blood cell counts, mental confusion and nausea; two experienced minor strokes, although one had a history of them. Once all the data on adenovirus are analyzed at the December 8 meeting, the RAC may recommend restrictions on its use, which will almost certainly slow down some aspects of gene-therapy research.

The meeting will be important for another reason: it will mark an unprecedented public airing of information about the safety of gene therapy—precisely the kind of sharing the RAC has unsuccessfully sought in the past. Officials say gene therapy has claimed no lives besides Jesse's. But since his death, there have been news reports that other patients died during the course of experiments—from their diseases, as opposed to the therapy—and that the scientists involved did not report those deaths to the RAC, as is required. This has created a growing cloud of suspicion over gene therapy, raising questions about whether other scientists may have withheld information that could have prevented Jesse's death. That question cannot be answered until all the data are analyzed. But one thing is certain: four years after the field was rocked by Varmus's highly critical evaluation, it is now being rocked again, this time over an issue more fundamental than efficacy—safety. "I think it's a perilous time for gene therapy," says LeRoy Walters, a bioethicist at Georgetown University and former chairman of the RAC. "Until now, we have been able to say, 'Well, it hasn't helped many people, but at least it hasn't hurt people.' That has changed."

No one, perhaps, is more acutely aware of gene therapy's broken promise than Mark Batshaw, the pediatrician who proposed the experiment that cost Jesse Gelsinger his life.

At fifty-four, Batshaw, who left the University of Pennsylvania last year for Children's National Medical Center, in Washington, is tall and gangly with slightly stooped shoulders and a shy smile that gives him the air of an awkward schoolboy, which he once was. As a child, Batshaw struggled with hyperactivity: He didn't read until the third grade; in the fourth, his teacher grew so irritated at his constant chatter that she stuck his chair out in the hall. The experience has left him with a soft spot for developmentally disabled children, which is how he has become one of the world's foremost experts in urea-cycle disorders among them OTC deficiency.

The urea cycle is a series of five liver enzymes that help rid the body of ammonia, a toxic breakdown product of protein. When these enzymes are missing or deficient, ammonia—"the same ammonia that you scrub your floors with," Batshaw explains—accumulates in the blood and travels to the brain, causing coma, brain damage and death. OTC deficiency is the most common urea-cycle disorder, occurring in one out of every 40,000 births. Its genetic mutation occurs on the X chromosome, so women are typically carriers, while their sons suffer the disease.

Severe OTC deficiency is, Batshaw says, "a devastating disease." Typically, newborns slip into a coma within seventy-two hours of birth. Most suffer severe brain damage. Half die in the first month, and

half of the survivors die by age five. Batshaw was a young postdoctoral fellow when he met his first urea-cycle-disorder patient in 1973, correctly diagnosing the disease at a time when most other doctors had never heard of it. Within two years, he and his colleagues had devised the first treatment, a low-protein formula called keto-acid. Later, they came up with what remains standard therapy to this day: sodium benzoate, a preservative, and another type of sodium, which bind to ammonia and help eliminate it from the body.

But the therapy cannot prevent the coma that is often the first sign of OTC and ravages the affected infant. By the time Batshaw joined the faculty at Penn in 1988, he was dreaming of a cure: gene therapy. Patients were dreaming, too, says Tish Simon, former co-president of the National Urea Cycle Disorders Foundation, whose son died of OTC deficiency three years ago. "All of us saw gene therapy as the hope for the future," Simon says. "And certainly, if anybody was going to do it, it had to be Mark Batshaw."

Gene therapy became a reality on September 14, 1990, in a hospital room at the National Institutes of Health, in Bethesda, Maryland, when a four-year-old girl with a severe immune-system deficiency received a thirty-minute infusion of white blood cells that had been engineered to contain copies of the gene she lacked. Rarely in modern medicine has an experiment been filled with so much hope; news of the treatment ricocheted off front pages around the world. The scientist who conducted it, Dr. W. French Anderson, quickly became known as the father of gene therapy. "We had got ourselves all hyped up," Anderson now admits, "thinking there would be rapid, quick, easy, early cures."

Among those keeping a close eye on Anderson's debut was Jim Wilson, a square-jawed, sandy-haired midwesterner who decided to follow his father's footsteps in medicine when he realized he wasn't going to make it in football. As a graduate student in biological chemistry, Wilson had taken a keen interest in rare genetic diseases. "All I did," he says, "was dream about gene therapy."

Today, as director of the Institute for Human Gene Therapy at the University of Pennsylvania, Wilson is in an excellent position to make that dream a reality. Headquartered in a century-old building amid the leafy maple trees and brick sidewalks of the picturesque Penn campus, the six-year-old institute, with 250 employees, state-of-the-art laboratories and a $25 million annual budget, is the largest academic gene-therapy program in the nation. In a field rife with big egos, Wilson is regarded as first-rate. "Present company excluded," Anderson says, "he's the best person in the field."

Batshaw was banging on Wilson's door even before Wilson arrived at Penn in March 1993, and within a month they were collaborating on studies of OTC-deficient mice. Their first task was to develop a vector. Adenovirus seemed a logical choice.

There had been some early problems with safety—a 1993 cystic fibrosis experiment was shut down when a patient was hospitalized with inflamed lungs—but Wilson and Batshaw say they figured out how to make a safer vector by deleting extra viral genes. Adenovirus was the right size: when its viral genes were excised, the OTC gene fit right in. It had a "ZIP code," on it, Batshaw says, that would carry it straight to the liver. And while its effects did not last, it worked quickly, which meant that it might be able to reverse a coma, sparing babies from brain damage. "It wasn't going to be a cure soon," Batshaw says, "but it might be a treatment soon."

The mouse experiments were encouraging. Mice that had the therapy survived for two to three months even while fed a high-protein diet. Those that lacked the treatment died. "It wasn't subtle," Wilson says. "We felt pretty compelled by that." But when the team contemplated testing in people, they ran smack into an ethical quandary: who should be their subjects?

To Wilson, the answer seemed obvious: sick babies. Arthur Caplan, the university's resident bioethics expert, thought otherwise. Caplan says parents of dying infants are incapable of giving informed consent: "They are coerced by the disease of their child." He advised Wilson to test only stable adults, either female carriers or men like Jesse, with partial enzyme deficiencies. The National Urea Cycle Disorders Foundation agreed. When Batshaw turned up at their 1994 annual meeting asking for volunteers, so many mothers offered to be screened for the OTC gene that it took him four hours to draw all the blood.

By the time Mark Batshaw and Jim Wilson submitted their experiment to the Recombinant DNA Advisory Committee for approval, the panel was in danger of being disbanded. Varmus, the NIH director, who won the Nobel Prize for his discovery of a family of cancer-causing genes, had made no secret of his distaste for the conduct of gene-therapy researchers. He thought the science was too shoddy to push forward with human testing, and it bothered him that so few experiments were focusing on ge-

netic diseases. It irked him to have to sign off on protocols the RAC approved, and it irked him even more to see biotech companies touting those approvals, like some kind of NIH imprimatur, in the business pages of the papers. "Some days," says Dr. Nelson Wivel, the committee's former executive director, who now works for Wilson at Penn, "it felt as though the RAC was helping the biotech industry raise money. Dr. Varmus hated that."

At the same time, the pharmaceutical industry and AIDS activists were complaining that the RAC was redundant: the FDA already reviewed gene-therapy proposals. So in mid-1995, after seeking the advice of an expert panel, Varmus reorganized the RAC, slashing its membership from twenty-five to fifteen and stripping it of its approval authority—a decision that, some say, has enabled gene-therapy researchers to ignore the panel and keep information about safety to themselves. "The RAC," complains Dr. Robert Erickson, a University of Arizona medical geneticist who served on the panel, "became a debating society."

The Batshaw-Wilson protocol was among the last the committee would ever approve. The plan was for eighteen adults (nineteen eventually signed up, including Tish Simon, but the last patient was never treated, because of Jesse's death) to receive an infusion of the OTC gene, tucked inside an adenovirus vector, through a catheter in the hepatic artery, which leads to the liver. The goal was to find what Wilson calls "the maximum tolerated dose," one high enough to get the gene to work, but low enough to spare patients serious side effects. Subjects would be split into six groups of three, with each group receiving a slightly higher dose than the last. This is standard fare in safety testing. "You go up in small-enough increments," Wilson explains, "that you can pull the plug on the thing before people get hurt."

The experiment stood in stark contrast to others that had earned Varmus's scorn. It was paid for by NIH, which meant it had withstood the rigors of scientific peer review. It was aimed at a rare genetic disease, not cancer or AIDS. It was supported by plenty of animal research: Wilson and his team had performed more than twenty mouse experiments to test efficacy and a dozen safety studies on mice, rhesus monkeys and baboons. Still, it made Erickson, one of two scientists assigned by the RAC to review the experiment, uneasy.

He was troubled by data showing that three monkeys had died of a blood-clotting disorder and severe liver inflammation when they received an earlier, stronger version of the adenovirus vector at a dose twenty times the highest dose planned for the study. No one had injected adenovirus directly into the bloodstream before, either via the liver or otherwise, and the scientists admitted that it was difficult to tell precisely how people would respond. They planned to confine the infusion to the right lobe of the liver, so that if damage occurred it would be contained there, sparing the left lobe. And they outlined the major risks: bleeding, from either the gene-therapy site or a subsequent liver biopsy, which would require surgery; or serious liver inflammation, which could require an organ transplant and might lead to death.

Both Erickson and the other scientific reviewer thought the experiment was too risky to test on asymptomatic volunteers and recommended rejection. But in the end, Batshaw and Wilson prevailed. They offered up Caplan's argument that testing on babies was inappropriate. And they agreed to inject the vector into the bloodstream, as opposed to putting it directly into the liver. That decision, however, was later reversed by the FDA, which insisted that because the adenovirus would travel through the blood and wind up in the liver anyway, the original plan was safer.

The RAC, in such disarray from Varmus's reorganization that it did not meet again for another year, was never informed of the change.

Jesse Gelsinger was seventeen when his pediatric geneticist, Dr. Randy Heidenreich, first told him about the Penn proposal. He wanted to sign up right away. But he had to wait until he was eighteen.

Paul Gelsinger was also enthusiastic. A trim forty-seven-year-old with intense blue eyes, Gelsinger, who makes his living as a handyman, gained custody of his four children nine years ago, when he divorced their mother, who suffers from manic depression. He had been having some difficulty with Jesse then; the boy was in the midst of an adolescent rebellion and was refusing to take his medicine. "I said: 'Wow, Jess, they're working on your disorder. Maybe they'll come up with a cure.'"

Jesse's was not a typical case of OTC deficiency: his mutation appears to have occurred spontaneously in the womb. His disease having been diagnosed when he was two, Jesse was what scientists call a mosaic—a small portion of his cells produced the missing enzyme. When he watched what he ate and took his medicine, he was fine. But one day last December, Paul Gelsinger arrived home

to find his son curled up on the couch. He had been vomiting uncontrollably, a sign, Paul knew, that Jesse's ammonia was rising. Jesse landed in the hospital, comatose and on life support. When he recovered, he never missed another pill.

On June 18, the day Jesse turned eighteen, the Gelsingers—Paul, Mickie and the children—flew to Philadelphia to see Paul's family. They played tourists, visiting the Liberty Bell and the Rocky statue, where Jesse was photographed, fists raised, a picture that would circulate in the newspapers after his death. On the twenty-second, they went to the University of Pennsylvania, where they met Raper, the surgeon, who explained the experiment and did blood and liver-function tests to see if Jesse was eligible. He was, and his treatment was scheduled for the fall. Jesse would be the youngest patient enrolled.

On September 9, Jesse returned to Philadelphia, this time alone. He took one duffel bag full of clothes and another full of wrestling videos. Paul Gelsinger planned to fly in a week later for the liver biopsy, which he considered the trial's most serious risk.

The treatment began on Monday, September 13. Jesse would receive the highest dose. Seventeen patients had already been treated, including one woman who had been given the same dose that Jesse would get, albeit from a different lot, and had done "quite well," Raper says. That morning, Jesse was taken to the interventional-radiology suite, where he was sedated and strapped to a table while a team of radiologists threaded two catheters into his groin. At 10:30 A.M., Raper drew 30 milliliters of the vector and injected it slowly. At half past noon, he was done.

That night, Jesse was sick to his stomach and spiked a fever, 104.5 degrees. Raper was not particularly surprised: other patients had experienced the same reaction. Paul Gelsinger called; he and Jesse talked briefly, exchanging I love yous. Those were the last words they ever spoke.

Early Tuesday morning a nurse called Raper at home; Jesse seemed disoriented. When Raper got to the hospital, about 6:15 A.M., he noticed that the whites of Jesse's eyes were yellow. That meant jaundice, not a good sign. "It was not something we had seen before," Raper says. A test confirmed that Jesse's bilirubin, a breakdown product of red blood cells, was four times the normal level. Raper called Gelsinger, and Batshaw in Washington, who said he would get on a train and be there in two hours.

Both doctors knew that the high bilirubin meant one of two things: either Jesse's liver was failing or he was suffering a clotting disorder in which his red blood cells were breaking down faster than the liver could metabolize them. This was same disorder the scientists had seen in the monkeys that had been given the stronger vector. The condition is life-threatening for anyone, but particularly dangerous for someone with Jesse's disease, because red blood cells liberate protein when they break down.

By midafternoon Tuesday, a little more than twenty-four hours after the injection, the clotting disorder had pushed Jesse into a coma. By 11:30 P.M., his ammonia level was 393 micromoles per liter of blood. Normal is 35. The doctors began dialysis.

Paul Gelsinger had booked a red-eye flight. When he arrived in the surgical intensive care unit at 8:00 Wednesday morning, Raper and Batshaw told him that dialysis had brought Jesse's ammonia level down to 72 but that other complications were developing. He was hyperventilating, which would increase the level of ammonia in his brain. They wanted to paralyze his muscles and induce a deeper coma, so that a ventilator could breathe for him. Gelsinger gave consent. Then he put on scrubs, gloves and a mask and went in to see his son.

By Wednesday afternoon, Jesse seemed to be stabilizing. Batshaw went back to Washington. Paul felt comfortable enough to meet his brother for dinner. But later that night Jesse worsened again. His lungs grew stiff; the doctors were giving him 100 percent oxygen, but not enough of it was getting to his bloodstream. They consulted a liver-transplant team and learned that Jesse was not a good candidate. Raper was beside himself. He consulted with Batshaw and Wilson, and they decided to take an extraordinary step, a procedure known as ECMO, for extracorporeal membrane oxygenation, essentially an external lung that filters the blood, removing carbon dioxide and adding oxygen. It had been tried on only 1,000 people before, Raper says. Only half had survived.

"If we could just buy his lungs a day or two," Raper said later, they thought "maybe he would go ahead and heal up."

The next day, Thursday, September 16, Hurricane Floyd slammed into the East Coast. Mickie Gelsinger flew in from Tucson just before the airport closed. (Pattie Gelsinger, Jesse's mother, was being treated in a psychiatric facility and was unable to leave.) Batshaw spent the day trapped outside Baltimore on an Amtrak train. He ran down his cell

phone calling Raper; when it went dead, he persuaded another passenger to lend him his. The ECMO, Raper reported, appeared to be working. But then another problem cropped up: Jesse's kidneys stopped making urine. "He was sliding into multiple-organ-system failure," Raper says.

That night, at his hotel, Paul Gelsinger couldn't sleep. He left his wife a note and walked the half mile to the Penn medical center to see Jesse. The boy was bloated beyond recognition; even his ears were swollen shut. Gelsinger noticed blood in Jesse's urine, an indication, he knew, that the kidneys were shutting down. How can anybody, he thought, survive this?

On the morning of Friday the seventeenth, a test showed that Jesse was brain dead. Paul Gelsinger didn't need to be told: "I knew it already." He called for a chaplain to hold a bedside service, with prayers for the removal of life support.

The room was crowded with equipment and people: seven of Paul's fifteen siblings came in, plus an array of doctors and nurses. Raper and Batshaw, shellshocked and exhausted, stood in the back. The chaplain anointed Jesse's forehead with oil, then read the Lord's Prayer. The doctors fought back tears.

When the intensive-care specialist flipped two toggle switches, one to turn off the ventilator and the other to turn off the ECMO machine, Raper stepped forward. He checked the heart-rate monitor, watched the line go flat and noted the time: 2:30 P.M. He put his stethoscope to Jesse's chest, more out of habit than necessity, and pronounced the death official. "Good-bye, Jesse," he said. "We'll figure this out."

Wilson reported the death immediately, drawing praise from government officials but criticism from Arthur Caplan, who says they should have made the news public, in a news conference. In the weeks since, the Penn team has put every detail of Jesse's treatment under a microscope. It has rechecked the vector to make certain it was not tainted, tested the same lot on monkeys, reexamined lab and autopsy findings. Wilson's biggest fear was that Jesse died as a result of human error, but so far there has been no evidence of that. "That's what's so frightening," French Anderson says. "If they made a mistake, you would feel a little safer."

The death has rattled the three doctors in various ways. Wilson has asked himself over and over again whether he should have done anything differently. "At this point, I say no, but I'm continuing to re-evaluate constantly." He has been besieged by worry, about the morale of his staff, about whether his institute's financial sponsors would pull out, about whether patients would continue to volunteer, about whether he would lose his bravado—the death knell for a scientist on the cutting edge. "My concern," he confessed, over dinner one night in Philadelphia, "is, I'm going to get timid, that I'll get risk-averse."

Raper has thrown himself into his work, trying to live up to his promise to "figure this out." There are a number of possible explanations, he says: the vector may have reacted badly with Jesse's medication; Jesse's status as a mosaic may have played a role; or perhaps the early testing in monkeys, which showed that the stronger vector had deleterious side effects, was more of a harbinger of danger than the doctors realized. An answer may take months, but he is determined to find one; only by understanding what happened to Jesse, and how to prevent it in others, can the research continue. "That," Raper says, "would be the best tribute to Jesse."

Of the three, Batshaw seems to have taken it the hardest. He is not a particularly religious man, but a few days after Jesse died he went to synagogue to say Kaddish, the Jewish mourner's prayer. He struggles with the idea of personal responsibility. He has cradled many a dying child in his career, but never before, he says, has a patient been made worse by his care. "What is the Hippocratic oath?" Batshaw asks rhetorically, looking into the distance as his fingers drum the tabletop. He pauses, as if to steel himself, and says, "I did harm."

Paul Gelsinger does not hold the doctors responsible, although he is acutely interested in knowing what other scientists knew about adenovirus before Jesse died. He has experienced a deep spiritual awakening since losing his son; in dying, he says, Jesse taught him how to live. He speaks frequently of God, and of "purity of intent," which is his way of saying that Jesse demonstrated an altruism the rest of us might do well to emulate. "I hope," he said on the mountaintop that Sunday afternoon, "that I can die as well as my son has died."

Further Resources

BOOKS

Bellenir, Karen. *Genetic Disorders Sourcebook.* Detroit: Omnigraphics, 1996.

Curiel, David, and Joanne T. Douglas. *Adenoviral Vectors for Gene Therapy.* Boston: Academic Press, 2002.

Phillips, M. Ian. *Gene Therapy Methods.* San Diego, Calif.: Academic Press, 2002.

PERIODICALS

"Assessment of Adenoviral Vector Safety and Toxicity: Report of the National Institutes of Health Recombinant DNA Advisory Committee." *Human Gene Therapy* 13, no. 1, January 1, 2002, 3–13.

WEBSITES

"Gene Therapy." Available online at http://www.ornl.gov /TechResources/Human_Genome/medicine/genetherapy .html; website home page: http://www.ornl.gov (accessed March 22, 2003).

"Gene Therapy." A *NewsHour with Jim Lehrer* Transcript, December 8, 1999. Available online at http://www.pbs.org /newshour/bb/health/july-dec99/gene_therapy.htm; website home page: http://www.pbs.org (accessed March 22, 2003).

Lehrman, Sally. "Genetic Medicine: Prescription for Conflict. The Topic In-Depth #1: The Safety of Clinical Trials." *The DNA Files.* October 2001. Available online at http://www .dnafiles.org/about/pgm14/topic1.html; website home page: http://www.dnafiles.org (accessed March 22, 2003).

National Health Museum. "Gene Therapy: An Overview." Available online at http://www.accessexcellence.org/AB /IWT/Gene_Therapy_Overview.html; website home page: http://www.accessexcellence.org (accessed March 22, 2003).

"Breaking the Code"

Radio broadcast

By: National Human Genome Research Institute

Date: December 2, 1999

Source: National Human Genome Research Institute. "Breaking the Code." A *NewsHour with Jim Lehrer* Transcript. Available online at http://www.pbs.org/newshour/bb/health /july-dec99/dna_12-2.html; website home page: http://www .pbs.org (accessed March 22, 2003).

About the Organization: The National Human Genome Research Institute (NHGRI) was established in 1989 to carry out the role of the National Institutes of Health (NIH) in the International Human Genome Project (HGP). The HGP was developed in collaboration with the United States Department of Energy (DOE). ∎

Introduction

The human genome refers to the full complement of DNA in a human being. It is spread across twenty-three pairs of chromosomes. Identical copies of each chromosome reside in every one of the trillion or so cells that make up the human body. Along each chromosome are arranged about 5,000 to 6,000 genes, or a total of around 140,000. Each gene is composed of varying sequences of four nucleotides: adenine (A), cytosine (C), thymine (T), and guanine (G). Different sequences of As, Ts, Cs, and Gs are responsible for the entire range of life on earth.

The seeds for the Human Genome Project began in the late 1980s with, perhaps surprisingly, the U.S. Department

A team of international scientists, including Dr. Nobuyoshi Shimizu, deciphered the genetic code of a human chromosome, called chromosome 22, which opens new possibilities for treatments of diseases ranging from schizophrenia to heart disease. © REUTERS NEWMEDIA INC./CORBIS. REPRODUCED BY PERMISSION.

of Energy (DOE). At a DOE meeting in 1986, several scientists discussed the possibility of sequencing the human genome. With knowledge of the sequence, they reasoned, it might be possible to determine if there had been increases in the gene mutation rate among survivors of the atomic bombs dropped on Hiroshima and Nagasaki, Japan, at the end of World War II (1939–1945). This is something that the DOE was very interested in knowing. Genes may be mutated, or changed, throughout our lives by *mutagens,* such as radioactive energy (as from an

atomic bomb), environmental chemicals, or ultraviolet light. The scientists wanted to know if the atomic bomb survivors and their descendents had more gene mutations than other people.

The Human Genome Project (HGP) began in 1990 as a collaboration between the DOE and the National Institutes of Health (NIH). The technical goals of the HGP project were to sequence the entire human genome, identify all the genes in human DNA, and make the information available to scientists, researchers, and doctors in academia and private industry around the world.

The human genome is discussed as if there was only one. Actually, there are more than six billion different human genomes in the world, one for each person except for identical twins. But even six billion variations on a theme represent only a minute portion of the whole genome. The vast majority of the human genome is in fact the same, so it makes sense to refer to *the* human genome.

On December 2, 1999, the heads of the DOE and the NIH announced that researchers had succeeded in determining the sequence of As, Ts, Cs, and Gs for one complete human chromosome, chromosome 22. At least thirty-five different diseases, such as leukemia and schizophrenia, have been linked to chromosome 22.

Significance

In 2001 the "draft sequence" of the entire human genome was published. The draft sequence will be turned into a "completed sequence," chromosome by chromosome. Gaps are filled in and uncertainties are cleared up until a certain level of preciseness is achieved (one error in ten thousand nucleotides). Then, the sequence is called *completed.* Researchers believe that such a high-quality sequence is critical for understanding the biology behind such disorders as heart disease, cancer, and diabetes. By early 2003, researchers for the Human Genome Project had completely sequenced four human chromosomes: numbers 14, 20, 21, and 22.

Scientists believe there will be profound implications for the practice of medicine once the human genome is completely sequenced. Diagnostic tests that can predict an individual's risk for particular diseases and their responsiveness to drugs are the first benefits that may be realized from the deciphered genome. The next benefits will come from "functional genomics"—understanding the function of each gene and how specific gene mutations cause disease. This part will not be quick or easy, but the rewards will be significant. Mutated genes are responsible for over four thousand hereditary diseases, such as cystic fibrosis or Huntington's disease. In some cases, a single misplaced letter among three billion can have lethal consequences. Gene therapy and the development of targeted drugs to fix a specific molecular abnormality will come later.

Legal and ethical implications will arise from the knowledge of the human gene sequence. As the understanding of genomes advances to the functional genomics stage, it will be possible to determine which diseases a person is genetically predisposed to. Testing for predisposition to such disorders as depression, heart disease, or obesity may one day encourage those at risk to adjust their lifestyle to prevent future illness. However, this increased knowledge raises red flags for many people, for it may also be used by employers or insurance companies to discriminate against those with higher risk of disease. Further out in the future, some ethicists worry that eugenics—using principles of genetics to "improve" humankind—may come into favor.

Primary Source

"Breaking the Code" [excerpt]

SYNOPSIS: Francis Collins, director of the National Human Genome Research Institute, and Dr. Bruce Roe, a lead researcher on the Human Genome Project, answer questions about what it meant to obtain the first completed genetic sequence of a human chromosome.

Susan Dentzer: For nearly a decade, scientists have been attempting to decipher the so-called book of life, the sequence of billions of molecules of DNA that constitute humans' genetic makeup. Yesterday, researchers involved in the international human genome project announced that one chapter of the book was now essentially complete. Dr. Harold Varmus, director of the National Institutes of Health, described the accomplishment.

Dr. Harold Varmus: As this chart indicates, there are, of the 24 volumes of the human encyclopedia that we mentioned earlier, chromosome 22, volume 22, is now filled in. In each of these volumes there are many chapters that tell us profound information about essentially the entire human body plan and the diseases that affect all those organs. . . .

Jim Lehrer: And to Ray Suarez.

Ray Suarez: One of the lead scientists on the new research joins us. Bruce Roe is professor of chemistry and biochemistry at the University of Oklahoma. Also with us is Dr. Francis Collins, who directs the National Human Genome Research Institute, part of the National Institutes of Health.

Well, Dr. Collins, as the leader of the project, when you hit a milestone like this, do you stop, catch your breath, take stock or do you start on chromosome number 23 or 21?

Dr. Francis Collins: Well, it's hard not to take a moment at least to experience this milestone because it is a pretty historic moment. Never before have we seen laid out in front of us the entire landscape of a human chromosome, or any mammalian chromosome, for that matter. And it does give one pause to stare at this. I have to tell you, when I looked at this entire sequence, it gave me chills. It was really a moment where you realize how far we have come, this whole sequence in front of us. Now, we have a lot of work to do. It was one of the smallest ones. We want to get all of the rest of them done in the next two and a half years, maybe less, so we'd better not celebrate too long, we have to get back in the lab and keep the job going.

Ray Suarez: Professor Roe, I know I'm supposed to be excited about this but I'm not sure why. Maybe you could break it down for us and tell us what this wonderful new tool can help us do.

Bruce Roe: Well, this wonderful new tool actually tells us the location of roughly 700 or 800 genes on the chromosome and it tells us some of the landmark features of the chromosome—the regions that are involved this . . . segment . . . of the chromosome that cause genetic diseases, the regions that map for cancer genes, that regions that have various genes for mental retardation. Now that we know what the structure of the complete chromosome is, we can go about pinpointing many, many more of the genes that are involved with diseases. It's interesting that there are almost 40 different genetic diseases that have been found on human chromosome 22 or related to chromosome 22, and of those, we only know about two-thirds of what—the actual point on the chromosome that's altered during that genetic disease. We know that many diseases map within a million units of one gene or another that cause a disease, but now that we have this complete blueprint, the complete sequence in front of us, those scientists that are interested in these diseases in determining what the features are that cause those disease can then go and look directly at those genes that are on the chromosome.

Ray Suarez: But don't you have about a billion of those letters, those C, G, A, and T's. There's an awful lot of chaff there, isn't there, along with the diseases and the clues that could help you find the things you're looking for?

Bruce Roe: But the chaff is that, that you want to call it, is, to me, the most intriguing and interesting thing. That's what creates for us our individual differences, those regions of the genome that people think of are junk DNA or something like that are really not junk but those are what allow genes to get expressed at different levels and the differences between humans, our genes are actually pretty much identical but how those genes are expressed and at what level they're expressed, that's what gives us our individual differences. . . .

Ray Suarez: Professor Roe, this gives us what we need to know to start inquiring about making modifications but it doesn't bring us closer to being able to know what to do yet, does it?

Bruce Roe: No. I think that what this gives us is this gives us the ability to, besides discover what the actual genes are that cause some genetic diseases, it also gives us the ability to detect these genetic diseases earlier. This will help us with earlier detection of cancer and earlier detection of different forms of mental retardation and then to classify them so that we can know how to treat them and how to make life a higher quality for people who are afflicted with various genetic diseases. I don't see down the road these kinds of genetic manipulations in the very near future. I'm sure that somehow that will happen, but I think that for the present time, we're really looking for the positive aspects of early detection of diseases and then more directed treatments for those genetic-based diseases that right now many of them are intractable to treatment.

Dr. Francis Collins: Let me jump in there because I think, in fact, that's what everybody's question is. Okay, so you've got this instruction book, what are you going to do with it? The things that come out of genetic research fall in a certain predictable pattern as far as the time line. As soon as you've identified a gene that's involved in a particular disorder, you then have the opportunity to figure out who's at risk, to develop a diagnostic test. In many instances, that alone can be very useful—

colon cancer, for instance. If I know I'm at risk for that because there's a glitch in my DNA in a particular gene, then I'm going to be motivated to go through that medical surveillance to pick up that first evidence, that little polyp in the colon while it's still possible to remove. And that's a curative therapy. Even though it's a diagnostic and a surveillance strategy, it works. Over the longer term, though, the real excitement and the reasons that every pharmaceutical company now has a genomics division is the absolute confidence that these gene discoveries give you a window into the inner-most workings of disease in a way that we've never had before. The blockbuster drugs of the future are all going to be built on the genome project and the insights that come out of that.

Ray Suarez: Well, I'm glad you mentioned those pharmaceutical companies because not more than a couple of miles from here is a place called Solera Genomics which is, in effect, racing your team to complete the handbook and would like to start patenting your discoveries, while you're taking the approach that this is something that should be given to humankind over the Net and through other sources.

Dr. Francis Collins: So this is a complex issue. Genomics will not reach its benefit without a vigorous partnership between universities and the private sector. We want the pharmaceutical companies and the biotechnology industry to be plunging into genomics and they are, that's great, because that's how products get developed. Where it gets more complicated is at what point along this pathway from very basic science to a product that you're going to offer to the public is it appropriate to begin to attach intellectual property constraints. The publicly funded Genome Project believes that the fundamental information about the human genome, the shared inheritance of humankind, if you will, is so basic and for the most part not very well understood that we ought to put it out there. So we do. Every 24 hours it goes up on the Internet and any scientist that wants to work with it can do so. If they get a good idea, they can run with it, and there's nothing getting in their way. On the other hand, as that gets moved into a circumstance where these discoveries turn into ideas that look like they would be pharmaceuticals, something the public needs but where patents are often important to provide an incentive to a company to do the kind of investment it takes, hundreds of millions of dollars to bring a drug to the market, then we have no problem at all with intellectual property kicking in. The argument sort of falls down to at what point along that road to discovery should you start to put up the toll booths? We believe they ought to be reserved for a fairly late step in that pathway but there are understandable business plans out there and I understand the marketplace and maybe it's good we have competition here. We'll see how it turns out. The publicly funded effort aims to, by next spring, have 90 percent of the sequence in the public domain and once it's there, it's there.

Ray Suarez: Quickly, Professor Roe, are you ready to get back to work?

Bruce Roe: I was in the lab today. It was really quite exciting. Everyone was at the bench and we collected another million bases today. Things are moving forward, and we're moving forward with new vigor because this is one of the most important projects that's ever been done in the public sector, and we need to get this data out there, as Dr. Collins said, a lot of pharmaceutical houses are anxiously awaiting our data and a lot of scientists at other universities are awaiting it. So, yes, we're back in the lab full steam ahead.

Ray Suarez: Professor Bruce Roe, Dr. Francis Collins, thanks a lot.

Bruce Roe: Thank you.

Dr. Francis Collins: Thank you.

Further Resources

BOOKS

Cooper, Necia Grant. *The Human Genome Project: Deciphering the Blueprint of Heredity.* Mill Valley, Calif.: University Science Books, 1994.

Marshall, Elizabeth, L. *The Human Genome Project: Cracking the Code Within Us.* New York: F. Watts, 1996.

Ridley, Matt. *Genome: The Autobiography of a Species in 23 Chapters.* New York: HarperCollins, 1999.

PERIODICALS

Bendall, Kate. "Genes, the Genome and Disease." *New Scientist,* February 17, 2001, 1–5.

Gavaghan, Helen. "Human Genome Sequences—a Potential Treasure Trove, but How Useful?" *Bulletin of the World Health Organization* 79, June 2001, 583.

Nerlich, B., R. Dingwall, and D. D. Clarke. "The Book of Life: How Completion of the Human Genome Project Was Revealed to the Public." *Communication Abstracts* 26, no. 2, 2003, 155–298.

WEBSITES

Aparicio, Samuel A.J.R. "How to Count . . . Human Genes." *Nature Genetics* 25, no. 2, 129–130. Available online at http://www.nature.com/cgi-taf/DynaPage.taf?file=/ng/journal /v25/n2/full/ng0600_129.html; website home page: http:// www.nature.com (accessed March 25, 2003).

Human Genome Project Information. Available online at http:// www.ornl.gov/hgmis/; website home page: http://www.ornl .gov (accessed February 27, 2003).

National Human Genome Research Institute. "Talking Glossary of Genetic Terms." Available online at http://www.genome .gov/glossary.cfm; website home page: http://www.genome .gov (accessed March 7, 2003).

"Explosive Growth of a New Breed of 'Cyberchondriacs'"

Survey

By: Humphrey Taylor

Date: 1999

Source: Taylor, Humphrey. "Explosive Growth of a New Breed of 'Cyberchondriacs.'" *The Harris Poll #11, February 17, 1999.* Available online at http://www.harrisinteractive.com /harris_poll/index.asp?PID=34; website home page: http:// www.harrisinteractive.com (accessed March 16, 2003). ■

Introduction

In February 1999, the Harris Poll surveyed 1,009 "online" American citizens about whether they used the Internet to get health information. The results of Harris Poll #11 provided a glimpse of how the 88 million Americans online in 1999 used the Internet for health care information. The poll found that all racial, ethnic, and socioeconomic groups used the Web to get health-related information. Women were more likely than men to surf the net for information about medicine and health. Women tended to look for general health information while men were more likely to search for answers to specific health questions. Prescription drugs and weight control were two of the most popular subjects people researched. The Web also made it easier for people to get information about "sensitive health issues." People who were hesitant or ashamed about discussing such issues as mental health diseases or sexually transmitted diseases

An increasing number of people turned to the Internet and its numerous medical websites for information on illnesses during the 1990s.
© MAMBO/CORBIS SYGMA. REPRODUCED BY PERMISSION.

with their doctors could find information anonymously on the Internet.

The poll showed that the vast majority of people were helped by the health information they found on the Internet. Some learned that their conditions were not as serious as those faced by other people with the same illness; others were frightened to learn all of the possible outcomes of their condition. Many took the information they learned to their doctors for verification and discussion. Often, armed with more information, people felt more able to take care of themselves and fight their disease.

Significance

The Internet empowered Americans. It improved the way people took care of themselves through diet, nutrition, exercise, and stress reduction. Armed with information gleaned from the Web, Americans were more knowledgeable and responsive when illness struck, enabling them to be a part of the decision-making process along with their doctor. The Internet allowed people to share their stories and find comfort and knowledge in the stories and prognoses of others. As the burden of health care responsibility was shifted to the patient in the 1990s,

the Internet provided a needed tool. More and more Americans received health care from Health Maintenance Organizations operating under strict insurance rules. Many people left doctors offices with lingering questions after office visits that were too short. Being able to find health information on the Internet filled an important role in the health care system.

Many doctors had concerns about the kind of health information their patients were getting from the Web and how they were using it. One worry was that people would self-diagnose and self-medicate based on Internet information. However, most people consulted with their doctors. Many in the medical profession were wary about inaccurate medical information on the Web, since no one regulates the content of Internet sites and anyone can develop a Web page that looks credible. However, very few people reported harmful effects from using the Web. Most people were aware of the warnings about inaccurate information and had their own system of distinguishing good sites from bad ones: whether the site was trying to sell something, when the site was last updated, the source of information, and confirmation of information at one or more other sites. Medical professionals say the best advice is to use the Internet to supplement physician-provided information but not let it substitute for a doctor's experience and training.

Primary Source

"Explosive Growth of a New Breed of 'Cyberchondriacs'" [excerpt]

SYNOPSIS: A Harris Poll taken in 1999 shows 60 million people, about 30 percent of the U.S. population over the age of eighteen, surfed the Web to find information about medicine and health.

- 60 million adults searched the Web for health care information last year.

- 91% found what they needed.

- Depression, cancer, allergies, bipolar disorder, arthritis, high blood pressure, migraine and anxiety disorder top the list of diseases they are interested in.

Sixty million people searched the World Wide Web for health care information in the last twelve months. The growth of the Internet arguably the fastest growing new technology in history has generated explosive growth of people who search the Web for healthcare information related to specific diseases. We call these people "cyberchondriacs."

Altogether 68% of the people on-line say they used the Web in the previous twelve months to look for "healthcare information related to any particular disease or medical condition." Other Harris data show that the on-line population (from home, office, school or elsewhere) has risen to 44% of adults (i.e. eighty-eight million people). "Cyberchondriacs," who use the Web to search for healthcare information, therefore account for 68% of those eighty-eight million or 60 million adults.

These are the results of a nationwide *Harris Poll* of 1,009 people who were surveyed on-line between January 8 and 11, 1999. The survey was based on the new *Harris Poll Online* methodology which uses the world's largest consumer panel (over 2.5 million adults). The data were weighted to ensure they represent the entire on-line population.

The value and success of the Web is remarkable; nine out of every ten (91%) of these people say that the last time they searched the Web for health care information, they found what they wanted.

The diseases which generate the greatest use of the Web are depression (19% of cyberchondriacs), allergies or sinus (16%), cancer (15%), bipolar disorder (14%), arthritis or rheumatism (10%),

high blood pressure (10%), migraine (9%), anxiety disorder (9%), heart disease (8%) and sleep disorders (8%).

Many Web sites contain multiple linkages, but the sites people believe they referenced most often were those of medical societies (40%), patient advocacy group or support groups (32%), pharmaceutical companies (20%) and hospitals (16%).

If people had visited more than one of these sites, they found the most helpful ones belonged to medical societies (36%), and patient advocacy or support groups (32%).

The scale of these numbers is staggering. Furthermore, other data suggest that rates of Web utilization are increasing much faster than the amazing growth of the on-line population—which has increased from 9% to 44% of all adults over the last four years. Not only are more people going on-line; they are doing so much more often.

Note:

1. The data in this on-line poll were weighted by region, sex, age, education, race/ethnicity, income and Internet usage to be representative of the total on-line population (90 million people).

2. Based on telephone surveys of 2,000 adults in November/December 1998, Harris estimates that 44% of all adults are on-line, at home, in the office, or in a school, library, or other locations.

Table 1

Used Web to Look for Health Care Information?

Base: All adults on-line (Estimated by Harris to be 88 million people)

"In the last twelve months, have you ever used the Web to search for, or look at, health care information related to any particular disease or medical condition?"

	Total (%)
Yes	68
No	32

Table 2

Did You Find What You Needed?

Base: Used Web to search for health care information

"The last time you did this, did you find what you thought you needed on the Web or not?"

	Used Web (%)
Yes, found	91
No, did not find	8
Don't know/Refused	1

■■■

Table 4

Whose Web Pages Did You Look At?

Base: Used Web to search for health care information

"The last time that you used the Web to look for this kind of information, can you remember if you looked at Web pages put out by any organization in the following list? [Check all that apply]"

If More than One Answer Ask:

"On the Web pages you referenced, which *one* organization's web page was most helpful?"

	Used web %	Most helpful if two or more categories used %
A pharmaceutical or drug company	20	15
A hospital	16	11
A medical society	40	36
A patients advocacy or support group	32	32
None of the above/ Other	26	6

Methodology

The data in this Louis Harris poll was conducted January 8 to 11 among a nationwide cross section of 1,009 on-line adults. Computer users were drawn from our panel of 2.5 million on-line adults and invited to by E-mail to participate in the poll at a web site. The results were weighted to include region, sex, age, education, race/ethnicity, income and Internet usage and to be representative of the total population (90 million) on-line in the United States.

Based on telephone surveys of 2,000 adults conducted in November and December of 1998, Harris estimates 44% of adults are on-line at home, in the office, school, library or other locations. In theory, with a sample of this size, one can say with 95 percent certainty that the results have a statistical precision of plus or minus 3 percentage points of what they would be if the entire adult population had been polled with complete accuracy.

Further Resources

BOOKS

Pauline, David. *Netdoctor: Your Guide to Health and Medical Advice on the Internet and Online Services.* New York: Dell, 1997.

Wallace, Patricia, M. *The Psychology of the Internet.* New York: Cambridge University Press, 1999.

Winters, Paul, A. *The Information Revolution: Opposing Viewpoints.* San Diego, Calif.: Greenhaven, 1998.

Wood, Sandra M. *Health Care Resources on the Internet.* New York: Hawthorne Information Press, 2000.

PERIODICALS

Licciardone, J.C., P. Smith-Barbaro, and S.T. Coleridge. "Use of the Internet as a Resource for Consumer Health Information." *Communication Abstracts* 26, no. 2, 2003, 155–298.

WEBSITES

"Assessing the Quality of Internet Health Information." Available online at http://www.ahcpr.gov/data/infoqual.htm; website home page: http://www.ahcpr.gov (accessed March 14, 2003).

Journal of Medical Internet Research. Available online at http://www.jmir.org (accessed March 19, 2003).

Pew Internet and American Life. "Vital Decisions: How Internet Users Decide What Information to Trust When They or Their Loved Ones Are Sick." May 22, 2002. Available online at http://www.pewinternet.org/reports/toc.asp?Report=59; website home page: http://www.pewinternet.org (accessed March 16, 2003).

"Quality of Health Information on the Internet: Enabling Consumers to Tell Fact from Fraud. Available online at http://www.ahcpr.gov/qual/hiirpt.htm; website home page: http://www.ahcpr.gov (accessed March 14, 2003).

National Report on Human Exposure to Environmental Chemicals

Report

By: Centers for Disease Control and Prevention

Date: 2001

Source: Centers for Disease Control and Prevention. *National Report on Human Exposure to Environmental Chemicals.* Atlanta, March 2001.

About the Organization: The U.S. Centers for Disease Control (CDC), an agency of the Department of Health and Human Services, is the premiere authority on U.S. health matters, especially those pertaining to infectious disease. The federal agency began in 1946 as the Communicable Disease Center, with the mission to fight malaria and typhus in the Deep

South. The CDC, headquartered in Atlanta, Georgia, includes a dozen centers and institutes across the United States. ∎

Introduction

Rachel Carson is credited with bringing the hazards of toxic pollution to the attention of the American public in her 1962 book *Silent Spring,* which documented the danger of the powerful pesticide DDT (dichloro-diphenyltrichloroethane). DDT was applied directly to people during World War II (1939–1945) to control malaria and typhus. DDT is neurotoxic, meaning its toxic effects are targeted at the brain and central nervous system. It was banned in the United States in 1973.

By the 1990s, Americans had become much more aware of potential toxic substances lurking in the environment. Most arise from electricity production, automobile exhaust emissions, manufacturing industries, incinerators, pesticides, herbicides, and fertilizers. However, even such mundane things as cooking fumes, carpets, and copy machine toner contain toxic chemicals. Several federal laws, such as the *Toxic Substance Control Act* and the *Federal Insecticide, Fungicide, and Rodenticide Act,* are meant to protect human health, wildlife, and the environment from toxic substances.

It is important for federal agencies like the U.S. Centers for Disease Control (CDC) and the Environmental Protection Agency (EPA) to know exactly what toxic substances humans are coming into contact with and which ones are actually getting into our bodies. Toxic substances can be inhaled into the lungs, ingested through the mouth, or absorbed through the skin. Once inside the body, the toxic substance itself or a metabolite will end up in blood and eventually in urine.

In the 1990s, technological advances in molecular biology and analytical chemistry allowed the CDC to measure small amounts of many chemicals directly in blood and urine samples. Before this, the CDC measured blood levels of only one or two substances, such as lead. They estimated exposure to most other things by the levels found in air, water, or soil. The first *National Report on Human Exposure to Environmental Chemicals* measured twenty-seven chemicals in four main groups: metals, tobacco smoke, organophosphate pesticides, and phthalates.

One of the toxic metals the CDC checked for was mercury. The effects of this toxic metal are targeted at the brain and central nervous system. Because of its unique property—the only metal that exists as a liquid at room temperature—mercury was used in a wide variety of products, such as batteries, fungicides, and electrical switches. Mercury is also emitted into the air from coal-fired electric power plants.

We are exposed to mercury from eating fish. Mercury is emitted into the air and travels through the atmosphere until it falls back to the earth in rainwater and from there, into lakes, rivers, and oceans. Bacteria in the water convert it into a more toxic form called methylmercury, which makes its way up the food chain to accumulate in larger fish. Even fish from pristine lakes contain mercury. Many states have fish consumption advisories that provide guidelines for how much of certain types of fish it is safe to eat.

Significance

The first *National Report on Human Exposure to Environmental Chemicals* provided information about the levels of twenty-seven chemicals in the blood or urine of the U.S. population. The CDC looked for four main groups of substances: metals, including lead, mercury, cadmium, and uranium; one metabolite of tobacco smoke, cotinine; the metabolites of pesticides such as diazinon, parathion, and chlorpyrifos; and metabolites of the ubiquitous compounds called phthalates, present in many common everyday products.

The results of the report helped the CDC, the EPA, and others zero in on potential health threats from the measured toxic substances. The importance of monitoring the public's exposure to toxic substances is illustrated by the metal lead, which affects the brain and nervous system. Lead poisoning can lead to learning and behavior problems, headaches, and even seizures and death. In the early 1970s, data on lead concentrations in the blood of Americans was very high, helping persuade Congress to enact laws mandating the removal of lead from gasoline in 1972. In turn, blood lead data gathered between 1976 and 1990 indicated that the ban on leaded gasoline had worked, as blood lead levels were much lower. The 1999 report also checked for lead and found that, except for a small segment of children, blood lead levels were even lower than they had been around 1990. Still worrisome, though, were the lead levels for poor urban children, who are usually exposed to lead from old buildings where lead-based paint still on the walls is chipping and peeling away. These results allowed the CDC to focus on providing health treatments for urban children and signaled to the EPA the need to remove the source of the problem.

Reports on human exposures to toxic substances have proven extremely helpful to scientists, medical professionals, and the government. The CDC released a second national exposure report in early 2003, which quadrupled the number of toxic chemicals measured to 116. The CDC intends to collect data on the levels of toxic substances in American blood and urine every year and to include a greater number of chemicals when possible. As data is collected over the years,

The U.S. government began investigating possible chemical and radiation exposure of military personnel after the 1991 Gulf War. Many veterans have experienced ill effects since their service in the Gulf, and some of their children born since the war have birth defects. **AP/WIDE WORLD PHOTOS. REPRODUCED BY PERMISSION.**

researchers will be better able to protect humans from toxic exposures.

Primary Source

National Report on Human Exposure to Environmental Chemicals [excerpt]

SYNOPSIS: Some of the major findings of the 1999 CDC report, such as the levels of chemicals present in the blood and urine of Americans, are outlined in the following excerpts.

First-time Information about Exposure Levels for the U.S. Population

The 1999 Report provides measures of exposure for levels of 27 chemicals in the U.S. population that are based on blood and urine samples obtained from people participating in NHANES 1999. For three chemicals—lead, cadmium, and cotinine—CDC has previously assessed the population's exposure through NHANES, and this Report provides new data for the 1999 calendar year. The Report provides information for the first time about the U.S. population's exposure to 24 additional environmental chemicals (metals, organophosphate pesticides, and phthalates). Because the sample size in one year of NHANES is relatively small and because the 1999 survey was conducted only in 12 locations across the country, data from additional years of the survey will be needed to confirm these findings. . . .

Decline in Blood Lead Levels among Children since 1991–1994

Since 1976, CDC has measured blood lead levels as part of NHANES. Results presented in the Report for 1999 show that the geometric mean blood lead level for children aged 1–5 years has decreased to 2.0 micrograms per deciliter (µg/dL), from 2.7 µg/dL, the geometric mean for the period 1991–1994. This decrease documents that blood lead levels continue to decline among U.S. children when considered as a group, highlighting the success of public health efforts to decrease the exposure of children to lead. However, special populations of children at high risk for lead exposure (e.g., those living in homes containing lead-based paint or lead-contaminated dust) remain a public health concern.

Reduced Exposure of the U.S. Population to Environmental Tobacco Smoke

Cotinine is a metabolite of nicotine that tracks exposure to environmental tobacco smoke (ETS) among nonsmokers. Higher cotinine levels reflect more exposure to ETS, which has been identified as a known human carcinogen. From 1988 through 1991, as part of NHANES III, CDC determined that the median level (50th percentile) of cotinine among nonsmokers in the United States was 0.20 nanograms per milliliter (ng/mL). Results from the 1999 Report showed that the median cotinine level among people aged 3 years and older has decreased to less than 0.050 ng/mL—more than a 75% decrease. This reduction in cotinine levels objectively documents a dramatic reduction in exposure of the general population to ETS since 1988–1991. However, since more than half of American youth are still exposed, ETS remains a major public health concern.

Better Assessment of Children's and Women's Exposure to Mercury

The 1999 Report provides important new data about blood mercury levels among children aged 1–5 years and among women of childbearing age (16–49 years old). The geometric mean of blood mercury levels among children (0.3μg/L) was about 25% of the geometric mean of blood mercury levels among women of childbearing age (1.2μg/L). Compared with an adult, the fetus and child are usually more vulnerable to the effects of metals. Consequently, when addressing mercury exposures, health officials are particularly careful to protect the fetus and child. The Report provides data for children and levels for women of childbearing age that reflect levels of mercury to which the fetus is exposed. Scientists will use these new data to better estimate health risks for the fetus, children, and women of childbearing age from potential sources of mercury exposure.

Setting Priorities for Research on Phthalates

Phthalates are compounds commonly used in consumer products such as soap, shampoo, hair spray, and many types of nail polish. Some phthalates are used in flexible plastics such as blood bags and tubing. Animal research has focused on evaluating reproductive effects of phthalates. For the 1999 Report, CDC scientists measured metabolites of seven major phthalates. Di-2-ethylhexyl phthalate

Threats of chemical exposure may come from the home or the workplace, as evidenced by one company's storing of chemicals noted as "extremely hazardous" by the Environmental Protection Agency. **AP/WIDE WORLD PHOTOS. REPRODUCED BY PERMISSION.**

(DEHP) and di-isononyl phthalate (DINP) are the two phthalates produced in greatest quantity, with diethyl phthalate (DEP) and dibutyl phthalate(DBP) produced in much lower quantities. However, data from the Report showed that levels of metabolites of DEP and DBP were much higher in the population than levels of metabolites of either DEHP or DINP. These new data have prompted CDC to conduct additional studies to explain these findings by examining the pathways by which these phthalates get into people's bodies. The data also indicate that health research needs to focus on DEP and DBP, given that levels of their metabolites are much higher in the general population than metabolite levels of phthalates produced in the largest quantities.

Further Resources

BOOKS

Colborn, Thomas, Dianne Dumanoski, and John Peterson Myers. *Our Stolen Future: Are We Threatening Our Fertility, Intelligence, and Survival? A Scientific Detective Story.* New York: Dutton, 1996.

Davis, Devra Lee. *When Smoke Ran like Water: Tales of Environmental Deception and the Battle Against Pollution.* New York: Basic Books, 2002.

Whelan, Elizabeth, A. *Toxic Terror: The Truth Behind the Cancer Scares.* Buffalo, N.Y.: Prometheus, 1993.

PERIODICALS

Ott, W.R., and J.W. Roberts. "Everyday Exposure to Toxic Pollutants." *Scientific American,* February 1998, 86–91.

Wakefield, Julie. "Human Exposure: The Key to Better Risk Assessment." *Environmental Health Perspectives* 108, no. 12, December 2000, A558.

WEBSITES

National Library of Medicine. "ToxTown." National Library of Medicine. Available online at http://toxtown.nlm.nih.gov /main.html; website home page: http://toxtown.nlm.nih.gov (accessed March 17, 2003).

U.S. Agency for Toxic Substances and Disease Registry. Available online at http://www.atsdr.cdc.gov/about.html; website home page: http://www.atsdr.cdc.gov (accessed March 18, 2003).

U.S. Centers for Disease Control. *"Second National Report on Exposures to Environmental Chemicals.* The U.S. Centers for Disease Control. Available online at http://www.cdc .gov/exposurereport; website home page: http://www.cdc .gov (accessed March 17, 2003).

World Wild Life Fund. "Toxic Chemicals." World Wild Life Fund. Available online at http://www.worldwildlife.org /toxics/progareas/ed/index.htm; website home page: http:// www.worldwildlife.org (accessed March 16, 2003).

10

RELIGION

DENNIS A. CASTILLO

Entries are arranged in chronological order by date of primary source. For entries with one primary source, the entry title is the same as the primary source title. Entries with more than one primary source have an overall entry title, followed by the titles of the primary sources.

Important Events in Religion, 1990–1999

1990

- The *New Revised Standard Version of the Bible,* the first translation into English that attempts to be gender neutral, is published.

- On April 17, in *Employment Division, Department of Human Resources of Oregon v. Smith,* the Supreme Court rules that two members of the Native American Church are not entitled to unemployment benefits. They had been fired from their jobs as drug and alcohol counselors after using peyote in a religious service.

- On June 4, in *Westside Community Board of Education v. Mergens,* the Supreme Court rules that public schools must give student-led religious groups the same access to school facilities allowed to other student groups.

- From June 12 to June 14, after nearly two decades of coordinated effort, fundamentalists take undisputed control of the Southern Baptist Convention.

- On June 25, the Central Conference of American Rabbis (Reform Judaism) votes to allow all rabbis to serve, regardless of sexual orientation.

- On July 4, Christian Scientists David and Ginger Twitchell are convicted in Boston of manslaughter in the death of their two-year-old son, Robyn, in 1986. The Massachusetts Supreme Court overturns their conviction in 1993 on a technicality but states that parents have a legal duty to provide medical care for their children.

- On September 29, the Washington National Cathedral, whose construction began on September 29, 1907, is formally dedicated by President George Bush.

- On December 14, former television evangelist James Orsen Bakker is found liable for $130 million in damages in a class action suit on behalf of 145,000 "lifetime partners" in his PTL Club. In 1989 he had been sentenced to forty-five years in prison for defrauding PTL members.

1991

- On May 1, Pope John Paul II issues the encyclical *Centesimus Annus* (On the Hundredth Anniversary of Rerum Novarum), urging capitalist nations to right the injustices within their economic systems.

- From May 9 to May 11, six thousand "moderate" Southern Baptists meet in Atlanta to organize the Cooperative Baptist Fellowship to provide a place for people who are no longer comfortable with, and whose ideas differ from, the increasingly conservative direction taken by the Southern Baptist Convention.

- From June 4 to June 6, the Southern Baptist Convention cuts all funding to the Baptist Joint Committee on Public Affairs, a religious liberty watchdog agency of several Baptist denominations, because its stand on several church-state and other issues are at odds with the leadership of the SBC.

- On August 16, after a month-long anti-abortion protest at a clinic in Wichita, Kansas, President George Bush calls the tactics of Operation Rescue "excessive."

- On September 22, the general public is allowed access to some of the Dead Sea Scrolls material for the first time when the Huntington Library in San Marino, California, puts its three hundred photograph negatives on display.

1992

- On June 12, April Ulring Larson of the LaCrosse (Wisconsin) Area Synod of the Evangelical Lutheran Church in America becomes the first female Lutheran bishop in the United States.

- On June 24, the Supreme Court rules in *Lee v. Weisman* that public schools may not include prayers as part of their graduation ceremonies. President Bush calls for a constitutional amendment to permit public prayer in school.

- From August 17 to August 21, Pat Robertson and the Christian Coalition dominate the Republican National Convention and its platform; Patrick J. Buchanan uses the phrase "culture wars" to describe the conflict of values in American society.

- In October, Randall Terry, founder and leader of the activist, pro-life, anti-abortion organization Operation Rescue, says in a pamphlet that voting for Bill Clinton in the presidential election is a sin.

- On November 16, the Roman Catholic Church issues a new catechism that includes a statement that the Jews as a group were not responsible for Christ's death.

1993

- On February 28, agents of the Bureau of Alcohol, Tobacco, and Firearms (ATF) storm the Branch Davidian compound near Waco, Texas, in order to arrest David Koresh and investigate charges that the religious group is stockpiling weapons. Four agents are killed in the botched raid.

- On March 10, Dr. David Gunn is killed by anti-abortionist Michael Frederick Griffin while entering a Pensacola, Florida, clinic where abortions were performed. Griffin claims that a vision from God led him to murder Gunn, but he is convicted and sentenced to life in prison on March 6, 1994.

- On March 26, R. Albert Mohler Jr., is elected president of the Southern Baptist Theological Seminary in Louisville, Kentucky.

- On April 13, the outspoken religious journal *Christianity and Crisis* publishes its last issue.

- On April 19, the Branch Davidian compound near Waco, Texas, is destroyed by fire as Federal Bureau of Investigation (FBI) agents try to end a fifty-one-day standoff. Nearly everyone inside is killed.

- From June 6 to June 8, ten thousand people attend Global Vision 2000 in Washington, D.C., to honor the one hundredth anniversary of the arrival of Swami Vivekananda (Narendranath Datta) in the United States. He began the Hindu Vedanta movement in this country.

- On June 7, in *Lamb's Chapel v. Center Moriches Union Free School District*, the Supreme Court rules that public schools allowing secular groups to use their facilities after school hours must grant equal access to religious groups.

- On June 11, in *Church of Lukumi Bablu Aye, Inc. v. City of Hialeah*, the Supreme Court overturns a Hialeah, Florida, ban on animal sacrifices because it discriminated against practitioners of Santeria.

- From August 28 to September 5, the Second Parliament of the World's Religions convenes in Chicago a century after the first meeting. Six to eight thousand people attend, representing two hundred different religions, including Native American, Rastafarian, and other groups.

- In October, the Evangelical Lutheran Church in America issues its controversial report on human sexuality.

- On October 27, the Religious Freedom Restoration Act is passed in the Senate by a vote of ninety-seven to three and is approved by the whole Congress on November 16. The bill is a response to the Supreme Court decision in *Employment Division, Department of Human Resources of Oregon v. Smith* (1990).

- From November 4 to November 7, the feminist "Re-Imagining Conference," sponsored by several mainstream denominations, outrages some when it includes a worship experience directed to Sophia, the feminine Wisdom of God.

- On November 7, as the Roman Catholic Church prepared to discuss clerical sexual abuse, Cardinal Joseph Bernadin is accused of the crime by Steven Cook, a former seminarian who claimed to have recovered memories of the experience. Bernadin denied the accusations and Cook recanted completely in March 1994.

- On December 15, Steven Spielberg's movie, *Schindler's List,* opens, raising public awareness of the Holocaust.

1994

- On February 26, five members of the Branch Davidian community are found guilty of aiding and abetting in the voluntary manslaughter of federal officials in connection with the ATF raid on February 28, 1993.

- On June 27, in *Board of Education of Kiryas Joel Village School District v. Louis Grumet*, the Supreme Court declares the creation of a public school district solely for learning disabled and handicapped Hasidic Jewish children to be unconstitutional.

- On July 29, Dr. John Bayard Britton, a physician at the Pensacola (Florida) Aware Woman Center for Choice, and James H. Barnett, his escort, are murdered by Paul Jennings

Hill, a former Presbyterian minister seeking to stop abortions.

- On September 21, the television show *Touched by an Angel,* featuring angels helping people straighten out their lives, premieres on Columbia Broadcasting System (CBS).

- In December, Jim Bakker is released on probation. In 1991 his sentence was reduced to eighteen years, making him eligible for parole after serving five.

1995

- The Church at Pierce Creek, New York, loses its tax-exempt status for publicly endorsing and opposing candidates in 1992. Randall Terry of Operation Rescue was a member. Pat Robertson's American Center for Law and Justice defended the church in court.

- In January, the *Memphis Commercial Appeal* reports that a fire that had destroyed an area church the previous week might have been connected to fires at three black churches in western Tennessee a year earlier, beginning a nationwide media focus on the plight of black churches attacked by racially motivated arsonists.

- On March 30, Pope John Paul II issues the encyclical *Evangelium Vitae* (The Gospel of Life) in which he condemns abortion, in vitro fertilization, birth control, and euthanasia. He also says that the death penalty is rarely, if ever, necessary in modern society.

- On May 17, the Christian Coalition releases its "Contract with the American Family."

- From June 15 to June 17, the National Conference of Catholic Bishops issues a statement critical of the United States for its participation in the international arms trade.

- On June 21, the Southern Baptist Convention formally apologizes for its history of racism.

- On June 29, in *Ronald W. Rosenberger v. Rector and Visitors of the University of Virginia,* the Supreme Court decides that the University must give the same funding to student-run religious publications as to student-run secular publications.

- On July 5, the Presbyterian Church (U.S.A.) says that all clergy must be faithful in marriage or celibate in singleness; this allows nonactive homosexuals to be ordained.

- On October 16, Louis Farrakhan (Louis Eugene Walcott) leads the Million Man March in Washington, D.C.

1996

- On March 28, the Central Conference of American Rabbis passes a resolution endorsing civil marriages for homosexuals.

- On May 15, an Episcopal Church court dismisses heresy charges against Bishop Walter C. Righter for his 1990 ordination to the diaconate of Barry Stopfel, who was in a committed homosexual relationship. The court says that there was "no clear doctrine" involved.

- On June 12, the Southern Baptist Convention votes to boycott Disney movies, theme parks, and other entertainment outlets in part because the Disney Company recognizes homosexual relationships for insurance purposes. The Catholic League for Religious and Civil Rights began the boycott on March 28, 1995.

- On October 16, the Public Broadcasting Service (PBS) airs the first of ten episodes of *Genesis: A Living Conversation with Bill Moyers.*

- On November 6, Ruth Hoffman becomes the first ordained woman in the Christian Reformed Church.

1997

- From January 17 to January 19, the Landmark Conference on the Future of Buddhist Meditative Practice in the West meets in Boston.

- On February 14, the First Baptist Church of Berryville, Arkansas, announces that it will close its daycare center within the month because its existence encourages women to work outside the home, contrary to the church's understanding of biblical teaching.

- On March 26, thirty-nine members of the Heaven's Gate religious organization commit suicide in their home near San Diego. They anticipated being taken to a higher level of being in a flying saucer supposedly trailing the Hale-Bopp comet.

- On May 24, the Dalai Lama dedicates the Great Buddhist Hall at the Chuang Yen Monastery in New York; it contains the largest statue of Buddha in the Western Hemisphere.

- On June 23, the Supreme Court overturns *Aguilar v. Felton* (1985), allowing public school teachers to provide remedial instruction for disadvantaged students attending religious schools.

- On June 25, the Supreme Court finds the Religious Freedom Restoration Act (1993) unconstitutional. The Court asserted that the act unduly burdened state and local governments by forcing them to recognize individual rights not specifically guaranteed in the Constitution.

- On September 17, the television show *Nothing Sacred,* about an inner-city Roman Catholic church dealing with issues such as abortion and clerical celibacy, premieres on the American Broadcasting Company (ABC) network. Protests about the show begin before its premiere and lead to its cancellation six months later.

- On October 8, the movie *Seven Years in Tibet* is released. It is based on the story of an Austrian mountaineer's introduction to Tibetan Buddhism and the Dalai Lama; it also introduces Buddhism to millions of Americans.

- On December 25, *Kundun,* a movie that focuses on the life story of the Dalai Lama, is released.

1998

- On March 13, United Methodist pastor Jimmy Creech is acquitted of violating denominational policy by officiating at a same-sex marriage.

- On March 16, the Roman Catholic Commission for Religious Relations with the Jews issues *We Remember: A Reflection on the Shoah.*

- From March 28 to April 5, at the World Conference of the Reorganized Church of Jesus Christ of Latter-Day Saints, Linda L. Booth and Gail E. Mengel become the first women appointed to the Council of Twelve Apostles.

- On June 6, the Southern Baptist Convention votes to add a clause to the *Baptist Faith and Message,* stating that a wife should submit graciously to the leadership of her husband.

- On August 10, Kay Ward becomes the first female bishop in the Moravian Church of America.

- On August 11, United Methodist Church Judicial Council says that same-sex marriages cannot be endorsed by the church and that pastors conducting such marriages can be punished.

- In September, after a twelve-year-long audit, the Internal Revenue Service (IRS) revokes the tax-exempt status of Pat Robertson's Christian Broadcasting Network (CBN) because of "intervention in political campaign activities" in 1986–1987.

- On October 4, the Evangelical Lutheran Church in America, the Presbyterian Church, the Reformed Church, and the United Church of Christ celebrate full communion for the first time.

- On October 16, anti-gay protestors, some of them Christians, demonstrate outside the funeral of twenty-one-year-old Matthew Wayne Shepard, a gay student at the University of Wyoming who died October 12 after having been beaten on October 7.

- On October 23, Dr. Barnett Slepian, an obstetrician who performed abortions, is killed at his home in Buffalo, New York.

- On October 27, President Bill Clinton signs the International Religious Freedom Act. The bill is intended to combat religious persecution overseas, calls on the president to assign an ambassador to monitor religious freedom outside the United States, and authorizes the imposition of diplomatic and economic sanctions against any country that violates the religious rights of its citizens.

- On December 18, Disney releases the feature-length animated movie, *The Prince of Egypt,* a fictionalized account of the story of Moses.

1999

- In February, Jerry Falwell warns in his *National Liberty Journal* that Tinky Winky, a character on the children's television show *The Teletubbies,* promotes homosexuality.

- On April 20, two students at Columbine High School in Colorado kill twelve students and a teacher, then commit suicide. Among the dead is seventeen-year-old Cassie Bernall, who reportedly was asked by the killers if she believed in God and was shot when she answered, "Yes, I believe in God."

- On August 11, the Kansas Board of Education decides that the state will no longer test students on evolution, though it may still be taught.

- In September, feminist professor and scholar Mary Daly is fired by Boston College for refusing to allow men into her classes.

• On September 9, Robert A. Seiple, Ambassador-at-Large for Religious Freedom, presents to Congress the first annual Report on International Religious Freedom, documenting harsh treatment of religious groups in 194 countries.

• On September 15, having already killed two people, Larry Gene Ashbrook opens fire on a group of young people meeting at the Wedgewood Baptist Church in Fort Worth, Texas, saying, according to one witness, "It's all bulls__, what you believe." He kills five worshipers and injures seven others before killing himself.

• On December 13, the Supreme Court decides that the state of Vermont was acting constitutionally by subsidizing secular but not religious private education.

"Prosperity Gospel: A New Folk Theology"

Essay

By: Joe E. Barnhart

Date: 1990

Source: Barnhart, Joe E. "Prosperity Gospel: A New Folk Theology." In *Religious Television: Controversies and Conclusions,* edited by Robert Abelman. Norwood, N.J.: Ablex, 1990, 159–161, 162.

About the Author: Joseph Edward Barnhart has been a professor of philosophy and religion studies at the University of North Texas since 1974. He received a Ph.D. in philosophy from Boston University in 1964. He serves on several editorial boards and has authored numerous articles and books, including *The Billy Graham Religion* and *Jim and Tammy: Charismatic Intrigue Inside PTL.* ■

Introduction

The 1990s witnessed a great increase in attention to religion in the media, according to a survey funded by the Pew Charitable Trusts and conducted by the Center for Media and Public Affairs and the Ethics and Public Policy Center. The study examined a random sample of 2,365 stories that appeared from 1969 through 1998 in major print media *(The New York Times, Washington Post, Time, Newsweek, U.S. News & World Report),* as well as the ABC, CBS, and NBC evening newscasts. The study found that national media coverage of religion doubled during the 1990s. It also found that religious observance among major media journalists also doubled from 1980 to 1995.

Religious news dealt primarily with political issues rather than matters of faith or spirituality. When it did deal with spirituality, the majority of the reports concerned Eastern or other non-Christian religions. Thus, despite this increase of religious coverage in the media, dissatisfaction with the nature of that coverage allowed televangelism to remain strong in the 1990s. Some observers portrayed the "liberal" media as hostile to Christian values, and televangelists claimed that people who wanted to get a Christian perspective on the news and religion needed to turn to their programs.

Despite the scandal that led to the fall of Jim and Tammy Faye Bakker's PTL ("Praise the Lord") ministry in 1987, numerous other televangelists remained popular in the 1990s, including Jerry Falwell, Rex Humbard, Jack Van Impe, Pat Robertson and the 700 Club, Robert Schuller and his Crystal Cathedral, and Oral Roberts' City of Faith program. These programs are generally conservative and evangelistic in nature, transplanting the nineteenth century's old-style camp-meeting revivals to the twentieth-century medium of television.

Significance

The selection below is from Chapter 13 of *Religious Television: Controversies and Conclusions,* entitled "Prosperity Gospel: A New Folk Theology." It deals with one of the most popular messages of televangelism, that is, that God wants to bless all of his faithful abundantly. In return for faithfulness to the Lord, which is usually understood to be contributions to that particular television ministry, God will bestow health, happiness, and wealth. In other words, contributions to the program are not only a religious act but a wise financial investment that can reap great rewards.

This message is a revival of the Gospel of Wealth, which had flourished in the late nineteenth and early twentieth centuries, when the social standing and popularity of businessmen was high. Theologically, it saw wealth as the result not only of hard work but also of God's blessings. The accumulation of great wealth was not viewed negatively as the product of greed and selfishness but was rather a sign of God's favor. Possessing wealth was not only acceptable for Christians but was in fact their duty. The Gospel of Wealth also urged those who had accumulated wealth to use that wealth for noble purpose and to further God's word.

In a modern-day version of this view, Jim Bakker once claimed that God can only bless us in proportion to what we give to him. Taking a teaspoon, which represented small donations, and going over to a pile of coins, he showed that with such a small gift God would be limited in how much he could bless the donor. But, grabbing a coal shovel, he claimed that if the gift was large, then God's blessings would be proportionately greater.

Primary Source

"Prosperity Gospel: A New Folk Theology" [excerpt]

SYNOPSIS: Religious leaders have used various media to communicate their messages. Developments in technology, such as the printing press, radio, and television, have all made enormous impacts on religion. In the 1990s, televangelism, despite scandals in the 1980s, was still an effective tool for religious conservatives. It remains to be seen what impact cable and the Internet will have on evangelism in the twenty-first century.

The New Folk Theology

Folk theology has always played a major role in religious movements because it is communicated directly to the laypeople in their own language. One of the most successful folk theologies was developed by John Wesley, 18th-century founder of the Methodist movement. In the 16th century a leading voice of the Protestant Reformation, Martin Luther, preached and penned a folk theology that has survived 5 centuries. Folk theology distinguished itself by responding to practical crises in the faith of a great portion of the populace. It is neither systematic nor intended to be scholarly theology. It is deliberately devotional, motivational, and inspirational. It may also function to communicate a moral challenge or to make sense of a social and moral crisis that many laypeople have been thrown into because of historical circumstances.

There is little question that Jim Bakker, Pat Robertson, and Oral Roberts have contributed to the emergence of a new folk theology. It goes under several names: The Gospel of Health and Wealth, Prosperity Theology, Deliverance Theology, or the Gospel of Success. Its principal 20th-century roots trace back to the swashbuckling faith healers of the big tent and to popular God-wants-you-to-get-to-the-top sermons that reflect the theme of Norman Vincent Peale's best seller, *The Power of Positive Thinking.*

There is one key difference between the major modern proponents of the Gospel of Health and Wealth, on the one hand, and Martin Luther and John Wesley, on the other hand. Whereas Wesley and Luther had training in historical theology, Bakker and Roberts have none. Pat Robertson attended a seminary, but there is little indication that he has a great knowledge of the world of Biblical scholarship. Whereas Wesley and Luther could engage the theologians and Biblical scholars of their time in meaningful exchange, the big-time television charismatics appear to have avoided testing out their new theology in scholarly give-and-take exchanges.

The Prosperity Gospel of Bakker, Robertson, and Roberts is based on the following chain of arguments or premises from the faith healing tradition: First, God has supreme power over everything, including Satan, who plays a major role in the thinking of Pentecostals. Second, God does not want anyone to be sick. In only rare cases, God may cause someone to be ill, but only for the purpose of demonstrating his healing power. Third, Satan and his underworld

Television evangelist Pat Robertson in 1992. **REUTERS/ARCHIVE PHOTOS, INC. REPRODUCED BY PERMISSION.**

sycophants are the prime cause of disease and illness. Fourth, God can overcome the power of the demons *if* the diseased and afflicted develop a proper relationship with God. Fifth, the gift of healing that Roberts, Robertson, and Bakker claim to have is double-barreled. It allows them (a) to make war on Satan and demons (even exorcising them when they have possessed someone), and (b) to inspire and instruct the infirm and diseased so that they may establish a "right relationship" with God and thereby open up the channels of healing.

As simple as it may seem, at least on the surface, Prosperity Theology takes the points above and inserts the phrase *economic hardship* or its equivalent in the place of *disease and illness.* In the place of *wholeness* or *health,* it substitutes *economic prosperity* and even *wealth.* In short, God can heal both the body and the bank account. According to this gospel, Jesus' death on the cross gained at least 3 victories for true believers: Deliverance of the soul from sin and hell, deliverance of the body from Satan and disease, and deliverance from poverty and economic hardship in this life.

The modern advocates of this new Prosperity Theology turn to Scripture for supportive proof texts.

In John 10:10, Jesus is quoted as saying, "I am come that they might have life, and that they might have it more abundantly." In his books and on television, Pat Robertson relates stories of how believers set failing businesses back on the mountaintop of abundance and success by exercising great faith in Jesus and by contributing to Robertson's ministry. Oral and Richard Roberts are also fond of such testimonials. For Jim Bakker, Pat Robertson, and Oral and Richard Roberts, God has infallibly laid out steps that, if taken by Christian believers, will lead them to certain financial prosperity. A favorite scriptural text of the Bakkers is Philippians 4:19: "But my God shall supply all your needs according to His riches in glory by Jesus Christ." Among the most successful television prophets of profit is the hard-selling Bob Tilton, who prays into the camera and loves to quote Deuteronomy 8:18: "But thou shalt remember the Lord thy God: For it is He that giveth thee power to get wealth." For people like Tilton, God intends wealth to go directly to Christian believers, not to sinners and unbelievers. And to reinforce this belief, he quotes again a Biblical text: "A good man leaves an inheritance to his children's children, but the sinner's wealth is laid up for the righteous" (Proverbs 13:22). . . .

The Media and the Message

When televangelists elect to go on television daily, they wittingly or unwittingly commit themselves to becoming disciples of the Gospel of Prosperity. The financial needs of the daily program virtually require that they embrace the new folk-theology. Gifts of seed-faith are the late 20th-century indulgences essential to maintaining the structure of daily television ministry. Unlike the system of indulgences in the days of Martin Luther (which were designed to maintain the Roman hierarchy's superstructure), the modern Prosperity Gospel does not promise that the gifts will transfer a soul from purgatory to heaven. Rather, the promise entails a transfer from failure, sickness, and financial defeat to health and prosperity in the here-and-now.

Further Resources

BOOKS

Fore, William F. *Television and Religion: The Shaping of Faith, Values, and Culture.* Minneapolis, Minn.: Augsburg, 1987.

Inbody, Tyron. *Changing Channels: The Church and the Television Revolution.* Dayton, Ohio: Whaleprints, 1990.

Newman, Jay. *Religion vs. Television: Competitors in Cultural Context.* Westport, Conn.: Praeger, 1996.

Ministry to Persons with AIDS
Booklet

By: Robert J. Perelli

Date: 1991

Source: Perelli, Robert J. *Ministry to Persons with AIDS: A Family Systems Approach.* Minneapolis, Minn.: Augsburg/Fortress Press, 1991, 18–20.

About the Author: Rev. Robert J. Perelli (1949–) was born in Buffalo, New York. An ordained Catholic priest, he is a member of the Eudist religious order. He received his Doctor of Ministry degree from Andover Newton Seminary in Pastoral Theology and Clinical Studies in 1989. He founded AIDS Family Services in Buffalo in 1989. ∎

Introduction

The first cases of AIDS occurred in the United States in 1981. When the scope of the AIDS epidemic first became known, some religious conservatives used the prevalence of the disease among gays as an opportunity to condemn homosexuality. In 1988, televangelist Pat Robertson stated on the *700 Club:* "Homosexuality is an abomination. The practices of those people is appalling. It is a pathology. It is a sickness, and instead of thinking of giving these people a preferred status and privacy, we should treat AIDS exactly the same way as any other communicable disease." Later, in 1995, Robertson claimed that AIDS-infected homosexuals posed a threat to Christians, saying: "[Homosexuals] want to come into churches and disrupt church services and throw blood all around and try to give people AIDS and spit in the face of ministers." It was further claimed that AIDS was God's punishment for the evils of homosexuality. Such remarks compounded the tragedy of those suffering from this disease.

The possibility of contracting AIDS, either directly through sexual contact or indirectly through contact with infected blood, created a great deal of fear and caused those with AIDS to be regarded as the lepers of the twentieth century. Religious groups were divided in their response, just as they were about leprosy centuries ago. Just as some saw the diseased as unclean threats to society who must be shunned, others reached out to those suffering from the illness. While caring for the sick has been a central work for religious groups, it was complicated in this case by the views held by most denominations regarding homosexuality. Even religious groups that supported the care of homosexuals with AIDS wanted to be clear that doing so was not an endorsement of the homosexual lifestyle.

Significance

One example of a caring response to this illness is the AIDS National Interfaith Network, founded in 1988, which works directly with two thousand faith-based ministries. In fact, while the popular perception is that churches and other religious groups are doing little about AIDS, a study by the AIDS National Interfaith Network and Public Media Center showed that of the thousands of AIDS organizations operating in the country, five thousand were the direct efforts of people of faith and faith groups.

The excerpt below is written by the founder of one of these faith-based AIDS ministries. Father Robert J. Perelli, a Catholic priest belonging to the Eudist religious order, founded AIDS Family Services in Buffalo, New York. This organization assists individuals, couples, and families affected by AIDS or HIV through a variety of services. It offers group therapy services for family, friends, and partners of those with AIDS. Other group-counseling sessions are held for gay/bisexual men living with HIV/AIDS. In its literature, the organization states: "Many difficulties that people experience may be addressed in group psychotherapy. In fact, group psychotherapy is often a preferred mode of treatment. These difficulties may include dissatisfaction with family relationships, work, social or romantic life, emotional problems such as depression and anxiety, stress related to sexual identity, substance use and abuse, and HIV prevention. Although individual challenges may be varied, group members often enjoy some commonality with other members." Pastoral care services are also provided within the parameters of the person's faith tradition, including memorial services and remembrance rituals.

Caring for the sick has long been a work of religious groups. In practically every American city, the first hospital was established by a religious community. Religious communities have also regarded homosexuality as a sinful lifestyle. In addressing the health crisis brought on by the AIDS epidemic, many members of religious communities have condemned the homophobia that has hampered the response to this disease.

Primary Source

Ministry to Persons with AIDS: A Family Systems Approach [excerpt]

SYNOPSIS: In the excerpt from Father Perelli's *Ministry to Persons with AIDS: A Family Systems Approach,* the difficulties encountered by pastoral counselors in dealing with gay persons with AIDS is addressed. These difficulties include lack of knowledge, fear, and homophobia. He also emphasizes the need for the pastoral counselor or caregiver to interact with the family of the sick person. Appearing as a sidebar is an excerpt from Jorge E. Maldonado's *Guide To HIV / AIDS Pastoral Counseling.*

Some pastors may feel uneasy dealing with the gay PWA because of the conflict between the theology of pastoral care of the sick and the teaching on homosexuality and homosexual activity. These people can be reinforced in their ministry if they take to heart the church's teaching about Jesus' compassion and forgiveness. This is not to imply that the gay PWA needs to be forgiven for being gay, but rather that the pastoral counselor or caregiver needs to accept the gay PWA at whatever point he is at in his journey of faith—a journey that almost always includes a walk with forgiveness.

Once pastoral counselors or caregivers can face their own homophobia, they will need to be courageous because criticism for working with PWAs will probably follow. People will question the clergy-person's sexual orientation, motives, and orthodoxy. That is one way people project their own homophobia on others. Pastoral counselors or caregivers would be naive not to take this into consideration before they begin a public ministry to the PWA and FWA. Equally naive would be the minister who entered this field without a support system of other people who minister to the PWA and FWA, or without superiors and family members who are understanding, accepting, and supportive (Shelp and Sunderland 1987, 93–94).

Pastoral counselors or caregivers also need to face their fear of serious illness and death. AIDS can be a horrible death to witness. One never knows the course that it will take: wasting, dementia, severe pain, long and repeated hospitalizations, an almost incomprehensible sense of loss and grief, an ever-increasing need for care often ending with the need for round-the-clock attention. Caregivers must be aware of all these possibilities and anticipate their own needs so that they will be capable of walking with the FWA on this often long and painful journey. The pastoral counselor may need a supportive environment where he or she can process the feelings that come from watching young men die in their prime. This supportive environment could take the form of a personal therapist or a support group of other professionals from the field. Either way, it would be to the minister's advantage to build some form of support into his or her work with the FWA.

The lack of true knowledge about the spread of AIDS can be one of the most powerful contributors to the spread of "AfrAIDS." "AfrAIDS" is the catchword for the irrational and uninformed fear of being contaminated by the AIDS virus. Even the medical profession, with all its knowledge about epidemiology

"The Pastoral Counsellor"

Not all those who wish to be counsellors for HIV/AIDS are equipped for the task. Pastoral counsellors working with HIV/AIDS-affected people should have certain characteristics. Some of these are part of the person, others are the fruit of their formal or non-formal education, still others are acquired by specific training.

Counsellor's Personal Resources

The prospective counsellor is invited to reflect on his/her personal resources: opinions, feelings, attitudes, strengths and weaknesses before entering training or doing counselling.

The following questions should be considered:

- What might be painful for me in my work with HIV-infected people?

- Have I thought about my own death?

- Have I thought about my own risk of HIV infection?

- What is it about people with HIV infection which might be upsetting for me?

- What are my personal limitations in working with people with HIV/AIDS?

- What are my strengths and qualities for working with people with HIV/AIDS?

- What views might I have, for example, on homosexuality, infidelity, prostitution, polygamy, etc.?

- How would I handle objections to this work from my own family, neighbourhood or congregation?

- How would I handle aggression, anger, hostility?

- What is my interest in committing myself to this work?

- How would I handle someone with very rigid views?

- What other questions should I ask myself?

Consulting with Others

Pastoral counsellors might also consult with other people within and outside the church network in order to clarify their own views about these issues. Your own views and beliefs will inevitably influence how you counsel. Self-awareness of this kind may help you to become aware of your own constraints, strengths and biases.

Some useful questions to consider prior to entering into training, or doing counselling, may be:

- Is there someone I know and whom I respect, to whom I could go for a personal conversation when I may feel stuck, depressed, angry or upset?

- If I cannot think of such a person right now, where could I go to try to find someone?

- What would be an appropriate way to approach this person?

- What would be some of the hindrances in approaching him/her, and how could I overcome them?

SOURCE: "The Pastoral Counsellor." In Maldonado, Jorge E., ed. *Guide to HIV/AIDS Pastoral Counseling.* Geneva, Switzerland: AIDS Working Group World Council of Churches, 1990.

and its techniques for isolation, is not exempt from irrational fears of contracting AIDS. The pastoral counselor or caregiver must know that AIDS is difficult to transmit, and he or she must communicate that knowledge by the ease in which he or she cares for the PWA. There is nothing more alienating for a hospitalized PWA and his family than having the minister enter the room unnecessarily covered from head to toe. The minister must know how to deal with the hospital staffperson who insists that the visitor follow complete isolation procedures. By the same token, the minister must be aware that on many occasions, isolation procedures are for the good of the patient, not the visitor. Therefore, the visitor must act in a way that will protect the PWA from any opportunistic diseases (such as the common cold) to which he or she may subject the pa-

tient. The minister must know when precautions are necessary and when they only add to the PWA's feeling of alienation.

If the pastoral counselor or caregiver discovers that he or she has great difficulty with homophobia, death, and contamination, it may be advisable that he or she make a referral to a minister who does not feel overly threatened by these pressures. It may make a difficult situation worse by treating the PWA like a leper, even if such behavior is not intentional (Dupree and Margo 1988, 2).

Lastly, the pastoral counselor or caregiver needs to have a strong sense of his or her own spirituality. Gay people with AIDS often have traveled much farther in their spiritual journey than their peers. This is due to the double pressure they feel from being a member of a sexual minority and from facing a life-threatening disease. Helpers, especially those from the religious community, need a mature and well-grounded spirituality if they want to provide authentic care to the PWA and FWA (Fortunato 1985, 119).

Further Resources

WEBSITES

"AIDS and Religion in America." Available online at www .aidsfaith.com/convocation/guide.asp; website home page: http://www.aidsfaith.com (accessed April 11, 2003).

"AIDS and Religion Without Moral Judgements." Available online at www.dignityusa.org/aids/aids98.html; website home page: http://www.dignityusa.org (accessed April 11, 2003).

"Council of Religious AIDS Networks." Available online at www.aidsfaith.com/convocation/paperidx.asp; website home page: http://www.aidsfaith.com (accessed April 11, 2003).

"Just War and the Burdens of History"

Magazine article

By: Alan Geyer

Date: February 6, 1991

Source: Geyer, Alan. "Just War and the Burdens of History." *The Christian Century*, February 6–13, 1991.

About the Author: Alan Francis Geyer is an ordained Methodist minister. He received his S.T.B. and Ph.D. from Boston University, and at the time of this article was professor of political ethics at Wesley Theological Seminary. ∎

Introduction

From 1980 to 1988, Iraq and Iran engaged in a long, bitter war. Since the United States had recently recovered its hostages from the American embassy in Iran, it looked favorably upon Saddam Hussein's attack on the fundamentalist Islamic regime in Iran and supplied him with weapons. After a long stalemate that included the use of chemical weapons, the war came to a close after eight years. One reason for the stalemate was the Reagan administration's attempt to sidestep a congressional ban against funding the contras in Nicaragua by secretly selling arms to Iran.

After the war, Saddam was left with a large army and huge debts. His solution was to invade oil-rich Kuwait, which Iraq had claimed in the past as part of its territory. As the United States and the United Nations began to build up military resources to respond to this invasion, a discussion occurred in the United States on the applicability of the Just War Theory to this situation.

The Just War Theory, a part of Christian social teaching back to St. Augustine in the fifth century, holds that while war should be avoided, under certain circumstances going to war may be permitted as the lesser of two evils. The Just War Theory specifies seven criteria that must all be met before it is morally permissible to go to war. These are (1) the war must be fought for a just cause; (2) only a competent authority can declare war; (3) the war must be fought for a right intention, that is, for the just cause and no other war aims; (4) war must be the last resort; (5) the cost of the war must be proportionate to the worth of the value of the just cause; (6) there must be probability of success; (7) the goal is to restore a peace preferable to the peace that existed before the war.

Significance

It might seem odd that an ethical debate over whether a war is just should matter in the latter part of the twentieth century. It should be remembered, however, that world opinion is important in international relations and is taken into account by leaders of nations, including dictators. Even Adolf Hitler, for example, made the claim on September 1, 1939, that he attacked Poland in self-defense after Polish border guards had fired on German troops (although his justification was false given that Germany had sixty divisions near the border with Poland).

The debate on whether to use military force against Iraq in 1991 took place in many venues, including radio talk shows, newspaper columns, and the floor of Congress. In its February 6, 1991 issue, *The Christian Century* magazine presented the views of two authors—James Turner Johnson, a professor of religion at Rutgers, and Alan Geyer, a contributing editor to *The Christian Century* and professor of political ethics and ecumenics at Wesley Theological Seminary.

Although both employed Just War criteria to assess the morality of using force in the Gulf War, they reach different conclusions. Johnson argued that all seven criteria for going to war were met and that with the use of new, high-accuracy weapons, the two criteria to be observed during a war, discrimination and proportionality, were met. Geyer, on the other hand, claimed among other things that the criterion of last resort had not been satisfied because other nonviolent means such as economic sanctions had not been given enough time. His article stating this position appears below.

On the whole, an invasion of one nation by another seemed by itself sufficient justification to many for the war. In 2003, even in the absence of such an overt act of hostility by Iraq, the terrorist attacks on the United States on September 11, 2001, resulted in less discussion on the justice of the second war.

Demonstrators march in protest against the Persian Gulf War on January 26, 1991. The U.S. Capitol building can be seen behind them. © NAJLAH FEANEY/CORBIS SABA. REPRODUCED BY PERMISSION.

Primary Source

"Just War and the Burdens of History"

SYNOPSIS: The Just War Theory has been an important part of Christian social teaching since the early Church. While challenged by changes in military technology and tactics, it continued, as seen in the article below, to be an important guide to determine the justice of going to war in the 1990s.

Just War and the Burdens of History

Christian reconnaissance of the hellish war in the Middle East would do well to recall the plenitude of biblical perspectives shared by both pacifists and nonpacifists. An ineluctable imperative for nations as well as persons—so say the Hebrew prophets and Jesus and Paul—is that repentance is usually the precondition of reconciliation.

Repentance over the Persian Gulf War is in very short supply just now. Indignation over the brutalities of Saddam Hussein, inordinate pride in the newest wonders of military technology, and sanctimonious "new world order" rhetoric all conspire to overwhelm any confessional impulse. Not only the burdens of the distant past (such as centuries of

Christian assaults on both Islam and Judaism) now compel a confessional stance by American Christians. What must not be lost to memory are the specific entanglements of U.S. policy in the events leading up to Saddam Hussein's August 2 assault on Kuwait, as well as the U.S. course of escalation between August 2 and January 15.

The invocation of just war criteria in the present conflict can be truly an exercise of justice only if the burdens of history are taken seriously. Too often those criteria have rationalized military reactions to only the last in a series of events steeped in moral ambiguities.

There are surely enough iniquities on the part of the Saddam Hussein regime to commend the justice of a firm response. But the case for a *just cause* is made morally ambiguous by recalling these things:

- the tens of billions of dollars of U.S. arms poured into almost every country in the Middle East, the most combustible region in the world;

- the U.S. double-standard concerning nuclear proliferation, with the Middle East presenting the most likely scenario for nuclear war;

- the lack of a disciplined energy policy in the 1980s, making the U.S. more driven to military action to safeguard oil resources;

- backsliding on promises of a homeland for the Palestinians, thus handing Saddam Hussein his most powerful political weapon;

- neglect of any serious effort in the past 20 years to develop a genuinely multinational United Nations peacekeeping force;

- the July 25 assurance by the U.S. ambassador to Iraq that the U.S. would not take sides in Iraq's disputes with Kuwait.

The norm of *just intent* has been scrambled since the November elections by the escalation of U.S. objectives: from 1) defense of Saudi Arabia and economic sanctions, to 2) deployment of an offensive force of a half-million troops, to 3) massive assault on Iraqi cities that has destroyed not only military facilities but the infrastructures of energy, communications and transportation upon which civilian life depends, to 4) the demand for unconditional surrender.

The administration's claim that offensive military action was a *last resort* is highly questionable on two grounds. With regard to economic sanctions, two former chairmen of the Joint Chiefs of Staff, six former secretaries of defense, and a near-majority of the U.S.

Senate had urged a much more patient and protracted sanctions campaign while voicing grave reservations about the costs and ultimate consequences of military action. With regard to diplomacy, the administration's claim that it had gone "the last mile for peace" is belied by the fact that Iraqi leaders were offered only threats and no incentives, even to the point of denying them any possibility of "face-saving." This macho style, along with the refusal to accept European proposals for a wider conference on the Middle East, hardly amounts to constructive diplomacy.

The criterion of *legitimate authority* was finally finessed by United Nations and congressional resolutions. However, the UN mantle and repeated invocation of a "new world order" are tainted not only by the unilateralism of military decision and command but by a long list of U.S. defaults concerning the authority and efficacy of the UN. That list includes U.S. repudiation of the jurisdiction of the World Court, its crippling nonpayment of dues, and its obstruction of a consensus on most global issues.

Prior to January 15, some of us argued against offensive military action on consequential grounds, appealing to the traditional requirements of a *reasonable hope of success, discrimination* and *proportionality*. Without making confident predictions, we nevertheless imagined the dangers of a wider war enveloping Israel, the collapse of restraints on targeting and weapons, massive casualties, the mounting hostility of Palestinians and other Arab peoples, millions of refugees, the bankruptcy of the U.S. economy, the shattering of our body politic, and protracted terrorism. Since January 15 these imaginings have not become less credible.

There are enormous public and even pastoral pressures to suspend political debate and support the president and U.S. forces. Our churches would indeed do well to maintain a more compassionate ministry to military personnel and their families, both now and after this war, than was the case in the Vietnam tragedy. But the very definition of pastoral ministry must be stretched to include the recovery of our own involved history through congregational and ecumenical forums, the counteracting of stereotypes, and the anticipation of policies and ministries for the huge tasks of postwar reconstruction. Even more, ministry must make public witness for a ceasefire, to stop the killing and start genuine negotiations at last.

Perhaps negotiations could begin to construct the elements of an authentic new world order by strengthening the peacemaking instrumentalities of the UN in the Middle East. That effort might include: 1) an arbitration panel to review Iraqi-Kuwaiti claims concerning access to the Persian Gulf and oil operations; 2) a regional plan to curb the arms trade and eliminate weapons of mass destruction; 3) a standing peacekeeping force composed primarily of contingents from middle and smaller powers; 4) a comprehensive international conference on Middle East conflicts; and 5) the launching of regional economic institutions to help overcome the enduring poverty and inequalities among Middle Eastern peoples.

Further Resources

BOOKS

Elshtain, Jean. *But Was It Just?: Reflections on the Morality of the Persian Gulf War.* New York: Doubleday, 1992.

Geyer, Alan. *Lines in the Sand: Justice and the Gulf War.* Louisville, Ky.: Westminster/John Knox Press, 1992.

Hallet, Brien. *Engulfed in War: Just War and the Persian Gulf.* Honolulu, Hawaii: Spark M. Matsunaga Institute for Peace, University of Hawaii, 1991.

"Physician-Assisted Suicide Shows No Mercy"

Magazine article

By: Jeremiah J. McCarthy

Date: November 1992

Source: McCarthy, Jeremiah J. "Physician-Assisted Suicide Shows No Mercy." *U.S. Catholic,* November 1992, 14–16.

About the Author:: Rev. Jeremiah J. McCarthy was ordained a Catholic priest for the Diocese of Tucson, Arizona, in 1972. He has served as president/rector of St. John's Seminary in Camarillo, California, and is currently director of Accreditation/Institutional Evaluation for the Association of Theological Schools in the United States and Canada. He is the author of *A Catholic Guide to Healthcare Decisions* (1990). ∎

Introduction

One of the great blessings of advances in medical technology has been the ability to prolong life. These technologies include organ transplantation, respirators, antibiotics, and intravenous feeding. Patients now are living despite accidents or diseases that only a few decades ago would have resulted in death. The disadvantage of this is that while the body may be kept functioning, pain, a lack of mobility or reasoning capacities, or some other debilitating factor may lead to a poor quality of life. While the debate over euthanasia has been a long-standing one in the field of ethics, the issue became suddenly more prominent in 1990, when a retired Detroit-area pathologist, Jack Kevorkian, assisted an Alzheimer's patient in committing suicide.

More deaths followed. In many cases, the individuals did not suffer from a terminal disease. Much of the debate centered on pain management, with those opposing physician-assisted suicide being accused of cruelty by allowing the patient to suffer needlessly. This revealed that for many people fear of pain was greater than their fear of death. In fact, no religious group ever taught that patients should continue to live only to suffer. It was deemed morally permissible for doctors to give strong, even lethal, levels of painkillers to patients, as long as the primary purpose was to alleviate suffering. Physician-assisted suicide was different in that the intended purpose was not pain management but the death of the patient.

For the most part, the position of faith communities on euthanasia was the same as their position on suicide—that it is a wrong against one's dignity and nature, it harms the community, and it violates the sovereignty of God. Some faith communities in Protestant Christianity and in Reformed Judaism, however, have stressed the dignity of the individual as a free decision maker, which would include the timing and method of one's death.

Significance

The most vigorous opposition to euthanasia in general and physician-assisted suicide in particular has come from the Roman Catholic tradition. Pope John Paul II described euthanasia as an example of what he called a culture of death that in his view has come to permeate Western societies. Euthanasia is viewed as a manifestation of social views that have abandoned the protection of life and lent support to liberalized abortion and capital punishment. While in American politics, the issues are divided politically, with liberals favoring euthanasia and abortion rights and conservatives favoring capital punishment, in Catholic social teaching these seemingly disparate issues are all part of the same basic attitude— the elimination of the weak and unwanted members of society.

Religious groups in general express concern for patients who may be in vulnerable positions because of their illness or their lack of social and economic resources. There is fear that patients who cannot afford expensive treatment, for example, will be pressured to accept euthanasia. A few liberal theologians, on the other hand, have argued that euthanasia is not a contradiction but rather a culmination of the religious values of compassion, mercy, and love. By combining these goods to respect for the individual's self-determination, they argue that it is morally possible to allow euthanasia.

Primary Source

"Physician-Assisted Suicide Shows No Mercy" [excerpt]

SYNOPSIS: The excerpt below is from a 1992 article in *U.S. Catholic* magazine. Written by Father Jeremiah McCarthy, it emphasizes that putting people out of their misery is not the Christian response to suffering. A copy of the article had been sent to a representative sampling of the magazine's readership. The vast majority of them believed that it was wrong for a physician to counsel suicide (92 percent), that extreme pain should be handled by medication rather than suicide (93 percent), and that they would not consider suicide if terminally ill (82 percent).

In 1990 Dr. Jack Kevorkian, a Detroit physician, helped Janet Adkins, who was suffering from Alzheimer's disease, to die by the administration of a lethal injection. Michigan authorities charged Kevorkian with murder, but the charge was dismissed by a judge because Michigan statutes do not criminalize assisted suicide. Adkins died in the back of an old Volkswagen bus as the 54-year-old woman simply pressed a button to activate Kevorkian's suicide machine, which he calls a *mercitron*. Of the three liquids administered intravenously, the last, potassium chloride, stopped Adkin's heart. This well-publicized case raises troubling and profound questions. What are the moral limits to the value of autonomy? Should anyone have the right to end life by means of suicide? Do physicians have a professional obligation to assist in such a decision? . . .

For many of us, modern medicine is a brilliant accomplishment of human intelligence and skill. Dedicated health-care professionals, assisted by awesome technology, are now able to provide care and sustain life almost indefinitely. And here is precisely where the shadow side of the blessing of our technical skills falls. As we each face our final hours, we are understandably concerned about being hooked up to machines, being a burden upon our loved ones, losing control over our lives, and maintaining our dignity till the end. These are legitimate concerns, and a Catholic ethics of care is an excellent response to them.

As my mother was nearing the end of her battle with liver cancer, she and I had a special moment in our family kitchen. With a twinkle in her eyes, she looked at me with great tenderness and said, "Son, live as long as you can, and die when you can't." With the assistance of some wonderful hospice nurses and the loving care of her beloved hus-

A rally protesting against Dr. Jack Kevorkian and assisted suicide, in Philadelphia, March 22, 1999. The protestors' black robes and masks of Dr. Kevorkian's face are intended to make them look like Dr. Kevorkian in the form of the Grim Reaper. AP/WIDE WORLD PHOTOS. REPRODUCED BY PERMISSION.

band, Michael, and her 11 children, my mother died at home on Good Friday.

It was a genuine blessing for us to be with my mother as she gave us strength to go on. In supporting and caring for us as she prepared to meet God, she allowed us to give back some of the love she had so richly lavished upon all of us. Her example brought home to me in a powerful way the special gift of our dying brothers and sisters and how important it is for all of us to deeply share the terrors and fears of death so that we may know how to live while we are dying.

For us Catholics, life is a precious gift from a God who is passionately and madly in love with us. As James Joyce proclaims so boldly in *Finnegan's Wake,* "Catholicism means, Here Comes Everybody!" Every second of our existence is charged with grace; and every life, no matter how young or old, no matter how well or ill, no matter how rich or poor, is loved tenderly and forever by the Lord who made us.

Such a grand vision is beautifully captured in the Vatican's "Declaration of Euthanasia" (June 1980).

This instruction reminds us that life is a gift and we are to be proper stewards of this gift. And clearly implied in the notion of stewardship are the exercise of appropriate responsibility for our health and well-being and, especially, the use of prudent judgment concerning medical treatment.

Euthanasia, or mercy killing, is defined by the Vatican's instruction as any action or omission that is directly intended to end life. Suicide severs links with others so definitively and with such finality that it is seen as an action that is profoundly disruptive to community life and the social context of our human lives.

However, one should not conclude that the "Declaration of Euthanasia" renders a harsh and judgmental verdict upon those who have tragically ended their lives through suicide. These wounded spirits are enfolded in the arms of God for whom "mercy is, as it were, God's other name" (Pope John Paul II, *Dives in Misericordia,* "On the Mercy of God"). Invariably almost all suicides are actions of persons in acute psychological distress and are properly understood by public safety and health-care professionals as a cry for help. Physician-assisted suicide is not assistance but rather callous abandonment of distressed and suffering brothers and sisters.

One of the cardinal ethical principles guiding the practice of medicine is the axiom: first, do no harm. Physicians enter into a special relationship with each patient, a covenant that commits them to act for the benefit of the patient. Physician-assisted suicide subverts this crucial moral principle and turns the doctor into an agent of death rather than a caring professional in the service of life. The erosion of this trust would be an incalculable loss to the confidence patients should have in the medical profession.

Euthanasia is any action or omission that has as its express purpose the direct ending of human life. There is an alternative to euthanasia and physician-assisted suicide. The alternative is improved pain-management strategies and better communication between physicians and patients concerning the provision of medical care and the appropriate withdrawal of treatment.

As individuals, we can maintain dignity and control without fearing the prospect of excessive technology or severe pain. The medical profession is now able to provide excellent pain management—especially for end-stage illnesses, and all of us need to be informed of the principles governing the ethical withdrawal of medical treatment. The Vatican declaration clearly establishes that sufficient pain medication can be administered to the dying person for comfort even though the dosage carries with it the unintended and regrettable side effect of shortening the patient's life.

Moreover, medical treatment can be withdrawn when it becomes disproportionate, that is, when it no longer provides sufficient medical benefits for the patient. To facilitate this communication concerning the management of one's medical care, various legal instruments are now available, including the Durable Power of Attorney for Health Care (DPAHC).

The DPAHC can be a valuable tool since it authorizes a relative or friend to direct the course of one's medical care when the individual becomes "incompetent," or no longer able to express his or her medical concerns to a doctor. Both the Catholic Health Association and local Catholic hospitals can provide further information on these advanced directives. A version of the DPAHC that incorporates Catholic life principles is available from the Archdiocese of Los Angeles in California.

In summary, my argument against physician-assisted suicide is that it represents the cruelest form

of abandonment of our suffering brothers and sisters. Moreover, it is an unnecessary response to the problem of pain and the control of one's medical care.

The alternative to this approach is the sane, Catholic instinct of care and trust in God. We need to campaign for more supportive services for the dying and the loved ones who care for them. Our national health policy needs to reflect this serious need by providing for more hospice care and home visitation by health-care professionals.

Above all we must learn how to be caring companions of one another's life journey. Saint John the Evangelist tells us that " . . . standing by the cross of Jesus were his mother, his mother's sister, Mary the wife of Clopas, and Mary Magdalene" (John 19:25). The example of these holy women richly instructs us about the kind of community we must be to combat the despairing isolation represented in the movement for euthanasia. Sound public policy is served well by an ethics of care. It is the right response to the ethics of abandonment inscribed in physician-assisted suicide.

Further Resources

BOOKS

Active Euthanasia. Chicago: Park Ridge Center, 1991.

Manning, Michael. *Euthanasia and Physician-Assisted Suicide: Killing or Caring.* New York: Paulist, 1998.

Melton, J. Gordon. *The Churches Speak on—Euthanasia: Official Statements from Religious Bodies and Ecumenical Organizations.* Detroit, Mich.: Gale, 1991.

James Dunn and Dean M. Kelley to President Clinton, March 11, 1993

Letter

By: James Dunn and Dean M. Kelley

Date: March 11, 1993

Source: Dunn, James, and Dean M. Kelley. Letter from James Dunn and Dean M. Kelley to President Clinton. Reprinted in Lewis, James R., ed. *From the Ashes: Making Sense of Waco.* Lanham, Md: Rowman and Littlefield, 1994, 237–239. ■

Introduction

The Book of Revelation, the last book of the New Testament, apocalyptically describes the transformation of Heaven and Earth into a new Heavenly Jerusalem. It contains many vivid images, including the Four Horsemen of the Apocalypse, the unleashing of various calamities upon the earth, and the vindication of the faithful. For centuries, many Christians have taken these images literally and have looked for signs of the coming end of the world when, after the unleashing of the plagues, disease, famine, and other disasters, the glorious Second Coming of Christ will occur. This view is known in Christian theology as millennialism.

One person anticipating these events was William Miller (1782–1849), a self-educated farmer from New York State. After rigorous study of the Bible, Miller came to the conclusion that the second coming of Christ and the end of the world would occur sometime around 1843. Miller became associated with Joseph Himes (1805–1895), who popularized Miller's views. Tens of thousands came to believe in the imminent Second Coming of Christ, and many sold their property and quit their jobs in anticipation of this event. There was great disappointment when Christ did not arrive on the original date of March 21, 1843. The fervor of those desiring this event to take place was so great that most were willing to maintain their hope when another date was proposed, October 22, 1844. While most became disillusioned after this second disappointment, some continued to believe that the Second Coming had taken place but in a spiritual rather than physical manner. This became the basis of the Adventist Church. While there are many different Adventist groups, the largest being the Seventh-Day Adventists, all share strong millennial beliefs.

Significance

One of the smaller of these Adventist groups was a sect called the Branch Davidians. The origins of this group can be traced to Victor Houteff, who became acquainted with the Seventh-Day Adventist Church in 1918 at a revival meeting and soon became an active member. In 1929, claiming to be God's divine messenger, he claimed that the church's teachings were inaccurate and called for reform. Houteff's relations with the Seventh-Day Adventists became strained, and in 1935 he and eleven followers founded the Mount Carmel Center near Waco. In 1942, his group broke completely from the larger denomination and called itself the Davidian Seventh-Day Adventist Association.

The group went through further splinterings and numerous leadership changes. One of these splinter groups, the Branch Davidians, took control of the Mount Carmel property in 1965. Through it all, however, it maintained its strong views on the imminent Second Coming of Christ and the end of the world. Such views attracted a young man named Vernon Howell, who joined the Branch Davidians in 1981. Seven years later, when the group's leader, George Roden, was sent to jail for con-

tempt of court, Howell took control of Mount Carmel and the Branch Davidians. He then renamed himself David Koresh and claimed to be the seventh angel who breaks the seven seals of the scroll referred to in the Book of Revelation, bringing about the end of the world.

On February 28, reports from former Branch Davidian members detailing child abuse led the federal government to raid Mount Carmel. The raid turned into a fiasco, which resulted in loss of life on both sides and the beginning of a siege of the compound. The situation became tense, featuring a dramatic military buildup by the federal government, which did not understand that such a show of force would feed into the end-of-the-world views of this millennialist group and make a peaceful resolution impossible.

Primary Source

James Dunn and Dean M. Kelley to President Clinton, March 11, 1993

> **SYNOPSIS:** The Second Coming of Christ is an important belief in Christianity. In fact, the delayed Parousia, or Second Coming, was the first major theological issue in the early Church. Millennialism, a movement in Christianity that puts a great emphasis on the Second Coming and the end of the world, has been prominent in American religious history. A tragic example of this in the 1990s was the destruction of the Branch Davidian compound in 1993. The letter below, dated March 11, 1993, shows attempts by religious leaders to alert the government to the dangers of a heavily armed confrontation with the Branch Davidians. The warnings were unheeded, and when government forces moved on the compound on April 19, the resulting conflagration killed most of those inside.

March 11, 1993

The President
The White House
Washington, D.C.

Dear Mr. President:

Please demilitarize the confrontation in Waco, Texas. It does not call for hundreds of heavily armed federal employees and Abrams tanks waiting for a showdown.

We are concerned that more people will be killed before the protracted encounter in Waco is over. Is there not some way to stand down from this standoff without throwing more lives after those already lost? We are reluctant to judge from a distance the tactics of law-enforcement personnel who have been asked to risk their lives in the line of duty, since we are informed only by sensationalized media cover-

The Branch Davidian compound near Waco, Texas, on February 28, 1993. Federal agents have surrounded the compound and can be seen crouching behind automobiles for cover. © AYDELOTTE, ROB/CORBIS SYGMA. REPRODUCED BY PERMISSION.

age, but we wish to urge a different way of thinking about this problem.

The law enforcement agencies are not being helped to understand this situation by the many anti-cultists on the scene uttering their shrill cries about "destructive cults" and "hostages" being held in "captivity" by a "cult leader" using "mind control." Neither they nor the officers seem to have any real understanding of what is involved in a high-energy religious movement, where the members are drawn into a tight circle of devotion and commitment to a charismatic leader whose spiritual insight and guidance they value more than life itself. The leader may seem eccentric or egotistical to outsiders, but there is no law against that.

Threats of vengeance and the mustering of troops and tanks are but proof to the "faithful" that the powers of the world are arrayed against them, evidence of their importance in the cosmic struggle—confirmation of their worst fears and validation of their fondest prophecies. Their level of commitment to their faith is higher than most other people give to anything and is therefore very threatening to oth-

ers. To invade a center of energy of that kind is like sticking a finger in a dynamo. Whether it explodes or implodes, the result will be tragic for all. The ordinary strategic calculus of physical combat is as useless here as it was in understanding how the followers of the Ayatolla Khomeini could overthrow the Shah of Iran.

According to the press, some anti-cultists are claiming that they have been working for months on the Davidian "problem" with the federal agency that mounted the attack, which suggests that they helped to shape the conceptualization that led to the scenario of disaster. Central to their definition of the situation is the notion of "mind control"—that there is a technique for controlling the human will at a distance without use of force or threat of force, and that "cult" leaders have this power (though no one else seems to) and can use it to gain and keep and manipulate followers. This hypothesis is not generally accepted in the relevant disciplines of psychology and sociology [see the rejection of "expert" testimony to this effect for this reason by the federal district court of the Northern District of California when it was offered by the defense as justification for criminal

A military helicopter flies past the smouldering ruins of the Branch Davidian compound on April 20, 1993. © SAN ANTONIO EXPRESS NEWS/CORBIS SYGMA. REPRODUCED BY PERMISSION.

conduct, *U.S. v. Fishman,* 745 F. Supp. 713, 719 (1990)], and it ill prepares those whose lives are at stake to understand what they are up against.

We are deeply distressed to suspect that an approach that should—at most—have been a last resort was used as the first resort. What opportunity were the members of the religious group given to surrender peaceably or to accede to arrest—if that was required—without violence? (A former prosecutor is quoted as saying that they did not resist an earlier investigation and arrest—*New York Times,* March 9, 1993.) This situation is not a problem that can be handled either with force or with arguments over biblical interpretation. It is better let alone as much as possible until it either runs down or stabilizes as a more conventional religion (as did the Mormon movement and the Christian faith itself, both of which began with a small group of faithful followers whose leader was killed by the authorities—in Joseph Smith's case by a band of militia after his arrest and jailing in Carthage, Illinois).

It would be even more tragic if the government has invested so much money and credibility in this no-win situation that it cannot be satisfied with less

than a total eradication of the offending sect (without ever explaining what offense justified the assault in the first place). And if there must be a "victory" to save face for the government, can it not be brought about in a humane way? Surely there are technological means of immobilizing resisters without slaughtering them—and others—in the process. In any event, the public that is paying for all of this deserves a fair and objective post mortem on how this debacle ever developed.

Yours sincerely,
Dean M. Kelley
Counselor on Religious Liberty
National Council of Churches

James Dunn
Baptist Joint Committee

Further Resources

BOOKS

Long, Robert. *Religious Cults in America.* New York: H.W. Wilson, 1994.

Samples, Kenneth. *Prophets of the Apocalypse: David Koresh and Other American Messiahs.* Grand Rapids, Mich.: Baker Books, 1994.

Wright, Stuart. *Armageddon in Waco: Critical Perspectives on the Branch Davidian Conflict.* Chicago: University of Chicago Press, 1995.

"Blessed Absalom"
Song

By: Harold T. Lewis

Date: 1993

Source: Lewis, Harold T. "Blessed Absalom." *Lift Every Voice and Sing, II.* New York: Church Hymnal Corporation, 1992.

About the Author: Harold T. Lewis (1947–) clergyman and teacher, started out as a social worker in New York City and later became an overseas missionary in Honduras. During the course of his career, he served at several different churches, as well as teaching at theological seminaries. He was the author of *In Season, Out of Season, A Collection of Sermons, Yet With a Steady Beat: The Afro-Amer Struggle for Recognition in the Episcopal Church, Christian Social Witness,* and *Elijah's Mantle.* He wrote the words for "Blessed Absalom" in 1992. ∎

Introduction

Africans first arrived in Virginia as slaves in 1619 and by 1750 numbered over 100,000 in that colony, although it should be remembered that there were a few free African American farmers. Religious instruction for slaves was limited by owners, who did not want to give the slaves time off for education and were concerned that baptism might be regarded as the basis for freedom. Some even believed that the slaves had no souls. In time, Baptist and Methodist preachers gained access to the slaves on the understanding that baptism did not confer freedom. A major impetus to missionary work among the slaves was the religious revival known as the Great Awakening, which swept the colonies before the Revolution. By 1790, a fifth of the Methodist Church was made up of African Americans. In the early nineteenth century, revivalism and its camp meetings maintained this evangelistic zeal.

Of all the biblical images converted slaves gained from Christianity, the most powerful was that of the Exodus. This story of God's dramatic intervention to bring about the freedom of Israel resonated with the slaves. It not only sustained their hopes during the Antebellum period but would continue to inspire them during the struggle for freedom in the civil rights movement under their Moses, Dr. Martin Luther King Jr.

The segregation of African Americans in churches led to the establishment of independent African American churches. In 1816, the African Methodist Episcopal

Church was founded in Philadelphia and by 1836 had 7,500 members. It founded the first African American magazine in 1841 and acquired Wilberforce University in 1856. This church was followed by other independent black churches, including the African Methodist Episcopal-Zion and the National Baptist Convention. The independent black churches allowed African Americans to forge a unique form of Christianity. A prominent example of this was in the area of music, especially the Negro spirituals.

Significance

In the late 1950s and early 1960s, the African American churches, allied through the Southern Christian Leadership Conference, confronted racism during the civil rights movement. In the 1990s, the churches continued to be the place to get things done in and for the African American community, despite some difficulties. A 1992 report funded by the Lilly Foundation entitled *The Black Church in America* stated: "some observers have lamented the black church's loss of members and prestige. Scholars and ecclesiastics have blamed secularization, the decline of the family and the pull of the suburbs for the diminishing size and status of African American congregations. But even if African American churches are facing problems that have plagued their white counterparts for more than a decade, they are still the strongest institutions left in many inner-city neighborhoods." A major reason for this is the vibrant spirituality of African American Christianity, a spirituality that sustained the community through slavery and the struggle for civil rights.

African American spirituality is a vibrant faith experience. Drawing on African roots and American revivalism, it features powerful preaching and soulful music. It was a spirituality that saw the community through slavery and energized it in the struggle for civil rights. It places trust in God the Liberator, who is always ready to lead his people from bondage to freedom.

Further Resources

BOOKS

Abbington, James. *Readings in African-American Church Music and Worship.* Chicago: GIA Publications, 2003.

WEBSITES

"A Look at African-American Spirituality." Available online at www.gracemillennium.com/sojourn/spring99/html/nantambu.html; website home page: http://www.gracemillennium.com (accessed April 11, 2003).

"Spirituality of African-American Pastors." Available online at www.pcusa.org/research/monday/aaspmm.htm; website home page: http://www.pcusa.org (accessed April 11, 2003).

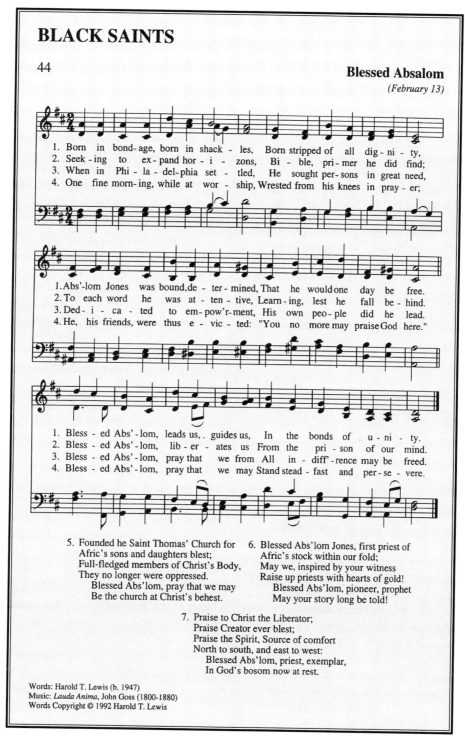

BLACK SAINTS

44

Blessed Absalom
(February 13)

1. Born in bond-age, born in shack - les, Born stripped of all dig - ni - ty,
2. Seek - ing to ex-pand hor - i - zons, Bi - ble, pri-mer he did find;
3. When in Phi - la - del-phia set - tled, He sought per-sons in great need,
4. One fine morn-ing, while at wor - ship, Wrested from his knees in pray - er;

1. Abs'-lom Jones was bound, de - ter - mined, That he would one day be free.
2. To each word he was at - ten - tive, Learn - ing, lest he fall be - hind.
3. Ded - i - ca - ted to em-pow'r-ment, His own peo-ple did he lead.
4. He, his friends, were thus e - vic - ted: "You no more may praise God here."

1. Bless - ed Abs' - lom, leads us, . guides us, In the bonds of u - ni - ty.
2. Bless - ed Abs' - lom, lib - er - ates us From the pri - son of our mind.
3. Bless - ed Abs' - lom, pray that we from All in - diff' - rence may be freed.
4. Bless - ed Abs' - lom, pray that we may Stand stead - fast and per - se - vere.

5. Founded he Saint Thomas' Church for
Afric's sons and daughters blest;
Full-fledged members of Christ's Body,
They no longer were oppressed.
Blessed Abs'lom, pray that we may
Be the church at Christ's behest.

6. Blessed Abs'lom Jones, first priest of
Afric's stock within our fold;
May we, inspired by your witness
Raise up priests with hearts of gold!
Blessed Abs'lom, pioneer, prophet
May your story long be told!

7. Praise to Christ the Liberator;
Praise Creator ever blest;
Praise the Spirit, Source of comfort
North to south, and east to west:
Blessed Abs'lom, priest, exemplar,
In God's bosom now at rest.

Words: Harold T. Lewis (b. 1947)
Music: *Lauda Anima*, John Goss (1800-1880)
Words Copyright © 1992 Harold T. Lewis

Primary Source

"Blessed Absalom"

SYNOPSIS: The document above is a hymn whose words were written by Harold T. Lewis entitled "Blessed Absalom." It tells the story of an early African American named Absalom Jones, who ministered in Philadelphia and founded Saint Thomas' Church. In addition to telling the story of a devout man, the hymn is also an excellent example of how the powerful theme of liberation from bondage continues to animate African American spirituality. REPRINTED FROM *LIFT EVERY VOICE AND SING II: AN AFRICAN AMERICAN HYMNAL*. THE CHURCH HYMNAL CORPORATION, 1993. WORDS BY HAROLD T. LEWIS. MUSIC BY JOHN GOSS. WORDS COPYRIGHT © 1992 BY HAROLD T. LEWIS. REPRODUCED BY PERMISSION.

Declaration Toward a Global Ethic

Declaration

By: World Parliament of Religions

Date: 1993

Source: Bettenson, Henry, and Chris Maunder, eds. *Documents of the Christian Church,* 3rd ed. New York: Oxford University Press, 1999.

About the Organization: In 1893, in connection with the Columbian Exposition being held in Chicago, the World Parliament of Religions was held. The 1893 Parliament had marked the first formal gathering of representatives of Eastern and Western spiritual traditions. Today, it is recognized as the occasion of the birth of formal interreligious dialogue worldwide. In 1993, on the one hundredth anniversary of this historic event, another World Parliament of Religions was held. ■

Introduction

Interreligious conflict and religious persecution have long been problems in human relations. Major examples in history have been the persecution of Jews by Hellenizing Greeks, the Roman persecution of Christianity, the Crusades, and the Thirty Years War. Today anti-Semitism is still virulent, as well as religious conflicts in the Middle East, Africa, and Asia. In 1992, for example, Hindus in Delhi, India, destroyed a sixteenth-century mosque, setting off a week of rioting between Hindus and Muslims that killed over a thousand people.

While such tragic conflicts make headline news, examples of interfaith cooperation and unity rarely do. In the United States, thirty-three Protestant denominations came together in 1908 to form the Federal Council of Churches, which continues today as the National Council of Churches in Christ. Americans were also prominent in the formation of the World Council of Churches. Charles Mott took a leading role in the World Missionary Conference in 1910, and Bishop Charles Brent was active in the Life and Work movement of the 1920s. These movements came together with others in 1948 to form the World Council of Churches, the largest continuing ecumenical organization today.

In the 1960s, the Roman Catholic Church gathered in the historic Second Vatican Council (1962–1965), which, in addition to renewing Catholic faith and practices, also had a strong ecumenical spirit as well. In the decrees of Vatican II, Catholic leaders expressed regret for Christian disunity and accepted blame for their part in this problem. They also abandoned the old idea of state-supported religion and stressed that it was the duty of governments to support religious liberty as a civil right.

Finally, the bishops renounced anti-Semitism and rejected the notion that all Jews bore the guilt for the death of Jesus, saying rather that it was the responsibility of a few living in the past.

Significance

While most of the ecumenical movement to date has been in the area of improving relations between Christians, the most significant event featuring virtually all religions was the World Parliament of Religions, which met in Chicago in 1893 in conjunction with the Columbian Exposition. This was the first formal assembly of representatives from Western and Eastern faith traditions.

In 1988, two monks from the Vivekananda Vedanta Society of Chicago suggested organizing a centennial celebration of the 1893 World's Parliament of Religions, resulting in the establishment of the Council for a Parliament of the World's Religions (CPWR). The event took place as scheduled in 1993, again in Chicago, with eight thousand people from all over the world coming together to celebrate diversity and harmony and to explore religious and spiritual responses to critical issues of common concern.

At the 1993 Parliament, the assembly approved a document entitled *Declaration Toward a Global Ethic,* which is included below. In seeking unity, the parliament did not seek to establish a single new religion or philosophy. Rather, it called for consensus on certain values, standards, and attitudes on which all religious groups could agree. Establishing such a global ethic was seen as the fundamental first step for putting behind the old order of war, poverty, and hunger, and establishing a global order that would promote human rights, freedom, justice, and peace, and preserve the environment.

It was also decided to gather again in 1999 in Cape Town, South Africa. The 1999 Parliament attracted seven thousand participants from over eighty countries, including the Dalai Lama. In 2001, it was decided that a World Parliament of Religions should convene every five years to further religious dialogue and cooperation.

Primary Source

Declaration Toward a Global Ethic [excerpt]

SYNOPSIS: The United States has been a leader in the ecumenical movement. Considering that it was the first nation to forgo an established, state-supported religion and to allow full religious freedom, this was appropriate. The most comprehensive and ambitious ecumenical endeavors have been sponsored by the World Parliament of Religion, first held in 1893 and revived in 1993. The following is an excerpt from its 1993 Declaration.

The Parliament Of The World's Religions: *Declaration Toward a Global Ethic,* **from the Parliament of the World's Religions**, 1993. Küng, Yes *to a Global Ethic,* 13–15

[This gathering of world faiths celebrated the centenary of the ground-breaking Parliament in Chicago, 1893. Representatives of world faiths had met again to pray for global peace at the instigation of John Paul II, at Assisi in 1986. The editor of the volume quoted from here is the Roman Catholic dissident Hans Küng. His well-known thesis is that, without a shared approach by the world religions, important social and ethical questions could not be tackled effectively by religion, and this would render a sense of global order and shared values impossible.]

We women and men of various religions and regions of Earth therefore address all people, religious and non-religious. We wish to express the following convictions which we hold in common.

- We *all* have a *responsibility for a better global order.*

- Our involvement for the sake of human rights, freedom, justice, peace, and the preservation of Earth is absolutely necessary.

- Our different religious and cultural traditions must not prevent our common involvement in opposing all forms of inhumanity and working for greater humaneness.

- The principles expressed in this global ethic can be affirmed by all persons with ethical convictions, whether religiously grounded or not.

As *religious and spiritual persons* we base our lives on an Ultimate Reality, and draw spiritual power and hope therefrom, in trust, in prayer or mediation, in word or silence. We have a special responsibility for the welfare of all humanity and care for the planet Earth. We do not consider ourselves better than other women and men, but we trust that the ancient wisdom of our religions can point the way for the future.

After two world wars and the end of the cold war, the collapse of fascism and nazism, the shaking to the foundations of communism and colonialism, humanity has entered a new phase of its history. Today we possess sufficient economic, cultural, and spiritual resources to introduce a better global order, but old and new *ethnic, national, social economic, and religious tensions* threaten the peaceful building of a better world. We have experienced greater technological progress than ever before, yet we see that world-wide poverty, hunger, death of chil-

Dr. Hans Kung (left) signs a copy of his book for one of his supporters (right) during the Parliament of the World's Religions in Chicago, 1993. **AP/WIDE WORLD PHOTOS. REPRODUCED BY PERMISSION.**

dren, unemployment, misery, and the destruction of nature have not diminished but rather have increased. Many peoples are threatened with economic ruin, social disarray, political marginalization, ecological catastrophe, and moral collapse. . . .

On the basis of personal experiences and the burdensome history of our planet we have learned

- that a better global order cannot be created or enforced by laws, prescriptions, and conventions alone;

- that the realisation of peace, justice, and the protection of the earth depends on the insight and readiness of men and women to act justly;

- that action in favour of rights and freedoms presumes a consciousness of responsibility and duty, and that therefore both the minds and hearts of women and men must be addressed;

- that rights without morality cannot long endure, and that there will be *no better global order without a global ethic.*

By *a global ethic* we do not mean a global ideology or a *single unified religion* beyond all existing religions, and certainly not the domination of one religion over all others. By a global ethic we mean a *fundamental consensus on binding values, irrevocable standards, and personal attitudes.* Without such a fundamental consensus on an ethic, sooner or later every community will be threatened by chaos or dictatorship, and individuals will despair.

Further Resources
BOOKS

Snodgrass, Judith. *Presenting Japanese Buddhism to the West: Orientalism, Occcidentalism, and the Columbian Exposition.* Chapel Hill, N.C.: University of North Carolina Press, 2003.

WEBSITES

"Envisioning the Dynamics of a World Parliament of Religions." Available online at http://laetusinpraesens.org/docs /parldyna.php; website home page: http://laetusinpraesens .org/ (accessed April 11, 2003).

"Reflections on the World Parliament of Religions." Available online at www.ubfellowship.org/archive/sfj/world_parliament .htm; website home page: http://www.ubfellowship.org/ (accessed April 11, 2003).

Louis Farrakhan's Remarks at the Million Man March, October 17, 1995

Speech

By: Louis Farrakhan

Date: October 17, 1995

Source: CNN. Louis Farrakhan's Remarks at the Million Man March, October 17, 1995. Available online at www-cgi.cnn.com/US/9510/megamarch/10-16/transcript /index.html; website home page: http://www.cgi.com (accessed February 17, 2003).

About the Author: Louis Farrakhan (1933–) was born Louis Eugene Walcott in the Bronx, New York, and was raised in Boston, in the West Indian section of Roxbury. Originally planning a career as an entertainer, he heard Malcolm X speak in 1955 in Roxbury and Elijah Muhammad in Chicago in 1956. He joined the Nation of Islam, changing his name first to Louis X and later to Louis Farrakhan. He became the leader of the Nation of Islam in 1977. ∎

Introduction

The U.S. Muslim population is approximately five million, and in time it will equal the size of the American Jewish population. It is a diverse community of Arabs, Asians (such as Pakistanis and Indonesians), Africans, and African Americans. There is no national organization uniting the Muslim community in the United States, but there are major Islamic centers in Washington, Toledo, Detroit, and New York City. The center in Washington, D.C., includes a beautiful mosque, library, classrooms for study, and administrative offices; it is open for daily prayer and offers lectures and publications on the literature, philosophy, religion, and art of Islam. By the 1990s, Muslims had established more than six hundred mosques and centers across the United States.

A Muslim community that is unique to the United States is the Nation of Islam. This African American religious community was founded in Detroit in 1930 by Wali Farad Muhammad (born Wallace D. Ford). In re-

action to the racism facing African Americans when they moved North, the Nation of Islam combined black pride and Islam. Farad gathered eight thousand members in Detroit and in 1931 founded Temple Number 1. Temple Number 2 was founded in Chicago.

Farad disappeared in 1934, and leadership of the community was taken over by Elijah Muhammad (born Robert Poole), the son of a Baptist minister. Elijah Muhammad claimed that Allah had communicated his will to him, which he wrote down in a book called *The Supreme Wisdom,* as well as further revelations in the journal *Muhammad Speaks.* Elijah Muhammad taught that all nonwhite people belonged to the tribe of SHABAZZ, which is descended from the patriarch Abraham. The goal of the Nation of Islam is to unite all these people.

Significance

Among Elijah Muhammad's most important converts were Malcolm X and Louis Farrakhan. Malcolm Little (1925–1965) joined the Nation of Islam while in a prison cell. He took the name Malcolm X to signal his lost African heritage. He became a public figure during the 1960s, although he separated himself from the Nation of Islam before his death. This was largely the result of his experience of the international character of Islam while on pilgrimage, which differed with Elijah Muhammad's nationalist version.

Louis Farrakhan joined the Nation of Islam in 1955. From 1956 to 1965, he was the minister of Muhammad Temple No. 11 in Boston. In 1965, after the death of Malcolm X, Farrakhan was appointed by Elijah Muhammad to take charge of Temple No. 7 in New York City. After Elijah Muhammed's death in 1975, the movement split. One branch, under the leadership of W. Deen Muhammad, the fifth son of Elijah Muhammed, moved closer to the beliefs and practices of Islam as it is practiced in most of the world. This group, which would later change its name to the American Muslim Mission, is the largest African American Islamic movement. In 1977, Farrakhan took control of the Nation of Islam and returned it to the original views of Elijah Muhammad. While he remains the most recognizable Muslim leader in the United States, many American Muslims would claim that the Nation of Islam under his leadership is not representative of either immigrant or converted Islam in the United States.

Despite these theological differences, Farrakhan remains an African American leader with a large following and great influence. This was demonstrated in 1995 when he organized the Million Man March in Washington, D.C., as an opportunity for black male fellowship, as well as to call attention to injustices against African

Minister Louis Farrakhan speaks at the Million Man March in Washington, D.C., October 17, 1995. **REUTERS/MIKE THEILER/ARCHIVE PHOTOS. REPRODUCED BY PERMISSION.**

Americans in the United States. The excerpt below is from a speech he gave at the event.

Primary Source

Louis Farrakhan's Remarks at the Million Man March, October 17, 1995 [excerpt]

SYNOPSIS: The Nation of Islam is a unique expression of the Muslim faith in the United States. Under the leadership of Elijah Muhammad and later Louis Farrakhan, its nationalistic bent has led it to be regarded as unorthodox by other Muslims, who stress that Islam is a universal religion embracing all nationalities. Still, Farrakhan has become a major voice in the African American community, as evidenced by the Million Man March in 1995.

FARRAKHAN: So, we stand here today at this historic moment. We are standing in the place of those who couldn't make it here today. We are standing on the blood of our ancestors. We are standing on the blood of those who died in the middle passage, who died in the fields and swamps of America, who died hanging from trees in the South, who died in the cells of their jailers, who died on the highways and who died in the fratricidal conflict that rages within our community. We are standing on the sacrifice of the lives of those heroes, our great men and women that we today may accept the responsibility that life imposes upon each traveler who comes this way.

We must accept the responsibility that God has put upon us, not only to be good husbands and fathers and builders of our community, but God is now calling upon the despised and the rejected to become the cornerstone and the builders of a new world.

And so, our brief subject today is taken from the American Constitution. In these words, Toward a more union. Toward a more perfect union.

Now, when you use the word more with perfect, that which is perfect is that which has been brought to completion. So, when you use more perfect, you're either saying that what you call perfect is perfect for that stage of its development but not yet complete. When Jefferson said, "toward a more perfect union," he was admitting that the union was not perfect, that it was not finished, that work had to be done. And so we are gathered here today not to bash somebody else.

We're not gathered here to say, all of the evils of this nation. But we are gathered here to collect ourselves for a responsibility that God is placing on our shoulders to move this nation toward a more perfect union. Now, when you look at the word toward, toward, it means in the direction of, in furtherance or partial fulfillment of, with the view to obtaining or having shortly before coming soon, eminent, going on in progress. Well, that's right. We're in progress toward a perfect union. Union means bringing elements or components into unity.

It is something formed by uniting two or more things. It is a number of persons, states, etcetera, which are joined or associated together for some common purpose. We're not here to tear down America. America is tearing itself down. We are here to rebuild the wasted cities. What we have in the word toward is motion. The honorable Elijah Muhammad taught us that motion is the first law of the universe. This motion which takes us from one point to another shows that we are evolving and we are a part of a universe that is ever evolving.

We are on an evolutionary course that will bring us to perfect or completion of the process toward a perfect union with God. In the word toward there is a law and that law is everything that is created is in harmony with the law of evolution, change. Nothing is standing still.

It is either moving toward perfection or moving toward disintegration. Or under certain circumstances doing both things at the same time. The word for this evolutionary changing affecting stage after stage until we reach perfection. In Arabic it is called Rhab. And from the word Rhab you get the Rhaby, or teacher, one who nourishes a people from one stage and brings them to another stage. Well, if we are in motion and we are, motion toward perfection and we are, there can be no motion toward perfection without the Lord, who created the law of evolution.

And is the master of the changes. Our first motion then must be toward the God, who created the law of the evolution of our being. And if our motion toward him is right and proper, then our motion toward a perfect union with each other and government and with the peoples of the world will be perfected. So, let us start with a process leading to that perfect union must first be seen. Now, brothers and sisters, the day of atonement is established by God to help us achieve a closer tie with the source of wisdom, knowledge, understanding and power.

For it is only through a closer union or tie with him, who created us all, with him who has power over all things that we can draw power, knowledge, wisdom and understanding from him, that we maybe enable to change the realities of our life. A perfect union with God is the idea at the base of atonement. Now, atonement demands of us eight steps, in fact, atonement is the fifth step in an eight stage process.

Look at our division, not here, out there. We are a people, who have been fractured, divided and destroyed because of our division now must move toward a perfect union. But let's look at a speech delivered by a White slave holder on the banks of the James River in 1712.

Sixty-eight years before our former slave masters permitted us to join the Christian faith. Listen to what he said. He said, "In my bag I have a fool proof method of controlling black slaves. I guarantee everyone of you, if installed correctly, it will control the slaves for at least 300 years. My method is simple. Any member of your family or your overseer can use it. I have outlined a number of differences among the slaves and I take these differences and I make them bigger. I use fear, distrust, and envy for control purposes."

I want you to listen. What are those three things? Fear, envy, distrust. For what purpose? Control. To control who? The slave. Who is the slave? Us. Listen, he said, "These methods have worked on my modest plantation in the West Indies and they will work throughout the south.

Now, take this simple little list and think about it. On the top of my list is age. But it's only there because it starts with an A. And the second is color or shade. There's intelligence, sex, size of plantation, status of plantation, attitude of owners, whether the slaves live in the valley or on a hill, north, east, south or west, have fine hair or course hair, or is tall or short.

Now that you have a list of differences I shall give you an outline of action. But before that, I shall assure you that distrust is stronger than trust. And envy is stronger than adulation, respect, or admiration.

The black slave after receiving this indoctrination shall carry it on and will become self-refueling and self-generating for hundreds of years. Maybe thousands of years. Now don't forget, you must pitch the old black male against the young black male. And the young black male against the old black male.

You must use the female against the male. And you must use the male against the female. You must use the dark skinned slave against the light skinned slave. And the light skinned slave against the dark skinned slave.

Further Resources

BOOKS

Alexander, Amy. *The Farrakhan Factor: African-American Writers on Leadership, Nationhood, and Minister Louis Farrakhan.* New York: Grove, 1998.

Singh, Robert. *The Farrakhan Phenomenon: Race, Reaction, and the Paranoid Style in American Politics.* Washington, D.C.: Georgetown University Press, 1997.

White, Vibert. *Inside the Nation of Islam: A Historical and Personal Testimony by a Black Muslim.* Gainesville, Fla.: University Press of Florida, 2001.

Just As I Am

Autobiography

By: Billy Graham

Date: 1997

Source: Graham, Billy. *Just As I Am: The Autobiography of Billy Graham.* New York: HarperCollins, 1997.

About the Author: William Franklin Graham Jr. (1918–) was born in Charlotte, North Carolina. He was ordained a Southern Baptist minister in 1939 at the age of twenty-one and, after serving as a minister in a traditional congregation, became an itinerant preacher. His revival meetings became tremendously successful, and he is today perhaps the most widely recognized Protestant religious leader in the United States. ∎

Introduction

Billy Graham was born four days before the Armistice ending World War I on the family dairy farm in Charlotte, North Carolina. As a young boy growing up during the Great Depression, he learned the value of hard work on the family farm. Young Billy was also an avid reader and found time to spend many hours in the hayloft reading from his grandfather's library.

In the fall of 1934, at age sixteen, Graham had a profound religious experience. Significantly, it was by way of a traveling evangelist, a man named Mordecai Ham, who visited the Charlotte area to conduct revival meetings. Through Ham's preaching, Billy made a personal commitment to Christ. This set Graham's life on a new track. Abandoning his earlier dreams of playing professional baseball, Graham decided to become a minister. He was ordained in 1939 by a church in the Southern Baptist Convention and later attended the Florida Bible Institute (now Trinity College) and Wheaton College in Illinois. In 1943, he graduated from Wheaton and married Ruth McCue Bell, a fellow student who had spent the first seventeen years of her life in China with her missionary family.

After graduating from Wheaton, Graham briefly served as a traditional minister at the First Baptist Church in Western Springs, Illinois. Soon, however, he became a traveling evangelist, the same kind of ministry that had led to his conversion. In 1945, he joined Youth for Christ, an organization founded to minister to youth and servicemen during World War II. Another turning point in his career came in a mission in Los Angeles in 1949, which launched Graham into national prominence. Originally scheduled for three weeks, the meetings drew ten thousand and were extended to more than eight weeks. This led to the founding of the Billy Graham Evangelistic Association.

Significance

In summing up the purpose of his work, Graham simply stated: "My one purpose in life is to help people find a personal relationship with God, which, I believe, comes through knowing Christ." This focus, combined with integrity, dignity, and an inspiring preaching style, led Billy Graham to become the most widely known and respected evangelist of his time.

Graham has preached his message to over 210 million people in more than 185 countries and territories. Hundreds of millions more have been reached through television, video, film and webcasts. The many works of the Billy Graham Evangelistic Association have included: *Hour of Decision,* a weekly radio program broadcast around the world on Sundays for over fifty years; the daily *Decision Today* radio program aired by approximately two hundred stations in the United States and Canada; television specials broadcast in prime time six times annually; a newspaper column, "My Answer," which appears in newspapers across the country with a combined circulation of more than five million readers; *Decision* magazine, the official publication of the association, with a circulation of 1.4 million; and a film production company, World Wide Pictures, which has produced and distributed over 130 productions. Graham himself has written over twenty books.

Reverend Billy Graham gives a sermon in Oklahoma City on April 23, 1995, shortly after the bombing there. © WALLY MCNAMEE/CORBIS. REPRODUCED BY PERMISSION.

Primary Source

Just As I Am [excerpt]

SYNOPSIS: Among Graham's books is his autobiography, *Just As I Am,* an excerpt of which appears below. In this work, he reflects on his humble beginnings as the son of a dairy farmer in North Carolina and his nearly sixty years of ministry around the world. One the most notable things about Graham's career has been his universal appeal and ability to rise above partisanship. This is demonstrated in the passage below. While Graham had strong relationships with conservative political leaders, he was also able to relate to those whose views he did not entirely agree with, such as those of President Clinton. Not only was he able to maintain a relationship with Clinton, but when the United States experienced the terrible tragedy of the Oklahoma City bombing in 1995, it was fitting that Billy Graham should be called upon to speak at the memorial service.

After Clinton's election, some people criticized me for agreeing to pray at his inauguration. On certain issues, the new President had taken stands that disconcerted those who were morally more conservative, including some evangelical Christians. I felt it was important to keep my commitment to pray, however, even if I did not agree with everything he held. I also felt a warm personal affection for Mr. Clinton, whatever his viewpoints.

I also wanted to assure Mr. Clinton of my prayers, for no President stands outside the need for God's constant help and guidance. That is one reason I have always agreed to lead prayers on such occasions whenever asked. Furthermore, the Scripture commands us to pray "for kings and all those in authority, that we may live peaceful and quiet lives in all godliness and holiness. This is good, and pleases God our Savior" (1 Timothy 2:2–3). When the Apostle Paul wrote those words, a pagan emperor ruled the Roman Empire, but that did not nullify the command. I asked one person who tried to dissuade me, "Are you saying you don't think Mr. Clinton needs our prayers, or that we shouldn't pray for him?"

The night before the 1993 National Prayer Breakfast—Clinton's first as President—Ruth and I stayed at the White House. The Clintons had the governor of Hawaii there too. At dinner that evening, Hillary Clinton had me to her right and the governor to her left; they talked much of the time about health care, a deep concern of the First Lady's. Ruth sat at the other end of the table on the President's right. My sister Jean and her husband, Leighton Ford, were also dinner guests. It was a delightful and informal time, almost like a family gathering. The next morning, the President and I both got up early and had quite a talk while he was getting ready for his morning run.

Afterward we went together to the Washington Hilton for the National Prayer Breakfast. My good friend Doug Coe (who has done so much in his quiet way to work with leaders and to foster the Prayer-Breakfast movement in the United States and many other countries) escorted us to the platform. I found the sincere words of both Vice President Al Gore and President Clinton acknowledging their need of God's guidance very moving.

Two events from President Clinton's first term in office will always remain in my memory.

The first occurred in 1995, shortly after the tragic bombing of the federal office building in Oklahoma City. By any standard, that bombing—which resulted in the deaths of 168 men, women, and children, and injury to hundreds more—was a senseless, barbaric act. The whole nation was in a state of shock, but no one was touched so deeply as the citizens of Oklahoma City and the state of Oklahoma.

The day after the bombing, I received an invitation to participate in a special memorial service for the victims of the disaster from Governor Frank Keating and his wife, Cathy. Just a few weeks earlier she had been taken to our San Juan, Puerto Rico, Crusade by Laura Bush, wife of Governor George Bush of Texas. Mrs. Keating was coordinating the Oklahoma service. President and Mrs. Clinton came also, and in his simple but deeply moving words he extended his and his wife's sympathy to those who had suffered the loss of a loved one. By his presence and his speech, he also conveyed to everyone in Oklahoma the clear message that the whole nation was standing with them in their grief.

I spoke also to the assembled crowd—one of the most difficult things I have done in my life—telling them frankly that I did not understand why God allowed things like this to happen. Our knowledge is limited, I pointed out, and there are some things we will never understand this side of eternity. I reminded them, however, that even though we do not understand, God does not change. He is still the God of love and mercy; and in the midst of our sorrow and pain, we can turn to Him in faith and trust.

Further Resources

BOOKS

Strober, Gerald S. *Billy Graham, His Life and Faith.* Waco, Tex.: World Books, 1977.

Wellman, Sam. *Billy Graham: The Great Evangelist.* Philadelphia: Chelsea House, 1999.

Wooten, Sara McIntosh. *Billy Graham: World-Famous Evangelist.* Berkeley Heights, N.J.: Enslow, 2001.

"Foundress, Missionary, Bride of Christ: Mother M. Angelica"

Magazine article

By: Ellen Rice

Date: March 1998

Source: Rice, Ellen. "Foundress, Missionary, Bride of Christ: Mother M. Angelica," *Catholic Dossier*, March–April 1998.

About the Author: Ellen Rice was assistant to the editor of *Catholic Dossier* magazine at the time this article appeared in 1998. She also contributed "The Myth of the Spanish Inquisition" in 1996. *The Catholic Dossier* was a conservative Catholic bimonthly periodical edited by Ralph McInerney and located in San Francisco, California. The magazine is no longer in publication. ■

Introduction

Catholics have been part of many of the major developments in the media. In the 1920s and 1930s, Father Charles Coughlin of Detroit, the "Radio Priest," was a master of that medium. Coughlin originally used the radio for the dual function of raising money for a new church, the Shrine of the Little Flower, and to combat anti-Catholic attitudes by the local Ku Klux Klan. He became very successful, some would say too successful. He turned to politics and later anti-Semitism before he was silenced by his bishop with the support of the Vatican. In the 1950s, in the early days of television, Bishop Fulton Sheen's series *Life Is Worth Living* was also a very successful use of a new medium to communicate a religious message.

In both cases, however, this early success was not followed up after the pioneer ceased broadcasting. It was not until the 1980s and 1990s that the next major Catholic media figure gained prominence: Mother Angelica, a Roman Catholic nun whose cable Eternal Word Television Network became a major force in religious broadcasting.

Mother Angelica was born in Canton, Ohio, on April 20, 1923 as Rita Antoinette Rizzo. She became a Franciscan nun and in 1946 was one of the founders of a monastic community in Canton. In 1962, she founded Our Lady of the Angels Monastery outside of Birmingham, Alabama. This community is a part of the Poor Clares of Perpetual Adoration. In 1978, Mother Angelica was interviewed on a Chicago religious station. This experience prompted her to tape a series of programs that aired on Pat Robertson's Christian Broadcasting Network, as well as to appear on Jim Bakker's PTL Club.

Significance

Mother Angelica taped her shows at the local Birmingham television station until it aired a film in 1981 called *The Word* about a forged Gospel that she regarded blasphemous. She decided to start her own television studio, called the Eternal Word Television Network. Starting with $200 and broadcasting out of a garage, EWTN received its FCC license in 1986 and became a hit on cable. In time, her network would reach 50 million households. The question remains, however, whether Mother Angelica's recent departure from EWTN because of health problems will have the same result on Catholic broadcasting on cable as Coughlin's and Sheen's retirements from radio and broadcast television did.

EWTN, like other popular religious broadcasters, promotes traditional values and becomes a place for those seeking spiritual comfort in a changing world. A major reason for its success is that much of that change has occurred within the Catholic Church itself over the past four

Mother Angelica during a 1995 program on the satellite television network she founded, the Eternal Word Television Network.
© CAMPBELL, WILLIAMS/CORBIS SYGMA. REPRODUCED BY PERMISSION.

decades. Many of the reforms introduced by the Second Vatican Council (1962–1965) were, especially those in the liturgy, unsettling to many Catholics; an example was the replacement of the Latin mass by mass in the vernacular, or the native language spoken by the people in the community. This discomfort has been compounded by Catholic liberals who felt that the church did not go far enough and who advocate, for example, optional celibacy for priests and the ordination of women.

Wearing a traditional nun's habit and speaking in a blunt, no-nonsense manner, Mother Angelica would criticize those she felt to be leading the Catholic tradition astray. While expressing loyalty to the leadership of the church, in particular Pope John Paul II, she was not afraid to bring to task any bishop she felt to be too liberal. This has made her a hero of the conservative Catholic press, an example of which is given in the excerpt below.

Primary Source

"Foundress, Missionary, Bride of Christ: Mother M. Angelica"

SYNOPSIS: As Father Charles Coughlin was to radio and Bishop Fulton J. Sheen was to broadcast tele-

vision, so was Mother Angelica to cable television in the 1980s and 1990s. In addition to being a powerful force in religious television, she has also been an important factor in the struggle between liberals and conservatives in the post–Vatican II Catholic Church.

Any time is a good time to celebrate the work of Mother Angelica. Her most visible apostolic endeavor is EWTN global television network, which is good news for 50 million households in the United States alone, and many more overseas. Short-wave radio network WEWN, recently made available on AM/FM, and an Internet supersite round out her apostolate, which is becoming the new gold standard in religious broadcasting.

God has bestowed a richer blessing through the labors of Mother Angelica: the flourishing of the religious communities that she herself has founded. In 1962, she built Our Lady of the Angels Monastery, using money raised from selling fishing lures. Her community of sisters is an autonomous monastery of the Poor Clares of Perpetual Adoration (P.C.P.A.), an order founded in Paris, France on the exact day that Pius IX promulgated the doctrine of the Immaculate Conception. Like so many modern orders, adoration of Jesus in the tabernacle is a central part of their spiritual life.

Like St. Francis of Assisi, who founded the Poor Clares many centuries ago, preaching to the multitudes has come naturally to the nuns at Our Lady of the Angels. In the early 1970s they began printing Mother Angelica's writings using their own press, built and financed from scratch.

Mother Angelica was soon discovered as a TV star, and by the late 1970s she hosted two shows on the Christian cable network, CBN. A local TV studio was provided to Mother Angelica as the site to tape her shows, until that fateful day when the station manager decided to air a blasphemous film, *The Word*. When he absolutely refused to yank the program, Mother Angelica declared that she would neither sign a contract with his station, nor continue to use his studio. Never mind that no other studios existed within 100 miles. In a moment of heated resolve, Mother Angelica declared that she would build her own studio, buy her own equipment, and tape her own shows! Eternal Word Television Network was born. The Poor Clare sisters eagerly set about turning the garage into a studio, and Mother Angelica procured her own satellite. Their meager resources of $200 were multiplied as donations poured in from around the country.

By 1987, EWTN had outgrown both the garage and the community's resources. The apostolate was so large that Mother Angelica instituted an order of priests and brothers, the Missionaries of the Eternal Word, who are totally devoted to evangelization using state-of-the-art media technology. More important, she established them to offer Mass and give the Sacraments to the Poor Clares and the frequent visitors at the Monastery.

What accounts for the flourishing of Mother Angelica's two apostolates—the religious communities and the mission through the airwaves? She is a great believer in what she calls "the theology of risk." She says, "Every thing today revolves around feasibility studies. Just suppose Jesus had decided to do a feasibility study on whether or not He should have chosen those twelve apostles."

Risk, going out on a limb to do God's work, is not to be understood as rashness. Mother Angelica's risky entrepreneurial and foundational ventures have always been grounded in a strong sense of union with Christ, her spouse. On the occasion of professing her vows in 1947, she sent a wedding invitation to her mother, signed "Jesus and Angelica." Indeed, the raising of Our Lady of the Angels deep in the Bible Belt was the fruit of a promise she made to her Spouse during her young years in the convent. When Sister Angelica was injured in a freak accident as she scrubbed floors with an unwieldy scrubbing machine, she was told she had a 50/50 chance of never walking again. She prayed and promised Jesus that if she could walk again she would build Him a monastery, and one in the South, at that!

Mother Angelica is a role model of risk-taking in these days when the Holy Father has asked us to shout the Gospel from the rooftops. She is also an important example to a needy and growing group—the children of broken homes. Rita Rizzo, the child who would become Mother Angelica, suffered the absence of her father from earliest memory and the trauma of divorce when only six years old. She and her mother, Mae Rizzo, though innocent, suffered poverty and ostracism as a result. Mother Angelica recalls the sewer rats in their apartment and the gigantic holes in her shoes. Because of her faith Mae Rizzo resisted the thought of remarriage, knowing all along this would have brought financial security. She kept up her struggling dry-cleaning business, where Rita would become a delivery driver at the age of eleven. Amidst this hardship, Rita turned to God. To this day she credits divine favor for her inexplicable recovery from an abdominal ailment as a girl. Rita

also learned to be aggressive in asking for what she needed. She it was who would find her mother the job that would alleviate their strict poverty.

Surely the entrepreneurial spirit in Mother Angelica could have propelled her to Wall Street or the boardrooms of the best corporations. After a childhood of extreme poverty, she chose a life of detachment and dependence on God, rather than choosing to aggrandize wealth using her own wits. Her mother would later join the community at Our Lady of the Angels, and live in prayer and thanksgiving until her death. God has certainly blessed Mother Angelica, her mother—and millions of TV watchers and radio listeners—a hundred-fold.

Further Resources

BOOKS

O'Neill, Dan. *Mother Angelica: Her Life Story.* New York: Crossroad, 1986.

WEBSITES

Eternal Word Television Network. Available online at http://www.ewtn.com (accessed April 11, 2003).

"Mother Angelica: Healed and Reviled." Available online at www.aquinas-multimedia.com/catherine/angelica.html; website home page: http://www.aquinas-multimedia.com (accessed April 11, 2003).

"Is Religion Possible? An Evaluation of Present Efforts to Revive Traditional Tribal Religions"

Essay

By: Vine Deloria Jr.

Date: 1999

Source: Deloria, Vine, Jr. "Is Religion Possible? An Evaluation of Present Efforts to Revive Traditional Tribal Religions." In *For This Land: Writings on Religion in America,* edited by James Treat. New York: Routledge, 1999, 261–265.

About the Author: Vine (Victor) Deloria Jr. (1933–) is a Native American author and activist born in Martin, South Dakota. He received a master's degree in theology from Lutheran School of Theology and a law degree from the University of Colorado. Among his many writings are *Custer Died for Your Sins: An Indian Manifesto* (1969) and *God Is Red* (1973). ∎

Introduction

There are as many forms of Native American spirituality as there are Native American tribes. The Crow creation story, for example, has the Creator sending away all the peoples brought to life except for the bravest, which happened to be the Crow. Communities have also varied considerably, from the urban, highly sophisticated societies of the Aztecs with their temples and human sacrifices to the animistic religious practices of the hunter-gatherers of the eastern woodlands, such as the Algonquins and the Iroquois. Some feature one supreme being, while others have multiple spirits. The Seneca, for example, explain good and evil through the existence of twin gods. The good god created the good things of the world, while the evil god created all the things that would bedevil a person living in the forests of the Northeast—gnats, mosquitoes, rivers that flow only one way and are broken up by rapids, and corn that grows smaller than it should.

Despite this variety, many common themes run throughout all Native American religion. One of the most significant is the idea that all life is interconnected. For Native Americans, everything is sacred and all living things are related—not just human beings but also four-legged and winged brothers and sisters, as well as those who crawl. This connection to nature can be seen in the many Native American creation stories, from that of the Sioux with White Buffalo Calf Woman to the role of the elk in the Osage creation account. A common Native American religious symbol has been the sacred pipe, popularly known as the "peace pipe." It is prominent in religious ceremonies and to solemnize agreements. Giving a pipe to another person creates a strong bond between the two. The French missionary/explorer Father Jacques Marquette was given one by the Illinois to protect him from attack on his travels down the Mississippi.

Significance

Vine Deloria Jr., a Native American writer, made a big impact with his first book, *Custer Died for Your Sins: An Indian Manifesto,* published in 1969. The book took the United States to task for its treatment of Native Americans and called for a new relationship that preserved the dignity of his people and gave them a means of economic independence. While critical of the federal government, which caused dependency by means of the reservation system, he opposed the integration of Native Americans into American society, a plan that might look egalitarian on the surface but would mean the elimination of Native Americans as a distinctive culture. There needed to be a relationship with the United States that guaranteed the economic viability of the Native American peoples while at the same time preserving their identity and culture. In other words, Deloria articulated the dilemma that has faced the Catholics, Jews, and Muslims: how to preserve one's unique way of life from the Old World while at the same time becoming a part of the United States. What is

unique about the Native American dilemma, of course, is that while these other groups brought their beliefs and practices to a new land, Native Americans are conquered peoples trying to preserve their identity.

To be a part of American society and yet preserve one's own distinctive beliefs and practices has been important for every immigrant group. It is even more important for Native Americans, who have no other homeland to go to in order to reclaim their cultural and religious heritage. As can be seen from this excerpt below, spirituality is an important part of the survival of Native American identity.

Primary Source

"Is Religion Possible? An Evaluation of Present Efforts to Revive Traditional Tribal Religions" [excerpt]

SYNOPSIS: In the following excerpt, Deloria expresses the difficulty of preserving and revitalizing Native American religion. He touches on the phenomenon of a new kind of white conquest. While in the past whites took Native American land, Deloria warns of New Age religion robbing them now of their spiritual heritage. New Age appropriation and misuse of Native American religion is, he seems to be saying, as bad, if not worse, than the appropriation and pollution of Native American land by the European invaders.

Many Indians are irritated, and justly so, with the wholesale appropriation of American Indian rituals, symbols, and beliefs by the non-Indian public. Several national magazines and newspapers and a myriad of pamphlets, posters, and bumper stickers proclaim the wonders of studying with the likes of Wallace Black Elk, Richard Erdoes, Sun Bear, Lynn Andrews, Edward McGaa, and a host of lesser luminaries in the New Age/Indian medicine man circuit. Even the staid Christian churches are busy trying to revamp their doctrines and programs to fit with the new interest in Indian religious ideas. Ecologists of all stripes including the self-appointed "Deep Ecologists" claim a kinship with traditional Indian beliefs so that one would wonder whether the tribes did not in fact win the Indian wars and expel the hated invaders from their homelands.

A few knotty problems do exist. The Pope at some point must choose between the Indian and Chicano versions of California history and classify Junipero Serra as a psychopath or a saint. Other Christian denominations must explain why, after five hundred years of persecution and neglect, they are now identifying Indian saints and beloved of the faith—people they would never have allowed in their ecclesiastical deliberations when they were alive. And Indians must determine whether adding a pipe and sweat lodge to organizational banquets and annual meetings necessarily blesses the programs and policies of the participating groups.

In short, Indian traditional religious affairs are a complete disaster area.

We must, if possible, dig beneath the rhetoric and poetry of present expressions of religiosity practiced by Indians and their admirers and examine whether or not there is any substance in the popularity of Indian traditions and whether or not something useful and constructive can be derived from present activities. This subject can be examined from almost any perspective but it is useful to sketch out the claims that are being made in the name of Indian religions and ask what impact these claims have on people's lives. The subject has a certain urgency because Congress will consider comprehensive legislation designed to protect traditional Indian religions in this session and it would be good to begin clarifying exactly what we are asking Congress to protect.

A persistent claim made by the Indians who allege to be practicing traditional ceremonies, on behalf of non-Indians and urban Indian clients, is that they have been instructed by their elders in these rituals and have been told by the same elders that they must go forth and proclaim the truth—often before the apocalyptic end of the present world and the initiation of the next world. Some of these claims, made in letters to me, smack more of the *Acts of the Apostles* than any instructions I have ever heard from tribal elders. If we accept these claims as true, we are basically saying that traditional Indian religions have become missionary-minded and now seek converts in a larger intercultural context. This claim is contrary to every known tenet of any tribal tradition but it may be a new revelation given at the end of this world.

Unlike Western religions which sought to convert a selected number of true believers and convince them that a particular interpretation of planetary history was correct, tribal religions were believed to be special communications between spirits and a specific group of people. The admonition given with the teachings and rituals instructed this particular group of people to faithfully perform ceremonies and act responsibly within the land and historical time period in which they existed as a people. Prophecies which gave the people signs of the impending end

Native American scholar and author Vine Deloria, Jr., in 1996.
REPRODUCED BY PERMISSION OF VINE DELORIA JR.

of each world, in those cases in which worlds were created and destroyed, often accompanied the ceremonies. No demand existed, however, for the people to go into the world and inform or instruct other people in the rituals and beliefs of the tribe. The people were supposed to follow their own teachings and assume that other people would follow their teachings. These instructions were rigorously followed and consequently there was never an instance of a tribe making war on another tribe because of religious differences. Thus the situation of today is a radical departure from everything we have known about traditional religion. . . .

The message which seems to underlie the practice of New Age and popular Indian religion is that everything is related. A subsidiary doctrine is that everything is circular and within this sacred circularity are the four directions which have a certain degree of power when invoked by creating a "medicine wheel"—made popular by Hyemeyohsts Storm's *Seven Arrows*. It does not seem that this idea, relationships with corresponding use of geometrical directions and figures allocating possible sources of sacred energy, is particularly revolutionary or something that needed to be contained within the specific

The mystic Rowena Kryder on Mt. Shasta around 1994. In an example of the cooption of Native American traditions by non-Native Americans, she is dressed in her vision of a Native American spirit. © CATHERINE KARNOW/CORBIS-BETTMANN. REPRODUCED BY PERMISSION.

tribal tradition. Indeed, Albert Einstein advocated the same proposition in articulating his theory of relativity and while he did not specifically apply it to plants, animals and people, he did suggest that all measurements and perhaps even all experiences were possible within a specific framework of the physical world that admitted that the universe did not contain isolated entities. So if we feel that traditional religions have been harmed in some specific way by informing people outside the tribe, then traditional religions must not have contained very many truths at all.

Use and abuse of the sweat lodge, sun dance, and pipe are another matter altogether. The sweat lodge is not exclusively Plains tradition and in fact some version of the sweat lodge was prevalent in Scandanavian countries long before they had Christianity. It has become an intertribal, inclusive ritual in which in many places the predominant number of people taking part are non-Indians. Before we get overly exercised about the universality of the sweat lodge we should remember that many tribes use it as purification prior to engaging in other ceremonies which have a deeper significance. If we admit that the minimum benefit and participation of people today in the sweat lodge is simply purification it does not appear that this violation of traditional religion is detrimental. . . .

Use of the pipe is also serious and complicated. Many non-Indians possess pipes for purely secular reasons and pipe making is an income-producing arts and crafts form that is not likely to be brought under control at this point in time. A strange melding of tradition and modern excitement has created a very confused situation with respect to the pipe. In the old days almost everyone had their own pipe and it was smoked as much for social enjoyment and hospitality as for religious purposes. Today we hear that some people are "Pipe Carriers" as if possessing a pipe initiated an individual into some secret brotherhood which stood apart from everything else. Many of the non-Indians using the pipe allege to be commissioned "Pipe Carriers" and then perform a bewildering variety of motions with the pipe, passing them off as special ceremonies which they claim to have been authorized to perform. They therefore get the benefit of having some obscure office within a traditional religion while escaping the necessity of actually having to live a fully committed religious life.

At the level I have seen many Indians and non-Indians use the pipe, I cannot find much real disrespect and exploitation. They light it, say a few prayers, and pass it around the group asking each person to say a prayer or mumble "All my relatives." In some cases this simple set of actions invokes behavior of great respect by the non-Indians, more respect sometimes than they allocate to their own traditions and practices. In a society totally ravaged by greed and individualism one would hope that the pipe would bring a better sense of community and sharing and if any progress is made along these lines we should be grateful for what the pipe is able to accomplish. . . .

Much of the difficulty that Indians have today with the appropriation of Indian rituals and teachings is the superior attitude which non-Indians project once they have made some acquaintance with things Indian. In most cases they have a sneering, self-righteous posture which communicates the message, to Indians and non-Indians alike, that they know all about Indian religion. It is this message, often communicated with arrogant body language, that infuriates many Indians because, seeing the effect of the transmission of ideas and ritual objects, Indians see how their tradition has been perverted. The non-Indian appropriator conveys the message that Indians are indeed a conquered people and that there is nothing that Indians possess, *absolutely nothing*—pipes, dances, land, water, feathers, drums, and even prayers—that non-Indians cannot take whenever and wherever they wish.

Non-Indians, accused of appropriating Indian religious ideas and sacred objects, often respond that religion is for sharing and some of the New Age Indian medicine men excuse their abuses by insisting that they are simply sharing these ideas and objects. Here we have a basic watershed in interpretation that needs to be seen in its real colors. Western religions insist that they have "Good News"—the gospel—that it is for everyone, and that it must be shared. The problem is that the ideas are shared but nothing else. Thus dispossession of Indians from their lands is excused by the argument that non-Indians brought Christianity and therefore the exchange was an even bargain. Indians are therefore put in a position where we must share with others—everything—but they need not share with us.

Further Resources

BOOKS

Bonvillain, Nancy. *Native American Religion.* New York: Chelsea House, 1996.

Hartz, Paula. *Native American Religions.* New York: Facts on File, 1997.

Klots, Steve. *Native Americans and Christianity.* New York: Chelsea House, 1997.

Surveying the Religious Landscape

Surveys

By: George Gallup Jr., D. Michael Lindsay

Date: 1999

Source: Gallup, George, Jr., and D. Michael Lindsay. *Surveying the Religious Landscape: Trends in U.S. Beliefs.* Harrisburg, Pa: Morehouse, 1999, 43–47.

About the Author: George Gallup Jr. (1901–1984) was born in Jefferson, Iowa. Trained as a journalist, he earned his Ph.D. from the University of Iowa in 1928. His dissertation, *A New Technique for Objective Methods for Measuring Reader Interest in Newspapers,* laid the foundation for his future career as a professional pollster and public opinion statistician. In 1935, he founded the American Institute of Public Opinion. ■

Introduction

The 1990s witnessed increasing diversification in American religion. In 1960, Will Herberg published *Protestant-Catholic-Jew: An Essay in American Religious Sociology.* At that time, with the nation on the verge of electing its first non-Protestant president, recognizing that Catholics and Jews were an established part of American religion was a significant development. While it took over three centuries for the Protestant establishment to make allowance for other groups, the last three decades have witnessed an even greater surging of diversity.

While in the 1950s 67 percent of Americans were Protestants, this figure declined to 56 percent by 1987. The trend continued into the 1990s, with the speculation that by the early twenty-first century Protestants will no longer make up a majority of the population. The Catholic population increased from 24 percent in 1950 to approximately 29 percent in the 1990s, with Hispanics making an increasingly higher proportion of its members. The Jewish population has remained at 3 to 4 percent.

The most significant development in this time period has been the increase in the number of Americans who belong to a religious groups other than of Herberg's "Protestant-Catholic-Jew." In the 1990s, 8 percent of the population said they belong to a faith other than Protestant, Catholic, or Jew. This is triple the percentage from the 1950s. This is the result largely of the relaxation of immigration laws, which has resulted in a great increase in the number of people coming to the United States from Asia, the Middle East, and Latin America. The most significant increases have been in the various branches of Buddhism, Hinduism, and Islam in the United States. This increasing diversity has been noted in the *Encyclopedia of American Religion,* which listed 1,200 different religious groups in its 1978 edition, 2,000 in the 1989 edition.

Significance

While religion in the United States changed very dramatically from the 1950s to the 1990s, what remained the same was that the United States was still a very religious country, especially compared with Europe. This is clearly reflected in the book *Surveying the Religious Landscape: Trends in U.S. Beliefs,* a portion of which is excerpted below. This 1999 book, co-authored by George Gallup Jr. and D. Michael Lindsay, addressed eight major areas: Religion and Trends, Religion and Beliefs, Religion and Practice, Religion and Experience, Religion and Attitudes toward the Church, Religion and Ethics, Religion and Society, and Religion and Youth.

The decade of the 1990s saw a further numerical decline in the Protestant numerical majority in the United States. Buddhist, Hindu, and Muslim communities became increasingly prominent. American religion, however, continued to be a good example of the notion that the more things change, the more they stay the same. While the face of American religion changed, the fact remained that Americans continued to be a religious people.

Primary Source

Surveying the Religious Landscape [excerpt]

SYNOPSIS: The passage excerpted is from the third section on Religion and Practice. Three forms of spirituality were studied in particular—prayer, study of Scripture, and charitable giving. The text below comes from the section dealing with prayer. According to the surveys taken, nine out of ten Americans pray, with 75 percent doing so daily. The vast majority pray alone (87 percent) and in a conversational manner to God (56 percent). For those who pray, virtually all believe that these prayers are heard (97 percent) and answered (95 percent). The five most popular subjects for prayer were: family's well-being (98 percent), world peace (83 percent), safety during travels (81 percent), loved ones who have died (79 percent), and the nation or homeland (76 percent). While a significant number did pray for victory in athletic events (23 percent), far fewer prayers were devoted to acquiring material possessions (18 percent) or for harm to come to enemies (5 percent).

Religion and Practice

Although 95% of Americans claim some religious tenets, a much smaller segment of the population practices their religious faith on a consistent basis. Three prevalent forms of spirituality include prayer, study of Scripture, and charitable acts of service. As Benjamin Franklin once remarked, "Serving God is doing good to man, but praying is thought an easier service and therefore more generally chosen." Indeed, prayer is the spine that holds up all other forms of American spirituality.

Over 90% of Americans today pray, and three in four U.S. adults pray on a daily basis. Most often they pray silently and alone, and nearly one-third of the population always prays before a meal (29%). Common subjects of these prayers involve the well-being of an individual's family, giving thanks, asking for strength or guidance, or asking for forgiveness. Americans also pray for very specific requests such as getting good grades, attaining victory in athletic events, or winning the lottery. Although some might denounce these types of prayers as self-serving or pretty, they also reveal the prevailing American notion that prayer is a means by which humans acquire. For most Americans, prayer is petition. Nearly all who pray contend that their petitions have been

answered in the past (95%); consequently, a number of Americans trust the power of prayer.

A robust majority of people in this country pray on a daily basis (75%), but only 15% read the Bible with the same frequency. Another 20% of the population read the Bible at least once a week. Most of them (69%) read the Bible alone. Individuals claim that the primary benefit of Scripture reading is that it makes them feel closer to God. Seventy-six percent of the nation says that reading the Bible helps them commune to a greater extent with God. Adults also cite the feeling of peace and finding meaning in life as primary benefits of reading Scripture.

The Chinese characters for "crisis" stand for both "danger" and "opportunity." Many Americans believe times of crisis provide good opportunities for deeper religious growth and spiritual development. Nearly everyone (94%) believes that more time spent in prayer, meditation, or reading the Bible is an effective way to allay personal depression. Almost nine out of ten U.S. adults (87%) think a pastor or religious leader can offer effective support and encouragement during bouts of depression. Not nearly the same number of people actually pursue these activities during the melancholy seasons of life. For example, the percentage of Americans who seek the help of a pastor during times of discouragement plummets a dramatic sixty points from those who think it would be a good idea (87% think it is a good idea; 27% actually do it). Eight out of ten Americans do find solace in prayer during times of crisis. Women are more inclined to seek spiritual solutions (such as prayer or Bible reading) to crises. Likewise, non-Whites respond to troubles by seeking spiritual solutions much more often than Whites do.

Almost four out of five adults (79%) received some form of religious training as children. An even higher percentage of society's most educated members, individuals with postgraduate education, experienced some form of religious training. Nearly all Americans—regardless of their own experience—would want their children to receive some form of religious instruction. Eighty-nine percent of adults express this desire. Generally, the strongest consensus on this matter arises from the Midwestern and Southern states of the Union. Strong majorities of both Protestants and Catholics wish for some form of religious education for their children.

For many Americans personal piety manifests itself through charitable giving. Gallup research reveals that three-fourths of Americans contributed food, clothing, or other property within the twelve months prior to the survey. Seventy percent contributed monetarily to non-church organizations, and 60% gave money to churches. People are much more willing to contribute material goods than they are to offer their time. Only 42% of the nation reported serving as unpaid volunteer workers for some charity within the last twelve months. Americans clearly prefer to give to charities that benefit the local community—59% compared to 11% benefiting the nation and 12% helping the world.

Involvement in small groups greatly bolsters the likelihood of an individual's practicing his or her personal faith. Princeton University sociologist Robert Wuthnow calls the small group movement in this nation a "quiet revolution." With almost half of the nation's population participating in small groups of some type, many faith communities are employing them as a means to develop greater spiritual disciplines within their congregations. Two members in three of all small groups—not just those that are church-related—say their groups lead them closer to God. For a majority of them (57%), the Bible has become more meaningful to them as a result of their group experience. Many—but not all—church-related small groups center around study of Scriptures and prayer. Wuthnow's landmark study estimates that there are more than 900,000 Bible study groups and 800,000 adult Sunday school classes in the United States today, and more are beginning every year.

In his 1948 text, *The Shaking of the Foundations,* theologian Paul Tillich declared the following:

> People sometimes say, "This is right in theory, but it doesn't work in practice." They ought to say, "This is wrong in theory and consequently it is wrong in practice." There is no true theory which could be wrong in practice. This contrast between theory and practice is contrived by people who want to escape hard and thorough thinking. . . . This is true of the history of science, morals and religion."

Certainly, American pragmatists have driven a wedge between theory and practice in the minds of many people. Within the religious arena, this wedge represents the distinction between religious belief and spiritual practice. Gallup research would indicate that the greatest chink in the bulwark of American religion is the lack of spiritual practices and disciplines actively exercised by religious adherents. Consider, for instance, the following statistic: 93% of Americans have a copy of the Bible or other Scriptures in their household, yet only 42% of the nation can name even five of the Ten Commandments. Spir-

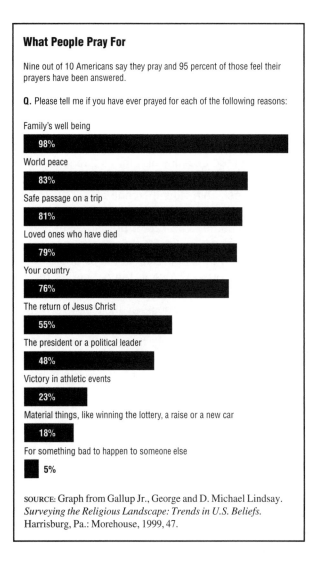

What People Pray For

Nine out of 10 Americans say they pray and 95 percent of those feel their prayers have been answered.

Q. Please tell me if you have ever prayed for each of the following reasons:

Family's well being
98%

World peace
83%

Safe passage on a trip
81%

Loved ones who have died
79%

Your country
76%

The return of Jesus Christ
55%

The president or a political leader
48%

Victory in athletic events
23%

Material things, like winning the lottery, a raise or a new car
18%

For something bad to happen to someone else
5%

SOURCE: Graph from Gallup Jr., George and D. Michael Lindsay. *Surveying the Religious Landscape: Trends in U.S. Beliefs.* Harrisburg, Pa.: Morehouse, 1999, 47.

ituality in America may be three thousand miles wide, but it remains only three inches deep.

Prayer

Nine out of ten U.S. adults say that they pray. Nearly all who pray think their prayers are heard (97%) and are answered (95%). Three persons in four pray daily. An additional 15% of adults claim that they pray at least weekly. Nearly all who pray believe that their prayers are heard by a supreme being such as God, Jesus Christ, Jehovah, or the Lord. Some differences in the objects and subjects of prayer exist according to religious preference. For example, Protestants are more likely than Catholics to pray for forgiveness (88%), personal salvation (80%), and for their country (80%). Catholics, on the other hand, are far more likely to pray for relatives who have died (95%). Saying grace or giving thanks to God before meals appears to be a fairly common practice in American homes. Protestants are somewhat more likely than Catholics to say they always or frequently say grace before meals, by a margin of 56% to 43%.

People pray for myriad reasons. From asking for the family's well-being to praying for the president and our nation's leaders, Americans offer prayers on a wide range of topics. Nearly half of those who pray say they started because of family influences (47%). The family continues to mold people's current praying practices. Thirty-four percent of adults in this country report that they pray most often at bedside or in bed; another 23% report praying elsewhere at home. By contrast, only 10% report praying the most when they are in a house of worship. Church influences are reported by one in ten people as the primary cause of prayer, and another 10% say they were led to prayer because of their beliefs. Prayer continues to exercise a pervasive influence over the lives of Americans. Among those who pray, 86% of the people believe that their prayers make them better persons. For most Americans prayer is something that originates in the family, is centered in the home, grows in importance, and generates feelings of peace and hope.

A majority of 55% of those who pray say that, compared to five years ago, prayer is now more important to them. Only 1% say it has become less important, and 43% judge it has remained about the same. Those who worry that young people are becoming less religious will be relieved to discover that young adults lead the nation in supporting the ever-increasing importance of prayer.

Most who pray (95%) contend that their petitions have been answered. Among those who say this, nearly all suggest the way they have been answered is in feeling more peaceful (96%) or hopeful (94%). Many declare that they got what they prayed for (62%), and others felt prayer resulted in divine inspiration or a feeling of being led by God (62%). About one in four (23%) reports hearing a voice or seeing a vision as a result of prayer.

In the end, 86% of those who pray believe their prayers make them better persons, and 77% are satisfied with their prayer life.

Further Resources

BOOKS

Bednarowski, Mary Farrell. *The Religious Imagination of American Women.* Bloomington, Ind.: Indiana University Press, 1999.

Leege, David C. *Rediscovering the Religious Factor in American Politics.* Armonk, N.Y.: M.E. Sharpe, 1993.

Lewis, James R. *Perspectives on the New Age.* Albany, N.Y.: State University of New York, 1992.

Introduction to *The Flowering of the Soul*
Essay

By: Lucinda Vardey

Date: 1999

Source: Vardey, Lucinda. "Introduction." *The Flowering of the Soul: A Book of Prayers by Women.* New York: Ballantine, 1999, 26–29.

About the Author: Lucinda Vardey (1949–) was born in London, England. She is a Roman Catholic writer. Her other writings include *Belonging: A Questioning Catholic Comes to Terms with the Church* (1989), *Mother Teresa: A Simple Path* (1995), and *An Anthology of Contemporary Spirituality* (1996). ∎

Introduction

Religion in the United States has been male dominated for most of its history. The Protestant Reformation had criticized monastic separation from the world and stressed that the proper role for women was in the family. St. Paul's statements regarding women being silent in church were strictly interpreted, and women had no opportunity to be heard in the churches. There were a few exceptions, however, among the Shakers, Quakers, and Christian Scientists. The struggle for a broader role for women was more difficult in the major denominations. In 1850, Oberlin granted the first theological degree to a woman, Antoinette Brown, who was later ordained in 1853 in the Congregationalist Church. Over time, women became more prominent in church and society through their participation in the temperance, abolitionist, and prohibition movements.

In the twentieth century, the movement toward woman's ordination gained further momentum. In 1970, the Lutheran Church in America and the American Lutheran Church permitted the ordination of women, while the more conservative Missouri Synod did not. The Episcopal Church in 1976 ruled that women could be ordained priests and in 1989 ordained its first female bishop, Barbara C. Harris. Neither the Roman Catholic nor the Orthodox churches ordain women to the priesthood. In 1972, the first Reformed rabbi was ordained, Sally Priesand.

In addition to ordination, another women's issue in religion was inclusive language in the scriptures and liturgy. Feminist theologians pointed out the problems with religious language that spoke of the "fatherhood of

God" or the "brotherhood of Man," claiming that this inhibited female spirituality.

Significance

As the role of women in religious communities has grown, there has also been a great increase in writings on women's spirituality. For the most part, this spirituality is a reinterpretation of Western monotheistic traditions. The concept of God having a male gender is rejected, and God is not referred to using male pronouns. Feminist spirituality often will also reject images of God perceived as authoritarian, parental, or disciplinarian (patriarchal characteristics) and instead emphasize "maternal" attributes such as nurturing, acceptance, and creativity.

A more radical version of feminist spirituality that emerged in the latter part of the twentieth century was associated with the rise of Neopaganism. Some feminists find the worship of an all-loving goddess or goddesses, rather than a god, to be more consonant with their views. The collective set of beliefs associated with this is sometimes known as *theology* as opposed to *theology*.

Lucinda Vardey's *The Flowering of the Soul: A Book of Prayers by Women* was one of the many responses in the 1990s for readings in the area of women's spirituality. The dedication reads: "In memory and gratitude for St. Catherine of Siena and for all women who pray." The book is divided into six sections: Introduction, Devotion, Supplication: The Requests, Surrender: The Responses, Contemplation, and The Fragrant Flowering of the Soul. Among the many women spiritual writers included in the book are Teresa of Avila, Hildegard of Bingen, Mother Teresa, Edith Stein, Simone Weil, Rosemary Radford Reuther, Elizabeth Cady Stanton, Harriet Beecher Stowe, and Riane Esler.

Primary Source

Introduction to *The Flowering of the Soul* [excerpt]

SYNOPSIS: The following excerpt is from the introduction to Vardey's anthology, in which she describes the search for a feminine image of God that goes beyond established archetypes.

Towards a Feminine Image of God

In her essay "The Long Journey Home: Reconnecting with the Great Mother," Riane Esler wrote, "Slowly, I also began to understand how, as a woman, I was in a miserable situation if I only have a God who's a Father, a King, a Lord. It implies that the only relationship I can have with the male deity is indirect. If we as women are to access the divine

Boticelli's *Madonna and Child*. The Virgin Mary is the most familiar and powerful feminine image in Christian faith. © FRANCIS G. MAYER/CORBIS. REPRODUCED BY PERMISSION.

in us, then a female deity, a divine Mother, is essential."

As Edith Stein taught that women have a responsibility to live, work, and express ourselves above all as "the image of God," for many women this image remains unclear. The contemporary American theologian Rosemary Radford Reuther wrote that women have not had a direct relationship with God, due to the monotheistic religions' promotion of male hierarchy. As a result, women were made to feel inferior because of being "connected to God secondarily, through the male." This image is still promoted and upheld particularly in the Catholic teachings, in that the representatives of God's covenant were males and "sons." Even though there are some women teachers who advocate replacing males with females—like replacing the word "son" with "daughter"—this is really only promoting the hierarchical single model of placing one sex over the other. The answer is in partnership between the two.

Naturally we have a way to go in seeking the feminine image of God beyond the established archetypes. As an example, the images of feminine holiness for Christian women have been confined to holy motherhood. Through the dogmatic teachings about Jesus' mother, Mary, being a perpetual virgin, girls were led to believe that feminine holiness meant being stainless of any sin of sexual desire or carnal experience. The other promoted image was of the repentant whore, which Christ's closest woman companion, Mary Magdalene, represented (even though we have no historical or scriptural fact to support this judgment). Mary Magdalene has become a vital symbol for Christian women as she was a woman who had an intimate and loving relationship with her Lord, and he loved her enough in return to seek her first after his resurrection. Mary Magdalene is a hopeful archetype for women who aspire to be "in the image of God," although the perception of her tainted past has made her seem lacking in holiness. Recent speculation, however, has suggested that she and Christ were married and that the marriage at Cana was theirs. Even if this is historically or scripturally inaccurate, the possibility of this idea of her being Christ's wife allows us to seek a place of equality and partnership as women with Christ.

Yet Christ also signifies, and taught, human partnership with God. For many women, Christ's humanity encompasses a pronounced femininity in balance with his masculinity; this brought hope and acceptance to those who were lost in a hierarchical heritage. His teachings and example, in fact, still instill hope, even though the rules of the institutional churches formed in His name tend to be lacking in balance and in feminine virtues. . . .

Before we explore the places to find Her, it is imperative to see where Her manifestations have occurred in the collective consciousness of the past. Divine feminine spirit is recorded in ancient literature and scripture under a variety of names and manifestations. First, there are the agents for Her spirit, like those in the Greek and Roman myths (Aphrodite/Venus, who is the goddess of love; Artemis/Diana, the hunter; and Athena/Minerva, the goddess of many counsels). There are the mother of corn, Demeter/Ceres, and the goddess of the earth, Gaia. Second, there are the consorts of the gods in various religions—Lilith, and Hera, and the Hindu goddesses Sarasvati (the goddess of speech and learning), and Kali (the "black" goddess, who represents the destructive aspect of the Divine), and last, the Buddhist bodhisattva consorts—Kuan Yin (the goddess of compassion) and the playful Tara (the goddess

who is in all nature and at the doors of life and death). Third, there are the humans—biblical women like Miriam and Sarah, and the Christian and Eastern saints, many of whose words are in this book and who by their actions, words, and work bring divine life into the concrete reality of matter and every day. Mary, the mother of Jesus, also has been an effective mediator between the realms of heaven and earth. It is believed that she, in her role as mother of divinity, has the mighty power to be heard and responded to by Christ, and so she is petitioned to intervene in the lives of Christian believers. She has been portrayed as Queen of Heaven, the Star of the Ocean, and the Sorrowful Mother (grieving for our world). In effect she has been placed in the role of Goddess, because of her supreme status and because she was God's chosen vessel as mother of Christ.

Further Resources

BOOKS

Chittister, Joan. *The Friendship of Women: A Spiritual Tradition*. Franklin, Wisc.: Sheed and Ward, 2001.

Labowitz, Shoni. *God, Sex, and Women of the Bible*. New York: Simon and Schuster, 1998.

Roberts, Wendy. *Celebrating Her: Feminist Ritualizing Comes of Age*. Cleveland, Ohio: Pilgrim Press, 1998.

"Jewish Education in the United States"

Study

By: Jack Wertheimer

Date: 1999

Source: Wertheimer, Jack. "Jewish Education in the United States." *American Jewish Year Book, 1999,* edited by David Singer. New York: The American Jewish Committee, 1999, 4–5, 112–113.

About the Author: Jack Wertheimer (1948–) was born in New York City. He received his master's degree and Ph.D. from Columbia University and is currently a faculty member in the Department of Jewish History at the Jewish Theological Seminary in New York, where he is the Joseph and Martha Mendelson Professor of American Jewish History. His writings include *The American Synagogue: A Sanctuary Transformed* (1987) and *A People Divided: Judaism in Contemporary America* (1993). ∎

Introduction

In Europe, the Jews had been expelled from Spain in 1492 and Portugal in 1497. The largest and most prosperous of the communities established by these refugee Spanish and Portuguese Jews was in Amsterdam. The United Netherlands was the only country in western Europe in which Jews could dwell legally. In 1630, the Dutch conquered Recife and the area around it in eastern Brazil. Recife offered many opportunities for Jews, and many emigrated there from Holland and elsewhere to form a large and flourishing community. In 1654, the Portuguese recaptured Recife, and the Jews had to leave. Some of the refugees went north to the Dutch colonies in the Caribbean, where Jewish communities already existed. Many returned to Amsterdam. And some landed in New Amsterdam, the future New York City. Thus, in this very roundabout manner, after being forced to uproot constantly because of racial and religious prejudice, Judaism was planted in what would become the United States of America.

By the time of the United States' independence, there were approximately 2,500 Jews in the United States, with settlements in New York, Newport, Charleston, Savannah, Philadelphia, and Richmond. In the beginning, these Jewish immigrants were "Sephardim," that is, Jews originally from Spain and Portugal. These Jews were soon joined by others, the "Ashkenazim," that is, Jews from Germany and Poland. From the beginning, the American Jewish community was itself diverse and contributed to the overall diversity of the new nation. American Jews also struggled over the degree to which they should assimilate into American culture. The Orthodox made very little accommodation, believing that to become assimilated in an overwhelmingly Christian country would result in the loss of Jewish identity. Reformed Judaism, established in 1885, was open to assimilation, while the Conservatives sought a middle path between the old ways and the new.

Significance

Later, in addition to the divisions of Orthodox, Reformed, and Conservative, there was added a fourth means of being Jewish in the twentieth century with the founding of Reconstructionism by Mordecai Kaplan in 1935. Kaplan argued that Reconstructionism was not a religion, as the term was generally understood, but rather a religious civilization. He described the breakdown of the Jewish community in the United States and called for the reconstruction of central Jewish communities that would coordinate the various activities being performed by Jewish organizations, both secular and religious. In his opinion, nonreligious Jews were to have as much a place in such a community as Orthodox, Reform, and Conservative Jews.

Such diversity, particularly the many different answers to the question of what it means to be American and Jewish, provided a daunting task to preserving Jewish identity. In response to this, the American Jewish community supported an extensive educational system. In addition to Hebrew language and religious schools, this system included many institutions of higher education, such as Brandeis University, Hebrew Union, and Jewish Theological Seminary of America.

The American Jewish community has made significant contributions to American society out of proportion to its small size. This is especially true in the area of philanthropic, charitable, and educational endeavors. A perennial challenge to this community has been to maintain its identity in an environment that is overwhelmingly non-Jewish. This has been a major concern for Jewish education.

Primary Source

"Jewish Education in the United States" [excerpt]

SYNOPSIS: The selection below, from an article written by Dr. Jack Wertheimer, appeared in the 1999 edition of the *American Jewish Year Book*. Entitled "Jewish Education in the United States," it surveyed the history of Jewish education in the United States and analyzed the challenges facing it. Some of the problems are common to other religious groups in the United States that struggle to maintain a belief system in an increasingly secular world. Others are unique to Judaism. While becoming a more accepted part of American society, the downside of assimilation has been an increase in intermarriage and the potential loss of Jewish identity. Considering the overall picture, Wertheimer concluded that the Jewish could be proud of the educational system they established.

The challenge of strengthening Jewish education is enormous because the field itself is so vast and complicated. Jonathan Woocher, a leading national spokesman on Jewish education, has taken the measure of its expansive dimensions: "American Jews today spend more than $1.5 billion annually to maintain an educational system that includes 3,000 schools and thousands more educational programs held in a wide variety of institutional settings. The system involves close to 50,000 teachers and more than a million Jews who study regularly—almost half of them young people between the ages of three and eighteen." Since this farflung network of autonomous schools and programs is primarily governed and funded through local initiatives in hundreds of Jewish communities throughout the United States, the field of Jewish education is highly diffuse. From a qualitative perspective, the situation is even more complex, for, as Woocher also notes,

A group of young Jewish children learn about Passover while attending Ramaz Hebrew Day School in New York. AP/WIDE WORLD PHOTOS. REPRODUCED BY PERMISSION.

American Jews maintain a "love-hate relationship" with Jewish education: on the one hand, a broad consensus that Jewish education stands as the final bulwark against powerful tides of assimilation; on the other, a "perception of failure and mediocrity in the system," prompting some to question the wisdom of "pouring additional dollars into the very enterprise that has brought American Jewry to its current sorry condition."

The upgrading of Jewish education—long a preoccupation of insiders—has taken on particular urgency since the release of the 1990 National Jewish Population Survey, which found that younger American Jews identify less intensely than their elders with fellow Jews, the organizations of the Jewish community, and Israel and, most dramatically, that by the late 1980s, more than half of all Jews were marrying outside the faith. "That figure served as a wake-up call to the American Jewish leadership," observed John Ruskay, a top executive of the New York Jewish community. Many analysts of the 1990 study also arrived at the conclusion that "the only serious antidote the Jewish community can muster to stem the escalating rate of intermarriage and other forms of assimilation" is Jewish education. As noted by the Commission on Jewish Education in North America, "the responsibility for developing Jewish identity and instilling a commitment to Judaism . . . now rests primarily with Jewish education." . . .

Conclusion: Great Expectations

It is instructive to situate our discussion of Jewish education within the larger field of American religious education. To what extent are the concerns of Jewish educators different from those of their Christian counterparts? And how does the system of Jewish education compare to Protestant and Catholic structures?

A recent listing of 19 religious high schools—Protestant, Catholic, and Jewish—in the Seattle area provides an illuminating perspective on the second question. Among the data presented are enumerations of the hours per week students engage in mandatory religious instruction. Only one of those schools reported that it required more than ten hours per week—the Northwest Yeshiva, the only Jewish day school in the sample. Three others offered six to ten hours, and the rest five hours or fewer, of religious instruction. Virtually all Protestant and Catholic religious high schools in this sample thus offered the same or fewer hours of religious instruction as do Jewish supplementary schools that meet two to three times per week—and only a fraction of the hours devoted to such subjects by Jewish day schools. While it is extremely difficult to get national statistics, a few surveys of Protestant and Catholic religious schooling suggest that there is nothing unusual in the Seattle figures. A study of Catholic parochial high schools in different sections of the country found that only one period per day was devoted to religious instruction—the equivalent of under five hours per week.

Jewish supplementary education is also more intensive than its Christian equivalents. Indeed, as the figures on religious day schools make evident, most Jewish students enrolled in such schools receive a more intensive education—five to six hours per week—than do Protestant and Catholic children enrolled in private religious all-day schools. Supplementary religious education in Christian settings tends to be limited to Sunday school. By contrast, one-day-a-week religious education has steadily eroded in the Jewish community in favor of more intensive forms of Jewish education.

The major weaknesses of Jewish education are evident in Christian schools too. A wide-ranging survey of religious education in six mainline Protestant denominations, encompassing a sample of over 560 churches, estimated that only 60 percent of children in churches are involved in religious education. By contrast, the percentage of all Jewish children receiving a Jewish education—not only ones who affiliate—is higher. Moreover, the dropout rate from church schools is exactly parallel to the pattern in Jewish schools: in both there is a steep decline during the junior and especially senior high-school years. In Protestant mainline churches, some 17 percent drop out between grades nine and ten. . . .

While such a comparison might reassure some within the Jewish community about the relative health and vitality of the field of Jewish education, it should, in fact help clarify the extent to which the enterprise of Jewish education differs radically from Christian religious schooling. Simply put, Jewish education addresses a multiplicity of goals and therefore must provide students with many more skills, greater know-how, and more wide-ranging understanding than does Christian religious education. In part this results from the complex nature of Jewish identity, a mix of religious and ethnic components—both of which must be integrated into the lives of young people. And in part it results from the nature of Jewish life in the United States, where Jews constitute a minority striving to sustain a distinctive religion and culture.

Further Resources

BOOKS

Bryan, Nichol. *Jewish Americans.* Edina, Minn.: Abdo, 2003.

Butwin, Frances. *The Jews in America.* Minneapolis, Minn.: Lerner, 1991.

Diner, Hasia. *Jews in America.* New York: Oxford University Press, 1999.

11

SCIENCE AND TECHNOLOGY

CHRISTOPHER CUMO

Entries are arranged in chronological order by date of primary source. For entries with one primary source, the entry title is the same as the primary source title. Entries with more than one primary source have an overall entry title, followed by the titles of the primary sources.

Important Events in Science and Technology, 1990–1999

1990

- On April 24, the space shuttle *Discovery* puts the Hubble Space Telescope (HST) into orbit around Earth.

- On May 22, Microsoft releases Windows version 3.0, which sells close to thirty million copies in a year; Windows becomes the industry standard in consumer operating systems.

- On June 1, U.S. president George Herbert Walker Bush and Soviet premier Mikhail Gorbachev sign a bilateral agreement to stop producing chemical weapons and to begin destroying stocks of agents by the end of 1992.

- In September, American geneticist W. French Anderson performs the first gene therapy on a four-year-old girl with an immune-system disorder called Adenosine Deaminase (ADA) deficiency.

- In October, the Human Genome Project (HGP) begins to map all human genes on their respective chromosomes.

1991

- Linus Torvalds, a student at the University of Helsinki, writes the code for the open-source Linux operating system and releases it over the Internet under a free public license.

- On April 3, the U.N. Security Council approves a Gulf cease-fire that includes stripping Iraq of its chemical and biological weapons.

- On August 14, scientists report that a worldwide band of volcanic dust from the eruptions of Mount Pinatubo (June–July 1991) in the Philippines could temporarily cool the climate worldwide.

- On September 26, four men and four women begin a two-year stay inside a sealed-off structure in Oracle, Arizona, called "Biosphere Two."

1992

- On March 6, a computer virus called "Michelangelo" strikes thousands of personal computers around the world.

- In April, University of Michigan anthropologist Milford Wolpoff disagrees with molecular biologists that Homo sapiens arose in Africa as little as 100,000 years ago. Rather Wolpoff believes that sapiens emerged throughout the world between 1 million and 500,000 years ago as populations of early man interbred with one another in Africa, Europe, and Asia.

- From May 7 to May 16, three astronauts from the *Endeavor* space shuttle walk in space for the first time, retrieving and repairing the Intelsat-6 satellite. Their walk lasts 8 hours, 29 minutes.

- In June, the U.S. Army begins collecting blood and saliva samples from all new recruits to create a genetic fingerprint of each soldier. The Army hopes genetic data will ease the identification of soldiers killed in combat.

- On June 9, the largest environmental summit opens in Rio de Janeiro, Brazil, with representatives from 178 nations.

- On June 28, two earthquakes hit southern California, including the third strongest in the United States during the twentieth century, registering 7.4 on the Richter scale.

- On September 12, NASA launches the space shuttle *Endeavor* with a crew that includes Mark C. Lee and N. Jan Davis, the first married couple in space.

- In September, American pharmaceutical firm Merck agrees to pay the Costa Rican National Institute of Biodiversity (*El Instituto Nacional de Biodiversidad,* or INBio) $1 million over two years for the right to search for new drugs in the tropical forests of Costa Rica.

- In October, American and British scientists unveil a technique for testing embryos *in vitro* for genetic abnormalities such as cystic fibrosis and hemophilia.

1993

- Curbside recycling increases 85 percent since 1988 in the number of U.S. communities that recycle.

- On January 3, Russian president Boris Yeltsin and U.S. president George H.W. Bush sign the Start II Treaty, aimed at eliminating about two-thirds of nuclear weapons in their nations.

- In February, the National Center for Supercomputing Applications (NCSA) releases the first version of Marc Andreessen's "Mosaic for X" web browser. There are some fifty Web servers.

- In March, George Washington University researchers clone human embryos and nurture them in a petri dish for several days.

- In March/April, the first issue of *Wired,* a magazine covering computers, the Internet, and culture related to high technology, is published.

- On April 30, the European Organization for Nuclear Research (CERN, *Conseil Europeen pour la Recherché Nucleaire*) announces that World Wide Web technology will be free for everyone.

- On May 6, the Pentagon shelves the Strategic Defense Initiative (SDI, or "Star Wars"), the futuristic defense program of former president Ronald Reagan.

- On June 16, biochemists at the U.S. National Cancer Institute announce that they have found at least one gene on the X chromosome and thus inherited from the mother that predisposes a person to homosexuality.

- In August, Marc Andreessen and coworkers release five versions of Mosaic for Macintosh and Windows. Windows NT is introduced.

- In September, an international research team, led by Daniel Cohen of the Center for the Study of Human Polymorphisms (*Centre d'Etude du Polymorphisme Humain,* or CEPH) in Paris, produces a map plotting some genes on all twenty-three pairs of human chromosomes.

- In September, NCSA releases a working version of the Mosaic browser for all common platforms: X, PC/Windows, and Macintosh.

- On September 6, Canadian Peter de Jager warns in *Computerworld* that computers with a binary code for the year may not function when 2000 begins.

- On December 9, U.S. astronauts finish a five-day repair on the $3 billion Hubble Space Telescope.

1994

- The revised open-source operating system Linux 1.0 is released over the Internet.

- On January 10, President Bill Clinton announces a deal under which Ukraine would give up its nuclear arsenal, the third largest in the world.

- In February, Bovine Growth Hormone (BGH), a genetically engineered hormone that boosts milk production in cows by as much as 15 percent, goes on sale after nearly ten years of legal battles.

- On February 11, five astronauts and a cosmonaut return to Earth aboard *Discovery* after the first joint U.S.-Russian space shuttle mission.

- On February 15, North Korea ends a year-long standoff with the International Atomic Energy Agency (IAEA), allowing inspectors to check seven declared nuclear plants.

- In March, Marc Andreessen and colleagues leave NCSA to form "Mosaic Communications Corporation," which soon becomes "Netscape Communications Corporation."

- On April 23, physicists at the U.S. Department of Energy's Fermi National Accelerator Laboratory in Chicago find evidence for the existence of the subatomic particle known as the top quark, the last of six quarks, the building blocks of all matter.

- From May to June, Marc Andreessen and coworkers create the original Netscape Navigator Internet browser. There are some fifteen hundred Web servers.

- In July, scientists discover three planets orbiting the dim remnants of a star that exploded long ago, evidence of a solar system beyond our own.

- In July, nearly two dozen mountain-sized chunks of the fragmented comet Shoemaker-Levy 9 crash into Jupiter, creating two-thousand-mile-high fireballs that are visible from backyard telescopes on Earth. Scientists learn about Jupiter's atmosphere, comets, and how a similar impact on Earth sixty-five million years ago might have killed off the dinosaurs.

- On December 15, Netscape Communications Corporation releases its graphical browser, Netscape Navigator 1.0. Within four months 75 percent of all Net users access the web using the Netscape browser.

1995

- Scientists record the hottest year to date, a fact some claim as evidence of global warming.

- On January 2, astronomers discover the most distant galaxy to date using the Keck telescope at the W. M. Keck Observatory in Mauna Kea, Hawaii. The galaxy is fifteen billion light years from Earth.

- On March 14, Norman E. Thagard becomes the first U.S. astronaut to fly in a Russian rocket on a mission to the Mir space station.

- In May, researchers at Duke University Medical Center transplant hearts from pigs into baboons. The hearts allowed the baboons to survive a few hours, proving that cross-species transplants are possible.

- On May 6, American molecular biologists Craig Venter and Hamilton O. Smith publish a paper in Science announcing their map of the entire genome of *Haemophilus influenzae,* a virus.

- On June 14, Congress passes the Communications Decency Act (CDA), part of the Telecommunications Reform Act, intended to regulate "lewd and obscene" content on the World Wide Web.

- In July, Sun Microsystems introduces Java, a miniaturized programming language.

- In August, a group of schoolchildren on a biology field trip in Minnesota discover deformed frogs, causing fear that insecticides, other toxins, and global warming are degrading the environment.

- On August 24, Microsoft releases Windows 95.

- On October 3, a jury acquits former football star O. J. Simpson of double murder in a high-profile trial. The jury discounted DNA evidence that fingered Simpson.

- On December 7, a probe from the spacecraft Galileo enters Jupiter's atmosphere.

- On December 10, NASA scientists receive the first data from the space probe Galileo—a message beamed over 2.3 billion miles (3.7 billion km).

1996

- On February 1, both houses of Congress approve the Telecommunications Reform Act, including the CDA.

- On February 8, President Clinton signs the Telecommunications Reform Act into law. On the same day, the American Civil Liberties Union (ACLU) and nineteen other groups file suit challenging it as a violation of the First Amendment's guarantee of free speech.

- In March, the Environmental Protection Agency (EPA) approves for sale genetically modified corn, known as Bt corn.

- In March, the U.S. Department of Agriculture releases in Florida the first genetically engineered insect, a predator mite to eat mites that damage strawberries and other crops.

- In April, farmers plant the first gene-spliced crops.

- In April, Genzyme Transgenics announces the birth of Grace, a transgenic goat carrying a gene that produces BR-96, an antibody being tested to deliver anticancer drugs.

- On August 6, Congress convenes the first hearing on the Y2K problem, focusing on how federal agencies will prepare their computers for the year 2000.

- On August 13, the Galileo space probe indicates that there may be water on one of Jupiter's moons. The water is frozen and so unable to support life.

- On September 25, NASA biochemist Shannon W. Lucid returns home after spending six months aboard the Russian space station Mir, earning her the title of America's most experienced astronaut.

1997

- U.S. farmers plant genetically modified soybeans on more than 8 million acres and genetically modified corn on more than 3.5 million acres.

- In February, researchers at PPL Therapeutics, in Virginia, announce the birth of a transgenic calf named Rosie, whose milk contains alpha-lactalbumin, a human protein that contains essential amino acids, making it nutritious for premature infants who cannot nurse.

- In March, the Hale-Bopp comet comes within 122 million miles of Earth.

- On April 21, the ashes of 1960s LSD guru Timothy Leary and *Star Trek* creator Gene Roddenberry are blasted into space in the first space funeral.

- On May 11, the IBM supercomputer Deep Blue makes chess history by defeating Garry Kasparov, the first time a computer beats a reigning world champion.

- On June 26, the U.S. Supreme Court rules the Communications Decency Act, meant to regulate "indecent" material on the Internet, a violation of the First Amendment's guarantee of free speech.

- On July 4, the U.S. Pathfinder space probe, carrying the Sojourner rover, makes a historic landing on Mars.

- On July 11, American molecular biologists Anne Stone and Mark Stoneking announce that Neanderthal DNA is too dissimilar to our DNA for Neanderthal to be our direct ancestor. Neanderthal's place in human lineage remains controversial.

- On October 2, scientists deliberately freeze their ship, the Canadian icebreaker *Des Groseilliers,* into the Arctic ice for a yearlong study of changes in weather in the Arctic.

- In December, representatives from 160 countries meet in Kyoto, Japan, to discuss climate change and agree to diminish the release of greenhouse gases that may cause global warming by the year 2012.

1998

- In January, molecular biologist Craig Venter, head of the biotech company Celeva, announces plans to decode the entire human genome by 2001, years ahead of the Human Genome Project deadline.

- On January 16, NASA approves former astronaut John Herschel Glenn, Jr., age seventy-six, for an October shuttle flight.

- On January 21, former University of California mathematics professor Theodore John Kaczynski pleads guilty to being

the anti-technology Unabomber in exchange for a sentence of life in prison without parole.

- On January 24, the National Research Council, of the National Academy of Sciences, conducts a workshop on failed stars and super planets.

- In February, 21.74 inches of rain fall on Santa Barbara, California, its highest monthly total on record. Scientists speculate that this deluge is the result of global warming.

- On February 2, President Bill Clinton names Eileen M. Collins as the first woman to lead a U.S. space mission.

- From February 22 to February 23, El Niño-powered storms hit Orlando, Florida, spawning tornadoes that kill at least thirty-six people and damage or destroy scores of buildings.

- On February 26, the last total solar eclipse of the millennium is visible from the Western Hemisphere.

- On March 5, NASA releases initial findings of the *Lunar Prospector.*

- In May, molecular biologists announce that DNA testing proves that U.S. president Thomas Jefferson had at least one child with Sally Hemings, one of his slaves.

- In May, India performs five underground nuclear tests, despite strong international disapproval. Pakistan answers with tests of its own.

- On May 19, a failure of its onboard control system causes the Galaxy IV satellite to rotate out of position, disrupting pager and television service for millions of people in the U.S. and the Caribbean, as well as some ATM services for banks.

- On June 4, space shuttle *Discovery* docks with Russian space station Mir to collect astronaut Andrew Thomas after he spends four months aboard Mir.

- On June 6, the National Research Council holds a forum in Los Angeles on the risk of an asteroid striking the earth.

- On June 21, University of Hawaii scientists, using a variation of Ian Wilmut's "Dolly" technique, clone a mouse, creating not only dozens of copies but three generations of clones.

- On June 25, Microsoft releases Windows 98.

- On July 30, Monica S. Lewinsky hands over to Independent Counsel Kenneth W. Starr a dress she alleges may contain evidence of a sexual relationship with President Clinton. DNA analysis of semen stains on the dress match DNA from a blood sample given by Clinton.

- From September 23 to October 1, NASA sponsors Challenge Mission, an eight-day deployment of the Carpenter Space Analog Station on the sea floor off Key Largo, Florida.

- On October 28, President Bill Clinton signs into law the Digital Millennium Copyright Act.

- On October 29, space shuttle *Discovery* launches with Senator and former astronaut John Glenn, seventy-seven, aboard as a payload specialist.

- In November, two research teams succeed in growing embryonic stem cells.

- On November 15, young people aged ten to sixteen from fifty-four countries gathered in Cambridge for the Massachusetts Institute of Technology (MIT) Junior Summit '98.

- On November 17, the Leonid meteor shower, said to be the most intense meteor shower in thirty years, occurs, threatening five hundred satellites circling Earth.

- On December 9, scientists announce the nematode worm, *caenorhabditis elegans,* as the first animal to have its entire genome mapped.

1999

- Fifty-eight hundred pairs of bald eagles flourish in the Continental United States; the birds are removed from the endangered species list.

- On March 26, the "Melissa" computer virus impairs e-mail systems around the nation and affects 19 percent of U.S. corporations, but causes little permanent damage.

- On April 2, police arrest David L. Smith for creating the Melissa virus. They had tracked him using the same technology that allows his virus to spread.

- From April 25 to April 27, International Data Group, one of the largest technology consultants in the world and publisher of high-tech periodicals, sponsors the first Enter Tech conference in Carlsbad, California, bringing together Silicon Valley and Hollywood executives to explore the union of technology and movies.

- On April 30, *Science* publishes two companion articles indicating that the deformities of the so-called "sentinel frogs" found in Minnesota and other states are caused by a parasite, not by global warming or insecticides as was thought.

- In May, researchers discover signs of premature aging in the cells of Dolly, the first sheep cloned from the cell of an adult ewe.

- On May 5, Microsoft releases Windows 98 Special Edition.

- In June, the computer virus "Worm.Explore.Zip" infiltrates systems around the nation through e-mail, burrowing into software, erasing files, and shutting down networks.

- In July, New York City has its warmest and driest July on record, with temperatures climbing above 95 degrees F (35 degrees C) for eleven days. Scientists blame the heat on global warming.

- In August, U.S. Attorney General Janet Reno heads the Working Group to address the issue of cybercrime.

- In November and December, on-line holiday sales triple from the total of $73 million in 1998 to $3.17 billion.

- On December 20, in New Orleans, Jazz, an endangered African wildcat, becomes the first mammal to be born from a frozen embryo implanted in the womb of a common species, in this case a house cat.

Jurassic Park
Novel

By: Michael Crichton

Date: 1990

Source: Crichton, Michael. *Jurassic Park*. New York: Alfred A. Knopf, 1990, 66–69.

About the Author: Michael Crichton (1942–) was born in Chicago, Illinois, and he earned a B.A. in anthropology in 1965 from Harvard University, and an M.D. in 1969 from Harvard Medical School. He turned to writing rather than the practice of medicine. His novels focus on the implications of scientific developments. His fiction has garnered awards and has been the source of several popular films. ∎

Michael Crichton, December 1990. Crichton's novel *Jurassic Park* involved scientists cloning dinosaurs to populate a "dinosaur zoo." © DOUGLAS KIRKLAND/CORBIS. REPRODUCED BY PERMISSION.

Introduction

In 1953, American chemist James D. Watson and his British counterpart, Francis Crick, identified deoxyribonucleic acid (DNA) as the molecule of heredity. They described its structure as a spiral ladder with each rung composed of two of the four nucleotide bases—adenine, thymine, guanine, and cytosine. Adenine always bonds with thymine, and guanine with cytosine. The nucleotide bases bond one atop another to create the DNA ladder structure. Half a strand of DNA might be the sequence thymine, cytosine, cytosine, guanine. The other half must be adenine, guanine, guanine, cytosine.

The commercial possibility of DNA emerged in the early 1970s when American chemist Hamilton O. Smith and other researchers discovered a class of enzymes that can cut out sequences of nucleotide bases. Each enzyme cuts out a unique sequence. Enzyme A, for example, might cut out only the sequence thymine, adenine, adenine, cytosine—whereas enzyme B might cut out only the sequence guanine, guanine, guanine. These enzymes allowed scientists to cut out sequences of nucleotide bases from one organism and transfer them to another, creating a genetically engineered organism. In 1980, the U.S. Supreme Court ruled that scientists and corporations could patent a genetically engineered organism, giving them the exclusive right to market their organisms.

Significance

Michael Crichton examines the consequences of the commercialization of genetic engineering in his novel *Jurassic Park*. In the novel, scientists at International Genetic Technologies Inc. (InGen) of Palo Alto, California, isolated DNA from fifteen species of dinosaur remains, using the DNA to engineer live versions of these long extinct animals. A wealthy entrepreneur, John Hammond, built a zoo to house these dinosaurs and planned to open it to the public, reaping huge profits.

Geneticist Lewis Dodgson, of Biosyn Corporation of Cupertino, California, speculated that Hammond could charge as much as $5,000 per visitor. The lure of such profits was too great for Dodgson to resist. Although he acknowledged that patents protected InGen's dinosaurs, Dodgson intended to circumvent these patents by pirating InGen's dinosaur DNA and changing the sequence of nucleotide bases enough so that no one would know that he had stolen the DNA from InGen. Biosyn's board of directors authorized Dodgson to steal InGen's dinosaur DNA in hopes of profiting, as InGen and Hammond surely would.

Although *Jurassic Park* may strike readers as fanciful, it has a serious message. The lure of profits was corrupting scientists (as it had Lewis Dodgson), Michael Crichton believed, who sought any means of genetically engineering an organism of commercial value. Crichton believed the commercial potential of genetic engineering had caused scientists to value profits more highly than the pursuit of knowledge.

In Crichton's opinion, the danger of this attitude was acute because no government agency had the mandate or ability to monitor biotechnology research in thousands of corporations and universities throughout the United States. This lack of oversight gave scientists carte blanche to act as they wished without fear of consequences. Dodgson typified this new attitude, as he was willing to steal DNA from another company and pass a modified version of it as his own—secure in the knowledge that no one would detect the theft.

Crichton worries that while the benefits of genetic engineering should extend to everyone, patent protection concentrates these benefits in corporations and universities. Biotechnology does not serve humanity, but rather corporations and venture capitalists. Biotechnology has become an extension of capitalism, which places profits, rather than science, above all else.

Primary Source

Jurassic Park [excerpt]

SYNOPSIS: In this excerpt InGen has isolated DNA from the fossils of fifteen dinosaur species, using it to restore these long extinct animals to life. In-Gen and John Hammond were building a dinosaur zoo that would heap profits on them. Lewis Dodgson of Biosyn intended to steal DNA from InGen, engineer dinosaurs of his own, and profit as InGen would.

Target of Opportunity

The Biosyn Corporation of Cupertino, California, had never called an emergency meeting of its board of directors. The ten directors now sitting in the conference room were irritable and impatient. It was 8:00 p.m. They had been talking among themselves for the last ten minutes, but slowly had fallen silent. Shuffling papers. Looking pointedly at their watches.

"What are we waiting for?" one asked.

"One more," Lewis Dodgson said. "We need one more." He glanced at his watch. Ron Meyer's office had said he was coming up on the six o'clock plane from San Diego. He should be here by now, even allowing for traffic from the airport.

"You need a quorum?" another director asked.

"Yes," Dodgson said. "We do."

That shut them up for a moment. A quorum meant that they were going to be asked to make an important decision. And God knows they were, although Dodgson would have preferred not to call a

meeting at all. But Steingarten, the head of Biosyn, was adamant. "You'll have to get their agreement for this one, Lew," he had said.

Depending on who you talked to, Lewis Dodgson was famous as the most aggressive geneticist of his generation, or the most reckless. Thirty-four, balding, hawk-faced, and intense, he had been dismissed by Johns Hopkins as a graduate student, for planning gene therapy on human patients without obtaining the proper FDA protocols. Hired by Biosyn, he had conducted the controversial rabies vaccine test in Chile. Now he was the head of product development at Biosyn, which supposedly consisted of "reverse engineering": taking a competitor's product, tearing it apart, learning how it worked, and then making your own version. In practice, it involved industrial espionage, much of it directed toward the InGen corporation.

In the 1980s, a few genetic engineering companies began to ask, "What is the biological equivalent of a Sony Walkman?" These companies weren't interested in pharmaceuticals or health; they were interested in entertainment, sports, leisure activities, cosmetics, and pets. The perceived demand for "consumer biologicals" in the 1990s was high. InGen and Biosyn were both at work in this field.

Biosyn had already achieved some success, engineering a new, pale trout under contract to the Department of Fish and Game of the State of Idaho. This trout was easier to spot in streams, and was said to represent a step forward in angling. (At least, it eliminated complaints to the Fish and Game Department that there were no trout in the streams.) The fact that the pale trout sometimes died of sunburn, and that its flesh was soggy and tasteless, was not discussed. Biosyn was still working on that, and—

The door opened and Ron Meyer entered the room, slipped into a seat. Dodgson now had his quorum. He immediately stood.

"Gentlemen," he said, "we're here tonight to consider a target of opportunity: InGen."

Dodgson quickly reviewed the background. In-Gen's start-up in 1983, with Japanese investors. The purchase of three Cray XMP supercomputers. The purchase of Isla Nublar in Costa Rica. The stockpiling of amber. The unusual donations to zoos around the world, from the New York Zoological Society to the Ranthapur Wildlife Park in India.

"Despite all these clues," Dodgson said, "we still had no idea where InGen might be going. The

Two dinosaurs hide in bushes in a scene still from *Jurassic Park* (1993), the movie based on Crichton's book. The film made an even larger audience question the consequences of the commercialization of genetic engineering. THE KOBAL COLLECTION/AMBLIN/UNIVERSAL. REPRODUCED BY PERMISSION.

company seemed obviously focused on animals; and they had hired researchers with an interest in the past—paleobiologists, DNA phylogeneticists, and so on."

"Then, in 1987, InGen bought an obscure company called Millipore Plastic Products in Nashville, Tennessee. This was an agribusiness company that had recently patented a new plastic with the characteristics of an avian eggshell. This plastic could be shaped into an egg and used to grow chick embryos. Starting the following year, InGen took the entire output of this millipore plastic for its own use."

"Dr. Dodgson, this is all very interesting—"

"At the same time," Dodgson continued, "construction was begun on Isla Nublar. This involved massive earthworks, including a shallow lake two miles long, in the center of the island. Plans for resort facilities were let out with a high degree of con-

fidentiality, but it appears that InGen has built a private zoo of large dimensions on the island."

One of the directors leaned forward and said, "Dr. Dodgson. *So what?*"

"It's not an ordinary zoo," Dodgson said. "This zoo is unique in the world. It seems that InGen has done something quite extraordinary. They have managed to clone extinct animals from the past."

"What animals?"

"Animals that hatch from eggs, and that require a lot of room in a zoo."

"What animals?"

"Dinosaurs," Dodgson said. "They are cloning dinosaurs."

The consternation that followed was entirely misplaced, in Dodgson's view. The trouble with money men was that they didn't keep up: they had invested in a field, but they didn't know what was possible.

In fact, there had been discussion of cloning dinosaurs in the technical literature as far back as 1982. With each passing year, the manipulation of DNA had grown easier. Genetic material had already been extracted from Egyptian mummies, and from the hide of a quagga, a zebra-like African animal that had become extinct in the 1880s. By 1985, it seemed possible that quagga DNA might be reconstituted, and a new animal grown. If so, it would be the first creature brought back from extinction solely by reconstruction of its DNA. If that was possible, what else was also possible? The mastodon? The saber-toothed tiger? The dodo?

Or even a dinosaur?

Of course, no dinosaur DNA was known to exist anywhere in the world. But by grinding up large quantities of dinosaur bones it might be possible to extract fragments of DNA. Formerly it was thought that fossilization eliminated all DNA. Now that was recognized as untrue. If enough DNA fragments were recovered, it might be possible to clone a living animal.

Back in 1982, the technical problems had seemed daunting. But there was no theoretical barrier. It was merely difficult, expensive, and unlikely to work. Yet it was certainly possible, if anyone cared to try.

InGen had apparently decided to try.

"What they have done," Dodgson said, "is build the greatest single tourist attraction in the history of the world. As you know, zoos are extremely popular. Last year, more Americans visited zoos than all professional baseball and football games combined. And the Japanese love zoos—there are fifty zoos in Japan, and more being built. And for this zoo, InGen can charge whatever they want. Two thousand dollars a day, ten thousand dollars a day . . . And then there is the *merchandising.* The picture books, T-shirts, video games, caps, stuffed toys, comic books, and pets."

"Pets?"

"Of course. If InGen can make full-size dinosaurs, they can also make pygmy dinosaurs as household pets. What child won't want a little dinosaur as a pet? A little patented animal for their very own. InGen will sell millions of them. And InGen will engineer them so that these pet dinosaurs can only eat InGen pet food. . . ."

"Jesus," somebody said.

"Exactly," Dodgson said. "The zoo is the centerpiece of an enormous enterprise."

"You said these dinosaurs will be patented?"

"Yes. Genetically engineered animals can now be patented. The Supreme Court ruled on that in favor of Harvard in 1987. InGen will own its dinosaurs, and no one else can legally make them."

"What prevents us from creating our own dinosaurs?" someone said.

"Nothing, except that they have a five-year start. It'll be almost impossible to catch up before the end of the century."

He paused. "Of course, if we could obtain examples of their dinosaurs, we could reverse engineer them and make our own, with enough modifications in the DNA to evade their patents."

"Can we obtain examples of their dinosaurs?"

Dodgson paused. "I believe we can, yes."

Somebody cleared his throat. "There wouldn't be anything illegal about it. . . ."

"Oh no," Dodgson said quickly. "Nothing illegal. I'm talking about a legitimate source of their DNA. A disgruntled employee, or some trash improperly disposed of, something like that."

"Do you have a legitimate source, Dr. Dodgson?"

"I do," Dodgson said. "But I'm afraid there is some urgency to the decision, because InGen is experiencing a small crisis, and my source will have to act within the next twenty-four hours."

A long silence descended over the room. The men looked at the secretary, taking notes, and the tape recorder on the table in front of her.

"I don't see the need for a formal resolution on this," Dodgson said. "Just a sense of the room, as to whether you feel I should proceed. . . ."

Slowly the heads nodded.

Nobody spoke. Nobody went on record. They just nodded silently.

"Thank you for coming, gentlemen," Dodgson said. "I'll take it from here."

Further Resources

BOOKS

Belcher, Brian, and Geoffrey Hawtin. *A Patent on Life: Ownership of Plant and Animal Research.* Ottawa, Ontario, Canada: IDRC, 1991.

Busch, Lawrence, et al. *Plants, Power and Profits: Social, Economic, and Ethical Consequences of the New Biotechnologies.* Cambridge, Mass.: Basil Blackwell, 1991.

Shay, Don, and Judy Duncan. *The Making of Jurassic Park.* New York: Ballentine Books, 1993.

PERIODICALS

Fineman, Howard. "Jurassic Park, 2002." *Newsweek,* November 11, 2002, 32.

Mongkolporn, Usanee. "Biotech Patents Up." *Nation,* June 11, 2002, 14–15.

WEBSITES

Beard, Carla. "Jurassic Park Teaching Resources." Available online at http://www.fayette.k12.in.us/~cbeard/jp (accessed July 15, 2003).

"Biotech: Ethics & the Industry." Strategis. Available online at http://strategis.ic.gc.ca/SSG/bb00001e.html; website home page: http://strategis.ic.gc.ca (accessed July 15, 2003).

Hinde, Tony. "Jurassic Park." Hinde Sight. Available online at http://www.ozcraft.com/scifidu/jurasic.html; website home page: http://www.ozcraft.com (accessed July 15, 2003).

"JPDB." Jurassic Park Database. Available online at http://www.jpdatabase.net (accessed July 15, 2003).

Jurassic Park. Available online at http://www.jurassicpark.com (accessed April 29, 2003).

"Jurassic Park Institute." Available online at http://www.jpinstitute.com/ (accessed July 15, 2003).

"The Recent African Genesis of Humans"

Magazine article

By: Allan C. Wilson and Rebecca L. Cann

Date: April 1992

Source: Wilson, Allan C., and Rebecca L. Cann. "The Recent African Genesis of Humans." *Scientific American* 266, April 1992, 68–73.

About the Authors: Allan Charles Wilson (1934–1991) was born in Ngaruawahia, New Zealand, in 1934, and immigrated to the United States in 1955, where he served thirty-five years as professor of biochemistry at the University of California at Berkeley. He received a MacArthur "Genius" Award, was a visiting professor at Harvard University, St. Louis University, the Massachusetts Institute of Technology, and universities in Israel and Kenya, and was nominated for a Nobel Prize.

Rebecca L. Cann received a Ph.D. in genetics from the University of California at Berkeley in 1982. She is professor of genetics and molecular biology at the University of Hawaii. Her research centers on quantifying the genetic diversity and the spread of diseases among Polynesians and endangered Hawaiian birds. ∎

Introduction

During the 1990s, scientists debated with unusual fervor the time and place of modern human origins. The debate pitted biochemists against paleoanthropologists. At issue was whether scientists could learn more about human origins by studying genes (molecules that code for traits) as biochemists did, or by studying fossils as paleoanthroplogists did.

Until 1967, paleoanthropologists monopolized the debate. That year, American anthropologist Vincent M. Sarich and biochemist Allan C. Wilson announced that humans accumulated mutations—chemical changes to deoxyribonucleic acid (DNA), the molecule of heredity—at a constant rate. This constancy allowed them to calculate back to the time when a single gene pool existed—after which diverged the line leading to humans and the line leading to the African apes, the two species of chimpanzee and the gorilla. This single gene pool must have been the common ancestor of humans and the African apes and had lived five million years ago, announced Sarich and Wilson. Their work implied that humans had originated in Africa because it was home to the African apes. Sarich and Wilson's announcement stunned paleoanthropologists, who had thought that the common ancestor of humans and the African apes lived between thirty million and one hundred million years ago.

Significance

No less stunning was the work of Wilson and Rebecca L. Cann. Whereas Sarich and Wilson had used DNA in a cell's nucleus in calculating the time of divergence between the lines leading to humans and African apes, Wilson and Cann used a second source of DNA—that in mitochondria, the sites in a cell that metabolize energy. Unlike nuclear DNA, mitochondrial DNA (mtDNA) passes through only the maternal line. Males contribute no mtDNA to offspring.

Like nuclear DNA, mtDNA accumulates mutations, allowing Wilson and Cann to calculate back to the time

when all modern humans shared the same mtDNA. This would have been the time when modern humans arose. Wilson and Cann stunned paleoanthropologists by announcing that modern humans arose not 500,000 years ago, as some thought, but only 200,000 years ago. Additional mtDNA studies fixed the date even later, at 100,000 years ago.

Equally dramatic, Wilson and Cann found the greatest diversity of mtDNA among Africans, implying that their populations were the oldest among modern humans, as they had more time to accumulate the most mutations. Modern humans must, therefore, have arisen in Africa between 100,000 and 200,000 years ago. Beginning about 100,000 years ago, they migrated into western Asia and later to Europe, the rest of Asia, Australia, and the Americas.

Wilson and Cann's work implied that modern humans replaced more ancient populations as they migrated with little or no interbreeding. These conclusions generated controversy. Even if modern humans originated in Africa, the frequency with which they have sex makes improbable the notion that they did not interbreed in large numbers with populations of early man. Moreover paleoanthropologists believed that a recent African origin of modern humans does not agree with the fossil evidence, the subject of the entry "The Multiregional Evolution of Humans."

Primary Source

"The Recent African Genesis of Humans" [excerpt]

SYNOPSIS: In this excerpt Allan C. Wilson and Rebecca L. Cann argue that evidence from mtDNA put the origin of modern humans between 100,000 and 200,000 years ago in Africa. Thereafter they settled the rest of the world, replacing populations of early man with little or no interbreeding.

Genetic Studies Reveal That an African Woman of 200,000 Years Ago Was Our Common Ancestor

In the quest for the facts about human evolution, we molecular geneticists have engaged in two major debates with the paleontologists. Arguing from their fossils, most paleontologists had claimed the evolutionary split between humans and the great apes occurred as long as 25 million years ago. We maintained human and ape genes were too similar for the schism to be more than a few million years old. After 15 years of disagreement, we won that argument, when the paleontologists admitted we had been right and they had been wrong.

Once again we are engaged in a debate, this time over the latest phase of human evolution. The paleontologists say modern humans evolved from their archaic forebears around the world over the

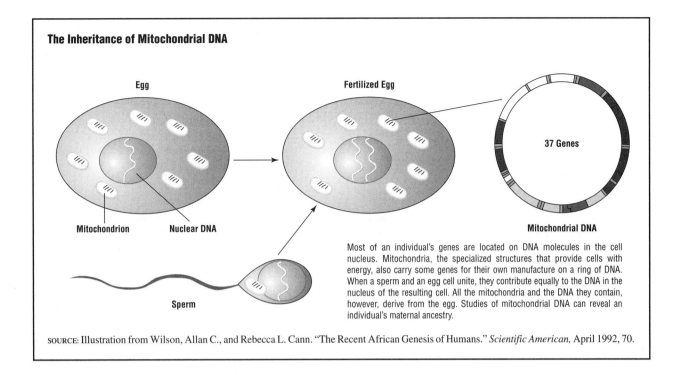

The Inheritance of Mitochondrial DNA

Egg

Fertilized Egg

37 Genes

Mitochondrion   Nuclear DNA

Mitochondrial DNA

Sperm

Most of an individual's genes are located on DNA molecules in the cell nucleus. Mitochondria, the specialized structures that provide cells with energy, also carry some genes for their own manufacture on a ring of DNA. When a sperm and an egg cell unite, they contribute equally to the DNA in the nucleus of the resulting cell. All the mitochondria and the DNA they contain, however, derive from the egg. Studies of mitochondrial DNA can reveal an individual's maternal ancestry.

SOURCE: Illustration from Wilson, Allan C., and Rebecca L. Cann. "The Recent African Genesis of Humans." *Scientific American,* April 1992, 70.

past million years. Conversely, our genetic comparisons convince us that all humans today can be traced along maternal lines of descent to a woman who lived about 200,000 years ago, probably in Africa. Modern humans arose in one place and spread elsewhere.

Neither the genetic information of living subjects nor the fossilized remains of dead ones can explain in isolation how, when and where populations originated. But the former evidence has a crucial advantage in determining the structure of family trees: living genes must have ancestors, whereas dead fossils may not have descendants. Molecular biologists know the genes they are examining must have been passed through lineages that survived to the present; paleontologists cannot be sure that the fossils they examine do not lead down an evolutionary blind alley.

The molecular approach is free from several other limitations of paleontology. It does not require well-dated fossils or tools from each part of the family tree it hopes to describe. It is not vitiated by doubts about whether tools found near fossil remains were in fact made and used by the population those remains represent. Finally, it concerns itself with a set of characteristics that is complete and objective.

A genome, or full set of genes, is complete because it holds all the inherited biological information

of an individual. Moreover, all the variants on it that appear within a population—a group of individuals who breed only with one another—can be studied as well, so specific peculiarities need not distort the interpretation of the data. Genomes are objective sources of data because they present evidence that has not been defined, at the outset, by any particular evolutionary model. Gene sequences are empirically verifiable and not shaped by theoretical prejudices.

The fossil record, on the other hand, is infamously spotty because a handful of surviving bones may not represent the majority of organisms that left no trace of themselves. Fossils cannot, in principle, be interpreted objectively: the physical characteristics by which they are classified necessarily reflect the models the paleontologists wish to test. If one classifies, say, a pelvis as human because it supported an upright posture, then one is presupposing that bipedalism distinguished early hominids from apes. Such reasoning tends to circularity. The paleontologist's perspective therefore contains a built-in bias that limits its power of observation.

As such, biologists trained in modern evolutionary theory must reject the notion that the fossils provide the most direct evidence of how human evolution actually proceeded. Fossils help to fill in the knowledge of how biological processes worked in the past, but they should not blind us to new lines of evidence

Reconstruction of a Neanderthal female, 1992. The head is based on actual fossilized skulls while the body is a modification of casts made from living people believed to have the same build. NEG./TRANSPARENCY NO. DF CC-4745, COURTESY THE LIBRARY, AMERICAN MUSEUM OF NATURAL HISTORY.

or new interpretations of poorly understood and provisionally dated archaeological materials.

All the advantages of our field stood revealed in 1967, when Vincent M. Sarich, working in Allan Wilson's laboratory at the University of California at Berkeley, challenged a fossil primate called *Ramapithecus.* Paleontologists had dated its fossils to about 25 million years ago. On the basis of the enamel thickness of the molars and other skeletal characteristics, they believed that *Ramapithecus* appeared after the divergence of the human and ape lineages and that it was directly ancestral to humans.

Sarich measured the evolutionary distance between humans and chimpanzees by studying their blood proteins, knowing the differences reflected mutations that have accumulated since the species diverged. (At the time, it was much easier to compare proteins for subtle differences than to compare the genetic sequences that encode the proteins.) To check that mutations had occurred equally fast in both lineages, he compared humans and chimpanzees against a reference species and found that all the genetic distances tallied.

Sarich now had a molecular clock; the next step was to calibrate it. He did so by calculating the mutation rate in other species whose divergences could be reliably dated from fossils. Finally, he applied the clock to the chimpanzee-human split, dating it to between five and seven million years ago—far later than anyone had imagined.

At first, most paleontologists clung to the much earlier date. But new fossil finds undermined the human status of *Ramapithecus:* it is now clear *Ramapithecus* is actually *Sivapithecus,* a creature ancestral to orangutans and not to any of the African apes at all. Moreover, the age of some sivapithecine fossils

Reconstructions of a *Homo erectus* male and female, 1992. The reconstructions were made for the Hall of Human Biology and Evolution at the American Museum of Natural History. NEG./TRANSPARENCY NO. DF 68-118A, COURTESY THE LIBRARY, AMERICAN MUSEUM OF NATURAL HISTORY.

was downgraded to only about six million years. By the early 1980s almost all paleontologists came to accept Sarich's more recent date for the separation of the human and ape lines. Those who continue to reject his methods have been reduced to arguing that Sarich arrived at the right answer purely by chance.

Two novel concepts emerged from the early comparisons of proteins from different species. One was the concept of inconsequential, or neutral, mutations. Molecular evolution appears to be dominated by such mutations, and they accumulate at surprisingly steady rates in surviving lineages. In other words, evolution at the gene level results mainly from the relentless accumulation of mutations that seem to be neither harmful nor beneficial. The second concept, molecular clocks, stemmed from the observation that rates of genetic change from point mutations (changes in individual DNA base pairs) were so steady over long periods that one could use them to time divergences from a common stock.

We could begin to apply these methods to the reconstruction of later stages in human evolution only after 1980, when DNA restriction analysis made it possible to explore genetic differences with high resolution. Workers at Berkeley, including Wes Brown, Mark Stoneking and us, applied the technique to trace the maternal lineages of people sampled from around the world.

The DNA we studied resides in the mitochondria, cellular organelles that convert food into a form of energy the rest of the cell can use. Unlike the DNA of the nucleus, which forms bundles of long fibers, each consisting of a protein-coated double helix, the mitochondrial DNA comes in small, two-strand rings. Whereas nuclear DNA encodes an estimated 100,000 genes—most of the information needed to make a human being—mitochondrial DNA encodes only 37. In this handful of genes, every one is essential: a single adverse mutation in any of them is known to cause some severe neurological diseases.

For the purpose of scientists studying when lineages diverged, mitochondrial DNA has two advantages over nuclear DNA. First, the sequences in mitochondrial DNA that interest us accumulate mutations rapidly and steadily, according to empirical observations. Because many mutations do not alter the mitochondrion's function, they are effectively neutral, and natural selection does not eliminate them.

This mitochondrial DNA therefore behaves like a fast-ticking clock, which is essential for identifying recent genetic changes. Any two humans chosen randomly from anywhere on the planet are so alike in most of their DNA sequences that we can measure evolution in our species only by concentrating on the genes that mutate fastest. Genes controlling skeletal characters do not fall within this group.

Second, unlike nuclear DNA, mitochondrial DNA is inherited from the mother alone, unchanged except for chance mutations. The father's contribution ends up on the cutting-room floor, as it were. The nuclear genes, to which the father does contribute, descend in what we may call ordinary lineages, which are of course important to the transmission of physical characteristics. For our studies of modern human origins, however, we focus on the mitochondrial, maternal lineages.

Maternal lineages are closest among siblings because their mitochondrial DNA has had only one generation in which to accumulate mutations. The degree of relatedness declines step by step as one moves along the pedigree, from first cousins descended from the maternal grandmother, to second cousins descended from a common maternal great-grandmother and so on. The farther back the genealogy goes, the larger the circle of maternal relatives becomes, until at last it embraces everyone alive.

Logically, then, all human mitochondrial DNA must have had an ultimate common female ancestor. But it is easy to show she did not necessarily live in a small population or constitute the only woman of her generation. Imagine a static population that always contains 15 mothers. Every new generation must contain 15 daughters, but some mothers will fail to produce a daughter, whereas others will produce two or more. Because maternal lineages die out whenever there is no daughter to carry on, it is only a matter of time before all but one lineage disappears. In a stable population the time for this fixation of the maternal lineage to occur is the length of a generation multiplied by twice the population size.

One might refer to the lucky woman whose lineage survives as Eve. Bear in mind, however, that other women were living in Eve's generation and that Eve did not occupy a specially favored place in the breeding pattern. She is purely the beneficiary of chance. Moreover, if we were to reconstruct the or-

dinary lineages for the population, they would trace back to many of the men and women who lived at the same time as Eve. Population geneticists Daniel L. Hartl of Washington University School of Medicine and Andrew G. Clark of Pennsylvania State University estimate that as many as 10,000 people could have lived then. The name "Eve" can therefore be misleading—she is not the ultimate source of all the ordinary lineages, as the biblical Eve was. . . .

Because our comparisons with the chimpanzee data showed the human mitochondrial DNA clock has ticked steadily for millions of years, we knew it should be possible to calculate when the common mother of humanity lived. We assumed the human and chimpanzee lineages diverged five million years ago, as Sarich's work had shown. We then calculated how much humans had diverged from one another relative to how much they had diverged from chimpanzees—that is, we found the ratio of mitochondrial DNA divergence among humans to that between humans and chimpanzees.

Using two different sets of data, we determined the ratio was less than 1:25. Human maternal lineages therefore grew apart in a period less than 1/25th as long as five million years, or less than 200,000 years. With a third set of data on changes in a section of the mitochondrial DNA called the control region, we arrived at a more ancient date for the common mother. That date is less certain, however, because questions remain about how to correct for multiple mutations that occur within the control region.

One might object that a molecular clock known to be accurate over five million years could still be unreliable for shorter periods. It is conceivable, for example, that intervals of genetic stagnation might be interrupted by short bursts of change when, say, a new mutagen enters the environment, or a virus infects the germ-line cells, or intense natural selection affects all segments of the DNA. To rule out the possibility that the clock might run by fits and starts, we ran a test to measure how much mitochondrial DNA has evolved in populations founded at a known time.

The aboriginal populations of New Guinea and Australia are estimated to have been founded less than 50,000 to 60,000 years ago. The amount of evolution that has since occurred in each of those places seems about one third of that shown by the whole human species. Accordingly, we can infer that Eve lived three times 50,000 to 60,000 years ago, or roughly 150,000 to 180,000 years ago. All our estimates thus agree the split happened not far from 200,000 years ago.

Those estimates fit with at least one line of fossil evidence. The remains of anatomically modern people appear first in Africa, then in the Middle East and later in Europe and east Asia. Anthropologists have speculated that in east Africa the transition from anatomically archaic to modern people took place as recently as 130,000 years ago.

Further Resources

BOOKS

Lewin, Roger. *Bones of Contention.* New York: Simon & Schuster, 1987.

——. *In the Age of Mankind: A Smithsonian Book of Human Evolution.* Washington, D.C.: Smithsonian Books, 1988.

——. *Principles of Human Evolution: A Core Textbook.* Malden, Mass.: Blackwell Science, 1998.

Smith, Fred H., and Frank Spencer, eds. *The Origin of Modern Humans.* New York: Alan Liss, 1984.

PERIODICALS

Ayala, Francisco J. "The Myth of Eve: Molecular Biology and Human Origins." *Science,* December 22, 1995, 1930–1936.

Bailey, William. "Hominid Trichotomy: A Molecular Overview." *Evolutionary Anthropology,* 1993, 100–108.

Begun, David R. "Relations among the Great Apes and Humans." *Yearbook of Physical Anthropology,* 1994, 11–64.

Moore, William S. "Inferring Phylogenies From mtDNA Variation: Mitochondrial-Gene Trees versus Nuclear-Gene Trees." *Evolution,* 1995, 718–726.

Pilbeam, David. "Genetic and Morphological Records of the Hominoidea and Hominid Origins: A Synthesis." *Molecular Phylogenetic Evolution,* February 1996, 155–168.

Pritchard, J.K., and M.W. Feldman. "Genetic Data and the African Origin of Humans." *Science,* 1996, 1548–1549.

Rogers, Alan R. "Genetic Evidence on Modern Human Origins." *Human Biology,* February 1995, 1–36.

Rogers, Jeffrey. "The Phylogenetic Relationships among Homo, Pan, and Gorilla." *Journal of Human Evolution,* 1993, 201–215.

Ruvolo, Maryellen. "Molecular Evolutionary Processes and Conflicting Gene Trees: The Hominoid Case." *American Journal of Physical Anthropology,* 1994, 89–114.

Stoneking, Mark. "DNA and Recent Human Evolution." *Evolutionary Anthropology,* 1993, 60–73.

——. "In Defense of 'Eve'." *American Anthropology,* 1994, 131–141.

Stringer, Christopher B. "The Emergence of Modern Humans." *Scientific American,* December 1990, 98–104.

Templeton, Alan R. "'Eve': Hypothesis Compatibility Versus Hypothesis Testing." *American Anthropologist,* March 1994, 141–155.

——. "The 'Eve' Hypothesis: A Genetic Critique and Reanalysis." *American Anthropologist,* 1993, 51–72.

WEBSITES

Brookfield, John. *Mitochondrial 'Eve.'* Routledge. Available online at http://www.fitzroydearborn.com/Samples/Genesmp2 .pdf; website home page: http://routledge-ny.com/ (accessed July 15, 2003).

Holsinger, Kent. "An Example: Mitochondrial Eve." Available online at http://darwin.eeb.uconn.edu/eeb348/lecture-notes /coalescent/node3.html; website home page: http://darwin .eeb.uconn.edu (accessed July 15, 2003).

"The Human Origins Program." National Museum of Natural History. Smithsonian Institution. Available online at http:// www.mnh.si.edu/anthro/humanorigins; website home page: http://www.mnh.si.edu (accessed July 15, 2003).

Marks, Jonathan. "Mitochondrial Eve." University of North Carolina at Charlotte. Available online at http://www.uncc .edu/jmarks/2141/mtEve.pdf; website home page: http:// www.uncc.edu (accessed July 15, 2003).

Walker, Phillip L., and Edward H. Hagen. "Human Evolution: The Fossil Evidence in 3D." Department of Anthropology. University of California, Santa Barbara. Available online at http://www.anth.ucsb.edu/projects/human; website home page: http://www.anth.ucsb.edu (accessed July 15, 2003).

"The Multiregional Evolution of Humans"

Magazine article

By: Alan G. Thorne and Milford H. Wolpoff

Date: April 1992

Source: Thorne, Alan G., and Milford H. Wolpoff. "The Multiregional Evolution of Humans." *Scientific American,* 266, April 1992, 76–81.

About the Authors: Alan G. Thorne received a Ph.D. in anthropology from the University of Sydney in 1963, where he taught human anatomy at its medical school. He is currently associated with the Department of Archaeology and Natural History at the Australian National University's Institute of Advanced Studies. He has unearthed fossils of early man at Kow Swamp and Lake Mungo, Australia. He is an authority on the indigenous people of Australia.

Milford H. Wolpoff (1942–) was born in Chicago, Illinois, and received a Ph.D. in anthropology from the University of Illinois at Urbana in 1969. He taught at Case Western Reserve University before becoming a professor of anthropology at the University of Michigan in 1977. He has won research grants from the National Science Foundation, the National Academy of Sciences, and the Committee for Scholarly Exchange with the People's Republic of China. ∎

Introduction

During the 1990s scientists quarreled over the time and place of modern human origins. Biochemists under-

Dr. Milford H. Wolpoff holds a skull in a lab room. Along with Dr. Alan Thorne, Dr. Wolpoff argued against the "Eve" hypothesis that all modern humans are descendants of one African woman. BOB KALMBACH, UM PHOTO SERVICES. REPRODUCED BY PERMISSION.

stood that deoxyribonucleic acid (DNA), the molecule of heredity, accumulates mutations (chemical changes to DNA) at a fixed rate. The DNA in mitochondria (mtDNA), the sites in a cell that metabolize energy, accumulate mutations faster than DNA in the nucleus of each cell, allowing scientists to make finer gradations in time with mtDNA than with nuclear DNA. By comparing the differences in mtDNA among modern humans, biochemists could calculate back to the time when humans' mtDNA had yet to accumulate any mutations, when all shared the same mtDNA. This time would, therefore, have been the origin of modern humans, which biochemists fixed between 100,000 and 200,000 years ago. Moreover, as Africans have the greatest diversity of mtDNA, their population must be the oldest—having accumulated the most mutations, meaning that modern humans arose in Africa between 100,000 and 200,000 years ago. They only later settled the rest of the world, replacing more ancient populations of early man with little or no interbreeding between modern and premodern people.

Paleoanthropologists relied on fossils rather than DNA, which they interpreted in light of Charles Darwin's theory of evolution by natural selection. Darwin believed that organisms evolve with their environment. But be-

cause the environment is static for long periods of time and changes only slowly, Darwin believed, evolution must be gradual. Modern humans must, therefore, have evolved several hundred thousand years ago in an innumerable series of small steps.

Significance

The multiregional model of human evolution of Alan G. Thorne and Milford H. Wolpoff contrasted with the biochemical approach. "Once again the molecular geneticists have entered the fray, attempting to resolve it [the debate over the time and place of modern human origins] in favor of the African hypothesis with a molecular clock," wrote Thorne and Wolpoff. "Once again their help must be rejected because their reasoning is flawed," an unusually sharp statement from what purports to be a dispassionate, scientific article. Thorne and Wolpoff fault biochemists for ignoring the fossils of early man, which indicate that early man (presumably *Homo erectus,* the immediate ancestor of modern humans, many paleoanthropologists believe) left Africa some one million years ago to settle Europe and Asia, including Indonesia and, later, Australia. In Europe, Asia, Africa, and Australia, these early men evolved into modern humans over the next one million years. Modern humans, therefore, evolved neither in one place, nor at a sharply defined time.

A corollary of this belief, wrote Thorne and Wolpoff, is that the races of modern humans sink roots one million years into the past, and are, therefore, fixed. Thorne and Wolpoff claim that races "maintain their physical differences despite interbreeding." This is an extraordinary statement. Interbreeding between blacks and whites yields offspring intermediary in characteristics from their parents, implying that race is a matter of semantic convenience, rather than the biological reality Thorne and Wolpoff suppose.

If Thorne and Wolpoff are right, genetic differences should separate human races because they arose over one million years—enough time to accumulate mutations that would separate one race from another. Yet, no such differences exist. Humans of all ethnicities and places share the same sequence of nucleotide bases (the building blocks of DNA) thousands of bases long. Even in regions of DNA where humans differ, these differences do not break down by race. In a DNA strand of some 330 nucleotide bases where humans differ, they differ by eight nucleotide bases on average, regardless of ancestry. Two whites differ by eight nucleotide bases in this region, and one white and one black also differ by eight nucleotide bases. At the level of the gene, no such entity as race exists. Although Thorne and Wolpoff chided biochemists for ignoring the fossils of early man, they ignore the genetic evidence that weakens their theory.

Primary Source

"The Multiregional Evolution of Humans" [excerpt]

SYNOPSIS: In this excerpt Alan G. Thorne and Milford H. Wolpoff assert that fossils of early man demonstrate that archaic humans (presumably *Homo erectus*) left Africa one million years ago. They settled in Europe, Asia, and, later, Australia, where they evolved into modern humans over the next one million years. Modern humans, therefore, evolved neither in one place, nor at one sharply defined time.

Both Fossil and Genetic Evidence Argues That Various Human Groups Arose Where They Are Found Today

Today the paleoanthropological community is again engaged in a debate, this time about how, when and where modern humans originated. On one side stand some researchers, such as ourselves, who maintain there is no single home for modern humanity—humans originated in Africa and then slowly developed their modern forms in every area of the Old World. On the other side are workers who claim that Africa alone gave birth to modern humans within the past 200,000 years. Once again the molecular geneticists have entered the fray, attempting to resolve it in favor of the African hypothesis with a molecular clock. Once again their help must be rejected because their reasoning is flawed.

Genetic research has undeniably provided one of the great insights of 20th-century biology: that all living people are extremely closely related. Our DNA similarities are far greater than the disparate anatomic variations of humanity might suggest. Studies of the DNA carried by the cell organelles called mitochondria, which are inherited exclusively from one's mother and are markers for maternal lineages, now play a role in the development of theories about the origin of modern human races.

Nevertheless, mitochondrial DNA is not the only source of information we have on the subject. Fossil remains and artifacts also represent a monumental body of evidence—and, we maintain, a much more reliable one. The singular importance of the mitochondrial DNA studies is that they show one of the origin theories discussed by paleontologists must be incorrect.

With Wu Xinzhi of the Institute of Vertebrate Paleontology and Paleoanthropology in Beijing, we developed an explanation for the pattern of human evolution that we described as multiregional evolution. We learned that some of the features that distinguish major human groups, such as Asians, Australian Aborigines and Europeans, evolved over a long period, roughly where these peoples are found today.

Multiregional evolution traces all modern populations back to when humans first left Africa at least a million years ago, through an interconnected web of ancient lineages in which the genetic contributions to all living peoples varied regionally and temporally. Today distinctive populations maintain their physical differences despite interbreeding and population movements; this situation has existed ever since humans first colonized Europe and Asia. Modern humanity originated within these widespread populations, and the modernization of our ancestors was an ongoing process.

An alternative theory, developed by the paleontologist William W. Howells of Harvard University as the "Noah's ark" model, posited that modern people arose recently in a single place and that they subsequently spread around the world, replacing other human groups. That replacement, recent proponents of the theory believe, must have been complete. From their genetic analyses, the late Allan C. Wilson and his colleagues at the University of California at Berkeley concluded that the evolutionary record of mitochondrial DNA could be traced back to a single female, dubbed "Eve" in one of his first publications on the issue, who lived in Africa approximately 200,000 years ago. Only mitochondrial DNA that can be traced to Eve, these theorists claim, is found among living people. . . .

The hominid fossils from Australasia (Indonesia, New Guinea and Australia) show a continuous anatomic sequence during the Pleistocene that is uninterrupted by African migrants at any time. The distinguishing features of the earliest of these Javan remains, dated to about one million years ago, show they had developed when the region was first inhabited.

Compared with human fossils from other areas, the Javan people have thick skull bones, with strong continuous browridges forming an almost straight bar of bone across their eye sockets and a second well-developed shelf of bone at the back of the skull for the neck muscles. Above and behind the brows, the forehead is flat and retreating. These early Indonesians also have large projecting faces with massive rounded cheekbones. Their teeth are the largest known in archaic humans from that time.

A series of small but important features can be found on the most complete face and on other facial fragments that are preserved. These include such things as a rolled ridge on the lower edge of the eye sockets, a distinctive ridge on the cheek-bone and a nasal floor that blends smoothly into the face.

This unique morphology was stable for at least 700,000 years while other modern characteristics continued to evolve in the Javan people. For example, the large fossil series from Ngandong, which recent evidence suggests may be about 100,000 years old, offers striking proof that the Javans of that time had brain sizes in the modern range but were otherwise remarkably similar to much earlier individuals in the region.

The first inhabitants of Australia arrived more than 60,000 years ago, and their behavior and anatomy were clearly those of modern human beings. Their skeletons show the Javan complex of features, along with further braincase expansions and other modernizations. Several dozen well-preserved fossils from the late Pleistocene and early Holocene demonstrate that the same combination of features that distinguished those Indonesian people from their contemporaries distinguishes modern Australian Aborigines from other living peoples.

If the earliest Australians were descendants of Africans, as the Eve theory requires, the continuity of fossil features would have to be no more than apparent. All the features of the early Javans would need to have evolved a second time in the population of invaders. The repeated evolution of an individual feature would be conceivable but rare; the duplication of an entire set of unrelated features would be unprecedentedly improbable.

Northern Asia also harbors evidence linking its modern and ancient inhabitants. Moreover, because the similarities involve features different from those significant in Australasia, they compound the improbability of the Eve theory by requiring that a second complete set of features was duplicated in a different population.

The very earliest Chinese fossils, about one million years old, differ from their Javan counterparts in many ways that parallel the differences between north Asians and Australians today. Our research with Wu Xinzhi and independent research by [Geoffrey] Pope demonstrated that the Chinese fossils are less robust, have smaller and more delicately built flat faces, smaller teeth and rounder foreheads separated from their arched browridges. Their noses are less prominent and more flattened at the top. Perhaps the most telling indication of morphological continuity concerns a peculiarity of tooth shapes. Prominently "shoveled" maxillary incisors, which curl inward along their internal edges, are found with unusually high frequency in living east Asians and in all the earlier human remains from that area. Studies by Tracey L. Crummett of the University of Michigan show that the form of prehistoric and living Asian incisors is unique.

This combination of traits is also exhibited at the Zhoukoudian cave area in northern China, where fully a third of all known human remains from the Middle Pleistocene have been found. As Wu Rukang of the Chinese Academy of Sciences has pointed out, even within the 150,000 or more years spanned by the Zhoukoudian individuals, evolutionary changes in the modern direction, including increases in brain size, can be seen. Our examinations of the Chinese specimens found no anatomic evidence that typically African features ever replaced those of the ancient Chinese in these regions. Instead there is a smooth transformation of the ancient populations into the living peoples of east Asia.

Paleontologists have long thought Europe would be the best source of evidence for the replacement of one group, Neanderthals, by more modern humans. Even there, however, the fossil record shows that any influx of new people was neither complete nor without mixture. In fact, the most recent known Neanderthal, from Saint-Césaire in France, apparently had the behavioral characteristics of the people who succeeded the Neanderthals in Europe. The earliest post-Neanderthal Europeans did not have a pattern of either modern or archaic African features. Clearly, the European Neanderthals were not completely replaced by Africans or by people from any other region.

Instead the evidence suggests that Neanderthals either evolved into later humans or interbred with them, or both. David W. Frayer of the University of Kansas and Fred H. Smith of Northern Illinois University have discovered that many allegedly unique Neanderthal features are found in the Europeans who followed the Neanderthals—the Upper Paleolithic, Mesolithic and later peoples. In fact, only a few Neanderthal features completely disappear from the later European skeletal record.

Further Resources

BOOKS

Aitken, Michael. *The Origin of Modern Humans and the Importance of Chronometric Dating*. Princeton, N.J.: Princeton University Press, 1993.

Brauer, Gunter, and Fred H. Smith. *Continuity or Replacement: Controversies in Homo sapiens Evolution*. Frankfurt, Germany: A.A. Balkema, 1992.

Eikle, Edward M., ed. *Current Issues in Human Evolution.* San Francisco: California Academy of Sciences, 1996.

Lewin, Roger. *Bones of Contention.* New York: Simon & Schuster, 1987.

———. *In the Age of Mankind: A Smithsonian Book of Human Evolution.* Washington, D.C.: Smithsonian Books, 1988.

Lewin, Roger. *Principles of Human Evolution: A Core Textbook.* Malden, Mass.: Blackwell Science, 1998.

Smith, Fred H., and Frank Spencer, eds. *The Origin of Modern Humans.* New York: Alan Liss, 1984.

PERIODICALS

Aiello, Leslie C. "The Fossil Evidence for Modern Human Origins in Africa: A Revised View." *American Anthropologist,* 1993, 73–96.

Ayala, Francisco J. "The Myth of Eve: Molecular Biology and Human Origins." *Science,* December 22, 1995, 1930–1936.

Begun, David R. "Relations among the Great Apes and Humans." *Yearbook of Physical Anthropology,* 1994, 11–64.

Frayer, David W. "Theories of Modern Human Origins: The Paleontological Test." *American Anthropologist,* 1993, 14–50.

Klein, Richard G. "Anatomy, Behavior, and Modern Human Origins." *Journal of World Prehistory,* 1995, 167–198.

Lahr, Marta M. "The Multiregional Model of Human Origins." *Journal of Human Evolution,* 1994, 23–56.

Lahr, Marta M., and Robert Foley. "Multiple Dispersals and Modern Human Origins." *Evolutionary Anthropology,* 1994, 48–60.

Pilbeam, David. "Genetic and Morphological Records of the Hominoidea and Hominid Origins: A Synthesis." *Molecular Phylogenetic Evolution,* February 1996, 155–168.

Stringer, Christopher B. "The Emergence of Modern Humans." *Scientific American,* December 1990, 98–104.

Templeton, Alan R. "'Eve': Hypothesis Compatibility Versus Hypothesis Testing." *American Anthropologist,* March 1994, 141–155.

———. "The 'Eve' Hypothesis: A Genetic Critique and Reanalysis." *American Anthropologist,* 1993, 51–72.

WEBSITES

"The Human Origins Program." National Museum of Natural History. Smithsonian Institution. Available online at http://www.mnh.si.edu/anthro/humanorigins; website home page: http://www.mnh.si.edu (accessed July 15, 2003).

Marks, Jonathan. "Mitochondrial Eve." University of North Carolina at Charlotte. Available online at http://www.uncc.edu/jmarks/2141/mtEve.pdf; website home page: http://www.uncc.edu (accessed July 15, 2003).

Walker, Phillip L., and Edward H. Hagen. "Human Evolution: The Fossil Evidence in 3D." Department of Anthropology. University of California, Santa Barbara. Available online at http://www.anth.ucsb.edu/projects/human; website home page: http://www.anth.ucsb.edu (accessed July 15, 2003).

Ebola: A Documentary Novel of Its First Explosion

Novel

By: William T. Close

Date: 1995

Source: Close, William T. *Ebola: A Documentary Novel of Its First Explosion.* New York: Ivy Books, 1995, 28–33.

About the Author: William T. Close was born in Greenwich, Connecticut, and received an M.D. from Columbia College of Physicians and Surgeons in New York City in 1951. In 1960, he began practicing medicine in the Congo, Africa. While in Africa, he witnessed the first Ebola outbreak in 1976, and the second in 1995. Between 1994 and 1996 he helped secure funds for rebuilding the Congo's aging hospitals. He now practices medicine in Big Pines, Wyoming. ∎

Introduction

In 1798, Anglican cleric Thomas Malthus wrote that war, famine, and disease check population growth. The third is potent when it erupts in epidemics. The most famous was the fourteenth century's Black Death that many, though not all, historians and epidemiologists attribute to bubonic and pneumonic plague, both bacterial infections. The Black Death originated in China, whose merchants brought it to Europe in 1347. During the next four years, it killed up to one-half of Europe's population, and created widespread hysteria. Stories abound of towns wiped out, of corpses decomposing in streets with no one to bury them. Cremation was the only way to keep abreast of the number of corpses.

Similar horrors visited the twentieth century. At the end of World War I (1914–1918), influenza, a viral infection, swept across the globe killing some thirty million people, millions more than had died in the war. In 1976, a mysterious disease killed hundreds in Zaire, the Sudan, and the Congo in only weeks before vanishing. The disease first erupted along the Ebola River in northern Congo (hence the name Ebola for the disease). Ebola, later discovered to be a viral infection, terrified people because it killed as many as 90 percent of those who contracted it, and because of its rapid spread through a population. In 1995, Ebola again erupted in Zaire, killing hundreds more before it vanished as abruptly as it had appeared. The 1995 outbreak made headlines throughout the world.

Significance

William T. Close witnessed Ebola's eruption in Zaire, as he desperately tried to care for its victims. In this excerpt from *Ebola: A Documentary Novel of Its First Explosion,* he describes the first casualty of the disease, Mabalo Lokela. Mabalo had come to a medical

A nurse in the necessary protective gear stands outside an isolation ward, Gozon, Ivory Coast, December 10, 1995. Inside, a Liberian man is held under quarantine after being diagnosed as the latest victim of an Ebola outbreak in Africa. AP/WIDE WORLD PHOTOS. REPRODUCED BY PERMISSION.

clinic in Zaire with a fever, headache, and muscle aches. The attending nurse suspected malaria, a common tropical disease with these symptoms, and gave him a shot of quinine. Within days he was too weak to move and was bleeding from the mouth, nose and anus. He died one week after receiving the shot of quinine. Close recalls the panic and helplessness that gripped people, for the disease had no cure.

The danger is that Ebola might spread across the globe as influenza had in 1918 and 1919. This peril is

acute because commerce has connected all regions of the world. Jets and ships crisscross the globe, making it possible for lethal viruses and bacteria to cross national boundaries and oceans in hours. An Ebola outbreak in the thinly populated countryside of Zaire cannot kill more than a few hundred people. Were the disease to erupt in New York City or San Francisco, however, thousands, perhaps even millions, of people might die.

Modern medicine has given humans vaccines, antibiotics, and the illusion of having eradicated epidemics, at least in the United States and Europe. Ebola reveals that medicine has yet to vanquish epidemics, particularly in poor regions of the world, and even affluent nations are at risk. The truth may be that the United States is little more prepared for an Ebola outbreak than Europe was for the Black Death.

Primary Source

Ebola: A Documentary Novel of Its First Explosion
[excerpt]

SYNOPSIS: In this excerpt, William T. Close describes the symptoms of Ebola and its first casualty, Mabalo Lokela, in Zaire. The disease began as a fever, headache, and muscle ache. Within days, Mabalo was too weak to move. Bleeding from the mouth, nose, and anus, he died only a week after he had sought treatment at a medical clinic.

Masangaya pulled up a stool and sat next to his friend. Mabalo's temperature was 39.5°C (103.5°F), blood pressure normal, but his pulse was 130. His breathing was rapid and shallow, his skin dry and hot. He was hunched over on the edge of the cot with his eyes closed. Mbunzu stood next to a screened window that let in the early morning light. She chewed on the corner of a handkerchief balled up in her fist.

Masangaya encouraged Mabalo to open his eyes. The whites were red with bloodstained crusts in the corners. Using a small flashlight, he examined Mabalo's mouth; his tongue was dry and coated with thick green mucus. Dull gray patches of exudate covered his soft palate and the back of his pharynx. After listening to Mabalo's heart and lungs, Masangaya helped him lie back on the cot. His fingers explored the teacher's abdomen, finding tender areas over the liver and spleen where even gentle pressure made Mabalo tighten up.

Mbunzu reminded him, "He has had nivaquine and quinine over the past few days."

Masangaya sat back and thought for a moment. "He must have something more than malaria, although malaria is bad enough and can make a man this sick. But the injections should have made him better, if malaria was the problem. He will be more comfortable and I can take care of him better if we put him in the private room off the medical ward. He needs fluids and stronger medicine."

The move was made, and Masangaya started an IV of saline. He handed Mbunzu some pills. "Give him these slowly with little sips of water. I hope he can keep them down. I will check back in a while."

Other patients were waiting for the medical assistant, but Masangaya wanted to talk to Lucie about Mabalo. He told them he would return soon as he hurried over to the maternity pavilion.

"Good morning, Sister. Working early this morning," he said, as they shook hands.

"Like you," she answered, smiling at him. "Have a seat."

"Mabalo's very sick."

"Vero told me about him last night. I'm glad he came to see you on his own."

"Mbunzu must have carried him over. He was too weak to climb the two steps into my office." He paused. "The malaria shots have not helped."

"That is strange. What will you do?"

"I hospitalized him, started an IV, and gave Mbunzu some chloramphenicol and aspirin to get into him. I do not know what he has, but the rehydration should help."

"You don't think he was given native medicine by a *féticheur*?" she asked.

"I doubt it; he is as Westernized as I am. But, of course, one can never really be sure." He raised his eyebrows and cocked his head like the sisters did sometimes when they spoke of African ways.

Later in the day, when Masangaya gave Mabalo another liter of fluid, the patient was passing black watery stool. The first IV had done little to relieve his dehydration.

During the night, his abdominal cramps became even more severe, doubling him up, and making him cry out. He vomited dark brown bile that looked like coffee grounds and continued to pass tarry liquid in the bed. Mbunzu washed him and changed the sheet over the rubber mattress. It was a long night, and she was relieved when dawn crept into the room through the window.

Masangaya and Lucie came in early. The room reeked of vomit and fecal blood. Mabalo was on his side in the fetal position.

"He just fell asleep," whispered Mbunzu.

Quietly, Lucie replied, "We will be back later." They left, and she followed the medical assistant into his office.

"A little coffee?" asked Masangaya, lighting a small oil burner under a blackened kettle.

"Why not," replied Lucie.

"At least he is resting," said Masangaya, rinsing out two cups in the cold-water sink next to his desk. "I don't know what else to do. I am afraid we might lose him."

"Oh, *mon dieu*! I hope not. But like you, I cannot think of anything we haven't tried."

Masangaya reached into the medicine cabinet for a can of Nescafé. Lucie gazed around the small office as spartan as her own. A canvas army cot covered with a stained pad was next to the wall behind her; a plain wooden table and chair filled the space at the other end; and under a narrow window, an old metal cart for the burner and its kettle made up the furnishings. The only personal effect was a faded photograph in a cheap metal frame hanging above the table. It showed a smiling group of young African and European students posing next to a plump older white couple in front of a café in Brussels.

Lucie watched Masangaya preparing the coffee. This big man—the backbone of the hospital—had been trained in Léopoldville, where the practical aspects of medicine and surgery were stressed. Afterward, because of his high grades, the Belgians awarded him a scholarship to the Institute of Tropical Medicine in Antwerp. He had run the Yambuku hospital for the past six years. The hair at his temples was turning white. To the sisters he was an effective and compassionate man, soft-spoken, and easier to work with than most of the young doctors that passed through the mission hospitals and thought they had the answers to everything.

Masangaya's reputation for good care was widespread, and people came from far to see him. The villagers considered him a learned elder with special knowledge of diseases and white man's remedies. Unlike many Western doctors and nurses, he was not in conflict with the traditional healers. He knew that they had important roles to play in the lives of the people. Masangaya was called "*monganga*"—an expert in white medicine.

"When he awakens I will give him more antibiotic and more saline. How is our supply of IVs?" he asked, handing Lucie a cup.

"We have one case of liter bags left. I will ask Vero to radio Lisala for more," replied Lucie. She sipped her coffee thoughtfully. "When Sophie—I mean, Mbunzu—wakes up, I'll send her home. Mabalo's mother can sit with him today. Mbunzu needs to nurse her baby; she can come back this evening."

"That's good. But remember, Mabalo is a *mokumi*—an honorable man. There will be many visitors."

"We should not allow them in the room," said Lucie firmly. "There's not much space, and it will be very hot."

"We cannot keep them out. If Mabalo is dying, and I think he is, they will want to be with him. He is esteemed as a teacher and a judge and will continue to be important to all of us when he becomes an ancestor."

"I know you are right," said Lucie, "but . . ." Masangaya turned to face her. His irritation showed for an instant, then he smiled. She handed him her cup. "Thanks for the coffee. I have to get back to my pregnant women," said Lucie, knowing that discussion would be useless.

■ ■ ■

During the day, Mabalo's mother sat next to her son's bed. His friends and fellow teachers, the president of the cooperative, and his neighbors came, packing into the little room. Some sat on the other bed; others leaned against the wall or squatted on the floor. Each one watched silently for a time, then took their leave of Mabalo's mother, holding their right forearm with their left hand in a sign of respect. Their place was taken by a person from the group waiting outside the ward for his turn to sit with the teacher and keep the vigil with others. Each new visitor coming into the crowded room shook hands all around, then approached Mabalo, taking his hand and saying softly, "*Mbote, mokumi.*" The stifling heat seemed unnoticed. No one spoke; their presence alone sufficed to mark their affection.

And so the day passed. Toward evening. Mbunzu returned to relieve Mabalo's mother, the visitors left, and she was again alone with her dying man.

Mabalo was now too weak to turn over in bed. Mbunzu washed him when he soiled himself and wiped the bloody mucus that oozed from the corner of his mouth. Pulling the chair over she sat next to the bed, resting her elbows on the mattress, and spooned drops of water between his cracked lips. His hand wavered when he tried to reach up and touch her face. She held it and pressed it to her

cheek. He smiled and she rocked gently, holding on tight as her tears washed over their fingers.

The door opened. Veronica tiptoed in and put her arm around Mbunzu who, burying her face in the nun's skirt, poured out her misery in soul-racking sobs. Veronica prayed for the agony to end. Slowly the light faded, and Vero helped Mbunzu onto the other bed. She lit the lantern on the table and tiptoed out. Mosquitoes and clumsy moths gathered around the smoky lamp. Mabalo's labored breathing was the only sound in the little room. Outside the open window, all was quiet except for thunder rumbling in the distance. Around midnight Mabalo's mother returned and lay on a mat under his bed.

During the small hours of the morning, Mabalo went into a coma. Mbunzu, her head resting in her arms on his bed, was asleep. Suddenly she awakened with a start and stared at Mabalo. Then throwing back her head and raising her fists to the ceiling, she let out a long cry of anguish. Mabalo's mother, awakened by Mbunzu's scream, threw herself on her son's dead body and wailed, "*Papa akufi, akei!*" He is dead, he is gone! Friends who had been sleeping outside came in and fell on the body, sobbing. One of them ran to Masangaya's house. Mabalo died just one week after receiving the shot of quinine.

Further Resources

BOOKS

Klenk, Hans-Dieter, ed. *Marburg and Ebola Viruses.* New York: Springer, 1999.

Peters, Clarence J., and James W. LeDuc, eds. *Ebola: The Virus and the Disease.* Chicago: University of Chicago Press, 1999.

Preston, Richard. *The Hot Zone.* New York: Random House, 1994.

PERIODICALS

"Ebola Vaccine Agreement Expanded to Include Marburg, Lassa Vaccines." *Genomics & Genetics Weekly,* September 20, 2002, 16.

Greer, Michael. "Effective Anti-Ebola Agent May Work by Augmenting Interferon Output." *Drug Week,* September 6, 2002, 16–17.

"Production Set for Ebola, Marburg, Lassa Vaccines in Human Clinical Trials." *Biotech Week,* November 13, 2002, 37.

WEBSITES

"Ebola Haemorrhagic Fever." World Health Organization. Available online at http://www.who.int/inf-fs/en/fact103.html; website home page: http://who.int (accessed July 15, 2003).

"Ebola Hemorrhagic Fever." Association of State and Territorial Directors of Health Promotion and Public Health Education. Available online at http://www.astdhpphe.org/infect/ebola.html; website home page: http://astdpphe.org (accessed July 15, 2003).

"Ebola Hemorrhagic Fever." Centers for Disease Control and Prevention. Available online at http://www.cdc.gov/ncidod /dvrd/spb/mnpages/dispages/ebola.htm; website home page: http://www.cdc.gov (accessed July 15, 2003).

"The Ebola Virus." Available online at http://ebola.cjb.net (accessed July 15, 2003).

Hessler, Robert. "Ebola Virus Links on the Web." Available online at http://www.iohk.com/UserPages/amy/ebola.html; website home page: http://www.iohk.com (accessed July 15, 2003).

The Journal of Infectious Diseases, vol. 179, supp. 1, February 1999. Available online at http://www.journals.uchicago .edu/JID/journal/contents/v179nS1.html; website home page: http://www.journals.uchicago.edu (accessed July 15, 2003).

Russell, Brett. "Ebola Information." Available online at http:// www.brettrussell.com/personal/ebola.html; website home page: http://www.brettrussell.com (accessed July 15, 2003).

AUDIO AND VISUAL MEDIA
Ebola: The Diary of a Killer. Princeton, N.J.: Films for the Humanities & Sciences, 1998.

The Road Ahead

Nonfiction work

By: Bill Gates

Date: 1995

Source: Gates, Bill. *The Road Ahead.* New York: Viking, 1995, 8–11.

About the Author: William Henry (Bill) Gates III (1955–) was born in Seattle, Washington, and wrote his first software program at thirteen. He computerized his high school's payroll system and founded Traf-O-Date, a company that sold traffic-counting systems. In 1975, he left Harvard University to found Microsoft Corporation, a software firm, with his friend Paul G. Allen. Microsoft's meteoric rise brought Gates wealth and controversy for his alleged anticompetitive practices. ∎

Introduction

In 1975, Bill Gates and his friend Paul G. Allen founded Microsoft (short for microcomputer and software) Corporation. During the 1970s, they refined the programming language Beginner's All-purpose Symbolic Instruction Code (BASIC) and created other languages. This work brought Microsoft to the attention of International Business Machines (IBM), which, in 1980, invited Microsoft to create the operating system for its first personal computer (PC), the IBM PC. Microsoft bought an operating system from a competitor, simplified it, and named it Microsoft Disk Operating System (MS-DOS). In 1981, IBM and Microsoft unveiled the IBM PC with MS-DOS as its operating system.

In *The Road Ahead* (1995), Microsoft founder and president Bill Gates asserted that the Internet would be to the 1990s what Gutenberg's printing press was to the Middle Ages. © JIM LAKE/CORBIS. REPRODUCED BY PERMISSION.

Other computer manufacturers followed IBM in licensing MS-DOS as their operating system. By 1990, Microsoft had sold more than 100 million copies of MS-DOS. Not content until he had a monopoly on operating systems, as industrialists John D. Rockefeller and Andrew Carnegie had monopolized the refinement of petroleum and the manufacture of steel in the nineteenth century, Bill Gates developed several versions of the Windows operating system during the 1980s and 1990s. By 1993, Windows 3.0 sold some one million copies per month, and nearly 90 percent of PCs used Windows or MS-DOS.

By the mid-1990s, Microsoft recorded annual profits of 25 percent, and its income surpassed two billion dollars in 1996. As he had cornered the market on operating systems, Gates sought a monopoly on Internet browsers, developing Internet Explorer to capture market share from Netscape Communications Corporation, developer of the browser Netscape Navigator. Gates combined Windows and Internet Explorer in a single package; computer manufacturers that wanted Windows also got Internet Explorer included free, and thus had no incentive to buy Netscape Navigator. Netscape chief executive officer Jim Barksdale charged Microsoft with trying to force Netscape out of the market—a position the U.S. Justice Department echoed in filing suit against Microsoft. The 1990s ended with the case pending.

Significance

Whatever his private thoughts, Bill Gates projected a public image of confidence, writing in *The Road Ahead* of his innate optimism. He noted that the PC had already changed how Americans worked and predicted it would soon change how they lived. He envisioned a future in which information, no matter how esoteric, would be available online. His optimism led him to disagree with critics who worried that the PC would widen the chasm between the affluent and the poor, that it would make many jobs obsolete or redundant, or that it could not solve the intractable problems of famine and disease.

Like World Wide Web inventor Tim Berners-Lee, Bill Gates understood the PC's potential, through the Internet, to liberate and empower people, allowing them to configure their lives as they saw fit. Gates wrote that people would be able to watch news or entertainment when they wanted and for the duration they chose. No longer would networks dictate such matters. Should an item of news interest someone, he or she would be able to request more detail about the topic. For example, people would be able to read an online menu from a restaurant they wished to visit, learn how food critics had rated the restaurant, and check its sanitation record or the crime rate in the restaurant's city. Only imagination would limit what we want to know and how we wish to live our lives.

Primary Source

The Road Ahead [excerpt]

SYNOPSIS: In this excerpt, Bill Gates notes that the PC has already changed how Americans work, and predicts it will soon change how they live. He envisions a future in which information, no matter how esoteric, will be available online.

The information highway will transform our culture as dramatically as Gutenberg's press did the Middle Ages.

Personal computers have already altered work habits, but they haven't really changed our lives much yet. When tomorrow's powerful information machines are connected on the highway, people, machines, entertainment, and information services will all be accessible. You will be able to stay in touch with anyone, anywhere, who wants to stay in touch with you; to browse through any of thousands of libraries, day or night. Your misplaced or stolen cam-

era will send you a message telling you exactly where it is, even if it's in a different city. You'll be able to answer your apartment intercom from your office, or answer any mail from your home. Information that today is difficult to retrieve will be easy to find:

Is your bus running on time?

Are there any accidents right now on the route you usually take to the office?

Does anyone want to trade his or her Thursday theater tickets for your Wednesday tickets?

What is your child's school-attendance record?

What's a good recipe for halibut?

Which store, anywhere, can deliver by tomorrow morning for the lowest price a wristwatch that takes your pulse?

What would someone pay for my old Mustang convertible?

How is the hole in a needle manufactured?

Are your shirts ready yet at the laundry?

What's the cheapest way to subscribe to *The Wall Street Journal?*

What are the symptoms of a heart attack?

Was there any interesting testimony at the county courthouse today?

Do fish see in color?

What does the Champs-Élysées look like right now?

Where were you at 9:02 P.M. last Thursday?

Let's say you're thinking about trying a new restaurant and want to see its menu, wine list, and specials of the day. Maybe you're wondering what your favorite food reviewer said about it. You may also want to know what sanitation score the health department gave the place. If you're leery of the restaurant's neighborhood, perhaps you'll want to see a safety rating based on police reports. Still interested in going? You'll want reservations, a map, and driving instructions based on current traffic conditions. Take the instructions in printed form or have them read to you—and updated—as you drive.

All of this information will be readily accessible and completely personal, because you'll be able to explore whatever parts of it interest you in whatever ways and for however long you want. You'll watch a program when it's convenient for you, instead of when a broadcaster chooses to air it. You'll shop, order food, contact fellow hobbyists, or publish information for others to use when and as you want to. Your nightly newscast will start at a time you determine and last exactly as long as you want it to. It will cover subjects selected by you or by a service that knows your interests. You'll be able to ask for reports from Tokyo or Boston or Seattle, request more detail on a news item, or inquire whether your favorite columnist has commented on an event. And if you prefer, your news will be delivered to you on paper.

Change of this magnitude makes people nervous. Every day, all over the world, people are asking about the implications of the network, often with terrible apprehension. What will happen to our jobs? Will people withdraw from the physical world and live vicariously through their computers? Will the gulf between the haves and have-nots widen irreparably? Will a computer be able to help the disenfranchised in East St. Louis or the starving in Ethiopia? There are some major challenges that will come with the network and the changes it will bring. . . .

I've thought about the difficulties and find that, on balance, I'm confident and optimistic. Partly this is just the way I am, and partly it's because I'm enthusiastic about what my generation, which came of age the same time the computer did, will be able to do. We'll be giving people tools to use to reach out in new ways. I'm someone who believes that because progress will come no matter what, we need to make the best of it. I'm still thrilled by the feeling that I'm squinting into the future and catching that first revealing hint of revolutionary possibilities. I feel incredibly lucky that I am getting the chance to play a part in the beginning of an epochal change for a second time.

Further Resources

BOOKS

Cusumano, Michael A., and Richard W. Selby. *Microsoft Secrets: How the World's Most Powerful Software Company Creates Technology, Shapes Markets, and Manages People.* New York: Free Press, 1995.

Edstrom, Jennifer. *Barbarians Led by Bill Gates: Microsoft From the Inside.* New York: Henry Holt, 1998.

Ichbiah, Daniel, and Susan L. Knepper. *The Making of Microsoft.* Rocklin, Calif.: Prima Publishers, 1992.

PERIODICALS

Cohen, Adam. "Demonizing Gates." *Time,* November 2, 1998, 58–61, 66.

"Microsoft on Custom XPs." *PC World,* December 2002, 25.

Weisman, Robert. "Former Netscape Executive Marc Andreessen Discusses Technology Innovation." *Boston Globe,* November 11, 2002, C2.

WEBSITES

Kramer, Dave. "A Brief History of Microsoft on the Web." Microsoft Corporation. Available online at http://www.microsoft.com/misc/features/features_flshbk.htm; website home page: http://www.microsoft.com (accessed July 15, 2003).

Microsoft Corporation. Available online at http://www.microsoft.com (accessed July 15, 2003).

AUDIO AND VISUAL MEDIA

The Business: The Rise and Rise of Bill Gates. Princeton, N.J.: Films for the Humanities & Sciences, 1998.

Reengineering the Business. Princeton, N.J.: Films for the Humanities & Sciences, 1997.

Darwin's Black Box: The Biochemical Challenge to Evolution

Nonfiction work

By: Michael J. Behe

Date: 1996

Source: Behe, Michael J. *Darwin's Black Box: The Biochemical Challenge to Evolution.* New York: Simon & Schuster, 1996, 18–22.

About the Author: Michael J. Behe received a Ph.D. in biochemistry from the University of Pennsylvania in 1978, and he is a professor of biological sciences at Lehigh University. His research focuses on the interaction between deoxyribonucleic acid (DNA) and proteins. He is an authority on protein evolution. He is also a leading advocate of the Intelligent Design argument. ∎

Introduction

During the last two centuries, science and religion have clashed over evolution. Religious opposition arose first in Europe as early as 1809, the year French naturalist Jean-Baptiste Lamarck proposed that all life evolved from primitive ancestors. More vigorous and long lasting was the opposition that arose in the United States in the mid-nineteenth century and remains a religious and political force today—a century after European clerics abandoned their opposition to evolution.

Conservative Christians insisted on a literal reading of Genesis: the earth and life are only some six thousand years old; and at the beginning of time, God created the universe and all life, including humans, in six days. This biblical account denied the evolution of life, fundamentalists (those who insist on a literal reading of scripture) believed.

The first wave of opposition to evolution crested in the 1920s. Texas governor Miriam Ferguson issued an

Michael Behe, 1996. His characterization of the chemistry of vision as "irreducibly complex" is used as an argument for the Intelligent Design view of life's origins. **PHOTOGRAPH BY GEOFF SPEAR. REPRODUCED BY PERMISSION.**

executive order forbidding public schools from using textbooks that referred to evolution, and in 1925 the Tennessee legislature banned the teaching of evolution in public schools. Biology teacher John Scopes defied the law, and attorney Clarence Darrow and Baltimore journalist H.L. Mencken used the trial to expose fundamentalists' intolerance and ignorance of science.

The failure of their attempt to ban the teaching of evolution in public schools led fundamentalists to adopt a second strategy. They proposed that creationism (a literal reading of Genesis's creation account) was a scientific theory and, as such, merited a place in public school curricula alongside evolution. The California State Board of Education in 1972 and legislatures in Arkansas and Louisiana in the early 1980s mandated that public schools teach creation science alongside evolution. The late Harvard University biologist Stephen Jay Gould led a distinguished group of scientists and philosophers of science in exposing creation science as a fraud; it was religion belief, and not science. A state court struck down the Arkansas law; and in 1987 the U.S. Supreme Court struck down the Louisiana law mandating the teaching of creation science in public schools.

Significance

Since this defeat, fundamentalists have crafted a third strategy: the chemistry of even the simplest bacterium is too complex to have evolved. An intelligence (God) must, therefore, have designed life. This is the Intelligent Design argument, whose most forceful advocate is Michael J. Behe, a Catholic who denies a religious agenda and a connection to fundamentalists.

In *Darwin's Black Box* he outlines in four pages the chemistry of vision—in which light strikes the retina, setting off a cascade of molecules, all of which must interact in sequence and with precise timing to enable an animal to see. The deletion of a single molecule or an interruption in the timing of the interaction between molecules will prevent an animal from seeing. That is, the chemistry of vision is "irreducibly complex": all components of a system must function perfectly, or it fails.

Nature could not have built this system or any like it, step by step, as Charles Darwin's theory of evolution by natural selection requires because nature would have no advantage to select (sight over blindness) until the entire system was complete. If nature could not have assembled the chemistry of vision (and, by implication, the chemistry of innumerable other processes of life, several of which Behe discusses in other sections of *Darwin's Black Box*) then God must have assembled these systems, Behe argues.

Fundamentalists have elevated Behe's argument to prominence. In 2002, they tried to persuade the Ohio Board of Education to adopt Intelligent Design as one of its standards, a move that would have led Ohio's public schools to add it to their curricula. Although the board refused, it also did not endorse the teaching of evolution in public schools. After two centuries of debate, evolution remains controversial.

Primary Source

Darwin's Black Box: The Biochemical Challenge to Evolution [excerpt]

SYNOPSIS: In this excerpt Michael Behe outlines the chemistry of vision—in which light strikes the retina, setting off a cascade of molecules all of which must interact in sequence and with precise timing to enable an animal to see. The deletion of a single molecule or an interruption in the timing of the interaction between molecules will prevent an animal from seeing. That is, the chemistry of vision is "irreducibly complex": all components of a system must function perfectly, or it fails.

The Vision of Biochemistry

To Darwin, vision was a black box, but after the cumulative hard work of many biochemists, we are now approaching answers to the question of sight. The following five paragraphs give a biochemical sketch of the eye's operation. . . . Don't be put off by the strange names of the components. They're just labels, no more esoteric than *carburetor* or *differential* are to someone reading a car manual for the first time. Readers with an appetite for detail can find more information in many biochemistry textbooks; others may wish to tread lightly. . . .

When light first strikes the retina a photon interacts with a molecule called 11-*cis*-retinal, which rearranges within picoseconds to *trans*-retinal. (A picosecond is about the time it takes light to travel the breadth of a single human hair.) The change in

The First Step in Vision

A PHOTON OF LIGHT CAUSES A CHANGE IN THE SHAPE OF A SMALL ORGANIC MOLECULE, RETINAL. THIS FORCES A CHANGE IN THE SHAPE OF THE MUCH LARGER PROTEIN, RHODOPSIN, TO WHICH IT IS ATTACHED. THE CARTOON DRAWING OF THE PROTEIN IS NOT TO SCALE.

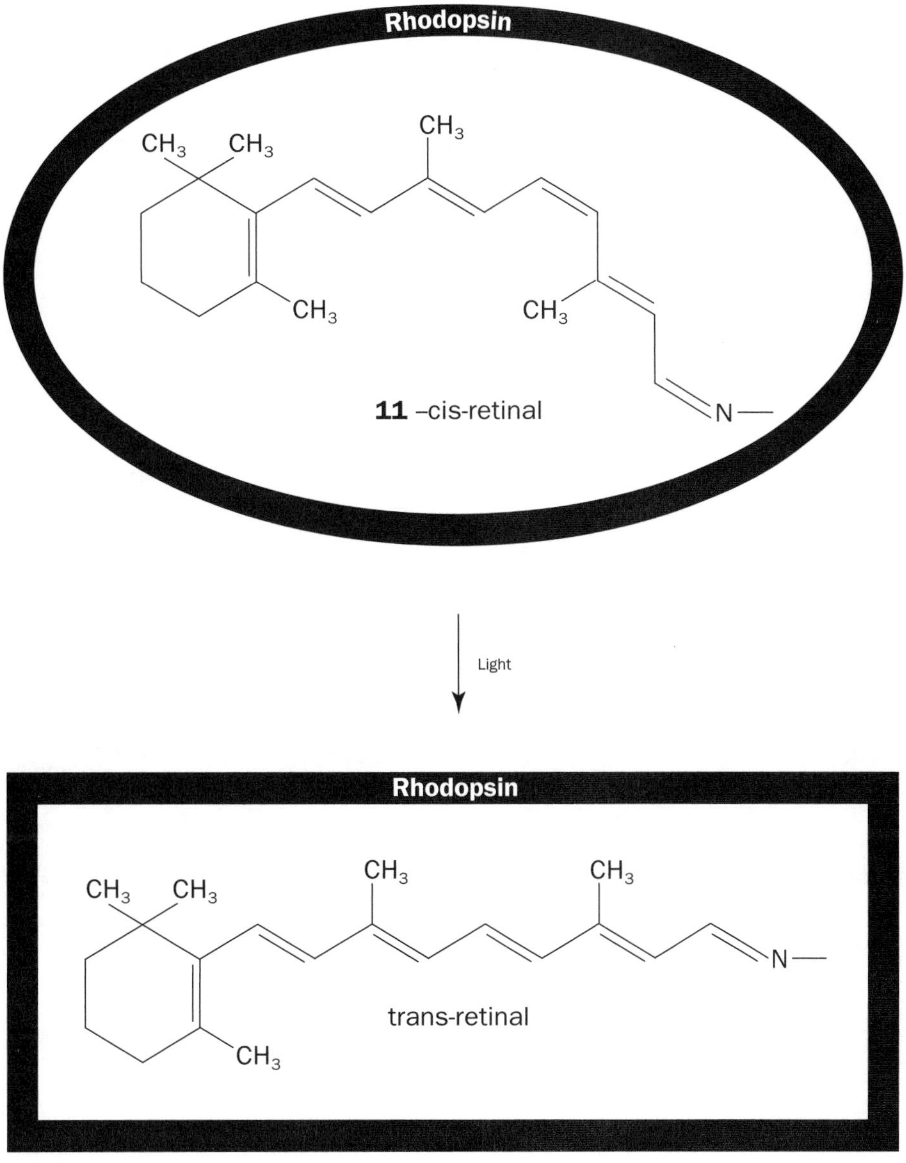

SOURCE: Figure 1–2 from Behe, Michael J. *Darwin's Black Box: The Biochemical Challenge to Evolution.* New York: Simon & Schuster, 1996, 19.

the shape of the retinal molecule forces a change in the shape of the protein, rhodopsin, to which the retinal is tightly bound. The protein's metamorphosis alters its behavior. Now called metarhodopsin II, the protein sticks to another protein, called transducin. Before bumping into metarhodopsin II, transducin had tightly bound a small molecule called GDP. But when transducin interacts with metarhodopsin II, the GDP falls off, and a molecule called GTP binds to transducin. (GTP is closely related to, but critically different from, GDP.)

GTP-transducin-metarhodopsin II now binds to a protein called phosphodiesterase, located in the inner membrane of the cell. When attached to metarhodopsin II and its entourage, the phosphodiesterase acquires the chemical ability to "cut" a molecule called cGMP (a chemical relative of both GDP and GTP). Initially there are a lot of cGMP molecules in the cell, but the phosphodiesterase lowers its concentration, just as a pulled plug lowers the water level in a bathtub.

Another membrane protein that binds cGMP is called an ion channel. It acts as a gateway that regulates the number of sodium ions in the cell. Normally the ion channel allows sodium ions to flow into the cell, while a separate protein actively pumps them out again. The dual action of the ion channel and pump keeps the level of sodium ions in the cell within a narrow range. When the amount of cGMP is reduced because of cleavage by the phosphodiesterase, the ion channel closes, causing the cellular concentration of positively charged sodium ions to be reduced. This causes an imbalance of charge across the cell membrane that, finally, causes a cur-

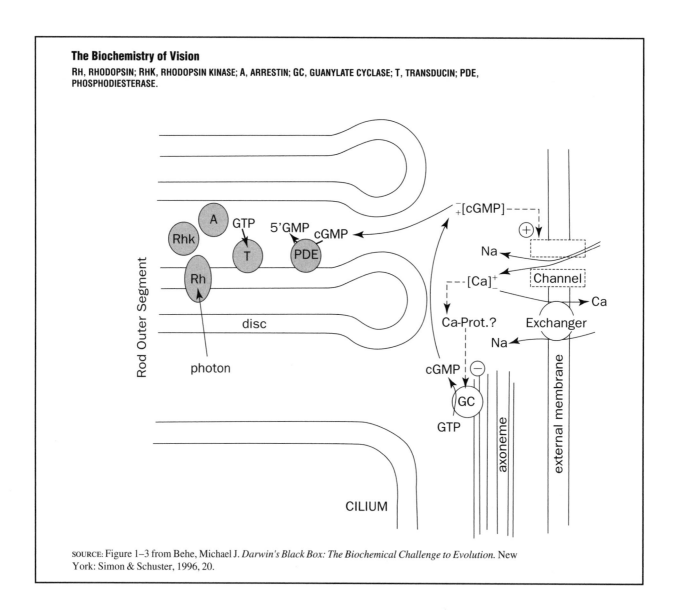

The Biochemistry of Vision

RH, RHODOPSIN; RHK, RHODOPSIN KINASE; A, ARRESTIN; GC, GUANYLATE CYCLASE; T, TRANSDUCIN; PDE, PHOSPHODIESTERASE.

SOURCE: Figure 1–3 from Behe, Michael J. *Darwin's Black Box: The Biochemical Challenge to Evolution.* New York: Simon & Schuster, 1996, 20.

rent to be transmitted down the optic nerve to the brain. The result, when interpreted by the brain, is vision.

If the reactions mentioned above were the only ones that operated in the cell, the supply of 11-*cis*-retinal, cGMP, and sodium ions would quickly be depleted. Something has to turn off the proteins that were turned on and restore the cell to its original state. Several mechanisms do this. First, in the dark the ion channel (in addition to sodium ions) also lets calcium ions into the cell. The calcium is pumped back out by a different protein so that a constant calcium concentration is maintained. When cGMP levels fall, shutting down the ion channel, calcium ion concentration decreases, too. The phosphodiesterase enzyme, which destroys cGMP, slows down at lower calcium concentration. Second, a protein called guanylate cyclase begins to resynthesize cGMP when calcium levels start to fall. Third, while all of this is going on, metarhodopsin II is chemically modified by an enzyme called rhodopsin kinase. The modified rhodopsin then binds to a protein known as arrestin, which prevents the rhodopsin from activating more transducin. So the cell contains mechanisms to limit the amplified signal started by a single photon.

Trans-retinal eventually falls off of rhodopsin and must be reconverted to 11-*cis*-retinal and again bound by rhodopsin to get back to the starting point for another visual cycle. To accomplish this, *trans*-retinal is first chemically modified by an enzyme to *trans*-retinol—a form containing two more hydrogen atoms. A second enzyme then converts the molecule to 11-*cis*-retinol. Finally, a third enzyme removes the previously added hydrogen atoms to form 11-*cis*-retinal, a cycle is complete.

The above explanation is just a sketchy overview of the biochemistry of vision. Ultimately, though, *this* is the level of explanation for which biological science must aim. In order to truly understand a function, one must understand in detail every relevant step in the process. The relevant steps in biological processes occur ultimately at the molecular level, so a satisfactory explanation of a biological phenomenon—such as sight, digestion, or immunity—must include its molecular explanation.

Now that the black box of vision has been opened, it is no longer enough for an evolutionary explanation of that power to consider only the *anatomical* structures of whole eyes, as Darwin did in the nineteenth century (and as popularizers of evolution continue to do today). Each of the anatomical

steps and structures that Darwin thought were so simple actually involves staggeringly complicated biochemical processes that cannot be papered over with rhetoric. Darwin's metaphorical hops from butte to butte are now revealed in many cases to be huge leaps between carefully tailored machines—distances that would require a helicopter to cross in one trip.

Thus biochemistry offers a Lilliputian challenge to Darwin. Anatomy is, quite simply, irrelevant to the question of whether evolution could take place on the molecular level. So is the fossil record. It no longer matters whether there are huge gaps in the fossil record or whether the record is as continuous as that of U.S. presidents. And if there are gaps, it does not matter whether they can be explained plausibly. The fossil record has nothing to tell us about whether the interactions of 11-*cis*-retinal with rhodopsin, transducin, and phosphodiesterase could have developed step-by-step. Neither do the patterns of biogeography matter, nor those of population biology, nor the traditional explanations of evolutionary theory for rudimentary organs or species abundance. This is not to say that random mutation is a myth, or that Darwinism fails to explain anything (it explains microevolution very nicely), or that large-scale phenomena like population genetics don't matter. They do. Until recently, however, evolutionary biologists could be unconcerned with the molecular details of life because so little was known about them. Now the black box of the cell has been opened, and the infinitesmal world that stands revealed must be explained.

Further Resources

BOOKS

Barrow, John D., and Frank J. Tipler. *The Anthropic Cosmological Principle.* New York: Oxford University Press, 1986.

Hanson, Robert W., ed. *Science and Creation: Geological, Theological, and Educational Perspectives.* New York: Macmillan, 1986.

Kitcher, Philip. *Abusing Science: The Case against Creationism.* Cambridge, Mass.: MIT Press, 1982.

Larson, Edward J. *Trial and Error: The American Controversy Over Creation and Evolution.* New York: Oxford University Press, 1985.

Morris, Henry M., ed. *Scientific Creationism.* San Diego: Creation-Life Publishers, 1974.

Shapiro, Robert. *Origins: A Skeptic's Guide to the Creation of Life on Earth.* New York: Summit Books, 1986.

Whitcomb, John C., and Henry M. Morris. *The Genesis Flood: The Biblical Record and Its Scientific Implications.* Philadelphia: Presbyterian and Reformed Publishing, 1961.

Zetterberg, J. Peter, ed. *Evolution Versus Creationism: The Public Education Controversy.* Phoenix: Oryx Press, 1977.

PERIODICALS

Callaghan, Catherine A. "Evolution and Creationist Arguments." *American Biology Teacher,* 1980, 422–427.

Cavanaugh, Michael A. "Scientific Creationism and Rationality." *Nature,* May 16, 1985, 185–189.

Gatewood, Willard B. "From Scopes to Creation Science: The Decline and Revival of the Evolution Controversy." *South Atlantic Quarterly,* 1984, 363–383.

Gould, Stephen Jay. "The Verdict on Creationism." *The New York Times Magazine,* July 19, 1987, 32–33.

Joyce, Gerald F. "Directed Molecular Evolution." *Scientific American,* December 1992, 90–98.

Miller, Kenneth R. "Life's Grand Design." *Technology Review,* February/March 1994, 29–32.

Nelkin, Dorothy. "The Science-Textbook Controversies." *Scientific American,* April 1976, 33–39.

Numbers, Ronald L. "Creationism in 20th-Century America." *Science,* November 5, 1982, 538–544.

"Ohio Science Curriculum Guidelines Question Evolution." *Ohio Schools,* November 2002, 5.

Scott, Eugenie C., and Henry P. Cole. "The Elusive Scientific Basis of Creation 'Science.'" *Quarterly Review of Biology,* March 1985, 21–30.

WEBSITES

Carol, Robert Todd. "Intelligent Design." The Skeptic's Dictionary. Available online at http://skepdic.com/intelligentdesign .html; website home page: http://skepdic.com (accessed July 15, 2003).

Institute for Creation Research. Available online at http://www .icr.org (accessed July 15, 2003).

"Intelligent Design? A Special Report Reprinted From *Natural History* Magazine." Actionbioscience.org. Available online at http://www.actionbioscience.org/evolution/nhmag.html; website home page: http://www.actionbioscience.org (accessed July 15, 2003).

"Intelligent Design and Evolution Awareness (IDEA) Club." University of California, San Diego. Available online at http://www-acs.ucsd.edu/~ideal; website home page: http:// www-acs.ucsd.edu (accessed July 15, 2003).

Intelligent Design Network. Available online at http://www .intelligentdesignnetwork.org (accessed July 15, 2003).

Intelligent Design URC. Available online at http://www.idurc .org (accessed July 15, 2003).

"Michael J. Behe, Ph.D." Lehigh University. Available online at http://www.lehigh.edu/~inbios/behe.html; website home page: http://lehigh.edu (accessed July 15, 2003).

Origins. Available online at http://www.origins.org (accessed July 15, 2003).

In Contempt

Memoir

By: Christopher Darden

Date: 1996

Source: Darden, Christopher. *In Contempt.* New York: ReganBooks, 1996, 315–319.

About the Author: Christopher Darden (1956–) was born in Richmond, Virginia, and graduated from the University of California Hastings College of Law in 1980. The next year he joined the Los Angeles County District Attorney's Office in Los Angeles, California, where he served fifteen years. He was a prosecutor in *The People of the State of California v. Orenthal James Simpson.* He later became an associate professor of law at Southwestern University School of Law. ■

Introduction

In *The Biotech Century,* American science writer Jeremy Rifkin asserts that the science of deoxyribonucleic acid (DNA), the molecule of heredity, is reshaping the world. Our legal system is an example of DNA's power—for it can confirm innocence and guilt wherever a crime scene has physical evidence that yields DNA.

The science undergirding DNA's use in our courts is straightforward. DNA is a spiral ladder, each rung containing two of the four nucleotide bases: adenine, guanine, cytosine, and thymine. Adenine always bonds with thymine, and guanine with cytosine. If half a strand of DNA (as one ascends the ladder) is thymine, thymine, cytosine, guanine, the other half must be adenine, adenine, guanine, cytosine. This example underscores that DNA is built by linking together nucleotide bases, as a ladder is built—by adding rung upon rung.

Each human, except identical twins, has a unique sequence of nucleotide bases in the nucleus of each cell in the body. DNA, therefore, is a genetic fingerprint of each person. Scientists can map the sequence of nucleotide bases of anyone given blood, hair, skin, or any other part of that person.

In a criminal investigation, where physical evidence yields DNA, scientists build sequences of nucleotide bases thousands, and even tens of thousands, of bases long. Alternatively, if they are fortunate, scientists may recover a sequence of nucleotide bases from a region of DNA where humans vary by several bases. In this instance, a sequence of several hundred bases will suffice. Several sequences of bases from a crime scene are matched against nucleotide bases extracted from a defendant. If they match, sequence by sequence numbering into the thousands or more of nucleotide bases, the likelihood that the DNA from the crime scene came from the defendant is near certainty. On the other hand, DNA sequences that do not match by even a single nucleotide base confirm a defendant's innocence. For the DNA from the crime scene to be that of the defendant, the match must be exact, nucleotide base by nucleotide base.

Significance

The most celebrated use of DNA evidence in the 1990s was for the 1994–1995 trial of Orenthal James (O.J.) Simpson for the murder of his ex-wife, Nicole Brown, and Ronald Goldman, an aspiring actor who arrived at Brown's home at the wrong time. During the trial, wrote Christopher Darden, the prosecution "presented perhaps the most impressive scientific evidence ever offered in a criminal trial." Blood at the crime scene, in Simpson's Bronco and in his home all yielded DNA, some of which matched the DNA of Nicole Brown, some Ronald Goldman, and the rest O.J. Simpson. "At Nicole Brown's condo, three blood samples . . . matched Simpson's blood," wrote Darden. "One of the drops had a one in 170 million chance of being someone else's."

Yet the jury acquitted Simpson, demonstrating that defense attorneys can persuade a group of men and women with a poor grasp of the science of DNA to doubt the validity of DNA evidence. Many people, including some of the trial's participants, have written at length about the role of race in the trial. This view has some truth, but it misses the larger point that too many Americans, including those on the Simpson jury, have a poor knowledge of science—not extending beyond an eighth or ninth grade course in earth science, a course in which students in too many public schools do little more than memorize, regurgitate, and forget vocabulary. Darden came close to this insight when he wrote "And yet, all along, we had a feeling that the science was coming up short with these jurors." Ironically, the jurors, rather than the science, came up short.

Thomas Jefferson, one of the eighteenth century's leading scientists, had envisioned an America in which all Americans, even those from humble backgrounds, would understand science well enough to keep abreast of current developments. The Simpson trial demonstrated that Americans have fallen far short of Jefferson's ideal. Science, as it has grown in complexity, has become the province of a small elite of highly trained practitioners. The Simpson trial demonstrates that our public schools must do better in educating Americans about science. Democracy grows weak when scientific knowledge concentrates among a minority of men and women. Jefferson's insight is as valid today as it was more than two centuries ago.

Primary Source

In Contempt [excerpt]

SYNOPSIS: In this excerpt Christopher Darden outlines the DNA evidence that identified O.J. Simpson

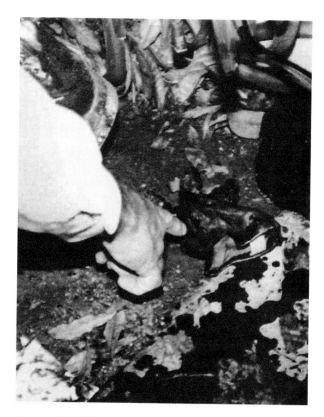

Detective Mark Fuhrman points to the infamous bloody glove found near the body of Nicole Brown Simpson, Los Angeles, June 12, 1994. Despite the tremendous amount of scientific evidence against him, O.J. Simpson was acquitted of the double murder of his ex-wife and Ronald Goldman. **AP/WIDE WORLD PHOTOS. REPRODUCED BY PERMISSION.**

as the murderer of Nicole Brown and Ronald Goldman. Yet he feared that this evidence failed to convince the jury.

Through May and early June, the Los Angeles County District Attorney's Office presented perhaps the most impressive scientific evidence ever offered in a criminal trial. For six weeks, we presented a solid and high wall of physical evidence: blood, hair, and fiber evidence from *three* separate sites—and showed that it would be impossible to fabricate or plant.

In the second week of May, we called Robin Cotton, the director of Cellmark Diagnostics of Maryland, the preeminent DNA lab in the country. With Woody Clarke asking intelligent but understandable questions, Cotton spent three days explaining DNA and the tests used to identify it. We received much criticism for the exercise from experts who said that we didn't need to teach jurors about a combustion engine to teach them how to drive.

They were right that the science lesson—like much of our evidence—took too long to present. No

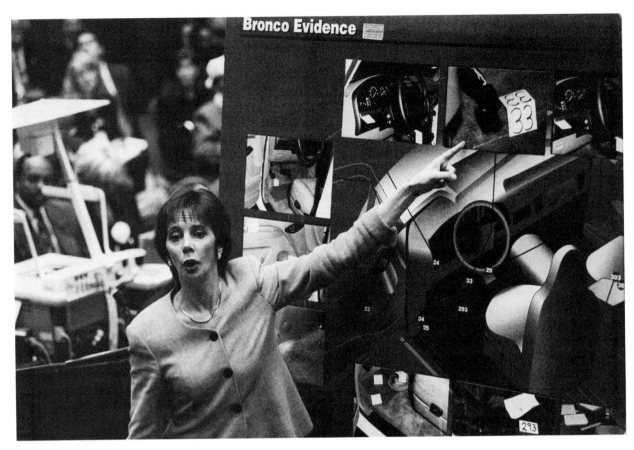

Prosecutor Marcia Clark points to an evidence chart during the O.J. Simpson trial, Los Angeles, September 29, 1995. The trial marked the most celebrated use of DNA evidence to link a suspect to the scene of a crime. **AP/WIDE WORLD PHOTOS. REPRODUCED BY PERMISSION.**

matter how simple Cotton tried to make it—"DNA is that part of the chromosomes that carries the information that programs an organism from the point of conception"—the complex theories still seemed to bore the jurors, who could hardly be blamed for their impatience by that point. Throughout the trial, I was trying to speed up testimony, but in this case, Woody and Rockne Harmon hoped to teach the jury just how conclusive this evidence was and how impossible it would have been to fabricate.

By the time Cotton finally got around to tying the blood at the murder scene to Simpson, and the blood at his estate and in his Bronco to Ron and Nicole, the experts criticized us for "anti-climactic" and "undramatic" testimony. I couldn't believe it. These were numbers! How sexy can you make numbers? We gave them the murderer and the pundits wanted drama! The case's transformation was complete: This was no longer a murder trial, it was a TV movie. Now, the critics had spoken. The second act, they said, needed more drama.

Instead, we presented facts. After Cotton, we called Gary Sims, of the California Department of

Justice, which had done DNA tests independent of Cellmark and had come to the same conclusions. When these two witnesses were done, we had presented a trail of evidence as conclusive as a videotape of Simpson committing the murders. More conclusive, in fact. It would have been more likely for a person who looked exactly like Simpson to show up on videotape than for the blood to have been from someone else.

It was the same evidence that had convinced me to take the case, that had convinced me that this wasn't a case about racial prejudice, but one about two brutal murders.

After cutting and slashing two people, O.J. Simpson left one of his gloves at the murder scene, along with his shoe prints, his hat, some of his blood and hair. At Nicole Brown's condo, three blood samples (at least eight separate drops of blood) matched Simpson's blood. One of the drops had a one in 170 million chance of being someone else's.

At Simpson's estate, O.J.'s blood was in his driveway and foyer, while Goldman's blood was on the glove alongside his house, and O.J.'s and Nicole's blood was on the socks in his bedroom. The blood was spattered on the socks—nineteen separate blood spots right around the ankles, where blood would likely splash as Simpson hacked at the victims and then walked through the pools of their blood. There were also blood smears at the tops of the socks, where he'd pulled them off his feet. The chance that the blood was someone else's besides Nicole's? One in 21 billion. Ron's? One in 41 billion. Pretty significant figures when there are only 5.5 billion people in the world.

In Simpson's Bronco, Nicole's blood was mixed with O.J.'s on the carpet. Goldman's blood was on the console, and a mixture of the blood of all three was elsewhere on the console.

Tests were done at two different labs. Contamination was impossible. And in all this testing, no other blood was found. In these lakes of blood, there were identifiable traces of only three people: Ron, Nicole, and O.J. Simpson.

Each time a defense attorney stood, his story became more absurd and contradictory. The attorneys argued vast incompetence and then argued a sophisticated conspiracy—all by the same people. If they couldn't find tiny mistakes in a witness's testimony—like missing staple holes—then the witness became part of a conspiracy that they insinuated spread even to the D.A.'s office, a huge plot apparently masterminded by one racist junior detective and carried out by people who had never met one another before.

During the science testimony, Scheck was the best at this duplicitous attack, asking hypothetical questions with no basis in fact and no evidence that anything he asked had ever happened. He attacked the numbers from Cellmark by bringing up mistakes made at the lab in 1989. He could find no errors in the analysis done on this case and so he had to go back six years and talk about problems that had already been addressed at the lab.

Rockne Harmon was Scheck's mortal opposite, a Vietnam vet who exuded military precision in the courtroom as he used DNA to convict criminals. Scheck was a Legal Aid-style lawyer who used the same technology to set them free. They had battled before, and once, while giving a slide presentation at a conference, Harmon had shown a photograph of Scheck and Neufeld and said "the princes of darkness."

Harmon went after some of Scheck's groundless theories, asking Sims—of the DOJ lab—if DNA could be contaminated by airborne particles, a theory Scheck had droned on about for hours.

"Now, can DNA fly?" Rock asked. "I mean, there are no scientific studies that have shown that, are there?"

"No," Sims said. "I don't think it has wings."

"How about if it's from a bird—can it fly? Does the DNA of an athletic person have any greater athletic prowess than that of a dead person?" Harmon asked. Scheck objected strenuously.

Like good seconds, Neufeld and Clarke argued as strongly as Scheck and Harmon, once getting into it over an unpublished letter by some experts questioning the value of forensic DNA. Neufeld wanted to introduce the letter as evidence and Woody argued that it had nothing to do with the case.

As they climbed all over each other, [Judge] Ito snapped again. "Get your checkbooks out. Right now! I'm not going to tolerate this thing any more."

He fined them each $250, but Woody didn't have any money on him. Earlier, Marcia had paid me back some money she'd borrowed on our trip to San Francisco—a few hundred dollars in an envelope that I still carried in my pocket. I stood, reached inside my pocket, pulled out the envelope, and gave Woody $250.

It wasn't until I sat down that I heard the buzz in the courtroom. By the time the day was over, there was a rumor about a prosecution slush fund that I, apparently, controlled from my coat pocket. It was ridiculous, but I wasn't going to explain the truth, that the money was given to me by Marcia to pay her half of our weekend getaway.

As May turned into June, the defense stepped up its ridiculous claims—like the theory that the blood under Nicole's fingernails might point to another suspect. They spent days talking about it, and we spent days refuting it. In this case, DNA showed it was Nicole's own blood. But with these kinds of arguments, by the time we settled the issue, I was afraid that enough noise had been made to distract and confuse the jury.

With every witness in this case, the defense spent days on cross-examination, giving the appearance of inconsistencies by the mere volume of questions they asked. And I have to believe that we played into their hands in some respects, trying to anticipate their attacks, spending too long debunking ridiculous theories.

Still, the science was overwhelming. Experienced lawyers were amazed at the amount and the level of scientific evidence we had against Simpson. Vincent Bugliosi, who prosecuted the Charles Manson family, said we could throw away 80 percent of our evidence and still get a conviction. Never in our legal system has so much blood and DNA evidence been amassed against one defendant.

One in 6.8 billion! That blood in Simpson's socks was Nicole's blood; there was no other explanation. One in 170 million! That blood at the scene was Simpson's; no other explanation.

And yet, all along, we had a feeling that the science was coming up short with these jurors. They watched matter-of-factly, as if the positive identification of Simpson's blood at the murder scene had no more meaning than Kato Kaelin's recalling what they ate at McDonald's.

There was some vital connection between the physical evidence and Simpson that was escaping these jurors. The science was too ethereal. We needed something concrete and visual, something to give life and meaning to these astronomical numbers.

Further Resources

BOOKS

Clark, Marcia. *Without a Doubt.* New York: Viking, 1997.

Dershowitz, Alan M. *Reasonable Doubts: The O.J. Simpson Case and the Criminal Justice System.* Thorndike, Maine: Thorndike Press, 1996.

Deutsch, Linda. *Verdict: The Chronicle of the O.J. Simpson Trial.* Kansas City, Mo.: Andrews and McMeel, 1995.

Gibbs, Jewelle Tayor. *Race and Justice: Rodney King and O.J. Simpson in a House Divided.* San Francisco: Jossey-Bass, 1996.

PERIODICALS

Chidley, Joe, and Anne Gregor. "O.J.: The Sequel." *Maclean's,* February 5, 1996, 50.

Figueroa, Ana. "O.J. Simpson's Latest Innocent Plea." *Newsweek,* February 28, 2000, 38.

Grabe, Maria E. "Narratives of Guilt: Television News Magazine Coverage of the O.J. Simpson Criminal Trial." *Howard Journal of Communications,* January 2000, 24–26.

WEBSITES

"Crime Scene Investigation Books: DNA." Available online at http://www.crime-scene-investigator.net/dna-books.html; website home page: http://www.crime-scene-investigator.net (accessed July 15, 2003).

"DNA Evidence." High Impact Training Solutions. Available online at http://www.hits.astcorp.com/les/dna.htm; website home page: http://www.hits.astcorp.com (accessed July 15, 2003).

The Evaluation of Forensic DNA Evidence. The National Academies. Available online at http://books.nap.edu/books /0309053951/html/index.html; website home page: http:// www.nationalacademies.org/ (accessed July 15, 2003).

"Forensics: DNA Evidence." Crime/Punishment. Available online at http://crime.about.com/cs/dnaevidence; website home page: http://crime.about.com (accessed July 15, 2003).

Meeker-O'Connell, Ann. "How DNA Evidence Works." How Stuff Works. Available online at http://howstuffworks .lycoszone.com/dna-evidence6.html; website home page: http://howstuffworks.lycoszone.com (accessed July 15, 2003).

Understanding DNA Evidence: A Guide for Victim Service Providers. Office of Justice Programs. Department of Justice. Available online at http://www.ojp.usdoj.gov/nij/dna _evbro/; website home page: http://www.ojp.usdoj.gov (accessed July 15, 2003).

"We're Going to Talk About Forensic Science and Mention the O.J. Simpson Trial Just This Once!" The Why Files. Available online at http://whyfiles.org/014forensic; website home page: http://whyfiles.com (accessed July 15, 2003).

"What Every Law Enforcement Officer Should Know About DNA Evidence." National Criminal Justice Reference Service. Available online at http://www.ncjrs.org/nij/DNAbro /intro.html; website home page: http://www.ncjrs.org/ (accessed July 15, 2003).

William J. Clinton to the Heads of Executive Departments and Agencies, March 4, 1997

Memo

By: Bill Clinton

Date: March 4, 1997

Source: Clinton, William J. Memorandum to the Heads of Executive Departments and Agencies, March 4, 1997. Available online at http://grants1.nih.gov/grants/policy/cloning_directive .htm; website home page: http://grants1.nih.gov (accessed July 16, 2003).

About the Author: William Jefferson (Bill) Clinton (1946–) was born in Hope, Arkansas, and was a Rhodes scholar at Oxford University in England between 1968 and 1970. In 1973, he graduated from Yale University Law School and taught at the University of Arkansas Law School until 1976. A Democrat, he won election in 1978 as Arkansas's governor, and he became the first Democrat to serve two full terms as U.S. president (served 1993–2001) since Franklin D. Roosevelt (served 1933–1945). ∎

Introduction

In February 1997, Scottish scientist Ian Wilmut electrified the world by announcing that he and team of researchers had cloned a sheep. "The science is the easy part," lamented American journalist Jeffrey Kluger in March 1997. Although the technical difficulties can be formidable, Kluger is right that the concept of cloning any animal, including a human, is straightforward. A scientist who wishes to clone a human must extract an egg from a woman (any egg from any woman will do). He or she must then remove the egg's nucleus, inserting in its place the nucleus from any somatic (nonsex) cell from the person (P) the scientist wishes to clone. The egg now contains a full complement of twenty-three pairs of chromosomes (forty-six total), and neither can be, nor needs to be, fertilized. The scientist implants the egg in the womb of any woman, and barring a miscarriage, nine months later she will give birth to a clone of P.

Yet the ethics of cloning a human are anything but straightforward. Instead, controversy engulfs the debate. As in the case of evolution, religion and science are at odds. "I can't think of a morally acceptable reason to clone a human being," wrote Richard McCormick, a Jesuit priest and professor of Christian ethics at the University of Notre Dame. The fear is that the cloning of a human reduces the mystery of life to technical proficiency in manipulating the genes in a cell. Rather than the poetry of Genesis, in which God forms man from the earth and breathes life into him, science has reduced life to a chemistry that researchers can duplicate in the laboratory. "It's a horrendous crime to make a Xerox of someone," wrote American science writer Jeremy Rifkin. "You're putting a human into a genetic straitjacket. For the first time, we've taken the principles of industrial design, quality control, predictability and applied them to a human being."

Significance

This argument resonated with President Bill Clinton, a Southern Baptist of conservative religious views. On March 4, 1997, he issued an executive order banning the use of federal funds in the cloning of humans. He also reiterated his charge to the National Bioethics Advisory Commission to report to him within ninety days on the legal and ethical issues of cloning a human.

Scientists chafed at these restrictions. American physicist Richard Seed announced in January 1998 his intention to clone a human within eighteen months, and he hinted that Clinton and those who supported his views were hindering scientific progress. Seed's argument implied that scientists, rather than policymakers, had the right to direct science.

Yet this is not an easy argument to make. The relationship between science and the federal government stretches back to the ideas of Thomas Jefferson and Benjamin Franklin, both of whom assumed that the federal government would fund science—and that this funding would give policymakers control over the direction of science. The first large federal investment in science came in 1862, when Congress created the U.S. Depart-

ment of Agriculture (USDA) and the agricultural and mechanical colleges. Since then, presidential appointees to the USDA have set the scientific agenda at the agency. Seed's position notwithstanding, federal funding has long given U.S. policymakers control over science. Clinton simply exercised the power that presidents have had since Abraham Lincoln signed the bill creating the USDA. If Seed or any other American scientist is to clone a human, he will need to do so with private funds. Whether private investors are interested enough in cloning a human to fund it is unclear. We may not know the answer for years.

Primary Source

William J. Clinton to the Heads of Executive Departments and Agencies, March 4, 1997

> **SYNOPSIS:** In this executive order, President Bill Clinton banned the use of federal funds in the cloning of humans. He also reiterated his charge to the National Bioethics Advisory Commission to report to him within ninety days on the legal and ethical issues of cloning a human.

March 4, 1997

For Immediate Release
Memorandum for the Heads of Executive Departments and Agencies
SUBJECT: Prohibition on Federal Funding for Cloning of Human Beings

Recent accounts of advances in cloning technology, including the first successful cloning of an adult sheep, raise important questions. They potentially represent enormous scientific breakthroughs that could offer benefits in such areas as medicine and agriculture. But the new technology also raises profound ethical issues, particularly with respect to its possible use to clone humans. That is why last week I asked our National Bioethics Advisory Commission to thoroughly review the legal and ethical issues associated with the use of this technology and report back to me in 90 days.

Federal funds should not be used for cloning of human beings. The current restrictions on the use of Federal funds for research involving human embryos do not fully assure this result. In December 1994, I directed the National Institutes of Health *not to fund the creation of human embryos for research purposes.* The Congress extended this prohibition in FY 1996 and FY 1997 appropriations bills, barring the Department of Health and Human Services from supporting certain human embryo research. However,

President Bill Clinton seated at his desk in the White House Oval Office, 1993. On March 4, 1997, President Clinton issued a memo banning the use of federal funds for cloning humans. THE LIBRARY OF CONGRESS.

these restrictions do not explicitly cover human embryos created for implantation and do not cover all Federal agencies. I want to make it absolutely clear that no Federal funds will be used for human cloning. Therefore, I hereby direct that no Federal funds shall be allocated for cloning of human beings.

William J. Clinton

Further Resources

BOOKS

Howard, Ted, and Jeremy Rifkin. *Who Should Play God? The Artificial Creation of Life and What It Means to the Future of the Human Race.* New York: Dell Publishing, 1997.

Rifkin, Jeremy. *The Biotech Century: Harnessing the Gene and Remaking the World.* New York: Putnam, 1998.

Silver, Lee M. *Remaking Eden: Cloning and Beyond in a Brave New World.* New York: Avon Books, 1997.

PERIODICALS

"Christian Legal Society Asks U.S. Senate to Act on Opportunity to Prevent Human Cloning." *Health & Medicine Week,* September 2, 2002, 7.

Coghlan, Andy. "Race Is on to Stop Human Cloning." *New Scientist,* September 28, 2002, 11.

"Doctor Defends Human Cloning Experiment." *Genomics & Genetics Weekly,* September 13, 2002, 10–12.

Evans, John H. "Religion and Human Cloning." *Journal for the Scientific Study of Religion,* December 2002, 747–759.

Kluger, Jeffrey. "Will We Follow the Sheep?" *Time,* March 10, 1997, 14–18.

WEBSITES

Best, Steven, and Douglas Kellner. "Biotechnology, Ethics, and the Politics of Cloning." Graduate School of Education and Information Studies. University of California, Los Angeles. Available online at http://www.gseis.ucla.edu/faculty/kellner /papers/biotechdem.htm; website home page: http://www .gseis.ucla.edu (accessed July 16, 2003).

Clonaid.com: The First Human Cloning Company. Available online at http://www.clonaid.com (accessed July 16, 2003).

"Cloning Discussion Scenario." Strategis. Available online at http://strategis.ic.gc.ca/SSG/bb00008e.html; website home page: http://strategis.ic.gc.ca (accessed July 16, 2003).

Human Cloning and Human Dignity: An Ethical Inquiry. The President's Council on Bioethics. Available online at http://www.bioethics.gov/reports/cloningreport/index.html; website home page: http://www.bioethics.gov (accessed July 16, 2003)

Human Cloning Foundation. Available online at http://www .humancloning.org (accessed July 16, 2003).

Kerschen, Arthur. "Human Cloning: The How to Page." Biofact Report. Available online at http://www.biofact.com /cloning/human.html; website home page: http://www.biofact .com (accessed July 16, 2003)

Wachbroit, Robert. "Genetic Encores: The Ethics of Human Cloning." School of Public Affairs. University of Maryland. Available online at http://www.puaf.umd.edu/IPPP/fall97 /Reportcloning.htm; website home page: http://www.puaf .umd.edu (accessed July 16, 2003).

"Neandertal DNA Sequences and the Origin of Modern Humans"

Journal article

By: Matthias Krings, Anne Stone, Ralf W. Schmitz, Heike Krainitzki, Mark Stoneking, and Svante Pääbo

Date: July 11, 1997

Source: Krings, Matthias, et al. "Neandertal DNA Sequences and the Origin of Modern Humans." *Cell,* 90, July 11, 1997, 21–28.

About the Authors: Matthias Krings has been a research scholar at the Frobenius-Institute of the Johann Wolfgang Goethe University in Germany, a research fellow at the Max Planck Institute of Evolutionary Anthropology in Leipzig, Germany, and a fellow at the University of Munich's Zoological Institute in Munich, Germany.

Anne C. Stone received a B.A. from the University of Virginia in 1989, and an M.A. (1992) and Ph.D. (1996) in anthropology from Pennsylvania State University. She was a postdoctoral fellow at the University of Arizona between 1997 and 1998. Since 1999, she has been an assistant professor of anthropology at the University of New Mexico.

Ralf W. Schmitz is a professor at the Institute for Prehistory and Protohistory in the Department of Early Prehistory and Quaternary Ecology at the University of Tübingen in Germany. An archeologist, he is an authority on Neanderthal and modern human burial sites.

Heike Krainitzki is curator at the Rhineland Museum in Bonn, Germany. She is an authority on the prehistoric people of Europe, including Neanderthals and modern humans.

Mark Stoneking (1956–) received a Ph.D. in genetics from the University of California, Berkeley, in 1986. After serving as staff scientist at the Human Genome Center in Berkeley, California, and teaching at Pennsylvania State University, since 1999 he has been a professor at the Max Planck Institute for Evolutionary Anthropology in Leipzig, Germany. In 2000, he was elected as a fellow of the American Association for the Advancement of Science.

Svante Pääbo (1955–) was born in Stockholm, Sweden, and received a Ph.D. in biology from the University of Uppsala, Sweden, in 1986. Between 1986 and 1987, he was a postdoctoral fellow at the University of Zurich in Switzerland. Between 1987 and 1990, he was a postdoctoral fellow at the University of California, Berkeley. Since 1990, he has been a professor of biology at the University of Munich in Munich, Germany. ∎

Introduction

In 1859, Charles Darwin announced that all life evolved from primitive ancestors. He restricted himself in *On the Origin of Species* (1859) to a single sentence on human evolution, a caution that did not deter British naturalist Thomas Henry Huxley and German naturalist Ernest Haeckel from publishing books in the 1860s on human evolution. Darwin joined the debate in 1871 with *The Descent of Man.* Yet the three had little fossil evidence of human evolution. Amateur fossil hunters had found the remains of early man in 1829 in Belgium, and, in 1848, in Gibraltar, but had not recognized the antiquity of the find.

The crucial find came in 1856, when quarry workers unearthed a partial skeleton in Germany's Neander Valley (hence the name Neanderthal, or Neandertal, man). Local teacher Carl Fuhlrott identified the bones as the remains of a robustly built early man. Since this discovery paleoanthropologists have debated Neanderthal's relationship to modern humans for nearly 150 years. One possibility is that Neanderthals were the immediate ancestors of modern humans. A second is that Neanderthals were a side branch in evolution, remaining separate from modern humans and becoming extinct without issuing any further species. A third is that Neanderthals were a side branch that interbred with modern humans in western Asia and Europe. Thus, modern humans would con-

Dr. Mark Stoneking. Dr. Stoneking was part of a research team that discovered that Neanderthals are not our ancestors. **PHOTO BY GREG GRIECO. © 2003 GREG GRIECO. REPRODUCED BY PERMISSION.**

tain Neanderthal genes, even though Neanderthals themselves went extinct.

During the twentieth century, the accumulating fossils established Neanderthals in western Asia and Europe by 150,000 years ago, perhaps earlier. Modern humans, the fossil evidence suggests, evolved in Africa about 130,000 years ago, migrating to western Asia 100,000 years ago and to Europe 40,000 years ago. Thus modern humans could not have evolved from Neanderthals in western Asia or Europe, though the two might have interbred in both places. The fossil evidence left unclear whether modern humans evolved from Neanderthals in Africa.

With the fossil evidence unable to provide an unequivocal answer, molecular biologists sought the answer in genetic comparisons of Neanderthals and modern humans. Were modern humans the immediate descendants of Neanderthals, they would carry Neanderthal genes in large numbers. Comparison, therefore, should show few

Matthias Krings, Bonn, Germany, July 11, 1997. Krings poses with parts of a skull found in 1857 in the Neander Valley, near Dusseldorf, Germany. Krings and five other researchers performed DNA tests showing Neanderthals were a different species than humans. AP/WIDE WORLD PHOTOS. REPRODUCED BY PERMISSION.

differences between Neanderthal genes and modern human genes. Were Neanderthals a separate branch that did not interbreed with modern humans, they should differ in genes more than any two modern humans differ. The intermediary position— that Neanderthals were a side branch, but interbred with modern humans— should yield more genetic differences than any two modern humans differ, but only by a small number.

Significance

Yet Neanderthals had vanished in western Asia and Europe thirty thousand years ago and had left no fossil trail in Africa. Few geneticists believed Neanderthals of such antiquity would contain any deoxyribonucleic acid (DNA), the molecule of heredity, for comparison with modern humans.

In 1997, an American-German team of researchers led by Matthias Krings stunned scientists by announcing the extraction of DNA from the famous 1856 Neanderthal skeleton. DNA exists in two locations in a cell: the nucleus—the center of a cell that contains information that tells a cell what to manufacture; and the mitochondria—

the parts of a cell that metabolize energy. Krings and his colleagues extracted mitochondrial DNA (mtDNA) from the Neanderthal skeleton.

DNA is a spiral ladder, with each rung containing two of the four nucleotide bases (large, carbon-based molecules): adenine, guanine, cytosine, and thymine. These bases are in a sequence unique to each person. (Only identical twins share the same sequence of nucleotide bases.) Krings and his colleagues compared a strand of mtDNA from the Neanderthal skeleton with mtDNA from 2,051 modern humans. The Neanderthal mtDNA strand had only 328 nucleotide bases. Fortunately, these bases were from a region of mtDNA in which modern humans differed from one another by eight nucleotide bases on average, and in which one would, therefore, expect differences between Neanderthal mtDNA and modern human mtDNA. Neanderthal mtDNA and modern human mtDNA differed by twenty-eight nucleotide bases, Krings and his colleagues announced, nearly four times more than any two modern humans differed in their mtDNA. These differences, they concluded, were too great for Neanderthal to have been the immediate ancestor of modern humans, or to have interbred with modern humans. Neanderthal had been a side branch that went extinct without issue.

Krings and his colleagues have made a strong case that Neanderthals were not ancestral to modern humans, but the issue of interbreeding is harder to resolve. The ancestors of the 1856 Neanderthal had not interbred with modern humans, at least not in large numbers, as Krings and his colleagues concluded. It is possible, however, that other Neanderthals in Europe and western Asia interbred with modern humans, perhaps in large numbers. Given the frequency with which humans have sex, either with one partner or several, some anthropologists find it improbable that humans coexisted with Neanderthals for tens of thousands of years without interbreeding in large numbers. Additional mtDNA comparisons may resolve this issue.

Primary Source

"Neandertal DNA Sequences and the Origin of Modern Humans" [excerpt]

SYNOPSIS: In this excerpt, Matthias Krings and his colleagues announced that Neandertal mtDNA and modern human mtDNA differed by twenty-eight nucleotide bases out of 328 bases, nearly four times more than any two modern humans differed in their mtDNA. These differences, they concluded, were too great for Neandertal to have been the immediate ancestor of modern humans, or to have interbred with modern humans. Neandertal had been a side branch that went extinct without issue.

Summary

DNA was extracted from the Neandertal-type specimen found in 1856 in western Germany. By sequencing clones from short overlapping PCR products, a hitherto unknown mitochondrial (mt) DNA sequence was determined. Multiple controls indicate that this sequence is endogenous to the fossil. Sequence comparisons with human mtDNA sequences, as well as phylogenetic analyses, show that the Neandertal sequence falls outside the variation of modern humans. Furthermore, the age of the common ancestor of the Neandertal and modern human mtDNAs is estimated to be four times greater than that of the common ancestor of human mtDNAs. This suggests that Neandertals went extinct without contributing mtDNA to modern humans.

Introduction

Neandertals are a group of extinct hominids that inhabited Europe and western Asia from about 300,000 to 30,000 years ago. During part of this time they coexisted with modern humans. Based on morphological comparisons, it has been variously claimed that Neandertals: (1) were the direct ancestors of modern Europeans; (2) contributed some genes to modern humans; or (3) were completely replaced by modern humans without contributing any genes. . . . Analyses of molecular genetic variation in the mitochondrial and nuclear genomes of contemporary human populations have generally supported the third view, i.e., that Neandertals were a separate species that went extinct without contributing genes to modern humans. . . . However, these analyses rely on assumptions, such as the absence of selection and a clock-like rate of molecular evolution in the DNA sequences under study, whose validity has been questioned. . . . An additional and more direct way to address the question of the relationship between modern humans and Neandertals would be to analyze DNA sequences from the remains of Neandertals. . . .

Determination of the Neandertal mtDNA Sequence

The entire sequence of hypervariable region I of the mtDNA control region (positions 16,023 to 16,400; was determined. . . .

Sequence Comparisons

When the Neandertal DNA sequence is compared to the human reference sequence, 27 differences are seen outside the heteroplasmic cytosine homopolymer. . . . Of these 27 differences, 24 are transitions, two are transversions, and one represents an insertion of a single adenosine residue.

The Neandertal sequence was compared to a collection of 2051 human and 59 common chimpanzee sequences over 360 bp of the sequence determined from the Neandertal (positions 16,024 to 16,383). Among the 27 nucleotide differences to the reference sequence found in this segment, 25 fall among the 225 positions that vary in at least one of the human sequences, and one of the two remaining positions varies among the chimpanzees. Thus, the types of differences observed (e.g., an excess of transitions over transversions), and the positions in the Neandertal sequence where they occur, reflect the evolutionary pattern typical of mtDNA sequences of extant humans and chimpanzees.

The Neandertal sequence was compared to 994 contemporary human mitochondrial lineages, i.e., distinct sequences occurring in one or more individuals, found in 478 Africans, 510 Europeans, 494 Asians, 167 Native Americans and 20 individuals from Australia and Oceania. . . . Whereas these modern human sequences differ among themselves by an average of 8.0 ± 3.1 (range 1–24) substitutions, the difference between the humans and the Neandertal sequence is 27.2 ± 2.2 (range 22–36) substitutions. Thus, the largest difference observed between any two human sequences was two substitutions larger than the smallest difference between a human and the Neandertal. In total, 0.002% of the pairwise comparisons between human mtDNA sequences were larger than the smallest difference between the Neandertal and a human.

The Neandertal sequence, when compared to the mitochondrial lineages from different continents, differs by 28.2 ± 1.9 substitutions from the European lineages, 27.1 ± 2.2 substitutions from the African lineages, 27.7 ± 2.1 substitutions from the Asian lineages, 27.4 ± 1.8 substitutions from the American lineages and 28.3 ± 3.7 substitutions from the Australian/Oceanic lineages. Thus, whereas the Neandertals inhabited the same geographic region as contemporary Europeans, the observed differences between the Neandertal sequence and modern Europeans do not indicate that it is more closely related to modern Europeans than to any other population of contemporary humans.

When the comparison was extended to 16 common chimpanzee lineages . . . the number of positions in common among the human and chimpanzee sequences was reduced to 333. . . . This reduced the number of human lineages to 986. The average number of differences among humans is 8.0 ± 3.0 (range 1–24), that between humans and the Neandertal, 25.6 ± 2.2 (range 20–34), and that between humans and chimpanzees, 55.0 ± 3.0 (range 46–67). Thus, the average number of mtDNA sequence differences between modern humans and the Neandertal is about three times that among humans, but about half of that between modern humans and modern chimpanzees. . . .

Age of the Neandertal/Modern Human mtDNA Ancestor

To estimate the time when the most recent ancestral sequence common to the Neandertal and modern human mtDNA sequences existed, we used an estimated divergence date between humans and chimpanzees of 4–5 million years ago . . . and corrected the observed sequence differences for multiple substitutions at the same nucleotide site. . . . This yielded a date of 550,000 to 690,000 years before present for the divergence of the Neandertal mtDNA and contemporary human mtDNAs. When the age of the modern human mtDNA ancestor is estimated using the same procedure, a date of 120,000 to 150,000 years is obtained, in agreement with previous estimates. . . . Although these dates rely on the calibration point of the chimpanzee-human divergence and have errors of unknown magnitude associated with them, they indicate that the age of the common ancestor of the Neandertal sequence and modern human sequences is about four times greater than that of the common ancestor of modern human mtDNAs. . . .

Implications for Modern Human Origins

Both pairwise sequence comparisons and phylogenetic analyses tend to place the Neandertal mtDNA sequence outside modern human mtDNA variation. Furthermore, the divergence between the Neandertal mtDNA sequence and the modern human mitochondrial gene pool is estimated to be about four-fold older than the diversity of the modern human mtDNA gene pool. This shows that the diversity among Neandertal mtDNA sequences would have to be at least four times larger than among modern humans in order for other Neandertal sequences to be ancestral to modern human sequences. Thus, although based on a single Neandertal sequence, the present results indicate that Neandertals did not contribute mtDNA to modern humans.

These results do not rule out the possibility that Neandertals contributed other genes to modern humans. However, the view that Neandertals would have contributed little or nothing to the modern human gene pool is gaining support from studies of molecular genetic variation at nuclear loci in humans. . . . It is also in agreement with assessments of the degree of morphological difference between Neandertal skeletal remains and modern humans . . . that would classify Neandertals and modern humans as separate species.

Given the placement of the Neandertal mtDNA sequence outside the range of modern human mtDNA variation, it can be used as an outgroup in phylogenetic analyses to assess the geographic origin of the human mtDNA ancestor. Initial claims that Africa was the most likely geographic source of contemporary human mtDNA variation . . . were challenged by subsequent reanalyses that found the original phylogenetic analyses to be inadequate. . . . However, new methods of phylogenetic analysis have continued to support an African origin of human mtDNA variation . . . as has the use of a nuclear mtDNA insertion as an outgroup. When the Neandertal mtDNA sequence is used to root a neighbor joining tree of modern human mtDNA sequences . . . the first three branches consist exclusively of African sequences. The Neandertal mtDNA sequence thus supports a scenario in which modern humans arose recently in Africa as a distinct species and replaced Neandertals with little or no interbreeding.

Implications for Neandertal Genetics

It is interesting to compare the mtDNA date for the divergence between Neandertals and modern humans of 550,000 to 690,000 years ago with dates derived from other sources of information. For example, the fossil record indicates a likely minimum date for the divergence between modern humans and Neandertals of 250,000–300,000 years . . . while the archaeological record also puts the divergence between modern humans and Neandertals at about 300,000 years. . . . A date of over 500,000 years for the molecular divergence between Neandertal and human mtDNAs is in excellent agreement with the palaeontological and archaeological record since the divergence of genes is expected to predate the divergence of populations by an amount that reflects the level of polymorphism in the ancestral species. . . . Thus, if the palaeontological and archaeological estimates for the divergence of the Neandertal and human populations are accurate, and the mtDNA estimate for the molecular divergence is also accurate, this would indicate that the diversity of the mtDNA gene pool in the ancestral species (presumably Homo erectus) from which Neandertals and humans evolved, was at least as great as that of modern humans.

Further Resources

BOOKS

Bowler, Peter J. *Theories of Human Evolution.* Baltimore: Johns Hopkins University Press, 1986.

Dobzhansky, Theodosius. *Mankind Evolving.* New Haven, Conn.: Yale University Press, 1962.

Leakey, Richard E., and Roger Lewin. *Origins: What New Discoveries Reveal About the Emergence of Our Species and Its Possible Future.* New York: Dutton, 1977.

Lewin, Roger. *Bones of Contention.* New York: Simon & Schuster, 1987.

———. *In the Age of Mankind: A Smithsonian Book of Human Evolution.* Washington, D.C.: Smithsonian Books, 1988.

———. *Principles of Human Evolution: A Core Textbook.* Malden, Mass.: Blackwell Science, 1998.

Shreeve, James. *The Neanderthal Enigma.* New York: William Morrow, 1995.

Smith, Fred H., and Frank Spencer, eds. *The Origin of Modern Humans.* New York: Alan Liss, 1984.

Stringer, Christopher B. *In Search of the Neanderthals.* London, England: Thomas and Hudson, 1993.

Tanner, Nancy M. *On Becoming Human.* New York: Cambridge University Press, 1981.

Tattersall, Ian. *The Last Neanderthal.* New York: Macmillan, 1995.

Trinkaus, Erik, and Pat Shipman. *The Neanderthals.* New York: Alfred A. Knopf, 1993.

PERIODICALS

Graves, Peter. "New Models and Metaphors for the Neanderthal Debate." *Current Anthropology,* 1991, 255–274.

Hublin, John J. "A Late Neanderthal Associated With Upper Paleolithic Artifacts." *Nature,* May 16, 1996, 224–226.

Kahn, Patricia, and Ann Gibbons. "DNA From an Extinct Human." *Science,* July 11, 1997, 176–178.

Klein, Richard G. "Neanderthals and Modern Humans in West Asia." *Evolutionary Anthropology,* 1995/1996, 187–193.

Schwartz, Jeffrey H., and Ian Tattersall. "Significance of Previously Unrecognized Apomorphies in the Nasal Region of *Homo neanderthalensis.*" *Proceedings of the National Academy of Science,* October 1996, 10852–10854.

Smith, Fred H. "The Neanderthals: Evolutionary Dead Ends or Ancestors of Modern People?" *Journal of Anthropological Research,* 1991, 219–238.

Stringer, Christopher B., and Robert Grun. "Time for the Last Neanderthal." *Nature,* June 27, 1991, 701–702.

Weaver, Kenneth F., et al. "The Search for Early Man." *National Geographic,* November 1985, 560–629.

WEBSITES

"The Human Origins Program." National Museum of Natural History. Smithsonian Institution. Available online at http:// www.mnh.si.edu/anthro/humanorigins; website home page: http://www.mnh.si.edu (accessed July 15, 2003).

"Lucy in the Earth." A Science Odyssey. Available online at http://www.pbs.org/wgbh/aso/tryit/evolution/lucy.html; website home page: http://www.pbs.org/wgbh/aso/ (accessed July 16, 2003).

Walker, Phillip L., and Edward H. Hagen. "Human Evolution: The Fossil Evidence in 3D." Department of Anthropology. University of California, Santa Barbara. Available online at http://www.anth.ucsb.edu/projects/human; website home page: http://www.anth.ucsb.edu (accessed July 15, 2003).

Mars *Pathfinder* Science Results

Photographs

By: National Aeronautics and Space Administration (NASA)

Date: October 1997

Source: Photri Microstock. Available online at http://mars.jpl.nasa.gov/MPF/ops/prm-thmb.html; website home page: http://mars.jpl.nasa.gov (accessed July 30, 2003).

About the Organization: In 1958, Congress created NASA to recapture U.S. leadership in the space race after the Soviet Union (U.S.S.R.) stunned the United States and the world, in 1957, by launching the world's first intercontinental ballistic missile and satellite, *Sputnik.* NASA launched the first probes to Mars in 1964 and landed the first man on the moon in 1969. NASA launched the first space shuttle in 1981, and landed *Pathfinder* and *Sojourner* on Mars in 1997. NASA planned subsequent probes to Mars in 2003 and 2005. ∎

Introduction

American astronomer Percival Lowell stimulated interest in Mars. Through his telescope at the Lowell Observatory at Flagstaff, Arizona, Lowell in the 1890s believed he saw a network of canals. Intelligent beings must have built them, he reasoned, evidencing that Mars once harbored life and, perhaps, still did.

During the space race between the United States and the U.S.S.R., both nations sought to expand their knowledge of Mars. In 1958, Congress created NASA to lead the American charge into space. In 1964, NASA launched *Mariner 3,* the first of its probes intended for Mars. Technical problems scuttled *Mariner 3,* a loss that did not deter NASA from launching *Mariner 4* in November 1964. In July 1965, it flew within 6,000 miles of Mars—photographing Mars' surface in more detail than any telescope on Earth could hope to achieve. These photos showed Mars to be cratered like the moon. *Mariner 4* detected an atmosphere only 1 percent as dense as Earth's. In 1969, NASA launched *Mariner 6* and *7* for Mars.

Primary Source

Mars *Pathfinder* Science Results

SYNOPSIS: The first of these three photos shows *Sojourner* on its approach to a Martian rock nicknamed "Yogi" on July 9, 1997. To the rover's immediate left is the smaller rock called "Barnacle Bill." At the lower left corner of the image is the ramp used by *Sojourner* to drive off *Pathfinder*. Other photos from *Pathfinder* and *Sojourner* reveal that wind has eroded Martian rocks, further evidence of Mars' atmosphere. COURTESY OF PHOTRI MICROSTOCK. REPRODUCED BY PERMISSION.

Two years later, Soviet probe *Mars 3* landed a capsule on Mars during a dust storm that disabled the capsule after twenty seconds. In 1974, Soviet probe *Mars 5* orbited Mars, detecting a weak magnetic field on the planet—implying that Mars had once had a radioactive core that melted rock and metals, including iron in its interior. The movement of molten iron inside Mars generated a magnetic field.

Meanwhile, in 1972, *Mariner 9* became the first U.S. probe to orbit Mars, sending back more than 7,000 photos of its surface. *Mariner 9* revealed that Mars had volcanoes, evidence that Mars had once had a radioactive core whose pressure and heat vented through volcanoes, evidence that *Mars 5* corroborated. In 1975, NASA launched *Viking 1* and *2,* both of which set landing craft on Mars. The crafts tested soil samples and

rock, and the probes relayed photos back to Earth, *Viking 2* until 1980.

Significance

NASA crowned these efforts, landing *Pathfinder* on Mars on July 4, 1997. *Pathfinder* released *Sojourner,* the first automated rover, to analyze and photograph soil and rock. The first of the accompanying photos shows *Sojourner* on its approach to a Martian rock. Other photos from *Pathfinder* and *Sojourner* reveal that wind has eroded Martian rocks, further evidence of Mars' atmosphere. Other rocks display pits and pebbles alongside them that scientists believe wind may have dislodged from larger rocks. Between July 4 and October 7, *Pathfinder* and *Sojourner* relayed some 16,000 photos to Earth, the largest collection from a single probe.

Primary Source

Mars *Pathfinder* Science Results

Close-up of the rock "Yogi," taken by *Sojourner* on July 9, 1997. *Sojourner* used its Alpha Proton X-Ray Spectrometer (APXS) instrument to conduct a study of Yogi's chemical composition. The rover's track marks are also visible in the foreground. Multiple soil mechanics experiments were performed by *Sojourner*'s cleated wheels at this location. COURTESY OF PHOTRI MI-CROSTOCK. REPRODUCED BY PERMISSION.

Primary Source

Mars *Pathfinder* Science Results

One of *Sojourner*'s two front cameras took this image of several large rocks on July 10, 1997. The lander and its deployed rear ramp are at the upper left. The rover was near the rock "Yogi" when the image was taken. COURTESY OF PHOTRI MICRO-STOCK. REPRODUCED BY PERMISSION.

That year NASA's Mars Global Surveyor began orbiting Mars with the objective of mapping its entire surface. With these maps, NASA scientists hoped to identify landing sites for probes they intended to launch in 2003 and 2005.

The exploration of Mars, from *Mariner 4* to *Pathfinder,* reveals that Mars was once like Earth in having liquid water, a radioactive core, and active volcanoes. These conditions, along with an atmosphere, may have permitted the evolution of microbial life, a humble step well below the intelligent beings Percival Lowell had envisioned. Some scientists believe a Martian asteroid contains tiny etchings left by microorganisms, though others contend these etchings resemble those on lunar rock, where no life existed. Even if Mars once harbored life, scientists believe none now exists on the barren, arid planet.

Further Resources

BOOKS

Hamilton, John. *The "Pathfinder" Mission to Mars.* Minneapolis, Minn.: Abdo & Daughters, 1998.

Pritchett, Price. *The Mars "Pathfinder."* Dallas, Tex.: Pritchett & Associates, 1998.

Shirley, Donna. *Managing Martians.* New York: Broadway Books, 1998.

PERIODICALS

Arvidson, Raymond E., et al. "The Surface of Mars." *Scientific American,* March 1978, 76–89.

James, J.N. "The Voyage of *Mariner IV.*" *Scientific American,* March 1966, 42–52.

Wilson, Nigel. "Shark Bay May Hold Clue to Life on Mars." *Australian,* November 13, 2002, 4.

WEBSITES

"Mars Atmospheric and Geological Imaging." Lunar and Planetary Laboratory. University of Arizona. Available online at http://www.lpl.arizona.edu/IMP; website home page: http://www.lpl.arizona.edu (accessed July 16, 2003).

"Mars Missions—Past, Present, and Future." Available online at http://mars.sgi.com (accessed July 16, 2003).

"Mars *Pathfinder.*" Live from Earth & Mars. Available online at http://www-k12.atmos.washington.edu/k12/mars/pathfinder.html; website home page http://www-k12.atmos.washington.edu/k12 (accessed July 16, 2003).

"Mars *Pathfinder.*" MarsNews.com. Available online at http://www.marsnews.com/missions/pathfinder; website home page: http://www.marsnews.com (accessed July 16, 2003).

Williams, David R. "Mars *Pathfinder* Images." National Space Science Data Center. National Aeronautics and Space Administration. Available online at http://nssdc.gsfc.nasa.gov/planetary/marspath_images.html; website home page: http://nssdc.gsfc.nasa.gov (accessed July 16, 2003).

Williams, David R. "Mars *Pathfinder* Project Information." National Space Science Data Center. National Aeronautics and Space Administration. Available online at http://nssdc.gsfc.nasa.gov/planetary/mesur.html; website home page: http://nssdc.gsfc.nasa.gov (accessed July 16, 2003).

"*Pathfinder* Arrives at Mars." SpaceViews. Available online at http://www.seds.org/spaceviews/pathfinder; website home page: http://www.seds.org/spaceviews (accessed July 16, 2003).

"14 Answers From Garry Kasparov"

Interview

By: Garry Kasparov
Date: 1997
Source: Kasparov, Garry. "14 Answers From Garry Kasparov." Interview by Spiros Tzelepis. Available online at http://users.otenet.gr/~tzelepisk/yc/kasp.htm; website home page: http://users.otenet.gr (accessed July 15, 2003).
About the Author: Garry Kasparov (1963–) was born in Baku, Azerbaijan, a former Soviet republic. At nine, he won a semifinal of the Blitz championship for adults in Baku, and at twelve he won the Soviet Junior Championship, the youngest player to win this title. In 1980, he won the World Junior Championship and, in 1985, rose to be the world's highest-ranked chess player, a position he held into the early twenty-first century. ∎

Introduction

The fascination with computers stems, in part, from the possibility that humans might build computers with an intelligence equal to or greater than their own. Should computers reach such a stage, they would presumably think and behave like humans and even display emotions. Many people doubt computers will ever exhibit these capabilities, but Tulane University mathematical physicist Frank J. Tipler disagrees.

Tipler attributes the inability of computers to think and behave like humans to the fact that they do not yet have the memory or speed of the human brain—able to code some 10^{17} bits of information in its memory and to process information at 10 trillion floating point operations per second (flops). Today's computers cannot match these numbers, though Tipler expects them to equal these numbers by 2030.

At that date, assuming Tipler is right, computers will be able to pass a test British mathematician and computer scientist Alan M. Turing devised in 1950. He imagined two rooms, one with a person and the other with a computer. Someone outside these rooms attempts to engage the occupants of both rooms in conversation in hopes of distinguishing the person from the computer. But, if after months of dialogue, he cannot identify which room contains the person and which the computer, he must conclude that the computer has equaled humans in language—implying that it has equaled humans in intelligence.

Chessmaster Garry Kasparov ponders his next move against IBM's Deep Blue, Philadelphia, February 13, 1996. Then the number-one-ranked chess player in the world, Kasparov ended up beating the supercomputer, 4-2. He lost a rematch the following year. AP/WIDE WORLD PHOTOS. REPRODUCED BY PERMISSION.

Significance

Already computers can simulate human thought and behavior in that computer scientists can program them to play chess, an activity that had previously been unique to humans. In this respect, computers can pass a modified Turing test. Again imagine two rooms, one with a person and the other with a computer. Someone outside the rooms sits at a table holding a chessboard and pieces. He plays several games, some in command of the white pieces and others in black. If game after game both computer and person respond with clever moves, the person outside the room will be unable to distinguish between computer and human.

International Business Machines (IBM) designed computer Deep Blue that in February 1996 played six games against Garry Kasparov. Deep Blue shocked people around the world by beating Kasparov in the first game. The defeat demoralized Kasparov, though he later admitted that the loss helped him by forcing him to treat Deep Blue as an opponent, not a machine. That is Deep Blue had passed the essence of the Turing test, for Kasparov was treating it as human. Thereafter, he concentrated on positioning his pieces in areas of the board that

gave Deep Blue only a few options. Kasparov, thus, could predict Deep Blue's moves, and he won four of the next five games to win the series, 4-2.

The defeat spurred IBM to upgrade Deep Blue, and a rematch was held in May 1997. Deep Blue could now consider 200 million positions per second, twice its previous speed. Kasparov won the first game, but resigned the second. Analysts demonstrated that he might have played the game to a draw, a realization from which Kasparov said he "never recovered." After three draws, Deep Blue won the final game to take the match, 2-1, demonstrating that a computer can match the human brain when it faces a task with a large, but still finite, set of possibilities.

Primary Source

"14 Answers From Garry Kasparov"

> **SYNOPSIS:** In this interview, Garry Kasparov admitted that Deep Blue had been a formidable opponent, one that displayed "No emotion, no fatigue—just a computing monster." He found it difficult to play an opponent that never tired, that noise or the audience could not distract, and that never suffered a headache.

World Chess Champion Reveals Himself

Garry Kasparov is one of the most successful professional chess players and has held the title of world champion for many years. Given the fact that chess is "a hot issue among many teenagers" I decided to present him in this interview. Surely, chess is a very productive way of spending one's free time and besides it helps to develop one's ability to think. Moreover, young people nowadays need role models who promote hard work as a way to succeed. Finally, Garry Kasparov is the champion who some years ago fought against Deep Blue, the computer manufactured by IBM for this purpose. I had always been curious to find out about how he felt when he has playing against a machine and in this interview, I found the answer.

Which was your first contact with chess?

At home in Baku when I was about four years of age.

What is it like to be a professional chess player?

It is very fulfilling.

How did you decide to do this in your life?

It just evolved.

How do you feel when playing chess?

Mostly good, unless I blunder.

What does chess represent for you?

It is the core of my life.

Is it just a profession or a passion?

It is both.

Some years ago, the whole world was watching anxiously your game with Deep Blue, the computer constructed by IBM. What do you think about this game?

I won one and I lost one game to "Deep Blue." I am a little disappointed that IBM did not make the experiment public.

Starting from this point, I want to ask you about the relationship between machines and us.

i. Do you think that such machines can be more capable of a human brain?

Only in some instances.

ii. Can they replace us?

Humans will always control machines.

iii. How was this game different from all the others you have played?

No emotion, no fatigue—just a computing monster.

How did you feel when your opponent was not a human but a computer?

A machine never gets tired. It does not get distracted by the audience or noise. To the best of my knowledge it never gets a headache.

Is it something you would do again just for the experience?

Yes, I would do it again, but as more of a scientific study.

What qualities should a chess player have in your opinion?

Desire, Drive, Intelligence, Access to Competition and a little Good Fortune does not hurt.

How can these be acquired?

With hard work.

Does the factor of cleverness matter in chess, or it is something one can learn through practice?

I believe that anybody can work hard and become a good player. To become a champion takes talent.

What would you say to the youth who love chess and maybe some of them want to follow your steps?

You can only have one #1, but thousands of people can enjoy a very high standard chess by working hard.

Further Resources

BOOKS

Fjermedal, Grant. *The Tomorrow Makers: A Brave New World of Living-Brain Machines.* New York: Macmillan, 1986.

Goodman, David, and Raymond Keene. *Man Versus Machine: Kasparov Versus Deep Blue.* Cambridge, Mass.: H3 Publications, 1997.

Khodarkovsky, Michael, and Leonid Shamkovich. *A New Era: How Garry Kasparov Changed the World of Chess.* New York: Ballantine Books, 1997.

Lanton, Christopher G., ed. *Artificial Life.* New York: Addison-Wesley, 1988.

Penrose, Roger. *The Emperor's New Mind: Concerning Computers, Minds, and the Laws of Physics.* Oxford, England: Oxford University Press, 1989.

Tipler, Frank J. *The Physics of Immortality.* New York: Doubleday, 1994.

PERIODICALS

Bell, Gordon. "Ultracomputers: A Teraflop Before Its Time." *Communications of the Association for Computing Machinery,* August 1992, 27–47.

Boyce, Nell. "Chips vs. the Chess Masters." *U.S. News & World Report,* October 7, 2002, 70–72.

Turing, Alan M. "Computing Machinery and Intelligence." *Mind,* October 1950, 433–462.

WEBSITES

"Crushed by Deep Blue, Kasparov Lashes Back at IBM." CNN. Available online at http://www.cnn.com/WORLD/9705/11/chess.update; website home page: http://www.cnn.com (accessed July 16, 2003).

"Deep Blue—Kasparov." Available online at http://www.rebel.nl/db-gk.htm; website home page: http://www.rebel.nl (accessed July 16, 2003).

"Kasparov vs. Deep Blue: The Rematch." IBM. Available online at http://www.research.ibm.com/deepblue; website home page: http://www.research.ibm.com (accessed July 16, 2003).

Schmidt, Charles F. "Chess, Deep Blue, Kasparov and Intelligence." Rutgers University. Available online at http://www.rci.rutgers.edu/~cfs/472_html/Intro/ChessContents.html; website home page: http://www.rci.rutgers.edu/ (accessed July 16, 2003).

The Biotech Century

Nonfiction work

By: Jeremy Rifkin

Date: 1998

Source: Rifkin, Jeremy. *The Biotech Century.* New York: Jeremy P. Tarcher/Putnam, 1998, 1–4.

About the Author: Jeremy Rifkin holds degrees in economics from The University of Pennsylvania's Wharton School of Finance and Commerce, and in international affairs from Tufts University's Fletcher School of Law and Diplomacy. He has written fourteen books on the implications of scientific and technological developments. He is founder and president of the Foundation on Economic Trends in Washington, D.C. ∎

In *The Biotech Century* (1998), Jeremy Rifkin says that notions of self, society, parenthood, free will, and progess will change dramatically in the next 25 years. © **WALLY MCNAMEE/CORBIS. REPRODUCED BY PERMISSION.**

Introduction

During the history of life the transmission of genes has been vertical, that is, from parents to offspring through sex. This mechanism holds for all species of plants and animals. During the past thirty years scientists have begun to amass the knowledge and technique to transfer genes horizontally, that is, between two organisms of the same generation. An example would be the transfer of genes from one human to another (excluding the transfer through sex) or from a tomato plant to an oak tree or perhaps from a mosquito to a human. One can multiply examples ad infinitum.

The horizontal transmission of genes requires the ability to isolate a gene or complex of genes which code for desirable traits. The genes that code for the production of protein in a wheat plant are an example of a desirable trait. A scientist who has identified these genes must then use an enzyme or enzymes to remove these genes from the chromosome or chromosomes on which they reside. The process is akin to cutting out a triangle from a sheet of paper, with the triangle analogous to the desired genes and the rest of the paper analogous to genes that have no immediate interest to the scientist. The scientist must then insert the genes into the organism of choice, again using an enzyme or enzymes. The process is akin to stitching a piece of cloth into a larger fabric.

Scientists might wish for example to insert genes for high protein production, obtained from the wheat plant mentioned above, into plants of great variety, certainly into the staples corn, rice and potatoes.

Other genes transfers may have little value. Should scientists insert the genes that code for blue eyes into other humans? The premise that blue is the best color for human eyes is not self evident on aesthetic grounds. Nor is it self evident that a particular color of hair or skin is preferable to another. Such gene transfers would demonstrate the technical skill of scientists, but these transfers would carry the danger of reinforcing prejudices about human appearance. Although the science of gene transfer is value neutral, its application can run the gamut from beneficial to benign to malicious.

Significance

Jeremy Rifkin believes the power to transfer genes between species has created a new era in history, one that will transform the world more "in the next several decades than in the previous one thousand years." By 2025, corporations will hold patents on the 100,000 genes in the human genome, farmers will grow feed in bacteria baths rather than soil, and scientists will clone animals and humans, and, perhaps, create human-animal hybrids. Parents might conceive their children in test tubes and grow embryos in artificial wombs. People might buy genetic readouts of themselves, allowing them to identify their risk for disease. Scientists will use computers to amass "biological databases."

Yet it may be too soon to gauge biotechnology's promise. In 1998, American physicist, Richard Seed, announced his intent to clone a human within eighteen months. Five years later Seed has yet to deliver on his word. The issue of human cloning demonstrates that Americans have misgivings about biotechnology. Their opposition to human cloning led President Bill Clinton (served 1993–2001) in 1997 to ban the use of federal funds to clone a human.

Even innocuous uses of biotechnology have frightened Americans. In 1996, Monsanto unveiled Bt corn. Its genes for resistance to the European corn borer occur naturally in some corn plants. All Monsanto did was concentrate them in a single variety of corn. Monsanto did not, therefore, introduce foreign genes into Bt corn. For millennia humans have eaten corn with some or all of the genes for borer resistance. Despite the safety of Bt corn, environmentalist labeled it "Frankenfood." Media coverage of their rallies led Monsanto to withdraw Bt corn.

If Americans are unwilling to accept even tame uses of biotechnology, they may not be ready for the sweeping changes Rifkin forecasts. Rather than embrace biotechnology, Americans may oppose it and such opposition may stall biotechnology. The twenty-first century will be the biotechnology century, as Rifkin proclaims, only if Americans overcome their fear of it.

Primary Source

The Biotech Century [excerpt]

> **SYNOPSIS:** In this excerpt Jeremy Rifkin expects that by 2025, corporations will hold patents on the 100,000 genes in the human genome, farmers will grow feed in bacteria baths rather than soil, scientists will clone animals and humans, and, perhaps, create human-animal hybrids. Parents might conceive their children in test tubes and grow embryos in artificial wombs. People might buy genetic readouts of themselves, allowing them to identify their risk for disease. Scientists will use computers to amass "biological databases."

Never before in history has humanity been so unprepared for the new technological and economic opportunities, challenges, and risks that lie on the horizon. Our way of life is likely to be more fundamentally transformed in the next several decades than in the previous one thousand years. By the year 2025, we and our children may be living in a world utterly different from anything human beings have ever experienced in the past.

In little more than a generation, our definition of life and the meaning of existence is likely to be radically altered. Long-held assumptions about nature, including our own human nature, are likely to be rethought. Many age-old practices regarding sexuality, reproduction, birth, and parenthood could be partially abandoned. Ideas about equality and democracy are also likely to be redefined, as well as our vision of what is meant by terms such as "free will" and "progress." Our very sense of self and society will likely change, as it did when the early Renaissance spirit swept over medieval Europe more than seven hundred years ago.

There are many convergent forces coming together to create this powerful new social current. At the epicenter is a technology revolution unmatched in all of history in its power to remake ourselves, our institutions, and our world. Scientists are beginning to reorganize life at the genetic level. The new tools of biology are opening up opportunities for refashioning life on Earth while foreclosing options that have existed over the millennia of evolutionary history. Before our eyes lies an uncharted new landscape whose contours are being shaped in thousands of biotechnology laboratories in universities, government agencies, and corporations around the world. If the claims already being made for the new science are only partially realized, the consequences for society and future generations are likely to be enormous. Here are just a few examples of what could happen within the next twenty-five years.

A handful of global corporations, research institutions, and governments could hold patents on virtually all 100,000 genes that make up the blueprints of the human race, as well as the cells, organs, and tissues that comprise the human body. They may also own similar patents on tens of thousands of micro-organisms, plants, and animals, allowing them unprecedented power to dictate the terms by which we and future generations will live our lives.

Global agriculture could find itself in the midst of a great transition in world history, with an increasing volume of food and fiber being grown indoors in tissue culture in giant bacteria baths, at a fraction of the price of growing staples on the land. The shift to indoor agriculture could presage the eventual elimination of the agricultural era that stretched from the neolithic revolution some ten thousand years ago, to the green revolution of the latter half of the twentieth century. While indoor agriculture could mean cheaper prices and a more abundant supply of food, millions of farmers in both the developing and developed world could be uprooted from the land, sparking one of the great social upheavals in world history.

Tens of thousands of novel transgenic bacteria, viruses, plants and animals could be released into the Earth's ecosystems for commercial tasks ranging from "bio-remediation" to the production of alternative fuels. Some of those released, however, could wreak havoc with the planet's biosphere, spreading destabilizing and even deadly genetic pollution across the world. Military uses of the new technology might have equally devastating effects on the Earth and its inhabitants. Genetically engineered biological warfare agents could pose as serious a threat to global security in the coming century as nuclear weapons do now.

Animal and human cloning could be commonplace, with "replication" partially replacing "reproduction" for the first time in history. Genetically customized and mass-produced animal clones could be used as chemical factories to secrete—in their blood and milk—large volumes of inexpensive chemicals and drugs for human use. We could also see the creation of a range of new chimeric animals on Earth, including human/animal hybrids. A chimp/hume, half chimpanzee and half human, for example, could become a reality. The human/animal hybrids could be widely used as experimental subjects in medical research and as organ "donors" for xenotransplantation. The artificial creation and propagation of cloned, chimeric, and transgenic animals could mean the end of the wild and the substitution of a bioindustrial world.

Some parents might choose to have their children conceived in test tubes and gestated in artificial wombs outside the human body to avoid the unpleasantries of pregnancy and to ensure a safe, transparent environment through which to monitor their unborn child's development. Genetic changes could be made in human fetuses in the womb to correct deadly diseases and disorders and to enhance mood, behavior, intelligence, and physical traits. Parents might be able to design some of the characteristics of their own children, fundamentally altering the very notion of parenthood. "Customized" babies could pave the way for the rise of a eugenic civilization in the twenty-first century.

Millions of people could obtain a detailed genetic readout of themselves, allowing them to gaze into their own biological futures. The genetic information would give people the power to predict and plan their lives in ways never before possible. That same "genetic information," however, could be used by schools, employers, insurance companies, and governments to determine educational tracks, employment prospects, insurance premiums, and security clearances, giving rise to a new and virulent form of discrimination based on one's genetic profile. Our notions of sociality and equity could be transformed. Meritocracy could give way to genetocracy, with individuals, ethnic groups, and races increasingly categorized and stereotyped by genotype, making way for the emergence of an informal biological caste system in countries around the world.

The Biotech Century could bring some or even most of these changes and many more into our daily lives, deeply affecting our individual and collective consciousness, the future of our civilization, and the biosphere itself. The benefits and perils of what some are calling "the ultimate technology frontier" are both exciting to behold and chilling to contemplate. Still, despite both the formidable potential and ominous nature of this extraordinary technology revolution, until now far more public attention has been focused on the other great technology revolution of the twenty-first century—computers and telecommunications. That's about to change. After more than forty years of running on parallel tracks, the information and life sciences are slowly beginning to fuse into a single technological and economic force. The computer is increasingly being used to decipher, manage, and organize the vast genetic information that is the raw resource of the emerging biotech economy. Scientists working in the new field of "bioinformatics" are beginning to download the genetic information of millions of years of evolution, creating a powerful new genre of "biological data banks." The rich genetic information in these biological data banks is being used by researchers to remake the natural world.

The marriage of computers and genes forever alters our reality at the deepest levels of human experience. To begin to comprehend the enormity of the shift taking place in human civilization, it's important to step back and gain a better understanding of the historic nature of the many changes that are occurring around us as we turn the corner into a new century. Those changes represent a turning point for civilization. We are in the throes of one of the great transformations in world history. Before us lies the passing of one great economic era and the birth pains of another. As the past is always prelude to the future, our journey into the Biotech Century needs to begin with an account of the world we're leaving behind.

Further Resources

BOOKS

Alberts, Bruce., ed. *Molecular Biology of the Cell.* New York: Garland, 1989.

Belcher, Brian, and Geoffrey Hawtin. *A Patent on Life: Ownership of Plant and Animal Research.* Canada: IDRC, 1991.

Busch, Lawrence, et. al. *Plants, Power and Profits: Social, Economic, and Ethical Consequences of the New Biotechnologies.* Cambridge, Mass.: Basil Blackwell, 1991.

Fox, Michael W. *Superpigs and Wondercorn: The Brave New World of Biotechnology and Where It All May Lead.* New York: Lyons & Burford, 1992.

Kenney, Martin. *Biotechnology: The University-Industrial Complex.* New Haven, Conn.: Yale University Press, 1986.

Krimsky, Sheldon. *Biotechnics & Society: The Rise of Industrial Genetics.* New York: Praeger, 1991.

Rudolph, Frederick B., and Larry V. McIntire, eds. *Biotechnology: Science, Engineering, and Ethical Challenges for the Twenty-First Century.* Washington, D.C: Joseph Henry Press, 1996.

Whelan, William J., and Sandra Black, eds. *From Genetic Experimentation to Biotechnology: The Critical Transition.* Chichester, England: Wiley, 1982.

PERIODICALS

Leahy, Stephen. "Biotechnology Hope and Hype." *Maclean's,* September 30, 2002, 40–43.

Mongkolporn, Usanee. "Biotech Patents Up."*Nation,* June 11, 2002, 14–15.

WEBSITES

BIO: Biotechnology Industry Organization. Available online at http://www.bio.org/ (accessed July 16, 2003).

Bio-IT World. Available online at http://www.boi-itworld.com (accessed July 16, 2003).

"Biotechnology: An Information Resource." National Agricultural Library. U.S. Department of Agriculture. Available online at http://www.nal.usda.gov/bic; website home page http://www.nal.usda.gov (accessed July 16, 2003).

"Biotechnology: Ethics & the Industry." Strategis. Available online at http://strategis.ic.gc.ca/SSG/bb00001e.html; website home page: http://strategis.ic.gc.ca (accessed July 16, 2003).

"Biotechnology Information Directory Section." Cato Research. Available online at http://www.cato.com/biotech; website home page: http://www.cato.com (accessed July 16, 2003).

Council for Biotechnology Information. Available online at http://www.whybiotech.com/ (accessed July 16, 2003).

National Center for Biotechnology Information. Available online at http://www.ncbi.nlm.nih.gov/ (accessed July 16, 2003).

"Interview Transcript: Richard Seed, Physicist"
Interview

By: Richard Seed

Date: 1998

Source: Seed, Richard. "Interview Transcript: Richard Seed, Physicist." Interview by CNN Chicago Bureau. Available online at http://www.cnn.com/CNN/bureaus/chicago/stories/9801/cloning/index1.htm; website homepage: http://www.cnn.com (accessed October 5, 2002).

About the Author: Richard Seed holds a Ph.D. in physics from Harvard University and has worked in embryology for fifteen years. He transferred the first human embryo from a pregnant woman to the womb of an infertile woman, an achievement he published in 1983. He has also studied the development of embryos in cattle. ∎

Introduction

In February 1997, Scottish scientist, Ian Wilmut, electrified the world by announcing that he and team of researchers had cloned a sheep. Suppose B is a clone of A. By definition A and B must share every gene in common, as is the case with identical twins. To think of A and B as identical twins may, however, mislead the reader. Identical twins are born at the same time. This is untrue of A and B.

To clone a human, a scientist must extract an egg from a woman. (Any egg from any woman will do.) He must remove the nucleus from the egg, inserting in its place the nucleus from a somatic (non sex) cell of the person (P) he wishes to clone. The egg now contains a nucleus with every gene in P. The egg cannot be fertilized, and does not need to be, because it already has the full complement of twenty-three pairs (forty-six in total) of chromosomes of a human, specifically of P. The scientist now implants the egg in the womb of any woman, and, in the absence of miscarriage, she will give birth nine months later to a clone of P. If P is forty at the time of his clone's birth, then forty years separate P and his clone; and in only this respect is a clone not the identical twin of its genetic equivalent. With this stipulation in mind one may think of a clone as a "time-lag identical twin."

Significance

Ian Wilmut's cloning of a sheep demonstrates that no scientific barrier exists to impede the cloning of any animal, including humans. In January 1998, Richard Seed announced his intent to clone a human within eighteen months. Four couples, he said, "have expressed some interest." He disagreed with President Bill Clinton's (served 1993–2001) condemnation of any attempt to clone a human, saying he saw no "real moral considerations." Seed wanted to clone a human because of its "intellectual challenge," its "contribution to science and technology," and its "advancement of the human race." He stressed his desire to please parents with the birth of a healthy child, who would presumably be a clone of a parent or sibling. He had enough money to begin cloning someone, but not enough to finish, he admitted.

That Seed had yet to clone a human as of 2003 suggests he still lacks funds, but most scientists understand that if he does not succeed someone else will—if not in the United States then in one of Europe's well-financed laboratories. Ethicists worry that scientists and the public at large have not thought through the implications of cloning a human. Suppose, for example, parents have a child who needs a bone-marrow transplant to survive and that they decide to clone the child because they know the child's immune system will not reject the clone's bone marrow, a perfect match. What ethical principles should guide the parents? That bioethicists, scientists and policymakers cannot agree on an answer suggests how far ethics lags behind science. The pace of scientific advance was so rapid at the end of the twentieth century that all but the most informed ethicists and policymakers have lost hope of staying abreast of it.

Primary Source

"Interview Transcript: Richard Seed, Physicist"

SYNOPSIS: In this interview Richard Seed announced his intent to clone a human within eighteen months. He expected no personal gain, but rather to advance science and human welfare. The purity of his intentions led to his disappointment in President Bill Clinton's condemnation of human cloning. Seed had enough money to begin cloning someone, but too little to finish.

His Goal . . .

"My personal target is to produce a two-month pregnant female in a year and a half's time. I don't always make my targets but the target is a year and a half and that mainly is to indicate we're not talking about a huge project. We're not talking about 5 to 10 years. What we intend to do is basically duplicate in humans what was done by Scottish researchers in sheep."

His Motivation . . .

"Number one is intellectual challenge, number two is a contribution to science and technology, and number three is advancement of the human race."

His Beliefs . . .

"Well, I happen to disagree with the President rather strongly. He has sent a bill as you know to

Physicist Richard Seed at a press conference, Tokyo, Japan, December 1, 1998. In 1998, Seed announced plans to open an animal fertility clinic and also revealed his intention to clone a human by the end of the century. **AP/WIDE WORLD PHOTOS. REPRODUCED BY PERMISSION.**

Congress to ban cloning. I personally don't even think it will reach the floor of either house of Congress. I don't think it will pass and I don't think there are any real moral considerations. I believe in God. I want to emphasize that. I am a Christian. I am a Methodist. I believe that man will become one with God.

"Basically, I mean man will develop the technology and the science and the capability to have an indefinite life span, and goes with that is the capability to have an unlimited knowledge. It's the next step from animal cloning.

"My biggest worry is the occurrence of chromosome abnormalities, but there is in place an enormous and incredible technology to study and analyze chromosomes, and there to detect any abnormalities. There is also an incredible ability to do DNA testing, as you know. You can evaluate DNA, and for instance identify different individuals by DNA testing. So that's a direct evaluation of the chromosome.

"Initially people are always frightened, both the populace and the legislatures and the leaders are

Dolly, the first cloned sheep, in her pen at the Roslin Institute, Edinburgh, Scotland, December 1997. By successfully cloning a sheep, Dr. Ian Wilmut brought the ability to clone a human within reach of the scientific community. AP/WIDE WORLD PHOTOS. REPRODUCED BY PERMISSION.

most often frightened by technology, not just technology but any new human activity, even mechanical devices, even politics. They frighten and the people are scared and sometimes abhorrent. Most human events go through three phases of growth. First is the fear and abhorrence, and the second phase is sort of a tolerance, acceptance, and passivity, and the third phase is enthusiastic endorsement.

"Human cloning is a legitimate treatment for certain types of human infertility, specifically when both the husband and the wife do not produce fertile sperm or fertile eggs and that's probably 10 to 15 percent of infertility."

The Couples Who Might Participate . . .

"We have four couples lined up or four couples whom we discussed the issue with and who have expressed some interest. I'm not ready to proceed with a formal informed consent but we will do that, and I plan to get it all on camcorder in addition to writing.

His Interpretation of the Sheep Experiment . . .

"I will reinterpret the paper for you. Yes, they had 200 embryos with 200 unfertilized eggs which they attempted to fertilize. The important point, they produced a live lamb on the first try, the very first try. And if you look at the data very carefully he only put in 17 embryos in the part of the trial that counts. Now, any time you can do a new experiment and succeed on the first try you got something that basically is easy. I don't think that I've ever succeeded in the first try of any techno thing I've tried. I think it took Steptoe and Edwards, to produce the first invitro fertilized pregnancy made almost a hundred tries. That was 20 years ago. So first try success now, I'm giving you a different viewpoint from the published literature."

His Credentials . . .

"I've worked in embryology for almost 15 years. I have a few published papers and we did five or six years of work in cattle, and I was responsible for the first human embryo transfer, the first human embryo transfer taken from a fertilized female donor and transferred into an infertile recipient female. This was published in 1983 and it created a mini-storm of protest and now it is not a popular process, but embryo transfer with invitro fertilization and everything you can think of doing with invitro fertilization is simply accepted as a routine procedure.

"My biggest concern is for chromosome abnormalities. And there is a large technology that exists that was not generally appreciated even by my fellow scientists that you can evaluate in enormous detail from a few sample cells, you can evaluate in enormous detail the chromosome normality.

"It's an unpleasant subject, but you cannot force anybody to have an abortion, you cannot force anybody not to have one, as you know, but we would like the couples to know if a pregnancy occurred and an abnormality was observed that we would recommend an abortion. Now I also would like to emphasize that you look at the microscope the first five days of the growth process when you put the nucleus in the empty human female egg. It then starts growing. If everything works out right, you'll get one cell division, two, four, eight, 16. Finally, after 5 days it grows up into a very particular and dramatic shape called a blastocyst. A simple visual observation under the microscope can watch this process. And when you have a blastocyst you are able to evaluate the embryo, and it is really a 5 day old embryo, and you are able to evaluate microscopically very carefully. So the main occurrence of abnormalities occurs in the first 5 days and you don't get a blastocyst. As a matter of fact, the main problem is you put the nucleus in the processed, unfertilized egg and nothing happens so that's what happens most of the time.

If Something Goes Wrong . . .

"That would disturb me enormously. That's my biggest worry. That would be unfortunate. It would also be unfortunate for the technology. But after you get hundreds of happy, healthy babies then an abnormality can be accepted. There is one Down's Syndrome baby produced in Europe by in vitro fertilization on the ground, and the parent was not even advised to get an abortion, they didn't even test for it, which is rather strange.

What Would Make Him Happy?

Oh that's very easy. Half a dozen healthy happy bouncing baby clones. And healthy, happy parents. That's very easy. I think when there's half a dozen healthy happy bouncing baby clones and they're shown on your television network, public opinion will change.

The Cloning Process . . .

Well, it's a fairly simple technical process. You take an unfertilized ovum with a little needle and ultrasound guidance. You extract an unfertilized egg from a human female. It's a painless office procedure, using ultrasound, the big advance. This is a part of in vitro fertilization. You get the unfertilized egg with a small microscopic needle. You suck out all the genetic material that is in it, and that is fairly easy to do because it's all in one location, it's underneath the polar body, but we don't have to discuss that. It's fairly easy to find it and suck it out. You stick in the various simplest terms, and you get an adult nucleus from some other cell in the body, and you do some processing to it, and you stick it into the unfertilized egg, you insert it with another similar small microscopic glass needle and then you give it a little electric shock. And then you culture it for 5 days. And that is very important because at the end of culturing if you have been successful you will have a hundred cells, what's called a blastocyst which is a very particular kind of structure which you can examine easily under the microscope and that assures you, that doesn't assure you but it gives let's say 90 or 95 percent assurance that you have a normal, healthy embryo. Mostly, nothing happens. You stick the nucleus in the unfertilized egg and you get nothing. It lays there like a stone."

The Cost . . .

"Well that's easy to answer in the sense that in vitro fertilization charges now run $4,000 to almost $20,000 per try, and I would expect after a hundred or two hundred successful clones, that the price would be in that range. It's quite expensive and I would expect the same thing to apply. In the beginning, who knows. I can't say what the charge can or will be. The first clone is going to cost one or two million dollars to create. I don't think anybody is going to be willing to pay a million or two million dollars, or their first clone might even be lucky and get it done free."

His Financing . . .

"I'm talking to some people, and I have enough to get started but not enough to finish the project. I need some more money. And I hope to get it. I'm talking to a few people, talking to people who are still talking back. I talked to some people who are not talking back who are not at all interested."

In Defense of Accusations That He Is "Preying on Desperate Couples" . . .

"No, actually I think that's laughable. It's like saying that doctors are preying on desperate cancer patients when they operate on them. But some people are infertile and you're attempting to treat the infertility. I don't think that's a serious consideration. A serious consideration is, as I told you, is chromosome abnormality, and I'm going to use all the technology available to make sure that does not occur. The rest of it is just, as far as I'm concerned, a lot of hard work. Although the chromosome detection is also a lot of hard work. There's not much creativity left to clone a human."

Further Resources
BOOKS
Howard, Ted, and Jeremy Rifkin. *Who Should Play God? The Artificial Creation of Life and What It Means to the Future of the Human Race.* New York: Dell Publishing, 1997.

Rifkin, Jeremy. *The Biotech Century: Harnessing the Gene and Remaking the World.* New York: Putnam, 1998.

Silver, Lee M. *Remaking Eden: Cloning and Beyond in a Brave New World.* New York: Avon Books, 1997.

PERIODICALS
"Christian Legal Society Asks U.S. Senate to Act on Opportunity to Prevent Human Cloning." *Health & Medicine Week,* September 2, 2002, 7.

Coghlan, Andy. "Race Is on to Stop Human Cloning." *New Scientist,* September 28, 2002, 11.

"Doctor Defends Human Cloning Experiment." *Genomics & Genetics Weekly,* September 13, 2002, 10–12.

Evans, John H. "Religion and Human Cloning."*Journal for the Scientific Study of Religion,* December 2002, 747–59.

Kluger, Jeffrey. "Will We Follow the Sheep?" *Time,* March 10, 1997, 14–18.

WEBSITES

Best, Steven and Douglas Kellner. "Biotechnology, Ethics, and the Politics of Cloning." Graduate School of Education and Information Studies. University of California, Los Angeles. Available online at http://www.gseis.ucla.edu/faculty/kellner/papers/biotechdem.htm; website home page: http://www.gseis.ucla.edu (accessed July 16, 2003).

Clinton, William J. Memorandum to the Heads of Executive Departments and Agencies, March 4, 1997. Available online at http://grants1.nih.gov/grants/policy/cloning_directive.htm; website home page http://grants1.nih.gov (accessed July 16, 2003).

Clonaid.com: The First Human Cloning Company. Available online at http://www.clonaid.com (accessed July 16, 2003).

"Cloning Discussion Scenario." Strategis. Available online at http://strategis.ic.gc.ca/SSG/bb00008e.html; website home page: http://strategis.ic.gc.ca (accessed July 16, 2003).

Human Cloning and Human Dignity: An Ethical Inquiry. The President's Council on Bioethics. Available online at http://www.bioethics.gov/reports/cloningreport/index.html; website home page: http://www.bioethics.gov (accessed July 16, 2003)

Human Cloning Foundation. Available online at http://www.humancloning.org (accessed July 16, 2003).

Kerschen, Arthur. "Human Cloning: The How to Page." Biofact Report. Available online at http://www.biofact.com/cloning/human.html; website home: page http://www.biofact.com (accessed July 16, 2003)

Wachbroit, Robert. "Genetic Encores: The Ethics of Human Cloning." School of Public Affairs. University of Maryland. Available online at http://www.puaf.umd.edu/IPPP/fall97/Reportcloning.htm; website home page: http://www.puaf.umd.edu (accessed July 16, 2003).

"Monsanto Statement on Bt Corn: Environmental Safety and a Recent Report on the Monarch Butterfly, May 20, 1999"

Press release

By: Monsanto Company
Date: May 20, 1999
Source: Monsanto Company. "Monsanto Statement on Bt Corn: Environmental Safety and a Recent Report on the Monarch Butterfly, May 20, 1999." AG BioTech InfoNet.

Available online at http://www.biotech-info.net/monsanto_on_btcorn.html; website home page: http://www.biotech-info.net (accessed July 17, 2003).

About the Organization: In 1901, American drug company agent John F. Queeny founded Monsanto Chemical Works. From its origins as a saccharin manufacturer, Monsanto has grown to be one of the world's leading biotechnology and agrochemical companies. It specializes in the manufacture of herbicides, insecticides, and livestock feed and in the genetic engineering of insect-resistant corn, cotton, and potatoes. ∎

Introduction

In 1866, Gregor Mendel announced that particles (genes) code for traits. By the early twentieth century, scientists understood that genes code for traits through chemical pathways, implying that genes are molecules. In 1953, American chemist James D. Watson and his British counterpart, Francis Crick, identified deoxyribonucleic acid (DNA) as the molecule of heredity—describing its structure as a spiral ladder, with each rung composed of two of the four nucleotide bases: adenine, thymine, guanine, and cytosine. Adenine always bonds with thymine, and guanine with cytosine. The nucleotide bases bond one atop another to form the ladderlike structure. Half a strand of DNA might be the sequence thymine, cytosine, cytosine, guanine. The other half must be adenine, guanine, guanine, cytosine.

In the early 1970s, American chemist Hamilton O. Smith and other researchers discovered a class of enzymes that can cut out sequences of nucleotide bases. Each enzyme cuts out a unique sequence. Enzyme A, for example, might cut out only the sequence thymine, adenine, adenine, cytosine, whereas enzyme B might cut out only the sequence guanine, guanine, guanine. These enzymes allowed scientists to cut out sequences of nucleotide bases from one organism and transfer them to another, creating a genetically engineered organism. For the first time, scientists had the ability to engineer a plant or organism with a desirable trait.

The first genetically engineered organisms were bacteria with the ability to manufacture insulin or break down petroleum, and, thereby, clean up oil spills. In 1980, the U.S. Supreme Court extended patent protection, established by Article 1 of the U.S. Constitution, to genetically engineered plants and organisms. The ruling gave private companies exclusive right to the profits from a genetically engineered plant or organism.

Significance

In 1996, Monsanto and other companies inserted genes (strands of DNA) that code for resistance to the European corn borer, a corn pest since the 1920s, in a variety of corn (Bt corn). It saved farmers the expense of spraying insecticides in areas infested by the borer, es-

Cornfield, Hackettstown, New Jersey, August 1997. Bt corn—corn enhanced through biotechnology—protects the corn from insect pests and all but eliminates the need for pesticides. © JAMES LEYNSE/CORBIS SABA. REPRODUCED BY PERMISSION.

pecially the Midwest. Farmers throughout the Midwest planted Bt corn, though the Environmental Protection Agency (EPA) restricted the sale of some types of Bt corn (that may trigger allergies in humans) to use by livestock raisers. This restriction did not significantly impact biotechnology firms or corn growers because it applied to a very limited part of the total production of corn in the United States.

Bt corn appeared to hold promise for U.S. farmers, but environmentalists, in 1997, began a campaign to label it "Frankenfood." To add to the worries of chemical companies such as Monsanto, entomologists, in 1999, announced that Bt corn pollen was toxic to monarch butterflies.

Monsanto countered in this May 20, 1999, press release that the planting of Bt corn actually protected monarch butterflies and other insects, except the European corn borer, by eliminating the need for widespread insecticide use. Monsanto said they had merely concentrated the genes for borer resistance, genes that occur naturally in some corn, in a single variety of corn.

Monsanto's logic did not persuade environmentalists, whose rallies against genetically engineered crops gained momentum in 1999 and won widespread press. As the value of its stock fell in response to this criticism, Monsanto felt the impact of the environmentalists' efforts. This issue had gotten the attention of the general public.

Primary Source

"Monsanto Statement on Bt Corn: Environmental Safety and a Recent Report on the Monarch Butterfly, May 20, 1999"

SYNOPSIS: In this press release, Monsanto defends the development and planting of Bt corn.

"Bt corn" refers to corn that has been enhanced through plant biotechnology with a trait that protects it from damage against specific insect pests. Because of a protective protein that the corn produces, it is not damaged by insects like the European corn

Research released in 1999 suggested that Bt corn negatively impacts the growth and survival of the monarch butterfly. FIELD MARK PUBLICATIONS. REPRODUCED BY PERMISSION.

borer, which can have devastating and irreversible effects on corn crops.

Prior to the introduction of Bt corn, farmers typically controlled insect pests with conventional insecticides that get rid of both those damaging insects, as well as the beneficial and desirable insects (e.g., those that help control other pests that harm plants or spread plant diseases) present in the field. An important advantage of Bt corn is that these sprays are either reduced or eliminated; as a result, the effects on beneficial and other non-target insects also are dramatically reduced or eliminated. By reducing the use of broad-spectrum insecticides, Bt corn reduces the potential to harm non-target and beneficial species, and it reduces the impacts of agricultural inputs on the environment in general.

Nature Article

The May 20 issue of the journal Nature reports on a laboratory study conducted by Cornell University researchers that asserts a negative impact of milkweed dusted with pollen from Bt corn on the growth and survival of the non-target Monarch butterfly.

We take very seriously research on Monarch butterflies and other non-target species, as well as beneficial insects that help control pests in fields. Considered in total, research conducted in the field supports the safety of Bt crops for beneficial and other non-target insects. The laboratory study in Nature provides interesting information, but reflects a situation very different than that actually prevalent in the natural environment.

Monarch larvae feed almost exclusively on milkweed. The natural habitat for milkweed is prairies, fields and roadsides, not the middle of full grown and pollinating corn fields. In real life situations, the exposure of milkweed to corn pollen is very low because only a very small portion of milkweed grows in close enough proximity to corn fields for exposure to corn pollen. This information supports the conclusion of a very low likelihood of effect of Bt pollen on non-target insects like the Monarch butterfly in their natural habitats.

The principal author of this laboratory study has cautioned against drawing conclusions until more research and data have been collected and studied. Monsanto is very supportive of initiatives that lead to better understanding of insect-protected crops and non-target and beneficial insects. To that end, we are participating in an industry effort to support additional field research to reaffirm the lack of impact of Bt crops for these insects in their natural environment. We will continue to cooperate with researchers and the industry to support studies aimed toward better understanding of insect-protected crops.

Additional Editors' Reference Notes

- Over 40% of all chemical insecticides used in the United States are used on cotton plants. Use of Bt insect-protected cotton has eliminated the use of nearly 1 million gallons of broad spectrum chemical insecticides since it was first commercially grown in 1996. (1996: 250,000+ gallons, 1997: 300,000 gallons, 1998: 300,000+ gallons)

- According to a University of Alabama study the adoption of Bt cotton has reduced chemical insecticide use in their state to the lowest levels in over 40 years since the introduction of these chemical insecticides.

- In 1998 use of Bt insect-protected corn reduced or eliminated the use of broad spectrum chemical insecticides on some 15 million acres of U.S. farmland.

• Farmers growing Bt insect-protected potatoes on nearly 40,000 acres have reduced their chemical insecticides use by over 40%.

Further Resources

BOOKS

Belcher, Brian, and Geoffrey Hawtin. *A Patent on Life: Ownership of Plant and Animal Research.* Ottawa, Ontario, Canada: IDRC, 1991.

Busch, Lawrence, et al. *Plants, Power and Profits: Social, Economic, and Ethical Consequences of the New Biotechnologies.* Cambridge, Mass.: Basil Blackwell, 1991.

Fox, Michael W. *Superpigs and Wondercorn: The Brave New World of Biotechnology and Where It All May Lead.* New York: Lyons & Burford, 1992.

Kenney, Martin. *Biotechnology: The University-Industrial Complex.* New Haven, Conn.: Yale University Press, 1986.

Kloppenburg, Jack R. *First the Seed: The Political Economy of Plant Biotechnology, 1492–2000.* New York: Cambridge University Press, 1988.

Krimsky, Sheldon. *Biotechnics & Society: The Rise of Industrial Genetics.* New York: Praeger, 1991.

Rissler, Jane, and Margaret G. Mellon. *The Ecological Risks of Engineered Crops.* Cambridge, Mass.: MIT Press, 1996.

Rudolph, Frederick B., and Larry V. McIntyre, eds. *Biotechnology: Science, Engineering, and Ethical Challenges for the Twenty-First Century.* Washington, D.C: Joseph Henry Press, 1996.

Whelan, William J., and Sandra Black, eds. *From Genetic Experimentation to Biotechnology: The Critical Transition.* Chichester, England: Wiley, 1982.

PERIODICALS

Charman, Karen. "Genetically Engineered Food: Promises & Perils." *Mother Earth News,* October/November 2002, 74–83.

Golden, Frederic. "Who's Afraid of Frankenfood?" *Time,* November 29, 1999, 49–52.

Leahy, Stephen. "Biotechnology Hope and Hype." *Maclean's,* September 30, 2002, 40–43.

"Of Corn and Butterflies." *Time,* May 31, 1999, 80–81.

WEBSITES

Bessin, Ric. Bt-Corn: What It Is and How It Works. Department of Entomology. University of Kentucky. Available online at http://www.uky.edu/Agriculture/Entomology/entfacts/fldcrops/ef130.htm; website home page: http://www.uky.edu/Ag/Entomology/enthp.htm (accessed July 17, 2003).

"Bt Corn & European Corn Borer: Long-Term Success Through Resistance Management." University of Minnesota Extension Service. Available online at http://www.extension.umn.edu/distribution/cropsystems/DC7055.html; website home page: http://www.extension.umn.edu (accessed July 17, 2003).

"Butterflies and Bt Corn: Allowing Science to Guide Decisions." Agricultural Research Services. U.S. Department of Agriculture. Available online at http://www.ars.usda.gov/sites/monarch/; website home page: http://www.ars.usda.gov (accessed July 17, 2003).

"Research Q&A: Bt Corn and Monarch Butterflies." Agricultural Research Services. U.S. Department of Agriculture. Available online at http://www.ars.usda.gov/is/br/btcorn; website home page: http://www.ars.usda.gov (accessed July 17, 2003).

Tenuta, Albert. *A Grower's Handbook: Controlling European Corn Borer With Bt Corn Technology.* Ontario Corn Producers' Association. Available online at http://www.ontariocorn.org/growing/btguide.html; website home page: http://www.ontariocorn.org (accessed July 17, 2003).

Transgenic Organisms Discussion Scenario. Strategis. Available online at http://strategis.ic.gc.ca/SSG/bb00011e.html; website home page: http://strategis.ic.gc.ca (accessed July 17, 2003).

Weaving the Web

Nonfiction work

By: Tim Berners-Lee

Date: 1999

Source: Berners-Lee, Tim. *Weaving the Web.* San Francisco: HarperSanFrancisco, 1999, 2, 208–209.

About the Author: Tim Berners-Lee (1955–) was born in London, England, and graduated with honors from Queen's College, Oxford University with a degree in physics in 1976. After working for technology firms in England, he joined CERN, a scientific agency in Geneva, Switzerland, as a software developer in 1980. In 1989, he developed software that provided the foundation of the World Wide Web (WWW). He went on to direct the WWW consortium at the Massachusetts Institute of Technology (MIT) in Cambridge, Massachusetts. ■

Introduction

In 1962, MIT psychologist Joseph C.R. Licklider conceived of a network of computers. This idea, which would lay the foundation of the Internet, was to allow anyone with a personal computer (PC) to access data from another computer. An international network, the Internet, would surmount the barriers of geography. That year President John F. Kennedy appointed Licklider head of a research program at the Advanced Research Projects Agency (ARPA), an arm of the U.S. Defense Department that Congress created in 1958. The purpose of the agency was to recapture U.S. leadership in military technology after the 1957 Soviet launch of the first intercontinental ballistic missile and the first satellite, *Sputnik,* had led Americans to fear that the United States trailed the Russians in missile and satellite technology.

Under Licklider's leadership, ARPA created, in 1969, the first computer network (ARPANET), the forerunner of the Internet. By 1971, it linked eighteen computers and,

Tim Berners-Lee, Cambridge, Massachusetts, 1998. Inventor of the World Wide Web, Berners-Lee predicted that the Internet would redefine not only work, but leisure as well. **AP/WIDE WORLD PHOTOS. REPRODUCED BY PERMISSION.**

named Enquire after a book of advice *Enquire Within Upon Everything* that brought together information on an eclectic mix of topics. This eclecticism was to be the core of his program that was the foundation of the WWW, a system that retrieved information on the Internet.

Berners-Lee envisions the WWW as technology in its most potent sense, as a means by which humans can refashion their world—as humans have done ever since *Homo habilis* invented the first stone tools, and the first technology some 2.5 million years ago. Berners-Lee boasts of the Internet's freedom, of its strenuous defense of free speech, and of its unfettered access to information. "Knowledge is power," wrote the seventeenth-century British philosopher of science Francis Bacon. Today the Internet may be the world's most ubiquitous source of information, the foundation of knowledge. Anyone with a PC or with access to a library with PCs can send information about anything to anyone anywhere.

Berners-Lee's democratic vision had, by 1996, attracted some forty million people in 150 countries to the Internet. By 1999, it teemed with more than seventy million websites. This exponential growth was expected to fill the Internet with some six billion websites by 2010, an amount that would approach the global population. The Internet has emerged as a technology that may revolutionize culture, as much as did the Neolithic transformation of humans from hunter-gatherers to farmers some 10,000 years ago in western Asia.

by 1972, had fewer than twenty-five online sites. Meanwhile, in 1971, American computer scientist Raymond S. Tomlinson wrote the first electronic mail (e-mail); in 1972, Tomlinson sent e-mail to a recipient through ARPANET. Academics quickly came to use ARPANET and e-mail, and the National Science Foundation (NSF) financed its growth. During the 1980s, the NSF, the National Aeronautics and Space Administration, the National Institutes of Health, and United States and foreign universities linked to the Internet, and the private networks Prodigy, Compuserve, and America Online granted anyone access to the Internet for a fee. In 1990, the Defense Department relinquished control of the Internet, and the next year the NSF allowed private firms to do business on its network, which was a large component of the Internet. By then, the Internet had grown to include some 300,000 sites.

Significance

The democratic potential of the Internet to bring people together on an equal footing to share information attracted Tim Berners-Lee—who wanted to foster its growth as a vast, eclectic and decentralized bazaar of information. He developed a software program that he

Primary Source

Weaving the Web [excerpt]

SYNOPSIS: In this excerpt Tim Berners-Lee celebrates the WWW that he created and the Internet as technology that may give humans the power to refashion their world. He emphasizes the Internet's democracy, its defense of free speech, and its access to unfettered information.

Enquire Within Upon Everything

When I first began tinkering with a software program that eventually gave rise to the idea of the World Wide Web, I named it Enquire, short for *Enquire Within upon Everything,* a musty old book of Victorian advice I noticed as a child in my parents' house outside London. With its title suggestive of magic, the book served as a portal to a world of information, everything from how to remove clothing stains to tips on investing money. Not a perfect analogy for the Web, but a primitive starting point.

What that first bit of Enquire code led me to was something much larger, a vision encompassing the decentralized, organic growth of ideas, technology, and society. The vision I have for the Web is about anything being potentially connected with anything. It is a vision that provides us with new freedom, and allows us to grow faster than we ever could when we were fettered by the hierarchical classification systems into which we bound ourselves. It leaves the entirety of our previous ways of working as just one tool among many. It leaves our previous fears for the future as one set among many. And it brings the workings of society closer to the workings of our minds.

Unlike *Enquire Within upon Everything,* the Web that I have tried to foster is not merely a vein of information to be mined, nor is it just a reference or research tool. Despite the fact that the ubiquitous *www* and *.com* now fuel electronic commerce and stock markets all over the world, this is a large, but just one, part of the Web. Buying books from Amazon.com and stocks from E-trade is not all there is to the Web. Neither is the Web some idealized space where we must remove our shoes, eat only fallen fruit, and eschew commercialization.

The irony is that in all its various guises—commerce, research, and surfing—the Web is already so much a part of our lives that familiarity has clouded our perception of the Web itself. To understand the Web in the broadest and deepest sense, to fully partake of the vision that I and my colleagues share, one must understand how the Web came to be. . . .

There's a freedom about the Internet: As long as we accept the rules of sending packets around, we can sent packets containing anything to anywhere. In Unitarian Universalism, if one accepts the basic tenet of mutual respect in working together toward some greater vision, then one finds a huge freedom in choosing one's own words that capture that vision, one's own rituals to help focus the mind, one's own metaphors for faith and hope.

I was very lucky, in working at CERN, to be in an environment that Unitarian Universalists and physicists would equally appreciate: one of mutual respect, and of building something very great through collective effort that was well beyond the means of any one person—without a huge bureaucratic regime. The environment was complex and rich; any two people could get together and exchange views, and even end up working together somehow. This system produced a weird and wonderful machine, which needed care to maintain, but could take advantage of the ingenuity, inspiration, and intuition of individuals in a special way. That, from the start, has been my goal for the World Wide Web.

Hope in life comes from the interconnections among all the people in the world. We believe that if we all work for what we think individually is good, then we as a whole will achieve more power, more understanding, more harmony as we continue the journey. We don't find the individual being subjugated by the whole. We don't find the needs of the whole being subjugated by the increasing power of an individual. But we might see more understanding in the struggles between these extremes. We don't expect the system to eventually become perfect. But we feel better and better about it. We find the journey more and more exciting, but we don't expect it to end.

Should we then feel that we are getting smarter and smarter, more and more in control of nature, as we evolve? Not really. Just better connected—connected into a better shape. The experience of seeing the Web take off by the grassroots effort of thousands gives me tremendous hope that if we have the individual will, we can collectively make of our world what we want.

Further Resources

BOOKS

Abrams, Marc, ed. *World Wide Web: Beyond the Basics.* Upper Saddle River, N.J.: Prentice Hall, 1998. *This book is also available in electronic format online at http://ei.cs.vt.edu/~wwwbtb/book/ (accessed July 17, 2003).*

Benedikt, Michael, ed. *Cyberspace: First Steps.* Cambridge, Mass.: MIT Press, 1991.

Jones, Steven G. *Cybersociety: Computer-Mediated Communication and Community.* Thousand Oaks, Calif.: Sage Publications, 1995.

Turkle, Sherry. *Life on the Screen: Identity in the Age of the Internet.* New York: Simon & Schuster, 1995.

PERIODICALS

"Going Digital." *Time,* November 18, 2002, 89.

"The Next Web." *Information Week,* October 14, 2002, 34–39.

WEBSITES

Berners-Lee, Tim. "Tim Berners-Lee Discusses the Future of the Web." Interview by Ira Flatow. *Talk of the Nation,* November 1, 2002. Audio transcript available online at http://discover.npr.org/features/feature.jhtml?wfId=919751 (accessed August 4, 2003).

Connolly, Dan. "A Little History of the World Wide Web: From 1945 to 1995." World Wide Web Consortium. Available online at http://www.w3.org/History.html; website home page: http://www.w3.org (accessed July 17, 2003).

Gromov, Gregory R. "History of the Internet and WWW: The Roads and Crossroads of Internet History." NetValley. Available online at http://www.netvalley.com/intval.html; website home page: http://www.netvalley.com (accessed July 17, 2003).

"History of the Internet and the World Wide Web." Web Developers Virtual Library. Available online at http://www.wdvl.com/Internet/History; website home page: http://www.wdvl.com (accessed April 30, 2003).

"Internet & World Wide Web History." Electronic Software Publishing Corporation. Available online at http://www.elsop.com/wrc/h_web.htm; website home page: http://www.elsop.com (accessed July 17, 2003).

"The World Wide Web." European Organization for Nuclear Research (CERN). Available online at http://public.web.cern.ch/public/about/achievements/www/www.html; website home page: http://public.web.cern.ch (accessed July 17, 2003).

The World Wide Web History Project. Available online at http://www.webhistory.org/home.html (accessed July 17, 2003).

Zeltser, Lenny. The World Wide Web: Origins and Beyond. Available online at http://www.zeltser.com/WWW; website home page: http://www.zeltser.com (accessed July 17, 2003).

12

SPORTS

JESSIE BISHOP

Entries are arranged in chronological order by date of primary source. For entries with one primary source, the entry title is the same as the primary source title. Entries with more than one primary source have an overall entry title, followed by the titles of the primary sources.

Important Events in Sports, 1990–1999

1990

- On January 1, the University of Miami (Florida) Hurricanes claim the college football national championship with a 33-25 win over the University of Alabama Crimson Tide in the Sugar Bowl.

- On January 15, Joe Montana sets the National Football League (NFL) record for postseason touchdowns with numbers thirty and thirty-one, breaking Terry Bradshaw's record.

- On February 16, the NFL allows college juniors to become eligible for the draft by renouncing their remaining college eligibility.

- On June 10, Jack Nicklaus wins the Seniors Professional Golfers' Association (PGA) tournament.

- On June 11, forty-three year old Nolan Ryan, of the Texas Rangers, pitches his sixth no-hit game, a major league baseball record, against the Oakland Athletics.

- On July 17, the Minnesota Twins become the first major league baseball team to record two triple plays in one game.

- On August 1, Nolan Ryan wins his three hundredth game, beating the Milwaukee Brewers, 11-3.

- On August 17, Carlton Fisk, of the Chicago White Sox, hits his 329th home run as a catcher, a major league baseball record. He ends his career in 1993 with 376 home runs.

- On October 25, Evander Holyfield knocks out James "Buster" Douglas in the third round to become the undisputed world heavyweight boxing champion.

- On October 28, fourteen-year-old Jennifer Capriati wins her first professional tennis tournament, the Puerto Rican Open.

1991

- On March 2, Del Ballard, Jr., throws the most famous gutter ball in Professional Bowlers Association (PBA) history in the finals of the Fair Lanes Open. Needing only seven pins to win, Ballard hits the gutter instead, losing the thirty thousand dollar first prize.

- On April 21, Russell Maryland, a defensive lineman for the University of Miami (Florida), is the first player taken in the NFL draft, by the Dallas Cowboys.

- On May 1, Nolan Ryan pitches his seventh no-hitter, beating the Toronto Blue Jays, 3-0.

- On July 15, Sandhi Ortiz-Del Valle becomes the first woman to officiate a men's professional basketball game.

- On July 28, Dennis Martinez pitches a perfect game for the Montreal Expos against the Los Angeles Dodgers, winning 2-0.

1992

- On March 18, the use of instant replay in the NFL is not reapproved, stopping a six-year-old practice.

- On April 12, Fred Couples wins The Masters golf tournament in Augusta, Georgia.

- On April 26, the Indianapolis Colts select Steve Emtman, a defensive lineman for the University of Washington, as the first player in the NFL draft.

- On September 7, Commissioner of Baseball Francis T. "Fay" Vincent resigns under pressure.

- On September 9, Robin Yount, a shortstop with the Milwaukee Brewers, collects his three thousandth hit.

- On September 30, George Brett, an infielder for the Kansas City Royals, goes 4-4 to reach three thousand career hits.

- On November 29, Jerry Rice, wide receiver for the San Francisco 49ers, catches his one-hundredth touchdown pass.

1993

- On January 1, the University of Alabama Crimson Tide defeats the University of Miami (Florida) Hurricanes, 34-13, in the Sugar Bowl, to win the national championship.

- On April 14, Sheryl Swoopes scores a National Collegiate Athletic Association (NCAA) record forty-seven points in leading Texas Tech University to victory in the Division I-A women's basketball tournament championship game.

- On April 25, Drew Bledsoe, a quarterback for Washington State University, is the first NFL draft pick of the year, selected by the New England Patriots.

- On April 30, tennis star Monica Seles is stabbed by a rival's fan while playing in Hamburg, Germany.

- On May 22, Roy Jones, Jr., wins his first boxing title (middleweight) with a twelve-round victory over Bernard Hopkins.

- On September 16, Dave Winfield, an outfielder with the Minnesota Twins, gets career baseball hit number three thousand.

- On September 22, the Colorado Rockies complete their first home season with a major league baseball attendance record of 4,483,350 fans.

- On October 26, the NFL awards the twenty-ninth franchise to the Carolina Panthers.

- On November 13, the University of Notre Dame Fighting Irish beat the top-ranked Florida State Seminoles in college football, 31-24.

- On November 14, Don Shula breaks George Halas's career victory mark as an NFL coach with number 325.

- On November 30, the NFL awards the thirtieth franchise to the Jacksonville Jaguars.

- On December 17, the Fox Network outbids the Columbia Broadcasting System (CBS) for the rights to broadcast NFL games, ending a thirty-eight-year relationship between CBS and the NFL.

1994

- On January 1, the Florida State Seminoles beat the University of Nebraska Cornhuskers, 18-16, in the Orange Bowl for the national championship.

- On January 6, ice skater Nancy Kerrigan is assaulted while preparing for the U.S. figure-skating championships in Detroit.

- On February 7, Michael Jordan, who retired from professional basketball the previous October after leading the Chicago Bulls to three consecutive NBA championships, signs with the Chicago White Sox as a baseball free agent.

- On February 14, more than three hundred baseball players are awarded $59.5 million as baseball owners are penalized for "collusion."

- On February 18, Dan Jansen wins the gold medal in the 1000-meter speed-skating event in the Winter Olympics.

- On February 19, Bonnie Blair wins her third consecutive 500-meter speed-skating gold medal.

- On February 23, Baylor University announces it will leave the Southwest Conference to join the Big 8. Before the week is out three other Texas schools (Texas A & M, Texas Tech, and the University of Texas) also announce their departure from the league.

- On March 23, Wayne Gretzky, playing for the Los Angeles Kings, breaks Gordy Howe's career record (801) for National Hockey League (NHL) goals. He finishes his career in 1999 with 894 goals.

- On June 14, the New York Rangers win the NHL Stanley Cup for the first time since 1940.

- On June 22, the Houston Rockets win the first major-league title in the history of the city, as center Hakeem Olajuwon leads the National Basketball Association (NBA) franchise to victory.

- The U.S. team gets its first victory in World Cup soccer since 1950, defeating Colombia.

- On July 28, Kenny Rogers throws the first perfect game in the history of the Texas Rangers, against the California Angels.

- On August 4, the Bowl Alliance is formed, with different sites to host the college football national championship game on a rotating basis.

- On August 12, Major league baseball players go on strike at 12:45 A.M. to protest the owners' plan for a salary cap. The season is ended and the World Series is cancelled for the first time in ninety years.

- On August 15, an NFL record 112,376 spectators watch the "American Bowl" in Mexico City between the Dallas Cowboys and Houston Oilers.

- On September 12, the National Labor Relations Board (NLRB) awards NFL players $30 million in back pay from a lockout by owners at the end of a strike in 1987.

- On September 30, the NHL announces the delay of the start of its regular season.

- On October 19, the Duke University Blue Devils break the University of North Carolina Tar Heels 101-game unbeaten streak held by the women's soccer team.

- On October 31, tennis player Venus Williams, age fourteen, turns professional.

1995

- On January 1, the University of Nebraska defeats the University of Miami, 24-17, in the Orange Bowl to become the fourth team in Division 1-A to finish with a 13-0 record.

- On January 2, Penn State University defeats the University of Oregon, 38-20, in the Rose Bowl. Penn State coach Joe Paterno is the first coach to win the Rose, Orange, Cotton, and Sugar Bowls. The victory is Paterno's sixteenth bowl victory, an NCAA record.

- On January 16, Lenny Wilkins, the coach of the Atlanta Hawks, surpasses Red Auerbach as the winningest coach in NBA history, defeating the Washington Bullets, 112-90. This is Wilkins 939th win.

- On April 22, Ki-Jana Carter, a running back from Penn State University, is selected by the Cincinnati Bengals as the first player in the year's NFL draft.

- On May 6, long-shot Thunder Gulch wins the Kentucky Derby.

- On August 20, Jose Mesa, pitching for the Cleveland Indians, gets his 37th save in 37 opportunities, a major league baseball record.

- On September 6, Cal Ripken, Jr., an infielder for the Baltimore Orioles, plays in his 2,131st consecutive major league baseball game, breaking Lou Gehrig's record.

1996

- On January 2, the University of Nebraska Cornhuskers defeat the University of Florida Gators, 62-24, in the Fiesta Bowl to win the national championship.

- On February 9, an agreement is reached that will allow Art Modell to move his NFL franchise from Cleveland to Baltimore with the promise that Cleveland will have a new Browns team no later than 1999. Modell's new team will be named the Ravens.

- On February 29, the Dallas Mavericks set an NBA record with eighteen three-pointers scored in a game and twelve in a half.

- On April 30, the transfer of the NFL Oilers from Houston to Nashville for the 1998 season is approved.

- On August 16, in the first major league baseball game ever played outside of the United States or Canada, the San Diego Padres beat the New York Mets in Monterrey, Mexico.

- On September 18, Roger Clemens, pitcher for the Boston Red Sox, ties his own major league record of twenty strikeouts in a nine-inning game.

- On November 23, with a victory over Marquette University, Pat Summitt wins her six-hundredth women's college basketball game while coaching the University of Tennessee Lady Volunteers.

1997

- On January 1, the University of Florida defeats Florida State University, 52-20, in the Sugar Bowl to win the national championship.

- On January 26, the Green Bay Packers win the Super Bowl, defeating the New England Patriots, 35-21.

- On April 9, Tiger Woods wins The Masters with a record eighteen-under-par 270.

- On April 12, Randy "Roadhouse" Spizer, age sixteen, wins the "Best Trick" category of the Professional In-Line Skating Challenge in Orlando, Florida.

- On April 19, Orlando Pace, an offensive tackle for Ohio State University, is the first selection in the NFL draft; he is chosen by the St. Louis Rams.

- On May 6, University of Kentucky men's college basketball coach Rick Pitino announces his resignation to lead a professional team, the Boston Celtics, for a ten-year, $70 million contract.

- On June 8, the Detroit Red Wings win the Stanley Cup for the first time in forty-two years, defeating the Philadelphia Flyers, 2-1.

- On June 12, the San Francisco Giants beat the Texas Rangers in the first-ever regular season inter-league game.

- On June 28, Evander Holyfield wins a heavyweight fight against Mike Tyson when Tyson is disqualified for biting Holyfield's ear.

- On July 31, Mark McGwire, a first baseman, is traded from the Oakland A's to the St. Louis Cardinals.

- On October 9, after thirty-six years as basketball coach at the University of North Carolina, Dean Smith surprises fans by announcing his retirement.

- On October 25, Kevin VanDam wins his fourth Bassmasters tournament, and second of the season, with a three-day total of fifteen bass weighing forty-one pounds, fifteen ounces in the Virginia Eastern Invitational on Kerr Reservoir out of South Hill, Virginia.

- On October 28, the NBA announces the hiring of Dee Kantner and Violet Palmer as the first women to officiate in the major-league, all-male sport.

- On December 7, the University of North Carolina women's soccer team beats the University of Connecticut for its fourteenth NCAA title in sixteen years.

- On December 31, future major leaguer Orlando Hernandez, half brother of Livan who plays for the Florida Marlins, defects from Cuba.

1998

- On January 6, a split college football national title is announced, shared by the University of Michigan Wolverines (12-0) and the University of Nebraska Cornhuskers (13-0).

- On January 25, the Denver Broncos and quarterback John Elway win their first Super Bowl, defeating the Green Bay Packers.

- On February 11, Picabo Street wins the women's super giant slalom (Super G) skiing gold medal in the Winter Olympics.

- On February 20, Tara Lipinski wins the women's figure skating gold medal.

- On March 1, Venus Williams wins her first professional tennis singles title, in the IGA Tennis Classic.

- On March 3, Larry Doby, the first African American athlete to play in the American League, as an outfielder with the Cleveland Indians, is elected to the Baseball Hall of Fame.

- On March 8, Kraig Welborn of DeRidder, Louisiana, catches a fourteen-pound, eleven-ounce largemouth bass near Anacoco, Louisiana, breaking the world record for that species by three ounces.

- On March 29, the University of Tennessee Lady Volunteers win their third consecutive women's basketball championship.

- On March 30, the University of Kentucky defeats the University of Utah to win the NCAA basketball tournament.

- On April 12, Mark O'Meara wins The Masters.

- On April 18, Peyton Manning, a quarterback for the University of Tennessee Volunteers, chosen by the Indianapolis Colts, is the first selection in the NFL draft.

- On May 6, rookie Kerry Wood, a pitcher for the Chicago Cubs, strikes out twenty batters, tying a major league record, in a one-hitter against the Houston Astros.

- On May 17, David Wells pitches a perfect game, only the thirteenth in major league baseball history, for the New York Yankees against the Minnesota Twins.

- On May 24, Eddie Cheever wins the Indianapolis 500.

- On May 25, Princeton University wins its fifth lacrosse title of the decade, 15-5, defeating the University of Maryland.

- On June 14, Michael Jordan hits the game winning shot, as the Chicago Bulls beat the Utah Jazz to win the NBA championship.

- On July 9, Allan H. "Bud" Selig is elected to the permanent post as commissioner of major league baseball.

- On September 8, Mark McGwire breaks Roger Maris's single-season home run record, hitting number sixty-two.

- On September 20, Cal Ripken, Jr., benches himself, concluding his streak of playing in 2,632 consecutive baseball games.

- On October 13, the NBA cancels the first two weeks of regular season play, ultimately eliminating ninety-nine games from its schedule.

- On October 21, the New York Yankees win the World Series, defeating the San Diego Padres in four games, after winning 114 during in the regular season.

1999

- On January 1, the University of Tennessee defeats Florida State University, 23-16, in the Fiesta Bowl to win the national championship.

- On January 31, the Denver Broncos and John Elway win their second consecutive Super Bowl, defeating the Atlanta Falcons, 34-19.

- On February 5, the NBA schedule begins belatedly after the first work stoppage in its history.

- On February 14, Jeff Gordon wins the Daytona 500.
- On March 17, reversing an earlier decision, NFL owners adopt a modified instant-replay system as an officiating aid for the 1999 season.
- On May 22, Mia Hamm becomes the all-time leading scorer in international soccer with her 108th goal.
- On June 27, during the Summer X Games, Tony Hawk completes the first "900" in the history of skateboarding competition.
- On July 10, Brandi Chastain's penalty kick leads the U.S. team to victory in the Women's World Cup.
- On July 25, cyclist Lance Armstrong makes an amazing comeback after battling testicular cancer to win the Tour de France.
- On September 11, Serena Williams, younger sister of Venus, wins the U.S. Open women's singles tennis championship.
- On September 26, the Ryder Cup team, captained by Ben Crenshaw, makes the biggest comeback in the history of the competition to help the United States golf team defeat the European squad.
- On October 23, in the first meeting between NCAA Division I-A football teams coached by a father and a son, Bobby Bowden's Florida State Seminoles are victorious over his son Tommy Bowden's Clemson Tigers, 17-14.
- On October 25, Payne Stewart, winner of three major golf championships, dies with other passengers in a plane crash.
- On November 13, Lennox Lewis defeats Evander Holyfield in Madison Square Garden in New York to win the first undisputed heavyweight boxing championship in nine years.
- On December 26, Michael Jordan is selected by the Entertainment and Sports Programming Network (ESPN) as the greatest North American athlete of the twentieth century. Babe Ruth is ranked second.
- On December 31, Sherry Davis, the first female public-address announcer in major league baseball, is dismissed after seven years with the San Francisco Giants.

Shaq Attaq!

Autobiography

By: Shaquille O'Neal, with Jack McCallum

Date: 1993

Source: O'Neal, Shaquille, with Jack McCallum. *Shaq Attaq!* New York: Hyperion, 1993, 108–114.

About the Authors: Basketball star Shaquille O'Neal (1972–) is a nine-time National Basketball Association (NBA) All-Star. He was the top draft choice in 1992, leaving Louisiana State University after his junior season. In 1996, he was traded from the Orlando Magic to the Los Angeles Lakers, whom he helped to three consecutive NBA titles beginning in 2000. O'Neal has also endorsed many products, as well as producing and performing on rap albums and appearing in movies.

Jack McCallum is a senior writer for *Sports Illustrated.* He has authored several books, including *Unfinished Business: On and Off the Court with the 1990–1991 Boston Celtics.* On several occasions, his works have been included in the annual anthology *The Best American Sports Writing.* ∎

Introduction

Professional basketball in the 1990s was fraught with celebrity and team scandal, and unethical behavior. This was an enormous change from the sport that began in YMCAs in the late nineteenth century. Dr. James Naismith developed basketball in 1891 to create an indoor sport to fill the gap between fall football and spring baseball. The sport's popularity grew rapidly, with men's and women's teams springing up in colleges, high schools, and YMCAs across the United States.

These amateur teams prohibited "professionalism." Paid players were banned from their leagues. However, professional basketball slowly gained ground. The NBA was founded in 1946 as the Basketball Association of America (BAA). Though college basketball eclipsed its professional counterpart for many years, the NBA prospered, and good players began to garner high salaries. The advent of television, an effective medium to transmit the athleticism of the sport, boosted team and player salaries even higher and drew additional fans to the game. Women's professional basketball leagues appeared briefly in the late 1970s and again in the 1990s.

Men's basketball underwent important changes from its founding through the 1990s. There were no African American players when the BAA was founded in 1946. By the time the organization changed its name to the NBA in 1950, however, it had ended segregation. Former Harlem Globetrotter Nat Clifton was the first African American to sign with an NBA team. Later that same season, Earl Lloyd became the first African American to play in an NBA game. By 1958, there was at least one African American player on every NBA team.

Significance

By the 1990s, star players were common in the NBA. At the top of the heap was Shaquille O'Neal. Though he was preceded by a long list of outstanding Laker centers, including George Mikan, Kareem Abdul-Jabbar, and Wilt Chamberlain, O'Neal has commanded the spotlight like few others before him.

In 1996, the NBA selected O'Neal as one of the fifty greatest players in its history. In 2000, he became the first NBA player ever unanimously selected MVP. Between 1997 and 2002, he was selected to the All-NBA First Team four times. Between 1993 and 2002, he was selected to the All-Star team nine times. He was the regular-season scoring champ twice in the 1990s. In the 1999–2000 season, he was chosen the league's most valuable player by the media. He has been selected the MVP of the NBA finals three times, while leading the Lakers to championships in 2000, 2001, and 2002.

O'Neal's significance to basketball lies in his combination of skills and size. Since the mid-1990s, Shaq has easily been the most dominant center in the NBA. At 7'1" and 338 pounds, his height and power have allowed him to impose his will on most opponents. In addition, unlike many centers before him, Shaq also has the ability and agility to run the court. However dominant Shaq has been, his career demonstrates that having a great center does not always guarantee a great team. O'Neal was the center for the Orlando Magic, but the team never lived up to its potential, largely because of a subpar supporting cast. In Los Angeles, though, it has been a different story. Aided by highly skilled teammates, O'Neal has consistently led the team to success.

Primary Source

Shaq Attaq! [excerpt]

SYNOPSIS: In this excerpt, Shaq begins by discussing a game against the New York Knicks, and how he wanted to do better than New York's center, Patrick Ewing. Then he discusses a game against the Chicago Bulls, in which the Bulls beat the Magic handily, and a game with the Celtics, which the Magic won. The section concludes with O'Neal talking about a game against the Bulls in Chicago, which the Magic won.

Making Noise in Charles's House

The Knicks came to town on January 8 for a TNT game and it was really a big one for us. We had that one-point loss to the Pistons and a three-point loss to the Nets a few nights later and we really needed a win. There was a lot going on at this time. I was leading Patrick Ewing in the fans' balloting for All-Star center and it was a big story in New York because Patrick had been the starting center in the East for the last three seasons. There was even talk that the Knicks were going to hold kind of a "registration voting party" so more New York fans would support Patrick. I didn't get caught up in it but, before the game, Patrick said to one of our clubhouse attendants: "Can you believe Shaq is beating me?" Well, yeah, I could.

I told you I don't like to get caught up in the one-on-one matchup thing very much, but it was important for me to play better against Patrick than I did in Madison Square Garden in November. I knew I was a better player in January than I had been in November. And I know Patrick wanted to come to town and show up this rookie who was stealing some of his thunder.

Well, we beat them 95-94 in one of our best games of the season. That's because we got behind early, 22-10 and still trailed 79-67 in the fourth period but didn't give up and came right back at them. A lot of teams hate to play the Knicks, but I love it. There's lots of shoving, lots of banging, lots of talking. My kind of game.

Dennis Scott hit a big three-pointer at crunch time and I was really hot in the fourth period when I scored 11 of my 22 points and blocked three of Patrick's shots. Patrick had a short jumper at the buzzer to beat us but I was in his face and he missed. Afterward, he was pretty hot about it. "I got fouled before I got the ball and I got fouled when I took the shot," he said. That's not the way I saw it, of course. He had his arm wrapped around me and I was just trying to get around him to defend it. Anyway, what Patrick should remember is that I had five fouls a lot of the game and had to sit out much of the third period. It was typical—the loser was mad, the winner was glad. We finished pretty even statistically just like we did that first time in New York. He had 21 points, 12 rebounds, 1 blocked shot; I had 22, 13, and 5.

Shaquille O'Neal and actor Nick Nolte in a scene from the 1994 movie *Blue Chips,* which starred basketball superstar O'Neal. **THE KOBAL COLLECTION/PARAMOUNT/GREENE, BOB. REPRODUCED BY PERMISSION.**

Maybe playing the Knicks does wear a team out more than I realized because we looked worn out against the Pacers the next night and lost 104-88. I came close to a triple-double again (30, 20, and 8) but it didn't do us much good. And three nights after that was that first game against Michael and the Bulls that I started to tell you about in Chapter 1.

After Michael blocked that first shot on me, maybe everybody thought it was going to happen every time, because I only got nine more shots the entire game. I made eight of them but finished with only 19 points, which wasn't nearly enough as we lost 122-106. It was one of those games where I thought I could do a lot more but didn't get the chance. Part of the problem, I'll admit, was that Scottie Pippen came to double me every time, holding up those long, elastic arms that make him look like a prehistoric bird. And another part of the problem was Jordan, who was just waiting for me to get the ball so he could come and double me. A couple times I got the ball in the air and before I came down— whoosh!—it was gone, almost like that Vegas magician, David Copperfield, touched it with his cane. I turned around to see who it was and it was Jordan. You can watch a guy on TV and think he's quick, but Michael is much, much quicker in person. Michael

Shaquille O'Neal descends to the basketball court after a dunk in Atlanta, December 19, 1992. The 7'1" O'Neal took the NBA by storm and quickly became one of the league's dominant centers. © REUTERS NEWMEDIA INC./CORBIS. REPRODUCED BY PERMISSION.

only had 23 points, the number on his jersey, but they got a real good game from Horace Grant, who had 26 points. That's the way it is with championship teams—somebody falls down, somebody steps back up. I blocked one of Michael's shots but he made a noise like "Agg-hhh!" and they called it goaltending. When Michael Jordan goes "Agg-hhh!" the rest of the NBA says, "Mike, what's the matter?"

We went up to Boston for a game against the Celtics on January 15 and, naturally, everybody wanted to know what I thought about Boston Garden, like it was the Leaning Tower of Pisa or something. What I thought was, it's a building. But I do realize the tradition because it's one of the places my father always talked about. Playing there probably meant more to him than it did to me. I could see the banners. I could sense the tradition. I could still smell Red Auerbach's cigar smoke from thirty years ago.

The first thing I wanted to know when I got there was whether or not Larry Bird was around. Unfortunately, it turned out he was down in Florida at his vacation home. I guess even he doesn't like Boston

weather in the winter. Bird had retired right before the season, and I'm sorry I never got the chance to play against him.

It's funny, but when I was young I never used to like Bird. And it had nothing to do with the white-black thing because I'm not into that. I just thought that he was lucky. I saw him one time get the ball, fall on his back, shoot it over the backboard, and it went in. I felt some players were just lucky and he was one of them.

Also, when I was in Germany, I had a white kid I used to play one on one with a lot named Mitch Ryals, who thought he was Larry Bird. He was about 6'6' then and I was about 6'8' and he used to beat me all the time. I'd always pretend I was Dr. J., but Mitch was a lot closer to being Bird than I was to being Doc. Mitch was skinny like Bird, real slow, and he'd do the same things Bird did. Fake right and go left, up-and-under moves, take real crazy shots that went in, make people look silly and get them frustrated. I just couldn't stop his shot and I could never figure out why. I'm sure guys in the NBA used to say the same thing about Bird. "Man, I'm right in this slow dude's face and he's just killin' me." It was only later on when I realized that he was a hard worker, very fundamentally sound, and with a lot of skills. I've still never met him, but he said some nice things about me, and I appreciated it.

The Celtics are a great organization with lots of tradition, but I don't know whether I'd like to play forty-one games a season in Boston Garden. It was kind of cold out there in the beginning because of the ice that's right underneath the basketball court. I guess you get used to it, though. Robert Parish and I had a great battle. I had a couple monster dunks on him and he put in a couple of his tricky hooks and that rickety, high-arching fallaway jumper. In the third quarter I blocked one of his shots and his momentum carried him into the stands. He came back with catsup on his shorts.

I had one interesting call made on me. I blocked a shot by Kevin Gamble and a referee out by the midcourt line called a foul, even though the ref right next to the play saw it was clean. When I asked the ref about it, he said, "I thought you got him with your body." And I said, "Oh, we're making thought calls now?"

I didn't say it too loud, though.

We won by a pretty comfortable margin, 113-94. I had a pretty solid game with 22 points, 12 rebounds, and 4 blocked shots, but Parish had some nice numbers, too, with 19, 11, and 2. Scott Skiles had a good game for us, but the big story was Anthony Bowie, who played because Dennis was hurt, and scored 23 points. I was happy for A.B., who's a great guy, a great player to have on the team whether he's on the court or not. During the season we had this joke where we'd rub baby oil on ourselves and pose in front of the mirror like those body builder dudes. A.B. looks the best because he's got about 1 percent body fat. Anthony's a family man, and sometimes I even envy him a bit. I love his son, little A.B., I love his small daughter, Brook Ashley, and his wife, Michelle, is a nice lady. If I ever get married, I'd probably want to marry someone like her. She reminds me of my mother a little bit—real quiet, real sweet.

The way we knew we were really in control of the game was when Greg Kite shot a technical foul for us late in the game. It was a great gesture because Greg used to be a Celtic and everyone is always on his case about his bad free-throw shooting. I know how that feels. Compared to Greg, I sometimes look like Mark Price or Ricky Pierce at the line. But Greg made this one and the crowd loved it. Greg's another family man, lives a life completely different from my own, and we would never hang out. I see him at practice and games and that's it. But, in a way, that's what sports is all about. A lot of different types of people, people who don't necessarily have anything in common, coming together for one cause.

One other thing about Greg: He is probably the only person to have played against both Wilt and me. When he was a freshman recruit at UCLA about fifteen years ago Wilt still came over for pickup games even though he was in his forties. Greg said he didn't play much but he saw enough to tell me, "Shaq, you woulda chewed up Wilt and spit him out for lunch." Okay, he really didn't say that at all, but it sounded good, right, Greg?

On January 16 we went into Chicago and beat the Bulls 128-124 in one of the strangest games of the year. First of all, just beating the two-time defending champions at home is strange. But this is the game that Jordan went off with 64 points, the most I had ever seen anyone score, and we still beat them. You have a choice when you play Chicago and neither of the options is very good. You can double-team Jordan, try to hold him below, say, thirty points, and take the chance that he won't get the ball to Scottie, Horace, or B. J. Armstrong and have them all go off on you. Or you can just let Jordan get his

points by single-covering him and try to stop everybody else. First, we tried to double him, but he was too quick for us and got his shots off anyway. So then we decided to let him go and play solid defense on everyone else.

Believe it or not, he hurt his wrist in this game but came back with a wristband and just kept shooting. He wasn't talking at all, just shooting and shooting. I only got one of his shots all night and they called it goaltending. I knocked him down once, too, which the fans really don't like very much in Chicago. It's kind of like if you went up to Mickey Mouse and knocked him on his butt right in the middle of the Magic Kingdom.

Michael finally stopped shooting at forty-nine, which is a lot of shots, but Nick hit a big three-pointer to send it into overtime, and we outplayed them in the five-minute extra period. After the game Michael said: "We could learn something from the Magic. They kept battling and battling, and we were really complacent." Thanks, Mike. Of course, by the end of the year, you and the Phoenix Suns were the only teams battling and battling, and the Orlando Magic was watching you on TV.

I was real happy with my game there. I had 29 points and 24 rebounds, which is a big improvement over the game when they beat us in Orlando. Bill Cartwright, their center, said after the game that the Bulls had done everything in their power to shake me. The fans went at me big-time, the players doubled me hard, some of them talked a little trash, and I ignored it all. I love to hear that because, most of the time, that's what I try to accomplish out there. I love to ignore all the extra stuff, just focus in on what I have to do, and shut everybody up with my play.

After the game, Nick, who's from Chicago, took us to his club, which is called The Clique. We went upstairs to the VIP Room and just chilled. Michael and his good friend from the Bears, Richard Dent, came in, said hi and left. It was nice to come out on top of Michael in Michael's town, because it doesn't happen that much.

Further Resources

BOOKS

Brenner, Richard J. *Shaquille O'Neal & Larry Johnson.* Syosset, N.Y.: East End, 1993.

Grabowski, John F. *The Los Angeles Lakers.* San Diego: Lucent, 2002.

Hunter, Bruce. *Shaq Impaq.* Chicago: Bonus, 1993.

Jackson, Phil, and Charles Rosen. *More Than a Game.* New York: Seven Stories, 2001.

Kaye, Elizabeth. *Ain't No Tomorrow: Kobe, Shaq, and the Making of a Lakers Dynasty.* Chicago: Contemporary, 2002.

O'Neal, Shaquille. *Shaq Talks Back.* New York: St. Martin's, 2001.

Rappoport, Ken. *Shaquille O'Neal.* New York: Walker, 1994.

WEBSITES

Shaquille O'Neal official website. Available online at http://www.shaq.com (accessed April 8, 2003).

AUDIO AND VISUAL MEDIA

Los Angeles Lakers 2001–02 NBA Champions. Directed by Wil Lyman. USA Home Entertainment, 2002, VHS.

Shaq Round the World! CBS Fox Video Sports, 1998, VHS.

Shaquille O'Neal Larger Than Life. Directed by Samuel Jackson. CBS Fox Video, 1995, VHS.

Dominique Moceanu: An American Champion

Autobiography

By: Dominique Moceanu, as told to Steve Woodward

Date: 1996

Source: Moceanu, Dominique, as told to Steve Woodward. *Dominique Moceanu: An American Champion.* Bantam, 1996, 59–67.

About the Author: Dominique Moceanu (1981–) won the all-around title at the U.S. Gymnastics Competition in 1995 at age fourteen. She moved to Houston at age nine and began to train with Bela Karolyi, who had previously trained Olympic champions Mary Lou Retton, Nadia Comaneci, and Kim Zmeskal. At ten, Moceanu qualified for the junior national team, the youngest ever to do so. In 1996, she helped the U.S. team win the gold medal for gymnastics in the Atlanta Olympics. ∎

Introduction

More than any other sport, women's gymnastics has been criticized for pushing young girls into competition before they are emotionally and physically ready. Bela Karolyi, in particular, has come under fire for his string of ever-younger Olympic athletes and the incredible personal sacrifices they make in order to win competitions. Girls in early puberty, whose bodies have not yet matured, have natural advantages over teens just a few years older.

Women's gymnastics features a total of four events; the balance beam, floor, uneven bars, and vault. Six medals are awarded—one for each event, one for the individual with the highest cumulative score, and one for the team with the highest overall score. When fourteen-year-old Romanian Nadia Comaneci achieved the first perfect score ever awarded in Olympic gymnastic history

(men's or women's), she had been training with coach Bela Karolyi for a little over half of her lifetime. Just four years later, though she still captured two Olympic gold medals, Comaneci's body had matured to the point that she retired from amateur athletics after the Olympics. After Karolyi defected to the United States and began coaching American gymnasts, he helped Mary Lou Retton, at sixteen, win America's first women's gymnastics Olympic all-around gold medal in 1984. Retton retired the following year. After Kim Zmeskal won the all-around title at the American Gymnastics World Championships at fifteen in 1991, she was widely expected to perform well at the Olympics the following year. Her subsequent career as an amateur athlete, however, was plagued by injuries.

And, of course, there is the athlete whose performance under pressure triggered the largest wave of controversy: Kerri Strug. At eighteen, Strug tore two ligaments in her ankle on her first vault during the 1996 Summer Olympic competition; but, as gymnasts get two chances to vault, under urging from Karolyi she forced herself to vault a second time, since it looked as though the U.S. team would need her second vault in order to help secure an all-around gold medal (as it turned out her second vault was unnecessary for the victory, but she did not know that at the time). She was called a hero, but her coaches, Bela and Marta Karolyi, were criticized heavily. The experience brought scrutiny to the intense physical regime and social isolation experienced by young women gymnasts.

Significance

At fourteen, Dominique Moceanu was the youngest member of the U.S. gymnastics team, having won the individual all-around gold medal at the U.S. Nationals in New Orleans the year before. After the controversy surrounding Strug's vault, rulemakers later determined no gymnast under sixteen could compete in the senior circuit, a rule that would have effectively eliminated all of these child-stars from competition, including Moceanu. Many gymnasts argue that this age limit effectively limits them from performing at their physical peak. Advocates of the rule, however, argue that it keeps young girls from suffering debilitating physical injuries and social pressures while their bodies and minds are developing most rapidly.

Indeed, Moceanu's own personal history gives some force to those in favor of the age limit. By the time she was seventeen, Moceanu had run away from home and successfully sued for emancipation. She also privately settled a large financial suit against her parents that accused her father of squandering ten years of her earnings and trying to hire a hitman to kill two of her friends. She said her parents forced her to sacrifice everything for her gymnastic career, sometimes hitting her at events. A far cry from the upbeat champion's tale reproduced here, Moceanu's real life contained many dark moments. Though she was able to retain her gymnastics skills and maintain an active career, her years as a child prodigy caused her a great deal of emotional trauma before she turned twenty.

Primary Source

Dominique Moceanu: An American Champion
[excerpt]

SYNOPSIS: In this excerpt, Moceanu discusses two of the events in which she had to perform well to win the women's all-around gold medal at the U.S. Nationals in New Orleans in August 1995. First, she narrates her balance beam routine in detail, beginning with ripping off all of the padding from the uneven bars to prepare for the beam. Then she describes her floor excercise routine that vaulted her to winning the all-around gold medal.

The Balance Beam

The first thing I had to do after my bars routine was rip off all my padding and wrist guards and palm protectors. All that stuff is useless, even a hindrance, on the beam. The only thing I needed was a pair of beam shoes, and I quickly slipped them on and ran to get into place.

Many gymnasts perform on the beam barefoot. When I was younger, I did too. Then I developed a problem with the middle toe on my left foot. The skin underneath it cracked and split from the pressure of my routine. Since I worked out every day, it could never heal. You might think that a small sore spot on one toe isn't a big deal, but it's a great big deal when you're a gymnast. Each time I got on the beam, my toe began killing me. Finally it became so painful that I couldn't ignore it. (And I can ignore a lot of pain, through concentration and practice.)

As soon as I started wearing beam shoes, it made all the difference. My toe healed. Now I never have a problem. Beam shoes are a little like ballet slippers but with a more rigid bottom. When I wear them, I can't point my feet quite as well. I have to concentrate more to make sure the line of my foot looks fully extended, the way it should be. But they do what they're supposed to do: protect my feet.

Before the beam event, each gymnast gets a thirty-second touch, which is a very brief warm-up on the beam during which you can practice just a few skills. I did that, jumped down, and got ready to perform my routine.

To start my program, I took a short run off the springboard and did a pirouette onto the beam, landing with all my weight on my shoulders. This move is called the Silivas, after a Romanian gymnast named Daniela Silivas. She was a gold medalist on the beam at the 1988 Olympics. I think it's a great move, and it's a very dramatic beginning.

After the Silivas, I did a little roll, and then I was up on my feet, on a wooden beam only four inches wide, four feet from the ground. Every moment up there requires nothing less than total concentration.

I did a series of dance movements down to one end of the beam. These dance movements let the judges see my flexibility, balance, grace, and control. At the end of the beam, I turned so that my heels were about an inch and a half from the back edge. Usually there is a thin layer of chalk dust on the beam, so I make a tiny scratch mark with my fingernail during a practice. I use this mark to keep my bearings, and to stay away from the very edge.

From there I went into my flight series, always beginning with my left foot. (I am a left-footed gymnast who is right-handed most of the time. Strange but true!) The flight series began with a back handspring, hands on the beam as I made the rotation. Then I performed three consecutive layouts—no hands, just aerial backward flips—with a slight arch in my body position. This is usually the part that makes coaches and parents hold their breaths, but it wasn't the end of my routine.

I performed another series of dance movements, including my compulsory leap jumps for an added degree of difficulty. After the dance movements, I added something new: a back handspring into consecutive handstand pirouettes. It was a new skill, and no one else had done it in competition before. (If I decide to use it in the Olympics, it will be named after me. Someday, perhaps, little girls will be performing the Moceanu on the beam. That's so exciting to think about.)

During my whole beam routine, I was thinking of Marta. If I wanted to make her happy, I had to do well on the beam. I was so anxious not to disappoint her, not to disappoint myself. It's the event she loves the most, and I wanted to show her that I loved it too. Finally came my dismount. I flung myself into it with all my power, trying to keep a perfectly controlled landing. And I stuck! I could almost hear Marta's cries of happiness and encouragement as I threw my arms overhead.

And that made three routines down, one more to go: the floor exercise.

"Karolyi: I'm Old-Fashioned" [excerpt]

Steve: Who was your favorite gymnastic person while growing up? Why?

Bela Karolyi: There are two favorites. By physical standards, the most attractive was Nadia Comaneci. Her willingness to improve was also superior. Her personality was sturdy, balanced, strong. That made her an excellent person to work with. She was very cooperative, too.

Physically, she had great balance. She was very strong, very explosive. She had natural endurance and excellent coordination. These are the abilities you need in this sport, and I recognized them early when she was a child.

She had such coordination, and you needed that to do the complicated tasks in gymnastics.

The other gymnast was Mary Lou Retton. Of course, she's known very well here, because she was the first all-around champion in the United States. Her personality was the best, and the most adorable. She was a totally open personality, and she had a great way of relating to her coaches and teammates. I never had anyone like that before.

Physically, Mary Lou was also remarkable. Her explosiveness and strength were natural—and they came from her genes. This is a combination of coordination and explosiveness, which was very important in our sport, especially in events like vaulting. Everything happens in a fraction of a second and you need to bring it all together quickly.

Rick Jones: What gymnasts that you've coached have had the most unusual, "freakish" physical qualities?

Bela Karolyi: In my career, I had one athlete of Mary Lou's generation and her name was Lee Wisnezsky, and she had incredible explosiveness and strength—more than anyone I've ever had. That made her an outstanding vaulter. Unfortunately, her preparation was not up to the standard necessary, and after a couple years she gave up her high-quality performance.

Susan: Do you ever visit Hungary, and if you do what can you tell about Hungarian gymnastics.

Bela Karolyi: Recently I did visit quite a few times, following up a movie project. That allowed me to watch the preparation.

I am very familiar with Hungary, because I grew up in Romania, which borders it. Unfortunately, today they are not experiencing the same type of standard that they were experiencing in the '60s and '70s.

Rick Jones: So, Bela, would you genetically test young gymnasts to figure out which ones have the most potential? What do you think other coaches in other parts of the world would do?

Bela Karolyi: I'm old-fashioned, so that's something I would not be interested in doing. I still love to find and develop the young athletes in traditional ways. I like to watch the physical and mental growth. That has always been very exciting.

Personally, I would never do genetic research.

Around the world, it's been proven that anything that is easier and more efficient will be tried and picked up by others. Who would do it? I would not point a finger. But there is a great rivalry among the nations in the world, even the third-world countries.

Perhaps China would probably be one of the first countries, and with their (huge) population from which to choose the best gymnasts, that would be frightening.

Tick: If you could build the best gymnast, what would they look like physically?

Bela Karolyi: You want a lean body with nice and aesthetic muscle definition—not bulky muscles. Genetics is all about showcasing human beauty along with high-quality performance.

The ideal gymnast would be between 4 feet 7 and 5-2. I wouldn't be able to pinpoint an ideal height, however. It would be foolish to say that a gymnast above 5-2 could not be great.

Regarding weight, well, a 5-foot athlete should weigh over 100 pounds.

Of course, flexibility is very, very important. Flexibility is something you can work on, too, so it's not all genetic.

Greg: What is your favorite sport to watch other than gymnastics?

Bela Karolyi: It's one of those things that comes from my background, as a former athlete. I like track and field. I can see the pure athletic abilities. I like the hammer and shot put—I was a hammer thrower.

Rick Jones: Do you think the Europeans would be more willing to use some of this science?

Bela Karolyi: Unfortunately, the precedent with East Germany and the communist systems generated an incredible desire to create super athletes. This was forcefully done, sometimes to the detriment of their physical health. The Bulgarian weightlifting teams used steroids, too.

But now most of the countries are going away from that non-democratic system. I don't think they would be as willing to use the quick-fix system of creating good athletes as they did before.

SOURCE: Karolyi, Bela. "Karolyi: I'm Old-Fashioned." Interview by ESPN.com users. June 3, 1997. Excerpt available online at http://espn.go.com/otl/athlete/karolyi.html; website home page: http://espn.go.com (accessed July 16, 2003).

The Floor Exercise

After the first three events, I knew I was ahead by a small margin. If I could turn in a good floor exercise, I had a chance at a medal—possibly even a gold one. The floor routine is one of my very favorites—I'm filled with joy when I'm out there performing. More than any other event, it's a chance for me to show my stuff and engage the audience in my performance.

I was so excited about going out there and wowing the crowd that I didn't feel at all nervous or excited. A big change from my earlier meets! I had no worries. I'm not sure how that was true. It's probably hard to imagine facing the performance of your life, the one that will make or break you—and in front of tens of thousands of people, no less—and not feel hysterical, but it was definitely true for me.

I felt supremely confident. I knew I could do every trick, every move in my routine. They came easily to me after so many months of training. So when I headed out on the floor, I decided to show it off really big, really powerfully from the moment I saluted the judges. Even better, I was the last competitor in that event, so I could really go after the crowd. I was determined to get the attention of everyone in the arena.

Bela seemed to sense my mood, and he encouraged it. He believed I could deliver a great performance. "You can do it, Dominique, with no problem," he told me over and over. "You know you are the best. Show the people you are the best."

As soon as the music started I was psyched. Bela had chosen "Chantilly Lace" by the Big Bopper as my signature song, and I loved it. The catchy rhythm and fun words made me feel like snapping my fingers.

The floor exercise takes place on a square of carpet forty feet by forty feet. The object is to perform all your skills, using as much of the carpet as possible, without putting even a pinkie toe over the line.

I began with a dance sequence cued to the music, which led into a tumbling pass from one corner of the carpet to its opposite diagonal corner. In my routine that day, there were a total of four tumbling passes from corner to corner. I used handsprings, roundoffs, layouts, saltos, you name it. I nailed every one. On one of the passes I performed my trademark move, which is a little hop at the very end of the tumbling series. It starts with a handspring, front full twist, followed by a forward punch layout (no arms, body straight). On the landing after the layout,

Dominique Moceanu competes on the balance beam during the 1996 Olympic Games in Atlanta, Georgia. Moceanu was the youngest member of the 1996 U.S. Olympic gymnastics team, which won the gold medal. © DAEMMRICH BOB/CORBIS SYGMA. REPRODUCED BY PERMISSION.

instead of raising my arms to signal the finish, I jumped straight up into the air, landed, then went into my final pose. The crowd went crazy, clapping, whistling, calling my name.

(I picked that move up from Svetlana Boguinskaia, who had been training with me and Kerri Strug at Bela's. I noticed that when Svetlana practiced different passes on her floor routine, she did that little hop move at the end. She did this only in the gym, not in competitions. After a while I added it to my performance, just to give it a different look. Svetlana is planning to represent the Republic of Belarus in the Summer Games in Atlanta.)

As soon as I landed my final pose cleanly, I felt ecstatic. I felt in my heart that I would win the all-around. I had done my best.

Yes! I thought. The moment I've been waiting for my whole life is here! I could barely breathe as I waited for my floor exercise score.

Then it came: 9.80. I confess that I was a little surprised and disappointed. I felt that I had done

The U.S. women's Olympic gymnastics team waves to the crowd after being awarded the gold medal in the Women's All Around competition at the 1996 Olympic Games in Atlanta, Georgia, July 23, 1996. From left to right they are Amanda Borden, Dominique Dawes, Amy Chow, Jaycie Phelps, Dominique Moceanu, Kerri Strug, and Shannon Miller. AP/WIDE WORLD PHOTOS. REPRODUCED BY PERMISSION.

better than that. I guess the crowd agreed with me, because they booed the judges' decision.

But even that score was good enough to win the all-around gold medal—over a great gymnast and 1992 Olympic silver medalist, Shannon Miller from Oklahoma. I had a total all-around score of 78.45. Shannon's was 78.25.

There's no way to describe the excitement I felt at that moment, when I realized I had definitely won the gold. Bela rushed over and swept me up into one of his huge bear hugs.

"You did it!" he shouted into my ear. "You did it! You little sucker, you did it!"

I was melting with happiness to hear his words. And I knew that up in the stands, my parents and my little sister were happy for me and proud of me. I felt that they could really see what all their sacrifices and endless support had led to.

Dominique Moceanu, United States National Gymnastics Senior Champion.

It was a tremendous moment.

Further Resources

BOOKS

Durrett, Deanne. *Dominique Moceanu.* San Diego, Calif.: Lucent Books, 1999.

Gutman, Dan. *Gymnastics.* New York: Viking, 1996.

Karolyi, Bela, and Nancy Ann Richardson. *Feel No Fear: The Power, Passion, and Politics of a Life in Gymnastics.* New York: Hyperion, 1994.

Quiner, Krista. *Dominique Moceanu: A Gymnastics Sensation: A Biography.* East Hanover, N.J.: Bradford Publishing, 1997.

Retton, Mary Lou, et. al. *Mary Lou: Creating an Olympic Champion.* New York: McGraw-Hill, 1986.

Ryan, Joan. *Little Girls in Pretty Boxes: The Making and Breaking of Elite Gymnasts and Figure Skaters.* New York: Doubleday, 1995.

WEBSITES

"Dominique Moceanu." Hollywoodfirm.com. Available online at http://www.hollywoodfirm.com/Biographies/dominique_moceanu.htm; website home page: http://www.hollywoodfirm.com (accessed July 15, 2003).

Dominique Moceanu Online. Available online at http://www.dominique-moceanu.com (accessed July 15, 2003).

"Dominique Moceanu." Infoplease.com. Available online at http://www.infoplease.com/ipa/A0767284.html; website home page: http://www.infoplease.com (accessed July 15, 2003).

"Dominique Moceanu." USA Gymnastics Online. Available online at http://www.usa-gymnastics.org/athletes/bios/m/dmoceanu.html; website home page: http://www.usa-gymnastics.org (accessed July 15, 2003).

"Bay Area Bambino"

Interview

By: Mark McGwire

Date: April 1997

Source: McGwire, Mark. "Bay Area Bambino." Interview by William Ladson. *Sport* 88, no. 4, April 1997, 48–53.

About the Author: Mark McGwire (1963–) established a new rookie home run record with forty-nine home runs in 1987. Despite a number of injuries that caused him to miss a large number of games, he hit 155 home runs between 1995 and 1997. In 1998, McGwire established a new single-season home run record with seventy home runs (since broken by Barry Bonds). He retired after the 2001 season, due to foot problems. He has established the McGwire Foundation to help sexually and physically abused children. ∎

Introduction

Professional baseball started in 1869 with the Cincinnati Red Stockings. The National League was formed in 1876, with teams including the Boston Red Caps, and the St. Louis Brown Stockings. Ban Johnson formed the rival American League in 1901. Its teams included the Baltimore Orioles and the Milwaukee Brewers. The leagues competed until 1903, when the World Series between the champions of the two leagues began. Through the late 1910s, the same ball was used throughout the game and ballparks were very large. This contributed to few home runs being hit. In 1901 the champion St. Louis Cardinals only had thirty-nine home runs as a team (and finished fourth in homers). The early 1920s saw a more lively ball introduced in both leagues and the spitball outlawed.

Babe Ruth took full advantage of this change. Ruth already held the single season home run record of twenty-nine in 1919, and he hit sixty in a 154-game season in 1927. In 1935, Ruth ended his career with 714 home runs—an amazing total as the first six years of Ruth's career were spent as a pitcher and prior to the introduction of the livelier ball.

Ruth's single season home run record stood for thirty-three years, even though individuals challenged it from time to time. The person who came closest during that period was Hank Greenberg of Detroit, who hit fifty-eight in 1938. The 1961 Yankees featured two players on pace to break the record—superstar Mickey Mantle (the fan favorite to break Ruth's mark) and Roger Maris. Mantle finished with fifty-four, but Roger Maris broke Ruth's storied record by hitting sixty-one home runs. Maris, however, did not hit number sixty-one until the 159th game of the season (in 1961 the American League had expanded its schedule to 162 games). Baseball commissioner Ford Frick ruled that an asterisk would be put next to Maris's record, as he did not break Ruth's mark in the same number of games.

Significance

Maris's mark lasted into the 1990s. In 1994, a player's strike shut down baseball, causing fans to view the players as greedy. While there were substantive issues at stake, they did not prevent many fans from souring on baseball. Cal Ripken's pursuit of Lou Gehrig's consecutive-game streak revived some interest in 1995. The 1998 home run race between St. Louis Cardinal Mark McGwire and Chicago Cub Sammy Sosa drew even more fans back to the game.

As the 1998 season opened, interest in baseball still lagged. The baseball authorities decided that home runs would bring back fans, and so a livelier ball was introduced. The livelier ball coincided with expansion (and the related diluted pitching quality) and the opening of newer ballparks with hitter-friendly dimensions. In 1998, both Sammy Sosa and Mark McGwire chased Maris's home run record. McGwire broke both Ruth's and Maris's record before the 154th game of the season, eventually reaching seventy home runs for the year; Sosa hit sixty-six. Sosa and McGwire developed a very friendly rivalry, and their camaraderie and honor, along with the home run chase, revived interest in baseball. McGwire's record did not stand long, though, as Barry Bonds hit seventy-three home runs in 2001.

Primary Source

"Bay Area Bambino"

SYNOPSIS: In an interview conducted by William Ladson, Mark McGwire speaks about his personal success in the 1996 season, despite the fact that he had missed many games during his career. Ladson also notes the lack of success by the Oakland A's,

Mark McGwire of the Oakland Athletics hits a two-run home run while playing the Detroit Tigers at Tiger Stadium, June 18, 1996. AP/WIDE WORLD PHOTOS. REPRODUCED BY PERMISSION.

for whom McGwire played at the time. McGwire talks about the pressure on him, how he prepares for the game, and his mental attitude. He also discusses mentoring Jason Giambi—a player who signed with the New York Yankees in 2001—his teammates, his family, and suddenly becoming a leader of the team.

Due primarily to back and foot injuries, Oakland A's first baseman Mark McGwire has missed 274 games over the past four years. But he's made up for lost time. Last season, the 6-5, 250-pounder slugged a career-high 52 home runs in only 130 games at a major-league-record rate of one round-tripper every 8.13 at bats.

Despite McGwire's success, the A's have been mediocre at best. Since winning their last division title in 1992, the team is 264-318, a far cry from when McGwire and fellow Bash Brother Jose Canseco led the A's to three consecutive pennants and a World Series title from 1988 to 1990. When former teammate Terry Steinbach signed a free-agent contract with the Minnesota Twins this winter, McGwire was left as the only player remaining from those glory years, a distinction that seemed impossible back in 1991 when he hit a career-low .201.

"To tell you the truth, I thought I would be the first to go," says the 33-year-old McGwire. "Because of my poor season in '91, they wanted to get rid of me, but there were no takers."

Everyone, including *Sport,* wants a piece of McGwire now.

You've always hit the long ball, but not since your rookie year have you hit for such a high average. What are you doing differently at the plate?

I'm not doing anything differently with my body. It's a mental thing. I believe the game is 99 percent mental. Everybody has the physical abilities to get to the big leagues. It's the ones who have the mental toughness who stay for a longer period. I always knew I could hit for average. I did it in college and in the minor leagues. When you get to the big leagues, it's such a different level. It's a learning process.

As a rookie, you hit .289, but your average went down after that. What happened?

Pitchers made adjustments to me, but I wasn't making adjustments to them. I didn't realize this game was mental until my terrible season in '91. It taught me to wake up and smell the coffee. Sometimes people get complacent. Sometimes you get to a certain level and you think you don't have to work as hard. I'm not saying I didn't work: I'm saying I could have worked harder. I had a lot of personal problems on top of that. But when you get distracted from what you love to do, failure usually follows.

If you hadn't missed all those games the last few seasons, you might have 400 career homers by now and be a candidate for the Hall of Fame. Do you ever think about that?

(Laughing) I've never been a person to think, "what if." I don't think you succeed in life or sports if you sit back and say, "What if I did this?" You can't go back and get those days. As far as the Hall

of Fame goes, who plays this game to get into Cooperstown? You play this game because you enjoy it. You play this game because you're good at it. The Hall of Fame is icing on the cake after a great career. That never enters my mind. You have to deal with what's dealt to you. I was dealt a few years of injuries. I'm not the only player who's been through that. The only thing I can do is play 10 or 15 more years and they won't be talking about it.

How do you maintain such a positive attitude when it comes to talking about your injuries?

It's common sense. My father had polio at age 7. He never had a chance to play sports when he was a kid. When I look at my father, it makes my injuries so minuscule. So I never say, "what if."

In 1987, another year in which you were shooting for 50 home runs, there was friction between you and the media. Last year, the relationship was great. What was the difference between those two years?

When you're a rookie and you do what I did, I don't think anybody is prepared for the attention. I wasn't even supposed to make the club, let alone hit 49 home runs. There was a time last season when I was stressing out about the press. But in July or August, I talked to [former Baltimore Oriole] Bobby Bonilla in the outfield before a game and I asked, "How did Cal Ripken Jr. deal with all the attention when he was about to break the consecutive-games streak?" Bonilla said: "You know what, Cal enjoyed it. He accepted it. "I drove home that night after the game and I started thinking: "You know what? It makes a lot of sense." Why fight the press or why fight what's happening to you? It doesn't happen to everybody in the game of baseball. So accept it, enjoy it and have fun with it. I never stressed out about it again.

After injuring your right foot in the spring of '96, you thought about retirement but were talked out of it. How frustrating was that injury for you?

It was frustrating having a foot problem for the third year in a row. I thought about retirement because I didn't want to go through rehab again. I've been through enough peaks and valleys in my career and I didn't want to face it again. I don't like when today's athletes make rash decisions and they come back and say, "I really didn't mean that." So I'm one to sit back and soak things in and play things off friends and family. Basically they told me it would be the worst mistake of my life. I sat back and thought about it and said, "You're right." Then I said, "Let's go to rehab."

Mark McGwire smiles as he rounds the bases, St. Louis, Missouri, September 27, 1998. He has just hit the 70th and final home run of his 1998 season, breaking Roger Maris's previous record of 61. AP/WIDE WORLD PHOTOS. REPRODUCED BY PERMISSION.

Tony La Russa has said you became a better player after you went through rehab. Do you buy that?

Yes, because I became a better mental player. It was the first time in my life I got to sit back and watch the game of baseball. What better manager to watch than Tony? I watched the pitchers, watched the visiting batters. I learned a lot. In '92, I was just starting to use my mind. In '93 and '94, I was getting better until I got injured. In '95, I was injured, but I had a really good year.

Let's talk about the A's. How do you feel about losing Terry Steinbach and Mike Bordick to free agency?

Big losses. Real big losses. It's part of the game that players have no control over. If you want to have a championship team, you have to be strong at catcher and shortstop. It's going to be tough to replace those two.

How does it feel to have Jose Canseco as a teammate again?

I think he's gonna be great. People were comparing us to Mantle-Maris when we were together the first six years. Now we can continue where we left off.

The media still calls you two the Bash Brothers, but you don't like that nickname. Why?

I don't like living in the past. As far as I'm concerned, the Bash Brothers are over with. We had a great run, but you don't succeed as a person or as an athlete if you look to the past all the time.

You have become the leader of the team. Where did that quality come from?

I don't know. I'm basically a shy person. It's funny, I can play in front of thousands and thousands of people, but to stand up in front of a group of people and talk, I clam up. But I'm loud and boisterous in the clubhouse. I like to get on players. I played with some guys in my younger years that used to be like that. Dave Parker, Carney Lansford, Dave Stewart, Don Baylor, Reggie Jackson. I used to watch them when I was a young kid. Suddenly, I'm playing with them and learning from them. It just shows me how I've come around as a human being and a player. I use bits and pieces from all those guys and show the younger kids. Hopefully, the kids will look at me like I looked at those veterans.

You have taken teammate Jason Giambi under your wing. How much have you helped him?

I've taken him under my wing because I see a lot of myself in him. He's a great, young, raw talent, but he's yet to adapt to the mental part of the game. I've tried to talk to him about using his mind and pacing himself. The second half of the year was tough on him due to injuries and being tired. I think taking him under my wing, if you want to call it that, will help him out in the long run, and hopefully he won't have to go through the failures that I went through.

Speaking of failures, the A's haven't won anything since 1992. Did the team take the glory years for granted?

In '88 and '89, we didn't take it for granted. During the 1990 season, people did take it for granted. It bothered me that nobody ran on the field and jumped on top of each other after we won the AL West. It bothered me that guys trotted out there, shook each other's hand and said, "All right, here we go again, we're in another postseason." In turn, we lost the World Series again. We got smoked. Our team should have had three World Series rings in a row. But if you don't prepare yourself . . . I mean, what I know now I wish I knew back then. There's no way I would let that happen. I didn't watch the '96 World Series, but I could only imagine what those Yankee players were going through. First of all, what excitement the city puts behind their team. What excitement to know that you came back and swept the Braves. I can honestly say I didn't have that feeling.

You don't think the Oakland fans were behind the A's when they won the 1989 World Series?

The city was behind us. It was just on a different level. I look at the Yankee series and say, "I want to feel that." When we won the World Series, we had the earthquake. We had to respect the people who died. We had to respect what happened to northern California. We didn't get to celebrate the way the Yankees got to celebrate. No champagne. No parade. We had a rally. There'll always be an asterisk next to our '89 championship. If any ballplayer saw Game 6 of the '96 World Series, it would drive them to get to the postseason. I would love to have that feeling, knowing what I know now.

Knowing what you now know, what should the A's have done differently in the '88 and '90 World Series?

In '88, it wasn't like we weren't prepared. Let's face it, the home run by Kirk Gibson pretty much knocked the wind out of us. And I don't necessarily think it was the home run by Kirk Gibson that beat us. It was walking Mike Davis to get to Gibson. There was no room to walk Mike Davis. If Mike Davis hits a home run, he hits a home run. If you ask Dennis Eckersley, he'd probably say the walk to Davis bothered him more than the home run.

The A's and San Francisco Giants are mediocre teams. What is the state of Bay Area baseball?

I would like to say good, but to tell you the truth, it's tough. Because there's so much to do in the Bay Area and no thanks to the baseball strike, I don't think people are interested in the Giants and A's right now. The attendance reflects that. When they build that stadium in San Francisco for the year 2000, how are they going to attract those fans? We need a commissioner and we have to do a serious p.r. job to get fans back on our side—owners and players. Baseball is the national pastime, but right now people don't really care about baseball.

You're currently seeing a psychiatrist. What brought this on?

It was because of the season I had in '91. That was the turning point in my life as a person and a professional ballplayer. [Seeking help] made me the person I am today. It made me find out what I'm all about. I'm a much happier person than I was six years ago. People say: "Happier. You're a pro ball player." There are pro ballplayers out there who are not happy inside. There are a lot of people in general who can't face the music and look at them-selves in the mirror and say, "I like myself." I did, and that was the turning point. My psychiatrist taught me a lot of things about life and myself. I really believe that anyone who confronts his problems succeeds, and the ones who keep failing, you'll never hear from again.

Family Man

Every story that's written about you, your son Matt is mentioned. What does he mean to you?

Everything I do in the game is for him. We have such a great relationship. I could be away from him for a month or so and come back and it's like we just missed yesterday. The reason for the great relationship is because I have a great ex-wife. Not many people can say that. She has a great husband. Today, when people get divorced, they try to pull this and pull that. What does divorce really do? It affects the children. I think society, or children, are so screwed up today because of what's happening in the household among divorced parents. When I talk about this, people go, "You got to be kidding." I always see my son at her house. It's such a nice relationship, and the one who benefits from it is Matthew. He is so well-rounded. What he sees is that his mother is really happy with Tom. He also sees his father really happy with Matthew. He is raised in two happy households instead of one deteriorating household that is going to affect the kid throughout his life.

How do you and your ex-wife manage to have this great relationship?

It was just over time. Granted, the divorce wasn't easy. There were some hard times. I'm the first to admit that. I'm a totally different person than when I was married to Kathy. I know she sees that.

How are you different?

I'm different in every way. I know what I like, I know what I dislike. I know myself. When I was married to Kathy, I didn't know myself. Things have worked out. She met Tom. I couldn't be happier for her. Their baby daughter just turned a year old. Tom is a terrific stepfather. I couldn't ask for anything better.

Further Resources

BOOKS

McNeil, William. *Ruth, Maris, McGwire and Sosa: Baseball's Single Season Home Run Champions.* Jefferson, N.C.: McFarland, 1999.

Noden, Merrell. *Home Run Heroes: Mark McGwire, Sammy Sosa, and a Season for the Ages.* New York: Simon & Schuster, 1998.

Paisner, Daniel. *The Ball: Mark McGwire's 70th Home Run Ball and the Marketing of the American Dream.* New York: Viking, 1999.

Smelser, Marshall. *The Life that Ruth Built: a Biography.* Lincoln: University of Nebraska Press, 1993.

Stewart, Mark, and Mike Kennedy. *Home Run Heroes: Mark McGwire & Sammy Sosa.* Brookfield, Conn.: Millbrook Press, 1999.

Thornley, Stew. *Mark McGwire: Star Home Run Hitter.* Springfield, N.J.: Enslow Publishers, 1999.

WEBSITES
Gumby's Mark McGwire Online. Available online at http://www.mcgwire.com (accessed April 15, 2003).

The Mark McGwire Foundation for Children. Available online at http://rc.yahoo.com/promotions/mcgwire; website home page: http://rc.yahoo.com (accessed April 15, 2003).

AUDIO AND VISUAL MEDIA
MLB '98: the Record Breakers. Directed by Dave Check. New York: PolyGram Video, 1998, VHS.

Favre: For the Record
Autobiography

By: Brett Favre, with Chris Havel

Date: 1997

Source: Favre, Brett, with Chris Havel. *Favre: For the Record.* New York: Doubleday, 1997, 162–169.

About the Author: Brett Favre (1969–) grew up in the small town of Kiln, Mississippi, and attended the University of Southern Mississippi. Favre has won three NFL Most Valuable Player awards (1995, 1996, and 1997)—so far a feat matched by only one other player—and is the only player ever to throw thirty touchdown passes in four consecutive seasons. He also holds the record for most consecutive starts by an NFL quarterback. ■

Introduction

The National Football League (NFL) started in 1922 and had eighteen teams by 1924. Many of those teams no longer exist, including the Canton Bulldogs, the Oorang Indians, and the Pottsville Marrons. Early professional players had day jobs or jobs in the off-season. Professional football had to compete for coverage with college and high school football in many areas, and it had nowhere near the popularity of professional baseball, suffering because of the game's perceived roughness. In the early days, players performed on both offense and defense, often playing the entire game. The earliest teams were limited to sixteen players.

The Green Pay Packers enjoyed early success in the NFL, winning titles in 1929, 1930, and 1931. In the 1950s, teams expanded their rosters and players began to specialize on offense or defense. By the 1950s, most professional football players were being paid enough to work full-time as players, at least during the season. In the 1960s, the NFL merged with the rival American Football League (AFL), and league champions met in the newly created Super Bowl. It was in the 1960s when football replaced baseball, in the estimation of many, as America's most popular sport. The Packers, the NFL's third-oldest football franchise, won the first two Super Bowls, behind the leadership of quarterback Bart Starr. After their second Super Bowl win in 1968, however, the Packers struggled, failing to win their division from 1972 to 1995.

In 1992, Green Bay hired Mike Holmgren as its new head coach. Holmgren acquired Brett Favre as his quarterback in a trade with the Atlanta Falcons, and Favre led the Packers to the playoffs in 1993. In 1994 and 1995, the Packers advanced in the playoffs before losing both years in Dallas. Finally, in the 1996 season, the Packers made it to the Super Bowl, defeating the New England Patriots 35-21.

Significance

As of 2003, Green Bay has not won the Super Bowl since 1996. In 1997, the favored Packers lost Super Bowl XXXII to Denver. In 1998, they lost to San Francisco early in the playoffs. From 1998 through 2002, the Packers have had four winning seasons, but have not returned to the Super Bowl.

The one Packer constant has been Brett Favre. Favre has had a variety of teammates over the years. He's also had three head coaches: Mike Holmgren, Ray Rhodes, and Mike Sherman. The changes haven't hurt Favre, who has proved amazingly consistent and durable. He has started every game since 1992, now having started a record 173 consecutive regular season games and counting. Favre has thrown for over 42,000 yards and 314 touchdowns. He is third in touchdown passes in NFL history. He has led the NFL in passing yards once and in touchdowns three times. He also holds a several other Green Bay and NFL records.

Favre has also had a great deal of personal success. After suffering an addiction to prescription drugs, he has successfully stayed off painkillers and avoided a relapse. Given the public failures of some other sports figures to conquer chemical dependencies, his success is admirable.

Primary Source

Favre: For the Record [excerpt]

> **SYNOPSIS:** In this excerpt from his autobiography, Brett Favre starts off with a discussion of the early games of the 1996 season. He describes the ups and downs of the season, and compliments his teammates on their play. Favre also discusses how

he deals with the pain associated with football, noting that he now only uses Motrin and heavily emphasizing the nondrug methods he uses to deal with pain. He explains how a big win in St. Louis, following two mid-season losses, turned the Packers' season around.

We really got off to a fast start.

We outscored our first three opponents by 110-16. I didn't see that coming, but I wasn't surprised by it, either. Philadelphia came into Green Bay for a *Monday Night Football* game the week after the Tampa game. I knew Philly had a good team and I figured it would be a close game but we dominated them. Then we hammered San Diego the next week and I knew we were pretty good.

There were times in the Philly game when I'd just watch and go, "Damn, that's pretty impressive." I'm standing there on the sidelines watching our defense kick their ass, take the ball away from them, force turnovers. They couldn't piss a drop on offense. I was glad I was playing for the Packers. Then we'd go on offense and it was damn near picture-perfect.

That first *Monday Night* game was pretty exciting. It was real festive. Our fans were fired up and we felt like we earned the right to play our first *Monday Night* game at home in ten years. We won 39-13.

Then we went out the next Sunday and beat San Diego 42-10. Our defense made it easy for me. They really got after the Chargers' quarterback, Stan Humphries. I felt sorry for Stan. I wouldn't want to play against our defense. I had a good game and we put a lot of points on the board, which is what counts.

We were feeling pretty good about ourselves, but then we had to go to Minnesota, where Mike hasn't won since he arrived in Green Bay. Well, here's what happened at Minnesota: the same old shit. Something freaky always happens there. Their defense really pounded me. They played like it was their Super Bowl. But after George Koonce, one of our linebackers, intercepted a pass and ran it in for a touchdown, I thought the game was ours. Then the Vikings came back and they won it 30-21. We were still in the game despite only eight first downs, but they forced some turnovers, which is what they do best.

I was disgusted after the game.

Shit, I couldn't believe it. But then I started thinking well, we'll get them. It's the last game of the season and it's a long wait, but that's okay. I didn't think we'd win all sixteen games and that's what Mike said after the game. He said no one expected

us to be 16-0. Losses are going to happen. We may lose again.

I got sacked something like seven times. I was pretty sore. Every time I play them, I'm pretty sore. I was thankful to get home in one piece. I dealt with the pain by taking some Motrin. I was tired and I went to bed right away. Deanna and Brittany were in there, so I climbed right in with them. Usually I watch *SportsCenter,* but not that night. I didn't even care how the other teams did.

I got up the next day, worked out, and hopped in the whirlpool. That's how I dealt with the pain all season.

The next week, we kicked the shit out of the Seattle Seahawks. Then we beat the Bears and we were back on a roll, scoring a lot of points. After the Bears game we had the San Francisco 49ers coming to our place on Monday night. It was one helluva football game. We ended up winning 23-20 in overtime but we paid a price. We lost our best receiver, Robert Brooks, for the season.

Coming into the game, we knew San Francisco had the best defense we'd faced so far. Offensively, though, we didn't think they could move the ball that well against our defense.

We hit some big strikes early, but we couldn't capitalize on them. I hit Don Beebe down the sideline but he accidentally stepped out of bounds. Then I hit Keith Jackson on a big one and if he scored, it could've been a blowout, but he got tripped up and it turned around and worked against us. We didn't get seven. We had to settle for three and they came back to take the lead.

But we were still doing some things well.

I could see some things that were open if I got a little time to throw. I knew I couldn't drop back five or seven steps and pick the 49ers apart; they were too good for that. But I was confident Don could do some things. He ended up catching eleven passes for 220 yards.

In the third quarter, he scored on a long play that was controversial. Their safety, Merton Hanks, let him go by about 10 yards and I just threw it. Don dove for the ball and caught it and it looked like Hanks touched him while he was down, but Don got up and ran it in for a touchdown.

Good teams get breaks like that. How many times have we gone to Dallas and they get the breaks? And you go, "Oh, shit." Referees know a good team and if you start making plays, they start expecting them. More than likely if a shitty team

Brett Favre drops back to pass during Super Bowl XXXI, played January 26, 1997, at the Superdome in New Orleans. Favre threw for 246 yards and two touchdowns in leading the Packers to a 35-21 victory. © **WALLY MCNAMEE/CORBIS. REPRODUCED BY PERMISSION.**

makes a play, he's down. If a great team makes it, it's a touchdown.

We needed a field goal in the two-minute drill to get the game into overtime and I thought what the hell, this is what I like. I love the two-minute drill because I've got nothing to lose. It's like the last shot in a basketball game. You miss it, everybody goes, "Oh, damn." If you make it, everybody goes crazy.

I thrive on that.

It's like when you're young and running around out in the yard playing ball. I'm doing it at the line. Squareout. Hook-and-go. We practice the two-minute drill every week. It's the most fun we have at practice. That drive propelled us into overtime and Chris Jacke kicked a long field goal to win it.

We were pretty beat up after that game.

We had a bye week and we needed it. Then we won a couple more games before those back-to-back losses at Kansas City and Dallas. Those losses didn't surprise me. We had everybody hurt and morale was down. Offensively we had been doing so well and now we didn't know if we could do it. Not to men-

tion we were playing two great teams at their stadiums. It was bad scheduling.

It would've been tough if we had everybody healthy. We could've split, maybe, but I don't know who we would've beat.

Kansas City was playing well at that point and they had a great game on offense—probably better than they had all year. We couldn't beat their bump-and-run defense and they rushed the passer pretty well. I was down after that game, but not really upset. I said when we get our backs against the wall, we'll be fine.

Then we went to Dallas, and once again we couldn't piss a drop.

Some of our guys got upset when Barry Switzer, the Cowboys' coach, had them kick that last field goal without much time to play. They were ahead 18-6 and the game was over, but Switzer wanted to give Chris Boniol a shot at tying the NFL record. He made it and we lost.

The last play of the game I threw a pass and rolled out toward Dallas's sideline. The horn blew and I went over and congratulated Switzer and told him he did a great job. Reggie White was upset, but Switzer wasn't rubbing it in.

It was a 21-6 game. They didn't score a touchdown; we scored one. We kicked their ass; they kicked our ass. There wasn't much more to it. Their defense played well; so did ours. We stunk it up on offense and they didn't do much, either. So give the kid the field goal record. How often does a kid get to do that?

I mean, if you're going to be pissed, be pissed at the last six or seven times the Cowboys have beaten us, not at that game. Now, Reggie can do his thing and I can do mine, so there's no beef between us. He was on defense and he felt like they were rubbing it in, so that was his business. I didn't feel the same way.

No big deal.

Well, after that we got healthy again and we went on an eight-game winning streak. Pretty impressive.

We were 8-3 going into the St. Louis game down there, but we were still down because of the Dallas loss. That Doug Evans interception and return for a touchdown to start the second half was huge. It turned us around. It was like the fumble recovery and touchdown Craig Newsome made for us against the 49ers in the play-off game the year before.

We were still struggling on offense and Mike was dejected. We hadn't been doing anything on offense for a couple of weeks but it wasn't his fault. He just calls them. But he told Sherman Lewis to call the plays. They're pretty similar in the way they call them, but sometimes Sherm says screw it and he wings it a bit more. Mike tends to be a bit more conservative.

Anyway, Sherm scripted the first fifteen plays of the second half. It would be hard for anyone to tell who was calling them. About the only difference is Sherm likes to roll out and use play action a bit more. That's about it.

We came back to beat the Rams 24-9.

We're a good first-drive team because the coaches do such a good job of scripting plays. But I still love to call audibles because it's all me. Every once in a while I'll tell Mike a play is going to work. And when it works, your chest just swells up and you can tell everybody, "I told you so." And when it doesn't work, Mike will tell me he's never going to listen to me again. But that only happens about four or five times a year.

Sometimes I think about playing back when the quarterback still called his own plays. That would've been pretty cool. I don't know how good I'd be at it, but it would be fun. That's why I can't wait to be a coach someday and call the plays. It would be razzle-dazzle and all that. And I'd have to deal with some knucklehead quarterback, although I've already dealt with one before.

Me.

And when I'm a coach, I'm going to say to that young quarterback, "Look, I know. I've tried it myself. Now shut up and listen."

It would be tough to call the plays. It's way too technical out there. There are too many defenses to allow that. The fire zones and the man-to-man on one side and zone on the other, this guy dropping off—there's just too much to do.

Every once in a while, I'll call a play and the guys will say, "Oh, shit. That won't work." Well, what the hell do they know? I've got offensive linemen telling me a play won't work and I'm like, just block the play. Everyone's an expert.

Sometimes they'll come back into the huddle after a play and ask why I audibled on a certain play. I'll say I saw something and they'll say, obviously it wasn't the same thing I saw. Linemen really hate it when there's a pass called and they think we should run. They love to run block and hate to pass block.

They get over it.

That stretch of the last five regular-season games included a showdown with the Denver Broncos. Well, it didn't turn out to be such a big deal because John Elway didn't play. I was dejected at first, but then I decided we'd just go out and kick some butt anyway. And we really made a statement that day—with or without Elway. We beat them 41-6. If they would've had Elway, it would've been a different story, like 41-28. I'll give them four touchdowns and it still wouldn't have been enough.

I remember the play when Michael Dean Perry broke free and I stiff-armed him. Good players make good plays. Good teams make other teams look bad. We made Denver look bad and I really thought the Broncos would make it to the Super Bowl. I threw four touchdown passes that day.

It gave me thirty-four and LeRoy Butler came over in practice and said I needed to do something after I throw a touchdown pass because I do it so often.

"Let's do six-guns," he said.

I said what the hell is six-guns?

"You come over to me on the sidelines, we'll pull out six guns and make believe we're shooting and then we'll stick 'em back in," LeRoy said.

Fine. We did it.

Then he said, "Let's add something to it. Let's tap each other on the left shoulder twice after we put the guns away." So we did that. Then he wanted me to add some more stuff right before the Super Bowl, but he thought it over and said, "We probably shouldn't. You don't have enough rhythm."

I said, "You're right. We're pushing the limit as it is."

LeRoy's always making that shit up. He's got entirely too much time on his hands. He's cool to be around, though. He makes it fun out there. What the hell, I'm out there to have fun, too.

Further Resources

BOOKS

Cameron, Steve. *Brett Favre: Huck Finn Grows Up.* Indianapolis: Masters, 1996.

Ganz, Howard L., and Jeffrey L. Kessler. *Understanding Business & Legal Aspects of the Sports Industry, 2001.* New York: Practicing Law Institute, 2001.

Mooney, Martin J. *Brett Favre.* Philadelphia: Chelsea House, 1997.

Mottram, D.R. *Drugs in Sport.* London: Spon, 1996.

Piparo, C.A., and Cheryl Nathan. *Brett Favre: Quarterback Dreams.* Ridgewood, N.J.: Infinity Plus One, 1998.

Schaap, Dick. *Green Bay Replay: The Packers' Return to Glory.* New York: Avon, 1997.

Wolf, Ron Michael, and Paul Attner. *The Packer Way: Nine Stepping Stones to Building a Winning Organization.* New York: St. Martin's, 1998.

WEBSITES

"Brett Favre." *Packers.com.* Available online at http://www .packers.com/team/players/favre_brett; website home page: http://www.packers.com (accessed April 15, 2003).

AUDIO AND VISUAL MEDIA

Athletes and Addiction: It's Not a Game. Directed by Jim McKay. MTI Film & Video, 1990, VHS.

Brett Favre: The Field General. Directed by Roy Firestone. TMW Media Group, 1996, VHS.

"From Russia With Love"

Diary

By: Venus Williams

Date: 1997

Source: Williams, Venus. "From Russia With Love." Diary entries from 1997 visit to Russia. Available online at http:// www.venustennis.com/thevenusdiaries.html; website home page: http://www.venustennis.com (accessed April 15, 2003).

About the Author: Venus Williams (1980–) entered a tennis academy at age eleven, and broke into professional tennis at fourteen. She signed a $40-million-dollar endorsement deal with Reebok in 2001, becoming the highest-paid female product endorser. She won both Wimbledon and the U.S Open in 2000 and 2001, and became the world's top-ranked female tennis player in 2002. ∎

Introduction

When it originated, tennis was a game played by the rich. It was often played as "lawn tennis" in the 1890s. In lawn tennis, players stretched nets across open lawns and hit the ball to one another. Tennis was also a popular sport at country clubs, which hindered its appeal to the poor, the middle class, and to minorities.

The few African Americans who did gain footholds in tennis often did quite well. Althea Gibson was one of the first African Americans to excel at the sport. She won both Wimbledon and the U.S. Open in 1957 and 1958. She also won the doubles championship at Wimbledon three straight years, as well as doubles championships at the Australian and French Opens. After this, Gibson turned professional. There were, however, few endorsement deals and her tennis career soon faltered. She passed out of the limelight by the end of the 1960s. Gibson, however, became a hero both to sports fans and to civil rights activists. She proved that African Americans could achieve success in not only team sports but individual sports, if given the chance.

After Althea Gibson, few African Americans excelled in tennis. The sport remained the province of those with memberships at country clubs and those receiving private lessons. Though there were other excellent African American tennis players, including Arthur Ashe, few achieved superstar status. Then, in the late 1990s, Venus and Serena Williams took the tennis world by storm.

Significance

Born in Los Angeles in 1980, Venus Williams made her professional women's tennis debut in 1994—and was quickly recognized as a prodigy. Similarly, her sister Serena, born in Michigan in 1981, also displayed an early aptitude for the game, making her professional debut in 1995. The youngest of five daughters, the sisters grew up playing tennis at a Los Angeles park that also served as a gang hangout. Their extraordinary talent, however, caused the family to move to Florida where the girls could receive better training. There they were home-schooled and, outside of that, they trained with tennis coach Rick Macci. Venus turned professional in 1994 at age fourteen, and Serena in 1995, also at fourteen. Fans wondered if the sisters would end up like former tennis prodigy Jennifer Capriati, who crumbled under public scrutiny and parental pressure, ultimately facing drug charges and public humiliation.

By 1997, the Williams sisters were recognized as tennis stars. Their outspoken father, Richard, was determined to prevent his daughters from experiencing the same parental and public pressures as other teen prodigies. He has been publicly scrutinized for his unorthodox managerial style, but his methods seem to have worked. After Venus's trip to Russia in 1997, she continued to excel. She became the first African American since Althea Gibson to win Wimbledon. Together, Venus and Serena won the Wimbledon doubles championship. They were the first pair of siblings in one hundred years to play each other at Wimbledon, and the first sisters to meet in the U.S. Open. In 1999, they became the first African American doubles team to win at the U.S. Open. The sisters have won numerous awards and signed many celebrity endorsements, including Venus's $40 million Reebok contract—believed to be the biggest ever awarded to a female athlete.

Even with the Williams' sisters success in tennis, their father encourages them to excel in all areas. Richard Williams was quoted in the November 21, 1998, issue of *Jet* as saying, "My girls are very great players, and they'll win lots of tournaments, but I'll tell you what I tell them: Education is much more important. . . . You know what I wish? I wish they'd quit tennis and move on to other things. Tennis is a good way to make a million dollars, but they've done that already, and then some. They're so brilliant, they'll be great in anything they do." ("Richard Williams, Father of Venus and Serena, Says He Wishes His Girls Would Quit Tennis")

Venus Williams plays at Wimbledon, July 1, 1998. © BARRY GOMER/CORBIS SYGMA. REPRODUCED BY PERMISSION.

Primary Source

"From Russia With Love"

SYNOPSIS: Venus begins her diaries by complaining about Russia, but she eventually adopts a more positive tone. Her second diary entry focuses on her play and her experiences at a VIP dinner. The third entry discusses her meeting with Moscow's mayor, and in the fourth she discusses her interaction with her fans and her loss to Jana Novotna. She closes her diaries with a number of random thoughts and lists of her favorite things. [Editor's note: spelling and usage errors present in the original.]

Entry 1—10/27/97

Moscow is definitely not America, but it is not that bad. In comparison to other well developed countries, I would say that Russia is halfway there.

At first I did not like Moscow. It was too cold, the cars were too old (70% of the cars here are from the 60's and 70's) etc. I was being pessimistic and negative. I think it was because I have been in Europe for like twenty-seven days and I have never been away from the States this long.

Of course like every other major city in Europe, there is a McDonalds. I had to go. I wanted to see if they had any weird Russian food, like caviar and egg burger. When we got there it was just the opposite. Everything's the same, except the menu is in the Russian Cyrillic alphabet. Fortunately some people there spoke English. My back up plan was to order a Big Mac if no one spoke English. Who doesn't know what a Big Mac is? What else . . . OK. I do plan to go see the Russian Crown Jewels and maybe buy myself some. I have a real problem with

Serena Williams at the SuperPower Challenge Cup in Hong Kong, January 7, 1999. © AFP/CORBIS. REPRODUCED BY PERMISSION.

jewelry. I am liable to get out of control in a jewelry store. Other than that I've just been seeing the walls of my hotel room and hitting the courts everyday. The touranent really has a good player's eatery. There is this Swiss chef that runs the whole thing. He's a pretty nice guy. A good cook too.

At the tournament they have all these booths in this stadium. (This is the Olympic stadium from the Olympics in Moscow in 1980) Reebok has this booth with my picture on it. I was so happy about it because it is a good picture for once. Most every other picture I have circulating out there are double feature creature pictures!

Other than that everything is cool. One more thing, when Russians talk to you, or at least to me, they get really close to you. With some people you feel as if you are about to die because they have bad breath.

I hope I have not bored anyone, if I have than I am sorry. I'll write some more things tomorrow and I'll be more prepared.

Entry 2—10-28-97

Hey it's me. I am writing this at 9:20 pm on Tuesday, October 28, 1997. As usual I have waited to the last minute to do this, as I do with everything else, especially if its pressing. I always say I'll put off till tomorrow what I can do today.

Anyway, I just finished playing Elena Likhovtseva (I can't say her last name). I won 7-6 (3), 6-2. I lost serve twice. I HATE losing serve. It just makes me sick! I play Silvia Farina next. I have never played her before, but that's ok. I feel good. I went to this V.I.P. dinner last night. They had this show going on, with singing and dancing. The singer guy had a voice like Louis Armstrong. He was pretty cool. Anyway, Arantxa [Sanchez Vicario] was sitting at the table next to me, along with her mother and Louise Pleming, this funny Australian player. Well anyway, they were saying, "Venus, you want to sing, Venus you are going to sing, aren't you?" After about five minutes they were VERY SERIOUS. The tournament director was setting it up and before I knew it they were about to announce to the people dining that I was going to sing! I was like no, oh my God, WAIT! I was saying no. Then I said, "OK, maybe with my sister." They took that maybe as a yes and before I knew it they had the spotlight on my table and the music was starting. Now I am not a bad singer, I can hold a tune, but just to sing on the spur of the moment a song I did not know the words to? That's trama. I was about to have a stroke, because I had already had a heart attack. They chose the song by Louis Armstrong "What a Wonderful World." I know the chorus, but not the verses. I could not stop laughing and my voice had a high pitch because I was afraid to sing into the microphone. My mother saved me though. She has a great voice. She sang a lot of the song for me. After that Arantxa decided that we (me, Serena, Louise and herself) all should get on stage and do the Macarena. I agreed, because I LOVE to get down. Anyway I had to learn to do the Macarena before I got on stage. It was pretty fun. After that, Louise (who I believe had too much to drink) got up and started dancing with Arantxa's mom. Then they started to pull guys from the audience to dance with. Arantxa tried to set me up to dance with some guy but that was TOO much for me. I ended up not even eating dinner after all the stuff that happened.

Tomorrow we (all the players) have to go meet the Mayor of Moscow and then I will practice, then maybe I will go shopping (jewelry!). Anyway, Bye!

Entry 3—10/29/97

OK. The last two days I wrote, in my opinion, long essays. Today I will try and keep it short and simple, but that hardly ever happens.

This morning all the players went to visit Moscow's City Hall and Moscow's Mayor. He was very hospitable and he was very proud of Moscow's major sporting event, The Kremlin Cup. He seemed very enthusiastic about Moscow, it's history, it's future and all it's potential. A plate celebrating Moscow's 850th Anniversary (celebrated this September) was given to each player in attendance. That's all I have to say about that. Oh yeah, also, in the City Hall building, which is about 100 years old (quite a grand building) there were two authentic bear rugs. One with the head, one without the head. Very Russian.

Right now I am just hanging around the tournament site. It is 3:30pm, my court is at 6:30. I have a long wait. I'll just watch some matches. Right now Anke Huber is playing Dominic Van Roost on Center Court. Helena Sukova is playing Marijana Lucic on Court 1.

It is snowing here in Russia. I have never been in snow before. I have lived in California and Florida, both sunny places. I am finished writing now. I cannot think of anything else interesting to write. If I do, I'll write later. I think I'll take a nap.

Entry 4—10/31/97

For everyone that thinks that Russia does not have toilet paper you are wrong. Whenever I told people at home that I was going to Russia they all replied: "Oh my God, I had a friend that went to Russia and they told me that there isn't any toilet paper over there." Imagine my dismay when everyone relayed such fallacies.

I am continuously running into people who experience temporary insanity in my presence. Once, this guy who worked at the grocery store wanted to call his wife and let her talk on the phone with me; "Or she will never believe that I met you." WOW, huh? The worst thing is when people ask me; "Why didn't you win? You should have won that match." I just say; "Yeah, I know." Let me give all you readers some advice: Never tell an athlete that they should have won. We know. And it hurts us 10 times more than it hurts you. You go on with your life and you say: "Nice match, man that was epic." But us athletes we never forget it. Let's change the subject.

When I get home I definitely have to get to Fort Pierce (Florida). You see I have adopted a new sport, surfing. It is so fun but unfortunately I am not so good. I must admit I pose! So, if by chance you have read in an article that I surf that statement is inaccurate. I don't surf, I wipeout.

I'm not looking to attain world class skills, but I would like to know that when I paddle in for a wave I will not waste it. + all the time there are only guys in the lineup and they are all thinking this girl can't surf and they are right. I aim to prove them wrong even if it takes me 10 years.

~~~I lost my match today to Jana Novotna 7-5, 6-4. I have something to say about the match:

You do it to yourself
You do
And that's why it really hurts
You do it to yourself just you
You and no one else
You do it to yourself

The match was all about me, what I was going to make happen whenever I lose a match I just give it away. I do it to myself.

All credit to Jana though because she obviously was in her right mind today. I, on the other hand, was not.

OK. I am saying goodbye. I'll talk to you all later. The week is ending. Boo-hoo (tears)

Hello to all Radio Head fans. You all might have recognized the verse above from the song just off their album *The Bends.* That was my favorite song back in August of 1995.

I also want to say hello today to everyone named Martin.

~~~ I think that Louise Woodword is innocent. Justice was not served.~~~

Venus

Entry 5—11/02/97

OK everyone, this is my last entry. It's been a good week. I have enjoyed writing and I have enjoyed Moscow.

OK. First things first. This morning we went to Red Square. We saw St. Basil's Cathederal. It was beautiful. I am not too big on the aesthetic part of life, raving over arts like the Mona Lisa and such.

In some of the rooms, the walls were painted with flowers and every flower was different. It was very nice.

Next we went in to the Mausoleum to see the late great Lenin. He was sitting in a glass case all petrified and preserved. He looked like a wax figure. He really doesn't look that real. What can I say, it was a real Russian treat. Wasn't that lady Evita from

Argentina preserved too? I don't know. I was watching this documentary on her a while ago. I think she was preserved and buried also.

This is my question for the day:

Q. Why do all golfers wear hats.

A. I don't know, probably for advertisement.

This is my advice for the day:

Remember someone is always looking, and someone is always listening.

This is my golden rule because I tend to do crazy things like wild dances or exaggerated impersonations when I think no one is looking, but someone really is, and I end up feeling kind of silly.

Here are some of my favorites:

My favorite Shakesperian play is *McBeth*. I have read *Hamlet* and *Romeo and Juliet,* but I really don't like those. I haven't read the other tragedies yet like *King Lear* or *Orthello* nor have I read any of the Histories.

My favorite books are the *Shawshank Redemption, The Hobbit* and the *Lord of the Rings* trilogy by J.R.R. Toilken.

My favorite movie is *Shawshank Redemption.*

OK everyone. Unfortunately I have to go. It is 6pm and I am supposed to be downstairs to hitch a ride (Green Day) to the theater. We are going to see *The Sleeping Beauty Ballet.*

Good morning everyone today is Sunday November 2 and it is 9am. in Russia. I am leaving today at 1:10pm. I am flying to Chicago to compete in another tournament. I have been over-seas for 33 days (almost 5 weeks).

I have seen a lot in Russia. The place is replete with history that is very interesting. The art here is wonderful also, and the people are very talented. It is great that they are finally being given the chance to live a more free life, with the fall of Communism.

OK, that's enough of that.

Last night we went to see the ballet, like I told you earlier. The first ten minutes were ok, but after that they kept doing the same dances over and over. OK, maybe it wasn't the same dances but it sure did seem like it. The ballet lasted almost three hours. I secretly wished that the sleeping beauty would fall back into her sleep. The theater was beautiful, I must say. I think it was built in 1856, but don't take my word for it. OK. This is my last story for the week. Before Serena left on Friday for Chicago she made me promise that if I saw Gustavo Kuerten

that I would ask him if he wanted to play mixed doubles with her at the Australian Open. I said; "Sure, OK." because I was convinced that I would not see him. As it turns out I did see him. Any other time I would not have seen so much as a trace of him. Anyway, he and his coach came sauntering into the lunch room yesterday, to my dismay. I really didn't want to say anything to him, I didn't know the guy, Serena does. Anyway, to cut this boring story short, I made myself go over to his table and ask him about mixed doubles. It wasn't that hard. He is a real nice guy, pleasant. His coach is funny too. They are both great.

OK everyone this is the end of the line. It's been real fun. Last of all I want to say hello today to everyone named Antony, and to all Hole fans (Courtney Love's Band). Goodbye everyone! Until next time!!

Venus

Further Resources

BOOKS

Aronson, Virginia, and Elaine K. Andrews. *Venus Williams.* Philadelphia: Chelsea House, 1999.

Asirvatham, Sandy. *Venus Williams.* Philadelphia: Chelsea House, 2002.

Gutman, Bill. *Venus & Serena: The Grand Slam Williams Sisters.* New York: Scholastic, 2001.

King, Billie Jean, and Kim Chapin. *Billie Jean.* New York: Harper & Row, 1974.

Navratilova, Martina, and Mary Carillo Bowden. *Tennis My Way.* New York: Scribner's, 1983.

Rineberg, Dave. *Venus & Serena: My Seven Years as Hitting Coach for the Williams Sisters.* Hollywood, Fla.: F. Fell, 2001.

Wertheim, L. Jon. *Venus Envy: A Sensational Season Inside the Women's Tennis Tour.* New York: HarperCollins, 2001.

WEBSITES

"Venus Williams." *ESPN.com.* Available online at http://espn.go.com/tennis/s/wta/profiles/vwilliams.html; website home page: http://espn.go.com (accessed April 15, 2003).

AUDIO AND VISUAL MEDIA

Raising Tennis Aces: The Williams Story. Directed by Terry Jervis. Jervis Entertainment Media, 2002, VHS.

Smashing Ladies: The Legends of Women's Tennis. Pop Video, 1988, VHS.

Tara Lipinski: Triumph on Ice

Autobiography

By: Tara Lipinski, as told to Emily Costello

Date: 1997

Source: Lipinski, Tara, as told to Emily Costello. *Tara Lipinski: Triumph on Ice.* New York: Bantam Books, 1997, 67–78

About the Author: Tara Lipinski (1982–) won the Olympic gold medal in figure skating at fifteen, becoming the youngest ever to do this. She started ice-skating at six; and at twelve, she won a medal at the U.S. Olympic Festival. In 1997, she became the youngest world champion ever, breaking Sonja Henie's longstanding record. She was named 1997 Sportswoman of the Year, the youngest ever to receive that honor. She won the gold medal at the 1998 Olympics, then turned pro. ∎

Introduction

In 1927, Sonja Henie became the youngest winner of the women's figure skating World Championships, at fourteen years and seven months old; a year later, Henie was the youngest women's figure skating Olympic gold medalist at just fifteen years, ten months. She would hold those records for seventy years. Like many sports, women's figure skating has experienced a recent rash of young stars. Unlike women's gymnastics, however, the sport is not dominated entirely by girls in their early teens. Historically, women's figure skating champs have ranged from their late teens to their late twenties.

In 1990, figure skating eliminated the compulsories (for example, figure eights), assisting younger stars, who might not perform as well in compulsory events, but who could dazzle crowds with high jumps. With their lower centers of gravity, smaller women gain more altitude on jumps. This favors younger women, as does the fact that jumping ability decreases as their bodies grow.

The new requirement that a competitor be at least fifteen years old for Olympic competition did not seem to have any immediate impact. The 1992 Winter Olympics featured American star, Kristi Yamaguchi, in women's figure skating. The twenty-year-old star, whose personal hero is Dorothy Hamill, drew fans to the sport and brought glory to her country. Yamaguchi was roughly the same age as Hamill was when she won Olympic gold. And attention at the 1994 Winter Olympics was focused on the Tonya Harding–Nancy Kerrigan debacle. When a man hired by Harding's former husband attacked Kerrigan after a rehearsal for the national women's figure skating championships, he badly injured her knee. Though Harding denied any participation in the attack, she subsequently was convicted for not preventing the attack,

Tara Lipinski skates her long routine during the ladies free skate at the 1998 Winter Olympics in Nagano, Japan, February 20, 1998. Lipinski won the gold medal for her performance. **AP/WIDE WORLD PHOTOS. REPRODUCED BY PERMISSION.**

and Harding was stripped of her tainted national championship title. Kerrigan went on to have reconstructive knee surgery, and she won a silver medal at the Olympics. Kerrigan gracelessly insulted Ukrainian winner, Oksana Baiul, during the medal ceremony. At the time, Nancy Kerrigan was twenty-four and Tonya Harding twenty-two. Clearly, young stars were the least of competitive figure skating's problems.

Significance

Indeed, it would be skating's youngest stars who redeemed the sport four years later. Seventeen-year-old Michelle Kwan, and Tara Lipinski, at age fifteen and eight months, faced off gracefully at the 1998 Winter Olympics. Lipinski won the U.S. Ladies Singles Championship, and then the world championship in 1997. Many considered Lipinski's win at the world championships a fluke, and expected Kwan to defeat her easily at the Olympics. When Lipinski won gold, Kwan—who had also given an excellent performance—reasonably could have been upset. Not so. Whereas Kerrigan whined about losing the gold medal four years earlier, Kwan told reporters that she had not lost the gold, but won the silver. She congratulated Lipinski for an excellent performance and relished further opportunities to compete against her.

At fourteen years, nine months old, Tara Lipinski became the youngest gold medalist at the women's figure skating world championships in 1997. Then, a year later, at fifteen years, eight months, she won the gold in figure skating at the 1998 Nagano Olympics, again, the youngest ever in her sport to do so. Part of her success hinged on her performance of the difficult triple loop–triple loop combination, an addition to her program she discusses in her autobiography. She was the first women's skater to introduce that jump in either the world championships or the Olympics. Such success, however, did not come without a heavy toll. She and her mother lived in a different state from Lipinski's father, whom they both missed terribly. And Lipinski's body suffered some strain from her career, later requiring hip surgery. Just after her Olympic win, she turned pro in order to reduce the emotional pressure on her family and the physical stress on her body. Professional tours require a much less demanding training and performance schedule, and Lipinski has been happy with her decision.

Primary Source

Tara Lipinski: Triumph on Ice [excerpt]

SYNOPSIS: In this excerpt, Lipinski discusses her coach's decision to add the triple loop–triple loop combination to her routine just two weeks before the U.S. Postal Service Challenge in Philadelphia. Then, she discusses her anxiety at nationals, her confusion when Michelle Kwan got low scores, and her focus on putting on a good performance rather than on winning. Finally, she discusses her winning scores.

Triple Loop–Triple Loop

In late 1996 I signed up to compete at the U.S. Postal Service Challenge in Philadelphia.

About two weeks before the competition, Mr. Callaghan suggested that we replace the triple salchow–triple loop combination in my long program with a triple loop–triple loop combination.

I gave him a look. Triple loop–triple loop combinations are very tough. I wasn't sure I could pull one off.

"Let's just try," Mr. Callaghan said. "Because if you can handle the new combination, your technical scores will improve.

That sounded interesting!

"Okay," I agreed. "I'll try it." Inside, I had already decided to go after the combination one hundred percent.

Mr. Callaghan talked me through the jump combination.

I landed the very first one I tried! But there was a lot of room for improvement. Mr. Callaghan gave me some pointers.

I tried the jump combination again. And again. Sometimes I fell. Sometimes I "popped" one of the jumps, substituting a double for a triple at the last second. And then—*pow!* I did a beautiful triple loop–triple loop.

Mr. Callaghan and I both started smiling. I was really amazed. He had been right. I *could* do it.

"That wasn't so hard," he said.

I shook my head.

"Now we just have to get the new combination into your program."

That proved more challenging. Sometimes I landed the combination, and then the next time I'd fall or pop into a simpler combination. But over the next two weeks I kept practicing, so that by the time we left for Philadelphia, I felt comfortable with the triple loop–triple loop. Now all I had to do was land it in the competition.

The United States Postal Service Challenge was a pretty ritzy event. It was held in the brand new CoreStates center in Philadelphia, and lots of skating stars were there to compete as part of organized teams. I was on a team with Dorothy Hamill, Michelle Kwan, Dan Hollander, and Caryn Kadavy. We were skating against another team made up of Todd Eldredge, Paul Wylie, Tonia Kwiatkowski, and Rosalynn Sumners.

With all these Olympic and world medalists around, no one was paying much attention to me. That is, not until I landed my triple loop–triple loop. I became the first skater—woman or man—to land a triple loop–triple loop at a meet.

The reporters were suddenly buzzing around me. "How long did you practice the combination?" someone wanted to know.

"Two weeks," I said.

The reporters thought I was crazy. But what could I say? It was true!

National Champion

I was a bundle of nerves at the 1997 Nationals!

Being nervous goes hand in hand with competing, but when my parents, Mr. Callaghan, and I got to Nashville for the competition, I was *super* nervous. To help calm myself down, I did all the stuff I usually do to get ready—checked over my dresses, talked to my friends, and visualized my programs in my mind. Doing that stuff usually soothes my nerves and helps me focus. But this time it wasn't working.

On the Wednesday before the competition, I went to the Vanderbilt Children's Hospital to visit. Since it was right before Valentine's Day, I brought little valentines to pass out. The kids loved it. I was the only one having a hard time relaxing and enjoying myself.

I kept thinking about the competition. All the top American women in the sport had gathered in Nashville, and Mr. Callaghan thought four of us had a good chance at the top three spots: Nicole Bobek, Michelle Kwan, Tonia Kwiatkowski (who had finished eighth in the world the year before), and me. To make the World team, I was going to have to skate better than at least one of them.

For some reason, I got more and more nervous. I'm not quite sure where that feeling came from. My training in Detroit couldn't have been stronger. I had done well in the fall championship series. And I had been skating well in practice all week. Still, I just couldn't calm down.

On Friday—the day we were supposed to skate the short program—Mr. Callaghan spent extra time talking to me. I was beyond precompetition jitters. I was so nervous I thought something might be wrong with me.

Mr. Callaghan assured me nothing was wrong. He reminded me that I'd been nervous at the Nationals the year before. It was normal. As with every Nationals, it was time to test my technical, artistic, and mental abilities against those of the best American skaters.

Mr. Callaghan also told me that being nervous might even help me skate better.

Our talk reassured me, and I was determined to keep my nerves under control.

A phone call I received also helped. It was from the famous gymnastics coach Bela Karolyi. Mr. Karolyi phoned me at my hotel that afternoon. His advice sounded a lot like Mr. Callaghan's—he told me to just go out and skate the way I had every day in practice. It was an honor to talk to him, and knowing that he and so many people were behind me helped put me in a much better mental state.

The medal winners in ladies figure skating at the 1998 Winter Olympics in Nagano, Japan, February 20, 1998. Tara Lipinski, the gold medalist from the United States, is in front. She is followed by Michelle Kwan, the silver medalist, also from the United States, and Chen Lu, the bronze medalist from China. AP/WIDE WORLD PHOTOS. REPRODUCED BY PERMISSION.

Being in the right mental state when you're competing is crucial. And even though spectators always think I seem calm and collected when the pressure is on, controlling my emotions is something I'm still struggling with. For example, I've learned that it's important for me to have a goal when I go into a competition. Without one, I don't try my hardest. At the Nationals, my goal was to come in third.

But if I'm *too* focused on my goal, I get all nervous and my muscles tense up and nothing works. So while I try to set a goal and push myself to meet it, I also try to remember that I'll always have another chance.

By the time Friday night finally rolled around, I was much calmer. I kept reminding myself that if I

"Iron Will, Golden Dreams" [excerpt]

. . . It is with absolute faith in that possibility that she [Michelle Kwan] storms the ice each time out, a pursuit that has already established Kwan as America's next great figure-skating queen. Last year, at 15, Michelle won her first national championship, then stunned her more seasoned rivals by becoming the youngest American ever to win the world title. She is a prohibitive favorite to repeat that double, starting this week in Nashville, Tenn., and seems destined, just one year hence, to land on the gold-medal podium at the Winter Olympics in Nagano, Japan. "I know I'm supposed to be surprised by what I've accomplished," says Kwan. "But why should I be? Everyone says it happened so fast, but it didn't seem fast to me. I was out there every day, all the time working and working and skating well."

. . . Michelle is her own worst critic. Watching a videotape of herself, a dismayed Kwan groans, "Look at my arm. It looks like a chicken wing." And when she actually does skate badly, she exacts her own penance. During a recent practice run-through of her free skate, Kwan crashed to the ice on her final jump, a double axel. (Kwan's program may be the toughest ever performed by a woman; it has eight jumps, seven of them triples—and three jumps occur in the final minute, when most skaters are ice-bound with fatigue.) When practice ended, she repeated the double axel again and again until she was squeezed off the ice by the Zamboni circling her. "I've learned that winning isn't about miracles on ice," she said. "It's all about training."

What she hasn't learned on the ice has come from her parents, who immigrated to L.A. from Hong Kong in 1974. Danny went to work for Pacific Bell and ran a few businesses, including a Chinese restaurant. Estella was soon shuttling three kids to the rink. Ron, the oldest, was a hockey player and Karen a figure skater good enough to place fifth behind her sister at the Nationals last year. But it was the youngest, Michelle, whose talent and mind-set were unique. When Karen competed in the 1991 Nationals in Minneapolis, Michelle was forced to practice at a small outdoor rink. "Michelle was furious the whole time," recalls Danny. "She kept saying, 'I'm never doing this again. I'm not coming to just watch'."

Michelle made it to the 1992 Nationals, competing at the junior level and finishing a poor ninth. But soon after, without her coach's consent, she took—and passed—the test that would move the 11-year-old to the senior ranks. "I was flabbergasted that this 11-year-old would go ahead without my blessing," says Carroll. "And she wasn't exactly apologetic. She said she wanted to challenge herself against the best. What was I going to do, stand her in the corner for a month? I told her, 'Believe me, little girl, we have our work cut out for us'."

Kwan was always a natural leaper, but concedes, "I didn't even know what artistic was." Today her sense of theater and musical interpretation are remarkably mature. But the most dramatic change occurred after the 1995 Worlds, where Carroll thought Michelle, who finished fourth, deserved a medal. It was clear to Frank that the judges preferred grown-up ladies to his cute little girl, who had barely outgrown her Fred Flintstone Halloween costume. Kwan, who is now 5 feet 2 and 100 pounds, still fumes: "I hated when people said I was cute." Six months later, Michelle—hair up, eyebrows plucked, makeup layered on—skated out for her first performance of the fall season as the wickedly seductive Salome. "I knew it would work before she even took the ice," Carroll remembers, "when I heard people saying, 'Who is that girl with Frank?'"

A few months later "that girl" was world champion. Only the great Sonja Henie, who was 14, and Oksana Baiul, who was 15 but a few months younger than Kwan, have been younger ladies' champs [Lipinski's win would follow Kwan's by just a year]. This year Kwan has already won all six of her competitions, even defeating former Olympic champ Kristi Yamaguchi in their first head-to-head meeting. Kwan doesn't worry about "peaking too early"—in a season or a lifetime. "You can peak and then peak again," she says. "Peak is only in your head." But exhaustion isn't just a state of mind. With all the big-money offers, her agent Shep Goldberg says, "the hardest part today is learning to say 'No'."

SOURCE: Starr, Mark. "Iron Will, Golden Dreams." *Newsweek* 129, no. 7, February 17, 1997, 52–53.

---

didn't come in third, there would always be next year. I skated my short program, and it went really smoothly. I was *so* glad to be finished with the first part of the competition. My scores were pretty good, too. I ended up in second place.

On Saturday the pace of the competition picked up. The men skated their long programs in the afternoon. Todd placed first after the short program and held on to win the men's title after the long pro-

gram. I was really proud of him, but he wasn't happy with his performance. He really is a perfectionist! I think Todd skated great, but I respect him for having such high standards.

After the men finished, I started to get ready for my long program.

By the time the first of the women glided onto the ice, the Nashville Arena was packed with sixteen thousand extremely enthusiastic spectators. ABC Sports was covering the event. Television viewers across the nation were tuned in. My parents were there—somewhere up in the sold-out stands. Todd was watching on a television monitor in the athletes' lounge.

I was in a very up mood. My second-place finish the day before had boosted my confidence. I had the usual competition nervousness, but the extreme jitters I'd experienced earlier in the week were gone.

I reminded myself that if I wanted to go to the Worlds, I'd have to nail my long program. Even though I was currently in second place, Nicole, Tonia, and plenty of other terrific skaters would be trying to slip by me and snag the chance to go to Switzerland. There was no room for mistakes.

After we had all warmed up, I changed back into my running shoes. I had to skate last in my group, which for me isn't the greatest. I prefer to skate earlier, but I tried not to worry about it.

While the other competitors took their turns, I hung out in the locker room. I jogged in place to keep my muscles warm. And I tried to stay focused. Todd came out of the skaters' lounge. "It's just like every day in practice," he told me. "Go out and do your thing and you'll be fine."

"Thanks," I whispered, grateful for his advice and encouragement.

Finally it was almost my turn. I walked over to the ice. When I got to the boards, Michelle had just finished skating. As she came off the ice, I noticed that she didn't look at all happy.

Mr. Callaghan hurried up to me. "Okay, Tara," he said. "Just pretend it's another day at the rink."

I nodded. Mr. Callaghan always tells me the same thing right before I compete. It helps, but it's hard to pretend it's just another day at the rink when sixteen thousand people are crowded into the stands.

I started to step onto the ice, but Mr. Callaghan pulled me back.

"What's wrong?" I asked.

"Just wait a second," he replied.

I noticed what was bothering him. The crowd was booing.

"They're not booing at you," Mr. Callaghan reassured me.

No, it seemed as if the crowd was reacting to Michelle's scores, which had just come up. I looked

Michelle Kwan during her winning performance at the 1996 U.S. Figure Skating Championship in San Jose, California. **ARCHIVE PHOTOS. REPRODUCED BY PERMISSION.**

at them too. They *weren't* great, and I was a little confused. (Later I found out that Michelle had fallen three times during her program. She'd had a bad day.)

Of course, I knew instantly what that meant. If I skated really well, I might win!

Mr. Callaghan seemed to read my mind. "Don't try to win," he told me firmly. "Just do your work."

His words didn't surprise me. I remembered my experience at the Worlds the year before, when I'd gotten distracted by my thoughts about beating Midori Ito, had pushed too hard, had ruined the timing of my jumps, and had landed on my backside—several times. Big mistake.

So I tried to put the chance of winning out of my mind, and instead I concentrated on my program. When the crowd calmed down, I glided onto the ice. My music began to play. I started to skate.

My first jump was a double axel. I brought my arms in and my right leg up and thrust myself into the air. Tucking in tight, I spun around two and a half times before I came down.

My triple flip was next. It was huge! By then I was getting into the rhythm of my program. That jump felt perfect. And the audience rewarded me by clapping loudly.

Next came my triple Lutz–double toe loop. I nailed it!

The tempo of my music slowed. I had time to catch my breath. But I couldn't relax yet. My next jump was a tricky one: the triple loop–triple loop combination.

I pushed off the edge of my skate and flew into the first triple loop. I came down cleanly. So far, so good. Almost immediately I pushed off into my second jump, spun around one, two, three times, and landed solidly.

A cheer went up from the crowd. I started to smile. My program was going really well. And the crowd's support kept me psyched.

The rest of my program went by in a blur, but every jump and spin felt good. When I finished, the crowd went wild. They rose to their feet and applauded madly. It was a moment I'll never forget.

I was ecstatic. I had skated my very best.

Mr. Callaghan was waiting for me at the edge of the ice. "Great job, Tara!" he told me.

"Thanks," I said, beaming.

We walked over to the kiss and cry area, the nickname skaters have for the bench where you wait for your scores. We call it that because if you've skated well, everyone kisses each other; if you've skated badly, everyone cries.

Pretty soon my scores came up. At first I couldn't believe them! None of the judges gave me a mark lower than 5.8. Plus, I'd earned six technical marks of 5.9 and three artistic 5.9s. In other words . . .

I'd won! I was the new U.S. Ladies Singles Champion!

Further Resources

BOOKS

Christopher, Matt. *On the Ice With—Tara Lipinski.* Boston: Little, Brown, 1999.

Daly, Wendy. *Tara and Michelle: The Road to Gold.* New York: Random House, 1997.

Gutman, Bill. *Tara Lipinski: Queen of the Ice.* Brookfield, Conn.: Millbrook Press, 1999.

Kwan, Michelle, and Laura James. *Michelle Kwan, Heart of a Champion: An Autobiography.* New York: Scholastic, 1997.

Lipinski, Tara, et. al. *Totally Tara: An Olympic Journey.* New York: Universe, 1998.

Lovitt, Chip. *Skating for the Gold: Michelle Kwan & Tara Lipinski.* New York: Pocket Books, 1997.

Ryan, Joan. *Little Girls in Pretty Boxes: The Making and Breaking of Elite Gymnasts and Figure Skaters.* New York: Doubleday, 1995.

Wellman, Sam. *Michelle Kwan.* Philadelphia: Chelsea House Publishers, 1999.

WEBSITES

"Michelle Kwan: Artistry on Ice." Available online at http://www.wam.umd.edu/~valecrie/michelle.html (accessed July 15, 2003).

The Official Tara Lipinski website. Available online at http://www.taralipinski.com (accessed April 15, 2003).

US Figure Skating Online. Available online at http://www.usfsa.org (accessed July 15, 2003).

Playing Through: Straight Talk on Hard Work, Big Dreams, and Adventures With Tiger

Memoir

By: Earl Woods, with Fred Mitchell

Date: 1998

Source: Woods, Earl, with Fred Mitchell. *Playing Through: Straight Talk on Hard Work, Big Dreams, and Adventures With Tiger.* New York: HarperCollins, 1998, 161–167.

About the Author: Earl Woods (1932–), father of golfer Tiger Woods, played baseball at Kansas State University, where he was the first African American baseball player in the Big Eight Conference. He joined the army, served two tours in Vietnam, and retired in 1974. ∎

Introduction

Golf originated in Europe and was brought over to the United States in the late nineteenth century. Originally played at country clubs, it became a popular sport among the wealthy at the turn of the century. Most country clubs, however, excluded African Americans as members, so the only way African Americans could play golf was to become caddies at the clubs.

With the increase in leisure time in the 1950s, many middle-class Americans took up golf. Arnold Palmer was a central figure in extending the appeal of golf to the masses. Palmer had a huge following, dubbed "Arnie's Army." With this rise in the sport's popularity, many municipalities started building golf courses, and golf became much more accessible to the average person. Virtually all golfers remained white, however.

African Americans began to participate more in golf during the 1980s and 1990s. Also at this time, an increasing number of children were being encouraged to start sports early. Tiger Woods started golf at age two, hitting golf balls with Bob Hope on the *Mike Douglas Show,* and then playing competitive golf at the age of three. He started receiving golf instruction by four.

He won the U.S. Junior Amateur title three times, in 1991, 1992, and 1993, as well as won three consecutive U.S. Amateur Championships, and an NCAA title while attending Stanford. Tiger turned pro in 1996 and enjoyed immediate success, winning the Las Vegas Invitational, his fifth professional tournament. In 1997, he won the Masters, setting a new scoring record, and also won the Player of the Year award.

Significance

Since 1997, Tiger Woods has dominated golf, winning Player of the Year honors every year except 1998. He won three of golf's four major events in 2000, becoming the first golfer in fifty years to do so. He became the first golfer ever to hold all four professional major titles simultaneously. He has won over fifty events as a pro and has been the sport's top money winner since joining the tour. He is also one of sport's highest-paid product endorsers, earning more than seventy million dollars a year, more than virtually any other celebrity.

But Tiger's tremendous success has raised serious concerns about children's involvement in professional athletics. Some child prodigies succeed, but many others burn out quickly and have trouble adjusting to adult life. Jennifer Capriati, for example, broke into professional tennis in 1990 at the age of thirteen. She had some success, but then battled drug addiction and weight gain before regaining her tennis form in recent years. Some events have adopted minimum age limits, and the NBA has considered a minimum age limit of twenty. The problem of child athletes is particularly prevalent in basketball, where many drafted underclassmen and high school students fail to make, or stay, in the NBA. A key to success will be incorporating the parental skills demonstrated by Earl and Kultida Woods. Tiger held off joining the PGA tour to spend a year at Stanford, and he seems well adjusted and happy as a result.

Primary Source

Playing Through: Straight Talk on Hard Work, Big Dreams, and Adventures With Tiger [excerpt]

SYNOPSIS: In "The Rookie," chapter eight of *Playing Through,* Earl Woods begins by discussing why he was at the 1997 Masters, despite recent heart surgery. He also discusses some of Tiger's play at the Masters, and how he met Tiger at the eighteenth

Tiger Woods stands to the right of his father, Earl Woods, Long Beach, California, April 14, 2001. © **REUTERS NEWMEDIA INC./CORBIS. REPRODUCED BY PERMISSION.**

green. Tiger, after winning, credits his father with his victory. Earl discusses his relationship with Tiger, and how he tried to support him emotionally.

The Rookie

The adrenaline was pumping faster than the blood from my heart.

Could that possibly be my son, walking down the 18th fairway at Augusta National? He walked as if he didn't even notice his feet touching the ground. I guess that's what someone looks like when they're on Cloud Nine. It was the most surrealistic, magnificent moment I have ever witnessed.

It was already a foregone conclusion that Tiger was about to win his first Masters tournament. Now it was simply a matter of how wide the margin of victory would be and how many records would be shattered along the way.

I recall that I was totally, physically exhausted; the heart surgery two months earlier had completely sapped me of energy, and I just didn't have it strength-wise. Yet I was so exhilarated. And, most importantly, I was alive.

Under any other circumstance, I should have been at home, recuperating. But I just had to be there in Augusta, if only to watch from the distance of the clubhouse. Tiger knew how seriously ill I was, and it was weighing on him mentally; it had become tough for him to focus. When his mind isn't clear, it is difficult for him to play. So I needed to be with

Tiger Woods, moments after winning golf's Masters Tournament, Augusta, Georgia, April 13, 1997. Tiger won with a score of 270—a record low for the Masters. **ARCHIVE PHOTOS. REPRODUCED BY PERMISSION.**

him, just so he wouldn't worry about me, what my condition was, or how I was doing. He could see me every day, look me in the eye and know that I was OK and that he didn't have to worry about anything.

It had been my goal all along to make it to the Masters, to watch my son play there for the first time as a professional. . . .

And there I sat, staring at the screen in stunned amazement, my ailing heart pounding. As I saw him make a great putt on the 16th hole, I said to no one in particular: "Wow! He two-putted it from way on the right side of the green with about a 30-foot break." He had about a six-inch target in which he had to almost stop the ball, then allow it to change direction and trickle down the slope toward the hole. Too long, it picks up speed and goes off the green down the bank into the water. Too short, it takes a severe break and almost comes back to him. Amazing doesn't do it justice. It seemed unfair that anyone could possibly make that shot, but Tiger did.

Then I watched him at the 17th. By now it was clear Tiger would win, and members of the media began descending on the area around the final hole;

suddenly everyone wanted to interview me. I talked to the writers briefly, excused myself and walked over to the 18th green, where Tida [Tiger's mother] and I were positioned in front of the scoring tent. By then Tiger had teed off, and I kept waiting and waiting for him to show up near the green. I said to myself: "Oh, no, Tiger. You're not going to do something dramatic again on the 18th hole, are you?"

Sounding more like a giddy fan than a parent, I muttered aloud: "Where's Tiger?" Somebody answered: "He's way down the hill over on the left-hand side of the fairway." As if I had spotted an apparition, I exclaimed, "Oh, my gosh! That's Tiger!"

I saw this little white ball pop up out of a multitude of people—an absolute sea of human beings. The ball landed on the green.

"Well, that's Tiger, all right," I deadpanned.

And then, as if I was watching a dream, he emerged from the crowd, head high, right arm pumping in the air, smiling from ear-to-ear, acknowledging the thunderous cheers and chants from the gallery like a victorious politician.

It was sheer pandemonium, and for a frightening moment, I was really concerned for his safety. Tiger was stuck down there in that mob. Later, after I viewed the television tapes, I was horrified to realize that my concern was totally justified, because he had no security support at all as he headed to the fairway. He was even separated from his caddie. Tiger was lost in the mob, and lucky for us, it was a loving mob. One little kid darted right out of the masses, ran up to Tiger after he hit his shot and patted him on the back. At that point I thought: "Oh, God. Just for the grace of God, that could have been someone crazy."

But when Tiger broke free, I had instant relief from my anxiety. Now I was overwhelmed by an indescribable, awesome sense of pride. I thought, "This is his dream. I am watching him accomplish his dream!" It was beautiful to see as a parent. I didn't break down; I wasn't emotional at that point. I was simply observant.

Tiger walked up to the 18th green and acknowledged the crowd. I knew, however, that despite the commotion and excitement, he was still most concerned about sinking that final putt. And I was right. He was all business. He never lost his focus. He immediately went into his pre-putting routine—the routine he had performed so many times that it was automatic, no matter how critical the situation, no matter how great the stress—and forgot all about the crowds and other external distractions. He focused on this one putt, a very difficult, downhill, break-left putt—a double-breaking putt, to be exact. He ran it about four feet by the hole.

I said to myself: "There is no way he is going to miss this." Tiger just doesn't do things like that on the 18th green. Under adverse conditions, he just maintains his poise. He does things dramatically. He just raises his level of performance.

Sure enough, he drained it. Tiger had just won the Masters by a record 12 strokes.

First, Tiger shared a private moment with his caddie, Fluff Cowan.

Then, as Tiger came towards the scoring tent, he headed straight into my arms. . . .

Tiger later told the press, "What I think every time I hug my Mom or Pop after a tournament: It's over. I accomplished my goal. To share it with them is something special."

What an incredible thing to hear your child say.

For the record: Closing with a 69, Tiger finished at 18-under par, 270, the lowest score *ever* shot in the Masters. The score matched the most under par by anyone in any of the four Grand Slam events. His 12-stroke victory over his nearest competitor Tom Kite was not only a Masters record by three strokes, but the greatest winning margin in any major tournament since Tom Morris Sr. won the 1862 British Open by 13 strokes. He just went out and brought the course to its knees and beat it.

I will never forget the infectious smile on Tiger's face when he slipped his arms into the symbolic green jacket presented by defending Masters champion Nick Faldo. Tiger Woods, Masters champion! I liked the sound of that. . . .

With Tiger, everything is such an emotional rollercoaster. Ninety-nine percent of the time are highs for him, and you tend to have an unflappable faith in him, because you know he owns those last two or three holes of a tournament. Or he owns overtime. His willpower and his mental strength are so great that he just controls the whole situation. You expect these good things to happen. And, quite frankly, they do. It is beautiful to watch. His mental strength is improving all of the time. I notice it when I have been separated from Tiger for a month or so. When I see him again, I can tell he's tougher in some way; it's like watching ice harden.

I just hope that Tiger doesn't toughen himself up so much that he loses touch with his real emotions. Now, there is a fine line there.

Further Resources

BOOKS

Andrisani, John. *Think Like Tiger: An Analysis of Tiger Woods' Mental Game.* New York: G.P. Putnam's Sons, 2002.

Callahan, Tom. *In Search of Tiger Woods: A Journey Through Golf With Tiger Woods.* New York: Crown, 2003.

Gutelle, Andrew. *Tiger Woods.* New York: Grosset & Dunlap, 2002.

Macnow, Glen. *Sports Great Tiger Woods.* Berkeley Heights, N.J.: Enslow, 2001.

Owen, David. *The Chosen One: Tiger Woods and the Dilemma of Greatness.* New York: Simon & Schuster, 2001.

Rosaforte, Tim, et al. *Raising the Bar: The Championship Years of Tiger Woods.* New York: St. Martin's, 2002.

Sampson, Curt. *Chasing Tiger.* New York: Atria, 2002.

WEBSITES

Tiger Woods official website. Available online at http://www .tigerwoods.com (accessed April 15, 2003).

AUDIO AND VISUAL MEDIA

Tiger Woods: Heart of a Champion. Goldhil Video, 2000, VHS.

The Tiger Woods Story. Directed by LeVar Burton. Paramount Home Video, 1998, VHS.

"Charles Is Gone, but the Chuckies Aren't"

Editorial

By: Rick Reilly

Date: December 20, 1999

Source: Reilly, Rick. "Charles Is Gone, but the Chuckies Aren't." *Sports Illustrated* 91, no. 24, December 20, 1999, 152.

About the Author: Rick Reilly (1958–) is a senior columnist for *Sports Illustrated.* He has coauthored several books with celebrities, including Marv Albert and Wayne Gretzky, and has published two fiction books. He has been honored with six National Sportswriter of the Year awards. ∎

Introduction

In the past, athletes did not have their troubles as heavily publicized as today's stars. Teams and leagues actually went out of their way to conceal player misconduct. Ty Cobb allegedly once went after a fan, and also assaulted a man working on a street, but neither of those incidents was heavily publicized. Mickey Mantle's drinking episodes—he was often hung over for games—are now the stuff of legend, but, at the time, local sportswriters buried the news out of loyalty and respect to the former Yankee great.

There are many reasons for the extended reporting of off-field activities. Multiple media outlets—including

Charles Barkley, of the Houston Rockets, blows a sarcastic kiss to Seattle SuperSonics fans at a game in Seattle on May 11, 1997. Barkley's outrageous behavior both on and off the court prompted a notable sportswriter to name annual mock awards given to sports figures for dumb statements and obnoxious behavior after Barkley. AP/WIDE WORLD PHOTOS. REPRODUCED BY PERMISSION.

twenty-four-hour sports television channels, sports talk radio, and the Internet—compete for the attention of fans, greatly increasing the information available. There are more sports to cover, and a much wider range of topics deemed acceptable for public disclosure.

In the early stages of many professional leagues, players worked non-sports jobs in the off-season—especially the lower-paid players. Now, even those making the league minimum salary can afford to work only in their chosen sport. Fans find it more difficult to identify with professional athletes, and additional time demands are made on players. Thus, professional athletes are bombarded with requests for autographs and personal appearances. These athletes, often pampered for much of their lives, seem less concerned with satisfying the many demands of their fans and more concerned with satisfying themselves.

But athletes are not solely to blame. Sports fans are also unruly. Numerous times in recent years, fans have rushed onto college football fields and basketball courts during the action, pelted players with various objects, and assaulted referees. While some of this behavior is caused by exuberance, fan behavior has been dangerously out of control at times—especially at European soccer matches, where thousands have been killed over the years.

Significance

Part of the reason for the increased publicity of sports stars' off-field behavior is greater media attention and exposure. Several stars' actions, however, have merited the attention. Carolina Panthers wide receiver Rae Carruth was convicted of conspiracy to commit murder in the shooting death of his pregnant girlfriend, and in 2001 he was sentenced to at least eighteen years in prison. Many athletes have fathered children out of wedlock and failed to pay child support. One of the most notorious is the NBA's Shawn Kemp. As of 1998, Kemp had fathered at least seven illegitimate children, and a recent paternity suit against him estimated that he might have as many as twelve illegitimate children.

Some teams also seem to attract problems. In a single year, the NBA's Portland Trail Blazers had so many players arrested that some called them the "Portland Jail Blazers." Their troubles included players arrested for domestic assault, drug possession, and drunken driving.

Primary Source

"Charles Is Gone, but the Chuckies Aren't"

SYNOPSIS: In this article, Reilly notes that, although NBA star Charles Barkley is retired, "The Chuckies"—mock awards created by Reilly for obnoxious behavior by athletes and sports fans, and bestowed in "honor" of the colorful and outrageous Barkley—live on. Reilly goes on to relate dumb statements and obnoxious behavior by sports figures. Also chronicled are the antics of obnoxious sports fans. Throughout, the points are related with Reilly's characteristic humor.

'Tis a bleak day for sportswriters. We'll lose our appetite for the free pregame buffet, set our seat backs at half mast, sing dirges at the karaoke. The world's greatest quote has hung 'em up.

Charles Barkley ruptured the quadriceps tendon in his left knee last week, ending his NBA career with 23,755 points, 12,544 rebounds and 3,241 They Said Its. Sales of recording tape and notepads immediately plummeted.

But the Round Mound of Sound lives on in the Chuckies, the annual celebration of the people we would most like to chuck through a plate-glass window, just as Barkley once tossed an annoying but aerodynamic sports fan in Orlando. Asked if he had any regrets afterward, Barkley said, "I regret we weren't on a higher floor."

Really gonna miss that man.

The envelopes, please. . . .

Chicago Bears rookie Cade McNown, the former UCLA quarterback who, after pleading no contest to illegally possessing a handicapped parking placard, showed up for his first day of NFL training camp and, you guessed it, parked in a handicapped spot.

Evander Holyfield, who came out of his losing championship bout with Lennox Lewis as unmarked as a mobster's mistress. "It makes me think I should have fought a little harder," Holyfield allowed. "Maybe I'd be sore and sick, but I'd have the victory." And maybe we should ask for our money back.

Golden State Warriors forward Chris Mills and Dallas Mavericks forward Samaki Walker. In the dumbest NBA moment of the year, Mills attempted to make a layup at the wrong basket. Luckily, Walker fouled him as he went up. For them, a double pane.

Los Angeles Lakers center Shaquille O'Neal, who said, "I'm like the Pythagorean theorem. Not too many people know the answer to my game." Actually, Diesel, the answer is c^2. Feel free to hurl yourself through any sixth-grade classroom window and let the kids clue you in.

Auburn athletic director David Housel, who paid $500,000 to get the Tigers out of playing Florida State this fall. After football coach Terry Bowden resigned in October 1998, Housel said that without Terry on the Auburn sideline, playing against dad Bobby Bowden's powerhouse Seminoles didn't seem so appealing. Duh.

The Grand Viking, a.k.a. Minnesota Vikings fan Brian Siegmann, walked the streets of Eau Claire, Wis., asking, "Who's a Packers fan?" When one couple said, "Us!" Siegmann set the man's pants leg and the woman's jacket sleeve and hair afire. Neither fan was seriously injured. Hey, Grand, we're chucking you through the front window of the nastiest Harley bar in Green Bay. Ask if there are any Packers fans in there.

New York Knicks center Patrick Ewing, who refused to sign autographs for seriously ill kids from the Starlight Children's Foundation at a Thanksgiv-

Basketball star Charles Barkley threw a man through this plate-glass window on October 26, 1997, after the man tossed a glass of ice at him. AP/WIDE WORLD PHOTOS. REPRODUCED BY PERMISSION.

ing luncheon. "I don't sign on game days," Ewing explained. He was on the injured list at the time.

Denver police officers, who maced members of the Colorado State marching band as they stood in the Mile High Stadium stands trying to play the school fight song amid an unruly crowd. The police said they were worried the band was going to storm the field. Cover me, Fred, I'm goin' after the clarinetist.

Orlando Magic rookie Corey Maggette, who missed a game with an infected toe after a bad pedicure.

The Animal Protection Institute, which protested the fish-toss contest at games of the minor league Sacramento Steelheads. Contestants tossed a dead fish from a base line to second base, and closest to the bag won. When a head came off in one fan's hand, the API complained to the team. Uh, folks, one small detail: The fish were dead already! Where were you two days ago when they needed you?

Kevin Mitchell, former National League MVP, who was arrested on suspicion of hitting his father because Dad owed him rent. Kevin, as you smash through the window, remember, this will hurt us a lot more than it'll hurt you.

Cheryl Smith, wife of Missouri football coach Larry Smith, who stood on the sideline in the final quarter of Missouri's 66-0 loss to Kansas State berating her husband's players. Yo, Cheryl, much more of this and you're no longer Team Mom.

And, last, the Chuckie Chuckee we've saved for Chuckie to chuck himself, Bob Knight, Indiana basketball coach, who in October filled a friend with shotgun pellets while bird hunting. Knight said his finger slipped off the safety and hit the trigger.

Hey, Chuck, whatever you do, don't go to his shootaround.

Further Resources

BOOKS

Barkley, Charles, and Rick Reilly. *Sir Charles: The Wit and Wisdom of Charles Barkley.* New York: Warner, 1994.

Berger, Gilda. *Violence and Sports.* New York: F. Watts, 1990.

Klatell, David A., and Norman Marcus. *Sports for Sale: Television, Money, and the Fans.* New York: Oxford University Press, 1988.

Reilly, Rick. *The Life of Reilly: The Best of Sports Illustrated's Rick Reilly.* New York: Total Sports Illustrated, 2000.

Roberts, Michael. *Fans! How We Go Crazy Over Sports.* Washington: New Republic, 1976.

Sperber, Murray A. *Beer and Circus: How Big-Time College Sports Is Crippling Undergraduate Education.* New York: Henry Holt, 2000.

Whannel, Garry. *Media Sport Stars: Masculinities and Moralities.* London: Routledge, 2002.

WEBSITES

"Rick Reilly Archive." CNN/Sports Illustrated. Available online at http://sportsillustrated.cnn.com/inside_game/archives /rick_reilly; website home page: http://sportsillustrated.cnn .com (accessed April 18, 2003).

"One on One with Sheryl Swoopes, Houston Comets"

Interview

By: Sheryl Swoopes

Date: December 1999

Source: Swoopes, Sheryl. "One on One with Sheryl Swoopes, Houston Comets." Interview by Lorraine Berry. *Gball,* December 1999. Available online at http://www .gballmag.com/pp_swoopes.html; website home page: http:// www.gballmag.com (accessed April 20, 2003).

About the Author: Sheryl Swoopes (1971–) led Texas Tech University to the NCAA basketball title in 1993. In the championship game, she set a record with forty-seven points. She played on the gold medal-winning U.S. Women's basketball teams in the 1996 and 2000 Olympics. She plays on the Houston Comets, winners of the first Women's NBA (WNBA) championship in 1997. She was named MVP of the WNBA in 2000 and 2002. ∎

Introduction

The National Basketball Association (NBA) was founded in 1946 for male professional basketball players. The idea of a women's league, however, lagged far behind. Women's athletics in general received a huge boost with the passage of Title IX in 1972, a federal statute that prohibited discrimination on the basis of sex in educational facilities—applying both to academic and athletic endeavors. While this did not, on a practical basis, mean equal funding for men's and women's teams, it did greatly increase the number of women's teams at the high school and college levels, greatly increasing the number of women and girls playing basketball. A women's NCAA basketball tournament was started in 1982, and attendance steadily rose at that tournament each year. Women's basketball at some schools began receiving nearly as much attention and attendance as men's. After a short-lived attempt to establish the professional Women's Basketball League failed in the early 1980s, there was little interest in establishing a new professional league for women until the mid-1990s. Two rival leagues were established: the Women's National Basketball Association (WNBA), backed by the NBA and which played during the NBA's off season; and the American Basketball League (ABL), which played at the same time (late fall, winter) as the NBA. The ABL paid their players more, but the WNBA had better support. Both leagues began in 1996, but the ABL disbanded in 1998.

The WNBA, due in large part to its support from the NBA, which included help acquiring a television contract, is still in existence. In 2002, the Los Angeles Sparks won the WNBA title for the second year in a row. The WNBA now appears to have a relatively good chance for survival, at least for a few more years—fielding fourteen teams and averaging fourteen thousand fans per game during the 2002 finals.

Significance

Women athletes are paid less and have a lower profile, generally, than their male counterparts. The average WNBA player earns approximately $50,000, while the average NBA player earns $4.6 million. Women athletes also get less for their shoe endorsement contracts. Nike named a basketball shoe after Sheryl Swoopes (the Swoopes), with Swoopes receiving a six-figure contract.

Sheryl Swoopes (number 22) of the Houston Comets and Teresa Weatherspoon (number 11) chase after a loose ball in Game 2 of the 1999 WNBA Finals, Houston, Texas, September 4, 1999. Swoopes helped the Comets defeat the Liberty to win their third consecutive WNBA championship. **AP/WIDE WORLD PHOTOS. REPRODUCED BY PERMISSION.**

By contrast, high school phenomenon LeBron James—who had not yet played a single NBA game—signed an endorsement deal with Nike worth over $90 million dollars. These figures indicate the disparity in pay and endorsement contracts in men's and women's basketball.

Primary Source

"One on One with Sheryl Swoopes, Houston Comets" [excerpt]

SYNOPSIS: In this interview conducted by Lorraine Berry, Swoopes begins by discussing why she went to junior college and how she picked Texas Tech.

She also notes how she continues to improve her fundamental skills, how she started basketball, and what winning an Olympic championship means to her. She concludes by outlining her relationship with the other Houston Comets players.

After an awesome college career and an Olympic gold medal, Sheryl Swoopes is enjoying being a star to both WNBA fans and her two-year-old son.

Sheryl Swoopes would appear to have the Midas touch: She has been part of three teams that have won five golden championships. In 1993, Texas Tech won the NCAA Division I Championship, and

Sheryl Swoopes cuts down the net after leading the 1993 Texas Tech women's basketball team to the NCAA Division I championship, April 4, 1993, in Atlanta, Georgia. Swoopes scored forty-seven points and was named Tournament MVP. AP/WIDE WORLD PHOTOS. REPRODUCED BY PERMISSION.

Swoopes collected Final Four MVP honors after setting an NCAA championship game record with 47 points against Ohio State. In 1996, she was part of the USA Women's Basketball Olympic Team that took gold in Atlanta. Since then, she has been a dominant player for the Houston Comets, the only champions the WNBA has known, capturing titles in 1997, 1998, and 1999.

Swoopes also proved that being a new mom and a great athlete are not mutually exclusive activities. She gave birth to son, Jordan, in June, 1997, but still managed to play the last nine games of the Comets' first championship season. On February 2, however, Swoopes announced that she will NOT be playing for the U.S. Olympic Team in 2000. Citing her reluctance to bring Jordan on a three-month playing tour, culminating in the Sydney Games, she withdrew her name from consideration for the squad. . . .

Most people know that you were a star at Texas Tech, but don't know that you started your collegiate career at South Plains College, a junior college in

Levelland, Texas. Can you talk about why you took this path?

I initially signed to go play basketball at the University of Texas, a Division I school. I decided I didn't like it there and transferred. I didn't want to sit out a year [because of Division I rules that require an athlete to sit out a year of play if she transfers schools] and the only way I could avoid that was to go to a Division II school or a junior college. So I chose to go to junior college for two years. If I had to do it all over again, I'd do the same thing. Junior college definitely prepared me—not only in basketball but being out on my own, as well.

Do you think that junior college is a good option for a lot of girls out there?

It depends on how mature you are or what you're looking for—if you want to go far from home or close to home. In my case, I had never really been away from home. I'd always had my mom or someone else with me, so going to Austin [where the University of Texas is located] was a very major change. I would definitely recommend junior college because it prepares you for life—being out on your own, during the first year. Junior colleges are usually smaller than Division I schools so it allows you to adjust—adjust your schedule and your lifestyle to a bigger environment.

Why did you choose Texas Tech after South Plains?

Because it was close to home. My mom has always been my number-one fan, and it was very important to me that she was able to come up and watch me play throughout my college career.

Do you think your mom has had a big impact on who you are now?

Definitely. My mom has probably had THE biggest impact on who I am today.

What parts of your game are you working on the most right now?

I try to work on all areas of my game. I don't spend a lot of time worrying about offense because I'm the kind of player who feels that's going to happen when I get in the game. Right now, I'm focusing on my conditioning and weights—I'm trying to get stronger in my legs and my arms, and just be in really good shape. That's the most important part for me. When I get out on the court to play, I want to feel that I can go for 40 minutes non-stop and still feel that I'll be ready to play in overtime. When I get more into my serious workouts, then I'll start doing more drills with the basketball as far as dribbling, ball-handling, shooting, working on my defense, and stuff like that.

Bill Clinton's Remarks Honoring the 1992–1993 NCAA Men's and Women's College Basketball Champions, April 27, 1993

[This is a transcript of the speech President Clinton gave at 4:45 P.M. in the Rose Garden at the White House.]

Good afternoon. I want to apologize to the people who are here from North Carolina and Texas. I have been inside in a meeting with some Members of the United States Congress of both parties, some of whom are also here in the crowd, talking about the situation in Bosnia. And I got away as quickly as I could. I thank all of you for coming here.

It's a great honor for me as an ardent basketball fan to welcome to the White House two proud new national champions, the Tarheels of North Carolina and the Lady Raiders of Texas Tech, who won the men's and women's NCAA basketball championships.

The Lady Raiders have been stirring things up in West Texas for some time now, with back-to-back Southwest Conference titles, and this year, of course, they brought home Texas Tech's first national championship in any sport. It helps when you have a secret weapon in basketball whose name rhymes with "hoops." No doubt about it, Sheryl Swoopes turned in a tournament performance that was one for the ages. She averaged over 32 points a game and scored 47 points in the final, which is an all-time championship record for men or women in basketball finals. If anybody hasn't figured it out yet, I think women's basketball has arrived.

I'd also like to say that we have to make special mention of the coach of the Lady Raiders, coach Marcia Sharp, who is a four-time Southwest Conference Coach of the Year and who took a wonderful 11-year career at Texas Tech to new heights.

Then there are the Tarheels, one of whom had the grace to remind me that they waxed Arkansas in getting to the Sweet 16 [laughter]. There may not be many things you can depend upon in this world, but normally it is when "March Madness" rolls around, you can be sure that Dean Smith's Tarheels will be there at the final bell, with discipline and style as great as any you will ever see. Nineteen consecutive years in the NCAA, 13 trips to the Sweet 16, 9 times to the Final 4, 2 national championships. Even though I have to admit that I didn't pull for them in every game [laughter], I thought they were magnificent, true Carolina Blue champions.

I also want to say a special word of thanks to Eric Montross for not standing on the riser when I walked by. I felt small enough as it was [laughter]. I want to congratulate him and Donald Williams for the three-pointers that they made, and George Lynch for muscling out his opposition on the inside. As a matter of fact, I was thinking of asking George to stay around here for a few days and help me [laughter].

I want to say again that the thing I like about basketball and the thing I think our country needs more of is that you can't just win with great players; you have to have great teamwork. People have to understand each other's strengths and weaknesses and learn to work together in a consistent way. These two teams have done it and have done it magnificently, and it's a great honor for me to welcome them to the White House today.

I'd like to now invite the coaches to come up and say a few words.

[At this point, team members were introduced, and each team presented the President with a basketball.]

I want to invite all the people to come up here, and we'll all take a few pictures and everything. And I thank all of you for coming. I want to take a few minutes; then I've got to go back to my meeting. Thank you very much.

SOURCE: Clinton, Bill. Remarks honoring the 1992–1993 NCAA men's and women's college basketball champions, April 27, 1993. *Weekly Compilation of Presidential Documents* 29, no. 17, May 3, 1993.

Do you think it's important for girls to spend a lot of time working on their fundamentals?

I think it's the most important part of the game. To me, it's very important to be a complete player. I don't want people to look at me and say, 'Well, all Sheryl can do is shoot the ball. She can't play good defense.' Or I don't want them to say, 'Sheryl's a good defensive player but she can't score.' I think working on your fundamentals is the way that you become a complete player—you become an overall player. I think every young girl and young boy out there should focus more on the fundamentals. Players should be able to dribble, if they're right handed, just as good with their left hand as with their right. And that's the part of my game that I still want to work on.

Four years ago, why did you decide to join the WNBA and not the ABL?

At the time the ABL started, we were just coming off of a long tour with the national team and the Olympics, and I just wanted a break. The ABL wanted us to make a commitment to join them a month after the Olympics were over and I just wasn't ready for that. I wanted to take a little break.

When did you start playing basketball?

When I was seven years old, I played in a youth league called 'Little Dribblers.' I was not very good when we played, but I would recommend that any little girl out there who wants to become a basketball player should start at a young age. I did it for fun, it wasn't anything more than that. It was fun and I enjoyed it.

You've had lots of experiences winning: three WNBA titles, an Olympic gold medal, and an NCAA title. Of all of those, which is the most special to you?

All of them were very special to me, obviously. Winning a national championship in college was, I thought, the ultimate—the highest thing you could accomplish. So that was very special to me. Playing in the WNBA and winning three championships was also incredible. The first one, because I was out with my son, I didn't feel that I contributed as much. But to come back the next year, and again last year to three-peat and win three world championships was phenomenal. Words can't describe how excited I am about that. But I would probably have to say the Olympics meant a little bit more to me. Not only was I doing it for myself, my town, and my team, but I was doing it for my country. You've got everybody in the United States, hopefully, pulling for you and rooting for you and wanting to see you do well—wanting to see the U.S. win. So, it meant just a little bit more to me.

Do you hang out with the other Comets players?

I go shopping every now and again with a couple of team members. But usually, once the season starts and we're in the gym, we're working out—working hard—and when practice is over with, we're all ready to go home, do our own thing, and go our separate ways. But, we all get along very well. We're a very close-knit team.

Did the news about Kim Perrot break you down or make you a stronger person?

If it's possible, I think it did both. Any time you lose a teammate, a friend, obviously that's going to be very devastating and hard to deal with. I think if there's one good thing that came out of that it was Kim. Kim was a great person, a great friend, a great athlete, but I think with Kim's illness and her death, it brought the team a lot closer. We were like a family. It made me slow down a little bit and look at life and not take things for granted. One day you're perfectly healthy and everything's fine and the next day you're diagnosed with some type of an illness. And you never know what's going to happen, so you've got to make the most of every day.

Further Resources

BOOKS

Burby, Liza N. *Sheryl Swoopes, All-Star Basketball Player.* New York: Rosen Publishing House, 1997.

Burgan, Michael. *Sheryl Swoopes.* Philadelphia: Chelsea House, 2001.

Coyle, Maureen, et al. *Official WNBA Guide and Register.* St. Louis: WNBA Enterprises, 2002.

Gutman, Bill. *Shooting Stars: The Women of Pro Basketball.* New York: Random House, 1998.

Layden, Joseph, and James Preller. *Inside the WNBA: A Behind the Scenes Photo Scrapbook.* New York: Scholastic, 1999.

Ponti, James. *WNBA: Stars of Women's Basketball.* New York: Pocket, 1999.

Rappoport, Ken. *Sheryl Swoopes, Star Forward.* Berkeley Heights, N.J.: Enslow, 2002.

Whiteside, Kelly. *WNBA: A Celebration: Commemorating the Birth of a League.* New York: HarperHorizon, 1998.

WEBSITES

"Sheryl Swoopes." WNBA.com. Available online at http://www.wnba.com/playerfile/sheryl_swoopes/index.html; website home page: http://www.wnba.com (accessed April 20, 2003).

AUDIO AND VISUAL MEDIA

Carrington; Sisters of glory; Shelter; Sheryl Swoopes. Directed by Beth Engler. Troy, N.Y.: Sage Colleges, 1995, VHS.

Go for the Goal: A Champion's Guide to Winning in Soccer and Life
Guidebook

By: Mia Hamm, with Aaron Heifetz

Date: 1999

Source: Hamm, Mia, with Aaron Heifetz. *Go for the Goal: A Champion's Guide to Winning in Soccer and Life.* New York: HarperCollins, 1999, 64–67, 178–183.

About the Author: Mia Hamm (1972–) was named the U.S. female soccer athlete of the year four straight times. She earned a degree in political science at the University of North Carolina. In 1991, Hamm, one of the team's younger players, led the U.S. Women's Soccer team to a World Cup victory in the world championship. In 1999, Hamm was an important part of the U.S. Women's team that won the World Cup. Lucrative endorsement contracts followed. ■

Introduction

Known as "football" in most of the world, soccer was invented during the nineteenth century in England and, at first, was played mostly by men. The international championship of soccer is the World Cup. The World

Cup was first held in 1930, and is held every four years. The United States, though, generally has been less interested than the rest of the world in soccer, instead favoring American football. Immigrants to America played soccer in the late nineteenth century, but, across the nation, soccer generated less interest than other sports. As early as 1906, professional leagues formed, though most failed quickly. In the 1920s, a league formed that drew forty thousand fans to some matches, however the league folded during the Great Depression. Until the 1960s, most teams founded were ethnic teams, followed by their ethnic communities. In the late 1960s, the North American Soccer League was formed, and it survived (barely) until 1984. In the late 1980s, a number of soccer leagues started and failed—eventually leading to Major League Soccer, which has enjoyed some success.

Women's professional soccer got off to a slow start in the United States. Women's soccer in high school and college received a large boost from Title IX in 1972, which mandated a much greater degree of gender equality in athletics. Colleges began to form female varsity teams in the late 1980s, and interest grew. By 1999, 77 percent of universities offered women's soccer, and the National Collegiate Athletic Association (NCAA) awarded a women's soccer championship. In 1991, the first Women's World Cup was held, and the United States, using former collegiate players, won it. In 1995, a permanent women's national team formed to compete against other women's teams from around the world. The United States won the 1996 Olympics women's gold medal in soccer, as well as the 1999 World Cup. The Women's United Soccer Association (WUSA) was formed as a professional league in 2001, and had been fairly successful before suspending operations in September 2003.

Significance

Women's soccer and the WUSA have been very successful in drawing an increasing number of American fans to the sport. A higher percentage of colleges offer women's soccer (77 percent) than offer men's soccer (70 percent). While seemingly not that significant, it is unusual (and unheard of only thirty years ago) for any sport played by both men and women to have more women's programs than men's. Women's soccer has risen significantly in visibility over the past few years, and female soccer stars are probably better known among the masses in the United States then men's soccer stars—although men's soccer leagues are doing better financially. Most people have heard of Mia Hamm, but few could name a men's soccer star. Indeed, Hamm has been one of soccer's most famous names, and she has earned numerous endorsement contracts. She is also a genuinely talented player, and in *Go for the Goal* she discusses her efforts to build her talents into excellent skills.

Hamm's celebrity has been bolstered by a greater public interest in soccer. In previous years, soccer was seen as a foreign sport, imported into the United States. While soccer has not been fully embraced as an "American" spectator sport, it is accepted widely as an excellent participant sport—as evidenced by the tremendous numbers of youths playing the sport in leagues across America. "Soccer moms," not "baseball moms," became a highly desired demographic group for President Bill Clinton's (served 1993–2001) second presidential campaign. One reason for soccer's popularity is that either sex can play soccer, and the sport is less dependent on height and power for success than other traditional American sports.

Primary Source

Go for the Goal: A Champion's Guide to Winning in Soccer and Life [excerpt]

SYNOPSIS: In these excerpts, Hamm talks about the importance of trapping the ball, and her own struggle to master this extremely important skill. She then lists instances where the ability to trap has been a key factor to a successful game. Finally she discusses the importance of the goalkeeper to the team, as well as her only game at that position.

Trapping: The Ball Is Your Servant

. . . Ever since I started playing, trapping has been something I've had to work on, and to this day I still need improvement. At any position but especially at forward—the position I've played most of my life—the ability to hold the ball is vital to the success of your team. When the ball is passed to you, you must be able to keep control of it, so that your teammates can advance up the field and your team can get more players into the opponent's attacking third. The point is, whether you're intercepting a pass from an opponent, collecting one from your teammate, or just in the right place when the ball squirts out from a swarm of players, you rarely receive a perfect ball. The pass might not have the best pace, it might not be that accurate, or it might be bouncing a bit too much. Plus, you are almost always under pressure from a defender. Being able to bring the ball under control in order to make your next touch an efficient one can mean the difference between having the time to shoot and having your shot stuffed by a defender.

If you watched the 1998 World Cup from France, you were lucky enough to see what might be the ultimate trap, if there is such a thing. In the last minute of the quarterfinal match between Argentina and Holland, with the score 1-1, Frank de Boer hit a long

Mia Hamm celebrates after scoring a goal against Denmark in the early rounds of the 1996 Olympics, July 21, 1996. Hamm and her teammates went on to win the gold medal in women's soccer for the United States that year. AP/WIDE WORLD PHOTOS. REPRODUCED BY PERMISSION.

pass to Holland's star forward, Dennis Bergkamp. Dennis is everything you want in a forward. Strong and fast, he can hold the ball on the forward line and is a great finisher. On this play, Dennis was racing flat out with a defender at his side when the ball reached him. Effortlessly, he brought the ball down in the penalty box with the laces of his right foot and cut it back inside with his next touch, losing his defender in the process. Then, from a sharp angle, he struck a shot with the outside of his right foot, bending it into the far corner past Argentina's goalkeeper, Carlos Roa. Roa was no doubt stunned by the grace and simplicity with which Dennis could make such a difficult play. And to win the game and send his team to the semifinals, no less! The Dutch team swarmed him in a huge dogpile of orange jerseys. What a great soccer moment!

In college I had a similar moment of inspiration. The ball came over my inside shoulder, kind of like the pass to Dennis, and I brought it down out of the air smoothly as I cut at top speed toward the goal. With my next touch I took a shot, but unlike Den-

nis's, it went wide. No dogpile for me. Still, I remember being really surprised that I had even brought the ball under control in that situation. It wasn't something I'd planned, it just happened because of all the years of trapping practice and repetition in training and games. I remember thinking, "That was pretty good!" And I don't think that very often.

Acquiring skills is a process of evolution. When you get really good at the basics, they will become second nature, and one day the game will present you with a difficult ball that you bring under control without thought or trouble—a truly great feeling.

So I went from taking a ball in the gut and scoring to making a brilliant trap and missing the goal. Sometimes that's just how the game of soccer works. Still, the point was made with me. I'll take a great trap over a ball drilled in the 'ol breadbasket anytime, because as you move up the ranks in soccer, you are less likely to get gifts in front of the goal. You will need to be able to control that ball to be effective, to have more fun, and to help your team win. . . .

Goalkeeping: The Last Line of Defense

I know a few things about goalkeepers. First of all, I love to score on them. But what soccer player doesn't? Second, it's the most important position on the field and one of the most difficult. Third, there have been four players in the history of the U.S. Women's National Team who have played goalkeeper in a World Cup game. Mary Harvey played all the games at the 1991 Women's World Cup in China. At the 1995 Women's World Cup in Sweden, we had three players who played in goal: our starter, Briana Scurry; her backup, Saskia Webber—and me.

Yes, it's a little-known fact that I pulled on the gloves in Sweden. Until that time, my goalkeeping experience had been limited to some end-of-practice crossing drills where my teammates took great delight in nailing me with the ball, but I guess I saved a few, because somehow the coaches decided that it was I who should step between the pipes.

It went like this.

We were playing our second Women's World Cup match of the first round at Stromvallen Stadium in a little town called Gavle. We were ahead of Denmark, 2-0, in the waning moments of the game, when the unbelievable happened. Briana picked up a ball in the penalty box with no pressure on her and went to punt it up the field. It was a seemingly innocuous

"Briana Says:"

Courage in goalkeeping is so important. Many aspects of the position require that you stick your head into places most people wouldn't dare. Sometimes you get kicked in places any sane person definitely wouldn't want to get kicked in, but that's just part of the job.

You have to play every game with confidence, and that confidence has to be real, and it has to be evident to those playing with you and against you. You must have an aura about you that says, "Things are under control in *my* penalty box." All your catches must be solid, you must never be indecisive, and you must always rule the air! All good goalkeepers have this presence in the nets.

But no doubt, to be a good keeper, you must be willing to work at it and work hard. Goalkeeper training is physically demanding and very fatiguing. You are constantly hitting the ground, getting back up, and diving again. You must be one of the fittest players on the team. Your training is a bit different from that of the other players, as it is more anaerobic than aerobic, but goalkeepers should take pride in working harder than everyone else. You must still try to be a good long-distance run-

ner like your field-player teammates. Goalkeeping can also be painful, especially when you have Mia Hamm and Michelle Akers shooting at you mercilessly from 12 yards away.

If you get scored on—and every goalkeeper does—you must have the mentality to bounce back right away. Some goalkeepers lose their composure after they let a goal in, but the great ones shake it off because that next save might be the one that wins the game for your team. If you dwell on your mistakes, another ball will be whizzing past your ear before you know it.

Finally, as a goalkeeper, you must take pride in your responsibility to the team as the last defender. Your team must know that they can depend on you. Even on the National Team there are defensive breakdowns, and when the shots do come, your teammates need to know that you will be there to bail them out.

That kind of respect is not given. You have to earn it. The harder you fight for the team, the more ferociously they will battle for you.

SOURCE: Scurry, Briana. "Briana Says." In Hamm, Mia. *Go for the Goal: A Champions Guide to Winning in Soccer and Life*. New York: HarperCollins, 1999, 182–183.

---

play, one we've seen a thousand times before. Well, apparently as she went to punt, she barely stepped over the edge of the penalty box before releasing the ball. The linesman raised his flag, waved it around like they do, and the referee came running over. Usually the referee would just call a hand ball and give Denmark a free kick at the top of the penalty box. This referee, however, decided to interpret the rules a little too literally and gave Briana a red card for intentionally handling the ball even though there was no one near her!

We were all in a state of shock for a few minutes, and then our assistant coach, April Heinrichs, called me over to the sideline. April was the captain of the 1991 Women's World Cup championship team. She put her arm around me and said very calmly, because I'm sure she didn't want to freak me out, "Mia, we've used all our substitutes, and we're going to put you in goal. How do you feel about that?"

It didn't really register fully, and I replied, "Why don't you use a real goalkeeper?" After all, we had two on the bench.

"We've used all our subs," she repeated. And then it dawned on me: We had already used three field players as substitutes! The rules only allow for

three, and I was about to get some on-the-job training in the nets.

The first thought that entered my mind then was that Denmark still had a free kick from 19 yards out and they had a huge sweeper who could really crush the ball. Her name was Kamma Flaeng, and Kamma didn't fool around. Yes, my international goalkeeping debut was to face a free kick about as close to the goal as could be without it being a penalty shot from a woman who would like nothing better than to blast me halfway across the Atlantic.

I really don't remember what I was thinking at the time, but looking back, I realize I wasn't well positioned. I was too far behind the wall instead of shaded toward the open part of the net (that's goalkeeper talk, thank you). Well, wouldn't you know it? Kamma took a big run up and sent the ball sailing over the crossbar. I like to think I would have saved it anyway, but of course, we'll never know!

I ended up touching the ball just twice. I didn't have to make any flying saves. I collected a ball that came bouncing through the defense and punted it as far from goal as I could. For my last touch in goal, I smothered a low-liner off a crossed ball for my one credited save in Women's World Cup play.

Our sweeper, Carla Overbeck, came up to me after the game, and I think her words probably summed up the feeling of the whole team: "You know, Mia, I was pretty confident with you going back there—I mean, you're a good athlete—until I turned around and you looked about the size of a peanut in the goal." I think it was probably then that the defense made a silent pact to not let anyone shoot on me. I'm happy to say they did their job and we escaped with a shutout and the victory.

But even before my brief fling in the different-colored jersey, I had tremendous respect for goal-keepers and what they do. Goalkeepers are defined by how well they handle pressure. Depending on the game, they may not see much action, but then all of a sudden the ball comes flying at them, and their reaction can determine the outcome of the game. If they can make one big save, perhaps their teammates will remember. But if they allow a goal, no one will ever forget.

Further Resources

BOOKS

Christopher, Matt. *On the Field With—Mia Hamm.* Boston: Little, Brown, 1998.

Longman, Jere. *The Girls of Summer: The U.S. Women's Soccer Team and How it Changed the World.* New York: HarperCollins, 2000.

Miller, Marla. *All-American Girls: The U.S. Women's National Soccer Team.* New York: Pocket Books, 1999.

Rutledge, Rachel. *Mia Hamm: Striking Superstar.* Brookfield, Conn.: Millbrook Press, 2000.

Stewart, Mark. *Mia Hamm: Good as Gold.* New York: Children's Press, 1999.

WEBSITES

"Mia Hamm." Soccertimes.com. Available online at http://www .soccertimes.com/usteams/roster/women/hamm.htm; website home page: http://www.soccertimes.com (accessed July 15, 2003).

Mia Hamm Foundation website. Available online at http:// www.miafoundation.org (accessed July 14, 2003).

"US National Team Forward Mia Hamm Talks to Eurosport About Life in the Trenches." Soccer.com. Available online at http://www.soccer.com/euro/features/hamm.html; website home page: http://www.soccer.com (accessed July 16, 2003).

AUDIO AND VISUAL MEDIA

1999 Women's World Cup: Champions of the World. Spring City, Pa.: Reedswain/Trace Videos, 1999, VHS.

USA vs. China: The Final. Spring City, Pa.: Reedswain/Trace Videos, 1999, VHS.

It's Not About the Bike: My Journey Back to Life
Autobiography

By: Lance Armstrong, with Sally Jenkins
Date: 2000
Source: Armstrong, Lance, with Sally Jenkins. *It's Not About the Bike: My Journey Back to Life.* New York: G.P Putnam's Sons, 2000, 228–231, 247–248, 257–258, 260–261, 265.
About the Author: Lance Armstrong (1972–) became a professional triathlete at sixteen. He then was a successful bicycle racer, competing for the United States in the 1992 and 1996 Olympics, before being diagnosed with testicular cancer in 1996. He fought his way back from that disease and became only the second American to win the Tour de France. He has also become the first American to win that event five consecutive times (1999–2003). In 2002, *Sports Illustrated* named Armstrong Sportsman of the Year. ∎

Introduction

Disease and adversity have stricken many athletes in American history. One of the most famous was Lou Gehrig, who played 2,130 baseball games consecutively before amyotrophic lateral sclerosis (ALS) forced him to retire. Gehrig became so associated with the disease that it is now commonly called "Lou Gehrig's disease." Another athlete who had to overcome a great deal of adversity was golf's Ben Hogan, who was nearly killed when a bus hit his car. Hogan suffered a broken collarbone, ankle, rib, and pelvis in the accident. Hogan, however, not only played golf again, he won the U.S. Open only a year and a half later. In the United States considerable emphasis is placed on sports figures being larger than life, so often more focus is given to their triumphs over adversity than equally heroic deeds by others.

The Tour de France started in 1903. Its grueling route—on average it is 3,400 kilometers (2,113 miles) in length including mountainous stages—makes it the top bicycle race in the world. It began with predominately French riders, and the first American did not participate until 1981. The only U.S. biker to win the Tour de France before Lance Armstrong was Greg Lemond—who won in 1986, 1990 and 1991. Lemond accomplished his victories with French teammates.

Lance Armstrong initially became involved in bike races as a triathlete, a competition combining long-distance swimming, biking, and running. The most famous triathalon is in Hawaii, and is called "The Ironman." He enjoyed success as a triathlete, being named "Rookie of the Year" in 1988 by *Triathlete Magazine.* He found that he liked biking best, though, and began training with the U.S. Olympic team. Armstrong became a pro racer in 1992, and he participated in his first Tour de France in 1993, with French teammates. Armstrong's best finish in his first few years of that event was seventh. Armstrong also participated in the 1996 Olympics. Tragedy then soon struck: he was diagnosed with testicular cancer in late 1996.

Armstrong was not given a high chance of survival, and few thought that he would return to racing. Some authors have noted that Armstrong was given a 40 percent chance of survival, but Armstrong himself disclosed that his doctor, at the worst stage, gave him about a 3 percent chance. After recovery and chemotherapy, Armstrong took some time before deciding to return to racing, and he joined the team sponsored by the U.S. Postal Service Team in 1998. Armstrong took a significant pay cut from his previous salary, as few thought that he could win. Armstrong entered the race in 1999, and he discusses feelings throughout the race in this excerpt from his autobiography.

Significance

Armstrong not only won the Tour de France by a large margin in 1999, but he also set a new speed record, averaging 40.726 kph (25.306 mph). Armstrong won with the U.S. Postal Service Team, comprised mostly of Americans. This was truly a victory for America, who, generally, had not done well in bicycle racing. It gained some new fans for the sport, but mostly it earned Americans prestige in an sport traditionally dominated by other countries.

Lance also won the Tour de France in 2000, 2001, and 2002. In 2002, he was named *Sports Illustrated's* Sportsman of the Year. In that article, Lance related his intention to return to the Tour de France in 2003 and to ride in "a couple more" Tours before retiring. On July 27, 2003, Armstrong won his record-tying fifth consecutive Tour de France with a narrow sixty-one-second victory. He immediately announced that he planned to race again in 2004; anticipation quickly began mounting as the world waited to see if he could become the first rider ever to win six consecutive times.

Primary Source

It's Not About the Bike: My Journey Back to Life
[excerpt]

> **SYNOPSIS:** Armstrong first discusses his return to the Tour de France after recovering from cancer, the reaction to him, and how he won the yellow jersey (given to the leader) in the first stage. He then notes rumors accusing him of drug use, and how he won an important time trial, clinching his victory. He closes by noting his feeling as he rode into Paris as the winner, but how surviving cancer was more important than winning the Tour de France.

The Tour

. . . We arrived in Paris for the preliminaries to the Tour, which included a series of medical and drug tests, and mandatory lectures from Tour officials. Each rider was given a Tour "Bible," a guidebook that showed every stage of the course, with profiles of the route and where the feed areas were. We tinkered with our bikes, changing handlebars and making sure our cleats fit the pedals just right. Some riders were more casual than others about the setup of their bikes, but I was particular. The crew called me Mister Millimeter.

In the prerace hype, our U.S. Postal team was considered an outside shot. No one talked about us as having a chance of winning. They talked about Abraham Olano, the reigning world champion. They talked about Michael Boogerd, who had beaten me in the Amstel. They talked about Alexander Zulle of Switzerland and Fernando Escartin of Spain. They talked about who wasn't there, the casualties of the doping investigations. I was a footnote, the heartwarming American cancer survivor. Only one person seemed to think I was capable of it. Shortly before the race began, someone asked Miguel Indurain who he thought had a good chance of winning. Maybe he remembered our conversation in the elevator and knew how I had trained. "Armstrong" was his answer.

The first stage of the Tour was the brief Prologue, a time trial of eight kilometers in Le Puy du Fou, a town with a parchment-colored chateau and a medieval theme park. The Prologue was a seeding system of sorts, to separate out the fast riders from the slow and determine who would ride at the front of the peloton. Although it was only eight kilometers long, it was a serious test with absolutely no margin for error. You had to sprint flat-out, and find maximum efficiency, or you would be behind before you ever started. The riders who wanted to contend in the overall needed to finish among the top three or four.

The course began with a sprint of five kilometers, and then came a big hill, a long suffer-fest of 700 meters—a climb you couldn't afford to do at anything less than all-out. After a sweeping turn, it was a flat sprint to the finish. The course would favor a bullish rider like me, and it had also been perfect for the great Indurain, who had once ridden it in a record time of 8:12.

All told, it should take less than nine minutes. The biggest factor was the hill. You didn't want to spend all your energy in the first 5K sprint, and then die on the hill. Also, there was a strategic decision to be made: should I take the hill with a big

Lance Armstrong and another cyclist ride past the Arc de Triomphe on July 25, 1999. After recovering from cancer, Armstrong is moments away from winning the Tour de France with a record average speed. **AP/WIDE WORLD PHOTOS. REPRODUCED BY PERMISSION.**

chainring, or a smaller one? We debated the matter on and off for two days.

Johan was calm and exacting as he plotted our strategy. He broke the race down into wattages and split times, and gave me precise instructions. He even knew what my heart rate should be over the first sprint: 190.

Riders went off in staggered starts three minutes apart. Reports drifted back from the course. Frankie Andreu, my teammate, sacrificed himself with an experiment when he tried to climb the hill using the big ring. It was the wrong decision. By the

time he reached the top of the hill, he was done, blown. He never recovered.

Olano broke the course record with a time of 8:11. Then Zulle beat that with an 8:07.

It was my turn. When I'm riding well, my body seems almost motionless on the bike with the exception of my legs, which look like automated pistons. From behind in the team car, Johan could see that my shoulders barely swayed, meaning I was wasting no extra energy, everything was going into the bike, pumping it down the road.

In my ear, Johan gave me partial time checks and instructions as I rode.

"You're out of the saddle," Johan said. "Sit down."

I was pushing too hard, not realizing it. I sat down, and focused on execution, on the science and technique of the ride. I had no idea what my overall time was. I just pedaled.

I crossed the finish line. I glanced at the clock.

It read "8:02."

I thought, *That can't be right.*

I looked again. "8:02."

I was the leader of the Tour de France. For the first time in my career, I would wear the yellow jersey, the *maillot jaune,* to distinguish me from the other riders. . . .

I knew there would be consequences for Sestrière—it was almost a tradition that any rider who wore the yellow jersey was subject to drug speculation. But I was taken aback by the improbable nature of the charges in the French press: some reporters actually suggested that chemotherapy had been beneficial to my racing. They speculated that I had been given some mysterious drug during the treatments that was performance-enhancing. Any oncologist in the world, regardless of nationality, had to laugh himself silly at the suggestion.

I didn't understand it. How could anybody think for a second that somehow the cancer treatments had helped me? Maybe no one but a cancer patient understands the severity of the treatment. For three straight months I was given some of the most toxic substances known to man, poisons that ravaged my body daily. I still felt poisoned—and even now, three years after the fact, I feel that my body isn't quite rid of it yet.

I had absolutely nothing to hide, and the drug tests proved it. It was no coincidence that every time Tour officials chose a rider from our team for random drug testing, I was their man. Drug testing was the most demeaning aspect of the Tour: right after I finished a stage I was whisked to an open tent, where I sat in a chair while a doctor wrapped a piece of rubber tubing around my arm, jabbed me with a needle, and drew blood. As I lay there, a battery of photographers flashed their cameras at me. We called the doctors the Vampires. "Here come the Vampires," we'd say. But the drugs tests became my best friend, because they proved I was clean. I had been tested and checked, and retested.

In front of the media, I said, "My life and my illness and my career are open." As far as I was concerned, that should have been the end of it. There was nothing mysterious about my ride at Sestrière: I had worked for it. I was lean, motivated, and prepared. Sestrière was a good climb for me. The gradient suited me, and so did the conditions—cold, wet, and rainy. If there was something unusual in my performance that day, it was the sense of out-of-body effortlessness I rode with—and that I attributed to sheer exultation in being alive to make the climb. But the press didn't back off, and I decided to take a couple of days off from talking to them. . . .

A time trial is a simple matter of one man alone against the clock. The course would require roughly an hour and 15 minutes of riding flat-out over 57 kilometers, a big loop through west-central France, over roads lined with red tiled roofs and farm fields of brown and gold grass, where spectators camped out on couches and lounge chairs. I wouldn't see much of the scenery, though, because I would be in a tight aerodynamic tuck most of the time.

The riders departed in reverse order, which meant I would be last. To prepare, I got on my bike on a stationary roller, and went through all the gears I anticipated using on the course.

While I warmed up, Tyler Hamilton had his go at the distance. His job was to ride as hard and fast as he could, regardless of risk, and send back technical information that might help me. Tyler not only rode it fast, he led for much of the day. Finally, Zulle came in at 1 hour, 8 minutes, and 26 seconds to knock Tyler out of first place.

It was my turn. I shot out of the start area and streaked through the winding streets. Ahead of me was Escartin, who had started three minutes before I did.

My head down, I whirred by him through a stretch of trees and long grass, so focused on my own race that I never even glanced at him.

I had the fastest time at the first two splits. I was going so fast that in the follow car, my mother's head jerked back from the acceleration around the curves.

After the third time check I was still in first place at 50:55. The question was, could I hold the pace on the final portion of the race?

Going into the final six kilometers, I was 20 seconds up over Zulle. But now I started to pay. I paid for mountains, I paid for the undulations, I paid for the flats. I was losing time, and I could feel it. If I beat Zulle, it would be only by a matter of seconds. Through two last, sweeping curves, I stood up. I accelerated around the corners, trying to be careful not to crash, but still taking them as tightly as I could—and almost jumped a curb and went up on the pavement.

I raced along a highway in the final sprint. I bared my teeth, counting, driving. I crossed the line. I checked the time: 1:08:17.

I won by 9 seconds.

I cruised into a gated area, braked, and fell off the bike, bent over double.

I had won the stage, and I had won the Tour de France. I was now assured of it. My closest competitor was Zulle, who trailed in the overall standings by 7 minutes and 37 seconds, an impossible margin to make up on the final stage into Paris. . . .

The final stage, from Arpajon into Paris, is a largely ceremonial ride of 89.2 miles. According to tradition, the peloton would cruise at a leisurely pace, until we saw the Eiffel Tower and reached the Arc de Triomphe, where the U.S. Postal team would ride at the front onto the Champs-Elysées. Then a sprint would begin, and we would race ten laps around a circuit in the center of the city. Finally, there would be a post-race procession, a victory lap.

As we rode toward Paris, I did interviews from my bike and chatted with teammates and friends in the peloton. I even ate an ice-cream cone. The Postal team, as usual, rode in superbly organized fashion. "I don't have to do anything," I said to one TV crew. "It's all my boys."

After a while another crew came by. "I'd like to say Hi to Kelly Davidson, back in Fort Worth, Texas," I said. "This is for you." Kelly is the young cancer fighter who I'd met in the Ride for the Roses, and she and her family had become my close friends.

Finally, we approached the city. I felt a swell of emotion as we rode onto the Champs-Elysées for the first time. The entire avenue was shut down for us, and it was a stunning sight, with hundreds of thousands of spectators lining the avenue of fitted cobblestones and brick. The air was full of air horns and confetti, and bunting hung from every facade. The number of American flags swirling in the crowd stunned me.

Deep in the crowd, someone held up a large cardboard sign. It said "TEXAS."

As we continued to parade down the Champs, it gradually dawned on me that not all of those flags were the Stars and Stripes. Some of those waving pennants, I saw delightedly, were from the Lone Star State.

The ten-lap sprint to the finish was oddly subdued and anticlimactic, a formality during which I simply avoided a last freak crash. And then I crossed the finish line. It was finally tangible and real. I was the winner. . . .

The Cereal Box

The truth is, if you asked me to choose between winning the Tour de France and cancer, I would choose cancer. Odd as it sounds, I would rather have the title of cancer survivor than winner of the Tour, because of what it has done for me as a human being, a man, a husband, a son, and a father.

In those first days after crossing the finish line in Paris I was swept up in a wave of attention, and as I struggled to keep things in perspective, I asked myself why my victory had such a profound effect on people. Maybe it's because illness is universal—we've all been sick, no one is immune—and so my winning the Tour was a symbolic act, proof that you can not only survive cancer, but thrive after it. Maybe, as my friend Phil Knight says, I am hope.

Further Resources

BOOKS

Abt, Samuel, and James D. Startt. *Lance Armstrong's Comeback From Cancer: A Scrapbook of the Tour de France Winner's Dramatic Career.* San Francisco: Poole, 2000.

Armstrong, Lance, and Chris Carmichael. *The Lance Armstrong Performance Program: The Training, Strengthening, and Eating Plan Behind the World's Greatest Cycling Victory.* Emmaus, Penn.: Rodale, 2000.

National Cancer Institute. *What You Need to Know About Testicular Cancer.* Bethesda, Md.: National Institutes of Health, 1992.

Stewart, Mark. *Sweet Victory: Lance Armstrong's Incredible Journey, the Amazing Story of the Greatest Comeback in Sports.* Brookfield, Conn.: Millbrook Press, 2000.

Wilcockson, John, et. al. *The 2001 Tour de France: Lance x 3.* Boulder, Colo.: VeloPress, 2001.

WEBSITES

Lance Armstrong Online. Available online at http://www.lancearmstrong.com (accessed April 20, 2003).

AUDIO AND VISUAL MEDIA

Who Says We Can't Do It? Lance Armstrong's Journey. Cambridge, Mass.: Enterprise Media, 2002, VHS.

Lance Armstrong Racing for His Life. Dirted by Harry Smith and Tom Seligson. New York: A&E Home Video, 2000, VHS.

GENERAL RESOURCES

General

Anderson, Annelise Graebner, and Dennis L Bark. *Thinking About America: The United States in the 1990s*. Stanford, Calif.: Hoover Institution, 1988.

Bezilla, Robert, ed. *America's Youth in the 1990s*. Princeton, N.J.: Gallup International Institute, 1993.

Condon, Judith. *The Nineties*. Austin, Tex.: Raintree Steck-Vaughn, 2000.

Davies, Philip John, and Fredric A. Waldstein, eds. *Political Issues in America Today: The 1990s Revisited*. Manchester, U.K. & New York: Manchester University Press, 1996.

Dolbeare, Kenneth, and Linda J. Metcalf. *American Ideologies Today: Shaping the New Politics of the 1990s*. New York: McGraw-Hill, 1993.

Farley, Reynolds, ed. *State of the Union: America in the 1990s*. New York: Russell Sage Foundation, 1995.

Feldman, Elane. *Fashions of a Decade: The 1990s*. New York: Facts on File, 1992.

Gallagher, John, and Chris Bull. *Perfect Enemies: The Religious Right, the Gay Movement, and the Politics in the 1990s*. New York: Crown, 1996.

Haines, David W., ed. *Case Studies in Diversity: Refugees in America in the 1990s*. Westport, Conn.: Praeger, 1997.

Heath, Daniel, et al., eds. *America in Perspective: Major Trends in the United States Through the 1990s*. Boston: Houghton Mifflin, 1986.

Kallen, Stuart A., ed. *The 1990s*. San Diego: Lucent, 1999.

Kibbey, Ann, et al., eds. *On Your Left: Historical Materialism in the 1990s*. New York: New York University Press, 1996.

Lamis, Alexander P., ed. *Southern Politics in the 1990s*. Baton Rouge: Louisiana State University Press, 1999.

Lightman, Alan P. *Time for the Stars: Astrology in the 1990s*. New York: Viking, 1992.

Newfield, Christopher, and Ronald Strickland, eds. *After Political Correctness: The Humanities and Society in the 1990s*. Boulder, Colo.: Westview Press, 1995.

Wattenberg, Ben. *The First Universal Nation: Leading Indicators and Ideas About the Surge in America in the 1990s*. New York: Free Press, 1991.

Weisberg, Herbert F., and Samuel C. Patterson, eds. *Great Theatre: The American Congress in the 1990s*. Cambridge & New York: Cambridge University Press, 1998.

The Arts

Baker, Russell, et al. *Inventing the Truth: The Art and Craft of Memoir,* rev. ed. New York: Houghton Mifflin, 1998.

Bayles, David, and Ted Orland. *Art & Fear: Observations on the Perils (and Rewards) of Artmaking*. Santa Barbara, Calif.: Capra, 1994.

Bloom, Harold. *The Western Canon: The Books and School of the Ages*. New York: Harcourt Brace, 1994.

Collier, James Lincoln. *Jazz: The American Theme Song*. New York: Oxford University Press, 1993.

Cowan, Louise, and Os Guinness, eds. *Invitation to the Classics*. Grand Rapids, Mich.: Baker Book House, 1998.

Fadiman, Clifton, and John F. Majors. *The New Lifetime Reading Plan*. New York: HarperCollins, 1997.

Haskell, Barbara. *The American Century: Art & Culture, 1900–1950*. New York: Whitney Museum of American Art in association with Norton, 1999.

Hickey, Dave. *Air Guitar: Essays on Art & Democracy*. Los Angeles: Art Issues; New York: Distributed Art Publishers, 1997.

Hughes, Robert. *American Visions: The Epic History of Art in America.* New York: Alfred A. Knopf, 1997.

Kendall, Steven D. *New Jack Cinema: Hollywood's African-American Directors.* Silver Spring, Md.: J.L. Denser, 1994.

Korda, Michael. *Another Life: A Memoir of Other People.* New York: Random House, 1999.

Miller, James. *Flowers in the Dustbin: The Rise of Rock and Roll, 1947–1977.* New York: Simon & Schuster, 1999.

Penman, Ian. *Vital Signs: Music, Movies and Other Manias.* London & New York: Serpent's Tail, 1998.

Petroski, Henry. *The Book on the Bookshelf.* New York: Knopf, 1999.

Phillips, Lisa. *The American Century: Art and Culture 1950–2000.* New York: W.W. Norton & Co., 1999.

Werner, Craig. *A Change Is Gonna Come: Music, Race & the Soul of America.* New York: Plume, 1998.

Zeigler, Joseph Wesley. *Arts in Crisis: The National Endowment for the Arts Versus America.* Pennington, N.J.: A Cappella, 1994.

Business and the Economy

Bach, David. *Smart Women Finish Rich: 7 Steps to Achieving Financial Security and Funding Your Dreams.* New York: Broadway, 1999.

Buckingham, Marcus, and Curt Coffman. *First, Break All the Rules: What the World's Greatest Managers Do Differently.* New York: Simon & Schuster, 1999.

Carroll, Michael C. *A Future of Capitalism: The Economic Vision of Robert Heilbroner.* New York: Macmillan, 1998.

Collins, James C., and Jerry I. Porris. *Built to Last: Successful Habits of Visionary Companies.* New York: HarperBusiness, 1994.

Coyle, Diane. *The Weightless World: Strategies for Managing the Digital Economy.* Cambridge, Mass.: MIT Press, 1998.

Cusumano, Michael A., and David B. Yoffie. *Competing on Internet Time: Lessons From Netscape and Its Battle With Microsoft.* New York: Free Press, 1998.

Davis, Bob, and David Wessel. *Prosperity: The Coming Twenty-Year Boom and What It Means to You.* New York: Times Business, 1998.

Ehrenhalt, Samuel M. *Profile of a Recession: The New York Experience in the Early 1990s.* Albany, N.Y.: Nelson A. Rockefeller Institute of Government, State University of New York, 1992.

Elpel, Thomas J. *Direct Pointing to Real Wealth: Thomas J. Elpel's Field Guide to Money.* Pony, Mont.: HOPS Press, 2000.

Evans, Philip, and Thomas S. Wurster. *Blown to Bits: How the New Economics of Information Transforms Strategy.* Cambridge, Mass: Harvard Business School Press, 2000.

Gates, Bill, and Collins Hemingway. *Business @ the Speed of Thought: Using a Digital Nervous System.* New York: Warner, 1999.

Goldratt, Eliyahu M., and Jeff Cox. *The Goal: A Process of Ongoing Improvement,* rev. ed. Springfield, Mass.: North River, 1992.

Hagstrome, Robert G., Jr. *The Warren Buffet Way: Investment Strategies of the World's Greatest Investor.* New York: Wiley, 1994.

Johnson, Spencer. *Who Moved My Cheese?: An Amazing Way to Deal With Change in Your Work and in Your Life.* New York: Putnam, 1998.

Krugman, Paul. *The Age of Diminished Expectations: U.S. Economic Policy in the 1990s.* Cambridge, Mass.: MIT Press, 1990.

Lynch, Peter, and John Rothchild. *Beating the Street.* New York: Simon & Schuster, 1993.

Madrick, Jeffrey. *The End of Affluence.* New York: Random House, 1997.

Nelson, Bob. *1001 Ways to Reward Employees.* New York: Workman, 1994.

O'Neil, William J. *How to Make Money in Stocks: A Winning System in Good Times or Bad.* New York: McGraw-Hill, 1991.

Orman, Suze. *The Courage to Be Rich: Creating a Life of Material and Spiritual Abundance.* New York: Riverhead, 1999.

———. *The 9 Steps to Financial Freedom.* New York: Crown, 1997.

Petzinger, Thomas, Jr. *The New Pioneers: The Men and Women Who Are Transforming the Workplace and the Marketplace.* New York: Simon & Schuster, 1999.

Senge, Peter M. *The Fifth Discipline: The Art and Practice of the Learning Organization.* New York: Doubleday/Currency, 1994.

Stanley, Thomas J., and William D. Danko. *The Millionaire Next Door: The Surprising Secrets of America's Wealthy.* Atlanta, Ga.: Longstreet, 1996.

Thurow, Lester C. *Building Wealth: The New Rules for Individuals, Companies, and Nations in a Knowledge-Based Economy.* New York: HarperBusiness, 2000.

———. *The Future of Capitalism: How Today's Economic Forces Shape Tomorrow's World.* New York: Penguin Books, 1997.

White, Kate. *Why Good Girls Don't Get Ahead—But Gutsy Girls Do: Nine Secrets Every Career Woman Must Know.* New York: Warner, 1995.

Wolff, Michael. *Burn Rate: How I Survived the Gold Rush Years on the Internet.* New York: Simon & Schuster, 1998.

Websites

"ADM: Who's Next?" Online NewsHour, October 5, 1996. Available online at http://www.pbs.org/newshour/bb/business/october96/adm_10-15.html (accessed July 30, 2003).

"Billion Dollar Disasters." Available online at http://www.disasterrelief.org/Library/WorldDis/wdo1.html (accessed July 30, 2003).

"The Economics of the Microsoft Antitrust Case: A Post-Trial Primer." Available online at http://www.neramicrosoft.com/NeraDocuments/Analyses/aei_paper.htm (accessed July 30, 2003).

"Exports and Imports of Goods and Services, 1980–2010." Available online at http://www.infoplease.com/cgi-bin/id/A0855074.html (accessed July 30, 2003).

"Florida Freezes; West Floods." *Rural Migration News.* Available online at http://migration.ucdavis.edu/rmn/archive_rmn/apr_1997-03rmn.html; website home page: http://migration.ucdavis.edu/rmn/index.html (accessed July 30, 2003).

"Local 34 to Strike Wednesday; Local 35 Waits." *Yale Daily News.* Available online at http://www.yaledailynews.com/article.asp?AID=8201; website home page: http://www.yaledailynews.com (accessed July 30, 2003).

"Minnesota Milestones: Homelessness." Available online at http://www.mnplan.state.mn.us/mm/indicator.html?Id=29&G=32 (accessed July 30, 2003).

"North American Free Trade Agreement." Available online at http://www-tech.mit.edu/Bulletins/nafta.html (accessed July 30, 2003).

"President Clinton: The Largest Budget Surplus and Debt Pay-Down in History." Available online at http://clinton3.nara.gov/WH/Work/102899.html (accessed July 30, 2003).

"UPS Workers Brace for a Long Strike." CNN.com. Available online at http://www.cnn.com/US/9708/13/strikers.cope; website home page: http://www.cnn.com (accessed July 30, 2003).

Education

Alampi, Mary, and Peter M. Comeau, eds. *American Education Annual: Trends and Issues in the Educational Community.* Farmington Hills, Mich.: Gale, 1999.

Bankston, Carl L. *A Troubled Dream: The Promise and Failure of School Desegregation in Louisiana.* Nashville, Tenn.: Vanderbilt University Press, 2002.

Bernhardt, Regis, et al., eds. *Curriculum Leadership: Rethinking Schools for the 21st Century.* Cresskill, N.J.: Hampton, 1998.

Berube, Maurice R. *American School Reform: Progressive, Equality, and Excellence Movements, 1883–1993.* Westport, Conn.: Praeger, 1994.

Biklen, Sari Knopp, and Diane Pollard, eds. *Gender and Education.* Chicago: National Study of School Evaluation, 1993.

Chawla-Duggan, Rita, and Christopher J. Pole, eds. *Reshaping Education in the 1990s: Perspectives on Primary Schooling.* London & Washington, D.C.: Falmer Press, 1996.

Cheney, Lynne V. *Telling the Truth: Why Our Culture and Our Country Have Stopped Making Sense, And What We Can Do About It.* New York: Simon & Schuster, 1995.

Cook, Constance Ewing. *Lobbying for Higher Education: How Colleges and Universities Influence Federal Policy.* Nashville, Tenn.: Vanderbilt University Press, 1998.

Edelman, Marian Wright. *Lanterns: A Memoir of Mentors.* Boston: Beacon, 1999.

———. *Stand for Children.* New York: Hyperion, 1998.

Ehrenhalt, Samuel M. *Public Education: A Major American Growth Industry in the 1990s.* Albany, N.Y.: Nelson A. Rockefeller Institute of Government, 2000.

Ehrlander, Mary F. *Equal Educational Opportunity: Brown's Elusive Mandate.* New York: LFB Scholarly Publishers, 2002.

Epstein, Debbie, ed. *Challenging Lesbian and Gay Inequalities in Education.* Buckingham, U.K. & Philadelphia: Open University Press, 1994.

Higher Education's Landscape: Demographic Issues in the 1990s. New York: College Board Publications, 1995.

Kerr, Clark, Marian L. Gade, and Maureen Kawaoka. *Troubled Times for American Higher Education: The 1990s and Beyond.* Albany, N.Y.: State University of New York Press, 1994.

Koetzsch, Ronald E. *The Parents' Guide to Alternatives in Education.* Boston: Shambhala, 1997.

Kors, Alan Charles, and Harvey A. Silvergate. *The Shadow University: The Betrayal of Liberty on America's Campuses.* New York: Free Press, 1998.

La Morte, Michael W. *School Law: Cases and Concepts.* Boston: Allyn and Bacon, 2001.

Ladd, Helen F., Rosemary Chalk, and Janet S. Hansen, eds. *Equity and Adequacy in Education Finance: Issues and Perspectives.* Washington, D.C.: Committee on Education Finance, Commission on Behavioral and Social Sciences and Education, National Research Council, National Academy Press, 1999.

Levine, David, et al., eds. *Rethinking Schools: An Agenda for Change.* New York: New Press, 1995.

Lowe, Robert, and Barbara Miner, eds. *False Choices: Why School Vouchers Threaten Our Children's Future.* Milwaukee, Wis.: Rethinking Schools, 1993.

Means, Barbara, ed. *Technology and Education Reform: The Reality Behind the Promise.* San Francisco: Jossey-Bass, 1994.

Menand, Louis, ed. *The Future of Academic Freedom.* Chicago: University of Chicago Press, 1996.

Mickelson, Roslyn Arlin, ed. *Children on the Streets of the Americas: Homelessness, Education, and Globalization in the United States, Brazil, and Cuba.* London & New York: Routledge, 2000.

Newfield, Christopher, and Ronald Strickland, eds. *After Political Correctness: The Humanities and Society in the 1990s.* Boulder, Colo.: Westview Press, 1995.

Old, Wendie C. *Marian Wright Edelman: Fighting for Children's Rights.* Springfield, N.J.: Enslow, 1995.

Palestini, Robert H. *Law and American Education: A Case Brief Approach.* Lanham, Md.: Scarecrow Press, 2001.

Parsons, Michael D. *Power and Politics: Federal Higher Education Policy Making in the 1990s.* Albany, N.Y.: State University of New York Press, 1997.

Perry, Theresa, and Lisa Delpit, eds. *The Real Ebonics Debate: Power, Language, and the Education of African-American Children.* Boston: Beacon, 1998.

Pride, Richard A. *The Political Use of Racial Narratives: School Desegregation in Mobile, Alabama, 1954–1997.* Urbana, Ill.: University of Illinois Press, 2002.

Ravitch, Diane, and, Joseph Viteritti, eds. *New Schools for a New Century.* New Haven: Yale University Press, 1997.

Seller, Maxine Schwartz, ed. *Women Educators in the United States, 1820–1993: A Bio-Bibliographical Sourcebook.* Westport, Conn.: Greenwood Press, 1994.

Stegelin, Dolores A., ed. *Early Childhood Education: Policy Issues for the 1990s.* Norwood, N.J.: Ablex, 1992.

Sykes, Charles J. *Dumbing Down Our Kids: Why America's Children Feel Good About Themselves but Can't Read, Write, or Add.* New York: St. Martin's Press, 1995.

Tomlinson, Sally, and Maurice Craft, eds. *Ethnic Relations and Schooling: Policy and Practice in the 1990s.* London & Atlantic Highlands, N.J.: Athlone, 1995.

U.S. Department of Education. *Digest of Education Statistics, 1999.* Washington, D.C.: U.S. Government Printing Office, 1999.

Walling, Donovan R., ed. *At the Threshold of the Millennium.* Bloomington, Ind.: Phi Delta Kappa Educational Foundation, 1995.

Wiggins, Grant, and Jay McTighe. *Understanding by Design.* Alexandria, Va.: Association for Supervision and Curriculum Development, 1998.

Websites

Broadway, Bill. "Few Clear Answers on Commencement Prayers." WashingtonPost.com. Available online at http://www.washingtonpost.com/wp-dyn/articles/A99092-1999 Jun12.html; website home page: http://www.washingtonpost.com (accessed July 30, 2003).

"Evolution and Creationism in Public Education: An In-depth Reading of Public Opinion." People for the American Way Foundation. Available online at http://www.pfaw.org/pfaw/dfiles/file_36.pdf; website home page: http://www.pfaw.org (accessed July 30, 2003).

"History of Indian Education in the U.S." American Indian Education Foundation. Available online at http://www.aief-programs.org/history_facts/history.html#1920; webiste home page: http://www.aiefprograms.org (accessed July 30, 2003).

"Improving America's Schools Act of 1994." Available online at http://lamar.colostate.edu/hillger/laws/schools-94.html (accessed July 30, 2003).

John E. Peloza v. Capistrano Unified School District. Available online at http://www.talkorigins.org/faqs/peloza.html (accessed July 30, 2003).

National Security Education Program. Available online at http://www.ndu.edu/nsep (accessed July 30, 2003).

Native American Languages Act. Available online at http://www.ncela.gwu.edu/miscpubs/stabilize/ii-policy/nala1990.htm (accessed July 30, 2003).

Official Report of Columbine High School Incident. Available online at http://www.cnn.com/SPECIALS/2000/columbine.cd/Pages/TOC.htm (accessed July 30, 2003).

"Religion at School Revisited: Justices to Review Pregame Prayer Ban." WashingtonPost.com. Available online at http://www.washingtonpost.com/wp-dyn/articles/A10791-1999 Nov17.html; website home page: http://www.washingtonpost.com (accessed July 30, 2003).

Rosin, Hanna. "Court Appears to Extend Some School Prayer Boundaries." WashingtonPost.com. Available online at http://www.washingtonpost.com/wp-dyn/articles/A10193-1999Jul 18.html; website home page: http://www.washingtonpost.com (accessed July 30, 2003).

Fashion and Design

Barr, Vilma. *The Illustrated Room: 20th Century of Interior Design Rendering.* Dani Antman, ed. New York: McGraw-Hill, 1997.

The Fashion Book. London: Phaidon, 1998.

Feldman, Elaine. *Fashions of a Decade: The 1990s.* New York and Oxford: Facts On File, 1992.

Jodidio, Philip. *New Forms: Architecture in the 1990s.* Köln, Germany & New York: Taschen, 1997.

Martin, Richard, ed. *Contemporary Fashion.* New York: St. James, 1995.

Mulvey, Kate, and Melissa Richards. *Decades of Beauty.* London: Hamlyn, 1998.

Reid, Aileen. *I.M. Pei.* New York: Crescent Books, 1995.

Stegemeyer, Anne. *Who's Who in Fashion.* New York: Fairchild Publications, 1996.

Government and Politics

Barrilleaux, Ryan J., and Mary E. Stuckey, eds. *Leadership and the Bush Presidency: Prudence or Drift in an Era of Change?* Westport, Conn.: Praeger, 1992.

Bush, George H.W., and Brent Scowcroft. *A World Transformed.* New York: Random House, 1993.

Carter, Dan T. *From George Wallace to Newt Gingrich: Race in the Conservative Counterrevolution 1963–1994.* Baton Rouge: Louisiana State University Press, 1996.

Drew, Elizabeth. *On the Edge: The Clinton Presidency.* New York: Simon & Schuster, 1994.

Friedman, Thomas L. *The Lexus and the Olive Tree.* New York: Farrar, Straus & Giroux, 1999.

Gillespie, Ed, and Bob Schellhas, eds. *Contract With America: The Bold Plan by Rep. Newt Gingrich, Rep. Dick Armey and the House Republicans to Change the Nation.* New York: Times Books, 1994.

Gordon, Michael R., and Bernard E. Trainor. *The General's War: The Inside Story of the Conflict in the Gulf.* Boston: Little, Brown, 1995.

Gross, Martin L. *The Great Whitewater Fiasco: An American Tale of Money, Power, and Politics.* New York: Ballantine, 1994.

Grossman, Mark. *Encyclopedia of the Persian Gulf War.* Santa Barbara, Calif.: ABC-CLIO, 1995.

Kelly, Michael. *Martyr's Day: Chronicle of a Small War.* New York: Random House, 1993.

Patterson, Robert. *Dereliction of Duty: The Eye Witness Account of How Bill Clinton Compromised America's National Security.* Washington, D.C.: Regnery, 2003.

Posner, Richard A. *An Affair of State: The Investigation, Impeachment and Trial of President Clinton.* Cambridge, Mass.: Harvard University Press, 1999.

Renshon, Stanley A. *High Hopes: The Clinton Presidency and the Politics of Ambition.* New York: New York University Press, 1996.

Tiefer, Charles. *The Semi-Sovereign Presidency: The Bush Administration's Strategy for Governing Without Congress.* Boulder, Colo.: Westview Press, 1994.

Walker, Martin. *The President We Deserve: Bill Clinton, His Rise, Falls, and Comebacks.* New York: Crown, 1996.

Will, George F. *The Leveling Wind: Politics, the Culture, and the Other News, 1990–1994.* New York: Viking, 1994.

Woodward, Bob. *The Agenda: Inside the Clinton White House.* New York: Simon & Schuster, 1994.

Law and Justice

Abraham, Henry J. *Justices, Presidents, and Senators: A History of the U.S. Supreme Court Appointments From Washington to Clinton.* Lanham, Md.: Rowman & Littlefield, 1999.

Belsky, Martin H. *The Rehnquist Court: A Retrospective.* New York: Oxford University Press, 2002.

Douglas, John. *Mindhunter: Inside the FBI's Elite Serial Crime Unit.* New York: Pocket Books, 1996.

Hall, Kermit L., ed. *The Oxford Companion to the Supreme Court.* New York: Oxford University Press, 1992.

Harrison, Maureen, and Steve Gilbert, eds. *Landmark Decisions of the United States Supreme Court II.* Beverly Hills: Excellent Books, 1992.

Hill, Anita. *Speaking Truth to Power.* New York: Doubleday, 1997.

Kelly, Alfred H., Winfred A. Harbison, and Herman Belz. *The American Constitution: Its Origins and Development–Vol. II,* 7th ed. New York: Norton, 1991.

Klier, Barbara, Nancy R. Jacobs, and Jacquelyn Quiram. *Gun Control: Restricting Rights or Protecting People?* Wylie, Tex.: Information Plus, 1999.

Landes, Alison, ed. *Death & Dying—Who Decides?* Wylie, Tex: Information Plus, 1996.

Lawrence, Richard, and Christopher Lawrence. *School Crime and Juvenile Justice.* New York: Oxford University Press, 1997.

Mikula, Mark F., and Mabunda L. Mpho, eds. *Great American Court Cases.* Farmington Hills, Mich.: Gale Group, 2000.

Palmer, Kris E., ed. *Constitutional Amendments: 1789 to the Present.* Farmington Hills, Mich.: Gale Group, 2000.

Posner, Richard A. *An Affair of State: The Investigation, Impeachment, and Trial of President Clinton.* Boston: Harvard University Press, 2000.

Sifakis, Carl. *The Encyclopedia of American Crime.* New York: Facts On File, 2002.

West's Encyclopedia of American Law, 2d ed. 12 vols. St. Paul, Minn.: West Publishing Co., 1998.

Websites

"Los Angeles Police Officers' (Rodney King Beating) Trials." Available http://www.law.umkc.edu/faculty/projects/ftrials/lapd/lapd.html (accessed April 20, 2003).

"The O.J. Simpson Trial." Available online at http://www.law.umkc.edu/faculty/projects/ftrials/Simpson/simpson.htm (accessed April 20, 2003).

Oyez: U.S. Supreme Court Multimedia. Available online at http://www.oyez.com (accessed April 20, 2003).

"The Presidents of the United States." Available online at http://www.whitehouse.gov/history/presidents (accessed April 20, 2003).

U.S. Supreme Court Opinions. Available online at http://www.findlaw.com/casecode/supreme.html (accessed March 16, 2003).

Lifestyles and Social Trends

Berman, Morris. *The Twilight of American Culture.* New York: Norton, 2000.

Blakely, Edward J., and Mary Gail Snyder. *Fortress America: Gated Communities in the United States.* Washington, D.C.: Brookings Institution, 1997.

Borstelmann, Thomas. *The Cold War and the Color Line: American Race Relations in the Global Arena.* Cambridge, Mass.: Harvard University Press, 2001.

Brooks, David. *Bobos in Paradise: The New Upper Class and How They Got There.* New York: Simon & Schuster, 2000.

Chideya, Farai. *The Color of Our Future.* New York: Morrow, 1999.

Clausen, Christopher. *Faded Mosaic: The Emergence of Post-Cultural America.* Chicago: Ivan R. Dee, 2000.

Coontz, Stephanie. *The Way We Really Are: Coming To Terms With America's Changing Families.* New York: Basic Books, 1997.

Covey, Stephen R. *The 7 Habits of Highly Effective Families: Building a Beautiful Family Culture in a Turbulent World.* New York: Golden, 1997.

Diaz, Tom. *Making A Killing: The Business of Guns in America.* New York: New Press, 1999.

Fairclough, Adam. *Better Day Coming: Blacks and Equality, 1890–2000.* New York: Viking, 2001.

Faludi, Susan. *Stiffed: The Betrayal of the American Man.* New York: Morrow, 1999.

Fox-Genovese, Elizabeth. *Feminism Is Not the Story of My Life: How Today's Feminist Elite Has Lost Touch With the Real Concerns of Women.* New York: Nan A. Talese, 1996.

Gaslin, Glenn, and Rick Porter. *The Complete, Cross-Referenced Guide to the Baby Buster Generation's Collective Unconscious.* New York: Boulevard Books, 1998.

Gerstmann, Evan. *The Constitutional Underclass: Gays, Lesbians and the Failure of the Class-Based Equal Protection.* Chicago: University of Chicago Press, 1999.

Gross, Michael. *My Generation: Fifty Years of Sex, Drugs, Rock, Revolution, Glamour, Greed, Valor, Faith, and Silicon Chips.* New York: Cliff Street Books, 2000.

Hersch, Patricia. *A Tribe Apart: A Journey into the Heart of American Adolescence.* New York: Fawcett Columbine, 1998.

Hutchinson, Earl Ofari. *Beyond O.J.: Race, Sex, and Class Lessons for America.* Los Angeles: Middle Passage, 1996.

Jennings, Peter. *In Search of America.* New York: Hyperion, 2002.

Kallen, Stuart A., ed. *The 1990s*. San Diego: Greenhaven Press, 2000.

Kitwana, Bakari. *The Hip Hop Generation: Young Blacks and the Crisis in African American Culture*. New York: Basic Civitas, 2002.

Kozol, Jonathan. *Amazing Grace: The Lives of Children and the Conscience of a Nation*. New York: Crown, 1995.

LaPierre, Wayne R. *Guns, Crime, and Freedom*. Washington, D.C.: Regnery, 1994.

Lerner, Michael. *The Politics of Meaning: Restoring Hope and Possibility in an Age of Cynicism*. New York: Addison-Wesley, 1996.

Nava, Michael, and Robert Dawidoff. *Created Equal: Why Gay Rights Matter to America*. New York: St. Martin's Press, 1994.

Queenan, Joe. *Balsamic Dreams: A Short But Self-Important History of the Baby Boomer Generation*. New York: Henry Holt, 2001.

Rosenblatt, Roger, ed. *Consuming Desires: Consumption, Culture, and the Pursuit of Happiness*. Washington, D.C.: Island Press, 1999.

Scambler, Graham, and Annette Scambler, eds. *Rethinking Prostitution: Purchasing Sex in the 1990s*. London & New York: Routledge, 1997.

Sowell, Thomas. *Barbarians Inside the Gates—And Other Controversial Essays*. Stanford, Calif.: Hoover Institution Press, 1999.

Steele, Shelby. *A Dream Deferred: The Second Betrayal of Black Freedom in America*. New York: HarperCollins, 1998.

Tuch, Steven A., and Jack K. Martin, eds. *Racial Attitudes in the 1990s: Continuity and Change*. New York: Praeger, 1997.

Weiss, Michael J. *The Clustered World: How We Live, What We Buy, and What It All Means About Who We Are*. Boston: Little, Brown, 2000.

Websites

1990s General Images. Authentic History Center. Available online at http://www.authentichistory.com/images/1990s/general_1990s/1990s_images_01.html; website home page: http://www.authentichistory.com (accessed April 28, 2003).

"American Cultural History, 1990–1999." Available online at http://kclibrary.nhmccd.edu/decade90.html (accessed April 28, 2003).

"Chronology of the Equal Rights Amendment, 1923–1996." National Organization for Women. Available online at http://www.now.org/issues/economic/cea/history.html; website home page: http://www.now.org (accessed April 28, 2003).

"The Clinton Years." CNN.com. Available online at http://www.cnn.com/SPECIALS/2001/clinton/timelines/timelines.html; website home page: http://www.cnn.com (accessed April 28, 2003).

InThe90s. Available online at http://www.inthe90s.com/index.shtml (accessed April 28, 2003).

"Official Report of Columbine Incident." CNN.com. Available online at http://www.cnn.com/SPECIALS/2000/columbine.cd/frameset.exclude.html; website home page: http://www.cnn.com (accessed April 28, 2003).

"The O.J. Simpson Trial." Available online at http://www.law.umkc.edu/faculty/projects/ftrials/Simpson/simpson.htm (accessed April 28, 2003).

"Oklahoma City Tragedy." CNN.com. Available online at http://www.cnn.com/US/OKC/index.html; website home page: http://www.cnn.com (accessed April 28, 2003).

Origin of a Browser: The Netscape Museum. Available online at http://www.hnehosting.com/mirrors/Origin_of_a_Browser (accessed April 28, 2003).

"The Two Nations of Black America." Available online at http://www.pbs.org/wgbh/pages/frontline/shows/race (accessed April 28, 2003).

The Media

Andersen, Robin. *Consumer Culture and TV Programming*. Boulder, Colo.: Westview Press, 1995.

Ansolabehere, Stephen, Roy Behr, and Shanto Iyengar. *The Media Game: American Politics in the Television Age*. New York: Macmillan, 1993.

Anuff, Joey, and Ana Marie Cox, eds. *Suck: Worst-case Scenarios in Media, Culture, Advertising, and the Internet*. San Francisco: Wired, 1997.

Brinkley, David. *Everyone Is Entitled To My Opinion*. New York: Ballantine Books, 1997.

Brunsdon, Charlotte, Julie D'Acci, and Lynn Spigel. *Film and Politics in America: A Social Tradition*. New York: Oxford University Press, 1997.

Chiasson, Lloyd, Jr., ed. *The Press in Times of Crisis*. Westport, Conn.: Greenwood Press, 1995.

Collins, Jim, ed. *High-Pop: Making Culture into Popular Entertainment*. Malden, Mass.: Blackwell Publishers, 2002.

Crouch, Stanley. *Always In Pursuit: Fresh American Perspectives, 1995–1997*. New York: Pantheon Books, 1998.

Crossen, Cynthia. *Tainted Truth: The Manipulation of Fact in America*. New York: Simon & Schuster, 1994.

Doreski, C.K. *Writing America Black: Race Rhetoric in the Public Sphere*. Cambridge & New York: Cambridge University Press, 1998.

Douglas, Susan J. *Listening In: Radio and the American Imagination, From Amos 'n' Andy and Edward R. Murrow to Wolfman Jack and Howard Stern*. New York: Times Books, 1999.

———. *Where the Girls Are: Growing Up Female With the Mass Media*. New York: Times Books, 1994.

Dow, Bonnie J. *Prime-time Feminism: Television, Media Culture, and the Women's Movement Since 1970*. Philadelphia: University of Pennsylvania Press, 1996.

Drucker, Susan J., and Robert S. Cathcart. *American Heroes in a Media Age*. Cresskill, N.J.: Hampton Press, 1994.

Ebo, Bosah, ed. *Cyberghetto or Cybertopia: Race, Class, and Gender on the Internet*. Westport, Conn.: Praeger, 1998.

Ettema, James S. and D. Charles Whitney. *Audiencemaking: How the Media Create the Audience*. Thousand Oaks, Calif.: Sage Publications, 1994.

Fallows, James. *Breaking the News: How the Media Undermine American Democracy*. New York: Pantheon, 1996.

Ferguson, Robert. *Representing "Race": Ideology, Identity and the Media.* London & New York: Arnold, 1998.

Fineman, Martha A., and Martha T. McCluskey, eds. *Feminism, Media, and the Law.* New York: Oxford University Press, 1997.

Foege, Alec. *The Empire God Built: Inside Pat Robertson's Media Machine.* New York: John Wiley, 1996.

Foerstel, Herbert N. *Banned in the Media: A Reference Guide to Censorship in the Press, Motion Pictures, Broadcasting, and the Internet.* Westport, Conn.: Greenwood Press, 1998.

Folkerts, Jean, and Dwight L. Teeter Jr. *Voices of a Nation: A History of Mass Media in the United States.* New York: Macmillan, 1994.

Gabriel, John. *Whitewash: Racialized Politics and the Media.* London & New York: Routledge, 1998.

Greenwald, Marilyn, and Joseph Bernt, eds. *The Big Chill: Investigative Reporting in the Current Media Environment.* Ames: Iowa State University Press, 2000.

Gripsrud, Jostein. *The Dynasty Years: Hollywood Television and Critical Media Studies.* London & New York: Routledge, 1995.

Gross, Larry, and James D. Woods, eds. *The Columbia Reader on Lesbians and Gay Men in Media, Society, and Politics.* New York: Columbia University Press, 1999.

Grossberg, Lawrence, Ellen Wartella, and Whitney, D. Charles. *Mediamaking: Mass Media in a Popular Culture.* Thousand Oaks, Calif.: Sage Publications, 1998.

Hamlet, Janice D., ed. *Afrocentric Visions: Studies in Culture and Communication.* Thousand Oaks, Calif.: Sage Publications, 1998.

Hartley, John. *Popular Reality: Journalism, Modernity, Popular Culture.* London & New York: Arnold, 1996.

Johnson, Haynes, and James M. Perry. *Contemporary Views of American Journalism.* Chestertown, Md.: Literary House Press at Washington College, 1993.

Juhasz, Alexandra. *AIDS TV: Identity, Community, and Alternative Video.* Durham, N.C.: Duke University Press, 1995.

Kamalipour, Yahya R., and Theresa Carilli, eds. *Cultural Diversity and the U.S. Media.* Albany, N.Y.: State University of New York Press, 1998.

Kiesler, Sara, ed. *Culture of the Internet.* Mahwah, N.J.: Lawrence Erlbaum Associates, 1997.

Koppel, Ted. *Off Camera: Private Thoughts Made Public.* New York: Knopf, 2000.

Kounalakis, Markos, Drew Banks, and Kim Daus. *Beyond Spin: The Power of Strategic Corporate Journalism.* San Francisco: Jossey-Bass, 1999.

Kraus, Elisabeth and Carolin Auer. *Simulacrum America: The USA and the Popular Media.* Rochester, N.Y.: Camden House, 2000.

Kurtz, Howard. *Media Circus: The Trouble With America's Newspapers.* New York: Times Books, 1993.

Leslie, Paul, ed. *The Gulf War as Popular Entertainment: An Analysis of the Military-Industrial Media Complex.* Lewiston, N.Y.: Mellen, 1997.

Lewis, Lisa A., ed. *The Adoring Audience: Fan Culture and Popular Media.* London & New York: Routledge, 1992.

Lipschultz, Jeremy Harris. *Free Expression in the Age of the Internet: Social and Legal Boundaries.* Boulder, Colo.: Westview Press, 2000.

Lull, James, and Stephen Hinerman, eds. *Media Scandals: Morality and Desire in the Popular Culture Marketplace.* New York: Columbia University Press, 1997.

Mermin, Jonathan. *Debating War and Peace: Media Coverage of U.S. Intervention in the Post-Vietnam Era.* Princeton, N.J.: Princeton University Press, 1999.

Moeller, Susan D. *Compassion Fatigue: How the Media Sell Disease, Famine, War, and Death.* New York: Routledge, 1999.

Munson, Wayne. *All Talk: The Talkshow in Media Culture.* Philadelphia: Temple University Press, 1993.

Paletz, David L. *The Media in American Politics: Contents and Consequences.* New York: Longman, 1998.

Rather, Dan. *Deadlines and Datelines.* New York: Morrow, 1999.

Remnick, David, ed. *The New Gilded Age: The New Yorker Looks at the Culture of Affluence.* New York: Random House, 2000.

Rodriguez, Clara E. *Latin Looks: Images of Latinas and Latinos in the U.S. Media.* Boulder, Colo.: Westview Press, 1997.

Ross, Karen. *Black and White Media: Black Images in Popular Film and Television.* Cambridge, Mass.: Polity, 1996.

Rushkoff, Douglas. *Media Virus!: Hidden Agendas in Popular Culture.* New York: Ballantine, 1994.

Shawcross, William. *Murdoch: The Making of a Media Empire,* rev. ed. New York: Simon & Schuster, 1997.

Sloan, William David, and Emily Erickson Hoff, eds. *Contemporary Media Issues.* Northport, Ala.: Vision Press, 1998.

Smith, Erna. *Transmitting Race: The Los Angeles Riot in Television News.* Cambridge, Mass.: Harvard University Press, 1994.

Solomon, Norman, and Jeff Cohen. *Wizards of Media Oz: Behind the Curtain of Mainstream News.* Monroe, Maine: Common Courage Press, 1997.

Sommerville, C. John. *How the News Makes Us Dumb: The Death of Wisdom in an Information Society.* Downers Grove, Ill.: InterVarsity Press, 1999.

Stark, Steven D. *Glued to the Set: The 60 Television Shows and Events That Made Us Who We Are Today.* New York: Free Press, 1997.

Torres, Sasha, ed. *Living Color: Race and Television in the United States.* Durham, N.C.: Duke University Press, 1998.

van Dijk, Teun A. *Racism and the Press.* London & New York: Routledge, 1991.

Willis, Jim. *The Age of Multimedia and Turbonews.* Westport, Conn.: Praeger, 1994.

Woodhull, Nancy J., and Robert W. Snyder. *Media Mergers.* New Brunswick, N.J.: Transaction Publishers, 1998.

Websites

"The 1980s and 1990s on CNN" (CNN Video Almanac). Available online at http://www.cnn.com/resources/video.almanac/ (accessed April 28, 2003).

"1990s News." Available online at http://www.authentichistory.com/audio/1990s/1990s_news_01.html; website homepage: http://www.authentichistory.com/ (accessed April 28, 2003).

"Lines in the Sand." Available online at: http://lcweb.loc.gov/rr/print/swann/herblock/sand.html; website homepage: http://www.loc.gov/rr/print/swann/herblock/ (accessed April 28, 2003).

Medicine and Health

Atkins, Robert C. *Dr. Atkins' New Diet Revolution.* New York: Evans, 1996.

Bender, Arnold E. *A Dictionary of Food and Nutrition.* NewYork: Oxford University Press, 1995.

Duffy, John. *From Humors to Medical Science: A History of American Medicine.* Urbana: University of Illinois Press, 1993.

Fumento, Michael. *The Myth of Heterosexual AIDS.* New York: Basic Books, 1990.

Golub, Edward S. *The Limits of Medicine: How Science Shapes Our Hope for the Cure.* New York: Times Books, 1994.

Haiken, Elizabeth. *Venus Envy: A History of Cosmetic Surgery.* Baltimore: Johns Hopkins University Press, 1997.

Hannaway, Caroline, Victoria A.Harden, and John Parascandola, eds. *AIDS and the Public Debate: Historical and Contemporary Perspectives.* Amsterdam & Washington, D.C.: IOS Press, 1995.

Howell, Joel D. *Technology in the Hospital: Transforming Patient Care in the Early Twentieth Century.* Baltimore: Johns Hopkins University Press, 1995.

Kraut, Alan M. *Silent Travelers: Germs, Genes, and the "Immigrant Menace."* New York: BasicBooks, 1994.

Kubler-Ross, Elisabeth, and David Kessler. *Life Lessons: Two Experts on Death and Dying Teach Us About the Mysteries of Life and Living.* New York: Scribner, 2000.

Mental Health: A Report of the Surgeon General. Rockville, Md.: U.S. Public Health Service, 1999.

Ott, Katherine. *Fevered Lives: Tuberculosis in American Culture since 1870.* Cambridge, Mass.: Harvard University Press, 1996.

Professional Guide to Diseases. 6th ed. Springhouse, Pa.: Springhouse, 1998.

Raymond, Janice G., Renate Klein, and Lynette J. Dumble. *RU 486: Misconceptions, Myths, and Morals.* Cambridge, Mass: Institute on Women and Technology, 1991.

Rhodes, Richard. *Deadly Feasts: Tracking the Secrets of a Terrifying New Plague.* New York: Simon & Schuster, 1997.

Rosen, George. *A History of Public Health.* Baltimore: Johns Hopkins University Press, 1993.

Rosenberg, Charles E. *Explaining Epidemics and Other Studies in the History of Medicine.* Cambridge & New York: Cambridge University Press, 1992.

Rosenberg, Charles E., and Golden, Janet, eds. *Framing Disease: Studies in Cultural History.* New Brunswick, N.J.: Rutgers University Press, 1992.

Rothman, David J. *Strangers at the Bedside: A History of How Law and Bioethics Transformed Medical Decision Making.* New York: BasicBooks, 1991.

Rothman, Sheila M. *Living in the Shadow of Death: Tuberculosis and the Social Experience of Illness in American History.* New York: BasicBooks, 1994.

Rowe John W., and Robert L. Kahn. *Successful Aging.* New York: Pantheon Books, 1998.

Samuels, Sarah E., and Mark D. Smith. *Norplant and Poor Women: Dimensions of New Contraceptives.* Menlo Park, Calif.: Henry J. Kaiser Family Foundation, 1992.

Tomes, Nancy. *The Gospel of Germs: Men, Women, and the Microbe in American Life.* Cambridge, Mass.: Harvard University Press, 1998.

United States Presidential Advisory Committee on Gulf War Veterans' Illnesses, *Presidential Advisory Committee on Gulf War Veterans' Illnesses: Final Report.* Washington, D.C.: Government Printing Office, 1996.

Websites

Frontline: The Kevorkian Verdict. Available online at http://www.pbs.org/wgbh/pages/frontline/kevorkian (accessed April 28, 2003).

The History of Medicine: 1966–Present. Available online at http://www.medhelpnet.com/medhist10.html (accessed April 23, 2003).

Mammography—History of the Mammography. Available online at http://www.gemedicalsystems,com/rad/whc/mswhhis.html (accessed April 28, 2003).

Medicine and Madison Avenue—Timeline. Available online at http://scriptorium.lib.duke.edu/mma/timeline.html (accessed April 28, 2003).

National Health Security Plan Table of Contents. Available online at http://www.ibiblio.org/nhs/NHS-T-o-C.html (accessed April 28, 2003).

Norplant. Available online at http://www.csua.berkeley.edu/monac/norplant.html (accessed April 28, 2003).

The Official Mad Cow Disease Home Page. Available online at http://www.mad-cow.org (accessed April 28, 2003).

Online NewsHour: Hong Kong Flu—December 16, 1997. Available online at http://www.pbs.org/newshour/bb/health/july-dec97/flu_12-16.html (accessed April 28, 2003).

Partial Birth Abortions—All Sides of the Issue. Available online at http://www.religioustolerance.org/abo_pba.htm (accessed April 28, 2003).

RU-486: The Abortion Pill. Available online at http://www.cbctrust.com/RU486.96.html (accessed April 28, 2003).

Surgeon General's Reports on Smoking and Health, 1964–2001. Available online at http://govpubs.lib.umn.edu/guides/surgeongeneral.phtml (accessed April 28, 2003).

United States Cancer Mortality From 1900 to 1992. Available online at http://www.healthsentinel.com/Vaccines/DiseaseAndRelatedData_files/she (accessed April 28, 2003).

Religion

Armstrong, Karen. *A History of God: The 4000-Year Quest of Judaism, Christianity, and Islam.* New York: Knopf, 1993.

The Book of J, translated by David Rosenberg, interpreted by Harold Bloom. New York: Grove-Weidenfield, 1990.

Brown, Raymond E. *The Death of the Messiah: From Gethsemane to the Grave: A Commentary on the Passion Narratives in the Four Gospels.* New York: Doubleday, 1994.

Bstan-'dzin-rgya-mtsho, the Dalai Lama XIV. *Ethics for a New Millennium.* New York: Riverhead, 1999.

Dietrich, Donald J. *God and Humanity in Auschwitz: Jewish-Christian Relations and Sanctioned Murder.* New Brunswick, N.J.: Transaction Publishers, 1995.

Drosnin, Michael. *The Bible Code.* New York: Simon & Schuster, 1997.

Foltin, Richard T. *Religious Liberty in the 1990s: The Religion Clauses Under the Rehnquist Court: A Consultation.* New York: American Jewish Committee, 1994.

Friedman, Richard Elliott, trans. *The Hidden Book in the Bible.* San Francisco: HarperSanFrancisco, 1998.

Funk, Robert W., Roy W. Hoover, and the Jesus Seminar, eds. *The Five Gospels: The Search for the Authentic Words of Jesus: New Translation and Commentary.* New York: Macmillan, 1993.

Hoge, Dean R., et al. *Vanishing Boundaries: The Religion of Mainline Protestant Baby Boomers.* Louisville, Ky.: Westminster/John Knox Press, 1994.

Johnson, Luke Timothy. *The Real Jesus: The Misguided Quest for the Historical Jesus and the Truth of the Traditional Gospels.* San Francisco: HarperSanFrancisco, 1996.

Jurgensmeyer, Mark. *Terror in the Mind of God: The Global Rise of Religious Violence.* Berkeley: University of California Press, 2000.

Kamenetz, Rodger. *Stalking Elijah: Adventures With Today's Jewish Mystical Masters.* San Francisco: HarperSanFrancisco, 1997.

Morreale, Don, ed. *The Complete Guide to Buddhist America.* Boston: Shambhala Publishers, 1998.

Moyers, Bill. *Genesis: A Living Conversation.* New York: Doubleday, 1996.

Nayang, Sulayman S. *Islam in the United States of America.* Chicago: Kazi Publishers, 1999.

Norris, Kathleen. *Amazing Grace: A Vocabulary of Faith.* New York: Riverhead, 1998.

Perry, Bruce. *Malcolm: The Life of a Man Who Changed Black America.* New York: Talman, 1991.

Reed, Ralph. *Politically Incorrect: The Emerging Faith Factor in American Politics.* Dallas: Word Publishers, 1994.

Warner, Michael. *American Sermons: The Pilgrims to Martin Luther King Jr.* New York: Library of America, 1999.

Wertheimer, Jack. *A People Divided: Judaism in Contemporary America.* New York: Basic, 1993.

Science and Technology

Berners-Lee, Tim, and Mark Fischetti. *Weaving the Web: The Original Design and Ultimate Destiny of the World Wide Web by Its Inventor.* San Francisco: HarperSanFrancisco, 1999.

Bishop, Jerry E., and Michael Waldholz. *Genome: The Story of the Most Astonishing Scientific Adventure of Our Time—The Attempt to Map All the Genes in the Human Body.* New York: Simon & Schuster, 1990.

Dyson, Esther. *Release 2.0: A Design for Living in the Digital Age.* New York: Broadway Books, 1997.

Eldredge, Niles. *Life in the Balance: Humanity and the Biodiversity Crisis.* Princeton: Princeton University Press, 1998.

Ferris, Timothy. *The Whole Shebang: A State-of-the-Universe(s) Report.* New York: Simon & Schuster, 1997.

Gates, Bill, with Nathan Myhrvold, and Peter Rinearson. *The Road Ahead.* New York: Viking, 1995.

Gleick, James. *Faster: The Acceleration of Just About Everything.* New York: Pantheon, 1999.

Gold, Thomas. *The Deep Hot Biosphere.* New York: Copernicus, 1999.

Gould, Stephen Jay. *Bully for Brontosaurus: Reflections in Natural History.* New York: Norton, 1991.

———. *Dinosaur in a Haystack: Reflections in Natural History.* New York: Harmony, 1995.

———. *Eight Little Piggies: Reflections in Natural History.* New York: Norton, 1993.

———. *Full House: The Spread of Excellence From Plato to Darwin.* New York: Harmony, 1996.

———. *Leonardo's Mountain of Clams and the Diet of Worms: Essays on Natural History.* New York: Harmony, 1998.

Greene, Brian. *The Elegant Universe.* New York: Vintage Books, 2000.

Hawking, Stephen. *Black Holes and Baby Universes and Other Essays.* New York: Bantam, 1993.

Horgan, John. *The End of Science: Facing the Limits of Knowledge in the Twilight of the Scientific Age.* Reading, Mass.: Addison-Wesley, 1996.

Hyatt, Michael S. *The Millennium Bug: How to Survive the Coming Chaos.* Washington, D.C.: Regnery, 1998.

Kauffman, Stuart. *At Home in the Universe: The Search for Laws of Self-Organization and Complexity.* New York: Oxford University Press, 1995.

Kurzwiel, Ray. *The Age of Spiritual Machines: When Computers Exceed Human Intelligence.* New York: Viking, 1999.

Lemonick, Michael D. *Other Worlds: The Search for Life in the Universe.* New York: Simon & Schuster, 1998.

Lewin, Roger. *Principles of Evolution: A Core Textbook.* Malden, Mass: Blackwell Science, 1998.

Maddox, John. *What Remains to Be Discovered: Mapping the Secrets of the Universe, the Origins of Life, and the Future of the Human Race.* New York: Martin Kessler, 1998.

Mullis, Kary. *Dancing Naked in the Mind Field.* New York: Pantheon, 1998.

Negroponte, Nicholas. *Being Digital.* New York: Knopf, 1995.

Rheingold, Howard. *Tools for Thought: The History and Future of Mind-Expanding Technology.* Cambridge, Mass.: MIT Press, 2000.

———. *The Virtual Community*. New York: Oxford University Press, 1994.

Rifkin, Jeremy. *The Biotech Century: Harnessing the Gene and Remaking the World*. New York: Jeremy P. Tarcher/Putnam, 1998.

Stephenson, Neal. *Cryptonomicon*. New York: Avon, 1999.

———. *The Diamond Age, Or, A Young Lady's Illustrated Primer*. New York: Bantam, 1995.

———. *Snow Crash*. New York: Bantam, 1992.

Stoll, Clifford. *Silicon Snake Oil: Second Thoughts on the Information Highway*. New York: Doubleday, 1995.

Talbott, Stephen L. *The Future Does Not Compute: Transcending the Machines in Our Midst*. Sebastopol, Calif.: O'Reilly & Associates, 1995.

Turkle, Sherry. *Life on the Screen: Identity in the Age of the Internet*. New York: Simon & Schuster, 1995.

Websites

"Bt Corn: What It Is and How It Works." Available online at http://www.uky.edu/Agriculture/Entomology/entfacts/fldcrops/efl30.htm (accessed April 28, 2003).

"Chess, Deep Blue, Kasparov and Intelligence." Available online at http://www.rci.rutgers.edu/cfs/472_html/Intro/Chess Contents.html (accessed April 28, 2003).

"Hubble Site—Gallery." Available online at http://hubblesite.org/gallery (accessed April 28, 2003).

"Human Cloning: The How to Page." Available online at http://www.biofact.com/cloning/human.html (accessed April 28, 2003).

Kramer, Dave. "A Brief History of Microsoft on the Web." Available online at http://www.microsoft.com/misc/features/features_flshbk.htm (accessed April 28, 2003).

"NASA: Mars Pathfinder Science Results." Available online at http://science.ksc.nasa.gov/mars/science/geology.html (accessed April 28, 2003).

National Center for Biotechnology Information. Available online at http://ncbi.nlm.nih.gov (accessed April 28, 2003).

"Neanderthal DNA." Available online at http://www.cs.unc.edu/plaisted/ce/neanderthal.html (accessed April 28, 2003).

"The Science of Crime: We're Going to Talk About Forensic Science and Mention the O.J. Simpson Trial Just This Once!" Available online at http://whyfiles.org/014forensic (accessed April 28, 2003).

The World Wide Web History Project. Available online at http://www.webhistory.org/home.html (accessed April 28, 2003).

Sports

Aaseng, Nathan. *Barry Sanders: Star Running Back*. Hillside, N.J.: Enslow, 1994.

Albert, Marv, and Rick Reilly. *I'd Love to But I Have a Game: 27 Years Without a Life*. New York: Doubleday, 1993.

Benedict, Jeff, and Dan Yaeger. *Pros and Cons: The Criminals Who Play in the NFL*. New York: Warner, 1998.

Burgan, Michael. *Sheryl Swoopes*. Philadelphia: Chelsea House, 2001.

Devaney, John. *Sports Great Roger Clemens*. Hillside, N.J.: Enslow, 1990.

Dickey, Glenn. *Sports Great Jerry Rice*. Hillside, N.J.: Enslow, 1993.

Feinstein, John. *A Good Walk Spoiled: Days and Nights on the PGA Tour*. Boston: Little, Brown, 1995.

Fireovid, Steve, and Mark Winegardner. *The 26th Man: One Minor League Pitcher's Pursuit of a Dream*. New York: Macmillan, 1996.

Guttman, Bill. *Jennifer Capriati, Teenage Tennis Star*. Brookfield, Conn.: Millbrook Press, 1993.

Halberstam, David. *Playing for Keeps: Michael Jordan and the World He Made*. New York: Random, 1999.

Hamilton, Scott. *Landing It: My Life on and off the Ice*. New York: Kensington, 1999.

Hirshberg, Dan. *John Elway*. Philadelphia: Chelsea, 1997.

Holyfield, Evander, and Bernard Holyfield. *Holyfield: The Humble Warrior*. Nashville, Tenn.: T. Nelson, 1996.

Layden, Joseph. *The Great American Baseball Strike*. Brookfield, Conn.: Millbrook Press, 1995.

Lee, Spike, and Ralph Wiley. *Best Seat in the House: A Basketball Memoir*. New York: Crown, 1994.

McManus, Patrick F. *Into the Twilight, Endlessly Grousing*. New York: Simon & Schuster, 1997.

Morrissette, Mikki. *Nancy Kerrigan: Heart of a Champion*. New York: Bantam, 1994.

Rains, Rob. *Mark McGwire, Home Run Hero* New York: St. Martin's Press, 1998.

Smith, Dean, et al. *A Coach's Life*. New York: Random, 1999.

Smith, Emmitt, and Steve Delsohn. *The Emmitt Zone*. New York: Crown, 1994.

Smith, Sam. *The Jordan Rules*. New York: Simon and Schuster, 1992.

Strenge, John. *Tiger: A Biography of Tiger Woods*. New York: Broadway Books, 1997.

Valvano, Jim, and Curry Kirkpatrick. *Valvano: They Gave Me a Lifetime Contract, and Then They Declared Me Dead*. New York: Pocket Books, 1991.

Wertheim, L. Jon. *Venus Envy: A Sensational Season Inside the Women's Tennis Tour*. New York: HarperCollins, 2001.

Will, George F. *Men at Work: The Craft of Baseball*. New York: Macmillan, 1990.

PRIMARY SOURCE TYPE INDEX

Primary source authors appear in parentheses. Page numbers in italics indicate images, and those followed by the letter t *indicate tables.*

Advertisements

Dockers Advertisement (Levi Strauss & Co.), *166*

"Will It Come to This?" (U.S. English, Inc.), *367*

Architectural designs

The Getty Center (Meier), *168*

Guggenheim Museum (Gehry), *173*

Monona Terrace (Wright), *170*

Autobiographies

Dominique Moceanu: An American Champion (Moceanu, Woodward), 603, 605–606

Favre: For the Record (Favre, Havel), 612–616

It's Not About the Bike: My Journey Back to Life (Armstrong, Jenkins), 641–644

Just As I Am (Graham), 516–517

My Life (Johnson, Novak), 344–346

A Season for Justice: The Life and Times of Civil Rights Lawyer Morris Dees (Dees, Fiffer), 274–277

Shaq Attaq! (O'Neal, McCallum), 598–601

Tara Lipinski: Triumph on Ice (Lipinski, Costello), 622–626

Book reviews

"A Fair Deal for the World" (Stiglitz), 86–88

"The New Demon" (Friedman), 71–72

Booklets

Ministry to Persons with AIDS (Perelli), 497–499

Cartoons

The Dilbert Principle (Adams), 349

See also **Political cartoons**

Charters

Charter of the New Urbanism (Congress for New Urbanism), 163–165

Clothing styles

The Grunge Look: Alice in Chains (Blair), *159*

Conference proceedings

"Experimental Cloning of Human Polyploid Embryos Using an Artificial Zona Pellucida" (Hall, Stillman), 449–450

Court cases

Ninia Baehr, Genora Dancel et al v. John C. Lewin (1993) (Levinson), 296–298

Debates

Presidential Debate, October 11, 1992 (Bush, et al), 217–220

Presidential Debate, October 15, 1992 (Clinton), 443–444

Declarations

Toward a Global Ethic (World Parliament of Religions), 510–511

Diaries

"From Russia With Love" (Williams), 617–620

Editorials

"Charles Is Gone, but the Chuckies Aren't" (Reilly), 630–632

"Sex Segregation and the War Between the States" (Epstein), 122–124

Educational treatises

Horace's School: Redesigning the American High School (Sizer), 104–109

Essays

Introduction to *The Flowering of the Soul* (Vardey), 527–528

"Is Religion Possible? An Evaluation of Present Efforts to Revive Traditional Tribal Religions" (Deloria), 520–523

"The Manifest Destiny of Anna Nicole Smith" (Carver), 360–362

"Prosperity Gospel: A New Folk Theology" (Barnhart), 494–496

"Worker Rights for Temps!" (Kelly), 363–364

Primary source authors appear in parentheses. Page numbers in italics indicate images, and those followed by the letter *t* indicate tables.

Primary source authors appear in parentheses. Page numbers in italics indicate images, and those followed by the letter *t* indicate tables.

Primary source authors appear in parentheses. Page numbers in italics indicate images, and those followed by the letter *t* indicate tables.

GENERAL INDEX

Page numbers in bold indicate primary sources; page numbers in italic indicate images; page numbers in bold italic indicate primary source images; page numbers followed by the letter t indicate tables. Primary sources are indexed under the entry name with the author's name in parentheses. Primary sources are also indexed by title. All primary sources can be identified by bold page locators.

A

AAUW (American Association of University Women), 109–112

report, **110–112**

Abortion

court cases, 308

fetal tissue research objections, 445–447

laws, 237–242

protests, *238*

Supreme Court decisions, 277–282

therapeutic cloning objections, 449

See also Roe v. Wade (1973)

Accessibility in architecture, 174–177, *176*

Acquired Immune Deficiency Syndrome (AIDS). *See* AIDS (Acquired Immune Deficiency Syndrome)

Acquisitions, corporate, 62–64, 90

Action for Children's Television (ACT), 115–116

Activist movements, 52, 337

Adams, Scott, 347

cartoon, *349*

nonfiction work, **349–350**

Adenoviruses in gene therapy, 470

Adkins, Janet, 438, 439–442

Advanced Research Project Agency (ARPA), Internet development, 65, 357, 589–591

Adventist Church, 505

Advertisements, assisted suicide, *441*

Advertising, 116

Advisory Committee on Blood Safety and Availability, 464

statement, **465–466**

AFDC, 220

Affirmative action, 128–131, 131–136

Africa

Ebola outbreaks, 551–555

human origins, 542–547, 548, 569–573

African Americans

artists, 37–40

education, 125–127, 128–131

families, 220, 221, 512–515

race tension, 10

religion, 508, 509, 512–515

Simpson trial, 299, 351, *352*

sports, 598, 616–620, 626–629

unemployment rates, 80

See also Ebonics (linguistics)

Aggression, effect of television violence, 115–116

Agreed Framework with North Korea, 226

Aid to Families with Dependent Children (AFDC), 220

AIDS (Acquired Immune Deficiency Syndrome)

in drama, 24–25

general population, 212–215, 343–344

homosexuality, 343, 496–499

in literature, 34–36

pastoral care, 496–499

treatments, 213, 458–461

Ailes, Roger, 423

Akers, Michelle, 639

Akron v. Akron Center for Reproductive Health (1983), 278

al-Qaeda (organization), 242–246, *244*

Alcohol and birth defects, 461–464

Alessi teapots, 188

Alfred P. Murrah Federal Office Building bombing. *See* Oklahoma City bombing

Alice in Chains (rock band), 158, *159*

Allen, Paul G., 555

Alternative music magazines, 161

Amazon.com, 390–392, *391*

America 2000. *See* Goals 2000: Educate America Act (1994)

American Association for the Advancement of Science, Project 2061, 148–151

American Association of University Women (AAUW), 109–112

report, **110–112**

American Civil Liberties Union, Reno v. (1997), 311–316, 396–399, *397*

American Foundation for the Blind, 199

Page numbers in bold indicate primary sources; page numbers in italic indicate images; page numbers in bold italic indicate primary source images; page numbers followed by the letter *t* indicate tables.

Page numbers in bold indicate primary sources; page numbers in italic indicate images;
page numbers in bold italic indicate primary source images; page numbers followed by the letter *t* indicate tables.

Page numbers in bold indicate primary sources; page numbers in italic indicate images;
page numbers in bold italic indicate primary source images; page numbers followed by the letter *t* indicate tables.

Page numbers in bold indicate primary sources; page numbers in italic indicate images; page numbers in bold italic indicate primary source images; page numbers followed by the letter *t* indicate tables.

Page numbers in bold indicate primary sources; page numbers in italic indicate images;
page numbers in bold italic indicate primary source images; page numbers followed by the letter *t* indicate tables.

Page numbers in bold indicate primary sources; page numbers in italic indicate images;
page numbers in bold italic indicate primary source images; page numbers followed by the letter *t* indicate tables.

Page numbers in bold indicate primary sources; page numbers in italic indicate images;
page numbers in bold italic indicate primary source images; page numbers followed by the letter *t* indicate tables.

Page numbers in bold indicate primary sources; page numbers in italic indicate images;
page numbers in bold italic indicate primary source images; page numbers followed by the letter *t* indicate tables.

Page numbers in bold indicate primary sources; page numbers in italic indicate images;
page numbers in bold italic indicate primary source images; page numbers followed by the letter *t* indicate tables.

Page numbers in bold indicate primary sources; page numbers in italic indicate images;
page numbers in bold italic indicate primary source images; page numbers followed by the letter *t* indicate tables.

Page numbers in bold indicate primary sources; page numbers in italic indicate images;
page numbers in bold italic indicate primary source images; page numbers followed by the letter *t* indicate tables.

Page numbers in bold indicate primary sources; page numbers in italic indicate images;
page numbers in bold italic indicate primary source images; page numbers followed by the letter *t* indicate tables.

Page numbers in bold indicate primary sources; page numbers in italic indicate images; page numbers in bold italic indicate primary source images; page numbers followed by the letter *t* indicate tables.

Page numbers in bold indicate primary sources; page numbers in italic indicate images; page numbers in bold italic indicate primary source images; page numbers followed by the letter *t* indicate tables.

Page numbers in bold indicate primary sources; page numbers in italic indicate images; page numbers in bold italic indicate primary source images; page numbers followed by the letter *t* indicate tables.

Page numbers in bold indicate primary sources; page numbers in italic indicate images;
page numbers in bold italic indicate primary source images; page numbers followed by the letter *t* indicate tables.

Page numbers in bold indicate primary sources; page numbers in italic indicate images;
page numbers in bold italic indicate primary source images; page numbers followed by the letter *t* indicate tables.

Page numbers in bold indicate primary sources; page numbers in italic indicate images;
page numbers in bold italic indicate primary source images; page numbers followed by the letter *t* indicate tables.